4 WEEKS Watkins, T. H. (Tom
H.), 1936-

Righteous pilgrim

$34.50

DATE			

10/90 ENT'D

© THE BAKER & TAYLOR CO.

RIGHTEOUS
P·I·L·G·R·I·M

RIGHTEOUS
P·I·L·G·R·I·M

The Life and Times of
HAROLD L. ICKES

1874–1952

T. H. WATKINS

HENRY HOLT AND COMPANY ■ NEW YORK

Published by Henry Holt and Company, Inc.,
115 West 18th Street, New York, New York 10011.
Published in Canada by Fitzhenry & Whiteside Limited,
195 Allstate Parkway, Markham, Ontario L3R 4T8.

Library of Congress Cataloging-in-Publication Data
Watkins, T. H. (Tom H.), 1936–
Righteous pilgrim : the life and times of Harold L. Ickes, 1874–1952
/ by T.H. Watkins. — 1st ed.
p.   cm.
Bibliography: p.
Includes index.
ISBN 0-8050-0917-5
1. Ickes, Harold L. (Harold LeClair), 1874–1952.   2. Statesmen—
United States—Biography.   3. New Deal, 1933–1939.   4. United
States—Politics and government—1933–1945.   I. Title.
E748.I28W37   1990
973.917'092—dc20
[B]   89-35746
                                                                       CIP

Henry Holt books are available at special discounts
for bulk purchases for sales promotions, premiums,
fund-raising, or educational use. Special editions
or book excerpts can also be created to specification.

For details contact:
Special Sales Director
Henry Holt and Company, Inc.
115 West 18th Street
New York, New York 10011

FIRST EDITION

Designed by Katy Riegel
Printed in the United States of America
Recognizing the importance of preserving
the written word, Henry Holt and Company, Inc.,
by policy, prints all of its first editions
on acid-free paper. ∞
1 3 5 7 9 10 8 6 4 2

Frontispiece courtesy of Elizabeth Ickes

This book is for Hutch.

Something hidden. Go and find it. Go and look behind the Ranges—
Something lost behind the Ranges. Lost and waiting for you. Go!

—Rudyard Kipling

Contents

Prologue   1

BOOK ONE: IN THE GARDENS OF THE MACHINE,
      1874–1933

PART I: THE ORPHANED SPIRIT

  1. Passions in a Small Place   9
  2. "Queen and guttersnipe of cities . . ."   22
  3. Prescribed Care   29
  4. In the Days of Fried Ham   35

PART II: AT THE CENTER OF THE WEB

  5. On the Street   55
  6. Urban Blights   59
  7. Exuberance and Wrath   64
  8. Tinkering with the Machine   74
  9. Triangulations   82
 10. The Case of the Missing Brain   93
 11. Travesties and Triumphs   100

PART III: TATTERED GUIDONS, PROUDLY BORNE

12. Progressive Declensions   113
13. The Road to Armageddon   125
14. Diminishing Returns   136
15. The House in Hubbard Woods   147
16. Escape to Paris   157

PART IV: THE MAKING OF A HAS-BEEN

17. Cutting Through the Smoke   175
18. Keeping the Faith   193
19. A Wall Against Despair   214

PART V: IN THE CRUCIBLE OF FEAR

20. Snuffing Out the Decade   229
21. ". . . at least 90% damn fool"   240
22. No Foundation   249
23. Waiting for Something to Turn Up   255
24. Hung for a Secretary   268

BOOK TWO: IN A KINGDOM OF PRIESTS, 1933–1952

PART VI: POWER AND AUTHORITY

25. "What Has This Man to Say to Us Today?"   287
26. The Inheritance   302
27. The Hundred and Twenty-two Days   325
28. The X Factor   354
29. Cheops Redux   367
30. Sorting Out the Public Weal   389
31. The Mourned and Unmourned Dead   402
32. Apostleship and Dissidence   410
33. On the Attack   430

PART VII: A DEPARTMENT OF CONSERVATION

34. The House That Ickes Built   447
35. Cries in the Wilderness   453
36. The Dust Cloud That Voted   473
37. Stewardship and Strife   484
38. Territorial Imperatives   495
39. The Most Forgotten American   530
40. Keeper of the Jewels   549
41. In the Arms of Disappointment   580

PART VIII: CURMUDGEON'S WAY

42. Love at the Headwaters   595
43. Inside Passages   608
44. Reductive Politics   618
45. Once in a Hundred Years   637
46. Family Business   654
47. Cycles of Darkness   663
48. Celebrating the Sphinx   676
49. A Distant Fire   698

PART IX: THE LAST ADVENTURE

50. Metamorphosis   723
51. Oil, Arms, and the Man   733
52. The Portals and Seams of Compromise   753
53. Interludes of Ink and Cowboys   760
54. A Species of Redemption   781
55. The Scent of Lilacs   805
56. The Rawest Proposition   823
57. Final Barricades   834

Epilogue   856

Acknowledgments   861
Notes   865
Sources   951
Index   975

Photographs follow pages 276 and 564.

RIGHTEOUS
P·I·L·G·R·I·M

Prologue

F OR MORE THAN forty years, Chicago's principal gateway to Washington, D.C., was the Norman magnificence of architect Solomon S. Beman's Grand Central Station. Built in 1890 at the corner of Harrison and Wells streets, it rose just a block and a half east of the turgid South Branch of the Chicago River. Behind the iron-framed masonry walls of the building's façade lay the carved mahogany and echoing marble expanse of the ticket lobby and waiting room, and beyond that one of the engineering marvels of its day: a thousand-foot balloon shed of glass and wrought-iron arched trusses, which vaulted hugely over trains that stretched along their platforms in the muted light, waiting.

It was here in the Grand Central train shed that the sleek, all-Pullman *Capitol Limited* of the Baltimore & Ohio Railroad stood, ready to haul its usual load of lobbyists and politicians from the Loop to Foggy Bottom. On the afternoon of Thursday, March 2, 1933, one of them was a man few people would have noticed as he weaved briskly through the crowded waiting room and out to the platform, his fedora clamped solidly on his head, his overcoat fanning out behind him, a fat briefcase in one swinging hand, and, in his wake, his imposing wife, their son Raymond, their ward Robert, and a porter earning whatever tip he would get by keeping close with the piles of luggage. The man was a short, slightly rotund, slightly rumpled character, bespectacled, sandy-haired, and pug-nosed, his square

face characteristically fixed in a look that could have been halfway toward
a scowl of outrage or hovering at the fringe of laughter—it was always
hard to tell which. His name was Harold LeClair Ickes, a politician-
lawyer and one of the mainstays of what little was left of the ragtag army of
midwestern Progressivism. He was on his way to Washington to attend
the inauguration of Franklin Delano Roosevelt as thirty-second President
of the United States and to be sworn in afterward by Justice Benjamin
Cardozo as Secretary of the Interior in Roosevelt's first cabinet. In less than
two weeks he would be fifty-nine, eight years older than his new boss.

The Chicago he was leaving this bitter March day was his adopted
hometown, his city, and he had given it some of the best that was in him.
But it was as crippled and beaten as the rest of the country now. Years of
grotesque extravagance during the 1920s had left the city with almost no
money and precious little energy to cope with the worst that these early
years of the Great Depression had already brought. For a long time the
city had been subsisting largely on warrants issued by the state of Illinois,
itself in dreadful shape. Teachers, police, and firemen had been laid off by
the hundreds; all city services had been cut to the marrow. (The Chicago
Public Library had not purchased a single book since May of 1931.) It was
a setting fraught with the irrational: James D. O'Reilly, a municipal
employee, had seen his home auctioned off in 1932 because he owed the
city thirty-four dollars in back taxes—the same city that owed *him* $850
in unpaid salary. People were living under bridges and sleeping in doorways, most of them ordinary citizens driven to desperation by conditions
far beyond their control.

So it was in most of the rest of the nation, which in the election of 1932
had put its hopes in a patrician Democrat from the Hudson River Valley
and former governor of New York, who would gather around him in his
cabinet and throughout his administration one of the most remarkable
collections of minds and skills ever to assemble in Washington. None of
these individuals knew precisely what they were going to do to remove
fear and restore hope. But they considered themselves innovative pragma-
tists, and were willing to try any likely avenue. "I am for experimenting,"
Harry Hopkins would remark, "trying out schemes which are supported
by reasonable people and see if they work. If they do not work, the world
will not come to an end." Already, newspapers were calling it the New
Deal.

It was to join this group of pragmatic crusaders that Harold Ickes was
now about to put his past behind him, closing the door forever on the
largest part of a life that had been a kind of quest from the beginning.
"No one can flatter himself that he is immune to the spirit of his own

epoch," Carl Jung once wrote. "Irrespective of our conscious convictions, each one of us, without exception, being a part of the general mass, is somewhere attached to, colored by, or even undermined by the spirit which goes through the mass." Ickes certainly did not consider himself immune to the spirit of his own epoch, and he already had spent the substance of his life in a stubborn and quite deliberate attempt to attach himself to the whole web of the world—a thirst for connection that had dominated both his personal and his professional lives to a degree that at times bordered on the pathological. The search in both areas of his life was weighted with such an intensely confused mix of hope, rejection, resentment, and despair that it had been exceedingly difficult—at times, impossible—for him to establish close relationships. Certainly not with his wife, Anna, an Illinois state assemblywoman in her third term now, as strong-minded and emotionally dysfunctional as her husband. From her and from everyone else he had demanded much, expected little, and was rarely disappointed in that expectation. Yet he had never stopped trying, and by sheer force of will and an incredible capacity for work—with a little luck thrown in for good measure—he had triumphed over a deprived background and his massive personality flaws to forge a career that had placed him smack at the center of the American Progressive movement and had made him a leading player in the always sprightly and sometimes vicious politics of his city. Along the way, he had become a colleague and intimate of Theodore Roosevelt, Gifford and Amos Pinchot, William Allen White, Judge Kenesaw Mountain Landis, Amos Alonzo Stagg, Clarence Darrow, Jane Addams, Paul Douglas, Edna Ferber, Hiram Johnson, Robert M. La Follette, and many others, a small army of "Bull Moosers" (in spirit if not always in fact) who had stood at the head of a middle-class revolution that was to inform most of this country's twentieth-century political life. At its core was a strain of optimism that was as old and as durable as the Republic itself, a conviction that men and women somehow could take hold of their government and shape it to great ends, great deeds, a vision to which Ickes, for one, would hold passionately to the day of his death and leave as his own most enduring legacy.

This was the inheritance Ickes carried with him as he settled into his compartment on the *Capitol Limited*. He was not a meditative man, but as the train lurched into motion he might have remembered the summer of 1894, when he had tried to leave the city and the trains had not been able to move for two days because of violence in the yards between antagonists in the great Pullman Strike. He might have remembered as well, glancing out his window toward the West Side as the train rattled slowly across the railroad bridge at Taylor Street, his relationship with Jane Addams and her Hull-House settlement complex twenty-five years earlier; and later, the killing of young Lazar Averbuch, or the garment workers' strikes that had shut Chicago down.

As the train stopped briefly to take on passengers at the Englewood depot five miles south of the Loop, he certainly would have remembered the drudgery in his uncle's drugstore. He might also have given some thought to his years of lonely struggle at the new University of Chicago in nearby Hyde Park, when both he and it were raw and unfinished, of the kindnesses of its president, William Rainey Harper, of himself and Anna and a graduate student named James Westfall Thompson and the strange alliance they would create for a time. He might have recalled, too, the stink and noise of the day when William Jennings Bryan made his "Cross of Gold" speech in the old coliseum on the grounds of the 1893 World's Columbian Exposition across Fifty-ninth Street from the university. He should have remembered that speech; listening to it had given him one of his most pungent introductions to an art he had tried to master ever since. And that was more than thirty-five years ago.

After leaving Englewood and crossing the sluggish Calumet River, the train would have picked up speed, moving purposefully across the narrow strip of land between Wolf Lake and the immensity of Lake Michigan, on past the few still-smoking steel mills of Gary, Indiana. East by southeast the *Limited* would be steaming, whistling into the darkness across the rich and troubled heartland of the nation, past fields of wheat and corn and barley that could find no price worth the selling, past farmhouses boarded up, abandoned, ready for auction, into and out of South Bend, and Fort Wayne, Indiana; Columbus, Ohio; Wheeling, West Virginia. By morning it would be grinding up into the tumbled Allegheny foothills just below Pittsburgh, the last long leg of the journey to Washington. It would have taken little here to remind him that he was in the country of his origins now, the hills and hollows of western Pennsylvania. Over breakfast coffee in the swaying dining car, he might have turned his mind to his grimy hometown of Altoona, a place he had revisited only once since the last burial in 1905, and he might have remembered, too—or perhaps just felt, like a pull on the heart—the labyrinthine connections of the disturbed and complex family into which he had been born.

Almost fifty-nine years earlier.

BOOK O·N·E

In the Gardens of the Machine

1874–1933

We and all the world in those days were deeply stirred. Our sympathies were responding excitedly to a sense of injustice that had become a part of the new glittering, gaudy machine age. Machines of steel and copper and wood and stone, and bookkeeping and managerial talent, were creating a new order. It looked glamorous. It seemed permanent; yet because some way the masses of the world, not the proletariat but the middle class, had qualms and squeamish doubts about the way things were going, discontent rose in the hearts of the people. . . . And the boss-hunters arose and the devil was to pay and no pitch hot, all across this lovely land of the free, this home of the brave.

—William Allen White, *Autobiography* (1943)

PART I

The Orphaned Spirit

I was born and lived for the first sixteen years of my life in a small city in central Pennsylvania. . . . I came to Chicago when I was sixteen and I have seen more or less of the further West. There is no comparison between the two. The spirit in the small eastern communities, as I know it . . . is mean and sordid and narrow as compared with the West. . . . If I had to pull up stakes now and change my home it would never occur to me to go east again.

—Letter to William Allen White, June 28, 1921

CHAPTER

· 1 ·

*Passions
in a Small Place*

J UDGE MCCUNE WAS a big man, physically and in the region of the heart. His people were Scotch, McEwens until some ancestor had corrupted the name to its nineteenth-century version. They were part of that determined band of Presbyterian immigrants, armed with the certitudes of Calvin and Knox, who had pushed into the wilderness of central Pennsylvania in the years following the Revolutionary War. Some of the family had moved up into the country of the Appalachian Plateau, where millions of years of erosion had left behind a mass of parallel ridges called the Allegheny mountains, whose narrow valleys, fed by a myriad of rivers, creeks, and rivulets, offered rich and productive soil.

Joseph McCune, the Judge's father, had gone all the way across the waves of mountains to settle near the hamlet of Frankstown north of Hollidaysburg in what would become Blair County. Situated in Logan Valley in the western foothills of the Alleghenies, watered mainly by the Little Juniata River, and shadowed by the rise of Lock Mountain to the east, it was especially good farmland. Joseph McCune became a leading citizen of Frankstown, serving for thirty-six years as a county judge, and he prospered; upon his death, family tradition had it, he left several farm properties and the sum of $10,000 in gold to his only son, Seth Robert. If so, there was nothing left of it by the 1870s but the old man's original farm and a patch of timberland in the mountains. This did not appear to bother the Judge overmuch, for by his lights he probably had done well enough for himself. He gave the lie to the common perception of the Scotsman as dour pinchpenny; he was generous and good-humored, with a booming, hail-fellow voice and a talent for friendship. He had served several terms as an associate county judge himself, and a measure of his popularity lay in the fact that it survived unimpaired a period in the 1840s when he had served as the Frankstown tax collector. He was enthusiastically political, too, in an age when partisan politics were as uncomplicated as they were passionately embraced, the gas that fueled the civic life of small-town America. He had been a good Whig and, after 1856, when all the antislavery, anti-South, and antiexpansionist sentiments in the nation had shaken down into a new party, a good Republican. These stern convictions he passed on to and nurtured in his children.

There were ten of them, brought into the world of the valley by his wife, Julyanna, a tiny, perpetually quiet woman almost lost in the shade of her husband, who stood nearly six feet tall and was almost as wide as he was tall. If the children got their politics from their father, they got their religion from their mother; the Judge, like most of the males of his day, looked upon religion as a necessary encumbrance to be endured tolerantly under the administration of the women of the family. Julyanna McCune did her duty, imposing on the household all the chilly doctrines of rigid Presbyterianism, a dogma that held that no earthly joy was to be trusted and that most of humankind, raddled with sin, inevitably would be denied access to Heaven no matter how hard it beat its puny fists against the gates. None of the McCune children ingested both politics and religion with greater fervor than Martha—called Mattie by the family— born in 1852. So profound a Republican was she, the story went, that she disgraced her Calvinist traditions by weeping openly when Senator James G. Blaine was defeated by Grover Cleveland in the Presidential election of 1884. Her religious feelings were no less intense, if somewhat less passionately expressed.

Both were the major portion of her dowry in 1872 when she married Jesse Boone Williams Ickes, a handsome young tobacconist from the railroad town of Altoona seven miles up the country road from Hollidaysburg. There is no record of what Mattie's parents thought of this match, but it could not have been easy for her mother to accept. In the first place, Jesse came of Baptist stock. In the second place, and worse, neither Jesse nor his father, John, took even this questionable branch of religion very seriously, although the father was known to mutter from time to time that "Hell is paved with Presbyterians," a tactic calculated to infuriate his daughter-in-law (it always worked). But Jesse was tall and slender and sported a sweeping mustache in the grenadier's fashion, curled up and sharply waxed at the tips. What is more, he probably had about him the reputation (later to be confirmed) of being something of a rake, and it is possible that Mattie—short, attractively plump, determined, and implacably serious—decided to straighten him out by marrying him. In any case, marry him she did, and went off to live with him in Altoona.

The roots of the Ickes family went even deeper into the soil of Pennsylvania than those of the McCunes. Jesse's people had arrived from Saxony as early as 1730, and at least one had founded the village of Ickesburg near Lancaster. They were of Germanic origin, with just enough touch of the Frankish to be reflected in an occasional middle name—"Loy," in the case of Jesse's father. His name bore another mark of distinction as well; one history of the region lists him as "Dr." John L. Ickes, although there is nothing in the record to suggest that he was either a doctor of medicine or a doctor of divinity. What is certain is that he was one of the earliest settlers of Altoona and had done well enough at farming to have gone into real estate, after a fashion, erecting a substantial frame building on the east side of town at the southwest corner of Twelfth Street and Ninth Avenue. Called the "Green Corner," the two-story structure served as a rental opportunity for various businesses on the street level and as a home for the Ickes family on the second floor. It was in the Green Corner that his father had set Jesse up in business selling notions, sundries, cigars, pipe tobacco, chewing tobacco, and Sweet Caporal and other popular brands of cigarettes, and it was surrounded by such noxious playthings of the devil that Mattie McCune Ickes set out to bring up a family.

Harold LeClair Ickes, his middle name a sprout from the family's obscure French connection, was born on March 15, 1874 (and because of that sprout, would be called "Clair" by his family and close friends for much of his life). Thirteen months before him had come brother John, and after him, in order, came sister Julia, brother Jesse Merrill, brother Felix, sister Amelia, and sister Ada Katrina. Two sisters and one brother survived to adulthood, and on one level or another at varying times in their lives, it was brother Clair who took care of them—just as, in the end, he took care of so much else.

"To understand the fashion of any life," it has been said, "one must know the land it is lived in and the procession of the year." The land in which Harold LeClair Ickes spent the formative years of his long life, this wooded, rolling western Pennsylvania country with its long valleys, dark hidden hollows, endless mountain ridges, tortured outcrops of primordial shale and limestone, sudden springs and chattering creeks and creeklets, had been permanently marked by civilization just twenty-five years before his birth, when functionaries of the Pennsylvania Railroad laid out a town in the northern end of the Logan Valley, an area called Tuckahoe Valley by the natives. The railroad called it Altoona, a corruption of the name of its model, the German railroad town of Altona, and until the economic imperatives of the latter half of the twentieth century reduced it to little more than a whistle stop on the Amtrak line, its seasons were punctuated quite as inexorably by figures on a timetable as they were by the soaking rains of spring or the dead hand of winter.

Eighteen forty-nine was not a good year for urban planning. The railroad's surveyors were practical men burdened by the weight of the Industrial Revolution, and they conceded not a thing to beauty. Altoona was to be a railroad town and it was as a railroad town that they laid it out, a gridiron of business and residential streets spreading over the valley floor and marching fearlessly up the slopes of the foothills. Dividing the streets in the hills from those in the valley was the roadbed for the line under construction from Harrisburg west to Pittsburgh (completed in 1854). On either side of the line running southwest to northeast and dominating the central part of town were the railroad's yards, 123 acres split into two sizable plots and set aside for the construction of a locomotive works, various shops, foundries, a wheelhouse, and roundhouses.

The Civil War has been called the first industrial war in history, at least on the North's side of the conflict, and it needed machines to do its work, among them locomotives, rail cars, and other paraphernalia of the age of steam—and Altoona could and did supply them. In the process the town blossomed and spread: by 1865 to more than eight thousand people; by 1870, to more than ten thousand; by 1875, a year after Ickes's birth, to more than fifteen thousand. And during the sixteen years of Ickes's residence there, Altoona would grow into a genuine submetropolis, with more than thirty thousand "industrious, frugal, well-informed, cheerful, and happy people," according to one civic hagiographer. As well, it boasted a number of macadamized streets, many churches, a privately owned gas works and a railroad-owned water company, electric street-lights and electric trolleys, a 150-room hotel (the Logan House, owned and operated by the railroad), six newspapers (including the *Blair County Radical,* an early underground sheet), scores of businesses, twenty-one doctors, an "opera house," schools, three principal banks, a sewerage system (though not until 1888), and "Whiskey Row," a section of Railroad Street given over to cheap taverns for the use of those too low on the social scale to drink comfortably at the Logan House bar.

And the railroad works, always the railroad works. By then, the city claimed they were the largest in the world, and more than one-third of the adult male population of the town was directly employed by them, the rest utterly dependent upon them. In 1880 alone, these works built eighty-five new locomotives (painted a dark green, with yellow stripes for freight and gold stripes for passenger engines), 106 passenger cars, and 3,781 freight cars.

There was pride in that, but Altoona was a company town, an industrial town invented and ruled inexorably by the enterprise that supported it, and it is safe to say that not all of its citizens—including a handful of blacks—were uniformly "cheerful and happy." It was a dangerous place, too. Maiming in the shops and yards was an everyday matter (there was a need for all those doctors), and death was a commonplace. So were the train wrecks that added to the death toll. "Living in a railroad town," one Altoona worker of the time remembered, "where wrecks were of almost daily occurrence, we had come to look on them with indifference."

And for all the technological amenities that ultimately came to the town, for all the natural beauty that surrounded it, Altoona remained an unrelievedly, stubbornly ugly place through the years of Ickes's growing up, many of its streets still unpaved, turning to boot-sucking mire with the spring rains, gutters running with raw sewerage, business-district buildings of bare brick, wood, or institutional stone, mundane workers' cottages bravely annotated with Victorian scrollwork, naked telephone and electric-light poles canted over the avenues, a few spindly, unhealthy-looking trees casting inadequate summer shade, and over it all the stink and noise and soot of progress unrestrained.

In the end, it was the ugliness of the town that Ickes remembered. "I believe that when I left Altoona in 1890," he recalled more than forty years after his departure, "the population was some 20,000 [actually, more than thirty thousand]. . . . The houses then as now were mostly of wood, built closely together. The smoke and gases from the railroad shops and the engines in the yards had a corroding effect upon the paint with the result that the town always had the appearance of badly needing a fresh coat." But there was another kind of ugliness fixed in his memory, one that had little to do with what the town looked like and much to do with his portion of its life. He hinted at it in an exchange of correspondence with William Allen White in 1921. White had sent him a copy of Victor

Murdock's *Folks,* a novel about life in Wichita, Kansas, praising its wholesomeness while damning Sherwood Anderson's *Winesburg, Ohio* for what White considered its distorted portrait of small-town life. Ickes did not fully agree. "Of course there isn't any doubt that *Folks* is much more wholesome than *Winesburg,*" he wrote.

> The one you would like to have your children read and the other you would keep out of their way, if possible. But it does seem to me that the two books deal with different kinds of people in two different types of towns. . . . I was born and lived for the first sixteen years of my life in a small city in central Pennsylvania. I don't believe Victor Murdock would have written *Folks* in the setting of my hometown, although he could have found some analogous characters there. I am afraid that Sherwood Anderson would have been able to duplicate there the stories he wrote about Winesburg. I wish I might be able to say that my hometown, as I remember it in the days of my youth, was more like Wichita than like Winesburg, but the sorry fact is it more nearly approximated Winesburg.

Ickes had reason for his memory. First of all, death must have colored it darkly—not just the impersonal deaths in the railroad yards that were the town's common inheritance, but deaths that cut close to the bone of his own life. There were more than a fair share of these. His step-grandmother Ickes (Jesse's mother had died long before Harold's birth, and John Ickes had remarried) was the first, dying when Clair was no more than four years old. "I don't recall the circumstances of her death," he said later, "but I shall never forget her funeral which ended in her own family's lot at Lancaster. We children were taken as a matter of course to this important ceremony and what a tremendously long, hot ride it was on the train. I was miserable for hours on [end] and quite ill on the way home. . . . Parents were not careful in those days," he added primly, "about subjecting children to extraordinary nervous and physical strains. The proprieties had to be observed." His grandfather Ickes was next, in 1881. ("I do remember my grandfather's last illness. I recollect that he lay for long days in the big double bed, which I think must have been a four poster, and then I remember that we were told he was dead.") The next decade saw, in succession, the deaths of his grandfather and grandmother McCune; his best boyhood chum, Charlie Moser (Ickes was close enough to the family to continue to write "Muzzy," Charlie's mother, for years afterward); and his infant sister, Ada Katrina. And then, the most devastating of all, his mother, carried up to Fairview Cemetery in 1890. Over the next fifteen years, Ickes would return for three more burials in the crowded family plot by the Soldier's Monument in that little necropolis on the hill—those of his father and two of his brothers.

If his recollection was embittered by the memory of all those shadows, it could not have been any less profoundly affected by the quality of his life at home before his mother's death put a finish to it. Mattie Ickes did her best, but circumstances and her own inflexible temperament were arrayed against her. Among other things, there was not enough money to support her large brood adequately. Jesse never did make much of a go as a tobacco merchant, and while John Ickes apparently was generous enough to make up for some of the slack, that ended in 1881 when he died. Any hopes the family might have had for a substantial inheritance were blasted when it was discovered that the old man had died intestate. The Green Corner building was seized by the courts and sold at auction, the slim proceeds divided among Jesse and his brother and sister. After renting various houses, Jesse spent most of his legacy in the construction of a small, two-story dwelling on a lot at 1518 Fifth Avenue. It was literally on the wrong side of the tracks, the windward side, with the air full of cinders and soot, sitting smack in the middle of the Fourth Ward on the east side of town, an area populated almost entirely by railroad laborers and their families and where, over the endless clatter of the yards, one could hear the sounds of a daily ritual eloquently described by one longtime Altoona railroad man: "In those days Altoona ate dinner in the middle of the day, and every noon you could hear housewives pounding steak all over town. The steak was laid on a board and hammered energetically with a potato masher. When it had been reduced to a pulp, it was fried brown and juiceless to be served with a thick gravy."

Not the least of Mattie's problems was her husband, who was turning out to be a shaky helpmeet. After the Green Corner left the family's possession (it ultimately went up in flames in 1885), and with it his tobacco business, Jesse took a job as a clerk in the counting rooms of Blake & Mackey's planing mill near the yards, an undemanding job that satisfied him even if it never quite satisfied the needs of his family—largely because of his own indulgences, if his son's memory was accurate: "I have always had a tremendous admiration for my mother. I have never known anyone who accomplished so much with so little to go on. It was always a major operation to get money out of Father. Not because he was stingy, but because he wanted it for his own pleasures." Those were considerable and various. Jesse was a dedicated joiner and, if a chronicler of 1883 can be credited, he had plenty of opportunities. Altoona, this reporter declared, boasted

> numerous moral and beneficial associations, in fact, all the secret and benev-
> olent societies usual in a metropolis. . . . Masonry is represented here by
> five organizations—two blue lodges, a chapter, a council, and commandery.

The Independent Order of Odd-Fellows embraces three lodges, an encampment, and three degree lodges of the Daughters of Rebekah. Two tribes (the Tammany and Winnebago) of Red Men, two lodges (Logan and White Cross) of the Knights of Pythias, two circles (Bethany and Rising Sun) of the Brotherhood of the Union of Pennsylvania (H.F.), two councils of the United American Mechanics . . . an association of the Independent Order of Philozatheans, and some temperance societies embrace the principal secret societies.

At one time or another, Jesse belonged to most of these, together with the Caravan Siesta of the Princes of Bagdad, something called the Haymakers' Association (he was "No. 364½"), and the Volunteer Firemen Association (although his son reported in *Autobiography of a Curmudgeon* that "It was a major family feat . . . to get my father up from a warm bed, dressed, and on his way to a night fire that was already lighting the sky"). He had the distressing habit of outfitting himself in the plumes, braid, and swords of one or another of these organizations on formal occasions, such as the numerous family funerals, a matter of considerable embarrassment to his wife. In truth, Jesse's memberships were useful principally in giving him an excuse to get out of the house at night to do whatever carousing he could find available in the Logan House bar or even along Whiskey Row. Jesse belonged to no temperance societies. "He drank," his son flatly remembered, "and at times he drank more than was good for him." And there was more: "He was attractive to women and as a very young boy I learned that he was not faithful to my mother. I suspect that his attentions to other women ranged far and wide."

Mattie's response to all this, since she was quite as powerless as any other woman in her time and place in life, was in a frenzy of devotion to the strictures of her religion, an obsession with politics of the Republican variety, endless work, helpless recrimination (but rarely within earshot of the children), and an unhealthy emotional reliance upon her second-born son, Clair, who became, sadly, inevitably, and at a very young age, very much the man of the house. His older brother, John, was difficult and irresponsible from the outset (and would remain so all of his life), demonstrating as little interest in family duties as his father. John also was something of a bully. He was bigger than the stubby little Clair and by Ickes's account pounded him regularly—until one afternoon, when by a happy accident the smaller boy managed to kick his brother in the testicles. The result was dramatic, gratifying, and permanent; John never bothered him again. Much of the care and even the discipline of the younger children thus fell to Clair.

And much else besides—running down to Shuff's Grocery on the corner of Fourth Avenue and Fifteenth Street to do the shopping, hauling wood, and building the morning fire in the kitchen, kneading dough, helping to cook, dusting, sweeping, waxing, changing diapers, rustling the children up for school, even ironing. And listening to his mother's complaints about his father, sharing games of "California Jack" (a form of blackjack), a highly suspect activity that they played in mutual guilt, learning from her lips the evils of the Democrats, the virtues of the Republicans, the brutal necessity of following the stony Presbyterian road with grim determination (a part of his mother's catechism that never quite took; he became a militant agnostic in college and stayed one, declaring that the Sermon on the Mount was as close to dogma as he cared to get).

Steeped in her own bitterness, Mattie probably had become something of a hysteric. That possibility certainly is suggested by one incident that took place when Ickes was fourteen years old (it may well have been after the death of baby Ada Katrina, which would make it more comprehensible, at least). Jesse came home more drunk than usual one night. After enduring his truculence for a while, Mattie came to her son and told him that she was afraid Jesse would beat her before the night was over. Clair had never seen his father become physically abusive, but he was worried enough to make his mother promise to come to him if she needed help, then stole his father's pistol and carried it upstairs. He stuffed it beneath his pillow on the bed he shared with his brother John, and spent quite possibly the worst night of his life, waiting. Nothing happened, and in the morning he replaced the gun. He and his mother never spoke of the incident again.

At the very least, the turmoil and uncertainty of his boyhood must have kept Clair off balance emotionally, and may have been the seedbed of the powerful contradictions that bloomed in later life. He accepted his place as a surrogate husband and father, rejoiced in his responsibilities and in the closeness he felt toward his mother—and at the same time resented her theft of his childhood, an anger that lasted. Forty years later he wrote: "It is not fair to a young child whose mind has not yet formed to be put under such a heavy responsibility as was laid upon me." He willingly mothered his brothers and sisters, even to some extent (in later years) brother John, the bully, and simultaneously could not fully conceal the irritation he felt even as he helped those three who survived stumble through their lives. The contempt he came to feel for his benighted father was indisputably powerful—some part of him probably would have pulled the trigger exultantly that night, in spite of the terror he said he felt in the possibility. But it was diluted by a thwarted love that was as deep as it was ancestral, the need of the son calling to the father for guidance, hope, heroism, identification, and he would look for these in other men all his life. Perhaps, then, the saddest portion of Ickes's recorded memories of his childhood is his tale of dressing himself up in the regalia of his father's various brotherhoods and marching about the house waving a sword that was too big for him.

It was not all unrelieved horror, of course. At a very early age, he learned of the escape that books could offer and he read, constantly, everything he could get his hands on, from the Bible, which he all but memorized (but only for the stories and the language, he insisted), to books smuggled in from the homes of friends (there was little in his own home that was not gravid with piety). He even managed to read books on Sunday, after the somber rituals of morning prayers, church services, Sunday school, and afternoon silences punctuated only by selected excerpts read aloud from the Bible (in none of which did the philandering Jesse participate). His mother did not approve of book reading on Sunday, of course, but Ickes got around this by reading only those things he brought home from the tiny Sunday school library, to which she could hardly object, even though some of it, Ickes was happy to learn, had little to do with religion.

Ickes remembered himself as a solitary child, with few friends, and it is true that he probably was more of a "lone wolf" (as he described himself) than most boys his age. Still, he also reported that he, his brother John (presumably after Clair had earned his respect by that kick in the groin), and Charlie Moser were a threesome as boys, and it is probable that he had more than a passing acquaintance with what the rest of the urchins of his neighborhood were up to. For young Clair, however, the best times were found beyond the neighborhood. When he was very little, his grandfather McCune would drive over in his buggy every now and then and take the boy away with him. That buggy was the disgrace of the family. The Judge had long ago removed its fringed top, on the grounds that he didn't like tops, and what little upholstery was left was ragged and patched. He refused to replace it. "They don't make buggies any more that are strong enough to carry me," he said. His grandson would sit on the left side of the tattered old seat, while the Judge would haul his bulk up into the buggy and sit on the right side, raising the seat like a teeter-totter. Off they would go, the boy perched at an elevated angle and snuggled against his grandfather's ample side. The Judge had sold the home farm in Frankstown by then, moving into Altoona, but sometimes they would drive over to visit the folks who now lived in the big old house where Ickes and his mother had been born, or up to the Cove, where one of the Judge's daughters and her husband worked shares on another farm.

Almost always to Hollidaysburg, where everyone knew the Judge and called him by name as they chatted their way through town, or out to the Poor Farm, in which the old man had a philanthropic interest.

And sometimes down to Newry, excursions Ickes remembered with the greatest affection. Here yet another of the Judge's daughters lived. She had married Alex Knox, who now ran a general store there and, with his son Sam, owned a number of farms, bred horses, and cut and bucked timber off some forest land they owned in the mountains. Cousin Sam took a particular liking to young Clair and, after the Judge died, would sometimes come up to Altoona and invite the boy down to stay with him and his wife. These were the truly good times. On his cousin's home farm he learned some of the basic rural arts: stacking hay, slopping the hogs, shucking corn, helping to milk the cows in the morning, herding them out to the pasture, bringing them back in the evening, and helping to milk them again. He learned to ride here, too, and was given his own horse for his own use. When he got older, his cousin sometimes would have him hitch up their own buggy and ride off on errands of various kinds. During several winters, he got to stay up in the logging camp, watching the hired lumberjacks pull the summer-cut logs out and sled them to the local sawmill. At home with the Knoxes, even religion had all the hard edges taken off it; there were the morning and evening prayers, but they lacked the desperate passion and intensity that gave them such grim weight in his own household. "I loved this life," he remembered. "There was a freedom and lack of restraint about it that filled my heart with joy. . . . I never had to be asked twice to go to Newry."

But he always had to go home again, back to duty, back to the mother whose needs he could not quite comprehend but which called to him, back even to the father who barely knew he was there. He discovered a measure of relief in beauty, some of it found, some of it created. The found beauty was in the mountains within easy reach and to which he made solitary escapes when he could. "I found real pleasure there," he said. "I loved to tread on soft moss along the course of a bubbling brook. I ate wintergreen berries and gathered nuts, chestnuts, walnuts, and butternuts, in season. I picked the wildflowers that blossomed so abundantly in that lovely country—wild crabapples, trailing arbutus, honeysuckle, dogwood, laurel, and rhododendron." The made beauty was at the rear of his house: "I cultivated a little flower garden in our backyard. In it I had some beautiful roses, the climate of that part of Pennsylvania being especially favorable for roses. I always had success with my flowers. None of my brothers or sisters was interested in this enterprise." And more: "Between the house and the adjoining house was a shady spot and there I built a rockery. I hunted rocks far and wide and carried them or conveyed them in a wheelbarrow. Next I made trips on foot over to the mountains, a distance of a mile or two, to dig leaf mold and carry it home in a basket to fill the interstices between the rocks. Last of all I brought back from the mountains ferns and other wild plants which I planted in my rockery and about it. When the whole thing was finished I was terribly proud of it."

Mattie took ill in the late spring of 1890, not long after her favorite son's sixteenth birthday. It began as a severe cold—they still called it the grippe in some of those parts—but it became gradually, steadily worse. She was only thirty-eight and tough, and her body fought the infection stubbornly, but it finally settled so deep in her chest that she was driven to her bed. One lung and then the other began slowly to fill. The family doctor came to see her regularly, but the antibiotics that could have cured her lay more than half a century beyond his competence and there was little he could do. If he stayed true to his instincts, and there is no reason to believe he did not, Clair attempted to take care of her and run the household simultaneously, too big a job for any one person. Mattie's sister Julia Custer came from Pittsburgh to help with the nursing, and by the end of May she was joined by another sister, Ada Wheeler from Chicago.

Early in June, Mattie began to decline alarmingly, and one day the sisters decided to bring Dr. George Smith of Hollidaysburg in for consultation (his first wife had been still another of the McCune sisters). There were as yet few telephones in the town, and Clair was sent on this mission. He ran across town to borrow a horse from Cousin Sam, who had moved into Altoona by that time, then galloped down the Hollidaysburg road he had ridden so often in his grandfather's eccentric buggy. "Uncle Doctor" hitched up his own buggy and came in, but only to pronounce the case hopeless. Mattie died that night of pneumonia.

Before she died, Mattie had discussed the family situation with Ada, who was childless, and had asked her to take in nine-year-old Amelia and, if he wished it, Clair. Jesse probably was not consulted in this matter, such decisions usually being made by the women of the family in those days, and it is likely that he did not really care one way or another. It was not much of a nest Clair would be leaving, and without his mother it lacked a center; he chose to go with his aunt Ada. She wrote her husband, Felix, and when he gave his assent, Clair packed up his and Amelia's things, some clothes, a few books, a handful of snapshots, all of which could easily have fit into a single string-tied cardboard box. John (until he grew old enough to get out on his own), Julia (until she married), Jesse Merrill (until he drowned in the Little Juniata in 1893), and Felix (until he ran away to the West) stayed behind with Jesse in the Fifth Avenue house.

One would like to think that this paltry leave-taking was brightened by a few of his own flowers pressed into his books. The flower garden and his little rockery were probably on his mind while he and the others waited one July morning for the train from Harrisburg to pull into the Altoona depot; he remembered more than forty years later that the ferns and the flowers were growing luxuriantly the day he left. Perhaps he hoped that someday there would be even better gardens, in other places. Possibly Chicago.

CHAPTER
· 2 ·

"Queen and guttersnipe of cities . . ."

THE YOUNG ICKES was heading toward a city that already was a legend, a reborn place that had started a new life itself only a few years before, one that served as a paradigm for the awesome hope, energy, and optimism that had made America what it was. Or so its more earnest citizens believed.

The city had gone to flames in the great fire of October 1871, seventeen straight hours of uncontrolled burning with from 250 to three hundred dead, ninety to one hundred thousand homeless, and 17,450 buildings destroyed over an area of 2,124 acres. Gone in less than two days—and in twenty years so triumphantly recreated that it seemed indescribable, though many people tried.

Theodore Dreiser tried with a frenzy. "This singing flame of a city," he wrote, borrowing shamelessly from Whitman, "this all America, this poet in chaps and buckskins, this rude, raw Titan, this Burns of a city!" Rudyard Kipling did not share Dreiser's passion: "Having seen it," he wrote in 1889, "I urgently desire never to see it again. It is inhabited by savages." But others disagreed. Jane Lippincott, a British visitor who did like it, called Chicago "the lightning city." Writing in *Munsey's* magazine in 1907, Newton Dent said it was "the first city of the world in many things. . . . Nowhere else is there such human voltage." And, of course, there was Carl Sandburg: "come and show me another city with lifted head singing so proud to be alive and coarse and strong and cunning . . . sweating, proud to be Hog Butcher, Tool Maker, Stacker of Wheat. . . ."

What was it, then, this "singing flame" of a city? First of all, it was big. The Chicago city limits stretched ambitiously for twenty-three miles along the western shore of the tongue of Lake Michigan, from Evanston in the north to East Chicago, Indiana, in the south, and almost ten miles to the west at their widest point. This capacious enclave spoke more for the hopes of the future than the reality of the present; it was by no means completely filled in and in fact much of it was still rural, or at least suburban, dotted with such names as Ravenswood, Lake View, Kenwood, Hyde Park, Englewood, Woodlawn, Roseland, Beverly, Morgan Park, Jefferson, Fernwood, Cicero—and, down by the shores of Lake Calumet, Pullman Town, the workers' utopia built by George Pullman, king of the railroad cars.

Closer to the shores of Lake Michigan, the city took on an indisputably urban character. The 1890 population of the city proper was more than 792,000 (the suburban population brought that total to more than 1.1 million), nearly 78 percent of whom were first- or second-generation hyphenated Americans. German Americans and Irish Americans had been the first sizable population of the foreign-born, most of them settling on the Near West Side between the north and south branches of the Chicago River and Western Avenue. As they prospered and moved into the lower-middle-class suburbs in the 1880s, nearly all the Irish and most of the Germans were replaced by a stewpot of nationalities, including some thirty thousand Poles, most of whom clustered in an area north of Chicago Avenue bisected by the east-west stretch of Division Street. The bulk of the remaining newcomers gathered in neighborhoods on both sides of Halsted Street running south to Twelfth Street and beyond. "Halsted Street," reformer Jane Addams wrote in *Twenty Years at Hull-House* (quoting herself from a speech given in the early 1890s),

is thirty-two miles long, and one of the great thoroughfares of Chicago; Polk Street crosses it midway between the stockyards to the south and the shipbuilding yards on the north branch of the Chicago River. For the six miles between these two industries the street is lined with shops of butchers and grocers, with dingy and gorgeous saloons, and pretentious establishments for the sale of ready-made clothing. . . . Between Halsted Street and the river live about ten thousand Italians—Neapolitans, Sicilians, and Calabrians, with an occasional Lombard or Venetian. To the south on Twelfth Street are many Germans, and side streets are given over almost entirely to Polish and Russian Jews. Still farther south, these Jewish colonies merge into a huge

Bohemian colony, so vast that Chicago ranks as the third Bohemian city in the world. To the northwest are many Canadian-French, clannish in spite of their long residence in America.

These hundreds of thousands of assimilating Americans made up the bulk of the city's working classes, but Chicago was not, like Ickes's Altoona, a one-industry town. Chicago made almost everything, and made it in abundance (including produce from the scattered truck farms enclosed within its generous borders). Still, a few enterprises were so immense that they dominated the economic life of the city—indeed, of a region encompassing thousands of square miles—to a degree unmatched anywhere else in the nation. There were the North Chicago Rolling Mills at the forks of the Chicago River, where the Bessemer Process had first been introduced on a wide scale in this country and where most of the steel rails in the United States were made. There was the McCormick Harvesting Machine Company, the sprawling climax of Cyrus McCormick's inventive genius, whose works along the South Branch of the river at Blue Island and Western Avenue covered twenty-four acres (in 1902, all of it would be taken over by the International Harvester Company). There were the Pullman Car Company works, an incongruous blend of serene landscaping, Gothic architecture, and smokestacks at the far south of the city, surrounded by the tidy brick cottages of Pullman Town, the village built by George Pullman to house and supply the needs of the families of the 2,500 workers who turned out sleeping cars for the nation.

Most dominant (and most redolent) of all were the stockyards; seven of them were scattered around the southern and western edges of the city, the biggest of all—the biggest in the world—being the Union Stock Yards, half a square mile of holding pens that could handle three hundred thousand hogs, seventy-five thousand cattle, fifty thousand sheep, and five thousand horses at a time, a place of "steam, dirt, blood and hides," where nearly thirty thousand men, women, and children worked at the business of killing and dressing animals for market. The complex was described with astonishment in 1884 by one visitor:

> 360 acres of land and forty miles of railroad track . . . in connection with all the railroads entering Chicago. . . . Fifteen miles of macadamized streets run through the yards, and forty miles of water and drainage pipes underneath. . . . If, for ten hours of every working day in the year, a constant stream of cattle at the rate of ten per minute, of hogs at the rate of thirty per minute, with the small addition of four sheep every minute, passed through these yards, it would fall short of the actual numbers brought to this market for sale, slaughter, or distribution!

In 1892 the actual number of slaughtered animals included 2.5 million cattle and five million hogs. The yards boasted the Exchange Building, a bank, restaurants, a hotel, and a fire department for their exclusive use; and around them on all sides sat the brick buildings of the great meat-packing giants—Armour & Company, Swift & Company, Libby, McNeill & Libby among them—that made up the little city within the city called Packingtown.

Add to all this the elevators and bathroom fittings coming out of the brass and iron foundries of Richard Teller Crane; the shipyards along the river; the lumberyards for white pine stripped from the North Woods of Minnesota, Wisconsin, and Michigan; the furniture factories; more grain elevators than there were anywhere else in the world; and the enormous retail and mail-order merchandise emporiums of Montgomery Ward; Sears, Roebuck; and Marshall Field, and one begins to comprehend the weight behind the words of the character in Henry Blake Fuller's contemporary novel of Chicago life, *With the Procession:* "This town of ours labors under one peculiar disadvantage: it is the only great city in the world to which all its citizens have come for the one common, avowed object of making money. There you have its genesis, its growth, its end and object; and there are but few of us who are not attending to that object very strictly."

The section of town where most of the money changed hands and where all its ancillary paper got shuffled around and about was called the Loop, where the Chicago River flowed from the south, met its north branch at South Water Street, then looped east to ooze its way into Lake Michigan. Between South Water Street on the north and Harrison Street on the south, Market Street and the river on the west and Michigan Avenue and the lakefront on the east, lay 170 square blocks that held in its banks and insurance companies one of the greatest concentrations of raw capital in the United States. These blocks also contained all of the city's greatest caravansaries, among them the Palmer House on Wabash Avenue, the Hotel Bismarck and the Sherman House on Randolph Street, the Leland and Richelieu hotels on Michigan Avenue, the Tremont House on Dearborn Street. Here the city's blizzard of major newspapers—the *Tribune,* the *Daily Globe,* the *Daily News,* the *Record,* the *Inter-Ocean,* the *Chronicle,* the *American,* the *Evening Post,* the *Herald,* the *Times*—and a flurry of lesser and foreign-language sheets were produced. Here sat the gray eminence of city hall and the Cook County Courthouse, taking up an entire block on Clark Street (in 1906, they moved to an even bigger, newer building on Randolph Street, where they remained) and the United

States Government Building (including the post office) filling another block on Dearborn Street. Here were the Custom House, the Railroad Exchange, the Board of Trade, the City Auditorium, the Chicago Art Institute, the Public Library, the City Club, the Union League Club, the Athletic Club, the Masonic Temple, and Marshall Field's huge department store on State Street. Here too were the better theaters (the Olympic, McVicker's, the Columbia), two opera houses (the Chicago and the Grand), and the higher saloons and restaurants (Chapin & Gore's, Rector's, Kinsley's, the Berghoff). Just a few blocks to the south were the lower barrelhouse bars, oyster bars, flophouses, dance halls, gambling dens, and bordellos of the "Levee" in the environs of lower Clark and Dearborn streets, a district that never closed and which numbered among its approximately two hundred brothels the Everleigh Club, an establishment operated with such sophisticated élan by the Everleigh sisters, Ada and Minna, that it was famous with sporting crowds all over the country.

But it was as a showcase of American architecture that the Loop achieved perhaps its greatest distinction in the 1890s. After the fire, the city had been rebuilt with an energy that amazed the world. During most of 1872, a visitor of the time reported, "There was built and completed in the burnt district of Chicago a brick, stone, or iron warehouse every hour of every working day." This was all quite admirable, but it carried with it a problem: the construction was largely horizontal and swiftly filled most of the available space in the Loop. There was nowhere to go but up, and that seemed impossible. The age of the skyscraper had begun, largely in New York, but Chicago's friable lakefront soil held no convenient bedrock on which to implant such wondrous—and heavy—expressions of Progress. Some refused to be discouraged, however. "Tall buildings will pay well in Chicago hereafter," wrote a real estate speculator in 1880, "and sooner or later a way will be made to erect them."

One was—and sooner rather than later. In 1881, John Wellborn Root—whose partner was Daniel H. Burnham—devised a Chicago-style foundation he called a "floating raft," a grid of steel girders laid flat across the bottom of a hole, and upon this raft his firm, Burnham & Root, erected Chicago's first skyscraper, the ten-story Montauk Building on West Monroe Street. After that, Chicago belonged to the architects, some of the greatest in American history. Burnham & Root went on to build the Rookery Building on LaSalle Street, described by architectural historian Carl Condit as "one of the final monuments of the art of masonry architecture," and perhaps their most famous monument, the Monadnock Block, a sixteen-story celebration on West Jackson Boulevard. Dankmar Adler and Louis Sullivan—Adler and Sullivan—adapted Root's floating raft for the foundation on which they placed the ten-story Auditorium Building on the lakefront, the especially magnificent thirteen-story Stock Exchange building on the corner of West Washington and LaSalle streets, and the Carson Pirie Scott store. For his part, William LeBaron Jenney (who had trained Sullivan, among others) contributed the ten-story Home Insurance building on the corner of LaSalle and Adams, a structure whose artful masonry exterior disguised a revolution—an interior skeleton of steel girders on which was hung the rest of the building, the so-called bird-cage technique that was adopted by the builders of skyscrapers all over the world, since it allowed them to build higher with less weight and greater strength. With these and a handful of other buildings, what came to be known as the Chicago School of architecture gave the city a skyline to match its considerable aspirations.

By the 1890s, for all the fact of its emerging and impressive skyline, the Loop appeared on the continental railroad maps of the day—including those produced by Chicago's own Rand, McNally & Co. on Adams Street—as nothing more than a tangled blotch of lines. There was good reason. After May 10, 1869, when the tracks of the Union Pacific met those of the Central Pacific at Promontory, Utah, the country acquired a truly national railroad system, almost all of whose lines sooner or later converged at Chicago in the heartland. Count the railroads whose rattling freight and passenger trains steamed into the city, almost all of them gone now but once the very lifelines of Chicago's growth: the Atchison, Topeka & Santa Fe; the Chicago & North Western; the Pittsburgh, Fort Wayne & Chicago; the Chicago & Western Indiana; the Chicago & Alton; the Chicago, Burlington & Quincy; the Chicago, Milwaukee & St. Paul; the Chicago, St. Paul & Kansas City; the Michigan Southern; the Chicago Central; the Wisconsin Central; the Illinois Central; the Pittsburgh, Cincinnati, Chicago & St. Louis; the Michigan Central; the Chicago, Rock Island & Pacific; the Louisiana Southern; the Wabash; the Baltimore & Ohio; the Grand Trunk. If there was romance in those names, and there are those who will insist on it, it contributed not a little to the transcendent image of the city its literary types worked so hard to render in words—"Player with Railroads and Freight Handler to the Nation," as Carl Sandburg put it.

There was less romance to be found in the city's internal transportation network, and no one looked for it there, but on its own scale it was no less impressive—and transcendently necessary. At the beginning of the decade, the horsecar lines that had proliferated after the fire and served as the city's principal system for almost twenty years still predominated in the district of the Loop. But these were supplemented now by eighty-two miles of cable-car lines, a system first developed in the 1870s for the horse-killing hills of San Francisco and whose cars were propelled by a cable moving through a slot embedded in the middle of the street. By 1890, too, the first electric streetcar line, this time based on a system developed and first put into use in Richmond, Virginia, in 1887, had opened along a stretch of Ninety-third Street near Pullman Town. Fear of overhead electric wires and the peril trolley cars posed to nervous pedestrians kept this modern improvement off the streets of the Loop until after the turn of the century, but by then electric trolley lines were serving almost every other district of the city, with more than 250 miles of track, most of it owned by the Chicago Consolidated Traction Company of Charles T. Yerkes. Another significant expression of the era was the development of elevated steam railways, the first of which began construction south from Twelfth Street to Jackson Park in 1890. By 1897 these, unlike the electric trolleys, had penetrated the heart of downtown, and to facilitate the movement of trains in and out of the district from all four points of the compass, an innovation called the Union Loop was installed, a squared circle of elevated tracks that wound up Wabash Avenue, turned left at Lake Street, went down Lake Street to Fifth Avenue (later named Wells Street), turned left again to Van Buren Street, then left once again back to Wabash, with switching points at three of its four corners for extensions out of the district—in short, a loop within the Loop. Of all the transportation systems in operation at the turn of the century, only the elevated would survive all the decades that followed, its dirty yellow girders straddling the avenues with an implacable ugliness that nevertheless spoke eloquently for the solid, practical visions of a city that once had "the grip of Caesar in its mind."

CHAPTER
· 3 ·

Prescribed Care

T HE CHICAGO OF 1890 was in a very real sense the inheritance awaiting Harold Ickes, and to that city he would devote the best part of the next forty-three years of his life. But when the train bearing him, his sister Amelia, and his aunt Ada Wheeler came in from Altoona via Pittsburgh that July day of 1890, it did not take them all the way to Grand Central Station at Fifth Avenue and Harrison Street. It left them off instead at the Englewood station at Wentworth Avenue and Sixty-third Street, a long way from the Loop, and it was at the Wheeler home a couple of blocks from his Uncle Felix's drugstore on Wentworth that Ickes unpacked the box containing his and his sister's possessions.

"I didn't like any of it," he maintained in *Autobiography of a Curmudgeon* more than half a century later.

> I missed my mother and my friends. I longed for Altoona. It was three years before I would admit that the skyscrapers of Chicago were as big and as architecturally satisfying as the three-story wooden buildings fronting on Altoona's own main street; that the homes of Chicago were as comfortable or as well built as those of the city from which I had come; or that even the wide spaces, the beautiful parks, or Lake Michigan itself could compare with the steep hills, the faraway mountains, or the artificial lagoon of Lakemont Park . . . between Altoona and Hollidaysburg.

He probably was disappointed. Chicago was a legend, and he must have traveled toward it with a sense of promise as well as pain, but here he was, settling in several stops short. It was tantalizingly close; by standing on a rooftop or climbing a tree he could have seen its skyline rising from the prairie less than five miles away, but it was several years before he got to know the heart of Chicago. In the meantime there was Englewood, at least a part of the city. And duty again.

Englewood was a pleasant enough place. The population was only a little short of that in Altoona, and it, too, was something of a railroad town, with eight major lines serving the Sixty-third Street depot. It was not incorporated as a city, but it was self-contained, with tree-lined residential streets, many of them paved, and a business section that stretched along Wentworth Avenue. There were no mountains at all and no creeks to speak of, but he would have had precious little time to enjoy them had they been there.

We do not know what Ada Wheeler said to her husband, Felix, in her letter from Altoona after Mattie's death, but it is likely she mentioned the fact that Ickes had dropped out of school the previous year to work in Irwin's Drugstore on Twelfth Avenue, experience that would have sweetened the prospect for Felix of inheriting a nearly full-grown foster son. In any case, Felix put the boy to work immediately in his own store (without salary, of course; Clair would earn his keep in the Wheeler household). It was a family operation. Shortly after marrying Felix (a widower without children), Ada had gone to school and obtained a license as a pharmacologist. It was she who filled the prescriptions, though her husband helped her out when things got especially busy, and in time even Clair would be trusted to mix a few chemicals. Felix handled the business end of the store, the purchasing of supplies and over-the-counter sales, while Clair served as general maintenance man, clerk, soda jerk, and delivery boy, opening the store every day but Sunday at six-thirty in the morning and, after a break for supper, remaining on duty until he closed it at ten in the evening. For three years these hours would be modified only by the time he spent at school.

School was Englewood High School, a four-story stone edifice built in a modified Queen Anne style and opened for use just two years before. Because Ickes had dropped out of the eighth grade to go to work, this great red pile of a building was his first real exposure to higher education; it probably intimidated the inexperienced boy, a condition heightened by the fact that it perched next to the campus of an even larger institution— the Normal School, a modest teaching college that must have seemed to him the very definition of higher learning. He was alone and lonely, very much the new kid in school, with little talent and even less time for making friends, a situation exacerbated by the fact that he was nearly two years older than anyone else in the freshman class. He also had no money to speak of; his uncle Felix paid him nothing for his work in the store and his father was the dry well he had always been: in answer to Clair's infrequent letters asking for help, Jesse would reply in almost unintelligible, obviously drunken scrawls, whining about his own poverty and sometimes signing off as "Your poor miserable father." His clothes were the shirts, pants, shoes, and one paper-thin overcoat he had brought with him from Altoona. These were augmented over the course of three years by socks, underwear, and at least one pair of new shoes provided by another of the numerous McCune siblings, this one Sam McCune, who worked in Chicago for the Illinois Steel Company. Even this casual generosity assaulted Ickes's always tender sensibilities, for it was offered in a heavy-handed manner with such remarks as "Well, I guess I will have to go and get this little beggar a pair of shoes." Ickes tells us, both in his *Autobiography* and his unpublished memoirs, that he kept a careful accounting of all this and later, when he was on his own, managed to scrape together enough to startle his uncle by paying him back every cent.

Altogether, his first year in Englewood was a misery he passed over quickly when recalling it in later life. But he was stubborn and full of grit as well as misery; he walked the mile from the drugstore to the school and back every day. His persistence was rewarded at the beginning of his second year when he first met two people who became important to his life. The first was Agnes Rogers, a teacher so young and pretty that Ickes mistook her at first for a member of the senior class. He was a seventeen-year-old sophomore by then, and the juices were running strong. It seems apparent that he developed a full-scale crush on Miss Rogers and it probably was his first. Nearly forty years later, he wrote a long letter of appreciation in which he told her: "I don't believe that you can possibly realize how much I owe to you. I am quite sure that you have never kept books on my obligation to you. But as I have grown older I have come more and more to appreciate what an influence you were in my life at a time when I was at loose ends, lonely, ill at ease and with no definite ambition or fixed intention with respect to my future." The letter was written in 1929, in yet another period of intense unhappiness, and in this fact may lie the measure of his boyhood infatuation with her: she had given him hope and solace once on a scale so important to him that he had reached out with touching romanticism in an effort to find it again thirty-seven years later.

The second person to enter his life at this point was Henry Adkinson, a schoolmate six months younger than Clair and a year ahead of him. Their only common ground at first was the walk to and from school, but this casual acquaintance soon developed into a friendship that gave Ickes a portion of the support and acceptance he spent so much of his life pursuing. Henry became the chum he had lost with the death of Charlie Moser, and the Adkinson family—like the Moser family before it— became the family he had never had (and would later work so hard to replicate). The Adkinsons took in this orphaned spirit with a natural generosity he never forgot.

Henry's father was a lawyer who dabbled earnestly in local Republican politics. During most of Ickes's high school years, he was battling over control of the Englewood ward with Charles S. Deneen, a superior manip- ulator who was just beginning a career that would lead him to two terms as governor and one as a U.S. senator. Within the family, Adkinson was, as Ickes remembered it, "Kindly, considerate, and jolly . . . a big brother to his two children," who loved nothing more than to roughhouse with them on the living room rug or the front lawn on Sunday afternoons. The other Adkinson child, Ruth, was the same age as Ickes's sister Amelia, and the family also included an aunt, Adkinson's live-in sister-in-law, Sylvia Magee. She was "one of the dearest women I have ever known," Ickes recalled. "She early took me to her heart and I became very much attached to her. In many ways she was a second mother to me and I always had for Aunt Sylvia, as I soon came to call her, a love and deep respect that I have not had for many people." The only thorn in this particular garden was Henry's mother, a strange woman who spent most of her time in her room, coming downstairs only to carp and complain with heavy sarcasm. She apparently detested Ickes, but he took comfort in the fact that she detested almost everyone, including her jolly husband. She was, Ickes said, "distrait."

Equipped with a borrowed family, a best friend, and the lovely Miss Rogers to moon over with that unrequited but perversely satisfying passion peculiar to adolescence, Ickes was better able to deal with the frustrations of adjustment. His second year at Englewood High School went by so smoothly that he decided, with the encouragement of Miss Rogers and his other teachers, to combine his junior and senior years so that he could graduate closer to his proper age group (had he not, he would have been getting out of high school at the age of twenty, a gloomy prospect). Miss Rogers was beginning to talk of his chances for college, something he had thought far beyond his possibilities, and visions of Cornell, where she had graduated, danced in his head.

It was at this juncture that his uncle Felix was struck by the sudden notion of becoming a doctor. For years, he had been prescribing across the counter, and since no one apparently had died as a result of these ministrations, he felt he possessed a gift. He was not, however, possessed of an education, and after applying to various schools had to settle for Hahneman Medical College, a local institution of homeopathic medicine with extremely liberal standards of admission. While he did not really subscribe to the principles of homeopathy, he carefully explained to his wife and nephew, the important thing was to get a degree. After that was accomplished, he could switch to allopathy and be respectable. He also carefully instructed Clair that it was now the boy's duty to drop out of school and help his aunt run the drugstore on a full-time basis; Felix himself would have little time for such things while studying. Clair felt momentarily trapped. All his life, the surest means of getting him to do something would be to accuse him of duty, and he might have complied with his uncle's desires. Fortunately, his aunt, who normally spent her energies keeping peace in the family at all costs, uncharacteristically rose up in Clair's defense and insisted that he be allowed to complete his education. He stayed in school. Ickes took a certain mean pleasure in remembering his uncle's pitiful struggles with the books at the desk he had appropriated from the boy (whose own studies were now relegated to the workbench behind the drug counter at the store). He once caught Felix preparing tiny cards to hide about his person in order to crib his way through an examination. Indeed, nothing ever came of his uncle's ambition.

Clair himself was in the meantime doing extraordinarily well. He held to his determination to double up his junior and senior years, in spite of the killing hours at the store, and even ran for class president and won, overcoming a powerful shyness and a terror of public speaking (it was Miss Rogers, unsurprisingly, who talked him out of both). Not even a bout with typhoid fever early in 1893 slowed him down appreciably, although it nearly killed him before he was able to use his convalescence to double up on all the studies he was already doubling up on. Nor was he slowed by one more family funeral in the spring. On April 23, his thirteen-year-old brother Merrill tried to lead a horse across the Little Juniata River, swollen with the spring runoff; the current was too much for him and the boy was swept away. For the seventh time Clair stood by a family graveside and listened to the grim words of Protestant solace that by now were all too familiar, then walked down Altoona's hills to the passenger depot. It would not be the final such trek.

Two crowning achievements in his senior year added immeasurably to his emerging self-esteem. During the course of that year, one of the Latin teachers fell ill. The principal applied for a substitute, but none was available. He turned to wonder student Clair Ickes, who remembered the event with undiminished pride forty years later:

> Of course I was keen to try it, but it was evident that Mr. Armstrong had misgivings as to my ability to keep the class in hand. To add to the zest of the occasion the class I was asked to take was the class I had entered with. When Mr. Armstrong ushered me into the room and announced that I would take the class even his presence could not restrain the titter that went up. He left me to my fate, but I noticed that once or twice during the period he hovered outside the door to find out how things were going. Fortunately, however, he did not have to intervene and for two full weeks I had the delightful experience of sitting behind a desk and teaching Cicero to contemporary youngsters who had entered high school with me.

His second achievement that year was the school's faculty choice of him to deliver the "Welcoming Address" at the graduation ceremonies. This, too, was a signal honor, but he accepted it with mixed feelings. He was nineteen years old, had completed four years of high school in three, and had even taught, if only for two weeks. But he was still without a suit; he had nothing to wear for the occasion. His aunt Ada had never been able to shake anything but loose change out of her husband for the children and she could do nothing to help. She and Clair petitioned Jesse (Clair going so far as to tell him he would refuse to take part if he did not have a proper suit), and his father finally parted with a few dollars. It galled him to do so, but Clair then turned to his uncle Sam McCune for the rest and was thus able to step up to the speaker's podium at the Englewood Presbyterian Church, where the graduation ceremonies took place, spiffily attired in a brand-new cutaway suit, whose effect was only slightly diminished by the fact that a good deal of the hair that had fallen out in patches during his bout with typhoid fever was only now beginning to grow back. On the program for the event, he was billed grandly as "H. Le Clair Ickes" and his twenty-minute oration was entitled "Egotism." The speech did not survive, and it is probably just as well. "Even when I think back now in the darkness of the night," he later wrote, "I am able to blush at the memory of that oratorical effort. What a speech!" He then joined his uncertain tenor to the school's male octet for a couple of songs and accepted his diploma with the rest of the class. His father did not attend.

CHAPTER

· 4 ·

In the Days of
Fried Ham

ICKES NOW FACED a monumental uncertainty about the rest of his life. He had the grades for Cornell, but Ithaca was impossibly distant and the tuition fees light-years beyond his ability to pay. The new University of Chicago over in Hyde Park was just an easy streetcar ride away, and he had taken, and passed, the three-day entrance examinations just in case something could be worked out. His friend Henry Adkinson, who had graduated a year ahead of him, was already there. But even the University of Chicago tuition was far beyond his means. His "job" in the drugstore was no help, since his uncle still refused to pay wages beyond the room and board he had already supplied for three years. Clair was determined not to ask for money again from his uncle Sam.

That left his father, a slim prospect but the only one in sight. Clair took a leave of absence from the drugstore and returned to Altoona for a few weeks that summer of 1893, hoping to badger his father into giving him at least enough money to get a start at the university. It was neither a happy nor a productive time. He found his sister Julia in the midst of a weepy, miserable adolescence, his brother Felix under the thumb of brother John, and Jesse, still following the habits that had driven Mattie to distraction, little more than a transient guest in the house on Fifth Avenue. "My father was not interested in my ambition," Ickes wrote a half century later, still nursing the memory of rejection, "and turned a stony ear to any and all appeals for help. . . . If I could have reached into the future for such an assortment of language as I came to acquire later, I might have been able to rattle a few reluctant dollars out of the pockets of a case-hardened parent." Wrapped in the cocoon of his alcoholism, Jesse remained unrattled, and his son returned to Englewood quite as poor as when he started out and with what by now must have seemed an intolerable burden of despair. He went back to work at the drugstore.

Then one day in the autumn, word came to him that one of the teachers at Englewood—a Professor Boyer—would be willing to take Clair to see William Rainey Harper, founding president of the University of Chicago. Boyer, who had been doing some work at the university and who knew Harper, apparently had heard of Ickes's plight from Miss Rogers. The boy snatched at the chance and during the interview must have impressed Harper with his earnestness and energy, if nothing else, for the president promised to give him enough work around the university to pay at least for his tuition—this in spite of the fact that Harper's own resources were limited.

That took care of part of the problem. But it still left him with board and lodging dependent upon his work in the drugstore. His uncle Felix, the failed medical student, had become more and more exacting, and Clair was certain that if he remained there it would leave no time free for his studies, much less for the work that was designed to satisfy his tuition needs. He had to get out. The means presented itself not long after his interview with Harper. He heard of an opening for an instructor to teach English grammar and composition in night-school classes for recent immigrants, most of them Scandinavians who had followed the waves of Italians, Jews, and Poles. Among the references he scratched together for his immediate application was one from J. E. Armstrong, his principal at Englewood High, who went so far in his enthusiasm as to exaggerate slightly Ickes's experience: "If I had a vacancy in my force of teachers I would trust him to do high school work. He is a fine scholar, excellent in executive ability and a hard worker. He made a splendid record as a student and frequently took classes while teachers were absent." He got the job.

Finally, by word of mouth he located free room and board with someone identified in his memoirs only as "Miss Montfort." She herself worked and needed someone to help with housework and in caring for her aged mother. Housework was something Ickes understood with a certain precision and it would consume little of his time. He took the room, moved out of the Wheeler house, and in mid-November, halfway through the autumn quarter, entered the university, a free and suddenly independent young man. As usual, he was starting a little behind.

᪥᪥᪥᪥

"Genius is but audacity," Mayor Carter H. Harrison proclaimed in the fall of 1893. "Chicago has chosen a star and, looking upward toward it, knows nothing it cannot accomplish." The site of this stirring observation was the Great White City, otherwise known as the World's Columbian Exposition, an extravagant celebration spreading over Jackson Park between Hyde Park and Lake Michigan. Ostensibly designed to commemorate the quadricentennial of the discovery of America by Christopher Columbus, it was in reality an expression of Chicago's vision of itself as the glittering exemplar of all that progress had wrought since 1492. Its ornate landscaping had been designed by Frederick Law Olmsted, architect of New York's Central Park, among other beautiful places; Augustus Saint-Gaudens, Daniel Chester French, and Lorado Taft had provided the sculpture; and, under the supervision of Daniel H. Burnham, its exhibit halls had been designed by some of the finest architects of the day, including Louis Sullivan, Charles McKim, Richard Morris Hunt, and Henry Ives Cobb.

It was all quite high-minded. Its enormous buildings housed instructive exhibits on progress as represented by developments in machinery, horticulture, agriculture, fisheries, fine arts, transportation, manufactures, and the liberal arts, among other things. By far the most popular part of the fair, however, was the Midway Plaisance, a mile-long strip designed to amaze and amuse with such exhibits as a Turkish village, a model of St. Peter's in Rome, an ideal "workingman's home," Irish industries, an East India bazaar, a street in Cairo, and the slightly scandalous "Little Egypt" (Fahreda Mahzar) and her troupe of Syrian dancers. But the most popular item in the Midway was the great Ferris wheel, the first and for a long time the biggest of its kind. It was the invention of engineer George Ferris, who intended it as America's answer to the Eiffel Tower, that lacework of structural steel that had dominated the Paris Exhibition of 1889. Called "the bridge on an axle" by one observer, this creaking steel behemoth could lift forty people 250 feet in the air in each of its thirty-six slightly swaying cars, giving them godlike views of the exposition grounds, the prairie, Lake Michigan, and the skyline of the Loop.

And, practically at their feet, along the edge of Fifty-ninth Street, lay the nascent campus of the University of Chicago. In 1893, the campus, built on ten acres of land donated by Marshall Field, still had a raw look to it. Newly planted saplings stood in two neat rows in the naked mall, whipped into submission by the wind off the lake. A large pool of standing water left over from the rains the previous spring still lay stagnant on the mall's western edge; the paths were dust or mud. The university had opened for business in 1892, but only five of the vaguely medieval buildings designed by Henry Ives Cobb (who won out in competition with Louis Sullivan, among others) had as yet been built— Cobb Hall, Kent and Ryerson laboratories, Walker museum, and Foster Hall. There were great, gaping spaces between them.

However embryonic, the school was a matter of considerable local pride. The old University of Chicago, founded in 1859, had closed in 1886 after a long period of financial difficulties. Its reincarnation in Hyde Park was largely the work of its president, William Rainey Harper, a rotund, bespectacled academic with a powerful religious bent who occupied much of his time in diligent and generally successful pursuit of money from that better-known Baptist, John D. Rockefeller. Harper was a biblical scholar of considerable reputation, and his university would be a hotbed of theological inquiry along strong Baptist lines, but he was no gelid fundamentalist; he believed passionately in the free exchange of ideas. Furthermore, he believed that education was for use and should be applied directly to the needs of the world, which were several and of sizable dimensions. He had proclaimed the motto of the "true university": "Service for mankind wherever mankind is, whether within scholastic walls or without those walls and in the world at large." With the same combination of relentless determination and charm that would extract more than a million dollars out of Rockefeller before he was through, Harper had assembled one of the most prestigious faculties in the country, its seventy-seven instructors and full professors including such luminaries as John Dewey in philosophy, Richard G. Moulton in literature, Thomas C. Chamberlain in geology, Frederick Starr in anthropology, John Franklin Jameson in American history, Ernest D. Burton in theology, Ludvig Hektoen in pathology and bacteriology, and—to assure that the students would remain *in corpore sano*—Amos Alonzo Stagg as director of the Division of Physical Culture. During Ickes's years, Harper would add Thorstein Veblen in political economy, Frank Tarbell in archeology, and Ferdinand Scheville in European history.

Harper also did his best to make the university as attractive as possible to a broad range of students, including the very poorest. He was a Republican in politics but a democrat in his educational convictions, and Clair Ickes was not the only young person he encouraged to work his way through college—there were so many, in fact, that he organized a board to administer their employment. In his decennial report in 1902, a little over three years before his death, he essayed a description of the kind of students his university produced, and self-reliance was prominent among the qualities he discerned:

> It has been a subject of general comment that the chief characteristics of the student body have been steadiness, sturdiness, strength, strong individuality, high ideals, and clear purposes. . . . The student constituency does not perhaps equal in outward polish that of one of the larger institutions of the East, but in ability to organize work, in skill of adaptation of means to ends, in determination of purpose to win, in readiness to make sacrifice for the sake of intellectual advancement, no body of students ever gathered together in this country, or in any other country, has shown itself superior to the student body of the University of Chicago.

Clair Ickes certainly would have qualified on the grounds of sturdiness, individuality, determination, and sacrifice, all of which he displayed in respectable quantities. Until his final year, in fact, his university experience was a horror of raw persistence. "I have often said," he wrote at one point in his memoirs, "that the price I paid for my education was too high and that, if I had it to do over again, I would not undertake it. I do not know whether this is true or not. . . . At any rate the thing is done and I am glad to have done it." There was little gladness in him at the time. He was not reduced to hard labor, but earning enough to keep himself going was a constant scramble that depleted his time and energies for study. His tuition work, paid at the rate of thirty cents an hour, at first consisted of screwing rubber tips to the legs of classroom desks, but later he worked as a runner in the university's telephone exchange and the president's office. He began to augment this in January 1894 by tutoring a high school student in Latin, which until he had to give it up in April brought in ten dollars a month. He enjoyed the pleasant eagerness of the English-language pupils in his night-school classes ("A nicer lot of people I would not care to teach," he would later say), but the teaching job, too, was exhausting. Finally, his duties at the Montfort house, while not especially demanding—consisting of running occasional errands, helping out in the kitchen, washing windows, and laying the morning fire—added their total to his load of work. He just managed to squeak through what was left of the autumn quarter with passing grades, then duplicated the effort in the winter quarter.

When the spring quarter began in April, the Sherwood School temporarily canceled its immigrant courses for a lack of sufficient students to support them and Miss Montfort informed him that she no longer had room for him. In true desperation he was driven back to the Wheeler household and work in the hated drugstore. He gritted his teeth, swallowed his bile, and stuck it out, though not without feeling the strain. For

Christmas 1893, his "aunt" Sylvia had given him a small, leather-bound diary (she would repeat the gift for each of his four college years). He was characteristically meticulous in making daily entries, and that for April 3, 1894, suggests the dimensions of his struggle: "I put in another very busy day today. My work is already beginning to tell on me. I am completely exhausted by bedtime and do not feel rested when I get up in the morning." He got through the spring quarter, which gave him roughly half a year's credits toward his degree, but he and his uncle were arguing constantly by then and Clair could no longer abide Felix's surly demands and pinchpenny whining. Perhaps on the theory that if he were going to retrogress, he might as well retrogress all the way, he quit his job, gave up hope of studying through the summer quarter, and got on the train for Altoona.

After stopping off in Pittsburgh to visit his aunt Julia and her family ("Pittsburgh is the dirtiest city in creation," he informed his diary on July 10), he arrived in Altoona on July 14. It was a visit of mixed emotions, though on the whole pleasant enough—particularly in contrast to his life during the past several months. Brother John, he was happy to learn, was gone, having gotten a job at Illinois Steel in Chicago through the good offices of their uncle Sam McCune, and while sister Julia continued her complaining, his younger brother Felix proved a lively companion who was touchingly grateful to be out from under the harsh control of John and now to be given the kind of fatherly attention he, like the rest of the Ickes children, never got from Jesse. Clair and the boy took long walks in the woods, during which the older brother imparted guidance and wisdom gleaned from his twenty years of life on the planet. The summer was tainted, however, by the onerous chore of making his financial needs for the next college semester clear to a father who so far had demonstrated little interest in helping out. And the long, vindictive arm of Felix Wheeler reached out to touch him even here—this time by a letter telling him never to enter the Wheeler household again (he was swiftly instructed by his aunt Ada to ignore her husband's injunction). Felix also had a couple of messages for Jesse: the first demanded the sum of eight dollars a month for all the time that Amelia had lived with the Wheelers; when Jesse refused, the second letter demanded that he take the child back (apparently Ada Wheeler once again intervened, for Amelia remained in Englewood).

In September Clair returned to Chicago and reentered the university. The night-school courses had been reinstated at Sherwood, and he had once more been hired. The university continued to give him work, and Sylvia Magee found him an unheated upstairs room in a ramshackle house she owned south of Fifty-seventh Street within an easy walk of Sherwood School. He would share kitchen privileges with an old former cook of the Adkinsons' who was allowed to live in the house for nothing. So was Ickes. Even his father apparently had been sufficiently persuaded by Clair's summertime pleas to promise to cut into his contributions to the fleshpots of Altoona by sending his son an occasional five-dollar bill.

On December 31, as the last pages of his 1894 diary presented themselves for comment, he felt moved to sum up the year in an epiphany that attempted to subvert the bleak drudgery of his everyday life with injections of forced optimism that could not have convinced even himself:

> While the past year had many disappointments for me, yet it had also many blessings. I was disappointed in not being able to continue my college course throughout the year owing to the fact that my night school did not last very long. The three months that I spent in Mr. Wheeler's employment were a sore trial to me but I forgot it all in the pleasure of my visit home [Clair was never able to bring himself to call Wheeler "Uncle Felix"]. My visit home was, on the whole, full of pleasure, and the fact that I won the love of Pa and Felix was especially gratifying to me. As a result I can influence Felix for good and Pa has helped me more than he ever did before. . . . I have made fewer enemies and more friends this year than usual and, thanks to Aunt Sylvia's influence, I perceive in myself a better boy than I have been. Undiscouraged by the rebuffs of 1894 I look forward to better things for 1895. . . . While I do not regret the estrangement that exists between Mr. Wheeler and me, yet Amelia's position is a source of constant mortification to me.

This dismal chronicle was repeated through most of his second and third years at the university. He was forever hard at it, forever hard against it, and always just a beat behind everyone else. He was exhausted much of the time, and in the autumn quarter of 1894 had been "conditioned" (the equivalent of failure, though correctible) by his instructor in elementary French. Harper, who had taken a liking to the boy, did his best, eventually even writing Clair's father on March 11, 1895:

> A notice was sent you that your son had failed in one of his courses of the autumn quarter. I write to say that after investigating the case, the reason for the failure is very plain. He has been compelled to do too much outside work, such as teaching in night school. This has not left him time for doing the best work. I should like to suggest that if possible you render him some additional help. He is an exceptional boy, with high ideals, good ambitions, and is a general favorite with us. He is a boy of whom you may be justly proud and whom you can well afford to assist.

If Jesse answered this letter there is no record of it, and his help, such as it was, continued to arrive sporadically. The teaching job came and went and came again, depending upon the number of students in any given session, and at one point Clair took to selling, placing an advertisement in the student paper, the *Chicago Weekly,* that declared that H. L. Ickes was the "sole agent" for the sale of "university insignia pins, solid gold at $2.00 apiece, for the W. J. Feeley Co. of Chicago." Later, he would try commission sales of a new bicycle—the "Racycle"—but did no better with this gadget than with the insignia pins. He tried to borrow money from a childless and well-off cousin in Altoona. "He declined to help," Ickes remembered angrily, "writing to me about the virtues of independence and self-support as if I hadn't forgotten more about those particular virtues than he had ever learned." When the prospect of another winter spent in the unheated upstairs room in Sylvia Magee's tenement proved unbearable, he took a shared room with Henry Adkinson near the university, saving money by walking everywhere he went and by taking only one meal a day at a tiny restaurant near Stagg Field, the university's brand-new athletic stadium. The diner was operated by a woman the students called "Mother" Ingram. "Her food was good," Ickes recalled, "and her portions fairly generous. My one meal I took at the noon hour and I always bought according to quantity rather than quality. Fried ham was my customary dish because with the fried ham I could get all the bread and butter I wanted and so managed to get along." This repast cost him fifteen cents a day. His only apparent recreation was playing on the scrub team in basketball and getting in an occasional tennis game. At about this time he began to suffer fits of self-contempt and depression—coupled with periodic insomnia; all would haunt his life in later years. "I despair of myself," he wrote in his diary on March 28, 1895. "I am getting more cynical and unworthy every day. . . . How I wish I could be as I was when a boy." And on March 29: "I was listless and melancholy all day. . . . Dined on bread and milk."

Nevertheless, slowly, almost imperceptibly, he emerges from this dreary, anonymous moil and, in his junior year, becomes suddenly visible—a late bloomer, but blooming with a vengeance. At the beginning of the winter quarter, 1896, his photograph appears in the *Chicago Weekly* as one of the four "Chicago Representatives in the Iowa Debate." (Chicago won, the *Weekly* reported, though Ickes himself apparently served only as an advisory member of the team during the debate.) His brown hair, fully recovered from the ravages of fever three years before, is parted straight down the center of his head in the fashion of the day, combed to either side in winglike branches. He wears one of his own

university insignia pins on the lapel of his high school graduation suit,
and his bow tie is slightly askew. He is nearly twenty-two and at least as
old as his companions, but appears much younger, his look of wistful
innocence betrayed slightly by a sardonic lift at the corners of his mouth.
He does not look undernourished—in fact, a little pudgy (his official
physical measurements taken by Amos Alonzo Stagg that year put him at
150.8 pounds on a small-boned frame a little under five feet, eight inches
in height, with a waistline of 30.5 inches).

In addition to his membership in the Debating Club, he joined the
editorial board of the *Chicago Weekly* in the spring quarter and in the
summer quarter was raised to associate editor with the chore of producing
the "Majors and Minors" column every week, a collection of flotsam
regarding tea dances, faculty news, club meetings, and the like. He
played a diligent game of tennis, and while he was not good enough to
make the school team, he did found and manage the University of Chicago
Intercollegiate Tennis Association and organized its first annual tournament in the spring of 1896 (and again in 1897), with the encouragement
of Stagg. He also served on Stagg's track team as a specialist in the mile
walk, though he claims no victories in his memoirs. (Stagg's spotty
records for this period bear out this unhappy fact.)

This would seem quite a sufficiency of extracurricular activities, given
his murderous schedule, but he was already beginning to probe the
mysteries of the avocation that would occupy most of his life. In a move
his mother would have applauded, he joined the University Republican
Club, "a pretty slim affair," as he described it in his *Autobiography*, which
nevertheless fed his growing fascination. He and classmate L. Brent
Vaughan were chosen delegates to the annual convention of the American
Republican College League held in Madison, Wisconsin, early that summer. Vaughan ran for president of the League during the convention and
lost; Ickes did *not* run for treasurer (he insists) yet was nominated and
elected. He must have liked this taste of office—the first he had enjoyed
since his senior year at Englewood High—for upon their return to the
university, he immediately challenged his friend Vaughan for the presidency of the Republican Club and won. He was on hand as an observer
when the Democrats came to town for their Presidential nominating
convention in July 1896. "The Democratic politicians are thicker than
flies in harvest time," he informed his diary. "It is almost impossible to
get through the crowd at the Palmer House."

His new eminence soon got him a ticket to an even better show—that
taking place in the convention hall itself. On one memorably humid
afternoon he walked into the cavernous Chicago Coliseum, a relic of the

now-vanished Exposition, climbed to his seat near the rafters, peered nearsightedly over a coatless sea of humanity to the tiny figures on the podium in the far distance, and bore witness. "I was nearly steamed," his entry for July 8 says, "but stuck it out. The platform was adopted after a hard fight and pledged the party to the support of free silver. Bryan of Nebraska made a speech for silver that carried the audience with him, and nearly stampeded the convention for him." What the political tyro had witnessed was William Jennings Bryan's theft of the convention's heart (and ultimately its nomination) with a single thundering line from a long and powerful oration: "You shall not press down upon the brow of labor this crown of thorns; you shall not crucify mankind upon this cross of gold!" The experience did not make a Democrat of Ickes, but he never forgot it.

His political exposure widened in a heady excursion later that summer. A canny young student entrepreneur by the name of Kelso hit upon the notion of selling bas-relief depictions of the profile of Ohio governor William McKinley, Bryan's Republican opponent, and to promote his merchandise hit upon the even more ambitious notion of presenting one to the candidate himself in Canton, where he could be found upon a kitchen chair on his front porch receiving thousands of well-wishers and giving stolidly orthodox Republican speeches all summer long. But Kelso needed some sort of official presenter. Ickes, as head of the University Republican Club, was both suitable and available. So at Kelso's expense, he and a fellow officer stuffed themselves into an upper berth on an eastbound train, Kelso stuffed himself and his bas-relief into the lower berth, and the trio rattled off to Canton. After a long hot wait in a long hot line on the trampled grass of the McKinley front lawn, Ickes was finally able to thrust the commemorative chunk of masonry at the governor with a few appropriate remarks. McKinley received it graciously and introduced Ickes to the editor of the *Canton Evening Repository,* his campaign's official newspaper. Ickes allowed as how he was a faithful reader of the "Suppository," a malapropism that gave McKinley, whose demeanor rarely slipped out of a portly and benign solemnity, a healthy chuckle that was not shared by the editor.

That November, Ickes marked his first Presidential ballot for McKinley, a winner. Then, with the contrary instinct that was to characterize his political life, marked his first gubernatorial ballot for John Altgeld, a radical Democrat—and a loser. He admired Altgeld as a man, he explained in his autobiography more than forty years later, and the Democrat's position on social issues was enough to drive him to this electoral *volte face:* "How the *Chicago Tribune* and others had smeared this

humane and courageous man because he had fought for the underdog. . . . So far as I could see, Altgeld stood about where I wanted to
stand on social questions. . . . On the other hand, Altgeld's Republican
opponent, John R. Tanner, did not appeal to me, so I started my active
political life by voting at the same election for a conservative Republican
candidate for President and a radical Democratic candidate for governor."

Altogether a busy and satisfying period for the poor boy from Altoona.
But he was infected by more than the virus of politics that spring and
summer of 1896. At first, he says in his unpublished memoirs, he
worshiped from afar, like any proper pre-Edwardian romantic:

> She was said to be the richest girl in college and she probably was. . . .
> Romantic tales were told of her and her wealth and social standing which had
> the effect of setting her somewhat in a class by herself. Certainly it was clear,
> even to my inexperienced eye, that she dressed more richly and in better taste
> than any other girl on the campus. . . . I wished that I might be introduced
> to Miss Wilmarth, but I never suggested it to anyone, nor did anyone to me. I
> realized that she traveled in an orbit so different and so far removed from mine
> that we might never meet.
>
> Then one day as I was mounting the first floor flight of stairs leading from
> the main floor of Cobb Hall I looked up and saw Miss Wilmarth descending
> in the middle of the stairway . . . and just as I was about to pass her, of course
> without any sign of recognition, she bowed and spoke my name. With a swish
> of her skirts she was gone, and if I didn't stand spellbound, with gratified
> astonishment, it was because my momentum was great enough to carry me on
> and up to the floor above. Of course I was mightily set up and when I got back
> to our room and related the incident to Henry Adkinson I could see that,
> sweet-natured as he always was, he was really jealous.

"Miss Wilmarth" was Anna Wilmarth, and she was indeed rich—
certainly by Altoona standards. Her father, Henry W. Wilmarth, had
come to Chicago in the prefire days at the age of nineteen and by the time
of his death from acute alcoholism in 1885 had conjured a fortune out of
the manufacture of lighting fixtures and from investments in real estate
(the home in which Anna was born on January 27, 1873, for example, was
on the site of what became the Congress Hotel). Her mother, Mary Hawes
Wilmarth, was a stern woman of probity and good works. She would
become the founding president of the Chicago Women's City Club and
president of the Consumers' League, already had strong interests in the
Mental Hygiene and Legal Aid societies, and had been one of the principal
supporters of the settlement work Jane Addams and Ellen Gates Starr had
been doing at Hull-House since 1889. Anna had attended the old South

Division High School and Miss Hersey's School in Boston, and then had spent some time at a French boarding school in Paris before matriculating at the University of Chicago a few weeks before Clair Ickes. She lived with her mother at the Auditorium Hotel, a most fashionable address.

She was a young woman who would have been described as handsome rather than beautiful—a little taller than Ickes, full-bodied but not yet plump, she carried herself with an imposing grace, shoulders back, notable bosom forward. Her dark auburn hair was invariably worn carefully piled atop her head, which added to her considerable stature. If her jaw was rather too strong and her mouth too often set in a stern line, her eyes were dark, deep, and compelling—the sort of eyes whose glance could stop a man's heart at twenty paces, as they obviously had stopped that of Clair Ickes on the stairwell of Cobb Hall. She was a remarkably solemn young woman, little given to gaiety and apparently without much humor.*

Anna gave every appearance of being quite as certain of her place in the scheme of things as Clair Ickes was profoundly uncertain of his. He had made some headway in the social graces since Englewood High, but not much. The young women of his acquaintance, he reported, "seemed to pay no attention to my appearance. They overlooked my clothes, just as they did my shyness and my self-defensive brusqueness. I began to know some of the girls in my classes and I got better acquainted with them at the dormitory receptions or at the few informal dances at Rosalie Hall that I went to when I could muster the small admission charge. But it was Anna Wilmarth who really liberated me socially." They shared a class in one of Ferdinand Scheville's courses in European history and in March Ickes took advantage of their "introduction" on the stairs of Cobb Hall. He began seeking her out at receptions and at some of the informal dances. After a Dramatic Club function, he noted in his diary, "We danced until nearly one o'clock. . . . Miss Wilmarth is a great dancer. I had a first-rate time." He was then invited by Anna to a luncheon at the Auditorium Hotel ("We had an out of sight time and a daisy feed."), and a week later he asked her to go to the next informal dance with him. She accepted—and to substantiate her democratic convictions did not insist upon a carriage, which she knew he could not afford.

They continued to see each other on increasingly promising dates—a band concert with her mother in attendance, a dinner alone at Chapin & Gore's, and, finally, she invited him to spend a weekend with her and her

---

*She retained these attributes all her life. During an interview in February 1985, I asked Raymond Ickes what single word he would use to describe his mother. He thought for a moment, then replied, "Austere."

mother at Glen Arden, their summer home on the shores of Lake Geneva, Wisconsin. ("I . . . will go if I have to walk," he vowed to his diary.) Not him alone, of course; that would have been unthinkable in the 1890s—or at least a far stronger indication of her interest in him than she was yet willing to demonstrate. Three other young people had been invited, among them a long-haired and rather poetic-looking young graduate student by the name of James Westfall Thompson, who was making something of a name for himself in medieval studies. Still, Ickes could— and did—take some encouragement from the fact that when they all arrived at the railroad station in the village of Lake Geneva, Anna consigned her other guests to the family carriage while in two separate trips she herself drove Ickes and Thompson the three miles to the house in a small dog cart. He contrived other ways to be alone with her again during that weekend and by the last evening he was as smitten as he would ever be. "This afternoon," he rejoiced in his diary on July 26, "we managed to row over to the Golf Club House between showers. Miss W. rowed me over in her boat. If I stayed here much longer I would be a married man. I was glad to see Thompson leave this evening. After he went Miss Wilmarth and I read Vergil and had quite a tête-à-tête until very late. She could put her clothes in my trunk if she wanted to." Before leaving the next day he persuaded her to send him a small photograph of herself and made a date to take her to the first football game of the season. If he had not returned to the university with a suddenly light heart after that weekend, he would have been less than human, or young.

Still, money remained a problem—not that he had suddenly grown profligate. He was now keeping a detailed account of his expenses at the back of his college diaries; those for 1895 showed a grand total of $318.28 spent for everything; those for 1896 dropped to $292.17; by the end of 1897—after his graduation—he would have squandered another $454.82 on himself. Thinking about his straits could drive him down just as certainly as a blow to the skull. Even the receipt of the promised photograph of Anna ("I flatter myself that I am the only man in college who has her picture") could not hold depression at bay for long. "I am horribly blue," he wrote on August 29. "I am very much discouraged to find myself without a cent in pocket or prospect after six years of long work." On August 30 he wrote, ". . . went home and went to bed, utterly depressed in spirit."

In spite of what he clearly believed was a condition of near penury, he was in fact slightly more secure than during his previous three years, largely through the continued interest of William Rainey Harper. The university had put so many of its poorer students on the payroll by then that there was no longer enough work to cover fully Clair's tuition (forty dollars a quarter now), but Harper had written a very distant but well-to-do cousin of the boy, Mrs. Susan Harding, in one more effort to raise money: "I can recommend no more satisfactory expenditure of four or five hundred dollars than the giving or lend [*sic*] of that amount to him. I am sure you will pardon the liberty I have taken in presenting this case. Permit me to say that I have done it upon my own suggestion." When that failed, Harper made arrangements with the registrar's office that allowed Ickes to work off what he could of the tuition during the year and to pay the remainder after graduation.* His night-school teaching remained sporadic, but when he taught now he was being paid fifty dollars a month. Finally, by some miracle, his father had been persuaded to send him five dollars a month beginning early in 1896, and while the promise to pay had not always been validated by the actual payment, it was more of a commitment than Jesse had ever shown before. When Henry Adkinson joined Alpha Delta Phi and moved into the fraternity house, Clair shared a room and a double-decker bed in Snell Hall with an equally hard-pressed classmate, William Otis "Billy" Wilson, continued to take his meals of fried ham at Mother Ingram's place, and saved trolley fare by walking. He was not comfortable, but there was no longer any danger that he would be forced back to the drugstore and a meanly triumphant Uncle Felix.

But on September 28 he suffered a powerful blow to his psyche when Henry Adkinson told him about a newspaper story that Anna and her mother would soon be off to Europe for a year. "This rather broke me up," he wrote, and when it was confirmed by Anna herself the next day, the news made him "frightfully blue." At dinner on October 4 he extracted permission to write her while she was gone, and about two weeks after she left he mailed off his first weighty missive: "I sent her six big pages of closely written stuff. It cost me ten cents to send it, but I cheerfully spent that amount on it." He then immersed himself in work. Billy Wilson was managing editor (the top job) of the *Chicago Weekly* by then, and on October 1, 1896, "Harold LeClair Ickes" appeared on the masthead as assistant editor. His beat was sports, and that issue contains the first lengthy example in print of the Ickesian prose style—a full-column report on the results of the Chicago-Eureka game (Chicago 46, Eureka zip). An excerpt is instructive: "The men are improving in tackling," this

---

*He graduated owing the university $116.68. It took him until June 20, 1899, to pay this off, but pay it off he did.

specialist in the mile walk sternly reported, "although some of them still persist in tackling around the scalp lock. A little practice at a tackling bag would do these men lots of good. Herschberger is by no means a sure man at full on the defensive, as several times lately he has failed to stop his man when there was absolutely no excuse for not doing so." A week later, he was after the fullback again: "Herschberger is making too many costly fumbles this year. Time after time he fumbles without rhyme or reason when a mere novice at the game would have no difficulty catching the ball." From the beginning, Ickes's journalism was of the fearless variety. (There is no evidence to suggest that the hapless Herschberger ever wandered over to Snell Hall for a little chat with the reporter, and it probably was a good thing that he did not.) Ickes would continue in this position on the *Weekly* until his final quarter in the spring, when he became managing editor himself.

After several more budget-wrecking letters sent to Europe, he finally received a "nice long letter" from Anna on December 4 in which he professed to discern homesickness (for him, surely). He wrote back immediately, but this letter was followed by an even longer silence, and by the end of February he was feeling the full anguish of the uncertain lover: "I cannot understand why Anna Wilmarth does not write to me," he complained on February 25, 1897. "I wrote to her before the holidays and have been looking for a letter for some time now. I am sure that I said nothing at which she could have taken offense, and as I say, I am at an utter loss to understand it. With most girls I wouldn't care so much but I like her extremely and would not for the world have anything come between us. She is one of the finest and best girls I have ever known." There still was nothing by Thursday, March 4: "I cannot understand it and will write if I do not hear from her by Sunday." He did not hear from her, and he did write again. Still no answer.

He did hear from his father, however. Early in February, Jesse had sent a terse note (with no money) to the effect that he was now out of a job. On March 12, his son reported in his diary, that unemployment was explained:

I got a letter yesterday from father and, much to my surprise I found enclosed a $5 bill. He has been sick under a doctor's care. He expressed the greatest interest in me and seems to be considerably worried over my prospects. It is extremely gratifying that I have won father's love and respect as I believe I have done. Up to the time that I entered college he did not like me and rarely expressed any interest in me. This was due to the fact that, more than any of the rest, I had defended mother against him. Finally, however, I won his respect, mainly because, I think, I showed him that I was trying to make a man of myself, and without any help from anyone.

In the void created by Anna's silence, he clutched at the thin straw of his father's sudden concern and took what solace he could from it, but soon that, too, would be inadequate to his needs. On March 25 the lack of communication from Anna was explained with bitter finality. That evening James Westfall Thompson, the graduate historian, invited him to dinner at the Quadrangle Club, the first and most prestigious on campus. (Ickes, needless to say, did not belong.) Ickes barely knew Thompson, and did not much like what he did know, believing him snobbish and more than a little precious. But someone in his position did not turn down invitations to dinner at the Quadrangle. Puzzled, he went. After dinner, over a game of pool in the billiard room, Thompson curtly explained the situation: "You have doubtless heard it reported that I am engaged to Miss Wilmarth. Well, I am." Ickes had heard no such thing, and listened thunderstruck as Thompson went on to explain that he would be leaving for London at the end of the quarter. He and Anna would be married there in July. Ickes somehow offered the requisite congratulations and the two of them finished their game of pool like gentlemen, whereupon Ickes thanked him for the dinner and returned to his shared room and the lonely upper berth of his double-decker bed. "I . . . tried to read myself to sleep," he told his diary in an entry made several days after the fact, "but failed. I then turned out the gas but I tossed about for hours before I fell into a fitful broken sleep. That expression 'Well, I am' rang through my head all night and I have not been able to drive it out since. . . . I am a fool, an ass of the most approved sort for believing that she cared for me. . . . Why did she encourage me? Why did she let me go on when she must have seen my condition? I am a fool."

It would have been little comfort for Clair to have known that both the pain he felt and the words he chose to express it were the common inheritance of all thwarted lovers, universal to the point of cliché. What he did know, as many others did not, was that work was a cure that would not fail him, a certain antidote to depression. He threw himself into a caldron of activity. He had remained president of the University Republican Club, and late in March was once again chosen as a delegate to the convention of the American Republican College League (though not until after a nasty floor fight put up by his former friend, L. Brent Vaughan), and during the convention was reelected treasurer. More significantly, he also became embroiled, albeit at the lowest levels, in the Chicago mayoral election that spring. At issue was the question of corruption—as it almost always would be in Chicago—specifically, the bribes allegedly being spread around among the members of the city council and the state legislature by Charles Tyson Yerkes, owner of the Chicago Consolidated Traction Company, in a campaign to win long-term extensions of his streetcar franchises, of which he possessed a near monopoly. Yerkes, who had been convicted of fraud and embezzlement and had served a prison term in Philadelphia before bringing his talents to Chicago, was an arrogant, boastful, and utterly ruthless individual whose open contempt for all that they held sacred drove Chicago's civic reformers into an inchoate fury. In 1897 they put their hopes behind John Maynard Harlan, an idealistic young lawyer and son of John Marshall Harlan, a justice of the U.S. Supreme Court. Harlan failed to capture the nomination of the Regular Republicans, who were under the firm control of the machine captained by councilman Martin B. Madden of the Second Ward, so he decided to run as an independent. His Democratic opponent was Carter J. Harrison II, who was determined to carry on the political dynasty created by his recently assassinated father.

For the impressionable Ickes it was a fearfully exciting business. Responding to a call for Harlan volunteers, he dropped his classes long enough to work in the central precinct office in downtown Chicago for a few days preceding the election, standing before a map festooned with pins, sending out other volunteers to various precincts as they were needed. Before long he was demonstrating his take-charge instincts with a confidence unmatched by experience; he was, in fact, a little insufferable, as exposed by himself in his diary entry for April 3: "They don't seem to know how to run things down at headquarters. I was put in charge of my department and today two or three men tried to boss me. I sat down on the most obstreperous of the lot and told him to let me alone, as I knew what I was doing. I got along better after that." It was all for naught; Harlan garnered more votes than the Regular Republican candidate, but both were roundly defeated by Harrison and the Democrats. It had, however, given Ickes his first whiff of the seductive stench of street-level politics in a context of absolute Good locked in sweaty combat with absolute Evil, and to his whole-souled but unsophisticated intelligence, it all smacked of the very guts of life. Somewhat refined by the practical cynicism that comes with age and experience, this impression would remain with him for the rest of his life.

He returned to his classes for the final stretch toward his A.B. degree, organized the second annual Intercollegiate Tennis Tournament, continued to put out the *Weekly,* did his chores around the university, taught his night-school students, walked his mile regularly for Amos Alonzo Stagg,

and, with Billy Wilson, organized the first Illinois chapter of Phi Delta
Theta, of which he was chosen president by Billy and the handful of others
who joined up. As it became clear that he would safely garner all the
credits necessary to graduate, he might have looked back upon his
education with some satisfaction. Out of thirty-nine courses taken over
the four years, he had been "conditioned" in only one (and had made up
that default). He would finish with more A grades (eight) than D's (six);
most of the rest were C's, but there was a healthy scattering of B's among
them. And if his place in the class was too low to be mentioned, he
nevertheless had managed against powerful odds to acquire as elegant a
collection of intellectual furniture as he could have gotten in any university in the land. He had four quarters of Greek and French and two of
Latin behind him, in all of which he generally excelled; he had four
quarters of European and American history and four of English composition and literature; three of political economy and sociology (including
"Folk Psychology" and "Primitive Social Control"); two each of mathema-
tics, philosophy, political science, and biblical literature; one of geology;
and no less than six in his favorite discipline, anthropology—general,
physical, and cultural, including studies of Mexico, Japan, and the
Pueblo Indians of the American Southwest. His enthusiasm for anthropology, in fact, was such that Professor Frederick Starr later recommended
him for a graduate scholarship; his grade average of C-plus in the subject
was not good enough, however, and his application was rejected.

In mid-June he sent his last issue of the *Chicago Weekly* to press without
a word of farewell to his readers, and a few days after that he graduated.
No member of his family attended the ceremonies. Unwitnessed by
family, he "marched up with the rest of my class, was handed a diploma,
which said in Latin that I was entitled to all the privileges of a batchelor
[*sic*] of arts degree, then I walked off the platform into the wide world as
poor as when I had entered college and without the slightest idea of what I
was going to do."

PART II

At the Center of the Web

I was the spider at the center of the web, the dynamo running the machine, and there seemed to be no limit to my energy or to my capacity for work.

—Unpublished Personal Memoirs, 1936

CHAPTER

· 5 ·

On the Street

O N JULY 9 the *Altoona Morning Tribune* reported that "H. L. Ickes, a student at the Chicago university, arrived home last night on the Philadelphia express." The paper also had reported his graduation as a member of the "class of '97, consisting of 128 graduates, both ladies and gentlemen," so if he did not return in what could be called a triumph, he did arrive with a faint whisper of public accolade. There must have been some satisfaction in having escaped anonymity in his hometown, and while he tells us little of that final Altoona summer, he probably had a fairly decent time in spite of his penury and a hugely uncertain future. There were boating and swimming to be had up at Lakemont Park, open for four years now and far and away the most popular summer spot in the region. Stanley's Opera Company offered performances of *The Pirates of Penzance, The Chimes of Normandy, Said Pasha, Billy Taylor, Mascot,* and Offenbach's *La Périchole* at the Lakemont Park Theatre throughout July, all at a price even Ickes could afford, and the Altoona City Band played for dances at the park's Casino on Wednesdays, Fridays, and Saturdays during most of the summer.

Still, it must have been strange coming back to his father's house following graduation. There is no mention of Jesse's activities in the memoirs, but we can safely assume that little if anything had changed in that regard. For the most part, Jesse had left the position of fatherhood vacant and his second-oldest son had long since filled it, at least for the younger children. While still in college, Clair had stepped in twice to assume the role. During his summer visit in 1894, he had learned from neighbors that his brother John's treatment of the young Felix had crossed the line from discipline to brutality; among other things, John had taken to stripping the boy naked, beating him, and locking him in the attic. John was no longer living in Altoona by the time Clair learned of this. Upon his return to Chicago, Clair had gone to John and threatened to pummel him personally if he ever touched Felix again. John promised to leave the boy alone. Even so young, Ickes must have been impressive in anger.

He got the opportunity to exercise it again shortly before graduation. He had returned to his room at Snell Hall after classes one day to find his sister Amelia waiting for him. She had walked all the way in from Englewood to tell him that Uncle Sam McCune—he who had provided the Ickes underwear in high school—had taken to dropping in at the Wheeler household to nag her constantly, and that the previous evening he had struck her. Amelia was then fifteen. Ickes had sent her back home with carfare, then went to the Englewood house that evening after dinner. When Sam came by on another disciplinary mission, Ickes told his uncle he would have no more of it. "In some heat I went on to assure him that if he ever laid hand on her again I would come over and thrash him," Ickes said in his memoirs. "I was bigger than Uncle Sam and stronger and he wasn't a very courageous soul anyhow. He almost cringed, he was so apologetic, and he never troubled her again."

Such manly rituals undoubtedly gave him satisfaction, but they were small compensation for the loss of any true sense of home. The Wheeler household had been only a little better than a boardinghouse, and the happiness he had found with the Adkinsons was something borrowed. Certainly there could have been little home feeling to be found in the house on Fifth Avenue in Altoona, with its troubled ghosts, his father lost in the mists of alcohol, his sister Julia tearfully doing her duties and bemoaning the unfairness of life, his brother Felix, having been a most unhappy boy, rapidly evolving into an even unhappier young man. And even this disturbed household was on the verge of disintegration. Shortly after Clair returned to Chicago at summer's end, Felix who—not surprisingly—had a history of running away, escaped for good, leaving high school at the age of seventeen and disappearing somewhere in the West. In November, Julia met and married A. Clinton Hazard, a local foundry worker. Jesse, considerate to a fault, promptly sold the family house and moved in with the new bride and her husband to insure that his daily needs were met. He was forty-nine years old.

"We are a curious and not a very pleasant family," Ickes remarked forty years later.

Back in Chicago, Ickes took a room at his fraternity house on credit, then borrowed a few dollars from Billy Wilson, who was working as a clerk in a law office. With this gelatinous foundation beneath him, he began casting about for something to do with his life. One afternoon he encountered James Westfall Thompson on the street. Thompson had secured a minor teaching position at the university, he told Ickes, and he and Anna were living at the Del Prado Hotel while looking for a permanent home. He invited Ickes to stop by some afternoon for tea, and two days later, he did. He and Anna greeted each other in a perfectly civilized though exquisitely formal manner—"Mrs. Thompson" and "Mr. Ickes"—and during the course of the conversation, Thompson suggested that Ickes apply for a high school teaching position somewhere. Ickes had his doubts, but went ahead and put his name in at an agency. Nothing came of this lukewarm effort, but during a subsequent visit Thompson suggested the possibility of newspaper work. Ickes admitted that his experience on the *Chicago Weekly* pointed in that direction. Thompson knew George Sikes, an editorial writer for Victor Lawson's *Chicago Record,* an Independent Republican sheet, and spoke to him of the graduate. So it was that Ickes began his brief career as a newspaper reporter—or "newshawk," as he preferred to remember it.

It was a felicitous decision, however casually made. This was the beginning of the golden age of American newspaper journalism, a period that extended from about 1890 to World War II, after which the world of journalism, like every other world, changed forever and not always for the better. The men and women whose names survived that remarkable era are invariably described as "legendary," and they defined the reporter's breed for all time—Ring Lardner, Damon Runyan, Gene Fowler, Ray Stannard Baker, Ida Tarbell, Elizabeth Cochran (Nellie Bly), Dorothy Thompson, Stanley Walker, George Ade, Lincoln Steffens, Heywood Broun, Eugene Field, Grantland Rice, Sherman Duffy, Ben Hecht, Charles MacArthur, and a dozen more, all of whom would have seconded H. L. Mencken's memories of his early days with the *Baltimore Sun:* "I was at large . . . with a front seat at every public show, as free of the night as of the day, and getting earfuls and eyefuls of instruction in a hundred giddy arcana, none of them taught in schools."

Ickes himself might have seconded the memories of Ben Hecht, who entered the Chicago branch of this frenzied trade not too many years behind him:

> My years in Chicago were a bright time spent in the glow of new worlds. I was a newspaper reporter. . . . I haunted streets, studios, whore houses, police stations, courtrooms, theatre stages, jails, saloons, slums, mad houses, fires, murders, riots, banquet halls and bookshops. I ran everywhere in the city like a fly buzzing in the works of a clock, tasted more than any fly belly could hold, learned not to sleep (an accomplishment that still clings to me) and buried myself in a tick-tock of whirling hours that still echo in me.

Ickes remembered his four years as a newspaperman with a similarly passionate fondness, although his career was rather more sedate than that of Hecht. Still, it was hugely important to his life, for if Hecht and a hundred others found literature in the experience, Ickes found politics. Even that took him awhile. He started at the *Record* as a lowly space writer, paid at the rate of five dollars a full column of printed copy; the first week, the city editor's copy shears clipped him down to a total of seventy-five cents. He persevered, and in a few weeks Sherman Duffy, then assistant sports editor of the *Tribune* and a fraternity brother, talked him into coming over to the rival paper. Here he was soon making as much as thirty-five dollars a week doing space writing on a beat that included the campus of the University of Chicago. In the fall of 1898 he was seduced back to the *Record* by the offer of a steady salary of twenty dollars a week, a byline, and a position as assistant sports editor. His specialty was football, reporting on the weekend's college games every Monday morning (the caliber of his newspaper writing, it might be noted, was reminiscent of his work for the *Chicago Weekly,* and it is a kindness not to reproduce it here). This satisfied him until sometime in 1899, when the position of assistant political editor under Malcolm McDowell opened up. Ickes went after the job, got it, and entered the very homeland of his soul.

CHAPTER
· 6 ·

Urban Blights

I F ICKES DID NOT become an habitué of those whorehouses and police precincts of the Loop that colored the lives and attitudes of Hecht and his cronies, he did become an intimate of the wardrooms, shysters' offices, government cubbyholes, and convention halls of the peculiar profession called politics—and by his own account learned quite as much from the experience. "There was nothing gentle about big city politics in those days," he wrote in *Autobiography of a Curmudgeon,*

> even from the standpoint of one who was only writing about it. It was the plug-ugly, the heavy-handed manipulator of ballots, the man who could smell out the loot and get to it first, who was in the saddle. He played the tune to which the "businessman in politics" and the stuffed shirts danced, and for which they paid. No softy could meet him or give him orders except on his own terms. . . . I learned to be a realist. I discovered, from my place in the press box, that the ebb and flow of surface political sentiment did not . . . give any true indication of the violent cross currents that run just a little deeper. I became cynically wise to the selfishness and meanness of men when their appetites are involved. . . . I found out, too, that there are men and women who often serve the common good at great self-sacrifice and without any hope of or desire for political reward or even without any, except condemnatory, public recognition of themselves.

If anything, Ickes's evaluation of Chicago politics in the 1890s was probably too kind. British reformer William T. Stead, editor of the *Review of Reviews,* came to see the World's Columbian Exposition and stayed to marvel at a system "built upon bribery, intimidation, bulldozing of every kind, knifing, shooting and the whole swimming in whiskey." He also put it all in context: "Here we have asserted in its baldest and plainest form the working principle on which the smart man of Chicago acts. Everything that is not illegal is assumed by him to be right . . . so long as it is permitted by law or so long as they can evade the law by any subterfuge, they consider they are doing perfectly all right. They believe in the state; they have ceased to believe in God."

Chief among the godless were the aldermen of the city council, as cheerful a set of boodlers as could be found in any city in the land. It was estimated that a seat on the city council came attached to the possibility of anywhere from $15,000 to $25,000 in graft yearly, and one reform group declared that no fewer than fifty-seven of the sixty-eight aldermen from the city's thirty-four wards were on the take. Although coming decades would demonstrate that the love of boodle, like love of mother, country, and the flag, crossed all political lines, most of the aldermen at this time were Democrats, but not even Carter H. Harrison II, the Democratic mayor who had so trounced John Maynard Harlan in 1897, could stand them. The citizens of Chicago, he wrote in his political memoirs, "from lack of interest, supineness, from absolute stupidity had permitted the control of public affairs to be the exclusive appendage of a low-browed, dull-witted, base-minded gang of plug-uglies with no outstanding characteristic beyond an unquenchable lust for money, with but a single virtue, and that not possessed by all, a certain physical courage which enabled each to dominate his individual barnyard."

Harrison may have despised these lowlifes, and fought them when he could, but like any other successful politician he used them when he had to. That was how things got done. Nothing had demonstrated this solid reality more than Harrison's struggle with the forces of corruption as embodied in the person of Charles Tyson Yerkes. By all odds the traction king probably had been the most hated man in Chicago, a sentiment shared by everyone. "He is not safe," Marshall Field had told his fellow businessmen. The opinions of those who had to use his streetcars for transportation would have been expressed more colorfully. Cars were chronically in short supply and poorly maintained. Service was erratic, infrequent, and slow; typically, any car that did clatter down one of his forty-seven separately incorporated lines would be stuffed with angry patrons, most of them dangling precariously from a grip on the straps—

possibly contemplating the fact that since Yerkes denied them the privilege of transfer from one of his lines to another, they might have to pay three or four individual fares in order to lurch to their destinations. When asked why he didn't at least put more cars on his lines, Yerkes had replied with arrogant simplicity, "Why should I? It's the people who hang to the straps who pay you your big dividends."

This reply had become common knowledge by 1897. So had the bribes he had scattered through the Illinois legislature in order to grease passage of "eternal monopoly" bills that would have granted his companies ninety-nine-year franchises. The offer of a $500,000 bribe, it was said, had not been enough to prevent Governor John Altgeld from stamping a veto on every one of the monopoly bills. When similar bills—trimmed down to forty-year franchises this time—failed in the next session of the legislature because of public pressure, Yerkes did manage to squeeze through the Allen Law, which conveniently switched authority to the Chicago City Council by giving this august body the latitude to grant streetcar franchises via city ordinance. Several months into Harrison's first term, the aldermen had succumbed to Yerkes's generous persuasion and authorized just such an ordinance, which then had to be approved by the electorate. Yerkes was not a stupid man; he knew his reputation in Chicago was comparable to that of Attila the Hun, so he bought the *Chicago Inter-Ocean* and used its columns in an attempt to change his image and promote the manifold advantages of his streetcar service. As an added weapon against the opposition of Harrison, who had taken to the streets to avow his firm intention of vetoing the ordinance should it be passed, Yerkes also began to spread money around among the various ward heelers.

Astonishingly enough, this proved his undoing. Two of those ward bosses—perhaps the two most powerful in the city—were "Bathhouse John" Coughlin, a saloon keeper and pious acolyte of the steam bath, and Michael "Hinky-Dink" Kenna, a dapper genius of street-level organization. Kenna's own fame was such that it got the attention of none other than H. G. Wells, who interviewed him for *The Future in America,* published in 1906. "Now Alderman Kenna is a straight man," Wells wrote, "the sort of man one likes and trusts at sight, and he did not invent his profession. He follows his own ideas of right and wrong, and compared with my ideas of right and wrong, they seem tough, compact, decided things. He is very kind to all his crowd. He helps them when they are in trouble . . . he helps them to find employment . . . he stands between them and the impacts of an unsympathetic and altogether too-careless social structure in a sturdy and almost parental way. . . . And whenever you want to do things in Chicago you must reckon carefully with him."

Kenna and Coughlin represented the First Ward, a political satrapy that included the bordellos and gambling dens of the Levee. Their influence was considerable, and after much thought regarding the subtle practicalities of the Yerkes situation, the pair had brought their conclusion to Mayor Harrison. "Mr. Mayor," said Coughlin, "I was talkin' a while back with Senator Billy Mason and he told me, 'Keep clear of th' big stuff, John, it's dangerous. You and Mike stick to th' small stuff; there's little risk and in the long run it pays a damned sight more.' . . . Mr. Marr, we're with you. An' we'll do what we can to swing some of the other boys over." True to their word, when Yerkes dropped by Coughlin's Silver Dollar saloon (Coughlin's tribute to the free-silver policies of William Jennings Bryan) a few days later to hand over a $150,000 bribe to the pair, they turned him down. And early in 1898, when all the votes were counted (and, where necessary, improved, as was the custom), the franchise ordinance was solidly defeated. After the expenditure of millions of dollars, Yerkes finally gave it up in 1899, philosophically selling off most of his streetcar companies for a reputed $20 million and retiring to a Fifth Avenue mansion in New York City to spend the rest of his days (he died in 1905) admiring his collection of fine art, including a thirty-thousand-dollar portrait of himself.*

Harrison's victory over the perfidious Yerkes had enabled him to win easy reelection in 1899. But while he was personally "a respectable figure," as Ickes said of him, he was still a Democrat, which to the city's slowly growing reform element was a condition quite as dangerous and incurable as consumption and to be avoided at all costs. That left the Republicans, but as Ickes described them, they were no less boss-ridden; and if not so flamboyantly corrupt, it probably had less to do with rectitude than with the lack of opportunity:

> It happened that the Republicans, at the time that I went to work for the *Record,* were being welded into a strong and militant machine under questionable but able leadership. Four men stood out—William Lorimer, who had worked his way up from driving a streetcar to dominate the Republican organization in the West Side wards that included the Democratic strong-

---

*Corruption and a dilapidated streetcar system were not Yerkes's only legacies to the city that had made him. Shortly after the University of Chicago opened in 1892, he had donated enough money for the construction of one of the most advanced observatories of the day. Situated at Lake Geneva, Wisconsin, the University of Chicago's Yerkes Observatory was dedicated in 1897. He also achieved a brand of immortality when novelist Theodore Dreiser chose him as the model for the character of Frank Cowperwood in *The Financier* (1912), *The Titan* (1914), and *The Stoic* (1947), a trio of overwrought but historically interesting morality tales.

holds; Henry L. Hertz, a Danish immigrant who had become the political overlord of the Republican Northwest Side wards where the Scandinavian elements were most in evidence; James Pease, who was in control of Lake View, which was overwhelmingly native Republican; and T. N. ("Doc") Jamieson, who ran things in the equally strong independent Republican territory of Hyde Park where I lived.

In the lower rank of political leaders were Fred A. Busse, later Mayor of Chicago, whose power was confined to the near North Side; Charles S. Deneen, soon to be State's Attorney and then Governor and United States Senator, a Lorimer lieutenant who was rapidly building a political principality in the Englewood wards; Tom Braden and Arthur Dixon, who had entrenched themselves in the near South Side wards embracing the "black belt"; Fred Blount, vice president of John R. Walsh's Chicago National Bank, who represented the financial and business interests, but who was an active politician in his own right; John M. Smyth, who owned a big department store in West Madison Street, and Graeme Stewart, a wholesale grocer, who was useful chiefly as window dressing—one of those typical American citizens of business and social standing who occasionally is in politics but seldom of it, who thinks that he is on the inside, who is ostentatiously consulted, and who is pushed forward when the electorate becomes restless and good-government-minded, but who really knows very little, and, in the end, is without influence.

However cynical and patronizing, this description from his *Autobiography* is as good a brief summary of the Republican situation at that time in Chicago as exists anywhere. But left undescribed here were men and women made of stronger stuff than a Graeme Stewart. They were informed, committed, stubborn, influential across a broad spectrum of the city's life, and determined to shake the filth out of it. In Ickes's memory they did not stack up all that well as individual human beings. "I confess that I liked and enjoyed the company of the crooks," he wrote. "They had real human qualities—most of them." On the other hand, "The reformers were aloof and austere. They had a veneer that was like the polish on a slab of granite, and contrasted unfavorably with the warm joviality of the Irish political chieftains." That may well have been; nevertheless, it was with these veneered citizens that he chose to spend the substance of his professional life, and it might be instructive here to take a closer look at the movement from which they sprang and which they embodied so austerely.

CHAPTER

· 7 ·

Exuberance and Wrath

T HE AMERICAN CIVIL WAR, whatever else it may have accomplished,
released forces long held in partial restraint by tradition, by the limits
of economic opportunity, by the complex saraband of political maneuver-
ing and compromise that had kept the North and the South from each
other's throats for more than a generation even as they effectively stifled
the political hopes of the emerging West. Once released, these forces, for
good or ill, could not be called back. Nor were they fully spent during the
war itself. After Appomattox, Howard Mumford Jones has written, "It
was as if the enormous energy concentrated by the Civil War, not satisfied
with killing or wounding a million men or more, could not check itself at
the peace but went on to gigantic verbal clashes over reconstruction,
industry, politics, and theology. Never was oratory more orotund, propaganda more reckless, denunciation more bitter, reform more strident. . . .
A people thus verbally unrestrained must have been filled with exuberance and wrath."

Indeed. Exuberance had obliterated the Indian "menace" that lay west
of the Mississippi, had latticed the land with railroads, had built a cattle
kingdom, had brought an agricultural civilization to the Great Plains,
had gouged gold, silver, and copper out of mines that would have fired the
envy of King Solomon, had built cities unlike those anywhere on earth
and had filled them with millions of immigrants, new blood for the new

land. Free enterprise—never so free as its disciples claimed or would have liked, but free enough—had brought the industrial revolution to full flower, had become the poltergeist of progress, the Great Disturber, moving things around and about, building up and tearing down, shivering the timbers of the social, economic, and political structure of this ship of state.

Exuberance, then, but also wrath. Too many people felt left behind, trapped, oppressed. For every J. P. Morgan whose banking monolith financed industrial production, there were a million laborers who would have echoed the words of a Chicago workingman in 1887. "Land of Opportunity, you say," he told an inquiring and patriotic reporter. "You know damned well my children will be where I am—that is, if I can keep them out of the gutter." For every E. H. Harriman, whose railroads hauled the produce from the American heartland, there were a million farmers who would have cheered the anger of the agricultural utopian, Ignatius Donnelly, in 1892:

> Corruption dominates the ballot-box, the Legislatures, the Congress, and touches even the ermine of the bench. The newspapers are largely subsidized or muzzled, public opinion silenced, business prostrated, our homes are covered with mortgages, labor impoverished and the land concentrated in the hands of the capitalists. . . . A vast conspiracy against mankind has been organized. . . . If not met and overthrown at once it forebodes terrible social convulsions . . . or the establishment of an absolute despotism.

"Plutocracy" was the word such men used to define what they saw as the greatest economic evil of their times: the concentration of wealth in the hands of men like Morgan and Harriman, of the Rockefellers, Vanderbilts, Carnegies, Huntingtons, Du Ponts, Whitneys, Fisks, and Astors of the country, and, yes, Chicago's own George Pullman, Philip Armour, Richard Teller Crane, Marshall Field, and, most assuredly, Charles Tyson Yerkes. And "trust" was the word they gave plutocracy's most pernicious expression—the "Lumber Trust," the "Railroad Trust," the "Oil Trust," the "Coal Trust," the "Sugar Trust," those combinations of capital that served to drive up prices and drive down competition and keep the workingman, the farmer, and all others of the oppressed firmly at the bottom of the economic pyramid. A simpleminded view, perhaps, but no more simpleminded than the response of the "plutocrats" themselves. Those with a powerful religious bent ascribed their lofty position in life to divine intervention, recalling the words of the Reverend Henry Ward Beecher of Brooklyn, New York: "God has intended the great to be great and the little to be little." If that was not authority enough, they could—

and did—turn to the "social Darwinism" carved out of poor Charles Darwin's thoroughly apolitical *Origin of Species* by philosopher Herbert Spencer. The basic rule of human life, like that of all species, Spencer said, was survival of the fittest; therefore, those at the top of the pyramid got there because they were the best. The pious John D. Rockefeller believed it, and taught it solemnly to the children of his Sunday school class: "The American Beauty rose can be produced in the splendor and fragrance which bring cheer to its beholder only by sacrificing the early buds which grow up around it. This is not an evil tendency in business. It is merely the working-out of a law of nature and a law of God."

Simplistic conviction on both sides left little room for compromise but a great deal for violence. And it had come, with greater frequency, greater intensity. In 1873, when Jay Cooke & Company failed, taking with it more than five thousand businesses and throwing hundreds of thousands out of work across the nation, desperate men organized into gangs of thugs and wandered the countryside, terrorizing rural communities, raping, pillaging, burning, and looting—and, in at least one instance, stealing an entire train (on the Rock Island Line). This random violence grew during the bad years that followed, with 5,830 business failures in 1874, 7,740 in 1875, 9,092 in 1876, almost 9,000 again in 1877. In that year, most of the country's railroads decided to take action, lest the value of their dividends decline; they promptly ordered an across-the-board 10 percent cut in wages. The railroad workers took action in turn, going out on strike and laying waste to railroad yards from Canada to California, battling with local police and state militia alike; in Pittsburgh alone, twenty-five people were killed, and 125 locomotives, two thousand cars, a grain elevator, two roundhouses, and the Union Depot were destroyed. From that point forward, the business of America was punctuated constantly by strikes, walkouts, police actions, militia skirmishes, the destruction of property, the systematic violation of constitutional law by the authorities, and, on both sides, mayhem and murder. In the year following the financial panic of 1893, an estimated 750,000 workers across the country were on strike at one time or another.

There was a terrible power in all this anger, and to many observers it seemed that it might disembowel the two-party system itself, leaving the country in the hands of anarchy, communism, or socialism—or all three (definitions were rarely precise). What else could one expect of the Populists, that agglomeration of peckerwood dirt farmers from the beaten South, failed homesteaders from the West, syndicalists, labor agitators, and vague dreamers of social perfection who had never had to meet a payroll in their lives? These were not Nice People, and they were not nice at the top of their lungs. They gathered in Omaha, Nebraska, in the sweltering summer of 1892 and cried out against the plutocrats, against the trusts, against the Vanderbilts and Morgans, against the Democrats and the Republicans, against the labor slavery of the cities, the mortgage slavery of the farms; they demanded the popular election of U.S. senators, an eight-hour day, the nationalization of railroads, a living wage, the right of collective bargaining, a graduated federal income tax with the heaviest percentages carved out of the incomes of the rich, an end to land monopoly, and the institution of referendum and initiative. Power, they bellowed, must be put back in the hands of the People, as God and Thomas Jefferson had intended it. They put up their own man and ran him for President on the Populist ticket. He lost, but the infection had taken hold; ten congressmen, five senators, and three governors (including John P. Altgeld in Illinois) sympathetic to the Populist cause were elected that year. And if the Populist Party itself soon disintegrated from the weight of too many internal conflicts and contradictions, one of those who embodied its principles, William Jennings Bryan, the "boy orator" of Nebraska, captured the Presidential nomination of the Democrats in 1896 and in the ensuing election garnered more votes than any Presidential candidate in history—save his opponent, William McKinley.

Bryan and the principles he carried with him like so many cockleburs on a hayseed's coat terrified the people in the middle, those who were not hardscrabble farmers, swarthy laborers, broken-tongued immigrants, or plutocrats, and it was these people who had beaten him at the polls. Some of them had taken to the hustings themselves to do it. Among them was Theodore Roosevelt (not poor, but no plutocrat either), former assemblyman for the state of New York, former U.S. Civil Service commissioner, currently police commissioner of New York City, and soon to be assistant secretary of the navy. He had stumped the country for McKinley that fall and spoke for a generation of people in the middle when he decried labor violence, the corruption of the cities, the dangerous insanity of socialism, the insidiousness of foreign ideas and foreign elements, and, above all, the threat of Bryanism and all its works. On October 15 he had brought his message to the Chicago Coliseum, where more than thirteen thousand people crowded to hear him give voice to their fears. "It is not merely schoolgirls that have hysterics," he proclaimed. "Very vicious mob-leaders have them at times, and so do well-meaning demagogues when their minds are turned by the applause of men of little intelligence." He had been told that there was a large contingent of students from the university in the audience (among them a very attentive Harold LeClair Ickes), and so he spoke a direct warning to them to avoid "the visionary social reformer . . . the being who reads Tolstoy, or, if he possesses less intellect, Bellamy and Henry George, who studies Karl Marx and Proudhon, and believes that at this stage of the world's progress it is possible to make everyone happy by an immense social revolution, just as other enthusiasts of a similar mental caliber believe in the possibility of constructing a perpetual-motion machine."

It is safe to speculate that virtually every reformer in Chicago was in the Coliseum that day (including a few Roosevelt probably would have considered visionary). Even then, TR's reputation (considerably exaggerated) as a one-man regiment battling the forces of urban corruption preceded him wherever he went, and he was always a good draw, particularly among those who were struggling to find a political and philosophical middle ground between the arrogant greed of high capitalism and the revolutionary forces that would shred the very fabric of the Republic. They had seen, in the streets of their own city, too many indications already of what the future might hold if that middle ground could not be found. They could remember, many of them, Chicago's own violence of 1877, when railroad workers and mobs of the unemployed had rioted for three days, with eighteen deaths and scores of injuries to rioters and policemen alike. They certainly could remember the McCormick Harvesting Machine Company strike of 1886, when proclaimed anarchists— *anarchists!*—had grown so presumptuous as to hold public meetings, including one called by the *Arbeiter Zeitung,* the radical German newspaper, for the evening of May 4 at the Haymarket on Randolph Street between Desplaines and Halsted. During the speechmaking a body of police moved in to break up the meeting, and a sputtering bomb had arched over the crowd and exploded in the midst of the police, killing seven of them and unknown numbers of civilians. Eight men had been tried and convicted of complicity in the bombing and four of them had gone to the gallows for it, including August Spies, editor of the *Arbeiter Zeitung;* one of them had killed himself in jail by biting on a dynamite cap. The death sentences of two of the remaining prisoners had been commuted to life imprisonment by Governor Richard Oglesby; all three surviving prisoners were pardoned by Governor John P. Altgeld in 1893. Some people also remembered, a bit uncomfortably, that the evidence against the eight had been insubstantial at best and that no specific guilt for the act itself had ever been firmly established.

There were other portents even closer in time to that Coliseum rally of 1896. On the evening of October 28, 1893—just hours after he had informed the opening-night audience at the Columbian Exposition that "Chicago has chosen a star" and that "Genius is but audacity"—Mayor

Carter H. Harrison, Sr., had been assassinated on his own doorstep by a pathologically audacious and disappointed office seeker. A few months after that civic horror, the city had experienced the bloodiest strike in its history.

It was perhaps symbolically appropriate that this strike had begun in Pullman Town on the shores of Lake Calumet, for this village was the definitive expression of plutocratic benevolence, hailed the country over as one of the great social experiments of all time. But George Pullman was no airy philanthropist; he had spent five million dollars in the construction of Pullman Town to demonstrate, he said, "that such advantages and surroundings made better workmen by removing from them the feeling of discontent and desire for change which so generally characterize the American workman, thus protecting the employer from the loss of time and money consequent upon intemperance, labor strikes and dissatisfaction which generally result from poverty and uncongenial home surroundings." It was merely good business sense that drove him, he admitted cheerfully; this was illustrated by the fact that the Pullman Land Association, an ostensibly independent corporation with no connection with the Pullman Car Works, was put in charge of the town and was expected to show a profit. It did. Workers paid 20 to 25 percent more for the privilege of living in one of Pullman's neat brick cottages than the equivalent anywhere else in the city. Prices in the company stores and shops in the pleasant surroundings of the town's mall were higher than anywhere else, and even the price of a ticket at the Pullman theater and the fee for the Pullman library were exorbitant, compared to elsewhere in the city. "We are born in a Pullman house," one worker complained, "fed from the Pullman shop, taught in the Pullman school, catechized in the Pullman church, and when we die we shall be buried in the Pullman cemetery and go to the Pullman hell." (But not the Pullman saloon or liquor store; these were prohibited in Pullman Town, and workers had to walk to the nearby village of Kensington for a drink.) They stayed only because it was commonly believed that the company gave preference to its own tenants when work was slack.

Pullman's benevolent instincts came to a halt at the bottom line. When orders for his railroad cars fell low enough to threaten the sanctity of the profit margin, he cut wages and hours. This might have been anticipated by his workers; what was not expected was his refusal to lower the monthly rent on the company cottages (which he continued to insist were under control of the Land Association, not his factory, a claim that deceived no one). When the workers sent a committee to point out to him that many of the men were taking home as little as seven cents a week after deductions for rent and purchases from the various company stores, Pullman refused to meet with them, fired every member of the committee, and had them and their families thrown out of his cottages the following morning. (This wondrous intransigence stirred the amazed indignation even of millionaire industrialist Marcus A. Hanna—William McKinley's chief supporter in 1896—who told fellow members of Cleveland's Union League Club that "A man who won't meet his men halfway is a God-damn fool." On May 11, 1894, three thousand men walked out of Pullman's shops.

Though many of Pullman's workers were secret members of the young American Railway Union, the walkout was a wildcat impulse. Eugene Debs, the union's president, knew that his organization was in no position to carry out a strike successfully and three times early in the walkout attempted to get Pullman to talk about a settlement. Pullman refused, and the union finally voted to initiate a boycott of Pullman cars on June 26; unless the manufacturer agreed to arbitrate, the union said, no train with a Pullman car in it would be allowed to move after that date. He refused and the boycott commenced, and if most trains did in fact move, it was only because they were heavily guarded by police, special deputies, state militia, and finally federal troops sent in by President Grover Cleveland—and many of these had not moved without mob violence, which inevitably spread from the railroad yards to the city streets in the usual riot of destruction and burning.

Young Harold L. Ickes, trying to get back to Altoona that summer, got his first exposure to the brutal reality of urban discord. "I tried to go home this afternoon," he wrote in his diary for July 6, "but found that the trains were not running over the B & O. . . . The RR strike has been getting worse and worse. Troops are coming from a distance." He had no better luck the next day: "I could not get home today. The soldiers and the mob had a 'scrap' in which some of the mob were killed." Finally, on July 8: "I . . . got out of Chicago today but under a guard of soldiers. There were long lines of burnt cars all along the tracks. Policemen and soldiers were stretched all along the tracks."

The strike was quickly broken, as Debs had feared (he went to jail, for the first of many times), and on August 2 the Pullman factory was open for business again. At least twelve men had died. Three years later, so did George Pullman; as his will directed, his casket was placed in a room-sized pit and completely covered in cement reinforced with steel girders. Even in death, he remained immovable.

Chicago settlement worker Jane Addams remembered that terrible summer of 1894 well, and in 1912 gave it the cool analysis characteristic of her orderly and kindly mind. Pullman, she said, had been a "modern Lear," who "assumed that he himself knew the needs of his men, and so far from wishing them to express their needs he denied to them the simple rights of trade organization." He had "cultivated the great and noble impulses of the benefactor, until the power of attaining a simple human relationship with his employees, that of frank equality with them, was gone from him." It was a failing common to those of Pullman's instincts, she emphasized. "Lack of perception is the besetting danger of the egoist . . . and philanthropists are more exposed to this danger than any other class of people within the community. . . . In so far as philanthropists are cut off from the influence of the *Zeit-Geist,* from the code of ethics which rule the body of men . . . so long as they are 'good to people' rather than 'with them' they are bound to accomplish a large amount of harm." Finally: "It sometimes seems as if the shocking experiences of that summer, the barbaric instinct to kill, roused on both sides . . . can only be endured if we learn from it all a great ethical lesson."

Jane Addams, though she doubtless would have dismissed the notion out of hand, was herself an ethical lesson—and if she was "good to people," she most assuredly was also "with them." Born to privilege in Cedarville, Illinois, in 1860, she had been raised up and educated in all the prim imperatives of Victorian ladyhood—"a little charity, a lot of culture, and travel in Europe," as one historian has described it. She was, however, born with curvature of the spine, and this disability, combined with fits of depression, kept her periodically bedridden for as long as six months at a time. But during an 1887 trip to England with Ellen Gates Starr, a friend from her college days at Rockford Academy, she encountered the Toynbee Hall Settlement, a center of social work in the Whitechapel slums of London. She and Miss Starr returned to America determined to establish just such a place in the heart of an American city. They chose Chicago, and after months of searching found a dilapidated survivor of the fire of 1871 on Halsted Street between Polk and Ewing; it would serve as their own Toynbee Hall. However decrepit, the place had good bones, and once restored it served very nicely as the heart of a complex that grew to five additional buildings by 1900, all of them designed in the Queen Anne fashion of Toynbee Hall itself by architect Allen Bartlit Pond (ultimately, there would be twelve structures filling the entire block). It was called Hull-House.

Here was the very core of poverty, the fetid contradiction of urban America. Politically, the section was known as the Nineteenth Ward; in humanitarian terms, it was a lime pit. "The idea underlying our self-government breaks down in such a ward," said Miss Addams (as she would be addressed all her life) in one of her early fund-raising speeches.

> The streets are inexpressibly dirty, the number of schools inadequate, sanitary legislation unenforced, the street lighting bad, the paving miserable and altogether lacking in the alleys and smaller streets, and the stables foul beyond description. . . . The houses of the ward, for the most part wooden, were originally built for one family and are now occupied by several. . . . Rear tenements flourish; many houses have no water supply save the faucet in the back yard, there are no fire escapes, the garbage and ashes are placed in wooden boxes which are fastened to the street pavements.

With a magnificent stubbornness that would later inspire British labor leader John Burns to canonize her as "the only saint America had produced" and in 1930 win her the Nobel Peace Prize, she reached out to this collection of hovels and brought into the warmth and safety of Hull-House battered wives, homeless children, and child prostitutes; she fed the hungry, taught the uneducated, nursed the sick, employed the unemployable as grass-roots social workers, formed neighborhood associations, established boys' clubs, petitioned landlords, police, city officials, politicians, businessmen, and the rich with a cool, quiet, professional, irritating, and often successful persistence that gained her plenty of enemies but whole divisions of supporters, most of whom idolized her.

It was around Miss Jane Addams and the work at Hull-House that the bulk of the Chicago reformers coalesced—in spirit and often in fact—seeking solutions to the political and economic anarchy that threatened to destroy their world. They were a noteworthy collection themselves. Most closely related to Hull-House itself in the 1890s were Miss Addams's companion, Ellen Gates Starr; the architect, Allen Bartlit Pond; Helen Culver, Charles Hull's niece, who owned the original mansion and much of the land around it and who had given Miss Addams a free permanent leasehold on the property; Mary Kenney, an Irish worker and trade-union organizer, who established a neighborhood boarding club for working women with the help of Hull-House financing; Florence Kelly, who would become the pioneer inspector of factories for the state of Illinois; Julia Lathrop, who began her long career in social work at Hull-House; and Dr. Alice Hamilton, who made such a name in the field of public health during her years in Chicago that she became the first woman professor in the history of Harvard Medical School.

Those who hovered at the edge of this remarkable world, giving money, lending their names and influence, sitting on committees, and sometimes volunteering for active service in the complex itself, included a representative sampling of the city's social, intellectual, financial, and political elite: William Rainey Harper, until his death in 1906; Julius Rosenwald, senior partner in the firm of Sears, Roebuck; Louise de Koven Bowen, a socialite widow who had once used her influence to get herself appointed garbage inspector for the Nineteenth Ward and whose fury over conditions was such that more than half the city's sanitation-inspection bureau was fired; Lyman Gage, president of the First National Bank and founder of the Civic Federation and the Municipal Voters League; Cook County judge Orrin N. Carter, who would challenge the regular Republicans for the gubernatorial nomination in 1900 (and lose); Charles Crane, son of the bathroom magnate Richard Teller Crane, who gave his own money away like a fool at a fire and once even persuaded his reluctant father to donate $100,000 to Hull-House for a nursery; Victor Lawson, owner of the *Chicago Record* and Ickes's employer; Mrs. Potter Palmer, of the Palmer House Palmers; Anita McCormick Blaine, daughter of Cyrus McCormick; Dr. Henry Baird Favill, president of the City Club and the Chicago Tuberculosis Institute; a handful of young Independent Republican hopefuls, like John Maynard Harlan; and, finally, Clair Ickes's lost love, Anna Wilmarth Thompson, who with her mother, Mary Wilmarth, was one of the staunchest benefactors of Hull-House.

These and other righteous pilgrims were Chicago's contingent of middle-class activists (middle class in their basic values, no matter how rich some of them may have been) who would in time rise up and join with like-minded reformers the country over to carry the banners of the crusade called Progressivism, perhaps the most important third-party movement in American history. For now, as an old century gave way to a new, these good people would largely confine themselves to the manifold shortcomings of Chicago. And if he later denigrated many of them as impractical *naïfs* lost in the jungle of urban politics or cold fish with little fellow feeling for those whom they were determined to save, Clair Ickes became very much a part of them, embraced their values as his own, took on their indignation and their principles, befriended them, stood up for them, promoted them, and fought for them. Long after most of them were dead or lost to conservatism or apathy, he would still be at it, often standing alone on the barricades, wrapped in the certitudes they had given him.

CHAPTER
· 8 ·

Tinkering with the Machine

T HE YEAR 1900 saw the young political reporter for the *Chicago Record* pulled out of the local scene that had begun to fascinate him and thrust into the frenzy of a Presidential election year. It was assumed that it would be McKinley versus Bryan again: Presidents are rarely denied a second nomination by their party, and the Democrats had no one in the offing who could draw the votes that Bryan could. The most interesting development on the horizon was the emergence of a national hero from "the splendid little war," Theodore Roosevelt, now governor of New York, whose regiment of Rough Riders had distinguished themselves in Cuba at the battles of Las Guasimas and San Juan—especially San Juan, when Lieutenant Colonel Roosevelt had led his horseless cavalry in assaults on Kettle Hill and San Juan Heights. Roosevelt, it was said, was a shoo-in as McKinley's running mate, and there were even rumors that his friends might stampede the convention in Philadelphia and get him nominated in McKinley's stead. That would have been news indeed, and Victor Lawson enlarged the *Record*'s crew for the June 19 convention session by sending Ickes east to Philadelphia with William E. Curtis, George Ade, Malcolm McDowell, and cartoonist John T. McCutcheon.

Lawson might as well have saved his money. McKinley was routinely nominated and Roosevelt was swiftly drafted for second place on the ticket in spite of Mark Hanna's anguished cry: "Don't any of you realize that there's only one life between this madman and the Presidency?" From Ickes's point of view, the Philadelphia convention was noteworthy mainly for the presence of his father, Jesse. In fact, for Ickes the most noteworthy political event of the previous year may have been Jesse's election as city controller of Altoona. It had been Jesse's second attempt to get elected to something (he had vainly sought a seat on the city council fifteen years before), and apparently all the years of glad-handing and good fellowship at the Logan House bar and his numerous organizational ties had finally paid off—he whipped his Democratic opponent 3,021 to 2,609. Not only that, he had been reelected in 1900, and perhaps as a gesture of filial pride in spite of himself, Ickes had gotten his father a ticket to the Philadelphia convention. They even managed to spend some time with each other, and if it was less than the warmest of family reunions, it had its moments, at least as Ickes remembered it: "He was delighted and he and I had a very good time together in Philadelphia, even if my duties were so heavy that I did not see much of him. . . . I have always been glad, not only that I was able to give him a bit of pleasure, but that we had an opportunity for an association in circumstances that were not strained and out of which, I am sure, both of us developed a better understanding of and a higher regard for each other." (He then added, out of one of his many compulsions, the following unnecessary elaboration: "I have never felt that in this softening in later years of my attitude toward my father I have been disloyal in any respect to my mother. . . . I loved her devotedly during her life and I have loved her memory just as devotedly.")

From Philadelphia, the news team entrained for Kansas City to watch the Presidential cotillion of the Democrats. Hotel accommodations were inadequate, and they were forced to bed down in a single large room with a number of additional reporters in the heat that settles down over that prairie city like a stovelid every summer. "I was so hot, so uncomfortable, and so over-worked," Ickes reported in *Autobiography of a Curmudgeon,* "that I have never had a desire since to see Kansas City." There was little of substance to report; after some wrangling over the platform, Bryan was duly nominated and the campaign was launched. As he had in 1896, McKinley would campaign from his front porch in Canton while crowds mutilated his helpless lawn. Bryan, as he had in the previous campaign, would whistle-stop much of the nation, but this time he had the monstrously energetic Roosevelt to contend with. It was no contest: by November 3, Roosevelt had made 673 speeches in 567 towns in twenty-four states, while Bryan had only 546 speeches in 493 towns in eighteen states.

Ickes was sent to St. Paul to cover Roosevelt's opening campaign remarks and while there had the opportunity to meet the candidate for the first time. Ickes was in the company of Bernard J. Mullaney, a conservative reporter then working for the *Chicago Times-Herald*, and as he reported it, his fellow newshawk imparted an observation eerily reminiscent of Mark Hanna's yelp of outrage during the Republican convention: "As Mullaney and I loitered in the broad gallery of the hotel that overlooked the foyer, arm-swinging Roosevelt came striding toward us. He was alone, and we stopped him on the chance of getting something to write about. . . . When Roosevelt had gone on his way, Mullaney turned to me and said: 'That man's crazy, and it would be just his luck if McKinley should die and he became President.' "

If Roosevelt himself had anything interesting to say during that brief encounter, Ickes made no mention of it. For the rest of the campaign, he was assigned directly to the Republican National Headquarters to cover any developments that might issue from the office of the national chairman, Mark Hanna. Ickes grew to like the chairman in spite of his reputation as the plutocrat's plutocrat, an amoral man in love with power and capable of buying it when necessary. "Personally," Ickes wrote,

> Hanna was a likable man—short and squat, with a round, friendly face. The most distinguishing of his features were his eyes. They were full of life and vitality and power. . . .
>
> Hanna did not regard the prodigal use of money in campaigns as anything improper, especially if it were Republican money. . . . He was "saving" America from the dangerous radicals of the day, just as other representatives of privilege, both before and since, have justified corruption and bribery to maintain the established order as "a patriotic deed" in the "public interest."

Ickes admired the man's candor, if not his politics or his methods, and when the campaign ended and Hanna passed out sapphire scarf pins as mementos to the reporters who had covered his activities, Ickes accepted his cheerfully.

The nineteenth century ended with the Republic safely in the hands of McKinley, Roosevelt, and Hanna. But Ickes's place, so recently established, in that world would be badly shaken as the twentieth century began.

Another Altoona chapter was about to close, colored by a certain Stygian comedy. Late in January, 1901, Jesse Ickes had checked into the city hospital for treatment of a bladder infection. He grew swiftly worse, and by January 31 he was too weak to hold a pen. This was a matter of some consequence to the city employees of Altoona, for they could not get their paychecks until the authorizing warrants had been countersigned by Jesse as city controller. The *Altoona Evening Gazette* for February 1 explained the dilemma: "Yesterday a rubber stamp bearing the signature of Mr. Ickes was taken to his bedside with the batch of warrants for the salaries of city employees. The sick man feebly attempted to use the stamp signature, but in his weakened condition he found it impossible.

" 'I hope the boys won't be angry,' he said sadly, 'I can't help them out today.' "

Nor could he help the boys out the next day. By then, his doctors had concluded he had to have an operation that could only be performed in Pittsburgh, so early on the morning of February 1 they ordered him taken by ambulance the few blocks down to the railroad depot for the morning train to Pittsburgh. Unfortunately, a hospital bureaucrat discovered a rule prohibiting use of the hospital ambulance wagon for anything but deliveries *to* the hospital and chose this occasion to enforce it (perhaps he was a Democrat). After several hours, Jesse, by now delirious with pain, finally was loaded into a police patrol wagon and bounced through the rutted streets to a later train. He did not arrive at the Pittsburgh hospital until late that afternoon and died shortly after the operation on February 2, fifteen days short of his fifty-third birthday.

Clair, now an orphan in fact as well as in spirit, did not get to Pittsburgh until his father was already dead. Justifiably enough, he was in a fury over the way Jesse had been treated, and after he had accompanied his father's body back to Altoona and had seen the casket lowered into yet another grave in the Ickes family plot in Fairview Cemetery, he let it be known in newspaper interviews that a lawsuit was by no means out of the question. Most of the newspapers agreed that the hospital had been meticulous to the point of absurdity. Ickes did not, however, follow through on his threats, perhaps wanting nothing more than to put Altoona and all it signified behind him once and for all.

Close after his father's death came the demise of his newspaper career. In February, Victor Lawson sold the *Record* to Herman H. Kohlsaat, who had parlayed a single bakery, where he also sold sandwiches, into a string of cafeterias and a fortune he enjoyed by investing much of it in politics and newspapers (it was he who had sold the *Inter-Ocean* to Yerkes in 1897). In a newspaper tradition that already had become time-honored by the turn of the century, Kohlsaat promptly fired most of Lawson's old staff, then merged the *Record* with his *Herald*. Among those who were out on the street was ace political reporter Clair Ickes. Through the intercession of friends, he landed a place on the *Chronicle,* owned by John R. Walsh, a banker who contributed heavy oil to the Republican machine. Ickes did not find the paper's politics congenial; nor did he enjoy being relegated to general assignment reporting. After two weeks, he resigned to become secretary of the Citizens' Association, the oldest if the smallest of Chicago's reform organizations, with the mission of overseeing city expenditures to sniff out any traces of graft, waste, and extravagance. He never returned to newspaper work, though it was not the Citizens' Association that captured his heart; totaling up numbers regarding the profligate waste of paper clips and carbon paper in city government was not, he felt, the best use of either his talents or his energy. After a few weeks of it, he was ready for a change.

It came to him in the person of John Maynard Harlan, the ambitious standard-bearer of Independent Republicanism. During Ickes's newspaper days, with a shared interest in the intricacies of Chicago politics, he and Harlan had become reasonably close acquaintances. After the mayoral election of March 1901—when the seemingly eternal Carter H. Harrison II and the Democratic machine had beaten yet another regular Republican—Harlan and his Independents came to believe that 1903 might be his year. All agreed he needed not only funding but also an organization in place well ahead of any attempt at capturing the Republican nomination; the lack of both had helped to defeat him in 1897. Forty thousand dollars was raised and Ickes was hired at twenty-five dollars a week to lay the foundation for the campaign.

He took an obscure office in an old building in the Loop on the east side of Dearborn Street between Madison and Washington. This was the heart of the ward whose Republican workings were controlled by State Senator Fred Busse. Harlan lived in this district, too, and its delegates were the key to his nomination; unless he could control the delegates in his own ward, he had little chance of capturing support elsewhere in the city. Fortunately, Busse had been an early ally of Harlan, and Ickes and the candidate were counting on his backing when it came time to go public with the campaign. In the meantime, the quiet gathering of information was paramount. "My name appeared nowhere in the building," Ickes remembers, "and I had no telephone. A bare handful knew what I was doing. My friends at the university thought I had some kind of job downtown, and people downtown thought I was doing something at the university." (He was still living at his fraternity house, sharing a room with college friend Stacey Mosser.)

In the office, he combed newspapers and magazines, clipping and pasting into scrapbooks any and every item he could find that related to local political doings. He built a cross-indexed card catalogue that served as a swift guide not only to this material but also to the political geography of the city and especially Busse's ward, from the saloons, gambling dens, and brothels of the West Side to the posh apartment houses and mansions of Lake Shore Drive on the East. Of primary concern in this grubby work was anything having to do with the city's streetcar system, for the traction situation would be a major issue in the coming campaign—and in many to follow. The departure of Charles Tyson Yerkes had left a tortured legal and financial snarl that the courts would not fully untangle until 1942. More important, it had left the city's streetcars in the control of not one villain but many villains, whose manipulations were all that more difficult to track. The cars continued to be badly crowded and in dreadful repair, service remained execrable, fares were inconsistent and uncontrolled, and the city council was still bribed regularly. As a kind of sidebar to his work for Harlan, Ickes helped to found the Strap Hangers' League to publicize the traction outrage and lobby for its improvement (the possibility of municipal ownership of the system soon raised its socialistic head within this group); not coincidentally, the League would be one of Harlan's chief supporters.

On the street, Ickes retraced the routes he had followed as a newspaper reporter, wandering in and out of ward halls, saloons, county and municipal offices, wherever the spoor of politics led him, casually chatting with aldermen, lawyers, bartenders, bureaucrats, ward heelers, and precinct workers, filing data in his head and carrying it back to his office to plug it into his growing card catalogue. "I became a human sponge," he said. If nothing else, Harlan was sure to be the best informed of the candidates come 1903.

Among the sherds of information picked up during these excursions were rumors that Fred Busse, Harlan's erstwhile friend and supporter, might not be the rock they had supposed. As time went on, it became increasingly clear to Ickes that while he was painstakingly constructing a network for Harlan's use, Busse was busily knitting up the strands of support for Graeme Stewart, the "window-dressing" grocer-politician, as Ickes described him, who had decided to run for mayor. Ickes went to Harlan and told him it was time to confront Busse. Harlan at first refused to believe him, but when he discovered that he could neither get an appointment with Busse nor get him to talk on the telephone, he was persuaded. The pair finally encountered Busse one afternoon in the foyer of a downtown building and cornered him. Harlan was not a big man, but he was young, well-built, and angry. "Busse was fundamentally yellow," Ickes wrote, "as most betrayers are. At first he tried to bluff and hedge but finally, under pressure, he admitted the truth of what I had been telling Harlan. Instead of breaking him in two right there, as he could have done, Harlan stung him with a few verbal jabs and we contemptuously left the miserable creature cringing in the middle of the foyer."

Leaving Busse cringing most likely gave both of them pleasure, but it did not alter the situation. With the ward boss in control of the delegates that Harlan needed, he had no chance at the nomination. He was ready to give it up, citing, among other things, his wife's objection to the whole idea of politics. Ickes argued that if he dropped out of the race, no matter how hopeless it might be, the decision would be a permanent one; he would lose forever the support he had built up since 1897 and his political career would effectively be over. He had to show the good people of Chicago that he was willing to make a fight for it. Ickes, who it must be admitted had little to lose, was certainly ready to make a fight for it, and he prevailed; Harlan stayed in the race.

However reluctant he may have been to continue, once the decision was made, Harlan was magnificent, in Ickes's opinion. So was Ickes, in Ickes's opinion. In truth, he probably was. The heat of a campaign was his natural element, fighting for a cause that was just and right (even if hopeless) his personal path of glory. What is more, he was in charge—a position that brought him such simple joy all his life that it is not difficult to forgive him the posturing and hyperbole with which he often reported it. This was his pride and his definition, and he was good at it—tireless and bustling, able to juggle time and responsibilities with a fierce competence. He worked fifteen, sixteen, seventeen hours a day as campaign manager, press agent, general secretary, precinct worker, canvasser. "If there had been a band," he wrote

> I would have been it, too. And it would have been brass. . . . I rented the halls, arranged for the printing and distribution of handbills, took charge of the publicity, and combed the neighborhoods for influential citizens to preside at meetings. Whenever I failed in that, I introduced Harlan myself. At the outset of our speaking campaign I gave out press releases in the form of excerpts from Harlan's statements. Later, as the campaign steamed up, I prepared advance copies of his speeches, so that before his noonday meetings . . . all newspapers were supplied. This method was new then and we got wonderful publicity.

As the nominating convention approached, Harlan was speaking to as many as six audiences a day, in every possible setting from the stage of McVicker's Theater to crowded church basements.

It was furiously exciting, and it was futile. At the convention, Busse and the Republican organization "delivered to Graeme Stewart almost as one man." But Harlan had indeed proved his ability and his willingness to fight, and it would be remembered during the next campaign, in 1905.

Ickes had shown something, too, and Stewart's people asked him to take over publicity for the campaign to unseat Harrison. Their offer of fifty dollars a week was nothing to sneeze at in those days, and he accepted the job like a good professional. At first he took some comfort in Stewart's assurances that his position on the traction issue was "the same as John Harlan's," but it soon became clear to Ickes that Stewart had little knowledge of, and even less interest in, the subject. Ickes wrote thundering denunciations of streetcar companies regardless and handed them out to the press. He knew his reporters; they rarely checked a press release against what a candidate actually said, and his message got exposure in spite of Stewart's apathy. Not that this did any good; early in April the voters returned Harrison to the mayor's office. Among these voters was Clair Ickes, consummately the Independent Republican.

CHAPTER
· 9 ·

Triangulations

A<small>MONG THE CHILDREN</small> of alcoholics there often arises a powerful need for attachments, human connections that provide anchors in a shifting and unreliable emotional world. An alcoholic parent obliterates emotional security, and the child raised in such an environment frequently spends the rest of his life in an attempt to fashion his own security system by entanglements that sometimes contradict logic and rationality, demanding more of himself and those to whom he has become attached than the human animal is normally capable of giving. At its most virulent, this need can become pathological, creating misery, resentment, and despair for everyone concerned. None of that matters, however; it is the attachment that signifies, and it is the attachment that will be maintained and controlled at all costs.

There is no better explanation for what Anna Wilmarth Thompson and Harold LeClair Ickes, both the children of alcoholic fathers, now did with their lives, however unconsciously. Rationality certainly had nothing to do with it. The process began innocently enough. In 1899, Anna had given birth to a son and had burdened the child with the Christian name of Wilmarth. By then, she had also erected a comfortable home at 5747 Washington (now Blackstone) Avenue in a fashionable section of the city. (It was she who financed it, since Thompson, just beginning his academic career, was hardly better off than his erstwhile competitor, Clair Ickes.) Ickes was an occasional visitor, and by the time Wilmarth was two years old and talking, he had become "Uncle Clair" to the boy. Still, the relationship was casual enough, and Ickes says he was astounded when in 1901 Thompson came to pay a call on him at the fraternity house while Ickes was recovering from a bout with appendicitis. Thompson did not merely visit him; he became quite insistent that Ickes come and live with him and Anna while convalescing. Ickes, dumbfounded, just as insistently declined. That time.

Two years later, after Harlan's second defeat, Thompson came to him again. He informed Ickes that Anna had taken Wilmarth and herself off for a long visit with relatives in the South and that both of them wanted Clair to stay with James while she was gone. This invitation was somewhat more difficult to resist. For nearly six years Ickes had been living in the fraternity house with Stacey Mosser, a good friend but one whose company probably was beginning to pall. The prospect of having his own room, with bath, in the best house that upper-middle-class Chicago luxury could offer must have been appealing. Money may also have been a consideration. Living as cheaply as he did, he probably had saved a fair amount from his various salaries, and he still had his share of his father's tiny patrimony to fall back on. Still, he was now putting his sister Amelia through the University of Chicago, having placed her own inheritance in trust for her, and the opportunity of living rent-free for a few weeks must have had its attractions, particularly now that he was out of a job. In any case, he packed up his things and moved in with James, as requested.

It was not likely that James had much, if anything, to say about all this. Who was or was not invited to stay at 5747 Washington Avenue was not his decision to make. Anna ran a tight household and made no bones about who was in charge of it. If anything, she viewed James's ability along these lines with monumental contempt, as revealed by an incident that had taken place the previous August while she and the child had been off on another trip. James had apparently informed her by letter that one of the servants had enjoyed the company of a visitor overnight without permission. He had done little about it, save reprimanding the woman gently. Anna was so enraged by the news that she sent him two letters by return mail. "My servants are *not* allowed company over night and Edith knows this perfectly," she wrote in one version. "She must have laughed at your very evident fear of her. It is all very well to be kind but not at another's expense and it simply means that you could not brace up and face the situation." She then had added, "And oh, how hard it is for me to be patient with just that sort of moral coward. . . . Don't moan about how good we have been to her—that's nonsense. Just lay down the law and make her see you mean it. . . . Oh, boy, if you could only know how my heart sinks when you show yourself so unable to brace up to a situation." The second version was hardly better: "If by the 16th I do not hear from you that you have *tried* to be a man I will write from here and dismiss her. . . . I am tempted to do as other women do. Close my house when I go away and leave you at the mercy of clubs. If you are afraid you may tell Edith that I have written only I warn you that if you do she will despise you as I do. For Heaven's sake James be a *man*. I *hate* a coward."

Whatever James may truly have felt about Ickes's visit, he and Clair got along comfortably enough, probably because they saw little of each other outside the meals taken together; Ickes spent most of his time with political cronies, and Thompson was either teaching at the university or ensconced in his upstairs study, reading and writing. It must have been with some regret that Ickes prepared to leave just before Anna's return in August. But James would have none of it, he told him. He and Anna had determined, he said, that Clair should continue to live with them until he chose to marry. "As there was not the slightest prospect of my marrying," Ickes remarked in his memoirs, "this seemed a remote contingency. I was not paying attention to any girl and I had no desire to marry. I had found that I could get along quite comfortably without a woman in my life. This is as good an occasion as any," he went on,

> for me to say that until after I had been out of college for some time I had not lost my "virginity." I must have been about twenty-four or twenty-five years old when this occurred. Then for a couple of years I had sporadic sexual experiences, but as in no instance were my emotions involved, I got no spiritual satisfaction out of them, even if I did have physical relief. With my background I could not be other than ashamed of these experiences and I had come to the decision that I would resume my continence and maintain it until I married. But marriage was still in the indefinite future.

Ickes made polite noises of refusal to Thompson's offer, but James was adamant (one can only assume that he was under strict orders not to let Ickes escape) and finally talked him into staying at least until Anna got back. When she arrived, she fixed those powerful dark eyes on him and added her own insistence. Her home was his home, she said. Nor would she accept any rent; that would have put her in the position of someone forced to take in boarders, a condition beneath her station in life. Ickes tells us he was terrified of losing his independence; he also tells us that he succumbed.

One of the principal attractions in this situation may have been the child Wilmarth. He was an engaging and affectionate little boy, and Ickes held a tender regard for children all his life. The child got little enough love from his father, most of whose affections were relegated to the complexities of the Middle Ages, and he turned to his Uncle Clair with an endearing and flattering devotion. Even so, after a few weeks Ickes began to have misgivings; there was more going on here than met his not very perceptive eye, he tells us. There certainly was—much more. In the first place, James himself apparently had gotten up enough nerve to tell Anna that her obvious regard for Clair—and apparently his for her—was not appreciated, for sometime later that summer she had written him from Martha's Vineyard, where the family kept a summer place. In contrast to her earlier letters, this one was admirable in its restraint; what is more, it professed to offer James a choice:

> As for Mr. Ickes, I believe you are wrong, but whether you are wrong or not, you know me well enough to know that, my friendship once given, I cannot withdraw it. He may make me suffer some day but he can never hurt my soul as distrust would. It is out of my power to stop caring [for Clair] but it is not out of my power to prevent any worry to you and if you have withdrawn the friendship, loyalty and love which you once professed for him . . . he must go out of your house. That is only right.

Thompson was not stupid enough to take this offer at face value, any more than he was deluded by the reference to "his" house. He did not ask Ickes to leave. But he must have made his feelings known to Anna privately from time to time, possibly even violently, for in the middle of September Anna wrote to Thompson's brother, Wayne, in New York, asking his advice. Wayne Thompson's reply reveals yet another ingredient in this operatic stew:

> It does no good to say "I thought," or "I told you so" but all the same I was afraid of James' actions and in his attitudes towards Clair, who is as fine a fellow in my opinion as ever drew breath, I was positive. . . . The substance of my opinion on that part of it is—no matter how unpleasant it becomes for you and Clair, and it will eventually be extensively so, do not let him leave the house. Keep him right there and even if things get so bad that he feels he must go make him stay. Confide in him if you think best. He will never betray you and will stand by you through thick and thin. . . . James is a mental and a physical coward as well as moral. It is hard for me to say that about my own brother, but I believe it.

Ickes had also written Thompson's brother independently, asking "what was what" at 5747, and Wayne's reply was even more strident:

For the sake of a woman in trouble and especially when that woman is Anna, whom both of us owe so much, it is the duty of at least one of us to remain in the house. If you can not see your way clear to stay then I must return to Chicago. Anna is *unsafe* in the house with James. He is a moral and physical coward and to a certain extent mental. . . . But with a man in the house of your moral courage and force to back up your physical ability he is, and ever will be, afraid to go too far. But if Anna is left alone, defenseless with him, I dare not say to what limits he will go. It is hard indeed for me to write these things about my brother but I believe all I write and more.

Duty called and Ickes stayed. If Wayne Thompson's exhortations had not been enough, Anna's soon would be. One night when James was off at a historical conclave and the two of them had returned from an evening at the theater, Anna unburdened herself in the kitchen over cheese and crackers. Before he knew what was happening, Ickes remembered,

she was telling me that she was very unhappy and had been so from the day that she had married James. In considerable detail she told me of their life together from the beginning. He not only had been inconsiderate; he had been brutal to her, that is, brutal on the highly sensitized plane on which they lived. He had no regard for her feelings; he was not interested either in her or in Wilmarth; history was the only thing that intrigued him and she was persuaded that he had married her because her money would make it easy for him to live the kind of a life that he wanted to live. On several occasions he had struck her.

Any resistance he may have felt dissolved in the face of this direct appeal, redolent with the memory of the night his mother had come to him fifteen years before. He could not leave now even if he had wanted to—and it is likely that at the deepest core of him he did not want to. Here was a tangle of attachment that had powerful, if unrecognized attractions, and he and Anna fed on it, each of them convinced of their calm control over a situation that in fact left them helpless before the force of their darkest instincts. It was, in short, a most unhealthy scenario in which they had become the players, and it ran for an extraordinarily long time. For his part, Thompson apparently decided to make the best of a very bad thing. As his wife and Clair grew inexorably closer, he retreated deeper and deeper into the world of kings and commoners, princes and paupers, of dynastic squabbles and court intrigues hardly more deranged and complicated than the history being made under his own roof.

This was the last gasp of the Victorian age, and all the parties involved turned an implacably civilized face to the world outside the house at 5747

Washington. Clair was soon accepted by unknowing friends and relatives as just another member of the family—rather like a distant cousin who made himself useful around the house.

In the autumn of 1903, Ickes decided to enter the University of Chicago Law School, and it was Mary Wilmarth, Anna's mother, who staked him to this second stage of his education with quarterly loans of $180 at 5 percent interest. (All were subsequently repaid, he takes time to note in his unpublished memoirs, although he does not mention the loan in *Autobiography of a Curmudgeon.*) The Law School had opened just a year earlier, in 1902. Organized by Joseph H. Beale, on loan from the faculty of the Harvard Law School, the school's philosophy and curricula were strongly influenced by the new "case method" of instruction established at Harvard by Christopher Columbus Langdell; as such, students learned their law less from the traditional study of treatises on "principles" than from the detailed analysis of actual cases in which those principles had been revealed and applied. This would equip them, Langdell had written, not only with a theoretical knowledge of the doctrines of law but with "such mastery of these as to be able to apply them with constant facility and certainty to the evertangled skein of human affairs." It was excellent training for any lawyer with a bent for political and social service, and the practical application of theory was a discipline especially attractive to Ickes, who viewed himself all his life as a hard-nosed pragmatist—however baroque his personal life may have been. At twenty-nine, he was older than all of his fellow students and some of his professors, but he attacked these studies with the ferocity he brought to almost everything; he would manage to graduate cum laude in 1907.

Not without interruptions, however. One of these was an infection early in 1904 that required an operation to remove the mastoid bone in back of his left ear. He refused to go to the hospital for this—the memory of what had happened to poor Jesse may have been too fresh—so it was done on a kitchen table in an upstairs room at 5747. The incision was a long time healing, and one day while he was recuperating, Anna came to his bedroom. They had a violent argument over some forgotten point. During the course of this battle, Ickes's incision exploded with blood—he ascribed it to the stress of the argument and the tension that built up as he manfully held his own temper—and it took two doctors and several hours of packing and pressure to stop the hemorrhaging. Even after the wound finally healed, he continued to have periodic discharge from the ear and there would be two more operations, during the last of which, in January

1907, the middle ear was entirely removed, leaving him almost completely deaf on the left side.

School was interrupted again early in 1905, when John Harlan asked him to become his campaign manager for one more try at the mayoralty. Remarkably enough, this time Harlan had the Republican nomination assured even before he started. In his *Autobiography*, Ickes attributed this happy circumstance to the cynical manipulations of the Republican machine: "The Republicans had reached the conclusion that the only way they could permanently purge their ranks of John Harlan was to make him their candidate in 1905." Unfortunately for both Harlan and Ickes, the seemingly invulnerable Carter H. Harrison II had finally been beaten for the Democratic nomination, his successor being the enormously popular and eminently respectable Judge Edward F. Dunne of the circuit court bench. Even with the Republican nomination in hand, then, Harlan once again seemed doomed. This did not deter Ickes. "A fight was, after all, a fight," he remembered, "and I had not had a good one for a long stretch— two years in fact. Besides, a miracle might happen."

Just when the fight began heating up, a wire came for him informing him that his runaway brother Felix, who had finally surfaced as a participant in the Tonopah and Goldfield mining excitements of Nevada, was desperately ill with typhoid fever. Because he felt he was needed in the campaign—and possibly because he had recovered from the same disease himself when he was younger and underestimated the seriousness of the situation—Ickes decided not to go to his brother. Anna went in his stead, arriving at the Carson City hospital just before Felix died. She brought the young man's body back to Chicago, and from there his brother Clair took it to Fairview Cemetery in Altoona. It was the last family burial in the quiet, familiar place; and it would be many years before Ickes returned to his hometown.

Back in Chicago, depression settled over him. Though Ickes worked as if there was every reason for hope, Harlan was defeated by Dunne on April 4, just as his campaign manager had expected. What was worse, Harlan had showed himself ambivalent during the campaign toward the question of municipal ownership of the streetcar system and compounded this weakness afterward by accepting the offer of a ten-thousand-dollar retainer and $2,000 a month from federal court judge Peter S. Grosscup to represent the "people's" interests in the snarl of litigation over traction franchises and ownership that followed the death of Charles Tyson Yerkes. Given the common assumption that Grosscup was firmly in the grasp of the traction companies, Ickes says, he considered this the equivalent of going to work for the companies themselves:

I pleaded with him not to destroy the faith of those thousands of young men and others in the city who had followed him in his fights and who still believed that he had been right. On this subject, I became emotional, because I felt it deeply. Tears trickled down my fast leathering cheeks and I noticed some in my former leader's eyes, too. All afternoon I wrestled with him, but his mind was made up. . . . From that moment our paths separated. We shook hands and I went home, greatly disturbed, heartsick, almost ready to give up.

There was more pain awaiting him at home that spring. By then he and Anna had concluded that they were in love. He assures us that there was nothing sexual in their relationship, and given their mutual high-mindedness there probably wasn't—certainly nothing that approached consummation. Still, it is not difficult to imagine steamy protestations of love and furtive hand-holding from time to time, all of which would have left them weak with guilt and frustration. He begged her to leave James. Not yet, she replied; she was not ready for that. In the meantime, James was off to France that summer, having completed two plays in his upstairs study—"When Henry IV Was King" and "The Balance of Power"—both of which were duly registered with the copyright office, apparently the only public attention they ever received. He would be pursuing evidence for a book on the Huguenots, and Anna and Wilmarth would be joining him in Paris. Ickes remained in the house with Anna until her departure, a breech of Victorian protocol that apparently disturbed no one.

Ickes was otherwise disturbed, however, and his agitation grew worse as the summer wore on. He began to make demands, among them that Anna was "never to live again with James as his wife," as he phrased it, and that when they returned she and James should have separate rooms in the house. James in fact had shown little sexual interest in Anna for quite some time, she told Ickes, a claim substantiated by her closing remarks in the letter she had written to James from Martha's Vineyard sometime in the summer of 1903: "My sole claim to your consideration seems to be as the mother of your boy. I accept the position so many another woman before me has found herself relegated to and humbly sign myself the affectionate mother of your son." However, she promised Clair that she would make the rejection officially mutual in France. While she was gone, Ickes spent the weeks in a frenzy of worry that she would change her mind or that James would insist upon the continued exercise of the conjugal rights he had lately taken to ignoring. He need not have worried; Anna kept her word and James accepted the situation with outward aplomb. When they returned to Chicago, he kept their big upstairs bedroom and Anna moved down the hall to a smaller one. Ickes continued to pressure her to make an even more final decision, and she continued to put it off. At some point she got it into her mind that James was destined to die soon—of natural causes, Ickes tells us hastily—a feeling she clung to with an intensity that finally persuaded her that it was a psychic vision, and she began exploring its significance with various mediums around town.

While Anna pursued her metaphysical investigations, Ickes busily sublimated his frustrations. He continued to cultivate his political associations after returning to law school in the summer quarter of 1905, largely through the Strap Hangers' League ("We Want Seats, Not Straps," its letterhead proclaimed), of which he was now treasurer. He became an active member of the Chicago City Club and the University Club, remained one of the alumni officers of his fraternity, and sat on the governing board of the fraternity house. He began a lengthy political correspondence with James Harlan, John's brother, who had been chairman of the federal Interstate Commerce Commission, a string of letters that amounted to a running commentary on political developments in the city and state as Ickes saw them. (Among these developments, early in 1907, was the bitter news that Mayor Dunne, of whom Ickes generally approved, had been beaten in the mayoral election by Republican boss Fred Busse, whom Ickes had never forgiven for his betrayal of John Harlan in 1903.)

He also had taken up with four new friends, each of whom he had met during the campaign of 1905 and all of whom would play an important part in his political life for many years: Charles H. Merriam, a young professor of political science at the University of Chicago; Donald Richberg, who had entered the university as a student in 1897, the year of Ickes's graduation, then had gone on to take a degree at Harvard Law School after his own graduation; and Raymond and Margaret Dreier Robins, rapidly earning reputations as radical leaders in the community of Chicago reformers. Of them all, it was Raymond and Margaret who would come to be most important to him, both as friends and as allies. There was much to admire in both. New Yorkers by bir h—Raymond had been born on Staten Island in 1873 and Margaret in Brooklyn in 1868—they had come together via widely divergent paths. Raymond, who later acquired the lifelong title of "Colonel" from his Red Cross work in World War I, had been raised with cousins in Florida. At the age of eighteen, he had formed a phosphate mining company, sold it almost immediately to a Wall Street firm, and taken to wandering, ending up in

Colorado as a working miner and a card-carrying member of the militant Western Federation of Miners, led by William D. ("Big Bill") Haywood. In 1894 he had decided to become a lawyer so that he could climb to leadership in "the mighty reforms of the coming crisis when the poverty and misery of this western world rise in their blind might."

He returned to Florida, took his degree, and moved to San Francisco, where he opened an office and also campaigned vigorously for William Jennings Bryan. When news of the gold strikes in the Yukon set all of San Francisco to trembling in 1897, he joined the rush north, across the Chilkoot Pass of Alaska and down the Yukon River to Dawson, in Canada's Yukon Territory. After three luckless years of prospecting there, he joined another rush back over the mountains and two thousand miles across Alaska by the Iditerod Trail to Nome at the edge of the Bering Sea, where, it was said, a man could wash the gold right out of the sands of the frigid beach. It apparently was true for Robins; he returned to the States in 1900 with enough money to buy a four-thousand-acre estate called Chinsegut Hill in Florida. He also returned with a commitment to Christ as reformer, the Redeemer who "drove the money changers out of the temple and befriended the whore." He became a lay preacher (and later a full-fledged evangelical minister in the Men and Religion Forward movement) and in 1902 moved to Chicago. There he worked simultaneously at the Chicago Municipal Lodging House and the Northwestern University Settlement House until 1905, when Mayor Dunne appointed him to the Chicago Board of Education, together with Miss Jane Addams and other prominent reformers.

He and Margaret had met in New York during one of his many speaking tours in 1904, and married a year later. Although each was independently wealthy (Margaret's father had left her a large inheritance from his iron-making business), they moved into a tenement flat in Chicago's Seventeenth Ward, a West Side neighborhood whose slums were quite as fetid as those that surrounded Hull-House itself. The decision was mutual, for Margaret's reformist instincts were no less finely honed than those of her husband. While engaged in the kind of charity work expected of women of her class—and especially unmarried women of her class—she had become involved with the Women's Municipal League of New York, and had helped to transform it into an activist group seeking passage of social legislation. In 1904 she and her sister Mary had joined the New York branch of the National Women's Trade Union League, formed in 1903 during the annual meeting of the American Federation of Labor. Margaret swiftly became president of the branch and was soon permanently committed to its goals of organizing women workers and bettering their wages, hours, and working conditions through collective bargaining. These were the basics of a decent life for working women, she believed, but trade unionism in her mind had broader social importance. "Beyond these is the incentive for initiative and social leadership," she once said. "The union shop calls up the moral and reasoning faculties, the sense of fellowship, independence and group strength. In every workshop there is unknown wealth of intellectual and moral reform." She brought these convictions to her marriage, and swiftly became president of the National League as well as its Chicago branch, which she had founded. She would hold both positions until her retirement in 1922.

Raymond and Margaret Robins had acquired the kind of importance in the community to which Ickes himself aspired with such single-minded persistence. He became particularly close to the somewhat flamboyant Raymond, whose handsome, charismatic presence must have had an almost seductive quality to someone as little graced or experienced in the social arts as Ickes. Throughout their long relationship—even during their most bitter arguments—there remained in Clair's feelings toward Raymond an inescapable and touching note of gentle envy, as if the flashy adventurer represented an ideal Ickes might hope to emulate but never hope to equal.

In any case, Ickes would need the help of those like Raymond and Margaret as he struggled to broaden his participation in the life of the city. At the end of March 1907, a little over two months after his final mastoid operation, he took his bar examinations for the state of Illinois. Possibly because of that operation, he went into the examination room in some fear. "When I started in that first morning session," he confessed in his memoirs, "it was all I could do to keep control of myself. I had taken with me a half pint bottle of whiskey. At one stage I was afraid that I would have to throw up the sponge. So I went into the toilet and took a good swig of straight whiskey. This restored my nerve to the extent that I was able to finish that session and the subsequent ones." When the results were published a few days later, he was even more relieved to learn that his desperate measure had enabled him to count himself among the 40 percent who had passed. He could now take to practicing law.

CHAPTER
· 10 ·

*The Case of
the Missing Brain*

H AROLD LECLAIR ICKES, attorney-at-law, did not bring to his new
profession a consummate love of the law as an institution. No one,
then or now, would confuse him with that other Chicago attorney,
Clarence Darrow, who even by 1907 had established himself as perhaps
the greatest defense lawyer in the country.

But what Ickes did bring to his new career was entirely his own: a
quick if not subtle mind, an extraordinary ability to grasp and sort out
detail, a high level of concentration, the doggedness that went with that
concentration, and, above all, a powerful conviction that the law was a
tool, not a chalice. A tool useful to his ambitions, certainly; but just as
certainly a tool to be used to further the causes in which he had come to
believe so acutely. By his own account, this was the principal reason he
never made much money as an attorney. "I simply hated to render bills for
services and when I did they were usually for totally inadequate
amounts," he said in his memoirs, then added somewhat grandly: "I
suppose that my attitude toward professional life, whether the profession
be that of law or medicine or the church, is a perfectly silly one, but I
believe that professional men ought to be servants of humanity, outposts
of civilization." One could note skeptically, as some of his later critics did,
that at least part of this attitude of high altruism stemmed from the fact
that at no point in his career was he actually dependent upon his law

practice for the necessities of life; these had pretty much been taken care of from the moment he moved in with the Thompsons. On the other hand, it is equally clear that the use of the law as a vehicle to accumulate money was a notion that bored him; for whatever reasons, he would much rather spend his energies and his expertise in the defense of good causes and in the promotion of men and women who would represent those causes politically. That, in any case, is what he did with most of his time for most of his life.

For quite a while after passing the bar, however, he had little reason to speculate on the conflict between money-making and public service; he achieved very little of either. It was not much of a practice at first. He had a shingle, but no place to hang it, save his room at 5747 Washington. This problem was temporarily solved when John Harlan offered him the use of his brother's space in the Harlan law offices downtown for as long as James remained in Washington with the ICC. Although Anna immediately retained him for what minor legal work she required, his first genuine client was the Great Northern Egg Company, a speculative outfit run by a former high school and college friend who was trying to corner the egg market (he failed). Raymond and Margaret then had him draw up their wills, a satisfyingly complicated task. He also handled the legal work when Margaret organized the Chicago branch of the National Women's Trade Union League, and he later became the branch's legal counsel, helping to draft state bills legislating a ten-hour day for women. When Mayor Busse attempted to remove Raymond and other radicals from the Board of Education, Ickes advised them on legal procedures and political strategy (none of which worked, unfortunately; Busse prevailed). With Robins and Charles H. Merriam he drafted a "corrupt practices act" and attempted to get it adopted in a new city charter under consideration; when that failed, he helped to organize the opposition to the charter, which the voters rejected in November 1907.

Early in 1908, Ickes decided it was time for a vacation—less from his not very onerous workload, probably, than from the emotional pressure tank at 5747. In January he took the eight-year-old Wilmarth with him to the little resort of Magnolia Springs, Alabama, where they spent the month fishing and doing nothing much. Ickes returned in reasonably good spirits. "I have not started seriously to practice law again," he wrote a fraternity brother on February 5, "but I am casting about with a view to determining just what form my legal activity shall take in the immediate future. I am undecided whether to open an office of my own and starve, or whether to try to get a position licking postage stamps at $5 per."

He was rescued from this ignominious (and unlikely) fate when a turn of events placed him at the center of another of Chicago's spasms of social trauma, this one featuring the kind of hysteria that had soiled the city's image after the Haymarket bombing of 1886. Anarchy—or the fear of it—combined this time with anti-Semitism to produce a situation that threatened to widen the chasm between Chicago's Jewish community and the rest of the city, perhaps beyond repair—and it is no exaggeration to say that the timely skills of Harold Ickes went a long way toward preventing that outcome.

It began at about nine o'clock on the morning of Monday, March 2, 1908. Chief of Police George Shippy and his family had just finished breakfast and the chief was preparing to leave for work; his driver was outside, hitching up the horse. Before he could depart, Shippy was called to the door, where a young man stood waiting to see him. The chief later reported to the newspapers that because of the man's "foreign cast of features," "cruel lips," and "defiant glare" he could immediately tell that "he was up to some wrong. The swarthy, undersized, but muscularly developed young man looked to me like an anarchist." On the strength of this, the chief said, he immediately seized the man, who twisted away from him, pulled a gun, and was able to shoot the chief's son and his driver, James Foley, both of whom had come running at the sound of the disturbance, before Shippy could get out his own pistol and gun the stranger down. The young man (who apparently had taken a bullet from Foley, too) died on the way to the hospital; Shippy's son and Foley later recovered.

The alleged assailant, it turned out, was an eighteen-year-old Russian Jew by the name of Lazar Averbuch (although his death certificate listed him as "Jeremiah" and the newspapers for several days gave him such names as "Lazarus," "Harry," and "Jerry"). He had come to this country only three months before to join his sister, Olga, who reported that her brother had just taken a job as an accountant for an egg dealer in Iowa and had gone to the chief's house that morning because he assumed that he would have to get some kind of travel permit or endorsement from Shippy before leaving; such was the practice in the old country, she said. For their part, the newspapers were ready and willing to believe the chief's story and the chief's theory. The *Record-Herald* instructed its readers on March 3 that "the greater proportion of anarchists are Russian Jews, and these are said to have had the doctrine of death to all officials by torch and knife and bullet ground into them ever since infancy." Against this perceived terrorism, state and local officials went into action immediately, organizing an "Anarchy Bureau" to banish "reds from the city."

Their tactics were of the strong-arm variety, as described in a solemn indictment by Miss Jane Addams just two years later:

> It was, to our minds . . . most unfortunate that the Chicago police in the determination to uncover an anarchist plot should have utilized the most drastic methods of search within the Russian-Jewish colony composed of families only too familiar with the methods of the Russian police. Therefore, when the Chicago police ransacked all printing offices they could locate in the colony, when they raided a restaurant which they regarded as suspicious because it had been supplying food at cost to the unemployed, when they searched through private homes for papers and photographs of revolutionaries, when they seized the library of the Edelstat group and carried the books, including Shakespeare and Herbert Spencer, to the city hall, when they arrested two friends of young Averbuch and kept them in the police station forty-eight hours, when they mercilessly "sweated" the sister, Olga, that she might be startled into a confession—all these things so poignantly reminded them of Russian methods that indignation, fed both by old memory and bitter disappointment in America, swept over the entire colony.

Fearing that hysteria might spread and merge with violence, Miss Addams called for an emergency meeting at Hull-House. Ickes, who attended with Anna and her mother, remembered it as rather a small meeting that included Julius Rosenwald of Sears, Roebuck, and S. S. Gregory, past president of the American Bar Association, among other reformers. During the meeting, it was agreed that one of the most important things to be done was to appoint an attorney to represent Averbuch's sister at the inquest, scheduled for March 24.

In an interview given in 1949, Ickes recalled that Miss Addams had some difficulties along this line:

> She . . . said, "I am afraid of trouble. I am afraid of clashes with the police, and that would be a terrible thing for the Jews themselves. Now what can we do about it?" We were all sympathetic. . . . She said, "Mr. Gregory, will you take the case?" Mr. Gregory said, no, he could not. . . . I understood that because Mr. Gregory had been a junior lawyer in the anarchist trial [after the Haymarket bombing], and it took him a good many years, fighting years, to overcome the handicap that that meant to his practice.
>
> She turned to one or two other lawyers. They couldn't do it. . . . I could see that she wasn't quite happy about it. . . . She said, "Well, Mr. Ickes, I guess we will have to ask you to take it." And I did.

A fund of $2,000 was established, most of it coming from Julius Rosenwald with the proviso, according to Ickes, that Rosenwald's name not be used in connection with the case.

With this rather timid support behind him, the tyro lawyer went to work. In order to demonstrate to the agitated colony that Olga Averbuch's interests were being represented, it was determined that a second autopsy must be made by doctors of her own choosing. (The coroner's office had already done a swift autopsy and had just as swiftly buried the body in the city's potter's field—without ceremony, which had done nothing to ease tension among Orthodox Jews; it had been disinterred and given a more proper Jewish burial at Ridgelawn cemetery on March 12.) Ickes made the necessary arrangements to have the body exhumed once again and examined by a pair of volunteer pathologists to see if the coroner's office had missed anything.

It had—a bullet in the back (the coroner's office had found only three in the body). It also had misappropriated something, it turned out, and as Ickes watched the proceedings in the amphitheater of the operating room in a small morgue attached to the cemetery, a sudden, worried conference took place among those performing the autopsy, then some attendants hurriedly left. When Ickes asked what was going on, he learned that the police, with the coroner's permission, had allowed doctors at Presbyterian Hospital to borrow a piece of the boy's body during the first autopsy on March 2. It had never been returned, and the attendants were now on their way to retrieve it. The purloined part had been the boy's brain, which surgeons at the hospital had wanted to have a look at, presumably to satisfy their curiosity regarding the structure of an anarchist brain as opposed to, say, that of a Presbyterian.

The brain was soon replaced, but such slipshod treatment of a human part was not only callous, it was illegal, and if the newspapers ever got wind of it the political career of Coroner Peter Hoffman, a product of Mayor Fred Busse's machine, would be ruined. This was the tool Ickes had needed. Even if he could hardly prove Averbuch's innocence at the inquest on March 24, he could at least make sure the newspapers were provided with no more fodder for hysteria. The night before the inquest Ickes went to see Hoffman and made it clear that if the police tried to inflame public opinion further by claiming Averbuch had been a raging anarchist bent on assassination—in spite of the lack of any evidence to prove such a thing—Ickes would make a point of questioning Hoffman at length in regard to the missing brain. "He went perfectly white," Ickes remembered. The ploy worked; during the testimony of the principals the next day, the word "anarchist" was notable by its absence, and if Shippy and his driver were officially exonerated of any wrongdoing, they had at least provided little incitement to journalistic riot. The police took the pressure off the Russian-Jewish colony and the newspapers went on to better things.

One distressing chore remained: no one had yet written Averbuch's mother back in Russia to tell her of her son's death. His sister Olga could not bring herself to do it, so Ickes was prevailed upon. His letter demonstrated uncommon grace:

> At the request of your daughter Olga I am writing you this letter to tell you some news in regard to your son Jeremiah, that will be extremely painful for you to hear. . . .
>
> Your son Jeremiah came to his death in a very sad way. It seems that on the morning of March 2nd, he called at the house of our chief of police. Why he called we do not yet know, but the chief of police thought that he was an Italian anarchist and shot him. Your son died on the way to the hospital.
>
> Many people here in Chicago felt that your son Jeremiah came to his death unjustly. . . . We do not want you and your family . . . to believe that we do not have justice in this country. We feel that what has happened has been in the nature of a terrible accident. . . .
>
> I hope that you and the rest of your family will realize that your daughter Olga, here in this country, is in need of your greatest kindness and sympathy, and that on her account you will bear this severe blow as bravely as you can, and in trying to comfort her and give her courage, comfort yourselves.

A few months later Shippy died. While the facts of the case never did come out, Ickes's theory, which he says was corroborated after Shippy's death by his assistant chief of police, Herman F. Scheuttler, was that Shippy, well-known as a heavy drinker, had been up late and drinking the night before the shooting (the chief did not, in fact, get home from a party until two that morning, the newspapers reported). When he saw Averbuch, he mistook the dark-complexioned young man for a hit man sent over by a gang of Sicilian crooks with whom he had been having difficulties. In a panic exacerbated by a hangover, Shippy opened fire, and his son and the driver were inadvertently wounded in the hail of shakily directed bullets. Averbuch himself, Ickes said, probably had come to the chief's house for precisely the reasons his sister claimed—to obtain a work or travel permit. The gun he was alleged to have used must have been planted by the police.

However murky the circumstances, the Averbuch affair struck a tender nerve in Chicago (and, in fact, in the country as a whole: Averbuch's "assassination attempt" made the front page of nearly every major newspaper in the nation). In the opinion of at least one later commentator, Ickes's arm-twisting in regard to the missing brain was instrumental in keeping the situation under control: "The already savage press might have published more rumors, half truths, and lies about Averbuch, Jews, Judaism, and immigrants, resulting in the accelerated polarization between groups in Chicago. Harold L. Ickes . . . may not have been an

'Emil Zola,' but Julius Rosenwald received full value for his $2000 investment in Averbuch's (and perhaps his own?) defense."

This nasty episode had one personally nasty repercussion for Ickes. John Harlan, who still entertained political ambitions, had grown nervous about his office's association with a known defender of anarchists. He asked Ickes to leave. Ickes did, but with a bitterness that rankled for the rest of his life. Though they never completely severed their relationship, it cooled to the point that they saw very little of each other from then on; Harlan had not only betrayed the best hopes Ickes had had for him, he had now betrayed Ickes personally.

CHAPTER

·11·

Travesties and Triumphs

WITH THE CONCLUSION of the Averbuch case, Ickes settled down to what was to be a fairly quiet year, its legal highlight being a case he took at the behest of Miss Addams. In it, he represented the Illinois Birth Control League in its effort to establish a free clinic in Chicago. The city had denied the organization a permit, but Ickes filed a writ of mandamus and the lower court granted the permit; the city appealed, however, and the appellate court reversed the decision. On a personal level, the high point seems to have been a visit to the Rocky Mountains. His memoirs are casual as to dates here, but he mentions spending at least parts of three summers on the pioneering dude ranch operated by Howard, Alden, and Willis Eaton in the Big Horn Mountains of Wyoming, and a pair of family photographs—one of them dated September 1908—shows this intimate of streetside saloons and covens of ward heelers happily perched on a horse with a string of similarly delighted tourists somewhere in the West. This was probably one of the horseback trips Howard Eaton regularly conducted into Yellowstone National Park every summer. "All of us—young men and young women—rode horseback and slept either in tents or in tarps," Ickes wrote. "No matter how hard it rained or how cold it was I was never driven into a tent or to a hotel any night. I prided myself on sticking it out, even although on one occasion we were in one camp for three full days on account of a driving rain which finally seeped through the protecting tarpaulin and got into my blankets. And every night was cold. . . . But I loved all of it."

If Ickes found 1908 a relatively quiet time, James Westfall Thompson, who continued robust in spite of Anna's dark fantasies, had been busy. He finished his book that year and successfully negotiated its publication by the University of Chicago Press in May 1909. Entitled *The Huguenots: Catherine de Medici and Philip the Second, 1559–76* it firmly established his reputation in the field and is still considered a standard work of scholarship for that period. Whatever satisfaction he might have taken, however, was effectively blasted a month later as his world came tumbling around his ankles.

It was a sexual incident—or at least the accusation of one—that did this presumably chaste man in. Earlier in 1909, following the dictates of one of her whims of steel, Anna had brought a young girl home with her from the Chicago Home for the Friendless, one of the charitable institutions with which she was involved. The girl's name was Frances Shook and her mother had placed her in the Home in a desperate attempt to keep the child away from her drunken and abusive father. Anna announced that she intended to adopt Frances; the mother had already given her consent. James and Clair, each of them disconcerted at the idea of further complicating an already difficult family life, raised objections. These had with Anna their usual effect, which is to say none, and in the end Clair handled the details of the adoption.

Frances, who was about thirteen at this time and quite appealing, was put in an upstairs bedroom adjoining a bathroom shared by James. This may have been a bad idea. "It must have been fairly early in 1909," Ickes wrote in his memoirs, "that I got home from the office one day to be met by Anna in a state of great excitement. Taking me into a quiet part of the house she told me that Frances had been to her that day with a most extraordinary story. The night before, James had gone into Frances's room and, putting back the covers of her bed, had put his fingers between her thighs."* Furthermore, Frances had told Anna, "it had happened on another occasion, but she had doubted the evidence of her senses at that time because she was not sure that she had been awake or was merely dreaming."

In spite of the girl's troubled background, Anna and Clair apparently never seriously questioned her story. Things moved rather swiftly after

---

* Ickes edited this sentence very carefully. In his first, dictated version, Thompson had "put his hand on her." This was changed to "put his fingers between her lips." He thought better of that, finally, and revised it again to "put his fingers between her thighs." By whatever sentence structure, it was clearly a sexual gesture.

this. Anna went to James and told him that she wanted a divorce immediately. To his reply that she had no grounds, she explained she most certainly did. When he denied the accusation, she refused to believe him and threatened to make it public if he resisted the divorce. He capitulated almost instantly—less an admission of guilt, probably, than a recognition that the accusation alone, if it became generally known, would ruin him. Ickes, to his credit, apparently kept his mouth shut about the incident, even when sorely tempted. When Mrs. Wilmarth, who had always liked James and who had been told none of the details, took his side in the crisis, Ickes felt moved to respond, writing her on June 24 in vigorous defense of Anna: "She has refused to talk even to her closest friends although the result is that she has had to submit to much unjust criticism when by a word she could win the approval and approbation of all. The uttering of that word, however, would blast James' personal life and professional career and she is protecting him at personal cost just as she has done for the past twelve years."

Both James and Clair moved out of 5747 Washington Avenue the day before the bill of divorcement was filed by John Maynard Harlan, who had risen above his fear of anarchist associations and was serving as Anna's attorney in the case. Ickes took a room at the University Club downtown. James probably stayed somewhere near the university. It was a very difficult time for him, for in spite of all the bonds of secrecy, at least part of the truth apparently had gotten out, as such things usually do, and he found himself suddenly very alone. When he gently inquired as to the university's position in the matter, Henry Pratt Judson, who had become president after the death of William Rainey Harper, replied with something less than a ringing endorsement:

> There are two separate questions. The first is whether you were in fact guilty of the incident which has made the ground of the court action—granting the divorce. Of course if the reply were in the affirmative you could not continue with the university. I am more than ready to believe the negative. The second question is as to the effect on the university of the present situation, assuming that the court has held you guilty of such conduct, but that no defense can be made public. There can be no doubt that the effect will be to injure the university in the public estimation. I do not know that it is possible to explain what has been done amiss. I wish that it could be done. You know, I am sure, that you have my entire sympathy.

On the strength of this oleaginous "support," James resigned his position as an assistant dean on September 30. In the end, the divorce was granted without sensation, and perhaps on the theory that the public had a short attention span, Judson ultimately rehired James. By then he had remarried and was probably working very hard at trying to forget he had ever met Anna Wilmarth. Thompson went on to a long and distinguished career as one of the world's outstanding scholars in the field of medieval and Renaissance history. He stayed with the University of Chicago until 1933, when he accepted an offer from the Berkeley campus of the University of California. He wrote and taught there until his death in 1941. For her part, Anna ripped almost all of the photographs of him out of the family albums and spent most of the rest of her life in an earnest attempt to disguise the fact that the first marriage had ever taken place. The effort was largely successful.

If Clair Ickes, the still handsome but swiftly aging suitor, thought that Thompson's departure and the subsequent divorce were suddenly going to clear the tangled path of love, he was soon disabused of the notion. At thirty-seven, Anna was beginning to put on weight and dignity in about equal proportions—her person would grow increasingly heavy with both as the years wore on—and the questionable nature of her relationship with Clair and the disreputable atmosphere surrounding the divorce seemed to dredge up previously untapped reserves of ponderous respectability. On the grounds that people would think she had divorced James just to get at Clair, she refused to marry him until Thompson himself was safely wed. Instead, she had a house built in Evanston, and sometime in 1910 she moved to this woodsy suburb with Wilmarth and Frances, leaving Ickes to commute there from his rooms at the University Club.

As for Ickes, he had plenty to occupy him, for he was beginning one of the busiest and most productive periods of his life. Back in February 1909 he had helped to organize the campaign of his friend Charles Merriam for a seat on the city council and in April had seen him win. This victory inspired him to go after a seat himself—his first and only serious attempt at elective office. In November he laid the groundwork for this move, running for election as Republican precinct captain for the Second Ward. In spite of the opposition of Mayor Fred Busse's crowd and largely with the help of Chauncey Dewey, Republican committeeman for the Second Congressional District, he won. Unfortunately, Dewey's clout apparently extended no further, and in March 1910 Ickes's bid for the aldermanic nomination failed. At the end of April, however, he probably got some pleasure from a headline splashed across the front page of the *Tribune:* "DEMOCRATIC LEGISLATOR CONFESSES HE WAS BRIBED TO CAST VOTE FOR LORIMER FOR UNITED STATES SENATOR." Republican boss William Lorimer, one of Fred Busse's closest friends and supporters, had been elected to the U.S. Senate by the Illinois State Legislature in 1909. While it was commonly assumed that such elections often were bought outright, this was one of the few times in history when the accusation was made specific and public. It caused a splendid stir among the good people of the state, particularly in Chicago, and Ickes strode busily into the middle of it.

In June 1910 the good people called for a political conference in Peoria to consider the Lorimer incident and its ramifications for the city and the state. Called "Decency's Army" by supportive newspapers and "The People's Conference" by themselves, one hundred people showed up, among them Ickes, who had helped to plan the program as the group secretary. At the end of the conference the officers issued a public statement that called for the direct election of U.S. Senators (no surprise here), primary elections, the establishment of initiative, referendum, and recall, a statewide "corrupt practices" act by which to facilitate the prosecution of just such offenders as Lorimer and the legislators he had purchased, and a stronger state civil service law. Ickes himself emerged from the conference as one of the "Committee of Seven" to direct a campaign to elect state legislators pledged to the Peoria demands.

As for the Lorimer scandal, which had been made public by legislator Charles White (he sold his information to the *Chicago Tribune* for $3,250 when an attempt to extort $75,000 out of Lorimer failed), White and several other legislators were later indicted but none were ever convicted. Lorimer himself almost got away with it. In March 1911 the U.S. Senate solemnly voted to allow him to keep his seat. But a few days after the vote, Herman Kohlsaat, in the pages of his own *Record-Herald,* declared that he had personal knowledge of at least $100,000 having been spread among the legislators by Lorimer's people. This apparently was a sum big enough to offend the dignity of the Senate, and this august conclave later booted him out.

Four months after the Peoria conference, as the legal representative of both Hull-House and the Chicago branch of the Women's Trade Union League, Ickes was embroiled in one more civic disturbance. On September 22 a small group of seamstresses protested a piecework reduction from four cents to three and three-fourths cents, walking out of Shop No. 5 of the enormous clothing works of Hart, Schaffner and Marx at the corner of Market and Monroe. These women were only a handful of the nearly forty-five thousand clothing workers in Chicago, half of them women and girls and most of them Jewish, Polish, Italian, and Lithuanian immigrants. They were not even a large part of the eight thousand workers at the Hart, Schaffner and Marx plant. But dissatisfaction over sweatshop conditions and wages had been simmering throughout the garment industry for some time, and the small walkout soon became a major strike directed by the United Garment Workers of America (predecessor of today's ILGWU). By the end of October, twenty-seven thousand workers had left their sewing machines and cutting benches, and picket lines were up all over the city.

As the strike wore on and winter approached, Hull-House and the Women's Trade Union League joined forces with the United Charities of Chicago to provide food, coal, and medical services for the workers on the street, and Ickes helped coordinate the gathering and distribution of goods. Picket-line arrests began to mount (there would be over four hundred such arrests before it was over more than four months later), and the authorities, according to Ickes's memory, carried these out with an unseemly enthusiasm: "The police would sound riot calls, club the pickets, rush up and throw the striking women into patrol wagons, taking occasion, in doing so, to twist their arms and ankles in such a way [as] to hurt them so that they were incapacitated for days." Not all the pickets were immigrant women; many were some of Chicago's finest, including Anna, whose mother stood ready to post bail for her and all the others, while Clarence Darrow stood ready to defend them in court. For the most part, Ickes says, the police "were careful to keep their hands off the 'society' women who were picketing," but on one occasion they got carried away and rounded up Ellen Gates Starr, Jane Addams's associate at Hull-House. Mary Wilmarth put up bail for her, and Ickes was asked to defend her, Darrow being overloaded at the time.

The case did not come to trial until after the strike had ended in February 1911, marked by the deaths of two strikers, mass funeral processions through the streets (during the second of which the mourners were attacked by police), and a precedent-setting arbitrated settlement with Joseph Schaffner, president of Hart, Schaffner and Marx. Miss Gates was acquitted of assault charges swiftly enough. The prosecution's case was weak to begin with, and it got no stronger when Ickes had the tiny woman stand up next to the hulking clod of a policeman who claimed she had attacked him. "She looked like a pygmy compared with the giant," he remembered, "and a titter went through the courtroom. At that point the case was lost." Much to his disappointment, Miss Gates and Miss Addams decided not to press charges of false arrest.

Things were looking up for the reformers. Back in September, before the beginning of the strike, Ickes had gotten himself elected a delegate to the state Republican convention and had helped to engineer passage of a statewide platform that adopted most of the Peoria Conference doctrines. And in the November Illinois elections, no less than 111 legislators who promised to support those doctrines were sent to the State House in Springfield. Moreover, it looked as if the reform wing of the Republican Party in Chicago at last had a genuine chance at getting its own man into the mayor's office. But first it had to pick its man. Apparently Ickes already had him: Alderman Charles H. Merriam. The sometime professor of political science had already distinguished himself on the city council by attacking the visible corruption of the Busse administration on a regular basis and by heading up the council's watchdog Bureau of Public Efficiency, which kept an eye on city expenditures. On the train back from the state Republican convention in September, Ickes said, he first broached the idea to Merriam. The young alderman said he would do it if no one better could be found and if Ickes promised to manage his campaign if he got the Republican nomination. Ickes gave his word.

That was how he would later remember it. In fact, it appears that the question of Merriam's candidacy did not arise until November, and probably not at the direct intervention of Ickes. "The trouble with our movement," he had written to Charles R. Crane as late as November 23, "is that we have no candidate. From the point of view of those who are interested in getting a decent mayor, I do feel that Fisher [Walter L. Fisher, who was being courted at that time] should make up his mind. . . . The important thing to me is not whether this man or that leads the movement . . . but that a movement would be led by someone against Busse and it is just as important that this movement should be started and pressed vigorously whether success or failure awaits it at the polls." However it came about, Merriam did finally consent to be the candidate and Ickes was chosen to lead his campaign for the nomination.

For the first time, Ickes enjoyed the heady experience of having a solid organization to work with and a sufficiency of money. Charles Crane became chairman of the Merriam Campaign Committee, whose other members included Julius Rosenwald, Walter Fisher, and Ickes's track coach at the University of Chicago, Amos Alonzo Stagg. Crane, whom Ickes described as "the one in a million who would contribute to a cause that he believed in even if he knew that it was hopeless," lived up to his reputation by contributing $50,000 to the Merriam kitty; Rosenwald gave $30,000, and another $50,000 ultimately came in from various sources. Under the direction of Ickes and Fletcher Dobyns, the support groups left over after John Maynard Harlan's 1905 campaign were stitched together into the Young Men's Progressive Republican Club, which borrowed its name from the National Progressive Republican League, formed in January in Washington, D.C. The League soon had twenty thousand members registered at Merriam headquarters in the

Grand Pacific Hotel on LaSalle Street. As an added measure of support—less important in those days than it would later become, but still significant—Ickes got the Chicago Federation of Labor to endorse Merriam publicly. He set up a speaking schedule that took his candidate into every ward in the city, made speaking engagements for such useful orators as Rosenwald and Raymond Robins, held numerous press conferences, and passed out campaign literature, most of it written by himself, all with the frenzied diligence of a Salvation Army worker. By the end of January, even most of the city's newspapers were taking the campaign of the "schoolmaster in politics" seriously.

Apparently, Mayor Fred Busse concluded that it would be futile to struggle against this suddenly rising tide. He announced that he would not be a candidate for reelection. In league with William Lorimer, who was disgraced but not yet thrown out of the Senate, he threw his *pro forma* support behind John R. Thompson as the nominee, while the machine, under the control of Governor Charles S. Deneen, put its weight behind a candidate from the city's Polish wards, John P. Smulski. The two new candidates started late and split the opposition. On February 27 the city's first election under the new statewide primary law gave Merriam a plurality of twenty-eight thousand votes, four thousand more than the combined total of his opponents. Among the notes of congratulations that Ickes graciously received was one he must have particularly treasured. It came from James Hamilton Lewis, a considerable power among the Democrats in the state, who told Ickes that his Merriam campaign was "one of the finest pieces of strategy and political work I have ever observed."

Ickes would have been happier, probably, if the Democrats had just left it at congratulations. Unfortunately, what they did was nominate Carter H. Harrison II for his fifth term, and Harrison was going to be somewhat more difficult to handle than the spineless Busse. He was still remembered as the man who had taken on Charles T. Yerkes and beaten him, and in spite of the scandals that had plagued his various administrations between 1897 and 1905, he continued to exude the aura of the reformer. He also had the full and still very considerable power of the Democratic machine as his rod and his staff. Ickes and Merriam had no such comfort. The Republican machine, in the persons of Lorimer, Busse, Deneen, Postmaster Daniel A. Campbell, and former Cook County sheriff James Pease, neither expressed nor offered any meaningful support. Ickes had known this would be the case, and he felt that Merriam might just get the entire city behind him if he scorned the regular Republicans as a bunch just as grimily corrupt as the Democrats. Merriam was not convinced. In his own memoirs, he explained that "on the one hand we were unwilling to entrust the regular party organization with the entire conduct of the campaign, but if we ignored them entirely they would of course assume a hostile attitude." They were going to assume a hostile attitude in any case, Ickes argued, and "if we hewed to our own line, instead of delivering ourselves to the payroll boys, they would be facing us and therefore in no position to stab us in the back." But Merriam decided to court the regulars. "I have always thought that he lost the election for sure then and there," Ickes said.

Whatever the reason and the blame, Merriam did indeed lose to Harrison on April 4, 177,997 votes to 160,672. Ickes says he took it philosophically, but that is doubtful. Thirty-two years later, there was still too much bitterness left:

> If a candidate wins, he gets the credit. If he loses, the manager gets hell. Shortly after the election we held a powwow of our volunteer workers at the Grand Pacific Hotel. There were a few men in the organization who had been selected by me but who were not unwilling to take advantage of his defeat to ingratiate themselves with Merriam by covert criticism of me. Even in those days, I was a good deal of a lone wolf and ran on my own power. I did not much care whether people liked me or not. I made a speech at that "get together."... I declared publicly that Merriam had not been defeated by Harrison, but by a Republican Governor, Deneen; a Republican Senator, Lorimer; and a Republican Mayor, Busse. The effect of the speech was to make some people shy away from me, but I had told them the truth whether they liked it or not.

Some of them must have liked it. By the end of the summer, the lone wolf had taken the Young Men's Progressive Republican Club and molded it into the Illinois Progressive Republican League. Out of this was carved the Chicago Progressive Republican League, of which the man who did not care whether people liked him or not was elected president.

Ickes was now securely linked with a genuine political force. He was, in fact, one of its leaders, with every reasonable hope that his power and influence would grow. His other quest for connection, however, was not going as smoothly. "We were still talking about getting married," he says of Anna and himself in his memoirs, "but the date seemed no nearer than it had ever been while the situation between us was becoming more and more difficult." They fought frequently.

> I have often had a bitter and caustic tongue when angry and Anna had a temper and an ability to hurt that were not to be despised. There were

altogether too many flareups, followed by customary reconciliations, not to have warned both of us that it would be a mistake for us to marry. However, we were sincerely devoted to each other and I know that I felt, and I suspect that Anna did too, that we were irrevocably tied to each other. . . . I made up my mind that as long as Anna wanted to marry me I could not honorably withdraw.

Duty again, self-imposed, as it so often was. But more than duty, in spite of his astringent memories of it. One cannot help but believe that each of these unlikely partners derived satisfactions from the relationship that were felt at the level of bone marrow, so deeply were their needs buried. Snarled in complications and contention, the attachment between these two stubborn souls was a bond so powerful that death alone could break it.

Their wait to make it official ended a little over five months after the Merriam campaign. One day that summer of 1911 the society columns carried a small notice to the effect that James Westfall Thompson had married one Martha Landers of Indianapolis, Indiana. Anna and Clair made their own moves with equal discretion. Since Anna wanted to be married at Glen Arden on Lake Geneva, at the end of August Ickes went up to the appropriate county seat in Wisconsin and obtained a license, and on September 16 they gathered at Glen Arden, with the two children; Anna's mother; Raymond and Margaret Dreier Robins; Dwight Perkins (an architect friend of the family who would later build them a house, to his everlasting regret); Perkins's wife, Lucy; Stacey Mosser, Ickes's old college chum; and three or four other friends. Robins performed the marriage rites under the aegis of one of the three denominations he was licensed to serve. (Ickes, the militant agnostic, does not tell us which.)

A few weeks later they sailed for Europe on a ship of the Hamburg-American line, with Wilmarth, Frances, and the children's nurse, Ida Erisman. Ickes remembered the wedding more tenderly than the honeymoon. In the first place, he was instantly seasick (he would be a dreadful sailor all his life, probably as the result of his missing middle ear). In the second place, shortly after sailing Anna marched into their stateroom and announced that she was a thirty-eight-year-old (almost thirty-nine) pregnant lady, and she was furious about it. "People will think that we got married just for that," she said, meaning sex. "Well, what if they do?" Ickes replied. "Fundamentally, isn't that what people get married for?" They fought, Ickes remembered, from one end of Europe to the other for the next two months.

PART III

Tattered Guidons,
Proudly Borne

*I have been over-taxing my strength and living on my nerves for years
now and there come times when I wonder how much longer I can keep
going. When I was a bachelor I didn't care and was willing to expend
myself in a way that I do not now feel that I have the right to do. . . .
Your word about little Raymond touches me deeply. I have built him a
sand pile in the back yard as the result of which I have come to the
conclusion that I am a better carpenter than I am a politician.*

—Letter to Raymond Robins, April 24, 1914

CHAPTER

· 12 ·

Progressive Declensions

W HILE ICKES, Baedeker in hand, squabbled with Anna through the
countrysides of France, Belgium, and Holland in the late fall and
early winter of 1911, two men in America were playing out the nasty end
of a long friendship, with consequences to the nation and to the clutch of
Republican activists, Ickes prominent among them, who would soon find
their imaginations seized by the powerful appeal of Movement.

All William Howard Taft had ever wanted to be was a justice of the
Supreme Court of the United States. Instead, his immensity now occupied
the White House. He had been groomed for that position by Theodore
Roosevelt, who had expected the large, genial man with a mustache the
size of a whisk broom to carry out the policies and programs established
during the seven years of his own administration, during four of which
Taft had faithfully served him as secretary of war. As time went on and the
election year of 1912 grew closer, however, the Colonel became increasingly convinced that Taft was genially betraying that inheritance. The
disaffection had begun not long after the elections in November 1908.
Three months before the inauguration, Roosevelt had sent Taft a Bible
with some passages in Ecclesiastes marked for his perusal: "Yea, I hated all
my labor which I had taken under the sun: because I should leave it unto
the man who shall be after me/And who knoweth whether he shall be a
wise man or a fool?" This was a joke, but as with so much else about the
ebullient President, his jokes tended to have a hard edge.

The edge began to show itself—though not publicly yet, and not to Taft—when the President-elect decided not to keep most of the Roosevelt cabinet. The dismissal of Secretary of War Luke Wright, who had accepted the position under Roosevelt only after assurances by him that he would be reappointed by any succeeding Republican administration, and James Garfield, the conservation-minded Secretary of the Interior, who had been given similar assurances, especially galled Roosevelt. "Jim," he told Garfield in January 1909, "something has come over Will, he is changed, he is not the same man."

Then Taft fired Gifford Pinchot in 1910; nothing could have been better calculated to persuade the righteous that Taft and his entire administration finally had fallen into the clutches of those very "malefactors of great wealth" against whom Roosevelt and his people had pitted themselves with such bright zealotry for nearly eight years. Pinchot was chief forester of the United States, head of the U.S. Forest Service, an agency created by Roosevelt in 1905 and one that reflected in its purest form his belief in the stewardship role of government. Roosevelt may have been closer to Pinchot and Garfield than any other two men in his administration. For his part, Pinchot, a tall, emaciated man whose haggard look suggested that he was constantly ravaged by the flames of conviction, worshiped Roosevelt. The President himself believed that Pinchot admired his predatory instincts above all else. "He thinks," he had told Archie Butt, his administrative assistant, "that if we were cast away somewhere together and we were both hungry, I would kill him and eat him, *and I would, too.*"

Pinchot passionately desired to see Roosevelt return to the White House, and there is every indication that he engineered his own dismissal in hopes of creating a final break between Taft and his mentor. That some sort of conflict would develop within Taft's administration regarding the proper use and administration of natural resources was inevitable the minute the President named Richard Achilles Ballinger to replace James Garfield as Secretary of the Interior. Pinchot knew Ballinger. The former mayor of Seattle had been appointed commissioner of the General Land Office during the Roosevelt administration, and that had soon been revealed as a major mistake. Ballinger was quite as committed to the proposal that such public resources as timber land, coal land, and grazing land should be turned over to private interests as Roosevelt, Pinchot, and Garfield were committed to the idea that these lands should be retained in public ownership and their commodities carefully parceled out under a permit and royalty system. Furthermore, Ballinger had vigorously opposed the creation of Chugach National Forest in southern Alaska in

1907, a project particularly dear to Pinchot's heart. After a year of perpetual bickering, Ballinger had resigned.

Then he was back, and Pinchot was not happy. When Louis Russell Glavis, the young head of the Portland Field Division of the General Land Office, came to him in the summer of 1909, Pinchot gave a sympathetic ear, for his tale concerned Richard Ballinger, Glavis's boss, and it did not reflect well upon that upright man. At issue were certain coal lands in Alaska. Under the provisions of an 1873 amendment to the General Mining Law of 1872, private claims to public coal-bearing lands were limited to a quarter section—160 acres—and the number of individual claims that could be consolidated under single ownership were limited to four. This was inconvenient, especially in Alaska, where individual entre- preneurs devoutly wished to stake claims to coal lands at ten dollars an acre, then turn around and sell them at a handsome markup to the Alaska Syndicate, a conglomerate controlled by the Guggenheim and Morgan banking interests. This was monopoly writ very large indeed, and to prevent it, Roosevelt had withdrawn from public entry some one hundred thousand acres of coal lands in the territory in 1906.

That had left about nine hundred coal-mining claims pending, among them thirty-three that had been entered by an Idaho man, Clarence Cunningham, for himself and thirty-two friends, several of them well acquainted with Ballinger. As commissioner of the General Land Office, Ballinger had ordered Glavis to approve these claims; Glavis had ob- jected, maintaining that the minute he did so the claims would be sold to the Alaska Syndicate in a previously agreed-upon arrangement, a clear violation of law. Ballinger had backed off, and shortly afterward had resigned and gone back to his law practice in Seattle—from which city he was soon bombarding his successor with letters requesting the validation of the Cunningham claims. They were still blocked by Glavis's insistence that the whole thing was a transparent fraud, however, when Ballinger subsequently became Secretary of the Interior, at which point he expedited matters by ordering Glavis off the Cunningham case. It was then that Glavis had gone to Pinchot, since several of the claims were staked in Chugach National Forest—and while the administration of mining claims in national forests was under the jurisdiction of the Interior Department's General Land Office, not the Department of Agriculture's Forest Service, what happened in his national forests was of proprietary concern to Pinchot. The chief forester advised Glavis to make a complete report of his findings and conclusions in the matter and take it directly to President Taft up at the summer White House in Beverly, Massachusetts.

Taft read the report, though he was too busy playing golf to see Glavis personally. The President was furious—not at Ballinger but at Glavis and Pinchot for stirring up trouble and calling his man's integrity into question. He ordered Ballinger to prepare a rebuttal, and on September 13, 1909, sent him a letter exonerating him and authorizing him to fire Glavis, which was promptly done. He also wrote Pinchot, rather gently urging him not to pursue the matter further and not to consider any such rash act as resignation. Taft knew full well that if Pinchot resigned it would be viewed as a final break between him and Roosevelt, with the consequent loss of any remaining support his administration might hope to have from the liberal Republicans. Pinchot was not easy to shut up, however, and he had no intention of resigning. By the end of September, Taft was afraid that he was losing control of the situation. "I am convinced," he wrote his brother, "that Pinchot with his fanaticism and his disappointment at my decision in the Ballinger case plans a coup by which I shall be compelled to dismiss him and he will be able to make out a martyrdom and try to raise opposition to me on the Ballinger issue."

Taft may have been a political *naif,* but he was guessing pretty close to the mark here. Over the next several weeks, as Glavis reproduced his charges in an article for *Collier's Weekly,* as the newspapers followed the intricacies of the story avidly, and as both sides began to call for a congressional investigation, Pinchot wrote in detail to Roosevelt (the former President was on safari in Africa), made himself available to the press, and gave a speech at the University Club in New York that was, not accidentally, widely quoted and reprinted: "There is," he said, among other things, "no other question before us that begins to be so important, or that will be so difficult to straddle, as the great question between special interest and equal opportunity, between the privileges of the few and the rights of the many, between government by men for human welfare and government by money for profit, between the men who stand for the Roosevelt policies and the men who stand against them." As the requested congressional investigation prepared to get under way after the turn of the year, Taft ordered all officials in the Executive Department to keep silence on the Ballinger case. This included Pinchot, but when the chairman of the Senate Committee on Agriculture and Forestry asked him for a letter regarding the Ballinger case, Pinchot sent it right along. The letter, which was read aloud in the Senate, supported Glavis's interpretation of the facts and called him a "most vigorous defender of the people's interest." Forced against the wall, Taft called the letter an example of insubordination "almost unparalleled in the history of the government" and on January 7 dismissed the country's chief forester. Pinchot rushed home with the letter of dismissal and waved it at his mother. "Hurrah!" that good lady cried.

Whether deliberately fashioned or not, Pinchot's expulsion from the Taft administration, with accompanying furbelows in the national press, had indisputably served the purpose of highlighting the split in the Republican Party. The outrage felt by liberal Republicans the country over was innocent of suspicion that Pinchot had acted in anything but the best interests of the American public and had been summarily thrown out at the behest of those determined to bilk the people of their patrimony. Certainly, Harold LeClair Ickes had seen it that way from his vantage point in Chicago. "It would be offensive," he had written Pinchot's brother, Amos, on January 14, 1910, "to offer or feel sympathy for a man of your brother's strength of character and ability to take care of himself in any situation. So I will not commit the offense of offering or feeling sympathy for him, but I do feel sorry as a citizen that one of the most loyal, disinterested and able officials that the government has ever had should have been so treated by his government, as has your brother." Pinchot's reply on the seventeenth revealed an unmistakable glow of satisfaction: "We have reached a point where open war is the only safe and conservative course, and the war is on. If Mr. Taft can by an unexampled feat of contortion, reach down to his boot straps and yank himself out of the embarrassing situation into which he has plunged himself in spite of everything his friends could do, he will be backed up by the public, but this seems too much to hope for in a gentleman of his build."

Like any other war, this struggle for the allegiance of the Republican electorate was a good deal more complex than it appeared to be on the surface. The rolling boil of discontent that had bubbled up Ickes and the rest of the Chicago reformers was a national phenomenon of great force, but it lacked definition. At its most elemental levels, the movement was an inchoate mix of indignation and that yearning for a perfect world that had fired the Utopian experiments of the nineteenth century—Brook Farm, New Harmony, and all the rest. It had produced, then abandoned, the Populist Party, stripping that short-lived agrarian eruption of some of its most useful dicta—the direct election of senators; initiative, referendum, and recall; primary elections—and making them its own. It had colored the attitudes and supported the goals of the labor movement, even while recoiling in horror from its excesses and its violence. It had toyed with the gaseous certitudes of Fabian socialism, exported from England by Sidney and Beatrice Webb and the Bloomsbury crowd, and had entertained the rather more rigid doctrines of Karl Marx. It would soon embrace the competing psychoanalytic theories of Sigmund Freud, Carl Jung, and Alfred Adler.

The movement could be profoundly moved, and often was, usually by the magazine press, which was emerging as a major force in American life. "Exposure," George W. Alger wrote in the *Atlantic Monthly* for August 1907,

> forms the typical current literature of our daily life. . . . They expose in countless pages the sordid and depressing rottenness of our politics; the hopeless apathy of our good citizens; the remorseless corruption of our great financiers and businessmen, who are bribing our legislatures, swindling the public with fraudulent stock schemes, adulterating our food, speculating with trust funds, combining in great monopolies to oppress and destroy small competitors. They show us our social sore spots, like the three cheerful friends of Job.

The drumbeat of exposure had sounded relentlessly through most of the first decade of the new century. In the pages of *McClure's Magazine,* Lincoln Steffens had laid bare the shame of Chicago, St. Louis, Minneapolis, New York, San Francisco; the meticulous Ida Tarbell had written a history of Standard Oil that was all the more devastating for its scholarship; and Ray Stannard Baker had taken on corruption of the coal miners' union. Stockbroker Thomas Lawson had informed the readers of *Everybody's Magazine* that Wall Street was a nest of vipers, and Charles Edward Russell told those same readers of the machinations of the beef trust. William Randolph Hearst's *Cosmopolitan* commissioned David Graham Phillips to explain "The Treason of the Senate," while *Collier's* offered Samuel Hopkins Adams on patent-medicine frauds. *Munsey's, American Magazine, Hampton's,* the *Independent*—these and a half-dozen other mass-circulation magazines compulsively ripped the lid off American institutions, a performance from which, contemporary historian Mark Sullivan claimed, "the average man got . . . both satisfaction and fun."

The average man, whoever that may have been, also got a scattering of triumphant heroes along the way. In Cleveland a streetcar millionaire named Tom Johnson abandoned the laissez-faire enthusiasms that had made him a rich man, took up the mantle of reform, got himself elected mayor, and through three consecutive terms produced what was commonly described as the best-governed city in America. In Wisconsin, Robert M. ("Battling Bob") La Follette, after serving quietly as a U.S. congressman for ten years, dropped his mild-mannered façade to take on the malefactors of entrenched capitalism, emerging first as governor, then, in 1906, as a U.S. senator, a seat he would own until his death in 1925. In Nebraska a young lawyer named George W. Norris, not even a native of that state, challenged a Bryanesque Democrat for his district's congressional seat and beat him—then exercised a decidedly liberal bias within the ranks of the regular Republicans throughout a forty-year career in Congress, no less staunch a defender of the people than any progressive in the land. Out in California, another young lawyer named Hiram Johnson waved the bloody shirt of the Southern Pacific Railroad's time-dishonored rule over his state's politics and in 1910 became its governor.

The reformist wave swept through other states—notably, New York, New Jersey, Michigan, Iowa, North Carolina, Texas, and, as we have seen, Illinois—and such was its force that its protagonists could be forgiven the conviction that they were the spokesmen of the future. Yet even as a group of them gathered in Washington, D.C., in 1910 to put a name to their persuasion—the National Progressive Republican League—the movement already had developed a schism, a split within the split, that would destroy it. In its most influential expression, the philosophy that lay behind the split came out of the convoluted mind of Herbert Croly, who, in 1909, had emerged as the pundit of Progressivism with the publication of *The Promise of American Life*. The modern reform movement, he argued, was mistaken in its belief that "no more than moral and political purification" was needed to make the existing system work perfectly. In ridding that system of the corrupting power of the plutocrats, the reformers believed they would "cleanse, oil, and patch a piece of economic and political machinery, which in all essentials is adequate to its purpose." Wrong, he said; the system itself was outmoded and inadequate to a new age, and passion alone could not alter it: "Reform exclusively as a moral protest and awakening is condemned to sterility."

What to do, then? First, the reformers must recognize the fact that the industrial system against which they railed with such moral fervor was not only inevitable but in fact was capable of great good. America offered the businessman limitless opportunities and plenty of elbow room in which to operate. But it also fostered a "more severe, more unscrupulous, and more dangerous competition" that gave him little choice "between aggressive daring business operations, and financial insignificance." Self-preservation, then, drove him to the corruption of local governments and to all those business practices—trusts, interlocking directorships, mergers, and the like—which tended to monopoly and infuriated the reformers. But it also produced a marvelous efficiency in the production and distribution of goods to the great mass of the public and created "an economic mechanism which is capable of being wonderfully and indefinitely serviceable to the American people."

But not under the present system of government. The second thing the reformers must realize, Croly said, was that the diffusion of power, the splintered and incoherent nature of Jeffersonian politics, had erected a system that was incapable of dealing with the new economic order on its own terms. If it was easily corrupted, this was because it was essentially weak, inadequate to the task of regulation and control. It depended altogether too much on local government, which encouraged the development of individual political fiefdoms ruled over by bosses who were less evil than humanly opportunistic. Jeffersonian politics must therefore be abandoned, Croly said; in its place must arise a kind of Hamiltonian centrality in which the power of local governments, state and municipal, was reduced to the barest essentials necessary to the business of daily life. All other power would be vested in the federal government, which, through the tools of taxation and regulation, would encourage the best that was in the economic order and curb what was worst.

He called it the "New Nationalism." Filtered through the twisted intelligence of other men in other places, of course, it was a system of government that would be called fascism (and Croly would live long enough to be sickened by this outcome). But in 1909 he had no suspicion of such possibilities. Neither did those who greeted *The Promise of American Life* on its publication. Judge Learned Hand, no less, told Croly that he was "lost in a maze of admiration at your excellent work"; *The Bookman* called it "the most remarkable book on this subject that has appeared since Bryce's *American Commonwealth*"; it was handsomely reviewed in all the other major publications; and Theodore Roosevelt, having been informed by Croly in the book that he embodied all that was best in the New Nationalism, dashed off an admiring letter, then snatched the phrase and took it as his own.

Most of the old-line liberal reformers, of course, were not much for theory. If they had been told that *The Promise of American Life* was the manifesto of a new philosophy whose orderly doctrines would come to dominate political and social thought and render their own movement impotent, they would not have been persuaded. In the meantime, there were things to be done—mainly, the task of turning the rascals out of office.

The chief rascal, it was commonly agreed among them by 1911, was William Howard Taft. Their first choice as a replacement was Theodore Roosevelt, "Teddy" to millions (though he hated the nickname himself), the cowboy-aristocrat, the killer of big game on two continents, the writer of history, the hero of San Juan Hill, the consummate political animal whose heart nevertheless remained pure. Even before the progressives started calling themselves Progressives, his two administrations between 1901 and 1909 had given their hopes vigorous articulation on a number of fronts. Businessmen, Roosevelt had said, needed "education and sound chastisement," and he had provided some measure of both. He had resuscitated the moribund Sherman Anti-Trust Act of 1890 and waved it threateningly, like one of his big sticks. (All he ever really did do, in fact, was wave it, but if it did not appreciably slow what Croly described as the inevitability of bigness, the gesture at least threw caution into the hearts of the plutocrats.) He had persuaded Congress to put teeth into the Interstate Commerce Commission, particularly in the matter of railroad regulation, to pass a meat-inspection act and a pure-food-and-drug law, and an antiquities act to stop the vandalizing of prehistoric Indian sites for the trinket market. He had forced coal owners into arbitration during a national coal strike. Using the forest reserves clause of the General Reorganization Act of 1891, he had withdrawn 148 million acres of forests from public entry under the various land laws and had placed them in the care of Gifford Pinchot and the Forest Service. Using other powers, he had also withdrawn eighty million acres of coal lands (including those one hundred thousand in Alaska), 4.7 million acres of phosphate lands, and 1.5 million acres of water-power sites. He had given his full support to passage of the Newlands Act authorizing the construction of federal irrigation projects in the West, one of whose goals was the breakup of land monopoly and the fostering of the small family farm. He had Booker T. Washington in to lunch at the White House (the first time ever for a black man) and had appointed Oscar Straus to his cabinet as Secretary of Commerce and Labor (the first time a Jew had been appointed to the cabinet). "If I am fighting against plutocracy," he told a reporter late in his administration, "it is because I am the enemy of Socialism and Anarchism. . . . Plutocracy is the best ally of Socialism and Anarchism. I am in my way a conservative, and that is the reason why I attack plutocratic abuses."

It was not a perfect alliance, this partnership between Roosevelt and the Progressives, whether they recognized it or not. In the first place, he did not like the negativism of the investigative press. During a Gridiron Club dinner on March 17, 1906, he had dipped into John Bunyan's *Pilgrim's Progress* and lifted out a quote with which to characterize the crusading journalist as "the Man with the muckrake, the man who could look no way but downward with the muckrake in his hand; who was offered a celestial crown for his muckrake but who would neither look up nor regard the crown he was offered but continued to rake to himself the filth of the floor."

Clearly, he was not comfortable with the scruffy passions of the ideologues. Nor was he inflexible when dealing with the plutocracy itself. During the financial panic of 1907, J. P. Morgan, Henry Clay Frick, and Judge Elbert Gary—representing the interests of the United States Steel Corporation—had made a proposition to the President. The Tennessee Coal and Iron Company, they said, was in trouble; the price of its shares had taken a terrible tumble. More important, a major New York brokerage house was holding a large block of Tennessee shares as collateral for a loan to the company. If the price began to fall so suddenly that other shareholders began to dump their Tennessee stock, the brokerage house would fail and so would most of the Wall Street firms behind it. Morgan and his colleagues offered to prevent such wide-scale ruin by having U.S. Steel buy a controlling interest in the fast-expiring coal and iron company, paying twice the face value of the stock. This would also bring one more very useful company into the maw of U.S. Steel, and the trio wanted to know whether Roosevelt would consider this a violation of the Sherman Anti-Trust Act and have his Justice Department try to halt the takeover. After thinking about it, Roosevelt decided that it was "no public duty of mine to interpose any objections," and the merger had gone through. In spite of his anti-plutocratic stance, Roosevelt's action in this case was consistent with his beliefs. Like Croly, whose book substantiated many of Roosevelt's long-held convictions, he saw nothing inherently corrupt in bigness, provided it could be turned to the national good. "Combinations in industry," he proclaimed in a 1910 speech outlining "his" New Nationalism (a speech Croly himself may have helped to write), "are the result of an imperative economic law which cannot be repealed by political legislation." The proper goal of government, then, "lies, not in attempting to prevent such combinations, but in completely controlling them in the interest of the public welfare." This he obviously believed he had done in giving his imprimatur to the takeover of the Tennessee Coal and Iron Company.

So Roosevelt did not mirror precisely the concerns of the grass-roots Progressives. Nevertheless, they were committed to him as the embodiment of their ideals, which was how most of them chose to see him, and he did little to discourage the image. And they wanted him back as their President. For quite a while, even after the firing of his friend Pinchot, Roosevelt was not at all certain that he wanted to come back, especially since it would mean a direct challenge to his protégé Taft. The President had repaired some of the damage shortly after Richard Ballinger himself had resigned under pressure a year after Pinchot's departure. In his place, Taft had appointed Walter L. Fisher, a conservationist and friend of Pinchot. Roosevelt, who had backed and filled and refused to commit himself during 1910 in spite of his growing dissatisfaction, continued to do so through most of 1911. As late as the last week of October, he had written to William Allen White that his friends should do anything in their power "to prevent any movement looking toward my nomination, no matter what the circumstances may be." There was every indication that he meant it, and many top Progressives began to look in the direction of Senator La Follette.

At that juncture, Democratic zeal combined with Taft's ineptitude to produce the final break between the two men. In the spring of 1911 a committee chaired by Democratic congressman Augustus O. Stanley of Kentucky decided to investigate the U.S. Steel–Tennessee Coal and Iron Company affair. Unsurprisingly, the committee concluded that Roosevelt had at least been duped by and may even have conspired with J. P. Morgan and his gang in their takeover of the small company, which the Democrats declared was clearly illegal. Roosevelt defended himself with characteristic vigor, calling the investigation an obvious partisan attempt to smear him. There matters might have rested. But at about the same time, Taft's Attorney General, George Wickersham, who fancied himself far more of a trust-buster than Roosevelt had even pretended to be, launched a whole series of antitrust suits in spite of Taft's nervous remonstrances that perhaps Wickersham was being just a little "too energetic." Taft soon regretted that he had not been more forceful with his zealous lieutenant, for on October 26 Wickersham filed suit against U.S. Steel over its purchase of Tennessee Coal and Iron. Roosevelt learned about it the next day in *The New York Times,* and he was not pleased—particularly when a section of the story entitled "Roosevelt Was Deceived" was followed by an excerpt from the suit: "The President [Roosevelt] was not made fully acquainted with the state of affairs in New York relevant to the transactions as they existed. If he had been fully advised he would have known that a desire to stop the panic was not the sole moving cause, but that there was also the desire and purpose to acquire the control of a company that had recently assumed a position of great significance." This indictment stopped just short of calling Roosevelt a damned fool, and he laid it directly at Taft's doorstep. "Taft was a member of my Cabinet when I took that action," he wrote in high fury to James Garfield. "We went over it in full and in detail. . . . He was enthusiastic in his praise of what was done. It ill becomes him either by himself or through another afterwards to act as he is now acting." From that moment on, there was no question but that Roosevelt would be back in pursuit of the White House.

Taft knew it. "If you were to remove Roosevelt's skull," he said gloomily, "you would find written in his brain '1912.' "

CHAPTER

· 13 ·

The Road to Armageddon

GESTATION MUST HAVE been much on the mind of Clair Ickes during the first few months of 1912. Had he enjoyed a poetic bone in his body, which he did not, he might later have made a good deal of the fact that both his wife and the political movement with which he was becoming ever more closely identified were preparing to give birth that year—and would do so within hours of each other.

It would be hard to say which of the two pregnancies was the more difficult. Anna was thirty-nine years old and at least three months pregnant when they returned from Europe early in January. Being with child in the middle of a Chicago winter was not a condition any woman would have welcomed, and Anna's age and her supremely taut sensitivity did not make the situation or the child any easier to bear. She was uncomfortable most of the time and let her husband and everyone else around her know it. Furthermore, she became obsessed with the possibility that the child might be born prematurely—"a seven-month baby," as she put it—and worried that people would then have living proof of their suspicions that she and Clair had succumbed to carnality before marriage. In his inimitable fashion he tried to reassure her, he tells us in his memoirs: "I argued that, whatever people might say or think about me, no one who knew her would imagine for a moment that she had yielded to a human weakness even if she had experienced one. She admitted the force of the argument, but continued to insist that people would be glad of such an excuse as a seven months baby would offer to drag her reputation in the dirt."

Ickes kept his temper (he says) and waded into the comforting tide of the Progressive movement then building toward its own delivery. On the local level, he found that the Illinois Progressive Republican League had been courting folly during his absence. It had endorsed for the state senate two men—Walter Clyde Jones and Hugh S. Magill—whom Ickes believed lacked both the experience and the voter appeal necessary to beat the regular Republican candidates in the upcoming primary elections. The endorsement had been engineered by Medill McCormick, brother to Robert McCormick, who was coeditor of the *Chicago Tribune,* cousin to Joe Patterson, the *Tribune's* other editor, and a man Ickes would always consider a lightweight in politics as in anything else. Ickes refused to participate in the Jones-Magill campaign and had the satisfaction of watching both men go down to defeat.

In the meantime, singly and in groups, Progressives from all over the land were making pilgrimages to Theodore Roosevelt's home at Sagamore Hill or to his offices at *Outlook* magazine in Manhattan, pleading with him to take leadership of the National Progressive Republican League and, more important, to announce his candidacy for the nomination. Finally, on February 25, in response to a letter from seven Progressive governors, the ex-President tossed the gauntlet:

> I will accept the nomination for President if it is tendered to me. . . . One of the chief principles for which I have stood, and for which I now stand, and which I have always endeavored and always shall endeavor to reduce to action, is the genuine rule of the people, and therefore I hope that so far as possible the people may be given the chance, through direct primaries, to express their preference as to who shall be the nominee of the Republican Presidential Convention.

This tone of orotund restraint did not long survive primary defeats in New York, Indiana, Michigan, and Kentucky; in the New York primary, Roosevelt cried "fraud" and linked Taft directly to corrupt bossism in that state.

He found better fortune in Illinois, largely through the efforts of the state's Progressive Republican League, Clair Ickes heavily involved, and especially the Chicago branch of the League, Clair Ickes presiding. Just before the April primary, Roosevelt was scheduled to speak at a rally in the Chicago Auditorium, and Ickes was dispatched to New York so that he could accompany the candidate west to Chicago and fill him in on the local situation. It was his first meeting with Roosevelt since the chance encounter during the campaign of 1900, and he remembered it fondly for the rest of his life. "En route to Chicago," he wrote in his *Autobiography,*

> I was invited to have breakfast with Roosevelt. All through the meal he talked
> politics in his vivacious and eager way. It was a great occasion for me. I was
> reminded, when his breakfast was served, of the rumors of excessive drinking
> on his part. Fruit, a large order of oatmeal, an extra allotment of specially
> cooked whitefish, a man's portion of bacon and fried potatoes, large quan-
> tities of toast, and two cups of coffee—I reflected that no heavy drinker could
> stow away a breakfast like that.

Heavy drinker or not (and at least one report claimed TR could put it
away with the best of them), Roosevelt had the stomach of a cowhand;
unfoundered, he stepped off the train and into an auditorium that "was
packed to suffocation," as Ickes described it. "It was a great meeting,
with the Colonel at his best, denouncing the political bosses and the big
interests that were seeking to deny the rank and file of the Republican
party the chance to nominate their own choice for President. I listened
with enthusiasm." He was not alone in his enthusiasm; in the primary
election, Roosevelt won nearly every precinct in the state. He went on to
take Pennsylvania, too, in spite of the efforts of Philadelphia boss Boies
Penrose and his gang of political thugs, and as delegates began to stream
into Chicago for the convention on June 18, the Progressives could take
some satisfaction in knowing that even if their man was denied the
nomination they were in a position to make themselves heard, loud and
clear.

And so they did. Edna Ferber, newspaperwoman and short story writer
(and soon to be playwright and novelist), was present:

> There never was such a national political convention. . . . The Republican
> convention hall was never for one minute anything but a mass of screaming,
> shouting, stamping, hooting maniacs. . . . Screaming women in the galleries
> . . . howling men on the delegation floor; shouts of "Liars! Thieves!" directed
> at Elihu Root [convention chairman], at Governor Hadley of Missouri [a rival
> for the nomination], at anyone who attempted to raise his voice from the
> speakers' platform. Ten thousand men during one solid week made noises
> such as animals fighting for their lives in a jungle would have considered
> unjustified. As the Roman aristocracy from the vantage point of their gar-
> landed loges looked down upon bloody gladitorial combats, so Chicago
> society and its out-of-town Social Register guests in chiffons, flower-laden
> hats and Palm Beach suits surveyed the hoarse-voiced gesticulating frenzied
> mob rampaging on the floor of the Republican convention called to nominate
> a man for President of the United States of America.

Roosevelt's people fought Taft's people all the way down the line—over
the seating of delegates, over the election of the convention chairman, over

the platform—sometimes quite literally; fistfights were common, and in anticipation of just such violence the railing of the speakers' platform had been wound with barbed wire, covered over with bunting, in case the groundlings should attempt to attack the ramparts. But Taft's people had the power; it was their delegates who got seated, it was their chairman who got elected, and it was their platform that would be adopted. By the afternoon of Saturday, June 22, the outcome was predictable, but the Progressives and Roosevelt made it clear that they were in it for the duration. Given the podium, delegate Henry Allen of Kansas told the convention, "We have fought with you five days for a 'square deal.' We fight no more. We plead no longer. We shall sit in protest and the people who sent us here shall judge us." He then read a statement from Roosevelt:

> A clear majority of the delegates honestly elected to this convention were chosen by the people to nominate me. Under the direction, and with the encouragement of Mr. Taft, the majority of the National Committee . . . with scandalous disregard of every principle of elementary honesty and decency stole eighty or ninety delegates, putting on the temporary roll call a sufficient number of fraudulent delegates to defeat the legally expressed will of the people. . . . I hope that the men elected as Roosevelt delegates will now decline to vote on any matter before the Convention. I do not release any delegate from his honorable obligation to vote for me if he votes at all; but under the actual conditions I hope that he will not vote at all.

Most of them did not. When the final roll call was finished at 10:35 P.M. that Saturday night, Taft received 561 votes, Roosevelt 107, La Follette 41; there were 344 abstentions. Most of Roosevelt's delegates and almost all of his gallery supporters had in fact left altogether by the time the final roll call was taken. All day, in ever-larger bunches, they had been marching out through the stone fairy-castle gates of the Coliseum, under the big arch of its electric sign, carrying their banners and signs and hopes down Wabash Avenue to Orchestra Hall less than a mile away. By midnight there were three thousand of them gathered there, singing, speechifying under the direction of their own chairman, Governor Hiram Johnson of California, waiting for their man to make an appearance.

According to Ben Hecht, then a reporter covering the story for the *Tribune,* Roosevelt was in his suite in the Congress Hotel, milking this hour for all that was in it. "He sat on a couch," Hecht later wrote in his memoirs, *A Child of the Century,* "beaming and tossing whisky after whisky down his gullet. He also pretended to be writing a speech. He grinned at us, ordered us to stop whispering, chewed up his pencils, drew comic elephants on the note paper, opened a second bottle of whisky and wrote nothing."

When Roosevelt finally stood and announced that he was ready to show himself to the crowd at Orchestra Hall, Hecht raced ahead of him and wedged himself into the press box. He had been watching Roosevelt drink steadily for at least two hours, he claimed, and he was concerned that his hero (the Colonel had captured even Hecht's cynical heart) would stagger from the wings of the hall's stage and make a fool of himself. Hecht needn't have worried:

> He came not out of any stage wings like a tardy actor but straight off the street into the auditorium—and alone. He walked down the center aisle as casually as some wayfarer hoping to find a seat. And he walked as sure-footedly as a mountain goat. . . . Up the three thousand leaped and out of them came a roar that lasted for seven minutes—the longest, loudest unbroken roar ever to that time heard under an American roof. . . . Why they roared, I know not then or now, nor why I roared, nor why the roar would not end but seemed to feed on this erect and grinning figure with teeth flashing from behind a walrus mustache. It grew louder like a succession of Wagnerian chords. Without rhyme or reason we stood roaring, our throats turned to megaphones of love. . . . I have no memory of what Teddy said, when finally he spoke. I remember his voice as almost a comic squeak. And I recall his fist sawing the air as he orated. But his words were unimportant, to the three thousand as well as me. We sat back glutted, voiceless and blissful. We had beheld a hero.

Ickes missed it—all of it, the lights and the screaming in the Coliseum, the march down the streets, the explosion of love at Orchestra Hall. Roosevelt and the Progressives had bolted the Republican Party without him and he would regret it all his life. But duty had once again laid its long, heavy arm on him. "I dearly wanted to be at least a spectator of those historic events," he said in his memoirs, "but I never even suggested to Anna the possibility of my going even for a brief moment. Not only would I not have dared to make such a suggestion, but I really doubt whether I would have gone if she had volunteered the suggestion herself. I felt that my duty was to be with her to help her all that I could and she wanted me at home, in Evanston, day after day until the baby should come." That happy event occurred late on the morning of June 23, less than twelve hours after Roosevelt's triumph at Orchestra Hall. It had been a long and arduous labor for Anna, and Ickes had sat in attendance during all the dark hours of it, giving her his hands to grip as she worked her way through the deepest waves of pain. The child was a boy, and they named him Raymond Wilmarth, after Raymond Robins, who had officiated at their marriage, and Anna's father.

As the child's christening would suggest, Raymond and Margaret

Dreier Robins were by then the closest friends Clair and Anna had, a relationship that became one of the few things they could share without reservation—though not without the full load of psychological baggage they brought to nearly everything. Admiration must have mixed with envy, for Raymond and Margaret were a profoundly loving couple whose affection for each other was openly and passionately expressed—almost cloyingly so—a living model for the kind of marriage Clair and Anna might have hoped to have and were so far from enjoying.

This formidable pair, who apparently never had a major disagreement over anything of importance, also had become a power in their own right, and not just locally. As such, they were not only good friends but invaluable allies as Ickes deliberately struggled to find his own niche within the Progressive movement. With nearly a decade of municipal politics behind him, he had pretty firmly established himself in Chicago itself, particularly after he had been elected president of the Chicago Progressive Republican League. His friendships and connections were all the right ones locally—Raymond and Margaret, Charles Merriam, the Harlan brothers, Charles T. Crane, Julius Rosenwald, Donald Richberg, Jane Addams, Judge Edward F. Dunne, even Medill McCormick, however much he disliked the man—and certainly his marriage to Anna, with its attendant connections, had done him little harm. Altogether, it had not been a bad showing.

But he wanted more; all his life he would. As early as 1907, he had tried to reach out for connection to the larger political world with his regular letters to James Harlan; these were designed to establish himself as a reliable analyst not only of the local political scene but of politics in general. As the troubled coalition called the Progressive Party slowly began to come together, he had broadened that correspondence considerably, with much the same ambition in mind. By 1912 he was writing regularly to a wide scattering of Progressive leaders—Amos Pinchot in New York, William Allen White and Henry Allen in Kansas, Chester Rowell and Hiram Johnson in California, James Garfield in Ohio— hundreds of letters, finally, outlining in exquisite detail his considered judgments regarding the movement and the men and women who powered it, most certainly including himself. There was nothing particularly weighty about these judgments. Abstract theory was not his strong suit (there is no indication that he ever read *The Promise of American Life,* for example), but he had developed a strong, practical eye for tactics, and when they could be divorced from any personal involvement, his observations of men and their motives were generally sound. In time, they would become almost as valued by others as they were by himself. In the meantime, he was building a constituency, and he worked at it with the grinding persistence that characterized his pursuit of anything that interested him.

Now that Raymond was safely born and Anna preoccupied with the infant and her recovery from the ordeal of the labor, Ickes was free to return to the thick of things—and things were thick indeed. The first order of business was to give form to the void created when the Progressives marched out of the Coliseum and down Wabash Avenue to Orchestra Hall on June 22. The new party, born of impulse and anger, had to be institutionalized, given civilized shape and respectability, and to that end a convention call had gone forth the day after the great walkout. The date chosen was August 5 and the place the Chicago Coliseum, still draped with Republican bunting—and barbed wire, exposed when Progressive crews began redecorating the place. "We were hopping-mad when we discovered that barbed wire," William Allen White remembered. "It was a symbol of all the fraud and force and shenanigans and duress which we had encountered in the Republican national convention a few weeks before. When we decorated the Coliseum we took off the barbed wire and replaced the bunting." The candidate himself (there would be no other) arrived the day before and almost immediately furnished the party with a nickname whose irreverence fitted the occasion, as William Allen White remembered it:

> Reporters asked Colonel Roosevelt, when he first arrived in Chicago for the convention, how he felt. He called out lustily, snapping his teeth, batting his eyes and grinning like an amiable orangutan:
> "I feel as strong as a bull moose!"
> From that hour we, who followed in his train, were Bull Moosers, and proud of it.

The next day, eighteen hundred delegates marched back through the gates of the Coliseum, beneath the head of an enormous stuffed bull moose that someone had mounted under the electric sign. Hiram Johnson of California proudly waved a banner that read: "I want to be a Bull Moose, / And with the Bull Moose stand, / With antlers on my forehead, / And a Big Stick in my hand." Ickes was in attendance this time, along with his mother-in-law, Mary Wilmarth; his best friend, Raymond Robins; his Hull-House client, Jane Addams; and his soon-to-be law partner, Donald Richberg. On the surface, there was a town-meeting atmosphere to this convention, a sense of coziness and familiarity, of good friends come together in a common cause, with just a touch of religious fervor (the meeting started with a long prayer and was punctuated by hymn-singing from time to time). As William Allen White saw them, these were the good people personified:

> Here were the successful middle-class country-town citizens, the farmer whose barn was painted, the well paid railroad engineer, and the country editor. . . . We were, of course, for woman suffrage, and we invited women delegates and had plenty of them. They were our own kind, too—women doctors, women lawyers, women teachers, college professors, middle-aged leaders of civic movements, or rich young girls who had gone in for settlement work. Looking over the crowd, judging the delegates by their clothes, I figured there was not a man or woman on the floor who was making less than two thousand a year, and not one, on the other hand, who was topping ten thousand. Proletarian and plutocrat were absent.

Well, almost absent. George W. Perkins and Frank Munsey were there, and those two alone were enough to subvert the common joy of unity that trembled and sang through the next two days. Perkins, chairman of the new party's executive committee, was the gray eminence, with gray eyes, gray mustache, graying brown hair, and gray alpaca suits, a Wall Street man through and through, vice president of the New York Life Insurance Company, a Morgan partner, and a power in the U.S. Steel and International Harvester trusts. Nevertheless, he considered himself as good a Progressive as any man, one who actually had read Herbert Croly's *The Promise of American Life* and had taken to his heart the perceived need for partnership between big business and big government. "The great question of the day," he had told a *New York Times* reporter in 1910, "is whether we shall go on with a war between corporations and the people which is certain to do neither any good." He was there because he was a close friend and supporter of Roosevelt, and he would be a principal contributor to party funds. So was Frank Munsey, the millionaire publisher of *Munsey's Magazine* and himself a big investor in U.S. Steel. If anything, Munsey's faith in the link between government and industry was even deeper than that of Perkins. "My observation and reasoning as I study these problems at home and abroad," he had written Roosevelt,

> leads unerringly to the conclusion that the state has got to . . . take on a more personal guardianship of the people. The people need safe-guarding in their investments, their savings, their application of conservation. They need encouragement, the sustaining and guiding hand of the state. They need the German system of helping them to save money for their old age. It is the work of the state to think for the people and plan for the people—to teach them how to do, what to do, and sustain them in the doing.

The people, however—at least most of those sweltering with their Bull Moose badges in the Chicago Coliseum that August—had no such chilling ambitions for society. They wanted good, clean government. They wanted nationwide preferential primaries, nationwide direct election of U.S. senators, nationwide initiative, referendum, and recall; they wanted female suffrage, a short ballot, civil service reform, the limitation and public disclosure of campaign contributions, the exclusion of federal officeholders from campaign politics, an eight-hour day for the workingman and -woman, a tariff commission to stimulate free trade; they wanted, most emphatically, a good, strong, specific antitrust law, one that went beyond even the Sherman Act to list concrete offenses for which corporations could be indicted.

This last was the only major bone of contention, but it was a big one. It stuck in the craws of the money men, Perkins and Munsey, as well as such other conservative Progressives as Senator Albert J. Beveridge and, some feared, Roosevelt himself. Farthest away on the other side of this issue were the left-wingers, William Allen White, the Pinchot brothers, Senator Robert M. La Follette, Henry Allen, and Harold Ickes, among others. For two days the platform committee wrangled and perspired in a room in the Blackstone Hotel, Perkins and even Roosevelt scuttling back and forth between this room and Roosevelt's suite, until a compromise plank was achieved. It was pretty limp; it not only made no mention of strengthening the Sherman Anti-Trust Act, it openly acknowledged that "the concentration of modern business, in some degree [is] both inevitable and necessary for national and international business efficiency." It was a clear triumph for Perkins and his people, but some Progressive imp managed to sully it. When the chairman of the platform committee got up to offer the agreed-upon platform to the convention at large, it was the bellicose antitrust plank of the left-wingers that got read into the record. Perkins rose to his feet in a fury, kicked back his chair, and left the hall. It took several hours of backstage persuasion on Roosevelt's part—together with the promise that all official campaign literature would carry his version of the antitrust plank—to keep Perkins and his bankroll in the party.

The incident was an object lesson in the uses of raw power. It also exposed, for anyone who cared to notice, the lethal split that was draining away the party's credibility like an open wound that refused to heal. Woodrow Wilson noticed, and he would make the most of it. As president of Princeton University, and then as governor of New Jersey, he had appropriated the dogma of the Progressive movement and made it respectable, even though Democratic. It was that aura of respectability (and the support of William Jennings Bryan) that had enabled him that summer to wrest the party nomination from Champ Clark, the favored candidate, and it was that respectability that gave force to the reforms he promised to carry into the Presidency. He called it the New Freedom, and he would hammer its message home with as much passion as his Presbyterian heart allowed him, contrasting it with the insidious potential of Roosevelt's New Nationalism:

> Perhaps this new and all-conquering combination between money and government would be benevolent to us, perhaps it would carry out the noble programs of social betterment, which so many credulously expect of it, but who can assure us of that? Who will give bond that it will be generous and gracious and pitiful and righteous? What man or set of men can make us secure under it by their empty promise and assurance that it will take care of us and be good?

With these dark questions clouding their own movement, with Wilson himself ripping at the trusts, at monopoly, at corruption and greed, with Taft and Roosevelt condemned to split the Republican vote, the Bull Moosers were doomed.

No matter—not that August, anyway. Not with a fine, vigorous, righteous platform to contemplate, not with the hymns sounding in the ear, not with the Greatest Man in America as a candidate—with Hiram Johnson, the second-greatest man, as his running mate—not with more than a decade of fighting for all that was right and holy. If the guidons they carried were somewhat tattered by now, the Progressives gathered in the sweaty heat of the Chicago Coliseum did not know it, or did not want to, and they would continue to bear them proudly to the lists. On the evening of August 6, Roosevelt stood before them, chin thrust out, fist sawing the air, his earnest falsetto rising and falling through thousands upon thousands of words of a "Confession of Faith" that finally achieved a ringing conclusion:

> Six weeks ago, here in Chicago, I spoke to the honest representatives of a convention which was not dominated by honest men; a convention wherein sat, alas! a majority of men who, with sneering indifference to every principle of right, so acted as to bring to a shameful end a party which had been founded over a half-century ago by men in whose souls burned the fire of lofty endeavor. Now to you men, who, in your turn, have come together to spend and be spent in the endless crusade against wrong, to you who face the future resolute and confident, to you who strive in a spirit of brotherhood for the betterment of the nation, to you who gird yourselves for this great new fight in the never-ending warfare for the good of humankind, I say in closing what in that speech I said in closing: We stand at Armageddon, and we battle for the Lord.

They cheered him again and again, and they sang to the tune of "The Battle Hymn of the Republic":

The moose has left the wooded hill,
His call rings through the land.
It's a summons to the young and strong
To join with willing hand:
To fight for right and country;
To strike down a robber band,
And we'll go marching on.

And then they cheered again. Clad in the armor of innocence, they marched to the slaughter.

CHAPTER
· 14 ·

Diminishing Returns

I WON'T PRETEND that we didn't awaken the day after election with a bad headache," Ickes recalled in *Autobiography of a Curmudgeon*. Wilson had beaten his sundered opponents nicely—435 electoral votes to only eighty-eight for Roosevelt and an inglorious eight for Taft. In fact, it was Taft who should have had the largest headache the morning after; Roosevelt had beaten him 4,126,020 popular votes to 3,483,922.* If nothing else, this demonstrated to the Progressives the truth of their conviction that the new party had the strength to carry the future, particularly if it could win back the apostate votes it had lost to Wilson and the Democrats this go-around.

Their hope was predicated on the feeble assumption that the reformist impulse of the Wilsonian Democrats was an aberration that would not last, and that right-thinking American voters would trot back into the fold of the Progressives as soon as they discovered that fact. But it was not an aberration. "The Nation has been deeply stirred," Wilson said in his inaugural address, "stirred by a solemn passion, stirred by the knowledge of wrong, of ideals lost, of government too often debauched and made an instrument of evil. The feelings with which we face this new age of right

---

* This in spite of a would-be assassin's bullet that had staggered but not stopped Roosevelt on October 14. It is a tribute to the man's nearly demented physical courage that he insisted on making a scheduled speech before entering a hospital for treatment.

and opportunity sweep across our heart-strings like some air out of God's own presence, where justice and mercy are reconciled and the judge and the brother are one." He meant it. Before his first administration was done, this Jeffersonian reformer had engineered many of the changes the old Progressives had been calling for since the turn of the century—an income tax; the Federal Reserve Board; the Federal Trade Commission; an eight-hour day for workers on interstate railroads; major tariff reductions; the exclusion from interstate commerce of any trade items produced by child labor; a workmen's compensation act for federal employees; the La Follette Act, improving working conditions for sailors; and, cruelest blow of them all, the Clayton Anti-Trust Act, generally regarded as a truly rational and workable means of controlling the excesses, if not the continuing growth, of business combination. Finally, he had bravely appointed a Jew—a radical Jew, at that—to the Supreme Court: Louis Brandeis, who would serve long and honorably and become an American institution. By 1914 even Herbert Croly, who continued to worry himself over the shadow of Thomas Jefferson's influence, had a good word to say for Wilson. Writing in the pages of the *New Republic* (he had become its founding editor that year), he allowed as how "the present Congress should be credited with the most remarkable record of any Congress since the Civil War," and went on to say that "the credit is largely due to Mr. Wilson." A major shift in American politics had taken place, and while the steadily diminishing numbers of old-line reformers could take credit for having inspired it in the first instance, they were rapidly being left behind.

Within two years, with former Progressives drifting into the camp of the Wilsonian Democrats or back to the ranks of the regular Republicans, the Bull Moose Party was little more than a skeleton articulated at the joints by a handful of diehards. Ickes now was one of the principal leaders, even though he claimed in *Autobiography of a Curmudgeon* that he recognized the dimensions of the problem at the time: "Everyone knew that the Progressive Party was disintegrating, but no one in Illinois knew so well as I how numerous and widespread our defections were. . . . It was up to me to put on as cheerful a face as I could, to keep a stiff upper lip and get out of the situation all that I could for the men and women who faithfully had gone down the line." Perhaps—but it is just as likely that he was far from ready to concede defeat, and in fact had every hope that the party could still be molded into a potent and permanent force, if not as an independent entity, then at least as the moving spirit within the Republican Party. He had far too large an emotional investment and too much at stake by then to believe otherwise, for even as the party began its long slide into oblivion, he rose within it to a genuine position of power.

Shortly after the August convention, Medill McCormick—by then vice chairman of the National Progressive Republican Party—had asked him to take over from John Bass as party chairman of Cook County. Ickes had accepted, and largely because of his work the county was one of the few in the state that had gone for Roosevelt in the election. On November 14 he organized a mass dinner at the Chicago Auditorium so that the Progressives could celebrate the formation of the Bull Moose Party, which many, like Ickes, still believed would replace the Republicans altogether, despite the result of November 5. More than a thousand people showed up to hear, among other things, a few verses dashed off and read by Donald Richberg, who admitted to a literary inclination (he had already had two autobiographical novels published: *The Shadow Man* in 1911 and *In the Dark* earlier in 1912). Richberg's cheerful screed purported to narrate the decline of the Republicans under the righteous assault of the reformers, and read in part:

> *"I am not dead," the elephant rolled up one bloodshot eye;*
> *"I may lie prostrate on the ground but yet how well I lie!*
> *"My eyes are blurred; I cannot hear men shouting in my ears;*
> *"But what of that! I have been blind and deaf for many years. . . ."*

> *Loud shrieked the tortured elephant: "Bring on the funeral wreath!*
> *"My tusks have been extracted and made into Teddy teeth.*
> *"Oh, where, where are the doctor men who tied me up last June,*
> *"When I had fits and tried to dance to the Progressive tune?"*

This brave evening was otherwise a success, for which Ickes could, and did, take credit. In December he was elected the party's state chairman for Illinois and promptly engineered the appointment of Raymond Robins as chairman of the state central committee (on which he, Charles Merriam, and Medill McCormick, who had won reelection as a state assemblyman, also sat). A few months later, Jane Addams asked Ickes to act as her proxy on the executive committee of the national party (whatever else might be said of the Progressives, they were structured to a fare-thee-well). This, in effect, gave Ickes four major positions in the new party—Cook County chairman, state chairman, member of the state executive committee, and proxy of the national executive committee (he would be elected to a permanent position on the national committee in his own right in 1915). All of this gave him the satisfaction of being able to deal as an equal with such other high-level Progressives as Amos Pinchot, Chester Rowell, William Allen White, and George Perkins, in addition to Medill McCormick and the other locals. And he would not hesitate to do so.

In the meantime, he had also become a law partner. Shortly after the election, Donald Richberg was appointed to direct the party's Legislative Reference Bureau in New York, an agency whose idealistic goals were later described by Richberg himself: "During the transition period between the almost purely parasite lawyer of today and the social counselor of tomorrow legislative reference bureaus may serve as postgraduate schools in which young lawyers may be brought in touch with the needs of their generation in the way of jurisprudence." He was reluctant to leave his overworked and ailing father, John Carver Richberg, alone with the duties of the law office they had shared since 1905, so he asked Ickes to join them as a full partner. Early in 1913 the firm in the Rector Building became Richberg, Ickes & Richberg. As Richberg recalled it in his own autobiography, *My Hero,* he had taken something of a chance: "My father was a man of strong convictions and irascible temper. He was also a conservative Democratic politician of considerable influence. As is well known [Richberg was writing in 1954], Ickes was a man of somewhat uneven temper, an intense partisan of any cause which he espoused and definitely a reformer of the type far from agreeable to my father's disposition. Yet, strange to say, they managed to get along together."

This amiable circumstance probably stemmed from the fact that Ickes spent too little time in the office for conflict to develop. As he had with his private practice, he used the law partnership mainly as a foundation for his sorties into the world of politics and reform; he was usually too busy to irritate old Mr. Richberg. Unfortunately, he was also too busy to bring in much business. When Donald Richberg returned from New York early in 1914, having decided that he could not make ends meet on the puny salary the party was able to give him, he found the firm intact but hardly flourishing. The situation did not improve much over the next year. Like Ickes, Richberg had little interest in the law as a business venture. Unlike Ickes, however, he had no independent source of income and was constantly on the shorts. In November he turned to Ickes for a five-hundred-dollar loan to meet personal expenses, then struck him up for another five hundred dollars in February. Ickes, who was a soft touch for friends and relatives all his life, paid over both instantly and without any fuss, inspiring an emotional note from Richberg after the second loan: "For what you did today and for your attitude in doing it I have a sense of deep appreciation which I want to put in black and white. At rare intervals one meets a friendliness that imposes not only an obligation to do the right thing, but a desire to do a fine thing oneself. For this impetus as well as for the immediate aid I am most grateful."

The firm's shaky business foundation suffered a nearly fatal blow in 1915, when Richberg's father was felled by a stroke. In desperation,

Richberg and Ickes took in two more partners, each of whom was more interested in law as a profession than as a platform: Morgan Davies and John S. Lord. Within a few months, the firm had prospered enough for it to take larger, more elegant quarters on the eighteenth floor of the Harris Trust Company Building at Clark and Monroe streets, one of the second generation of Chicago skyscrapers. After an unsuccessful bid for a seat on the circuit bench that year as a Progressive-Republican fusion candidate, Richberg himself began to contribute somewhat to the firm's solvency by becoming Special Council to the city of Chicago in its litigation efforts to obtain rebates from the People's Gas Light and Coke Company, an outfit under the control of Thomas Alva Edison's former assistant Samuel Insull, by now one of the power plutocrats of the nation. The following year he also took on the job of master in chancery for the circuit court of Cook County.

Ickes's own career was not moving quite so smoothly, however satisfying it may have been on the surface. As far as the Illinois Progressive Party was concerned, he was fighting his way toward the helm of a sinking ship. In 1913 the local party managed to get four aldermen elected to the city council, Merriam among them, but Carter H. Harrison still sat secure in the mayor's chair. On the state level, Ickes was locked in a struggle over control of the State Central Committee with Medill McCormick and his wife, Ruth—now head of the Illinois Legislative Reference Bureau and, many believed, the real brains of the family. Ickes had the votes to beat them ("The organization was in our hands and we intended to use it for the good of the party," he proclaimed), but both the McCormicks would ultimately slip back into the comforting arms of the regular Republicans, taking many Progressives with them. The pair did manage to put Ickes in an awkward position in August of that year. Ickes had decided to campaign for an appointment by the governor to the State Utilities Board, and the McCormicks promptly put forward the name of Raymond Robins for the job. Ickes then pulled out. "The matter," he primly wrote the governor's secretary, "has been made the subject of a bitter factional fight within the Progressive Party and while this of itself is not a thing of much concern to me, I do feel reluctant to be regarded, even by my political enemies, as scrambling for a political job."

Robins did not get the appointment either, but had he, it is questionable whether he would have been able to fulfill his duties. While in England that July, he had suffered a bad fall and would be a long time recovering. By April of the following year, he was still feeling so poorly that he wrote Ickes from Chinsegut Hill in Florida to resign as chairman of the Central Committee.

"Now that your decision has been made don't let it worry you," Ickes replied with the deference that was characteristic of their relationship at this time. "I don't like the note of discouragement that crept into your letter. I don't know of any one who has accomplished more that is worth while at your age than you have. If I had done as much myself I might be more willing to retire than I am and after all you are only beginning. You are just coming into your full powers and what matters the loss of a few months, or even two or three years, in a lifetime."

Three months later Robins had recovered sufficiently for Ickes to persuade him to run for a U.S. Senate seat on the Progressive ticket.* It was the last major office for which the Illinois Progressive Party would put up a candidate, and Ickes and the rest of the diehards probably were counting heavily on the female vote that year—the first in the state's history, and one of the few in the country. A female suffrage bill had been passed by the state legislature and signed into law by Governor Edward Dunne late in 1913. On February 3, 1914, the first day of registration, 153,897 women in Chicago alone had entered their names on the voter's lists.

Despite the women's vote, however, Robins was defeated in November. Medill McCormick did make it back to the state legislature, although it would be his last campaign as a declared Progressive. In Chicago itself, the situation was even worse. Ickes and the Progressives were able to put up their own candidate for the Republican mayoral nomination in 1915, but he was roundly defeated in March by William Hale ("Big Bill") Thompson, who was being touted as a reformer by the regular Republicans. Ickes despised Thompson, who had served undistinguished terms as a city alderman and a county commissioner. "He loved to go in state to football games, play poker, get drunk, and chase women," Ickes said of the big man in his memoirs. Ickes worked against Thompson, in spite of the fact that Thompson was getting considerable Progressive support from other quarters—including those inhabited by Medill McCormick and his wife. "My disgust was unbounded," Ickes reported in his *Autobiography,* "to think of men and women who had voted for principle since 1912 being attracted to this political *symplocarpus foetidus* in the mistaken belief that a flickering and sickly flame was a real beacon of civic righteousness."

Thompson won the mayoralty in June, then almost immediately proceeded to justify Ickes's bad opinion. On September 27 the Chicago

---

* After ratification of the Seventeenth Amendment to the Constitution in 1913, U.S. senators were no longer elected by state legislatures, but by popular vote.

garment workers once again went on strike (not including the eight thousand happily-unionized workers at the Hart, Schaffner and Marx plant, whose president, Joseph Schaffner, had by now become one of organized labor's rare industrial champions). This time they were led by the young Sidney Hillman, beginning a career that would see him emerge as one of the giants of the modern labor movement. Twenty thousand workers walked off their jobs and the streets soon rang with the kind of violence that had characterized the strike of 1910—as before, most of it perpetrated by the police. Thompson's attitude encouraged it. When Hillman led a delegation of prominent citizens to the mayor's office early in October to plead with the city government to mediate the strike, Thompson refused to see them, while on the street outside the police took up billy clubs and went after the crowd of workers that had accompanied the delegation. By the end of the month, strikers—at least half of them women—were being clubbed and shot at regularly (two would die and more than eight hundred would require medical treatment before it was over), but Thompson still refused to intervene. He remained unmoved even after Margaret Robins and the Women's Trade Union League organized a Citizens' Mass Meeting (Ickes was its publicity chairman) in November at which his intervention was demanded. Hillman, his union out of money, finally declared an end to the strike on December 12. It was, nonetheless, a partial victory: eighty-seven shops employing some five thousand workers had signed agreements with the union by then.

On the national front, the party's condition was hardly any better. "The Progressive party was tottering to its deathbed," Ickes recalled, "although its ghost was to walk for some little time." He knew exactly who was to blame for this sorry fact (and *someone* had to take the onus; Ickes's need for villains was quite as powerful as his need for heroes): George W. Perkins. He was encouraged in this conviction by Amos Pinchot, who, if anything, detested the financier even more than did Ickes. The Progressive Party, Pinchot had written Ickes a few weeks after the 1912 elections, was

falling more and more into the hands of two men, Mr. Perkins and Mr. Munsey. Our whole program of social and industrial justice is a good deal of a fraud if we do not tackle the trust question. Mr. Perkins, as chairman of the Executive Committee, has become the mouth piece of the party. Mr. Munsey . . . believes that the trouble with the country is . . . that the working classes are too well paid and work too short hours. . . . In other words, the party is, to a great extent . . . in the hands of two men who are fundamentally opposed to the realization of the real purpose . . . for the party's existence.

Ickes agreed that "our chief danger as a party lies in the prominence . . . of George W. Perkins," and described its leadership as "George W. Perkins and a push button." He suggested that Gifford Pinchot would make a much better leader (Amos did not challenge this notion) and that some tactful means ought to be found to restructure the national and executive committees to reduce Perkins's power.

Tact was not prominent among Amos Pinchot's virtues. In May 1914 his own resentment of Perkins rose to such a boil that he decided to challenge the committee chairman head-on. In an effort to gain support for this move, he circulated a ten-page "confidential memorandum" to Ickes and others that indicated Perkins as a tool of the trusts and called for his immediate removal as chairman of the Executive Committee and treasurer of the party. But Roosevelt, still the spiritual head of the party, while ostensibly keeping himself at Olympian remove from its grubby struggles, made it clear he would support Perkins. In the face of this, even Ickes backed off. Pinchot's movement aborted, and he noisily resigned from the party.

Perkins's power was indeed considerable, and as the Presidential election year of 1916 drew closer it became increasingly apparent what he was up to, however obliquely: he had abandoned any hope that the Progressive Party could ever maintain itself as an independent force and was now determined to haul it back into the Republican fold. Ickes and the other diehards saw this as a malign intent to subvert the goals of the reformers, and certainly Perkins had demonstrated himself throughout the brief history of the party to be much less radical than most of the rank and file. Still, it was not ideology but survival that probably motivated him—his own survival as an architect of national politics and, to give him credit, the survival of those moderately progressive beliefs he sincerely held and earnestly hoped would ultimately be adopted by the Republican Party.

If he succeeded, it would be over the dead bodies of the old-line Progressives, who now pinned their future to another third-party run by Roosevelt. Roosevelt himself was ambiguous at best, negative at worst, regarding the idea, and remained so right to the final moment. On the last day of April 1916, Ickes threw a major luncheon for Roosevelt at his new home in Hubbard Woods, to which he invited all the leading Progressive lights of Chicago. Roosevelt sparkled, chortled, declaimed—and committed himself to nothing. He then went off to Kansas City and had a long talk with William Allen White, at the end of which, White remembered, the Colonel was firm: "No, White, I just musn't do it. As things look now, it would be more than the Progressives ought to ask of me!"

It was not that Roosevelt was willing to leave the Republic in the hands of Woodrow Wilson. In fact, he hated Wilson with an intensity that was almost pathological in its adolescent passion. Wilson, among other Rooseveltian descriptions, had become that "infernal skunk in the White House." In Roosevelt's eyes, the President had not only purloined the dogma of the New Nationalism—and calling it the "New Freedom" was a particularly scurvy trick—he had twisted and perverted it to his own cheap ends. To Roosevelt, moreover, Wilson was clearly a moral and physical coward; when the guns of August 1914 began the long mutilation of Europe, their thunder sounded in Roosevelt's very soul. "The just war," he had once declared, "is a war for the integrity of high ideals. The only safe motto for the individual citizen of a democracy fit to play a great part in the world is service—service by work and help in peace, service through the high gallantry of entire indifference to life, if war comes on the land." It galled his martial sensibilities to hear Wilson say that Americans should remain "impartial in thought as well as deed" in regard to the European conflict. The situation grew almost intolerable for Roosevelt when German submarines sank the British liner *Lusitania* on May 7, 1915, with the loss of 1,198 lives, including 128 Americans. "President Wilson," he said, turning to Scripture again, "has earned for the nation the curse of Meroz for he has not dared to stand on the side of the Lord against the wrongdoings of the mighty."

No, Roosevelt wanted Wilson defeated well enough and would go to any lengths to assure it. But he knew that he probably had little chance of doing it himself as the candidate of the Republican Party; in 1912 he had sinned mightily against all that party politics held dear, and it was not likely he would be forgiven. In fact, as the convention month of June approached, it became more and more likely that the Republicans would go for Charles Evans Hughes, a dour associate justice of the U.S. Supreme Court. Still, Roosevelt was a politician, a species that feeds entirely on hope, and he had no intention of spoiling whatever chance there might be by linking his name directly to the Progressives. When it came right down to it, as a matter of fact, by then he was ready to abandon the Progressives altogether. Like Perkins, he had little faith in the party's strength and was not willing to insure Wilson's reelection by running as a third-party candidate and splitting the Republican vote to Wilson's advantage. A few days before the resurgent Bull Moosers began gathering at the Chicago Auditorium (the Republicans coalesced at precisely the same time over at the Coliseum), he gave Perkins a letter of rejection to be read to the convention at the proper time.

Ickes, Raymond Robins (who was promptly elected chairman of the convention), Hiram Johnson, Donald Richberg, Gifford Pinchot, and the rest of the Progressive radicals had their own plans—and, like Roosevelt, hopes that refused to recognize the odds. Their scheme was simple: to nominate Roosevelt before the Republicans could settle on a candidate and thus force them to endorse Roosevelt themselves in order to avoid the third-party split. The Progressives were willing to compromise: they would go so far as to reject whomever might be chosen as their own nominee for Vice President and take that of the Republicans instead. They were counting heavily, of course, on being able to persuade Roosevelt to accept the nomination, believing, as William Allen White put it, that "Roosevelt . . . would not desert them. In that week more than at any other time in his career Theodore Roosevelt was a little tin god to his idolators. Not at any time in 1912, not even when he escaped an assassin's bullet, was he so vividly lifted in the hearts of his followers as the hero-god of their hopes."

Perkins had hopes, too—first, that the Republicans would, by some miracle, actually nominate Roosevelt and he could then persuade the Progressives to accept the inevitable and fuse with the mother party. Failing that, he had the even more unlikely dream that he could persuade them to accept Hughes as a fusion candidate. He withheld Roosevelt's letter for fear that if he read it to them they would instantly nominate someone, anyone, out of sheer rage and frustration. Through one rancorous conference after another (at one point, he and Ickes were locked in a screaming match for several hours), Perkins and his people attempted to keep the diehards from making their move.

Things proceeded in spite of him. Committee meetings soon produced a platform, which was swiftly adopted. Donald Richberg was installed with a telegraph operator in the Coliseum, sending word of the Republican doings to White and another telegraph operator in the Auditorium. When the message came that the Republicans were beginning to make their nominating speeches, White sent word to Ickes, who spread it among the conspirators. Bainbridge Colby (a New York lawyer who would soon become Wilson's Secretary of State), out of order, asked the chair for recognition. Robins gave him the floor. Perkins, on the podium, suddenly must have realized what was happening. He leaped to the speaker's stand and tried to interrupt Colby. Robins firmly pushed Perkins back into his chair and Colby proceeded to nominate Theodore Roosevelt. The Auditorium burst into a ten-minute howl, then the nomination was passed by the thunder of "Aye!" from the floor. John M. Parker, former governor of Louisiana, was quickly accepted as the Vice-Presidential candidate.

In due course the Republicans indeed nominated Hughes. It was at this juncture that Perkins pulled Roosevelt's letter from his pocket and read it to the convention. "The last words, 'But your candidate I cannot be,' " White remembered, "fell upon them like a curse. For a moment there was silence. Then there was a roar of rage. It was the cry of a broken heart such as no convention ever had uttered in this land before. Standing there in the box I had tears in my eyes, I am told. I saw hundreds of men tear the Roosevelt picture or the Roosevelt badge from their coats, and throw it on the floor. They stalked out buzzing like angry bees."

Anticlimax, then. On July 10, as a gesture of conciliation, Perkins saw to it that Ickes, James Garfield, Chester Rowell, Oscar Straus, and Everett Colby—hard-nosed Progressives all—were named to the Republican National Campaign Committee, and Garfield and Ickes were placed in charge of the Hughes western campaign headquarters in Chicago. The regular Republicans then proceeded generally to ignore the advice and counsel of their rebellious colleagues, while the Progressives, as Ickes wrote Rowell in California, promised one another to "to keep in touch . . . until such time as a national organization again seemed practical." On the evening of November 3, as everyone soon learned, Charles Evans Hughes went to bed convinced that he had taken California—and with it, enough electoral votes for the Presidency. He woke up to learn that he had in fact lost the state—and the election. Wilson won with 49 percent of the popular vote and 277 electoral ballots; Hughes had 46 percent and 254 electoral ballots. Once again, in November, Ickes gathered around him what Progressives he could find. He knew what they had to do, he told Rowell again. They had to get behind Hiram Johnson for the elections of 1920: "Hiram Johnson will be the one man who looms in that territory and he must be taken into consideration as a presidential possibility." Brave words, but the year 1920 must have seemed as far away as the next turn of the century to Ickes by that time.

CHAPTER
· 15 ·

The House
in Hubbard Woods

O N APRIL 24, 1914, writing to Raymond Robins about his decision to resign as Central Committee chairman, Ickes went on to unburden himself—at least partially—for one of the few times in his life. "I told Anna some time ago," he wrote,

> that it was my firm intention to resign as County Chairman. She had not suggested anything of the sort and, on the contrary, she wants me to give as much of my time and strength as I feel I ought to give, to the party. I came to the conclusion, however, because my health was and had for some months been pretty rotten. While I kept going it was under the lash of the spirit and I began to realize that unless I began to let up a complete break would inevitably come from which I might not recover for years, if at all. I have been over-taxing my strength and living on my nerves for years now and there come times when I wonder how much longer I can keep going. When I was a bachelor I didn't care and was willing to expend myself in a way that I do not now feel that I have the right to do. . . .
>
> Your word about little Raymond touches me deeply. I have built him a sand pile in the back yard as the result of which I have come to the conclusion that I am a better carpenter than I am a politician. He has a glorious time in there shut off by wire fence and gate from too friendly dogs. During these latter days I have been trying to go home early occasionally to garden and then Raymond comes out to "help Poppy." I wish you could see him. He is

exceedingly active now and talks clearly and distinctly. . . . We are all as
crazy about him as we have been and he seems to grow dearer every day.

There was much to be read between the lines of this, if Robins had
been so inclined. Probably he was not, for it is unlikely that either he or
Margaret had any reason to suspect that the married life of Clair and Anna
was anything but normally placid. Through all the decades of their
regular correspondence with these two, not once did either of the Ickeses
let their pain show from under a cloak of careful respectability. At times,
the effort must have called for superhuman restraint, for if even half what
he tells in his memoirs is the uncluttered truth, not just a memory twisted
out of shape, their life together was more often than not an emotional
charnel house.

Their fights continued, worse now than even before the marriage.
Ickes accepted full blame for his share of temper, but reported that

> Anna had one advantage over me at such times. If a quarrel was more than
> unusually bitter and prolonged she could develop an astonishing case of
> hysterics. She would throw herself about on the bed or the floor, screaming
> and moaning, until she became incoherent and semi-cataleptic. . . . For a
> long time these states actually frightened me and there was no self abasement
> to which I would not willingly subject myself in order to bring her out of
> them.
>
> Then Anna would strike me. When she was quarrelling she had a disposi-
> tion to stand as near to me as possible, glaring at me, and suddenly she would
> hit me with her open hand full in the face. More than once she broke my
> glasses. Since the first blow was usually a precursor to others I would then
> seize and hold her wrists until she had quieted. Some times I would force her
> to sit in a chair or lie on the bed until she had regained self control. Later she
> was to characterize these acts of mine as "striking her" or "abusing her
> physically," but it was too deeply ingrained in me that a man should never
> strike a woman.

"We quarreled about everything," he says in another section of the
memoirs,

> my friends, my clubs—although I never was a club man in any real sense of
> the word—my business associates, my political interests, my flower gar-
> den. . . . We quarreled about the children, about her mother and especially
> about my mother, against whom Anna had conceived a bitter and vindictive
> hate, although she had never seen my mother nor known of her except from
> my lips. . . . It would not be credited if I should recite the bitter, cruel and
> slanderous things that Anna used to say about my mother.

For several years—at least long enough for Anna to suffer two
miscarriages—these gargantuan struggles, he tells us, would often end in

the moist frenzy of sexual passion. ("Psychologically there seems to be a sexual aspect to quarrels between a man and a woman," he says with overwhelming innocence.) In time, this too would end, by his own decision: "I have always been repelled by the thought of sexual intercourse between a man and a woman who do not love each other and so, when I finally came to the definite conclusion in my own mind that I no longer loved Anna and could never love her again, I was determined, if I could, to desist from this intimate relationship with her." The disclaimer, not very convincing to begin with, is shattered when he later informs us that after several years of self-imposed celibacy ("this life was playing havoc with my nerves") he began to take up with other women—women whom he did not love and who did not love him. Probably it would not stretch the limits of either biography or psychology to suggest that the withdrawal of his favors from Anna was essentially an act of aggression: deprived by tradition (middle-class folks did not do such things) and his own inhibitions of the opportunity to slug her back, he was getting at her in one of the few ways left open to him.

It was not, in any case, a marriage made in heaven, but it would endure. He put the thought of divorce out of his mind, he says, first because of the children. It is always permissible to suspect this, but in Ickes's case there may have been a measure of truth in it, simply because his need for the children—at least for Wilmarth and Raymond—may have been at least as great as their need for him. Wilmarth, nicknamed Mike after his schoolmates had taken to calling him "Microbe" because of his small size, had been an ingratiating child and was growing up to be a sweet-natured if somewhat tempestuous youth. His adolescent forays into independence did not sit well with Anna, Ickes reported; she could love her children freely only so long as she could control them—after that, it was a bitter struggle for dominance. Increasingly, it was to his stepfather that the boy turned for emotional solace, as he did one afternoon when he was about twelve. After a battle with his mother, during which she had slapped the boy, Clair took him on his lap, put mothering arms about him, and let him cry (this shattered all principles of child-rearing, of course, which hold that one parent should not subvert the discipline of the other, but even if Ickes had known this, it is not likely that he would have cared—the boy had come to *him* to be held). When he was older, perhaps fifteen, Wilmarth disappeared while on an obligatory visit to his real father. It was Ickes who tracked him down after several frantic weeks. He found him working in a farm field in Winnipeg, of all places, and when Ickes called to him, Wilmarth turned and ran—straight toward his stepfather's waiting arms.

If Clair's love for Wilmarth was real, his love for Raymond was absolute—and during the boy's childhood years, at least, it was unsullied by the strain of competition that clearly marked his relationship with Wilmarth. Or so he tells us:

> . . . if Raymond loved me he loved his mother with equal devotion. As a matter of fact I think that he loved her more than he did me and I did not resent it. It seemed to be perfectly natural that a boy should love his mother more than his father. It gave me pleasure to feel that in a life where there was manifestly little active joy there should be the satisfaction that Anna derived from Raymond. Instinctively we both protected him. We co-operated together for his welfare and, naturally, we kept scrupulously from him any intimation that we did not love each other as much as he thought that we did.

This happy circumstance began to deteriorate when the solemn, remarkably articulate little boy—"Ick," his parents called him—entered his adolescent years, but for a time the child did inspire the best that was in both of his parents.

Not as much could be said for poor Frances, who was now a young woman and having a bad time of it with both of them. Anna's powerful need to control those about her was her least endearing characteristic, and Frances got the full weight of it. Anna attempted to govern every aspect of the girl's life; Frances resisted, as any healthy adolescent would; and the upshot was a relationship that alternated between thunderous battles and sullen silences on the part of both women. Clair tiptoed around this particular situation like Caspar Milquetoast, unwilling to arouse Anna's jealous wrath—which came to the fore, he says, whenever he paid the slightest bit of attention to the girl. He simply absented himself, and Frances got no solace from him.

Raymond and Wilmarth, then, played a major role in keeping Ickes from divorcing Anna. Another reason, he says, "was Anna herself. She had already been divorced once and a second divorce would have hit her terribly hard indeed. I felt that, not only as the mother of my son, but as the woman whom I had married in the circumstances in which I had married her, it was my duty to endure." We can believe this, I think—at least a good part of it. His readiness—indeed, eagerness—to accept responsibility and the dictates of what he perceived as his duty was chronic all his life. However onerous it may have seemed at times and however long-suffering his endurance, his nearly obsessive adherence to duty brought with it powerful benefits that went a long way toward obliterating the helplessness of his childhood: if so much of his world was so utterly dependent upon him for its well-being, indeed its very survival, was he not then firmly established at the center of it?

ଯାଯାଯାଯା

Until early 1916 this periodically tormented household kept its residence
in the Evanston house that Anna had built in 1910. Ickes did not
particularly like living in Evanston—"never . . . a very friendly place,"
he noted—and convinced Anna that they should build another house in
another town. Late in 1914 they found a seven-acre plot of land in
Hubbard Woods, part of the township of Winnetka just north of Evanston. The land was heavily wooded throughout and included a number of
great oak trees hundreds of years old; just three minutes away by foot lay
Lake Michigan, and the passenger depot of the Chicago & Northwestern
was quite as close. It was a splendid piece of country and they bought it.

It was here they planned their house. Anna's old friend Dwight Perkins
was chosen as the architect, although he had made his reputation in the
building of schools, not houses; in 1905 he had been appointed chief
architect of the Chicago school system and in 1909 had constructed Carl
Schurz High School on Milwaukee Avenue and Addison Street, still
considered a masterpiece of educational design. Perkins would live to
regret taking on the Ickes assignment, but Clair and Anna had a wonderful time. "While building this house," he wrote,

> Anna and I worked more happily together than in any other matter. I felt that
> she had good taste and she respected mine. Even when there was an original
> difference of opinion over details we always ended in perfect accord. Some-
> times I yielded to her and at other times she yielded to me; but in all of such
> instances each was satisfied with the judgment of the other. The result was a
> house into which the thought and feelings of both of us entered in full
> measure. I have never seen a house that I liked as well as this one.

Ground was broken for the house in the early spring of 1915, and from
the beginning Ickes felt that his personal supervision was necessary to its
completion. "Every Sunday morning," he remembered,

> almost without exception, from the time that the house was started until it
> was finished, I would go over it very carefully and, usually, I would take an
> earlier train a couple of times during the week and go right through to
> Hubbard Woods to spend an hour or two at the site before going home. The
> result was that I kept very close track of the building and gave it a closer
> inspection even than the architects. One contractor told me that he wished
> that he could hire me as an inspector because nothing escaped me. Perhaps he
> was just kidding me.

Yes, perhaps he was.

The firm of Perkins, Fellows & Hamilton was regularly informed in exquisite detail of all those things that did not escape him. These were numerous. At one point he "discovered" that a fireplace in the already half-built sun porch was not properly centered on the wall and ordered it ripped out and restructured the way he decided he wanted it ("I never regretted that decision or the extra cost it put us to"). Most of his complaints, however, were of a comparatively minor nature, if endless. Closet shelves were "badly bungled," bathroom and fireplace tiles were cracked, the flooring squeaked, the molding in the dining room was all wrong, the plate warmer in the butler's pantry was "inadequate," the linoleum in the kitchen was improperly stretched, one of the transoms was incorrectly installed ("In the circumstances I do not expect to be called upon to pay for rectifying this mistake"), the radiators were sloppily painted, the supply pipes to the sitz bath were asymmetrical, the bathtubs drained poorly, so did the flower boxes, there was a leak in the slate roof. . . . The litany of memoranda to Perkins continued long after the family had taken residence, until the two men were barely speaking to each other. (On two occasions, Ickes hung up the telephone on Perkins, later explaining by letter that Perkins's failure to supply him with one blueprint or another was the cause: "I do not suppose that this was done deliberately, but if you had deliberately set out to try to the breaking point my already over-strained and, at best, not any too resolute patience, you could not have hit upon anything more likely to have the desired effect." This was probably by way of an apology.) Unsurprisingly, when it came time to build a gardener's cottage and a garage-cum-living quarters for a chauffeur and his wife, Perkins was not the architect chosen for either job.

The house had just been finished when Ickes gave his luncheon for Theodore Roosevelt at the end of April 1916. Ickes probably regretted that he had not also finished his landscaping and his flower gardens by then, for this was the portion of his life in Hubbard Woods that he would come to love above all others, the most satisfying expression of the childhood impulse that had moved him to create beauty in the grimy surroundings of working-class Altoona. After World War I his efforts would acquire a measure of regional fame, but even within a year of moving into the house, he had accomplished much: "I have never seen anywhere as lovely a spring garden as I developed just to the west and southwest of the house where I had thousands of mertensia and daffodil bulbs, which were a glorious sight when they were in bloom. . . . I also went in for peonies in a big way, buying only the ones that ranked 8 or above, according to the ranking of the American Peony Society and sometimes paying as high as $50 for a single new root."

While his top-of-the-line gardens were beginning to be laid out in the summer of 1916, Clair and Anna began filling the place with people, until it eventually took on the character of a small colony. In addition to the two of them and the three children, there were Ida Erisman, the nurse; Eric and Ruth Magnuson, the chauffeur and his wife; three house servants; and the first of the two gardeners to occupy the gardener's cottage over the years. That would appear to have been a sufficiency, but within two years the entourage would be enlarged by two more permanent residents. The first was Anna's cousin, Tom Gilmore, who came to live with them at Anna's invitation when his wife took herself and their daughter to New York in an attempt to break into show business. It was to be a temporary arrangement until Gilmore's wife returned or he found another place to live. In the end, he stayed with them for nearly fifteen years, a faded, unobtrusive man who held some sort of low-paying job in the city and loved to practice target shooting and play billiards; he would teach Raymond how to do both. (If Ickes perceived the striking similarity of Gilmore's situation to the one he had occupied in the Thompson household for so many years, he does not reveal it.)

The second addition to the household came about under even stranger circumstances—although quite characteristic of this family. After her second miscarriage, it became clear that Anna was not likely to bear any more children. She worried that "little Ick" would grow up without companionship his own age (they were having the boy tutored, not educated in public schools), and decided that they should find and bring into the family another little boy, much as she had brought in Frances. This was a bit more responsibility than even Clair was willing to assume without objections, but his everlastingly stubborn wife insisted and he finally caved in. ("Anna had learned nothing from the adoption of Frances," he remembered, "and apparently I hadn't either. . . . I was thoroughly tired of fighting. I was a coward even when the best interests of my own son were involved.") After a couple of unsuccessful experiments when Raymond was about four (Raymond has the vague memory that one of them was named Glenn), Ickes found a boy being offered for adoption by a finishing school in New York City that did social work on the side. His name was William Francis Jones, he was a little over two months younger than Raymond, and upon meeting Ickes he climbed immediately into his lap and put his arms around his neck. This first impression survived even Ickes's discovery a few weeks later that the boy's father had been an alcoholic who had died drunk and his mother a slattern who had disappeared after her husband's death. The boy was inserted into the Ickes family troupe and his name was changed to Robert, presumably to sever any connection with his scurvy past (Ickes does not otherwise explain the change).

If one includes the servants, there were now fourteen in residence in Hubbard Woods—but if this extended family gave him satisfaction, he could not bring himself to admit it. As he had complained in his letter to Raymond Robins in 1914, emotional stress—from both his public and his private lives—had played havoc with his health, which had never fully recovered from his mastoid operation of 1907. He had suffered from periodic migraine headaches ever since, and on top of that he was a dedicated insomniac (both headaches and insomnia would haunt him for the rest of his life). Even Donald Richberg, who was not given to much charity in his reminiscences, could bring himself to admire Ickes's fortitude under the circumstances:

> There is much to be said in extenuation of the temperamental qualities of Harold Ickes. He had suffered for many years from several varieties of ill health, particularly from a mastoid disease which several operations had failed to relieve. From this and other causes he had persistent insomnia and anyone who has been harassed by sleepless nights will understand the ragged condition of one's nerves in the following days. Indeed, it was always a surprise to me, and evidence of his strength of character, that Ickes remained only a moderate drinker, since the temptation to relieve jangling nerves with soporific doses of alcohol must have always been with him.

Remarkably enough, given his family history, alcohol apparently was the least of his problems, though strength of character probably had little to do with it; if he had more than two or three drinks at a sitting, his headaches usually would assault him with a fury that often incapacitated him. On the other hand, in his later years he would come to depend upon nightly doses of various "sleeping powders" in combination with whiskey to an extent that at least bordered on addiction.

For whatever specific reason, he was soon mired in the first of several Stygian depressions that would overcome him for long periods and from which there never seemed to be escape—although they always passed. This, at least, is how he remembered these years nearly a quarter of a century later:*

> I slept apart from Anna. I had ceased having intercourse with her. I went to the office as early as possible and got home as late as possible. And, after the customary 6:30 dinner, I went to bed as early as possible. Every morning my spirits lifted when I got beyond the point of recall on my way to the train.

* When I asked Raymond Ickes whether chronic depression was the sort of thing his father could have experienced, he replied, "Yes, it is. I don't know the extent of the depression—let's just call it mildly depressed—unhappy, not infrequently. No question about it."

Every afternoon my heart began to grow heavy as the clock inexorably approached the time when I would have to leave the office, and by the time I got home all my defenses were in front of me and I crouched behind them alert but depressed. . . .

I never played with the idea of suicide. . . . But I did wish for death— constantly and longingly—although undoubtedly I would have instinctively fought against it if I had thought that it was impending. I wished that an accident might carry me off without too much lingering in pain. I was living like an automaton. I had no ambition; I even came to the point where I had almost given up my interest in politics; and while I could not take my own life or even divorce Anna, in order that I might have a chance at life, I did not care to live.

Ickes may or may not have cared to live, but he did live, and, being alive, could not prevent himself from having an interest in politics, no matter how depressed he might feel. He was a political animal, which, to borrow from Wallace Stegner, can be defined as a body that will go on circulating a petition even with its heart cut out. The petition in question here was the draft of a call for a major Progressive conference to be held in mid-March, 1917. The draft had been composed by William Allen White and late in December 1916, Ickes distributed it with a covering letter asking for comment to the long list of active Progressives he had been accumulating and maintaining for several years now (unofficially, he had become a kind of general secretary for the more radical wing of the party). He received more than five hundred replies, all of them enthusiastic. This response, Ickes reported to James Garfield, made it clear that "some such movement as ours is absolutely necessary if the Republican Party is to have any chance in the national field in the immediate future." The apparent hope of Ickes was that such a conference might give the radicals the opportunity to snatch control of the party from the grip of George W. Perkins and his gang and place it in the hands of someone like Hiram Johnson—and if the struggle also coughed up Harold LeClair Ickes as Johnson's right-hand man, it would not have broken his heart. In any case, with new leadership the Progressives could reenter the Republican Party as a coherent force willing and able to restructure the GOP from top to bottom—to "progressivize" it, as Ickes described the process. Preferably with Perkins left out of things altogether. To ensure this right from the start, Ickes urged that the formal call for a conference be issued without Perkins's signature.

Perkins was too fast for him. During the Republican Executive Committee meeting on January 17, 1917, the dapper financier blandly outlined all of the Progressives' numerous complaints regarding the Republican leadership and even more blandly made a motion to merge the

Executive Committee with the 1916 campaign committee, complete with all the Progressives, including Ickes, who had been put on the committee as an empty gesture in July. The Republicans listened to Perkins's recital of their failings with growing irritation, then promptly responded to his motion by voting to retain the Executive Committee precisely as it had been structured *before* the campaign. This left— surprise!—Perkins as the only "progressive" member of the Executive Committee and, by powerful implication, the last hope the Progressives had to influence Republican Party policy at the upper levels.

Ickes sputtered, but there was not much he could do about it. Most of his allies now began to express reservations about even having a conference, much less issuing its call without Perkins's signature. After a few days even Ickes began to make compromising noises, suggesting the possibility of some kind of deal. This had to have galled him, and it must have been with enormous relief that he received strong encouragement from Hiram Johnson at the beginning of February. Go ahead and issue the call, Johnson said. The sooner the better. With or without Perkins's signature. Johnson was Ickes's kind of fighter, and he responded in kind on February 2, bravely proclaiming that he was "willing to go ahead regardless of Perkins and also regardless of any fight which he might make on us or any lineup he might be able to effect against us. I am, and have been strongly opposed to Perkins signing the call and if that means a fight with Perkins . . . then I would say let the fight come. I believe we will have to have a showdown with him sooner or later anyhow and it might be just as well to clear the decks at the start."

He never got the chance. February 2, as it happened, was the very day that President Woodrow Wilson decided to sever diplomatic relations with Germany, and on February 3 the President went before Congress to announce his decision and to warn Germany that if any American ships were sunk or American lives lost from that point forward, further steps would be taken; he did not have to specify what those steps might be. Six weeks later, the American ships *City of Memphis* and *Illinois* were torpedoed and sunk by German submarines and on the evening of April 2, Wilson went before Congress once again, this time to ask for a declaration of war. On April 6, after rancorous debate, Congress granted the President's request.

CHAPTER
· 16 ·

Escape to Paris

E VEN FOR ICKES, politics had to defer to the exigencies of combat. He
wired Wilson immediately, congratulating him for a war message
that "was a wonderful statement of the ideals for which, as a nation, we
stand and for which we are willing to fight," and offering his services in
any capacity the President might think appropriate. This was *pro forma,* of
course. His age—he was forty-three by now—and his missing middle ear
(not to mention a career devoid of the faintest whisper of military experience) would have precluded any involvement with the armed forces.
Nevertheless, with many another middle-aged American male of that
time, he felt the pull of this large event and wanted to be part of it,
somehow, some way. Unlike La Follette and George Norris—both of
whom had spoken against the declaration of war in the Senate—and a
number of other Progressives, Ickes had no pacifist inclinations. He was,
in fact, downright bellicose. On April 2, in responding to a mailing he
had received from something called the Emergency Peace Federation, he
took the occasion to express contempt "for the emotional drunkenness of
the professional pacifist who is thinking less of his country and of the
future of our civilization than of whether the calcium light is showing to
the audience in clear and bold outline, his pseudo-heroic and tragic
features."

Ickes volunteered his executive abilities in a number of directions in an effort to get overseas—or even to serve on the home front—but none of them led anywhere. By May he was generally discouraged, writing to an acquaintance that "ever since the war was declared I have been trying to wish my services upon the government or State in some executive capacity. I have volunteered right and left, but so far without success. I have even seriously thought of trying to enlist in the Officers Training Corps, but I hate like the deuce to be turned down on a physical examination and I am pretty certain that is what would happen."

Ickes's struggles to find a wartime place for himself finally were rewarded, at least temporarily, in September—but under circumstances that must have seemed odd even to him: his good angel here was none other than Samuel Insull, a man who was well on his way toward fully assuming the bespattered mantle of Charles Tyson Yerkes as the principal *bête noir* of the Chicago reformers.

The similarities between the two men, however, existed largely in the imaginations of the reformers. In the first place, Insull exercised more real power in the state and city than Yerkes had ever enjoyed, and if his arrogance was quite as pronounced he satisfied it through a methodology so slick it made the efforts of Yerkes look like the slimy bumblings of a Neanderthal. Insull did not believe in open bribery, holding with the theory that no man was ever bought just once. He believed in persuasion and, when that failed, employment; both had served him well and both had greater effectiveness in the long term than the crude distribution of money. In the second place, while Yerkes was a man ruled almost entirely by avarice, Insull was a true visionary with a powerful belief in himself as the harbinger of progress—and at this stage of his career, at least, it would have been difficult to give him the lie on that point. He was the man who had electrified Chicago.

In 1881 this British expatriate had gone to work for Thomas Alva Edison in Menlo Park, New Jersey. He had been hired to be the great man's flunky—his personal secretary, in effect—but within a matter of months had made himself so valuable to the inventor that his career accelerated at a rate that was meteoric even by the standards of that go-ahead age. In 1889 he emerged as second vice president of the newly formed Edison General Electric Company, in charge of all manufacturing and sales, and three years later, when J. P. Morgan reorganized the corporation as General Electric, he was offered the same position at a salary of $36,000. He was thirty-two years old. Insull accepted the position, but only temporarily. By then he had developed his own theories about how the electric business in this country ought to be run and was anxious to put them into action with a freedom denied him as a mere vice president. With that ambition in mind, in July 1892 he accepted a position as president of the relatively tiny Chicago Edison Company— and immediately acquired a controlling interest in the outfit with a loan from Marshall Field, who admired promising young men.

Unlike most of those in the business of generating and selling electricity, who considered it a specialized "luxury" item and charged for it accordingly, Insull believed in power to the people—*all* the people—and through a combination of reliable delivery systems, cheaper rates, steady expansion and improvement of facilities, mergers and acquisitions, and an aggressive campaign of public education regarding the virtues of electricity over those of gas, had wired almost the entire city and built a benign but absolute monopoly with the company he now called Commonwealth Edison. Moreover, he had expanded his network far beyond Chicago itself; through his subsidiary, the Middle West Utilities Company, he was delivering electricity to 131,000 customers in thirteen states.

Insull was now even something of a railroad tycoon on the local level. Several years before, the city's various elevated railway companies had decided to merge into one for reasons of efficiency and needed six million dollars to integrate the lines. Commonwealth Edison was happy to loan them the money, with stock in the new organization as security; later, it loaned them a little more money, with a little more stock as security, and after that even more money with more stock as security. All these loans came due in July 1914, and the el companies could not pay—except in stock, four-fifths of all their stock, in fact, and Insull's Commonwealth Edison now owned all the city's elevated railroads. True to his conviction that decent service was both practical and profitable, Insull promptly reduced and rationalized fares, instituted a universal transfer system, repaired and replaced decrepit equipment, cleaned and redecorated the stations, demanded courteous public service from his employees, and maintained friendly and generous labor relations. Not long after that, Insull acquired a number of the interurban lines as well and introduced similar improvements.

If this was monopoly, it was the kind of monopoly whose efficiency and ideal of service appeared to justify the arguments of Herbert Croly's *The Promise of American Life,* and only Insull's control of the People's Gas Light and Coke Company, assumed in 1913, gave the reformers much of a target for their alarums and excursions. This company had a sordid and generally corrupt history, and while Insull eventually would clean it up and straighten it out in his own way and in his own time, a considerable backlog of complaints would impede his efforts. Chief among these was the belief of the reform element on the city council that the company had overcharged its customers outrageously for years and that element's determination to force rebates amounting to millions of dollars. It was to spearhead this campaign that the city had hired Donald Richberg, Ickes's law partner. Insull fought back; in his view what was past was past and not his responsibility. The contention would wind on for years without resolution, more of an irritation to Insull than any sort of serious inconvenience.

Otherwise, Insull's power and prestige were unchallenged. So were his patriotism, expressed with a fervor common to converts, and his commitment to the Allied war effort, enhanced by his British origins. When President Wilson asked all governors to create state councils of defense to work under the aegis of the National Council of Defense, Governor Frank Lowden immediately turned to Insull to organize and direct the Illinois contingent. Once this became public knowledge, Ickes began using his various political connections in an attempt to get himself appointed to the council. Probably, he was counting heavily on the fact that he and Insull knew each other, at least slightly, and that Insull owed him a small favor. Two years earlier, Ickes had gone to Insull's office at the magnate's request. "He was at great pains to sell himself to me," Ickes recalled. "I was struck by the man's forceful personality. There was no doubt, whether you agreed with him or not, that he was a real man, one to be reckoned with if you crossed his path." What Insull wanted to know was whether Ickes would speak to Charles Merriam, then still on the city council, and broach the idea of a meeting between him and Merriam to discuss the People's Gas Light and Coke Company affair. True to form, he also offered to put Ickes on retainer for this and future services. Ickes declined the offer ("I had no desire to be part of his legal string"), but did agree to talk with Merriam. He did so, and Merriam acceded to a meeting, though for one cause or another it had never taken place.

This tenuous connection failed to place him on the council, but he continued to pester his cronies (Insull's aides came to refer to him as "That man Itches") until Insull was finally moved to make him chairman of the Neighborhood Committee, the council's principal propaganda arm, in September 1917. "It is not an army that we must shape and train for war," President Wilson had said early on. "It is a nation." Ickes did his best for Illinois. After seven months of the kind of frenzied activity that had become his trademark, he could make a satisfying report to Chairman Insull:

The Neighborhood Committee was organized with the purpose of encouraging and stimulating the patriotic sentiment of the State. Its work has been carried on the theory that it is better to make the doubtful and unpatriotic citizen patriotic by means of education than to repress him and leave him still unpatriotic. . . .

It would be difficult to estimate the number of neighborhood and larger patriotic meetings that have been held in the State under the auspices of the Neighborhood Committee, but such meetings, on a conservative estimate aggregate at least 800. These meetings have been of various sizes, but by their means we have reached all kinds of citizens in all parts of the States. The work carried on by the Neighborhood Committee through these patriotic mass meetings has had a considerable influence in helping to tone up the patriotic sentiment of the State and to bring our citizens into closer harmony with the policy of the government in prosecuting the war.

One of the devices used by the Neighborhood Committee to "tone up" patriotic sentiment, it should be mentioned, was a "Loyalty Pledge" card which citizens were encouraged to sign. It is a little unnerving to note that Ickes, a profoundly dedicated civil libertarian all his life, enthusiastically endorsed the use of these cards. Wartime breeds these kinds of excesses, however, and on the other side of the ledger it should also be noted that while he served as their chairman, none of the Illinois neighborhood associations ever degenerated into an anti-German vigilante group—as similar organizations did in several other states.

Years later, while dictating his political memoirs, Ickes denigrated this episode in his life. The work, he said, was "not thrilling. I had organized so many public meetings in my life and had issued so many statements and interviews that it just seemed to me like a very dull political campaign. Moreover, I was not persuaded that what I was doing was at all important. The vast majority of the People were loyal to the Government, during the war in any event." His main ambition was still to get closer to the war itself.

It could have been argued that the Ickes family was doing more than its share already. Anna had taken to knitting socks and sweaters for the soldiers ("Anna was really expert as a knitter, the only physical thing that she was ever able to do"). Wilmarth, who turned eighteen shortly after the U.S. entered the war, enlisted in the army as a private and by April 1918 had emerged as a sergeant of artillery in the Black Hawk regiment. "He has a bully captain and is very happy," Ickes wrote to Clinton Hazard, his sister Julia's husband. "In fact we are both very proud of him." He was proud of Harold Hazard, too, he added. He had been very fond of his namesake nephew ever since his birth to Clinton and Julia in 1899—just a few months behind Wilmarth—and had maintained a savings account for the boy ever since. In March 1918, after allowing young Harold to live at Hubbard Woods long enough to establish Illinois residency, Ickes had persuaded his old political rival Medill McCormick—now a Republican congressman-at-large—to sponsor the lad for Annapolis.

The family regiment was rounded off by Frances. As soon as war was declared, and over Anna's objections, she had enlisted as a Red Cross nurse's aide. After several months of hospital training in Chicago she got her orders for France. Since Anna stubbornly refused to demonstrate any approval, it was Clair, who had spent so many years ignoring the girl, who accompanied Frances to New York to see her off that winter. German submarines still made the Atlantic crossing a risky business, and Ickes determined to make things right between Frances and himself before she entered those dangerous waters. "But she had built up pretty strong defenses," he recalled. "She was withdrawn into herself and was very reserved. Moreover, as I was to learn . . . she was suspicious of me. Naturally, she wondered why I should show any interest in her after I had treated her so indifferently for so many years." He persisted, however, and late on the night before her departure, in her room in the Belmont Hotel, he got through: "We sat and talked for a long time and finally I broke down her reserves. For long hours we talked. At the end, sitting in my lap and with her head on my shoulder, she sobbed out how desperately unhappy she had been and how much she resented her mother's treatment of her." They were, he reports, fast friends by the time she sailed the next night. (Frances was probably twenty years old at this time and not unattractive. Given that fact and Ickes's ridiculous conjugal situation, it is impossible to dismiss the probability of a strong undercurrent of sexuality at work here. It is equally probable that it never got expressed any more passionately than the avuncular hugging Ickes described. Had anything openly sexual ever occurred between them, it is not likely he would have hinted at the possibility, as he does here.)

By now he was in a powerful funk indeed. Frances would soon be in the thick of things, and Wilmarth's regiment surely would be sent over before long. Charles Merriam was now an army officer, Raymond Robins was on his way toward becoming a colonel in the American Red Cross, and even his friends William Allen White and Henry Allen of Kansas, both of them older than himself, had suited up for the Red Cross and been sent overseas. He envied them all. "Not only, like Frances, was I anxious to get away from home, caring little whether I ever got back or not," he remembered, "I was seriously interested in the war and a violent partisan of the allied powers." In true desperation, he finally turned to the YMCA, an organization that heretofore had held no particular attractions for him, since it was quite as militantly Christian as he was militantly agnostic.

Still, the YMCA needed overseas workers to administer the distribution of good cheer, patriotic sentiments, magazines, newspapers, wholesome books, Bibles, candy, doughnuts, coffee, and other demonstrations of love and support from the folks back home to the boys of the AEF. Sometime early in April 1918 he applied for an administrative position, stipulating his desire to be sent overseas, and by the middle of the month had secured it. He immediately resigned as chairman of the Neighborhood Committee, ordered himself a tailor-made uniform, and late in May boarded a ship for France. Not even his eternal seasickness could dampen his enthusiasm, for escape was blooming in his heart.

Ickes went through the final six months of World War I like a man released from prison. For the first time in his life he had cut the cords of duty that had bound him for so many years—and never mind that he had tied most of the knots himself. For these few months he was free—free of the demands of Hubbard Woods, free of the mind-numbing pursuit of political prominence, free of the wife who lurched about their bedroom in cataleptic tantrums, free of the terror of inferiority that drove him to reach beyond his natural capacities. Not since his final year in college had he been so plainly happy.

Still, a world without something in it to make him angry would have been incomprehensible to him. The YMCA bureaucracy provided him with this necessary ingredient. Shortly after his arrival in Paris, he and the rest of the new personnel were given formal indoctrination: "We spent a few days listening to lectures of the most superficial type," he remembered.

> We were told things that sensible adult men and women might have been expected to know as a matter of course. All of this seemed to be a waste of time, but of little moment one way or the other. There was one man, however . . . who was a blatant, fire-eating, professional CHRISTIAN. He ranted in good old Evangelical style, apparently on the theory that if we didn't have religion of his sort we ought to have it; or, if we did have it, it ought to be more fervid and explosive. In utter disgust I listened to him one day saying that every time a YMCA secretary talked to a soldier he should first speak of "God, mother, sister." I actually felt like puking.

The organization itself made him equally nauseated. It was, he said, "really a mess. It consisted of a lot of eager amateurs, many of them 'Christers' who were doing a job too big for them and for which they had neither experience nor training; but who, nevertheless, were puffed up with a sense of their own importance. It made no difference to these underlings that I had had a distinct understanding in Chicago, without which I never would have joined." The "understanding," which may have been clearer to him than to the YMCA officials, was that he would be given a major assignment immediately, together with autonomy to run things pretty much as he saw fit. But when he was finally able to see E. C. Carter, head of the YMCA operations in France, no assignment was available, although Carter held out the possibility that Ickes might be sent to London to direct operations there. In the meantime, he suggested that Ickes take a tour of the various canteens established near the front lines, so that he might get an idea of how things were set up. This would not be difficult. The front lines were getting closer every day, as the Germans had launched what would be their last major offensive of the war on May 27, pushing deeper into France on a broad line that extended ninety miles from Lens in the north to Reims in the south; some of the heaviest fighting was taking place just a little over fifty miles from Paris. The city itself was subjected to periodic air raids of questionable military effectiveness but considerable psychological impact.

Before leaving the city Ickes made contact with Frances, who was working at a field hospital near the Bois de Boulogne. These were excitable days, shadowed by the fearful possibility that German troops might come goose-stepping down the road to Paris at any time, and the two of them discussed the situation at considerable length. Frances, he said, "would not desert her post and I would not have suggested it. However, there had been a good many stories of rape by German soldiers and I did not want such a fate to befall her. Neither did she when she frankly faced the possibility." Ickes accordingly hunted up a doctor acquaintance from home and, after hearing the problem, she gave Frances a small bottle of morphine tablets. With this grim mission accomplished, Ickes took his leave of Paris.

A few days later he found his war and got his baptism by gas and shell only forty-five miles east of the city, in the rolling, wooded hills just north of the Marne River. Arriving there on his canteen tour, he asked a lieutenant in the Signal Corps if he could accompany the officer to the front. The lieutenant agreed and they set out.

Topping a rise, they looked down on the tiny village that was their destination, bathed in moonlight and smoke. It was under bombardment. "The sound of the artillery became closer and closer," Ickes wrote to Anna on June 20, "and we could hear the bursting of the high explosive shells as they went through the air. Fortunately, none of them came near us and we bore right ahead." On the outskirts of the village, they entered a small wooded area full of smoke. Ickes, with his pharmacy-trained nose, detected the smell of chlorine gas, but the lieutenant refused to believe him. "The odor was suspicious to me—very—and I kept insisting there was gas about. Finally he took a good long smell and began to get his gas mask on in a hurry." Ickes fumbled his way into his own mask and, looking like a pair of large insects, the two men dog-trotted through shot and shell to a ruined stone building, where the Signal Corps communications center was bivouacked in the basement. There Ickes spent the night on a cot while the German bombardment grew in intensity. "I continued to lie there, scared, but afraid to show that I was afraid," he wrote in the *Autobiography.* "I did not close my eyes all night. . . . Finally all firing ceased, and then the ambulances began to go back and forth in earnest with their burdens of hurt humanity. At daybreak I went outdoors. I could still smell chlorine gas but it didn't seem too bad. . . . Tied near what was left of a stone barn were horses laboring heavily under the gas that had been their lot during the attack. One or two of them looked pretty badly off. The day wore on. A heavy mist lay over the ground. One venturesome bird from a branch of a dead tree twittered a note of hope for a world that would be different . . . where men would not maim and destroy each other because of a madman or two."

On this melancholy note, he returned to Paris, his curiosity satisfied. The YMCA still had no suitable assignment for him, and he had just about decided to give it up and try once more to get into the Red Cross when he encountered Henry Allen, the Red Cross inspector from Kansas. When Ickes told his old Progressive compatriot of his inclinations, Allen laughed and told him that he himself was about to get out of his Red Cross uniform and into that of the YMCA.*

With the prospect of working with Allen at hand, Ickes changed his mind. Together the two of them marched into Commander Carter's office, where they both were assigned to the Thirty-fifth Division, composed of troops from Kansas and Missouri; Allen would be division secretary, Ickes his business manager. "I am very happy over this assignment," he wrote Anna, "and Allen seems to be too. . . . Allen is an ideal man for the job he is to take. Won't it be corking to be with him? For once I was on the right spot at the right moment."

The Germans did their best to kill him before he and Allen could get

---

* Allen had let his name be entered as the regular Republican candidate for the governorship of Kansas (even in wartime Progressives were toppling from the ranks like soldiers on a hot parade ground). He and William Allen White, who had by this time returned to the States, had discerned a plot within the Red Cross officer corps to discredit him in some fashion before the election, so he was getting out before the saboteurs had a chance to do their dirty work (the paranoia, at least, remained purely Progressive).

on the road to join the Thirty-fifth. Several times a week enemy planes would come wobbling through the night skies over Paris to drop their loads, and one night a load came close to the hotel in which he was still living. Frances was staying there as well, as she usually did when he was in town, and when the raid started, Ickes went to her room. He described the scene for Anna:

> I was in Frances' room when she remarked that she could hear a German plane and craned my neck out to see what I could, stepped back a foot and stood there facing the window and looking out.
>
> And then it came. There was a great roar, a rushing downward of flame, an enormous crash, a glare of dull light and the sound of rent stone and timbers and of broken glass. The hotel building shook, glass fell about the room but not touching me, from one of the windows and I stood there, wanting to get away from it all but not at the moment knowing where to go.

The bomb had dropped on the building directly across the street, killing two people but leaving Ickes and Frances (who had ducked under the bedcovers at the first flash) unscathed. Sitting in the woodsy quiet of Hubbard Woods, Anna must have found this thrilling reading, but it may have aroused more than the wifely concern and admiration it was clearly designed to inspire. Harold (she rarely called him Clair) seemed to be spending a great deal of time with Frances over there, out of Anna's sight. And in Frances's room.

By the time Allied armies had beaten back one more German attempt to break through their lines on July 15, Allen and Ickes had established YMCA headquarters in the town of Saulxures in the Vosges mountains, a long way from the heat of the action. The Thirty-fifth was being given a rest, and the two YMCA officers were not averse to having one themselves. "Here Henry and I were to have a long stay," Ickes remembered, "but we were comfortably established in the two best rooms in the 'best' hotel, where, if dirt was plentiful and the plumbing of the most primitive, we nevertheless found good food and I discovered as fine a variety of rich red Burgundy as I have ever drunk." This hard duty was relieved by trips to nearby Nancy in search of ever-missing supplies. One item in particular demand and in perpetual short supply were plugs of chewing tobacco to soothe the nerves of the Missouri troops (Ickes suspected theft on the part of some of his Christian brethren), and he was forced to make repeated trips all the way to Paris to get these, during which occasions he invariably took hotel rooms for himself and Frances.

This pleasant interlude lasted for nearly a month, interrupted finally when the Allied forces began their own major offensive early in August. Things then started getting moved around and about in a hurry, including the Thirty-fifth. Before long, the Thirty-fifth found itself part of an assault force that numbered more than 650,000 men, most of them Americans. Among them was Wilmarth, whose artillery regiment had finally been sent over at the end of August. "I have just heard that Wilmarth's division is here," Ickes wrote Anna on September 3. "I shall work out some way to get to Wilmarth in a few days. Unfortunately we are moving now and that will tie me up temporarily. I am eager to see him and I shall cable you just as soon as I have positive news."

He found him, but the reunion was brief, for the American divisions, together with the French II Colonial Corps, were swiftly being deployed in a shallow V around three sides of the German fortifications at St. Mihiel. In the early morning hours of September 12 a stunning barrage shattered the dark, and at 5:00 A.M. the assault began. It was a furious success; in just six days, the Germans were driven out of St. Mihiel and across the Côtes de Meuse to the Woevre Plain. Some fifteen thousand prisoners, 247 guns, and more than two hundred square miles of French territory had been captured. "Among these troops, no time was allowed for cheering," military historian S. L. A. Marshall has written.

> They were back at trench warfare on a front boiling trouble round the clock. Troops in support took over the old German positions. They were everywhere booby-trapped and lice infested. The enemy's abandoned ammunition dumps lay in no-man's land. Still under guard by sudden-death detachments, they had to be raided and destroyed. Roads, ripped apart by the bombardment, had to be rebuilt under fire. There was no lack of material; where villages had been, there remained only rock piles.

Allen and Ickes found themselves in a terror of confusion and incessant motion, which continued over several weeks. The Thirty-fifth had been broken up for the offensive that followed, with units scattered through the bloody, smoking forest of Argonne from Verdun to Dun-sur-Meuse. Following them were the various YMCA personnel. Finding and servicing the needs of this diaspora along roads cratered from shelling and choked with traffic was a nightmare Ickes never forgot—sleeping in the mud and dung of barns, in haymows, in open fields, eating where and when they could and sometimes not at all, drinking quite a lot of whatever fell to hand, like common soldiers. He had a splendid time.

So did Allen, until coming down with diphtheria in the latter part of October, just as the units of the Thirty-fifth got relieved and moved to a rest area near Nancy. He was removed to a pup tent in the middle of the field by himself (the disease in those days was still a killer and highly contagious), where, as Ickes remembered it, "they sluiced large doses of antitoxins into his back every day." In early November, while recovering and still too weak to get around without having his knees buckle under him, Allen discovered that he had been elected governor of Kansas. He wanted to stick it out in France until the war ended, but Ickes persuaded him that he owed it to the people of Kansas, even if he was now a regular Republican, to get back home as soon as he was able to travel comfortably. Ickes himself was so thoroughly sick of the YMCA bureaucracy by then that he had resolved to pull a few of the several strings he had accumulated and get himself into the army as a Quartermaster Corps officer. He commandeered a car and the two men drove back to Paris.

There they took rooms in the Hotel Continental overlooking the Rue de Rivoli and the Tuileries Gardens. Sometime after 11:00 A.M. on November 11, Ickes was standing on his balcony when crowds began streaming out of the Metro station and spilling into the street below him, waving little tricolor flags, shouting and singing. Word quickly spread through the hotel that an armistice had been signed and the guns were silent all along the front. By evening the streets of Paris were dense with French civilians and soldiers of three nationalities, dancing with the excitement of overpowering relief. Ickes had joined the catharsis by then. "I saw not one exhibition of ill nature the entire evening," he wrote Anna the next day. "You were jostled, crowded, almost trampled under foot, but no one minded. And everyone kissed everyone else. It was the greatest kissing carnival the world has ever seen and yet it seemed entirely proper and in order."

Allen, still weak but now anxious to get home, took passage a few days after the Armistice. Ickes, who swiftly mopped up his business with the YMCA (and did not go into the army), could have joined him, but did not. He had decided to rest up in Paris for a few weeks. More than exhaustion made him linger, however; he was now struggling with a terrible ambivalence. Almost from the moment he had stepped off the boat in France, he had started sending dispatches to the west, to Anna, long, frequent letters scratched out in his forceful stroke on squares of YMCA stationery. Anna apparently had not looked upon his European excursion with any enthusiasm (not even accompanying him to New York to see him off), and if she had followed her usual patterns she had let him know it. From the beginning, there is a wheedling, conciliatory tone in his letters that suggests she provided him with a substantial load of guilt to carry around with him in Paris. "When I come home to you," he wrote on July 3, "I will be spiritually improved. I am trying to remedy my defects of character and temper over here—all with a view to my home-coming. I want to make you happy and I want you to find in me all the love and gentleness and consideration that you would want in a husband." Those sentiments were typical, and so were the extraordinary expressions of love with which all of the letters were festooned; reading them, it is impossible not to believe that they were written from the heart. June 2: "I love you my dear wife, with all my heart and soul. . . . I love you, love you, love you." Later that same day: "All that I said in my letter of this morning I meant, and much more. I have been lonely and homesick for you even in the midst of war." June 9: "At this hour you are probably just turning over for your final morning nap, bless you. I can see the tender green of the oaks, and the filtering sunlight and hear our wren's cheerful song, and I wish, oh how I wish, I were with you." July 3: "My Loved One: Why did I ever come so far away from you? Three more letters have just come . . . and I want to come to you and take you in my arms and assure you of my love and devotion." September 9: "Dear, dear Anna, this letter goes to you from a heart full of love. I love you, dear one."

These vibrant sentiments, of course, do not track with his memoirs, in which he tells us that he was miserable with Anna, that their marriage was a travesty from which he yearned to escape, that he had sought the overseas YMCA assignment to accomplish this, and that he had hoped, at some vaguely conscious level, to be blasted painlessly off the earth. Which the lie and which the truth? Almost certainly, neither was a lie and both were the truth. His marriage was, much of the time, ludicrous and painful, a maelstrom of obligation and misery that fed his depression and self-pity. This was the part he chose to remember and emphasize. Conversely, separated from her by several thousand miles of ocean and surrounded on all sides by the reality of impending death, this was the part of his marriage he chose to ignore—or, if not ignoring it, hoped would magically improve somehow, cauterized by war and separation. There is even the suggestion, in the passionate, relentless insistence of his declarations of love, that he was somehow trying to *will* happiness into his crippled marriage from the surreal environment of a war zone.

If so, Anna apparently was not responding in kind. None of her letters to him has survived, but there are strong hints in some of his responses that her own letters bristled with complaints more often than with protestations of abiding love. "Dearest," he wrote on July 3 in apparent answer to one such grievance, "no one could influence me against you, if he tried to do so." Again on July 9: "How could you feel as you did about these additional things in my bank box, dearest? There is nothing there that you may not freely see at any time. I am so sorry you should take such an attitude. . . . [There] was nothing private about them so far as you are concerned." And again on September 9:

> Dear, dear Anna, I wonder why you assume that I have some deep laid political plans . . . ? As I wrote you before, I have done literally nothing in a political way since I left New York. I have no plans for the national campaign that I am conscious of and necessarily none that I have confided in anyone. I am glad to be away from politics and I didn't come over here to play politics of any sort. If my plans are unknown to you it is because they are equally unknown to me since I haven't any plans. . . . I don't see how you could even temporarily feel that I had left you "holding the bag for political ends." I have never played politics for selfish personal reasons, least of all at your expense and certainly my coming over here has not the remotest political connection of any sort, personal or otherwise.

And finally, on November 19:

> I never said, implied or meant to imply at any time that you were unwilling to forgo things on account of the war. My heart is too full of admiration for you in every particular with respect to the war for me even to feel any criticism. I can't imagine what I could have said that caused you to wonder what I might mean. . . . It is a pleasure for me to say again that I regard you as an unselfish and truly patriotic citizen in this war. I don't see how you could have done any more than you have; I know you could not have been justly criticized if you had done much less. You have my admiring love.
> —Harold.

That rather stiff conclusion may be the anger creeping back in again. The war was over, and the realization that things had not changed, were probably never going to change, may have begun to undermine his fond hopes. In any case, he was suddenly in no hurry to get home. Neither was Frances. Ickes had wangled her a position in the YMCA, and sometime in December she was sent to Nice, where she would remain for the next several months. Before she left, Ickes asked her to give him the bottle of morphine tablets. He had it with him when he finally boarded ship at the end of the year, and he says, "I carried it with me all the way to Chicago and kept it in a secret place for many years when it became lost." Having these in his pocket gave him a kind of mordant comfort when the ship docked in New York. "Anna had written that she would meet me," he remembered. "I did not want to see her until the inevitable last second. I did not go to the rail until we were ready to tie up. Then my eyes quickly found her. She looked terrible. She had been suffering too; that I could plainly see. And yet with the best intention in the world, my heart did not warm up to her or even go out to her as a woman who was undoubtedly in great stress of mind."

The reunion was not a success. They had no sooner gotten into a taxi, he reports, than she accused him of having had a gaggle of mistresses in Paris. Then she accused him of having taken Frances as a mistress. "Here was hell with a vengeance," he said.

> That night at the Belmont Hotel I did what a man will do almost to the end with a woman who is legally his wife and from whom he has been away for a long time [vows of abstinence apparently forgotten—then or in the remembering of it]. My embraces seemed to soothe and quiet her for a while, but, in the middle of the night, she was up, dashing about the floor and upraiding me in a loud voice for misdeeds in Paris. . . . I lay in my bed and let her rage. I did not even stir when she dramatically charged at the window with a threat of suicide on her lips. I knew perfectly well that she would not do anything, and what would it matter anyhow, except that she would be released and I wouldn't.

Anna did not jump.

The next day, Ickes went around to Theodore Roosevelt's office to pay his respects, only to be told that Roosevelt was in the hospital. He decided not to go see his old hero, and by the time he and Anna stepped off the train in Chicago, the Colonel was dead. So were a lot of things.

PART IV

The Making of a Has-been

I don't believe anything can be done to stir up the interest of the younger citizens through any educative effort on the part of those of us who are, and probably ought to be, regarded by the younger generation as "has beens." Some day some issue will arise that will appeal to the consciences and stir the imaginations of the youth of the land, but what that issue will be or how or when it will arise I cannot attempt to predict. We live in a discouraging time.

—Letter to S. J. Duncan-Clark, November 6, 1929

CHAPTER
· 17 ·

Cutting Through the Smoke

"Make no little plans," Daniel H. Burnham had instructed the city of Chicago. "They have no magic to stir men's blood and probably themselves will not be realized. Make big plans; aim high in hope and work, remembering that a noble, logical diagram once recorded will never die but long after we are gone will be a living thing." The occasion of this punditry had been Burnham's employment in 1906 by a group of businessmen and civic leaders, later incorporated as the Commercial Club, to stir the blood of Chicago by redesigning the place. With his associates Edward H. Bennett and Charles H. Moore, the architect fell to with a will, and in 1909 the Commercial Club published the result as the "Chicago Plan." The following year, it was submitted to the voters and approved as the official blueprint for all future public works in the city.

In keeping with Burnham's sentiments, it was no little plan he had produced. It projected a population by the middle of the twentieth century of 13,250,000. It called for the creation of great highways encircling the city, of a rationalized and coherent system of public transportation, of the reconstruction of Michigan Avenue and Halsted Street as the city's chief north-south arteries, and the construction of broad new diagonal boulevards that cut straight through to the heart of the Loop. It dreamed of a magnificent park system and a network of parkways to connect one with the other, of public buildings grouped and centralized for the convenience of the citizenry, of museums and art galleries and other cultural institutions sitting in the midst of landscaped beauty, of residential housing for the poor and the working classes that furnished both dignity and comfort. And it dreamed of a limitless future for this "empire crying glory in the mud," as Theodore Dreiser had described the city. For, the plan stated, "consideration is given to the fact that in all probability Chicago, within the lifetime of persons now living, will become a greater city than any existing at the present time; and that therefore the most comprehensive plans of today will need to be supplemented in the not remote future. Opportunity for such expansion is provided for."

Precious little of this had gotten done by the end of World War I (precious little ever would), but what little was done became ammunition in Mayor William Hale Thompson's bid for a second term in November 1919.* "Caesar Augustus found Rome a village of wood and brick," a handout from the mayor's office declaimed. "He left it a marvelous city of stone and marble. William Hale Thompson found Chicago with many unsightly spots, congested streets and a lack of recreation facilities; he is making it a city beautiful with wider thoroughfares, monumental buildings and all modern conveniences." Never mind that these accomplishments had come about in spite of—not because of—his supremely venal administration. Never mind that in 1918 the Republican machine had rejected his attempt to win the nomination for U.S. senator, favoring Medill McCormick instead (who also won his election bid in November). Never mind that his blustering opposition to the Allies throughout the war (his Anglophobia was such that ten years later he would offer to punch the King of England "on the snoot") had embarrassed the entire city and incited editorials in the *Chicago Tribune* that grumbled of treason. Never mind that in less than four years the city's surplus of $3 million had magically become a deficit of $4.5 million. And never mind that Big Bill had formed an alliance with Big Jim Colosimo, a former street sweeper who now ran an underworld network of gambling and prostitution out of offices in "Colosimo's," his popular restaurant and nightclub on Wabash Avenue in the heart of the "New Levee" between Eighteenth and Twenty-second streets, and that as a result saloons all over the city now boasted slot machines in every unoccupied corner.

Criticisms of him and his administration, Thompson maintained, were criticisms of the city, acts of urban disloyalty. He organized the Chicago Boosters Club, which extorted a million dollars from businessmen by suggesting future difficulties with their licenses if they did not

* The mayoralty had been changed from a two-year to a four-year term in 1915.

come up with the cash. Garish posters publicizing the town—and, not incidentally, its mayor—sprouted throughout the city. "A booster is better than a knocker!" proclaimed one. Another, presumably a favorite with Thompson, admonished citizens to take "All hats off to our mayor, Big Bill, the Builder." To shore up his political base, he passed himself off as the champion of the oppressed in the wards of the lower South Side, where tens of thousands of black war workers had settled, moving up from the sharecropper society of the Deep South in search of hope; instead, they had found a ghetto, and Thompson was quick to exploit their misery.

All this made the hackles of Harold Ickes twitch almost from the moment he stepped off the train from New York on January 1, 1919. "Like an old fire horse," he remembered, "I smelled burning and I began to paw the floor of my stall. In the spring following my return from France I began to look about for someone—anyone—who might beat 'Bluffing Bill' Thompson." He bethought himself of U.S. District Court Judge Kenesaw Mountain Landis, a Tennessee-born jurist who had once imposed a fine of $29,240,000 on Standard Oil for accepting rebates; the fine had been reversed on appeal, but the judge had earned the everlasting respect of the Progressives.* Ickes went to his old employer, Victor Lawson, now publisher of the *Chicago Daily News,* and got Lawson's promise of support for Landis, then walked over to the Federal Building to broach the subject with the potential candidate. "He was hearing a case," Ickes recalled,

> but he left the bench and came into the chambers. He was always a very dramatic, picturesque figure. Even then he had prematurely gray hair, a lean Lincolnesque face and a lithe, quick motion to his body. We sat down at his desk. Around three edges . . . stood thin plugs of chewing tobacco. He explained that he stood them thus in order to dry. Taking one plug in his hand he said: "Ickes, this is the sweetest tobacco that you have ever put in your mouth, take a plug."

The only tobacco that Ickes had ever put in his mouth had been in the form of cigarettes, of which he was a moderate smoker, and he declined the offer. He then presented his own offer. "Ickes," the judge replied with vigor, "I would just as soon have you ask me to clean a shithouse."

In the end, it was Charles Merriam who decided to challenge Thompson for the nomination. Merriam still believed that it had been Ickes's astringent attitude toward the regular Republican machine that

---

* The judge entered the national spotlight again at the beginning of 1920, when he was appointed baseball commissioner. It was the Chicago White Sox who got him there. During the World Series of 1919, the team's bush-league performance had aroused suspicions; it was soon discovered that several of the team's players had taken bribes and they would forever after be known as the "Black Sox." It was the mission of Landis to clean the game up. He did, too.

had cost Merriam the election in 1911, and he neither consulted with his former campaign manager nor asked him to take part. In both his memoirs and the *Autobiography,* Ickes insisted that he remained unhurt by this deliberate snub, but that seems hardly likely. Among other reasons to disbelieve it was the undisguised satisfaction he displayed in reporting the inept fumblings of those who did manage the effort and Merriam's consequent trouncing by Thompson in the primary election in April.

After that, Thompson squeezed out a win in June with a plurality of 21,000 votes, largely because of support from the "Black Belt" of the South Side. He soon had the opportunity to return the favor, had he chosen to do so. Late in July a black teenager waded over an invisible color line on a Lake Michigan beach. He was promptly stoned and drowned by white youths. A policeman leaped into action by arresting a black man, after which a crowd of blacks streamed onto the beach, followed by a battalion of police. A black man took a shot at the police, who gunned him down. Sporadic violence continued for the next several days, with gangs of whites cruising through the South Side in automobiles, shooting and assaulting blacks on sight. Thompson's police force did little to interrupt this urban blitzkrieg, and not until twenty-six people (only one white among them) were dead and hundreds injured did he consent to ask Governor Frank Lowden for state troops to put an end to it. "Chicago," the *Tribune* editorialized on July 31, "is disgraced and dishonoured."

Political developments on the national scene were only a little less seamy than those afflicting Chicago, at least from Ickes's point of view. The squeeze play that had been put on the Progressives by the regular Republicans in 1916 had taken on the dimensions of permanence by the end of the war. As a party, the Progressives were long dead, and as an effective voice within the circle of Republican power, they had been rendered impotent. To Ickes's mind, nothing more thoroughly demonstrated this sorry fact than the appointments made to the Republican National Committee by its new chairman, Will H. Hays (who would later achieve lasting fame as president of the Motion Picture Producers and Distributors of America and author of the group's "code" regarding acceptable material), and it probably did not cool his temper much to learn that he was not among them. Of the twelve additions made outside the regular Republican ranks, Ickes found only two on whom he could look with favor, William Allen White and Henry Allen. What was worse, Hays had included his old nemesis in the selection. This pleased him not at all, and he let Hays know it on December 12:

I find with respect to these twelve outsiders that while six may be classified as former progressives only four are known so nationally, and of these four two are George W. Perkins of New York and Walter Brown of Ohio. It would have been franker, and the result would have been exactly the same, if, instead of appointing Walter Brown, you had simply designated George W. Perkins and given him two votes. And as to Mr. Perkins you are not the astute political leader that I have imagined if you believe that he represents any real progressive sentiment. . . .

Progressives practically everywhere since 1916 have learned the bitter lesson that while their votes and support are courted their voice within the party councils isn't any more desirable than it was from 1912 to 1916. We are wooed in the public speeches of the politicians; we are told that no books are being kept and that no discrimination will be made; we are assured that when the candidates soliciting our support are elected to the offices they aspire to they will recognize former progressives on a fair and equitable basis; party managers, with honeyed words, tell us that the party can't succeed without us. . . . But when we come to face the facts we find that they do not square with the assurances held out.

Hays responded to this blast three weeks later by inviting Ickes to join the National Committee's subcommittee on policies and platform. ("Most earnestly urge your acceptance by wire," the honeyed words of his telegram said. "Want your help in this very much.") Ickes replied by night letter on January 2, 1920: "I appreciate compliment but frankly I am not persuaded that Committee on Platform will or can be really influential. . . . If time permits and you consider it worth while to advise me proposed personnel of committee what scope of its activities will be method of selecting its executive committee and probable personnel of executive committee I will be glad to consider the matter." Ickes was being coy here; most likely, he had no intention of contributing anything to this soiled committee under any circumstances, and Hays never was able to talk him into it.

By then, he had already laid his political plans for 1920. In spite of his declaration in November of 1916 that Hiram Johnson—now Senator Johnson—"must be taken into consideration as a presidential possibility," and in spite of the fact that he had renewed his steady correspondence with the "Chief" early in 1919, Johnson did not lie at the center of those plans. Instead, Ickes had decided to cast his lot with Governor Frank Lowden. This move, he tells us in the *Autobiography,* was all for Johnson's sake: "Much to my surprise, Lowden had made a first-rate Governor and, at the moment, I could see nothing in the offing remotely resembling Illinois delegates for Hiram Johnson. So I adhered to Lowden with the distinct understanding that if he failed of nomination, he would make no attempt to deliver me to another. I told him frankly that Johnson was my real choice. Lowden, in turn, assured me that he would rather throw his strength to Johnson than to any of the reactionary candidates. So I went along." He went along so far as to become secretary of Lowden's Illinois Campaign Committee. This was done, he assured an inquisitive Henry Allen, in order to get a sprinkling of Progressive delegates into the Republican National Convention in June. What is more, he wrote Allen, Johnson knew all about it and approved.

But Johnson didn't know all about it. At best, this—like the rest of Ickes's labored apologetics in the matter—was wishful thinking; at worst, it was a plain lie. Ickes wanted to be a delegate to the national convention and he realized his chances were far better with Lowden than with Johnson. Moreover, he knew, as did most intelligent observers, that the regular Republican leadership was far from ready to forgive Johnson his participation in the bolt of 1912 and the insurgency of 1916, and no matter how well he might do in the upcoming primaries, the leadership would prevent his nomination by whatever means necessary. Finally, Johnson's stubborn isolationism, curiously enough, not only increased the disaffection of most of the party's conservative elements but alienated him from many of its handful of liberals as well. One of the sections of the Treaty of Versailles that had ended the war was Article Ten, proposing the creation of a League of Nations to insure a permanent peace. It was largely the work of President Woodrow Wilson, the last remnant of the idealistic "Fourteen Points" he had attempted to impose on the Allies as the framework of the treaty. There was much popular support for the League, including some from a few anti-Wilson Progressives like William Allen White and Ickes, and to stir it up, Wilson had stumped the nation in September, driving himself so hard that he suffered a stroke that left him all but helpless and the nation in charge of a "regency" headed by his wife. It still remained for the Senate to ratify the treaty, and within that body sentiment was, at best, mixed. Democrats, generally speaking, were for the League, believing it to be the planet's only hope that World War I would indeed go down in history as "the war to end all wars." Republicans, among them many of the fallen-away Progressives, were generally against it, believing that Article Ten's stipulation that all signatory nations agreed to respect and preserve the territorial integrity and political independence of all League members from outside aggression would once more entangle the United States in the ancestral squabbles of Europe. Still, as a gesture to public concern, however misguided they believed that opinion to be, opposition leaders—

Senator Henry Cabot Lodge of Massachusetts at their head—
condescended to ratify the treaty, but with reservations that would have
stripped the United States of any moral or legal obligation to adhere to the
provisions of Article Ten, leaving the League of Nations a paper tiger. But
Johnson would not even go this far; he did not want the League endorsed
by the United States in any way, shape, or form, and would remain an
"irreconcilable" isolationist through most of the rest of his long career in
Congress, at the cost of a political base that grew narrower as the years
passed.

Ickes may have discerned this weakness early. In June he had written
Johnson that the Senate should "hold their noses and vote to approve the
covenant because the American people are honestly and idealistically in
favor of a League of Nations and this is the best that can be obtained."
Over the next several months, Johnson would, at least briefly, bring Ickes
around to his opinion, but this shared conviction was still not enough to
keep Ickes from going with Lowden. Regardless of his lifelong contention
that he enjoyed supporting the underdog, Ickes had been with too many
losers in his time. He wanted a winner, and Lowden's chances appeared
excellent. He had been a good and popular governor during the war
months, and if he was a bit more reform-minded and independent than
the machine politicians would have preferred, his wide popular support
made him a good deal more than a dark horse. As 1920 warmed up,
Lowden's only real competition seemed to be Johnson (who would never
be endorsed by the party's leaders) and General Leonard Wood, Theodore
Roosevelt's commanding officer in the Spanish-American War, lately the
army's chief of staff, and, some said, Roosevelt's heir-apparent. Standing
in the shadows just behind the limelight were Herbert Hoover, former
director of the Committee for the Relief of Belgium and head of Wilson's
Food Administration, an able man whom no one considered a serious
contender; and Senator Warren G. Harding of Ohio, whom many considered a rude joke. Even further back, in deeper shadows yet, lurked Justice
Charles Evans Hughes, Governor Calvin Coolidge of Massachusetts, former President Taft, and even—though almost entirely invisible—
Governor Henry Allen of Kansas, who was busily removing the last taint
of Progressivism from his person.

Against this lineup, Governor Lowden was a distinct possibility—and
if Ickes hooked up with him early on, who knew what might develop?
This was a perfectly rational political decision, and Ickes need not have
harried himself about it; it was no more or less than what any practical-
minded person would have done under the circumstances. But it did not

square with his self-image as the disinterested idealist in politics, and guilt would not let him admit that he was looking out for himself. Hence the tortured justifications; hence the lies. Fortunately, he would be given the chance to redeem himself before the year was out.

In the meantime, William Allen White was not entirely comfortable in his position on the National Committee. He worried about how he and the handful of ensconced Progressives might carpenter a few appropriately liberal planks into the party platform; left to their own devices, he feared, the regulars would erect something that William McKinley could have sat upon comfortably. At the end of March, he proposed to Ickes that they travel together to New York to confront Hays and get his clearance for a meeting of Progressives who would, ideally, hammer out a liberal program that could be folded into the party's general platform. The idea of asking permission for such a meeting must have greatly irritated Ickes. That last December he had vainly tried to set up a conference of Progressives himself, and in one of his letters of persuasion to Henry Allen had expressed his continued belligerence:

> The standpatters don't respect anything that they don't have reason to fear and that is pretty much human nature generally. If we are afraid of ourselves and doubt our right to get together and discuss party and political matters is it to be supposed that the standpatters will fear us and voluntarily ask us to a real participation in party affairs? You never got anything in this life that you didn't go after and the progressives of the country won't get anything merely by lying down and asking the standpatters to feel generous towards us because of our self effacement.

But Allen and the others would not move without the endorsement of the Republican leadership; increasingly, Ickes found himself nearly alone in his crusade against the party establishment.

Nevertheless, he temporarily closed a damper on the coals of his antagonism and journeyed to New York with White, where the two of them overcame Hays's fear that such a meeting would give the impression that the party was once again threatened with an open split. Ickes offered Hubbard Woods as the meeting place and promised that the gathering would be held in the strictest secrecy. So it was that on April 30 a motley band of Progressives slipped into Chicago one and two at a time from all points of the compass like conspirators, then took the cars of the Chicago & Northwestern for the Hubbard Woods station, where they were met throughout the early morning by the Ickes chauffeur and transported to the big house. Among the twenty or so in attendance were such Ickes familiars as James Garfield, Gifford Pinchot, Donald Richberg, White, Chester Rowell, and Margaret Robins (Raymond was on the road), together with a few less well-known to him—Ogden Mills, who came as Hays's official representative; advertising tycoon Albert J. Lasker; Wyoming governor Robert Carey; and Henry C. Wallace of Iowa (who would soon serve as Secretary of Agriculture, a position his son, Henry A., would hold during FDR's first two terms). Henry Allen, nursing tender hopes for the nomination, was pointedly absent.

Hays need not have been concerned that this group would function as a cabal; it was instead a mess of conflicting opinions whose participants Ickes could barely force himself to feed with proper hospitality. "We went into session about ten in the morning," he remembered,

> and I must say that my dear friend, William Allen White, made a perfectly rotten chairman. He didn't seem to have any particular things he wanted the conference to consider and every one talked all around Robin Hood's barn. We had provided luncheon, but after luncheon we went back into the living room for another session. Hour followed hour and still the flow of talk continued. Late in the afternoon Anna said to me that apparently we would have to ask all of our guests to stay for dinner and she didn't know where the food was to come from. However, she and the servants got busy and we managed to serve an adequate dinner.

In reporting the proceedings to Raymond the next day, Margaret Robins was somewhat more detailed in her own complaints. Of White, she wrote, "We might just as well have had a tortoise," and, she added,

> Either Mr. Mills and Mr. O'Laughlin did not know the purpose of the meeting or they had come to balk it. These men planned to read to us ten or fifteen reports of the various committees of the Policies Committee and when Harold or Gifford Pinchot ventured to suggest that we had come for a discussion we were lectured to as if we were school children. . . . It beat the band!! We were told to be good and silent. . . . I inquired very politely of the chairman whether we might not discuss some principles touching some of the problems confronting us in America, politically and industrially. Both Mr. Mills and Mr. O'Laughlin protested: principles could not and ought not to be discussed before studying the reports so carefully prepared by the Committee!! There was a howl from the multitude and Mr. Mills moved that we have a recess to give Mrs. Robins time to formulate her questions. Sweetheart mine, after that we had a merry time. . . . I was sorry I had to leave early, as I would have given a lot to discuss it all with Harold and Don Richberg.

She apparently missed very little. "The total and net result of the meeting," Ickes announced disgustedly in his *Autobiography,* "was nothing. Our deliberations, so far as I could judge, had not the slightest effect upon the platform that was later adopted at the Chicago convention." As disappointing as this Progressive conclave may have been, Ickes might have done well to remember it with more fondness; it was the last such meeting in the movement's history.

If the Republican National Committee had chosen the second week in June for the 1920 nominating convention in an attempt to escape the ghastly heat that had stunned the last two Chicago conventions, the tactic did not work. Providence supplied the entire Midwest with an unseasonable heat wave that week, and as the 984 voting delegates, including Harold Ickes, the gentlemen and ladies of the press, and the usual collection of gallery spectators filtered into the Coliseum's glass-roofed amphitheater the first morning, they were already sweating. They would be streaming by the end of the day—by the end of every day for five days, in fact, as the temperature climbed to a daily high of 100 degrees or more and held there for hours. Day after day, Edna Ferber recalled nineteen years later, "the sun beat down on the bald heads and heat-suffused faces of the delegates. . . . I idly wondered why we were known as the white race when we really were pink. The men sat in their shirt sleeves and as the sweltering week wore on they shed collars, ties, even shoes in some cases. It was the American male politician reduced to the most common denominator." She was working for United Press International now, and had eight years of the cynical journalist's trade behind her, but she remained as innocently Progressive in her sympathies as she had been in 1912. Like many, she probably considered the fetid environment of the convention hall symbolically convenient, for, she remembered, "There I saw the brewing of as poisonous a political mess as any party ever stirred up in the history of the United States government."

The common assumption made then and later by those who like their politics neat, with the heroes and villains cleanly drawn, was that the convention was plainly rigged and its outcome the work of political gangsters—bosses—whose only interest was in how well their pockets might be lined. The bosses were there in force, true enough, as they always were, and they did what work they could, as they always did. But to conclude that they were in control of the proceedings at any given moment during those five overwrought days would be to ignore the deranged nature of convention politics in general and of this convention in particular. The Republican Presidential nomination of 1920 was not rigged; more accurately, it was, as Lucius Beebe once described the twentieth century in general, a street accident, with similarly inelegant results.

When the convention opened on Tuesday, June 8, primary elections had pledged 125 delegates to General Leonard Wood; 112 to Hiram Johnson; 72 to Ickes's man, Governor Frank Lowden; and 39 to Senator Warren G. Harding. Seventy-two were pledged to various favorite sons. The rest—564—were uncommitted. A total of 493 would be necessary to win the nomination. Tuesday was given over to opening remarks and convention business, including the selection of its chairman, Senator Henry Cabot Lodge, and the deliberations of the Platform Committee, which continued through the early hours of Thursday morning. This body, unsurprisingly, did not produce a revolutionary manifesto, although William Allen White, Medill McCormick, and a few others did manage to insert some liberal sentiments in sections granting the right of collective bargaining to labor, approving equal pay for women, and disapproving child labor, together with a promise at least to consider the diplomatic recognition of communist Russia and a mild endorsement of the idea of a world court. An aging Senator Elihu Root contributed a plank regarding the League of Nations that White said was "fearfully and wonderfully made. It meant nothing except that it frankly did mean nothing, and we accepted it. It was that, or defeat on the floor." Thursday's session lasted only long enough for Lodge to announce that a platform had been achieved. On Friday morning the nominating speeches began. What with demonstrations, seconding speeches, and the nomination of a few favorite sons, it was late afternoon before a final "The man who . . ." ceased echoing in the great hall. "After reading these nominating speeches," a reporter for the *Boston Transcript* wrote, "Washington, Lincoln, Grant, Roosevelt, Julius Caesar, and Napoleon feel like pretty small potatoes."

Three days of caucusing, trade-offs, and persuasion were reflected on the first ballot, which began shortly after five that evening. Wood led with 287½, followed by Lowden with 211½, Johnson with 133½, and Harding with 65½; Hoover brought in a dismal 5½. On the second ballot, Wood lost two votes, Lowden gained 48. The juggling continued through the third and fourth ballots, with Wood ending up at 314½ to Lowden's 289. And there, or very near there, it seemed apparent, was where the votes were going to remain. (Harding had slid to 61½ and Johnson, after gaining on the second and third ballots, had dropped back to 140½.) The deadlock between Wood and Lowden, as William Allen White put it, had "clinched and set like a bone." Over a chorus of nays—most from Lowden's people, who hoped for a run toward their man on the next ballot or two—Lodge forced an adjournment until ten o'clock the following morning.

Enter now the stuff of legend. Back in February, Harry M. Daugherty,

Harding's campaign manager, had ventured a prediction to a pair of reporters in New York: "I don't expect Senator Harding to be nominated on the first, second, or third ballot," he said, "but I think about eleven minutes after two o'clock on Friday morning of the convention, when fifteen or twenty men, bleary-eyed and perspiring profusely from the heat, are sitting around a table some one of them will say: 'Who will we nominate?' At that decisive time the friends of Senator Harding can suggest him and can afford to abide by the result." Daugherty's little bit of bravado was uncannily close to the mark. After the adjournment Friday night, Suite 404 of the Blackstone Hotel, National Committee headquarters during the convention, became the scene of much cigar smoke and speculation. For six hours, party leaders and hangers-on streamed in and out of the suite, discussing ways in which the deadlock might be broken or, failing that, who indeed they might nominate in the stead of the two leaders. Harding's name came up repeatedly through the night. There was, on the face of it, little to commend him. He was a glad-handing, tobacco-chewing boozer. (William Allen White had encountered him in front of an elevator door during the convention looking "disheveled," with "a two-days' beard"; altogether, White said, "the model I saw there at the elevator door looked like the wreck of the *Hesperus*.") When he was not suffering from a hangover, his shock of white hair and substantial paunch gave him the look of a statesman, but this was largely surface; he had read little of substance in his life, and his notion of intellectual pursuit was normally confined to draw poker or the composition of banal editorials for his own *Marion* (Ohio) *Star*. Finally, his moral condition was, at best, questionable, and rumors of a long-time sexual affair (later confirmed) hung about him as stubbornly as the smell of tobacco and bourbon.

A sorry prospect, one which few but Daugherty himself could endorse with any real enthusiasm; yet, as Francis Russell, Harding's best biographer, has put it, "However many times the political cards were shuffled and dealt and discarded, somehow the Harding card always remained." He was from the key state of Ohio, looked good (when not drunk or recovering from a drunk), was popular with his colleagues in the Senate, was so free from the stain of any reformist inclinations that he positively glittered, was too timid in his opinions to cause anyone much trouble, and could be trusted to take direction. By two o'clock Saturday (not Friday) morning, the party elders had run through all the options, and even Henry Cabot Lodge, a strong Wood advocate, was convinced that Harding was the only recourse. "There ain't any first-raters this year," Connecticut's senator Frank Brandegee explained to one reluctant participant. "This ain't 1880 or any 1904; we haven't any John Shermans or

Theodore Roosevelts; we got a lot of second-raters and Warren Harding is the best of the second-raters."

By the time the convention reconvened at 10:00 A.M., the word had spread that the leadership wanted Harding, but it still took nearly eight hours, one adjournment, another six ballots, and considerable trading and arm-twisting to bring it off—yet bring it off they did. Psychic exhaustion, William Allen White claimed, was as responsible as anything else for the outcome: "I believe now," he recalled a quarter of a century later,

> that the death of Theodore Roosevelt and the rout of his phalanx of reform, together with the collapse of Wilsonian liberalism when America rejected the League of Nations . . . all created in my heart a climax of defeat. My purpose was enervated. Indeed, the whole liberal movement of the twentieth century . . . was tired. The spirits of the liberals who called themselves Progressives were bewildered. The faint-hearted turned cynics. The faithful were sad and weary.

When, on the tenth ballot, Pennsylvania cast the vote that put Harding over the top, Edna Ferber remembered all the fine Progressive convictions that had sustained her for the previous eight years and mourned their passing: "Now, in the trumped-up fanfare that followed the nomination of Harding I felt these beliefs being torn from me as a child, helpless, is bereft of her toys. I knew that I was going to cry. I tried hard not to. Perhaps I was weary, nervous, a little hysterical from the noise and the heat and the excitement. But I knew deep down that it was the horrible pain of disillusionment in my country and my people that was making me weep."

Delegate Harold Ickes was not bewildered or weary; neither did he weep. He was furious, and he bellowed. When Senator Joseph Frelinghuysen of New Jersey offered the customary motion to make the nomination unanimous, Ickes's harsh midwestern yelp of outrage cut through the noise and smoke into history: "*No!*" Unperturbed, Lodge ruled that the anointing of Harding was indeed unanimous.

Later that Saturday evening, after Calvin Coolidge had been nominated as Harding's running mate and the final blow of the gavel had fallen, a handful of weary Progressive tigers gathered at the University Club for a desultory postmortem. All of them agreed, Ickes remembered, that Harding was a dreadful man who did not deserve the Presidency. Almost all of them nevertheless admitted that they would support the ticket. They thought, Ickes said, "that we either had to go along or go dead. We just couldn't get off the reservation every four years." Ickes, who would rather have been dead, announced that he could go off the reservation—and would. Pinchot expressed the hope that the Progressive remnants—most of them together in that very room—would at least keep in touch by regular correspondence. Ickes, who had been the group's unofficial corresponding secretary for years by now, said that he did not think there would be much point in "keeping up any further pretense and corresponding as progressives when progressive principles had been completely abandoned." Depressed and disintegrating, the last remnant of the Progressive Party said its farewells.

Two weeks later, Henry Allen wrote Ickes in one final effort to get him to go along. Ickes's response on June 30 discouraged any further attempts. Harding, Ickes wrote, was nothing more than a "complascent [sic] instrument ready for manipulation by the big special interests. He is a platitudinous jellyfish whose election I would regard as distinctly detrimental to the best interests of the country. I can't let you tell me I ought to be a good boy and support for president a man upon whom the Lord conferred a bunch of wet spaghetti instead of a back bone without my letting out some sort of yell of anguish."

Early in July, the Democrats out in San Francisco went one up on the Republicans in convention confusion. President Wilson, terribly ill, was not a candidate, although his ever-loyal Secretary of State, Bainbridge Colby, made noises about submitting his name in nomination. That impulse was soon squelched by party leaders, but this did little to smooth the subsequent proceedings. Early on, just as in Chicago, a deadlock arose between two of the strongest candidates, Senator William Gibbs McAdoo and Attorney General A. Mitchell Palmer. And, just as in Chicago, a compromise candidate finally slid out from the shuffled and reshuffled deck—Governor James Cox of Ohio, a colorless Wilsonian liberal. This time, however, it took no less than forty-four ballots to bring in sufficient votes. As Cox's running mate, the convention then nominated the thirty-eight-year-old Assistant Secretary of the Navy, Franklin D. Roosevelt.

In Chicago, Ickes looked upon this result, found it generally good, and began honing his maverick instincts. A few weeks before the Democratic gathering, he tells us, he had suggested to George Brennan, who had by then emerged as Chicago's principal Democratic boss, that the Democrats would do well to nominate Roosevelt for the Vice Presidency. He certainly had the right name to bring in a few Progressive votes, Ickes pointed out. (Like TR, Roosevelt had made a fairly good, and very public, Assistant Secretary of the Navy; furthermore, he was TR's cousin and had married the former President's niece, Eleanor.) And, he might have added, Roosevelt's name on the ticket could partially offset the fact

that most of TR's branch of the family had come out in support of
Harding (Theodore Roosevelt, Jr., in fact, would become Harding's
Assistant Secretary of the Navy, such being the nature of American
political alliances). Ickes's endorsement of Roosevelt almost certainly did
not have any influence on the decision made in San Francisco (nor does he
claim that it did, in spite of Brennan's respectable position in the Democratic ranks), but the outcome just as certainly reinforced his conviction
that it was time to jump completely clear of the Republican Party—at
least on the national level.

Shortly after the convention, he went to Brennan again and asked him
to set up an interview with Cox. Brennan complied, and early in August,
Ickes met with the governor in Dayton, Ohio. "Cox didn't measure up to
my conception of a Presidential candidate," he remembered, "but he
greatly outpointed Harding. Besides, he shot straight. He did not regard
public office as a private bust. Moreover, he seemed to be sound on
Progressive issues, and he assured me that while he believed in Wilson's
League of Nations, it was not his intention to make an issue of it during
the campaign, or to push it if he should be elected." Upon his return to
Chicago, Ickes scribbled out a long statement in support of Cox and in
opposition to Harding and gave it to the press for release on August 19.
This screed's most notable virtue was an eloquent stab at Harding, whose
nomination, Ickes wrote,

> was a distinct shock to the progressive thought of the country. It is impossible
> for a real progressive to support the man who called Roosevelt "the Aaron
> Burr of the Republican Party" and declared that "when the progressives come
> back into the Republican party they would have to come on their knees."
> Harding presents himself not as a candidate in his own right but as a mimic
> attempting to act McKinley's role. McKinley had his Hanna; Harding must
> have his. Who is it to be?

Cox did in fact make the League of Nations an issue in his campaign
almost immediately, but this did not noticeably detract from Ickes's
support (which would suggest that his opposition to the League was not a
very firmly held conviction). Ickes joined the Cox-Roosevelt Progressive
Republican League, began an extensive letter-writing campaign on his
own hook, and when the Democratic campaign committee printed up
several thousand copies of his statement, he sent three thousand of them to
the people on his list at his own expense. He also culled Harding's
editorials from back issues of the *Marion Star,* pulling out usefully deroga-
tory items concerning progressivism's heroes, TR and Hiram Johnson, as
well as the Progressive Party in general; these also were printed up as a
pamphlet by the Democratic committee and went off to Ickes's list.

Throughout, he kept up a running correspondence with Johnson, even though the "Chief" had come out in support of the Harding-Coolidge ticket; since both of them were looking to 1924 as Johnson's big hurrah, Ickes considered this a forgivable expedient. "To date," he wrote on September 11,

I have received 256 letters from progressives in various parts of the country commenting upon my statement on behalf of Cox. Of these 256 I find that 114 are against Harding. . . . It is safe to say that from 85 to 95% of the 114 have made up their minds to support Cox. . . . On that basis of the letters that have come to me my opinion is confirmed that if Harding is elected (and I always have expected him to be elected) it will be really on account of the anti-democratic drift in the country and the revulsion from the Wilson administration. Regardless, however, of who is elected next November I am very much encouraged by the large proportion of former progressives who are still willing to do their own thinking and stand by their own convictions.

For Ickes, this election was simply not personally crucial; he was playing the game largely for the sake of it, his real interest lying four years down the road. About some things, however, he was not indifferent. One of these was A. Mitchell Palmer, who had been appointed Attorney General of the United States by Wilson in February 1919.

The year following the end of the war was a time of considerable social upheaval, punctuated by sometimes violent labor strikes (including that of the entire Boston police force, the successful suppression of which had first brought Calvin Coolidge into national prominence), shadowed by the bloody Bolshevik revolution in Russia, sullied by lynchings in the South and by race riots in Chicago and elsewhere, and capped off by a series of bombings scattered from Manhattan to Seattle, each of them perpetrated by small groups of agitators or even single individuals of varying political or antipolitical persuasions. Much of the public, encouraged by most of the national press, added all this up and concluded that revolution was afoot and the Republic in peril of being overthrown by an international conspiracy. This was the great Red Scare of 1919–20, and one of those utterly convinced that a vast revolutionary program was in effect was Wilson's attorney general. Palmer had his reasons, to give him his due: on June 2, 1919, the front of his house on R Street in Washington had been shattered by a bomb thrown by an agitator who had died in the act (parts of this luckless revolutionary had landed on the steps of Franklin Roosevelt's home across the street). In August, Palmer established an antiradical division within the Justice Department, with a young J. Edgar Hoover at its head, and early in November began a series of raids, during which many of the stipulations of the Constitution of the United States were high-handedly ignored or violated with intent. Armed with blanket warrants, Palmer's agents, accompanied by local police, broke into private homes, union halls, and political gatherings all over the country, rounding up thousands of people, citizens and aliens alike, holding them without counsel or communication with anyone, and turning them over to a cooperative court system for kangaroo trials (249 aliens, most of them innocent of any actionable crimes, were also deported). Near the end of this mindless reaction, on a single night in January 1920, more than four thousand suspected members of the Communist Party had been arrested in thirty-three cities across the nation (although membership was not illegal). Not since 1861, when President Abraham Lincoln suspended *habeas corpus* at the onset of the Civil War, had the Constitution been so thoroughly bent—and never with so little reason: there was, of course, no conspiracy loose on the land, international or otherwise, and as soon as this became sufficiently clear, public opinion shifted and responsible officials were able to put an end to it.

It was over, but not forgotten. Those who applauded Palmer's efforts made up the bulk of the following that had made possible his bid for the Democratic nomination in July, but his actions had left behind a healthy residue of plain disgust on the part of many more, some of whom saw in this exercise of frenzy a clear illustration of what Wilsonian liberalism had brought the nation to. Among them was Ickes, who let George White, chairman of the Democratic National Committee, know his feelings the instant he heard a rumor that Palmer had been booked for a number of speeches in support of the Cox-Roosevelt ticket: "I hope," he wrote to White on September 17,

> these reports are inaccurate because I cannot think of anything that would make it more difficult for voters like myself to support the Democratic national ticket. . . . The Wilson administration reached its lowest ebb when Mr. Palmer was appointed Attorney-General. I regard him as the greatest menace to our American Institutions and political system who has occupied prominent political office within my recollection. A few more A. Mitchell Palmers, or a little more of the one A. Mitchell Palmer, and we would have open rebellion in this country. He is a greater menace than "Big Bill" Haywood. He is a true anarchist. Instead of performing his sworn duty to uphold the constitution and laws of the United States he has cynically ignored our constitution and violated our laws. He has denied to citizens their constitutional right and has outraged the sense of justice of the American people. He should have been impeached and driven from office long since.

Warren G. Harding would have agreed, after a fashion. Not that he held any profound emotions regarding the sanctity of the Constitution.

But contention of any sort made this large, timid man nervous. "Too much," he would remark in one of his few public statements on the subject of the communist menace, "has been said about Bolshevism in America." He was sick of quarreling and violence, sick of reform and agitation, sick of the whole messy process by which change was effected in this country, and he was convinced that his countrymen agreed with him. "America's present need," he had said in a speech back in May 1920, "is not heroics but healing; not nostrums but normalcy; not revolution but restoration; . . . not surgery but serenity." He may or may not have been right about what Americans needed—but he apparently was right about what they wanted. On November 2, 1920, Harding was elected President of the United States, 16,152,200 popular votes to 9,147,353 for Cox and 919,799 for Eugene V. Debs (sitting in prison for antiwar activities). Harding had captured the largest percentage of votes in the history of Presidential elections up to that time.

"Here," Harold Ickes said, "was reaction with a vengeance."

CHAPTER
·18·

Keeping the Faith

A S PRESIDENT-TO-BE, Harding may have offered the country what he chose to call "normalcy," but what the country got in the decade that began with his election can only be described rationally as one of the most abnormal periods in our modern history. If the United States of America had been a human being, instead of a tangled agglomeration of individual dreams and aspirations, it would have been diagnosed as manic-depressive in the years of the sputtering twenties. On the surface, the times glittered with a frantic energy, the nation's people released from a ghastly war and now breaking restraints that had bound society for more than a century. In response to the Eighteenth Amendment to the Constitution—the Prohibition Amendment—which became law on January 16, 1919, and the National Prohibition Act—the Volstead Act—which gave muscle to enforcement and became law on October 28, Americans invented the cocktail party and the speakeasy, learned what a proper martini was, and became a nation of lawbreakers. While the country did not precisely discover sex in this period, Americans did learn to read about it, talk about it, explore it, and analyze it, and even—though not quite so widely as is commonly supposed—do something about it. Henry Ford, who had already given them wheels with the Model T, gave them the rumble seat with the Model A; the movies gave them something to do with their eyes, and the *Saturday Evening Post* informed their intellects. From economics, they learned what a down payment was and how to buy stock on margin; from religion, they learned that Christ would have been an advertising man; from philosophy, they learned that morality was relative; from politics, they learned not to expect very much. It was, newspaperman Gene Fowler said, "a world of Nevertheless."

Too glib a description, of course; there were currents of intelligence and moral and philosophical strength at work, or the nation would never have survived the period. But these were far from dominant, and only the inevitable hangover would bring them to the forefront when the binge was over. In the meantime, all this unchained and undirected energy had its darker, depressive side, a powerful strain of cynicism, apathy, and indifference. Nowhere was this condition reflected more precisely than in the widespread decline of social and political concern, even among many of the old reformers.

Disillusionment drove some, like Walter Lippmann, who had cut his ideological and philosophical teeth with Herbert Croly and the *New Republic,* into a detached analysis of democratic principles and purposes; theory, not practice. Others, like Croly, sought help in mysticism and a search for moral foundations, and others, like the old muckraker Lincoln Steffens, looked to Russia for the visions that had failed them here; in the new communist states, Steffens said, people believed passionately that the "future is coming; it is in sight; it is coming, really and truly coming, and soon. And it is good." Disillusionment drove still others, a handful of young writers whose work would come to dominate American letters, clear out of the country to lead expatriate lives on the wrecked European continent in search of something—cultural certitudes, Art, themselves. And it drove those with less rarefied sensibilities into an ironclad selfishness. Near the end of the decade, among that class of women who had once been the very bone and sinew of Chicago reform, a University of Chicago sociologist did a survey of social attitudes and found little more than complaisance. The response of one interviewee was typical: "Dr. W. at the University of Chicago wanted me to go down there on the West Side where all those horrible slums are to see 'real life.' I wouldn't do it. They're too dirty and besides its [sic] too dangerous. I can't see how anyone would get a kick out of doing that. Merely the idea of it is nauseating to me."

Against such pathology, the career of Harold Ickes stands as a glowing counterpoint. For all his posturing as the wise old cynic in his *Autobiography,* in matters of politics and public affairs he remained throughout the decade as solidly, unquestioningly progressive in his instincts as he had been when he had first discovered them a quarter of a century before. True cynicism was impossible in him, apathy and indifference alien to his nature. He refused to flex with the times. He would not slide into the easy embrace of regular Republicanism, as his friends William Allen White and Henry Allen had done, nor would he lose confidence in the essential strength of the traditional democratic process, as his friend Raymond Robins did. Robins, like Lincoln Steffens, returned from Russia to spread the good news all over the country: "I made a bully good talk on Lenin and Ideals and Principles of the Bolshevick [*sic*] Revolution," Robins wrote Margaret from Cleveland after one speech. "It got over in great form. The folks so hypnotized that there were no questions." For fifteen years, when not proselytizing for the Outlawry of War, an international peace group, or calling for the United States to join the League of Nations, Robins would spend most of his energy in trying to persuade the American government to grant diplomatic recognition to the Soviet state. Ickes had no argument with Russia (and in time would himself call for recognition) or with communism itself, though he held no illusions that it was either workable or desirable in the United States. His own goals for his city, state, and nation were the same simple dreams that had given definition to his entire adult life, transcending his massive personality flaws, his weaknesses, his flaming ambition, his anguished marriage, his profound insecurities: clean government, the preservation of the Bill of Rights, the uplifting of the underdog, and fair play for every citizen. Whatever else one might say of this complex and difficult man, through the twenties— as through the rest of his life—he stayed a righteous pilgrim. He kept the faith.

Chicago and Illinois suffered their own, peculiarly virulent strain of the national disorder, with Big Bill Thompson running the city and a powerful clutch of reactionary politicians running the State House in Springfield. Thompson's alliance with the underworld satrapy of Big Jim Colosimo, forged during the years of his first administration, had solidified by the early twenties. Colosimo, with the nervous Irishmen, "Bathhouse" John Coughlin and "Hinky Dink" Kenna, firmly under his indelicate thumb, delivered the votes of the First Ward and all necessary graft payments; Thompson delivered protection from undue harassment on the part of his obedient and well-lubricated police force. This arrangement continued even when the increasingly competitive and lucrative bootleg industry brought about some personnel changes among the gangland entrepreneurs: Colosimo was murdered in his own restaurant one night on the order of his faithful torpedo, Johnny Torrio, who then took over the operation; Torrio, for his part, was then badly wounded and driven out of town by *his* faithful torpedo, Alphonse Capone, a.k.a. Al Caponi, a.k.a. Al Brown, "dealer in second-hand furniture." Capone, crude, ruthless, and effective, with powerful links to the national Mafia and the Unione Siciliano, introduced murder as one of the tools of the political process and extended it outside the confines of the First Ward; during one aldermanic election in the Nineteenth Ward, for example, an anticrime candidate for the city council and five ward heelers were gunned down in the street by Capone's henchmen.

Meanwhile, a majority in the Illinois State Legislature saw the rising tide of conservatism as an opportunity to gut the state of nearly all the progressive legislation that had been adopted since the turn of the century. The means these ambitious lawmakers came up with was the writing of a new state constitution to replace that of 1879, and on October 22, 1922, they presented it to the people for a referendum scheduled early in December. It was quite a document. Among other provisions, the new constitution provided for Bible-reading in the public schools; empowered the state's attorney general to go into any local jurisdiction and make arrests without showing cause to any court; gave life tenure to justices on the state supreme court and enabled them to appoint, switch, or remove at will judges in the lower court system; amended the right to bail to exclude those accused of capital crimes; reduced taxes on corporate stocks and bonds; established universal conscription for the state militia with no exemptions on religious or conscientious grounds; and enabled the attorney general and any two additional state officials to gerrymander— redistrict—the political divisions within the state according to their own lights and over any objections on the part of the legislature. It also eliminated the teachers' pension fund, the graduated state income tax, and the political instruments of initiative and referendum, and included stipulations that effectively prohibited any future amendments to itself. About the only thing the proposed constitution did not seek to mutilate was female suffrage—and this, probably, only because suffrage had become national law with ratification of the Nineteenth Amendment to the federal Constitution.

The legislators had overstepped themselves in their enthusiasm, misreading the political situation and forgetting to take into account the opposition of the old-line Progressives, most of whom, after all, were not dead and who still exercised some considerable—if sporadic—influence across the state. At or very near the head of these was Harold Ickes, who went to work immediately, organizing the People's Protective League, eliciting active support from such liberal veterans as Charles Merriam,

Clarence Darrow, Donald Richberg, and even Amos Alonzo Stagg, and directing a blistering propaganda effort. It was one of his finest hours: statewide, the new constitution was crushed by a plurality of more than 700,000 votes; in Cook County alone, it was defeated 541,206 to 27,874. A triumphant Ickes grandly announced to the newspapers that the victory clearly indicated the rebirth of the "progressive movement . . . that was halted temporarily by war."

Not exactly, but obviously there was life remaining in the reformers yet, at least at the local level, and it would soon be demonstrated once more—again with Ickes leading the way. By 1923 the city of Chicago was so paralyzed by corruption and violence that it was hardly functioning as a city at all. Like the constitution of 1922, the situation was too much for even an apathetic public to swallow without gagging. Big Bill Thompson was not a very smart man, but neither was he comatose; early in 1923 he detected a certain loss of popularity, and decided not to challenge fate. He announced that he would not be a candidate for a third consecutive term. Nor did he offer his own hand-picked candidate to the Republican machine. Senator Medill McCormick stepped into the breech, put forward the name of Postmaster Arthur C. Lueder, and secured his nomination. McCormick by then had made his peace with the regular Republicans, and his sponsorship of Lueder was more than enough to drive Ickes and most of the old Progressives into the camp of the Democratic candidate, Judge William E. Dever, a former alderman, a close associate of former mayor and governor Edward F. Dunne, a liberal, and a practicing Roman Catholic.

Ickes organized the Independent Dever Club, with offices in the Morrison Hotel, and was elected chairman of the group, whose officers and executive committee included Raymond and Margaret Robins, Anna, Charles E. Merriam, and Stacy Mosser, his old college friend, among the thirty-six former Progressives willing to assume Democratic spots for a while and serve the cause of Judge Dever. (Donald Richberg, for once, did not take an active part; he had become general council to the Brotherhood of Railway Workers the previous year and that duty, with his continuing litigation work for the city against Samuel Insull, apparently kept him out of things.) This term, however, the usual battle between the Democratic and Republican machines was colored o'er by the sickly cast of bigotry. It was not a phenomenon confined to Chicago. Anti-Catholicism had once again reared its head in American society, as it had done periodically since the 1830s. This time, it was promulgated most effectively by a resurgent Ku Klux Klan, which had capitalized on various discontents after the war to build its membership to a claimed 1.5 million across the nation. Some of the Klan's greatest strength lay in the rural districts of Ohio, Illinois, and Indiana, and if it did not get any real foothold in Chicago itself, both Ickes and Dever believed the group's sentiments crept into the city's mayoralty contest, aided by Lueder (a Protestant of Lutheran persuasion) and his people who, they felt sure, were spreading bigotry's poison with a broad brush. The Independent Dever Club (itself almost entirely Protestant) decided to counterattack by forcing the issue into the open. Thomas D. Knight, one of Lueder's chief supporters, responded to Ickes's consequent public charges that Knight himself had taken part in the smear by calling him "a plain liar," and similar gutter-level exchanges on both sides made the last two weeks of the campaign uglier than was normal even by Chicago standards.*

Neither Klan slander nor a considerable investment of money and personal effort on the part of Medill McCormick was enough to do serious damage to Dever's wide and truly bipartisan support, and Raymond Robins, for one, anticipated an easy success. "I am very tired tonight," he wrote Margaret (who was sitting out the election in Chinsegut Hill) on April 2, the night before the election, "but have a great gladness in the sureness of Victory. Do you realize that I have not been inside the City Hall since the election of Fred A. Busse in the spring of 1907 some sixteen years!" The next morning, he appended a typically overwrought postscript: "I wish you were here this morning to go down to our polling place to vote for dear old Bill Dever—Alderman Bill Dever, Hissonner Jedge Dever, THE HONORABLE WILLIAM E. DEVER MAYOR OF CHICAGO! Its [*sic*] raining heavily," he added more calmly. "This is good democratic weather and the Irish and the Ku Klux Klan will have to fight it out. Most of the respectables will stay at home."

In the end, Dever beat Lueder by more than 100,000 votes, one of the largest pluralities in recent Chicago memory. Dever himself ascribed much of the win to Ickes and the work of the Independents; Ickes was willing to accept this, and his pleasure doubtless was magnified by the defeat of his old rival, Medill McCormick, whose influence in the city was badly shaken. (The defeat of his man in 1923 would be followed by a more

---

* It probably was during this campaign that Ickes had a personal run-in with the Ku Klux Klan, as reported by Raymond Ickes. When he was about eleven, Raymond says, he and his father stopped at some unremembered town in Ohio to watch a local Klan parade during a trip: "We were standing in the front rank, and along came this parade of peaked-hooded characters. Ahead of it was an individual carrying the American flag. As the flag passed—as was the custom in those days—Dad took off his hat. As soon as the flag had gone by, he put it back on again. A minute or two after that, one of these thugs came alongside, reached over and got Dad's hat, and said, 'Take off your hat—I'm an American.' Dad said, 'I'm an American, too, you son-of-a-bitch!,' hit him in the face and retrieved his hat."

direct blow in 1924: he was turned back in a bid for renomination to his U.S. Senate seat. On February 25, 1925, he would commit suicide.) Not that the victory meant all that much, in the long run. Thompson had left behind a legacy that Dever never was able to get fully under control. Capone, for his part, simply moved operations to the city of Cicero, one of the few nearby suburbs that had escaped the municipal embrace of Greater Chicago, installed his own people in the Cicero city hall, and continued to reign untouched. He could afford to bide his time. So could Big Bill Thompson, for that matter. They would both be back.

Even as Ickes savored the triumph of the Dever campaign, he found himself in the middle of one more snarl of frustration. Late in the summer of 1922, probably at the request of Jane Addams (herself a friend of Mary White Ovington, the organization's chairman of the board), he agreed to become president of the Chicago branch of the National Association for the Advancement of Colored People. As it had for most Chicagoans, the fragility of the relationship between blacks and whites in the city had come home to him with shocking force during the violence of 1919. He had reacted then like a good Progressive: when he heard that Governor Frank Lowden might appoint a commission to look into the situation, he wrote offering his support and some recommendations of his own: "I think the idea is a good one. It seems to me such a Commission, with good results, could go beyond the mere studying of the race problem with a view to making recommendations. Couldn't a permanent body be created which, in addition to making investigations and recommendations, could actually act as a commission on conciliation in instances where the feeling has become tense and where a better understanding is needed in order to avoid such friction?" The question of race, he concluded, "is one of the most important matters facing us today. It should be approached humanly and sympathetically." Nothing came of his suggestion, but his concern remained high enough for him to accept this new chore with a hope that something substantial might be done. Unfortunately, this expectation was linked to the assumption he apparently held that the NAACP branch was a viable, even vigorous group requiring little more of him than the use of his name. If so, he was swiftly disabused, as he told Miss Addams two months later:

> So far as I have been able to find out there is really no such organization. . . . I discovered this, much to my chagrin, some time after I had consented to take the presidency of the local branch. . . . I found, as a matter of fact, that only a paper organization existed. There haven't been any meetings of the Executive

Committee; there is no membership and apparently no effort has been made to build up or retain a membership. . . . There is no money in the treasury and the woman who acted as Secretary of the Association has a claim for unpaid salary.

Ickes tried, in so far as time allowed. He scratched together a new, if somewhat reluctant, Executive Committee. (One of its members, Mrs. Irwin Rosenfels, responded to his letter of invitation with a hasty note: "I have little time to give to this work now but for the present, I'll go on the Executive Committee. I know that few people are willing to serve here.") Of all his closest friends and colleagues, only Mary McDowell and Jane Addams consented to serve. In October he got some organizing help from Robert W. Bagnall, director of NAACP branches in the New York office, who came west firmly believing "that Chicago should have at least 5000 members of the Association, and that there should be a working program which would keep the members interested during the entire year." He returned to New York six weeks later, leaving behind a membership that could be counted in the hundreds, not thousands, most of whom soon fell away. Ickes did talk the national office into paying for a full-time executive secretary, a young black man named Morris Lewis, whose most successful achievement was the organization of an antilynching rally early in June 1923; Ickes got Raymond Robins to speak, and the well-attended meeting raised $879.50 in membership fees, donations, and pledges. That, unfortunately, was the high point. Membership continued to wane, money was next to impossible to raise (later that same June, Ickes sent out sixteen letters to his rich friends asking for donations, bringing in a total of $135), and the infrequent Executive Committee meetings at no time showed full attendance. In February 1924, Lewis resigned to become circulation manager of the *Chicago Defender,* the city's black newspaper. Ickes stayed on as president of the increasingly moribund branch until November, when he, too, gave it up.

"I don't know what is the matter with our Chicago branch," he wrote Bagnall shortly before his resignation.

Some of us have thought that our officers were too high-brow and that we could not make the right appeal to the rank and file of the colored people of Chicago. Mr. Morris Lewis has expressed the opinion that the real difficulty is that the colored people of Chicago have no real grievances. Be the cause what it may, the fact is that your own efforts here, covering a considerable period two years ago, followed by the prolonged activity of Mr. Lewis, have not only failed to build up the local organization, but have not even sufficed to keep it from going backward. So far as I can see no blame attaches to any individual or group for this state of affairs.

Perhaps not. Yet the city's progressive contingent could have taken some of the onus for an attitude of apparent indifference; even among these good men and women, old prejudices died hard. It would be a long time before the liberal white community would be ready and willing to take up the cause of black people with any real enthusiasm. It is probable, however, that the black rank and file of Chicago was itself unwilling at this time to make an issue of its circumstances. Morris Lewis's perhaps desperate analysis of the situation should have been amended: black people in the city had no cause for which they were yet willing to die. Most of them, Lewis and Ickes both should have remembered, were fresh from the South, from a culture that did not go out of its way to encourage self-expression on the part of its black people; what it did do, more often than not, was hang them for it, and the memory of the bloody riots of 1919 and the visible and violent presence of a reborn Ku Klux Klan in the countryside all around them gave Chicago's blacks plenty of reason to believe that the same thing could happen even up north in Freedomland. In any case, it would be many years before the NAACP would be able to secure a firm and permanent position in Chicago.

Another good cause in the early twenties gave Ickes more satisfaction, if its own portion of frustration (most of it self-imposed this time). His involvement in this instance came about through the intercession of Anna, who had been keeping herself quite as busy as her husband, though perhaps less noisily. She had always been active in public affairs, of course; she had been helping support Hull-House and the Women's Trade Union League for years, sat on the boards of a number of charities, had participated in the garment workers' strikes, had joined with her mother to help found the Women's City Club in 1910, and had played a continuing role in the movement that led to the formation of the Progressive Party. (And, it should be remembered, it had always been Anna's money—over which she had given him control—that had enabled Harold to pursue his political career as erstwhile kingmaker.) After Raymond's birth in 1912, Anna had cut back on much of her activities for a time, but after war's end and her mother's death in 1919 she had plowed right back in. By the early twenties, her own full plate included most of her old alliances plus memberships in the Fortnightly Club, the Women's University Club, the Winnetka Women's Club, the Society of Mayflower Descendants, the League of Women Voters, the National Consumers League, and the Chicago Women's Club—and in 1920 she had even taken to the stump in South Dakota in support of the Cox-Roosevelt ticket (with no better success than Ickes had enjoyed in Illinois).

Anna had also acquired a passionate interest that would sustain her for the rest of her life and to which she would devote herself with much the same relentless energy that Harold gave to his own pursuits. Possibly beginning as early as 1916, periodic attacks of asthma had driven her to seek the high, dry air of New Mexico for relief, and after repeated visits she fell in love with the broken, beautiful desert country just east of Gallup. Sometime in the early twenties she built a small adobe house in the tiny outpost of Coolidge on the edge of the Navajo Indian reservation, not far from Bertram I. Staples's famous trading post, Crafts del Navajo. The simple, geometrically spare adobe stood on a plateau at an elevation of fifty-five hundred feet, with a view to the south of the pinon-covered Zuñi Mountains and to the north of a forty-mile line of sandstone cliffs that changed from lavender to orange to red with the passage of the sun. With this house as her base, Anna launched her career as an amateur anthropologist, studying the cultures of the nearby Navajo and Zuñi tribes and of the Pueblo people of the Rio Grande Valley a little over one hundred miles to the east. By the end of the decade she would be hard at work on a book about her observations. It was her fascination with the Indians of the Southwest that inspired her to take a seat on the Indian Welfare Committee of the General Federation of Women's Clubs, and it was through this connection that she and Harold were first introduced to John Collier and his consuming interest in the plight of the Indian.

The intense, ascetic Collier, a devotee of the works of Nietzsche and the early *Gestalt* psychologists, was a reformer in the mold of Raymond Robins, an enthusiast of mysticism and capacious Utopian dreams, and, like Robins, utterly committed to the uplifting of sorrowful humanity. He had worked for the Associated Charities of Atlanta, had been executive secretary of the People's Institute of the Cooper Union in New York City, had worked for the California State Immigration and Housing Commission, and finally, until 1922, had been an instructor in social science at San Francisco State Teachers' College (today, California State University at San Francisco). While working in New York, he had been a regular (with such others as Walter Lippmann and Herbert Croly) at the Greenwich Village salon of Mabel Dodge; this formidable lady had since removed herself to Taos, New Mexico, married Antonio Luhan, a Pueblo Indian, and in her own enormous timber-and-adobe house in that ancient village had reestablished herself as the intellectual doyenne and patronness of a sexually and politically liberated collection of writers and artists. (Anna Ickes was acquainted with these blithe spirits well enough, and consequently had as little to do with them as possible.) During 1921, at Mrs. Luhan's invitation, Collier and his family had spent several months living among the Pueblos, an experience that forged in him so strong a sense of identification with the Indians that it bordered on neopantheism. He was an easy mark, then, when in 1922 Stella M. Atwood of the General Federation of Women's Clubs asked him to go to work as a "research agent" for the Federation on behalf of Indian rights. At issue was an attempt by a number of New Mexico ranchers to nullify the title to lands guaranteed to the Pueblo Indians by the Treaty of Guadalupe-Hidalgo in 1848 and subsequently affirmed by various Executive Orders. The spokes-man of the ranchers in Congress was Senator Holm Olaf Bursum, himself a ranchman from Socorro, New Mexico, who had been elected to fill the vacancy created when his friend, Albert B. Fall, left the Senate to become Secretary of the Interior in the Harding administration. In 1922, Bursum had introduced legislation ostensibly designed to resolve in an impartial manner long-standing disputes between white ranchers and the Indians over land and water rights, but in fact the Bursum bill would have stripped the Pueblo villages of much they had held since before the arrival of the Spanish early in the seventeenth century. The Harding administra-tion, in the person of Fall, owner of the enormous Three Rivers Ranch of New Mexico's Tularosa basin, gave the bill its full support, and to counteract this, Collier and Antonio Luhan organized the Indians into the All Pueblo Council. By spreading the word through Francis Wilson, a Santa Fe attorney with good connections in Congress, they managed to block the bill for that session. A version of it, however, was immediately introduced into the House when Congress reconvened in January 1923, while on the other side of the Hill, legislation more favorable to the Indians (and largely drafted by Wilson) was placed before the Senate by a Democratic senator from New Mexico with the extraordinary name of Andrieus Aristieus Jones. To testify against the House bill and for the Senate bill, Collier led a troop of Indians north.

Along the way, the delegation made a number of stops to drum up support. One of these was at Chicago, where James W. Young and Henry Stanton of the J. Walter Thompson advertising firm gave Collier and half his Indians a luncheon at the Cliff Dwellers Club. The other half of the delegation was appropriated by Anna Ickes for a parallel luncheon at the Chicago Women's Club (of which she was now vice president). Harold, whose interest in Indian matters, largely moribund since the days of his anthropological studies at the University of Chicago, had been rekindled by Anna's work, attended the Cliff Dwellers luncheon and came away a passionate convert to the cause. "A more moving tale of wrongs wantonly committed and proposed against a peaceful, law-abiding and self-respecting group of people I have never listened to," he wrote Hiram Johnson that very afternoon. "The story as told by Mr. Collier, if spread broadcast throughout the country, ought to make every decent American's face burn with shame for the injuries that have been and are proposed to be committed in his name and in the names of his fellow citizens. Voluntarily I gave Mr. Collier a note of introduction to you. . . . I can honestly say that there is no one in the U.S. Senate who can make this fight as you can make it. It is a fight for human rights against knavery, oppression and greed." Johnson supported the Jones bill, and while it never got out of committee, neither did the anti-Pueblo bill in the House.

In order to wage a proper fight, Ickes was convinced, one needed a proper organization, so he forthwith set about helping to put together the Chicago Indian Rights Association, with his old Democratic enemy Carter H. Harrison installed as chairman and Anna as treasurer. Although giving the general impression that he pretty well ran the organization over the next ten years, Ickes himself held no title beyond membership on the board. (Other notable board members included editorial cartoonist John T. McCutcheon, a crony from his newspaper days, and Edgar Lee Masters, author of *Spoon River Anthology.*) At about the same time, in New York, Collier, Robert Ely, president of the New York Economic Club, and Dorothy Straight, cofounder (with her husband, Willard) of the *New Republic* under Herbert Croly's editorship, organized the American Indian Defense Association, with Collier as executive secretary. Ickes immediately joined, and at the invitation of Collier became a charter member of the AIDA's board of directors.

It was an abrasive alliance, as were so many in Ickes's life. Not long after taking his seat on the association board, Ickes began to promote the idea of gathering into one huge conference all groups that claimed to speak for the Indians, earnestly believing that only organization on a national scale could effectively protect the rights and interests of all Native Americans (although they were not yet called that). Collier opposed the idea on the equally earnest grounds that such organizations—of which there were scores by now—were too various, too well-established, and too accustomed to their own way of doing things to willingly give up their autonomy; better, he said, to seek their cooperation, not attempt to ingest them. Neither man was willing to give an inch in his position, and over several months they exchanged increasingly ill-tempered letters, each accusing the other of bad faith, intransigence, and a stubborn refusal to face the facts or fairly entertain the other man's point of view. Ickes, perhaps because he had more practice at invective, was particularly violent in his language; near the end of this squabble, in August 1923, he informed Collier that as executive director he had been "stupid and shortsighted," and went on to conclude that "You have failed in your leadership in this movement to such a degree that I, for one, would hesitate to follow you anywhere further." When Collier fired attorney Francis Wilson over a disagreement, Ickes resigned from the AIDA's board of directors.

Before the year was out, however, Ickes was back on the board, helping Collier and the AIDA to defeat yet another piece of Bursum legislation, this one called the Indian omnibus bill, which would have done to all Indian-held lands what the earlier bill would have done only to the lands of the Pueblos. Through most of the rest of the decade, while the Chicago Indian Rights Association and the AIDA generally cooperated, Ickes and Collier maintained a relationship that was sporadically troubled by bouts of anger and suspicion and in no way hinted at the deep personal and professional friendship it would become in later years, one that would bring this accolade from Collier in his memoirs: "Here was a great man; and in government and in American society today, there are very few equally great."

Greatness, however, continued to elude Ickes through the twenties, though he made one more effort to get Hiram Johnson's long-awaited train under way, with himself securely on board. For a while during the latter part of 1922 and the first several months of 1923, it did seem that Johnson had at least an outside chance at the Republican nomination. Harding's popularity of 1920 appeared to be slipping by the last quarter of 1922, according to public opinion polls, and the enthusiasm the electorate had demonstrated for upright conservatism was not reflected in the congressional elections in November: before the elections, the Republican majority in the House had been 300 to 130; after the elections the figures plummeted to 221 against 212. Farm prices had not kept pace with the general prosperity of the new consumer society, with its disdain of thrift, its growing dependence upon marketing and advertising campaigns, its growing white-collar class of middle-level managers, its passion for speculation in everything from bucket-shop securities to southern California real estate. On the farms people were hurting, and they were expressing their hurt by a scattering of open revolts that bore an unsettling resemblance to the anger of the nineteenth-century Populists. Nor was the labor movement convinced it was getting its fair share, and strikes burst into headlines all over the country. Finally, a certain stench was beginning to issue from various quarters in the administration.

From the Department of the Interior, for example. Secretary Albert Fall's open support of the anti-Indian legislation of his friends in Congress had offended almost no one but John Collier, Ickes, and the relatively small band of others similarly interested in the cause of the Indian. Fall's handling of the nation's naval oil reserves was another matter. Back in the years preceding American entrance into World War I, Presidents Taft and Wilson had established under the administration of the Interior Department three major oil reserves for the future use of the navy—Buena Vista Hills and Elk Hills in California's San Joaquin Valley, and Teapot Dome in east-central Wyoming. In 1920, not convinced that the Interior Department was doing all it could to protect these reserves, Secretary of the Navy Josephus Daniels persuaded President Wilson to transfer all three of them to the navy. They did not stay there long. Shortly after taking office in 1921, the new secretary of the navy, Edwin N. Denby, who did not want the responsibility, persuaded Harding to transfer them back to Interior, where Secretary Fall received them with equanimity.

In the spring of 1922, Fall concluded two sweet deals which he steadfastly maintained were to the profound benefit of the United States. On April 7 he granted a twenty-year lease on the Teapot Dome Reserve to old friend Harry F. Sinclair, owner of the appropriately named Mammoth Oil Company. In return, Mammoth Oil would pay to the government royalties ranging from 12.5 percent to 50 percent—not in money but in certificates that could be exchanged for the purchase of gasoline, fuel oil, and the construction of storage tanks for the navy. The Secretary had not asked for any bids on this transaction; he had gone straight to Sinclair, and the deal had been accomplished in secret. Eight days later, and more openly, he accepted a bid from another old friend, Edward Doheny, owner of the Pan-American Petroleum and Transport Company, this one in connection with the Elk Hills Reserve. In exchange for six million barrels of crude oil from the reserve, Doheny's company would construct storage tanks for the navy at Pearl Harbor in the Hawaiian Islands. In December this agreement was amended to give Doheny's company unlimited drilling rights in the reserve in exchange for building even more tanks, plus a refinery and a pipeline for the navy's exclusive use. These contracts, Fall announced, would not only assure the navy of a ready supply of oil on demand but would give them storage facilities that the Congress, in its shortsightedness, had consistently refused to authorize.

There were those who did not see it that way, among them Gifford Pinchot—now governor of Pennsylvania—who had never lost his interest in the conservation of the country's natural resources, and a young associate of his, Harry Slattery, who had served as secretary of Pinchot's National Conservation Association from 1912 to 1917. To such as these, Fall's actions were nothing less than open giveaways of public resources, and they and a few others loudly proclaimed their suspicions that more than the needs of the navy had been on Fall's mind. In Congress, Senator Robert M. La Follette requested all relevant materials in connection with the Doheny and Sinclair leases. Fall supplied a truckload of papers, and as the aides of Montana senator Thomas J. Walsh of the Committee on Public Lands began slowly to sift through the mounds of documents in the summer of 1922, suspicions began to mount. When Fall chose to resign early in 1923, pleading ill health and the press of personal business, he left under a cloud—a small cloud, to be sure, but a cloud nevertheless.

There were genuine thunderheads elsewhere in the administration. Late in 1922, it was revealed that high-living Colonel Charles R. Forbes, Harding's appointee as director of the Veterans' Bureau, had been selling off millions of dollars' worth of hospital supplies at cut-rate prices to a private firm and had awarded hugely inflated hospital construction contracts to a few select companies. For all of this, of course, "Charlie," as he was fondly known throughout the administration, got a very fat cut. When his scam was discovered, he left the country and telephoned his resignation, which Harding accepted. ("My God, this is a hell of a job!" Harding wailed to William Allen White during an interview at this time. "I have no trouble with my enemies, I can take care of my enemies all right. But my damn friends . . . my God-damn friends, White, they're the ones keeping me walking the floor nights!") Then there was Harry M. Daugherty, Harding's campaign manager, now his Attorney General, and Daugherty's inseparable sidekick, Jess Smith. Jess, it was said on good authority and with increasing frequency, was Daugherty's bag man for the distribution of favors and the collection of bribes. And over in Daugherty's Federal Bureau of Investigation, it was rumored with equal confidence, Director William J. Burns and his associate Gaston Bullock Means had their own system of corruption in place and functioning smoothly. Finally, on March 3, 1923, Charles Cramer, former general counsel for the Veterans' Bureau, put a newspaper clipping regarding the Forbes scandal in a book of Oscar Wilde's poems near the lines "All my life's buried here/ Heap earth upon it," and shot himself. A little over two months later, Jess Smith took a pile of Justice Department documents and his and Daugherty's personal correspondence home with him, burned it all, and put a gun to his own head.

Harding, it seemed clear, was in terrible trouble, and when Ickes wrote to Johnson on April 10 to say "It is my dearest wish to see you President and I will be only too happy if I can contribute in some small way to that result," he was not merely being uncharacteristically gracious; he believed that Johnson could be nominated and elected and that he, himself, could help make it happen. That hope received a dreadful blow the evening of August 2, when Harding died in San Francisco while returning from a junket to Alaska. The straitlaced (and straight-faced) Calvin Coolidge was duly sworn in as President, and no matter how hard the administration's opponents might try, he could not effectively be tarred by the sins of his predecessor. Like most Vice Presidents, Coolidge had been kept sublimely ignorant of the inner workings of the Harding administration, and when subsequent investigations began to reveal one malefactor after another like cockroaches exposed to a sudden kitchen light, his disgust was genuine. "There are three purgatories," he said to Secretary of Commerce Herbert Hoover at one point, "to which people can be assigned: to be damned by one's fellows; to be damned by the courts; to be damned in the next world. I want these men to get all three without probation."

One of them was former Interior Secretary Fall. On October 22, the Senate Committee on Public Lands began hearings on the Doheny and Sinclair leases at the Elk Hills and Teapot Dome reserves. During the hearings, Edward Doheny himself cheerfully admitted to having loaned Fall $100,000 without security or receipt and that the money had been considerately hand-delivered to the Secretary by Doheny's son in a newsworthy black satchel. It was a pittance, Doheny said, nothing one friend wouldn't normally do for another, and it had no connection with his contract for the Elk Hills lease. Harry Sinclair, as it happened, had been an even more openhanded friend. Between May 1922 and January 1923, again without security or a single piece of signed paper between them, Sinclair had loaned Fall a total of $304,000. He, too, insisted that this money was untainted by any secretarial favors. Fall, who looked increasingly sick, wretched, and guilty with each appearance before the committee, piously agreed with both men. In the meantime, Senator Burton K. Wheeler, Thomas J. Walsh's companion senator from Montana, began investigating Attorney General Daugherty, and as the testimony of the Wheeler hearings began to mount, Daugherty's resignation finally was demanded by Coolidge.

Coolidge's ability to remain unspattered was going to make things difficult enough, Ickes knew, but Johnson himself was going to be a major problem. In spite of Ickes's urging that soon was not soon enough, Johnson did not admit even privately that he would be a candidate until the middle of August, and refused to make his decision public until the middle of November. All this gave Coolidge too much time to firm up his position, Ickes felt; nor was he happy when Johnson left the situation in Illinois and the Midwest in a state of uncertainty, returning to California in August and remaining there for months. He was even less happy when Johnson stuck to his decision to have TR's 1904 campaign manager, Frank Hitchcock, as his own national campaign manager, even though Ickes had told him that it would be better to "take a chance on some wide awake, aggressive man, who has his spurs yet to win in the national field" (it is not difficult to imagine whom Ickes had in mind). Still, Ickes did his duty, talking advertising man Albert J. Lasker and William Wrigley, Jr., son of the chewing-gum king, into contributing $25,000 each to Johnson's war chest, opening up a Johnson headquarters, and otherwise busying himself in full confidence that he would be placed in charge of the Illinois campaign. Illinois, after all, was one of the three states utterly necessary to success (New York and California being the other two), and Ickes knew as much about its political byways and culs-de-sac as anyone then alive.

It did not happen. For the rest of 1923 it did not happen. Hitchcock appointed no one else to handle the Illinois campaign, but refused to consider Ickes, whom he did not like. Illinois drifted, and so did Johnson, who disliked making administrative decisions. Astonishingly, Ickes put his own hurt feelings and growing irritation to one side and continued his work, lining up support from the old Progressives where and when he could. His commitment to Johnson was resolute, perhaps reinforced by a measure of guilt for having "abandoned" the senator in 1920, and personal, as such things usually were with Ickes. "I am for Johnson," he wrote Henry Allen on November 24, "because, other things being equal, I prefer to support one of the old crowd that went through the Progressive fight with us and stuck to the end. Whoever has kept the Progressive faith still has with me as large a credit balance as I am able to meet."

Allen, who had become solidly conservative by now, remained unmoved, and Ickes was having trouble with even the radical side of the ledger. Donald Richberg, for example. The two of them were seeing less and less of each other and were growing farther apart politically. For one thing, the law partnership had disintegrated. In 1921, Morgan Davies had suffered a mental collapse and later killed himself by jumping out of a window while under treatment at Presbyterian Hospital. Shortly afterward, a new partner, Charles Cobb, joined with John Lord to ask for Richberg's resignation because one of the firm's best clients had complained that Richberg's work for the Railway Brotherhood gave the partnership a hue of red radicalism. Richberg left in some bitterness. Ickes stayed on, although he had stood up for Richberg, only to leave a year later himself, ultimately taking offices in the new State Bank Building on West Monroe Street. For another thing, Richberg's politics had in fact shriveled down to a hard leftist knot, and he and Ickes found it increasingly difficult to share common interests or goals. By the end of 1923, Richberg had decided to give his support to the radical machine of Senator Robert M. La Follette.

Raymond Robins, though remaining friendly enough, proved a similar problem. Johnson wanted Robins's support very much, but by his lights it came attached to a very high price tag. Ever since August, Robins had been cultivating Coolidge in hopes the new President would announce his support of Robin's current obsession, the Outlawry of War campaign. He would give up this effort and join Johnson's team only if the senator was willing to abandon his isolationist principles and publicly endorse the Outlawry of War. Johnson could not bring himself to do this. Ickes tried to mediate between the two, but it was hopeless; neither would soften his stand, and Robins ultimately was lost to Coolidge, even though the President himself remained ambivalent on the peace issue.

Ambivalence also continued to mark Johnson's treatment of Ickes. His erstwhile campaign manager was working very hard for him, but the effort was almost entirely unofficial and without authority, even in Illinois. It also was harried by constant backbiting from Hitchcock, who otherwise paid very little attention to what was going on in the state and even on those rare occasions when he did come to Chicago managed to slip in and out of the city without even contacting Ickes. Johnson, who may have been harboring some resentment over Ickes's support of Lowden four years before, refused to interfere. By the last week of January 1924, Ickes was fed up: on the twenty-ninth he officially resigned his unofficial position. "Hitchcock," he told Johnson, "has been determined from the start that I not get in and you have permitted him to have his way. There are extremes which even devotion and deep affection cannot be required to go." This finally galvanized the candidate, who promptly overruled his national manager and offered the Illinois campaign to Ickes. He accepted, and Hitchcock vanished from the state for the rest of the campaign.

It was far too late by then. Ickes probably knew this at the time he took the job. On the same day he had written Johnson, he had also written Robins in a gloomy vein: "I don't mind being licked in a fight where all our resources are brought to bear, but I cannot regard with equanimity a division of forces that ought to be together, resulting in the picking off of one small detachment after another and leading to the final annihilation of separated groups and the further entrenchment of the common enemy."

This unhappy state of affairs slowed him down, but it did not stop him. In the nine weeks in which he had left to work, he managed to get a slate of Johnson delegates admitted to the ticket and persuaded a reluctant Johnson to leave California for speaking engagements around the state. Nevertheless, Johnson lost the Illinois primary on April 8 by 120,000 votes, and a grand total of six Johnson delegates (himself among them) were all that Ickes would carry with him to the convention in Cleveland (Chicago, for a wonder, being passed over this term, perhaps because the memories of the 1920 fiasco were just too bitter). This gathering took place on June 10 and was swiftly done. It was dominated by businessmen ("The business of America," Coolidge had said, "is business," and he believed it) who controlled it so thoroughly that a stolid conservative platform was adopted. Coolidge was nominated on the first ballot with a minimum of noise in just three days.

"The Republican Party is the party of reaction," Ickes told a colleague on June 13, "bitter as that conclusion must be to those of us who have been hoping against hope and fighting like damn fools to make it something else. We see in 1924 the party so reactionary as to make the party in 1912 liberal by comparison." In August a collection of disaffected Progressives and radicals of varying political affiliations gathered under the banner of something called the Conference for Progressive Political Action and nominated La Follette as a third-party candidate; the coalition traveled under the name of the Progressive Party but otherwise bore only the slightest resemblance to the crusade of 1912. For their part, the Democrats, after a singularly nasty struggle between the supporters of New York governor Alfred E. Smith and those of Senator William Gibbs McAdoo, chose a conservative corporation lawyer by the name of John W. Davis as their candidate; it took them 103 ballots.

For a while, Ickes found himself without a candidate he could reasonably support. He certainly was not going to back Coolidge; he disliked the rigid La Follette personally; and he could not quite bring himself to support the conservative Davis. Both Donald Richberg, who had written much of La Follette's platform, and Congressman John N. Nelson, La Follette's national campaign manager, urged him to go to work for the new Progressive Party. He declined. He also rejected similar overtures that came to him from the Democratic camp.

Raymond Robins, who was rarely unaware of his importance in the world, was convinced that Ickes did not declare for La Follette only because Robins himself would not. After a visit to Hubbard Woods on August 11, he informed Margaret that "Harold does not come out for La Follette largely because [La Follette] has practically no support among the old Progressives either here or in the country generally. [Ickes] needs me just as a drowning man needs a plank—and if I do not move into the La Follette camp he is not worth very much to them. And that's THAT!" That, as a matter of fact, was not that. Ickes's motives were a good deal more complicated, as he outlined them in a letter to Hiram Johnson a month later. "I have never seen such a peculiar campaign as this one," he wrote.

> My own belief is that Coolidge, from present indication, will be re-elected. . . . Looking further ahead my belief is that if Coolidge is reelected there will be a natural drifting together of the La Follette Progressives and the Democrats. The Republican Party will then be the conservative party and the new Democratic Progressive Party will be the Progressive Party. I know how many flaws can be picked in this statement and yet it seems to me, largely speaking, the present natural trend. In talking with George Brennan the other day I found that he had made the prediction in private conversation that if Davis was defeated the democratic party would never again nominate a conservative for president.
>
> If I shall decide to cast my lot in the La Follette forces openly, I will do so with the idea that I am definitely out of the Republican Party. . . . Naturally, I have a very real hesitation in taking a step politically that is likely to change radically my whole political life. . . . But when I see Raymond and . . . Garfield and Henry Allen, and even dear old Gifford Pinchot, falling on their bellies to lick the hand that has struck them I am filled with inexpressible disgust and an almost overpowering inclination to pack my playthings and go off with the lunatic fringe.

Circumstances almost forced his hand. Late in September a group of former Bull Moosers, led by Robins, Allen, Garfield, and Ruth Hanna McCormick, issued a furious statement blasting La Follette's Progressive Party as a radical travesty of the Roosevelt brand of progressivism and a real danger to America. Ickes was livid and apparently could barely hold himself in check when Robins came calling again a few days later. "I don't know when I have spent a drearier evening," Raymond told Margaret on October 3. "Harold is impossible and although I was prepared for all sorts of ugly statements I was not prepared for quite such dullness. I think the trouble is that the only things he can say are so nasty that if he wants to be nice he must be dull. [Anna] is greatly distressed—Harold said he was coming out in a statement for La Follette but I have not seen one to date."

He soon would. On October 4, Ickes erupted for publication: "I challenge these former Progressives," he growled in a widely circulated statement of his own,

> who recently sang their hymn of hate against La Follette to disclose their real purpose and at the same time give a frank account of what they have done during the past four years to uphold the Roosevelt tradition. . . . I agree that

La Follette does not represent the political ideals of the Republican Party in 1912. But neither does any other political group in the country today. . . . It has become the fashion since 1912 to claim to be a "Progressive." The Progressive label has been affixed where it is in fact a contradiction in terms. And Raymond Robins, Ruth Hanna-McCormick, Henry Allen, and their associate protestants, are not free from responsibility for this situation. Four years ago, in the name of Roosevelt and Progressivism they flung themselves headlong into the Harding camp, loudly calling upon all other progressives to follow them. Nor has their record during the past four years shown vigilance or even interest in upholding the fair fame of progressivism and the cherished name of Roosevelt. The good dog progressivism has been asleep in a curious kind of a kennel with a curious breed of pups.

In spite of this denunciation—which was more of a defense of Roosevelt than an endorsement of La Follette in any case—Ickes finally voted for Davis, accepting the least of three evils.

CHAPTER

· 19 ·

A Wall Against Despair

COOLIDGE BEAT DAVIS by a margin of nearly eight million votes to begin the era of what was called "Coolidge Prosperity." His victory also appeared to end the career of Harold Ickes as an important—or even visible—influence on the national political scene. Ickes had lost with Johnson and with Davis all in the same year, and it did not seem likely that he would ever again get the chance to participate on even the *losing* side in a Presidential race. With Coolidge's win, he told Johnson, "Mediocrity is king and it is a virtue to be lacking in initiative, forcefulness, qualities of leadership or even average ability. That president is the greatest in our history who can almost qualify as a deaf mute." He then appended his own political epitaph: "As an active force in politics it seems to me that my future is all past."

Not entirely. He came out of the starting box again less than two years later, though not at the Presidential level and not with much happier results. In August 1926, the discovery that Frank Smith, chairman of the Illinois Public Utilities Commission and a Republican candidate for the Senate, had accepted $125,000 in campaign money from Samuel Insull set the embers flaming again in the hearts of the dwindling number of Illinois reformers, Ickes in the lead. Even though the senatorial election was only a little over two months away, they decided to put their own Independent Republican candidate up to challenge both Smith and the

Democratic candidate, George Brennan, Ickes's old acquaintance. They chose Hugh Magill, now general secretary of the International Council of Religious Education, and Ickes became his campaign manager. It was a noisy, difficult fight, not only against Insull's money and influence but against the considerable power of the state Anti-Saloon League, which supported the "dry" Smith on the grounds that he was far more likely to beat the avowed "wet," Brennan, than Magill, and never mind Insull's pernicious corruption of the city and state. Smith easily won in November. (Rumors that Insull had "purchased" his election followed this Mr. Smith to Washington, however, and the Senate refused to accept his credentials. The seat remained vacant until the elections of 1928, when it was filled by Otis F. Glenn.)

The dust had barely settled around this disaster when another presented itself. With a dreadful inevitability, William Hale Thompson offered himself as a candidate once again for the mayoral election of 1927 and was swiftly nominated by the Republican Party. Thompson was counting heavily on support from Insull, who had learned to cordially dislike William Dever when the incumbent mayor spearheaded an unsuccessful attempt to put all public utilities under municipal ownership. Thompson also found confidence in the fact that a large segment of the city's population resented Dever's sporadic attempts to enforce Prohibition; if Illinois as a whole was "dry" enough to have elected Frank Smith, Chicago as a whole was unashamedly "wet" enough to want to stay that way, even if it meant the return of a feral alliance between city hall and the underworld empire of Al Capone. Against this possibility, Ickes helped stitch together an independent coalition called the "People's Dever for Mayor Committee," with himself as chairman, and launched a series of broadsides at Thompson, the Republican machine, and, with special relish, Insull. The effectiveness of his committee, however, was severely weakened by competition from a similar, more conservative independent group made up of bankers and others unwilling to endorse any major assault on Insull himself (too many of them owed him money or had invested in one or another of his many companies). More often than not, the two committees worked at cross purposes. The result was a divided and disorderly opposition over which Thompson and the Republicans trampled on the way to an easy victory in June.

During the next year's Presidential campaign (in which he took no active part at any level), Ickes voted for Democrat Alfred E. Smith, who promptly lost to Herbert Hoover. In the end, it was his own wife who kept Ickes from being connected to what threatened to be an unbroken string of losers. In 1924, Anna had been elected to serve a term on the board of trustees for the University of Illinois. She enjoyed the work in Springfield, was good at it, and was no more averse to public prominence than her husband. ("I told her the other day," Ickes wrote Johnson in November 1924, "she was the real politician in the family.") She was having such a fine time, in fact, that in the fall of 1927 she decided to run for a seat in the Illinois General Assembly. Ickes backed up her decision immediately—it would keep her in Springfield much of the time, he noted in his memoirs—and took over the management of her campaign, even though she insisted on running as a regular Republican. "I never ran a more helpless or politically ignorant person for public office," he remembered with ill grace.

> I had to spell out the abc's for her, telling her precisely what to do, what to say and what not to say. . . . One thing must be said to Anna's credit and that was that she took it in quite good part when I told her that I could not, in any circumstances, go to her speaking engagements with her; that she must stand on her own feet and avoid the impression that she was merely running as my candidate. She was quite gallant about this. . . . She had another good point as a candidate and that was her direct and brief speeches. She never tried to orate and she made a point of presenting facts. This she did without tiring her audience or annoying the men candidates, who would have resented it if a woman had cut in on the time they wanted to devote to spread-eagling.

Anna won the nomination on April 10, 1928, and the election in November, not a little because Raymond and Margaret Robins managed to persuade the Anti-Saloon League to support her in spite of the fact that her husband was a "wet" and she was, at best, only a moderate "dry." She would win again in 1930 and 1932—for both of which campaigns Ickes would again serve as her manager—and even he had to admit that she deserved her victories on merit alone. "As a matter of fact," he conceded,

> Anna did do a good job. She was more than usually intelligent; she had all the money that she needed and she had a high-minded attitude toward the public service. . . . She got along well with the men at Springfield because she never made any appeal to them on the basis of her being a woman. I liked this about her and so did her associates to the degree that she became quite a favorite and they were willing to help her when she needed help. None of them tried to give her a bum steer either. They treated her like one of themselves for whom they had respect and the relationship was quite satisfactory.

There was a sneaking pride in Anna here that he could not quite suppress even in memory; at the same time, the irony inherent in the situation could not have been lost on him, then or later. Anna's star was on the rise at precisely that moment when his appeared to be fading, and a powerful hint that he was beginning to feel this can be discerned in a

letter he wrote to S. J. Duncan-Clark of the *Chicago Evening Post* on
November 6, 1929:

> I don't believe anything can be done to stir up the interest of the younger
> citizens through any educative effort on the part of those of us who are, and
> probably ought to be, regarded by the younger generation as "has beens."
> Some day some issue will arise that will appeal to the consciences and stir the
> imaginations of the youth of the land, but what that issue will be or when it
> will arise I cannot attempt to predict. We live in a discouraging time. . . .
> The man who ventures to raise his voice today to question the accepted order
> of things is a hardy soul indeed. At his peril will he criticize any public policy
> or any political trend that has the support of the conservative newspapers
> and there are few newspapers that are not conservative. He will be called
> names and derided and misrepresented. Even fellow reformers will turn
> against him.

There is little question as to who he believed this victim to be.

On the Ides of March, 1924, just a little over three weeks before Hiram
Johnson's grinding defeat in the Illinois Presidential primary, Harold
LeClair Ickes had turned fifty. This is a watershed year for any man, but it
was perhaps more pointedly so for Ickes; it began what may have been the
most troubled decade in his personal life. Politically—and with Ickes it is
always difficult to separate politics from the person—it was a long ride
downhill. The year before there had been a celebration in the headquarters
of the Independent Dever Club; but during 1924 and the eight years that
followed there would be little to cheer about. This would not keep him
from fighting, but as time went on, it was increasingly only the fight
itself that brought reward to his soul, and that could not help but give
even his joy a bitter taste. And, at fifty, time was his enemy; he would
never run out of windmills, but he might run out of strength.

In his account of these struggles there is a haunting tone of loneliness.
There were fewer and fewer of the old veterans who would stand with him
now, and fewer still to take their places. He gives us to believe that he did
not care, that he was the "lone wolf" who relished his independence. If
anything he ever said in his life was a barefaced self-deception, this is it.
His need to belong, to be part of—if at all possible, to lead—something
larger than himself was one of the single most powerful drives of his
existence. He was not a man comfortable in isolation, and he never would
learn to be. But the happy band of warriors who had marched beneath the
stuffed bull moose at the Chicago Auditorium in 1912 was no more, and
nothing had come along to replace them. And if Ickes could not lead, he

wanted heroes who would at least lead *him*—and he was fast running out of these, too. John Harlan, the first, had long since drifted away. Charles Merriam, the second, had become querulous and impatient with him; he had not even been able to talk Merriam into participating in any significant way in the Magill and Dever campaigns of 1926 and 1927. Theodore Roosevelt, the third, was dead—though as a charter member of the Theodore Roosevelt Memorial Association, Ickes did his best to keep at least the myth of the man alive. Hiram Johnson, the fourth, was still in this world, but it seemed ever more likely that he would never get beyond the Senate; if Ickes continued to support him and play to his fantasies, it was mostly for the sake of old times—and the lack of anyone to fill Johnson's shoes.

There is another dirge that runs through this section of the memoirs, one more straightforwardly expressed than his loneliness: his conviction that he has given far more than he has received. This lapse into self-pity would be easier to denigrate if the record did not support him. He did give more than he got; but it was to a very large degree because he simply could not let himself ask for much. His isolation was more than political, and it was aggravated by an inability ever to let himself be seen as vulnerable. Still bound by the emotional ganglia of a childhood environment that had demanded but not provided strength, he could not—dared not—give a hint that he was anything less than indestructible, because he might not be. This shield (he would later institutionalize it as the way of a curmudgeon) may have been necessary to his survival—in his own mind, at least—but it made it terribly difficult for him to nurture the kind of sharing that is one of the hallmarks of any true friendship. "I don't think he *had* any close friends to whom he would feel he could turn with openness and candor and with the defenses down in case of pain or trouble," his son Raymond has said. "I don't know of any." But if he could not ask, he could at least give, and there were plenty of those who could—and did—come to *him* in time of pain and trouble, and he always offered them what he could. He could not do otherwise, and he usually did it with grace; there were many people in his life who had reason to think well of him for it.

Not that all of them did. Many simply could not cut through his argumentative style, his impatience and flares of short-lived temper to the person lurking insecurely behind it all. Many did not try, and some who did try gave it up as a bad idea. Others can only be called small-minded, even ungrateful. It is both sad and symptomatic that while Ickes continued to think of Raymond Robins as a friend—perhaps his best friend—in spite of their growing and probably insurmountable political differences,

Robins did not respond in kind. For all his Christian piety and dedication to good works, Robins himself had an ego that was the size of a small city and he was not the most generous-hearted of friends. Even in 1914, when their relationship was at least bound by a commonality of interests and when Ickes had for once revealed some of his pain and depression in his letter of April 24, Robins had ignored it, too full of himself to bother with his friend's anguish. By the twenties, Robins's regard had degenerated into contempt, expressed in one whining letter after another to Margaret. Invariably, the hospitality he found at Hubbard Woods fell short of what he believed he deserved. On one visit, he reported in outrage, he had actually been forced to carry his own bags through falling snowflakes on the three-minute walk from the train station to the house. "They are bum hosts!" he wrote. "I would like to have them on the Hill Top and give them every courtesy and let them know what real hospitality is *Once* and then never again to see them! . . . Anna would drive me crazy & Harold to drink if I know much of either." In fact, it would be many years before either of the Ickeses ever saw Chinsegut Hill; during the 1920s they were invited only once—by Margaret, not Raymond—and could not make it on that occasion. (Margaret, it should be pointed out, was a more tolerant spirit, and she would remain especially close to Anna for the rest of her life.)

Robins, then, was a pretty thin reed on which to lean for solace, even if Ickes had been so inclined. Nor was there much available support at Hubbard Woods. He and Anna had achieved, at best, an accommodation that allowed each to pursue separate lives outside the home and function as necessary together within it. He still slept on the screened porch, pleading his insomnia, and avoided Anna's bed as much as possible (though he admits to occasional lapses now). He continued his hit-or-miss sexual adventures, he tells us in the memoirs, but none had any lasting quality and he gives no details. Only once, apparently, was the dreary placidity of those latter years of the marriage shaken. In September 1925, Harold left the house in a fury, taking a room at one of his clubs and refusing to return unless he could live in the house on the "footing of Tom Gilmore." In a brief note, Anna sternly informed him that

> I can only consent to your return on the footing of my husband, the children's father, and a responsible head of this household. . . . My work began today under this severe strain and I cannot write as I would. I cannot subject myself to another shock of this kind, or another such humiliation before servants . . . and others. Until I can be somewhat assured that I shall not be required again to undergo these I must not take you back. I need not tell you how deeply I care for you.

On large, ragged sheets of yellow paper ripped out of a notebook, Ickes replied to this with a pen dipped into the core of an active volcano. "I agree that responsibility to my home and children is equal to yours," he sputtered,

> but that responsibility I cannot discharge if you are permitted longer to exhaust my energy and absorb my strength. . . . If you have been humiliated it has been of your own doing. Lately you have been gradually discarding the armor of good breeding and have been willing that the world should view your sores. Moreover, you chose to ignore repeated warnings that the end was at hand. You have dared me to leave; you have ordered me to leave. . . . No you need not tell me how deeply you care for me. I *know*. My wrecked ambitions, my cynicism, my friendlessness and lonliness [*sic*], my indifference to life itself all testify to your love and wifely consideration.

Somehow, they worked through this particularly nasty patch (perhaps his letter was never sent; the sheets were never folded, as they would have to be if they were ever jammed into an envelope). But the family was riven with other trouble in these years. Frances never did return to live again at Hubbard Woods after the war. Over Anna's objections, she took her own apartment, got herself a job, and later became Mrs. Requa Bryant; she and her husband did not spend a lot of time with the Ickeses, though she and Harold remained close. Wilmarth did return after the war, but did not promise to amount to much. "Very perceptive, very warm individual," his half-brother Raymond remembers. "I was very fond of him." At the same time, he adds, "He was certainly a butterfly—he'd skip from flower to flower and take a little sip of nectar here, another there, and never get very deep into any one of them. Very attractive, he had a lot of friends, most of whom my parents seemed to think were unfortunate influences on him. A fairly fast crowd." He went to Northwestern for a year while living at Hubbard Woods, then gave that up and got a job as head of the neckware department at a haberdashery store, spent most of his free time with his friends, and dipped lightheartedly into the small capital his grandmother had left him upon her death.

While on a two-week vacation at Pike Lake in northern Wisconsin, Wilmarth met and fell in love with Betty Dahlman, "young and pretty and modest and intelligent," as Ickes described her in the memoirs, who lived in Milwaukee with her father and two younger sisters, Anna and Jane (Mrs. Dahlman was hospitalized most of the time for a mental disorder). Wilmarth proposed, and Betty accepted. The question of where they were to live came up. Anna wanted to build them a house on the Hubbard Woods property; Ickes agreed with the children that it would be better for them to have someplace more removed, so insisted that he and

Anna buy a house for them on Walden Road in Winnetka, for which Wilmarth agreed to pay rent, with an option to buy. Though the house was only a few minutes away from Hubbard Woods by car, Anna, Ickes says, never forgave him this betrayal.

Shortly after the wedding—held in the great hall at Hubbard Woods—Wilmarth fell behind on the rent, then lost his job. Ickes let the rent slide and, when several months of diligent searching had failed to land Wilmarth another job, he cosigned a loan to a pair of Wilmarth's friends that enabled them to buy a going concern, the General Printing Company of Chicago. In exchange, they made Wilmarth a full partner in the enterprise and gave him a drawing account as a salesman, even though he had no experience whatever; Ickes was to sit in as chairman of the board until the loan was paid off by all three partners; and to watch over things in his absence, he had his secretary, May Conley, placed on the board. Over the next few years, Wilmarth produced three children with Betty, Ickes remembered, but very little in the way of business for the company. He spent his afternoons at the Palmer House and many of his evenings gambling and otherwise having a good time in the best tradition of the twenties, and he continued to fall behind on his rent, rarely made payment on anything more than the interest on his share of the company's loan, and, when his partners were forced to reduce his drawing account, sold off the stock his grandmother had left him and continued his grasshopper ways.

If Wilmarth was disappointing, Robert was a calamity—but it is hard to put much blame on him. Never formally adopted, he could not have helped feeling like the odd child out. His was apparently a nature that demanded physical affection for assurance, but his foster parents, who were not normally demonstrative with any of the children, rarely if ever provided it. Raymond, who says that he and Robert were never very close—even though that was the reason his parents had brought Robert into the family—remembers him as an "unhappy boy," and adds: "Robert was always pretty much of a trial to my parents. I think it's probably true that they didn't like him very much, although neither of them would have admitted it." It probably did not help much that while playing mumblety-peg when he was eleven or twelve years old, Robert stabbed himself in the left eye with a careless spin of the knife. He was rushed to the hospital, but the eye could not be saved, and he wore a glass eye in that socket for the rest of his life. It is not too surprising, then, to learn from the memoirs that Robert spent much of his teens getting into one kind of scrape or another—including drinking sprees that at least once required Ickes to take a long drive up into Wisconsin in order to bail him out of jail. He did badly in all of the several secondary schools to which he was sent—including the well-known Fountain Valley School in Colorado for one term—and he pretty clearly seemed destined to follow no particular career or purpose in his life.

Raymond was another matter. Even to his father's hypercritical eye, his son was developing along satisfactory—if occasionally rambunctious—lines. He was an active boy who built himself up through wrestling and heavy exercise into a well-muscled young man. He became a skilled amateur boxer, fighting successfully as a welterweight and, coached by Tom Gilmore, Anna's live-in cousin, he also became an expert marksman. Throughout his teenage years, he spent as much time as he could in New Mexico with his mother, and when not consorting with his Navajo friends in New Mexico, or exploring the woods and lake shore in and around Hubbard Woods, which he loved with a passion similar to that of his father, he attended the Avon Old Farms School in Connecticut. He was not a model student, having little patience for discipline, but he did well enough to graduate. Only once did he bring any real trouble to his parents. During one Thanksgiving visit to the school, Anna somehow got wind of a rumor that Raymond (a very good-looking young man) had been fooling around with the school nurse (it was true enough, Raymond admits, but adds that his mother never had anything but her finely tuned suspicions to go on). Anna, unsurprisingly, was swollen with fury; she sent lurid telegrams to her husband, then went to the dean and got the nurse quietly fired—so quietly that Raymond himself never learned the reason why she had left. Raymond's father took the tiny scandal more philosophically, even with a hint of fatherly pride, and in any event his son regained whatever (if anything) he may have lost in his father's estimation by this escapade when he chose the University of Chicago as his college and passed the entrance examinations. Ickes approved with some vehemence: "At the time that Raymond was called upon to make his choice Chicago was one of the two or three great universities in the country, if indeed it did not outrank all of them scholastically. Thus it was one of the five or six great universities in the whole world. Moreover, under a vigorous and highly intelligent new young President, Robert M. Hutchins, it had embarked upon an educational experiment which seemed to me to be very much worth while."

The outer ring of the Ickes family also contributed to the emotional tone of these crepuscular years. Of his sister Amelia, he had heard little for years. He had put her through the University of Chicago until she left school to marry a man who turned out to be a philanderer. Ickes loathed the man, a sentiment he was never reluctant to express, and he and his younger sister (who had taken to using her first name of Mary after her wedding) had a falling out that endured for many years. It would not be until the mid-thirties that she and Ickes would begin to communicate again on a regular basis. Brother John was another matter; after a long absence, he had resurfaced, looking for money. In the years after Altoona, John had worked for U.S. Steel in Chicago, had fought in the Spanish-American War, had taken a degree at the Kent College of Law, had drifted into New York, gotten married, divorced, then married again to a woman whose first husband had shot her in the skull and left her for dead—grounds for divorce even in New York. He dabbled in the law and got involved in a number of oddball schemes, including a revolutionary new oil burner in which he begged Ickes and Anna to invest. They passed over this opportunity, which was just as well since it went nowhere, but Anna did invest in a comic-opera libretto John had written, which, along with other plays, never got produced. When John finally could not support himself and his wife, Ickes put him on a monthly allowance for a time in New York, then persuaded him to move back to Chicago, where he got him a low-level job in Mayor Dever's administration. John accepted this position, though it was beneath him, then immediately began pestering his brother to use his influence to get him a better job or, failing that, a succession of raises—petitions that continued through the next several city administrations, though John never did rise very high in Chicago's bureaucracy. Altogether, Ickes notes with little pleasure, he had invested eight thousand dollars in the brother who had used him like a punching bag as a child.

He probably invested that much or more in sister Julia and her husband Clinton Hazard, though he makes no mention of this in his memoirs—probably because he believed them more deserving of help and felt true pity for their condition. Clinton had been a good, hard-working man, a laboring man, all his life. When an accident in his shop left him permanently disabled, he and Julia, herself never in the best of health, were reduced to living off a tiny relief check from the Pennsylvania Railroad. Clinton apparently had tried to keep this from his brother-in-law, but in November 1928 a cousin of Clinton's wrote Harold, outlining the situation:

> I am very much worried about Clinton who does not seem to be coming back and he is so brave through it all and Julia is so wonderful that my hat is off to both of them. . . . I am wondering, without any talk with Julia or Clinton on this subject, whether you can suggest anything that will be to their advantage, and I hope you will pardon my taking up this question with you, my thought being to do anything in the world I can for these cousins who are very dear to me.

Julia was not especially dear to her brother—but she and Clinton were family, and they were in trouble. They were immediately factored into the Ickes family welfare system. "Dear Clair," Julia wrote (she was one of the few people left who still called him that)—apparently after one delicate attempt to turn him down had been rejected—"your letter of recent date is a hard one for me to answer. In the first place I cannot see why it is up to you to provide for us, even though you are so willing and gracious in the giving. It is more than hard to realize that after all these years of striving and honest effort that Clinton and I have proven to be failures." It is to Ickes's credit that in all the years he "provided" for the couple, in no single surviving letter does he give a hint that he believes them "failures" or that his help is anything but a temporary leg up until Clinton can get back to work, which he never was able to do.

Some grace under pressure, then, a wall of help lifted up against despair. The barrier kept the black clouds from overwhelming him, too; there was help in the helping. A powerful yearning for the might-have-been may have come over him suddenly at this time. In the spring of 1929 Ickes attended a meeting of the alumni of Englewood High School to discuss the raising of a fund to help poor but promising students complete their secondary education. The school must have seemed smaller to him now (they always do), but it probably still smelled the same, redolent with chalk dust and disinfectant soap, varnish, and the residual stench of ten thousand wet winter coats. He may have caught a pharmaceutical whiff on himself, too, at least in memory. Uncle Felix and Aunt Ada were long dead (he had handled her tiny affairs without charge for several years after Felix's death), but he could not have helped but remember with a certain pain those years in the drugstore when he was the poor but promising student who could have used the kind of help they were now discussing. It is certain that he remembered the supportive, the beautiful Miss Agnes Rogers; he got her address from a friend who had kept in touch with her. (She now lived in Rochester, New York, presumably retired.) Two weeks later, he sat down and composed his touching letter to her:

> I hope you are psychologist enough to understand how a man who is under deeper obligation to another than he can ever hope to repay, and who has had in mind literally hundreds of times during many years the purpose of getting into communication with that other, should nevertheless fail utterly to do the thing that he ought to have done and has wanted to do. . . . There have been in my lifetime two or three persons who have given definite trends to my life and in so doing have helped to form my character and to make me whatever I

happen to be. You are one of this exceedingly small group. And if I haven't done for myself all that I should have done under the encouragement and impetus given to me by you and others, my failure does not minimize my indebtedness to you or disparage the great gifts to me of your interest, encouragement and help.

He apologized a few more times, then exposed his life—his education, his law work, his political ups and downs, above all, the terrific struggle he had undergone as a young man clawing his way up in the world. There was no mention of Anna or the children, or even a hint that he was married. He finally brought himself up short at about two thousand words: "When I started this letter I didn't expect to write a long biographical sketch. What I really want to know is about yourself." If Miss Rogers ever answered the letter, her reply has vanished.

Whatever he had been reaching for in this astonishing apologia, it was beyond his grasp. For that and everything else that now seemed beyond him there was the finely tuned sublimation, always sublimation, the mind kept too busy to devour itself. When politics or the civic barricades proved inadequate to this by themselves, he could always turn to his stamps. He had begun to collect them casually at first, but nothing ever stayed casual with him for long. In 1926 he began to make occasional purchases from the Scott Stamp & Coin Company in New York, one of the biggest dealers in the business. From there, he soon branched out to other dealers in other cities, and then there were scores of letters going out all over the country and the world; this was *serious* philately, and he kept at it doggedly for years, the colorful squares neatly inventoried, mounted, arranged and rearranged, the albums filling up and piling up.

If not the stamps, then the gardens. In Hubbard Woods he had his own country, and he made it shout with beauty, filling it with flowers— flowers at the front of the house, at the back of the house, on both sides of the endless driveway, everywhere you looked an explosion of color like laughter in a crowded theater. Peonies, mertensia, and daffodils, crocuses, roses, and narcissi; and dahlias, a celebration of dahlias: "We developed our own varieties," he remembered, "and every Summer . . . we had a great mass of glorious blooms down by the gardener's cottage on Tower Road. People by the hundreds used to come out to see these dahlias on Saturdays and Sundays until the traffic at that section of Tower Road became a considerable problem." He even developed his own varieties— one so outstandingly beautiful that someone got hold of a few tubers without his knowledge and the flowers started showing up all over Winnetka. That was bad enough, but when a nursery called Mission Gardens started selling the tubers as the "Winnetka Beauty" he took action: he filed for a patent. It took two years, one exasperated lawyer, and numerous applications to the Department of Agriculture, but he received the first patent ever issued for a dahlia. He called it the "Anna W. Ickes Dahlia" and immediately got out an injunction against Mission Gardens.

"Like Ferdinand the Bull," he exclaimed in his *Autobiography*, "I love flowers! I always have. I won't say that I would rather be a florist than a fighter, and yet I wouldn't want the choice put up to me in earnest." Here was a world he could plan, shape, nurture, and control, a world governed by sun and soil, the predictable cycles of germination, death, regeneration, things he had understood in his bones since childhood. "He'd come home from the office in the afternoon—sometimes fairly early in the afternoon," son Raymond remembers, "and go out in the garden and work on those long summer evenings, and he'd be out there until dark."

And then the dark would turn him back to the house.

PART V

In the Crucible of Fear

Few people seem to be aware of the degree to which our political fiber has been softened. Especially prior to the recent stock market debacle all too many have been content to jazz while their heritage was being stolen."

—Speech before the Progressive
Conference, March 12, 1931

CHAPTER

· 20 ·

Snuffing
Out the Decade

I F THEY CARED to put out of mind the condition of the city's politics and
national image—the one still in the grip of William Hale Thompson,
the other regularly besmirched by such rancid gangland spectacles as the
St. Valentine's Day Massacre of 1929—Chicagoans did not have to look
very far for evidence that their city had reaped its full share of prosperity
as the decade of the twenties skittered to a close. That evidence was the
forty-story Civic Opera Building, which rose like an enormous throne
above the Chicago River and the new double-decked North Wacker
Drive, itself a demonstration of progress and one of the few portions of
Daniel Burnham's grandiose plan for the city that ever achieved reality.
The Opera Building was nearly ready to be topped off in the fall of 1929.
The Civic Opera already had begun preparations for its first
performance—Rosa Raisa singing *Aïda*—scheduled for November 4,
and Samuel Insull's people were busily packing up supplies and equipment for the move to offices in the new building.

It was Insull's brainchild. In 1927 he had become the Civic Opera's
principal sponsor. The Chicago company, like opera companies everywhere, was a consistent money-loser, even after a season under the direction of the incomparably flamboyant and popular Mary Garden. Insull
saw the solution to this situation in a new building that would combine a
3,700-seat auditorium with office space whose rental would support the

opera company. With that in mind, he had selected a site on the river, floated a ten-million-dollar stock sale to the city's music lovers to finance the beginning of construction, gave a mortgage on the remaining $10 million it would take to complete the job to the Metropolitan Life Insurance Company, and had broken ground in February 1928. His own companies would be the first and most prominent tenants, and to smooth the opera company's way, he donated $300,000 of his own stock to it.

Insull could afford such gestures in 1929. If the Civic Opera Building stood as one more architectural symbol of Chicago's growth, it also stood quite as handsomely as a totem for the seemingly endless growth of Insull's business empire. Even for the expansive twenties, even for the astonishing Insull, that empire was enormous. It began with the tiny Chicago Edison Company in 1892, but by 1929 it had swollen to include Commonwealth Edison, an almost absolute monopoly in Chicago; People's Gas Light and Coke Company, still going strong after several years of harassment from Ickes's former partner, Donald Richberg; Public Service of Illinois, serving electricity and gas to three hundred communities in the state; Midland Utilities Company, a holding operation whose subsidies provided electricity and gas to seven hundred communities in Indiana; North American Light and Power Company, serving the towns around St. Louis; and the biggest of them all, the Middle West Utilities Company, whose several hundred subsidiaries aggregated a worth of more than $1 billion and served five thousand communities in thirty-two states. And, of course, Insull still controlled the elevated railroads of Chicago, as well as three interurban electric lines serving its suburbs.

He wanted more, and in December 1928 hit upon what seemed like a wonderful way to get it. He created an investment company he called Insull Utilities Investments (IUI), traded stocks in his old companies for a controlling interest in the new, then placed the rest of the IUI stock on the market at a value of $12 a share. The results were nearly immediate and indisputably remarkable: IUI stock opened on January 17, 1929, at $25, closed that day at $30, jumped to $80 by the end of spring, and to more than $150 by the end of summer. Infected by the same contagion of enthusiasm, stock in Commonwealth Edison went from $202 to $450 in the same period, and in Middle West from $169 to $529. During one fifty-day period that summer, Insull securities climbed in value at a rate of $7,000 a minute, and by the end of September, the increase amounted to more than $500 million. Insull's personal fortune now came to more than $150 million. "My God," he told an associate. "A hundred and fifty million dollars! Do you know what I'm going to do? I'm going to buy me an ocean liner!" He did not buy an ocean liner; what he did do was form yet another holding company, this one called Corporations Securities Company of Chicago, and toss its stock into the manic spiral of speculation.

The game had a lot of participants by then. Millions of Americans had been playing for years. They were encouraged—indeed, goaded—in this direction by an insistent ululation that the American potential was limitless, that economic growth was permanent, that the bandwagon of progress had room enough for anyone with the vision and fortitude to hop aboard. It was the age of the big sell, the first great era of advertising. "Today," wrote Paul M. Mazur in his 1928 book, *Prosperity: Its Causes and Consequences*, "American prosperity exists through intensive selling. Let him who would destroy that foundation consider the cost of such an act of Samson upon the pillars of the temple of American business." As Zelda Fitzgerald, who with her husband, Scott, came to symbolize the decade's sometimes charming, sometimes destructive insouciance, remembered, "We grew up founding our dreams on the infinite promises of American advertising. I still believe that one can learn to play the piano by mail and that mud will give you a perfect complexion." And in the pages of that eminently middle-class institution, the *Ladies' Home Journal*, financier John Raskob declared, "Everybody ought to be rich," explaining that if an individual saved a mere fifteen dollars a month and invested carefully in the stock market, there was no reason on earth why at the end of ten years he would not be worth at least $80,000.

It was in the arena of the stock market, in fact, that this romance of the possible was played out with greatest intensity—though some would call it frenzy. There had never been a decade like it; there never would be again. In 1919 the New York Stock Exchange had seen 1.5 million shares traded, a figure so high that it caused worry among the ever-cautious but nearly powerless members of the Federal Reserve Board. By the middle of the decade, three million shares a day was a common figure and there were those who talked confidently of a five-million-share day in the not-too-distant future. In the period of greatest activity, from 1926 to 1929, the daily average top price for the 25 leading industrial stocks rose from $186.03 to $469.46, an increase of about 250 percent. Those kinds of figures had brought some three million Americans into the game by 1929.

And why not? Any number could play, and as many as one million investors entered the market on margin—that is, their brokers sold them stock with a down payment of only 10 or 15 percent; the rest of the value of the stocks in the customers' names stood as a loan from the brokers. For their part, the brokers borrowed from the banks to buy the stocks they would sell on margin to individuals. As long as the market continued to climb, everyone in this cunning saraband stood to make money: the customers by selling their stocks at just the right time; the brokers through their commissions and the interest they charged the customers against the unpaid balance of the stock loans; and the banks through the interest—as high as 15 or 20 percent—they charged the brokers. In September 1926 such brokers' loans totaled $3.2 billion; by September 1929 they came to $8.5 billion—a figure that takes on its properly impressive dimensions when compared to the entire national debt of the United States at that time: $16.9 billion. For those who looked askance at such a concentration of capital, Henry Harriman Simmons, president of the New York Stock Exchange, had words of calm assurance. Brokers' loans, he said in a speech in May 1929, were "the safest form of investment in this country." Furthermore, that was where the money belonged, for to divert "the enormous masses of capital today invested in stock market loans" into industry or commercial businesses would "produce a huge rise in commodity prices, inflation of inventories, and an artificial business boom." The stock market, he concluded, was a kind of safety valve to relieve the pressure built up by the presence of too much money in the country. Keep it coming, he said.

And it did keep coming—much of it through the kinds of investment trusts put together so successfully by Samuel Insull in Chicago. These paper institutions built nothing, manufactured nothing, and sold nothing real; they existed purely to own and trade stocks. Fortunes were realized as if by magic in the realm of the trust, and by the end of 1928 one a day was being formed, quite often oozing out of the membrane of another, rather like the reproductive mechanism of amoebas: the owner or owners of one investment trust would organize another, arbitrarily issue a predetermined number of stocks in the new company, trade stocks in the old company for a controlling share in the new company, offer remaining stock for sale to the public, and almost invariably end up with a huge new paper profit in the new paper company—and then, frequently, repeat the process. By September 1929 there were more than five hundred such trusts worth billions of dollars. In and on paper.

The whole business added up to the greatest bull market of all time, and millions of people found it impossible to resist—including Harold LeClair Ickes, who first joined the game not long after the war. "It was during those terrible days after I had come back from France, when I did not care whether I lived or died, that I started to speculate," he said in his memoirs. "There was a time when I was speculating like a crazy fool." Most of his activity in the beginning was limited to the commodities market—wheat, corn, oats, cotton, and lard—and after he nearly took a beating in 1921, he cut back on his holdings. "I was frightened," he wrote, "and I decided not to extend myself again, but to keep within moderate limits." It was all a kind of hobby, he tells us, not unlike his stamp collecting or even his gardening: "I found that I was having the diversion that I so desperately needed. As I stood in Slaughter's [A. O. Slaughter and Company, his intriguingly named brokerage house] watching the boys mark up the changing prices I could forget what a hell I had left behind at Hubbard Woods and what a hell I was going back to."

But speculation was not gardening; there was a dangerously seductive quality to it, and Ickes was more than ready to turn his good ear toward the Lorelei song of Coolidge prosperity, however much he despised the man himself:

> When the great boom days came in the Coolidge Administration I lost my head like many others. I bought like a crazy man. At one time I had over a quarter of a million dollars in paper profits. In the meantime, I had been drawing down heavily against my profits. I had paid off the mortgage on Hubbard Woods. I had bought the Walden Road property [for Wilmarth and Betty]; I had bought real estate over in Northfield and I bought heavily in bank stocks. . . . These were exciting days and I was spending money with a free hand. It was out of the stock market that I financed the General Printing Company; it was out of the stock market that I could give Anna all of the extra money that she wanted. One year, according to my estimates, she spent $10,000 on herself alone.

For a time, it seemed he was going to emerge a big winner, for he made at least one intelligent play before circumstances shut the game down. Beginning sometime in 1928, greed again overcoming contempt, he had begun to purchase shares in Insull's Middle West Utilities Company, which was then selling at about $400. It was a wise investment, as such things go, for at about that time Cyrus Eaton, of the Cleveland investment firm of Otis and Company, began a raid on all Insull stocks, driving them up (and forcing Insull ultimately to borrow heavily from New York banks to stave off the buccaneering operation). Ickes continued to buy, until he had five hundred shares of Middle West, which he held for a couple of weeks, then sold, taking out a clean profit of fifty thousand dollars. As he later remembered it, he would have done well to sell the rest of his stocks at the same time ("I would have cashed in a cool quarter of a million at least"). But he let them ride, secure in the conviction that his Insull dealings had illustrated his brilliance in such matters. He was not alone in this hubris. If things were this good, the cry seemed to be, how could they not get better? As late as October 15, Professor Irving Fisher of Yale was moved to issue a statement that would haunt him the rest of his

life: "Stock prices have reached what looks like a permanently high level."
This in spite of the fact that in September 1929 the market in stock
leaders had broken, then rallied, then broken again, with RCA falling
thirty-two points, General Electric more than fifty, and U.S. Steel nearly
sixty. For a time, the one thing that apparently would not break was
Fisher's kind of optimism. The declines were called "technical readjust-
ments." But they continued throughout that month and into October,
slowly, inexorably building toward panic as one large trader after another
lost his nerve and began selling off major blocks of holdings. Finally,
beginning on October 24—"Black Thursday"—speculation was "technically readjusted" clear through the floor of the market.

When the New York Stock Exchange opened its doors for business that
day, brokers were immediately flooded with sell orders from all over the
country. Prices fell in spurts of as much as a point a minute all morning,
sometimes as much as five points between sales—an unheard-of phenomenon. The clamor on the floor of the exchange became so frenetic that
officials closed the visitors' gallery for fear that observers might run
screaming into the street and panic the crowd that had gathered there,
staring at the closed doors, muttering, wondering. Inside, everything
was dropping—U.S. Steel from $205\frac{1}{2}$ to $193\frac{1}{2}$, General Electric from
315 to 283, RCA from $68\frac{3}{4}$ to $44\frac{1}{2}$. Shortly after noon, a consortium of
financiers—Charles E. Mitchell of National City Bank, Albert H. Wig-
gin of Chase National, William C. Potter of Guaranty Trust, Thomas W.
Lamont of J. P. Morgan and Company, and Richard C. Whitney, vice
president of the Stock Exchange—met in the Morgan offices across the
street. In an effort to interrupt the downhill slide, they formed an
investment pool and Whitney strolled through the crowd back to the
Exchange and ostentatiously began buying large blocks of stocks at prices
higher than those being currently quoted. The tactic seemed to work, for
the market closed that day with the stock leaders down an average of only
ten points. But 12,894,650 stocks had been traded—more than at any
time in history—and in the wake of the day, hundreds of thousands of
small investors lay ruined.

On Friday and Saturday (then a half day) trading was comparatively
calm and the market seemed to have steadied. It was an illusion. On
Monday, October 28, 9,912,800 shares were exchanged, almost all of
them losers—losses that single day were more than during the entire
week of Black Thursday. The bankers met again Monday night, and when
he emerged, Thomas W. Lamont told reporters that the situation "retained hopeful features." But it did not. "Bankers, brokers, clerks, messengers were almost at the end of their strength," Frederick Lewis Allen

wrote two years later. "For days and nights they had been driving themselves to keep pace with the most terrific volume of business that had ever descended upon them. It did not seem as if they could stand it much longer. But the worst was still ahead."

That worst was Tuesday. Within thirty minutes of the opening, three million shares were dumped on the market; by noon, eight million had been traded; by closing, 16,410,030 had gone across the board. Almost everything took terrible losses on this Black Tuesday; the Dow-Jones Industrials dropped forty-eight points; over the entire board the average loss was twenty-five points. In a little over one month—from the middle of September to October 29—$32 *billion* in equities had vanished. "Never," wrote historian William E. Leuchtenberg, "was a decade snuffed out so quickly."

In Chicago, as elsewhere in the country, rumors had it that the air was full of falling bodies in the aftermath of October 29. No such instance, in Chicago at least, was ever documented. In any case, Harold Ickes would not have been among the suicides, even if he did have an alarming susceptibility to depression. Incredibly, his fortunes, such as they were, survived the worst of 1929. He does not tell us the nature of his investments, except for describing his brief and profitable flier in Middle West Utilities, but they must have been among the very few that did not crumble immediately while a clamorous gaggle of the desperate gathered to watch the board in Slaughter's during those days. As late as the summer of 1930 he remained unconcerned enough about his financial condition to make one more attempt to put his marriage on a more comfortable footing. "Anna and I had been having desperately bad times at home," he recalled. "She kept nagging at me to close my law office and, finally, in desperation I agreed to spend the summer with her and Raymond and Robert in New Mexico, in what she called her 'dream house.' "

It was one of Ickes's few trips to the New Mexico house (there may have been no more than three over more than ten years), and in spite of his continued unhappiness with Anna, it may have been one of their more enjoyable times together. Anna's love for the pastel-colored, light-struck country of the American Southwest was deep and infectious, and she was at her best in these surroundings. Raymond's own love for the land was quite as powerful; the house in Coolidge was now a second home to him, and he had become thoroughly Indianized, living in a small hogan behind the house, sporting around the countryside with his young Navajo friends, bedecking himself with silver-and-turquoise jewelry. With both

Anna and Raymond so clearly happy, it should have been difficult for even the often sullen Harold to resist enjoying it all. He did get out into the Indian country for the first time himself this summer, though he leaves us with no impressions of either the land or the people he met there; Raymond remembers that his father took particular pleasure in watching his son fight and win a few bouts on the local boxing circuit. Still, one suspects that the situation back home continued to worry him, for the few surviving photographs from this trip show him with an irritated scowl that may not have been caused entirely by the relentless sun of New Mexico. "I feel morally certain," he later wrote, "that if I had not taken that trip I would have come out of that stock market adventure, not only without any loss, but probably with a profit."

His moral certainty notwithstanding, it is unlikely that he would have been more able than anyone else to come out of the mess with a profit; as it happened, only a happy combination of luck and one intelligent move managed to keep him from being ruined like so many others. He had justification for worry down in New Mexico. The market, after a period of minor recovery in the spring of 1930—the "Little Bull Market," it was called—slumped once again in May, then again in June. By the end of the summer it was in full disarray. "It was on my way back [from New Mexico] that the market really began to go to pieces," he wrote.

When I reached Chicago it was in desperate shape. While I would have sold stocks on the way down if I had been there I really felt that after such a severe break, at least a normal reaction was about due. This is the wishful but dangerous thinking of every speculator. So I spent days with quaking diaphragm watching the stock market go lower and lower than anyone anticipated it could possibly go until, in order to protect my account, I had to sell pretty close to the bottom. . . .

In time it became a question of liquidating everything that I had as rapidly as I could. I had a fortunate break at this time. I had bought some State Bank of Chicago stock which had brought me some stock dividends until I owned about 300 shares. . . . Then it [the State Bank] merged with the Foreman National Bank and the stock began to soar. It went up and up. The Foremans guaranteed that they would pay not less than $1000 a share for every share of the State Bank stock offered. . . . So I offered my stock. The president of the State Bank came to my office to beg me not to sell. He assured me that the stock would go much higher and that the officers hoped that they would carry with them some of their own stockholders. . . . But thank God I sold. I received my check from the Foremans for $300,000 when the whole financial world was quaking. . . . Later both the State and Foreman [banks] went to pieces and never recovered. I hurried to the First National Bank where I paid off a loan of about $250,000 and the balance of $50,000 I turned in to my account with the Slaughter firm.

"In the end," he concludes this cautionary tale, "I came out with practically no impairment of capital." Perhaps so, but the capital in question was essentially Anna's, and he was not going to get off the hook without impairment of another sort, emotional pain inflicted by Wilmarth. It was not their first run-in about money, nor would it be the last, and in none of these instances did either man dip into any reserves of character, compassion, or rationality. They always squabbled meanly on the question of money, and if Wilmarth was motivated almost entirely by the simplest greed, the righteous tone that his stepfather invariably took in describing these encounters suggests that the poor boy from Altoona still lurked guiltily somewhere within him, reminding him that he was living off someone else's money and that he was, at best, presumptuous to think he had any right to control its disposition. When in doubt of your position, the saying goes, attack—which is what Ickes usually did, quite often to good effect.

The ugliness takes on a melancholy shade when it is remembered that Ickes believed that he and Wilmarth had become close in the troubled household in Hubbard Woods and that the young man had become a kind of emotional ally in the continuing struggle with Anna. Harold had little respect for Wilmarth's lack of initiative or his careless attitude toward responsibilities, but he tells us that he continued to love him in spite of these failings: "I was devoted to him and, so far as I could see, he reciprocated my feelings. Wilmarth was always somewhat shallow in his affections—in fact, he was rather shallow in all of his emotions—but I never had any doubt that he was very fond of me and loyal to me." He first began to wonder at the depth of Wilmarth's feelings, he says, shortly after his stepson returned from the war and entered Northwestern. He was still living at home then and Ickes had purchased for him a car and had put him on an allowance that he considered sufficient to cover "not only every convenience, but every comfort and even luxury." But Wilmarth wanted an increase, and when he did not get it, he turned on his stepfather. Driving together in the car one day, he accused him of having "robbed" him and Raymond of their share in the estate of the long-dead Grandfather Wilmarth. The share in question had been established when Anna was left some property on State Street in her father's will, property on which her annual rental income was limited to eighteen thousand dollars; any income above that amount was vested as an inheritance for her children, should she have any (which, of course, she ultimately did). Ickes convinced Anna, and after her the estate judge, that by another interpretation of the will the remaining income was a contingent remainder, not truly vested, and that it could and should be released to Anna. He then had renegotiated the lease on the property so that Anna could realize an income of forty thousand dollars a year from it. All of this struck Ickes as perfectly reasonable, even while admitting that if it had not been for his action, Wilmarth, Raymond, and possibly even Frances (not Robert, since he was never formally adopted) would have inherited the property and all accumulated excess income on the death of Anna. He pointed out to Wilmarth, probably more testily than he confesses in his memoirs, that the children would get the entire estate when he and Anna died, and that it would be substantially enriched by the infusion of forty thousand dollars a year. Wilmarth, unconvinced, continued to sputter angrily about it until his attention was diverted by something else.

But the memory must have continued to simmer in Wilmarth's bosom, for the anger nastily percolated to the surface when Ickes returned to Chicago at the end of the summer of 1930 to find his investments in tatters. When he realized the trouble he was in, Ickes called Wilmarth into his office to explain the situation, on the grounds that his stepson had the right to know. He also informed Anna. Both of them appeared to take the news calmly enough, but a few days later Wilmarth slammed into Harold's office and informed his unamused stepfather that Anna had given her son authority to wrest control of her property and her money away from her husband. "A hot discussion developed," Harold says (and we can believe him), "during which my back began to get stiffer and stiffer. Finally, in an unconvincing manner, he struck my desk with his fist and shouted at me: 'Dad, I command you to do this.' Thoroughly angry by this time I said to him: 'You get the hell out of here.' I think that he was more than ready to leave . . . and out he rushed with the statement that he was going to Winnetka to put it up to his mother."

They were waiting for him when he got home and another hot discussion ensued. "Of course Anna had the right to do what she pleased with her own property, but, after all, she had given it into my hands and had told me more than once that I could do what I pleased with it. The three of us had a dreadful scene that afternoon." When they refused to back off, Harold played his trump card:

Finally, I demanded from Wilmarth payment of the balance due on the joint and several note of himself and his partners [for the General Printing Company]. His partners had been making me monthly payments while Wilmarth had merely been keeping up his interest. I told him that the note was past due and that, according to its terms, I could forfeit all of the outstanding stock which I held as collateral, take over the business and oust him and his partners. . . .

Wilmarth turned white and acted the part of the coward. Anna offered to buy the note from me. I refused. Then she offered to pay me double its value. I told them I wouldn't sell it at any price. She begged me not to ruin Wilmarth and I told her that if Wilmarth would mind his own business I would be content to let things go on as they were.

In the end, Ickes says, Wilmarth succumbed to tears (he was thirty-one years old at the time) and Ickes reassured him that he would continue to let the note ride. "I was anxious to get back on the old personal basis with Wilmarth," he rather stunningly recalls. "For a while he was self-conscious, but within a short time, on the surface at least, matters with us were as they had been before."

They were not, of course. The encounter could not have been other than humiliating to Wilmarth, and Ickes, not especially sensitive to the moods of others at the best of times, was overlooking an entire sargasso sea of unhappiness here. Wilmarth was a deeply troubled young man. And, at about this same time, he had been having a steamy and expensive affair with a woman from New York. When his wife, Betty, confronted him on the point, he broke off the affair and sent the woman home to Manhattan—then drove out to some obscure railroad crossing, parked his car on the tracks, and waited for a Chicago & Northwestern train to come along and kill him. He lost his nerve at the last minute, drove back to Winnetka, and told his mother about it. She in turn told Harold. None of them apparently ever told Betty and neither Harold nor Anna, it appears, ever suggested that Wilmarth seek help.

CHAPTER

· 21 ·

" . . . at least 90% damn fool"

I CKES HAD MORE than financial and family troubles to irritate his psyche as the wreckage of one decade washed over into the new. It is symbolically appropriate that for him these months were dominated by one more fruitless struggle against the evils of capitalistic bloat and that the adversary in question was none other than Samuel Insull, who remained the kingpin of Chicago in spite of the crash of '29. "Insull is the supreme utility and political boss of these parts," Ickes wrote Raymond Robins in July 1930.

> His man Ettleson [Samuel Ettleson, Insull's political lawyer and chief "corporation counsel" to Mayor William Hale Thompson] has been the de facto mayor of this fair city practically since Thompson was elected. He owns the city council, the state legislature and the Illinois Commerce Commission. The governor of the state, the lieutenant governor of the state, the speaker of the house of representatives, the mayor of the city of Chicago, the president of the county board are all eager to carry out his slightest wish.

For Ickes, as for the rest of the tiny clutch of old-line Progressives left in the land, Insull sat in his Opera Building enthroned as the exemplar of everything that was polluted in the economic flux of America (and never mind the irony in the fact that Ickes at one point in his brief investment career had made fifty thousand dollars off the Insull companies). What is more, Insull had come to characterize as no one before him the ancient and unholy alliance between money and politics, for if his methods remained sophisticated when compared to the callow corruption of those who had gone before him, in the view of the Progressives his power was all the more malevolent for its refined character. Insull, William Allen White wrote in 1932, "had to be in the politics of at least twenty states in order to hold his great financial web from being torn to pieces. He typifies all that went wrong in October, 1929. He was greater than the others, but morally he is typical."

The issue that arose at the end of the twenties was once more variation on a very, very old theme: traction. Late in 1927, the owners of Chicago's five remaining streetcar companies, Leonard Busby and Henry Blair—heirs to the rattletrap legacy of Charles Tyson Yerkes—found that they had managed most of their antique operations to the brink of receivership just as the twenty-year franchises granted the companies in the elections of 1907 were coming up for renewal. Busby and Blair had come to Insull and had asked him to take over the crippled lines, as he had assumed control of all the elevated railroads so many years before. That kind of merger required special legislation from the statehouse in Springfield, something even Insull could not accomplish quickly. The immediate need, then, had been to arrange for fare increases and temporary franchise extensions to keep the lines going for a couple of years. That taken care of, Insull instructed one of the many law firms at his bidding to draw up five separate bills for the state legislature's approval. These would have provided for unification of all lines, regulation by a city commission, long-term extensions, compensation to the city, the construction of a fully integrated subway system, and dictatorial control by Samuel Insull. The bills were introduced in due course, but when word came back to him that outright bribes would be required to assure their passage, Insull erupted. That was not his style, he said. Perhaps not, but it was the style of the Illinois state legislature—or at least a good part of it—and the bills did not pass.

In 1928, to resolve the impasse, Judge James Wilkerson of the federal district bench appointed a group of citizens headed by James Simpson, chairman of the board of Marshall Field and Company and a longtime personal and business supporter of Insull. The group dubbed itself the Citizens' Traction Settlement Committee and was instructed to study the streetcar situation for a few months and come up with a recommendation. Early in 1929 the committee produced a report that offered a plan almost identical to that put forth by Insull's lawyers in 1927, although it did include one particularly interesting addition: the combined lines would be given an "indeterminate" franchise, which meant that at any time the city of Chicago could exercise an option to buy out the system. It also would require not only enabling legislation from the legislature, but a regulatory ordinance from the Chicago City Council and a popular referendum to put a cap on it. Appropriate legislation was accordingly introduced in the statehouse in the spring. Although the elections of 1928 had brought in a better class of people—including Anna Wilmarth Ickes—Insull had every confidence that the veneer of respectability given the enterprise by the formation of the citizens' committee would be enough to assure the legislation's passage this time around.

Not if Harold Ickes had anything to do with it. He joined this newest traction fight at the instigation of one of Charles Merriam's colleagues at the University of Chicago—Paul H. Douglas, a young professor of economics who was beginning a long and admirably varied career in public service, which would end with three terms in the U.S. Senate. When, after the citizens' committee report was issued, Insull's people claimed a valuation of $264 million for the combined properties, Douglas was hired by a group of progressive-minded real estate men to investigate the validity of the claim. It did not take him long to discover that as much as $135 million of that valuation was purest fabrication. He wrote in his own memoirs:

> The valuation of $167 million claimed for the surface lines included most of the cost of the original horse-car system, which had long since gone the way of all flesh; the cost of the cable car system that had replaced the horsecars and had also been scrapped; the cost of the first trolley system, which had already been largely obsolete when a twenty-year franchise was granted in 1907; the cost of the second trolley system, built under the 1907 franchise, plus an additional 15 per cent allowed upon this cost, but with no deduction for the physical depreciation of the properties incurred during twenty-some years of use. . . . In the list of physical properties, we actually found horses itemized that had departed this life many decades before, together with tracks and cars that had long since disappeared.

Setting aside the fact that this artificial bloat would give the whole of the Insull companies an injection of false value, which would enhance (and doubtless cause a rise in) the value of their stocks, Douglas concluded that placing a value of $264 million on the combined systems would, in effect, make the requested "indeterminate" franchise a permanent license; at that price, the city could never afford to exercise its option to buy out the lines. Douglas, Merriam, and a few of their colleagues decided to oppose this bit of financial witchery. Being Chicagoans, they organized; this group was called the People's Traction League, and Douglas turned to Ickes to head it up. Ickes became chairman, but the organization was but a pale reflection of those hyperkinetic groups that had coalesced for the betterment of the body politic in the years before the war. Ickes found it difficult to gather any substantial membership. "We even reached into the political sepulchre," he wrote Raymond Robins, "and dragged forth Carter Harrison and Edward F. Dunne." These worthies—both very old by now—served as honorary chairmen, their presence being titular and thus not particularly effective. The executive committee of the group included only thirteen members at any one time, and of these, Paul Douglas, the youngest, was by far the most active—and even his efforts would have to end in the spring of 1930, when he left Chicago to take a teaching position at Swarthmore College. Still, he worked diligently while he could. "I was given the roles of economic expert, chief witness, and spokesman for the group," he wrote. "All that spring and summer . . . I was kept busy testifying before the state legislature and the City Council, speaking before civic groups, and preparing statements."

However busy Douglas may have been, it was nearly the end of July 1929 before the League had been organized sufficiently even to make its presence officially known to the newspapers. Of these, only the two William Randolph Hearst papers, the *Herald-Examiner* and the *American*, supported the League's efforts, and then only when the publisher himself could be distracted from the demands of completing his unintentionally comic tribute to unfettered wealth at San Simeon in California. The first round had already been lost by the time the *Herald-Examiner* announced in a banner headline that "Leading Citizens Organize to Fight to Save City's Traction Rights" on July 29. Back in June, the statehouse had passed the enabling legislation with a minimum of fuss and the struggle moved now to city hall. When an editorial in the *Chicago Daily News* informed the city council that "the city is now emancipated from the control of the Illinois Commerce Commission and that leaves it genuine autonomy in transit," Ickes called upon his old law partner, Donald Richberg, now a member of the League's executive committee, for a response he could send to the papers. Richberg complied, writing that the notion that the enabling legislation returned autonomy to the city of Chicago was nonsense. No matter what the city decided in regard to any attempt at regulating the term and conditions of any traction franchise finally granted Insull's consolidation, the Illinois Commerce Commission, a body conceded to be under the perpetual sway of Insull and his people, retained—in the language of the enabling legislation itself—full veto power. "The right to lock the stable door and chase the horse after it has been stolen," he wrote, "is less valuable than control of the stable door right now, while the horse is still inside. But the enabling legislation gives the Illinois commerce commission the key to the stable door."

A series of painful hemorrhages at the site of his old ear operation again forced Ickes to take to his bed for most of August, but by the last week of September he was well enough to respond with one of his most eloquent outbursts when the Citizens' Traction Settlement Committee decided to appoint a subcommittee to aid the City Council's Committee of Local Transportation and its own subcommittees to study and report out on the enabling legislation. "Judge Wilkerson," Ickes thundered to the press,

> on behalf of the security holders of the traction companies, appointed a so-called Citizens Committee. This committee necessarily cannot represent anyone except the security holders. Now this committee, without authority, has appointed a new committee called the "Deadlock Committee." We may expect in time that the "Deadlock Committee" will create a "Gordian Knot" Committee, which may then give birth to an "Ultimate Crisis" Committee and so on indefinitely. We don't know how many more committees are capable of being extracted from the pandora box originally opened by Judge Wilkerson, but we do feel sure that the people are tired of this clowning.

Probably they were. Ickes and the other League members were "Quixotic crusaders, voices crying in the wilderness," even the sympathetic social scientist Harold F. Gosnell reported seven years later. The traction issue was swiftly drawing to a close. On May 19, 1930, the city council with only one dissenting vote approved an ordinance based on the state legislation, which was then signed by Mayor Thompson and put on the ballot for a special referendum on July 1—just forty days away. Ickes had his work cut out for him, not only because there was so little time left, but because by his own account he was pretty much standing alone at this point. In June, when the City Club—an organization of which he had been a member for more than a quarter of a century—gave its support to the council ordinance, Ickes resigned in a fury: "Since I am not ready to join in what I regard as a base betrayal of the City of Chicago I must necessarily sever my connection with an organization that has decided to tread the easiest way uttering an excuse that is so flimsy as to be transparent." When the old Citizens' Association, of which he had briefly served as secretary at the turn of the century, did the same, he cut this group of old friends and colleagues adrift, too. Hearst's newspapers had lost interest in the long crusade, probably because it seemed hopeless by now. What is more, most of his companions of the old days were absent, and even those who had joined to fight Insull one more time had drifted away, some of them quite literally. "I never felt so much alone as I did during this last fight," he wrote to Raymond Robins in Maine when it was all over.

> You were not here; Merriam was in Europe; Paul Douglas was at Swarthmore College; Billy Kent [William Kent, an old Progressive soldier from San Francisco] was dead; Charles R. Crane was hither or yon; Walter Fisher had gone over to the enemy bag and baggage. Poor old John Harlan used to float in pretty often to tell me what great stuff I was putting out. But John Harlan has been a ghost for the last twenty-five years. Now he is more or less a bleary ghost. Don Richberg was in the fight, but he was carrying on from his own office and I from mine.

The defection of Walter Fisher was especially galling. Fisher, another ally from the prewar days—and Richard Ballinger's replacement as Taft's Secretary of the Interior—was a special consultant to the Chicago City Council on traction matters and had actually been the author of the traction ordinance the council finally approved on May 19. Beginning on June 22, Ickes had launched a series of newspaper attacks that were poisonous even by his own standards. "We are urged," he wrote in the first of these, "to accept the ordinance because the chief draftsman was Walter L. Fisher. Moses descending from Mount Sinai with tablets inscribed at the dictation of the Creator of the world was no more sacred an object in his time than is Walter L. Fisher today. Samuel Insull and his sycophants cannot do this man enough honor. Their estimate of his transcendent ability almost equals Mr. Fisher's estimate of his own ability." Fisher maintained a dignified silence in answer to this and the vituperation that followed (although Fisher's son later reacted so strongly and bitterly that Ickes was moved to apologize to both of them), but John C. Bowers, president of the Central Uptown Chamber of Commerce, was inspired to note in a release of his own that "so long as our traction situation was left in its present muddle Mr. Ickes was content to bask on the front porch of his palatial home in Winnetka and let Chicago take care of itself. But just as soon as some one tries to solve the traction question, Mr. Ickes rushes to Chicago, pulls off his coat, rolls up his sleeves and screams 'gray wolves.' "

While Ickes berated Fisher for his craven subservience and Insull for his corruption, and the supporters of the ordinance called Ickes a mean-spirited, headline-hunting spoiler, the practical-minded Insull greased the rails of traction with an admitted payment of $500,000 to precinct captains and their workers across the city in what his people described as a civic-minded effort to ease the burden of these political soldiers in having to work an off-year election. On July 1 the citizens of Chicago approved Insull's traction ordinance 325,837 to 56,590.

"I never had any illusions as to the result of the fight," Ickes assured Raymond Robins. "It was a foregone conclusion that we would lose and lose heavily. I have never seen a more perfect setup to put over any election." Then a note of sadness, together with the kind of inflated self-pity that crept into his correspondence with increasing regularity in these years:

> I have realized for several years now that I have merely been going along with my old interests because I was wound up many years ago and haven't been able quite to run down. . . . As I look back over the struggle of our generation I sometimes wonder if it has been worth while. We certainly haven't succeeded in planting the standard that we carried in advance of the line that we occupied at the beginning of the war. I think it can be demonstrated that, politically speaking, Chicago and Illinois are much worse off than they were when we volunteered the fight.

And yet, he added, "I haven't had sense enough to admit defeat and make the most of my remaining years for myself and my family. I suppose I always will be like that. I imagine that one has to be at least 90% damn fool to plunge headlong into every hopeless fight that calls for volunteers."

Well. One would have to be at least 90 percent damn fool to imagine Ickes retiring from the fray to putter about his house and gardens in Hubbard Woods and spend his golden years wrapped quietly in the embrace of a family that gave him fits more often than not. If the walls of righteousness had indeed been breached and abandoned all around him, Ickes intended to continue defending them till the fiery end. So it was that in spite of his repeated complaints about the futility of it all, March 11 and 12, 1931, found him in Washington, D.C., as one of the featured speakers at a "Conference of Progressives to Outline a Program of Constructive Legislation dealing with Economic and Political Conditions for Presentation to the first Session of the Seventy-Second Congress." His speech before this ponderous conclave was called "Representative Government," and if it reiterated some of the helplessness he had begun to feel, it still rang with the vigor he could never quite suppress:

> Few people seem to be aware of the degree to which our political fiber has been softened. Especially prior to the recent stock exchange debacle all too many have been content to jazz while their heritage was being stolen. The dialogues of Amos and Andy have been more worth while than discussion, however eloquent and well-informed, on the tariff or the plight of the farmers.
>
> The plea of the courageous and incorruptible public officer seeking popular support of vitally essential policies, has not been audible above the whispered proposition of the bootlegger. . . .
>
> Leadership and courage will be required in this absolutely essential fight

for the return of representative government. The gray wolves of privilege and the coyotes who skulk on the fringe for the leavings will not easily give ground. The booty is too rich and succulent to be given up without a struggle.

It would have been of some comfort to Ickes had he known that in the traction battles of 1929–30 he had suffered his last political defeat and Insull had won his last political victory (his last victory of any kind, for that matter). In November 1930, Anna won her second term in the Illinois State Assembly with Harold at the helm of her campaign once again. That same election saw the resounding defeat of Ruth Hanna McCormick, widow of his old adversary Medill McCormick. In 1928 she had won a seat in the House of Representatives, a victory that persuaded her to challenge Senator Charles Deneen for the Republican Senate nomination in 1930. She won the nomination but was badly beaten in November by her Democratic opponent, James Hamilton Lewis, whom Ickes supported vigorously, still playing the hard-nosed independent. ("I owed nobody an explanation when I continued to shift from party to party in search of the better candidate," he later cockily wrote.) Lewis, Ickes noted cheerily, "was too clever for her. I have never seen a campaign more adroitly run. His chivalry would not permit him to raise directly the issue of Mrs. McCormick's sex, but in no speech did he fail to make some such reference as 'the disarming lady who is opposing me,' without mentioning her name."

Even sweeter success came with the elections of the following year, when Big Bill Thompson's Chicago career was ended by another Democrat, Anton Cermak, an immigrant from Prague who had started life in Chicago as a pushcart peddler in the warrens off Halsted Street. "Tony," Thompson liked to jeer during the course of the campaign, "where is your pushcart at?" But Cermak beat him by a plurality of 194,267 votes, the largest such in Chicago history, and once again Ickes had happily jumped the traces to support and vote for a Democrat. There seemed little choice, for, as he wrote Hiram Johnson in April, Cermak was a "good executive" who knew "everything there was to know about the city and he is an indefatigable worker. Of course what will go on behind the scenes will perhaps not bear close examination, but even if he gives us an administration that is good only on the surface it will be a gain over Thompson."

It took somewhat longer for Samuel Insull to be brought down, but when he went it was swiftly and with profound reverberations. Throughout the worst months of 1929 and early 1930, all of the Insull operating companies—those manufacturing electricity and gas as well as running trains—continued to show healthy profits, and even the stock value of his investment trusts, unlike most such, held firm while the economic world disintegrated around them. But this was largely through the complex efforts of Insull's principal securities salesman, Fred Scheel, an adroit trader who juggled the buys against the sells with an extraordinarily delicate instinct for making the right moves at the right times. Unfortunately, a good deal of this exquisite manipulation involved the regular purchase of Insull stocks to maintain the price levels, and, as Scheel himself said, "You can't go on buying your own stocks forever. Sooner or later you run out of money."

The balance that Scheel had maintained through sheer effort was too fragile to survive the panic that hit the New York Stock Exchange in September 1931, when Great Britain announced that it was going off the gold standard. Within a week, the stocks of Insull Utilities Investment Company, Corporation Securities Company, Commonwealth Edison, and Middle West Utilities together dropped more than $150 million in value, and the losses continued inexorably in the days and weeks that followed. Frantically, Insull borrowed from this one to keep that one afloat, manipulated, dissembled, and in the end failed. Ever since 1928 and 1929, when he had borrowed heavily to buy off Cyrus Eaton's raid, the New York banks—particularly the Morgan banks—had held enormous quantities of Insull securities as collateral; now they had them all. After sending in teams of accountants to examine the Insull books, the banks forced IUI, Corporation Securities, and Middle West into receivership. By June 1932, Insull was left with nothing but his operating companies, including Commonwealth Edison, People's Gas, and Public Service, and on June 4 his creditors demanded his resignation from these and all the rest. On Monday, June 6, the utilities king of the United States went to his office in the Opera Building for the last time and spent most of the day formally resigning from more than sixty individual corporations. When he was done, he left the office to confront the mass of newspapermen waiting for him outside. "Well, gentlemen," he said, "here I am, after forty years a man without a job."*

---

* A few days later, Insull slipped into Canada and from there to Europe. In October he was indicted by a Cook County grand jury on several counts of embezzlement and larceny and in March 1933 was seized aboard a rented yacht in the harbor of Istanbul, Turkey, and brought back to the United States for trial—before Judge James Wilkerson, he who had appointed the Citizens' Traction Settlement Committee in 1928. The trial did not begin until October 4, 1934, and Insull was acquitted on November 24. He retired to France on a pension of $25,000 a year and dropped dead on a Paris Metro platform in July 1938.

CHAPTER
· 22 ·

No Foundation

S AMUEL INSULL WAS NOT the only one out of a job in 1932. If the crash
of '29 was high drama, the Depression that followed was a threnody—
muted, constant, stupefying in its persistence. It beggared understanding, even among those who might have been expected to comprehend it at
some level useful to the rest. Just a few days before his death in January
1933, Calvin Coolidge could offer only despondency. As President (and
inspiration) of what was touted as "Coolidge Prosperity," he had gone
along in his tight-lipped fashion for the ultimately ruinous joyride of the
twenties. Now he looked around him at disaster and could find nothing of
substance. "In other periods of depression," he said, "it has always been
possible to see some things which were solid and upon which you could
base hope. But as I look about, I now see nothing to give ground for hope,
nothing of man."

The soup kitchens, the bread lines, the apple sellers, the crowded,
dingy employment offices, the wasted, lined, hungry, haunted faces have
long since become part of the national iconography, the songs and stories
part of the national folklore, and memory and reconstruction have given
much of it an almost romantic gloss. Even the statistics that can be made
to march across the page have a callow impersonality that tends to numb
their impact.

But consider the numbers: there had never been anything like them.

In 1929 there had been a little under two million unemployed American workers out of a population of about 122 million; by the end of 1930 that figure had risen to more than six million, by the end of 1931 to more than ten million, by the end of 1932 to more than twelve million—just about 10 percent of the entire population. Per-capita income, adjusted for inflation, fell from $681 in 1929 to $495 in 1933. Salaries dropped by 40 percent, and at one point as many as 34 million people had no incomes at all—28 percent of the population. Millions wandered in search of jobs— in one year, the Southern Pacific Railroad estimated that it had thrown 683,000 transients off its boxcars. In New York, 40,000 people had to give up their telephones between 1929 and 1931. The Consumer Price Index dropped 18 percent between 1929 and 1933. More than 1,500 colleges had closed by 1933. The gross national product fell from $104 billion in 1929 to $41 billion in 1933. The 451,800 corporations still in business in 1932 had a combined deficit of $5.64 billion, and the 960 most successful corporations had to divide up a mere $300 million in net profits. Gross investments in the United States fell from $16.2 billion in 1929 to just $800 million in 1932, and in the stock market, brokers' loans went from the high of $8.5 billion in 1929 to $430 million in 1932. The issuance of corporate securities dropped 96 percent in the same period, and in 1932 General Electric and U.S. Steel were worth 8 percent of what they had been in 1929. General construction dropped 26 percent in 1930, 29 percent in 1931, and 47 percent in 1932. Business construction went from $8.7 billion in 1929 to $1.4 billion in 1933. In 1929, 659 banks had been suspended, with a loss to depositors of $77 million; in 1930, 1,352 failed, with losses of $237 million; in 1931, 2,294, with losses of $391 million; in 1932, 1,456, with losses of $168 million; and—before March—in 1933, 4,004, with losses of $540 million. And the farmers, always the farmers: During World War I they had expanded production beyond the wildest dreaming, for what seemed like good reason—wheat, for example, was bringing in $2.19 a bushel by 1919, corn $1.50, and cotton more than thirty-four cents a pound, almost triple the prewar prices for wheat and cotton, more than double the price for corn. But mortgage debt to finance that expansion had risen to $9.4 billion by 1925 and the prices that were supposed to last forever began an intermittent decline throughout the twenties. After 1929 they plunged to the bottommost levels—in 1932, wheat fell to thirty-eight cents, corn to thirty-two cents, cotton to less than six cents. Farm income across the board in 1932 was one-third that in 1929, and the parity index— the prices farmers received for all the products they sold compared to the prices they paid for everything they had to buy—went from eighty-nine in 1929 (itself not a very good figure) to a dismal fifty-five in 1932. Between 1930 and 1935, the average value of American farms fell from $7,625 to $4,823—and there were more than 750,000 foreclosure and bankruptcy sales in those years.

Still, the dry horror of statistics is inadequate to the story. It was about terror, not numbers, the terror of uncertainty, helplessness, inchoate frustration, despair; it was an anomie of spirit that left millions constricted by guilt and hopelessness. "The suddenly idle hands blamed themselves, rather than society," Studs Terkel noted in *Hard Times*. "True, there were hunger marches and protestations to City Hall and Washington, but the millions experienced a private kind of shame when the pink slip came. No matter that others suffered the same fate, the inner voice whispered, 'I'm a failure.' " As Elsa Ponselle, a Chicago schoolteacher, recalled, "The Depression was a way of life for me from the time I was twenty to the time I was thirty. I thought it was going to be forever and ever and ever. That people would always live in fear of losing their jobs. You know, *fear*. . . ."

Fear. It stank in Chicago as elsewhere, a fetor not even the wind whipping in off Lake Michigan could disperse. The Depression here took on a character of its own when it was discovered that the third Thompson administration, profligate like all the rest, had spent $23 million more in 1930 than it could hope to collect in taxes. Some fifteen hundred city employees were laid off—not the ward heelers and bureaucrats, of course, but teachers, firemen, police. And the teachers, as they usually do, got the shortest end of the already short stick. Those who were not fired got paid in city warrants that carried 6 percent interest. "A marvelous investment," Elsa Ponselle remarked. "But not for the teachers who had to take them for pay. They had to peddle those warrants for what they could get. It was a promise to pay when the city got some money. We didn't think we'd ever get paid." City employment dropped by half, payrolls by nearly 75 percent. In 1929 there had been 3,148 foreclosures in the city; in 1933 there were 15,201. Throughout the metropolitan area, 163 banks had failed. Land values dropped from $5 billion to $2 billion.

It had become a city of the homeless. In the first half of 1931 alone, nearly fourteen hundred families were evicted, and the sight of people standing miserably with their furniture on sidewalks in front of the locked doors of their apartment buildings became a Chicago commonplace. "While sitting in the Landlord and Tenants Court," Chicago Municipal Judge Samuel A. Heller remembered, "I had an average of four hundred cases a day. It was packed. People fainted, people cried: Where am I going?" To the streets, as they always had. On August 25, 1931, the

Urban League reported that "every available dry spot of ground and every bench on the west side of Washington Park between 51st and 61st Streets is covered by sleepers." When fall came, they took to more sheltered spots, as they had in the winter of 1930–31, when a reporter took note of the contrasts the city offered: "You can ride across the lovely Michigan Avenue bridge at midnight with the . . . lights all about making a dream city of incomparable beauty, while twenty feet below you, on the lower level of the same bridge, are 2,000 homeless, decrepit, shivering and starving men, wrapping themselves in old newspapers to keep from freezing, and lying down in the manure dust to sleep." When they did not sleep under the bridges, they congregated in the ingenious clutter of all the big and little "Hoovervilles" and "Hobovilles" scattered around the city wherever there was vacant ground to put them—makeshift, handmade out of packing crates and cardboard, corrugated tin, oil drums, and abandoned strips of tarpaper, grotesque villages of the desperate whose inhabitants were as tattered and ramshackle as the homes they had cobbled together.

Edmund Wilson saw this and more. It was 1932 when he came to Chicago, and the worst of everything that economic collapse can do to a people was visible throughout the West Side. "All around the social workers of Hull House," he wrote in *The American Earthquake*, "there today stretches a sea of misery more appalling even than that which discouraged Miss Addams in the nineties. This winter even those families who had managed to hang on by their savings and earnings have been forced to apply for relief." In one warren he found "an old man . . . dying of a tumor, with no heat in the house, on a cold day. His pale bones of arms lie crooked like bent pins; nothing is heard in the house but his gasping." In the crowded shelters for the homeless he found "faces that are shocking in their contrast to the environment here: men who look as if they had never had a day's ill health or done a day's careless work in their lives. Now they jump at the opportunity of spending a day a week clearing the rubbish off vacant lots or cleaning the streets underneath the Loop tracks." Down on South Wabash Avenue, he found the old Angelus Building, formerly the Ozark Hotel,

> seven stories, thick with dark windows, caged in a dingy mess of fire-escapes like mattress-springs on a junk-heap, hunched up, hunchback-proportioned, jam-crammed in its dumbness and darkness with miserable wriggling life. . . . There is darkness in the hundred cells: the tenants cannot pay for light; and cold: the heating system no longer works. . . . And now, since it is no good for anything else, its owner has turned it over to the Negroes, who flock into the tight-packed apartments and get along there as best they can.

And then, perhaps something near the ultimate horror: "There is not a garbage-dump in Chicago which is not diligently haunted by the hungry. Last summer in the hot weather, when the smell was sickening and the flies were thick, there were a hundred people a day coming to one of the dumps, falling on the heap of refuse as soon as the truck had pulled out and digging in it with sticks and hands."

Against this Stygian landscape and in spite of the fact that it could not feed or house thousands of its people, the city of Chicago prepared itself for another fair, this one to be financed by private business, built on four hundred acres of fill along the lakefront just south of Grant Park, and given the theme of "A Century of Progress." Perhaps in unconscious recognition that the century of progress in question had brought the nation to what many feared might be a permanently sorry condition, the architecture of this fair, unlike the Columbian Exposition of 1892–93, would not celebrate the classical forms of the past but seek to envision the outlines of the future. Rufus Dawes, president of the fair, explained that the stark, spare white buildings that would be arranged in geometric precision and accented with carefully placed flashes of color would represent the "spontaneous expression of the pride of citizens of Chicago," as well as offer proofs of man's "power to prevail over the perils that beset him."

Well, a fair has to stand for *something*, and the Century of Progress that began to be erected in 1932 may well have expressed that kind of faith as an antidote to fear. It seemed to echo, faintly, perhaps a little insistently, the note of possibility that had always lain at the heart of the city's appeal.

Now in bitter contrast to that ancient hope stood the gray reality of terror. Something in the city—in the country—had failed and neither memory nor words nor the architecture rising in the brave new imaginary world of the Century of Progress could mask it. It remained, barely held in check, so powerful and incomprehensible that often it was transformed into something else, something simpler that the individual could tolerate. So it was with James T. Farrell's Studs Lonigan, who walked the streets of Chicago in the thirties, stone-heavy with a fear that could only find expression in the shape of rage:

> He saw himself walking in the rain, wet and tired, with things crashing down on his head, being screwed at every turn, forced to do something. He saw himself walking south along State Street in the sloshing rain, past department stores, past attractive windows full of suits and ties and shirts and dresses and furniture and baseball bats and football suits and feminine lingerie and refrigerators. Walking past tall buildings full of people at work

who didn't have the troubles Studs Lonigan had. He looked at people on the street, their faces indistinct, and an unquenchable hate rose up in him, and he wanted to punch and maim and claw them. He caught a close-up view of a fat male face, a sleeping contentment in the features. There went another sonofabitch, another sonofabitch who had a job. . . .

CHAPTER

· 23 ·

Waiting for Something to Turn Up

E VERYWHERE THE PUNDITS argued numbers, sifting through the wreckage in search of cause and effect, in search of a way out of the confusion. In Washington the confusion was real enough. "No sooner is one leak plugged up than it is necessary to dash over and stop another that has broken out," President Herbert Hoover complained to his secretary, Theodore Joslin, in 1931. "There is no end to it." Hoover, after a career in which he had acquired a respectable personal fortune as a mining engineer in such far-flung places as Australia and South America, had achieved international prominence as head of the Committee for the Relief of Belgium during the first three years of World War I. Then he had been personally responsible for the feeding, clothing, and housing of millions of people made destitute by war. When the United States entered the conflict, he had become U.S. Food Administrator for War, and after the Armistice director-general of the American Relief Administration. In all of these endeavors he had demonstrated remarkable skill in obtaining and managing enormous amounts of money and supplies, and the efficiency of his operations was lauded the world over as the model of what could be accomplished when good works were married to the peculiarly American genius for administration. That reputation was enough to have made him a serious, if unsuccessful, contender for the Republican Presidential nomination in 1920 and more than enough to persuade the successful candidate, Warren G. Harding, to appoint Hoover to his cabinet as Secretary of Commerce. He had served in that capacity for seven and a half years, until his own successful run at the Presidency in 1928.

Now the economic world he had inherited and helped to direct was the metaphorical equivalent of the rubble he had witnessed in war-shattered Europe. He struggled manfully, if fruitlessly, to set things right. Even before the crash he had initiated a program of reform and his was a dedication to responsible government not seen since the first Wilson administration—expanding civil service protection, canceling oil leases on the public lands, investigating tax-refund fraud, launching a Commission on Conservation and Administration of the Public Domain (chaired by TR's Secretary of the Interior, James Garfield), signing the Agricultural Marketing Act in an effort to build a floor under farm prices, giving the massive Boulder Dam project in Arizona—which he had helped to bring into being as Secretary of Commerce—the full support of his engineer's heart, making repeated and increasingly public warnings against mindless speculation. Yet none of this had done anything to prevent disaster, and nothing he seemed to do after it came had any but the most temporary effect—not all of it good. In June 1930, for example, he had signed the radically protectionist Hawley-Smoot tariff act, which by 1932 had revealed itself as one of the most ruinous economic measures in the history of the modern world. Not only did it raise consumer prices in the United States by cutting off the flow of most cheap foreign goods (this at a time when consumer purchasing power already had been gutted by unemployment and falling wages); its wall against imports inspired other Western nations to erect their own in retaliation, and world trade soon descended into a pit of feral nationalism that all but strangled it and sent waves of collapse oscillating through both hemispheres.

Hoover, the self-made, self-reliant engineer, believed in the essential soundness of the capitalistic system, and he distrusted all governmental interference that could not clearly and inescapably be proved necessary. Even more, he denigrated the notion of direct government aid to the needy, except in the most extreme cases; volunteerism, he maintained, had fed the hungry in Europe and could do the same in America, and to resort to the public dole would be to eviscerate the best that lay within the sturdy American character. So he created the President's Committee for Unemployment Relief, which, working with local volunteer groups, was designed to feed the hungry without spending government money. It puzzled him when this did not seem to be enough, but he resisted anything more expansive—especially anything that might require congressional legislation. "The most dangerous animal in the United States," he told the Gridiron Club in December 1930, "is the man with an emotion and a desire to pass a new law." It was not surprising, then, that when Senator Robert Wagner of New York introduced a bill for direct federal relief, Hoover threatened to veto it. "Never before has so dangerous a suggestion been seriously made to our country," he declared, and the Senate rejected it. And when circumstances became so plainly dreadful that he was forced to sign a considerably watered-down version of Wagner's bill, he did so reluctantly and with trepidation for the soul of America.

Cooperation fired by confidence—that was the thing, he believed. Shortly after Black Tuesday, 1929, he had organized the National Business Survey Conference, whose members pledged not to cut wages (though in the end, most of them did). This, he was convinced, would encourage people to spend, and by spending save business from ruin. The government would do its part by launching an unprecedented program of public works—in 1931 alone, his newfound Public Works Administration (PWA) would inject $700 million into the economy. He issued statements designed to buck up the public spirit. To show "any lack of confidence in the economic future or the strength of business in the United States is foolish," he said. He called writer Christopher Morley to the White House for a chat. "What this country needs is a great poem," he told the astonished Morley. "Something to lift people out of fear and selfishness. Every once in a while someone catches words out of the air and gives a nation an inspiration. . . . I'd like to see something simple enough for a child to spout in school on Fridays. I keep looking for it but I don't see it. . . . Let me know if you find any great poems lying around." He was not joking; Hoover rarely joked.

Some read this aspect of his character as coldness and indifference. Ickes certainly did. He had met Hoover back in the days when Ickes was head of the Illinois Neighborhood Committee during World War I. He had gone to Washington then for a meeting with George Creel, Wilson's director of the Committee of Public Information, and Creel asked him to join Hoover and himself for lunch. "I did," Ickes recalled, "and that was the only time—I say it without a trace of regret—that I ever met Hoover. He monopolized the conversation and I forget what it was all about. Turning sideways and facing Creel, he never once looked in my direction or addressed a remark to me, after telling me, mechanically, what a great pleasure it was to meet me. It wasn't a pleasure at all. It was a bore. And so was he." This encounter—snub was how he always remembered it— did not make Ickes a good target for the letter sent him in December 1930 by Russell Doubleday, inviting Ickes to contribute ("no more than") one hundred dollars toward a nationwide advertisment expressing confidence in President Hoover. Ickes had a habit of answering such junk mail. "Your whole plan," he replied,

> I regard as ill-advised. I carry no picture in my mind during these last twelve or fourteen months of a calm, resourceful, able and experienced President steering the country into a safe port. On the contrary, I believe that President Hoover has been as scared and rattled as the rest of us. He has failed in leadership. . . . Waiving the question whether the language of the suggested advertisement does not outrageously twist the clear facts, it seems to me that such a venture at this time is both foolish and puerile. The country is tired of organized cheers to make it believe that it is not in a serious economic crisis or that even if it is it will soon emerge under the leadership of a man who is peculiarly wanting in qualities of leadership. . . . I must respectfully decline to join what appears to me to be either an act of stupidity or a reckless attempt to fool the people.

In that same month, Hoover asked Congress for considerably more than a hundred dollars. Still pursuing the conviction that the best way out of the situation was a working partnership between business and government, he sent down to the hill a message proposing the creation of a federal body that would be in a position to "facilitate exports by American agencies; make advances to agricultural credit agencies where necessary to protect and aid the agricultural industry; to make temporary advances upon proper securities to established industries, railways and financial institutions which cannot otherwise secure credit, and where such advances will protect the credit structure and stimulate employment." Congress responded with the Reconstruction Finance Corporation Act, which Hoover signed into law on January 22, 1932. He then called in former Vice President and now Ambassador to the Court of St. James's Charles Dawes to head the new agency, and the Reconstruction Finance Corporation (RFC) expeditiously began to spend the $2 billion Congress had appropriated—all of this on the basis of an early version of the "trickle-down" theory: give the money to aid those at the top, and as their enterprises recovered the benefits would seep down through the ranks of the middle class, then the working class, then, finally, the poor.

To finance the trickle down would put the national deficit at something close to an unprecedented 60 percent of the national budget, however, so the Hoover administration proposed a national sales tax to bolster income—a tax, of course, that would inflict the greatest hardship on those at the bottom of the trickle. But Congress had lately been hearing too much testimony like that offered by Mayor Frank Murphy of formerly auto-rich Detroit: "It used to be the wage earner alone who was

on the welfare lists. Now it is the skilled artisan and the cultured citizen."
The House killed the sales-tax bill by a margin of 223–153, and it was
never seriously proposed again. "There is no hope for the ineptitude of this
administration," William Allen White (who had voted for Hoover) wrote
to a friend. "For a man who has high intentions and a noble purpose, our
beloved President has a greater capacity for doing exactly the wrong thing
at a nicely appointed time than any man who ever polished his pants in the
big chair at the White House."

It is too much to say, as some did then and have since, that the nation
trembled at the lip of revolution, but it was in powerful trouble. "I feel
the capitalistic system is dead," John A. Simpson, president of the radical
National Farmers' Union, said. "It has as its foundation the principles of
brutality, dishonesty, and avarice." In the spring of 1932, Milo Reno,
former president of the Iowa Farmers' Union, organized the Farmers'
Holiday Association and began to lay plans for nationwide farmers'
strikes. And speaking for labor, William Green, president of the American Federation of Labor, said, "When despite every effort to get employment, men and women find no opportunity to earn their living,
desperation and blind revolt follow." On March 7, 1932, some three
thousand workers marched to the River Rouge factory of the Ford Motor
Company in Dearborn, Michigan, to present a list of demands; they were
greeted by police and Ford's own private force, and in the ensuing melee
the air was filled with stones, tear gas, and, finally, bullets. Four workers
were killed and fifty injured, and at the mass funeral five days later, the
Communist Party's "Internationale" was played beneath a red banner
featuring a likeness of Lenin. Throughout the country that spring, hundreds of hungry mobs organized to hijack meat and produce delivery
trucks and loot grocery stores. Out in Portland, Oregon, Walter Waters,
an unemployed veteran, began urging a march on Washington to demand
that Congress pay the "bonus" it had promised the nation's servicemen
with the Adjusted Compensation Act of 1924. Under the stipulations of
this law, each veteran of World War I was vested with an interest-bearing
policy whose amount depended on the length and nature of his service; the
policies could not be redeemed until 1945, when their average value
would be as much as one thousand dollars. If redeemed in 1932, the value
would have been only about five hundred dollars, but "General" Waters,
as he soon became known, and the hundreds, then thousands, of men in
the tatterdemalion "Bonus Army" that did in fact "march" by boxcar,
truck, bus, and foot into Washington that spring wanted it now. By June
there were at least twenty-five thousand men living in twenty-three
impromptu, quasi-military encampments scattered around the city, the

biggest of which was in Anacostia Park on the banks of the Anacostia River. The desperate men had come, Waters said, to demand their bonus from Congress, and they would not leave until they got it. On June 13 the House granted their request in a bill introduced by Wright Patman of Texas, and the proposition moved to the Senate. As thousands of men gathered below the steps of the Capitol, debate in the Senate continued into the evening. A vote did not come until nine-thirty; the bill was defeated 62–18. One of the eighteen, Senator Hiram Johnson, turned to a colleague. "This marks a new era in the life of our nation," he said. "The time may come when this folderol—these trappings of government—will disappear, when fat old men like you and me will be lined up against a stone wall." Not quite yet; outside, the men took the news in silence, then sang a chorus of "America" and drifted back to their camps to continue waiting.

That sense of waiting would characterize the mood of much of the country for months. As one newspaper feature reporter, Anne O'Hare McCormick, would say: "Un-American as it sounds, we are all waiting, waiting for something to turn up. . . . But why this paralysis of the intellect? Where are the big American brains to deal with unemployment, with group planning, with the ghastly cost of competition, with that hoary wheeze that supply balances demand, with the control of industry, with a modern credit system? Or are we to go on waiting for something to happen until it does?"

Something was beginning to happen in 1932, as a matter of fact, and it was beginning in Chicago, as such things had so many times before. On June 13, the day of the vote on the Bonus Bill, Republican delegates gathered in Chicago again for the quadrennial ritual of selecting their Presidential candidate (this time in the new Chicago Stadium on Madison Street, completed in 1929). As the convention started, it was a foregone conclusion that Hoover would be renominated, since no serious contender to oppose him had emerged. Coolidge had refused to consider the idea when approached by a group of businessmen who held the curious delusion that the reinstallation of its namesake alone would be enough to resurrect Coolidge prosperity. The last real hope of the ever-shrinking Progressive contingent of the party had been that Hiram Johnson finally could be persuaded to make a significant attempt at the nomination. Ickes had been especially active in trying to nudge the reluctant senator into the ring. "Dear Chief," he had written Johnson on January 22, 1932.

Since my return from Washington [from the Progressive Conference in March 1931] I have been more and more impressed by your strength in this state. Hoover is growing weaker day by day and no one is talking of any other candidate than yourself as a possibility against him. It is the consensus of opinion that you can defeat Hoover and that you are the one available man to do this.

I say in all sincerity that you can be nominated for President if you will only go into the fight. Never has there been such an opportunity for you to be President and never will there be such an opportunity again. . . .

In spite of this ardent clarion and all the others that had preceded and would follow it, in spite of similar letters to Johnson's wife, in spite of assurances from many others that what Ickes said was true, and in spite of their guarantee that a two-hundred-thousand-dollar campaign chest could easily be raised to finance the effort, Johnson had officially declined by mid-February. "Dear Hiram," Ickes wrote on February 16 (no "Dear Chief" this time around), "Your letter of February 13 was a shock and a disappointment to me. . . ."

Once Johnson had removed himself, Gifford Pinchot, the former chief forester of the United States and now in his second term as governor of Pennsylvania, decided to test the waters and persuaded Ickes to help him by writing a circular letter and sending it out to lists of names provided by the erstwhile candidate, who would then pore over the replies and conduct himself accordingly. Ickes participated in this semi-campaign more for old times' sake than out of any conviction that Pinchot's hopes were real. "Just between you and me," he had written William Allen White in March, "I agree with you that Gifford has not got a chance and that no one can take the nomination away from Hoover. . . . I did this because I am so fond of him, although I really did not want to do it. . . . But then, I always was an easy mark for my friends. If you want to be elected Pope, or something like that, just let me know and I will circularize all the crowned heads of Europe in your behalf." By May 5, Pinchot himself had become so discouraged by the tepid response from this effort that he told Ickes it would be "a pure waste of money to send out any more letters, and so I wish you would send back the names and let the thing go. It is perfectly clear to me that the big fellows are in control to such an extent that there is no use doing anything about the Republican Convention."

He was quite correct. Before the final gavel of a convention that H. L. Mencken called "the stupidest and most boresome ever," Hoover had won renomination with only twenty-eight delegates withholding support. "Well," Hoover said when he heard on the radio that he had won, "it was not wholly unexpected. Guess I will go back to the office now." Had he been in Chicago at the time, he might not have taken the news quite so phlegmatically, for if the ceremonials taking place inside the stadium could have been described as pedestrian, there was nothing dull about the crisis taking place outside, where the chattering of panic could be heard as a kind of ironic counterpoint. Pressure waves set in motion by the collapse of the Insull empire early in June had caused one suburban bank after another to cave in even before the convention started, and by the time it opened, banks in the Loop had begun to fail. On June 15, Charles G. Dawes had suddenly resigned as president of the Reconstruction Finance Corporation and had rushed to Chicago to see what, if anything, he might do to save his own bank, the Central Republic, one of the five most important financial institutions in the city. Ten days later, after the Republicans had packed their bags and left town, the Democrats began to assemble for their own nominating convention. One of them was Texas millionaire Jesse Jones, who arrived on June 25. One of the RFC board members, Jones soon found that Dawes and the other bankers in town had been able to do little or nothing to halt the dreadful crumbling. He later reported:

> From my hotel, that ominous Saturday morning, I walked through the Loop and watched the tail end of the week's terrible runs on the big downtown banks. Thousands of frantic, rumor-spreading depositors were still milling about every bank entrance in La Salle, Clark, and Dearborn streets. Bank lobbies swarmed with nervous customers. . . . Alarming rumors fanned the fears of the city's millions, of whom hundreds of thousands, being unemployed, had only their dwindling savings on which to exist and could not afford to lose their deposits or have them tied up.

The Central Republic Bank, he soon learned, was in particular trouble. On Sunday, Dawes called a meeting of the chief officers of all the Loop's biggest surviving banks, a meeting to which Jones was pointedly invited. Dawes told the assembled pinstripes that unless they could come up with some way to save his bank, he would not be able to open for business on Monday, with dire consequences to the rest of the banking community. The bankers turned to Jones, asking him to telephone President Hoover and request the approval of an RFC loan big enough to keep Central Republic open. Jones asked for a few hours to go over the bank's books first, then called Hoover that evening and recommended that the RFC lend the bank ninety million dollars—which Jones himself proposed to guarantee. Hoover agreed, the loan was expeditiously processed, and on Monday morning Central Republic opened its doors.

While details were sketchy, rumors of the RFC loan to Central Republic and the banking chaos that continued to rattle office windows in downtown Chicago during the sultry week that followed provided a suitable context for the proceedings of the Democratic National Convention. Whatever else it might have been, that convention would not be described as boresome. There was a powerful feeling among the delegates that the Republican era finally had ended and that—quite aside from the standard rhetoric and quadrennial dose of political adrenaline—they were, in fact, going to be choosing the next President of the United States. That conviction made the Democratic prize more seductive than ever, and there were plenty of contenders whose soldiers had gathered to do battle. "To the politicians who like action and plenty of it," New York's James A. Farley remembered,

> there was no disappointment at Chicago. The air was soon filled with charges and countercharges; rumors that this or that was about to happen flew thick and fast. The headquarters of the contending candidates were almost side by side in the Congress Hotel, and delegates and visitors alike were cordially welcomed by each camp in turn. Behind closed doors, the strategists of the contending armies were sitting for hours on end trying to devise methods of increasing their own voting strength while weakening that of their opponents.

Prominent among the hopeful were Alfred E. Smith, former governor of New York and unsuccessful candidate for the job in 1928; Newton D. Baker, Woodrow Wilson's Secretary of War and now a rich and successful corporation lawyer in Ohio; and John Nance ("Cactus John") Garner, Speaker of the House of Representatives and the favorite son of Texas.

But the man to beat in 1932 was Franklin Delano Roosevelt, governor of New York. Roosevelt had emerged on the national scene as one of the stellar products of a tradition that had somehow combined mercantile grubbing and politics to effect the closest thing to an aristocracy as it was possible to achieve in an ostensible democracy. He had grown up patrician on the Hyde Park estate called Springwood and had enjoyed all the privileges such a background provided. He emulated his famous cousin Theodore ("Uncle Ted" in family parlance), whose niece, Anna Eleanor Roosevelt, he had married in 1905, and in some respects his own career had paralleled that of TR. After being admitted to the New York bar in 1907, he worked as a law clerk for three years, then in 1910 ran successfully for the New York State Senate and served most of two terms in Albany—just as TR had more than twenty years earlier. In 1913, again like his cousin, he had been appointed Assistant Secretary of the Navy, a position he held until 1920, and in July of that year had been nominated for Vice President by the Democratic Party. That was where the parallels ended, of course, for in November he and his running mate, James M. Cox, had been soundly whipped by Harding and Coolidge.

A devastating attack of poliomyelitis in 1921 had nearly killed him and his political career, leaving him with a pair of withered and permanently paralyzed legs. This had slowed but not stopped him. In 1924, as chairman of the national Citizens' Committee for Alfred E. Smith, he had placed Smith's name in nomination at the Democratic National Convention. In 1928, after offering Smith's name to the Democrats once again, he had himself run for governor of New York—and had won. He won again in 1930, and from this highly visible platform, he launched his own campaign for the Democratic Presidential nomination. He was guided in this quest by the wizened, asthmatic, impossibly ugly, and obviously brilliant Louis ("Louie") McHenry Howe, a political strategist who worshiped FDR and had been with him in every election arena since 1912, and by James A. Farley, a large, affable Irish political workhorse who had functioned as Roosevelt's principal "field agent" since 1928. To the work of these two had been added the efforts of Samuel I. Rosenman, a young lawyer hired as a speechwriter, and Raymond A. Moley, a professor of political science at Columbia University who had been brought into the fold to develop ways of addressing major issues. To this end, in March 1932, Rosenman and Moley put together the elements of an advisory body that would come to be called the "brain trust," the most important members of which were Rexford G. Tugwell, an agricultural economist at Columbia, and Adolf A. Berle, a professor at the Columbia Law School specializing in corporation law. Roosevelt had his own generous portion of political intelligence, and despite his wheelchair and his crutches, the millstone of aristocratic wealth, the splenetic opposition of the Tammany wing of the party and such party regulars as National Committee chairman John J. Raskob and Roosevelt's old mentor Alfred E. Smith, and in spite of charges and investigations of fraud and corruption in his administration that had eaten away at the fabric of his public image, he had engineered a campaign of primary and state caucus victories that stunned the party establishment and had given him a sure hold on a majority of delegates as the convention opened on June 27.

The handsome collection of committed delegates that FDR's people had placed on the floor of the convention, however, fell far short of the two-thirds majority necessary for the nomination, and there was substantial opposition to contend with. Neither among those at the convention nor among those on the outside looking on was Roosevelt universally admired, at least as a potential President. Back in 1920, when he heard that Roosevelt had been nominated for the Vice Presidency, Walter Lippmann had been delighted. "When cynics ask what is the use," he had wired the candidate, "we can answer that when parties can pick a man like Frank Roosevelt there is a decent future in politics." And Lippmann had been one of those who had urged Roosevelt to run for the governorship of New York in 1928. But by the time FDR emerged as a contender for the highest office in the land, the columnist had changed his mind. "I am now satisfied," he wrote his own choice, Newton Baker, in November 1931,

> that he just doesn't happen to have a very good mind, that he never really comes to grips with a problem which has any large dimensions, and that above all the controlling element in almost every case is political advantage. . . . I am convinced that he has never thought much, or understood much, about the great subjects which must concern the next president, about such matters as the tariff, foreign policy, taxation, currency and banking. He is best on certain questions of social welfare, old age pensions, and that kind of remedial legislation, but on the real problems of statesmanship, my impression, from many long talks in the last few years, is that he is a kind of amiable boy scout.

Less than two months later, he went public with his genteel contempt, noting in his newspaper column that FDR was "a pleasant man who, without any important qualifications for the office, would very much like to be President."

Lippmann was not alone in such sentiments (journalist Elmer Davis, for one, said that Roosevelt was "a man who thinks that the shortest distance between two points is not a straight line but a corkscrew"), and it did not help matters when FDR's people almost sabotaged their own hopes by making a badly bungled effort to get the two-thirds rule rescinded. As late as Thursday, June 30, Roosevelt's fate at the hands of the convention was still so uncertain that his workers were nearly beside themselves with frustration and exhaustion. Louie Howe could most often be found prostrate on the floor of his hotel room in front of an enormous electric fan, gagging for breath and (as he often seemed) apparently near total collapse. Down on the convention floor, Farley was on his feet but not much better off, at least as he remembered it six years later:

> It was Thursday afternoon, and we were back in the Chicago Stadium listening to nine presidential candidates being placed in nomination by speaker after speaker, who unloosed what can only be described as a merciless and unholy flood of oratory. The afternoon wore on; there was a recess; we returned to another session at night; and still the hours were consumed by the endless chain of nominating and seconding speeches, to the accompaniment of the din, the uproar, and the unseemly noise which characterized the customary "demonstrations" for favorite candidates. Before it was ended, the

delegates, the visitors, the campaign managers and workers, and even the candidates themselves were driven almost to distraction. I can hardly recall a more nerve-wracking experience in my long association in politics.

As the hours crawled on, Farley sent messengers to the other campaign headquarters offering to eliminate all of Roosevelt's seconding speeches if the remaining speakers for the other candidates would do the same. "I learned something on that occasion," he wrote, "that perhaps we should have known before: a thorough-going Democrat will give you his support, his loyalty, his vote, and his money—but never his radio time. When a Democratic orator has his throat cleared and ready, holds his manuscript in his hand, and knows the folks back home are there at the radio, it's too much to expect him to give way. Our appeal was in vain."

The first ballot consequently did not begin until 4:28 A.M. July 1. As expected, Roosevelt fell short of a two-thirds majority. On the second ballot, he gained 11½ votes, still not enough, and on the third, another five—still short. "On the night they took three ballots," Sam Rayburn, John Nance Garner's floor manager, remembered, "I was under the platform with Arthur Mullen, Burt Wheeler, and Cordell Hull and some others. It was 6 o'clock in the morning, and everybody was hot and sweaty. Nobody had shaved and a lot of people were drunk. I told them, 'If you want to nominate Roosevelt, you'd better recess this convention and let people have some conferences and so forth.' " Rayburn's advice was followed, for his power was considerable. From the beginning it had been clear that if Roosevelt could get the votes from Garner's Texas and California delegations (Garner had won California by primary election), it would be enough to put him over the top, and Farley had already offered FDR's support of Garner as the Vice-Presidential nominee if the Texan would agree to release his delegates. Garner had no particular desire for the job of Vice President, which in fluent Texan he had characterized as being worth about as much as a "bucket of warm spit" (though some accounts insist that the bucket in question actually held "warm piss"). Still, he wanted a Democrat for President, any Democrat, and it seemed likely that a continued deadlock might seriously damage the election chances of whoever might finally emerge as the candidate; during the recess he agreed to Farley's deal, and at three o'clock told Rayburn to inform all delegates committed to him. Early that evening the two delegations met to vote on the proposition, and after heated discussion ultimately acceded to pressure from Rayburn. The convention reconvened at 9:00 P.M. and the fourth roll call began. When California's turn came, delegation leader William Gibbs McAdoo asked leave to address the convention, went to the podium, and over a cacaphonous mix of boos and cheering shouted, "California came here to nominate a President of the United States. It did not come here to deadlock this convention. California casts forty-four votes for Franklin D. Roosevelt." What followed was one of the swiftest bandwagons in American political history, and at 10:32 P.M., FDR was declared the winner with 945 votes. Shortly afterward, a telegram read to the floor informed the convention that the candidate—who possessed an exquisitely tuned instinct for the moment—would be flying in from Albany the next day to accept the nomination and address the delegates, the first time any candidate had done such a thing.

The next morning, Garner was duly nominated and chosen as Roosevelt's running mate, and after a turbulent nine-hour plane ride from Albany that apparently left every passenger but the candidate shaken, FDR arrived in Chicago at 4:30 P.M. Hundreds of thousands of cheering, waving people lined the streets through which Roosevelt's car drove on the way to the Chicago Stadium, and the stadium itself was a caldron of noise, klieg lights, and cameras as he took the podium. "Roosevelt," remembered White House correspondent Bess Furman, "gripping the parallel bars of a little stall made to aid him in public speaking, held his massive shoulders high. His upflung head was a gesture of challenge. As I stood there close to him, his triumph over physical affliction was a tangible thing." Then the cultured, amplified tones of what would soon become, through the magic of radio and films, the most widely known and well-remembered political voice in the life of an entire generation boomed out over the sea of upturned faces:

> The appearance before a national convention of its nominee is unprecedented and unusual, but these are unprecedented and unusual times. I have started out in the tasks that lie ahead by breaking absurd tradition. . . . Never before in modern history have the essential differences between the two major parties stood out in such striking contrast as they do today. Republican leaders not only have failed in material things, they have failed in national vision. . . . Throughout the nation, men and women, forgotten in the political philosophy of the government of the last years, look to us for guidance and for a more equitable opportunity to share in the distribution of national wealth. . . . Those millions cannot and shall not hope in vain. I pledge you, I pledge myself, to a new deal for the American people.

CHAPTER

· 24 ·

Hung for a Secretary

T HERE WAS NO QUESTION as to which of the two candidates would get the vote of Harold Ickes. He had supported Cox and Roosevelt in 1920 and he would support Roosevelt and Garner in 1932. "I had been head over heels for the nomination of Franklin D. Roosevelt for President," he wrote in *Autobiography of a Curmudgeon.* "I had followed his career and thought highly of him, although I had never met him personally." He had nothing more ambitious in mind than the tendering of his vote, however, and when Basil Manly, a veteran of the various La Follette campaigns, came to him a few days after the convention and asked him to organize an independent Republican group to promote Roosevelt's effort, he declined. "I told him that . . . I was through with politics, except for an occasional foray into a local campaign that would interest me, when I became too bored with myself." There were two such entertainments on hand in 1932. First, he had agreed to take on the campaign of Democrat Thomas J. Courtney in his bid to be elected Illinois state's attorney. Second, he would again be managing the State Assembly reelection campaign of Anna, who remained a straight Republican, though with Progressive leanings.

Since he had the considerable weight of Mayor Tony Cermak's Democratic machine to back him up in what appeared to be a strong year for Democrats the country over, Ickes anticipated little trouble in getting

Courtney elected. The situation with regard to Anna was a little less certain. He and Charles S. Deneen, the old warhorse of the regular Republican machine, had long since worked out an accommodation that allowed them to function together when it was advantageous to both, and this had helped Anna in her 1928 and 1930 campaigns. After Ruth Hanna McCormick's brief moment of glory in 1930 when she had wrested the Republican Senate nomination from Deneen (only to lose the election), the former Senator had stitched up his wounds and by 1932 had reemerged as the Republican power to deal with in Chicago. But when Ickes went to him this time to get his endorsement of Anna, he found one William Busse standing in his way. This Busse, a power in Anna's district, apparently was no relation to the Fred Busse who had given Ickes and John Harlan so much grief in 1903 and had gone on to serve as Chicago's mayor from 1907 to 1911, but he displayed the same tender regard for Ickes and his political interests. The two men loathed each other, and during the slate-making caucus early in 1932, Busse opposed the endorsement of Anna on the grounds that she was a dry, and that the farmers in her district (whose man he was) were for the repeal of Prohibition. Under the circumstances, he maintained, Anna could not win either the nomination or the election this time around.

"Busse and I nearly came to blows," Ickes said in his unpublished political memoirs.

> I told him that he did not know what he was talking about; that Anna had always led her ticket and that she would do so again notwithstanding anything that he might do. . . . I had despised him and his type for years and I really welcomed the opportunity of giving him both barrels in the presence of Deneen and his lieutenants. I told him what a self-seeking, prevaricating, double-crossing person he was and that he had always been willing to betray Deneen or any one else for his own advantage. Busse was livid with rage before I was through with him.

After a battle that had smacked satisfyingly of the good old days, Anna lost the endorsement ("Deneen was not man enough" to stand up to Busse, Ickes said) but did in fact lead her ticket in the primaries and easily captured the nomination. So did Thomas J. Courtney for the Democrats.

These concerns were fully occupying his time and attention when attorney Roscoe Fertich came out from New York in mid-July to repeat Basil Manly's request, this time from a higher authority: the Democratic National Committee itself. Fertich was harder to put off, and after several days of persistent argument, Ickes finally was persuaded to organize and head up what they decided to call a Western Independent Republican

Committee for Roosevelt.* After he agreed to take on the job, Ickes made a quick trip to New York, where he met with James Farley, now the new chairman of the Democratic National Committee (he had been elected to replace John J. Raskob at the convention's end); Frank Walker, the Democratic treasurer; and Arthur F. Mullen, an intimate of Senator George Norris and an adviser to the National Committee on western matters. Mullen advanced Ickes's Western Committee two thousand dollars, and Ickes returned to Chicago to open up an office in the Auditorium Hotel.

Meanwhile, he not only had Anna's campaign to deal with but Anna herself. She did not look upon his new responsibility with any enthusiasm; in fact, she claimed it would embarrass her and damage her chances of election in November. He replied, he tells us in *Autobiography of a Curmudgeon*, that

> I had always been as irregular as a rail-and-rider fence built without line or plummet. I wouldn't surprise anyone unless I suddenly decided to be regular. Besides, I had my principles, such as they were. I assured her that she was bound to be elected in spite of hell and high water. I must follow out with exactness the irregular political course that I had charted for myself. I had been sort of a wobbly Republican from the first and had become wobblier with the years.

Given the history of these two, the discussion was probably not quite as civilized as this account suggests. In any case, Anna remained opposed until Ickes hit upon an idea that would mollify her: he promised that if Roosevelt was elected, he would ask to be made commissioner of Indian Affairs in the new administration.

By all accounts, this was the first time it had occurred to him to seek any kind of position in the national government, and it could hardly have been better calculated to gain Anna's endorsement. Next to her work in the statehouse in Springfield, the plight of the Indians, particularly of the Indians of the Southwest, remained the major interest in her life, and she had become thoroughly disenchanted with the Hoover administration's handling of the situation, founded, as it was, almost entirely on simplistic notions of assimilation as the solution to all problems. In *Conservation in the Department of the Interior*, Ray Lyman Wilbur, Secretary of the Interior, and his executive assistant, William Atherton Du Puy, had spelled it out with purblind assurance:

---

* When finally pieced together, Ickes's committee included representatives from Illinois, Indiana, Ohio, Michigan, Wisconsin, Iowa, Minnesota, South Dakota, Nebraska, and Kansas. Clearly, it would more accurately have been called the *Mid*western Independent Republican Committee for Roosevelt.

Recent and exhaustive investigations have found that many of the Indians on reservations are habitually idle, distressingly poor, and consequently undernourished. . . . The trouble, say the experts, is "their lack of adjustment to the social and economic conditions of the prevailing civilization which confronts them." They do not earn enough of the white man's money properly to keep themselves going. The Indian must therefore be given money earning work to do. He must be put to work at the white man's tasks. That will doubtless lead to his final transformation and assimilation.

Wilbur also advocated the rapid transfer of responsibility for the Indian to the individual states and for the eventual elimination of the Bureau of Indian Affairs, a strategy even his own commissioner, Charles J. Rhoades, did his best to ignore studiously.

Anna's concern had to do less with policy matters, however, than with the nasty reality of the survival of individual Indians—surrounded as they were by a culture that at the moment was having trouble feeding a lot of the people of its own "prevailing civilization." There are few accounts (and none from Harold) of the work she had been doing out in New Mexico since the early twenties, but on September 23, 1931, she outlined some of the difficulties she faced on the ground in an unusually long and evocative letter to Margaret Dreier Robins:

Our Indians are already suffering. We can usually manage to save the nursing babies in spite of the severe undernourishment of the mothers, but weaning time is a time of horror, not altogether because of ignorance but because the only food available is totally unfitted for babies. The dreadful school conditions are being relieved a little under Mr. Rhoades. I have been bitterly disappointed in his administration but the publicity given the school conditions has resulted in a little more food a day and better food. . . .

We need so many things that there is almost a comic side to our efforts. For instance I want dreadfully a "bean washer" and hope to get courage to ask Mr. McCormick to get us one for a reduced price. If the Indians in one valley could have this they could market their beans anywhere and get good prices. . . . Then to jump to the other end of my list, a medicine man whom I value highly and who lives many miles from here and also from the bean valley, thinks he would be happy ever after if he could have a buffalo tail! In his clan a buffalo tail is mighty medicine. I have written to Mr. Parker of Lincoln Park [the Chicago zoo] about this but his buffalo always die with their tails on and the hide is much less valuable without the tail.

The prospect of having her own husband in charge of the fate of "her" Indians must have been attractive indeed; Anna forthwith withdrew her objections to Harold's Democratic taint and he was free to pursue votes for Roosevelt across his ten-state sphere of influence. Later in the campaign, she also agreed to serve on the national committee of the National Progressive League, formed by Senator George Norris of Nebraska as a place for Republicans to hang their hats for FDR. In fact, though Ickes kept himself characteristically busy organizing the standard run of speeches and rallies and issuing the standard blizzard of news releases, there was little that needed to be done by him or anyone else to assure Roosevelt's victory—certainly not after July 28, when hysteria and arrogance came together in Washington to produce the Bonus Army riots as the grim capstone to the brief, tortured career of Herbert Hoover as President of the United States.

Ever since Congress had adjourned without passing legislation to give the veterans their bonus money, the situation in the various encampments of the "BEF" (Bonus Expeditionary Force, as the Bonus Army now was called) had been growing more and more tense. At least half the veterans had left the District, but as the moist weight of summer began to bear down, there still were anywhere from eight to ten thousand left, including several hundred women and children. And members of the Communist Party—only a few, but enough to keep things stirred up and to revive the same fears of violent revolution that had led to Attorney General A. Mitchell Palmer's anticommunist raids in 1919. To his credit, Hoover was not among those prone to hysteria, and he quietly supported the efforts of Washington's conscientious and fair-minded Superintendent of Police, Pelham D. Glassford, to keep things under control.

But on the morning of July 28, Glassford himself was pelted with bricks in a skirmish with a number of veterans resisting eviction from some downtown buildings under construction; later that same day, a veteran was shot and killed and another mortally wounded during another such fight, and by midafternoon it was feared that Glassford's force of several hundred policemen would not be enough to quell any further rioting. Shortly after 2:30 P.M., Secretary of War Patrick J. Hurley conveyed orders from Hoover to General Douglas MacArthur, army chief of staff. MacArthur and his troops, the order stated, were to "cooperate fully with the District of Columbia police force which is now in charge," and were to "surround the affected area," clearing it without delay and turning over all prisoners "to the civil authorities." The directive went on to say, "In your orders insist that any women and children who may be in the affected area be accorded every consideration and kindness. Use all humanity consistent with the due execution of this order."

What Hoover did not realize was that MacArthur believed firmly in the preposterous claim of a secret army intelligence report that "the first bloodshed by the Bonus Army at Washington is to be the signal for a communist uprising in all large cities thus initiating a revolution. The entire movement is stated to be under communist control, with branches being rapidly developed in commercial centers." He took the President's order of July 28 and interpreted it to suit his highest mission. This, as he explained to his skeptical adjutant, Major Dwight David Eisenhower, was to save the country from "incipient revolution in the air." MacArthur dressed himself in his flashiest uniform, complete with ribbons and medals from World War I, took to the "field," and led a battalion of infantry, a squadron of cavalry, one platoon of tanks, and one machine-gun unit against the BEF, using tear gas, clubs, sabers, and bayonets to drive the rock-throwing, stick-wielding "troops" of the Bonus Army out of the downtown area, across the Eleventh Street and Anacostia bridges (this latter in violation of a direct order from Hoover and Hurley telling him to stop there), then into the huge encampment on the Anacostia River where, with a final push, the Bonus Army was dispersed into the country-side after its tents and shacks had been set afire. By evening, MacArthur's soldiers had completed the burning of the camp so that no Bonus Marcher would be tempted to return and his helpless soldiers, MacArthur reported primly, would not be forced to "bivouac under the guns of traitors."

Remarkably, while hundreds were injured, only one person died as the result of MacArthur's callous insubordination—a child who apparently succumbed to the effects of tear gas—but the political repercussions were such that he might as well have killed dozens.

Even though Hoover made (for him) an astonishingly bellicose campaign effort as the end drew near, the Bonus Army imbroglio added one more grotesque burden to an administration already sinking under the weight of circumstance and stupidity. On November 8, Roosevelt captured 22,815,530 popular votes and 472 electoral votes, winning forty-two states and beating Hoover by a little over seven million votes—almost precisely the margin by which Harding and Coolidge had beaten Cox and Roosevelt twelve years earlier. It was, Ickes said, "a great and glorious end," and he had a good deal to cheer about besides Roosevelt's victory: both Anna and Thomas J. Courtney had won, too; it was the first clean sweep for Ickes in his long political life.*

* He undoubtedly would have enjoyed writing Raymond Robins a triumphant "I told you so" letter at this point, since Robins, by now a firm Republican in his domestic politics, was a Hoover man. In September, near the end of a speaking tour in support of Prohibition, Robins had vanished. In the wake of the infamous kidnapping and murder of the Lindbergh baby the previous March, newspapers immediately broadcast speculations that Robins had been ab-

ꊛꊛꊛꊛ

There now ensued one of the most Byzantine quadrilles of all in a career that already had been marked by some notably complicated turns. Among other things, this dance highlighted the alarming tendency toward cannibalism that so often sapped the strength of the righteous and it centered on Ickes's struggle to become part of the Roosevelt administration as commissioner of Indian Affairs.

It began straightforwardly enough (at least on the surface) immediately after the election, when Charles de Young Elkus, an attorney from San Francisco, stopped by Ickes's office in the State Bank Building while on a visit to Chicago. He and Ickes had become acquainted through work in the American Indian Defense Association (Elkus was president of the northern California chapter of the AIDA), so he was a logical choice to be among the first to be told of his fellow attorney's ambitions. He received the news enthusiastically and promised to try to get Hiram Johnson's active support for Ickes when he returned to San Francisco. Elkus did consult with Johnson, who apparently approved of the idea but declined to make any overt suggestion to Roosevelt at that time. Elkus also informed John Collier, executive secretary of the AIDA and, as noted earlier, an occasional combatant with Ickes over Indian matters. In his own memoirs (written near the end of a long life and with many axes to grind), Collier said, "At the top of my list was Harold L. Ickes, who had been an able and vigorous champion of the Indian cause. And Ickes wanted the job. The only question I can recall coming up as to Ickes for Indian Commissioner, was whether he would be capable of the infinite patience which I knew an Indian Commissioner must exercise."

Unhappily, about the only truth in that statement was that Ickes wanted the job. Ickes was not only *not* at the top of Collier's list of candidates for the position, he was not even at the bottom of it; Collier was plainly appalled at the idea, and while he did not tell Elkus of his feelings for fear they would get back to Ickes, he did unburden himself in a swift

---

ducted and rubbed out by bootleggers. Ickes himself doubted this. "All I can say," he wrote William Allen White on September 23, "is that the friends who have known him the longest and most intimately discount the murder and kidnapping theories. My own guess is that something snapped inside his head. My daughter Frances is positive that she saw him in Adams Street near State Street the afternoon before the newspapers carried news of his disappearance. Of course this might be a case of mistaken identity, but she certainly knows Raymond. . . . She said he looked very badly which was the reason why she did not stop and speak to him." Three months later, Raymond was found living in North Carolina under another name. It was several months before he fully recovered his senses, and to this day no one knows the full details of his disappearance.

letter to Stella M. Atwood of the southern California chapter of the AIDA. Ickes would not do at all, Collier said, for "his personal idiosyncracies unfit him for the task which requires considerateness of co-workers, subordinates, cooperation with Congress and subordination of egotism." In another letter, this one to Lewis Meriam, a Brookings Institution economist and author of a 1928 book, *The Problem of Indian Administration*, he reiterated his objections, noting that Ickes was "personally impracticable, while as for his record in Indian matters, he has none." The fact was, Collier quite logically wanted the job for himself, or if he could not get it, for someone he could pretty generally control (which certainly would not include Ickes), and he had been working toward that end with political connections of his own ever since Roosevelt's nomination. To that effort he now would have to add attempts to head off Ickes's own bid for the position.

Ickes, of course, knew nothing (and never would learn) of Collier's efforts to sabotage his quest when he received word from Elkus that Collier had met with Senator Bronson Cutting and that the two of them had come up with the idea of promoting Ickes for the job of first assistant secretary of the interior, a more prestigious position that, not incidentally, would remove Harold as a contender for the slot Collier was after for himself. The idea understandably intrigued Ickes and he hopped on a train immediately when Collier invited him to Washington in December for a meeting with himself, Meriam, and Nathan Margold, a young protégé of Felix Frankfurter at the Harvard Law School and legal counsel to the American Civil Liberties Union on minority problems (including those of the Indian). By the time Ickes returned to Chicago a few days later, Collier was convinced that he had talked the office seeker out of pursuing the Bureau of Indian Affairs job and had turned him solidly toward the assistant secretaryship. He was partly right; what he did not yet know was that, after consulting with Hiram Johnson, Bronson Cutting, and a few others, Ickes had decided to go all out for the top job— that of Secretary of the Interior—though not quite so abruptly as he described in *Autobiography of a Curmudgeon*: "The notion came to me that if, for the first time in my life, I should go out for anything, I might just as well try to become Secretary of the Interior. It would be no more painful or fatal to be hung for a secretary than for a commissioner."

This, of course, was cabinet-level stuff and there were plenty of those who may have told him he was presumptuous to dream of getting it. Perhaps, but as he began to tick off to himself his qualifications for the job—as he almost certainly would have done—it must have seemed to him that he was at least as solid a candidate as anyone else he knew. He had a long acquaintance with the principles of conservation as injected into the bloodstream of the Progressive movement by such as Theodore Roosevelt and Gifford Pinchot, together with a decent respect for the value of public resources on the public lands. He had, too, a powerful affection for the beauties of the American landscape that had been instilled in him as a boy playing in the runs and hollows and woods of Pennsylvania and enlarged by a number of trips west to experience the splendors of Yellowstone, Glacier, and other national parks, the "crown jewels" of the nation's public lands system, at a time when few Americans of any kind and almost no politicians at all comprehended their full glory. He had an informed interest in the question of public power—not just power for the cities, but such region-wide proposals as the Muscle Shoals project in Tennessee, put forward with stubborn persistence by Senator George Norris year after year and just as stubbornly resisted by the kind of private utility interests Ickes had been fighting most of his public life. There was, of course, his longtime and even better-informed interest in Indian matters, which were part of Interior and which had brought him to this point in the first place. And if his bureaucratic experience was limited, he had demonstrated through one political campaign after another an uncommon skill at shuffling time, people, and priorities, administering a multitude of often conflicting elements and guiding them toward a single goal—not always successfully, but never incompetently. Finally, if there was any fifty-eight-year-old man in the United States of America who knew how to work harder than Harold LeClair Ickes of Chicago, he would have liked to have met him.

Such an evaluation of his own talents probably would have been a little exaggerated—but not by much, and his opinion would have been shared to a greater or lesser degree by many who knew him. He did qualify for the position. But so did Hiram Johnson and Bronson Cutting, in the opinion of the President-elect, and it was to these two that Roosevelt first offered the job. Johnson declined immediately, but to Ickes's sorrow did not put forward his old protégé's name as a possibility. Cutting tried to turn the job down, but Roosevelt asked him to think about it for a while before making a final decision and Cutting agreed. And there matters rested for weeks. No Progressive to whom Ickes turned, no matter how approving of his goal, was willing to interfere, and by the end of January he had just about given up the dream. "It was, of course," he lamented to Hiram Johnson on January 30, just a little over four weeks before the inauguration, "too much for me to hope that there was any chance of me realizing my ambition to be Secretary of the Interior. . . . Luck has never broken my way in political matters, but on the whole I have been content

Harold LeClair Ickes in April 1896, aged twenty-two and still going by the nickname of "Clair." This handsome, though damaged, portrait probably was done by his high school chum, Henry Adkinson. (*Harold McEwen Ickes*)

At the top left of this page is the farmhouse of Ickes's grandfather, Seth McCune, photographed in 1935. It was here that both Ickes and his mother were born; the people in front are unidentified. (*Blair County Historical Society*) At top right is young Clair himself, looking worried and a little irritated even at the age of four. (*Harold McEwen Ickes*) Below left is Mattie Ickes, the boy's mother, at sixteen, shortly before her marriage to the footloose Jessie. (From *Autobiography of a Curmudgeon*) Directly left is Jessie Boone Williams Ickes, the boy's father, ornamented with his volunteer fireman's badge. (*Harold McEwen Ickes*)

The Ickes's little house on Fifth Avenue, Altoona, probably in 1885. At left is sister Amelia (also known as Mary), in the middle is sister Julia, and at the right is brother John. (*Harold McEwen Ickes*)

Above is a scene along Eleventh Avenue, Altoona, in 1883. (*Blair County Historical Society*) The big-eyed child at the left is our hero, shown here in his new high school graduation suit, furnished through the infuriating but unavoidable generosity of his uncle Sam McCune. (*Harold McEwen Ickes*)

At the top is the University of Chicago campus as seen from the great Ferris Wheel of the World's Columbian Exposition, 1893. Directly above, sitting on the right, Ickes managed to appear both wistful and vaguely sardonic in a sitting with the other "Chicago Representatives in the Iowa Debate." (Both, *University of Chicago Archives*)

Looking appropriately high-minded, Ickes poses for his first college portrait, probably taken sometime in 1895. (*Harold McEwen Ickes*)

Anna Wilmarth, the object of Ickes's youthful desire. "She was said to be the richest girl in college," he remembered forty years later. (*Ann Ickes Carroll*)

Triangulations: Above, Harold, Anna, and young Wilmarth at Martha's Vineyard in the brief period before Anna's first marriage collapsed; at right, Anna, baby Wilmarth, and James Westfall Thompson, reluctant father and indifferent husband—and soon to be relieved of both responsibilities. (Both, *Ann Ickes Carroll*)

Overleaf: A bird's-eye view of the business district of Chicago—the Loop—in 1893. (*Chicago Historical Society*)

Directly left: Anna, Wilmarth, and the golden-tressed Frances in a moment at 5747 Washington Street. (*Ann Ickes Carroll*) Bottom left: Mary Wilmarth, the infant Raymond, and Anna in the garden of the Evanston house, 1913. (*Raymond Ickes*) Bottom right: Harold decked out in his tailored YMCA uniform, ready for the worst World War I could offer. (*Elizabeth Ickes*)

Opposite, in a more peaceful mode, he poses with Raymond at about the age of three. (*Raymond Ickes*)

The streetside politician and habitué of the ward halls and lawyers' offices in which the protocols of Chicago's civic life were forged sits (fourth from left) with apparent ease upon a horse somewhere in the West in 1908; the photograph probably was taken on one of his excursions into Yellowstone National Park. (*Ann Ickes Carroll*)

Above, Ickes resides at the center of the web, running Theodore Roosevelt's Cook County campaign from a desk in Chicago; the pin in his lapel, appropriately enough, is that of a bull moose. (*Harold McEwen Ickes*) At the right is the Bull Moose candidate's running mate, Hiram Johnson, seen here with Ickes sometime in the 1920s, when all the fine Progressive dreams were done. (*Elizabeth Ickes*)

Above: Harold and Anna locked in gentle combat on the patio of her adobe house outside Coolidge, New Mexico, 1930. (*Ann Ickes Carroll*) Left: The house in Hubbard Woods, 1930. (*Raymond Ickes*)

Both of these portraits of domestic tranquillity were taken in 1930 in the Hubbard Woods house. Above, following family tradition, Harold reads "'T'was the Night Before Christmas" on Christmas Eve; left to right: Anna, Wilmarth, Frances, Harold, Raymond, and Robert. At the right is a photograph worth at least a thousand words. (Both, *Raymond Ickes*)

Harold LeClair Ickes, March 2, 1933, cleaning out his desk and stuffing his briefcase in preparation for departure to Washington, D.C. (*The Franklin D. Roosevelt Memorial Library*)

to labor in the ranks and do what I could for the common good." As far as he knew, FDR had never heard of him.

But Roosevelt had. Sometime between nomination and election, Rexford G. Tugwell and Roosevelt had engaged in a long conversation that would have startled Ickes had he known of it—and probably would have irritated him as well. Roosevelt, Tugwell was to write,

> showed real concern about a third group now being identified in the press. These were professed supporters of his own cause who had met recently at the call of Senator George Norris and had organized as a National Progressive League. Producing a clipping that described the meeting, he called attention to the names. Besides Norris, there were Bainbridge Colby, Amos Pinchot, William Draper Lewis, Francis Henry, Ray Stannard Baker, Felix Frankfurter, and Harold Ickes. . . . It was an honor roll, he said, from old wars. This fellow Ickes, he had heard, had tried to persuade them last spring that they ought to endorse Gifford Pinchot for another third-party presidential run. . . . Nothing had come of it; most of them were disillusioned by now, knowing that victory by any third party was most unlikely. . . .
>
> He went on to say a good deal more about the old progressives. . . . They were a wonderful people, but they did have the general characteristic of complete unreliability. They were individualists who never really granted leadership to anyone. . . . What it said in the *Times*—he referred to the clipping—was that they had gone to this Washington meeting at Norris' call, and that the Senator reported for them, when it was over, that what this country needed was another Roosevelt in the White House. He would be happier about that, Roosevelt said, if he didn't recall that when there had been a man of that name in the White House, the progressives had found him unsatisfactory, or many of them had. They could never be counted on for support. Besides, the bonds holding them together were weak.

In spite of this combination of contempt, insight, and rank misinformation, Roosevelt knew that he needed the "old progressives" if his administration's programs were to have the wide support necessary for anything to get done in Congress. That was why he had offered the Interior post to Johnson and then to Cutting, and why he continued to wait for Cutting's answer as the year turned and the weeks dragged closer to inauguration. It was also why he and Raymond Moley decided to include two Progressives on a team to discuss the international economic situation in February. To this end, Moley called Johnson, Cutting, and Senator Robert M. La Follette, Jr.—"Young Bob," who had moved into the Wisconsin Senate seat on the death of his father in 1925. He asked them to confer and come up with two names. They did, and one of the names they offered was that of Ickes. "I discussed this with Louis Howe," Moley remembered, "and he growled in his characteristic way, 'There isn't any such name as Ickes. There must be some mistake.' But there was such a name and I reached him on the telephone. I asked him to come to New York for conferences . . . on February 21."*

"Of course I could," Ickes says he responded. And in one last grasp at Secretary of the Interior, he decided to stop off for a day or two in Washington on his way to New York to see what was up. "I called on Senator Cutting one Sunday afternoon at his home," he recalled in yet another of his unpublished memoirs, "to learn that he had seen Roosevelt again . . . and had definitely declined the invitation to go into the Cabinet as Secretary of the Interior. I also learned that, as was the case with . . . Johnson, he had not been asked to make a suggestion and therefore did not feel at liberty to do so." He had a desultory dinner with Hiram Johnson and his wife that night, and the next day, feeling increasingly desperate, he sent identical telegrams to Newton Jenkins, Gifford Pinchot, and Donald Richberg: "Am persuaded Roosevelt wants to appoint Progressive and leading Progressive Senators, notably Johnson and Cutting are prepared to urge me if Roosevelt asks them for suggestions. Would appreciate it if you feel like wiring promptly both Roosevelt and Moley suggesting me as Progressive possibility and particularly urging that Progressive Senators referred to be consulted." Pinchot wired back his regrets, but Jenkins did as he asked (although nothing in the record suggests that either Roosevelt or Moley ever saw his telegram). Richberg apparently wired only Moley and did so without mentioning Ickes's name, merely informing the doubtless puzzled brain-truster in a vague fashion that he was available for consultation should Roosevelt wish to contact him.

Pinchot, Ickes always suspected, was after some sort of cabinet position himself and did not want to queer his chances. Richberg explained his own strange actions in a long, stiff-necked letter to Ickes several days later, saying that Ickes's telegram had "in effect asked me to take myself entirely out of the cabinet picture so that you might put yourself in" and "placed me in a very difficult position." Ickes scratched a furious "Hooey!" at the bottom of Richberg's letter and promptly dictated a memorandum for posterity that noted particularly that the only positions for which Richberg had ever been mentioned were those of Attorney General and Secretary of Labor and that he had not sent his telegram until it was general knowledge that these jobs had gone to Senator Tom Walsh and Frances Perkins, respectively.

---

*It was not long before this date, it should be noted, that FDR had nearly been shot—very like his cousin Theodore in 1916. While in Miami on February 15, he had attended a rally of American Legionnaires and a crazed Italian bricklayer by the name of Anthony Zangara attempted to assassinate him. He missed Roosevelt but got Chicago's mayor, Anton Cermak.

Six months earlier, Ickes had not even known he wanted this job; now he wanted it possibly more than anything he had ever wanted in his life, and it seemed to be slipping away from him in spite of his best, his most frantic efforts. Not even knowing exactly what he had in mind, he wandered over to the Capitol Building Monday afternoon and ran into Roscoe Fertich. Ickes was spilling his woes to the patient Fertich when Arthur H. Mullen, who had financed the opening of an office for the Western Independent Republican Committee, came into view and Fertich suggested they talk to him about Ickes's problems. Mullen listened with equal patience and gave it as his opinion that Ickes would make a fine Secretary of the Interior. More important, he agreed to call Roosevelt and tell him so. The three men got into a cab and went to Democratic National Headquarters, where Mullen put through a call to New York. The President-elect was not available, but Mullen scheduled another call for seven that night.

By then, Ickes was on his way to New York and never did learn whether Mullen got through to Roosevelt, though he later believed he must have. From his hotel the next morning (the Roosevelt Hotel, appropriately enough), Ickes called Moley, who came over to get him and took him to FDR's Manhattan home on East Sixty-fifth Street, where Roosevelt and the economic conferees were gathering in the second-floor library. "We had all been standing," Ickes remembered,

> and as I started to sit down the President-elect said "Is Mr. Ickes here?" I made my presence known. Then followed a short conference. . . . As a matter of fact, a good deal of the discussion was well over my head. I said nothing at all during the conference although Bernard M. Baruch . . . and one or two others had some remarks to make. I observed during the conference that Roosevelt kept eyeing me closely but I thought nothing of it. At the conclusion . . . we all filed around Roosevelt's chair to shake hands with him and bid him goodby. I was at the head of the stairs about to go down to the ground floor when one of his secretaries came out and asked me if I were Mr. Ickes. He told me that the "Governor" would like me to wait until he had finished a little talk with Mr. Baruch. After he was through with Baruch I was taken into Mr. Roosevelt's study. He invited me to sit down in a chair close to him and then he said to me, in substance: "Mr. Ickes I want to ask your advice. You and I have been speaking the same language for the last twenty years and we have the same outlook on affairs. I am having difficulty in finding a Secretary of the Interior. I offered it to Johnson and Cutting but they both declined. I particularly want a western man. Above all other things, I want a man who is honest and who knows how to say 'No.' I have about come to the conclusion that the man I want is Harold L. Ickes of Chicago."

Harold L. Ickes of Chicago was momentarily stunned, he tells us, stunned apparently to the point of incoherence even in memory of the moment: "All during my life I had had to work very hard and what I got out of life for surprise awards such as this had been few and far between. Of course, there had never been anything like this."

Roosevelt told him that he still had not completely made up his mind and would have to talk to a few other people about him, including Johnson and Cutting, but that Moley would call him at seven that night at his hotel and tell him the decision. "I was as nervous as could be the rest of that day," Ickes remembered. He went to a movie in the afternoon to get his mind off the long hours until seven. Charles E. Merriam, his old on-again, off-again ally in the urban struggles of Chicago, also was staying at the hotel, as it happened, and took Ickes to a speakeasy of his acquaintance, where he had a "badly needed" cocktail, followed by "a delicious dinner with a bottle of excellent imported French wine." Back at the hotel, it was not until sometime between seven-thirty and eight o'clock that Moley finally called, and even then it was only to say that he would be by shortly to pick Ickes up.

"On the way up to 65th Street, Moley did not say in so many words that my going into the Cabinet was a settled thing, although I was justified in concluding that it was," Ickes continued in his unpublished memoirs, which remain the best source we have for this crossroads of his life.

> However, my nervousness did not diminish. Shortly after I reached the President-elect's house I was taken to the second floor to a large room where people were coming and going, including Jim Farley whom I thus met for the second time. Shortly I was shown into Roosevelt's study. Frances Perkins, to whom I had been introduced on the first floor, was there ahead of me. After asking whether we had met each other, the President remarked in that wonderfully gracious manner that he had: "It is nice to have the Secretary of Labor meet the Secretary of the Interior here tonight."

So it was done—not quickly and not well ("one of the most casual appointments to a Cabinet position in American history," Moley called it). But done. Ickes returned to Chicago the next day, February 22. The inauguration was scheduled for March 4, just eleven days away, and there was much to be done and not much time left in which to do it. Anna, it was decided, would come to Washington only for necessary ceremonies, returning to Illinois until the expiration of her State Assembly term in 1934. She would not run for a fourth term. Harold would take a suite of rooms in the Mayflower Hotel on Connecticut Avenue in Washington until they were ready to rent or buy a home in the area. Raymond would continue to live in Hubbard Woods while attending the University of Chicago and Robert would stay with him when on leave from his studies at Lake Forest College. Harold would close his law office in the State Bank Building permanently. May Conley, his secretary since 1912, had decided that she could not leave her mother; she would stay behind in another job Ickes had obtained for her (although she would join him again after her mother's death).

There was no celebration in Winnetka, Raymond remembers. Everyone in the family was very pleased with the appointment, but there was no celebration, no champagne or frivolity. There should have been. There should have been delight, exuberance, enthusiasm, friends and relatives crowding in to the great hall of the house. There should have been an excitement to match the distance of the journey the new Secretary of the Interior had made from the little house on Fifth Avenue in Altoona, from the grime and cacophony of the railroad yards, from the disgrace of a drunken father, from poverty, exhaustion, obsession, loneliness, desperation, duty, pain, and the haunted stones in Fairview Cemetery. All his life he had fought to *participate* in the world around him, to have that world embrace him, take him in, listen to him, respect him, even—though he would never admit it—love him. He once had expressed pleasure in being what he called "the spider at the center of the web." Now he would be at—or at least near—the center of the most important web in the world. There should have been a measure of joy taken in the survival and the triumph.

There should have been some note of melancholy, too, some sadness mixed in with the uncelebrated satisfaction. If something was beginning, something also was ending. The house in Hubbard Woods, for instance. It is fair to say that he had loved three things above all others in his life so far: his mother, his son, Raymond, and the house in Hubbard Woods, the house he had brought into being with such intensity that sometimes it may have seemed to him that he had nailed it together with his own hands, the house whose gardens he had planted with an artist's eye for all the colors of life, the house that once, briefly, had held what there was left of hope in a dimming and bitter marriage. Now he would be leaving it, and something in him must have known he would never live there again.

And there should have been sadness for the city, too, that great, noisy, wounded beast of a place to which he had given so much of . . . something. If not love, call it a devoted fascination, a furious affection that demanded from it all the best it had to give, and when it failed him, demanded it again and again. As the brave buildings of the Century of Progress were readied for opening day that coming summer, he must have known that he would never live in this city again, either.

There should have been some of all of this in the face that comes down to us from this moment, the only one we have from this moment. It is in a UPI photograph. He is in his office for the last time, standing in shirt-sleeves at his desk and stuffing a briefcase full of papers. There should be something there that we can see, but there isn't. The face is preoccupied, busy, cannot be read. Harold L. Ickes has a train to catch.

BOOK
T·W·O

In a Kingdom of Priests

1933–1952

*I sometimes wonder, as I cross this enormous land, if a sort of grisly
game is not going on; if the land is not destroying the people who inhabit
it as the people who inhabit it are destroying the land. A magic
continent, a peculiar treasure, stuffed with riches, millions in it are
starving in the midst of plenty. Slash down the forests, drain the rivers,
till the land and let it lie there turning to destructive dust. Perhaps that
still small voice that could be heard above the sound of the meadow lark
is drowned out now by the iron-throated machines. Or perhaps in this
quivering electric continent no one listens now. Yet the words are there,
so clear if we pause to hear. Now, therefore, if ye will obey my voice
indeed, and keep my covenant, then ye shall be a peculiar treasure unto
me above all people; for all the earth is mine; and ye shall be unto me a
kingdom of priests and an holy nation.*

—Edna Ferber, *A Peculiar Treasure,* 1939

PART VI

Power and Authority

If this administration plan of the President goes through, it will mean that instead of having less power, I will have greater power and will really outrank all the other men. . . . This will be a surprise to a good many people who have been proclaiming that I was to have a back seat and an inconspicuous part in the new program. It is a surprise to me, too.

—from the *Diary*, April 21, 1935

CHAPTER
· 25 ·

"What Has This Man to Say to Us Today?"

W HEN HAROLD, Anna, Raymond, and Robert pulled up in front of
the Mayflower Hotel in a pair of cabs the afternoon of Friday, March
3, 1933, it was a bleak and snowless urban landscape that offered itself,
the naked limbs of pin oaks and red oaks etching random black lines
against a gray sky along Connecticut Avenue. It had been a hard winter
for trees as for people. Forecasts called for sunny skies to brighten the
inauguration on Saturday, but there was little now to indicate that
possibility. In Washington, as elsewhere, winter seemed to be a permanent condition that year, and city-room philosophers were not averse to
drawing comparisons with the nation's moribund economic state, which
had degenerated steadily since the brief "recovery" of early 1930.

In Washington, however, some citizens apparently held more regard
for trees than for people. On February 19 the *Washington Herald* had
reported the results of a meeting of the Federation of Citizens' Associations, which had by a vote of fifty-seven to fifteen affirmed its opposition
to a congressional bill authorizing the city to borrow $2.5 million from
the Reconstruction Finance Corporation for the relief of the destitute.
Since the same federation recently had approved a huge loan to expand the
city's parkland, the *Herald* reporter noted, this decision amounted to a
declaration: "Sixteen million for the purchase of parkland, but not one
cent of borrowed money to feed the starving." The federation also decided,

the story went on, that "any special relief necessary to care for the starving and needy in Washington could be provided by the new Congress."

In truth, Washington was singularly proud of its greenery, having, some would have said, precious little else to brag about. It called itself "The City of Trees," a sobriquet it had been able to seize upon largely because of the benign dictatorship of Alexander Robey ("Boss") Shepherd in the 1870s. In 1871 Congress—under whose rule the District of Columbia was governed—had instituted a territorial form of government, concluding that the old mayor-council structure had encouraged corruption and slipshod administration. The cumbersome new government included a governor, a Board of Public Works, a legislative council of eleven members, a legislative body of twenty-two members, and one voteless delegate to Congress. Shepherd, a local builder, became vice president and executive officer of the Board of Public Works (and later, very briefly, governor of the city). Believing in civic betterment, Shepherd immediately set about bettering things with more enthusiasm than regard for the niceties of governance. He laid sewers, paved streets, built parks, installed water systems, erected streetlights. And planted trees, perhaps as many as sixty thousand trees—maples, poplars, lindens, elms, sycamores, ashes, oaks, and more. In a little over two years he effectively transformed much of the city, while putting it $22 million in debt. Concluding that the territorial form of government had encouraged at the least slipshod administration, in 1874 Congress abolished the office of governor and instituted a commission to run the city (Shepherd was not invited to participate). Four years later, with the Organic Act of 1878, Congress moved again, setting the District up as a municipal corporation.

Both corruption and slipshod administration had remained, of course, since this was a major American city. But so had the trees. By 1915, *National Geographic,* a hometown publication, could describe Washington as a city "where a mighty forest is growing in the midst of metropolitan life," and in 1932 civic hagiographer Earle Kauffman declared: "Today in Washington the visitor may find more than two thousand varieties of trees and shrubs, representing nearly two hundred distinct species. It holds . . . more different kinds of trees and shrubs than any city on earth."

That may have been, but the "mighty forest" was looking pretty thin in the last week of February and the first week of March, 1933, too thin to shield effectively the fact that for all its shrubbery and institutional architecture the nation's capital city was an urban planner's nightmare, giving weight to its reputation as a place that combined northern hospitality with southern efficiency. Just three years later, the great WPA guide, *Washington: City and Capital,* would render a critical description that could have been applied to the city at almost any period of its history, and certainly in 1933:

> The noble scheme of a Federal city, created as an entity, falls asunder; and the grand avenues of L'Enfant seem more significant on paper than in reality. Flanked by impressive edifices near the center, they proceed uncompromisingly toward the outskirts, often through humdrum and desultory regions, where staid Government employees contrive to pass the less august half of their lives. Even squalor lurks close to the Capitol. The effect is incongruous and depressing. . . . When the Capital should have afforded an example of excellence in the design and disposition of its living quarters, it serves instead to emphasize once more the unapproachable dignity of government, and the dominance of institutions over men.

The people on whom institutional dominance rested most heavily, of course, were black; there were a little over 132,000 black people in Washington in 1930, and while this number represented only 27.1 percent of the city's total population of nearly 487,000, it was the poorest and most powerless portion. A handful of these had managed to gain precarious footholds in the Negro middle class, but most were agonizingly poor, many of them jammed into the narrow, fetid slums that had been created throughout the central city when landlords discovered the profit to be made by converting backyard gardens into tenements in the years following the Civil War. These were the infamous alley dwellings of Washington, the Capital's "Secret City" about which popular guidebooks and Board of Trade publications had nothing to say in spite of the fact that hundreds of heatless, lightless, waterless, and toiletless houses and apartments were tucked cunningly into urban crannies within crawling distance of some of the principal institutional landmarks of the city, not excluding the White House. Washington's blacks were also daily reminded that the nation's capital was a southern town, segregation being maintained with almost the same rigidity there as anywhere in the South. "Whites Only" and "No Colored" signs sprouted like angry flowers throughout the city, and where there were no signs there were understandings that were not challenged by any black person without risk. Only in the reading rooms of the public library and the Library of Congress, on trolleys and buses, or in Griffith Stadium, where all were welcome to watch the Senators lose, were black people allowed to share space with white. "Long live King Baseball, the only monarch who recognizes no color line," an editorial in the black newspaper, the *Daily American,* had proclaimed in 1924. (The reference was to the stadium, of course, not the sport, which was segregated with Draconian inflexibility.)

Depression recognized no color line either, but the racial indifference of fate was little comfort to Washington's black community. It was hurting, as was the entire city. For a time, it had seemed that Washington might escape the worst effects of the economic disaster, largely because of a massive public-buildings construction effort that had been set in motion by Calvin Coolidge, of all people, in a message to Congress in December 1925. Congress had responded with the Public Buildings Act of May 25, 1926, which called for the construction of an enormous complex of government offices called the Federal Triangle along Constitution Avenue (then B Street) and Pennsylvania Avenue between Sixth and Fourteenth streets, which included new buildings for the Department of Commerce, the Bureau of Internal Revenue, the National Archives, and the Department of Labor, among others. Later plans for this and other areas of the District would add new buildings for the Department of Agriculture and the Supreme Court, an addition to the House Office Building, and such other oddments as completion of the Tomb of the Unknown Soldier, a National Arboretum, development of Union Station Plaza, and improvement of the Mall.

By 1931, however, only the buildings for the Federal Triangle and the Department of Agriculture and new wings for the Smithsonian's Museum of Natural History had been authorized. While these projects indisputably swelled the numbers of the employed, many of the laborers were from outside the District (including hundreds of black workers imported from areas of the Deep South, where paycheck expectations were even lower than in Washington), and these government construction efforts could not quite make up for the decline in private building, investment in which had fallen from nearly $48 million in 1929 to less than $35 million by the end of 1930. Faced by continuing and increasingly visible poverty, Congress in February 1931 had authorized another $8 million for the building program, adding to the scheme schools, street paving, water mains, sewers, and bridges. For the rest of 1931 and through the spring of 1932, things had been looking up: somewhere between nine thousand and ten thousand new jobs had been filled, and the city was punctuated everywhere by the reassuring clatter and bustle of construction work.

The respite did not last. Even as the thousands of Bonus Army marchers had begun to filter into Washington in June 1932, the federal budget ax was preparing to fall. It came down on July 1, and the cuts devastated this company town—salaries were pared, obligatory furloughs were instituted, reductions in force (RIFs, one of the oldest and least loved of Washington's agglomeration of acronyms) affected every department of government, and Hoover announced plans to cut another $700 million from the following year's budget. One estimate has calculated that the federal budget cuts for that year directly affected one family out of every three in the city. Indirectly, the cuts sapped the income of local businesses, forcing scores into failure, including four major banks. The budget for the District stipulated $350,000 for local relief, but that had to be augmented by another $625,000 by the end of the year. Even that was not enough; with tens of thousands now unemployed, the amount of welfare money a single family could receive was limited to one hundred dollars a year—and even that mite was so burdened with restrictions that only a portion of the needy could receive it. Some three thousand people suffering from malnutrition and diseases related to inadequate diet were admitted to the already overcommitted facilities of Gallinger Hospital, and Freedman's Hospital experienced a similar load. Private attempts to deal with misery on such a scale were bravely earnest. Vegetable gardens were planted in vacant lots; old clothes and shoes were collected, repaired, and distributed; the *Washington Herald* spearheaded a school lunch program. The Community Chest drive for 1932 went all out, but could not make its goal. The Board of Trade, on February 23, inaugurated a "Renovize Washington" campaign by appointing a five-man committee to undertake a survey of the city to encourage homeowners to renovate their dwellings with labor provided by the army of the unemployed and with low-interest loans of five hundred dollars from a pool of $500,000 established by the District Bankers' Association; the Board of Trade estimated that as many as twenty-five thousand people could be at least temporarily employed in such a campaign, but nothing much ever came of it.

Nothing much seemed to come of anything, and as inauguration day approached, frustration and helplessness fed anger and cynicism in Washington, just as it did in much of the rest of the country. "I am not bitter about losing my home," an anonymous letter writer told Betty Norwell in her "Federal Merry-Go-Round" column for the *Washington Herald*. "I realize the real estate men of Washington are not in business for their health, and if they want to put the screws on at a time like this, that is their privilege. However, I have lost all love of country, and I don't teach my children patriotism. I couldn't teach a child who has been evicted from his home patriotism. . . . There must be many like myself, not Communists; just American citizens whose government doesn't give a damn about them." Members of Congress doubtless would have argued that they cared deeply. Just as certainly, the letter writer would have remembered that members of both houses recently had solemnly voted against any salary cuts for themselves and would not have been surprised that when the House adjourned *sine die* on Friday, March 3, it had not provided the District of Columbia with an appropriation for the upcoming fiscal year. Nor would it have improved his frame of mind when most of Washington's banks joined thousands across the country that same March 3 for a "bank holiday," closing their doors to business until further notice. In part of the business community, at least, there seemed to be some doubt whether many of the country's banks would ever reopen; the Washington Hotel Association, for instance, had posted notices on reservation desks all over the city to the effect that "Members find it necessary that, due to unsettled banking conditions throughout the country, checks on out-of-town banks cannot be accepted."

The assassination attempt on Roosevelt's life on February 15, 1933, had heightened the tension as Washington and the nation prepared for his inauguration. Anton Cermak, the mayor of Chicago who had taken the bullet meant for FDR, had lain close to death ever since, while the newspapers gave daily, increasingly grim reports on his condition (he finally would die two days after the inauguration).

In Washington, however, the deathbed watch for Cermak had to compete for front-page space with daily bulletins on the condition of the impending inaugural event, which the city anticipated with a mixture of celebration and anxiety. Estimates of the number of people who would be on hand for the inauguration, the parade, and the ball at the Government Auditorium (for which fifteen thousand tickets had been sold at fifteen dollars apiece by February 27) ranged from 150,000 to half a million. With the memory of the assassination attempt fresh, the entire metropolitan police force was called up for duty for the week of March 1 to March 7, and three hundred additional men from Philadelphia, New York, and neighboring communities were borrowed. The preceding week, the police had launched what they called an "inaugural roundup" of numbers operators and other lowlifes (though there was no indication that the force had inconvenienced any of the city's thirty-five hundred speakeasies). There was some particular worry that the tattered remnants of the Bonus Army might make trouble. A handful had set up headquarters in an abandoned building, and on February 23 their "Veteran's National Liaison Committee" had issued a formal protest against the choice of General Douglas MacArthur as grand marshal of the inaugural parade, citing his brutal rout of the BEF's troops the year before. The headquarters of the American Legion had issued a response, branding the protest as "unwarranted and undemocratic." As it happened, the veterans had nothing violent in mind, their hopes, like those of millions of others, resting firmly in the person of the President-elect and what he might do.

᭡᭡᭡᭡᭡

The object of all the hope and concern had left his governor's chair in
Albany for the last time on Wednesday, March 1, motoring down the
Hudson River Valley to New York City, where thousands had lined
Riverside Drive to cheer him into Manhattan. In Washington there had
been much speculation over the question of whether Roosevelt would fly
down from New York, as he had flown to Chicago the previous June.
Front-page news that Wednesday had announced the arrival of a special
four-seater flying boat at the Anacostia Naval Station. It had been built for
the new President at the behest of the navy by the Douglas Aircraft
Company in Santa Monica and seemed a clear indication that FDR would
be the first President to fly since his cousin Teddy had gone up for three
minutes and twenty seconds in an insectlike contraption in 1910. In fact,
Roosevelt had chosen to come down by special train, and he arrived at
Union Station at 9:28 P.M. on March 2, too late to attend a concert given
by the Marine Band that evening at the Pan-American Union Building,
where he could have heard the first performance anywhere of "The Franklin D. Roosevelt March," composed by his chosen Secretary of the Treasury and amateur musician, William H. Woodin. Deprived of that
pleasure and surrounded by some three hundred Secret Service men and
District policemen, Roosevelt had settled into a suite on the seventh floor
of the Mayflower, next to one occupied by James Farley and three floors
above one occupied by Harold, Anna, Raymond, and Robert Ickes.

In spite of their proximity, Ickes and Roosevelt apparently did not even
glimpse each other during the next thirty-six hours. There would have
been little time for chat even if they had met. Roosevelt had a full day on
Friday, including a meeting with Herbert Hoover in the White House at
four that afternoon. He was not looking forward to it. For weeks, Hoover
had been trying to persuade Roosevelt to endorse various schemes designed to reverse the continuing economic slide, but the President-elect
had steadfastly refused to commit himself, fearing that his administration
would be trapped in a snare of Hooverian ineptitude if he did not keep his
distance. Hoover was still trying. His most recent efforts had been
directed at convincing Roosevelt that he join him in declaring an official
national bank holiday. Roosevelt had the same thing in mind, but he
wanted the declaration to come from him alone, and he had refused,
arguing that whatever holidays might be needed to save the banking
system could be declared by individual governors on a state-by-state basis.
(Early Saturday morning, as it happened, an FDR adviser, Raymond
Moley, and incoming Treasury Secretary Woodin would persuade New

York's new governor, Herbert Lehman, to do precisely that, without FDR's knowledge but with his later endorsement.) Hoover stubbornly brought the subject up again during the teatime meeting Friday afternoon, but Roosevelt just as stubbornly remained adamant and the meeting ended badly. Upon rising to leave, FDR remarked that he would understand completely if Hoover was too busy on this last day to return his call. Hoover, exhausted and frustrated, marched stiffly to the door and said, "Mr. Roosevelt, when you have been in Washington as long as I have been you will learn that the President of the United States calls on nobody."

"It's been very pleasant, but we must go now," Eleanor Roosevelt said, getting her husband out of there.

Newspaper predictions to the contrary notwithstanding, the weather was unpromising on Saturday morning, with overcast skies and the promise of a cold rain to come. That did not discourage inauguration watchers. More than 250,000 of them had journeyed to Washington, including more than a hundred ragged teenage boys who had hopped a freight into town the night before, only to be met at the Washington yards at Fourth and T streets by a contingent of police who had been informed that "a freight train full of rabid Reds, aching for trouble" was on its way from northern Pennsylvania. "The train stopped," a reporter for the *Herald* wrote, "and from under the rods, from the top of the cars, from behind bales of merchandise hopped the lads, most of them under 21. They scuttled from box car to box car, but the cops managed to round up about 60 of them. Seventy-five of them escaped."

Herbert Hoover himself was about to escape, but he took little joy in it. He had been awakened at one-thirty Saturday morning by a telephone call from Eugene Meyer, publisher of the *Washington Post* and governor of the Federal Reserve Board, who had claimed that reserves were almost gone and had begged Hoover to close the banks with or without Roosevelt. Hoover had refused, then returned to a fitful sleep. Shortly after he woke, he learned that the New York Stock Exchange had opened as usual for Saturday trading—only to close immediately, as did the Kansas City Board of Trade and even the Chicago Board of Trade, which had not closed on a business day since 1848. "I do not know how it may have been in other places," Louise Armstrong remembered in *We Too Are the People* (1938), "but in Chicago, as we saw it, the city seemed to have died. There was something awful—abnormal—in the very stillness of those streets. I recall being startled by the clatter of a horse's hooves on the pavement as a mounted policeman rode past." As he dressed that morning, Hoover turned to an aide: "We are at the end of our string," he said. "There is nothing more we can do."

Roosevelt's mood was not as grim, but it was clearly somber. He was withdrawn, apparently engaged in some deep interior dialogue, as he got into an open car outside the Mayflower a little before ten with his mother, his wife, his son James, and his son's wife, Betsy, for the short drive to St. John's Episcopal Church, the "church of the Presidents," on Lafayette Square across Pennsylvania Avenue from the White House. In the nave of the church about one hundred people—including the members of his cabinet and their families—were waiting for the President-elect, standing as he and his own family entered pew fifty-four at the front. After everyone sat, Endicott Peabody, the venerable rector of Groton, FDR's prep school, entered with Robert Johnson, rector of St. John's. Peabody had been asked by Roosevelt to conduct the service, and the old man had chosen a program based on the Order for Morning Prayer, modified by the addition of "O God Our Help in Ages Past" and "Faith of Our Fathers," two of FDR's favorite hymns. At the end of the service, Peabody prayed, "O Lord . . . we heartily beseech Thee . . . to behold and bless Thy servant, Franklin, chosen to be President of the United States." Roosevelt remained bowed in his own silent prayer for several moments after Peabody's "Amen," then reached down to lock the braces on his legs and rose to shuffle out of the church on the arm of his son James. He returned briefly to the Mayflower, and from there went down to meet Hoover at the White House for the ride to the Capitol and the inauguration ceremonies.

Outside the church, in the meantime, the remaining members of the little congregation scattered to make their ways to the Capitol as best they could. Harold, Anna, and the boys, like other foresighted folk, had rented a limousine with chauffeur and drove off in style. Those who had not been so clever were left to the callow mercies of Washington's four thousand cabdrivers, many of whom were cheerfully overcharging their out-of-town customers in spite of dire warnings from the police department and the Taxi Commission. There were far too few taxis to handle the crowds in any case, as Frances Perkins and Henry Wallace, the incoming secretaries of Labor and Agriculture, learned when they tried to get one to share. It took an agonizingly long time to flag one down, and when they finally did, the vehicle could only creep along for much of the ride. Terrified that they would miss the inauguration, the two finally jumped from the cab when it could go no farther, climbed over a police barrier, and galloped awkwardly over the wet Capitol lawn to the back of the building, emerging a few moments later in the front—only to find that their seats had been taken. They sat where they could.

Roosevelt's own ride had not been frantic, but it had possessed its own levels of tension. Protocol demanded that the outgoing and incoming Presidents should ride together in an open car down Pennsylvania Avenue from the White House to the Capitol, but either man probably would have been willing to forgo the honor. Except for one brief twitch of a smile and a request at the end that FDR find room for a friend of Hoover's on the federal bench (Roosevelt would comply), the outgoing President sat silently for the whole ride, his face set in the characteristic dead scowl that may or may not have played a part in the outcome of the election in 1932. After trying to make light conversation with a man who had little talent for it under the best of circumstances, FDR finally gave up. Then, as he later told his secretary, Grace Tully, "I said to myself, 'Spinach! Protocol or no protocol, somebody has to do something.' The two of us simply couldn't sit there on our hands, ignoring each other and everyone else." He took his silk hat off and began waving it at the friendly crowds along the avenue, flashing his smile like a semaphore.

At the Capitol, he and Hoover entered the west side of the Senate wing and split up, Hoover going into the President's Room to sign or pocket-veto a few final bills, Roosevelt into the office of the Military Affairs Committee next door, where he looked over the inaugural address that he, Raymond Moley, Samuel Rosenman, and Louis Howe had been working over intermittently since early February. At the last minute, he scribbled a new lead—"This is a day of consecration"—then at noon went into the Senate Chamber to watch as a few new senators and Vice President John Garner were sworn in, after which Charles Curtis, Hoover's Vice President, gaveled the last session of the Senate of the Seventy-second Congress to an end *sine die*. Roosevelt and Hoover then prepared to make their appearances under the canopy of the inaugural platform.

Waiting for them were tens of thousands of people who filled the twelve thousand seats of the special stands that had been erected for members of Congress and their families and friends, the 624 seats reserved on benches for the press, and the seatless Capitol Plaza, where children and a few adventurous adults ornamented the limbs of leafless trees while below them at least one hundred thousand people stood, filling the grounds like a dark ocean. Eleanor ("Cissy") Patterson, editor of William Randolph Hearst's *Washington Herald* (and cousin to Colonel Robert McCormick of the *Chicago Tribune* and sister to Joseph Patterson of the *New York Daily News*) was there and had a good seat in the press section. "You get your seat outside in the Capitol Plaza," she reported in the next morning's *Herald,*

> on one of those long pine benches, close below the platform where President-Elect Roosevelt is to speak. The long, long wait begins. The cold creeps down, creeps along your bones. . . . The sky is gray. Gray clouds sagging, full of rain and snow. . . .
>
> The Marine Band right in front of you doesn't play. Waiting. Everybody, everything waiting. Did you hear the siren of an ambulance? Yes. People question each other with their eyes. Could anything have happened? . . . .
>
> And then, suddenly, Mr. Hoover. Very pale his face is. Yes, and a tragic face. I have seen people once or twice, standing at the brink of an open grave with that same look of despair. . . . And then you see the bold profile of another man. Young, fresh, colored, yet gray at the temples. Roosevelt. . . .
>
> The cheering is scattered. The crowd is dead serious. Stricken. Still. None of that roisterous welcome. For what has this man to say to us today?

Roosevelt had left his wheelchair to walk the last yards to his place at the rostrum on the arm of James. His left hand on the old Dutch Bible that had been in the family for generations, his right hand raised, he faced Supreme Court Chief Justice Charles Evans Hughes, who had dreamed of the Presidency once himself, who had refused when Hoover had urged him to resign rather than serve with the dangerous Roosevelt. Duly sworn, FDR turned to speak. "The famous smile flashes once," Damon Runyon wrote, "when he first faces his audience, then is gone."

It was not a long address, nor did it quite cry revolution, as some had expected (hoped, feared), but it attempted to make up in firmness and eloquence what it lacked in detailed analysis and specific programs. Clearly, Roosevelt wanted his listeners to remember the spirit, if not necessarily the substance, of what it was he had to say to the people this day. "This is a day of national consecration," he began, amending vocally his written amendment of an hour before. "I am certain that my fellow Americans expect that on my induction into the Presidency I will address them with a candor and a decision which the present situation of our Nation impels." First, he said, "let me assert my firm belief that the only thing we have to fear is fear itself—nameless, unreasoning, unjustified terror which paralyzes needed efforts to convert retreat into advance." Still: "Only a foolish optimist can deny the grim realities of the moment." We were a rich nation, he said: "Plenty is at our doorstep, but a generous use of it languishes in the very sight of the supply." He blamed it on "the rulers of exchange" who had "failed through their own stubbornness and their own incompetence, have admitted their failure, and have abdicated.

Practices of the unscrupulous money changers stand indicted in the court of public opinion, rejected by the hearts and minds of men." At issue here, he said, was a question of values: "Happiness lies not in the mere possession of money; it lies in the joy of achievement, in the thrill of creative effort. The joy and moral stimulation of work no longer must be forgotten in the mad chase of evanescent profits."

Beyond a change in ethical standards, he said, "This Nation asks for action, and action now." The country's primary goal must be "to put people back to work . . . treating the task as we would treat the emergency of war. . . ." In agriculture, he called for a national program of "redistribution" to "provide a better use of the land for those best fitted for the land." He said that the costs of government must be reduced, that the banking and investment systems must be monitored and regulated by the federal government, that the balance of trade had to be redressed, and that the nation's foreign policy must be firmly founded on "good neighbor" principles. These were the "lines of attack" which his administration would be following, he said. "I am prepared," he promised, "under my constitutional duty to recommend the measures that a stricken Nation in the midst of a stricken world may require." And if that did not work: "I shall not evade the clear course of duty that will then confront me. I shall ask the Congress for the one remaining instrument to meet the crisis—broad Executive power to wage a war against the emergency, as great as the power that would be given to me if we were in fact invaded by a foreign foe." He could do no less, he said in conclusion. The people had "registered a mandate." They wanted "direct, vigorous action." They had made him "the present instrument of their wishes. In the spirit of the gift I take it."

Only then did the crowd break out into loud applause and full-throated cheering. At no point during the speech had FDR been seriously interrupted. "It was very, very solemn," Eleanor Roosevelt said of the moment, "and a little terrifying. The crowds were so tremendous, and you felt that they would do anything, if only someone told them what to do." Raymond Moley, who had been listening with his head down and his hat dangling between his knees, turned to Frances Perkins. "Well," he said, "he's taken the ship of state and he's turned it right around." Olive Clapper, the wife of newsman Raymond Clapper, said that the speech had "thrilled us into forgetfulness of the cold. Our shivers were those of amazement, of inspiration, of new courage."

Others were less impressed. The speech, outgoing Secretary of State Henry Stimson said, "was full of weasel words." Edmund Wilson was kinder, though hardly inspired himself. Even when "one reads them later," he wrote, "the phrases of this speech seem shadowy—the echoes of

Woodrow Wilson's eloquence without Wilson's exaltation behind them. The old unctuousness, the old pulpit vagueness." In her own diary, Beatrice Berle, the wife of Roosevelt adviser Adolf Berle, indicated that Edmund Wilson may not have been the only one who was unmoved: "We heard Roosevelt's speech pushing through the Capitol grounds as the other half of the population was pushing away—bored. It was a great speech . . . most timely and dramatic though the crowd showed no indication it thought so."

The crowds in Washington, whichever way they may have been pushing, were not the only ones who heard Roosevelt's words that day, however. This inauguration was given greater radio coverage than any event in history up to that time. Both NBC and CBS, showing signs already of the communications monsters they would become, had spared no resource, and beginning at nine-thirty that morning nearly two hundred stations across the country had been crackling with reports from NBC's Graham McNamee, Floyd Gibbons, David Lawrence, and Arthur Godfrey, and CBS's Bob Trout, Ted Husing, H. V. Kaltenborn, and Boake Carter, among others. Reporters were tied into hookups that had been scattered at strategic points throughout the city in an effort to cover everything from Roosevelt's departure from the Mayflower in the morning to the inaugural ball that night. NBC had strapped heavy mobile units to the backs of two of its strongest correspondents and had installed more elaborate mobile equipment in five open cars; for its part, CBS had the oracular voice of Kaltenborn issuing from a blimp. And at the top of the Washington Monument shortwave equipment broadcast the endless details of this quadrennial American ritual to the cities of any nation in the world equipped to hear them.

The central moment in all this ancestral network hype was Roosevelt's inaugural address, and tens of millions of Americans were consequently privileged to draw their own conclusions regarding its virtues or faults. It is not impossible that for most of them the speech had the same power that one listener could still feel more than forty years later: "It was a talk the nation had not heard in my lifetime. I felt not merely the words— arousing, challenging, unexpected—but the tone and the great courage and the strength of the man behind them. How fortunate are those of us who lived at that time and were touched, ever so slightly, by this gigantic force in our history."

After the address Herbert Hoover shook Roosevelt's hand, then swiftly made his way to a car that took him to Union Station and a train for New

York (upon his arrival at Pennsylvania Station, he told reporters that he fully intended to sleep for forty-eight straight hours). He and Roosevelt never met again. For his part, the new President had every intention of seizing the day and wringing from it all the pleasure that he could. FDR loved a parade, and one of the most stupendous in American history went by him for three hours that afternoon as he sat on the reviewing stand in the Court of Honor on Pennsylvania Avenue in front of the White House. Among the 30,224 individuals who marched or rode past him were generals and admirals, soldiers, sailors, and marines, cavalry regiments and American Indians, governors from states that had gone Democratic in 1932 and delegations of one kind or another from every state, including Tammany Tigers from New York (Alfred E. Smith waving his famous derby to great cheering), the musicians from forty bands, and thirty beautiful local girls perched like blossoms atop MGM's "Studio on Wheels." Overhead, the *Washington Herald* reported, more than a hundred "fighting planes roared out of the East and soared above Pennsylvania Avenue from the Capitol to the White House. . . . The giant [airship] U.S.S. *Akron* and an Army dirigible formed a stately escort for the roaring planes."

The parade was so long that FDR could not stay for all of it. At dusk he went into the White House, where Eleanor was already greeting the first of a thousand guests invited to a reception at which tea and sandwiches— and only tea and sandwiches—were being served. FDR went upstairs to supervise the swearing in of his new cabinet. At two that afternoon Vice President Garner had left the inaugural festivities and returned to the Senate Chamber in the Capitol. There he had called the first Senate session of the Seventy-third Congress to order, the first and only item of business being the confirmation of Roosevelt's cabinet nominations. Only Republican senator James Couzens of Michigan had had much to say in regard to any of the nominees, questioning the thoroughness with which William H. Woodin had divested himself of stocks and other holdings in preparation for assuming office as Secretary of the Treasury. Couzens's remarks had been ridden over without significant delay, and a vote for confirmation taken and passed for all nominees. Garner had then recessed the session and returned to the reviewing stand. Now FDR called all his appointees to the Oval Room to be sworn in *en masse* for the first time in history.

Frances Perkins remembered that Roosevelt first introduced Justice Benjamin J. Cardozo, who would do the honors, then said, "I hope you don't mind being sworn in on my old Dutch Bible. You won't be able to read a word of it, but it's the Holy Scriptures all right." Beginning with Cordell Hull as Secretary of State, FDR called the name of each person, who was then sworn in by Cardozo and handed a certificate of office by the beaming Roosevelt. "As I looked about the Oval Room while awaiting my turn to be sworn in," Ickes remembered fifteen years later, "I felt almost like a stranger in a strange land. . . . While it was impossible to appraise, on such a brief and formal occasion, the potentialities of the nine men and one woman who, as members of his Cabinet, were to follow the leadership of the new President in tackling the most serious economic situation in which the country had ever found itself, it was clear that the captain himself, as he sat at his desk, was courageous, competent, and confident."

After handing out the last certificate, the President welcomed them all to the administration. "No cabinet," he said, "has ever been sworn in before in this way. I am happy to do it because it gives the families of the new cabinet an opportunity to see the ceremony. It is my intention to inaugurate precedents like this from time to time." The cabinet then dispersed for dinner and the inaugural ball. "By this informal little touch," James B. Farley (sworn in as Postmaster General) remembered, "the Chief Executive had successfully converted what is usually a stiff and pompous ceremonial into a friendly, happy occasion that was appreciated by everyone present. A man who wouldn't feel pleased under the circumstances would have to be either a humbug or a stuffed shirt."

FDR himself ate at a buffet downstairs with seventy-five members of both branches of the Roosevelt clan. He did not attend the inaugural ball down at the immense Government Auditorium on Constitution Avenue. Eleanor attended, however, as did the cabinet members and their families, Harold Ickes in white tie and tails, Anna in a gray gown, black coat, black hat trimmed at the back with small gray flowers, and a soft gray fur—two square people of medium height who could not have stood out in a crowd that overwhelmed the auditorium's seating capacity of thirteen hundred, each member of which seemed to be out to vindicate the old saw that Democrats, if nothing else, knew how to have a better time than Republicans. "The inaugural ball that night was bedlam," newspaperwoman Bess Furman remembered. "I never came so near to getting crushed in all my life. . . . When we at last emerged into the midnight air, my evening wrap was torn beyond repair, and the old pumps that I had had sense enough to wear were ready to be junked." She was lucky. Not long after her escape, the *Herald* reported the next morning, four women had fainted when the "pleasure mad crowd" jammed the doorways trying to get out of the sweltering auditorium and the riot police had to be called in to straighten things out.

So began the New Deal.

CHAPTER
· 26 ·

The Inheritance

W ORK BEGAN IMMEDIATELY, for Ickes as for the rest of the new
administration. The new cabinet officers barely had time to inspect
their offices on Sunday before Roosevelt called them all to the White
House. It was after that meeting that Ickes dictated the first entry in the
diary he was to keep with religious fervor for the rest of his life, a work
that would grow to nearly five million words and stand as one of the
central documents from the age of Roosevelt.* "President Roosevelt," he
said,

> called the members of the Cabinet, Vice President Garner, and Speaker-elect
> [Henry T.] Rainey to meet him at the White House at two-thirty to discuss

* Apparently it was Paul H. Douglas, Ickes's young colleague in the fight against Samuel
Insull, who had prodded him in this direction. On August 17, 1943, Ickes wrote to Douglas
(who was in the marines at the time): "I . . . remember that you insisted that I ought to keep a
day to day diary of occurrences here in Washington after I became a member of the Administration and you referred to the value to history of the diary that Gideon Welles kept during the
Civil War. I think that I can honestly say that I would not have undertaken a diary, at least
when I did, if it had not been for your suggestion. As it is, I have been quite faithful about it
and someday somebody will find parts of it at least interesting reading." Even though about
one-tenth of the whole thing was published in three volumes after his death as the "secret"
diary, there was little that was secret about it. Many people learned of its existence over the
years, and if some of them were made nervous by the knowledge, it is not likely that it would
have bothered its author much.

the acute banking situation and agree on a policy. We considered, and the President decided to issue, the Executive Order which will appear in tomorrow morning's papers, the effect of which will be to close every bank in the United States for a bank holiday of three days, to stop the exportation of gold, and put into effect other emergency regulations designed to stop the run on the banks and to prevent the hoarding of gold or gold certificates.

Conferring with his cabinet on these questions was largely a pro-forma matter on Roosevelt's part; after meeting with Secretary Woodin and Raymond Moley the morning of the inauguration he had already made his decision to close the banks and block the export of gold. By Sunday he had been assured by Attorney General Homer Cummings that he had the legal authority to do so under provisions of Section 5(b) of the Trading with the Enemy Act of 1917, an unanticipated but—given FDR's remarks about war during his inaugural address—symbolically appropriate use of the statute. Later that Sunday, after meeting with congressional leaders, he also decided to issue a proclamation convening the new Congress on Thursday, March 9, by which time Moley and Woodin had promised he would have an emergency banking bill to present. This proclamation was signed sometime late that night.

The proclamation for closing the banks and freezing the export of gold was not signed until one o'clock Monday morning, and then only after the sleep of Harold Ickes had been interrupted. He had returned to the Mayflower that night "dog tired," he reported in his diary, had "told the operator not to put through any calls unless one should come from the White House, and tumbled into bed. Just before midnight, Secretary of the Treasury Woodin called to ask authority to sign my name to cablegrams to the Governors of Alaska, Hawaii, and the Virgin Islands, with reference to the banking situation in those Territories which are under the jurisdiction of the Department of the Interior." Ickes gave his assent.

That telephone call in the dead of night was the first hint the new Secretary of the Interior received of the extraordinary dimensions of the responsibility he had worked so diligently to assume. He got an additional indication on Monday, his first regular working day. In his office in the Interior Building, an enormous neoclassical pile that sprawled over the entire block bordered by Eighteenth and Nineteenth streets and E and F streets, he spent his first hours putting his signature to routine paperwork and meeting the various department heads. At four o'clock he asked all the employees in the building to come up and be introduced to him. "They filed past me about twenty-five hundred strong," he noted in his diary for March 6, though if this number astonished and sobered him he made no record of it.

It should have, for the Washington contingent he met so briefly that afternoon represented less than 10 percent of a work force scattered over forty states and territories, more than thirty thousand full-time employees all told, together with about five thousand temporary workers. Interior's was one of the largest bureaucracies in the nation, perhaps the world, and arguably the most complex and least comprehensible—certainly, the least well-defined, having been dubbed years before "The Department of Things in General." Even when it was created, it was as the recipient of functions cheerfully discarded by the departments of Treasury, State, and War—the three Executive departments then in existence. It was something of a bastard agency that Ickes had been summoned to administer, and nothing that he learned during the first months of his tenure could have given him much comfort. Indeed, fifteen years later he was to say that rescuing it from obloquy was possibly the principal task that awaited him: "Perhaps I had aspired to become Secretary of the Interior because all my life I had been for the underdog. Here was the most discouraged and nagged-at major department of the Government. . . . Subsequent to [the Teapot Dome scandal] little had been done to restore the morale of Interior. It was a furtive and demoralized scapegoat, shame-stricken and apologetic, over which I was called to preside."

A good deal of this can be dismissed as hyperbole, an attempt to enhance the dimensions of what he had accomplished during his service as Secretary, unnecessary because his accomplishments were in fact remarkable. Nevertheless, if he exaggerated, it was not by much. From its beginning, the Department of the Interior had been a weak and raddled agency that had acquired the reputation, largely deserved, of an institution that combined incompetence and corruption in about equal portions.

The year was 1849, and the young nation, stretching toward continental destiny, had recently acquired an embarrassment of land with the conclusion of the Mexican War and the Treaty of Guadalupe Hidalgo in 1848. The new territory, together with that already acquired by the Louisiana Purchase in 1803 and by treaty with Great Britain (settling the ownership of the Pacific Northwest) in 1846, constituted most of what became America's trans-Mississippi empire (the last chunk would be added with the Gadsden Purchase of 1853, which filled things out in what would become southern Arizona). The new territory—1,817,527,000 acres— was the great stage on which the last great expression of the frontier experience in the history of the United States was acted out. Here were the territories of Kansas, Dakota, Nebraska, Wyoming, Montana, Utah,

Oregon, and New Mexico. Later divisions would create separate territories for Colorado, Nevada, Washington, and Arizona; California, being ahead of its time even then, became a full-fledged state in 1850.

Most of the nation celebrated this continental urge (the New England states and a few others, fearing the expansion of southern slavery, did not), but precisely what to do with all the land involved was a question that would lie at the heart of western development for generations. It was federal land, land owned by the government (and by extension, by every citizen) of the United States. This was America's landed inheritance, a patrimony of grasslands, forests, deserts, mountains, lakes, and rivers that possessed a greater abundance of natural resources and physical beauty than that enjoyed by any nation on the planet. Its fate, however, seemed likely to be the same as that which had befallen the three hundred million acres of public land that had lain between the original states and the Mississippi River: by the time of the Mexican War, these had disappeared from federal ownership—sold, most of them. From the start, this land had been perceived as commodity. "It is now no longer a point of speculation and hope," James Madison had written in the *Federalist Papers* as early as 1788, "that the Western Territory is a mine of vast wealth to the United States." Under proper management, he had said, it could be used "both to effect a gradual discharge of the domestic debt and to furnish, for a certain period, liberal tributes to the federal treasury." The discharge of debt and the enjoyment of tributes, it was anticipated, would each come from land sales, and after two decades of casual (and often venal) administration by Congress itself, tens of millions of acres had been handed over to speculators of one ilk or another at prices that brought more shame to Congress than ready cash to the treasury. As a reaction to its own maladministration, in 1812 Congress established the General Land Office in the Department of the Treasury. The duties of the new agency included the issuance of land warrants and grants, the scheduling of sales at various district land offices, the collection of money from such sales, the preparation and issuance of deeds and patents, and the maintenance of land records.

Speculation and corruption continued, as they would continue so long as land was money. But something else had risen in the years following the creation of the General Land Office, particularly when the conclusion of the War of 1812 opened the valleys of the Ohio and Mississippi rivers to settlement. "Cultivators of the earth," Thomas Jefferson wrote in 1812, "are the most valuable citizens. They are the most vigorous, the most independent, the most virtuous, and they are tied to their country and wedded to its liberty and interests by the most lasting bonds." The cultivators of the earth agreed wholeheartedly and proclaimed it the duty of the federal government to reward their virtue by placing land in their possession immediately, and at prices they could easily afford, with liberal credit terms available. As their numbers and political influence had grown, they got more and more of what they demanded—the minimum size of federal land units offered for sale fell from 320 to 160 and finally to 80 acres, while the purchase price dropped from two dollars an acre to $1.25—and if the government itself did not always offer credit, there were plenty of almost completely unregulated banks that would.

The clamoring hunger for federal land had climaxed in the several preemption acts, the purest expression of western influence the country had yet experienced. Contrary to all law, adventurous settlers (they were sometimes called "pioneers," but it was not always considered a compliment) had for years ventured out beyond the lines of settlement, squatting on and cultivating unsurveyed land to which they had no hope of legal title once civilization caught up with them and the land was surveyed and put up for sale by the General Land Office. No hope until preemption, that is. Simply stated, preemption would grant the squatter the right to buy the land he had settled at a minimum price, thus removing the possibility of his being evicted from land that presumably he had cleared, broken, and carved into a home with his own hands (as many did). In 1830, Congress institutionalized this idea with passage of the first Pre-Emption Act, which stipulated that squatters could buy for $1.25 the acre up to 160 acres of the land on which they sat. Designed as a temporary expedient, the law was much to the liking of the West; it was renewed four times between 1832 and 1841, at which point it was made permanent.

Preemption and the increasingly liberal land laws that had preceded it had brought settlement into the Ohio and Mississippi river valleys, together with speculation and a land-based boom-and-bust economy that ruined quite as many lives as it nurtured. What they had not brought was a sufficiency of tribute to the national coffers. As early as 1820, an alarmed Secretary of the Treasury reported that of the $47 million contracted for in the sale of nearly twenty million acres of federal land, more than $17 million remained uncollected. Nearly thirty years later, many millions more remained uncollected (and probably uncollectible), and as Secretary of the Treasury Robert J. Walker looked around his agency in 1848 and thought about the hundreds of thousands of settlers who almost certainly were going to carry tradition into the newly won trans-Mississippi West, bringing more grief than profit to the department, he decided that Treasury did not need the General Land Office. He recommended to Congress that it create a brand new department in the executive branch, a "Home" department like that in Great Britain, and that the General Land Office and all its responsibilities be placed there. While Congress was at it, he added, it might as well move the Patent Office out of the State Department, which had no earthly use for it, and the Pension Office and the Bureau of Indian Affairs out of the War Department, which was not equipped to administer either, and place all three of these, too, into the new department.

Congress agreed; on the evening of March 3, 1849, it passed a bill creating a Home Department (a name soon changed to Department of the Interior), and President James K. Polk signed it into law during the final hours of his administration. To the list suggested by Treasury Secretary Walker, Congress had added the Bureau of the Census, the administration of federal public buildings across the United States as well as charitable and penal institutions in the District of Columbia, the supervision of territorial governments, and the appointment and supervision of all federal district attorneys, marshals, and deputy marshals (there was not yet a Department of Justice). President Zachary Taylor appointed Thomas Ewing, a successful lawyer and former Secretary of the Treasury under Presidents William Henry Harrison and John Tyler, as the first Interior Secretary, and by December, Ewing was ready to announce his department's requirements for the Washington office: a permanent force of ten and a budget of $14,200. Over the next several months, he called for the establishment of an agricultural bureau within the department, the creation of a solicitor's office to handle legal matters, and a cadastral survey of public lands in California, Oregon, and New Mexico. While pursuing these worthwhile goals, he also managed, as a good Whig, to fire almost every Democrat he could find within the bureaus out of which his department had been formed, a practice that earned him the label of "Butcher Ewing" by opposition newspapers and the enduring enmity of the Democratic-controlled House of Representatives. A few weeks into the administration of Millard Fillmore following the death of Zachary Taylor in July 1850, Ewing had become a political millstone hanging heavy from the neck of the Whig Party, which was on its last legs in any case. He resigned under pressure, leaving behind him a disorganized wreck of a department whose legacy was best described by historian Norman Forness: "Secretary Ewing's great concern with party power and the execution of a ruthless patronage policy had not augured well for the office he administered. Rather than becoming a showpiece of administrative excellence, it became the battleground of political partisanship."

〖〗〖〗〖〗

Tradition firmly established, for the next eighty-odd years, the Department of the Interior presided over more than its fair share of what historian Vernon L. Parrington called "The Great Barbecue." Its Bureau of Indian Affairs never was able to deal adequately with one of the great conundrums of American history—how to reconcile principles with expediency as the Iron Age met the Stone Age on the North American continent— nor did it even try much of the time. It stank of corruption, cupidity, and cruelty almost from the beginning, and even the bureau's more benevolent efforts would bring the Indian to the edge of cultural disintegration and a level of poverty that was nothing short of devastating, even by Depression standards. Similarly, the General Land Office, understaffed and underfunded (and intermittently corrupt) throughout its lifetime, was incapable of stemming the inexorable subversion of the confusing welter of land laws under its supervision. There were almost three thousand of them, finally, beginning with the Ordinances of 1785 and 1787 and continuing down through the Pre-Emption Act of 1841 and the host of big and little laws that followed, chief among them the Swamp Land Act of 1850; the Homestead Act, the Morrill Land Grant Act, and the Pacific Railroad acts of 1862; the Timber Culture Act of 1873; the Desert Land Act of 1877; the Timber and Stone Act of 1878; the Enlarged Homestead Act of 1909; and the Stock-Raising Homestead Act of 1916.

Most of these liberal exercises had idealistic motives behind them, not the least of which was to place land in the hands of the landless, as in the Desert Land Act, the Timber Culture Act, and the various homestead acts; or to foster the economic development of the nation, as in the Swamp Land Act, the Timber and Stone Act, and the Pacific Railroad Act; or to finance higher education, as in the Morrill Land Grant Act. To some degree, the goals were met: between 1862 and 1902, for example, there were 1,728,761 claims made under the provisions of the Homestead Act of 1862 (although only 718,819 were held to full title, and those against odds that only superhuman effort could overcome); the transcontinental railroad did get built, as the Pacific Railroad Act of 1862 had intended (although the monopoly that its two components—the Union Pacific and the Central, later Southern, Pacific railroads—enjoyed went a long way toward validating Bernard DeVoto's later description of the American West as "the plundered province"); and land-grant colleges did get established throughout the nation (although many millions of the 130 million acres that were used to finance them ended up in the hands of speculators at prices considerably and conveniently lower than the $1.25 an acre that the Morrill Land Grant Act stipulated).

What the various laws did do, indisputably and expeditiously, was dispose of federal land. By the turn of the century, nearly four hundred million acres of the public domain west of the Mississippi had been sold or given away to private or corporate ownership, almost all of it under the unwatchful eye of the Department of the Interior's General Land Office. Much of the land went legitimately, but much of it with the kind of casual malfeasance described eloquently by historian Ray Allen Billington in his discussion of the Timber and Stone Act and its effect on the forests of the Pacific Northwest:

> It invited corruption; any timber magnate could use dummy entrymen to engross the nation's richest forest lands at trifling cost. Company agents rounded up gangs of alien seamen in waterfront boarding houses, marched them to the courthouse to file their first papers, then to the land office to claim their quarter section, then to a notary public to sign over their deeds to the corporation, and back to the boarding houses to be paid off. Fifty dollars was the usual fee, although the amount soon fell to $5 or $10 and eventually to the price of a glass of beer. By 1900 almost 3,600,000 acres of valuable forestland were alienated under the measure.

Similar chicanery had characterized the disposal of land under the other laws, but not all of the land got taken, legally or not. Among the millions of acres that remained were more than three hundred million in forests and grasslands. The condition of both was a matter of concern to those few who were beginning to look upon the nation's land less as a commodity to be sold than as a resource to be husbanded, among them George Perkins Marsh, whose *Man and Nature,* published in 1864, pointed out that the destruction of forest watersheds had obliterated complex civilizations in North Africa, the Arabian Peninsula, Syria, Mesopotamia, Asia Minor, and the Mediterranean, and warned that it could do the same for the civilization lately implanted on the North American continent.

There was reason for worry. By the last quarter of the nineteenth century, the forestland east of the Mississippi had long since been logged out—sometimes twice over—and while generally humid conditions had allowed much of the land to recover in second and third growth, erosion had permanently scarred many areas and unimpeded runoff during seasonal rains had caused such ghastly floods as that which destroyed Johnstown, Pennsylvania, in 1889. Now the forests of the West—not blessed, for the most part, with soils and climates that encouraged quick regrowth—were threatened by much the same kind of abuse. In addition to legitimate timber companies who consistently misused the land laws by clear-cutting entire claims without even bothering to remain around long enough to establish final title, many "tramp" lumbermen simply marched men, mules, oxen, and sometimes donkey engines onto a suitable (and vacant) tract of public forestland, stripped it, and moved out, knowing full well that apprehension and prosecution were generally beyond the means of the overcommitted General Land Office. As early as 1866, such instances of cheerful plunder had gutted many of the forests of the public domain; in that year, the surveyors-general of both Washington Territory and Colorado Territory earnestly recommended to the General Land Office that the forestlands in their districts be sold immediately, while there was something left to sell.

The forests were not sold, nor did they vanish entirely, but they did remain vulnerable to regular depredation. In 1877, Carl Schurz, a German-born naturalized citizen and the first Interior Secretary since the department's founding to perceive fully the necessity of intelligent federal land management, recommended to Congress that regulations be established for the "care and custody" of timberlands, "for the gradual sale of the timber thereon, and for the perpetuation of the growth of timber on such lands by such needful rules and regulations as may be required to that end." Congress ignored him. Twelve years later he recalled "a public opinion, looking with indifference on this wanton, barbarous, disgraceful vandalism; a spendthrift people recklessly wasting its heritage; a government careless of the future and unmindful of a pressing duty. But I found myself standing almost solitary and alone. Deaf was Congress, and deaf the people seemed to be." President Benjamin Harrison's Secretary of the Interior, John W. Noble, had better results. Like Schurz, he believed Congress had to be persuaded that the public forests needed protection; unlike Schurz, he was not above a little quiet legerdemain. On March 3, 1891, during the closing hours of the last session of the Fifty-first Congress, Noble caused a rider to be attached to an act "For the repeal of the Timber and Stone Act and for other purposes." (The abuses of this act had proved too onerous for anyone to tolerate, even most western congressmen, and it was certain to pass.) The rider, Section 24, was later called the Forest Reserve Clause: "That the President of the United States may, from time to time, set apart and reserve, in any state or territory having public lands wholly or in part covered with timber or undergrowth, whether of commercial value or not, as public reservations, and the President shall by public proclamation, declare the establishment of such reservations and the limits thereof."

This mild-mannered marvel tiptoed through to passage before Congress, particularly those members from the West, where most of the public forests lay, really had much of a chance to consider its implications. As one of the last acts of his administration, President Harrison withdrew thirteen million acres, and President Grover Cleveland added another twenty-one million before he left his second term in 1897. When understanding at last glimmered into life, a great howl arose in the West. Gifford Pinchot, then the young chief forester in the Department of Agriculture (the department had no forests to supervise at that time; Pinchot's job was to advise private landowners on proper forestry practices), found the anger understandable. The Forest Reserve Clause, "vitally important though it was," he wrote in *Breaking New Ground,*

> did not provide for the practice of Forestry on the Forest Reserves. It did not even set up a form of administration. It gave the Reserves no protection, and they had none, except as an occasional Agent might be spared from the meagre force of the Land Office. It merely set the land aside and withdrew it, legally at least, from every form of use by the people of the West or by the Government. . . . [T]he situation [the law of 1891] created was clearly impossible. Under it no timber could be cut, no forage could be grazed, no minerals could be mined, nor any road built, in any Forest Reserve. Legally at least, no man could even set foot upon a single one of them.

The situation did not sit well with the utilitarian-minded Pinchot, even though he had been one of the principal engineers of Cleveland's withdrawals, and in 1897 he helped write the language of the Forest Organic Act, passed on June 4. It stated the purposes of the reserves to be "to improve and protect the forest within the boundaries for the purpose of securing favorable conditions of water flow, and to furnish a continuous supply of timber for the use and necessities of citizens of the United States." The act also limited which kinds of trees could be taken from the forests, and required that each be "marked and designated" before cutting. That done, Pinchot then lobbied to have himself installed as chief forester in the Department of the Interior (without losing his place in Agriculture), from which post he hoped to wrest control of the forests from the inept administration of the General Land Office, dominated as it was by lawyers and Land Office agents entirely uneducated in and indifferent to the science of forestry.

Interior Secretary Ethan Allen Hitchcock was agreeable, but could not move the idea in Congress, largely because of opposition from the politically potent director of the General Land Office, who had no intention of turning control of the forests over to this young upstart. Pinchot then changed his tactics and, with the support of Hitchcock, began fighting

for the wholesale transfer of the forest reserves from Interior to his own
bureau in the Department of Agriculture, where he was slowly building a
cadre of trained foresters. It took eight years and, after September 1901,
the full weight of President Theodore Roosevelt's considerable influence,
but on February 1, 1905, a transfer bill became law. The 46,410,209
acres of forestland that had been withdrawn since 1891 were safely out of
the hands of the General Land Office.

Roosevelt would go on to withdraw more than 104 million more and
place these, too, under the protection of the new chief forester of the U.S.
Forest Service, Department of Agriculture, a position Pinchot held comfortably until his dramatic falling-out with Taft in 1910. By the time
Franklin Roosevelt became President in 1933, the forests for nearly thirty
years—with some lapses during the casual years of the twenties—had
been managed under the rigid utilitarian principles of stewardship established by Pinchot (whose influence on the management of the forests
continued powerful until the day of his death, in spite of the fact that he
never again held federal office).

The grasslands of the nation had enjoyed no such rescue. Beginning in
the years following the Civil War, the tall-grass prairies that spread west
to become the short-grass plains had been subjected to relentless use by
individual homesteaders and corporate farmers, by a cattle industry that
migrated north from Texas and Oklahoma to use the high-plains country
of the Dakotas, Montana, and Wyoming as an enormous feedlot, and by
the sheep industry, whose millions of animals chewed across the land like
"hooved locusts" (as John Muir called them). These three industries
systematically corrupted and subverted the various land laws, locking up
in single ownership huge blocks of land and squabbling among themselves over use and ownership for at least three generations, with no clear
winner emerging.

There had been one indisputable loser, however, and that was the land
itself. As early as the summer of 1886 and the winter that followed,
nature, as it has a way of doing, had given clear indications of the
consequences of abuse. That summer lay at the heart of one of the worst
droughts in the history of the West. Nevertheless, the cattle industry,
convinced that the boom of the 1880s was a permanent condition, packed
every animal on the land that it could, until it was being grazed far
beyond its carrying capacity. Millions of animals, then, were in a weakened condition when winter closed down on the region in the middle of
November. From then until early March, one scarifying blizzard after
another raked the northern plains. Millions of cattle died brutally, many
of them stacked in grotesque piles in the corners of the illegal fences

ranchers had erected to keep sheepmen and homesteaders off those portions of the public domain they had claimed as their own, with or without
the sanction of law. Fully three-quarters of all the herds of the West had
been destroyed, although the losses were so huge that no firm numbers
ever were tallied. And the land? Let Theodore Roosevelt, whose own
North Dakota ranching enterprise was wiped out, tell it: "The land was a
mere barren waste; not a green thing could be seen; the dead grass eaten
off till the country looked as if it had been shaved by a razor."

The signal that nature had broadcast in 1886–87 was ignored the
minute the land recovered sufficiently to support once again grazing and
industrial farming, both of which entered one more cycle of the boom-
and-bust traditions that would characterize them for all time. Not even
the winter of 1906–1907, which repeated the "Big Die-Up" of 1886–87
in many of its particulars, seemed to trip a learning mechanism. When
World War I created a sudden new market for wheat and cattle, the land
again was used beyond its limits—and not just in the high-plains country
this time, but everywhere in the West that something edible could be
made to grow or a cow or sheep could be led to a blade of grass. And in
spite of hard times in the West that periodically belied the permanence of
Coolidge prosperity, the grazing industry in particular continued its
assault on the land throughout the twenties, until by 1932 the
172,258,379 acres of "unappropriated and unreserved public lands" in
the eleven western states were carrying nearly eleven million cattle and
more than twenty-six million sheep—even while drought once again
began its arid creep across the West and denuded farmland and grazing
land alike started to drift and blow in the hot winds.

Except for the sporadic enforcement of the land laws, the General Land
Office had been every bit as powerless, even when inclined, to control the
use and prevent the abuse of the millions of acres of grassland under its
control as it had been with regard to the forests. It was in the business of
selling or giving land away, not managing it, and even this level of
involvement was too much for President Herbert Hoover, who would have
preferred getting the federal government out of the land business altogether. The individual states, he informed Congress in 1929, "are today
more competent to manage" the unappropriated lands "than is the Federal
Government. . . . For the best interests of the people as a whole, and
people of the western states and the small farmers and stockmen by whom
they are primarily used, they should be managed and the policies for their
use determined by state governments." Congress authorized Hoover to
appoint a Committee on the Conservation and Administration of the
Public Domain to study the question in December 1930. After several

weeks of deliberation, the committee concluded that the President was right. Bills to put this proposal into action were introduced in 1932, but Congress, preoccupied with the country's economic problems and, more important, the upcoming elections, gave them little more than cursory attention, and the remaining public domain of the United States did not get cooked in the pot of state ownership yet. In the meantime, the land continued abused when it was not neglected, hostage to greed and indifference.

However willing they may have been to relinquish control of the surface rights of the unreserved public domain to the states, even Hoover's commission and his Interior Department were not so conservative that they would have given up the federal government's share of the subsurface rights. With these, millions—perhaps billions—of dollars were involved, and Hoover's Interior believed that the government should continue to get a portion of revenues from the extraction of oil, gas, coal, and other deposits.

The federal government had not always been so perspicacious, giving up significant claim to such hard-rock minerals as gold, silver, and copper when the General Mining Act was passed in 1872. Like its predecessors, the Mining Law of 1866 and the Placer Act of 1870, the 1872 law was predicated on the assumption that mineral prospectors should be given free access to the public lands and that they should be allowed to develop any proven reserves with minimal interference from, and precious little revenue to, the government. Consequently, all that the government had received (would ever receive) from mining claims on the public lands, which had produced tens of billions of dollars of precious and semi-precious minerals since the discovery of gold in California in 1848, were modest filing fees and the sale of mining land at prices that ranged from $2.50 to five dollars an acre. Generations of lawyers were more fortunate. "The law is at once highly specific, wondrously vague, and maddeningly terse," its best historian has written, adding that "a statute so inadequately conceived in its details . . . has proved an enormously productive engine of litigation." (The Mining Law of 1872, one of the holiest of talismans for any western politician, is still with us in all its shoddy glory.)

Although the exploitation of coal, oil, and gas resources on the public lands proved somewhat more profitable to the government, it was not without its own share of confusion, litigation, and chicanery. Public coal lands, which became increasingly valuable as the railroad industry grew in the 1830s and 1840s, had been subjected to almost entirely uncontrolled depredation until 1864, when the first Coal Act stipulated that the General Land Office could sell them at auction to the highest bidder at no less than twenty dollars an acre. The next year, in an effort to control speculation, an amendment restricted auction sales to individuals already engaged in mining coal on units of public lands not to exceed 160 acres. In 1873 a third version provided that any citizen (or any individual who declared it his intention to become a citizen) could claim unreserved coal lands up to a maximum of 160 acres, while any association of individuals was privileged to claim as many as 320 acres; in either case, the fee was to be not less than twenty dollars an acre within fifteen miles of a railhead and ten dollars an acre beyond fifteen miles. Furthermore, those already mining coal from public lands could form an association of not less than four persons and could get access to as many as 640 additional acres at the same prices if they already had expended no less than five thousand dollars in work and improvements on their existing claims to demonstrate their intent.

Like the rest of the land laws, those regulating the sale of coal land were vulnerable to abuse, not the least example of which was the filing of coal-land claims in various national forests in order to get at timber. It was little help when the General Land Office consistently interpreted "no less than" to mean "no more than," refusing to gear its prices to the actual value of any given deposit and playing into the hands of speculators who could and did turn around and sell their claims to mining companies at prices many times higher than those that the government charged. The reluctance of the General Land Office may have stemmed from nothing more sinister than bureaucratic inertia, but by 1906, Theodore Roosevelt was determined to move things around and about to see that the government got a fair return for the public's resources. As one such move, he had legislation introduced for a bill stipulating that the government would retain ownership of all public coal lands and lease them on a per-ton royalty basis. Even before this revolutionary proposal entered the congressional lists (going down to defeat within a few months), the President ordered the withdrawal of about sixty-six million acres of potential coal land and instructed the Secretary of the Interior to investigate, classify, and place a fair value on them. Similar withdrawals were made by Presidents Taft and Wilson, until by the middle of 1916, 140,533,745 acres had been removed from entry under any of the public-land laws.

The body chosen to do the work of exploration, classification, and evaluation was one of the few generally admired agencies in the Department of the Interior: the U.S. Geological Survey (USGS), an outfit with considerable experience in the business of seeking out the lay of the land—and what lay *within* the land. It had been engineered into existence by Major John Wesley Powell, a one-armed government scientist who had led the first riverboat exploration of the Grand Canyon in 1869 and in the 1870s had headed up the official survey of the Colorado Plateau Province. His was only one of four mutually independent government surveys then scratching around in the West, and in 1879 Powell convinced Congress that the surveys needed central direction and control to be fully efficient. Powell became head of the USGS himself in 1882, and by the time of his resignation in 1894 had established the agency as the epitome of what the best of government science could do and be.

The USGS went about its task of investigating the nation's public coal lands with a will that Powell (who died in 1902) would have approved, and by March 1907 it had studied and released back to land law entry twenty-eight million acres of Roosevelt's withdrawals as being too poor in coal reserves to be commercially mined. With the aid of a Land Classification Board, created in 1908, the Survey refined its efforts to such an extent that as early as 1909 it had placed a market value of $30,488,351 on 742,573 acres of coal lands—a valuation that added up to more than twice what the land would have brought in under the minimum prices of the 1873 law. And it paid off: between 1900 and 1907, there had been 1,285 coal-land entries on a total of 189,527.13 acres, the prices for which had averaged fourteen dollars per acre; between 1908 and 1914, however, there had been 2,372 entries on 355,418.95 acres for an average price of $16.91—the government had made more than one million dollars more than it would have under the old system.

Agitation for a leasing system continued over the years, however, advocates pointing out that a long-term leasing program could generate many millions more in income than short-term sales—and the government would simultaneously maintain some control over when and how a finite public resource would be used. Just such a system had been established for the coal lands of Alaska in 1914. By 1920 sentiment in Congress was so strong for the idea that even its western members had to concede that the withdrawn coal lands (more than sixteen million acres still had not been classified) were not likely to be released for development until a leasing system was in place. Contributing to this new sentiment had been the question of petroleum reserves. For years they had been "mined" under the provisions of the Placer Mining Act of 1870, for want of any more appropriate statute, but until the turn of the century, oil had been so minor a component of the national economy that few had concerned themselves with its value as a national resource. The rise of the automobile industry, the development of more efficient oil-burning loco-motives, and World War I, however, brought a more seemly regard. In 1909 the director of the Geological Survey pointed out that oil-rich public lands were disappearing into private hands so fast that the govern-ment might "be obliged to repurchase the very oil that it has practically given away." President Taft responded by temporarily withdrawing about three million acres of oil land, then—nervous about his constitutional authority to do so—asked Congress for legislation specifically authorizing such withdrawals. Congress gave him the Pickett Act of 1910, and under its provisions he withdrew enough additional oil land to form Naval Reserves 1 and 2 at Elk Hills and Buena Vista Hills in California; Wilson would add Reserve No. 3 at Teapot Dome in Wyoming in 1915, and later reserves would be established in Colorado, Utah, and Alaska.

As with the coal lands, it was becoming increasingly clear that the majority of Congress was never going to consent to the development of oil lands without some sort of leasing program, and so it was that Senator Reed Smoot of Utah, who had long opposed leasing, in 1919 introduced a mineral leasing bill that would apply to coal, oil, gas, oil shale, phosphate (useful in making fertilizer), potassium, and sodium. (Another mineral, potash, an important ingredient in the manufacture of explosives, had been given its own leasing law in 1917.) Smoot's bill became the Mineral Leasing Act, the first major change in the mining laws in nearly fifty years. Passed on February 25, 1920, it was signed into law by President Wilson. The government was now in the minerals business on a perma-nent basis, and in 1933 the new Interior Secretary Harold Ickes would find his office not only supervising the leasing program through the General Land Office but monitoring the state of the industry through the Department's Bureau of Mines; acting as the designated custodian of the records and files of the United States Fuel Administration, the Bi-tuminous Coal Commission, and the United States Coal Commission (on all of which the Secretary also held seats); and himself sitting as the designated chairman of the Federal Oil Conservation Board.

If the Mineral Leasing Act of 1920 was, as one historian has called it, "a belated effort to safeguard the remnants of the nation's lands . . . after a century and a half of speculation and exploitation marked by exalted references to manifest destiny and internal improvements," the Newlands Act of 1902 was in large part a belated effort to rectify the manifest shortcomings of the Homestead Act of 1862. That act had been passed to provide land for the small farmer, an individual perceived as the heart of what made America great, and on the face of it should have accomplished that worthy goal, for its terms were both generous and simple: for a small filing fee, a citizen (or soon-to-become citizen) could obtain title to 160 acres of public land (320 for a man and wife) if he lived on and cultivated it for five years. But the law had been conceived out of experience derived in the well-watered eastern third of the nation; west of the Mississippi River aridity was the central fact of existence, more so the farther west one went, and it was in the West that homesteading most frequently applied. Without irrigation, the fate of the small farmer was problematic at best. "It took a man to break and hold a homestead of 160 acres even in the subhumid zone," Wallace Stegner has written. "It took a superman to do it on the arid plains. It could hardly, in fact, be done, though some heroes tried it." By the 1890s the dryland farmers of the West who had survived—many of them anything but small, corporate farming having become a dominant force—had their gazes fixed upon and their palms extended toward the federal government in Washington. The government, they reasoned, had tried to provide land for the landless; why should it not now provide water for the waterless? Their timing was excellent: the Progressive Movement was beginning its first surge to power and the notion of perpetuating the Jeffersonian ideal was perfectly suited to the era. When Theodore Roosevelt assumed the Presidency in 1901, it was virtually certain that something would be done. That something had been the Newlands—or Reclamation—Act, named after its chief supporter, Congressman Francis Newlands of Nevada, and passed on June 17, 1902. The act stipulated the creation of the federal Reclamation Service as a department in the U.S. Geological Survey; the service's function would be to build dams and other irrigation works in the western states. The works would be designed to provide water to both public and private lands. To promote small farms and prevent the kind of land and water monopoly that had characterized western development, the act also specified that no farm family would be sold cheap federal water for more than 160 acres (later amended to 320 acres). Furthermore, the farmers had to live on and actually work the land in order to qualify; absentee owners need not apply. To receive federal water on any portion of his land, the farmer had to agree to sell off all acreage in excess of 160 (or 320) acres within ten years of signing a water contract with the government—and to sell it at prewater prices. "Not one dollar will be invested," Frederick Newell, the first director of the Reclamation Service, promised the members of the National Irrigation Congress in 1905, "until the Government has a guarantee that these large farms will ultimately be put into the hands of small owners, who will live upon and cultivate them."

Millions of dollars were, in fact, invested right from the start by the Reclamation Service, which became an independent agency in the Department of the Interior in 1907 and had its name changed to the Bureau of Reclamation in 1923. By 1933 twenty-five reclamation projects irrigating forty thousand farms on 1.5 million acres had been completed, chief among them Roosevelt Dam on the Salt River of Arizona, which at the time of its completion in 1911 was the highest in the world, rising 280 feet from bedrock to impound 1.5 million acre-feet of water.* Even more impressive was another Arizona reclamation effort: the Boulder Canyon Project, authorized in 1928 but, by 1933, just beginning the first phases of construction. Among its most stupendous features would be Hoover Dam (later called Boulder Dam; later still, Hoover again) on the Colorado, which would pile cement 730 feet above bedrock, with a crest of 1,180 feet spanning the river from Arizona to Nevada. Two enormous powerhouses would generate more electricity from falling water than any other hydroelectric project anywhere in the world, and, farther downriver, a huge irrigation ditch called the All-American Canal would carry water from the Colorado to the rich floodplain of the otherwise arid Imperial Valley of southern California. And engineers were dreaming of similarly outsized projects for the Columbia and Missouri rivers as well.

Exciting business—but there was a sour note. Like the Homestead Act whose hardships and inequities it had been conceived to alleviate, the Reclamation Act was twisted to fit convenience and its most revolutionary stipulation plainly ignored. First, the announcement that the bureau was about to develop an area did not so much bring forth the anticipated flood of small family farmers to apply for homesteads and cheap water as it attracted a gaggle of speculators who filed homestead claims by the truckload and signed water contracts with every intention of selling both at hugely inflated prices once water arrived—such sales more often than not going to outside corporations, not family farmers. Second, at least half the projects in the first thirty years of operation went to the benefit of those who already had owned land when the projects were authorized, often in tracts of several thousand acres in size. Third, many reclamation farms ended up being worked by tenant farmers, while the owners lived in places like San Francisco, Denver, and Los Angeles, a clear violation of law. Fourth, in 1926, responding to corporate pressures, Congress extended the repayment time for federal water to forty years, with no interest, which alone amounted to one of the largest federal subsidies in history. Finally, the political pressure from western interests that was placed on the bureau at every level from farm fields to the carpeted offices

---

* An acre-foot is enough water to cover an acre to a depth of one foot; it is 353,000 gallons or, as historian W. H. Hutchinson has said, "enough water to flush approximately 60,000 suburban toilets simultaneously."

of the Secretary of the Interior produced what can only be called one of the most glaring examples of bureaucratic nonfeasance in our history: not one single landowner getting federal water from federal reclamation projects had ever been forced to sell his excess lands as required by the law. By 1933, federal reclamation, the dream of social engineers, had become largely the province of federal dam-builders and corporate entrepreneurs, any one of whom would have found comfort in the brave anthropocentrism of reclamation advocate John Widtsoe in his 1928 book, *Success on Irrigation Projects:* "The destiny of man is to possess the whole earth; and the destiny of the earth is to be subject to man. There can be no full conquest of the earth, and no real satisfaction in humanity, if large portions of the earth remain beyond his highest control."

Elsewhere in the warrens of the big Interior building in Washington, Ickes might have found lurking a more benign attitude toward the land. Of all the land-management agencies in his department, in fact, there was only one that the new Secretary could have looked upon in full confidence that it did not perceive the American land as a commodity to be sold off or conquered to service the needs of economic progress: the National Park Service, one of the youngest agencies in Interior and almost entirely the creation of one singularly energetic man, Stephen Mather. Even before the Forest Reserve clause of 1891 had set in motion the withdrawal of public lands for sundry public purposes, Congress had been moved to establish the first national park in American history. This was a 2.2-million-acre region of scenic magnificence in the upper Yellowstone River valley of Wyoming, set aside in 1872 as "a public park or pleasuring ground for the benefit and enjoyment of the people." Over the next four decades, Yellowstone National Park had been followed by the congressional withdrawal of other areas so beautiful or geographically unique or commercially valueless that they were deemed suitable as parks—Yosemite, Sequoia, and General Grant in 1890; Mt. Rainier in 1899, Crater Lake in 1902, Mesa Verde in 1906, Grand Canyon in 1908, Zion in 1909, Glacier in 1910, and Rocky Mountain in 1915. In addition, under the provisions of the Antiquities Act of 1906, which empowered the President to withdraw lands by executive order if they contained valuable scientific, historic, or scenic treasures, Presidents Roosevelt, Taft, and Wilson had established sixteen national monuments, ranging from the 211,272-acre Dinosaur National Monument in Colorado-Utah to the seventeen-acre Tumacacori National Monument in Arizona.

Altogether, by 1916 nearly 7.5 million acres had been folded into what was called the National Park System, though there was in fact precious little system involved. There was no single director of the system, no single office in charge of the system, and no general law under which the system might be regulated and administered. In 1914, Wilson's Secretary of the Interior Franklin K. Lane received a letter from the "borax king," Stephen Mather, an old school chum, who complained about the poor management practices he had witnessed in Yosemite.* "Dear Steve," Franklin replied. "If you don't like the way the parks are being run, come on down to Washington and run them yourself." Mather, happily retired from the pursuit of money at the age of forty-seven, took him up on the challenge. Over the next two years, the new director put in prodigious hours and a great deal of his own money to improve the facilities of the parks, expand staff, increase public awareness and visitation, and lobby Congress for legislation that would place the system under the umbrella of a central agency. His efforts in the latter regard succeeded in 1916, with passage in August of the National Parks Organic Act, which established within the Department of the Interior the National Park Service to

> promote and regulate the use of the Federal areas known as national parks, monuments, and reservations hereinafter specified by such means and measures as conform to the fundamental purposes of said parks, monuments, and reservations, which purpose is to conserve the scenery and the natural and historic objects and the wildlife therein and to provide for the enjoyment of the same in such manner and by such means as will leave them unimpaired for the enjoyment of future generations.

Congress did not give Mather much with which to accomplish this tangled mouthful of majestic instruction: a salary for himself of $4,500 a year, with $2,500 a year for an assistant director, $2,000 for a chief clerk, $1,800 for a draftsman, and another $8,100 to spread around in salaries anywhere he thought it would do some good in Washington. In the field he received $30,000 a year for the management of each of the national parks and $166 for each of the national monuments. Undaunted, Mather set out to make over the National Park System, aided most notably by publicist Robert Sterling Yard, former editor of *Century* magazine (whose salary was paid out of Mather's pocket) and, after 1919, young Horace Albright, former superintendent of Yellowstone. To a great extent, Mather succeeded. Visitation to the parks increased from less than a million in 1916 to 3.7 million by 1933, largely because of Mather's

---

* Mather had made a fortune as a salesman for the Twenty Mule Borax Company of Chicago, had then retired, and now, at the age of forty-six, spent his time on various philanthropic projects, when not camping, hiking, and mountain climbing.

insistent publicity campaign and his aggressive construction of roads and visitor facilities.* Mather and Albright personally led repeated and very popular park junkets for newspapermen like Irwin S. Cobb, magazine editors like George Horace Lorimer of the *Saturday Evening Post,* philanthropists like John D. Rockefeller, Jr., and politicians like Representative Louis Crampton of Michigan, chairman of the House Appropriations Subcommittee for Interior—all of this essential, as Mather saw it, in building a constituency of support for funding and park expansion. He got both. By 1929, he had an annual budget of more than $9 million and another ten million acres in seven new parks and thirteen new monuments, not including Great Smoky Mountains and Shenandoah national parks, both of them authorized by Congress but still being pieced together from private lands by the time illness forced Mather's retirement.

Horace Albright succeeded Mather (who died in 1930), declaring it his goal to "consolidate our gains, finish up the rounding out of the park system, to go rather heavily into the historical park field, and get such legislation as is necessary to guarantee the future of the system on a sound permanent basis, where the power and the personality of the Director may no longer have to be controlling factors in operating the Service." The cult of personality may have ended, but the legacy from the large personality of Stephen Mather to the equally large personality of Harold L. Ickes was an agency whose health was good and whose integrity was unquestioned, an institution that went a long way toward validating the opinion of British Ambassador James Bryce that America's national parks were the best idea we ever had.

The five hundred million acres of federal land and the confusion of laws and agencies at work upon them made up what was far and away the largest responsibility of Ickes's job. But it was by no means the only one. By 1933 the Department of the Interior had lost the Bureau of the Census and the Patent Office to the Department of Commerce and the supervision of federal district attorneys, marshals, and deputy marshals to the Department of Justice, but had retained everything else and had gained even more—not merely the U.S. Geological Survey, the Bureau of Mines, and the Bureau of Reclamation, as noted, but such items as the territories of Alaska, Hawaii, and the Virgin Islands, none of them small matters.

---

* He was too successful for Yard, who believed the parks should remain in as primitive a state as possible; he broke with his benefactor and began to oppose him from a perch as director of the National Parks Association, which—ironically—Mather had helped him found in 1919.

Alaska, purchased from Russia in 1867, was a great immensity so underpopulated by U.S. citizens in the beginning that it had been administered at various intervals by the army, the Treasury Department's Customs Office, and the navy. The discovery of gold in Canada's neighboring Yukon Territory in 1897 and then in Alaska itself had wakened Congress to its significance, and it was given the status of an official territory and a civil government. It was still so remote and underpeopled in 1933, however, that much of it remained unexplored and most of it unsurveyed, and the principal administrative difficulties it presented were in the governing of its native population of Tlingit, Aleut, Athabascan, and Eskimo peoples.

The four large and nineteen small islands of the Territory of Hawaii, which voluntarily became a possession of the United States in 1898 and a territory in 1900, were, at a distance of seven thousand miles, even more remote from the homeland than Alaska, but they were more abundantly—and variously—populated, with 370,000 people, including 20,000 Hawaiian natives, or Kanakas, 25,000 Chinese, 65,000 Filipinos, 140,000 Japanese, and 65,000 Caucasians, most from the United States. With an economy firmly based on the production of pineapples, cane sugar, and happy tourists, and its government comfortably manipulated by a consortium of merchants called the "Big Five," Hawaii gave every outward appearance of Paradise. By contrast, the Virgin Islands, purchased for purposes of naval strategy from Denmark in 1917, were in very bad shape. Administered by the navy until they were turned over to the Department of the Interior by Executive Order in 1931, their population had actually decreased in the five previous years, from 27,000 to 22,000, and their economy was moribund.

In the summer of 1934, the Territory of Puerto Rico, with its own set of complexities, would be taken out of the control of the War Department and given to the Interior Department, too. In the meantime, among the other odd tasks that had fallen to the lot of the new Interior secretary were five that would prove to give him less grief than any other part of his job. The first was supervision of the Office of Education, placed in Interior in 1869. Its functions were devoted to the gathering and dissemination of statistics and other information deemed useful to the nation's educators and school systems, the administration of funds provided the land-grant colleges by the Morrill Act of 1862, the conducting of biennial education surveys, and the publication of a monthly periodical, *School Life*. More direct connections to education were provided by Howard University up by McMillan Reservoir, a fully accredited all-black university that had been established in 1867 and was now the largest such institution in the

United States, and by the Columbia Institution for the Deaf at Seventh Street and Florida Avenue in Washington. Founded by an act of Congress in 1857, the institution had grown to include not only the twelve-grade Kendall School, but Gallaudet College, a five-year college that was the only institution for higher learning for the deaf anywhere in the world. Finally, there were Freedmen's Hospital, established in 1865 as the hospital for the city's black population (and staffed largely by personnel connected to the nearby Howard University Medical School), and St. Elizabeth's Hospital, the largest federal hospital for the mentally ill in the United States, an entity of a hundred buildings sprawled over 160 acres on a bluff four miles from central Washington, complete with truck gardens, poultry pens, and a dairy herd. Fully half its forty-six hundred patients came from the service branches of the government—the army, navy, Marine Corps, and the like—while the other half came from the District of Columbia. There were those (Ickes often was among them) who looked around Congress from time to time and concluded that perhaps too many people had been left outside the walls of St. Elizabeth's.

Ickes would deal with these last five responsibilities usually only at budget time. There was very little corrupted or corruptible in them, and with few exceptions their administration would never prove to be a chore that sapped the considerable energies of the new Secretary. It was just as well, for he had a sufficiency on his plate already and would get more, much more, very shortly. Not that the prospect chilled him, he insisted in 1948. He was, he remembered,

> not only willing to undertake, I was eager for, the task. When I went to my office early in the morning of March 5, 1933, it was with the resolve that each day I would so conduct myself that, at the end of it, I would be able to put on my hat, close the door firmly behind me and say to myself, "Well, that was that." It was in this spirit that I finally reached for my hat on February 12, 1946, and said to myself, "To hell with it." The surprising thing is that there should have been such a long interval between.

CHAPTER

· 27 ·

The Hundred and Twenty-two Days

W HAT HAPPENED ON March 4," Anne O'Hare McCormick told her readers on March 19, "was more than a transfer of authority from one party to another. . . . It was a real transposition of power, so that instinctively people refer to the event as a change in government instead of a change of administration." Nearly two months later, she also detected a great change in mood from that air of somber anxiety that had characterized the city of Washington—indeed the country—in the weeks preceding Roosevelt's inauguration. The people, she said,

> are vivified by a strong undercurrent of wonder and excitement. You feel the stir of movement, of adventure, of elation. You never saw before in Washington so much government, or so much animation in government. Everybody in the administration is having the time of his life. So they say, and so you perceive as you watch the new officials . . . settling into this great business of national reconstruction. They dash from conference to conference, from hearing to hearing, briefcases bursting with plans and specifications. They are going somewhere, that is plain.

By then, she was writing from the core of what came to be called "The Hundred Days," that period from March 4 to June 16, 1933, which saw fifteen major new government programs muscled into existence, written up into legislative form by a handful of dedicated advisers in a frenzy of effort that often consumed eighteen to twenty hours a day for weeks on end, most of the proposed new laws then jammed through Congress so swiftly it sometimes seemed that Roosevelt had become the dictator the most stubborn mossbacks had always feared was his darkest ambition. As early as the March 22 issue of the *New Republic,* "T.R.B." seemed to look upon even this possibility with some equanimity:

> The speed with which the government of the United States has moved from democracy to dictatorship has more or less stunned the statesmen on the Hill, but it apparently has pleased nearly everyone else. As things stand today, Mr. Roosevelt has, in some respects, more power than any President under our Constitution ever had, except perhaps Mr. Wilson in wartime, and while some thoughtful men here are disturbed over what they call a surrender of its constitutional rights by Congress, the shadow of the national emergency stills their protest and controls their vote. And when the facts are considered it seems clear that nothing else could be done.

"We're fiddling along with more legislation," Hiram Johnson wrote his wife, "than any one man or any legislative body can accurately digest." Congress was not quite putty in Roosevelt's hands during this period, as legend usually has had it; much that got through to passage required long bouts of negotiations with those who exercised the most power on the Hill—namely, committee chairmen—and often superhuman efforts at persuasion, not infrequently by FDR himself. Still, there is no questioning the fact that at no other time in our history did so much new law get passed so swiftly. The first piece of legislation was an emergency banking act, passed less than eight hours after its introduction on March 9 as the first order of business for the special session of Congress FDR had called in the early morning hours of March 6. The law ended the bank holiday, allowing banks with liquid assets to reopen immediately and authorizing the reorganization of those in worse shape; gave the President control over the movement of gold; set up penalties for hoarding; authorized the issuance of new Federal Reserve notes; and, not incidentally, validated everything the President already had done.

With that act as a kind of opening wedge, over the next three months Congress ground out at varying speeds legislation whose sundry stipulations cut $400 million from the federal budget, established a Civilian Conservation Corps to put unemployed young men to work, repealed prohibition, set up a program of Federal Emergency Relief, authorized the emergency refinancing of farm mortgages, established a national agricultural policy, conferred on the President broad powers of monetary expansion, took the United States off the gold standard, provided for the unified agricultural and social development of the Tennessee River Valley by the federal government, attempted to stabilize the railroad industry, stated that full disclosure must accompany the issuance of new securities, made provisions for the financing and refinancing of home mortgages, reorganized the agricultural credit system, guaranteed bank deposits, separated investment banking and commercial banking operations, established voluntary price and wage controls throughout industry, validated the right of labor to organize and bargain collectively with management, put in place a public works program that made Hoover's seem paltry by comparison, and abrogated the gold clause in private and public contracts.

It was a storm of legislation, a hurricane of laws, a phenomenon unlike anything ever seen in this country before and not duplicated since. Even Edmund Wilson felt the energy that drove it all. Washington, he said, "is more entertaining than I have ever known it before, and more lively than at any time since the war. The last administration weighed on Washington, as it did on the entire country, like a darkness, like an oppressive bad dream, in which one could neither speak nor act; and the talk and animation in Washington today are a relief like waking up from a dream." And from the cluttered rolltop desk of William Allen White in Emporia, Kansas, came an exclamation to the new Secretary of the Interior, Harold Ickes: "These are grand days, worth living for!"

Ickes certainly would have agreed, though he had precious little time for celebration. While the winds of the hundred days buffeted him quite as profoundly as anyone in the administration—and more than most—he was busily stirring things up himself over at Interior. "The first thing to do, surely," he wrote in his *Saturday Evening Post* reminiscences in 1948, "was to clear away dead wood and recruit men of ability and character who had the same convictions that I had, men whom I could trust." Surely it was, and surely he did—but what he did not go out of his way to mention in 1948 was the extent to which patronage played a part in his selection of those to go and those to come. As one of the largest agencies in government, Interior was a prime arena for political payoffs. There was nothing unusual in this (it had been this way from its inception), nor was it considered particularly reprehensible. The new Roosevelt administration owed a lot to a lot of people, and from the first, Roosevelt used the opportunity to repay such debts with the Interior Department as coin; shortly after his inauguration, for instance, he sent the names of Theodore A. Walters, attorney general for Idaho and a protégé of Idaho senator William E. Borah, and Oscar Chapman, a lawyer in the Colorado firm of Senator Edward Costigan (and Costigan's campaign manager), to the

Senate as assistant secretaries of the Interior. Both had been confirmed swiftly. (Chapman would become a career man at the agency and would himself become Secretary of the Interior in 1949.)

Ickes took no umbrage at such "politicization" of his department by the Chief Executive; it would occasionally give him grief by saddling him with someone of little real use to him, but it was a fact of life in the Washington of his day and he learned to live with it—sometimes a little sullenly, to be sure. In fact, until the Hatch Act of 1939 attempted to put an end to the spoils system, Ickes, like other administrative heads, was not himself bashful about using his agency to provide jobs for deserving Democrats and a few Progressive Republicans, as well as for their families and friends, though he did resent the amount of time and energy it consumed. "I was under very great pressure this morning," he informed his diary on March 25,

> interviewing people, so that when one o'clock came I was thoroughly tired out. I seem to have an unusual proportion of job hunters. This is the most difficult aspect of this office, as it is of any public office where there is patronage to distribute. Of course, the people who come in to see me about it are nothing as compared to those who write me. Hundreds and hundreds of letters, bespeaking jobs either for the writers or for someone else, have to be answered every day.

Over time, the friends and relatives of Harold Ickes, too, were given jobs in his department, among them his son Robert; a niece (the daughter of his sister Mary); an old family friend, Ruth Hampton; and Jane Dahlman, the fresh-out-of-college sister of his daughter-in-law, Betty Dahlman Ickes. Among those outside the immediate Ickes circle who benefited from his largesse was the son of Secretary of Agriculture Henry Wallace, who was fortunate enough to have been looking for work while his father and Ickes were still speaking to each other on a regular basis.

Most of these kinds of appointments were to such low-level jobs as clerkships and secretarial positions, and whenever he found it necessary to mention them, Ickes always emphasized that he demanded quite as much from any of the individuals involved as he would have of anyone else in his department, and it probably was true. Other positions carried more weight, and Ickes seems to have made his decisions about most of these pretty firmly on the grounds of merit and competence, duly acknowledging political indebtedness where possible but often reaching outside the ring of patronage for his people. One of the first was Nathan Margold, appointed as Interior Department solicitor. A Jew of Romanian birth, the thirty-three-year-old Margold had been brought to this country by his parents in 1901 and was naturalized shortly after his graduation from the

City College of New York. He had been able to get into Harvard Law School in spite of university president Lawrence Lowell's rigid quota system for Jews, but had not been accepted by Lowell for appointment to the faculty after his graduation in 1923—an appointment urged on Lowell by Professor Felix Frankfurter, among others. Margold had gone on to become an assistant U.S. attorney for the southern district of New York, had taught at Harvard in 1927 and 1928 in spite of Lowell's anti-Semitism (though only on a temporary basis), had served as special counsel for the New York Transit Commission, and had been special counsel to the N.A.A.C.P. and legal adviser on Indian matters with the Institute for Government Affairs, the latter of which had brought him to Ickes's attention. Until his appointment to the municipal bench of the District of Columbia in 1942, Margold would serve his new boss brilliantly on both the professional and, from time to time, the personal levels. Felix Cohen and Charles Fahy, both of whom, like Margold, had been deeply involved in the question of Pueblo Indian rights in New Mexico, came in as the new solicitor's assistants.

Another, no less important (though in the end considerably less gratifying) appointment was that of Harry Slattery as one of his two personal assistants. The new Secretary had inherited E. K. (Ebert Keiser, but known to all as "E.K.") Burlew, who had been with the department since 1923. Burlew was a good detail man, swift and reliable, Ickes had concluded, an assessment borne out by Milburn Wilson, who joined the department later that year and remembered Burlew in action: "He was an extremely hard person, and a very quick person. . . . He was at Ickes' elbow all the time. Ickes could press a button, and almost anything he wanted, Burlew could come back in a very few minutes with it." Still, Ickes felt Burlew would be less valuable in matters of policy and general administration. For this, he turned to Slattery, whose credentials for the job were impressive. Born in Greenville, North Carolina, in 1887, the courtly, slow-talking, apparently imperturbable Slattery had become Gifford Pinchot's secretary in the Forest Service in 1909 and had left with his chief when Pinchot was fired by Taft. After several years as secretary of the National Conservation Association, a citizens' group Pinchot had founded in 1909 to keep an eye on the government's administration of the forests and the development of public power projects, Slattery became special assistant to Interior Secretary Franklin K. Lane in 1917, then in 1918 moved over to the Department of Labor as assistant to Labor Secretary William Wilson. During the twenties he had practiced law and served as counsel to the Boulder Dam Association, a lobbying group, and to the National Conservation Association, and in 1931 had become

Washington representative for the New York Power Authority. His connections, which included Senator George Norris and his old boss Gifford Pinchot, were as impressive as his credentials, and it was the connections as much as anything else, as Slattery remembered it, that got him the job with Ickes—though it had not been quite the job he apparently expected:

> Many friends of mine . . . had written President Roosevelt urging I be appointed an Assistant Secretary of the Interior. Louis Howe called me into the White House and phoned Ickes asking him to see me. A few days afterward, the Secretary called me over. He said: "Let's get along with the appointment." He called in the Chief Clerk to give me the oath as Personal Assistant to the Secretary and hastily a few officials and friends were summoned to the office to be present. . . . Ickes was not one addicted to ceremonies.

The Margold, Cohen, Fahy, and Slattery appointments had been pretty straightforward affairs. Not as much could be said for the appointment of John Collier as commissioner of the Bureau of Indian Affairs, which came about via many of the same Byzantine paths whereby Ickes had become Secretary of the Interior. When Ickes offered him the job—indeed, insisted that he take it—Collier wrote in his memoirs, the "proposal thoroughly dismayed me, and I asked for time to think it over." This was specious nonsense; the head of the American Indian Defense Association had been fighting for the job ever since he contrived to maneuver Ickes away from it earlier in 1933.

Even with Ickes out of the running and on his way toward the Interior post, it had been necessary to fight for it; the position of commissioner of Indian Affairs traditionally was one of the chief patronage plums, usually filled not so much on the grounds of what an individual could do for the Indians as on what he lately had done for some needy politician. Tradition had been modified somewhat this time around when the names of Nathan Margold and Brookings Institution economist Lewis Meriam, author of *The Problem of Indian Administration* (1928), had come up for discussion. Neither of these was a political hack, but Meriam had declared himself not interested in the job and Margold was removed as a possibility when he became Interior solicitor. Collier could have endorsed either man (and in communications with Roosevelt's people had mentioned them with himself as prime candidates), but he could not stomach the idea of Edgar B. Meritt, a certifiable hack as well as a moralizing bigot who had served during the Harding and Coolidge administrations as assistant commissioner and, among other things, had pushed for legislation that would have empowered the bureau to prosecute its charges for such violations as "unlawful cohabitation, fornication, seduction, carnal knowledge, incest, polygamy, lewdness, soliciting females for immoral purposes, and desertion of wife." By April, Meritt nevertheless had emerged as the leading candidate.

Ickes, who had already fired two holdovers in the bureau because of their attitudes toward the Indians (one had declared that eleven cents a day was more than enough to feed an Indian child), found Meritt quite as repellent as Collier did, but the former assistant commissioner came armed with the determined support of majority leader Senator Joseph T. Robinson of Arkansas; Meritt was an Arkansas native popular with local politicians and Robinson had a few debts to pay himself. By this time, however, the equally determined Ickes had decided that he wanted Collier. "My concern," he had written Indian advocates and Collier supporters Mr. and Mrs. Charles de Young Elkus of San Francisco on February 28,

> is to bring about the appointment of a Commissioner and Assistant Commissioner to whom I can entrust the administration of Indian affairs without having to bother about it myself. I am being subjected to a great deal of pressure from various quarters [an exaggeration probably; it was a little early for pressure] but I am hopeful that I will be given a free hand. . . . If I am, I have two friends in San Francisco who will not be disappointed in the result.

He still didn't like Collier much, but as he explained later to one of Collier's many enemies, he was willing to rise above animosity for the sake of the Indians:

> I think you know that I have had serious differences of opinion with John Collier. . . . I do believe, however, that no one exceeds him in knowledge of Indian matters or his sympathy with the point of view of the Indians themselves. I want someone in that office who is the advocate of the Indians. The whites can take care of themselves, but the Indians need someone to protect them from exploitation. I want a man who will respect their customs and have a sympathetic point of view with respect to their culture. . . . John Collier, with whatever faults of temperament he may have, has to a higher degree than any one available for that office, the point of view towards the Indians that I want in a Commissioner of Indian Affairs.

Unlike the man he wanted for the job, Ickes had little taste or talent for the devious (he would get better at it as he gained experience in the capital of deviousness), though he did have Margold and Cohen quietly draw up bills of particular against Meritt's candidacy and for that of Collier. Roosevelt, who concurred in the choice but had little enthusiasm for challenging Robinson so early in his administration, counseled patience. "I was willing to be at ease," Ickes remembered, "but I was determined not to make or recommend any other major appointment until Collier had been confirmed." By April 11 he still did not have an Indian commissioner when Marguerite ("Missy") LeHand, Roosevelt's ranking personal secretary, called him to say that the President would like him to come for afternoon tea with himself and Robinson. "After tea had been served," Ickes recalled

> the President, whose adroitness I had never recognized as clearly as I did later that afternoon, asked Senator Robinson how he had got along with Sen. Huey Long, of Louisiana. Robinson, on behalf of the Administration, had been hard put to it to defend the Roosevelt program against the attacks of one of the cleverest and ablest, if one of the most unscrupulous, senators who had ever sat in the upper chamber.
>
> Robinson lost no time in flexing his intellectual muscles. . . . Before such an audience, Joe really surpassed himself, while the President continued to play out the line until he was ready to give the jerk that would firmly fix the hook in the jaw of the fish.

The jerk on the line came just before it would clearly be time to leave and when Ickes had just about given up hope. Having stroked Robinson's ego with the skill for which he was well-known, the President remarked, almost casually, that he knew that Robinson had Meritt in mind for the Bureau of Indian Affairs job, but that he had received a lot of complaints about the idea from "women's organizations, Indian rights associations, and reformers generally. Now, I don't suppose you and I want to go up against that kind of opposition." Robinson, according to Ickes, "made some incoherent reply," upon which FDR moved in for the kill. "Well, I thought you would feel that way about it," he said. "I have been under pressure to name John Collier. And Harold Ickes, here, does not want Meritt. He does not believe that he can work with him. He wants Collier. Since he is to be responsible, I suppose that the thing to do is to let him have the man that he wants." Teatime ended and so did Robinson's sponsorship of his fellow Arkansan. Two days later, Roosevelt sent Collier's name down to the Senate, where, with Robinson's support, he was swiftly and unanimously confirmed.

As Collier's assistant, Ickes appointed an old acquaintance, William Zimmerman, a liberal-minded businessman from Indianapolis, and since the bureau had been a pit of corruption for much of its history, Collier's operation was further strengthened when Ickes chose Louis R. Glavis to head up Interior's Division of Investigations. Glavis, who had set in motion the Pinchot-Ballinger-Taft mess in 1909 with his charges against Interior Secretary Richard Ballinger over the Cunningham coal claims in Alaska, had gone into private law practice in San Francisco after his own dismissal and had acquired some expertise in Indian matters while serving from time to time as a research assistant for the Senate Indian

Investigating Subcommittee. Among Glavis's champions was Senator George Norris of Nebraska, who congratulated Ickes on the choice and suggested that FDR be persuaded to issue an executive order restoring the investigator's civil service status. "This, of course, will be of no benefit, in reality, to Mr. Glavis at the present time," Norris wrote, "but it would be the correction of a record in his favor, and would only be giving to him, after these many years, the exoneration from his removal by Secretary Ballinger." Ickes agreed and by the end of July the executive order had been signed and issued—a singularly ironic note, given the nature of events after Glavis and Ickes parted company a few years later in a split that was nasty even by the standards of an Ickes relationship. For now, however, all relationships were in place and functioning smoothly. Ickes, a "take charge" man if one ever lived in the earth, established the pattern of his operating style early and except on those rare occasions when his body failed him did not let up for the next thirteen years. Righteous, incorruptible, innocent of tact as always, he swiftly began earning the reputation that would inspire a *Time* magazine writer to call him "dog robber to the New Deal." No one could accuse him of sloth (and no one ever would). From the first day, he worked prodigious hours, twelve, fourteen, sixteen a day, in an age in which modern medical science had yet to conjure up the term "workaholic" or invest it with opprobrium. Virtually no slip of paper produced by the agency would escape his attention or go out without his direct approval. His mind was a trash barrel of facts and figures that he shuffled around with frantic energy, his presence a stubby, rumpled sprite that haunted all the cubbyholes of Interior, nose twitching at the smell of disloyalty, birdlike eyes narrowing at the suspicion of lassitude.

Although he used himself savagely (like most such personalities, he expected the same of others and was always a little puzzled when they balked), he had learned a few tricks over the years to keep the details from strangling his time. Such as his office, which was arranged as if to illustrate an article in a business magazine entitled, "How to Keep Things Moving." It was "hot as blazes" in the building (which, like most in those primitive days, was not air-conditioned) when Milburn L. Wilson showed up for his first interview with Ickes in the summer of 1933:

> His office was in one of the wings of the old Interior Building on about the fifth floor. As I remember it, he had his office in a long room and his desk was at the far end of the room. Instead of people waiting in an anteroom, they had a string of chairs right at the door, so that when you went in there you saw all of these people ahead of you there that were waiting. That gave you the feeling that this was an awfully busy man and that you were going to do your

business with him pretty fast. He was down at the far end of the room, so that you wouldn't hear the conversation that went on there when you were sitting next to the door.

Ickes would need all the tricks he could lay hands on, for if the commotion of the first hundred days of the New Deal was a hurricane, the tumult in the Department of the Interior was a whirlwind spinning in the eye of the bigger storm. Ickes had never been so plainly *busy* in his entire busy life. In addition to parrying the continuing assaults of job-seekers and making those appointments most immediately necessary to help him do his job, his activities during this period ranged from accepting a war bonnet from a band of Sioux Indians to sifting through piles of résumés in search of a new governor for the Territory of Hawaii, from attending the twenty-fifth anniversary dinner of the National Press Club to sitting in on meetings of the National Forest Reservation Commission to discuss the purchase of land to "round out" a number of national forests, from using his newfound influence to help squelch a bill in the Illinois state legislature that would have placed on the tax rolls any nonprofit organization in which "sedition" was taught to wielding an axe to come within $2.5 million of the budget cuts required of his department by the President's Economy Act (close enough, FDR said). There were luncheons and dinners to honor such dignitaries as the secretary of the treasury of Mexico or the Canadian ambassador, conferences to discuss the operation of Howard University, and confrontations with delegations objecting to everything from his closing of an Indian school to his changing the name of Hoover Dam to Boulder Dam for the Bureau of Reclamation's Colorado River Project.

And there were the regular cabinet meetings, usually held on Friday afternoons. In later years, Ickes would conclude that most of these served no real purpose. "The fact is," he observed in 1935, "that on important matters we are seldom called upon for advice. We never discuss exhaustively any policy of government or question of political strategy. The President makes all of his own decisions, and, so far at least as the Cabinet is concerned, without taking counsel with a group of advisers. . . . Our Cabinet meetings are pleasant affairs, but we only skim the surface of routine matters." In his memoirs for the *Saturday Evening Post,* he nevertheless described these useless gatherings in some detail:

> Customarily, the President was wheeled into the Cabinet Room by his bodyguard. . . . He was practically never on time. With his cigarette in its inevitable holder at a rakish angle, he would hold extended in his two hands the noon edition of a newspaper. As he reached the door, we all rose and stood respectfully until, with his strong arms and shoulders, he had swung himself

into his chair, which his attendant then pushed to the head of the table. Now
he was ready for business. It was a rare occasion indeed when he was not in a
good humor and ready to open the proceedings with some pleasant quip. . . .
Then he would turn to the Secretary of State, who sat immediately on his
right, and would say, in substance, "Well, Cordell, what have you got for us
today?" Following this, he would go down the Cabinet, skipping from one
side of the table to the other in order of precedence [established, generally,
according to the age of the department in question].

The meetings may have usually been a waste of time, but at least they
gave Ickes the opportunity to observe his colleagues (at least one of them,
in Ickes's view, would become an adversary well worth the watching) at
close quarters. They were a variegated bunch, only one of whom besides
Ickes would stay the full course. Cordell Hull ("the never-smiling Cordell
Hull," Ickes described him), the Secretary of State, was a former senator
from Tennessee, an elegant, white-haired southerner who looked like a
well-cared-for Warren G. Harding; in 1944, seventy-three, exhausted,
and not in the best of health, he would retire. To his left sat the well-liked
and musical Secretary of the Treasury, William H. Woodin, until his own
ill health forced him to take a leave of absence in October 1933, when he
was unofficially replaced by Henry Morgenthau, a gentleman farmer from
FDR's Hyde Park neighborhood who had worked for Roosevelt's gubernatorial administration in New York. Morgenthau, whose position became permanent when Woodin's health forced his resignation on January
1, 1934, was the only Jew in the cabinet, and as such was invariably and
irritatingly described as "sensitive" by most in this group of presumably
thick-skinned, often condescending Gentiles, though Ickes himself preferred "humorless." Secretary of the Navy Claude Swanson, a former
senator from Virginia and chairman of the Senate Naval Affairs Committee, was so old, Ickes noted, that he was "too feeble to get into his chair or
out of it without the help of his assistant"; that was fine by Roosevelt, who
intended to be his own Secretary of the Navy in any case, though Swanson
would retain his largely titular position until his death in 1940. George
Dern, Secretary of War and former governor of Utah, was even more of a
short-termer; he would die in 1936 and be replaced by his assistant,
Harry H. Woodring.

"The massive gum-chewing Jim Farley with brows unfurrowed, but
generally without interest except when a political subject was broached,"
Ickes remembered, sat on his left as Postmaster General until Farley and
Roosevelt split over the question of a third term in 1940. Homer S.
Cummings, a Connecticut lawyer and politician who had served as
chairman of the Democratic National Committee in 1919 and 1920, was

Attorney General, and, Ickes said, "with his Scotch canniness, presented a bland countenance upon which nothing legible was writ"; like most of those who had devoted themselves to the New Deal, Cummings's personal finances had suffered and he would resign in 1939 in order to make some money in private practice. Secretary of Commerce Daniel C. Roper, who had served the government in such capacities as vice chairman of the U.S. Tariff Commission and commissioner of the Internal Revenue Service before joining the Roosevelt administration in 1933, would take his own leave for purposes of money in 1938. Secretary of Agriculture Henry A. Wallace never did leave the Roosevelt administration (however Ickes may have wished it at one time or another), but he did leave the cabinet temporarily, becoming Vice President in 1940, then Secretary of Commerce in 1945; while he was at Agriculture, he and Ickes would be quarreling incessantly over the possession of the U.S. Forest Service, among other things, a situation that tended to color Ickes's memories of their time together in the Cabinet Room, where, he claimed archly, Wallace was "present in the flesh, but usually *in absentia* in spirit."

Only Frances Perkins, Secretary of Labor and Roosevelt's industrial commissioner in New York, would serve with Ickes in the cabinet all the way to the end of the Roosevelt years. (Ickes himself would be the only member of the original New Deal cabinet to hold his job for any length of time *after* Roosevelt's death.) Petite, sharp-minded, experienced, tough (she once had helped to disarm a man who was waving a loaded gun), generous-hearted, and utterly dedicated to the principles of the New Deal, "Madam Secretary," the first woman member of a United States cabinet, tended to annoy Ickes, who, however liberal his instincts and however much he genuinely may have respected any given woman's mind and experience, had trouble all his life accepting women as true equals, particularly women as strong-minded as Perkins. She talked too much, he said, "in a perfect torrent, almost without pausing to take breath, as if she feared that any little pause would be seized upon by someone to break in on her." (In fairness to Ickes, he was not the only man to complain of her loquacity.) He particularly (and revealingly) objected to her habit of jumping up at the end of cabinet meetings and hurrying to get in a word with the President. On one such occasion, he told his diary, she "pushed in ahead of everybody else and continued to talk and talk and talk, regardless of the fact that some of us were waiting for promised brief moments. I didn't get a chance to talk to the President at all. . . ."

While not an official cabinet member, Vice President John Nance Garner was FDR's principal link to Congress and consequently was invited to sit in on the meetings on frequent occasions. Dish-faced and usually smelling of bourbon and cigars, his tiny blue eyes flicking shrewdly from face to face as he dispensed opinions in a west Texas twang, Garner was the very embodiment of the canny country politician, and until his own Presidential ambitions became clear several years later, he won the rare approval of Ickes. As late as 1935, Ickes still thought of him as "a pretty substantial and sturdy character. I have come to feel a growing regard and respect for him. There isn't any doubt that he has the real interests of the country at heart."

If Ickes was sitting there reading the characters of his fellow cabinet members, they were reading him, too. To Henry Morgenthau, he was Washington's "tough guy." To Cordell Hull, he "was often quite far to the left and hence frequently out of line with many of us, and he had an unfortunate approach to problems which not infrequently antagonized others." After seven years of dealing with the Ickes approach, Henry Wallace in his own diary described him with some bitterness in 1940 as a "peculiarly twisted man." Frances Perkins, who either did not recognize or chose to ignore Ickes's chauvinism, was a good deal more kind. "I liked Ickes almost from the start," she remembered nearly twenty years later.

> He set his teeth very firmly, but he had that kind of a face. I remember looking at him and thinking that he had a very Anglo-Saxon face. . . . He looked like the kind of man who would be on Robin Hood's band of Anglo-Saxon men. . . . When he laughed, he had as laughing a face as I ever knew. He could laugh more heartily than most people can, and with a deeper involvement of all parts of his body in his laughter. His wit was very, very considerable. He was a very witty man and capable of repartee. . . . Ickes never left any doubt in anybody's mind that he could give as good as he took. So he had certain jolly qualities that were pleasant to know.

Frances Perkins may have been the only person on the planet ever to have thought of Harold Ickes as "jolly," though his harsh wit and gift of invective would in time become recognized as potent (indeed, pungent) administrative weapons. In the meantime, he found little to laugh about during most of these first months of the New Deal, though at least one development ultimately gave him satisfaction. That was the creation of the Civilian Conservation Corps, which, even if he did not conceive or control it, would prove to be one of the most useful adjuncts of his department's National Park Service operations and a part of the New Deal with which he would always be happy to be identified. By all accounts, the CCC, as it came to be known, was entirely FDR's idea. Frances Perkins remembered it as a "pipe dream" that the President introduced almost casually at an early cabinet meeting. FDR, she said, outlined a general proposal to offer jobs to unemployed young men to perform forestry work and other useful tasks in the national forests, at the national parks, and on other public lands. The young men, he said, would work out of camps that would be administered by the army. Ickes, who must have been having a bad day, interrupted at this point, as Perkins remembered it. "So this will be a military training proposition, will it?" he asked. "This will be forced military training. Take the poor fellows off the streets and put them into the military."

"Oh, no!" Roosevelt said, apparently horrified. "That must never be. That must never be!"

For his part, Henry Wallace remembered that he considered the whole thing a bad idea. "I thought it would be better to have these young people find work at regular jobs—that the economic system itself ought to be cured."

Nevertheless, in a memorandum of March 14, Roosevelt, who had been giving the idea much more thought than Perkins supposed, asked Wallace, together with Ickes for Interior, Perkins for Labor, and Dern for War, to constitute themselves an informal cabinet committee to "coordinate the plans for the proposed Civilian Conservation Corps. These plans include the necessity of checking up on all kinds of suggestions that are coming in relating to public works of various kinds. I suggest that the Secretary of the Interior act as a kind of clearing house to digest the suggestions and to discuss them with the other three members of this informal committee." With the memorandum, he included copies of draft legislation that had been patched together a few days before.

The committee met in Ickes's office the next day and returned its findings so swiftly there was little need for Ickes's "clearing house" function. In fact, the committee overstepped its assignment a bit by suggesting two additional courses of quick action with regard to relief— immediate federal appropriations for grants in aid to the various states for direct relief work, and the launching of a broad public works program. Both ideas had been in the discussion stage even before the inauguration, but this report was one of the first official written articulations of either. As for the CCC, Ickes and the rest felt strongly that it ought to be kept separate from both regular relief efforts and the suggested public works program. "We are of the opinion," the report read,

> that the work to be done by this Corps should be strictly limited to works which are not available as projects for public works, either by the National Government or the State governments, and that it is highly desirable that they should be specifically confined to forestry and soil erosion projects in the Bill.

To confine it to such projects specifically will overcome much of the growing alarm regarding the wisdom of this measure, and will serve to reassure those interested in the constructive permanent relief and stabilization of our population, that no enormous dislocation of population is anticipated with all of the social maladjustments which follow such a program. It will also relieve the minds of those who fear the depressing effect on the wage levels of free labor, due to the wide use of this recruited army, and also those who feel that works which should be done by contract by free labor will be progressively urged as suitable for the Conservation Corps, thus further limiting the opportunity to secure normal work and wages.

These concerns were addressed in FDR's message to Congress when the unemployment relief bill was introduced on March 21. He promised, first of all, early action on federal relief to the states and for public works legislation, then asked for immediate passage of legislation for the creation "of a civilian conservation corps to be used in simple work, not interfering with normal employment, and confining itself to forestry, the prevention of soil erosion, flood control and similar projects." The bill itself added the prevention and fighting of forest fires, the control of plant pests and diseases, and the construction and maintenance of trails and firelanes in the national parks to the list of CCC jobs. Over the objections of American Federation of Labor president William Green, who complained that the thirty dollars a month the program would pay the boys was too low, and socialist Norman Thomas, who said that such "workcamps fit into the psychology of a Fascist, not a Socialist state," Congress passed and Roosevelt signed the bill on March 31. As a sop to the AF of L's Green, Robert Fechner, a vice president of the International Association of Machinists, was appointed to head the agency as director of emergency conservation work, and the operation was divided among four departments: the army to build, outfit, and supervise the camps and provide food, clothing, and medical services for the workers; the Labor Department to enroll the workers; the Interior Department to see to their continuing education through its Office of Education and to supervise work projects in the national parks; and the Agriculture Department to be in charge of work done in the national forests, where most of the boys would be spending most of their time. To someone's worry that this division of responsibility would get confusing, Roosevelt, Perkins remembered, waved it off: "Oh, that doesn't matter. The Army and the Forestry Service will really run the show. The Secretary of Labor will select the men and make the rules and Fechner will 'go along' and give everybody satisfaction and confidence." So it seemed: at its height, the Civilian Conservation Corps would have as many as half a million young men in its ranks, and until World War II put an end to it, the agency became the only innovation of the New Deal to earn the unvarnished respect of nearly everyone.*

If his participation in the creation and operation of this new agency was generally a pleasant business, there was plenty left to try Ickes's patience, chief among the irritants the national oil situation, which was quite the snarl one would expect of an industry so purely exploitive and opportunistic that it provided the twentieth century a powerful hint of what the California Gold Rush must have been like more than eighty years before. Its already convulsive nature had only been exacerbated recently by two of the biggest oilfield discoveries since Edwin L. Drake had brought in his first well in Titusville, Pennsylvania in 1859: Oklahoma City in 1929 and the East Texas field in 1930.

Both fields had been overrun immediately by an unpalatable but entirely typical mix of corporate and independent producers, who sank well after well into the flat short-grass country of both states and wrangled constantly over claims and distribution in the market. As usual in such circumstances, the big corporate producers struggled to establish monopoly, using every means at their disposal, fair or foul, to achieve their ends, while the independents used fang and claw to sustain the Little Man's right to become his own corporation. Greed fueled both factions, of course, and the most troublesome consequence was overproduction, which destabilized prices and gave the entire industry a frenetic character that sent ripples of discord and uncertainty through the entire financial community.

For the most part, the independents wanted to produce without limit so that they could sell enough volume to keep their operations—most of them of the shoestring variety—going on a week-to-week or even day-to-day basis. But production throughout the nation exceeded demand by billions of barrels every year. In 1930, for instance, Interior Secretary Ray Lyman Wilbur, in his capacity as chairman of the Federal Oil Conservation Board, had announced that production had topped 5.03 billion

---

* The creation of the CCC served another useful function during these hundred days of the New Deal. In May, the Bonus Expeditionary Force, or what was left of it, once again made its presence known in Washington, about a thousand men showing up to demand their bonuses for service during World War I. Roosevelt had no intention of giving it to them, but he was equally determined not to repeat the disaster of the previous summer. He provided six hundred tents, complete with showers, latrines, and a mess hall where the men could get three free meals a day. When their number swelled to almost three thousand, he offered them jobs in the CCC, and Eleanor Roosevelt came to the camp for a friendly visit. As one marcher said, "Hoover sent the army; Roosevelt sent his wife." In the end, when it became clear that they were not going to get the bonus, twenty-six hundred men did indeed enroll in the CCC, and the remainder gave up the quest.

barrels, while there was demand for only 2.84 billion barrels. This kind of imbalance frequently had driven the price of oil down to as little as twenty or twenty-five cents a barrel. The situation had gotten so bad that as early as March 1929 even Hoover had been moved to act, closing the public domain to further leasing and canceling approximately 15,000 out of 20,260 outstanding oil and gas drilling permits; the public domain had not been reopened for two years, and then only under strict regulation.

Hoover's actions, of course, had no effect on private lands, where the oil continued to be sucked out at alarming rates. Both Oklahoma, through its Corporation Commission, and Texas, through its Railroad Commission, had attempted to impose restrictions on their immense fields, had even shut some of the producers down at one time or another, and had briefly imposed martial law to keep them down. Most of the corporate producers like Sinclair Oil, Shell Oil, and the various mutations of the Standard Oil Company backed such actions; indeed, there were those ready to insist that the public agencies were in fact controlled by these companies, and made not a move without their advice and consent. Most of the independent producers had fought the restrictions— sometimes by subterfuge, sometimes by violence, and sometimes by challenging state laws in the courts (though the laws were consistently upheld). And still the oil kept coming. By the end of 1932, the Oklahoma City field was producing 33,398,000 barrels a year, while East Texas was pumping a staggering 121,449,000 barrels, only a little under fifty-seven million barrels less than the entire state of California, the nation's largest producer. Equally staggering was the amount of oil being secretly produced in excess of state limits and sold off to cheapjack refineries; "hot oil," it was called, and in the East Texas field alone, it was estimated, 25.3 million barrels of it had been siphoned off illegally in 1932.

During the cabinet meeting of March 14, Roosevelt asked Ickes to call the governors of Oklahoma, Texas, and California—the three biggest oil producers—to see if they would be willing to attend or send representatives to a conference in Washington to discuss federal participation in an effort to control the production and distribution of oil. He did, and Governor William H. ("Alfalfa Bill") Murray of Oklahoma and Governor James ("Sunny Jim") Rolph of California agreed to send representatives; Governor Miriam Fergusson of Texas asked for time to think it over, later deciding to send someone. Ickes later added the name of Governor Alf Landon of Kansas to the list of invitees; Kansas was not quite in a league with the other states as an oil producer (it had produced only a little over 7.3 million barrels in 1932, compared to the nearly 230 million of Texas), but the participation of a Republican governor in the conference would have some political value. Landon promised that he would attend in person. In the meantime, J. Edward Jones, a New York lawyer and sometime representative of independent oil producers, got wind of the conference. Convinced, logically enough, that a conference that included only the representatives of the four major oil-producing states would insure the dominance of the big corporations in any discussions, he sent a telegram on March 16 to the governors of all twenty-one oil-producing states with this warning: "SUCH ISSUES AS REVOLVE AROUND MONOPOLIS-TIC PRACTICES THROUGH UNFAIR COMPETITIVE METHODS REGULATION OF PRODUCTION PRICE FIXING GOVERNMENTAL ACTIVITY RESPECTING INDUS-TRIAL CONDUCT ETCETERA WILL BE TREATED AT CONFERENCE STOP THESE MATTERS SHOULD NOT BE DISCUSSED FOR SOLUTION WITHOUT YOUR STATE BEING REPRESENTED."

As a result, by the time the conference opened on March 27, it had grown to include representatives of numerous state governments, to-gether with officials from the American Petroleum Institute (largely dominated by such corporations as Standard Oil); the Independent Petro-leum Association of America, which represented the moderate wing of the independent producers; a clutch of dissident independents led by Jones and California oilman John B. Elliott; and executives from various major oil companies. The first, though unofficial, meeting took place on Sunday night, before the conference opened on Monday morning, and it served as a precursor of future discord when William Boyd, president of the American Petroleum Institute, rose to introduce a resolution that he urged be adopted immediately. The resolution deplored the continuing overproduction of oil and called for federal control of production at the wellhead. Jones, present as the official representative for the state of Kentucky, made a speech against it, arguing that it was not domestic overproduction that was the problem, but the importation and sale of oil by the large corporations from their foreign operations, most of them in Mexico and South America. This was the standard plea of the more radical independents, even though the facts do not seem to have supported it; from 1932 to 1938, imported crude oil amounted to an average of between 4.3 and 5.6 percent of domestic crude production—and reex-ports reduced the net to between 2.3 and 4.2 percent. Nevertheless, Jones presented the argument passionately; then he and the rest of the radicals walked out while the remaining members passed the resolution.

The next afternoon, the governors' representatives, and Alf Landon as his own representative, met with Ickes in a sixth-floor office of the Interior Building. There the Secretary made a brief opening statement, then suggested that the group form a committee of five to meet with similar committees from big and little oil to see if some kind of agreement on federal action could be worked out. The representatives agreed, and Landon, who had said that he admired "the courage with which President Roosevelt has attacked the depression" and that his own participation in the conference was "one way in which a member of that species thought by many to be extinct—a Republican Governor in a Mid-Western state—can aid in the fight," accepted Ickes's offer to chair the committee. The Secretary then went downstairs to the department auditorium, where he performed another act of mitosis on the group of corporate oilmen and independents who were waiting to hear what he had to say. Form two committees of five men each, was what he had to say, and confer with the governor's committee upstairs. He and Frances Perkins, who at his request had accompanied him to both meetings, then went on to the White House. Here they met with Roosevelt; John L. Lewis, president of the United Mine Workers; Senator Carl Hayden of Arizona; and Congressman David J. Lewis of Maryland (no relation to the histrionic, bristle-browed John L., though himself a former mine worker) to discuss similar overproduction problems in the bituminous coal industry, as well as wage differentials and the horrific working conditions and antiunion sentiments of the industry as a whole. No committees were formed.

On Tuesday morning, Ickes received a delegation of radical independents headed by John B. Elliott and J. Edward Jones, even though the governor of Kentucky had removed Jones as his state's representative the day before, apparently not wanting to be seen as a troublemaker for the Roosevelt administration. They were, Ickes told his diary, "certainly all hot and bothered. They did a lot of haranguing and speech making. They really had a chip on their shoulders. In the end, I managed to find out that they don't want anything at all done to curtail oil production, but they do want action to break up the big oil combinations." Jones claimed that the chip was borne entirely by the Secretary. "As Mr. Ickes listened to Mr. Elliott," he wrote in 1939,

he very definitely began to exhibit a demeanor of anger and belligerency. His face became drawn and almost white. Finally he cut short Mr. Elliott by bursting out, as he turned directly toward me, that "if it hadn't been for Mr. Jones" the Conference would not have been so big. . . . "Mr. Jones," he stated, "went over my head by sending a telegram which implied that I had slighted the governors by not inviting them all. . . ." He then complained that "you independents" had "come down here" and caused trouble by bolting a meeting of oil men on Sunday so that "all the papers" on Monday morning carried news of a breakup of the Conference even before it had been officially called to order by him. Mr. Ickes was obviously a very wrought-up and angry man as he snapped his words in a severe, almost lecturing style.

It probably is safe to assume that chips appeared on many shoulders that morning. Ickes's demeanor very likely did not improve much when, as he reported to his diary, Elliott asked him for a private chat after the meeting's conclusion and proceeded to explain that he had an "in" with the Roosevelt administration. "On two or three occasions," Ickes said, "he threatened me rather crudely. He assured me that he was an old newspaper man . . . and that he knew how to take his case to the newspapers." Ickes does not tell us what his response was, but it can be imagined. Afterward, he went to a joint meeting of the three committees formed the day before, where a draft program for federal action was discussed. Ickes suggested the creation of yet another committee, this one made up of six individuals who would be assigned the task of coming up with concrete proposals, which would then be put into official form by Interior solicitor Nathan Margold.

That night, Jones and the other dissidents had a meeting at the Mayflower and formed the "Independent Petroleum Association Opposed to Monopoly." The next morning, they met again with Ickes. It was a good deal calmer, Ickes said (though Jones insisted that Ickes raised his voice at least once), but still, "The only concrete suggestion they had to make to meet the present emergency was that nothing at all be done. They think that everybody ought to be permitted to produce as much oil as possible, without restraint." Ickes then met again with the representatives of the governors, who, he said, "were beginning to feel neglected" (possibly because they had no committees to sit upon) and after that went into a joint session of the three five-man committees to consider the draft program that the committee of six and Margold had worked out. A final version was put together and taken back up to the governors' representatives, "where we pulled and hauled, and after a number of absolutely unnecessary and lengthy speeches had been delivered, the draft was finally approved on my plea that we conclude the matter and reach an agreement, if possible." Not quite done yet, though: "Then we went down to the auditorium, where we had a meeting of the committee of fifteen, the representatives of the governors, and others interested. Here, once more, the Margold draft was read and approved."

Finally, after conferring with Steve Early, President Roosevelt's press secretary, Ickes and Landon received the press and handed out their agreed-upon program for the control of oil production in the United

States. It was neither very long nor very revolutionary (a not-surprising development, given the number of committees involved in the whole procedure, remarkable even by Washington standards). It called for federal intervention, since, as Landon put it, "even the iron hand of a national dictator is preferable to paralytic stroke," and specifically asked Roosevelt to persuade all state governors to impose a moratorium on production in their "flush pools"—the huge producing fields like East Texas and Oklahoma City—until April 15 and to ask Congress for legislation that would ban the interstate shipment of "hot oil." After the press people had finished asking their questions, the conference finally disbanded.

"The last two or three days have been as strenuous as any I have ever gone through in a political campaign," the now fifty-nine-year-old Ickes wrote in his diary entry for March 29. (His birthday had come on March 15.) "I am thoroughly tired. . . . Whether or not we accomplished anything for the betterment of the oil industry and the good of the country as a result of the conference remains to be shown. At any rate, we worked hard at it and tried to keep as sane an outlook as possible on an intricate and difficult situation." Over the next several days, he would be gratified to receive congratulations for a job well done—not from Roosevelt, but from newspaper people covering the conference, who, he said, told him that he "had made more progress in three days than Dr. Wilbur had in as many months on a prior occasion in connection with the same matter." He had in fact performed with considerable skill in what has to be viewed as his first major challenge as Interior Secretary. Which is not to say that anything much came of it. On Friday, March 31, he met with FDR and laid out the results of the conference. Roosevelt asked him to draft a letter to the governors of the oil-producing states. That letter, sent on April 3 with a copy of the conference report and a copy of the minority report of the Independent Petroleum Association Opposed to Monopoly, made it clear that Roosevelt himself was not ready for dictatorship in the cause of oil conservation. "The President of the United States," it said, "has no authority to declare a moratorium such as is proposed and he might be regarded as infringing on the authority of the sovereign States if he should make the suggestion. . . . There seems to be a widespread feeling that an emergency exists in the oil industry calling for action and it is hoped that the Governors of the States affected, after consultation with each other, will take action appropriate to meet it." On the other hand:

I am of the opinion that the suggestion that the Congress pass legislation prohibiting the transportation in interstate and foreign commerce of any oil or the products thereof produced or manufactured in any State in violation of the laws thereof, is well considered. I am prepared to recommend such legislation to Congress as a contribution on the part of the National Government toward a solution of the difficulties in which the oil industry finds itself.

And then . . . nothing. For the next several weeks Roosevelt put off Ickes's inquiries regarding the proposed legislation for the control of hot oil. It was the Secretary's first exposure to the fact that what Roosevelt said he was going to do and what he actually did often were not one and the same thing. This time, the experience gave Ickes no pain to speak of; in times to come, it would give him plenty.

One of the reasons FDR was slow to act in this politically charged situation, apparently, was that he hoped to be able to discreetly fold proposals regarding the oil situation into legislation, which had slowly been building almost from the first day of his administration, that would create an agency to do for the recovery of the nation's industrial condition what the Agricultural Adjustment Administration (AAA), established by the Farm Relief Act of May 12, was supposed to do for its agricultural situation. "When former civilizations have fallen," Agriculture Secretary Henry Wallace had announced shortly after he came to Washington, "there is a strong reason for believing that they fell because they could not achieve the necessary balance between city and country." The AAA sought to achieve this balance by a complex system to control surplus production through price subsidies financed by a processing tax, marketing agreements to control the sale and distribution of specific products, government loans on storable crops, government purchase of some crops, stiffer controls on the export and import of foodstuffs, and other measures that entwined the federal government and American agriculture in a *Laocoön* of mutuality that would prove permanent.

Just that level of involvement, it was generally believed, would be necessary to the recovery of industry. Like the structure that largely governed the AAA, cooperation among industry, labor, and Washington, Roosevelt believed, should characterize industrial recovery; legislation would provide the machinery by which this interdeperlency could be established and maintained. In *The Democratic Roosevelt,* brain-truster Rexford Tugwell, who had been appointed an Assistant Secretary of Agriculture in the new administration and whose principal responsibility was overseeing the AAA, outlined FDR's thought: "Franklin, in common with a good many others, felt that the negative regulatory philosophy was obsolete, and that a more positive approach ought to be substituted for it.

Industry ought to accept the responsibility for decent social behavior, and it ought to be allowed to develop those common standards of practice which, if enforced, would eliminate the nonconforming few who persisted in 'unfairness.' "

The pressure to do *something* and do it on a grand scale was building in Congress. Senator Hugo Black of Alabama had introduced increasingly popular legislation for a thirty-hour work week, and senators Robert La Follette, Jr. (Wisconsin), Edward Costigan (Colorado), and Bronson Cutting (New Mexico) had cosponsored a bill calling for the expenditure of $6 billion in a public works program; Senator Robert Wagner of New York was busily working up a shopping list for the federal funds. Black's legislation terrified industry and Roosevelt feared that its passage would destroy any chances of cooperation from that quarter; the public works program appalled Lewis Douglas, FDR's supremely cautious director of the Budget, who could see the ultimate destruction of all the good (as he saw it) being wrought by the Economy Act.

With these threats to good order prodding him, Roosevelt turned to a small army of people for advice on how legislation should be shaped. These included Ickes, who on April 27 was appointed chairman of a cabinet committee—consisting of himself, Dern of War, Perkins of Labor, and Wallace of Agriculture—to go over the outlines of an administration bill for public works that would take the steam out of that under consideration in Congress. The worked-over draft, which itself called for an appropriation of five billion dollars, was read and discussed at the cabinet meeting on April 29, after which Perkins introduced a list of potential projects in several states. Roosevelt, who in spite of his reputation then and now remained essentially a fiscal conservative, paid particular attention to the list for New York, Ickes reported, and

> proceeded to rip that list to pieces and Miss Perkins was, in effect, put on trial, although she was not responsible for the list but simply presented it as a suggestion brought in by others. . . . There was no opportunity to go to Miss Perkins' rescue, much as I wanted to once or twice, not that she needed it, as she was perfectly able to handle it herself, but once or twice I did feel a bit sorry for her. . . . In the end, we got around to a discussion of the subject matter of the bill and made considerable progress. It is hoped to have the bill perfected and introduced in Congress within ten days.

In the meantime, Tugwell's fellow brain-truster, Raymond Moley—officially an Assistant Secretary of State now, but, like many of Roosevelt's people, also a kind of utility infielder wherever FDR felt he needed help—was given the assignment of talking with economists at the Brookings Institution and the U.S. Chamber of Commerce about legislation that would deal with industrial recovery. Tugwell himself helped to recruit people to work with a planning team in the Department of Commerce to come up with similar legislation. A third planning group developed in the Senate under Robert Wagner and his legislative team, and this task force, too, would come up with specific ideas. Finally, a tiny and entirely informal planning group developed when Moley encountered General Hugh Johnson and financier Bernard Baruch in New York one day. Johnson, who had served under Baruch on the War Industries Board during World War I, had been chairman of the board of the Moline Implement Company (maker of the famous Moline plow), an adviser on agricultural matters to the Roosevelt Campaign Committee, and was now, as Baruch himself described him, Baruch's "number-three man." Johnson had a reputation for brilliance, and on the spot Moley asked Baruch if he would "lend" the general to the government long enough for him to draft legislation for industrial recovery. Baruch assented, and Johnson immediately went to work in an office Moley found for him in the State Department building, where the general began pulling in ideas from all directions.

One of those who came to help him as a consultant on questions of labor was Donald R. Richberg, Ickes's old law partner and sometime friend. Richberg was not unknown in Roosevelt circles; in fact, during the cabinet meeting of March 14, Roosevelt had remarked that he was considering Richberg for an appointment either to the Federal Reserve Board or as Comptroller of the Currency and had asked Ickes if he knew him. "I said that I had known him for a great many years and that he was a brilliant lawyer," Ickes reported. When FDR inquired as to Richberg's banking experience, Ickes said he replied that "he had never had any actual banking experience but that he had an economic mind, and that both he and his father before him had represented for many years county appraisers, boards of assessors, boards of review, etc. I added that he had been my former law partner, and the President said: 'That ought to be enough recommendation for him.'" Given Richberg's mean-spirited refusal to endorse Ickes for Interior Secretary a few weeks before, one could even say that the recommendation was more than Ickes owed him.

Richberg still had no appointment, but his service to Johnson apparently was important enough for him to be included as a member of the committee that Roosevelt formed in early May to reconcile the two legislative drafts that had finally emerged: the Johnson-Richberg version and one pieced together by Senator Wagner's people in cooperation with the Commerce Department team under Assistant Secretary John Dickinson. Johnson, Richberg, Tugwell, Senator Wagner, Budget director Lewis

Douglas, Perkins, and Dickinson made up the new team, though Tugwell, Dickinson, and Perkins dropped out shortly after the meeting
started and left the remaining four to hammer out the final product. They
worked, Richberg remembered, "almost continuously for several days in
the office of the director of the budget who kept in close touch with the
President until we four had finally completed the bill which eventually
became, with a few revisions, the National Industrial Recovery Act."

Roosevelt had decided that a public works program should be folded
into general legislation, so the National Industrial Recovery Bill, introduced in its final form on May 17, would establish, in the section labeled
Title II, a Public Works Administration with an appropriation of $3.3
billion to finance major federal building projects throughout the country.
Title I would create a program to allow each industry to propose codes of
fair competition regarding prices and wages, such codes to be developed
by cooperative panels put together for the purpose or by trade associations
where they existed in any given industry; once approved by the President,
the codes would have the force of law and industries adhering to them
would then be exempt from the antitrust laws, and the President would
have the power to license businesses that complied with the law and to
impose penalties on those licensed businesses that violated the agreements. Title I also included two provisions that went beyond the semi-
voluntary code system. Section 9(c) applied itself to the question of "hot
oil," declaring it the government's right to prohibit interstate or foreign
trade in any oil that had been produced in excess of limits established by
such state agencies as the Oklahoma Corporation Commission and the
Texas Railroad Commission; enforcement authority was placed in Interior's Bureau of Mines and, later, the Petroleum Administration Board,
also an Interior body. Section 7(a), for its part, outlawed "yellow dog"
contracts (those in which an employee promised never to join a union) and
guaranteed labor the right to organize and to bargain collectively to
achieve improvements in wages, hours, and working conditions (Richberg always maintained that he and Johnson had originated what came to
be called "labor's Magna Charta," though his biographer notes that "the
evolution of Section 7a was a far more complex undertaking" involving a
good many more people whose ideas came together in this legislation for
the first time).

While the bill began making its way through Congress, being sniped
at perhaps more resolutely than any other single piece of legislation
during the Hundred Days, Roosevelt let it be known that he wanted
Hugh Johnson to run the program once it was enacted. This, Frances
Perkins later said, may have been a bad choice. While conceding his

brilliance, she had her doubts about the general's flamboyant style and apparent instability (he was well-known as a heavy drinker, though he claimed to have gotten his problem under control). During one early meeting shortly after Johnson had come to Washington at Moley's behest, she remembered, some worry was expressed that the Supreme Court might find many of the provisions under discussion to be unconstitutional should they be enacted into law. "Well, what difference does it make anyhow," Johnson said, according to Perkins, "because before they can get these cases to the Supreme Court we will have won the victory. The unemployment will be over and over so fast that nobody will care. We'll go on doing it somehow under some other name, because this is the answer." She also found him singularly agitated that day. "I remember that it was hot," she said,

> and he squirmed around in his chair like a restless child. He had no coat on. He'd get up and walk around. He'd run his hands through his hair. Then he'd come back and sit in his chair. . . . He finally pulled his legs up into the chair and stretched himself forward in a crouching position on the table. His arms from the elbows up, his fists, and his torso were leaning on the table. . . . It was the most ridiculous looking spectacle—face red, hair rumpled, and a curiously restless, uncontrolled, undisciplined look on his face—just kind of chewing his face to pieces, moving it all the time, as though he couldn't bear this.

This display, which probably meant that the general wanted a drink and wanted it *now*, Perkins found unnerving, and her confidence in the man did not improve when Bernard Baruch came to her after hearing that Johnson was FDR's choice. "I think he's a good number-three man," he told her, "maybe a number-two man, but he's not a number-one man. He's dangerous and unstable. He gets nervous and sometimes goes away for days without notice. I'm fond of him, but do tell the President to be careful." But Roosevelt had made up his mind; he asked Johnson to take the job and concurred in Johnson's own choice of Donald Richberg as the new agency's general counsel.

The act creating the National Recovery Administration (NRA) was finally passed and signed into law by Roosevelt on June 16, nearly a month after its introduction. Except for occasional meetings to discuss various potential public works projects, Ickes had had very little to do with the process after chairing the meeting of April 27—but now he was thrust into the middle of things, and for once apparently through no conscious effort on his part. Again, most of the story comes from the memories of Frances Perkins.

A few days before passage of the act, she remembered, she urged

Roosevelt not to give the administration of Title II and its billions of dollars to Johnson. She said it would be "hazardous." When FDR asked if she wanted to run it herself, she said, "Oh, mercy no. Far from it. . . . I don't know Harold Ickes very well. I don't know him any better than I know anybody else in the Cabinet, but I have been very impressed with his kind of punctilious, fussy, scrutiny of detail. . . . That's exactly what you want, I think."

Then, on the morning of June 16, she again met with Roosevelt, who told her that he thought she was right: he was not going to let Johnson run Title II, but confine him to Title I. He would give Public Works to the Interior Department to run.

> "Have you asked Ickes?"
> "No." (I remember he pulled his face down into that oval shape mouth that he always had when he knew he'd been bad. . . . I knew he felt guilty when he did that. I knew he knew he ought to have spoken to Ickes.)
> "Well, you know, I think you ought to speak to Ickes."
> "How can I? Hugh doesn't know yet."
> "You haven't told Hugh?"
> "No."
> "Oh, Mr. President!"
> "Well, I thought it would be better and he would be less hurt if we did it in a kind of an atmosphere of glory and praise."

In the end, they decided to have Johnson come over to the White House at the conclusion of the cabinet meeting that afternoon. He would then be asked in and told of the decision after being laved in the Rooseveltian praise for a while. Half an hour before the meeting, Perkins telephoned Ickes, who volunteered the information that he had heard that Johnson was not too stable and that the President should be careful.

"Now listen," Perkins said, "I haven't got too much time to tell you this, but the President is going to be careful. Because of the fact that he is going to be careful, he is going to appoint you . . . to be the administrator of Title II. . . ."

"The hell he is!" Ickes replied in apparent surprise. Then, in irritation: "He should talk to me."

Perkins mollified him and asked him to keep quiet about developments until Johnson himself was informed. During the cabinet meeting, FDR discussed the situation with regard to a split administration of the two titles of the NIRA, got an opinion from Attorney General Cummings on the legality of the idea, and expressed his view that it ought to be done. No one apparently dissented. At the conclusion of regular business, Johnson was called in and eulogized at some length for his fine work so far and given FDR's assurances that he had every confidence in the work Johnson would do as administrator of the NRA. As for Public Works, Roosevelt said, given the enormous workload required by Title I, he and the cabinet had decided that Johnson ought to be relieved from any responsibility for the "ordinary, routine" matters that would be involved in that program. Public Works would be administered separately—in fact, Roosevelt announced to the surprise of everyone but Perkins and Ickes, he was going to give the job to "that fellow down there," pointing to Ickes. "This is rather sudden, Mr. President," Ickes said.

Johnson said nothing—though his physical reaction was eloquent. "I saw Johnson beginning to turn color," Perkins remembered. "From having looked like a normal man, he began to look red, then dark red, then purplish. He was a very emotional man and his psychosomatic responses to his emotional disturbances were always very obvious. . . . I almost used to think his hair stood on end sometimes." Perhaps in an effort to stave off any outburst from the visibly disturbed general, Roosevelt continued to babble on for a few minutes, then made his preparations to leave. So did everyone else but Johnson, who sat in his chair, muttering. As Perkins stepped up to the President, Roosevelt whispered to her, "Stick with him, Frances. Don't let him talk to the press." She bundled the still-muttering Johnson into her chauffeured government car and drove him around Washington for at least an hour until he had calmed down. She then put him on a plane to Pittsburgh, where, ironically enough, he was scheduled to give a speech to a group of businessmen and announce the details of the NRA organization.

"It was clear that General Johnson was taken quite aback," Ickes said in his diary entry for that night, "since he had been counting on running both shows and had made commitments to many people. I was told afterward," he added, evidently oblivious to the little drama acted out by Perkins and Johnson after the meeting, "that he said to somebody that he might resign, but apparently he is going on with the work."

His account of events differs from that of Perkins in two other respects. First, he makes no mention anywhere of her telephone call telling him that Interior was going to get responsibility for Title II. Second, he says that while responsibility would indeed reside within the Interior Department, it was not him, personally, but Colonel Donald H. Sawyer, director of the Federal Employment Stabilization Board since 1931, who was made actual administrator of Title II that day. True, Sawyer would work out of an office in the Interior Department and would report directly to Ickes as chairman of the Special Board for Public Works, which Roosevelt had created by executive order on June 16 as one of his first administrative acts under the powers given him by passage of the NIRA. Nevertheless, as late as June 17, Ickes apparently was still not convinced that he was fully in charge. "[Louis] Howe called . . . to tell me that both he and Colonel McIntyre [Marvin H., one of FDR's personal secretaries] had made it clear to Colonel Sawyer that I was the real head of the public works program," he informed his diary that night. "I don't understand that this is the situation, or at any rate it is an exaggerated statement of the situation. I believe the President has not yet made up his mind as to what he wants as a final setup for public works, and may keep Sawyer on or he may substitute for him, or he may substitute for me as chairman of the commission."

All was made clear on July 5, when, during a luncheon meeting with Roosevelt and Commerce Secretary Roper, it was agreed that Sawyer lacked the administrative skills necessary to the job of directing Title II. Roper formally offered Ickes's name, FDR concurred, and Ickes agreed to take it on. On July 8, Roosevelt signed Executive Order No. 6198 appointing "Harold L. Ickes to exercise the office of Federal Emergency Administrator of Public Works." It was twenty-two days after the end of the Hundred Days, and the poor boy from Altoona had just been given responsibility for a budget larger than that for most European countries and the opportunity to remake much of America.

CHAPTER

· 28 ·

The X Factor

O N THE FACE of it, domestic matters between Harold and Anna had reached that plateau of unspoken accommodation that comes to so many marriages not made anywhere in the vicinity of heaven. Anna, certainly, showed every sign of comfortable resignation. She now had plenty to occupy her mind, in any case, what with her continuing duties in the Illinois state legislature, her charitable and club work in Chicago, her work with the Indians in New Mexico, and putting the finishing touches on the manuscript and galleys for her book, *Mesa Land: The History and Romance of the American Southwest,* scheduled to be published by Houghton Mifflin in November. Having a book in prospect can have a wonderfully mellowing effect on a person, and it is likely, too, that she was taking a good deal of pleasure from being the wife of a cabinet member in an exciting new administration, even if she would be spending more time in Springfield, Chicago, and New Mexico than in Washington over the next two years. During an interview on Sunday, March 5, a reporter for the *Washington Herald* found her in uncharacteristically girlish good spirits. "When it was suggested to Mrs. Ickes that her pictures didn't do her justice, she laughed and said, 'My husband has made a collection of them which he labels "Why Harold Ickes went to Washington." ' " Three days later, another reporter found Anna to be in the same good fettle shortly before returning to Illinois. She was described then as "one of those ageless women, brown-eyed, dynamic, with a bubbling sense of humor. . . . Despite a pleasant personality and ready laugh, you quickly sense that she is no person to be trifled with. She has a fighting glint in her eye and a firm upper lip." (Her husband doubtless would have found the latter part of that description to resemble more closely the Anna he knew.)

Anna took her bubbling good humor back to Chicago at the end of Ickes's first week on the job, and while she would come back for occasional visits of various lengths, she would not return permanently until her term in the state legislature expired in April 1935. In the meantime, Harold maintained the suite in the Mayflower for a few weeks, taking his breakfasts in the coffee room downstairs and his dinners at Harvey's just around the corner. Something was soon bubbling in him, too, and it was not his good humor (or his digestion). It apparently had been a long time between women. As he noted in his unpublished memoirs, there had been the occasional dalliance during the course of the twenties, but nothing that had lasted long or had meant much to him beyond the casual excitement of the moment. But Anna had no sooner departed before he received a telephone call from a woman he identifies only as "X" in his memoirs, and from that moment whatever calm his life possessed departed. He says he had known her for as long as thirty years, but had seen her only once in the last ten; she had been married then and the meeting had been brief. Even so, "a spark passed from her to me which made me aware that she was attractive physically, as well as alert sexually and that I would like to possess her." He had restrained himself, however, and had had no contact with her again until the telephone call in March 1933.

The spark flared the minute she came by the Mayflower to talk to him about getting her fiancé a job in the Interior Department (she had since divorced her first husband), the subject of her telephone call. In a week, they were in bed together, Ickes bound up in the coils of infatuation and simmering with an old-fashioned lust that drove circumspection from his mind. "X was without inhibitions," he remembered several years later, still with some awe.

> She was a physical little person who, freely, and with a total absence of self-consciousness, liked to make love. She was the mother of two children, but no one would have known that from her figure, which was smallish but very good and firm and compact. . . . It became more than a suspicion with me later that she had been intimate with more men than her husband, but on that side she was decidedly reticent and when a man is getting what he wants he isn't too inquisitive. It is easy to persuade himself that his own great attractiveness as a lover has overcome scruples that would not yield to anyone else.

His own scruples were put to the test and succumbed quite as swiftly. He did get the woman's fiancé a job in some obscure branch of the department in the "far middlewest," wherever that might have been, a circumstance she greeted with a laugh. "From that time on," he says, "our relationship was frankly that of lover and mistress. No woman ever played her part better than did she." And no older man ever gave himself over to a banal fantasy more completely than did he. "I became quite mad about X and very reckless," he says. "I had to have her, regardless of consequences, even if the consequences were the loss of my job. Here was something that I had wanted all my life and I was not going to give it up." He bought her a big diamond ring. He put her to work in her own office in the Interior Department (at what, he does not say), and found a job for the woman she and her children lived with as well. She came and went on several occasions to the suite at the Mayflower, and after April 5, when he moved to a small furnished home he rented from the counselor to the Danish legation at 1327 Thirty-third Street in Georgetown, he smuggled her in at every opportunity. He took her out to the country in his official car for long drives and ardent grapplings in the backseat, trusting utterly to the discretion of Carl Witherspoon, the government chauffeur who apparently earned every word of the encomium Ickes gave him in 1948: "Quiet, loyal, and devoted, this fine Negro from South Carolina had already served under seven secretaries. On merit alone I promoted him to the extent of my ability under the inflexible and not always reasonable personnel regulations of the Government. And he never failed me. I came to count him more friend than employee, and he worked for, and with, me long exhausting hours, until the unfortunate loss of one eye forced him to retire."

Near the end of the summer, the woman's fiancé became restless in his exile and she asked Harold to bring him back to Washington. Incredibly, he complied, and for a time the three of them functioned under the same government roof. ("He was one of the most unattractive men that I have ever seen," Ickes says, unsurprisingly. "He was mean and tricky and badly bred.") Not long thereafter, nasty anonymous letters began to appear in the mailbox of Ickes's mistress. Ickes persuaded her to ignore them. But then Anna began to receive her own set of letters while she was staying in New Mexico. "These," he says, "were to the effect that a certain member of the Cabinet was seen frequently in the company of a woman other than his wife; that she spent long hours at night with him in his home while his wife was in New Mexico, etc., etc." Anna sent them to him with assurances that while the letters did disturb her, she knew there was no foundation for them; she thought he ought to know about them, however, for his own protection.

Ickes tried to disregard the letters in the hope that the writer would tire of the game if he or she got no response. But they kept coming, in greater and greater numbers. Some were beginning to show up at several newspapers; at a dinner party, he reports, "Eugene Meyer [publisher of the *Washington Post*] . . . took me aside . . . and handed me one that he had received. They went to probably every office in Washington and to a number outside, including the *Chicago Tribune*. . . . These letters were so libelous that no newspaper would dare to print them, in the absence of court proceedings or other privileged status. Moreover, in those early days, most of the papers were willing to give me the benefit of the doubt." Nevertheless, they were coming in such numbers by the third week in August that he went to Louis Howe and told him about them (without admitting any truth to them, of course). "Colonel Howe," he told his diary for August 23, "assured me that I was only getting my turn, and that the enemies of the Administration, having had no chance to attack the President himself, make attacks successively on those supposed to be close to him." Howe put William H. Moran, chief of the Secret Service, on the job of trying to find out who was writing the letters and to put a stop to them when he did.

Meanwhile, Ickes was having other personal difficulties. While he was on firmer moral grounds with these than he was in the case of his sexual didoes, they were still complicated and nettlesome—particularly since circumstances forced him to discuss them with Roosevelt personally. The first of these additional burdens had to do with a Chicago lawyer named Lucius J. M. Malmin. Malmin, who had served as a judge in the Virgin Islands during the Wilson administration, now wanted to be named governor of the islands. As soon as the announcement of Ickes's appointment as Interior Secretary had been made, Malmin had come by his office in Chicago and told him that he intended to be the next governor of the islands. If Ickes did not comply, he threatened to petition the probate court with charges of fraud in connection with an estate case Ickes had handled. Ickes got rid of him and then called the Illinois state's attorney, asking for an immediate investigation of the charges in order to clear his name before assuming office; the state's attorney complied to the degree that he called Malmin into his own office, questioned him, and found to his own satisfaction that the judge had no grounds for any such petition. He told Ickes not to worry about it.

But Malmin had followed Ickes to Washington and by the middle of

July was beginning to make trouble again. He tried to get in to see Roosevelt, but failed; he then bearded Harry Slattery, Ickes's assistant, in the Interior Building, saying that if he was not appointed at least lieutenant governor of the islands he was going to go to the newspapers with his charges; what is more, he said, he would have Ickes disbarred in Illinois. In a desperate effort to get Malmin to make such threats in front of witnesses, Ickes interviewed him in the presence of Louis Glavis, his chief of investigations, and Theodore Mack, his stenographer; but Malmin was sweetness and light and could not be maneuvered into any incriminating remarks. Malmin went away, but in September was writing his own letters, these to Roosevelt as well as to Eleanor, making thinly veiled charges against Ickes and offering a way to avoid scandal. At a cabinet meeting on September 12, FDR tossed one of the letters to Ickes, together with the President's reply stating, as Ickes described it in his diary, "that he would not enter into any scheme to cover up anything affecting a member of the Administration, for if any member of the Administration had done what was not right, he should stand the consequences, and if he had not, he would doubtless know how to protect his good name." Ickes heartily endorsed the President's reply, but also asked him and Attorney General Cummings to make a formal investigation of Malmin's charges just to protect the administration, and FBI director J. Edgar Hoover was sent over by Cummings the next day to discuss the case and to pick up Ickes's files on Malmin.

That investigation, too, cleared Ickes of any wrongdoing, but Malmin would not let up. In October he called Harry Slattery; Slattery repeated the conversation in a memorandum to Ickes dated October 13:

"Is this Mr. Slattery? Well, this is your old friend Judge Malmin from Chicago back on your neck again. You know what I did to protect you and the secretary."

To which, Slattery said, "I replied I knew nothing about his protecting qualities."

"Well," said Malmin, "I thought from the beginning you were fish-eyed, thought yourself a diplomat and probably wore spats."

"This man," Slattery concluded in his note, "is clearly out of his mind."

But stubborn. As late as March 1934 he was still writing his letters. Ickes finally went on the offensive, filing his own formal charges with the Illinois Bar Association against Malmin and another Chicago lawyer who had joined with the judge in the enterprise. The case was heard in June, and Malmin and the other man ultimately were disbarred in a decision upheld by the Illinois Supreme Court two years later.

回回回回

Early in September 1933, Ickes and Anna had gotten together long
enough to lease a home at 4880 Glenbrook Road in the Spring Valley
section of the District; it was a spacious house with many trees, a nice
spread of lawn, and its own little creek, and it would be his home for the
next several years. He had little time or emotional latitude to enjoy it now,
however. While Malmin continued to hound him and the anonymous
letters regarding his mistress kept arriving in various mailboxes, New
York business interests decided to take a shot at him. On November 14,
Marvin McIntyre, FDR's secretary, came by to see him in his office after
dinner. He told him that Oliver Max Gardner, a former governor of North
Carolina now practicing law in Washington, had informed McIntyre that
afternoon that some of his clients had instructed him to bring suit against
Ickes for an unpaid account he still had with his old Chicago brokerage
house, A. O. Slaughter. At the time he had been offered the job in
Washington, Ickes had negotiated a deal with the outfit that would allow
the account to ride until he was able to pay it off. But now the firm had
been taken over by New York interests, a less accommodating bunch.
They wanted their money.

After the cabinet meeting the next day, Ickes handed Roosevelt his first
resignation. FDR refused it. "I know you," he said. "All of us have been in
trouble some time or other." He advised Ickes to settle out of court; if the
amount was more than he could handle, Roosevelt said he would be
willing to call in a few people and see if the money could not be raised
somehow. "Naturally I demurred strongly at such a suggestion," Ickes
told his diary. "I feel very much relieved at his altogether human and
friendly attitude," he added in one of his most touching comments on the
President. "Whatever may be the outcome, I can never forget his kindness
and understanding. I have never been given to hero worship [but he had],
but I have a feeling of loyalty and real affection for the President that I
have never felt for any other man, although I have had very deep attachments for other men."

Roosevelt continued to be remarkably supportive over the next several
weeks—including the rejection again of one more offer of resignation
when things got rough—as Ickes's personal secretary, Fred Marx, entered
into negotiations with Gardner. His clients claimed that Ickes owed a
total of $107,000, but that they would settle for fifty cents on the dollar.
Ickes got an independent audit that indicated he owed no more than
$11,000. On Roosevelt's advice, he tendered this amount, on the theory
that if the firm did not accept it they would have to pay all court costs if

they were not able to get the settlement they wanted in a suit. Gardner said he had made it clear to his clients that he had no desire to embarrass the administration and that if they insisted on bringing suit, he would refuse to handle it. His reluctance may have had to do with the fact that he was shortly to be appointed ambassador to Great Britain (he would die before being able to serve); in any event, his clients accepted the offer in January 1934 and the case was closed—only to reopen briefly in October, when a young reporter for the *Chicago Tribune* named John Boettiger questioned Ickes over allegations that he had, in fact, accepted money from the Democratic National Committee to pay off the account; Ickes denied it and the story dribbled into oblivion.

He would have wished for the same fate for the anonymous letters regarding his love affair, but they would not go away, nor could the chief of the Secret Service seem to track down their author. Ickes himself had begun to suspect his lover's fiancé, even though X assured him it was impossible. Truly desperate by now, he brought Louis Glavis into the investigation and the two of them cooked up a scheme to uncover the fiancé's wrongdoing: Ickes sent the fiancé south on a pretended assignment for a couple of days, while Glavis "made arrangements," as Ickes put it, to get into the man's apartment and search for evidence.

> I told Glavis particularly to look out for any used carbon paper because the letters that were sent out were always carbon copies; this in order to make it difficult to trace the typewriter. Triumphantly, one day Glavis brought in samples from the man's typewriter, which he had in his apartment and also some used carbons, which clearly revealed that the letters had been written on this typewriter and that these were the carbons that had been used. The evidence was absolutely unimpeachable.

The evidence may have been unimpeachable, but it also was certainly inadmissible, since the methods Ickes had used to obtain it *were* impeachable. As with many a government official before him, desperation had revealed a line visible only to himself that divided the rectitude demanded of his public affairs from that which governed his private life. In his memoirs Ickes demonstrates no guilt over what he had caused to be done, but he must have known that he had taken an extraordinary risk; if he had been caught out, the offer of resignation he would have been forced to make almost certainly would have been one that Roosevelt *would* have accepted. Nevertheless, he took yet another chance and called the man into his office, presented him with the evidence, and accused him of being the author of the letters. The man denied the accusation. "But he was guilty as hell and he knew that I knew it," Ickes recalled. "Naturally, his days in the department were over. Naturally, also, he wasn't in a position to make any trouble for me, or about the manner in which Glavis had secured the evidence." One has to wonder where on earth he got this breathtaking notion; it apparently never occurred to him that anyone disturbed enough to write poison-pen letters would be quite capable of bringing his accuser down with him. The fiancé did not succumb to the temptation, as it happened, but went quietly. "After our interview," Ickes says, "there never was another anonymous letter, which of itself was pretty conclusive proof that we had the guilty man."

He did not escape so easily the consequences of another move he initiated in this inelegant game—a gambit quite as deranged as the invasion of his rival's apartment, if less criminal. "This was no ordinary situation where I was willing quietly to seek physical satisfactions on an unemotional give and take basis," he wrote. "This time my emotions were deeply involved. I felt that, in the circumstances, the only fair thing, either to Anna or to X, was that Anna should know about X. . . . My love for X was deep enough, or so I believed, so that I felt that I owed it to her, as much as I did to Anna, to put all of my cards on the table." This classic expression of the husbandly impulse to expiate sexual guilt by dumping it on the hapless wife was offered on the night of Thursday, November 16, after the occasion of the first of Roosevelt's annual dinners for the cabinet.

Up to this point, it had been a generally good month for Anna. She had come to Washington to spend a few weeks with Harold early in October and on October 8 had held her first news conference in the big living room of the house in Spring Valley. "I am tremendously enthusiastic about the present Federal situation, as I have observed it," she told reporters. "There is now a most understanding set-up under John Collier, our new Indian Commissioner, from which we are hoping for great things out there in the Southwest. The Pueblo Indians need a change in medical attention and education, and the Navajos need land and water. Far from being a 'vanishing race,' their number is increasing rapidly." She must have enjoyed the solemn attention her words were given by the reporters, and could not have been displeased that she continued to get a good press (something her husband could not always count on, even so early in his Washington career). The reporter for the *Washington Post*, for example, wrote: "Poised and friendly, Mrs. Ickes submitted agreeably to a cross fire of questions from nearly a score of newspaper women. She gave the impression of perfect candor and when she didn't know the answer, said so." Further, *Mesa Land* had just been published to generally agreeable reviews.* The book deserved at least that much. It broke little new ground, but her analysis of the various Indian cultures of the Southwest was sound and if her prose fell several cuts short of that of Mary Austin or even Charles F. Lummis, both of whom had covered much of the same territory, she had her moments.

Whatever sense of well-being she may have gained from the publication of the book and the heady pleasures of being a cabinet wife were pretty thoroughly shattered the Thursday night Harold told her of his mistress. As he and Anna were undressing for bed just before midnight, Ickes remembered, "much as I hated to do it because Anna was happy over the dinner that we had attended, I told her bluntly that I was in love with another woman. . . ."

> I really felt sorry for Anna that night. It was a blow right between the eyes. At first it merely staggered her, but when she came to realize all that it meant she went pretty completely to pieces. . . . Subsequently, there developed for me at home the worst hell that I had ever known and yet I have never been able to blame Anna as I blame her for all of the preceding years when she continually forced me into a defensive and humiliating position with her imperious will.
>
> Now she was hurt both in her pride and in her affections. We would go through terrible scenes. Anna would become hysterical to a degree that I had never before witnessed. I would try to help her all that I could, but there was not much that I could do after I had told her that I had not loved her for many years. However, I did what I could and I was as gentle as I could be. I was never without a very real sense of guilt that she was suffering as she was.

Anna's state of mind did not prevent her from attending a dinner six nights later at the Turkish embassy, but she was clearly very disturbed. Not too long thereafter, following one particularly frenzied episode of recrimination, she took a small overdose of some sort of medicine, then called her doctor immediately. This cry for help was not sufficiently dangerous a gesture to be described as a suicide attempt, but it was unnerving nevertheless. At the doctor's advice, Anna entered a nursing home for a few weeks. "The quiet there did her good," Ickes convinced himself,

> and she came home in much better shape. Moreover, while there, she reconciled herself to an unchanged situation to a degree that seemed almost im-

---

* Neither earlier, at this time, nor at any time in the future did Ickes say a word about the composition or publication of *Mesa Land*. It is a puzzling omission. One suspects some peculiar jealousy, but on every other occasion that I know about, he was more than willing to give Anna her due for her very real accomplishments in the public world. But not here, apparently.

possible. She came back with a conviction that . . . in the end, she would win out over X; that all that she had to do was give me my head and that I would return to her. Her conclusions were not far wrong except that I never really came back to her except on the surface, which, however, made for a more tolerable life together.

Their son Wilmarth, who continued to be called into these imbroglios as a kind of referee, counseled them to get a divorce, according to Ickes. Anna would not even consider it, he says, nor was he in favor of it. This may have been because he was unwilling to subject her to the public disgrace of a second divorce, as he once claimed was his motivation during an earlier period of conflict, or it may have been because by this time his mistress was apparently beginning to have second thoughts about their relationship and where it was not heading. One afternoon, finally, she stormed into his office, threw the ring he had given her on the desk, said she was resigning, then left, driving down to the home of her fiancé's mother in southern Virginia. Three or four days later, she married the man. Not long thereafter, Ickes learned that the man had been sleeping with the woman all along, and that the two of them might even have gotten together numerous times in their respective offices in the Interior Department, a singularly unauthorized use of government property. This bit of turnabout shook Ickes badly enough to confess his pain to Anna. "She realized what a shock it was," he remembered, "and she was really tender and understanding about it. . . . If only Anna had used such tactics, even in a small degree, in less serious situations in the past, our married life might have been very different. On this occasion her tact was exemplary and her attitude all that anyone could ask for—much more considerate than I had any right to expect."

Quite so—particularly when he took up with the woman again a few months later, she having left her new husband and moved back to Washington. This time, he says, he kept his heart out of it and the relationship was purely a matter of sexual gratification. He did not rehire her at the Interior Department, but he did rent a small apartment in Georgetown for their trysts. After another few months the flames of lust finally guttered out and the two lovers drifted apart, this time with no apparent regrets (and no cruel and mindless confessions to Anna).

In years to come, Ickes's carnal adventuring became one of the accepted legends of the New Deal. In spite of frequent snatches of lurid speculation, however, almost all of it exercised many years after the fact, his affair with the mysterious Mrs. X is the only sexual excursion of his for which we have any real evidence. Two things seem to argue against his legend: first, he could not possibly have found the time or energy for as many pursuits as he was given credit for, and, second, if he had been the cocksman his reputation suggested, he almost certainly would have talked it up, or at least hinted at it, in his memoirs, which he did not do.

Whatever substance there may or may not have been to the stories of Ickes's prowess, the atmosphere in which they blossomed was very much in the temper of the times. Beginning with Roosevelt himself, whose long-term affair with Lucy Mercer would become widely known among many in the administration and whose relationship with Missy LeHand, his chief secretary, was a matter of frequent speculation among the prurient, rumors of fornication of one kind or another among the mighty were in the air fairly regularly. "There was more preoccupation with sex rearing its head all over the New Deal," Walter Trohan, *Chicago Tribune* correspondent and relentless gossip, claimed in his own memoirs, "than in preceding or succeeding administrations. . . . There were many young ladies in those days who played the games people liked to play with as much enthusiasm as New Dealers displayed in making over America." Sometimes rumor had considerable substance. Over in the offices of the NRA, for example, something almost certainly was going on between Hugh Johnson and his twenty-eight-year-old personal secretary, Frances ("Robbie") Robinson, who traveled everywhere with him, sat in on meetings ("as obtrusive as a certain type of wife," Ickes complained in his diary), and even shared an apartment with him—all of this on a salary a good deal above that specified in civil service guidelines for secretaries. When newspaper reporters called him on that point, the general said she was no "mere stenographer or secretary," which headlines the next day faithfully recorded as "more than a stenographer." "Boys," Johnson had complained, "you're hitting below the belt," a remark that did nothing to help raise the level of discussion.

The Johnson-Robinson affair, combined with the general's continuing drinking problem, had left things in a shambles at the NRA, Adolf Berle recorded in his daily memorandum to himself for August 3, 1934: "Bobby Straus reported that the N.R.A. was practically over; about one-half the men were resigning, largely because of the affair between Johnson and 'Robbie' . . . which has now reached an acute stage." Both Johnsonian indulgences provided Donald R. Richberg with ammunition in his efforts to get Johnson eased out of the NRA and himself installed as its virtual director, armament which Ickes's old law partner put to good use. By the end of September 1934, Johnson had tendered his resignation and Roosevelt had reorganized the upper levels of the NRA completely, establishing a National Industrial Recovery Board to administer it "subject to the general approval of the Industrial Emergency Committee," a body he had created by executive order on June 30—with Richberg as its head.*

Ickes had avoided Johnson's sordid fate, though perhaps not by much. In the same memorandum in which he commented on Johnson's troubles at the NRA, Berle noted that "A somewhat similar situation on rather the same lines seems to be going on in the Interior," and even Roosevelt's legendary reluctance to fire people might not have been enough to save Ickes if the illegal entry business had ever become public. In the end, he came away unscathed, publicly. But he was made to pay for his messy tangles nevertheless. Throughout a period in which he contrived to mingle the monstrous demands of a very complex job with the concerns of a personal life hardly less rigorous and complicated, he was plagued by insomnia so dreadful that not even the whiskey and powders he took to overcome it did any good. He was exhausted, even more short-tempered than usual, and generally so raddled with care that as early as the end of November 1933 even Roosevelt took notice. FDR insisted that Ickes spend a weekend with him at Warm Springs, the retreat the President owned in Georgia near the polio clinic he had established after his own survival of the disease. Ickes enjoyed the respite amid the bosky dells of the southern Appalachians, and found here even more evidence to support his growing admiration for the President, as he recorded in his diary:

> I have never had contact with a man who was loved as he is. To the people at Warm Springs he is just a big jolly brother. They swarm all over him and around him and their genuine affection for him is apparent on all occasions. On our drive Sunday afternoon we went clear out to the end of a knob where we had a wonderful view of the surrounding country. This was on his property and there we ran into a group of people, including Colonel McIntyre, who were having a beefsteak picnic. He couldn't get his car stopped before they all came swarming around it. . . . They climbed all over the car. One woman

---

* On the way to achieving his position of power over the NRA Richberg also managed to incur the wrath of Harold Ickes once again—and not without reason. Ickes and Charles Wyzanski, Jr., the Labor Department solicitor, had suggested to Roosevelt that he make Robert Hutchins, president of the University of Chicago, chairman of the National Industrial Recovery Board. Roosevelt liked the idea and instructed Ickes to sound Hutchins out. Hutchins agreed and went so far as to obtain a leave of absence from the university—only to have Richberg step in and block the appointment by stirring up the members of the board against Hutchins to the point where they threatened to resign if FDR gave him the job. Richberg apparently feared that his own power would be undermined if someone with the administrative skills of Hutchins were installed on the board; that, at any rate, was how Ickes saw it: "As the matter now stands," he wrote in his diary on November 4, 1934, "Richberg, through his . . . NRA Committee, is in pretty firm control of the situation and he will fight any man who threatens to jeopardize that control."

whose legs were badly crippled with infantile paralysis was hoisted onto my side of the car and sat on the edge of it with her feet in my lap while she led in the singing of two or three songs for the President. Then, happy and laughing, they all backed away from the car when he insisted that he had to leave them.

This happy interlude ended Sunday night, and for the next several months his diary entries include a scattering of complaints regarding sleeplessness, exhaustion, and general stress over his personal problems. It did not help matters when on December 11 he slipped on the ice outside his home and broke a rib so badly he had to spend the next three weeks in Bethesda Naval Hospital, where in a condition approaching constant fury he tried to work and recuperate simultaneously. "I continued to work hard at the hospital day after day," he wrote on January 2, 1934,

and I found it very tiring signing contracts and letters in bed, seeing people, and dictating in the intervals. The worst of my trouble was that I couldn't get a normal night's sleep. I would start in with a lot of whisky and end up with some soporific, with the result that the next morning I would feel very badly indeed. Friday morning, the twenty-second, I felt so tired out that I was almost desperate. I decided that I didn't care whether school kept or not, and that being so, I felt I might as well go to the Cabinet meeting that afternoon. Over the protests of the doctors I did go. When the President was wheeled into the Cabinet room and saw me, he stopped stark still and stared at me for a long interval and then remarked that it looked very much like insubordination. . . . He told me I ought to go back to the hospital and stay there and then when the doctors discharged me to go away for a couple of weeks' rest.

Ickes did return to the hospital, but shortly after Christmas checked himself out. "I had a tough argument with Captain McDowell, who had me in charge, and with Captain Munger, the head of the hospital. They said I was the worst patient they had ever had. They told me how displeased the President would be and so on, but in the end I prevailed and I came from the hospital to the office."

Work would save him. Work would fill the emptiness that lay within, would hold off depression, would shore up self-esteem, would numb physical and psychological pain, would stifle insecurity and camouflage an emotional life so stunted and unfulfilled that it left him prey to his own worst instincts. Work always had. And both the quantity and the quality of the work he was able to accomplish in this grim context are testaments to nothing less than a species of bravery; for this public servant, the survival to the end of each day with his wits fully intact often was a triumph of will over reality.

CHAPTER
· 29 ·

Cheops Redux

ONE WAY TO CONQUER reality is to systematize it, and few governmental organisms in history have been more intricately structured than the Public Works Administration (PWA) under Harold L. Ickes. It had to be. It was by far the largest single responsibility of all those that now lay in his hands, its dimensions suggested vividly by an image he or one of his amanuenses conjured up for use in *Back to Work*,* his account of the first two years of the PWA:

> Probably no member of that original PWA organization ever comprehended the magnitude of the fortune entrusted to it. It is fair to say that not one of them was able to visualize how much money 3 billion 300 million dollars really was. Few people can even encompass such a sum within their imaginations. It helped me to estimate its size by figuring that if we had it all in currency and should load it into trucks we could set out with it from

---

* Of the six books that appeared under his name as Secretary of the Interior, only *Autobiography of a Curmudgeon* was entirely his own work. The rest were outlined and drafted by various members of his staff, then placed in Ickes's hands for editing and rewrite. It was a procedure as common then as it is now, though the Hearstian press, in particular, liked to profess indignation from time to time that Ickes would put his name to prose not his own. Ickes being Ickes, he usually responded with indignation himself at charges of loose literary morality, and not without some justification: he spent a lot of time on these publications and the Ickes editorial touch was rarely a light one; the books consequently bear a stronger individualistic stamp than most public books written by public servants.

Washington for the Pacific Coast, shovel off one million dollars at every milepost and still have enough left to build a fleet of battleships. That's how much money 3 billion 300 million dollars is. That was the sum that the President had entrusted to us. It was up to the Public Works Administration to write whatever record, for good or ill, was to be made.

He had the money; now he needed the shovelers. Shortly after Roosevelt made his position official on July 8, 1933, Ickes appointed Colonel Henry M. Waite his deputy administrator. Waite had been brought into the planning process for the NIRA by Hugh Johnson even before the bill was introduced, and one of his principal chores had been to blueprint the kind of organization it would take to choose projects, evaluate their costs, allocate funds, guide construction and monitor wages and working conditions, guard against graft and theft, and in general ensure that the highest visions of the New Deal were sustained in the field. That effort was intensified under Ickes's prodding. First, they hired lawyers, many lawyers—more than one hundred for the Washington offices alone, headed up by chief counsel Henry T. Hunt, a former mayor of Cincinnati, and featuring one of the brightest young legal minds in the country, that of Benjamin V. Cohen, another of Felix Frankfurter's many protégés at Harvard, whose talents in the drafting of legislation would make him one of the most influential young men in the New Deal. (While Cohen was a student at the University of Chicago between 1910 and 1912, one of his heroes had been reformer Harold L. Ickes, and the young man did not lose regard for Ickes upon closer acquaintance; over time, he would become a good friend and eventually literary executor of Ickes's estate.)

After the lawyers came the engineers. Waite was an engineer himself, and, as Ickes put it, "proceeded to surround himself with engineers who had done great things. There were brought from the four corners of America men who had built bridges and dams and monumental buildings." Most of these big builders were assigned to individual units with responsibility for helping to develop additional great things along the lines of sewers, roads, tunnels, bridges, viaducts, water works, canals, streets and highways, city parks, public buildings, and a swarm of similar projects. Others were placed in the Inspection Division, a unit charged with monitoring adherence to PWA specifications. Louis Glavis was given principal responsibility for investigations into graft, fraud, and theft on any given project, while Michael W. Straus, a correspondent for the International News Service, was hired away to handle public relations.

Added to all these were platoons of accountants, clerks, stenographers, and typists, until there were more than 2,300 new people jammed into the Interior Building—so many that some smaller bureaus of the department had to find offices in other federal buildings (one of the first major projects funded by the PWA would be the construction of a new Interior building just to the south of the old one). Outside Washington, the nation was divided into ten regions, with a director and staff for each, while each state within each region was given a state engineer and a state advisory board of three members, together with necessary support staff. (The territories were lumped together into a single division in Washington.) These ultimately added another 3,735 people to the ranks of the new agency.

It was an enormous machine, the PWA; an organizational chart drawn up in August 1933 showed no fewer than eighty-three individual squares to be occupied by the more than six thousand employees involved. The only square not shown on the chart was that which held Franklin D. Roosevelt himself; it should have been included, for if Harold Ickes was the administrator of Public Works, it was Roosevelt who had the final word on every individual project to be financed by the PWA, whether it was a federal dam or a municipal sewerage treatment plant, a post office or a county road. Except for federal projects, which could be conceived, designed, and promoted by the agencies near the top of the chain, the road to approval was a long tortuous route that ended only in Roosevelt's office. A municipality that wanted to build a town bridge with PWA funds, for example, would first have to submit an application to the state advisory board and the state engineer for an outright grant or, as was most often the case, a grant combined with a long-term loan. If the engineer and the board approved the application, it would be passed on to the regional office. If the regional office approved it, the application was sent to Washington, where copies of it would be made and distributed to the appropriate engineering, legal, and financial departments for examination. The engineering department in charge of bridges would then determine whether there was a demonstrated need for the project and whether its specifications for labor and materials met the standards established by the PWA (prices for material and wages, in particular, had to be in line with those prevailing in any given area). The legal department would determine whether the city was meeting all local, state, and federal laws in its application, while the finance department would calculate whether the town was likely to be able to pay back any PWA loan in no more than thirty years at 4 percent interest, as the law required. Where necessary, Louis Glavis's people in the Division of Investigations would be sent into the field to interrogate the principals and generally sniff around in search of fraud. If the project staggered through each of these administrative swamps, it went up to Ickes himself, who would take it with his recom-

mendation for approval or rejection to the weekly meetings of the Special
Board for Public Works. If the board approved it, the application would
be summarized in some detail and placed in a project book—actually, a
thick manila folder—with a number of other projects. Once a week Ickes
would take the book to the White House, where he and Roosevelt would
go through the summaries and Roosevelt would make the final decision
regarding each project.

"The device that Mr. Ickes had set up was a very interesting one," John
Carmody, Ickes's successor at the PWA, remembered.

> It was important, it seems to me, that the President be aware of the scope and
> character of these projects. . . . But the device did another thing. It insured
> Mr. Ickes' talking to the President about once a week without the customary
> difficulty of getting through, getting appointments, persuading the Presi-
> dent's secretary each time that "This is important," and more important than
> something else. It got to be a routine so that it was very easy for him, and I
> think it was a very useful thing for him.

It was indeed, for it gave him access to the President's ear perhaps more
frequently and regularly than any other member of the cabinet—and not
always on matters relating exclusively to the PWA: Roosevelt himself was
prone to wandering off the subject, and often it was easy to get him
steered around to something else that might have been on the Secretary's
mind during any given meeting. And there would be quite a lot on the
Secretary's mind more often than not.

The first "book" taken into Roosevelt's presence was largely pieced
together from numerous loan applications that had been made to the
Reconstruction Finance Corporation, now under the direction of Jesse
Jones, one of the few high-level holdovers from the Hoover administra-
tion.* Some of these RFC loans would now fall under the aegis of the
PWA, and one of Ickes's first directives to his deputy administrator had

---

* Jones and Ickes would enjoy a typical long-term relationship that alternated between
cautious mutual respect and open conflict, particularly after Congress empowered the RFC to
purchase and market PWA bonds as one means of financing its projects. In his account of his
years with the RFC, *Fifty Billion Dollars,* Jones says he went out of his way to avoid
antagonism, setting up a program whereby any profit made for the sale of PWA bonds would
go back to the PWA, while any losses would be absorbed by the RFC. "I went to Secretary
Ickes' office," he wrote, "with my prepared proposal. All he had to do was accept it. He read it
and, as I recall, exclaimed: 'This won't even cost us a postage stamp!'

"I said: 'That's correct.'

"He asked: 'Where's the catch?'

"I replied that there was no catch, that it was simply cooperation between government
departments in the interest of the government. He signed the agreement, and the matter was
handled amicably between his department and ours."

been to go through them to find the appropriate applications. "The resultant search through the RFC records was swift and exhaustive," Ickes wrote in *Back to Work*. "Lights blazed in the Interior Building throughout most of the ensuing nights; groups of engineers and lawyers pored over the mass of documents relating to each of the hundreds of applications made to the RFC by municipalities all over the country, sifting, sorting, rejecting, approving. The building had some of the tense atmosphere of a general staff headquarters after a declaration of war. Indeed, we had declared war on depression!" Out of all this, twenty-four projects amounting to a little less than a million dollars in cost were tucked into a folder on July 12 and taken to Roosevelt, who approved them.

This was faster action than any regular PWA applications ever got, and it is probable that this first bunch was pushed through in a deliberate attempt to satisfy those who complained that the government was moving too slowly to meet the crisis in employment and relief. In spite of this first, well-publicized surge of activity, however, the Public Works Administration was no more built for velocity than was its administrator. There was simply too much money involved, and while Ickes came to despise the nickname of "Honest Harold" that his critics and friends alike pinned on him, he was determined that nowhere in his Department of the Interior would there ever be found a smell similar to that which had coiled through the place during Albert Fall's residence. No project would get to Roosevelt's desk before it had been comprehensively planned, meticulously examined for legal and financial soundness, then finally picked over by the Secretary himself, and if that meant that things moved more slowly than many wished, it could not be helped—and would not be apologized for. Many, perhaps most, of his critics, he wrote in *Back to Work,*

> have not and, in my opinion, never will be satisfied. The theory of public works as administered was sound but it has only a speaking acquaintance with the beliefs of those who considered PWA primarily an agency to distribute money. Even those who accepted the theory of public works as practiced by PWA found much fault with the lack of speed of the Administration. I have seen and heard PWA division heads damn the obstacles which they encountered as they sought to get projects under construction. I, myself, have cursed these hindrances, but even when tempted to break Federal, State or local laws to get work actually started, I realized that any such short-cutting would not only increase the difficulties in the long run, but would arouse widespread dissatisfaction.

There were those besides Ickes who thought his fussiness a good thing, including Henry Wallace, of all people. "Ickes was completely constipated with regard to public works, so many people thought," Wallace remembered in a kind of backhanded compliment. "Personally I think it was a good thing for Roosevelt that he had somebody like that sitting on public works. I don't know what guardian angel caused Roosevelt to select Ickes for that job."

Ickes firmly held that speed was less important than stability, permanence, and a fair return to the government for its investment. "What PWA sought to do," he said, again in *Back to Work,* "was to get honest work at honest wages on honest projects, which was a great deal more difficult task than giving away money. . . . PWA chose the harder course, and did so deliberately. It is still my belief that there is little to be gained in the long run from construction that cannot be economically justified." It was still his belief thirteen years later, too. "The duty of Public Works," he told the readers of the *Saturday Evening Post* in 1948, "was to build permanent and socially desirable projects that would be assets of the communities which they would serve many years in the future." Fully secured loans, he emphasized, were no less important to the PWA program than outright grants: "Thus we were, in effect, helping local governmental agencies to help themselves. This loan-and-grant method also resulted in bringing more money into circulation than the Federal Treasury itself could afford."

What was more, Ickes maintained that Roosevelt himself supported his cautionary view. He recalled a meeting with the President in which FDR had told him

> that he had been receiving some complaints about the tardiness of the program. He said that he recognized the almost insurmountable reasons for not getting off to a faster start. But this did not displease him. On the contrary, he said to me, "I do not want you to move any faster." He went on to explain that he was still hoping that there would be a quicker economic recovery than had seemed possible, in which event a "more deliberate carrying out of the Public Works program would mean money saved to the Treasury."

This partnership of purpose—which apparently is how Ickes viewed it— did not long survive the pressures of political expediency (with Roosevelt, few things ever did), but for nearly two years it did give Ickes the latitude to pursue his own vision of public works with comparatively little hindrance. It was no small vision.

"In the long run" was a phrase that was strung like a litany through the pages of *Back to Work*. In a town in which the exigencies of politics rarely if ever recognized any run longer than that which it took to gain and hold office, it demonstrated a philosophy guaranteed to provide contention—a prospect that struck little fear into Ickes's heart. It was for the long run that he wanted PWA projects built, and it was for the long run that most of them did get built, giving rise to New Deal historian William E. Leuchtenburg's description of Ickes as "a builder to rival Cheops."

Ickes doubtless would have enjoyed (and agreed with) the description, and not without justification. According to PWA figures, 19,000 individual projects in 3,040 of the nation's 3,073 counties and in all her territorial and insular possessions had been authorized by the spring of 1935, of which more than 11,500 were completed and nearly 5,500 under construction. "Including dependents of those gainfully employed on construction sites and in material production and transportation," *Back to Work* claimed, "it is estimated that at least 10,000,000 persons have been directly benefited by expenditures to increase the national wealth through construction of useful public works as a substitute for direct relief." Most of the projects were quite as durable as even Cheops might have liked; thousands are still with us, in fact, mute reminders of that brief moment in our history when the federal presence in American life was generally deemed more necessary than evil, and somewhere on most of these utilitarian monuments appear the words "Harold L. Ickes, Secretary of the Interior" as the stamp of immortality.

The projects were as daunting in variety as they were in number. They embraced 583 municipal water systems and 622 sewerage systems, including a $42 million sewer and waste-treatment complex built for the Chicago Sanitary District; 263 hospitals, including a $2.4 million, 700-bed marine hospital in New York City supervised by the National Public Health Service; 522 schools, including a $2 million expansion of facilities at Virginia State College for Negroes; and 368 street and highway projects, including $8.5 million in highway construction for the state of Wyoming alone. Virtually all PWA grants and loans were made to public agencies of one kind or another. A notable exception was the railroad industry—which in the expedient lexicon of the New Deal fell under the rubric of public service, particularly public passenger service, and thus was deserving of public aid. So it was that between June 1933 and June 1935 the PWA made a total of $200 million in loans to railroads, including $80 million to the Pennsylvania Railroad to electrify its line from New York to Washington, D.C., cutting its running time by forty-five minutes, and to build new electric locomotives in the aging shops of Ickes's old hometown of Altoona.

Altoona appreciated the work. So did many another town. In Florida, PWA money built a bridge across the bay at Apalachicola on the Gulf Coast; other PWA bridges crossed the Mississippi at Baton Rouge in

Louisiana and at Davenport in Iowa; in Michigan it built a courthouse for Kalamazoo, while in Kansas the city of Wichita got a new museum; out in California, new schools were built to replace those destroyed in the great Long Beach earthquake of 1933, and the city of Los Angeles got $11.6 million to build new dock facilities at Port Hueneme; in Texas, Lubbock got new dormitories for Texas Tech, Fort Worth got a new sanitation system, and San Antonio got new elementary and secondary school buildings.

Few cities worthy of the description could not point to at least one PWA project, even if it was merely a new post office building or public library. But no municipality could match the success of New York City in the PWA sweepstakes. This was unsurprising; Roosevelt had no particular fondness for the city, but a major part of his political strength came from there and it is in the nature of politics that debts will be paid. This in spite of the presence of Robert Moses, unsuccessful Republican candidate for New York governor in 1934, chairman of the New York State Council of Parks as well as the state's Emergency Public Works Commission, and a profound political enemy of Franklin D. Roosevelt whose antagonism was as fresh and vital in the middle of the decade as it had been during the years of FDR's gubernatorial term. In 1934, apparently ignorant of the fact that the two men hated each other, the newly elected mayor of New York City, Fiorello La Guardia, had appointed Moses head of the New York City Department of Parks and a member of the Triborough Bridge Authority, a body that was to supervise the construction (with PWA funding to the amount of $42.6 million) of a bridge designed to link the boroughs of Manhattan, the Bronx, and Queens. Moses had made it conditional that he be allowed to hold his state positions as well, making him one of the most powerful men in New York, which did nothing to raise FDR's opinion of him. "Jesus Christ," the Little Flower cried out to a friend when he fully understood the situation, "of all the people in the City of New York I had to pick the one man who Roosevelt won't stand for and he won't give me any more money unless I get rid of him. Jesus Christ, I had to pick the one that he hated. Jesus Christ!"

The mayor's agitation was justified. Roosevelt was determined to force the removal of Moses and he appointed Ickes as the instrument of his wrath. La Guardia, who feared the political power of Moses as much as he did that of Roosevelt (and with good reason), stalled, dissembled, and otherwise resisted as Ickes, with the aid of James Farley, Louis Howe, and other administration figures, pressed him to get rid of the man. At Roosevelt's insistence, Ickes finally issued a confidential order stating that the PWA would award no further money to any project whose supervising

authority included anyone who held a state or local office, a device clearly
aimed at Moses and one that threatened completion of the Triborough
Bridge, by then well under construction. Throughout, Ickes did his duty
like a good political soldier, but he had little stomach for it. "I don't know
Moses," he wrote in his diary for January 9, 1935, after Moses had
obtained a copy of the order and had leaked it to the press, which resulted
in a flaming public uproar in New York. "From all accounts he is a highly
disagreeable and unpleasant person, who is also tremendously efficient.
He has done great things for Greater New York and for the state in
developing a wonderful park system. . . . I never had any interest in this
enterprise. I think it is a great mistake on the President's part. . . . By
making a martyr of him we are only serving to build him up. But I have to
take it on the chin and act as if I liked it."

Not for too much longer: Moses, as tough and talented a bird as ever
held public position, used both the press and his political connections
(including Alfred E. Smith, once FDR's staunch friend, now his worm-
wood enemy) with so much skill that the pressure against Roosevelt
became too much for even his hatred to withstand. Doing their best to
disguise the full dimensions of the capitulation, Roosevelt and Ickes
contrived a letter to La Guardia that in the case of Moses "incidentally"
made an exception to the PWA order restricting funds. No one was
deceived, least of all the New York newspapers. "Ickes Backs Down on
Moses," the *Herald Tribune* headlined its March 12 story on the event,
then in an editorial celebrated "the grandeur of that handsome, outsized
white flag now floating above the offices of the PWA."*

In the end, despite the sea of malice that lay between FDR and Moses
and the meddling of Tammany politicians (successfully shielding all that
money from the talons of avaricious borough ward heelers was one of Louis
Glavis's proudest accomplishments), the PWA spent and loaned tens of
millions of dollars to tear things down and build things up in New York
between the summer of 1933 and the summer of 1935. Not only did the
Triborough Bridge get finished (Moses, La Guardia, Roosevelt, and Ickes,
all smiling stiffly, would share the platform at its dedication on July 11,
1936); so did eighteen miles of new subway system at a cost of
$23 million, the Lincoln Tunnel under the Hudson River at a cost of
$37.5 million, and three of the largest piers in the world at a cost of $1.2
million. Before the PWA program finally wound down at the end of the

* Ickes could never quite bring himself to dislike Moses as much as FDR did. Years later, he
even demonstrated some admiration when remembering the conflict of the New Deal years.
"There can be no doubt of the porcupinish disposition of Moses," he wrote. "And is he
clever! . . . He put it all over President Roosevelt and me in that squabble."

decade, the list would come to include the Queens–Midtown Tunnel, expansion of facilities at Bellevue Hospital, an enormous ferry house on Ellis Island, the Henry Hudson, Grand Central, Cross-Island, Gowanus, and Interborough parkways—projects dear to the heart of Robert Moses—and such low-income housing complexes as the First Houses of Manhattan's Lower East Side, the Williamsburg Houses of Brooklyn, the Boulevard Gardens Apartments of Queens, and the Harlem River Houses of West Harlem.

Ironically, these New York housing projects were among the few anywhere in the country that got built or financed by the PWA's Housing Division, which at the local level was frustrated by political manipulation and financial speculation and at the federal level by a court ruling that prohibited the government from the exercise of eminent domain for the construction of low-cost housing. Only forty-nine PWA housing projects were built or even started before September 1937, when Congress took housing out of Public Works and put it in the newly created U.S. Housing Authority, a nearly autonomous body in the Interior Department that required little time or energy from the Secretary, a situation he greeted with an entirely typical mixture of relief and resentment.

By contrast—at least until another court order later put a stop to the use of its funds for such purposes—the PWA's military program was an unqualified success. With an outright grant of $238 million, the U.S. Navy fell to the building of two aircraft carriers, one heavy and three light cruisers, four submarines, two gunboats, and twenty destroyers. Another $25 million went to the Coast Guard for the construction of five 165-foot and seven 328-foot cutters, four harbor tugs, nine patrol boats, and ten amphibian airplanes. In addition, the air sections of both the navy and the army got a total of $15 million for the purchase of 168 new planes, including sixty-four Martin bombers of the latest design (though not as late as the Stuka bombers busily being prepared in Hitler's Germany). In the meantime, the Corps of Engineers, the army's most visible peacetime presence, was turned to the task of completing such domestic improvements as a one-hundred-million-dollar project to dredge shipping channels and build levees, floodways, and other flood-prevention works through most of the watershed of the Mississippi River Valley, and a $7.7 million project to build levees around Florida's Lake Okeechobee (to the dismay of a later generation of conservationists).

All this bustling about with a multitude of projects scattered from Seattle to Savannah, Galveston to Galena, provided considerable satisfaction and a sense that something was indeed getting done to bring the nation back from the abyss of Depression. But there was a good deal more than mere busyness in the vision held by Ickes and most of his colleagues at work in Public Works and other vineyards of the New Deal. It was all, they liked to feel, part of a larger plan to restructure not only the physical condition of the nation, but its economic fabric as well—to provide for nothing less than the redistribution of wealth by harnessing the natural resources of what Edna Ferber called "a magic continent" and turning them toward what Ickes called "the goal of the greatest happiness for the greatest number of our people." Whether such a goal was practical was irrelevant; it was the nation's duty to attempt to reach it. "Utopian goals?" Ickes had asked in an article for the May 27, 1934, issue of *The New York Times Magazine.* "Yes, Utopian indeed, but I do not apologize for suggesting that Utopia is a proper goal for us to strive for and that we are worthy of such a realm if we can achieve it. We are a spiritual people, and life for us would not be worth living if we did not have this urge to reach for what will always seem beyond our reach. If we cannot have it for ourselves, we want it for our children, those projections of ourselves into immortality."

That the realm of perfection could be achieved only through planning was a given of the New Deal. To that end, Title II of the NIRA had set up a National Planning Board to which Roosevelt had appointed his uncle, Frederick Delano; Ickes's old friend from Chicago, Charles Merriam; economics professor Wesley C. Mitchell; and, as executive secretary, city planner Charles Eliot II. While it began studies on economic structure and land use, a concurrent group, the Mississippi Valley Committee— also an offshoot of the PWA—prepared studies on soil erosion, water use, and flood control in the Mississippi River Valley.

The National Planning Board issued its first report in June 1934, and among its recommendations was that a broader permanent committee be established, one better funded and staffed for the job of integrating the scattered programs of the New Deal into a central plan for economic development and land and water use. That was agreeable to Roosevelt, who had complained earlier that "We have been going ahead year after year with rivers and harbors bills and various other pieces of legislation which were more or less dependent, as we all know, on who could talk the loudest. There has never been any definite planning." Supported in his convictions by the Planning Board, on July 5, 1934, FDR issued Executive Order 6777—largely written by Ickes and his people—establishing the National Resources Board (which later enfolded within it the Mississippi Valley Committee as well as other, smaller planning committees). It would include the Secretary of the Interior as chairman, the secretaries of

Agriculture, War, Commerce, and Labor, and the Federal Emergency Relief administrator (Harry Hopkins), together with Delano, Merriam, and Mitchell from the now abolished National Planning Board. The new board's function, the executive order said, would be "to prepare and present to the President a program and plan of procedure dealing with the physical, social, governmental, and economic aspects of public policies for the development and use of land, water, and other national resources, and such related subjects as may from time to time be referred to it by the President."

Simultaneously, and on the same principles, Roosevelt asked Ickes to establish a National Power Policy Committee in PWA, whose duty would be to "develop a plan for the closer cooperation of the several factors in our electrical power supply—both public and private—whereby national policy in power matters may be unified and electricity may be made more broadly available at cheaper rates to industry, to domestic and, particularly, to agricultural consumers." Representatives from the Federal Power and Federal Trade commissions, the Army Corps of Engineers, the Bureau of Reclamation, and other government departments with an interest in power projects were asked to sit on this committee, and Ickes, again, was appointed as its chairman.

That over the next several years these committees did what committees do best—which is to issue voluminous reports and recommendations that outside circumstances usually make it all but impossible to implement—is less important than the quality of thinking behind their formation. There was in the New Deal a touching optimism—perhaps naïve, but no less noble for all that—in the conviction that planning, combined with the careful application of money and technology, could overcome almost any obstacle the vagaries of nature or the imperfections of human character might present. "Today it is builders and technicians that we turn to," wrote the irrepressible New Dealer David Lilienthal, still simmering with possibilities as late as 1944,

> men armed not with the axe, rifle, and bowie knife, but with the Diesel engine, the bulldozer, the giant electric shovel, the retort—and most of all, with an emerging kind of skill, a modern knack of organization and execution. When these men have imagination and faith, they can move mountains; out of their skills they can create new jobs, relieve human drudgery, give new life and fruitfulness to worn-out lands, put yokes upon the streams, and transmute the minerals of the earth and the plants of the field into machines of wizardry to spin out the stuff of a way of life new to this world.

All these men and tools were never quite enough, of course, to do everything that was expected of them, but for all its failings, it should be remembered that this kind of thinking got things done in a big way—never perfectly, sometimes badly, but almost always with a dimension of hope that is breathtaking to observe from the distance of more than fifty years.

Consider the Tennessee Valley Authority, one of the biggest things the New Deal ever accomplished and the inspiration for David Lilienthal's fervent exclamation above (by then, he was running it). It centered on the little town of Muscle Shoals on the Tennessee River in northern Alabama. At this spot the river water fell with spectacular force, and during World War I the War Department had started to build Wilson Dam to tap that power for the generation of electricity to run a number of nitrate plants for the making of gunpowder. The war ended before the dam was completed, but the site soon earned the regard of the old progressive-minded Republican, Nebraska senator George Norris, a longtime champion of federal public works projects, who saw it as a potential starting point for a wide system of federal dams to control the ravaging floods that swept through most of the Tennessee River Valley on an almost yearly basis. In time, he also began to push for the development of hydroelectric projects owned and operated by the government to ensure cheap electricity for one of the most oppressively poor sections of the country.

Throughout the twenties, Norris's campaign became a crusade, as he introduced legislation (twice vetoed) for the federal development of the river basin and successfully thwarted various attempts on the part of private interests (including Henry Ford) to gain control of the Muscle Shoals site. But it was not until the arrival of Franklin Roosevelt that the senator's vision came to fruition. In January 1933, Roosevelt and Norris had paid a visit to the spot; then, during a speech in Montgomery, FDR articulated his own scheme. Its breadth startled even the dreaming Norris:

> Muscle Shoals is more today than a mere opportunity for the Federal Government to do a kind turn for the people in one small section of a couple of States. Muscle Shoals gives us the opportunity to accomplish a great purpose for the people of many States and, indeed, for the whole Union. Because there we have an opportunity of setting an example of planning, not just for ourselves but for the generations to come, tying in industry and agriculture and forestry and flood prevention, tying them all into a unified whole over a distance of a thousand miles so that we can afford better opportunities and better places for living for millions of yet unborn in the days to come.

Roosevelt offered legislation to translate vision to reality on April 10, and on May 18 he signed a bill authorizing a new entity called the Tennessee Valley Authority to "construct dams, reservoirs, power houses, power structures, transmission lines, navigation projects, and incidental works in the Tennessee River and its tributaries."

A three-man board was established to administer the TVA. Arthur H. Morgan, an engineer, was named chairman of the board and would be responsible for the construction of dams and the implementation of educational programs and social planning in the valley. H. A. Morgan (no relation to Arthur), an agricultural scientist and president of the University of Tennessee, would be in charge of phosphate fertilizer production (a new use for the War Department's old nitrate plants) and agricultural policy. David Lilienthal, the third member of the board, was a lawyer and colleague of Donald Richberg and a specialist in public utility law; he would handle power policy. With a start-up grant of $50 million from the PWA and continuing funding over the next decade, the TVA constructed sixteen new dams—one of the biggest of them, up on the Clinch River, was appropriately named after George Norris—and reconstructed five old ones. It dredged and diked the Tennessee River and made much of it navigable for the first time in history, and its flood-control projects made hundreds of thousands of acres of bottomland safe for agricultural development (or at least as safe as floodplains ever get)—including that taking place on "demonstration" farms utilizing new techniques of tillage and soil conservation and a good part of the 150,000 tons of fertilizer produced annually by the TVA's Muscle Shoals facilities, whose phosphate plants were soon renowned throughout the world. By the beginning of World War II, a region in which electricity once had been something that most people—including many of those in the cities—had only read about and yearned after had a generating capacity of more than one million kilowatts and one out of every five farms was electrified at rates against which prices in the rest of the nation were measured for fairness.*

The dream as realized was impressive enough, even though it fell a

---

* These rates were established and enforced by the contracts through which TVA power was provided to utility companies owned by municipalities and farmers' cooperatives (private power companies were not allowed to tap into federally generated power—in fact, many private companies were bought out by the government). Neither the system—socialism!—nor the rates—unfair competition!—were looked upon favorably by the utility industry; nor did it much like the fact that its own rates were measured against those of the TVA. The industry had fought vainly to prevent passage of TVA legislation and would repeatedly, and again vainly, take to the courts to challenge the government's right to engage in the power business in the Tennessee Valley or anywhere else. For several years the point man in the industry's struggle against the government's presence in its bailiwick was the president of the Commonwealth and Southern Corporation, a utility company with numerous subsidiaries in the region and headquarters in New York. His name was Wendell Willkie, and he would be stirring things up considerably in a few years.

good deal short of what had been hoped for it. Life improved measurably for most and spectacularly for some of the more than four million people who lived in the region. Yet a policy struggle between the practical-minded Lilienthal and the somewhat visionary Arthur Morgan ultimately resulted in Morgan's bitter departure and with him any real hope that the indisputable engineering and agricultural marvels taking place in the valley would be matched by revolutionary social changes. Indeed, after the war years any pretense at social engineering faded to oblivion at the same time that the TVA's power generation bloated to more than twelve billion kilowatts, making it one of the largest producers of electricity in the world. There is more than a little irony in the fact that the electricity produced by this greatest of all of the New Deal's peacetime efforts at social change was put to perhaps its most important—certainly, its most dramatic—use at the government-built village of Oak Ridge, Tennessee, where during World War II it helped to separate uranium 235 from uranium 238 for an enterprise called the Manhattan Project.

No matter. The TVA was seen then and is remembered in many quarters today as the closest approximation of a Utopian world this democratic Republic ever accomplished. It was never duplicated, although the planners of PWA, in tandem with the Bureau of Reclamation and the U.S. Army Corps of Engineers, attempted the job in four great river basins west of the Mississippi with mixed results.

The first and most ambitious of these was the child of the Bureau of Reclamation, which had been busy in any number of directions during the period, putting tens of millions of PWA dollars to work in seventeen individual irrigation, flood control, and power-producing projects, including five—the Hyrum, Ogden River, Moon Lake, Sanpete, and Provo River—which with funding of $16 million essayed nothing less than the development of a coherent water-use system for the entire state of Utah. Even this shrank to niggardly proportions when compared to its extraordinary Colorado River Project, whose development would affect a watershed shared by seven western states and Mexico. The project's principal component, Boulder Dam, had been authorized by act of Congress in 1928. Taken by itself, the dam was a phenomenon—"the biggest dam built by anyone anywhere," as described by Frank Crowe, chief engineer for the Six Companies, the construction consortium that had won the contract. So it was: 726.4 feet high from its base, 1,244 feet long at its crest, 45 feet thick at the top, and 660 feet thick at the bottom, it was then the largest chunk of concrete ever poured. If it could have been weighed, it would have tipped the scales at more than 6.6 million tons. Down in the two enormous powerhouses that bracketed the two sides of the river at the bottom of the dam, nine turbines would use the power of falling water to generate more than 700,000 kilowatts of electrical energy when all of them were finally installed and placed on line—making the Boulder Dam complex the largest single hydroelectric facility in the world.

However overwhelming, Boulder Dam and its powerhouses were only part of the whole project. Other components included Parker Dam, a smaller wall of concrete that would be jammed into the river more than a hundred miles downstream. This, too, was a Bureau of Reclamation project built by the Six Companies; its reservoir, called Lake Havasu, would hold water for delivery to the Metropolitan Water District of Southern California through a 241-mile-long aqueduct being built by the district itself. To lift the water over hill and dale, the district had contracted for 36 percent of the power produced at Boulder Dam (the remainder went to the city of Los Angeles, the Southern California Edison Company, and the states of Arizona and Nevada). Even farther south, just above the Mexican border, the All-American Canal, designed to carry Colorado River water eighty miles across the desert to the fecund soils of the Imperial Valley, got under way in October 1933, while final plans for yet another dam—Imperial—were given the final touches (by 1941, all segments of the Colorado River Project would be in place and functioning).

All of this except the beginning work on Boulder Dam itself was still a matter of blueprints when Ickes became Secretary of the Interior, but it still required his immediate attention. For one thing, it gave him the opportunity to exercise the caution that would earn him his reputation for vigilance even before becoming administrator of Public Works. Early in May 1933, the Bureau of Reclamation opened bids for the delivery of 400,000 barrels of cement for Boulder Dam. Ickes rejected all of them because, as he explained in his diary, "except for a variation due to different freight rates, all the bids were identical." The action set up a storm of complaint on the part of offended cement manufacturers and inspired considerable ink in the newspapers, much of which was favorable and all of which he clearly relished. Another decision made at about the same time brought forth an even greater tempest, this time most of it in protest. In 1930, then–Interior Secretary Ray Lyman Wilbur had directed that the dam be referred to as Hoover Dam in honor of his President. On May 8, Ickes reversed Wilbur's directive, ordering the project henceforth and forever to be referred to as Boulder Dam. "The name Boulder Dam is a fine, rugged, and individual name," he explained to one inquirer. "The men who pioneered this project knew it by this

name. . . . These men, together with practically all who have had any
first-hand knowledge of the circumstances surrounding the building of
this dam, want it called Boulder Dam and have keenly resented the
attempt to change its name." All Republicans and most newspapers
believed Ickes had been motivated entirely by his detestation of Hoover,
and that revulsion probably did play a major part; still, both names had
been used interchangeably for years and Ickes stood his ground—Boulder
Dam it would remain until 1947, when an act of Congress officially
declared it Hoover Dam.

There were more serious problems than nomenclature that had to be
dealt with during the course of construction, however. One was the use of
scrip instead of cash to pay the workers, a device Wilbur's Interior
Department had allowed the Six Companies but one which smacked of
oppressive nineteenth-century company-town practices. Ickes ordered the
company to begin paying its workers in cash. By 1934 this threatened to
be a difficult assignment, because by then the ambitious project had just
about run through all that was left in the Reclamation Fund (financed by
the sale of public lands and by royalties from oil production on federal
lands in the western states). But Ickes solved that problem easily enough
by engineering the allocation of $38 million in PWA money to keep the
project going.

After that, things moved along without notable participation on the
part of the secretary until February 26, 1935, when the payroll records of
the Six Companies were seized by order of Attorney General Homer
Cummings. A former employee of the company had charged it with no
less than sixty thousand violations of the federal eight-hour law, which
required government contractors not to resort to overtime except in clear
cases of emergency; he also claimed that the books had been doctored to
cover up the violations, thus defrauding the government of more than
$300,000 in overtime penalties. Henry J. Kaiser, one of the Six Com-
panies partners and its chief liaison with Interior, denied the allegation of
fraud and maintained that the Boulder Dam project was exempt from
fines in any case because its construction, by its very nature, was a state of
constant emergency. "Every reason to believe that not a single day passed
without the existence of some kind of emergency," he wrote Ickes on
March 18. "This can be appreciated when *considering the five thousand men*
employed and the *unusually large construction items* involved in this project
[italics in original]." Ickes was not persuaded and the Department of the
Interior pushed for collection of the penalties. Kaiser was up to the
challenge. He hired a press agent to put together a crisis-filled narrative
called *So Boulder Dam Was Built,* and mailed thousands of copies to

members of Congress, government officials, and newspapers; he went on the radio and invited newspaper interviews to relate how the project's immense obstacles had been overcome, painfully, one by one; he subjected Interior to what Ickes irritatedly called "a telegraphic bombardment." The effort paid off: in February 1936, Interior finally agreed to a negotiated settlement that cost the Six Companies only $100,000 in penalties.

By then the dam was finished and the Six Companies had moved on to other things, including Parker Dam and the huge concrete piers of the San Francisco–Oakland Bay Bridge (another PWA-financed project). Boulder Dam itself had been dedicated on September 30, 1935, as the waters of Lake Mead slowly gathered behind all that concrete. Ickes gave the first speech that day and spoke for the hopes of a still stubborn dream: "Here behind this massive dam is slowly accumulating a rich deposit of wealth greater than all the mines of the West have ever produced, wealth to be drawn upon for all time to come for the renewed life and continued benefit of generations of Americans." Like the TVA, however, Boulder Dam never did live up to its promises; the wealth that Ickes saw rising with the waters of Lake Mead ended up in the hands of the few, not the many. Nevertheless, as one historian has written, completion of the Colorado River Project marked a turning point in natural resource policy.

> With its completion the Federal government emerged as the dominant agent in river basin development. It opened new vistas in the West because it was the first project to develop the resources of the basin in a planned, integrated way. It established the principal of the maximum development of hydroelectric power as part of all but a very few reclamation projects built after it. Improved agricultural production and expanded commercial and industrial opportunities were included as goals of multiple purpose reclamation and became established as parts of future Federal conservation policy. But Boulder Dam symbolized more than the utilitarian concerns of the progressive conservationists. It committed the government to expanding the benefits of the public funds invested in the nation's natural resources.

Ickes fondly hoped to duplicate this feat in other river basins. In that of the Missouri River, for instance, where by the spring of 1935 the Corps of Engineers, armed with $50 million in PWA funds, was busily completing the Fort Peck Dam, an earth-fill structure 3.68 miles long in eastern Montana that would impound much of the river's water in a reservoir stretching for 175 miles. Or in that of the Columbia River in the Pacific Northwest, where the Corps of Engineers was busy again with Bonneville Dam forty miles west of Portland. Some $30 million in PWA money would finance the completion of this long, low (fifty-four feet high) dam designed not only to make the Columbia River navigable as far upstream as the mouth of the Snake River, but to provide irrigation water and—especially—about 600,000 horsepower of hydroelectric energy to light an entire region at cheap government rates; other notable features of this dam were its fish ladders, built at a cost of $3.2 million to enable Pacific salmon to return to their spawning beds every year. The fish were granted no such courtesy on the second great dam of the Columbia, that at Grand Coulee on the river's upper stem. This was a Bureau of Reclamation project that had taken $63 million in PWA money to get under way early in 1934. As proposed, Grand Coulee Dam would have stood more than five hundred feet high with a crest 4,173 feet long and would have cost as much as $181 million to complete, which in both money and sheer bulk would dwarf even Boulder Dam. It certainly dwarfed the expectations of Congress, most of whose members objected strenuously to the allocation of so much money on a single project, even one its proponents claimed would pay for itself by the sale of federal water to irrigate 1.2 million acres of land in eastern Washington and by the sale of more than 1.2 million kilowatts of electricity. To calm the Congress, Roosevelt and Ickes decided to authorize a dam only 297 feet high—big enough to stand as a dam on its own, certainly, but even more important, also big enough to stand as the *foundation* for a dam that could easily be expanded to the five hundred feet originally proposed as soon as the political climate would allow it. (And by the time of Grand Coulee's completion in 1941, that is precisely what had happened.)

While the dams on the Missouri and Columbia rivers slowly stoppered those great western streams, the state of California inadvertently moved to provide Ickes and the Bureau of Reclamation with the largest water development effort in history up to that time—the Central Valley Project, designed to capture the flows of both the Sacramento and the San Joaquin rivers by several big and little dams and carry the water through canal systems to irrigate much of the six-hundred-mile length of the Great Central Valley from Redding in the north to Bakersfield in the south. In the beginning, the state planned to build all these waterworks—including such large dams as Shasta on the Sacramento and Friant on the Kern—itself, and to finance it, California's voters had approved a bond issue in 1933 of $130 million, itself the largest bond issue in history. Not long thereafter, the bottom collapsed under the bond market and the state could not sell its securities anywhere in the country. The great project was bankrupt even before it got started—but its scope and potential for planning on an immense scale proved irresistible to Roosevelt, who in December 1935 accepted the state's offer to let the Bureau of Reclamation finish it.

In the end, only the Central Valley Project (many of whose components are still not finished and may never be) came close to matching the grandiose urges of which the Colorado River Project had been the first major expression. Both Roosevelt and Ickes lobbied regularly for the rest of their terms in office for the creation of river valley authorities comparable to the TVA to control development in the watersheds of the Missouri, Columbia, and even the Arkansas, but Congress never authorized legislation that would embrace so capacious a vision. As with the TVA itself, the New Deal ultimately would have to settle for a dream that, if not deferred, was less than it might have been. Even shrunk to a size that could be accommodated by the political realities of the time, however, the dream changed the West forever.

Long before it became apparent that the largest visions of the New Deal would fall short of the hopes that had given them birth, Ickes had been forced to deal with other limitations. On February 7, 1935, he decided to send orders out to all state engineers not to accept any more project applications, noting that there were already more than three billion dollars in PWA projects in the works or awaiting approval. He had no money to continue his program beyond the levels already reached. This irritated and worried him. In addition, internal affairs had not gone as smoothly as they might have. As early as December 1933 he had begun to suspect that Colonel Waite, his deputy administrator at PWA, was too often overstepping his authority and had called him on the carpet, where he assured the colonel, according to his diary, "that I have every confidence in his character and ability and that I have a feeling of real affection for him, but that since the President had given me instead of him the particular responsibility as Administrator, since the country understood that I was Administrator, and since Congress would hold me responsible as Administrator, I would have to exercise the power that went with the responsibility." In spite of this stern but kindly reprimand, Ickes apparently continued to have his doubts about the colonel's loyalty, fortified in his suspicions by secret communiqués from his personal assistant, Harry Slattery, who was beginning to show an interest in office intrigue and conspiracy that would reach troubling levels in the years to come. "Very frankly," Slattery had written Ickes in a memorandum of July 13, 1934, "the clique that Colonel Waite and his aides have placed in Public Works . . . have used their positions to boost their friends and to pay off old scores on men who they knew were giving loyal service to you rather than to them. They have penalized every man who was not a member of their clique and who, back in the early days, were giving Mr. Burlew, Mr. Glavis and myself the inside on Public Works." Finally, in September 1934, Waite had resigned, taking a job in Cincinnati. It was all done in a friendly enough fashion (Ickes even threw a farewell dinner for him), but a shake-up at the top of his administration had potential as political fodder for his enemies, and the affair had been unsettling.

Furthermore, the administrator had been having trouble with one of his less endearing responsibilities, the subsistence housing program, a vaguely Utopian scheme that had been written into Title II of the NIRA by Congressman William B. Bankhead of Alabama. A Subsistence Housing Division had been set up within the PWA, given $25 million, and charged with the task of building model villages in which hard-working citizens could escape the concrete bogs of urban life and sustain themselves on the land. Ickes had been suspicious of this noble, ill-defined enterprise from the beginning, and his regard had not improved when Eleanor Roosevelt and Louis Howe, FDR's old campaign manager and now his general-purpose adviser, had decided to take a personal interest in it. So far as he could, Ickes had distanced himself from the whole business. Shortly after he had been hired to run the division, Milburn Wilson remembered, Ickes had told him "that since he was an extremely busy man in connection with the Public Works Administration, he wouldn't give this the personal attention that he would like to give it. He intimated that this was kind of a pet project of the President and Mrs. Roosevelt, and of Louis Howe and Senator Bankhead."

Of the twenty communities that got under way before FDR folded the program into yet another new agency, the Resettlement Administration, in April 1935 (much to Ickes's relief), Howe and Mrs. Roosevelt had chosen Reedsville (later renamed Arthurdale), West Virginia, as their own pilot project. "Sparing no expense is the first rule, and must be the first rule, in the development of any new project," Howe announced grandly during a radio address, and he and Mrs. Roosevelt had spared none at Reedsville. But they also had made a number of mistakes, such as ordering up prefabricated houses that would not fit on the foundations that had been poured for them, and the cost overruns, as a later age would call such phenomena, were enough to bother even Wilson, who was normally exceedingly casual about such matters. "I said to Colonel Howe, the first time I went over to visit with him, 'Do you think that I had better talk with Secretary Ickes about this?'

"Without any smile or the faintest expression on his face, he said in a very positive way, 'No. The less that fellow knows about this the better, as far as I'm concerned. Let me take care of him.' "

Howe was not able to keep the truth from Ickes, however, and as early as December 2, 1933, the Secretary remarked in his diary that "I am afraid that we are due for some criticism for our work there. In the first place, we undertook it too hastily. Colonel Howe, in a rash moment, told the President that we would start work within three weeks. . . . The result has been, in order to make good on this rash boast, that we have rushed ahead pell-mell. I am afraid we are spending more money than we have a right to spend." Except for some politic (for Ickes) remarks to Eleanor Roosevelt and FDR from time to time and increasingly frequent complaints in his diary, Ickes continued to maintain his distance from the Reedsville project, operating on the apparent theory that if and when the business went smash he had better make certain that the blame would not attach to the PWA.

Reedsville finally did stagger through to completion, though it never approached the dimensions Howe and Mrs. Roosevelt had hoped for it, and by then it had been taken out of Ickes's hands. Throughout 1934 and well into 1935, however, it was one more problem constantly nibbling at his vitals. In combination with the onerous task of trying to get rid of Robert Moses, the beginning of his long feud with the Department of Agriculture over possession of the national forests (see Chapter 37, "Stewardship and Strife"), his still aching ribs, his headaches and continuing insomnia, and the cloud of distractions provided by his anguished private life, such difficulties left him ill prepared to meet his competition with much grace. And there soon was competition of a high order, an increasingly caustic struggle for the control of billions of dollars and the consequent dominance whoever held that control would have over the shaping of the New Deal's most visible presence in America.

CHAPTER
· 30 ·

Sorting Out the Public Weal

AT ONE OF the first cabinet meetings, Frances Perkins remembered, Vice President Garner had succumbed to a thoroughly uncharacteristic burst of compassion. He pounded the table, she said, and practically shouted: "Mr. President! Mr. President! I've been through this campaign. I read our campaign book. It seems to me that we promised that we would do something for the poorer kind of people. That's what we promised— we'd do something for the poorer kind of people. By George! We've got to do it! And we've got to do it quick! . . . These poor devils are really suffering. . . . This can destroy our civilization."

However important the long-term view and however admirable Ickes's dedication in holding to it throughout his administration of Public Works, more immediate help *had* been needed, and it had come in the form of a lanky, slung-jawed horse player named Harry Lloyd Hopkins, a man who gave off, according to one observer, "a suggestion of quick cigarettes, thinning hair, dandruff, brief sarcasm, fraying suits of clothes, and a wholly understandable preoccupation." Hopkins had been serving as deputy director of New York State's Temporary Emergency Relief Administration since 1931, and shortly after Roosevelt's inauguration, he and fellow relief worker William Hodson had come down to Washington to meet with Frances Perkins, who had known both of them during her own service with the state government. They met at the University

Women's Club during a party so crowded, she recalled, that the three of them had to huddle on a bench beneath the stairs. Hopkins and Hodson had come with a comprehensive plan for national relief. "It was a good plan," she remembered. "It was well thought out. It was practical." Hopkins and Hodson thought that one or the other of them should run it. Perkins agreed, and "my prime obligation from that time on—to push this through."

Perkins arranged for a meeting between Hopkins and Roosevelt. FDR was preoccupied with trying to balance the budget at the time and reluctant to get the government involved in major relief expenditures. But the need could not be denied and Hopkins was persuasive. Roosevelt asked senators Wagner, Costigan, and La Follette to come up with legislation. By May 12 a bill creating the Federal Emergency Relief Administration (FERA) had been passed and signed into law. The act allocated the sum of $500 million, to be provided by the RFC, half for relief on a matching grant basis—one dollar of federal money for every three dollars of local money—half in the form of outright grants, and on May 20 the Senate confirmed the appointment of Harry Hopkins to spend it.

He was not bashful. Within hours of stepping into his office in the old Walker-Johnson Building on New York Avenue (an office still piled high with the cartons of the agency that was moving out to make room for him), Hopkins had gone through a set of RFC state loan applications that had not yet been acted upon and had approved five million dollars' worth of them. He then sent telegrams to state governors, informing them that they had a new friend in Washington and asking them to tell him what they needed. He was determined to get relief into the hands of the needy as soon as possible; when someone came to him at one point and offered an idea that would "work out in the long run," Robert Sherwood reported in *Roosevelt and Hopkins,* Hopkins's response was, "People don't eat in the long run—they eat every day." At the same time, Hopkins could be as tough-minded as Ickes himself. He demanded that the states do their part. "Every department of government that has any taxing power left," he wrote his state administrators early on, "has a direct responsibility to help those in distress." When the state legislature of Kentucky came up with no money for relief, Hopkins cut the state off from federal money. He turned down requests for extra money from Ohio, West Virginia, and even New York City when these complained of the difficulty of raising local funds. Try harder, he said in effect to these and others.

Nor did the FERA administrator believe in the dole as anything but a temporary measure. "As a nation," he wrote in *Spending to Save,* his 1936 counterpart to Ickes's *Back to Work,*

we were beginning to acknowledge that our economic distress was no overnight disaster which would recede some fine morning like the waters of a
flood. Direct relief might do to tide over a few months or a year, or even
longer. But millions had already been out of a job for several years. In
addition to want, the unemployed were confronting a still further destructive
force, that of worklessness. This feeling became articulate in many quarters,
but most particularly among the unemployed themselves. . . . Men who had
never in their lives asked for, or accepted, a cent of alms refused to believe that
the situation had gone into permanent reverse. It made no difference to them
in what pretty words the unattractive fact of their dependency was dressed. It
was charity and they didn't like it.

By the beginning of November 1933, when millions of people were
looking with little hope toward what promised to be the worst winter in
their lives, Hopkins had come up with the idea for a work-relief program
in which the federal government would finance various projects not
already under PWA jurisdiction, hiring people and putting them to work
instead of treating them like charity cases. He was convinced that he could
employ as many as four million people before the end of the year, and
proposed to do it by reallocating a large portion of FERA relief funds as
wages, making up the difference in what the ambitious new program
would cost by getting $400 million from the PWA. If everyone he
thought could be hired was hired, the money would be gone in three or
four months, but the work program would at least help people get
through the hardest part of the winter. Hopkins brought the idea to
Roosevelt, who liked it well enough to discuss it favorably during his
November 3 press conference: "There is a great deal to be said for it. . . .
It adds to the self-respect of the country, and we are trying to find out
whether a plan of that kind is a feasible thing to do." (When one of his
cohorts asked Hopkins whether FDR had approved the plan, he answered,
"Approved it, hell, he just announced it at his press conference!" It was a
forgivable exaggeration.)

On November 6, at Roosevelt's behest, Hopkins, Wallace, and Perkins
met with Ickes in his office to begin to work out the details of the new
program, which by now had been dubbed the Civil Works Administration (CWA). Ickes was somewhat worried about losing the $400 million,
but was generally amenable. The allotment, he told his diary, "would put
a serious crimp in the balance of our public works fund, but we all
thought it ought to be done. There was a general feeling that we really are
in a very critical condition and that something drastic and immediate
ought to be done to bolster the situation." He continued amenable five
days later when after another long meeting the program was fairly

launched. Even though it still would appropriate $400 million of PWA funds, Ickes took comfort in the fact that the CWA would not compete with the PWA in any serious way. "This organization will undertake no contract work," he sternly noted in his diary.

> It will put up no buildings. It won't build any sewers or water works or incinerators or bridges. But these men will be put to work on projects of a minor character. They will work thirty hours a week and they will be paid the wage scale set up in our public works program. After the meeting the newspaper correspondents were in and I made the statement for publication that any state or municipality withdrawing a project submitted to the Public Works organization for consideration in the hope or expectation that the Civil Works organization would do this work instead, free of cost, would not only not have such work done by the Civil Works organization, but that it might not again resubmit its project to the Public Works organization.

Having firmly established the boundaries of the CWA's limits, at least to his own satisfaction, Ickes was content to let Hopkins go about the business of putting people to work. And so Hopkins did: by the end of January 1934, when the funds finally neared exhaustion and he had to start the painful process of dismantling his own program (done by the middle of March), Hopkins had in fact put 4.25 million people on the payroll of the CWA. He was convinced that the project had proved its worth and he was determined to restructure the FERA so that it would emphasize work programs over simple relief at every possible turn. If he had known that this would in time make him and Ickes institutional rivals, it probably would not have deterred him.

The campaign began in earnest in the fall of 1934, as Hopkins laid out plans to employ an additional four million people through FERA work projects structured much like those of the now-defunct CWA. To do it, he calculated, he would need $250 million in additional funding. Before exploring ways of getting hold of such an amount with Secretary of the Treasury Henry Morgenthau, he went first to Roosevelt to outline his thinking. FDR startled him with the proposal that the government should take the work-relief program and institutionalize it on a massive scale. "The big boss is getting ready to go places in a big way," Hopkins exclaimed to a colleague later, and while driving to the racetrack with several of his people one afternoon elaborated on the possibilities of the moment: "Boys—this is our hour. We've got to get everything we want . . . now or never. Get your minds to work on developing a complete ticket to provide security for all the folks of this country up and down and across the board."

While the planners of the FERA fell to outlining a new program,

Hopkins and Ickes were directed by Roosevelt to work out the financial details with Henry Morgenthau, a cautious sort who today probably would be described as a fiscal conservative. It had been Morgenthau and Lewis Douglas—until Douglas's frustrated resignation on August 30, 1934—who had argued most consistently for the virtues of a balanced budget and the horrors of deficit spending. Morgenthau still held for a balanced budget, though he willingly modified his stand to make an exception for relief. Still, he insisted on precision from Hopkins and Ickes, and with their first meeting on the work-relief program on October 1, in the words of his biographer, he "demanded definitions of how much the government would spend, how fast, for what projects, and with what impact on unemployment. Unless those questions could be answered accurately, he said, the Treasury could not make plans to finance the program by taxation or by borrowing, nor could the government make progress toward a balanced budget."

Morgenthau never was able to force the two men to come up with facts and figures that satisfied him, but in the end it did not really matter; Roosevelt himself was in no mood to wait for precision—he wanted to announce the new program in his State of the Union address in January and made it clear that he would, no matter how the financial details finally worked out. Marriner Eccles, who would become governor of the Federal Reserve Board in January, was then Morgenthau's special assistant; he was a deficit-spending man whose instincts lay closer to those of Harry Hopkins than to those of his boss and in his memoirs he remained convinced that it was Hopkins and Ickes who had persuaded Roosevelt to take the plunge. After complaining about Morgenthau's rule that all contact with the President was off-limits to Treasury staff other than the Secretary himself, Eccles went on to render an uncommon tribute:

> With the Treasury staff reduced to silence, and with its chief whispering the language of economic orthodoxy, the initiative for a large-scale spending program went by default to two men whose roles exposed them to the charge that they were "playing politics with human misery." These two, Harry Hopkins and Harold Ickes, perforce had to play politics with human misery—if one wishes to call it that. Each day of their work they waded through the muck and mire of human distress. They knew better than most people that if politics was not played, if the government did not put an end to distress, then government as we had known it would be destroyed by social upheaval.

Roosevelt needed no prodding in that direction, however; by now he had given up any hope of a balanced budget. He wanted a program, and he wanted it now. Near the end of December, when Morgenthau repeated his

complaint that he still had no real figures to consider and urged
Roosevelt—not for the first time—to choose one man to run things
(preferably not Ickes, whom Morgenthau distrusted), the President, Morgenthau reported in his own diary, answered "in a very emphatic and
rather angry tone of voice: 'I will get a program within forty-eight hours. I
am going to get my program first and I will not settle as to who is going
to run it until I get my program.'" To that end, he loosely outlined a
work-relief plan in his State of the Union address on January 4, then went
on to ask Congress for $4 billion of new money and $880 million in
unused appropriations from other programs to finance it.

While Congress deliberated over the question, Ickes proved to be just
as fretful about who would run the program as was Morgenthau. He
became convinced that it might be Admiral Christian Joy Peoples, director of the Treasury Department's Procurement Division, or even Donald
Richberg, though Ickes apparently was the only person in Washington,
including Richberg, to whom such a notion had ever presented itself. "I
have no respect at all for Richberg's organizing ability," Ickes informed
his diary. "He would be swimming in waters that for him were un-
plumbed. Hopkins and I would do the work and he would get the credit."
To block this dreadful possibility, early in January he went to see Hopkins, who was at home recovering from the flu. Hopkins also had no love
for the idea of working under Peoples or Richberg, Ickes observed, "and if
he and I will only stick together on this, I feel confident that no attempt
will be made to force us to work under either." As insurance, he proposed
to Hopkins that they push to have a new cabinet position created—with
Hopkins filling it, of course—to head up a new federal agency into which
all the government's purely social services would be folded, including a
number of things from the Interior Department, like Subsistence Housing, for which Ickes had no particular fondness; Ickes, naturally, would
run everything else, especially Public Works. Or, Ickes said, possibly
Hopkins could go to work for him as deputy administrator of Public
Works, with special responsibility for Subsistence Housing and the supplying of labor for the various public works projects, including those
under the new program, however it worked out. Hopkins, perhaps weak
from illness, apparently did not rise up on his elbows to protest either of
these strategies, both of which offered him nothing but trouble and one of
which would have left him in a clearly secondary position to Ickes. No
matter; neither of the ideas went any further than his sickroom.

The question was still unsettled by April 5, 1935, when Congress
passed the Emergency Relief Appropriation Act, giving Roosevelt the
money he wanted and the latitude he needed to put it to use. Over the

next three weeks, FDR, Ickes, and Hopkins each tinkered with proposals for how the work program should be organized and operated. Ickes wanted a large organization firmly placed in Washington, with himself at its head (though he was not so crude as to state the latter condition outright); Hopkins, whose main interest remained in getting as many people to work as fast as possible, wanted a far more decentralized organization to run the program, and while he, too, would have headed it up, divisions at the state level would have had near autonomy in many respects, all in the interests of speed. Each viewed the other's thinking, of course, with a jaundiced eye, but of the two it must be said that Ickes reacted more vehemently. "He gives himself absolutely all the power there is," he complained to his diary when he first saw an outline of Hopkins's organizational plan on April 8. "It seems to me that he even arrogates to himself things that normally would belong to the President. This is the most sweeping and arrogant thing I have seen here." He immediately called in Slattery, Burlew, Ben Cohen, and Edward Foley, the PWA general counsel, and got them started on a draft that would reflect what he believed was the President's desire to have a strong central organization with a strong man at the head of it.

He also apparently had been muttering threats to resign if things did not work out as he wanted them to. He had made similar noises during congressional deliberation on the Emergency Relief Act, when it looked for a while as if amendments might prohibit PWA loans on any nonfederal project unless it could be shown that 51 percent of the money would go to labor costs. A compromise had reduced the requirement to 25 percent and had given FDR wide discretionary powers in its enforcement, so Ickes had subsided. Now he was unhappy again, particularly when newspaper reports began assuming that Hopkins would end up in charge of the work relief program, and an unhappy Ickes was not usually a quiet Ickes. On April 10, Thomas G. Corcoran came by to see him and calm him down, almost certainly at the behest of Roosevelt.

The wizened and worn-out Louis Howe, who had looked as if he were pounding on death's door for years, was by now in the last stages of emphysema (though he would not die for another year), and Corcoran was rapidly developing into Roosevelt's principal liaison with various elements of his administration and the leadership in Congress. He had proved himself particularly useful with regard to specific pieces of major legislation like the Emergency Relief Act, the National Labor Relations Bill (then under consideration, it would be signed into law on July 5), the Social Security Bill (signed on August 12), and the Public Utility Holding Company Bill (signed on August 26).

It was the utilities bill, largely written by Ben Cohen and designed to obliterate the kind of overweighted monopoly that Samuel Insull had enjoyed and Harold Ickes had opposed in Chicago, that had brought Ickes and Corcoran into close contact for the first time. The ebullient and professionally Irish Corcoran was another of Felix Frankfurter's "hot dogs" from Harvard Law; he had also clerked for Justice Oliver Wendell Holmes (who had died in March) and was an acolyte of Justice Louis D. Brandeis, one of the few friends the Roosevelt administration had on the Supreme Court. He had joined the administration in 1933 as a special assistant in both the Department of the Treasury and the Department of Justice, then had transferred to the Reconstruction Finance Corporation as a special counsel, a usefully vague position he held until he left Washington to enter private practice in 1941. He and Cohen, who was as gently quiet as Corcoran was boisterous, were roommates in a small house in Georgetown with a number of similarly underpaid young New Dealers (the "Little Red House" it was soon called by the press, a description considered particularly fitting by the administration's enemies, who imagined that the protocols of socialism were formulated behind the brick exterior of the place). The two young men had become fast, if unlikely friends, as well as close working partners in the toils of the New Deal. Together (Cohen "on loan" from the PWA), they had drafted the legislation that became the Securities and Exchange Act of 1934, and when Ickes gave Cohen the assignment of drafting utilities legislation for the study of the National Power Policy Committee, on which Interior held a seat, Corcoran was soon helping out with this, too—making Ickes's acquaintance and earning his respect along the way (as with Cohen, the relationship would blossom swiftly into an enduring friendship).

Ickes was predisposed to listen, then, when the young man came to call on April 9, particularly when Corcoran ("Tommy the Cork," Roosevelt dubbed him) argued that if Ickes were seriously considering resigning over the work relief question, it would be a terrible blow to the administration. "He said that I was the last hope of the Progressives in the Administration," Ickes told his diary, "and that if I would only manage to hang on for three or four weeks, he felt that everything would work out all right. . . . He said the President realizes that I am the spearhead of the Progressives. . . . He thinks further that the President knows he must have me in the new works administration as an assurance to the country that it will be honestly administered, and that he will want my help in the campaign next year." Thus assured of his importance in the scheme of things, Ickes stifled his muttering about resignation. For now.

Whether Roosevelt really considered his Secretary of the Interior to be the "spearhead" of the Progressives is moot; but there is no question that he wanted Ickes to stay and that he would indeed want to have the old Progressive's political skills, connections, and influence on hand when he ran for a second term. Just as certainly, all of Roosevelt's own political instincts told him that on the eve of an election year, the kind of swift, dramatic, and seemingly free-spending program that Hopkins appeared to offer had enormous advantages over the more stately institutional approach advocated by Ickes. As was his style more often than not, the President turned to deception to work his way through the dilemma. He gave Ickes to understand that his approach to the whole program was very much his own and that Ickes would in effect be running it, however the titular positions worked out. He convinced him of this even while setting up a structure that would make such an outcome all but impossible—and in fact would give Hopkins considerable power over Ickes.

Roosevelt divided the operation into three parts. A Division of Applications and Information, headed by Frank Walker, the executive director of the National Emergency Council, would receive all grant and loan applications that wanted to tap into the $4.8 billion of work relief money, sort through them, then pass along those that proved virtuous; it also would keep records, publish statistics, and in general monitor the program. The division to which the applications would be passed was the Advisory Committee on Allotments, made up of representatives from twenty-three groups, including the Forest Service, the U.S. Army Corps of Engineers, the American Bankers' Association, the U.S. Council of Mayors, and numerous other discrete elements of both government and society. It would meet once a week to discuss the various proposals, determine which qualified for approval, and decide which agency should be given responsibility for the project. Roosevelt himself would have a seat on the committee, although it would be chaired by Ickes. The final division was given the name of the Works Progress Administration (WPA) and would be run by Hopkins.*

Buried within the federalese of the Executive Order giving it birth were two provisions, both of them probably the deliberate invention of Roosevelt himself, that would prove to be the seeds of frustration for Ickes, though he did not immediately recognize them as such. Among the

---

* To his dying day, Ickes was convinced that Hopkins had chosen the name of the new agency in an attempt to get it confused with the PWA. "I have always thought that the similarity of initials was more than coincidental," he wrote in the *Saturday Evening Post* in 1948. "Was it a deliberate attempt to make WPA shine by reflected light? My friends could not unscramble them; my enemies did not want to." As it happened, however, Hopkins not only had not chosen the name (FDR probably had), he thought it was "terrible."

WPA's other duties, the order stated, would be the chore of prescribing rules and regulations with the approval of the President to "assure that as many of the persons employed on all work projects as is feasible shall be persons receiving relief." Another task was to "Recommend and carry on small useful projects designed to assure a maximum of employment in all localities." Neither "small" nor "useful" were precisely defined, though Harry Hopkins would never have difficulty identifying projects which fit this gossamer description. Nor did he have any uncertainty about what "maximum of employment" signified; both he and Roosevelt were determined to put no less than 3.5 million people to work before the onslaught of another winter.

Ickes, his ego soothed by FDR's repeated assurances that the two of them were thinking along similar lines, remained unconscious of the depths of the President's commitment to the creation of jobs, jobs, and more jobs. As a consequence, he thoroughly misread the situation. "If this administration plan of the President goes through," he crowed in his diary on April 19, "it will mean that instead of having less power, I will have greater power and will really outrank all the other men in the work-relief organization. This will be a surprise to a good many people who have been proclaiming that I was to have a back seat and an inconspicuous part in the new program." Two weeks later, he had modified his enthusiasm somewhat, though he remained confident: "Of course, in the end, Hopkins may appear as the outstanding man in the new organization. No one can predict one way or the other, but I am still Administrator of Public Works and in addition I am chairman of the committee to make the allotments. It will be Hopkins' duty to see that the labor is provided from the relief rolls and to keep track of the progress of the work on the projects."

That was not quite how Hopkins viewed his role, and with the tacit and sometimes the active support of Roosevelt, he made his presence felt in no uncertain terms from the moment of the first meeting of the Allotment Committee (on which he, too, held a seat) on May 7. The meeting was held in the Cabinet Room, and Ickes found himself "not without embarrassment" sitting in the President's chair to conduct the proceedings, the President himself sitting demurely in a chair to Ickes's right and a little back from the big table. Rexford Tugwell was there, sitting as the representative of the new Resettlement Administration. "It was a long meeting," he wrote in his own diary, one colored by

the political cross-currents and the general struggle for power which is going on. The announcements up to now make it fairly clear that Harry Hopkins and Frank Walker are really charged with making the Works Program work. With Ickes presiding, he was, of course, anxious to put across a number of his Public Works projects but they were pretty generally smothered. Harry's obvious effort is to think in terms of three and a half million men off the relief roll going to work with four billion dollars to be expended.

In spite of the bickering over individual projects between Ickes and Hopkins during the next several weeks—Roosevelt usually sitting back in his chair saying little or nothing—the committee managed to allocate some $3.5 billion of the money by the end of August. Still, neither man was happy. Hopkins complained that too much of the money had gone to agencies and programs that ought to have been funded out of the general treasury and that administrative bottlenecks were tying up what funds he had been given. "I have no money down here," he complained to one caller in mid-June. "I have no appropriations. We can't make any commitment about what we can do." For his part, Ickes objected to the fact that since most of his PWA projects were large-scale affairs, the committee insisted on going over each of them in detail, whereas Hopkins could submit a large number of his comparatively small projects at one time, asking for a lump sum to cover them all, and in the interests of time and sanity the committee would pass on them with only a cursory look at any individual project. He also felt that too often the two of them were competing for the same projects and that Harry got far too many of them—sometimes in a devious manner.

There was a touch of a persecution complex in Ickes's complaints; there also was a good deal of truth. Early on, Hopkins had agreed that in an effort to clarify matters, all projects costing more than $25,000 would be considered the province of the PWA, those costing $25,000 or less falling to the WPA. That would appear to have left such things as a million-dollar bridge project, say, firmly in the hands of the PWA—but not if one divided it up into forty individual projects, which Hopkins was entirely capable of doing when he wanted to create jobs in a given area. Furthermore, he was not above outright theft when he considered it justified, sometimes encouraging applicants to redefine their PWA projects so that they would fall under the purview of the WPA, other times prodding them to abandon PWA project applications altogether and submit only those for WPA. Thus a telephone conversation with Mayor Ed Kelly, Anton Cermak's successor in Chicago and no friend of Ickes (in spite of the fact that Harold's brother, John, still held his job with the mayor's administration and that for political purposes Kelly was forced to maintain superficially cordial relations): "Ickes wants to get a lot more of this money," Hopkins said, "and by implication take it away from me, which would mean, I think, that the President would be left in a hell of a jam. Ickes is very much opposed to things like [your] road project."

"He wants to do something that would take two or three years," Kelly said.

"Yes, he wants that sewage, etc."

"Yes, or the airport."

"Yes, and the result is you never get anybody to work."

"You think a wire [to FDR] about that other thing would work out all right?" (Kelly apparently wanted to persuade Roosevelt to approve his "road project" and other WPA jobs over the PWA projects Ickes was sponsoring.)

"I think it would. It wouldn't tie up directly, but indirectly. Tell him how much money, how many it would put to work."

Finally, Hopkins soon discovered that the clause in Roosevelt's Executive Order charging him with the responsibility of assuring "that as many of the persons employed on all work projects as is feasible shall be persons receiving relief" gave him the equivalent of veto power over any project that did not offer the opportunity to hire a sufficiency of what the administration called "unemployed employables." Precisely what a sufficiency might be was a matter of interpretation, of course, and Ickes suspected that Hopkins used his discretionary powers to gut the PWA and promote the WPA. "Hopkins holds up our projects for an indefinite period," he complained to his diary on August 6. "Some he approves and some he doesn't approve. He pretends to exercise judgment, but I suspect it is largely a matter of whim. [Fred E.] Schnepfe said . . . that he gives us just enough PWA projects to bait the hook for us and make us feel that we are getting something." Again, persecution complex mixed with reality here; while it is hardly likely that Hopkins operated by whim, he had in fact blocked no fewer than two thousand PWA projects worth $375 million before the end of the summer.

This would have been more than enough to test the patience of any man; it nearly shattered that of Ickes. "I am more disposed," he was writing by August 23, "where we can't agree with Hopkins that a project does belong to PWA, simply to let him have it. I am tired of squabbling with Hopkins over projects. After all," he added in a moment of self-righteous pity, "all I want is to build substantial projects and make money go as far as it can with as much coming back into the Federal Treasury as possible." He was nicely primed for explosion, then, when he received a curt note from FDR on the afternoon of Monday, August 26, that was just vague enough to be open to misinterpretation: "I am writing to inform you that, with respect to public works funds available for carrying out the purposes of the National Industrial Recovery Act . . . I desire that all future applications for allocations . . . be submitted to the Advisory Committee on Allotments, to be acted upon in the same manner and to the same extent as that committee acts with respect to allocations made under the Emergency Relief Appropriation Act of 1935." Ickes took this to mean that PWA allocations would be taken out of his hands entirely; so did the noon edition of the *Washington Star,* he learned later that afternoon, when someone showed him a copy. The paper had gotten hold of a copy of the letter and had laid the story out under a bluntly specific headline: "Ickes Is Shorn of PWA Power." This smacked of public humiliation and once again he made plans for a letter of resignation.

Before penning it in full fury, however, he called Hiram Johnson to tell him of his determination. Johnson sympathized with him, but urged him to confront Roosevelt directly before announcing his departure from the administration. Ickes called the President, who reacted with apparent astonishment to the anger of his Interior Secretary. Both Ickes and the *Star,* Roosevelt insisted, had misread his letter; he had no intention of taking control of PWA from Ickes. "He said the newspapers were cock-eyed," Ickes told his diary, "and that I mustn't be childish. I told him I wasn't being childish and that I had good reason to take exception to learning first from a newspaper about a matter vitally affecting my administration.

"I was pretty angry and I showed it. I never thought I would talk to a President of the United States the way I talked to President Roosevelt." In the end, while FDR did not go so far as to apologize (he usually managed to avoid this inconvenience by the exercise of charm that stopped short of admitting error), he did promise to have press secretary Steve Early put out a press release saying that his letter had been misinterpreted and that he planned no change in Ickes's status as PWA administrator. The release was duly issued and Ickes withdrew his threat, but the incident fed his always hungry insecurities, robbed him of sleep, and once again drove him to the edge of clinical depression. This at a time when the immutable wheel of his life was ready to lurch through another dark cycle.

CHAPTER

· 31 ·

*The Mourned
and Unmourned Dead*

I N HIS LIFE outside the office, the summer of 1935 had begun with the
promise of relative tranquillity colored slightly by melancholy. Both his
marriage and his career seemed to have survived the worst he could do to
them with his sexual antics and financial shortcomings. Anna's last term
in the Illinois state legislature had drawn to a close and she was prepared
to enter fully into Washington life, with the usual excursions into New
Mexico to work with her Indians and perhaps do some more writing. The
indefatigable Chicago spinster May Conley, his personal secretary of
secretaries since 1912, was once more by his side, her mother safely buried
in Chicago and she free once again to absorb the complaints and confi-
dences of his life—both in the weekly entries for his diary (a stenographic
duty she shared with Theodore Mack) and in the various personal and
professional reminiscences Ickes would spill forth over the years (which
she alone was privileged to record).

May Conley was not the only one who had returned. Raymond Robins,
the peripatetic reverend, had surfaced after his strange disappearance in
the fall of 1932 and by the spring of 1933 had recovered enough from
whatever ailed him to travel to Russia. Upon his return, he had come to
Washington to lobby the Roosevelt administration for recognition of the
Soviet government, which he still believed to be the hope of the world
(recognition in fact would come later that year), and on July 13 had

dropped by to see Harold. It was their first meeting since the disappearance, although they had been in communication: through the good offices of Postmaster General Jim Farley, Ickes earlier had been able to help Robins get his hands on some money he had deposited in a bank under the name he had taken while in his psychological limbo. Ickes was appalled at what he saw in July. "I was terribly shocked at his appearance and his manner," he remarked in his diary. "He looked much older, and while he tried to talk with his old-time vigor, it was easy to see he was putting on a lot of pressure. The old laugh and the old fire were entirely missing. . . . After he had been here a while, Gifford Pinchot came in and I called him in to the small private office where I had Raymond. . . . Gifford had exactly the same feeling about him that I had. . . . It has lain heavy on my heart ever since he was here."

Neither of them should have written Robins off so quickly. He soon was running true to form, wanting something from Ickes—first, a job for his nephew, John Dreier (Harold complied by placing young Dreier with the Subsistence Housing Division), then the use of his influence. In the spring of 1932, Raymond and Margaret had deeded their home and property at Chinsegut Hill in Florida to the Department of Agriculture for use as an agricultural experiment station, forest reserve, and wildlife sanctuary; under the terms of the agreement, the couple had been granted a life estate, which would enable them to live there until their deaths. (Margaret, suffering from rheumatic heart disease, apparently never left the place now.)

Since the arrival of the new administration, the Department of Agriculture, by Raymond's lights (he had been a Hoover man, after all), had treated one of its local employees badly and furthermore had not moved swiftly enough to complete various improvements on the property; the work was being done with a PWA grant, and he had been nagging Ickes to do something about both situations since the middle of 1934. "I saw Harold for a brief ten minutes," he wrote Margaret in April 1935.

> He is well and says his folks are well. I have never seen him look better. . . . I put the Sheets case to him for counsel. He said rather testily "Raymond I have nothing to do with the Department of Agriculture." I sought to put his cooperation on other ground, but without success. Now while this seems a little unfair and unfriendly, I want to say that he *is* one of the busiest men in Washington, and he feels this is a small matter when he is driven with large affairs. I still want to keep some sort of touch with him, despite his coldness and almost indifferent attitude.

Given the very real dimensions of the affairs Ickes was indeed driven by, he could be forgiven a certain testiness. In truth, he gave Robins's difficulties what time and attention he could over several months of prodding, most of the time with uncommon courtesy; in spite of a history of often rancorous political disagreements and Robins's sublime arrogance, Harold bore no grudges and maintained a residual fondness for this irritating man, who refused to accept Ickes's repeated pleas of helplessness with regard to a project within Henry Wallace's bailiwick. Robins was still after him at the end of July 1935, writing with his usual ornate effusions: "Congratulations! I have just finished 'BACK TO WORK.' It is a thrilling and splendid record of a vast and original achievement. You have here a more noble and enduring monument than can ever be built from granite or marble. It vindicates the prophecies and fulfills the hopes of your friends." Then: "Perhaps, if this be possible, the reading of 'BACK TO WORK' makes me more eager than before, that the P.W.A. projects on Chinsegut Hill Sanctuary should become a worthy witness to the usefulness, efficiency and honor of P.W.A. The setting is all that could be desired. . . . It now belongs to all the people and its equipment should be worthy of them."

A less annoying—but ultimately much sadder—reconnection with his past had been made in May. On May 2, as chairman of the Anniversary Committee of the Women's International League for Peace and Freedom—founded by Jane Addams in 1915—Anna had organized a huge dinner at the Willard Hotel on Pennsylvania Avenue to commemorate both the twentieth anniversary of the organization and the seventy-fifth birthday of the increasingly fragile doyenne of Hull-House. Harold had been a featured speaker at this occasion, together with Eleanor Roosevelt; Gerard Swope, president of the General Electric Company; Oswald Garrison Villard, who had become publisher of the *Nation;* Sidney Hillman, who had risen from the Chicago streets to become head of the Amalgamated Clothing Workers of America and one of the leading advisers to the Roosevelt administration on labor matters; and Dr. Alice Hamilton, who had served so long at Hull-House during the early years and was now well established in the firmament of the Harvard Medical School. Ickes and Mrs. Roosevelt, he noted in his diary with more than a little pride, had been the first and second speakers and both had been carried on the NBC network. "The hotel management said this was the biggest dinner ever given at the hotel," he added. "Five hundred people who wanted reservations were turned away and after dinner a good many people stood at the entrances to hear the speeches."

Less than three weeks later, Jane Addams was dead, the body whose failings she had refused to acknowledge finally betraying her. On May 21, Ickes entrained for Cincinnati, where he gave a dinner speech on public housing for the poor, then went on to Chicago, where he was met by young Raymond, who was still in residence at Hubbard Woods and now busy studying law at the University of Chicago. After giving another speech before fifteen hundred people gathered at a junior high school ("I made a great hit with the audience, if genuine and prolonged applause is any indication," he wrote in his diary), he and his son joined Charles Merriam for lunch at the old University Club, Ickes's home away from home for so many years. Then the three of them went down to Hull-House for Miss Addams's funeral, which was held in the court of that citadel of care she had created as a defense against hopelessness. Both Hull-House and the streets around it had filled with mourners, and Ickes found himself particularly moved by the purple ribbons of grief that had been strung from the Greek shops and restaurants along Halsted Street. Memories of his own clamoring young manhood in the warrens of the city probably gave special weight to this moment for him. "Dean Gilkey gave a good talk," he told his diary, "but it didn't seem to me that he quite rose to the occasion. However, I doubt whether anyone could have done so. There were a number of old friends and admirers of Miss Addams there, and all of us felt the occasion very deeply. She was a great spirit, gentle and simple, and yet able and with rare vision. I have never known anyone like her, nor shall I ever."

After the funeral, Raymond took him up to Hubbard Woods to have a look at the spring flowers. He was pleased to see that the mertensias and daffodils he had planted along the west and south of the house were blossoming handsomely. It still was too early for the dahlias.

In June, Harold and Anna took their last trip together, though it was more in the manner of a procession. On the afternoon of the fourteenth, his driver, Carl Witherspoon, drove Ickes and Anna north into Pennsylvania and across the mountains to Bedford. There they were met by a reception committee, complete with state motorcycle police, which accompanied them the last few miles into Altoona, where he was scheduled to give a Flag Day speech the next afternoon. It was the first trip back to the country of his boyhood in many years, and he was sobered by the changes he saw all around him as the little cavalcade of two limousines and two motorcycles sped over the mountains and through the winding hollows of early summer. In Newry, where in his childhood he had found the closest approximation of joy he may ever have known, his Uncle Alex's big barn and most of the capacious old farmhouse had been torn down—though he was touched to see that the well pump he had worked so often as a boy was still standing. In Hollidaysburg, his grandfather McCune's own sturdy farmhouse—the place where Harold and his mother had been born—was now rickety with age and abandoned, its windowpanes broken, its yard a mess of uncut weeds, its picket fence gap-toothed and sagging.

The Logan House Hotel, once the greatest caravansary in the whole region, was gone entirely, torn down for a parking lot in 1931; Harold and Anna would be staying at the new railroad hotel, the Penn-Alto. Most of Altoona's streets were paved now and choked with the automobile and streetcar traffic they had never been designed to accommodate. But the railroad yards still dominated the town—huge, dirty, shouting with noise, still providing most of the employment for a population now edging toward eighty thousand and still excreting the smoke and acidic grime that relentlessly ate away at the helpless exteriors of the town's buildings. "It really is one of the ugliest and most unattractive cities that I have ever seen," Ickes lamented. "[T]he whole town looks unkempt and down at the heels."

He had kinder words for the people: "The town really was most friendly and did the best it knew how to show that it was interested in and proud of me. They were very sincere, worth-while people." The townsfolk gave him and Anna a dinner at the Penn-Alto early Friday evening, then everyone gathered at Cricket Field on the edge of town, the only place big enough to hold the crowd that came to hear him. He would be speaking not only to the people standing before him on this balmy June night, but to much of the nation, his words broadcast over NBC in an age in which Flag Day was still widely and reverently observed. Slightly rumpled as always, his thin sandy hair gently blown by the summer breeze, almost entirely surrounded by the enormous microphones of the day, with his wife, his sister Julia and her husband, Clinton, and sundry town leaders on the bunting-draped podium behind him, the Altoona-reared Secretary of the Interior of the United States held his speech in one square, stubby hand and peered nearsightedly at it through his eyeglasses as he read, the flat, almost harsh voice taking on tone and pitch and emphasis as he warmed to the task of instructing his listeners on the meaning of the day.

"I am no stranger in a strange land as I stand before you," he told them. "I am a true Pennsylvanian at heart, proud of the traditions and of the heritage that are mine as a son of this State." And then he told them this, echoing the sentiments of his President: "In the midst of superabundance, there is want throughout the land. Something must be wrong." And this:

The oligarchs of America have devoted all of their energies and contributed all of their abilities to making themselves ever richer, with little regard for what was happening to the great mass of the people. It would be interesting to search the hearts of these men . . . to discover what the Stars and Stripes really symbolize to them. . . . There are those who insist that a beneficent despotism is the most perfect form of government, but for my part, I believe in the theory that it is better for a people to be badly governed by themselves than to be well governed by others.

And finally, the words coming hard and strong now, rising to conclusion:

Let it be the destiny of the American flag to symbolize to future generations, just as it does to us, those precious boons of liberty which have been handed down to us by our forefathers. . . . Let not some future historian write down the tragic fact that our children ever justly accused us of being so ignorant or unheeding that we passed on to them a flag which was no longer a symbol of freedom, equality, and justice, but a symbol rather of oppression and injustice through the denial of those liberties without which free political institutions cannot exist.

As heirs of a great past, it is within our power to be the progenitors of a great future. A true soldier of the Republic will uphold the Constitution in all its parts and insist that every citizen of the land shall have full enjoyment of all the rights and guarantees in that charter of liberty. . . . He will ever be acutely conscious that a man is fine and strong and truly patriotic in the precise degree in which he is considerate and humane and just.

The American Flag is the symbol of our free American institutions founded upon, and buttressed by, the rights that are guaranteed in the Constitution. Allow those rights to be destroyed or even impaired and while the American Flag may still have its purity of colors . . . it will not be the American Flag.

Flag-wrapped and righteous, he accepted their applause with a broad smile. As well he should have. This raspy credo of liberalism may not have been a landmark of literary craftsmanship, but the speech had the power of a long tradition behind it and the resonance that could only come from a man who believed every single word of it at the center of his troubled soul.

Anna would never hear another. On August 3, she returned to Chicago for a few days, then flew to Albuquerque for her annual pilgrimage to the little adobe house in Coolidge, taking along as a traveling companion Genevieve Herrick, a newspaperwoman and Interior Department publicity writer to whom Ickes had given the assignment of writing a series of articles on the Indians of the region. "Letters from Anna during the summer of 1935 went back to the old basis between us," he wrote in his unpublished memoirs.

She wrote to me every day and so did I to her. My letters were all dictated and I tried to keep her aware of what was passing in my life. I would usually close with a sentence or short paragraph in my own handwriting. She set great store by this, although I could not see that it meant much. . . . It was in her last letter, I think, that she said that she had had the happiest Summer of her existence, notwithstanding which she was looking forward eagerly to coming back to Washington. In a previous letter she had expressed the belief that she and I were now ready to go forward with "our own New Deal."*

On Saturday night, August 31, Harold was in his office, using the dictating machine to make his weekly diary entry, when one of his personal secretaries, Fred Marx, put his head in. "During all the time he had been with me," Ickes remembered, "Fred Marx had never showed up at night. . . . He looked queerly at me and I asked him what he was doing at the office. He started to speak and I could see that he had some bad news to break. I always want to have any bad news full force so I told him, impatiently, to tell me what he had to say."

What Marx had to say was that he had gotten a call from a local newspaperman, who had told him that Anna had been in an accident and had been rushed to St. Vincent's Hospital in Santa Fe. Harold immediately called the hospital and learned from an ambulance driver that Anna was dead. She had hired Frank Allen, her usual driver in New Mexico, to take her, Genevieve Herrick, and Ibrahim Seyfullah, a vacationing member of the Turkish embassy, up to the Taos Pueblo north of Santa Fe. On the way back, their car had been sideswiped by one traveling in the opposite direction, had swerved to the soft shoulder, then had rolled over several times. Anna had died instantly, her skull crushed. Allen, his skull also fractured, lingered only long enough to get to the hospital, then died. Both Miss Herrick and Ibrahim Seyfullah were so badly injured it took months for them to recover. The driver of the other automobile did not stop, nor was he ever found.

Ickes stayed late at the office, taking care of the necessities. He called

* Unhappy memories must still have eaten at her, however. In one of the dozens of family scrapbooks the Ickes kept, in the midst of various banal items from the midsummer of 1935, is pasted—with not even a hint of explanation—one of Dorothy Dix's "lovelorn" columns. In it, a woman ("Sidney M.") had written that her husband had been unfaithful. "I am financially independent," she wrote, "with money left me by my family, and the only plan I have thought of is to move my personal belongings to a furnished apartment in another part of the city some day while he is gone, leaving him a surprise-of-his-life note telling him I have decided to live my own life, traveling, visiting the children, doing more church work and civic work, and telling him he can bring his chosen to his home to work for him, wash, iron, and EARN her living. I feel I would be happier alone than with living with one I no longer trust. My love is dead. What do you think?"

"I think your plan is an inspired one," Miss Dix replied.

Congressman John Dempsey in Santa Fe and asked him to arrange for the shipment of Anna's body to Chicago. He called a friend in Winnetka to arrange for a funeral service at Hubbard Woods. He called his son Raymond, who was in the midst of a skeet-shooting championship; Wilmarth, who was vacationing with Betty and the children in Michigan; Frances, who was at home with her husband in Evanston; and Robert, who was working as a temporary ranger in Yellowstone National Park. He talked to various newspapers and wire services when they called. It was nearly midnight by the time he left for the house in Spring Valley.

The next day, Ruth Hampton came out to the house and chose a burial dress for Anna. Harold took the four-thirty train for Chicago, then drove up to Hubbard Woods, where the caretaker and his wife already had cleared out from the enormous front hall what little furniture had not been shipped to Spring Valley in 1933. On Monday, Harold and Wilmarth went out to Memorial Park Cemetery, where they chose a burial plot. Anna's body arrived at Hubbard Woods that afternoon and was prepared for the funeral. The service, presided over by Episcopal minister Ashley Gerhard of Christ Church in Winnetka, took place at three in the afternoon on Tuesday. Two hundred flower arrangements had been placed along the interior walls of the downstairs portion of the house. The coffin itself (closed because of Anna's injuries) was covered in a blanket of asparagus fern topped by a wreath of white asters and gladioli sent by the Roosevelts. It sat in a bay window open to the garden outside, where some four hundred camp chairs had been placed, in addition to the several dozen that sat in the great hall for relatives, friends, and members of the administration and other official folk. These included Eleanor Roosevelt, Harry Hopkins, several cabinet members, and Ed Kelly, mayor of Chicago.

The service was simple, brief, and, according to Ickes, almost emotionless. "It was the coldest funeral that I have ever attended," he remembered. "I did not even try to make myself believe that I possessed a grief that was not there. Nothing up to that time had made me so fully conscious that, so far as Anna was concerned, my feelings were absolutely dead. And I would not be a hypocrite by pretending to give the appearance of a sad and disconsolate widower before the gaping eyes of the curious." Only Robert wept as the casket was carried out of the house by him, Wilmarth, Raymond, Frances's husband, ReQua, Harold's old friend Stacey Mosser, and one of Anna's cousins, William McCrillis, while hundreds of the gaping curious jostled one another for a glimpse of Eleanor Roosevelt and other dignitaries. Some of Harold's flower beds got badly trampled in the crush, including portions of those in which special dahlias lifted their amber heads to the summer sun.

CHAPTER

· 32 ·

Apostleship and Dissidence

O N WEDNESDAY, Harold and Raymond started back to Washington in the government limousine, which Carl Witherspoon had driven out on Sunday. Ickes may have been feeling no grief, as he insisted, but did admit to his diary that he was "near the end of my nervous endurance and felt that I had to get away from Chicago." They arrived, after a grueling drive, at nine Thursday night and Ickes fell into an exhausted sleep that lasted well into Friday.

He would need the rest, for another crisis with Harry Hopkins was building. The middle of September 1935 was fast approaching and with it the deadline for allotting the $4.8 billion that had been authorized for the programs of the WPA and the PWA. Projects totaling almost $1.8 billion had been approved—or were in the process of being approved—by Hopkins's office as satisfying the requirement that sufficient numbers of the "unemployed employables" be put to work. They were all WPA projects; Ickes and the PWA had gotten not a cent of the n w money so far. At a press conference on Friday, September 5, while Ickes was resting after his return from Chicago, Hopkins told reporters that he expected more than two billion dollars in further applications to come into his office in the next week or so, which would consume all but about $900 million of what was left of the original $4.8 billion budget. When asked whether any of the two thousand PWA projects his office had rejected had much chance of being recast to satisfy the employment requirements and be resubmitted in time for approval, he replied, "I would not worry about that."

"What do you mean you would not worry?" a reporter asked. "It is a dead project, isn't it?"

"If it does not get through the mill, I assume so."

Ickes, who came into the office on Saturday to start catching up on his work, was given a report on the conference and decided that it represented a full-bore assault on the PWA, with consequences to FDR's reelection hopes in 1936 that he found worrisome. He apparently was encouraged in this belief by his new undersecretary, Charles F. West, former congressman from Ohio, who had been appointed by Roosevelt in August. West, Ickes informed his diary, "has received many complaints, some of a particularized nature, from different parts of the country with reference to the apparent scrapping of the public works program and the turning of the whole work-relief proposition over to Hopkins. . . . Later Tom Corcoran came in to see me. He is as much concerned about PWA as is West. We all agree that the way things are headed may mean political disaster for the President next year."

On Monday, Hopkins was called up to Hyde Park, where FDR was spending a few days, and Ickes worried about the implications of this until receiving his own summons on Monday night. At his regular press conference the next morning, he did not discuss anything in detail, but both his irritation and his worry were apparent. When a reporter asked if he would take up the "reported dispute with Mr. Hopkins," he replied, "I haven't seen or talked to Mr. Hopkins since I came back to Washington."

"Is it correct," another reporter asked, "that of 2,000 applications turned down, most were approved by PWA and then turned down by Mr. Hopkins?"

"Yes," Ickes snapped.

"Is it possible that you will push for their adoption in spite of Mr. Hopkins?"

"I have never yet predicted what I was going to do."

"Where does Mr. Hopkins' disapproval leave all these projects?"

"In suspense until there is a final decision."

"Will this visit," queried another reporter, "mark a showdown, would we be far wrong in saying?"

"Would it make any difference to you whether you were far wrong or not?"

After that nasty moment, the conference concluded with a brief exchange that summed up the situation quite handily.

"Do you want more time?" someone asked.

"No," Ickes said. "We do not need more time. What we need is money."

He did not get it. In the end, all the elaborate machinery of process and approval that had been erected to administer the $4.8 billion involved in the work relief program was abandoned to all intents and purposes during the course of a single afternoon in Hyde Park, New York; the endless meetings with their serpentine discussions, the rancorous public and private arguments, the manipulations and speculations of months, decisions seemingly made and accepted—in a few hours all of this was subsumed in the President's iron determination to put to work as many people as possible as soon as possible.

Ickes and his entourage, including West, arrived at Hyde Park late Wednesday afternoon. There was a birthday celebration that night for Missy LeHand, then on Thursday morning Ickes had a few minutes alone with FDR. "I told him that the program as at present outlined had me scared. I tried to make it very clear that I had no faith in the program and that I believed it might jeopardize his reelection next year. He was in a friendly mood, but it was clear that he had made up his mind to some sort of a compromise which wouldn't mean anything at all." In the afternoon, Ickes, Hopkins, Daniel W. Bell—acting in the capacity of director of the Budget ever since Lewis Douglas's resignation—and several others gathered for a budget meeting in the big library of the house. There, FDR did considerable damage to Ickes's hopes. PWA had more than $2 billion in applications pending; in spite of Ickes's heartfelt pleas, Roosevelt gave it only $200 million—and $184 million of *that* was carved out of the budgets for the PWA's Division of Housing and programs for Puerto Rico and the Bureau of Reclamation. Rexford Tugwell got $150 million for his Rural Resettlement program. Harry Hopkins and WPA got the rest of the money—in addition to final approval of all currently authorized WPA projects, as well as those in the works. In short, PWA got millions, WPA billions.

It was as thorough a defeat as Ickes could have feared, but he accepted it rather more sedately than might have been expected, probably more from exhaustion than from any sudden tractability. There was no offer of resignation, only a bitter sigh in his diary: "I was pretty sore and discouraged," he wrote, "but I have no option except to accept the President's decision." He took what comfort was available from FDR's further decision to remove Hopkins's veto power; in the future, Hopkins would merely provide unemployment figures for any community applying for grant money and Ickes would take these into consideration when

deciding whether it would be worthwhile to submit any PWA grant for
approval by the President. The Secretary remained grouchy enough,
however, to show no remorse when FDR complained that only a leak in
the Interior Department could explain the deluge of telegrams that had
come in objecting to threatened cutbacks in PWA funds. "I know there
has been a leak . . . and I know where the leak has been," Ickes told his
diary, "but I am not likely to discipline anyone who has been trying to
protect PWA from the onslaughts of Harry Hopkins."

Ickes returned to Washington on his shield, knowing full well that the
PWA was suddenly and irretrievably diminished. It would still demand
his time and attention. Thousands of projects across the country would
remain under construction for months and years to come, new ones would
be authorized, he would continue to fight for money, and hundreds of
millions of dollars more would be allocated and spent with meticulous
honesty until 1939, when the agency finally would be restructured into
little more than a caretaker body (at which point Ickes would be forced to
give it up). But no longer could he look upon himself as standing at the
controls of an enormous administrative machine whose power was unchallenged and whose capacity for reshaping and enriching the American
estate was nearly limitless.

For Roosevelt, too, the thirty months in office had been a mix of triumph
and defeat, as the politically attuned President attempted to steer a
sinuous middle way between the ranks of those who would have him
return forthwith to the days of laissez-faire economics and those who
demanded nothing less than revolution of one stripe or another.

During the elections of 1934, he had been granted what every President yearns for: a Congress in which his own party holds the whip.
Democrats had captured twenty-six out of the thirty-five senatorial contests, while their population in the House had increased to 322, giving
them a majority over the Republicans of 219 seats; moreover, Democrats
had won the gubernatorial contests in thirty-nine states. The result had
been, Walter Lippmann wrote the President in December, a "vote of
confidence . . . as magnificent as it was well earned." But the Seventy-
fourth Congress had proved less than the rubber stamp the New Deal's
critics had feared and FDR might have desired. For one thing, on January
29, 1935, the Senate, led by Hiram Johnson and the isolationist wing,
had voted 52 to 36 to reject a treaty that would have made the United
States a member of the Court of International Justice at the Hague
(popularly known as the World Court), this in spite of a special plea for

ratification from FDR. For another, when Roosevelt had made a personal appearance before Congress on May 22 to veto passage of a veterans' bonus bill, the House had overridden him that same day by a vote of 322 to 98, and the next afternoon the vote in the Senate had fallen just ten votes shy of the two-thirds necessary for override.

Both the outright defeat of January and the narrow victory of May had robbed the electoral triumph of 1934 of much of its sheen. There had been other difficulties, too, including the sweaty yapping of Louisiana's Senator Huey Long, "the Kingfish," whose support had been wooed in 1932 but whose growing power during 1935 had become both an embarrassment to democracy and a threat to the administration. To challenge what he saw as Roosevelt's failure to meet the demands of the Depression, Long had contrived the "Share the Wealth" program, one of a plethora of radical get-well-quick schemes that had been prescribed for the Republic by a gaggle of visionaries, ranging from Upton Sinclair's "End Poverty in California" (EPIC) program, upon which the novelist had run for governor of California in 1934 (unsuccessfully, but with a strength that had terrified the comfortable), to Dr. Francis Townsend's "Old Age Revolving Pensions" movement, which in less than two years had spread from Long Beach, California, across the nation, garnering a membership in "Townsend Clubs" that approached half a million by January 1935.

Long's program had been even more successful, largely because of the recruiting efforts of his talented acolyte, the Reverend Gerald L. K. Smith, who apparently worshiped Long nearly as much as he was supposed to worship Christ and who had spread the gospel of Share the Wealth throughout much of the South and Midwest. Unlike Townsend, however, who as yet had no political ambitions, Long had viewed the growing membership of his Share the Wealth societies as the foundation of a potent political force that would give him the strength to challenge Roosevelt himself in 1936. Not without reason: in the spring of 1935, Farley had estimated that Long might end up in control of as many as six million votes in any third-party attempt at the Presidency.*

This possibility had been frightful enough; it had taken on even more ghastly dimensions when wedded to the growing fear that Long would

---

* Ickes had not remained above the fray here. When reporters asked him his opinion of the Louisiana senator during his regular press conference on April 18, 1935, Ickes reported to his diary, "I remarked that the trouble with him was that he had halitosis of the intellect. This made a great hit with the correspondents." Long got back at him a few days later in the Senate, where he described the Secretary as "the Chinch-bug of Chicago"—and went on to call Farley the "Nabob of New York," Wallace "Lord Corn-Wallace, the ignoramus from Iowa," and Roosevelt "Prince Franklin," the "Knight of the Nourmahal [the *Nourmahal* was the Presidential yacht]."

join his movement with yet another radical crusade for reform, the National Union for Social Justice. This one, whose membership was claimed to be 500,000, was the invention of Father Charles Edward Coughlin, a Detroit priest whose weekly radio broadcasts over the CBS network reached somewhere between thirty and forty-five million listeners. At first a fervent supporter of the New Deal, Coughlin had grown disenchanted by what he saw as FDR's conservatism and in November 1934 had organized the National Union as "an articulate, organized lobby of the people." By the spring of 1935, there had been considerable speculation that Coughlin and Long would get together, and while it was never likely that either of these two outsized personalities would ever have taken to the notion of sharing power, neither of them had gone out of his way to deny the possibility. "I don't disagree with Father Coughlin very often," Long had told a reporter at one point. "I would almost say that we are working for the same principles."

Ickes had been worrying for quite a while about the possibility of some kind of radical movement becoming a major force. As early as September 1934 he had voiced his concern during a dinner party at Cissy Patterson's Italianate mansion on Dupont Circle. "I expressed the opinion," he told his diary,

> that the country is much more radical than the Administration and that it was my judgment that the President would have to move further to the left in order to hold the country. I said, as I have said on a number of occasions, that if Roosevelt can't hold the country . . . no one else can possibly hope to do so, and that a breakdown on the part of the Administration would result in an extreme radical movement, the extent of which no one could foresee.

And on March 4, 1935, he had been joined in his concern by none other than General Hugh Johnson, who had risen above his falling-out with Roosevelt to warn an audience of Democratic politicos in a private dining room at the Waldorf-Astoria that Long and Coughlin were not to be dismissed lightly. "They speak," he growled, "with nothing of learning, knowledge nor experience to lead us through a labyrinth that has perplexed the minds of men since the beginning of time. . . . These two men are raging up and down this land preaching not construction but destruction—not reform but revolution. . . . You can laugh at Father Coughlin, you can snort at Huey Long—but this country was never under a greater menace."

By the end of May 1935 Roosevelt had begun to take the menace seriously, having told intimates that he was thinking of some sort of device to "steal Long's thunder." In the meantime, however, the U.S. Supreme

Court had given the administration something else to think about. On the first Monday following the President's second State of the Union address in January, the court had ruled Section 9(c)—the "hot oil" provision of Title I of the National Industrial Recovery Act—to be unconstitutional on the grounds that the delegation of authority to the President to forbid the interstate shipment of oil produced in excess of state quotas was too vague. The administration and the Congress had countered the court's move with passage of the Connally Act in February, which very specifically gave the President such authority—exercised through the Interior Department's Petroleum Division. But on May 27 the Court had rendered another, more sweeping rejection of New Deal policy; in *Schechter* v. *United States* the Court struck down as unconstitutional the very heart of Title I—its code-making authority and its power to establish and enforce wage and hour provisions (Title II, which had established the Public Works Administration, was not affected by the decision). "The President has been living in a fool's paradise," Justice Louis Brandeis had told Tom Corcoran and Ben Cohen in his chambers after the decision had been handed down. "The Court unanimously has held that these broad powers cannot be exercised over matters within the States. All the powers of the States cannot be centralized in the Federal Government." Roosevelt himself had characterized it somewhat differently during a press conference on May 31: "We have been relegated," he had said, "to the horse-and-buggy definition of interstate commerce."

Bombarded from all sides with advice on precisely how to deal with the Court, Roosevelt decided to do nothing at all—at least for the time being. Instead, he called congressional leaders into his office on June 5 and, pounding his desk, demanded that they postpone their summer adjournment for 1935 until they had enacted the body of legislation over which they had been deliberating for months. Thus had been launched what came to be called the "Second Hundred Days," a period in which Congress passed some of the most dramatic laws of the New Deal—the National Labor Relations Act (the so-called Wagner Act), signed into law on July 5; the Social Security Act, signed on August 14; the Bituminous Coal Conservation Act (the Guffey Act), signed on August 23; the Banking Act, signed on August 24; the Public Utility Holding Company Act, signed on August 26; and the Wealth Tax Act, signed on August 31, shortly after which an exhausted Congress was allowed to escape the cruel and unusual punishment of working through most of a Washington summer.

Roosevelt was at Hyde Park, himself recovering from the long summer session, when he received the news that Huey Long had been assassinated on September 9 by one of his disaffected constituents. "The spirit of violence is un-American and has no place in a consideration of public affairs," FDR proclaimed in a public statement, "least of all at a time when a calm and dispassionate approach to the difficult problems of the day is so essential." Still, honest horror must have mixed with jubilation that what had appeared to be the most serious potential threat to his Presidency was now removed. This fact, in combination with his legislative triumphs of the summer and what he considered a successful resolution of the conflict between Ickes and Hopkins over the question of funding in September, had put Roosevelt in the mood for a happy processional, and he insisted that Ickes accompany himself; Hopkins; Colonel Edwin M. ("Pa") Watson, his personal secretary; Colonel Ross McIntyre, his personal physician; and Captain Wilson Brown, his naval aide, for a month-long voyage on the heavy cruiser *Houston* from San Diego, through the Panama Canal, and back up to Charleston, South Carolina.

Ickes, still smarting from his defeat at Hyde Park, did not want to go, but Roosevelt would not be refused, so on Thursday, September 26, the Secretary, accompanied by his son Raymond, boarded the Presidential Special with the rest of the entourage, which for the trip to San Diego would include Grace Tully, Missy LeHand, and press secretary Steve Early. After a stopover in Arizona to dedicate Boulder Dam, and another in California to allow Roosevelt to make a speech at the Los Angeles Coliseum, the party arrived in San Diego on October 2. Here, Early, Raymond, and the women said good-bye to the seagoing crew and returned east on the train. ("I was very glad to have had [Raymond] with me," Ickes wrote in his diary, "and I saw him depart with much personal regret. It has been an unusual pleasure for me to have him with me on his brief vacation. We seem to grow closer together as we grow older. There is undoubtedly a great bond between us.")

Ickes boarded the *Houston* the afternoon of October 2 and proceeded to have a grand time in spite of his sulk, his worry over work left behind, and his ever-present vulnerability to seasickness—which by some beneficence did not bother him this time out nearly as much as he had feared it would. If Roosevelt's invitation had been calculated mainly to win back the affection of his disgruntled Secretary of the Interior (and it probably was), the ploy worked. For the next three weeks, Ickes all but forgot the slights and setbacks of the past several months, losing himself in poker, blackjack, and fishing, marveling at his first sight of the mountainous desert landscape of Baja California, the startling white city of Panama with its background of dusty green jungle, the wonder of the Panama Canal, the stunning beauty of the Caribbean, with its waters of turquoise and azure and skies through which slid pearly mountains of clouds the size of small continents.

He even found himself able to endure in good spirit some heavy-handed needling. When the *Houston* made its way through the canal and anchored off Cristobal on the east coast of the Isthmus, a special edition of the ship's newspaper, *The Blue Bonnet,* was issued to mark the occasion. Much if not most of the kidding probably was the work of Hopkins, possibly in collaboration with FDR. "The Blue Bonnet," the paper's main front-page "story" proclaimed,

> is anxious to pay its respects to the President's two civilian aides aboard ship, Secretary Ickes and Hopkins. This paper remained neutral during the recent unpleasantness between these two apostles of the New Deal. However, we would be faithless to our readers if we failed to make a few pointed observations about their irrelative movements. We haven't seen much of Harold because the sea has been a little too much for him and just as he is about to heave into full view, his stomach gets in the way. He was born with the well-known silver spoon in his mouth (Hopkins is said to have remarked that it should have choked him then and there) and never worked a day in his life until Roosevelt put his name in a hat along with other contributors to the campaign and pulled his out.

Another "feature" of the edition reported on the expected completion of a PWA sewer project by 1945. "The only explanation given for this amazing burst of speed," the squib said, "was that the Secretary was at sea." Finally, the paper reported:

> The feud between Hopkins and Ickes was given a decent burial today. With flags at half mast—the band's trumpets muted—Pa freshly shaved—the Officers half dressed—the President officiated at the solemn ceremony which we trust will take these two babies off the front page for all time. Hopkins, as usual, was dressed in his immaculate blues, browns and whites, his fine figure making a pretty sight with the moondriffed sea in the foreground. Ickes wore his faded grays, Mona Lisa smile, and carried his stamp collection.
>
> The ceremony, tho brief, was impressive. Hopkins expressed regret at the unkind things Ickes had said about him and Ickes on his part promised to make it stronger . . . as soon as he could get a stenographer who could take it hot. . . . The President gave them a hearty slap on the back—pushing them both into the sea. "Full Steam Ahead," ordered the President.

Once they were safely anchored in Charleston harbor (though not until the *Houston* had been chased out of the Caribbean by a hurricane in the waters north of Haiti), Ickes noted that the trip had been more than worthwhile ("I slept better than I have for many, many months"), and cheerfully conceded the fact that "Harry Hopkins fitted in well with his easy manners and keen wit." This benign summation characterized a relationship that over the years would develop into something resembling a cautious but genuine friendship, at least as Ickes remembered it. "One day when Thomas G. Corcoran and Benjamin V. Cohen were lunching with me at Interior," he wrote in the *Saturday Evening Post* in 1948,

> Tom insisted that I should work out a *modus vivendi* with Harry. . . . Tom thought that I was so obstinate that I stood in my own way. He felt that there was room in the Administration for both Hopkins and me, and that we ought to accommodate ourselves to each other so far as possible. Tom's reasoning has always been persuasive with me, and I accepted his point of view. This was not difficult, because, despite the fact that Harry and I were fundamentally opposed on the subject of how much money should be spent on the program, and in what manner, I had always had a liking for him—the liking of a man who had grown up under Scotch-Presbyterian restraint for the happy-go-lucky type who can bet his last cent, even if it be a borrowed one, on a horse race. . . . We always got along well when we were together. Even during the periods when we were pretty much at each other's throats, battling with no holds barred, each for his own passionate convictions, there were occasions when we foregathered at the instance of the President. Brass knuckles would be left at the door, and, as the evening wore on, I would find that I, too, was succumbing to the blandishments of Harry's personality.

Still, early and late, each man always knew where he kept the brass knuckles and could get at them when he felt they were needed—and neither would ever hesitate to do so.

Ickes returned from the September 1935 Presidential excursion to bad news regarding another, older friend (though at times one hardly less irksome than Hopkins). On the afternoon of Saturday, September 21, Raymond Robins had fallen twenty-five feet to the ground from the top of a ladder he was using to prune a eucalyptus tree at Chinsegut Hill. Three of his vertebrae had been fractured and he was paralyzed and helpless from the waist down—temporarily, his doctors hoped at first. Ickes wrote Margaret immediately upon his return to Washington:

> It distresses me to learn of the long and painful siege that lies ahead of Raymond but it is a great relief to know that the doctors say that with time and care he will be quite himself again. Raymond has stamina and courage and he will pull through—of that I am sure. I want you to give him my affectionate regards and tell him that I wish there were something that I could do to ease his pain and shorten the period that will seem interminable before he is able to resume his normal activities.

But Raymond never would regain the use of his legs or control of his bodily functions and would be in and out of hospitals regularly for the rest of his life with various setbacks. There *was* stamina in the old stump speaker, however (in the end he would outlive both Margaret and Harold), and determination, as well as a sudden humility and a touching bravery to which Ickes responded with a whole-souled affection that finally and forever transcended whatever bitterness may have remained between them. For nearly twenty years more, the two old friends—while they rarely saw each other—would maintain a regular correspondence during which they would even manage to forge a political compatibility. "I have had a couple of letters lately from Raymond Robins," Ickes wrote in his diary in the middle of February 1937, "and they are from the Raymond Robins with whom I fought shoulder to shoulder in the days before he strayed off after the false gods of Harding, Coolidge, and Hoover. . . . It is fine to be marching side by side again with this old comrade, and I only wish that he were in condition physically to take part."

He could have used that kind of companionship even earlier, for if 1935 had tested his strength and fragile patience, 1936 would demand no less of him. Not the least of the pressures was the political situation facing Roosevelt as the election year dawned, one during which the Secretary would play an increasingly important role. On the face of it, hard times lay ahead for the administration, in spite of the legislative victories of the summer of 1935. The NRA lay in tatters in the wake of the Supreme Court decision of May, the body's Title I structure stripped of power. Ignoring pleas from Donald Richberg and others to introduce new legislation that would restructure the agency, FDR had merely asked Congress to approve its temporary extension as a skeleton organization whose principal duty would be to dissolve itself. Richberg had consequently resigned his NRA position on June 5, telling Roosevelt in a handwritten note accompanying his official letter "I feel that I am a burden rather than an aid to the accomplishment of your apparent aims."

On January 3, Roosevelt came out with what he described as a "fighting speech" in his annual message, once again taking on the "unscrupulous money-changers" who had earned his scorn in his first inaugural address:

> They steal the livery of great national constitutional ideals to serve discredited special interests. As guardians and trustees for great groups of individual stockholders they wrongfully seek to carry the property and the interests entrusted to them into the arena of partisan politics. They seek—this minority in business and industry—to control and often do control and

use for their own purposes legitimate and highly honored business associations; they engage in vast propaganda to spread fear and discord among the people—they would "gang up" against the people's liberties.

Three days later, in *U.S.* v. *Butler,* the Supreme Court struck again, this time in a 6–3 decision invalidating the Agricultural Adjustment Act, which, with the NRA, could be said to have been the very core of the New Deal. Roosevelt appeared to take this decision, like that with regard to the NRA, as a challenge rather than a defeat. "There isn't any doubt at all that the President is really hoping that the Supreme Court will continue to make a clean sweep of all New Deal legislation," Ickes told his diary after a meeting with Roosevelt on January 29, "throwing out the TVA act, the Securities Act, the Railroad Retirement Act, the Social Security Act, the Guffey Coal Act, and others. He thinks the country is beginning to sense this issue but that enough people have not yet been affected by adverse decisions so as to make a sufficient feeling on a Supreme Court issue."

The Court very nearly accommodated FDR. On February 17 it rendered an 8–1 decision in *Ashwater* v. *Tennessee Valley Authority* that endorsed the TVA's power to sell electricity—but did so on grounds so limited as to leave the TVA open to further suits that would not necessarily be decided in favor of the administration. Then on May 18 the Court invalidated the Bituminous Coal Conservation Act in a decision that specifically challenged the power of Congress. Justice George Sutherland, in writing the majority opinion, said that coal mining was "just as much a local activity as is farming or manufacture" and thus "the evils which come from the struggle between employers and employees" were not subject to congressional control under the interstate commerce provisions of the Constitution. Finally, lest it be assumed that this decision by implication validated the right of individual states to legislate such local matters, the Court promptly struck down New York's minimum wage law for women.

What to do about the Supreme Court, then, became a point of debate during much of 1936. From the start, Ickes had been for taking on the issue directly, even along the lines of a speculative plan outlined for him by Roosevelt on January 29 that would have obliterated the system of checks and balances altogether: "Congress would pass a law, the Supreme Court would declare it unconstitutional, the President would then go to Congress and ask it to instruct him whether he was to follow the mandate of Congress or the mandate of the Court. If the Congress should declare that its own mandate was to be followed, the President would carry out the will of Congress through the offices of the United States Marshals and ignore the Court." By one means or another (though it is unlikely that FDR was serious about this particular gambit), Ickes believed, Roosevelt was going to have to challenge the power of the Court and told him that "the President who faced this issue and drastically curbed the usurped power of the Supreme Court would go down through all the ages of history as one of the great Presidents."

But in spite of encouragement from Ickes, Wallace, and others in his political family, in spite of the Court's continuing assault on much that the New Deal held dear, in spite of private speculations on how to deal with the "horse and buggy" justices, Roosevelt refused to be pinned down on the question firmly enough for it to be anything more than a subtext during the campaign of 1936. One caution holding him back was his worry that he already had so offended the conservative element of the country—including that in his own party—that to take on the Supreme Court conservatives directly would be to encourage a response that might be wider and more dangerous than his candidacy could safely endure or might inflict wounds so deep they would cripple his administration even if he safely won the election in November.

Disaffected conservative Democrats—including such elder statesmen of the party as Newton Baker and John W. Davis, together with former Democratic National Committee chairman John J. Raskob and FDR's old friend and mentor Al Smith—had formed up under the banner of the American Liberty League as early as the summer of 1934 and by the end of 1935 were spending more money (much if not most of it from the coffers of industrialist Pierre S. Du Pont and his family) than the Republican Party in furious denunciation of the New Deal. The leaders of the league had decided to launch 1936 with a flourish, and on January 25 some two thousand of them gathered at the Mayflower Hotel in Washington to hear Al Smith give voice over the NBC network to their complaints about the New Dealers. "I was struck with Al Smith's bad radio voice," Ickes noted in his diary. "His utterance is so thick that at times it is difficult to understand. As a matter of fact, with the closest attention on my part there were words and phrases that were unintelligible to me." When not unintelligible, Smith's rantings had bordered on the comical, at times sounding like lines put in the mouth of a character in a Hecht-MacArthur satire. "It is all right with me," he had growled, "if they want to disguise themselves as Karl Marx or Lenin or any of the rest of that bunch, but I won't stand for their allowing them to march under the banner of Jackson or Cleveland. . . . Let me give this solemn warning: There can only be one capital, Washington or Moscow. There can be only one atmosphere of government, the clean, pure, fresh air of free America, or the foul breath of communistic Russia."

"It was perfect," Pierre S. Du Pont said of the speech. Other Democrats considered it perfectly contemptible. John L. Lewis called it the utterance of "a gibbering political jackanapes," and while the official response—also broadcast on NBC—from Senate majority leader Joe Robinson was more temperate than that from Lewis, it was still devastating. Smith, the former poor boy from New York's Lower East Side, he said, had presided over "the swellest party ever given by the Du Ponts," had "turned away from the [Lower] East Side with those little shops and fish markets, and now his gaze rests upon the gilded towers and palaces of Park Avenue." Within a few weeks it was accepted wisdom that the lunatic fringe of the Democratic Right had gone too far (Du Pont and others had even begun toying with the idea of backing Governor Eugene Talmadge of Georgia, one of the most virulent racists in American history and a man Ickes had characterized during a January press conference as "His Chain-Gang Excellency," noting further that "the more people in the country who see and hear Governor Talmadge, the better it will be for President Roosevelt or any man that he opposes").

That still did not let Roosevelt off the hook with more responsible Democrats who sincerely worried that the New Deal was drifting toward a collectivist state. Among these was Walter Lippmann, who in April submitted to former Budget director Lewis Douglas a "statement of principles" that he thought Douglas and other dissidents might use to influence Roosevelt's future course: "The record shows," Lippmann's declaration read in part,

> that this enormous concentration of power in the hands of appointed officials cannot be exercised wisely, that it is beyond the capacities of men to use that much power successfully, that it can lead only to waste, confusion, bureaucratic rigidity, and the loss of personal liberty.
>
> Holding these views, we cannot subscribe to the view that the monopolistic tendencies, which had official sanction from 1920 to 1932, were conducive to material efficiency, and we cannot subscribe to the view of those New Dealers who claim that their experiments in monopoly, restriction, and centralized political power are in the interests of the abundant life. We believe that the New Era and the New Deal are streams from the same source. The one fostered private monopoly in the name of national prosperity. The other has fostered state controlled monopolies in the name of the national welfare. We believe that both are an aberration from the basic principles upon which this nation has grown great and has remained free.

Lippmann, Lewis Douglas, and those who shared their sentiments could not so easily be written off as reactionaries like Smith and the Du Ponts, and Roosevelt doubtless considered it the better part of valor not to antagonize them further by pushing the conflict with the Supreme Court. In the meantime, other radical elements were gathering forces—namely, Father Charles Coughlin, Gerald L. K. Smith, and Francis Townsend. In the months following Long's death, which he called "the most regrettable thing in modern history," Coughlin had worked assiduously to build his National Union into a formidable political creature, and during the spring primary elections he used his voice and his organization in an open attempt to influence the vote in several states. By May he had decided to take his crusade beyond the state level; in collusion with William Lemke, a supremely conservative second-term congressman from North Dakota, he formed the Union Party and on June 20 went on the air to endorse Lemke as the new party's Presidential candidate. Shortly afterward, Gerald L. K. Smith, who had taken on the mantle of the dead Huey Long as head of the Share the Wealth movement and had forged a loose partnership with Francis Townsend's organization, held a press conference in Chicago and declared that he and Townsend would support Lemke and the Union Party.*

For their part, the Republicans witnessed a brief struggle for the nomination among the supporters of Governor Alf Landon of Kansas; Senator William Borah of Idaho; Frank Knox, Harold Ickes's friendly antagonist from Chicago, who had become editor of Hearst's *Chicago Daily News* in 1931; Senator Arthur H. Vandenburg of Michigan; and Herbert Hoover. Vandenburg was too little known, while Hoover's indisputably recognizable name still bore the dead weight of the Depression; both soon dropped from serious consideration. Borah at seventy-one was too old and far too liberal (in the tradition of the old Bull Moose Progressives) for the old-guard Republicans to swallow, and he entered the convention in early June carrying only twenty firm delegates with him. Knox, who spent the then-astonishing sum of $25,000 in winning the Illinois primary, was more acceptable, but still ran well behind Landon in the estimation of the party regulars. Landon was himself an ex–Bull

---

* In *Voices of Protest*, Alan Brinkley reports that when Lemke himself announced his candidacy, adding that the new party's convention would take place later that summer, newsmen joked that the convention had already taken place—in a telephone booth, with Lemke on one end of the line and Father Coughlin on the other. There *was* a real convention, however; it took place in Cleveland in August, and, according to reporter Jonathan Mitchell in the *New Republic*, was something akin to a camp meeting gotten out of hand: "They indulged in cries, shrieks, moans, rolling of the eyes and brandishing of the arms that—performed in their own family circles—would have caused their relatives to summon ambulances."

Mooser and was in sympathy with much of the New Deal's social programs. At the same time, however, he was a rigid conservative when it came to government spending and fiscal accountability. He intended to occupy the middle ground, having written in November 1935 that "I think four more years of the same policies that we have had will wreck our parliamentary government, and four years of the old policies will do the job also."

He was William Randolph Hearst's nominee; that much was certain. In that same November of 1935, Hearst; his chief editorial writer, Arthur Brisbane; and the *Washington Herald*'s editor, Cissy Patterson, had met with Landon in Topeka. While Cissy Patterson had her doubts ("Has this clean-living, simple man the power within him to guide our sorely troubled country out of its present wilderness? Has he?"), Hearst had come away in love with the Kansas governor and the columns of his newspapers henceforth were crowded with laudatory news and commentary on the Landon candidacy. This was the point hit upon most strenuously during a radio speech Ickes gave at Roosevelt's behest on the eve of the Republican convention; Landon, he said, was the captive of Hearst, who had ambitions to become a political boss of the dimensions of Mark Hanna, in spite of the fact that Landon was the least qualified of the Republican candidates (though he gently pointed out that none of them—including his old friend Knox—was any great shakes).

Ickes's scorn notwithstanding, on June 11 the Republican convention in Cleveland gave Landon the middle ground he had asked for, nominating him unanimously on the first ballot, with Knox getting the Vice-Presidential spot. For William Allen White, who had reluctantly joined the ranks of those who thought the New Deal had gone too far, Landon was a generally satisfying though less than exciting candidate, and there was an air of apologetics in a letter he wrote to Ickes on the subject on July 24. "Fundamentally," he said of Landon,

> he has nothing bad. He doesn't lie. He is more intelligent than the average. He is money honest and when he makes up his mind he has all the courage in the world and will go any distance without flinching. He has made a decent governor as governors go. . . .
>
> Landon has always been one of my boys. His bad qualities are a mulish stubbornness and a Napoleonic selfishness. But he knows what he is doing, and I have noticed as his power grows he is more and more candid about his progressive qualities. I think as he feels his hold stronger he will reveal more and more of what I am sure is his progressive reactions. This is pure hunch. . . . But I have been fooled on men before and may be fooled again.

The mosaic of opposition provided by Landon and Knox, Coughlin and his crew, the Liberty League extremists, and the more moderate Democratic dissidents gave the political scene a colorful patchwork quality as the date of the Democratic Party's own convention drew near. Roosevelt had no doubts as to his candidacy (at least so long as he kept the Supreme Court issue in the background); as early as February 7 he had assured Ickes that "he would be re-elected all right, but that the next four years would be very tough ones, with a crisis in 1941. . . . He said that he believed there would be a realignment of parties, and he pointed to the defection of Al Smith and Governor Talmadge as indicating a trend of that sort."

Roosevelt soon had another incipient defection on his hands—that of Ickes himself. The Secretary had borne up remarkably well under the steady barrage against the PWA, but just before the convention Roosevelt did him such genuine dirt that it drove Ickes to tender the second of his several "official" resignations. On March 17 he and the President had a meeting during which FDR "took a pad of paper and a pencil and proceeded to put down a lot of figures from which he tried to demonstrate to me that there would be a very large public works program during the coming year," Ickes reported to his diary. "He also said that in two or three years he wanted to discontinue the Works Progress Administration and turn it all into Public Works."

The air of skepticism apparent in his diary entry was justified, as he learned soon enough. Despite the President's assurances, of the $1.5 billion in work relief money Roosevelt asked Congress for in his budget message the very next day, not one nickel was requested for PWA projects; it would all go to Hopkins and the WPA. Ickes at first attempted to counter the President by endorsing (and possibly even engineering) a rebellion in the House, noting on April 25 that

> I was given a list of members of the House of Representatives who have signed a petition for the earmarking of $700 million of the proposed relief fund of $1.5 billion for PWA. This list contains one hundred and thirty-seven names. . . . I don't expect anything to come of this movement, but the fact that so many Congressmen should go on record is strong corroboration of my belief that if Congress were left free, it would vote overwhelmingly for PWA.

He may not have expected anything to come of it, but he stayed in close touch with Representative Alfred F. Beiter of New York, PWA's champion in the House, over the next several weeks, discussing strategy and possibilities of success regularly. It was from Beiter that he learned that Roosevelt had his own man attempting to influence Congress—none other than Ickes's subordinate, Undersecretary Charles West. Ickes had written West off some time before as being useless to him as any kind of genuine assistant, since the undersecretary spent most of his time serving Roosevelt as one more political liaison with Congress and state-level

Democrats across the country. That did not make Ickes any less furious, but when he called him on the carpet, West squirmed out of admitting anything. "I said that it was not fair to me for him to go up there as he had, considering his position in the Department," Ickes wrote. "He admitted that the President had put him in a very embarrassing position. . . . He protested his loyalty and hoped that I didn't doubt his sincerity. At this point I kept silent. He went on again to deprecate the WPA program and to tell what a fine job PWA had done. He was plainly on the anxious seat and I let him stew in his own juice."

Ickes did some stewing of his own, particularly when FDR made it clear during one of his press conferences that he would not buy the earmarking of any relief funds for PWA. In a subsequent meeting with the President, Ickes insisted that this amounted to a repudiation of the agency. Roosevelt denied any such implication. Ickes went on to complain that Hopkins had "sabotaged" the PWA by withholding approval of projects and had competed unfairly and even underhandedly with PWA from the beginning. "The President agreed with me on all these points," Ickes insisted in his diary. FDR then went on once again to conjure up a rosy future for the PWA through a complicated new financing system that would employ WPA funds. Ickes had his doubts, but left partially mollified. "I had gone to see the President with my mind fully made up that if there was no yielding on his part, my resignation would shortly follow," he wrote. "I think I made some progress with him, but whether anything can be worked out is still a matter of grave doubt."

In the meantime, Senator Carl Hayden of Arizona had introduced an amendment to the appropriations bill which—like the House petition—called for the allocation of $700 million for the PWA, and Ickes had his staff prepare testimony he could use during the upcoming Senate Appropriations Hearings. He was particularly determined to use figures that included estimates of indirect employment that had resulted from PWA projects, this in an attempt to counter Hopkins's argument that the PWA just did not put enough people to work. He had shown these figures to FDR at their meeting and the President had not objected to them. But during the cabinet meeting on May 14, Roosevelt went on the attack. "I don't know who had told him that I was expecting to go before the subcommittee as a witness," Ickes wrote, "although I had intended to do that at the conclusion of the Cabinet meeting. That he knew, there was no doubt, for he told me that he didn't want me to give any figures that he had not seen in advance. In this connection he told me that the figures I had submitted to him last Saturday were all wrong."

Ickes defended the accuracy of his figures and stated that it would be better not to testify at all if he could not be "full and free and frank." Roosevelt did not discourage him in this regard, but went on to emphasize that he did not want figures on indirect employment ever to be utilized to justify PWA projects. Ickes defended this tactic, too. "We hammered back and forth at each other on this subject," he wrote, "and it was plain to see that the President was not in the best of temper. Neither was I, if the truth be told. . . . I was pretty angry by this time. It was as clear as day that the President was spanking me hard before the full Cabinet and I resented that too." After the cabinet meeting, Ickes went back to his office and began dictating a letter of resignation, consulting with Slattery and Burlew in its preparation and even calling in a newspaperman friend from the *Evening Star* to get his thinking on the subject. By the time the letter was finished it had taken on the length and character of a South American *pronunciamento*, and not even a furious Ickes could bring himself to actually submit it. ("I did not think it was quite fair to kick the President in the face before closing the door.")

The next morning, consequently, he dictated another, gentler letter:

I find myself differing fundamentally with your work-relief program as extended and modified under the bill now pending before the Senate. As I see it, the passage of this bill as written will destroy the Public Works Administration, a purpose which was indicated in statements made by you at recent press conferences by which, in effect, you repudiated PWA and indicated a lack of confidence in me as Administrator. Little doubt of your attitude in this matter remains in my mind in view of your statement at the Cabinet meeting today when your orders made it impossible for me to respond to the request of the Senate Appropriations Committee to present a statement of what PWA has accomplished to date.

In the circumstances I have no option except to tender my resignation, both as Secretary of the Interior and as Administrator of Public Works. This I hereby do with my thanks to you for the opportunity that you have given me to serve the country and with profound regret that the situation makes this action necessary. I hope that you will accept this resignation, to take effect at your earliest convenience.

He signed it and dispatched it to Missy LeHand for delivery to the President that morning. However stiffly worded, the resignation was no more intended seriously than the verbal blusters he had been given to from time to time over the past three years. This was made clear later that same day when Ickes went to the White House for a lunchtime meeting with Roosevelt. When he walked into the room, he said, FDR "looked at me with an expression of mock reproach and then, without saying a word . . . handed to me a memorandum in his own handwriting as follows:

Dear Harold:

1. P.W.A. is not "repudiated."
2. P.W.A. is not "ended."
3. I did not "make it impossible for you to go before the committee."
4. I have not indicated lack of confidence.
5. I have *full* confidence in you.
6. You and I have the same big objectives.
7. You are needed, to carry on a big common task.
8. Resignation *not* accepted!

Your affectionate friend . . .

"I read this communication and was quite touched by its undoubted generosity and its evident sincerity of tone," Ickes concluded. He may have been touched, but he was not softened so much that he hesitated to put his case before the President once again, urging him, among other things, to get the appropriations bill amended in the Senate so that the $1.5 billion in relief money should go directly to the President for disposal, not to Hopkins. "I said that . . . it was not a good time for him to be thumbing his nose at the country as he would be doing if he allowed a bill to go through that would give Hopkins greater power and authority than had ever been given to anyone in history."

The bill was so amended and was passed by the House and Senate on June 19. What was more, in spite of FDR's opposition it allocated $300 million directly to the PWA which, with other funding through Jesse Jones and the RFC and WPA grants already agreed upon, gave Ickes's agency about $600 million to work with. It was, Ickes felt, a clear vindication: "While PWA doesn't get a great deal of money, what we do get is ours without any interference by Hopkins. . . . The important thing is that PWA is recognized as a going concern. . . . All told, I am quite satisfied with the way this matter has worked out." This happy resolution probably encouraged him in the future use of the threat of resignation to get his way or at least to make a point with a therapeutic flourish. Most of his colleagues looked upon the strategy as childish and upon Roosevelt's repeated refusals to accept such resignations as incomprehensibly tolerant. But Roosevelt understood perfectly well that these threats were little more than bargaining chips, and over time the two men would fall into the ritual of offering and rejection like players in a curious but familiar little drama. It is entirely possible that at some level both enjoyed it.

CHAPTER

· 33 ·

On the Attack

ROOSEVELT ALMOST CERTAINLY enjoyed the fact that he had gotten his nettlesome Secretary of the Interior calmed down in time for the Democratic National Convention in Philadelphia, which started a few days after he signed the appropriations bill. Ickes, although he was not yet a registered Democrat, would be attending as a delegate-at-large, having been elected to this post by the Illinois Democratic State Convention on May 1. The convention was *pro forma,* of course; despite the efforts of anti–New Deal Democrats, Roosevelt had no competition for the candidacy and even Garner would not be challenged seriously. The whole thing could have been taken care of in a matter of hours, but to deprive the Democratic rank and file of those noisy rituals that gave glitter to the political process would have been akin to taking mother's milk from a squalling infant—and, as historian Kenneth S. Davis has pointed out, Philadelphia merchants were expecting a session long enough to guarantee them a return on the investments they had made in the form of donations to the party. Both rituals and obligations were served over the course of five days, and when Roosevelt made his appearance to accept the nomination on June 27, the enthusiasm that had greeted him in Chicago four years before was nearly equaled. "Under a cloud-veiled moon," Arthur Krock wrote for *The New York Times,* in skies suddenly cleared of rain to a mass of more than 100,000 people gathered in the stadium of the University of Pennsylvania, and by radio to unnumbered millions all over the nation and the world, Franklin Delano Roosevelt tonight accepted the renomination of the Democratic party for President of the United States. . . .

The arrival of the President in the stadium was greeted by a real demonstration, as distinguished from the artificial efforts of conventions. One hundred thousand people rose and roared unmistakable acclaim as Mr. Roosevelt entered the platform on the arm of his eldest son and clasped the hand of Vice President Garner while "The Star-Spangled Banner" was sung.

If the high tenor of his speech can be taken as an indication of what sort of campaign he will conduct, Postmaster General Farley's prediction of the "dirtiest" contest of recent times will not be realized, so far as the chief protagonists of the parties are concerned, for Governor Alf M. Landon has implied the same tactics.

Roosevelt did indeed take the high ground, as he would during most of the campaign; like most first-term Presidents, he wanted to go in search of a second term sounding more like a statesman than a politician. His acceptance speech that night was garnished with phrases that resonated nicely without being inconveniently specific. "The royalists of the economic order," he said at one point, "have conceded that political freedom was the business of the Government, but they have maintained that economic slavery was nobody's business." At another point, he announced that "In the place of the palace of privilege we seek to build a temple out of faith and hope and charity." And finally, near his conclusion, appeared a statement that would be remembered almost as faithfully as his "nothing to fear but fear itself" in the inaugural address: "There is a mysterious cycle in human events. To some generations much is given. Of other generations much is expected. This generation of Americans has a rendezvous with destiny."

Ickes, who was by then completely won back to the Rooseveltian fold, wired the President that he considered the speech a wonderful thing, and during a subsequent meeting with him on July 1 told him again that "it was the greatest political speech that I have ever heard," as he reported to his diary. "I told him that, as the result of that speech, I would have to support him even if he should fire me." During this same love feast, Ickes remembered, "I asked the President what part he expected me to play in the campaign and he said he wanted me to attack. Later, just as I was leaving after luncheon, I told him that I hoped he would feel free to call upon me for anything that I could do at any time and he said again that I made such a grand attack that that was what he wanted."

Ickes was willing to oblige, and from the middle of July until the end of October, the campaign took precedence over most of the rest of his public (and a good deal of his private) time. Louis Howe had died at Bethesda Naval Hospital on April 21, and for the first time in his career Roosevelt would take principal charge of his own campaign strategy, though he would be abetted in the logistics again by Jim Farley. Farley was particularly anxious to use Ickes, and until Roosevelt himself started campaigning actively at the end of September, the Secretary became perhaps the most effective voice of those administration officials—Ickes, Henry Wallace, Homer Cummings, and, *ex officio,* General Hugh Johnson—that the President and Jim Farley had decided should most prominently sing the praises of the New Deal and bring to scorn its enemies.

For the next several months, while Roosevelt went about acting in a Presidential manner, Ickes and the rest would be dispatched from podium to podium, microphone to microphone, carrying the administration's message with a partisan vigor that was considered unseemly for the President himself to display. The Postmaster General also supplied them with copies of responses to a questionnaire he sent out to the ranks four times during the campaign, an astonishing total of thousands of reports from employees of the post office, the WPA, the PWA, and other government agencies, state party chairmen and county party chairmen, congressmen, senators, newspaper editors, and even selected members of fraternal orders—a kind of preelectronic polling system that enabled Farley to keep his finger on the pulse of the Democracy.

Ickes hardly had time to begin sifting through the first of this material before Louis R. Glavis resigned as director of investigations in the Interior Department, thereby resolving one election-year difficulty. Ickes accepted the resignation on July 9, he said, with "profound satisfaction, and, I believe, to the equally keen delight of practically everyone in the Department and in Public Works." Glavis had been a thorn in the side of the Secretary for some time by then—and, by extension, in the side of Roosevelt himself. His work had been invaluable and had gone a long way toward helping to establish the reputation of the PWA as incorruptible. But he was rigid, humorless, moralistic, and ready to believe the worst of anyone if given the chance; and his methods tended to be both ruthless and tactless, as did those of some of his subordinates. Ickes himself had been concerned about such zealotry for some time. "I am beginning to suspect," he had complained in a memorandum to Harry Slattery on November 22, 1934, "that some of our investigators are running a little wild. They are not only investigators, but judges, juries and executioners all combined in one. They must be made to realize that they are not sent out to get a man but to get the facts."

Almost from the beginning Glavis had demonstrated a talent for offending the powerful. Ordinarily this did not incur the wrath of his boss, who had some skill in that direction himself, but it had resulted in some awkwardness from time to time. Routine investigations into the troubled operations of the Subsistence Housing Division, for example, had drawn complaints about Glavis and Ickes's administrative assistant E. K. Burlew from Eleanor Roosevelt herself in 1934; word of these complaints had gotten to the press, and on July 2, 1935, Ernest Lindley of the *New York Herald Tribune* reported that Roosevelt had all but insisted on the dismissal of both men. "The story was a highly sensational one," Ickes commented in his diary. "It charged Glavis with wire tapping, with espionage [directed at] high Government officials, both inside and outside of the Department, and Burlew with disloyalty to the New Deal, with terrorizing employees in the Department, and with building up a machine of his own within the Department." Ickes had defended both men vigorously and Roosevelt had gone out of his way to deny publicly that he wanted them out. Burlew and Glavis then spent some time muttering about filing libel suits against Lindley. Ickes did not discourage them, but Roosevelt made it clear that he was against the idea and nothing ever came of it.*

That tempest had no sooner died down than Ickes found himself in a fight with Henry Morgenthau, again with Glavis at the root of things. In the middle of February 1935, seeking to make trouble for the administration, Senator Huey Long had accused Jim Farley of corruption and had introduced a resolution calling for Ickes to lay before the Senate any documents relating to an investigation Glavis had made of the awarding of a contract for a post office annex in New York City to a firm in which Farley had an interest. While the file showed that a letter from someone in the Post Office Department to someone in the Procurement Division of the Treasury Department (which was in charge of actually paying out allocated funds) had mysteriously been destroyed with the apparent complicity of Assistant Treasury Secretary Chip Roberts, who had handled the

---

* Glavis had in fact resorted to wiretapping during the first two years of PWA's operation, Ickes admitted without remorse in a statement made during the Senate hearings on the confirmation of Burlew as his First Assistant Secretary in January 1938. The telephones in question, Ickes insisted, were only those within the Department of the Interior, and while he had not specifically ordered them tapped, he clearly condoned the action as a legitimate investigative device.

contract for Treasury, there had been no evidence that reflected on Farley in any way, and Ickes had considered the case closed for some time. What he apparently did not know was that the firm had not technically qualified for a PWA contract at the time Roberts had authorized payment, that Glavis had taken this information to Senator Millard Tydings of Maryland, no friend of the administration, and that Tydings had gone to Morgenthau with it.

The Treasury Secretary had been "driven crazy," according to his own recollection, because his reputation had been "besmudged" by the implication that he had done something of which he was "entirely innocent." He had persuaded Tydings to go with him while he tracked down and confronted Roberts on the question. They had discovered the Assistant Secretary cleansing his pores in a Turkish bath. Roberts admitted that he had authorized payment to the firm in spite of its ineligibility and that he knew of the letter's disappearance; he also persuaded Tydings that Morgenthau and Farley had had nothing to do with it all, and when Morgenthau canceled the firm's contract and readvertised for new bids on the project, Tydings had let the subject drop. Roberts later had been persuaded to resign.

The incident left Morgenthau feeling less than friendly toward Glavis, though he apparently never told Ickes of the investigator's unorthodox and probably insubordinate contact with Senator Tydings. Morgenthau's regard for the man had not improved in February 1935 when he requested a look at the file Huey Long's Senate resolution had demanded and he found there a letter from Glavis to someone in Treasury questioning the legitimacy of the New York post office project. This, Morgenthau had decided, was evidence that Ickes had ordered an investigation of the Department of the Treasury, and during the cabinet meeting of February 15 the Treasury Secretary had, by his own account, gotten "very excited and demanded of Ickes what he meant by investigating the Procurement Division." Ickes had replied that he resented both the tone and the implication of the remark and heatedly denied that he ever had caused the investigation of any cabinet member's department. Nor had he ever seen the Glavis letter, he said with equal heat. Morgenthau scorned both denials. Finally, Roosevelt, who hated open displays of temper among his staff, pounded the table and demanded an end to the quarrel. When Morgenthau persisted in his complaints, the President turned to him angrily and said, "Don't you understand, Henry, that Harold says he knows nothing about it and that ends the matter."

"The President succeeded in stopping Morgenthau," Ickes told his diary, "but he did not improve his disposition any. For the balance of the

Cabinet meeting, which ran its full time, until four o'clock, he sat in his seat like a sulking child, glowering at me at intervals." A few days later Roosevelt turned over to the Senate all the documents in the case and not long after that a Senate committee declared Long's accusations to be frivolous and without merit, but the imbroglio had severely strained Ickes's relationship with Morgenthau, never very good to begin with in these early years (they would grow much closer during the war). While he continued to defend Glavis privately and publicly, by the end of 1935 Ickes had become increasingly worried. In November he called in a number of Glavis's principal investigators and told them, according to his diary, "that they ought to be very careful of their facts and not draw conclusions based upon incomplete or ex parte facts," and in December called in Glavis himself when rumors of his impending resignation began to circulate. Glavis admitted that he had considered an offer from another department but had turned it down. Ickes told his chief investigator, "very frankly as a friend," that "from his own point of view he could not afford to resign. I told him that he was cordially hated by nearly everyone in the Department and that the minute he stepped out everyone would be yapping at his heels."

This argument does not scan, and in spite of later reassurances to himself in the diary ("So far as Glavis' doing me any harm is concerned, I am not worried"), it is difficult not to suspect that Ickes was a good deal more concerned over the potential damage a disgruntled Glavis could do to him personally and to Roosevelt politically should he resign in an atmosphere of contention. It is unlikely that Ickes would have been alone in his worry (though there is no evidence that the situation had yet been discussed openly); Glavis was a certifiable fanatic, and who knew whose names were in his locked files?

Worry or not, however, it was becoming harder and harder for Ickes to avoid open conflict with the man. In the middle of March, the Secretary demanded the resignation of Glavis's chief assistant and *his* assistant for doctoring a report to him regarding the Division of Investigation's dogged—and, as it had turned out, unjustified—attempts to get the PWA's state director for Rhode Island fired over the awarding of a contract for the construction of the Rhode Island state airport. During a meeting with Glavis's assistant, according to a summary prepared for the record by Harry Slattery, "Considerable argument took place . . . during which the Administrator charged the Division of Investigations with building up a 'man-hunting organization and a 'system of espionage.' "

Shortly after this blowup Glavis vanished. In answer to Ickes's inquiries as to his whereabouts, Glavis's staff said he was at home, sick with a bout of laryngitis, but Ickes soon learned that he was in New York looking for a job as an expediter, or liaison man, for the city of New York on PWA's Midtown Tunnel project. "This has created a very serious situation," Ickes reported to his diary on April 4. "I cannot see how I could permit anyone connected with the PWA staff to resign and at once become the Washington representative of a PWA project."

By then Ickes was thoroughly disenchanted with Glavis—but not yet ready to ask for his resignation. "I am willing to continue him as Director of Investigations," he wrote, "but only under clearly defined and restricted powers. I will no longer put up with his highhanded methods." Three days later, he was questioned on the point at his regular press conference, but did his best to scotch any rumors of dissatisfaction.

"There seems to be considerable conjecture in the country about investigations by government agencies," one reporter remarked. "They frown on the activities of Glavis, particularly."

"No," Ickes said, "they welcome them."

"Who is 'they'?"

"Whoever they are."

"I hate to bob up with resignation rumors," another reporter commented, "but there is one concerning Glavis. Can you comment on it?"

"I have no comment on a non-existent fact, except to say that it is non-existent."

"You mean that Glavis will continue as Director of the Division of Investigations?"

"So far as I know."

Finally, he burst out with a remarkable single-sentence apologia of large investigating arms in government: "I think they are absolutely essential in a department like this where we have jurisdiction over public domain, mines, oil and all sorts of things, and if you will cast your mind back over the history of the past, you ought not to require much argument to convince you or anyone else it is necessary to have investigators all the time to watch the man who would steal that part of the public domain that he would like to have."

It was Roosevelt who came up with a way out of this increasingly tangled situation. On April 14 he told Ickes that he was going to recommend the appointment of Senator Hugo Black of Alabama to head up a Senate committee on campaign funds and that he wanted Glavis to go to work as Black's chief investigator. Could Ickes spare the man? Ickes admitted that, yes, he could spare him all right, and his relief was embossed in his diary entry for the moment: "As a matter of fact, if it works out this way it might relieve me of an embarrassing situation over here with respect to Glavis. I think Glavis wants to make a change and this would give him a change which would be to his advantage and credit without thought of any disagreement or misunderstanding." By early July the details had been worked out and Glavis accepted the new assignment, which would begin sometime in August.

There is no hint in the Ickes diary, published and unpublished, that Roosevelt had anything devious in mind when he proposed the Glavis transfer. But in a "Confidential Memorandum" for his personal files on August 24, FBI director J. Edgar Hoover revealed that the President apparently had been worrying about Glavis nearly as much as had Ickes and had accomplished a stratagem clearly designed to keep Glavis's claws retracted during the campaign: "In conversation with the President this morning, he informed me that the Glavis organization in the Interior Department is being broken up. He stated that he had had the position created for Glavis by the Senate Committee in order to find a place for him so as to get him out of the Department of Interior and so he would be occupied and not break out at the present time. He indicated that Glavis was most unsafe and had almost a self-persecution complex."

With this Byzantine (and typically Rooseveltian) scenario played out to a safe conclusion by spring 1936, Ickes was free to pursue the reelection of the President, and it was over the next several months that he vindicated Roosevelt's faith in him as a political animal and established himself as one of the New Deal's most potent campaign weapons. It began sedately enough with a cornerstone-laying speech on July 14 at the site of a new Wieboldt's department store in Chicago. "There can be no doubt that recovery has made enormous strides," he said, adding that people "have more money to spend because business is better in all parts of the country."* The rhetoric began heating up three days later at the Institute of Public Affairs at the University of Virginia, where he warned, "The people should beware of entrusting their government, now that they have rescued it at last from the grip of cold and heartless and sordid men, to any man whose repudiation of the money power has not been attested by the outpourings of hate of that same money power."

---

* Well, a *little* better. Unemployment had dropped from a high of 12,830,000 in 1933, but still stood at more than 10 million (in 1929, it had only been a little over 1.5 million); per-capita personal income had risen from $374 in 1933 to $535 (in 1929 it had been $705), but the per-capita amount that people were spending in places like department stores came to only forty-nine dollars (in 1929 it had been seventy-six dollars). The fact was, while the country had survived the worst years of the Depression with its economy generally intact, it was a long way from recovery—and indeed would not fully recover until the demands of World War II created an entirely new economic order.

As yet, he had made no specific reference to Alf Landon or—as he devoutly wished—to William Randolph Hearst's support of the Kansas governor. At a strategy meeting with Roosevelt, Steve Early, Marvin McIntyre, and several others on July 7, Farley remembered, it had been decided not to let Ickes "take out after Alf Landon" until Landon had made his acceptance speech (unlike Roosevelt, Landon had not been present at the convention that nominated him). Roosevelt was particularly strong on this point, fearing especially that if the Democrats made too much of the Hearst connection before the speech, Landon would disavow Hearst when he finally delivered it. "I think this is downright silly," Ickes had written in his diary on July 18. "Landon cannot repudiate Hearst now." Farley agreed with him, and on July 21 sent FDR a telegram, urging him to at least let Ickes get after Landon himself in a speech scheduled for the coming Friday:

WE WISH TO URGE WHAT WE BELIEVE TO BE IMPERATIVE IMPORTANCE ALLOW ICKES TO GO AHEAD WITH FRIDAY NIGHT SPEECH. . . . HE WILL MAKE NO ATTEMPT TO ANSWER LANDON BUT WILL SPEAK AS A FORMER REPUBLICAN AND GO DIRECT INTO QUESTION OF REACTIONARY REPUBLICAN LEADERSHIP. . . . HIS ONLY MENTION OF LANDON WILL BE TO POINT OUT HIS DEPENDENCE ON THAT LEADERSHIP. . . . NO ONE ELSE QUALIFIED TO JOB SO WELL AS ICKES AND WE ARE CONVINCED THAT HE SHOULD BE ALLOWED TO GO AHEAD AS ANNOUNCED.

But Roosevelt held firm, and it was not until August 4, after Landon's acceptance speech (in which no reference to Hearst was made) that Ickes was finally allowed to go on CBS to decry the Hearst connection. He did it with savage delight. The Republican platform, he said, "is the platform that William Randolph Hearst in one of his shrill editorials calls 'progressive.' . . . In the same editorial he laid down the law to the effect that the candidates for both president and vice president are also progressive. Well, who in the whole country, may I ask, has a better right to name the children than their father?" As for the governor himself, Ickes heaped contempt upon his self-description as "the everyday American" and "a practical Progressive": "Landon cannot at the same time be the candidate of the exploiting and of the exploited. Not even a 'practical' Progressive ought to be able to run with the hares and hunt with the hounds."

It was a theme he took to again on August 27, this time on NBC, in a speech grandly entitled "Hearst over Topeka," though he did not ignore Landon's own shortcomings:

It is notorious that the Republican Party was surprisingly shy of men who measured up to Presidential stature. There seemed to be none to fill the bill.

So Mr. Hearst proceeded to gear up his great publicity machine to make a candidate. Making bricks without straw was an easy task compared with the one in hand, but desperate situations require desperate measures. . . .

He [Landon] wants the country to conform to "the American way of life." Well, who doesn't? He reiterates this phrase as if he meant something by it, but in his mouth it is only a catch-phrase, a bit of empty rhetoric, a tinsel object designed to attract the attention of the unthinking. I haven't attempted to count the number of times that the Republican candidate and his running mate have used this expression—which also is a favorite of the Hearst press—but when Governor Landon, in particular, reaches a point in a speech where hope runs high that he is at last going to say something about the real issues of the campaign he can always be depended upon to wind up with some inanity.

"Hearst over Topeka" brought in scores of letters in response, almost all of them favorable. Both the *New York Daily News* and *The New York Times* carried the speech in full, beginning on the front page. Even more satisfying was the response of Representative Joe Martin, Landon's campaign manager. "Chairman Farley," he told a reporter, "is apparently trying to make good on one of his campaign promises . . . that this was to be a dirty campaign, and Mr. Ickes apparently has been glad to assume the role of chief mud slinger." Roosevelt, who was traveling in the Midwest and West to observe drought conditions firsthand, was so pleased that he did not insist that Ickes accompany the rest of the cabinet members to Salt Lake City for the interment of Secretary of War George Dern, who had died on August 24. Instead, he urged Ickes to stay in Washington and work on a speech he was scheduled to make on September 4 at the homecoming celebration and eightieth anniversary of Columbus, Nebraska.

The speech was written but never delivered. Ickes had no sooner gotten to his office the morning of August 31 than Mike Straus, his public relations director, walked in to tell him that H. L. Woolhiser, the village manager of Winnetka, had called to say that Wilmarth had been found dead in the downstairs bedroom at Hubbard Woods. It was precisely one year since Anna had been killed in New Mexico.

Wilmarth's behavior, never very stable under the best of circumstances, had been particularly erratic in the months following his mother's death. When Anna's will was read after the funeral, he had expressed no particular surprise that Harold had been given the bulk of the estate and had been named executor, nor had he seemed nonplussed by the fact that out of bequests totaling $11,000, Wayne Thompson, the brother of her first husband, had been left $5,000 and that Harold's sister Julia had received $2,500, while he and the other children got nothing. He must have been dissembling, Ickes later concluded, for Wilmarth soon got it into his head that because of the catastrophic relationship between Anna and Harold, she must have made a codicil to her will that cut Harold out and gave him, Raymond, Robert, and Frances everything. Raymond angrily refused to listen to such speculations, he remembers, but apparently Robert and Frances were willing to keep open minds on the subject while Wilmarth did some investigating.

His instincts had been correct, though they did him little good. He learned from the lawyer who had drawn up Anna's will that she had indeed installed a codicil shortly after Ickes had confessed his affair with Mrs. X. It had stipulated that Harold was to get only his statutory share in the estate and that Wilmarth, not Harold, was to be the executor. Unfortunately for Wilmarth's hopes, she had rescinded the codicil when she decided that she and her husband were on the road to reconciliation. "Well," he had told Robert bitterly after learning of this disappointing change of heart, "you and I are sunk; the old man gets everything."

If Wilmarth's hope had been for great gobbets of ready cash—and given his history as a gambler, it probably had been—he would have been in for some disappointment even if the codicil had survived. Not only did Anna leave a pittance of $971.65 in cash and promissory notes; her stock portfolio amounted to only $1,560 (and three of her four stocks, the probate report noted, "were probably not worth their face value"). The house in Hubbard Woods was assessed at $75,000, other property in the region (including the house on Walden Road for which Wilmarth had failed to pay the rent for years) was valued at a total of $21,000, and the State Street property in Chicago at a whopping $568,000 (though it was encumbered by a $190,000 mortgage taken out in 1926), but it was a terrible period for the sale of real estate and the $40,000 in annual rent produced by the State Street property was the only income Wilmarth could have expected. That would have done him no more immediate good than it did his stepfather, for most of what was left to be paid in 1935 had gone to satisfy the will's bequests (even there, Ickes had been forced to dip into his own funds to pay the balance not covered by the rent money). Finally, there had been the inheritance taxes. He may have gotten every-thing, Ickes had noted in his diary on September 13, 1935, "but what I don't see is where in heaven's name I am going to get enough money to pay the state and Federal inheritance taxes. It looks as if these taxes would run well over $100,000, and the only way I can get that money is by mortgages or sale of real estate, both of which are exceedingly difficult in these times." Those taxes, in fact, were to amount to only a little less than his estimate—$93,461.53 to be precise—and to pay them he would have to negotiate a new loan against the State Street property with the Northwestern Mutual Life Insurance Company.

Nevertheless, Wilmarth apparently had nursed the conviction that he had been done out of his inheritance in some fashion, adding this outrage to a list of old resentments and molding it all into full-blown hatred. "None of this I realized at the time," Ickes said in his unpublished memoirs, "or I would have tried to do something about it because I continued to be fond of him and wanted him to care for me." He realized Wilmarth's true feelings soon enough. Betty and the children spent most of each summer vacationing in Michigan, and since he had no servants of his own and did not feel inclined to take care of the house on Walden Road by himself, Wilmarth had taken to staying in the downstairs bedroom at Hubbard Woods when they were gone. It was here, apparently after several days of some kind of illness—a powerful depression is not unlikely—that he had shot himself with a service revolver on the anniversary of his mother's death.

He had left behind a note, shown to Ickes by Winnetka's chief of police after Ickes and Straus had flown out on Monday's noon plane. It was a rambling, nearly incoherent missive that indicated the young man was in a distraught condition as he wrote it. He insisted to Betty that he had not been drinking, but he almost certainly had. After assuring her that her grandfather's estate would be enough to take care of her and the children, he signed off with a vague complaint against "HL," presumably an oblique reference to Ickes.

Ickes overreacted. "I saw at once that the newspapers would give anything for this note," he remembered,

> because it would make a front page sensation. Personally, I was not able to figure out for some time just what Wilmarth meant. When I showed it to Betty it sounded incoherent to her and her explanation of it was that Wilmarth had probably been out of his mind when he wrote it. But it came clear to me, as other facts were brought to my knowledge, that here was the final attempt by Wilmarth, whom I had loved and who for many years had loved me, to strike me what might prove to be a mortal blow, considering my position in public life.*

* Back in 1933, Ickes had since learned, Wilmarth had somehow gotten hold of some of the letters written by the fiancé of Ickes's lover and had attempted to sell them to one of the Hearst newspapers. When Hearst was contacted at San Simeon, Ickes remembered, the publisher "said there were many things that he did not like about me, but that this would be hitting below the belt."

At Ickes's request, Frank Walsh, the Cook County coroner and an old political ally, agreed not to introduce the note as evidence during the inquest and both the chief of police and his assistant calmly lied when questioned about whether they had found anything. "They perjured themselves magnificently," Ickes remembered, "and I have always felt tremendously grateful to them. Nor has my conscience bothered me about this matter. After all, the note threw no light on Wilmarth's motives for his self-destruction; the only effect of it would have been that every newspaper in the country would have carried screaming headlines and for days would have speculated about what was back of the note."

Perhaps because the note had leached him of whatever affection he still felt, Ickes wasted as little emotional energy mourning the death of his stepson as he had that of Anna the year before. After simple, brief ceremonies, the body of the unhappy young man was interred in a grave next to his mother's at Memorial Park Cemetery, after which Ickes and Straus flew back to Washington and to the political world in which he functioned with far greater comfort and competence than he ever had in the murky, uncertain, and dangerous world of emotional relationships. Wilmarth's death rated only five quick sentences in his diary.

Then another horror less than a month later: his nephew Harold, the son of Julia and Clinton Hazard, also killed himself. Ickes had helped young Harold get into Annapolis and had helped him along in his career in the navy whenever and however he could through the years, but not even his position as Secretary of the Interior could do anything to alleviate his nephew's chronic high blood pressure, which finally had forced his retirement the year before. Apparently despondent, he, too, shot himself. Two deaths in the family within the space of weeks necessarily curtailed Ickes's political activities; in that more circumspect age, death was an event that still required a period of mourning even of someone not easily given to mourning, and Ickes turned down speaking assignments throughout the month of September.

By the time he was ready to take up the cudgel again in early October, Roosevelt himself had entered the fray, officially opening the campaign on September 29 with a speech before the Democratic State Convention in Syracuse, New York. "The task on our part is twofold," the President had said. "First, as simple patriotism requires, to separate the false from the real issues; and, secondly, with facts and without rancor, to clarify the real problems for the American people."

That may have been, but Ickes was more inclined toward raw sarcasm, if not rancor, and he devoted the better part of the last month before the election to laying it on with a heavy hand, or tongue. The "queer combination" of characters who were bent on Roosevelt's defeat, he told the Good Neighbor League in Columbus, Ohio, on October 9, was held together by "hatred of Roosevelt. He must be defeated at all costs. He is the greatest threat to special privilege that this country has known for at least a generation, and the beneficiaries of special privilege know how to fight. Try to take away from any man an unfair advantage and you will find a scratching, spitting wildcat on your hands." For an audience at the Democratic National Committee in Philadelphia on October 19, he "reviewed" something he called "Landon's Angels," an "opera buffa that is being staged throughout the country by the Republican National Committee." Landon, he said, was "the Kansas song-bird," Knox "the eccentric basso," Herbert Hoover Landon's "understudy," while "Comedy relief is supplied by Father Coughlin, Doc Townsend, and the Reverend Gerald L. K. Smith." That other Smith, Alfred E., came in for the greatest share of derision. He was, Ickes said, "the villain of the piece" who had

> wanted the leading part in that great American favorite—"Happy Days Are Here Again" and, failing to get it, sulked for a season and finally took a part in "Landon's Angels," even though it is scheduled to close on November 3 for lack of public support. . . . His hatred of President Roosevelt is a personal hatred—the hatred of a disappointed man. It is not a pretty spectacle he is making of himself as he goes about the country exposing the political sores of which he complains.

For a CBS radio audience on October 20 he explained that "Governor Landon is a changeling candidate. When he is in the East he is 'hail fellow well met' with Wall Street and the big interests, but when he turns his face westward again he tries to take on a progressive coloration and declares against the very policies that he has just enthusiastically endorsed." At Northwestern University the next day he built his speech around a campaign device utilized by Colonel Robert McCormick in the *Chicago Tribune*. For weeks the front page of the *Tribune* had warned that there were only so many days left in which to "save America." "You people," Ickes said, "who suffer from too much *Tribune* must know by now that there are only thirteen more days within which to volunteer to help Colonel Bertie to 'save America.' . . . My own conviction is that America has already been saved by Franklin D. Roosevelt and that the people know it."

In Altoona again on October 27, he lashed out at Gifford Pinchot, who, by Ickes's lights, had turned his back on his Progressive roots by declaring for Landon: "It is nothing short of tragic to witness a man of his background, in his declining years, perform an act of self-stultification that will inevitably be a blot upon his record in the pages of history." And finally, in a CBS radio address from Carnegie Hall in New York on October 28, he returned to what he viewed as Landon's schizoid condition: "What manner of man is this political Dr. Jekyll and Mr. Hyde? How can one know just where he stands on the hundred and one grave issues that confront the electorate? Shall we find the pea under the progressive or the reactionary shell?"

In the end, it was a very tiny pea indeed, and never mind the character of the shell that covered it. Ickes was quite right when he said that the people believed that Roosevelt had saved America—or at least had carried the country a long way in the direction of salvation. So was James G. Farley when he wrote to Claude G. Bowers, U.S. ambassador to Spain, on October 23 that "we expect a tremendous landslide. In my prophecy the Sunday before election I am going to claim everything west of the Hudson. Delaware, Pennsylvania, Michigan, Iowa, and Kansas are going to be close, but I think we will win them all." And so they did. On November 3, Roosevelt was reelected by a majority of 27,476,673 popular votes to Landon's 16,679,583; the President carried every state in the nation except Maine and Vermont.

"It is all over now," Ickes reported in his diary on November 7, "but even in retrospect the result is astonishing. . . . There has been nothing like it in the history of American politics." As for his own future in Roosevelt's second administration, he professed to a wondrous and thoroughly uncharacteristic serenity: "What the President has in mind with respect to his Cabinet or with respect to me in particular, I haven't the least idea. Probably he won't say or do anything until well along in January. In the meantime, we can do the worrying, if we are disposed to worry. For my part, I do not propose to worry." It is more than likely that he knew perfectly well that he had nothing to worry about; Ickes's performance during the campaign had been exemplary, and for all their periodic disagreements and the Secretary's everlastingly thin skin, there is no evidence anywhere that Roosevelt had ever considered replacing him at Interior. No, there was little question that Ickes would be in the new cabinet when Roosevelt was sworn in on January 20, 1935 (the inaugural date had been moved from March 5 with passage of the Twentieth Amendment), and he could be forgiven if he looked ahead to his own second term as an opportunity to put forward the one change in the structure of the American government that he truly believed would mark his place in history with greater force than anything else he had done or would ever do.

If Roosevelt would only let him.

PART VII

A Department of Conservation

In a very real sense, the argument of Agriculture, whatever surface appearances may be, is a personal argument. It is not only personal, it is offensive. That argument runs: Secretary Ickes cannot be trusted to administer the national forests because Albert B. Fall was Secretary of the Interior and you all remember Teapot Dome. If and when the Department of Agriculture shakes off from the Forest Service the heavy and prehensile hands of the lumber interests it may be more proper to argue that only a Secretary of Agriculture can be trusted to administer the national forests.

—Letter to Henry A. Wallace, June 25, 1935

CHAPTER
· 34 ·

The House That Ickes Built

I N DECEMBER 1934, Henry Salem Hubbell completed the official portrait of Secretary of the Interior Harold L. Ickes. It was a gentle
rendering, one that softened most of Ickes's hard edges and apparently
attempted to achieve the bland and inhuman quality typical of most
government portraits; if so, the artist was betrayed by the presence of one
slightly cocked eyebrow and the familiar satiric twist at one corner of the
mouth, both of which characteristics helped to illuminate the very real
and very complicated person behind all the oil. So did the props that Ickes
had chosen to be painted with—the preliminary plans for the new
Department of the Interior building.

Of all the buildings that Ickes caused to be built during his tenure as
administrator of Public Works, none was more important to him than the
one he erected to hold the offices of the greatly expanded (and consequently underspaced) Department of the Interior, and he had dedicated
quite as much time to its design and construction as he had to the house in
Hubbard Woods twenty years before—and for similar reasons. If the
house in Hubbard Woods can be said to have symbolized Ickes's escape
from rootlessness and poverty and his safe arrival in the haven of respectability, then the Interior Building symbolized for its builder the rescue of
his department from the disdain and obloquy with which it had been
tarred by Secretary Albert Fall. The department was to be invested with

new hope, and Ickes was determined that the home he made for it would not merely be the first major government building to get under way after the creation of the Public Works Administration, but that it would be the best.

The building had been authorized in early 1934 with a PWA grant of $12,740,000 for construction; another $1,435,422 had been allocated for the purchase of the land, a double block that covered the territory between Eighteenth and Nineteenth streets and C and E streets (D Street between Eighteenth and Nineteenth would be eliminated) just across Rawlins Park from the old Interior Building; the old and new buildings would be connected by a tunnel beneath the park. In June 1934, Ickes entered into a contract for the building's design with local architect Waddy B. Wood, who had designed numerous mansions and other buildings around town, including the Masonic Temple and the Chancery for the Chinese legation. Before Wood could get fairly under way, however, there would be one more contretemps with Henry Morgenthau and the Department of the Treasury. Morgenthau's comptroller general had complained that Ickes was not authorized to enter into any contract for the design or construction of any government building, including one for his own department; that authority, the comptroller general had quite correctly pointed out, lay with the Procurement Division of the Treasury Department. Morgenthau had taken the complaint to Roosevelt, and Roosevelt had told Ickes to work things out with Morgenthau. Ickes tried, by his own account. "I did talk it over with him," he wrote in his diary on November 15, 1934. "I told him that I was asking a personal favor, that it would not mean anything to him personally whether he built this building or not, but that it did mean a good deal to me. He said he was willing to do everything he could." But Morgenthau feared that it would undercut the authority of his own department if he let Interior have complete control, so without informing Ickes, he worked out an agreement with Roosevelt whereby the architect and the construction firm and all Interior Department employees connected to the job would be placed temporarily on the payroll of the Treasury Department's Procurement Division, although Ickes himself would continue to supervise design and construction without hindrance. "This should clear up the whole situation," Roosevelt had cheerily proclaimed in a note to both men, "and I see no reason why the work should not proceed . . . in the record-breaking time desired by the Secretary of the Interior."

Ickes had not been pleased but, in the interests of getting the job done, had decided to cooperate. From then on he had filled many of the interstices of time between all his other responsibilities with hours de-

voted to poring over plans for the building, offering numerous suggestions, criticisms, and demands, all of them designed to create what would
be at once the most comfortable and the most functional government
building in Washington. He remembered well the misery of his first
summer in Washington and had stipulated that the new building would
have central air-conditioning, making it the first government building to
enjoy this luxury. He, like everyone else in the department, had disliked
the cramped offices of the old Interior Building, so the typical office
among the twenty-two hundred rooms of the new building would be a
generous twelve feet eight inches by eighteen feet nine inches, with one
wall given over to tall double windows overlooking a courtyard; what is
more, the walls between most offices were specially designed sound-
proofed steel partitions that could be removed so that a room might be
enlarged to fit any need.

Other features directly attributable to the Secretary were the
escalators—again, a first for a government building—that connected the
basement with the first and second floors and facilitated the easy movement of four thousand employees, even at lunchtime; an auditorium two
stories high and 10,650 square feet in area; a library (though it was
utilized exclusively by the Office—and later Department—of Education
until 1948); a museum, formally opened to the public in 1938; an art
gallery for the display of student art from around the country; an Indian
arts and crafts shop, an enterprise, it was said, that had been suggested by
Anna; an enormous cafeteria for the employees, including an outdoor
dining area; an employees' lounge, complete with soda fountain; a gymnasium in the basement featuring a regulation-sized basketball court with
maple flooring; and, finally, a small but fully equipped radio station in the
north penthouse, which would go on the air with educational broadcasts
in 1937.

Throughout the building, wall space was left for bas-relief work and
murals, and over the course of more than a decade, paintings and other
decorative work commissioned by the Federal Arts Project of the WPA or
the Public Arts section of the Division of Procurement would embellish
almost every cranny of the building, from the cafeteria in the basement to
the main room of the south penthouse. None of it got done without the
personal approval of the Secretary himself, who wanted the work and the
responsibility of the Interior Department celebrated in art and who
exercised considerable influence over both the style and content of the
finished work. Not without contention, of course, including at least one
clash of aesthetics between the Secretary and Edward Bruce, chief of the
Painting and Sculpture Section of the Division of Procurement. When

California artist Millard Sheets submitted some panel work in 1937, Edward Rowen, chief of Interior's Painting and Sculpture Section, passed on Ickes's response:

> The Secretary expressed great respect for the quality of the work which you submitted but seriously questioned the appropriateness of the theme of "Air, Fire, Land and Water" in connection with his program of "Conservation." The panel of "Water" suggested to the Secretary the program of "Flood Control" which is not in the Department of the Interior. In the panel dealing with "Air" the Secretary explained that the Department of the Interior is the one Department in the Government that owns no airships and has nothing to do with airways.

Ickes suggested, instead, that the artist devote the four panels to the subjects of the Negro and the Indian. "In the case of the 'Negro,' " Rowen explained, "you could depict him living in a society without enlightenment and may make it rather sordid but no scenes of lynching should be included. The contrasting panel to this theme should deal with the advancement which has been made by the 'Negro' and might depict Howard University . . . or the contributions which Negroes have made to science, literature and art." As for the Indians, Ickes suggested that one panel be entitled "Woods Indians being uprouted [*sic*] out of their native haunts and brutally driven into an arid country by the United States Army," while the other, contrasting, panel should "depict the more enlightened treatment of the Indian in our own time."

Bruce was outraged at the Secretary's gall in daring to criticize the work of an artist. "It seems to me pretty revolting," he wrote Sheets, "that we have to deal with such a complete vulgarian as Ickes in taking on the chin the ridiculous comments on his ideas of art. . . . I don't know why we stand letting an utter vulgarian and ignoramous [*sic*] get by with things like that." Reluctantly, Bruce did admit that "I suppose there isn't any use in fighting him as he is bound to lick us, having the upper hand."

Precisely. Ultimately, Sheets did four panels depicting the contributions of black Americans to education, art, religion, and science, though they were not completed and installed until 1948. By then, the building was ornamented with a richness of theme unmatched by any government building in the nation: Henry Varnum Poor's forty-two-foot mural in the main corridor depicted the conservation of American wildlife, while Ralph Stackpole's bas-relief in the auditorium illustrated John Wesley Powell's river exploration of the Grand Canyon. Maynard Dixon's two murals in the south lobby of the fourth floor showed the Indian (*à la* Ickes) first as an adversary, then as a ward of the government. John Steuart Curry's murals in the main corridor of the fifth floor apotheosized the

Oklahoma land rush and the homesteader. Heinz Warneke's bas-relief in the auditorium showed Lewis and Clark on their way to the Pacific, while David McCosh's murals on the east and west walls of the third floor's south lobby depicted scenes in twelve of the national parks. Frank J. Mackenzie's huge painting on the west wall of the main corridor of the seventh floor showed the fruits of federal irrigation in the Salt River Valley of Arizona.

While devoting laudable amounts of time and attention to the needs of his employees and the quality of the building's artwork, the Secretary had not neglected the needs of the Secretary. Suite 6000, the Office of the Secretary, occupied more than fifty-seven hundred square feet on the sixth floor of the West Wing and included space for Ickes's support staff, including his stenographers and personal secretaries May Conley and Theodore Mack, as well as offices for Harry Slattery and E. K. Burlew. Ickes's private office, beautifully paneled in oak, floored with pegged black walnut boards of random widths and tones, and lighted by a pair of spectacular chandeliers the general size and configuration of wagon wheels, took up more than twelve hundred square feet. It also had attached to it a small kitchen, a bedroom, and a private bath for those nights when the Secretary could not bring himself to drive back out to the house in Spring Valley after one of his sixteen-hour days. These amenities would attract the avid and usually inaccurate regard of the press, the bathroom coming in for most of the attention. At least one reporter would describe it as a "gold and blue marble Roman bath suitable for a Turkish harem," though it was in fact a decently modest room with white fixtures and blue and white tiles; its most unusual—and less than sumptuous—feature was a shower separate from the tub.

The building was not ready for occupancy until the spring of 1937, though its official dedication had taken place on April 16, 1936. "As I view this serviceable new structure," Roosevelt had concluded his address on this occasion, "I like to think of it as symbolical of the Nation's vast resources that we are sworn to protect, and this stone that I am about to lay as the cornerstone of a conservation policy that will guarantee to future Americans the richness of their heritage." Ickes himself had hinted broadly that the building meant even more than that, at least to him. It would stand both as vindication and as harbinger: "This new building," he said, "represents much more to us than merely better and more desirable office space; it means something besides relieving the over-crowded conditions in our present building; it is a symbol to us of a new day." In the parlance of Harold L. Ickes, a phrase like "a new day" was not the vague generality it might have been in the mouths of most govern-ment officials; he meant something quite specific and quite revolutionary by it, and he would spend much of the rest of his career as Secretary of the Interior in bitter pursuit of the goal for which the phrase stood as talisman. This great government house he was building had been designed to hold a dream: the dream would be called the Department of Conservation and under an administrative mandate held and exercised by the Secretary of the Interior, it would be devoted exclusively to the preservation and wise management of all of the federal public lands of the United States. All of them. That was the dream. As always, reality would offer obstacles, long interruptions, and shorter but no less maddening distractions, yet for nearly thirteen years Ickes would not let it go, believing to the end that logic and the weight of history combined to make the big dream inevitable.

CHAPTER
· 35 ·

Cries in the Wilderness

THE WEIGHT OF HISTORY was pressing toward something, right enough, but no one as yet discerned precisely what it might be. It was called conservation, but the American conservation movement, barely half a century old, was poorly defined and riven with competing ideas. Ickes caught its flavor early on, though a little harshly. "The real trouble with the conservation movement in this country," he told the guests of the annual Game Conference Banquet on January 22, 1935, in a speech broadcast over NBC, "is that it is subdivided into small cliques and factions; it is not a cohesive, coherent movement. Forces that ought to be united and working for the common good, are so busy struggling for their own selfish interests, that, due to the resulting confusion of counsel, the exploiters are still largely having their wanton way with the natural resources of our America."

However disparate and contentious, the sundry factions of the movement were all branches of one or the other of two different trees that had grown, as it were, from the same soil. When it became apparent by the middle of the nineteenth century that the unrestrained exploitation of the natural world had consequences barely imagined and almost never acknowledged during most of human history, the realization helped to shape two schools of thought that would become fully formed by the 1930s. The one had its first major expression in 1864 in George Perkins

Marsh's *Man and Nature,* a book that would serve as a kind of bible for what would come to be called utilitarian conservation. Gifford Pinchot, who had given Marsh's philosophical points concrete reality in government, put it succinctly in *Breaking New Ground:* "The first duty of the human race on the material side is to control the use of the earth and all that therein is. Conservation means the wise use of the earth and its resources for the lasting good of men. Conservation is the foresighted utilization, preservation, and/or renewal of forests, waters, lands, and minerals, for the greatest good of the greatest number for the longest time." Human beings were God's chosen stewards of the land, and if they did not use it wisely and well, as Marsh had pointed out with historical examples, the results could be devastating; at its core, then, the principle of stewardship was a matter of enlightened self-interest. The doctrine fit particularly well with the social and political instincts of the Progressive Movement, for it implied that the stewardship of natural resources meant that the benefits of their use should accrue to all the people, not to just a handful of individuals or, even more reprehensibly, to a few large corporations. Again, Pinchot:

> Conservation is the application of common sense to the common problems for the common good. Since its objective is the ownership, control, development, processing, distribution, and use of the natural resources for the benefit of the people, it is by its very nature the antithesis of monopoly. . . . Monopoly on the loose is a source of many of the economic, political, and social evils which afflict the sons of men. Its abolition or regulation is an inseparable part of the Conservation policy.

With such principles as his underpinning and with the creation of a national constituency for government conservation programs as his goal, Pinchot had formed the American Conservation League in 1908. It was made up of about twenty small organizations, most of them concerned with water projects and river conservation; the coalition's president was Harold Ickes's old Progressive acquaintance Walter L. Fisher. When, however, it became clear that the organizations that made up the league were far too embroiled in their individual concerns ever to become the coherent voice Pinchot wished, he turned to an older group, the American Forestry Association, and attempted to shape it to his ends. But forces within that group resisted his efforts to turn it from a narrow interest in forest management to the more protean concepts of national conservation policy, particularly as they related to water and power projects and mineral leasing, so once again he formed an independent organization. This one was called the National Conservation Association, and while it continued in existence until the middle of the twenties, the group never did grow to a size or influence that matched Pinchot's ambitions for it.* Along the way, he had also watched with dismay as his Forest Service, under the direction of Chief Forester William B. Greeley, became more and more a tool of the lumber industry and less a practical steward of the land. (In 1928, Greeley would demonstrate the new alliance by leaving the Forest Service to head up the West Coast Lumbermen's Association.)

However difficult it may have been for Pinchot and others to establish a nationwide organization to express its philosophy in action—the "Gospel of Efficiency," one historian has characterized it—utilitarian conservation, embraced and propounded by a growing class of professionals like Pinchot, was a force that already had shaped public policy as few movements in American history ever had. Its energy had lain behind the various land law reforms of the late nineteenth and early twentieth centuries, had moved Presidents Harrison, Cleveland, and Theodore Roosevelt to withdraw from uncontrolled public use tens of millions of acres of forestland, and had inspired Roosevelt to put millions of acres of coal reserves off limits to private exploitation. It had given birth to both the Forest Service and the Bureau of Reclamation and for more than a decade had inspired annual meetings of the National Conservation Congress to discuss the use and misuse of national resources. Finally, it had given form to the movement for the development of public power from public water, and had led inexorably to the revolutionary Tennessee Valley Authority and to the huge river basin projects developed by the Bureau of Reclamation and the U.S. Army Corps of Engineers, largely financed by Ickes's Public Works Administration.

But there was another instinct at work, one at least as old as utilitarianism and for some just as persuasive. For want of a better word then or now, those who held to this contrary philosophy were called preservationists. And as Marsh was the prophet of utilitarianism, the sometime schoolteacher and essayist Henry David Thoreau was the oracle of the preservationist movement. In "Walking," a long essay written just three years before the publication of Marsh's *Man and Nature*, the peripatetic philosopher of Concord, Massachusetts, gave voice to an idea that challenged every conviction common to his time. "The West of which I speak is but another name for the Wild," he wrote,

> and what I have been preparing to say is, that in Wildness is the preservation
> of the World. Every tree sends its fibres forth in search of the Wild. The cities

* It was this organization which Harry Slattery served as secretary.

import it at any price. Men plow and sail for it. From the forest and wilderness come the tonics and barks which brace mankind. . . .

A town is saved, not more by the righteous men in it than by the woods and swamps that surround it. A town where one primitive forest waves above while another primitive forest rots below,—such a town is fitted to raise not only corn and potatoes, but poets and philosophers for the coming ages.

Unlike Marsh's book, Thoreau's musings, when noticed at all by those in power, were usually dismissed as the harmless natterings of a fool who spent too much time alone. But not by everyone, and among those who took him seriously was a hairy wood sprite by the name of John Muir, who became to Thoreau what Gifford Pinchot had been to Marsh. Even before he had read Thoreau, Muir had already discovered that his own salvation would be found in wildness. Born in Scotland in 1838, the son of a small farmer and itinerant preacher, Muir had spent his youth working the reluctant sandy soil of his father's two Wisconsin farms before escaping to an on-again, off-again education at the University of Wisconsin in Madison, and after that to a time of cheerful wandering that took him into the boggy wilds of southeastern Canada, then to a brief career as the foreman of a wagon-wheel factory in Indiana, then on a thousand-mile walk to the Gulf of Mexico. Here, after recovering from a fever that nearly killed him, he sailed for California, arriving in 1868. From San Francisco, he took a ferry across the bay to Oakland, then started walking again, marching all the way to the Sierra Nevada and the place that would become and remain the homeland of his heart for the rest of his life—the glorious trench called the Yosemite Valley.

This was where he forged the protocols of his own conviction that such places ought to be protected from the careless enthusiasms of human enterprise. In wilderness, he wrote, echoing Thoreau, "lies the hope of the world—the great fresh unblighted, unredeemed wilderness." In the 1870s and 1880s, his writings about the valley and the Sierra Nevada—as well as other wild places in the West, from Utah to Alaska—brought him the support of Robert Underwood Johnson, editor of *Century* magazine. With *Century* as his podium and Johnson as his most influential acolyte, Muir led the effort that established Yosemite National Park in 1890. Unfortunately, the new park did not include the valley itself; that remained in the hands of the state, which encouraged such unwild activities as stock raising on fenced ranges, logging operations, and the unregulated development of tourist facilities.

In 1892, Muir joined with a few other California mountain lovers to form the Sierra Club, one of whose principal goals was to protect Yosemite Valley and ultimately to add it to the federal park that surrounded it.

That campaign would take another thirteen years before achieving success. Along the way, Muir, as president of the small but energetic and effective little organization, became an early advocate of the creation of forest reserves. "The battle we have fought," he told the members of the Sierra Club in 1895, "and are still fighting, for the forests is a part of the eternal conflict between right and wrong, and we cannot expect to see the end of it." This sentiment brought him the friendly acquaintance of Gifford Pinchot and Theodore Roosevelt, and Muir's was one of the earliest and most influential voices urging Roosevelt to establish the Forest Service with Pinchot as its head.

However friendly at the outset, the relationship between Muir and Pinchot probably could never have flourished. A chasm of perception lay between them, a difference suggested by Pinchot in *Breaking New Ground* when he told of the time the two of them had encountered a tarantula on the rim of the Grand Canyon during a trip in 1896. Muir, Pinchot wrote in bemusement, "wouldn't let me kill it. He said it had as much right there as we did." In any case, whatever chance there might have been for a permanent friendship was effectively stifled shortly after the creation of the Forest Service in 1905, when Pinchot eagerly endorsed San Francisco's plan to build a dam on the Tuolumne River in a portion of Yosemite National Park called the Hetch Hetchy Valley. The project, the city's spokesmen said in a claim sure of a sympathetic hearing in a Progressive-minded era, would free San Francisco from the grip of monopoly in the delivery of its water supply and in the generation of its electricity. It also would flood the Hetch Hetchy Valley, destroying a place whose beauty many people—Muir among them—considered the equal of Yosemite's.

The Hetch Hetchy affair was the first (though by no means the last) pure conflict between the two schools of conservation thought—use and preservation—and it pitted Muir and Pinchot against each other with precision. It would take a permit from the Interior Department followed by an act of Congress to allow the breach of a national park. Muir begged Roosevelt to order James Garfield not to issue the permit; Pinchot just as vigorously urged him to allow Garfield to grant it. Pinchot won and the permit was granted, leaving the next step to Congress. Muir and the preservationists managed to block congressional action from 1909 until 1913—largely because Taft, furious with Pinchot after the Ballinger affair, did not give the proposal the weight of his approval. But when Woodrow Wilson became President, his chosen Secretary of the Interior was Franklin K. Lane, a former city attorney for San Francisco, and it was not long before the utilitarians won the day in Congress. Lane had a bill to develop Hetch Hetchy introduced and late in 1913 it was passed and signed into law. "The destruction of the charming groves and gardens, the finest in all California," Muir wrote to Sierra Clubber William E. Colby, "goes to my heart. But in spite of Satan & Co. some sort of compensation must surely come out of this dark damn-dam-damnation."

Muir died the following year, and with his passing much went out of the life of the preservationist movement. Even in the Sierra Club there had been a painful split between those who opposed the damming of Hetch Hetchy and those who felt it more politic to let the city have it, and the years of World War I and the stuttering twenties were not fruitful ground for anything so abstract as wilderness preservation. The Sierra Club gradually subsided into an agreeable association of amateur mountaineers whose formerly militant publication, the *Bulletin,* was now largely given over to articles on climbing techniques and natural history. For the most part, the pursuit of the primitive among conservation groups was now confined to Robert Sterling Yard's National Parks Association, an organization started when Yard and National Park Service director Stephen T. Mather decided the parks needed a citizens' group to help broadcast their beauties and garner political support. Since then, Yard and Mather had arrived at their split over the question of concessions, roads, and tourist facilities, and Yard spent the tiny resources of the group—its membership barely topped a thousand—in an endless storm of newsletters, broadsides, petitions, and pamphlets in complaint of what he perceived as the degradation of the primeval qualities of the national parks under the management of both Mather and his successor, Horace M. Albright. It was a showy effort, but almost entirely the work of a single man.

The situation with regard to wildlife conservation at the beginning of Ickes's tenure was similarly divided. A movement that took on color from both the utilitarian and preservationist philosophies, it had begun as a sportsmen's crusade in the late nineteenth century when a combination of greedy private hunters—"game hogs," they came to be called—and the destruction of habitat by agricultural and urban growth was seriously threatening the survival of several game and nongame species. These forces had nearly exterminated the bison, had driven the passenger pigeon and the Carolina parakeet to the edge of extinction (the last representatives of both would die in captivity in 1914), and had forced many states to establish closed seasons for the hunting of elk, pronghorn, bighorn sheep, mountain goats, woodland caribou, and many bird species—and for some species, such as the California tule elk, hunting was banned altogether.

The American Ornithologists' Union, founded in 1883 to study, identify, and classify bird species, established a committee for the preservation of North American birds and went so far as to formulate legislation that states might use to prohibit the killing of endangered species, but many felt that state-by-state efforts to preserve wildlife were demonstrably inadequate. Among the doubters was George Bird Grinnell, editor of *Forest and Stream* (precursor of today's *Field & Stream*), and in 1886 he proposed in the pages of his magazine the creation of a national organization for the protection of wild birds. He called it the Audubon Society, and within two years it had a membership of fifty thousand—too many for Grinnell and his small magazine staff to deal with. The organization was allowed to wither.

Eight years later the idea returned, though from a different direction, when a number of bird lovers in Massachusetts banded together to protest the destruction of heron habitats and the hunting of snowy egrets and other "plume" birds for the ornamentation of women's hats. They called themselves the Massachusetts Audubon Society, and within ten years the idea had taken hold in thirty-five other states, each of which was represented by an independent Audubon Society. The collective voice of these groups—with the support of the American Ornithologists' Union and Grinnell's *Forest and Stream*—was instrumental in the passage of the Lacey Act of 1900, which prohibited the interstate shipment of any birds killed in violation of state laws. The cohesion of purpose was formalized in 1905 when the various groups organized the National Association of Audubon Societies under the leadership of William E. Dutcher, who said the association's purpose would be to stand "as a barrier between wild birds and animals and a very large unthinking class, and a smaller but more harmful class of selfish people."

Meanwhile, Grinnell—who would serve as a member of the board of directors of the Audubon Societies—had gone on to engineer the formation of the Boone and Crockett Club, a group of wealthy eastern sportsmen whose most notable member was Theodore Roosevelt and whose stated purposes included the desire to "work for the preservation of the large game of this country, and, so far as possible, to further legislation for that purpose, and to assist in enforcing the existing laws." This clause was first vindicated in 1894, when the Boone and Crockett Club became the major force behind passage of legislation designed to protect the birds and animals of Yellowstone National Park by prohibiting the killing or transportation of any wildlife, as well as the removal of mineral deposits and the logging of trees (these regulations became applicable to all the parks with passage of the Organic Act of 1916).

In 1911 the Winchester Repeating Arms Company made the Audubon Societies an offer that Grinnell, for one, found difficult to resist: $25,000 a year in funding from the major gun companies in exchange for an intensified effort to preserve game birds. Until a stroke cut him down in 1910, Dutcher had spent the organization's limited funds with more enthusiasm than good sense and it could have used the money. With Grinnell and Dutcher's successor, T. Gilbert Pearson, pushing the idea, the board of directors accepted the proposal. Two weeks later, however, responding to pressure from those who feared that the organization would become hostage to the gun interests, Pearson asked the board to rescind its acceptance. Reluctantly, it did so. Winchester and the other companies went on to form their own group, the American Game Protective Association, and Grinnell, irritated by Pearson's timidity, devoted most of his time to the formation of an alliance between his Boone and Crockett Club and the new organization.

In 1913 these disparate interests had come together in a rare concerted effort to bring the protection and regulation of migratory birds under the interstate commerce clause of the Constitution. The idea was loudly opposed by states' rights advocates in the South and West, but in a move reminiscent of that which had established the Forest Reserve clause of 1891, a rider was attached to an agricultural appropriations bill in March 1913, slid past the attention of the opposition, and was signed into law by President Taft in the last, inattentive hours of his administration. Power to impose and enforce hunting seasons, bag limits, and other regulations governing the hunting of migratory birds was placed in the hands of the U.S. Biological Survey, a Department of Agriculture agency previously devoted almost entirely to scientific inquiries, predator control, and the titular administration of the several dozen federal wildlife refuges that had been established around the country under provisions of the Forest Reserve clause and the Antiquities Act of 1906 (many of the refuges were in fact "managed" by local Audubon societies, since the Biological Survey did not have the manpower for the job).

After the singular victory of 1913, the wildlife conservation movement, like the wilderness preservation movement, lost much of its edge for a time. The American Game Protective Association, largely financed by gun companies and an acknowledged spokesman for game hunting and little else, thoroughly dominated the administrative actions of the Biological Survey, while the National Association of Audubon Societies, under Pearson's cautious leadership, became increasingly torpid and politically moribund even as it grew in size. But in the twenties a number of militant amateurs stepped into the vacuum and stirred the movement as nothing had since the early years of the Sierra Club.

The first was Will H. Dilg, a Chicago advertising man who had joined with a group of fishermen and hunters at the Chicago Athletic Club in 1922 to form the Izaak Walton League. Dilg became the League's first president, a driven man whose sentiments John Muir would have found agreeable. "I am weary of civilization's madness," Dilg wrote at one point, "and I yearn for the harmonious gladness of the woods and the streams. I am tired of your piles of buildings and I ache from your iron streets. I feel jailed in your greatest cities and I long for the unharnessed freedom of the big outside." He left his advertising job and devoted the rest of his life (he died of throat cancer in 1927) to building the Izaak Walton League into the largest conservation organization of its time; by the time of his death, it had a membership of more than a hundred thousand in three thousand chapters in forty-three states, and its magazine, *Outdoor America,* had attracted the work of such prominent writers as Zane Grey, Gene Stratton Porter, Theodore Dreiser, and Emerson Hough, as well as illustrations from John Held, Jr., the chronicler of the Flapper Era. In 1924, Dilg used the resources of both the membership and the magazine to achieve the league's first major accomplishment—the passage of legislation establishing a federal wildlife refuge along three hundred miles of the Upper Mississippi River.

He also threw his support behind the efforts of another ardent wildlife protector, William T. Hornaday, head of the Bronx Zoo and president of the Permanent Wild Life Protection Fund, a cantankerous, equally driven man who used both his positions to further a single-minded crusade for the preservation of wild creatures. The object of his fury during the twenties was a bill that the American Game Protective Association and the U.S. Biological Survey had been pushing in every session of Congress since 1920—legislation that would establish a string of federal refuges along the flyways of migratory birds. The purchase and administration of the refuges would be financed by a federal hunting license, and they would be used as public shooting grounds, effectively reversing national policy with regard to wildlife sanctuaries. Citing the gun company funding of the American Game Protective Association, Hornaday erupted: "The sportsmen are led by the men and organizations *interested in killing*—with profits, salaries, and emoluments at stake. The *only* money available for our much vaunted 'protection' is the blood money derived from the annual sale of licenses to kill game!!" T. Gilbert Pearson of the National Audubon Societies, in an effort to retain the support of the hunting establishment for his organization, backed the refuge bill, but Hornaday and Dilg found powerful allies in Congress—among them Fiorello La Guardia, then a representative from Arizona—and while Hornaday ultimately was forced to resign as director of the Bronx Zoo because of his unauthorized vituperations, the bill was stalled so long that the gun companies finally gave up on the idea in 1926, going so far as to announce their withdrawal of support from the American Game Protective Association "in the belief," a spokesman said, "that it would 'improve the Association's amateur standing' in the eyes of the public."

One of those who had joined the campaign as a literary point man was a young newspaperman and free-lance writer named Irving Brant, whose long article on the controversy in the *New York Herald Tribune* had concluded that "bird sanctuaries should be permanent and inviolate." After the questionable refuge bill died from lack of nourishment from the gun companies, Brant joined with Hornaday and others to support legislation for the establishment of a string of refuges *without* shooting privileges or the federal hunting license and for the reduction of bag limits on ducks and geese. Both became law in 1929.

T. Gilbert Pearson had opposed this new refuge legislation and had refused to testify in favor of reducing bag limits. This brought forth the wrath of Willard G. Van Name, a biologist with the American Museum of Natural History in Manhattan, who in June 1929 appeared as the principal author of a pamphlet entitled *A Crisis in Conservation*. Without naming names, but making himself perfectly clear nonetheless, Van Name castigated a large, well-financed conservation organization "which owing to entangled alliances performs its work with inertia, incompetency and procrastination." Van Name was ordered by the director of the museum never to do such a thing again, and the director—a longtime supporter of Pearson's rule at the Audubon Societies—issued a statement declaring that "The Museum is . . . of the opinion that the alleged 'Crisis in Conservation' exists largely in the minds of the authors of this pamphlet." This statement, in turn, inspired the annoyance of Irving Brant, who by now was a regular contributor to *Forest and Stream,* no longer edited by George Bird Grinnell. In December 1929, Brant wrote an editorial for the magazine in which, as he recalled in his memoirs, "I presented the Audubon record on conservation and described so extensive an interlock between that body and the museum that (I said) the 'defense of the Audubon Society by the American Museum turns out to be a defense of the Audubon Society by the Audubon Society.'"

Van Name's seditious pamphlet also came to the attention of former suffragette Rosalie Edge, an Audubon Societies member, avid birdwatcher, and reluctant socialite who had time and energy to spare. She presented herself at the 1929 annual meeting of the Audubon Societies (held at the American Museum), normally sedate affairs presided over by Pearson and his old-line conservative supporters in the organization. "My entrance made a stir," she recalled, "though no one knew me. That was the trouble; no stranger was expected. This was a family party of directors and office workers, with a few delegates from Audubon societies of other states." She agitated the room considerably when she rose to ask Pearson for a response to Van Name's charges. He and others came to his defense, Edge asked a few more questions, and Pearson finally shut her down by calling the debate because lunch was getting cold. No official mention of the incident was ever made in *Bird-Lore,* the Societies' official publication, but word of it got around swiftly enough in the small world of conservation, and Brant called on her in New York. He was, he said, "impressed by her keen mind, fighting spirit, and devotion to conservation. In February I wrote to her that I was 'very much inclined to write a detailed history of Pearson's record.' She replied, 'Our need is a small committee to sponsor such pamphlets. . . . Would you like to be a member of such a committee?' "

He would, and so would Willard Van Name, William T. Hornaday, and Davis Quinn, another employee of the American Museum and an Audubon dissident. This minuscule organization was given the title of the Emergency Conservation Committee, and with Name's financial backing, Hornaday's extensive mailing lists—accumulated over twenty years of conservation agitation—Brant's pamphleteering talents, and Rosalie Edge's refined but implacable lobbying skills, it went after Pearson over the next several years with such unrelenting determination that membership in the Audubon Societies declined by 60 percent and Pearson was finally forced to resign in September 1934. Under new leadership, the organization changed its name to the National Audubon Society and took on some of the militancy it had possessed under Dutcher. "Slowly, painfully, still clogged with reactionary directors," Brant remembered, "the society fought its way back toward the high standards of its founders—standards which two hundred state and local Audubon societies and eleven thousand individual members had never abandoned. At last a miracle, physiologically impossible, was achieved in the field of morality: the National Audubon Society recovered its virginity."

The committee did not stop with the restoration of the Audubon Society's virginity, but went on to wage a brand of guerrilla warfare for three decades against all those who in its opinion were bent on abusing the land and the creatures who lived upon it. "The committee," Brant wrote with some pride, "fully deserved the charge leveled against it by provoked critics, that it was a small, self-appointed body without a parent. Quinn dropped out after a time, the changing membership never exceeded five, and Mrs. Edge and I were the only ones continuously in it during the thirty years of its existence." The pride was forgivable. Almost unknown outside the conservation community and the federal agencies that so often incurred its displeasure, overshadowed throughout its life by more prominent groups like the Sierra Club and—ironically—the National Audubon Society, the Emergency Conservation Committee repeatedly proved itself one of the most effective voices for the land in the history of the conservation movement.

If the movement for the unqualified preservation of land and wildlife was incoherent and shattered into factions outside the government at the beginning of Ickes's tenure, within the government it operated, at best, as a kind of fifth column. In the National Park Service, an admirable agency but one largely given over to the principle that access and enjoyment by humans should take precedence over the primitive character of the parks, the idea was all but invisible. In the Bureau of Reclamation and the General Land Office, the notion of preservation, if ever discussed, would have been dismissed out of hand. Unlikely as it may have seemed, the only agency in which the idea had found any kind of home at all was the Forest Service, that temple of Pinchot's firm utilitarian prejudices.

The sentiment, even more remarkably, had developed during Greeley's term as chief forester, a time in which the lumber industry had established itself as the dominant influence in national forest management. In 1918, Arthur Carhart, a professional landscape architect, had joined the Forest Service as a "recreational engineer," and the following year was given the assignment of developing recreation plans for Trappers Lake in White Mountain National Forest, Colorado. After several months of studying this untouched wild place, he concluded that the best thing to do with it was to leave it alone. His recommendation came to the attention of Aldo Leopold, the assistant forester for District 3 (an area that encompassed most of the Southwest), who had been thinking about the idea of wilderness preservation in the forests for some time. They met and talked, and Leopold persuaded Carhart to put their conclusions in writing. The problem, Carhart wrote in the consequent memorandum,

> was, how far shall the Forest Service carry or allow to be carried manmade improvements in scenic territories, and whether there is not a definite point where all such developments, with the exception perhaps of lines of travel and

necessary sign boards, shall stop. There is a limit to the number of lands of shore line on the lakes; there is a limit to the number of lakes in existence; there is a limit to the mountainous areas of the world, and in each one of these situations there are portions of natural scenic beauty which are God-made, and the beauties of which of a right should be the property of all people.

Carhart's recommendation with regard to Trappers Lake was endorsed by his superiors and the area was left unmarred. Two years later, Leopold outlined his own thinking on the subject of wilderness in an article in the *Journal of Forestry:*

> When the national forests were created the first argument of those opposing a national forest policy was that the forests would remain a wilderness. . . . At this time, Pinchot enunciated the doctrine of "highest use," and its criterion, "the greatest good to the greatest number," which is and must remain the guiding principle by which democracies handle their natural resources.
>
> Pinchot's promise of development has been made good. The process must, of course, continue indefinitely. But it has already gone far enough to raise the question of whether the policy of development (construed in the narrow sense of industrial development) should continue to govern in absolutely every instance, or whether the principle of highest use does not itself demand that representative portions of some forests be preserved as wilderness.

"By 'wilderness,' " he went on, "I mean a continuous stretch of country preserved in its natural state, open to lawful hunting and fishing, big enough to absorb a two weeks' pack trip, and be kept devoid of roads, artificial trails, cottages, or other works of man."* In October 1922 he recommended to his superiors that a 540,000-acre segment of Gila and Datil national forests in New Mexico be set aside as the Forest Service's (and the nation's) first administratively designated wilderness area "in order to preserve at least one place in the Southwest where pack trips shall be the dominant play." And on June 3, 1924, a few days after Leopold left Albuquerque to become director of the Forest Products Laboratory in Madison, Wisconsin, District 3 Forester Frank Pooler put into place the Recreational Working Plan that established the Gila Wilderness Area.

The idea first promulgated by Carhart and Leopold slowly began to take on a bureaucratic dimension. In 1926, L. F. Kneipp, chief of the Forest Service's Division of Lands and Recreation, did a survey of roadless areas in forests similar to the Gila Wilderness, found seventy-four tracts

---

*It is interesting to compare Leopold's language with that in the preamble to the Wilderness Act passed forty-three years later: "A Wilderness, in contrast with those areas where man and his own works dominate the landscape, is hereby recognized as an area where the earth and its community of life are untrammeled by man, where man himself is a visitor who does not remain."

totaling 55 million acres that qualified, and helped to formulate what
came to be called the "L-20" regulations—administrative directives that
allowed the chief forester to encourage the designation by district foresters
of "primitive areas" within their forest regions, areas that were to be kept
wild in their "environment, transportation, habitation, and subsistence."
By 1932 the list of primitive areas had grown to sixty-three, embracing
8.4 million acres. On the face of it, this was a truly revolutionary
development, one that received remarkably little opposition from those
development interests one might have expected to rise up in anger. In
fact, the designation of these areas got by without appreciable protest
mainly because they included regions so high and wild that they had
attracted little commercial interest from the beginning—and because the
designations were entirely at the discretion of district foresters; should a
commercial interest develop, there was little doubt that it would be
accommodated.

This was not good enough for another young forester. He was Robert
Marshall, a graduate of the New York State College of Forestry, owner of a
master of forestry degree from the Harvard Forest (a forestry training
center owned and operated by Harvard University) and a Ph.D. in plant
pathology from Johns Hopkins University, and one of a small group of
incipient rebels within the Forest Service establishment. He also was the
son of the highly successful New York lawyer Louis Marshall, who had
been instrumental in establishing New York State's Adirondack Park and
Forest Preserve in the 1880s and who had imbued his children with both a
powerful love of the outdoors and equally vigorous liberal instincts. In
Robert these were swiftly translated into an avowed socialism and a
suspicion of rank capitalism that discovered grounds for complaint in,
among other things, what free enterprise had done to the forests of the
nation—and was still doing. This sentiment brought him to the attention of Gifford Pinchot—by then enjoying his second term as governor of
Pennsylvania (while keeping in touch with forestry matters)—who, in
January 1930, asked Marshall to help draft a "letter to foresters." Its
recommendations would include the strict federal regulation of private
forests and "a greatly increased program of public forests." The young
man was happy to oblige.

But Marshall's vision went beyond the limited utilitarian considerations of Pinchot. He was a true disciple of Leopold's wilderness gospel
and, in one of the first letters between them, early in 1930, he had called
Leopold "the Commanding General of the Wilderness Battle." In February of that year, Marshall outlined his own thinking in "The Problem of
the Wilderness," an article published in *Scientific Monthly*. America was

losing its wild country, he said: "Just a few years more of hesitation and the only trace of that wilderness which has exerted such a fundamental influence in molding American character will lie in the musty pages of pioneer books and the mumbling memories of tottering antiquarians." It was necessary, right now, he said, to undertake a thorough study of the nation's wilderness needs and to be forthrightly radical in designating additions to the tiny resource already established by the Forest Service— "because," he said, "it is easy to convert a natural area to industrial or motor usage, impossible to do the reverse; because the population which covets wilderness recreation is rapidly enlarging, and because the higher standard of living which may be anticipated should give millions the economic power to satisfy what is today merely a pathethic yearning."

As young and relatively inexperienced as he was (he was twenty-nine in 1930 and had spent comparatively little time in the field), Marshall's thinking was provocative and his influence and contacts were such that he was asked to contribute a chapter on forest recreation needs in the so-called Copeland Report of 1932, an analysis of the nation's forests that Congress had requested in a resolution introduced by Senator Royal Copeland of New York. The report, "A National Plan for American Forestry," completed after the elections of 1932 and one of the first documents approved and passed on to the President by Secretary of Agriculture Henry Wallace, was radical in its own right, declaring that private ownership of forests had led to widespread degradation of watersheds and soil depletion and that state and federal governments should join in a program of acquisition that would place a total of 224 million acres of forestland in public ownership; furthermore, the report said, the Forest Service should be given broad powers of regulation on whatever private forests might remain. For its part, Marshall's contribution pointed out that in 1931 the national forests had drawn more than eight million recreation visitors and the national parks and monuments more than three million, that wilderness recreation was growing in popularity, and that

> a greatly increased amount of journeying in the wilderness may fairly be expected. It would seem reasonable, therefore, to establish as wilderness areas all tracts for which no definitely higher present utility exists. If in the future the use of these tracts does not justify their retention as wilderness areas, it will always be possible to cut them up with additional roads. But once roads are built, it will be very difficult to restore the wilderness.

Marshall went on to recommend that ten million acres of designated wilderness be added to the current system of primitive areas at once—all that he apparently felt could be put forth realistically in an official proposal. In *The People's Forests,* his own radical dream for the future published in October 1933, he was a good deal more ambitious, not only advocating the public ownership of no less than 562 million acres of forests but raising the wilderness ante to 27 million acres.*

Polemics and proposals were not enough for Marshall, however. As early as his 1930 *Scientific Monthly* article, he had been persuaded that "There is just one hope of repulsing the tyrannical ambition of civilization to conquer every niche on the whole earth. That hope is the organization of spirited people who will fight for the freedom of the wilderness." In January 1935 he joined with Aldo Leopold, Robert Sterling Yard, and a handful of other "spirited people"—among them Benton MacKaye, a planner with the TVA, and Bernard Frank, an economist with the Forest Service—to found The Wilderness Society. "The Wilderness Society does not plan a large membership or a fine establishment," Yard wrote in the first issue of the organization's magazine, *The Living Wilderness* (echoing Marshall's sentiments precisely). "A few hundred or thousand picked workers will suffice, represented in states where there is wilderness to save. We are picking our members now, studying the field, planning methods, mapping opportunities, meantime spreading abroad, through every member, the intense need of wilderness salvation." The other founders asked Marshall to serve as president of the Society. He decided to clear the idea with his boss, writing him that the organization was designed to fight "the propaganda spread by the American Automobile Association, the various booster organizations, and innumerable chamber of commerces, which seem to find no peace as long as any primitive tract in America remains open to mechanization," and that he did not feel that the presidential position would interfere with his government job. While his boss agreed with the goals of the new organization and held no affection for chambers of commerce, he did fear a conflict of interest; he suggested that it would be better for Marshall to do the work of a president and let someone else carry the title. Marshall concurred, officially remaining in the background, while funding the organization largely from his own pocket and effectively dictating its policies; the Society had no official president for its first ten years, though Yard served the function of a public voice as secretary and editor of *The Living Wilderness.*

The boss who had expressed his sympathies with the purposes of The

---

* It was the formidable Marshall's second book that year. The first was *Arctic Village,* the account of a year spent living among Eskimos and a few white prospectors in the tiny Alaska village of Wiseman. The book was published to warm reviews and became a Literary Guild selection for June.

Wilderness Society but had suggested that Marshall stay out of the limelight was not Henry Wallace, Secretary of Agriculture, but Harold L. Ickes, Secretary of the Interior.

Robert Marshall had been one of the earliest and most vocal supporters of John Collier for the job of commissioner of Indian Affairs, writing Ickes on March 28, 1933, that Collier was "so far ahead of any other possible candidate" that it would be nothing short of a "tragedy to the Indians if he were not appointed." In August 1933, Collier had rewarded this support by appointing Marshall—with Ickes's full approval—head of forestry, grazing, and wildlife management on the BIA's reservations. It was the beginning of a relationship between the young forester and the Secretary that would never reach the level of what could be called friendship, but one in which the two men shared—however unlikely such an alliance may have appeared on the surface—a common love of wilderness.

In holding that sentiment, Ickes was nearly alone among the New Dealers—at least at his level of service. Franklin Roosevelt was indisputably a dedicated conservationist, an amateur forester who had planted and tended half a million trees on his Hyde Park estate and who was fond of listing his occupation as "tree farmer" on various official forms. He was the first President since his cousin Theodore to embrace the concept of stewardship with a vigor that would establish it as deliberate national policy, and his understanding of the principles of conservation was both broad and deep. "A forest is not solely so many board feet of lumber to be logged when market conditions make it profitable," he told the Society of American Foresters in January 1935.

> It is an integral part of our natural land covering, and the most potent factor in maintaining nature's delicate balance in the organic and inorganic worlds. In his struggle for selfish gain, man has often heedlessly tipped the scales so that nature's balance has been destroyed, and the public welfare has usually been on the short-weighted side. Such public necessities, therefore, must not be destroyed because there is profit for someone in their destruction. The preservation of the forests must be lifted above mere dollars and cents considerations.

Furthermore, Roosevelt could and did recognize the value of recreation to the psychological well-being of the nation and would expand the national park and monument systems as no other President before him; he could even appreciate the spiritual character of the outdoors experience. At the dedication of Shenandoah National Park in the summer of 1936, he would speak movingly of those American families who would seek that summer, as in all the summers to come, the smell of the woods and the wind in the trees. They will forget the rush and the strain of all the other long weeks of the year, and for a short time at least, the days will be good for their bodies and good for their souls. Once more they will lay hold of the perspective that comes to men and women who every morning and night can lift up their eyes to Mother Nature. There is merit for all of us in the ancient tale of the giant Antaeus, who, every time he touched his Mother Earth, arose with strength renewed a hundredfold.

Nor were such words the convenient mouthings of the politician; they were the expressed belief of the man. Still, however sincere and deeply rooted, Roosevelt's brand of conservation was far closer to the utilitarian traditions of Gifford Pinchot than to the preservationist instincts of a Leopold or a Marshall. If he believed in stewardship, it was stewardship for human use; if he believed in recreation, it was a democratic recreation, one to be enjoyed by and available to all Americans, including those like himself who could only embrace the outdoor experience by automobile. There was, he emphasized in the Shenandoah speech, a powerful "need for recreational areas, for parkways which will give to men and women of moderate means the opportunity, the invigoration and the luxury of touring and camping amid scenes of great natural beauty." He had little sympathy for wilderness as an abstract idea, or much appreciation of wilderness landscape as pure aesthetic—particularly if it was not covered by trees. "It looks dead," he said after his first visit to the Grand Canyon.

His Secretary of the Interior shared with him a decent regard for stewardship in the name of human use; he would spend billions of dollars proving it. At the same time, Ickes brought to his job a fully formed and genuine appreciation of wild country that had been nurtured in him from his childhood days in the tangled, woodsy beauty of the land around his boyhood home of Altoona and reinforced by his trips to the West in the years before and after World War I. On March 3, 1934, he initiated a series of weekly broadcasts over NBC on the virtues of the National Park System. He began by recounting his first horseback trip into Glacier National Park with a friend in 1916, and if his description utilized every cliché he could lay hands on, it was no less valid as an illustration of his depth of feeling:

I love nature. I love it in practically every form—flowers, birds, wild animals, running streams, gem-like lakes, and towering, snow-clad mountains. All of these Glacier Park has—and much more besides.

Imagine a great valley literally massed with lovely flowers in full bloom. A riot of color. No formal garden this, meticulously planted with an iris here, a phlox there, and a peony yonder, but such a planting as only nature itself could plan or afford. As we went higher and higher into the mountains, the flowers, while of the same variety as those in the valleys, became smaller and smaller until way above the tree line where bitter winds blew constantly even in the bright sun and frost formed every night, we found some of these same flowers blooming on plants of alpine size. But the coloring! The higher up the mountains the flowers grew, the more vivid and deeply colored were the flowers, until one drew one's breath at their marvelous beauty!

This, from the man whose Bureau of Reclamation dams and sundry PWA projects would take hold of nature and shape it to human purposes as never before in history. But if he endorsed and promoted such uses, he would demonstrate repeatedly during his years as Interior Secretary that he was every bit as passionate in his determination to preserve the land in its wild state. It was a contradiction that apparently raised no questions in his own mind (although it did from time to time in the minds of both the utilitarian and the preservationist wings of conservation, each of which would periodically view him either as the worst enemy or the best friend conservation ever had, depending upon the issue at hand). With equal sincerity, he could stand and deliver a speech in San Francisco in October 1934 celebrating the delivery of the first water from the reservoir that had flooded John Muir's incomparable Hetch Hetchy Valley, declaring it a great moment for human vision and foresight, and less than four months later could stand before a conference of state park authorities in the Interior Department auditorium and defy his President and his own director of the National Park Service, who wanted to extend the Blue Ridge Parkway through Great Smoky Mountains National Park in what was billed as a "Skyline Drive." The beautiful Blue Ridge, choreographed by the National Park Service, built by the Interior Department's Bureau of Public Roads with CCC labor, and financed entirely by PWA funding, was just under construction as one of the showcase parkways of the New Deal; Ickes liked it well enough, but believed that it should go no farther than the northern boundary of the Great Smoky Mountains park, and said so at the state park authorities meeting in a statement that neither Bob Marshall nor Aldo Leopold would have been reluctant to endorse (a version of it would, in fact, be reprinted in two successive issues of *The Living Wilderness*):

I am not in favor of building any more roads in the National Parks than we have to build. I am not in favor of doing anything along the lines of so-called improvements that we do not have to do. This is an automobile age, but I do not have much patience with people whose idea of enjoying nature is dashing along a hard road at fifty or sixty miles an hour. I am not willing that our beautiful areas ought to be opened up to people who are either too old to walk, as I am, or too lazy to walk, as a great many young people are who ought to be ashamed of themselves. I do not happen to favor the scarring of a wonderful mountainside just so that we can say we have a skyline drive. It sounds poetical, but it may be an atrocity. . . .

I think we ought to keep as much wilderness area in this country as we can. It is easy to destroy a wilderness; it can be done very quickly, but it takes nature a long time, even if we let nature alone, to restore for our children what we have ruthlessly destroyed. . . .

There ought to be many exceptions when it comes to dealing with wilderness areas, with regions of natural beauty. We ought to resolve all doubts in favor of letting nature take its course. In a field where nature is preeminently the master artist, where nature can do much more than we can do with all our cleverness, with all of our arts and with all of our best efforts, we cannot improve but can only impair if we undertake to alter.

This was in the way of a manifesto, and he meant every word of it. The Great Smoky Mountains portion of the skyline drive was never constructed, and he consistently resisted the building of highways where he felt highways had no business being built. "We are making a great mistake in this generation," he told a group of road builders in his office early in 1937, as recorded by Marshall. "We are just repeating the same mistake in a different form that our forefathers have made. Instead of keeping areas . . . which will add to the wealth, health, comfort and well-being of the people, if we see anything that looks attractive we want to open up speedways through it so the people can enjoy the scenery at 60 miles an hour." He was quite as earnest about wilderness preservation. When Marshall established 4.8 million acres of designated wilderness on the Indian reservations before leaving Interior to become chief of the Division of Recreation and Lands in the Forest Service in the spring of 1937, it was with the encouragement of both Collier and Ickes. And in the great park battles to come, the Secretary—this hard-boiled refugee from the meanly pragmatic street warfare of Chicago politics—would repeatedly validate his position as one of only three Interior secretaries in American history to understand fully and value the importance of wilderness preservation to the spiritual and ecological well-being of the nation.*

Before that elegantly foresightful theme could fairly be established, however, there was something more immediate that had to be dealt with, a disaster that stood as one of the most telling examples since the "Big Die-Up" of the 1880s of what could result when human greed and ignorance would not acknowledge the limits of what the natural world could—or would—endure.

* The others were Stewart Udall and Cecil Andrus.

CHAPTER

· 36 ·

The Dust Cloud That Voted

NATURE, as George Perkins Marsh warned nearly seventy years before the beginning of the New Deal, has a way of making its points in dramatic fashion, and by the spring of 1934 it took no modern conservationist—whether of the Pinchot or the Muir variety—to figure out that something dreadful had gone wrong. The ground had been prepared for some kind of ghastly climax for more than a decade, and it began in the summer of 1930, when severe drought struck a wide band of America from Maryland and Virginia to Missouri and Arkansas. The next year the drought spread like an arid shadow into the Great Plains, and for most of the next decade drought combined with heat to transform the middle portion of America into a wretched caldron of blistered lands and blasted hopes.

Drought and Depression drove thousands from their farms to wander miserably in a diaspora that carried them west into the more fruitful valleys of the Pacific Coast, where they found a new kind of slavery as migrant farm laborers and a bitter immortality in John Steinbeck's *Grapes of Wrath*. Those who clung to the wasted land as long as they could had their misery emulsified forever in the work of photographers like Dorothea Lange and Arnold Rothstein or measured and mourned in the pages of official and unofficial reports from investigators like Lange's husband, sociologist and economist Paul Schuster Taylor, and newspaperwoman Lorena Hickok. Sent into the West by Harry Hopkins in the summer of 1933, Hickok found eight hundred families living on paltry state relief in Bottineau County, North Dakota, existing amid conditions that would be duplicated in one degree or another everywhere she traveled: "Their houses had gone to ruins. No repairs for years. Their furniture, dishes, cooking utensils—no replacements in years. No bed linen, and quilts and blankets all gone. A year ago their clothing was in rags. This year they hardly have rags."

It was not just the blind forces of an impersonal nature that had driven the land to ruin, however. The boom years of World War I had persuaded small farmers and large farmers alike to expand their operations tremendously, plowing under more and more of the soil-holding native grasses and planting the ground in wheat. When the drought and the winds came, the ground was exposed and fragile, mined of nutrition and beginning to vanish through erosion even before the spring of 1934. "Approximately 35,000,000 acres of formerly cultivated land have been essentially destroyed for crop production," the 1934 *Yearbook of Agriculture* (published in April that year) noted, going on to say that "100,000,000 acres now in crops have lost all or most of the topsoil; 125,000,000 acres of land now in crops are rapidly losing topsoil; and additional area is suffering from erosion in some degree."

But farming was only part of the problem. On about 850 million acres that lay west of the hundredth meridian, livestock grazing was the dominant use—and if the farmers of the Great Plains had overcultivated their land during the boom years, the graziers of the West had allowed their cattle and sheep to clip much of theirs clear to the desiccated soil. The situation was exacerbated when the arrival of the Depression drove stock prices down with sickening force—the average price of a cow fell from $58.49 in 1929 to $17.29 in 1934, of a sheep from $11.12 to $4.01. The response was to increase volume by putting more animals on the land. As a consequence, by the middle of the decade more than half the grazing land in the western United States was, by Department of Agriculture estimates, in a state of "extreme" or "severe" soil depletion. A little over 173 million acres of the total of 850 million were on the "vacant and unappropriated lands" of the public domain under the administration of the Interior Department's General Land Office, and on these, almost completely unregulated grazing had created severe and extreme depletion on closer to two-thirds of the land. The eighty million acres of grazing lands in the national forests were in better condition, some control over the use of the land having been exercised by the Forest Service since

1905—though even here nearly twelve million acres were in trouble.

More than forty-five million cattle, horses, sheep, goats, and even a few thousand hogs had been turned out on this public land. The effect was eloquently put forth by Harold Ickes in October 1934:

> An evil that is the twin of the destruction of our forests is the destruction of the public range through over-grazing. Herds of sheep and cattle, totaling more heads than the range can reasonably support, literally stand about hungrily waiting for a venturesome blade of grass to stick its head through the soil. . . .
>
> The result of it all is that our land, in wide areas, is being stripped of its covering of soil, or gullied beyond the possibility of redemption. . . .
>
> The seriousness of wind erosion was brought home very forcibly last May to those of us who live on the Atlantic Seaboard. We were made to appreciate by a natural demonstration that we will not soon forget, how our western plains . . . are being denuded of fecund top soil at an alarming rate.

The demonstration of which he spoke was impressive indeed, even terrifying to those nearest to it. "Dusty old dust," songwriter Woody Guthrie called it, and it curled up in black storms as high as mountains, boiling clouds of dust that rose, first, from the naked grazing lands of the West, then blew east across the plains, the winds stripping more and more exposed soil from the earth and lifting it into the otherworldly continent of dust that churned across the horizon to choke the lungs and obliterate light. Here is Beadle County, South Dakota, on Armistice Day (November 11), 1933:

> By mid-morning a gale was blowing, cold and black. By noon it was blacker than night, because one can see through night and this was an opaque black. It was a wall of dirt one's eyes could not penetrate, but it could penetrate the eyes and ears and nose. It could penetrate to the lungs until one coughed up black. If a person was outside, he tied his handkerchief around his face, but he still coughed up black. . . .
>
> When the wind died and the sun shone forth again, it was on a different world. There were no fields, only sand drifting into mounds and eddies that swirled in what was now but an autumn breeze.

In 1932 there had been fourteen regional dust storms that reduced visibility to less than a mile; in 1933, thirty-eight, including the Armistice Day storm whose dust blew all the way to New York City; in 1934 there had been only twenty-two, but none before it or after it matched the power of the storm of May 1934. Between May 9 and May 11, an estimated 350 million tons of soil were scooped up from Montana, Wyoming, Nebraska, and the Dakotas and carried eastward at jet-stream speeds approaching one hundred miles an hour. In Chicago that night, four pounds of dust for every person in the city drifted down and clogged the streets like filthy snow. On May 10, Washington, D.C. turned dark at midday, and the streetlights were on at noon in New York and Boston the next day. For the next forty-eight hours, ships in the Atlantic reported dust on their decks. And back in the heartland, one woman recorded in her diary at the end of May, "Life in what the newspapers call 'the Dust Bowl' is becoming a gritty nightmare." The nightmare would continue periodically for most of the rest of the decade.

It was to deal with one aspect of the problem that Ickes, acting under his authority as administrator of Public Works, had established a Soil Erosion Service within the Department of the Interior on August 25, 1933. Hugh Hammond Bennett, a soils scientist who had been working in the Department of Agriculture's Bureau of Soils since the first decade of the century, was transferred over to Interior to run the new agency. With a PWA grant of $10 million, Bennett set to work establishing a program whereby operations utilizing CCC labor were set up on cooperating farms to demonstrate such techniques as contour plowing and terracing to preserve soil.

Ickes was not allowed to keep the agency long. From the beginning, Henry Wallace believed this program should have been placed in Agriculture, not Interior, but had held off doing anything about it until a time when PWA funding for the program was scheduled to run out and it would have to be either renewed or abandoned. Late in 1934 he broached the idea to Ickes, who wrote in his diary, "I am half inclined to agree with him that it belongs in Agriculture, but the other day the President brought up the subject and I found him inclined to believe it belonged here."

If so, Roosevelt soon enough changed his mind, encouraged in that direction by both Wallace and Donald Richberg, who was then still executive director of the National Emergency Council. On February 28, 1935, Richberg responded to a Presidential inquiry on the subject by assuring FDR that he had the authority to make such a transfer, that the agency logically belonged in Agriculture, and that if it was going to be transferred, then it ought to be transferred immediately. "I have not taken this matter up with the Secretary of the Interior," he added, and we can believe him. Wallace put his own oar in a week later. "I have the feeling that Secretary Ickes has no illusions whatever as to the character of the functions of the Soil Erosion Service and where it belongs," he told Roosevelt, "but he is holding on to it because he thinks it is good trading stock."

On March 20, while Ickes was away on a tour of the Everglades, FDR decided he wanted the transfer accomplished immediately. Informed in Miami of the President's intentions, Ickes telegraphed an appeal for a delay, but to no avail. Roosevelt insisted that Ickes sanction a special meeting of the PWA board to authorize the transfer, without Ickes's presence. The Secretary agreed, in no good humor. On March 22 the meeting was held and the necessary resolution passed, and upon his return on March 23, Ickes signed the order making the transfer official. "I have no disposition to submit to many incidents of this sort," Ickes sputtered futilely in his diary.

A few weeks later, Congress passed the Soil Erosion Act, establishing a Soil Conservation Service as a permanent agency within the Department of Agriculture—though not without a little extra inspiration at least partially orchestrated by Hugh Bennett, the man slated to direct the program. Invited to testify before a congressional committee on the need for a permanent soil service, Bennett stalled his appearance until a dust storm that had originated in New Mexico reached Washington. "This, gentlemen," he then announced, indicating the dusty gloom outside the windows of the committee chamber, "is what I have been talking about!" The legislation was duly passed on April 19, and under Bennett and his successors, the agency would go on to establish itself as one of the most durable and best-loved programs of the New Deal. "Listen," one farmer told a reporter. "If this country could produce the trainloads of products that it did before we knew anything about how to farm this land, before we had put this great program into effect, what will it be capable of in the future?"

Even before he was deprived of the Soil Erosion Service, Ickes had acquired another agency to comfort him. This one, too, was designed to meet the crisis of land abuse of which the great dust storms served as grim reminders. Early in the first session of the Seventy-third Congress, Representative Edward Taylor of Colorado introduced a bill that would have given the Department of the Interior the power to regulate grazing on the appropriate lands of the public domain and the national forests. A long-time enemy of federal "intervention" in the business of the West, Taylor changed his mind in this instance, he said, "because the citizens were unable to cope with the situation under existing trends and circumstances. The job was too big and interwoven for even the states to handle with satisfactory co-ordination. On the western slope of Colorado and in nearby states I saw waste, competition, overuse, and abuse of valuable range lands and watersheds eating into the very heart of western economy." Ickes had testified in favor of the bill, but had objected to one provision that would have given individual states veto power over federal grazing regulations. As a result, the bill had never gotten out of committee.

Taylor reintroduced it immediately when the second session of the Seventy-third Congress began, this time without the provision regarding veto power. Roosevelt sent a letter to the appropriate House and Senate committees declaring his approval of the bill, and Ickes and Wallace joined forces in support of it in a rare expression of agreement—an accord that slowly weakened and finally collapsed as the bill went through the amendment process on its way toward passage.

The legislation delivered to the President for his signature in June 1934 empowered him to withdraw all 173 million acres of public domain from entry under any of the existing land laws, "pending its final disposal," thereby at least modifying the policy of systematic disposal that had governed the management of the public domain since the eighteenth century. Grazing districts that would embrace as many as eighty million acres were to be established—including lands withdrawn from Forest Service territory, if the President so determined. The Secretary of the Interior was empowered to formulate regulations for the protection and use of the lands within the districts, to issue ten-year permits for the grazing of livestock, giving preference to those individuals "within or near a district who are landowners engaged in the livestock business, bona fide occupants or settlers, or owners of water or water rights," and to determine the fees for such permits (in the beginning and for many years thereafter, five cents per cow per month and one cent per sheep per month).

In fact, the system was designed to limit any direct influence the Secretary or anyone else in Washington could exercise. Those who had painstakingly hammered out the final versions that had passed the House and Senate, been referred to conference committee, molded into an acceptable set of agreements, then given final approval, maintained that the people of the West had become bitter over what they considered the dictatorial rule of the Forest Service in its administration of national forest grazing privileges (which the West invariably considered "rights"). In the structure of administration that the law set up, therefore, the districts would be governed at least in part by an advisory board comprising seven cattlemen and seven sheepmen elected by the holders of grazing permits and one Grazing Service employee appointed by the Interior Department, preferably a local individual. Furthermore, state advisory boards similarly made up of those in the regions affected by the law would be established, and the Civil Service Commission was directed to prepare job descriptions for positions throughout the Division of Grazing—or Grazing Service, as it came to be called—that would emphasize practical field experience in the public land states, thus further ensuring that local influence would be exercised at the local level.

And, as final gestures to local concerns, Representative Pat McCarran of Nevada had engineered two important amendments. The first declared that no renewal of any permit "shall be denied, if such denial will impair the value of the livestock unit of the permittee, if such unit is pledged as security for any bona fide loan." The second stated, among other things, that nothing in the Taylor Grazing Act would restrict any state laws "heretofore enacted . . . or that may hereafter be enacted as regards public health or public welfare." The conference committee took some of the muscle out of the first addendum by adding a statement that no "permittee complying with the rules and regulations laid down by the Secretary of the Interior" would be denied renewal, and managed to neutralize McCarran's other addendum by adding its own: "*Provided,* however, that nothing in this section shall be construed as limiting or constricting the power and authority of the United States."

Any way one viewed it, the Taylor Grazing Act was a complicated bundle of compromises, and Wallace didn't like it at all, passing on to Roosevelt an assessment of the act written by his chief forester, Ferdinand A. Silcox, and recommending that the President not sign the legislation. "It is not now a conservation measure as originally designed," Silcox wrote. "Instead, it is a distribution measure, with the policy of ultimate distribution openly stated in the first sentences in the words 'pending its final disposal.'" Furthermore, Silcox went on, "The bill grants permanent and inalienable rights to the present users of the range, conferring upon them substantial property rights which the Secretary could neither diminish, restrict, nor impair. . . . In its original form, as approved by the Department [of Agriculture], the lands were not burdened by any such servitude." Finally, he maintained, McCarran's second amendment was not sufficiently watered down by the conference committee proviso—the states thus had, in effect, veto power over any regulation established under the provisions of the act and it was thereby rendered all but meaningless.

Both Interior's solicitor, Nathan Margold, and Attorney General Homer Cummings disagreed with this interpretation of the law, and on June 28, 1934, Roosevelt signed the Taylor Grazing Act. Five months later, worried that a sudden jump in the number of land entries under the Homestead Act and the Stock Raising Act were being made in an effort to frustrate the purposes of the new law before its provisions could be put in place, Ickes decided to recommend to Roosevelt that he exercise the power granted him under the act to withdraw all of the public domain from entry under the land laws—but not before the Secretary had a run-in with his newly appointed head of the Grazing Division. This individual was Farrington R. Carpenter of Colorado, a breeder of Hereford cattle and, as Ickes described him, "a graduate of Harvard and Harvard Law School, but he looks like a typical cow man." On Thursday morning, November 22, 1934, Ickes had called Carpenter, Slattery, and a few others into his office to discuss the withdrawal matter and the wording of the Executive Order to be submitted to the President. That afternoon, after his regular press conference, Ickes was maddened to learn that Carpenter had held his own meeting with reporters from United Press and the Associated Press and had not only told them of the proposed withdrawal but had actually shown them copies of the agenda of Ickes's meeting—all of this before Ickes himself had said a public word about it or even discussed it with Roosevelt. Called into the Secretary's office to explain himself, Carpenter, Ickes wrote, "naively said that he had told the newspaper correspondents that he was giving them this information in confidence. I raised particular hell. I wouldn't have been surprised if Carpenter had resigned and I confess I wouldn't have cared much. However, he assured me that he realized his mistake and that a similar one would not occur again." It was the beginning of yet one more troubled employer-employee relationship.

On November 24, Roosevelt signed the Executive Order withdrawing public-domain lands in twelve western states from entry under any of the land laws; a little over two months after that, he would withdraw lands in another twenty-five states.* By then, it was agreed among those who had crafted passage of the Grazing Act that eighty million acres was not enough; and by the end of the year, amending legislation that empowered the President to include as many as 142 million acres within grazing districts was passed without significant opposition.

* It was not quite as if a gate had slammed shut, however. The law required a period of public hearings in each of the grazing districts before full withdrawal could become official, and during the interim, a number of Stock Raising and Homestead claims continued to be made. Moreover, once the withdrawn lands had been inventoried and classified as to their most appropriate uses, those suitable for entry could he opened up again. Even so, from 1935 on, entries under any land laws dropped precipitously. In 1934, for instance, there had been 7,741 Homestead entries; six years later, the number had fallen to 383. Finally, it should be noted that the Territory of Alaska was exempted entirely from the provisions of the Taylor Grazing Act.

ⰓⰓⰓⰓⰓ

In February 1935, Ickes traveled to Denver to address a conference of westerners who were meeting to discuss public-domain policy under the Taylor Grazing Act. In his speech the Secretary attempted to reassure his listeners of the benign character of the law by wrapping it securely in the banner of Progressivism. "I want to emphasize," he told them,

> that the policy of the Federal Government, as expressed in this law, will be not only to protect and administer the range in the interest of your essential industry; it will be equally our policy to give to the small, independent stockman that protection which he so badly needs and which he has so sadly lacked in times past. The public range is to be devoted to the greatest good of the greatest number of those dependent upon it. Size will not count as against this dedication to the common good; political influence will be of no avail. In more ways than one, the Taylor Grazing Law is not merely a regulatory measure to upbuild and maintain the public range and to control its use in the interest of the stockmen of the nation. It is a Magna Charta upon which the prosperity, well-being and happiness of large sections of this great western country of ours will in the future depend.

Brave words, sincerely delivered and politely applauded, but as it happened, irrelevant. However necessary it had been to attempt some rational means of controlling the use of the public domain, and however difficult it had been to contrive and pass *any* sort of meaningful legislation in a Congress whose relevant committees were almost entirely dominated by western members dedicated to serving the interests and parroting the philosophies of those who controlled the economy of the West, the Taylor Grazing Act was seriously flawed by the very compromises necessary to its passage. Just as Wallace and Silcox had warned, the awarding of grazing permits on a preferential basis assured that those who already dominated local economies—often to the point of monopoly—would continue to do so. Furthermore, while the permit system was conceived as a means by which the number of animals on the land could be regulated, the virtual guarantee of renewal for permits used as collateral would entwine the permit system with the complexities of local economies and cripple its effectiveness as a regulatory device: every time an animal was taken from the land, the act would be perceived as a blow against property values. Finally, the concession of local participation through local boards assured, in the end, local control. Most of the advisory board appointees who were supposed to represent the interests of the Interior Department, after all, were men who were in the livestock business themselves, men who were derived from the local population and could not be expected to challenge their friends and neighbors with any consistency. Much the same could be said of the district managers who were chosen to administer the law in the field.

The director of the Grazing Service made no secret of where his own loyalties resided. "I am of the philosophy," Carpenter told the members of a Denver grazing conference in January 1935, "that the quicker land is put under private ownership, the better off the state to which it belongs will be. I am in favor of turning the government land over to the states and thence to the citizens as soon as possible." This statement—coming from a man who was charged with assuring the wise use of land that the government, his employer, had no intention of turning over to the states—was only slightly mitigated when he added, with apparent regret, that the grazing districts were "units of government, and thereby hangs a tale that may be with us for thousands of years." It is not surprising, then, to learn that in March 1937, as Ickes reported in his diary, he felt compelled to

> set up an Advisory Committee on Grazing on account of my recent discovery that Carpenter and Walters [Carpenter's assistant] have been more or less playing a game of their own with respect to grazing. In the matter of several appeals to the Department from decisions in the field the cases have been kicked around until the questions to be solved have become moot. Through this committee that I have set up I expect to keep a closer watch and a better control over the Grazing Division.

Neither his committee nor his later dismissal of Carpenter (who would go on to become a stockmen's lobbyist), however, would ever be able to get genuine control of the Grazing Service out of local hands. The administration of the law would remain an unresolved frustration throughout Ickes's tenure, forever hampered by its own structure and sniped at constantly by those western congressmen—led by the persistent and talented Pat McCarran—who resented even the little control the federal government managed to impose on lands that belonged to all Americans.

And the land itself? Imperfect as it was, the Taylor Grazing Act did make a difference. The abuses that had been perpetrated by what Carpenter called "free-loading on the public domain by the cowboys and the sheepherders" were effectively stifled by a permit system dominated by larger, more stable enterprises, and these, too, began to use their land with a little less greed and a good deal more intelligence under a program of what was, to a very large degree, self-regulation. Even so, much of the grazing land in the West would continue to be abused and much that was not would never fully recover from what had been done to it over all the decades of careless ignorance—not even in 1941, when the healing rains finally began to come again.

CHAPTER

· 37 ·

Stewardship and Strife

ACCORDING TO HIS MEMOIRS, at least, conservationist Irving Brant may have been the first to offer a proposition that would remain at the center of one of the longest, noisiest, and most controversial squabbles in the annals of American bureaucracy. On March 31, 1933, he says, he wrote to Roosevelt, urging a reorganization of the departments of Interior and Agriculture. In brief, he argued that such agencies as the Forest Service and the Biological Survey did not belong in Agriculture, which had no bureaucratic affinity for conservation matters, and that all *non*conservation agencies did not belong in Interior, since their presence merely confused an agency that should be devoted entirely to the preservation of land and wildlife. He proposed, therefore, that

> all bureaus primarily devoted to conservation be placed in the Interior Department, that all others be eliminated from it, and that the name be changed by congressional enactment to Department of Conservation. The change in name may appear superficial, but it is not. It will wipe out the mortgage claimed by the public land states, establish a new principle, set a new standard, centralize responsibility for it, and focus public attention upon that responsibility.

Whether Brant's letter planted the seed for the controversy is uncertain. What is certain is that the New Deal had hardly begun before Henry Wallace and Harold Ickes were locked in combat—usually polite, sometimes not so polite—over the question of whose department was better equipped to handle the conservation duties of the government. Reorganization was much in the air in the early weeks of the new administration. During his campaign, Roosevelt had declared that "Before any man enters my Cabinet he must pledge . . . complete cooperation with me looking to economy and reorganization in his department," and while he had actually demanded no such pledge, the Economy Act passed during the "Hundred Days" gave him broad authority for two years to reorganize the Executive Branch to suit his purposes. It was not at all inconceivable, then, that both Agriculture and Interior would face some juggling of responsibilities in the months to come.

Apparently, one of the earliest rumors was that the Forest Service would be moved out of Agriculture's bailiwick and be placed in Interior, just as Brant had proposed (though there is no evidence to suggest that the rumor stemmed from his letter of March). Ickes was not against the idea, but he got a rude shock on April 19, 1933, when, as he noted in his diary, a rumor had come to him that afternoon that "instead of the National Forests coming over here from the Department of Agriculture, the latest plan contemplates the transfer to Agriculture of the National Parks from this Department. As I am particularly interested in the National Parks, this is a matter of real concern to me and I hope it isn't true." That night, during an informal speech before the annual National Parks dinner of the American Civic Association, he was a good deal more forceful: "I heard the disturbing rumor this afternoon that it was proposed to transfer the Bureau of National Parks to the Department of Agriculture. I hope not. I am very fond of Henry Wallace. He is one of the ablest men in the Cabinet. But one who could not love the national parks more than I do, and I know he would give no better attention to them than I will."

Ickes could hardly have been made easy by Roosevelt's firm lack of opinion on the matter. "Should the Park Service go into the Department of Agriculture or should the Forestry Service go into the Department of the Interior?" the President mused after a question at a press conference later that spring. "Well, it is probable that at this particular time I won't do anything on that. I want to have a little more argument on that during the summer." He continued to do nothing about it during the rest of 1933, leaving both Ickes and Wallace slowly twisting in the wind of his ambiguity, each ready and willing to believe the worst of the other's plans.

While it was not in his nature to maintain a passive attitude for long, Ickes himself refrained from doing anything about it until March 7, 1934, when he bluntly asked Roosevelt where he stood on the question of transferring the Forest Service to Interior. When the President expressed some reservations about the political atmosphere, Ickes noted in his diary, "I told him that I believed the Senators and Congressmen are distinctly in favor of the move and pointed out to him the obvious advantages of such a transfer. He went into the matter in question in some detail and admitted that Forestry should be in this Department. In the end he said that if I could bring it about, it would be quite all right as far as he was concerned." Roosevelt's skill at persuading others that he was in agreement with them without ever quite coming out and stating it in so many words was one of his most useful and infuriating talents. It is possible that this apparent endorsement was one more exercise in Rooseveltian deception; it also is possible that Roosevelt meant what Ickes thought he meant. Ickes proceeded as if it were, in any case, opening discussions on the topic with his allies in Congress.

Enter Rexford Tugwell, who had been given chief responsibility for developing the reorganization plan for the Department of Agriculture that Roosevelt had called for early in January (although no specific recommendations regarding the Forest Service had been forthcoming from the President). Tugwell decided to get Ickes and Wallace together to discuss the situation openly, though he did not look forward to the meeting himself. "The old quarrel . . . between Interior and Agriculture," he wrote in his own diary on March 30, "has been threatening to break out all over again.

H. A. W. [Wallace] has been all steamed up to go for Ickes. . . . Altogether I dreaded the interview all week. Ickes opened up by proposing to assemble all land activities in Interior; H. A. W. countered by telling him he might as well suggest making Agriculture a bureau of Interior. The air was full of electricity for a few minutes. I then interposed a conciliatory remark that too much was at stake for them to get into an administrative quarrel. "You both," I said, "need to work together all the time against mutual enemies. And we must find a compromise.". . .

I begged Henry, at some risk, not to be too stiff about Forests as such, saying that we [Agriculture] might take over Public Lands together with all grazing activities in the Forests. This caught on. Henry offered Roads; Ickes offered Reclamation. . . .

I then suggested that we have Subsistence Homesteads and Soil Erosion. Ickes readily agreed. . . . At the last minute, H. A. W. tried to bargain for Indian Affairs but Ickes was adamant and I indifferent. But I did suggest that along with forests he ought to have wild life. So Biological Survey was understood to be going to him as we broke up. This will bring us Reclamation, Public Lands, Soil Erosion, and Subsistence Homesteads; together with a new grazing service to be set up. It will take away Roads, Forests and Biological Survey. For my part, I think it is a grand compromise.

So did Ickes, who apparently believed things were moving along swimmingly. On April 18, at a lunch he and Wallace had with FDR, Ickes noted, they "discussed with him the proposed interchange of some bureaus in our two departments and he seemed to be very much taken with the proposal, though he does not want to do anything about it during this session of Congress. This is a sound position for him to take," Ickes added, seeming to accept with equanimity the necessity of waiting until after the elections in November before any large moves could be made. When Senator Henry Ashurst, one of his strongest supporters in Congress, attached to the Taylor Grazing Act—which was then being ushered through Congress—an amendment that would have transferred the Forest Service to Interior by congressional mandate, Ickes did nothing to hinder it, but also nothing to further its advance (FDR, according to Tugwell, *did* intervene, making it known that he opposed the amendment, and it soon died).

Ickes held his patience until after the elections—until the middle of December, in fact, when he asked Tugwell and Wallace to come talk with him about the transfers. By then, Wallace had changed his mind. "I visited in May of '34 a great many forests . . . in the southwest," he recalled with spectacular vagueness, "and came back convinced that the proposal was not feasible." He did not explain further. Ickes later claimed that he had not known of Wallace's turnabout before the meeting, but in any case, as Tugwell reported it, he seems to have kept his temper well enough. Ickes was, Tugwell wrote

> still of the same mind and wanted us to go to the President with him. He suggested it again, he said, since the President had not turned it down but merely had thought it expedient to wait until after the election. H. A. W. was not at all enthusiastic about it, saying that he thought there were many grave political questions involved which Ickes tended to minimize and that on the whole he thought it would be better to keep the status quo. Ickes said that if Henry were not really for the change it would be a mistake to go see the President, but urged that it would be very much worth while to assure a complete conservation set-up under one head as well as to settle the old problems which have always tormented the relationships between the two departments.
>
> I said also that I thought it would be very important to have some of these important administrative questions settled and that there was a third alternative—which would be the setting up of a separate conservation department.

Ickes said that he wanted to keep all conservation matters in Interior. In fact, he added, he would like to have all such activities in the department put under the control of an undersecretary, and, Tugwell wrote, "hoped that I might come over to the Department of the Interior and be the Under Secretary there." It was now Wallace's turn to keep his temper.

Tugwell diplomatically said that Ickes's proposal was attractive, but not much of a likelihood, and the meeting ended with Wallace willing to go to see the President on the question but now adamantly opposed to any transfers. Ickes, perhaps as a result, had decided a meeting would be useless, stiffly explaining to Wallace a few months later that the Secretary of Agriculture "had made it so clear" that he was opposed to any transfer "that I didn't see what was to be gained by such a procedure. . . . In the circumstances, it is hardly to be wondered at that I came to the conclusion that if there was to be any logical rearrangement of bureaus as between our two departments, I would have to provide that machinery without any help from Agriculture and, in fact, in spite of the opposition of your department."

Ickes did not tarry long after the holidays to put the machinery in place and give it a kick start. On January 22, 1935, in his address to the American Game Conference Banquet in New York (a speech broadcast over NBC), he declared that the Forest Service and the Biological Survey should be placed in the Interior Department and that "if we are in the highest degree to protect, foster and prudently use our natural resources in the interest of all the people, the administration of conservation activities should be concentrated in one department, under a sincere conservationist, so that conflicts may be avoided, jealousies stilled, and an opportunity given to drive ahead along a broad front in the cause of conservation." The pronouncement stirred things up quite as much as Ickes doubtless hoped it would. "It seemed," Wallace remembered, "that Secretary Ickes felt that the Department of the Interior was the great conservation department of government. Of course Secretary Ickes himself was a great conservationist, but the Department of the Interior, previous to his coming, had, in considerable segments of its activities, been noted for the giving away and exploiting of natural resources rather than the conservation of them." The next day, responding to news stories celebrating a rift between the two departments, Wallace added, FDR "authorized me to say to the newspapermen that there is not now, nor has there been any intention of shifting the Forest Service and Biological Survey from the Department of Agriculture to the Department of Interior."

The lack of intention did not filter down to Harold Ickes, who by now was determined to make it happen. During a meeting with the President on March 25, he once again told Roosevelt that he would "like to have all the conservation activities in this Department." FDR countered by saying he was thinking about setting up a separate Department of Conservation, echoing both Brant and Tugwell. Ickes complained that a separate department

> would take over practically all of our activities and leave us nothing to do. I urged that the conservation activities ought to come to Interior. This was the natural place for them. He said that I was right and he suggested that I canvass the situation up on the Hill to see whether we could get the necessary legislation. . . . I then asked him whether I had his authority to go into this matter on the Hill and see what could be done, and he told me to go ahead.

By early April, on the theory, apparently, that Congress would be more likely to make the transfers if the vessel to receive them sounded more like the proper place to put them, his staff had drafted legislation that would have changed the name of Interior to the Conservation Department and would have given the President the power for two years to take bureaus out of other departments and place them in the renamed Interior Department. On April 13, Ickes asked Roosevelt if he could have the bill introduced in Congress. "All right, go ahead," Roosevelt replied, though he would not commit himself so far as to let Ickes tell his friends in Congress that the bill was an administration measure. Instead, he later suggested that Ickes tell the chairmen of the appropriate committees that they could "consult" with FDR on the legislation and that he would then tell them that it was "all right."

Ickes gave copies of the legislation to Senator James Hamilton Lewis of Illinois and Congressman John J. Cochran of Missouri, who then introduced the bill in their respective Houses. On May 17 the Senate Committee on Expenditures, with Senator Lewis as chairman, opened hearings on the bill. Ickes testified briefly and noted his surprise that Chief Forester Silcox and another Wallace aide had come down from Agriculture to voice its opposition. Ickes later described their testimony as "a metaphysical discussion of what conservation might mean" and was insulted. "I think," he wrote in his diary, "that if Wallace had wanted to oppose this bill, he should have appeared personally and not permitted subordinates to appear and catechize me." That was rectified during hearings before the equivalent committee in the House, where Wallace did make an appearance, as did General Markham of the U.S. Army Corps of Engineers, which apparently feared that it, too, might become one of the agencies to be moved into the newly named Department of Conservation. When Ickes objected, FDR promised to tell the War Department to pull General Markham out of the fight and to speak with Henry Wallace about his opposition. "I told him," Ickes said, "that it would be a simple matter to pass this bill if he would only crook his little finger."

Roosevelt's finger remained uncrooked, and if he indeed talked to Wallace, the Secretary of Agriculture paid not the slightest attention. He and Silcox were both in attendance at the House hearings the next day, complaining that while they hardly opposed granting the President power to reorganize the Executive, the real intent of the bill was to get Interior's hands on the national forests, even if the legislation made no specific mention of the Forest Service or even of the Department of Agriculture. For his part, Ickes denied any sinister intent, maintaining only that since his department had been "pre-eminent in conservation matters" for many years, the name change was both logical and deserved. To objections that tradition and past practice rendered the Department itself incapable of responsible stewardship—an argument that Wallace himself was fond of making—Ickes bristled. If the conservation of natural landscapes were placed in his hands, he said, his policies "would create protective grooves that any temporary transgressor in public office would find it difficult to free himself from," adding, "Now it may be that they do not want us to change from the Department of the Interior, so they can still throw Secretary Fall in our face. . . . No one is going to tie that dead cat on my neck and get away with it."

That night, he wrote, "The committee had to adjourn before I was through on account of a call for a quorum from the House, but I came away feeling that our position had been strengthened not only by what I said but by what Henry had said." But the Forest Service was not through. Silcox asked all his regional foresters to support local letter-writing efforts, urging them to use "discretion and finesse. There must be no wires, for example, signed by Forest officers. But the chances that the Bill may pass are so great that to prevent it immediate, definite, and planned action . . . must be taken." Gifford Pinchot took a hand against the bill, too, sending out some four thousand letters in opposition—ironically, most of them to the same list that he had provided in 1932 when he asked Ickes to institute a letter-writing campaign to drum up support for Pinchot's nomination as the Republican candidate.

The Forest Service's lobbying effort, coupled with Roosevelt's studied lack of support, did its work: on August 13, the House Committee on Expenditures rejected the bill by a vote of ten to five. Ickes did not give up hope, however. The bill was doing somewhat better over in the Senate, and on the same day the House committee voted against it, he received, at least temporarily, the support of one of the most influential conservationists in the federal bureaucracy, Jay Norwood ("Ding") Darling, editorial cartoonist for the *Des Moines Register*, former head of the Iowa Game Commission, a board member of the Emergency Conservation Committee—and now head of the Bureau of Biological Survey, one of the agencies Ickes was anxious to tuck under the wing of the Interior Department. A longtime critic of how the federal government managed its wildlife programs, Darling had been asked by Wallace to take over the bureau in the spring of 1934, and since then he had established within it a Migratory Waterfowl Division, had been instrumental in the passage of the Duck Stamp Act of 1934, which provided public funds for the maintenance of the new division's programs, had been tremendously effective in gouging appropriations out of Congress for the bureau, and had designated twenty-two new wildlife refuges totaling 840,000 acres. Darling came to see Ickes the day of the House vote. "There isn't any doubt that he believes as I do that all conservation activities should be concentrated in one department," Ickes wrote in his diary with some pleasure. "He said that if this wasn't done, conservation would go to hell."

Other conservationists were less supportive. Both the Izaak Walton League and the Society of American Foresters were against the name change (and the suspected transfers). The Foresters were particularly vigorous and public in their opposition, which earned their president, H. H. Chapman, a classic response from the Secretary, written less than a week after the House rejection of his bill. He had failed to take Chapman's opinions seriously, he said, "because your views, when expounded to independent thinkers, are so narrow in substance, so inaccurate in reasoning, and so arbitrary in their pronouncement that they are discredited on utterance. It seems that because of your comparative obscurity, the newspapers will not publish your stuff if it is lacking in vituperation or criticism, which I believe accounts for the character of your output."

He was still on the offensive—or at least prepared for it—after the first session of the Seventy-fourth Congress adjourned. "Congress will be in session again before we realize it and I want to be prepared to meet the attacks of the Forest Service on our Department bill," he wrote to Harry Slattery on September 30, 1935, just before giving his dedication speech at Boulder Dam. "I wish you would put one or two people to work making as thorough a study as possible of the Forest Service, with particular attention paid with reference to where it overlaps our Park Service and other services; where it has blocked the legitimate expansion of our Park Service; the money it spends, etc., etc. I want to be able, if necessary, to make out such a complete case against the Forest Service that we can put it on the defensive."

In January 1936, when the second session of the Seventy-fourth Congress convened, he marshaled his forces both to continue pushing the Senate bill along and to revive the House version that had succumbed to committee vote. "Secretary Ickes is pushing it [the legislation] personally with a vigor unequalled by the advocacy of any secretary for any bill within my fifteen years' experience in handling legislation in Congress," Robert Sterling Yard of The Wilderness Society wrote a colleague in Wyoming. "He has personally attended at least seven hearings, demanding a vigorous part in the fight against every opposition. He denies that its purpose is to get possession of the Forest Service, but does not deny that the bill will accomplish precisely that." Yard, with the covert support of Robert Marshall, the Society's backroom president (and Ickes's employee), had joined the ranks of those who opposed the Conservation Department bill, both because Yard had learned to despise the National Park Service and because the Society's origins largely derived from the "loyal opposition" of dissidents within the Forest Service. Yard did not trust Ickes's commitment to wilderness preservation and would spend much of the next nine years sniping at the Secretary. "I suggest," he told his correspondent on this occasion, "that you bring all the pressure you can through Congress, but please do not mention me."

Pressure was brought, from Yard's friend and from many other quarters, most certainly including the Forest Service. In February, after introduction of the bill to expand the Division of Grazing's territory, the Forest Service lobby even made a short-lived attempt to attach an amendment that would have transferred both the land and the Division to the Forest Service. That ploy was too clearly vindictive to get anywhere, however, and thanks to the manipulative skills of Majority Leader Joe Robinson, the Conservation Department bill itself was reported out from committee, voted on, and passed by the Senate on May 13. All Ickes needed now, he felt, was to get a rule in the House that would force the bill onto the floor for a vote, but this time Wallace managed to frustrate him. "I at once called the President and asked him if he would let me get a rule in the House," Ickes informed his diary. "He said he would." Two days later, Roosevelt told Ickes that he had sent word to Speaker of the House Joseph Byrns that he wanted a rule on the bill and that he thought it had a good chance of passage.

Ickes could allow himself a note of triumph, then, in a speech broadcast over the NBC Network the evening of May 16. He began by defending the past actions of the Interior Department, noting that "the real student of history knows during a long period . . . exploitation was a popular policy of government, and that the Department was only executing the laws of the Congress." Having established the fact that Interior

had only been following orders, he would have had his listeners understand further that things had changed since 1932, and that new times
demanded the creation of a Department of Conservation. "If I were one of
those interested in the continued exploitation of those few remaining
riches of mine and forest and stream and public domain," he said,

> I would resist with all my might any mandate by Congress that conservation
> should be made a principal function of Government under the charge of a
> responsible Cabinet officer. I would be satisfied with the irresponsible policy
> of division and spoliation that has prevailed in the past. I would want
> activities relating to conservation to remain scattered. I would encourage the
> misunderstandings, the jealousies, the overlappings, and the wasteful expen-
> ditures of public bands that have been like a posse comitatus, following each
> other with fitful lanterns while the thief that we were sent out to apprehend
> slips away to safety.

If Ickes was entertaining visions of success, he was soon jerked back to
reality. Roosevelt had either lied when he told his Secretary of the Interior
that he had sent word to Byrns that he wanted a rule on the Conservation
Department bill, or had sent down instructions buried in so much cottony
language that it was clear that he actually wanted nothing done. If word did
get to Joseph Byrns, in any event, it never got from Byrns to John J. O'Connor, chairman of the Rules Committee, which would have to pass on any
measure forcing the bill to the floor. When Ickes asked why Roosevelt had
apparently gone suddenly soft on the issue, the President explained that
Henry Wallace had warned him the bill would precipitate an election year
fight that he, Roosevelt, could not afford. Nevertheless, Ickes noted, Presidential secretary Marvin McIntyre later called and told him that the President was still going to push for a rule. "I do not believe it," Ickes wrote.

His skepticism was well placed. A week later, information came to
him that not only had Roosevelt not asked for a ruling, his people had
made it abundantly clear to Chairman O'Connor that the President was
actively opposed to a ruling. Once again, Ickes told his diary in tired
anger, Roosevelt had "broken faith" with him.

> He did it with respect to soil erosion; he has done it on other occasions; and
> now he has done it in a manner that affects me very deeply. Unfortunately,
> there isn't anything I can do about it. We cannot pass the bill without a rule
> and we cannot get a rule unless the President gives the word. I cannot go to
> the White House again with my resignation in my hands [he had just done so
> on May 14 over the PWA contretemps]. That would make me appear
> ridiculous.

Wallace and his Forest Service lobby had won the day. For the day.
Ickes would be back in a few months with another, better informed and

better orchestrated assault. At one level or another, Ickes firmly believed (and not without reason), both Wallace and the President had double-crossed him. To the very genuine conviction that his Department of the Interior would be a better steward of the land for the land's sake than the Department of Agriculture was now added the desire for personal vindication—and with that came a hard-edged, compulsive determination that would run like an angry subtext throughout the rest of his term, suppressed now and then by the press of other business or by events or by the demands and delights of his personal life, but never far beneath the surface, ready to be pulled up and thrust again and again into the middle of things.

CHAPTER

· 38 ·

Territorial Imperatives

AMONG THE DISTRACTIONS that would pull his attention away from the pursuit of the national forests was the administration of those territorial possessions placed in the care of the Interior Department. In the beginning, these included only Alaska, Hawaii, the Virgin Islands, and a few tiny island possessions in the Pacific Ocean left as booty from the Spanish-American War. But on May 24, 1934, acting under the mandate given him by the Economy Act of 1933, Roosevelt had taken Puerto Rico out of the control of the War Department and placed it with the other possessions in a new bureau within the Department of the Interior—the Division of Territories and Island Possessions. (Since they were considered to lie within a potential war zone even then, the Philippine Islands remained in the possession of the War Department.) To head up the new division, FDR appointed Ernest Gruening, a physician who had exchanged his first profession for that of journalism, becoming editor of the *Nation* and the *New York Post*. Gruening was a loyal Rooseveltian whom the President had chosen to represent the United States at the Seventh Inter-American Conference in Montevideo in 1933.

Alaska, jutting like a great fist from the northwest corner of the North American continent, isolated and populated almost entirely by Indians and Eskimos, demanded little of Ickes's time and attention until World War II, but with the other three major possessions, the Secretary inherited

various forms of grief that even the extraordinary energies of the New Deal
could do little to alleviate. One of the most frustrating situations was that
in Hawaii, the polyglot paradise of native Hawaiians and first- and
second-generation Japanese, Chinese, Koreans, and Filipinos ruled over
by a minority of mostly American Caucasians and fortified on the island of
Oahu by the presence of the navy at Pearl Harbor and the army at
Schofield Barracks outside Honolulu. In 1932, Interior Secretary Ray
Lyman Wilbur and his assistant, William Atherton Du Puy, gave the
islands a spectacular bill of health: "Despite all this mingling of races,"
they wrote,

> no unpleasant incidents of importance have developed. . . . Hawaii is a land
> of good feeling, toleration, happiness, pleasant living. Few communities
> approach more nearly to the ideal of self-government. Washington looks on
> with approval, lends a hand here and there, almost never exercises even a
> suggestion of civil authority. A far-away land and a strange and conglomerate
> people are being conserved in such a way as to produce a prosperous and
> happy community.

This bit of frabjous nonsense obscured the fact that the "prosperous
and happy community" of Hawaii was ruled with feudal implacability by
a handful of old white families, most of them descended from the missionaries who had come to save the islanders from themselves in the nineteenth
century and most connected, one way or another, to the consortium of
commercial enterprises that had ruled the local economy for more than
two generations. The consortium was called the Big Five, not always with
admiration: Castle & Cooke, Alexander & Baldwin, American Factors, C.
Brewer & Company, and the Theo. H. Davies Company. Led by Castle &
Cooke, the Big Five had established and maintained an economy based on
enormous sugar and coffee plantations and pineapple farms of industrial
dimensions, all of them worked by thousands of cheap field hands who had
been imported from the far corners of the Pacific Basin. This labor force
had been used with the casual brutality typical of plantation economies,
and after World War I the rise of a feeble unionism among Japanese and
Filipino workers had resulted in a handful of strikes as bitter and bloody as
anything the mainland had experienced, if on a smaller scale. But the Big
Five, with the cooperation of a local government unencumbered by any
federal interference, had managed to suppress these violent inconve-
niences, and by the beginning of the Depression the labor movement of
Hawaii was in a state of arrested development.

The social structure of the islands was quite as rigid as the economic
order. Novelist John P. Marquand, who spent the winter of 1932 in

Honolulu, remembered it with a precision gained from watching the civilization of New England at work and play for many years. "On the upper crust," he wrote, "was the decorous and snobbish civilization of the old island families, who had their great houses and their gardens on the mountain slopes outside the city, and their banks and offices with elaborate tropical planting downtown on Queen Street, their beach houses on the windward and their hunting lodges on the other islands." Below this layer, he said, was one made up of the parvenu rich, Hollywood types looking for an ersatz paradise, and below that, American and European flotsam that had drifted in from all points of the compass, "the beachcombers and the bums, the stranded sailors, the international drunks" settling into a seedy waterfront life of careless degradation. At the very bottom, of course, were "the slum dwellers and the inhabitants of the slatternly termite-ridden shacks in the regions away from the polite real estate developments." Honolulu, he said, "with its veneer of comfort and vulgar luxury," was "spread over an age-old basis of Oriental poverty—the melting pot of the Pacific which was never hot enough to melt."

Not very far beneath that veneer lay a pestilent racism, demonstrated by events that had begun in September 1931, when Thalia Massie, the well-connected wife of Lieutenant Thomas Massie, a naval submarine officer stationed at Pearl Harbor, left a drunken party at a Honolulu night spot and was later found wandering alone along Ana Moana Boulevard at midnight, dazed and bleeding, her jaw broken. She told police that she had been beaten and raped by five dark-skinned locals. At about the same time she was picked up, five young men—four native Hawaiians and one nisei (an island-born Japanese)—had been arrested after a street accident had inspired a drunken brawl. Thalia Massie identified two of the men as being among her assailants, and all five were charged with her assault. (The nisei was later released when he was able to prove he had been on another part of the island at the time of the alleged rape.)

In November the four accused rapists were brought to trial in an atmosphere of racial hysteria that would not have seemed out of place in some dank, river-bottom hamlet of Mississippi. Both island and mainland newspapers, spurred on by the glamorous fact that Thalia Massie's mother, Mrs. Granville Fortescue, was of noble southern birth and the niece of Alexander Graham Bell, reveled in lurid speculations concerning the safety of delicate white women surrounded by dark-skinned men of degenerate sexual appetites. And the navy, constantly looking for evidence with which to persuade Congress to place the government of the islands in the hands of a military commission, as in the Philippines, let it be known through one of its rear admirals that "Honolulu is not safe for wives and families of the Navy." In spite of the emotional tone of the proceedings, the prosecution offered a case so raddled by inconsistencies and contradictions that the jury spent four days and one hundred ballots before deciding that it could not decide. The jurors were dismissed, the defendants released, and a new trial was scheduled.

It was never held. On the morning of January 8, 1932, Joseph Kahahawai, one of the defendants, was kidnapped. Later that morning, police stopped an automobile after a furious, erratic chase across the island. At the wheel was Mrs. Granville Fortescue, Thalia Massie's mother, and in the back were Lieutenant Massie and another naval officer. At their feet on the floor of the car, wrapped and tied in a bloody sheet, was the body of Kahahawai. He had been shot in the spine. Reluctantly, a grand jury brought a bill of indictment, and in April Mrs. Fortescue, Massie, the other navy man, and another naval officer later arrested as a coconspirator were put on trial, charged with premeditated murder, and defended by none other than Clarence Darrow. Again, the atmosphere in and out of the courtroom quivered with racist overtones, most of the white population being locked in agreement that justice, however crudely, had been served by the acts of the new defendants and that they had done no more than what any right-thinking American would be forced to do when the system failed him. Remarkably, the jury did not buy the argument, at least not entirely; the four were convicted of manslaughter, a verdict that carried with it the potential of ten-year sentences—though the jury recommended leniency.

Even this relatively mild conclusion was too much for many, including more than a hundred members of the U.S. House of Representatives, who immediately signed a telegram to Territorial Governor Lawrence M. Judd, the descendant of missionaries and a longtime executive with Big Five companies. "We, as members of Congress," the telegram said, "deeply concerned with the welfare of Hawaii, believe that the prompt and unconditional pardon of Lieutenant Massie and his associates will serve that welfare and the ends of substantive justice. We, therefore, most earnestly urge that such pardon be granted." Many in the Senate agreed, although no collective telegram was sent. An emissary reported to the Hawaii Sugar Planters Association that "very conservative senators, both Republican and Democratic, want Hawaii made a military post, and that, generally in the Senate, the feeling is very intense against Hawaii and anything is likely to happen at any time."

Judd could not bring himself to issue a pardon in a case where guilt was so clearly established, but in the end did satisfy the purposes of "substantive justice" by commuting the sentences of the four to an hour and allowing them to "serve" this time by sitting around in his office one afternoon. To his credit, Judd took no pride in the decision. For the rest of his life, he said, he carried a "feeling of personal guilt in granting commutation in the face of threats by scores of congressmen and assorted public officials and newspaper publishers from coast to coast. I felt I should scrub my hands afterwards, even though the jury had recommended leniency."

It probably was with some sense of relief, then, that Judd tendered his resignation as governor in March 1933, recommending that President Roosevelt appoint as his replacement Joseph B. Poindexter, who had been made U.S. district judge for the Territory of Hawaii by Woodrow Wilson in 1917. But Judd's resignation was not formally accepted for almost a year. Ickes and Roosevelt were not unaware of the islands' "very delicate situation," as Ickes described it in a letter to a former Hawaiian resident. "As a result of recent unfortunate circumstances in Hawaii," he went on,

it is desired to name a man as Governor of sufficient strength of character to handle the situation, and of enough tact to inaugurate an era of better feeling between the different racial elements involved. . . . I would want to avoid any entangling alliances with the sugar interests or any other big interest which plays a dominating part in the political and social life of the Islands. In short, we want a man who is free, a man of standing, probity, of character and tact; a man who, while white himself, would approach the problems of the other strains with a sympathetic understanding.

This worthy goal was frustrated by the fact that the Organic Act establishing the territorial government had stipulated that no one could serve as governor who had not lived in the islands for at least two years. This codicil had been engineered in the interests of the Big Five, who wanted to scotch the possibility that some unfriendly administration might install a governor who was not in some way indebted to them and hence not inclined to be responsive to their desires. The stipulation had served them well in the past, and it continued to serve them. Ickes had legislation drafted that would have amended the Organic Act to allow Roosevelt to appoint a nonresident, but the Big Five's lobbyists easily blocked that in Congress, and the President and Ickes were forced to consider only those who had lived in Hawaii long enough to qualify—and to have been folded comfortably into the white world of the islands. After months spent sifting through possibilities, the search finally ended where it had begun—with Joseph B. Poindexter, who was inaugurated as governor on March 1, 1934. With that decision, the administration effectively abandoned the islands to a condition not far removed from status quo ante.

Roosevelt visited Hawaii for the first time in July that year. "In a fine old prayer for our country," he said on his departure,

> are found these words: "Fashion into one happy people those brought hither out of many kindreds and tongues." That prayer is being answered in the Territory of Hawaii. You have a fine historic tradition in the ancient people of the Islands and I am glad that this is so well maintained. You have built on it—built on it wisely—and today men and women and children from many lands are united in loyalty to and understanding of the high purposes of America.

The President had a great deal on his mind in 1934, and perhaps could be forgiven the fact that his words had no more to do with reality than had those of Wilbur and Du Puy two years earlier. Racial tensions in Hawaii remained high, and the embryonic labor movement, given a brief new life in the early months of the New Deal, was soon reduced to sullen, impotent anger by a combination of federal neglect and the continued economic totalitarianism of the Big Five and the social and political apparatus they controlled. In late 1937, an investigator for the National Labor Relations Board came to the islands to look into complaints that union organizers were intimidated. He found, he said, an entrenched and very effective system of antilabor surveillance conducted under the supervision of an entity called the Industrial Relations Committee, with offices in the Castle & Cooke building in downtown Honolulu. The head of the committee was former governor Lawrence M. Judd.

So it was, so it had always been, so it would generally remain until, as one historian has put it, "there cut the terrible swift sword of World War II."

If the people of Hawaii were in economic bondage to monopoly, those of the Virgin Islands were gripped by a poverty so overwhelming that it was almost incomprehensible. This scattering of about fifty volcanic islands—thirty-two of which belonged to Great Britain, the remainder to the United States—lay at the top of the Lesser Antilles, the island chain that curved up into the Caribbean Sea in a counterclockwise direction from the coast of Venezuela. Even on the three largest American islands, St. Thomas, St. John, and St. Croix, the topography was generally too rugged to provide much in the way of arable land; at the same time, the low-elevation mountain chains ran parallel with the prevailing winds, making them useless in the capturing of rain from passing cloud formations. Sugar cane was just about the only money crop that could be grown, and the poor soils and inconstant rainfall made even this a chancey undertaking. For a period in the nineteenth century, Charlotte Amalie on St. Thomas had been important as a cargo transshipment point and provisioning station, but the arrival of steam-powered vessels with greater speed and range than sailing ships had all but extirpated that business. By the time the United States decided to buy the islands from Denmark as a naval base during World War I, their economy was all but moribund.

Most of the approximately twenty thousand islanders were black, descendants of the West African slaves who had been carried in to replace the Caribs and other native peoples systematically exterminated by the European "discoverers" of the islands. Less than two thousand residents were white, including officials and employees of the United States government, a few American, Danish, and Scots families who owned 90 percent of the arable land, and a colony of a little under a thousand French whose ancestors had colonized a portion of the north coast of St. Thomas in the middle of the nineteenth century. The population of blacks had been gradually declining for nearly a century because of disease, malnutrition, and high infant mortality, a trend accelerated by outmigration to the mainland after citizenship was granted the Virgin Islanders in 1927. Nearly half of those who were left had settled on St. Thomas, most of them in Charlotte Amalie, where a few more jobs were available.

The majority of those who left the islands for the mainland United States were young male adults, leaving behind a family structure already severely crippled by centuries of slavery; by the middle of the 1930s, females in the island population exceeded males by about 15 percent and the average age of a male farmhand or tenant farmer on St. Croix, where most agriculture on the islands was practiced, was 51.8 years. Slave traditions also continued in the high rate of illegitimacy; more than half of all births were illegitimate—a legacy of the decades under which the production of children, whether sanctified by marriage or not, was endorsed and encouraged by slave owners. The same cultural inheritance made the islanders poor candidates for success under the principles of free enterprise and the work ethic. For three centuries, these people had watched the indolent, self-indulgent patterns of behavior typical of plantation society in which the purpose of wealth was to create leisure. As a consequence, the moment the average islander accumulated enough money to provide himself with some free time, he would cease working until the money was gone. This seemed perfectly logical to the islanders, but by American standards it made for bad work habits and unreliability, both of which characteristics (like the perceived "immorality" of the people) were immediately identified by most whites as racial, not cultural, attributes.

There had been only one major slave revolt in the history of the islands, that of 1733, when most whites were massacred and the blacks ruled themselves for about six months before Danish and French soldiers hunted down the insurrectionists and wiped them out (retribution was so cruelly vicious that, trapped at the edge of a cliff, three hundred blacks killed their women and children themselves rather than let the soldiers get their hands on them, then leaped into the sea). Since then, the population had been generally docile—although, as in most plantation cultures in which slavery had figured, memories of insurrection ran long and the almost subliminal presumption of imminent violence tended to shape white attitudes. The years of rule under the American navy—which, like the rest of the armed services, was heavily populated by southerners—hardly improved relations, as it enforced press censorship, made civil judicial appointments, deemed military personnel immune from prosecution by civil authorities, and dissolved the colonial councils that had provided what little self-government there was. To its credit, the navy also substantially improved sewerage and water-supply systems, built schools for about four thousand children, and all but obliterated malaria.

By the end of the 1920s, the onset of the Depression, the expense of maintaining a military base where it clearly was not needed, and pressure from such organizations as the National Urban League, the NAACP, and the American Civil Liberties Union combined to fuel a movement to take control of the islands from the navy and place it in the hands of a civil government. Early in 1929, Herbert Brown, head of the Bureau of Efficiency—an independent agency in the Executive Branch that had been established by Woodrow Wilson in 1916—was asked by Congress to study the situation in the islands. His report, issued the next year, envisioned a major rehabilitation program sponsored by the government, featuring the revitalization of the sugar cane industry on about twenty thousand acres of arable land; the government purchase of some of the largest sugar plantations and mills (many of which were bankrupt by then), and the institution of a homesteading program of small farms; the creation of an agricultural training center; a large public works effort, particularly for wells, reservoirs, harbor improvements at Charlotte Amalie, and road systems; tax incentives for investment from the mainland, an advertising campaign to tout the beauty of the islands as a tourist attraction, and a major overhaul of federal relief programs.

President Herbert Hoover, who had appointed Brown the head of the

Bureau of Efficiency, nevertheless had little hope that the plan would succeed. Shortly before the transfer from military to civil authority in February 1931, he visited the islands. From the back of a battleship, he publicly declared them to be "an effective poorhouse comprising 90 per cent of the people," going on to say that "Viewed from every point of view except remote naval contingencies it was unfortunate that we ever acquired these islands." Still, Brown's recommendations became the framework of recovery implemented by the islands' first civilian governor, Paul Pearson, father of columnist Drew Pearson and former promoter of the nationwide Chautauqua movement—although when Governor Pearson put in place a music and drama program patterned after those in Chautauqua, New York, he earned the permanent enmity of the practical-minded Brown, who, considering such things frivolous, began a concerted effort to get Pearson removed.

In spite of Brown's antagonism, Pearson, with the aid of a dedicated staff—led by Lieutenant Governor Lawrence Cramer, a professor of political science and a colleague of both Rexford Tugwell and Raymond Moley—had a program of rehabilitation functioning when Ickes took over as Secretary of the Interior, a program the New Dealers embraced with enthusiasm, convinced as always that the application of money, planning, purpose, and energy could swiftly rectify decades of economic and cultural impoverishment in one of the grimmest corners of America. They were persuaded that the Virgin Islands would be a kind of demonstration project of what the New Deal at its best could accomplish, and to that end, on February 23, 1934, Roosevelt established an advisory council for the islands, consisting of Charles W. Taussig, president of the American Molasses Company and an expert on the manufacture and trading of sugar; George Foster Peabody, a philanthropist and educator; Mordecai Johnson, president of Howard University; Walter White, director of the NAACP; Joanna Carver Colcord, a Red Cross officer; and for the government, Henry Wallace and Harold Ickes (Wallace would later be replaced by Rexford Tugwell). Less than two months later, a government corporation called the Virgin Islands Company (VICO) was chartered in St. Thomas with five trustees on its board of directors—Ickes (chairman), Assistant Secretary of the Interior Oscar Chapman, Governor Pearson, and representatives from the islands' business community and labor movement. Ultimately, most of the government's work in the islands would be done under the umbrella of the VICO.

If the highest hopes of the administration were never satisfied, though not for lack of trying, life in the islands improved somewhat between

1933 and the beginning of World War II. Financed at first by FERA funds and later by the WPA, a system of government-sponsored cooperatives for the manufacture of handicrafts was established, which at its height employed as many as seven hundred islanders, most of them women. PWA money built 190 miles of roads (though only fifty were paved) to facilitate the movement of tourists, and to house them, expended $120,000 in the construction of the Bluebeard Hotel on twenty-four acres overlooking the Caribbean on St. Thomas, a government-owned facility operated by private parties under a lease granted by the Department of the Interior. PWA funding also built schools and other public buildings, financed homesteads, and constructed some public housing (though, as on the mainland, the PWA's housing program was pretty anemic). The Rivers and Harbors Act of 1899 was extended to include the Virgin Islands, and harbor improvements at Charlotte Amalie were instituted. The CCC set up three camps on the islands and got to work building roads, digging drainage ditches, planting stands of mahogany and groves of coconut palms, preventing soil erosion, and constructing minor waterworks. After Ickes failed in efforts to purchase the assets of the bankrupt Danish Bank—the only one in the islands—Jesse Jones and the RFC helped set up and fund the Virgin Islands National Bank.

Finally, a few months after the repeal of Prohibition in December 1933, the VICO went into the liquor business. In September 1934, the federal government, with PWA funding, purchased the Bethlehem Estate, a twenty-two-hundred-acre enterprise on St. Croix complete with sugar mill, from the Danish West India Company, then leased it to the VICO. The Bethlehem operation, together with a few other government-owned facilities, would grow cane for sugar and molasses as the major part of its function, but it also began to distill federal rum—200,000 gallons of it by 1935, most of it sold to other companies for blending; after 1936, however, it became available in the American market under the Government House brand. In 1937, almost entirely because of rum sales, the VICO showed a profit of more than five thousand dollars and at least temporarily promised to be the one public agency of the New Deal that would pay for itself.

By then, Paul Pearson, though he had gotten much of the islands' rehabilitation program under way, was no longer governor, having been victimized by antagonisms and political machinations of a low order, both in the islands and on the mainland. His problems began when Ickes, in one of his first actions as Interior Secretary, fired the government attorney for the islands, George H. Gibson, a lazy and uncooperative holdover from the naval years whom Pearson and Cramer had never been able to persuade then Interior Secretary Lyman Wilbur to get rid of.* As Gibson's replacement, Ickes reluctantly accepted the appointment of Eli Baer, a Baltimore lawyer and a highly partisan Democratic supporter of Senator Millard Tydings, chairman of the Senate Committee on Territories and Insular Possessions. Before his first year was out, Baer was accusing both Pearson, a Republican, and the entire PWA administration in the islands of graft and inefficiency, detailing his charges in a letter to the Secretary. Ickes, ever mindful of the integrity of the PWA, sent Glavis down to the islands to investigate. The only charge that had any substance at all was that a native worker by the name of Leonard McIntosh had taken eleven dollars' worth of PWA lumber and $27.40 worth of cement to use in the construction of his own home. In return, he had repaired the office radio, using his own money for materials. This kind of casual transaction had been common in the islands for years and the arrangement had been approved by McIntosh's superior in the PWA. Ickes legitimately concluded that Baer's only motive was to discredit Pearson; he fired the attorney.

Pearson's difficulties were compounded, however, when Paul C. Yates, the governor's executive assistant, began stirring things up against him. Even though Yates was yet another Democratic partisan, Pearson had insisted on his appointment because the man was a good friend of Robert S. Allen, coauthor with Pearson's son Drew of the politically potent "Washington Merry-Go-Round" column. But in the summer of 1934, Yates had begun making the same kind of public charges as Baer, and in October Ickes had ordered him home. Yates resigned in outrage, cabling Steve Early at the White House that "I, together with other loyal Democrats, have been abused and crucified by a gang of reactionary and thieving Hoover Republicans."

The plot congealed further in January 1935. Another political appointment in the islands had been that of T. Webber Wilson, a Democratic constituent of Senator Pat Harrison of Mississippi, chairman of the powerful Senate Finance Committee. In the summer of 1934, Attorney General Homer Cummings had been persuaded by Harrison to appoint Wilson to a civil judgeship in St. Thomas. Wilson soon proved himself something of an embarrassment. When one of his earliest decisions was called into question by a reporter, he responded with astonishing arrogance: "I am responsible only to Homer Cummings and to God Al-

*According to an undated communication from Governor Pearson to Secretary Wilbur written sometime in November 1932, Gibson apparently had done no work and answered no communications from anyone since the navy had relinquished control of the islands to the Interior Department in February 1931.

mighty." Nor was he a Pearson man. Before his firing, Baer had instituted proceedings against the hapless Leonard McIntosh. In January 1935 the new government attorney appointed by Ickes, George Robinson, moved a *nolle prosequi*—a decision not to prosecute—in Judge Wilson's court on the grounds that McIntosh's "crime," if it was a crime, was too petty to warrant a trial. Wilson, who apparently perceived an opportunity to discomfit Pearson and the Roosevelt administration, promptly ordered Robinson to prosecute (as he was authorized to do under the civil code of St. Thomas) and when the attorney refused, held him in contempt, refused a jury trial for McIntosh, put witnesses on the stand, questioned them himself, and brought in a verdict of guilty, fining McIntosh two hundred dollars and calling him a combination of "Judas and Benedict Arnold."

Shortly after that singular decision, Assistant Interior Secretary Oscar Chapman and Ernest Gruening, head of the Division of Territories and Island Possessions, took a trip down to the islands to investigate the situation and returned, Ickes informed his diary, feeling "more strongly than ever that Judge Wilson is a thoroughly bad actor in the Virgin Islands and both are convinced that he ought to be removed at as early a date as possible. I share this belief." He shared it and expressed it openly, irritating both Cummings and Senator Pat Harrison, who had engineered Wilson's appointment. On February 19, hearing that Harrison had sent Roosevelt a complaining letter, Ickes went to see the senator. "I thought I would have it out with him face to face," he wrote.

> However, I didn't get anywhere and I came back with a very low opinion of Harrison. He doesn't fight things man-fashion. He was like an old, complaining woman and also, like a woman, he keeps running around in circles and coming back to the point of departure. He could not be made to face the issue. On the contrary, he kept whining about his grievances. He pretends to think that he has had no consideration at all at the hands of this Department and little courtesy when, after all, the only thing that is bothering him is my outspoken opposition to Judge Wilson.

The forces militating against Pearson finally coalesced in April 1935 when the Senate voted to authorize an investigation of his and the Interior Department's administration of the islands. The investigation would be conducted by Senator Millard Tydings's Committee on Territories and Insular Possessions. By personal intervention, Roosevelt managed to persuade Tydings to include Judge Wilson among those to be investigated. Furthermore, FDR reported to Ickes, in spite of the fact that the Secretary had fired the chairman's friend Baer, Tydings promised Roosevelt that the investigation would be impartial, that Ickes would be allowed to make an opening statement in defense of Pearson and the Interior Department, and that any witnesses called could be cross-examined by Ickes or his appointed representative.

Tydings lied. When the hearings opened on July 2,* the chairman refused to let Ickes have his opening statement and made it clear that witnesses would not be available for cross-examination. Denied a public forum in the Senate, Ickes decided that "we ought to fight back day by day through the newspapers, which is the only means available to us to meet the vague charges that are being produced before the investigating committee." He started with his press conference of July 9, which followed testimony given that morning by Judge Wilson (the judge had been "very suave and unctuous," Ickes told his diary).

"Have you plans to clean up the situation in the Virgin Islands?" a reporter asked.

"Oh, yes, I have plans," Ickes answered. "I have done a good deal. I have fired Gibson, Baer and Yates—that is a pretty good start." (Not strictly accurate, of course; Yates had resigned, not been fired.)

When asked why he had stated earlier that Wilson should be removed from office, he replied, "I think he ought to be removed for judicial misconduct."

"Can you explain that?"

"His conduct in the McIntosh case where he acted as prosecutor, judge and jury. His justification is that it is permitted under the Danish Court which we inherited, but it is utterly abhorrent to any ideas of Anglo-Saxon jurisprudence. . . . Then he is always haranguing the mob from the bench. . . . I think he is bringing the administration of American justice into disrepute in the Virgin Islands and that is the reason I think he should be removed."

He followed this blast a day later by releasing to the press a letter to Tydings in which he accused the senator of "whitewashing" Wilson and conducting a one-sided investigation. Tydings responded with his own letter, denying Ickes's charges and admonishing him to mind his own affairs: "If in the future you want to tell the United States Senate how to conduct its business you first get elected to that body, and for the present, confine yourself to the duties for which you were appointed."

Before Ickes could finish an answer to Tydings's answer, he was called to a meeting with Roosevelt on the morning of July 11. Vice President

---

*Paul Yates was scheduled to be the first witness, but on the morning of the hearing he encountered his former friend Robert S. Allen in a Senate corridor. Words were exchanged— among them "double-crosser" and "son-of-a-bitch"—and the smaller Allen beat Yates so thoroughly that he had to be hauled off to the hospital for repairs.

Garner, the President told him, was worried that the public quarrel over the Virgin Islands was threatening FDR's legislative program in Congress. He asked Ickes to refrain from making any further public statements on the subject, unless it was to defend himself against another direct attack from Tydings. Ickes agreed. Later that day, Roosevelt met with Tydings, Harrison, and Majority Leader Joseph Robinson. According to the report given Ickes by the President himself, FDR "went after Tydings very directly. He told him that he (Tydings) couldn't get away with the kind of an investigation that he had been running, that at the rate he was going he would soon constitute a Trinity since he was already judge and prosecutor." Perhaps. What seems clear is that a deal had been done and through it Pearson was done in as governor. His departure probably was inevitable by that time. Not only did he have mainland politicians lined up against him for partisan reasons; in the islands he was opposed by both the right-wing landowner class, which feared government competition in the growing of sugar and the distillation of rum, and the left-wing laboring class, which accused him of being a front man for the wealthy. This latter faction was dominated by the Roosevelt-Garner Club, a four-thousand-member organization that at one point in the affair had petitioned Congress for the impeachment of Pearson, Ickes, Glavis, and E. K. Burlew.

In any event, shortly after the meeting with Roosevelt, Tydings announced that the hearings were recessed, subject to a call by the chairman. The call never came. On July 16, Ickes had Pearson in to his office and told him that the President would like him to write a letter requesting that FDR give him a new post in some other government agency. Pearson balked at this, insisting that such an action would put an undeserved cloud over his administration. "I told him," Ickes said, "that I realized that he had been jobbed and that the whole situation was terribly unfair. I pointed out to him, however, the difficult situation in which he found himself." Pearson agreed that he had to go, but that he would like to see the President himself and persuade FDR to write a letter to *him* offering a new post. Ickes set up the meeting, FDR agreed to the proposal, Pearson was offered the position of assistant director of the Housing Division of the PWA, and on July 24 he formally resigned as governor of the Virgin Islands. In the meantime, Homer Cummings apparently cut a deal for T. Webber Wilson, agreeing to remove him from the Virgin Islands judgeship and appointing him instead to a spot on the Federal Parole Board—a position Cummings created by asking for the resignation of Dr. Amy Stannard, the only psychiatrist on the board. He justified this on the grounds that since only 4.3 percent of prisoners eligible for parole were women, it was not appropriate to have a woman sit on the board. This peculiar drawback, more than one critic pointed out, had never been cited before.

All together, the uncommonly sleazy political maneuverings that attended the New Deal's first years in the Virgin Islands brought credit to almost no one, unless it was Pearson himself. Ickes thought so, anyway. "My respect for Pearson went way up," he wrote. "He is a mild-mannered man, even to the point of gentleness, but his Quaker stability of character showed when the test came. Quakers have real moral courage, and that is the highest form of courage." The moral quality of the situation certainly did not improve with Pearson's departure. When Roosevelt put forth the name of Lieutenant Governor Lawrence Cramer as Pearson's replacement, Tydings once again swung into action, leading the opposition in the Senate on the grounds that what was needed was a clean sweep and Cramer was a Pearson man; there was even some sentiment for returning the islands to the navy.

The islands stayed in civilian hands and Cramer was approved by the Senate in spite of Tydings's efforts. One of the new governor's first and most significant acts was to help formulate the final details of an Organic Act for the islands that would replace all previous Danish law, provide for universal suffrage, and establish a representative form of government. But before this long-needed legislation had completed its journey through Congress, Judge Albert Levitt, appointed by Attorney General Homer Cummings to take Wilson's place, immediately antagonized the landowner-dominated civil councils by arbitrarily declaring all forms of law not compatible with the laws of the United States to be immediately invalid, a precipitous move that created both confusion and anger. The judge then alienated much of the black population of the islands by issuing a suspended sentence to a white man for raping his stepdaughter and on the same day sentencing a black man to five years in prison for attempted rape.

Cramer and Ickes, along with many others, raised a ruckus over Levitt's actions, and Cummings brought the judge back to the United States and put him to work in the Justice Department before he could do any further damage. The Organic Act passed on June 22, 1936, but Tydings quickly invited Levitt to testify against the governor in an effort to block the renomination of Cramer after Roosevelt's second inaugural. Tydings also took the occasion to hold up the nomination of William Hastie as the new government attorney to replace Levitt. Hastie, a former assistant solicitor in the Interior Department, was a black man, described by Ickes as "a fine person with a very real legal ability and judicial poise, whom we have been trying to get in there for some time." Although fully three-quarters of the government jobs in the islands had gone to blacks during Pearson's administration, a practice continued by Cramer, Hastie would be the first to hold such a high place. This did not sit well with southerner Tydings. However, as Ickes noted in his diary, "Tydings will be a candidate to succeed himself next year and there is a very large Negro vote in Baltimore." With that fact in mind, Ickes sent one of his black PWA investigators into Maryland to spread the word among black constituents that Tydings was out to get not only Cramer, a demonstrated friend of black people in the islands, but Hastie, a respected black attorney. Ickes also complained to Roosevelt both about Levitt and about the racist character of Tydings's opposition to Hastie. FDR, promising to have Levitt fired, called Senator Joseph Robinson and asked him to use his power as majority leader to bring Tydings to heel. These tactics must have worked, for Tydings subsequently and suddenly abandoned the fight and both Cramer and Hastie were approved.

With political turmoil seemingly behind him, Cramer set to work to consolidate the social and economic gains that had been achieved in spite of all the quarreling, and for nearly two years after passage of the Organic Act it seemed that at least some of the goals the New Deal had for the islands might become real: the VICO made a modest profit in 1937; homesteading, while limited, was generally successful where it was practiced; voter registration slowly rose to embrace a significant portion of the black population, and the stirrings of a nascent two-party system began to be felt; the craft cooperatives had expanded sales by more than 600 percent and tourist visits had risen to more than eleven thousand a year; and working and living conditions on all three American islands surpassed by far those on the neighboring British Virgins.

Then came drought, beginning in 1938 and continuing like a plague for the next five years. The VICO's profit of $5,195.85 at the end of 1937 dropped to a staggering loss of $86,420.66 at the end of 1938; for the rest of its existence, the government corporation would again show a profit only during three of the war years. With the loss of the VICO's profit went any hope that the islands would ever become self-sufficient; they were a dependency and would remain a dependency—a rebuke, critics of the New Deal said; a failure of circumstance, its allies insisted.

Cramer's political troubles paralleled those of the islands' economy. Among other things, the new legislature—still made up largely of the white landowning class—stubbornly refused to impose local taxes, determined to make the federal government pay most of the tariff for the support of the islands. This became particularly odious, in Cramer's view, when the same legislature voted salary increases for itself, an act he promptly vetoed.

He also began having troubles with Washington, especially with Ickes, who as early as January 1937 suspected Cramer of working behind the scenes to oust Ickes and get his friend Roy B. West installed in his place. Cramer had persuaded Ickes that the rumor was not true, but it created a mistrust between the two men that did not evaporate over time. When the Secretary received information in 1940 that racial tensions in the islands had reached dangerous levels—a frightening prospect, with the possibility of U.S. involvement in the European war growing closer with every passing week—he sent his own investigator down. This employee apparently believed everything he was told by those who were no friends of Cramer and sent back a lurid report of imminent uprisings, which he ascribed to slack administration. Ickes was soon convinced that the report was stuffed with politically motivated exaggerations and dismissed the investigator—but in a moment of what can only be described as stupidity, he gave the report to Cramer. Ickes thought of it as a conciliatory gesture, but Cramer was in no mood for conciliation, particularly after reading the report, and wrote the Secretary a letter he found so insulting that he asked Roosevelt to demand Cramer's resignation. FDR concurred and Cramer was out.

Cramer's replacement was another Cummings man, Charles Harwood, a former special assistant in the Justice Department and a federal judge in the Panama Canal Zone. He was not a popular choice in the Interior Department; Rupert Emerson, then director of the Division of Territories and Island Possessions, was disappointed after his first meeting. "I hope that time will prove me wrong," he wrote to a colleague, "but I have no impression that he either knew much about the islands now or would be much concerned to find out about them. My general sentiment was that he was an elderly gentleman who looked to this governorship as a means of spending his declining years in some tropical indolence." Ickes certainly agreed, and would later describe Harwood's appointment as "a tragic joke."

Harry Taylor, then administrator of St. Croix and the only remaining high-level official from the Pearson years, looked back on all the ruined hopes of the New Deal and found nothing to laugh about: "Never in my ten years in the Virgin Islands has there been such an accumulation and concentration of misfortunes and problems, and now all under the dark threatening cloud of . . . war."

〰〰〰〰

Ickes spent only three days in the Virgin Islands during his Caribbean inspection trip in January 1936, just long enough to get a superficial impression that conditions were measurably improved, especially on St. Croix, which, he wrote, "Certainly . . . had the appearance of being a fairly prosperous place." He had gained no such conviction during his tour of Puerto Rico several days before, especially the ghastly slums of San Juan. They were, he wrote,

> the worst slums that I have ever seen. The dwellings looked as if a breath would blow them over. They are thoroughly disreputable and disagreeable. Open sewage runs through the streets and around the buildings and there are no sanitary facilities at all. The children play in this sewage, which in many cases is covered with a thick, green scum. . . . Such slums are a reflection not only upon the Puerto Rican Government but upon that of the United States. It is unbelievable that human beings can be permitted to live in such noisome cesspools.

Poverty, concentrated and immediately visible (as the more scattered, rural poverty of the Virgin Islands often was not), was nearly the only characteristic shared by Puerto Rico with the Virgins. For one thing, this single island (the first in the chain called the Greater Antilles), lying just forty miles west of St. Thomas, possessed a population of more than 1.8 million people living on 3,421 square miles—roughly ninety times the number of people and thirty times the amount of land on all of the Virgin Islands put together. Second, about 500,000 acres of land on the island was commercially arable and a profitable three-crop economy was well established—cane sugar along the coast and in the river bottoms, coffee in the western mountains (which reached the respectable altitude of four thousand feet), and tobacco in the central and eastern highlands. Of the three, sugar was the island's dominant crop by far. More than 800,000 tons were produced annually, over half of this by four large corporations that controlled nearly 200,000 acres and operated eleven *centrals,* sugar-processing centers to which their own farmers as well as independent farmers, or *colonos,* brought raw cane. While the corporations were ostensibly native-owned, fully three-quarters of the capital that financed them came from American investment; by 1930 this amounted to about $120 million, one reason why there was no tariff on the importation of Puerto Rican sugar in the United States in spite of cries of foul from the producers of cane sugar in Hawaii, the Virgin Islands, and Cuba, and the producers of beet sugar on the mainland. During its best period, the industry was an excellent bet: for more than twenty years one corporation, the Fajardo Sugar Company, paid an average return on investment of 50 percent.

Another difference lay in political traditions. Puerto Rico had some. "The Puerto Rican is said to be an inveterate politician," Ickes wrote, and he was right. Unlike the people of the Virgins, who had gone from the oppression of slavery to the oppression of Danish civil government to the oppression of American military government and were only beginning to learn the art of politics by the middle of the 1930s, the Puerto Ricans had been at it for three decades. Military rule on the island had lasted only two years after the United States acquired it as one of the rewards of the Spanish-American War of 1898. The Foraker Act of 1900 extended civil government to Puerto Rico, and while it was answerable to the Bureau of Insular Affairs in the War Department and its governor and the heads of its six administrative departments were appointed to their posts by the President of the United States, with the advice and consent of the Senate, Puerto Ricans were authorized to elect a House of Delegates and a resident commissioner who would represent their interests in Washington. The government was liberalized even further with the Organic Act of 1917. The island officially remained in the portfolio of the War Department, but the people were declared citizens of the United States and could now elect members of a territorial senate and house of representatives. The governor, the attorney general, and the commissioner of education remained Presidential appointees, but the governor, subject to the approval of the Puerto Rican senate, could appoint the remaining heads of his administrative departments.

Within this relatively liberal context, the island's political life seethed with a complication of local interests and individualistic philosophies that much of the time was too volatile to be adequately described. By 1932, however, the sundry elements that went into the political scene had shaken down (for the moment, at least) to two major components and one minor. The first large party was an alliance formed between the Union-Republican Party (itself a coalition devised out of two older factions), made up of upper-level business and professional people, and the Socialist Party, the child of a vigorous trade-union movement led by Santiago Iglesias. While not entirely indifferent to the island's social problems, this alliance was interested mainly in improving business conditions and wages and saw its future closely tied to that of the United States— although it did advocate a far greater degree of autonomy than the current structure allowed, including the popular election of the Puerto Rican governor. The second large faction was that of the Liberal Party, forged by various radical dissidents who had fallen out with both the old Union

Party and the Socialist Party over the question of independence for Puerto Rico. The Liberals, who wanted independence, were led by Antonio Barcelo, an experienced politician and former leader of the Union Party, but their most popular spokesman was the young Luis Muñoz Marín, a graduate of the Columbia School of Journalism, contributor to the *Nation*, the *American Mercury*, and the *New Republic*, and editor of *La Democracia*, one of Puerto Rico's most influential newspapers.

The minor element in the political milieu of the island was the Nationalist Party, not only actively in pursuit of independence but increasingly (and violently) anti-American, as the Liberal Party was not. The sentiments of this party were reinforced early in 1932 by an extraordinarily offensive private letter written by Dr. Cornelius Rhoads, a Rockefeller Foundation physician working in a Puerto Rican hospital. The Puerto Ricans, his letter said, "are beyond doubt the dirtiest, laziest, most degenerate race of men ever inhabiting this sphere. It makes you sick to inhabit the same island with them . . . a tidal wave or something to totally exterminate the population is necessary. . . . I have done my best to further the process of extermination by killing off eight and transplanting cancer into several more." When the grotesque screed became public, Dr. Rhoads immediately explained it away as a deliberate parody of attitudes all too common among the American residents of the island, as it certainly must have been (no evidence that Rhoads had deliberately killed anyone was ever uncovered), but the Nationalists professed to see in it evidence of a conspiracy, which they exploited to good effect. *

For all the differences between the Virgin Islands and Puerto Rico, the common denominator of poverty remained—and it was fully as grim here as anywhere in the Western Hemisphere, complicated by religious traditions that forbade contraception and a cultural inheritance from centuries of Spanish colonial rule that had left a chasm between rich and poor so wide that it seemed permanent, as if it were a natural landmark. In a letter of early January 1935, Harold Ickes summed things up as well and as succinctly as anyone ever had:

> Puerto Rico . . . has been the victim of the *laissez-faire* economy which has developed the rapid growth of great absentee owned sugar corporations, which have absorbed much land formerly belonging to small independent growers and who in consequence have been reduced to virtual economic serfdom. While the inclusion of Puerto Rico within our tariff walls has been

---

*A final, very small, component in the political world of the island was provided by the Democratic Party, occupied almost entirely by a tiny, impotent knot of U.S. government workers and officials.

highly beneficial to the stockholders of these corporations, the benefits have not been passed down to the mass of Puerto Ricans. These on the contrary have seen the lands on which they formerly raised subsistence crops, given over to sugar production while they have been gradually driven to import all their food staples, paying for them the high prices brought about by the tariff. There is today more widespread misery and destitution and far more unemployment in Puerto Rico than at any previous time in its history.

To break up the pattern of land monopoly that Spanish tradition had created and American investment had perpetuated, a Joint Resolution of Congress on May 1, 1900, had restricted every corporation engaged in agriculture "to the ownership and control of not to exceed 500 acres of land," but this declaration had been enforced with the same regularity as the similarly motivated 160-acre limitation on federal water in the American West—which is to say, not at all. In Puerto Rico, as in most regions of the world in which single-crop agriculture was dominant, the rich owned the land that the poor planted and harvested—and, in Puerto Rico at least, the poor then gathered in slums where rickets, tuberculosis, and malaria contributed to a death rate that was one of the highest in the world.

The grimness of the situation had recently been aggravated by the intervention of nature—not drought this time, but two great hurricanes. The first, called San Felipe and considered the most powerful ever recorded up to that time, had torn through the island in September 1928, leaving more than three hundred dead and 200,000 without homes. The island had not fully recovered from that assault when the San Cipriano hurricane blasted the island in September 1932, killing 225 people and destroying the homes of more than 100,000.

Such was the social, economic, and political situation in Puerto Rico when the Roosevelt administration came to power in 1933, an amalgam whose misery, complexity, and passion would snarl the New Dealers in a tangle of frustration and lead with dreadful inevitability to the only instance of violence and death ever connected with the administration of Interior Secretary Harold L. Ickes.

In Puerto Rico, the Roosevelt years began badly and continued badly. By all accounts, the President's appointment of a new governor to replace the Republican, James Beverly, was one of the worst he ever made. Robert Gore, a former newspaperman and insurance executive and now an owner of newspapers in Florida, was one of James Farley's political soldiers and his appointment as governor of Puerto Rico apparently was payment for services rendered. Newspaperwoman Ruby Black, *La Democracia*'s Washington correspondent and one of Luis Muñoz Marín's principal American supporters, interviewed Gore early in May 1933 and described him in a letter to a friend in Puerto Rico as a man who "chews gum. He is short, baldish, plump with a dimple. The boys who know him tell me to warn you to nail down the furniture. He seems simple and honest, but if he is, how did he make millions?"

Gore, as it happened, was simple and honest, but also inept and seemingly incapable of making any move that did not have a political motive behind it—chiefly the desire to strengthen the position of the Democratic Party in Puerto Rico at the expense of the other factions, particularly the Liberal Party, which he and many other Americans perceived, however inaccurately, as anti-American. By August, his situation on the island was approaching the untenable. "They hate this new governor Gore, who seems to be a sap," an American woman in Puerto Rico wrote a friend on the mainland. "He drinks like a lord, and wants the people to have cock fights, and in selecting his cabinet asked every member to write their resignation, leaving the date in blank, so that he can kick them out, if not suitable, at his convenience. I am telling you that these Portoricans are seeing red and are ready to have him kicked out. . . . Well, whether Roosevelt recalls this man or not, remains to be seen, but there is trouble ahead."

There was, and on December 27, a little over two months after one dynamite bomb had exploded harmlessly at the governor's country estate at Jomomé and another had been disarmed at the governor's mansion in San Juan (both very likely the work of an extreme wing of the Nationalist Party), Gore offered his letter of resignation. Roosevelt accepted it on January 12, 1934, and almost immediately appointed Adjutant General Blanton Winship of the War Department to take Gore's place. Muñoz Marín, who had been elected to the Puerto Rican senate in 1932 and was rapidly becoming a power in the Liberal Party, was pleased. "I hope that mere politics can now be adjourned among Puerto Ricans," he wrote the President, "and I shall certainly bend all my efforts to that end, in order that the economic implications of the New Deal shall have as full an opportunity for beneficial application to Puerto Rico as possible."

That was what the Roosevelt administration wanted, too, and early in 1934 FDR appointed a three-member Puerto Rican Policy Commission headed by Dr. Carlos Chardon, chancellor of the University of Puerto Rico. The commission's charge was to come up with a rehabilitation plan for the island, and by the end of June it had done so, calling for the creation of a semipublic corporation similar to the Virgin Islands Company. This corporation would take over a large portion of the sugar industry on the island, including processing mills, and through its operations both stabilize and democratize the business of growing cane and processing sugar. Furthermore, the corporation would buy enough sugar, coffee, and tobacco land for the creation of as many as twenty thousand subsistence homesteads, together with the housing, animals, tools, and utilities necessary to keep them functioning as a means of growing staples and a few cash crops. Land monopoly would be eliminated, permanent employment for as many as seventeen thousand men created, a fund for social improvements established, ten thousand acres of eroded mountainside land reforested, and a public works program instituted, including dams, waterworks, and public power facilities, as well as the remodeling of the Hotel Condado in San Juan as the center of a revivified tourist trade.

And that, for a very long time, was that. The Chardon Plan, as it came to be called, vanished for months into a bureaucratic maze in which its presumptions and legal standing were analyzed, its proper administration debated, its financial implications studied, and its implementation called into question by conservative opponents on both the mainland United States and in Puerto Rico, where the Union-Republican/Socialist alliance led the fight against it.

While the Chardon Plan was being passed from hand to hand, Roosevelt set up an Inter-Departmental Committee for the Economic Rehabilitation of Puerto Rico—featuring Tugwell from Agriculture and Chapman from Interior, together with representatives from Hopkins's FERA and the Treasury Department—then at the end of July took Puerto Rico out of the Department of War and placed it in the newly formed Division of Territories and Island Possessions in the Department of the Interior. In August he appointed Ernest Gruening head of the new division. Gruening, who would soon be forced by circumstances into spending virtually all his time on Puerto Rican affairs, made no secret about where his sympathies lay; as editor of the *Nation,* he had been one of the first to publish the work of Luis Muñoz Marín, and the liberal young Puerto Rican senator would be a major influence during the first several months of Gruening's administration of affairs on the island. By January of 1935, Gruening grew impatient waiting for a resolution on the structure of Puerto Rican rehabilitation and decided to try to enforce the 1900 Joint Resolution of Congress regarding the limitation of land ownership to five hundred acres. With the full backing of Ickes, he proposed to Benjamin Horton, the attorney general in Puerto Rico, that the government immediately institute *quo warranto* proceedings against one of the

largest corporations, Eastern Sugar Associates. At about the same time—
and almost certainly in concert with Gruening—Muñoz Marín introduced and engineered the passage in the Puerto Rican senate of a resolution requesting the attorney general to enforce the five-hundred-acre law.

Horton, who found his political allies and friends among the sugar
interests, resisted. He was supported in this by Governor Blanton Winship, who was swiftly demonstrating a kinship with the Union-Republic/
Socialist alliance even deeper than Gruening's attachment to the
Liberals—and with it a single-minded determination to destroy the
disruptive Nationalist Party of Pedro Albizo Campos, an obsession that
would come to dictate the shape of his policy for the next several years. For
now, it would take the direct intervention of Roosevelt after nearly two
months of stalling on the part of the governor to persuade Winship to
order his attorney general to begin drawing up the necessary papers.
Meanwhile, Gruening laid plans to get Horton dismissed, and Muñoz
Marín expanded his own efforts by starting to formulate legislation for the
Puerto Rican legislature that would accomplish the task of enforcement.

On May 3, 1935, the Chardon Plan finally was given an administrative entity with the creation by executive order of the Puerto Rican
Reconstruction Administration (PRRA). Gruening was appointed administrator of the PRRA, while retaining his position as head of the
Division of Territories and Island Possessions. An opinion submitted by
Interior Solicitor Nathan Margold at Ickes's request observed that Gruening enjoyed a degree of autonomy under the law that would cloud the
Secretary's own responsibility for the island. Margold concluded that the
order gave Gruening "full control over the detailed administration of
the business of [the PRRA] and full power to act without the sanction of
the Secretary of the Interior, but . . . that the first paragraph of the order
makes it entirely proper that you initiate discussions with the Administrator and make such recommendations to him as you may deem appropriate." The tensions, political conflicts, and administrative confusion over
the next several months made this state of affairs, in the Secretary's view,
impossible, but it would not be until November 1936 that he would be
able to persuade Roosevelt to amend his order and place the PRRA
directly under his control—and by then he might have been forgiven if he
had not wanted it.

When Gruening finally achieved management of the rehabilitation
program on the island, it pitted him even more directly against Governor
Winship, who continued to use every means at his disposal to block
progress on the five-hundred-acre program. His opposition did not diminish when Horton was dismissed as attorney general in June 1936 and a

Puerto Rican, Rafael Fernández García, was installed in his place (against Winship's wishes) and began working with officials in the PRRA to develop both legislation and administrative machinery for the enforcement of acreage limitation. The governor, PRRA planner Earl Hanson remembered, simply could not help himself. He was "a southern gentleman in the finest sense of the word—correct, hospitable, polite, decent and pleasant in his personal relations. . . . Like thousands of his class, he was utterly bewildered by the New Deal and all it stood for. A retired general, he tried to do his duty as he saw it, but he was completely baffled by the PRRA, incapable of understanding its aims, its basic philosophy, and what it meant—or should have meant—to Puerto Rico." Gruening then and later was not so kind. The governor, he complained in a typically ornate memorandum to Ickes on July 15, 1935, was willfully standing in the way of progress: "frequent suggestions, recommendations, pleas, exhortations, injunctions, etc. that have to be sent and are usually ignored are the evidences of the hopelessness of trying to put over a . . . New Deal program with our local chief representative out of sympathy with it, and in any case lacking the ability to fight it through or the will to adapt himself to the wishes of the Administration which appointed him."

Working with someone empty of the passions of the New Deal was clearly difficult, but Gruening had problems of his own devising, too, among them a demonstrated lack of administrative skill and an arbitrary manner that brought him into conflict not only with people like Winship but with those who were otherwise ardent supporters of the very real goals he had for the PRRA. These individuals included Dr. Carlos Chardon. Gruening installed him as the regional director of the PRRA but gave him so little control over the legal, financial, and personnel operations of the organization that Chardon felt paralyzed, a situation that ultimately would lead to his resignation. Other Puerto Ricans in the organization were alienated by Gruening's policy of hiring young mainland American lawyers over qualified Puerto Ricans and paying them more than those few island lawyers that were hired. A final obstacle to the orderly progress of the PRRA was something over which Gruening had no control— money. For all its dedication to the principles of rehabilitation, the Roosevelt administration—largely because of resistance from Harry Hopkins, jealous of his own WPA's needs—consistently gave the PRRA far too little to carry out its most ambitious programs on anything but the smallest scale. In spite of considerable sound, fury, and general agitation, very little actually seemed to *happen.*

The frustration that attended all this bureaucratic and political infighting was not confined to the principals involved, of course; it filtered down to the people who had given their hopes to the promise of the New Deal, and the radical Nationalist Party took full advantage of this disappointment. Its influence steadily grew, particularly among the self-styled intelligentsia and the always volatile student population, and violence soon followed, especially during the first few weeks of 1936, an election year in Puerto Rico as it was on the mainland. Scattered incidents between young Nationalists and members of the Insular Police Force—still under the control of the War Department—had left eight Nationalists dead and several policemen wounded by the middle of February. Then, on the morning of February 23, Colonel E. Francis Riggs, chief of the Insular Police, was assassinated while emerging from Mass. The two Nationalist assassins were immediately captured and taken off to the police department where they were killed, according to the police, when they lunged for weapons.

Raids throughout the island two weeks later garnered Nationalist leader Pedro Albizo Campos and seven others who were taken into custody and charged with conspiring to overthrow the federal government in Puerto Rico—a federal offense ensuring that they would be tried in a federal court, not in local jurisdictions where intimidation might render a verdict of innocent (so the government reasoned) on a charge of conspiracy to commit murder. Ickes, the civil libertarian, was made exceedingly uncomfortable by this decision, admitting in a later letter to Roger Baldwin of the American Civil Liberties Union that "it would have been much better if the charge of being accessory to murder could have been brought," but going on to say that "The lives, not merely of government officials, but of peaceable citizens . . . are at stake. If assassinations cannot be stopped by ordinary legal processes, there will be no alternative but the highly undesirable one of declaring martial law." The eight men were brought to trial in July; after the first trial ended in a hung jury, an immediate second trial with a more carefully selected jury (ten Americans and two Puerto Ricans) convicted them and they were taken off to the local prison at the end of the month to await sentencing.

In Washington, meanwhile, a kind of panic seemed to have settled on the administration and Congress. Senator Millard Tydings asked Gruening to draw up legislation for him that would allow the Puerto Ricans to vote for or against immediate independence in the November elections. Gruening agreed that it should be done, he noted in a bleat of outraged virtue to Ickes,

although I am convinced that independence for Puerto Rico would be folly and that the Island could not sustain itself either politically or economically.

Our withdrawal would spell alternating periods of chaos and dictatorship. I venture this prediction without qualification. . . .

Nevertheless, it seems grossly unfair that the United States . . . should be subject to the charge that [it] is holding an alien people in bondage and should bear the onus of that charge in its international relations. . . .

If in the serious effort to remedy the economic situation in Puerto Rico, and to make the blessings of citizenship under our flag a tangible reality for the people of Puerto Rico, the United States has to contend with the unwarranted charge of exploitation and domination and finds itself resisted and sabotaged in this unselfish and praiseworthy purpose, it will be placed in a position that is wholly unjust and unfair to the American citizen and taxpayer. Moreover, it is in accordance with our oldest and finest tradition . . . that every people has a right to choose its form of government. If the people of Puerto Rico after being *fully apprised of the consequences of independence,* still desire to vote for it, they should be allowed to have it.

This outburst of "Let 'em eat independence!" apparently was accepted without comment by Ickes, who recommended at the cabinet meeting on March 18 that a bill allowing a vote for independence be drawn up by the Division of Territories and Island Possessions. "I strongly urged its immediate introduction," he wrote in his diary, "although it might not pass at this session of Congress, because of the quieting effect that I anticipated it might have on Puerto Rican public opinion."

When Tydings introduced the prepared legislation on April 24, Luis Muñoz Marín (who had not been consulted by anyone, including his friend Gruening) was appalled. No one was more eager for independence than he, but he recognized immediately the bald truth expressed by Gruening in his memorandum to Ickes: Puerto Rico was not ready to take on financial and political responsibility for itself so suddenly; he saw the bill as an essentially punitive measure that would cut the island adrift at a time when rehabilitation financed and directed by the resources of the New Deal was of far greater importance than a spurious independence that would destroy what little good had already been done. But Gruening was adamant—when a team of his own people, headed up by Earl Hanson, analyzed the economic impacts of the bill and concluded that it would "double and triple the island's prevailing starvation and could result in nothing short of chaos," he had every copy he could get his hands on destroyed. When Muñoz Marín not only refused to endorse the bill as written but actively and publicly opposed it, Gruening broke with him and with the Liberal Party in general. Before very many months, he would be allied with Governor Winship and courting the support of the Union-Republican/Socialist alliance that he had previously held in contempt. As the November elections approached, he instituted a program of sniffing out and either dismissing or disciplining members or supporters of the Liberal Party in the PRRA who were, as he viewed it, violating federal law by active politicking. For his part, Muñoz Marín denigrated Gruening's administration of the reconstruction agency. "The picture is this," he wrote Ruby Black on October 26, 1936. "The PRRA functions like a madhouse because Ernest, who does not know how to exercise authority, also does not know how to delegate it."

Nor did public peace ensue. Nationalist fervor, enhanced by the "martyrdom" of the party's leader, who languished in jail, only increased with the perceived "capitulation" of the American government. Student strikes and rioting took place on an unprecedented scale, and a growing radical element of the Liberal Party muttered threats to join with the Nationalists and convene a constitutional convention even before any referendum might be approved and scheduled by the American Congress (though none ever was during the Roosevelt years). Muñoz Marín struggled to keep events from overtaking the political process, but in the end was unable to prevent a disastrous split among the Liberals that gave the Union-Republican/Socialist coalition a majority in the November elections—and when Antonio Barcelo formally expelled Muñoz Marín and his followers from the Liberal Party later that month it left effective control of Puerto Rico's political structure in the hands of the coalition for the next several years.

By November the administration of the PRRA also was in a shambles, with dismissals, resignations, and recriminations epidemic. Early in December, Ickes sent one of his assistants, Leona Graham, down to the island to investigate the situation and she returned with evidence of "such amazing incompetence and extravagance" that the Secretary was able to persuade Roosevelt to put the PRRA under his direct control, then urged Gruening to resign as administrator before things got any worse. Gruening agreed, but won the concession from Ickes that he be allowed to go to the island for an "inspection tour," after which he would make a public statement to the effect that everything was in fine condition, then resign and confine himself to the administration of the Division of Territories and Island Possessions. He still had not made his inspection tour by the middle of February 1937, however, and Ickes was getting nervous, warning Gruening with heavy irony that "if there should be any sort of a flare-up in the PRRA in Puerto Rico, then your plan to resign because everything is going so well in that administration would have to go in the discard."

A flare-up did occur a little over a month later, and while it was not in the PRRA, its impact on the future administration of Puerto Rico was just as profound as if it had been. It took place in Ponce, a quiet port town on the southern coast of the island, on Palm Sunday, March 21. A group of about eighty unarmed "cadets" and twelve female "nurses" of the Nationalist Party's "Army of Liberation" had won permission from Ponce's mayor for a parade that day, but the morning of the event the city's chief of police prohibited it, lined the street with armed police, and installed at least one machine-gun emplacement on a balcony overlooking the proposed line of march. The cadets and nurses attempted to move in spite of an order to halt, someone fired a shot, and the police, including the machine-gunner, commenced general firing.

Within a few minutes, fourteen young people were dead and more than a hundred people wounded, six of whom would later die (including two policemen). Winship's report, filed two days after a cursory investigation, maintained that the Nationalists had fired the first shot, but no hard evidence ever emerged to prove that contention—and in fact, excellent news photographs clearly showed that the cadets were carrying no guns as they lined up to march, and just as clearly revealed policemen a few seconds later firing into a screaming, scattering crowd of marchers and spectators, none of whom appeared to be shooting back. Other photographs showed that almost all the dead and wounded (including the two policemen) had been shot in the back.*

After issuing the standard public announcements of regret over the incident and proclaiming their solemn intention to see that justice was done, the governments of Puerto Rico and the United States did their best to minimize the affair. The police would later arrest thirteen Nationalists, once again on conspiracy charges (the evidence against them remained so thin that they would be acquitted almost a year later). But Roger Baldwin and the ACLU were not satisfied that Winship and the Insular Police Department had any real interest in the truth. In April the organization hired the well-respected New York attorney Arthur Garfield Hays to head up a "Commission of Inquiry on Civil Rights in Puerto Rico" and sent the commission to the island to make a report on what the newspapers, with more justification than usual, were calling the "Ponce Massacre."

Even before the Hays commission issued its report on May 22, word began to leak out that its conclusions were not going to reflect well on the Winship government—and hence on the New Deal. The House of Representatives issued a resolution asking the Secretary of the Interior to furnish it with all information on the riot. With FDR's permission, Ickes—

* The photographs, in excellent condition, can still be seen in the Ickes Collection in the Manuscript Reading Room of the Library of Congress (Container 257, Secretary of Interior File).

perhaps with the intent of forestalling any congressional investigation that might ensue—sent a radiogram in naval code to Winship on May 21 suggesting in strong terms "that you request me as of your own motion to send to Puerto Rico an impartial and qualified board to conduct such an investigation as will bring to light all the facts." When the governor had not done what was asked of him by Monday, Ickes called him. According to a stenographic transcript of the conversation, Ickes asked Winship, "Did you get my radiogram, Governor?"

"I did," Winship replied, "and I don't want to do that. I think that would not be a very good thing at this time."

"Well, now, Governor, we are between the Devil and the deep blue sea. There is going to be an investigation and if we don't make it, somebody is going to make it."

"I am sending a memorandum to you. The attorney general [of Puerto Rico] and the best people are very much the other way about it."

"I don't doubt it but the best people are usually wrong, Governor, and after all, the people cannot be shot down the way they were at Ponce. . . . Governor, if lives are lost the way they seem to be lost in Ponce, it does not make a damn bit of difference to me whether they are irresponsible or responsible people. The government is supposed to protect the weak against the strong."

"We don't take these cases out of the hands of the courts."

"I am not taking anything out of the courts, but I have a right to inform myself of what has happened down there. I think it would be better for you to send me the request that I suggested, but if you don't want to do it, that is all right by me."

"I am not going to send it to you. Everybody was responsible and the thing has not had time."

"You talk about people who are responsible. Have I not a responsibility?"

"Of course you have."

"Then I am going to exercise it. That is all I have to say. Good-bye."

His next words on the subject were issued from a sickbed.

Ickes had been having even more than his usual trouble with insomnia for months, and no amount of whiskey and sleeping prescriptions seemed to help. Even worse, he had been having bouts of extreme exhaustion that sometimes drove him to his bed in a depressed state for two or three days at a time. His physical problems had been compounded on December 1, 1936, when he was severely bruised and his hand badly cut by flying glass in an automobile accident while on his way to make the cornerstone-laying speech at a new medical building at the University of Virginia that had been financed by PWA funding. Picked up by a passing car, he had wrapped his bleeding hand in a handkerchief and had gone on to make the speech as scheduled, but after seeing a doctor had gone to bed for three days. On December 10 he was a little less sore, but otherwise still feeling well below par. "There isn't any doubt that I am hanging over the ropes so far as my nerves are concerned," he told his diary. "I was in bad shape before that automobile accident and I have been much worse off since. I don't seem to be able to get hold of myself, although I am taking things as easily as possible and leaving my office about the middle of the afternoon each day."

By May 1937, under doctor's orders, he was spending much of his time at home. On Wednesday, May 26, he became even more tired than usual and took to his bed with a heart rate, by his own measurement, of more than a hundred beats a minute. His doctor came to the house and examined him and made an appointment for him with a heart specialist, then sent an assistant out to the house that night with a shot of morphine to help him sleep. By the time Ickes got to the heart specialist's office on Thursday afternoon, he was suffering the pain of a full-fledged heart attack. The doctor gave him morphine again, and he was ordered back to bed with what was diagnosed as a coronary thrombosis.

He did as he was told, but when Winship and Gruening came to Washington the next day, he called both of them to his house, where from his bed he reiterated his insistence on an investigation and, he said later, "Governor Winship said that he would request an investigation which was to come to me through Dr. Gruening with the latter's approval." On Monday, May 31, he was taken by ambulance to the Bethesda Naval Hospital. Here, doctors assured him that the damage to his heart muscle was relatively minor and that after five or six weeks of complete rest he should be able to return to work.

They did not know their man. While Slattery, Burlew, Assistant Secretary Chapman, and Undersecretary West formed a team to administer the various Interior agencies, they did not do so without the advice and consent of their boss, expressed in a steady flow of memoranda from his hospital bed, written down and carried back and forth by May Conley. Most of them had to do with the island situation. "What is happening in Puerto Rico matter?" he asked Burlew and Slattery on June 2. "Tell Gruening he ought to send in his resignation as Administrator of PRRA at once. My understanding with Gruening was that he would go to Puerto Rico at once; find out that everything was going along all right there and that he would then resign. It may be fatal for him to delay his resignation. I may not accept the resignation until I am back at the office again, but to avoid any mishap the resignation ought to be tendered at once."

The resignation was not forthcoming. On June 4, Ickes was told that Gruening and Winship had gone to see Tydings without consulting anyone in the department. Tydings was no friend to Ickes or the administration, and the Secretary was a good deal more furious than was probably beneficial to his condition. "This is flagrant insubordination," he erupted, "and I want both the Governor and Gruening to be told that that is my opinion. . . . If Gruening does not send me his resignation as Administrator I shall remove him at once. If a request does not come from Winship, through Gruening, for an investigation, I shall, notwithstanding that fact, order an investigation."

He would not get the chance. On June 7, the eight Nationalists convicted in connection with the assassination of Colonel Riggs in February 1936 were sentenced by U.S. District Court Judge Cooper to serve six to ten years at the federal penitentiary at Atlanta. A day later, Cooper was shot at by three or four unidentified men. This apparently threw the fear of insurrection into Roosevelt, who firmly "suggested" to Ickes that any investigation be postponed. "At this particular time," he wrote in a memorandum of June 9, "I am definitely convinced that the maintenance of Federal authority is the first consideration and that nothing be done until the Island thoroughly understands that Federal authority will be unhesitatingly maintained."

Ickes obeyed, but not without comment. "I hope," he replied, "that we do not find ourselves in that vicious circle where the Federal authority tramples upon or ignores constitutional rights, the people denied those rights resort to violence, and then the Federal authority, in order to assert itself, further denies civil rights."

The Secretary finally was able to pull a resignation out of Gruening on June 16. (Earl Hanson claimed that when the news of that resignation reached San Juan, "the entire staff of the PRRA, hundreds of men and women . . . poured out of their offices into the open air in a great, spontaneous demonstration of relief.") Ickes remained highly irritated with him. Just after dark on July 2, with the permission of his doctors, an ambulance took Ickes from the Naval Hospital to the Interior Building, where he was comfortably installed in his private suite, furnished with one of his own beds. One of his first acts in the following days was to bring Gruening in and put him in his place in front of Undersecretary West, Burlew, and Slattery:

I asked Gruening what he meant when at a conference held in West's office while I was in the hospital he read a memorandum from me and said that it was "the memorandum of a sick man." He replied that he thought that the memorandum showed irritation. I admitted that it did and told him that I was entitled to feel irritated. . . . I insisted that he meant more than this, that in fact his remark was designed to carry the impression that I was so sick that I didn't know what I was doing. He denied this emphatically.

Gruening also defended himself against charges of disloyalty and on "one or two other matters," Ickes wrote, "I . . . made it clear that I was not very much pleased with him." Gruening apparently endured all this like a good soldier, for he remained as administrator of the Division of Territories and Island Possessions for another two years before his growing interest in the affairs of Alaska led him to accept appointment as the territory's governor in September 1939. Ickes himself took over responsibility for the PRRA until October 1939, when it was folded into the Puerto Rico governor's office. Gruening's post at the Division of Territories and Island Possessions remained vacant until a suitable replacement was found in Harvard professor Rupert Emerson in April 1940.

By that time, the Secretary had also gotten rid of Governor Winship, who was finally persuaded to resign on October 31, 1939. Admiral William D. Leahy, chief of naval operations, took over the job on September 1 and held it until December 1940, when Roosevelt named him ambassador to France. Pennsylvania representative Guy J. Swope then took the position. Shortly thereafter, Ickes fired Rupert Emerson as head of the Division of Territories and Island Possessions for demonstrating an independent nature too reminiscent of Gruening. In the meantime, he had asked Rexford G. Tugwell—who had left the federal government in 1936—to head up a commission to look into the enforcement of Puerto Rico's five-hundred-acre law, which remained unenforced. When Swope expressed a desire to resign as governor of Puerto Rico and take over the Division of Territories and Island Possessions, Tugwell expressed a desire to become governor, and in August 1941 the deed was done.

The deranged saraband of responsibility in Puerto Rico ended with the arrival of Tugwell, who would remain until 1946. What the new governor found waiting for him was a political scene whose players had been shifted around significantly. Among other developments, Luis Muñoz Marín had made a comeback as head of the Popular Democratic Party, a hybrid born of the split that had torn the Liberal Party asunder in 1936, and in the elections of November 1940 the new party had won a majority. He promised Ickes and Tugwell his cooperation in the future administration

of the island, and even during the war years the new governor and the
resurgent political leader would do much to bring Puerto Rico a semblance of stability. Tugwell, who stayed on as governor for the next five
years, nevertheless had inherited responsibility for a land that would never
be entirely free of political violence—nor of the poverty that gave this
violence birth, a condition which nearly seven years of incomparably inept
and strife-riddled attempts at reconstruction had invested with the character of a kind of grisly joke. In July 1934, before creation of the PRRA,
there had been 643,327 people receiving some sort of relief. By the end of
1938, that number had grown to 1,121,035.

Understandably, the betrayal of hope represented by the New Deal experience in Hawaii, the Virgin Islands, and Puerto Rico does not come in for
much discussion in the standard histories of the era; the problems that
beset these island possessions, after all, were hardly representative of those
that afflicted the American mainland, nor was their destiny central to the
fate of the nation. Nevertheless, they demonstrated an aspect of economic
planning and social engineering that rarely was anticipated by the planners and the engineers and just as often overlooked by public philosophers
like Walter Lippmann, who in 1937 was worried that planning carried to
its logical ends could imperil democracy. By the nature of the task, he
wrote in an *Atlantic Monthly* article,

> planners must control the people. They must be despots who tolerate no
> effective challenge to their authority. Therefore civilian planning is com-
> pelled to presuppose that somehow the despots who climb to power will be
> benevolent—that is to say, will know and desire the supreme good of their
> subjects. . . . Thus, by a kind of tragic irony, the search for security and a
> rational society, if it seeks salvation through political authority, ends in the
> most irrational form of government imaginable—in the dictatorship of
> casual oligarchs.

What Lippmann overlooked and the planners did not anticipate was
that *sometimes it could not be made to work, no matter how benevolent the
intention, no matter how much money was spent, no matter how hard one tried.*
The quirks of greed, ego, vindictiveness, compassion, ambition, common
sense, and plain cussedness which were given room for expression in any
functioning democracy usually were enough to thwart the most grandiose
planning, no matter how cunningly devised. Against this wall of reality
some of the highest expectations of the planners were shattered, and with
them any chance of the oligarchy Lippmann feared. Probably, this was a
good thing for the nation in the long run, but it was dreadfully hard on

the planners, who were generally worn down by it as the decade of the thirties drew to a close. "Five years have seen the New Deal rise to a peak of hopeful enthusiasm and then settle down, where it is now, into a cautious and bewildered old age," United Press columnist Raymond Clapper wrote on March 4, 1938. "These have been five years of mingled successes and failures, of quick-changing and baffling currents. They have left Roosevelt not sadder but certainly wiser. He knows now there is no slide-rule formula for running a democratic country. If democracy is the easiest form of government to live under, it is the hardest to run."

CHAPTER
· 39 ·

The Most Forgotten American

THERE WERE OTHER ARENAS in which the best hopes of the New Deal's Progressive instincts discovered failure—one of them centering on perhaps the oldest continuing paradox in American history: the Indian and his place in the national life. "It is the nature of human ecology," anthropologist John Greenway has written, "that hunting-gathering and Neolithic peoples cannot survive against the onslaughts of expanding agriculturists. The fact that the Indians . . . managed to save not only their populating viability but also their pride and their culture, is a tribute to the psychic energy that made them and motivated them." The people of the United States are hardly the first agriculturists to have overrun the lands occupied by a subsistence culture, but we may well be the first people in history to have assumed a burden of guilt because of it. "The progress of our settlements westward," President James Monroe wrote in 1818, "supported as they are by a dense population, has constantly driven them back, with almost the total sacrifice of the lands which they have been compelled to abandon. They have claims upon the magnanimity and I may add, on the justice of this nation which we must all feel. We should become their real benefactors."

That sentiment, however earnest, was the child of an eastern environment, where even by 1818 the Indian "problem" was largely an abstraction. Out on the cutting edge of the frontier, it was no abstraction; it was a reality whose raw and sometimes bloody outlines could not be softened by rhetoric. The Indians occupied the land; the frontier wanted the land, demanded the land, would not be denied the land. And as the westward movement grew in force and political significance, its desires were accommodated. The government in Washington found itself compelled to do what its highest instincts said it could not do: dispossess an entire race of people. Therein lay the paradox. Paradox begat confusion, and henceforth confusion fed an amalgam of guilt, greed, promises, broken promises, and a desperate inability to reconcile the forces of history and conscience.

Responsibility for Indian matters was first placed in the Department of War in 1789, but it was not until 1824 that the department established the Bureau of Indian Affairs. In 1849, after the Five Civilized Tribes (the Choctaw, Chickasaw, Creek, Cherokee, and Seminole) had been forcibly moved west across the Mississippi River and any "uncivilized" Indians long since obliterated, subjugated, or chased out of the eastern United States, the bureau was taken out of the War Department and placed in the newly created Department of the Interior on the assumption that the presence of the military would no longer be required. That attitude swiftly changed as the line of white settlement moved across the Mississippi and met with sporadic Indian resistance in ugly skirmishes from the short-grass country of the Dakotas to the volcanic stones of northern California. Collectively dignified as the "Indian Wars," they culminated in the massacre of Sioux Indians at Wounded Knee in 1890. Still, nonlethal responsibility for the Indians remained in the hands of the Bureau of Indian Affairs, which, especially in the years following the Civil War, was directed by a succession of political appointees whose administrative skills often were matched by their venality and represented in the field by Indian Service agents frequently as corrupt as their masters in Washington.

Not that the tenderhearted had done the Indians much more good than soldiers or greedy bureaucrats. The question was one of assimilation, the assumption on the part of the reformers being that the Indian's best hope was to enfold himself within the dominant civilization. Christianization, education, citizenship, and the systematic erasure of tribal identity, native religion, and cultural traditions became the highest goals of reform, particularly during the last third of the nineteenth century. By then, most Indian peoples had been removed to immense western reservations carved out of lands for which white settlers had no immediate need. At best, this was a temporary expedient, in the view of the reformers. "The utter absence of individual title to particular lands," one of them wrote as early as 1857, "deprives every one among them of the chief incentive to labor and exertion—the very mainspring on which the prosperity of a people depends."

This definitive nineteenth-century perception of what constituted civilization was translated into an official program by the General Allotment Act of 1887. Under its stipulations, the President was authorized to make grants of reservation land to individual Indian heads of family (160 acres), single individuals over the age of eighteen (eighty acres), and each child in a family (forty acres); where grazing, not farming, would be the dominant use, larger allotments were made. All adult allottees would be granted citizenship as well. The land, untaxable by the states in which it lay, was to be held in trust by the government for twenty-five years, during which time each allottee was expected to learn the arts of farming and husbandry and otherwise divorce himself from his traditional feast-or-famine ways and become an Indian version of Jefferson's legendary yeoman. At the end of the twenty-five years, he would be given full title to his allotment. Until that time, he could neither sell nor lease it. "Surplus" lands—those left over after the allotments had been made—were to be sold by the federal government, the money held by the U.S. Treasury; the money would earn 3 percent interest, and it was from this that Congress would make appropriations each year for the administration of the program.

A grand design, and quite possibly—next to Prohibition—the most thoroughly misguided and unworkable reform measure in American history. With few exceptions, most Indians had little taste, experience, or talent for farming, and the attempts on the part of the Indian Service to bend them in this direction failed. By 1891 it was becoming clear that thousands of Indian families would not be able to sustain themselves on the land, and the law was revised to allow for leasing to white farmers and ranchers, which provided the Indians with at least some income, though in most cases it amounted to a pittance. Even for those Indians inclined to give it a try, Indian Service agents on many reservations frustrated the intent of the law, blocking the allotment of the best land so that it could be made available to white settlers for sale as surplus. Through such surplus sales, Indian holdings had declined from 138 million to 47 million acres between 1887 and 1934.

Because the lands were not subject to local taxation, many states in which the land was held refused to construct schools or roads or to provide judicial services for Indians. At the same time, Congress was consistently penurious in its own annual appropriations for the operations of the bureau, and the Indian Service, and all services, from education to medical help, remained at an abysmal level for years (there was no Indian medical service at all until 1909, for example). In 1906, because the Supreme Court had declared that the Bureau of Indian Affairs could not prohibit the sale of liquor to allottees since they were citizens, Congress passed the Burke Act, which delayed citizenship to the allottees until the end of the twenty-five-year trust period and consequently—and contradictorily—perpetuated the wardship status of the Indians that allotment was supposed to have eliminated (though at his discretion, the Secretary of the Interior could shorten the waiting period in individual cases). Finally, the 1887 General Allotment Act had been predicated on the assumption that the population of pureblood Indians would decrease through assimilation or death, leaving more and more land in the possession of fewer and fewer Indians through heirship. But the Indians did not cooperate; between 1890 and 1930, the population actually increased from 248,253 to 332,397; as a result, numerous Indian family heirs often found themselves holding shares of only one, two, or three acres out of the original allotments made two generations before. When these were sold or leased, the income came to pennies a person.

The General Allotment Act, then, with all good intentions, had instituted a kind of progressive poverty. By the 1920s tens of thousands of Indians were economically destitute and not only locked out of general American society but bereft of the cultural ties that had sustained them for generations, their ancient traditions weakened and in many cases broken altogether by the inexorable forces of bureaucracy and reform.

Under pressure from groups like the General Federation of Women's Clubs and John Collier's American Indian Defense Association, Coolidge's Interior Secretary Hubert Work—Albert Fall's successor—had been moved to commission the Institute for Government Research to do a study of the Indian situation. Financed by the Rockefeller Foundation and edited by Lewis Meriam of the Brookings Institution, it was subsequently published by the Johns Hopkins Press in 1928 under the title *The Problem of Indian Administration*. The highly critical report took Congress to task for appropriating too little money for education or medical services and attached the Bureau of Indian Affairs for operating overcrowded boarding schools it described as "grossly inadequate." It also came down with some force on the allotment program, which, it said, had "resulted in much loss of land and an enormous increase in the details of administration without a compensating advance in the economic ability of the Indians."

If he read the Meriam report, Hoover's Interior Secretary, Ray Lyman Wilbur, apparently did not believe it. He came to office determined to continue the allotment program as the surest means of forcing the Indian into the white world. Just like the child who takes too long to be weaned

(Wilbur was a physician), he told a reporter for the *Washington Star* shortly after taking office, the Indian must be pulled off the teat of government support; hand it "a pickle and let it howl," he said. His commissioner of Indian Affairs, Charles J. Rhoads, the man who would have to listen to the howling, moved cautiously, however, doing his best to improve conditions in health, education, irrigation, and other programs, while upgrading the personnel of his agency. But Wilbur left office just as didactic and close-minded as when he entered it, writing in 1932 that "The Indian should be developed into a self-respecting American citizen. The Indian stock should merge with that of the Nation. Individually the Indian should be prepared for life among the rest of us. The Indian Bureau should work itself out of a job in 25 years."

John Collier, Ickes's chosen commissioner of Indian Affairs, had no intention of letting the bureau work itself out of a job. From the moment of his confirmation by the Senate on April 21, 1933, he and his assistant William Zimmerman, Jr., invested the agency with new energy—and, as elsewhere in the agitated world of New Deal bureaucracy, the sense of purpose took on an almost frantic edge. "Even after twenty-five years," Zimmerman remembered in 1957,

> it is still easy to relive the first months of the new administration. There were endless meetings, inside and outside of working hours. In the evenings we sometimes met at Collier's apartment which was so sparsely furnished that some would sit on the floor. On a bright Sunday morning the meeting might be on a grassy point in Potomac Park. There was zest and fun in those meetings, but also always a sense of urgency, of fighting time, of doing things now, before it should be too late; but there was always a feeling of accomplishment.

Collier was determined that the bureau would be the vessel within which he would turn the administration of Indian affairs on its head, refuting history. The Indians should be given all the financial, medical, nutritional, and educational means necessary for survival and even prosperity; at the same time, they should be encouraged to celebrate their past, embrace their own cultures, and maintain tribal identity. It was a conviction that had come to him after his first weeks among the Pueblo Indians in the early 1920s. "The discovery that came to me there, in that tiny group of a few hundred Indians," he remembered in his florid prose, "was of personality-forming institutions, even now unweakened, which had survived repeated and immense historical shocks, and which were going right on in the production of states of mind, attitudes of mind, earth-loyalties and human loyalties, amid a context of beauty which suffused all the life of the group." That kind of cultural energy must be retained, he believed, as the essence from which the Indian's future was to be formed, and he made himself uncommonly clear in his first annual report: "No interference with Indian religious life or expression will be tolerated. The cultural history of Indians is in all respects to be considered equal to that of any non-Indian group. And it is desirable that Indians be bilingual—fluent and literate in the English language, and fluent in their vital, beautiful, and efficient native languages. The Indian arts are to be prized, nourished, and honored." So firmly did he hold these convictions and so repeatedly did he emphasize the value of Indian traditions that his enemies—and there would be many—were persuaded that he considered Indian civilizations superior to that of whites; they may have been correct.

Ickes probably did not always understand fully the sometimes labyrinthine philosophical musings of his commissioner (many people did not), but from the beginning he gave Collier the kind of uncritical support that he gave almost no one else serving under—or even with—him, this in spite of the contentious history between them. Ickes, Zimmerman remembered, was "a powerful stimulus. . . . In those first months before the tentacles of bureaucracy took hold, it was almost a daily routine for Mr. Collier and the Assistant Commissioner, each morning before nine, to dash up two flights of stairs to the Secretary's office and tell him quickly about the newest problems or get an answer to a vexing question."

Before long, Ickes would delegate virtually all responsibility for the bureau to Collier. Part of this rare accommodation must have stemmed from the fact that Ickes ultimately found himself just too busy with other matters to attempt to involve himself intimately in the administration of an agency whose complexities were more than a match for anything else in the Department of the Interior. As long as Collier appeared to be firmly in control, Ickes seemed content to let him run things. In addition, Collier's headlong defiance of tradition and his willingness to take on the perceived enemies of the Indians hammer and tongs must have appealed greatly to a man who was no stranger to windmill tilting himself. Certainly, Ickes had little more than informed contempt for what his and Collier's predecessors had accomplished. Nor was he willing to let Congress off the hook of responsibility. In June 1933 a congressional delegation came to call on the secretary with regard to the closing of an Indian boarding school. Shutting it down, the congressmen said, would release underfed, underclothed, and sometimes diseased Indian children into white schools. "It was urged," Ickes wrote in his diary, "that they would not get along happily with the white children. . . .

I pointed out that we had exploited the Indians from the beginning; that we had taken from them their lands; that we had robbed them right and left; that the diseases they were suffering from were due in a large measure to contacts with the whites and were not unrelated to undernourishment. I said that Congress wouldn't give us money for things needed to be done for the Indians; that Congress had assisted in despoiling them and that the man who was largely responsible for Indian appropriations in the House of Representatives for many years had gone publicly on record to the effect that eleven cents a day was enough to feed an Indian child.

Ickes doubtless found solace for his anger as he watched Collier and his people at work that first year of the Indian New Deal. Before his departure, Commissioner Rhoads had started to pull children out of the traditional boarding schools, long criticized as little better than psychological prisons in which the children were isolated and abused, placing students instead in community day schools designed to become part of reservation life; Collier accelerated that process. Within weeks, the new commissioner raised the number of Indians working in the Bureau's Indian Service to 1,785—30 percent of the total—including the appointment of an Indian to run the Klamath Indian Agency in Oregon, an unheard-of development in a field that had always been lily-white.

At the end of April, Collier asked Roosevelt to create a special division of the CCC for Indians, to be directed and manned entirely by Indians, and Roosevelt did so, establishing the department of Indian Emergency Conservation Work. Congress appropriated nearly six million dollars for the program, and within six months there were seventy-two IECW camps on thirty-three reservations. (Before being closed out by World War II in 1943, the IECW would employ about eighty-five thousand young Indians, not only putting them to work on simple construction and reclamation jobs, but training them in the operation of heavy equipment, erosion control, and other skills.) On May 25 the busy Collier persuaded Ickes to ask Roosevelt to issue an Executive Order abolishing the Board of Indian Commissioners on the grounds of saving the thirteen thousand dollars a year it took to support it. In fact, Collier considered the influence of this advisory board, long made up of Republican conservatives and supporters of the allotment program, to be pernicious and he wanted to be rid of it. FDR obliged, and Collier replaced the board with a kind of Indian Affairs "brain trust" made up of such people in his own agency as Robert Marshall, director of forestry in the Indian Service, and such outsiders as Ralph Linton, professor of anthropology at Columbia University.

Ickes made no objection when Collier went to Henry Wallace and

Rexford Tugwell for assistance in promoting cattle ranching on Indian reservations. With an allocation of $800,000 from the AAA, the bureau purchased purebred stock from white ranchers facing bankruptcy and used the animals to establish foundation herds on a number of reservations; within six years, Indian ranchers had increased from 8,627 to 16,624 and the number of cattle from 167,373 to more than a quarter of a million. Conversely, the AAA purchased surplus sheep and goats to relieve the grazing pressure on the land—especially on the Navajo Reservation in the Southwest, where generations of overgrazing had led to some of the worst erosion anywhere in the West. Tugwell's Resettlement Administration also funded the drilling of wells, administered five subsistence homesteads on reservation lands, financed canning and clothing factories, and purchased nearly a million acres of additional grazing land in the watershed of the Rio Grande for the use of the Pueblo and Navajo tribes.

As winter came on that first year, Collier got the War Department to provide tens of thousands of items of clothing—including 123,000 suits of woolen underwear—for his Indian wards. When Hopkins put together the FERA, the commissioner made certain that the Indian population was in line for relief payments; when the CWA and the WPA came along, Collier was there to see that jobs for Indians were included. At his urging (though it took little persuasion to move Ickes in this regard), the PWA built reservation schools, hospitals, irrigation works, sewerage systems, and museum centers for the display of Indian arts and crafts. Ickes was also persuaded to use an obscure law that authorized the Secretary of the Interior to "adjust or eliminate reimbursable charges" as a device to wipe out more than $12 million in past Indian debts for roads, bridges, irrigation works, and other developments on reservation lands.

All of this activity was both impressive and necessary, but Collier knew that it was essentially cosmetic. For reform to have any lasting effect, it had to be accompanied by a thorough overhaul of the system and philosophy of administration. To this end, on January 7, 1934, Collier and numerous other officials—including Nathan Margold, Charles Fahy, and Felix Cohen from the Solicitor's Office in the Department of the Interior—joined with the American Indian Defense Association and representatives from virtually every other white Indian interest group in the country for a conference on Indian legislation at the Cosmos Club in Washington (among the numerous private individuals also attending was Anna Wilmarth Ickes, in from Illinois for the occasion).

After a full day of speeches, presentations, and debate, the conference agreed upon sixteen points that should be addressed by congressional legislation. Among the most revolutionary of these was the call for the immediate repeal of the allotment system; the consolidation of existing trust lands, placing them under community ownership; the modification of heirship laws to relieve the problem of split estates and to further promote the concept of community ownership; the purchase of lands for landless tribes; the settlement of Indian claims against the government for lands taken without benefit of treaty and for unpaid treaty obligations; and the incorporation of Indian communities and the gradual transfer of many governmental powers from the Bureau of Indian Affairs to the incorporated towns.

On January 20, Collier summarized the conclusions of the Cosmos Club conference in a circular entitled "Indian Self-Government" and sent it to all his Indian agents, tribal councils, and a number of individual Indians with the suggestion that they discuss its points and get back to him in the following three weeks with their thinking in regard to legislation. The response was by no means unanimously in favor of change; those Indians who had come a fair distance on the road to Americanization or who had acquired a financial stake in the status quo raised various objections, as did many agents, some of them fearing the loss of power but some honestly worried that so profound a shift in administrative policy would merely confuse their charges. Collier nevertheless was convinced that it was time to act, and he and his people in the bureau collaborated with Cohen and Fahy from the Solicitor's Office to produce legislation; a little over a month later, the Indian Reorganization bill was ready. Collier and Zimmerman took a car down to the Hill on February 12, making a few last-minute changes on their copies as they went. Collier gave his copy to Representative Edgar Howard of Nebraska, chairman of the House Committee on Indian Affairs; Zimmerman gave his to Senator Burton K. Wheeler of Montana, chairman of the Senate Committee on Indian Affairs. Both men introduced the copies without making changes (Wheeler always claimed he never even read his copy).

At fifty-two pages, it was one of the longest pieces of legislation ever produced by the New Deal, with four titles dealing with most of the concerns expressed at the Cosmos Club conference. The first addressed the question of incorporating Indian communities and the transfer of some power from the federal government. The second outlined a program of higher education for Indians, particularly technical training. The third, and by far the longest and most complicated, repealed the allotment system and attempted to rationalize and consolidate the Indian land system under the principle of community, not individual, ownership, by—among other devices—compelling the exchange of existing allotments for shares of "equal value" in the tribal estate, and by the purchase of non-Indian lands within or adjacent to reservations, including allotments that had been sold after the trust period. The fourth and final title would have established a United States Court of Indian Affairs to handle all judicial matters regarding Indians, Indian lands, and reservations. The question of Indian claims was put aside for later, separate action.

Hearings before both committees on the Indian Reorganization bill (also called the Wheeler-Howard bill) began later that month. "It will be properly asked," Collier noted in his introductory statement, "what is the ultimate goal of this legislation? Does it contemplate for the Indian a permanent tribal status, isolation from the white man, collective or distinguished from individual enterprise, and nonassimilation into American civilization?

"The answer is a clear-cut one: No. . . .

"The future of the Indian tribes will be diverse, as their backgrounds and present situations are diverse. The bill will not predetermine their futures. It is they who should determine their own futures."

At the moment, however, the future of Collier's bill was in the hands of the U.S. Congress, and already it was in trouble. No one on the House committee had any substantial argument with the provisions regarding education, but while committee members were in agreement with the general goals of repealing the allotment system and Indian self-government, most expressed serious reservations about such specifics as the exchange of allotment lands for shares in the tribal estate and the question of whether Indian communities could be taxed by the state for services provided. The title dealing with the establishment of a separate judicial system for the Indians came under especially heavy fire, and by the time the hearings ended on February 27, it was clear that the bill had a long way to go before approval.

The situation in the Senate committee was even more troublesome. There was only one hearing on the bill in February, and that one did not discuss anything of substance because Senator Henry Ashurst of Arizona, presiding in the absence of Senator Wheeler, refused even to let testimony begin until Collier assured him that the bill would not allow for the expansion of holdings on the Papago Indian Reservation in his state to lands that the mining industry had an eye on. Ashurst also wanted the Papago lands reopened to mineral exploration under the provisions of the General Mining Law of 1872 (they had been closed since 1929, when the bureau had drawn a contract with several attorneys to help the Papagos make a claim on subsurface rights, still unresolved by 1934), and when he did not get what he regarded as satisfactory answers from Collier, the Senate hearings closed the day they began and would not be resumed until Ashurst formulated and introduced separate legislation in regard to the Papago lands.

In the meantime, considering the mixed response he had received from his circular of January 20 and the uncertain situation in the two committees, Collier decided to call a series of ten Indian "congresses" around the country, during which he and other bureau officials would explain the bill and attempt to answer questions and objections from Indian delegations from all affected tribes. Over the next several weeks, Collier attended seven of these congresses himself in a killing itinerary that took him from California to New Mexico, Arizona to Wisconsin, and during which he faced thousands of questions, many of them hostile, accusing him, the new bureau, and the bill of communism, socialism, and paganism, charges that would become more frequent as time passed. Still, largely because of promised amendments, votes taken during and shortly after the congresses showed that fifty-four tribes representing 141,881 Indians favored legislation, while twelve tribes with a population of 15,106 rejected it.

By the end of April the authors of the bill added more than thirty amendments to satisfy objections raised by the tribes. In the most significant of these, the exchange of allotment land for shares in the tribal estate would be made voluntary; mineral rights on allotted land would not revert to tribal ownership even when exchanged for estate shares; the division of lands under heirship would be continued as long as any given parcel did not become so small as to be economically useless; and no tribal assets could be disposed of without specific tribal consent. In this form, the bill was resubmitted for consideration.

In spite of strong letters of recommendation that Ickes and Collier persuaded Roosevelt to send the two chairmen, the legislation continued to crawl through both committees, bits and pieces of it being chopped off as it went. Meanwhile, rumors came to Collier that some aid and comfort was being provided the opponents of the bill by disgruntled bureau employees, and he asked Ickes to issue a singularly nasty memorandum to all employees on April 30:

> It was anticipated that there would be resistance to any plan designed to increase the protective features of the Indian policy and at the same time to decrease Federal overlordship; but it was not expected that employees of the Indian Service would deliberately attempt to obstruct the program that has been developed. . . .
>
> My purpose in addressing you is to notify all of those engaged in this scheme to defeat our program that a continuance will be under penalty of

dismissal from the Service. It is not intended to deny to any employee the freedom of expression or the right to petition Congress, but these privileges do not carry with them the right to interfere with administration by under-cover methods. . . .

If any employee wishes to oppose the new policy, he should do so honestly and openly from outside of the Service. This would mean his resignation. Any other course is unscrupulous.

This directive, which some recipients doubtless considered distinctly unscrupulous itself, probably was pointless. The members of Congress, Senate and House alike, did not need help from employees of the bureau to make their own revisions and deletions in the legislation. The bills that finally passed each house were merged into a single document after further revisions in conference committee at the end of May, and on June 18 signed into law as the Indian Reorganization Act, which was at best a pale reflection of Collier's original legislation. Title IV, which would have created a separate Indian court system, was deleted entirely. The allot-ment system was formally abolished and all remaining trust lands were incorporated into tribal ownership, but the exchange of existing allot-ments for shares in the tribal lands was made voluntary. Landless Indians were forbidden grants of land on reservations belonging to a different tribe; an annual appropriation of two million dollars was established for the purchase of non-Indian land to consolidate tribal holdings, but a stipulation allowing purchases in trust for individuals as well as tribes undercut the goal of community ownership. Community incorporation for business purposes was allowed, but required a petition signed by two-thirds of the community before the Secretary of the Interior could (at his discretion) grant the papers and a majority vote of the tribe before formal adoption, and Congress (at *its* discretion) could revoke any charter. Tribes were authorized to organize and write constitutions, but the scope of their provisions was limited and approval subject to the discretion of the Secretary. Finally, the act stipulated that it could go into effect for any given tribe only if that tribe endorsed it by secret ballot within one year. And, to Collier's everlasting disappointment, by the time final elections had been held, 172 tribes had accepted the act, but seventy-three had repudiated it, including the Navajo, the most populous tribe in the country. During the years of the New Deal, only ninety-three tribes ever adopted constitutions and only seventy-three ever incorporated them-selves.

Two large segments of the native population remained to be accounted for even after passage of the Indian Reorganization Act. First, the Indians of Oklahoma, who had been excluded from six major provisions of the act at the insistence of Oklahoma senator John William Elmer Thomas, who felt that the relevant portions of the act applied more appropriately to the reservation Indians of the Far West than to the more settled and "civilized" Indians of his state, many of whom had intermarried with white people. In addition to the Five Civilized Tribes, these Indians included scattered remnants of such tribes as the Kaw, Pawnee, Ponca, Ottawa, and Seneca, all of whom were bitterly poor and all of whom were now cut off from federal aid and other benefits (however hedged about with restrictions) provided by the Reorganization Act. Collier worked with Thomas and with Representative Will Rogers, Jr. (himself part Indian and by then chairman of the House Committee on Indian Affairs), to produce the Thomas-Rogers bill, an adaptation of the Reorganization Act revised to meet the special needs of the Oklahoma tribes. Introduced in April 1935, it went through much the same kind of painful metamorphosis as the Reorganization Act before being passed and signed into law in June 1936 as the Oklahoma Welfare Act. Under its provisions, nineteen Oklahoma tribes with a total population of 13,241 adopted constitutions during Collier's term as commissioner, while thirteen ratified charters of incorporation.

That left the Indians and Eskimos of Alaska, who remained out in the cold after passage of the Reorganization Act because of a mistake: the congressional conference committee, in rewriting various sections of the bill, had inadvertently left the Alaska natives out of Section 7, that part of the act that allowed for incorporation and, not least important, access to a revolving credit fund established by the act. The native peoples of the territory were easily enough forgotten, apparently; through some peculiarity of bureaucratic convenience, they had been placed under the administration of the Education Department after Alaska was taken out of military control in the 1880s and had not enjoyed the supervision of the Bureau of Indian Affairs until 1931, when an Executive Order finally put them where they belonged. Nor had they been included in the provisions of the General Allotment Act of 1887.

Legislative isolation ended in 1936, when a separate bill to rectify the oversight in the Reorganization Act of 1934 was drafted by Felix Cohen, introduced, and passed as the Alaska Reorganization Act in June 1936 with little opposition (Alaska was a very long distance from Washington). In addition to allowing for community incorporation and the adoption of constitutions, the act also authorized the Secretary of the Interior to create reservations from public-domain land in the territory (virtually all of which was public domain). Not only would this for the first time put the natives of Alaska on the same footing as the Indians of the contiguous forty-eight states, but as Ickes noted in a letter to Will Rogers, Jr., on March 14, "if native communities are to set up systems of local government, it will be necessary to stipulate the geographic limits of their jurisdiction. Reservations set up by the Secretary of the Interior will accomplish this." Ickes subsequently established six large Alaskan reservations, including the 1,408,000-acre Venetie Reservation in the shadow of the Brooks Range just north of the Arctic Circle. During the course of Collier's administration, forty-nine villages with a population of 10,899 natives joined the ranks of the Indian New Deal by adopting constitutions and charters of incorporation.

Collier had hoped that, as first proposed, the Indian Reorganization Act "would have a massive and dramatic nature, commanding the imagination of Indians and Congressmen alike." The first bill had been dramatic enough, certainly, but he clearly had overestimated the capacity for imagination in both groups, at least as far as something so complicated and far-reaching as this legislation was concerned. In the end, only the repeal of the allotment system came close to satisfying his highest hopes for the legislation.

Still, within the context of what was left him, Collier doggedly pursued his goal of creating "new collective advantages" for the Indians. In 1935 he persuaded Congress to pass legislation that authorized the Interior Department to create an Indian Arts and Crafts Board. The board, whose five appointed members served five-year terms, had fairly wide powers of research and promotion to aid in the production and marketing of Indian goods, including the authentication of each product and the use of a government trademark to foil imitations. Collier also established the Applied Anthropology Unit in the bureau and hired numerous social scientists whose task was not merely to study Indian cultures but to aid in educating the Indians themselves in the old traditions and to encourage their revival within individual tribes. (So important a part of the bureau's operations did this become that it gave rise to the definition of the typical Indian family as consisting of a husband, a wife, three children, and an anthropologist.) The same emphasis on traditional values lay behind Collier's endorsement of Robert Marshall's plan for the designation of sixteen wilderness areas on the reservations. "The Indian folk-like has not shredded away," he wrote in his 1937 order establishing the reservation wilderness system, "as have the other folk cultures of our country, in the face of a commercialism ruthless alike toward man and the wild creatures and toward the land, the earth. Yet increasingly, the Indian is encountering the competition and disturbances of the white race and the acquisitive society. The roadless areas are to save for the Indian places that are all his own, but also to save for the Nation some fragments of commercially unexploited wilderness."

The reference to what this order would do for the nation as a whole as well as for its Indian inhabitants had purpose behind it. This and other administrative actions were designed to illustrate the fact that a functioning civilization "must be a collaboration of local unique groups cooperating in order to intensify their significant individualities." This hymn of pluralism illustrated his conviction that Indian society must eventually stand as an example for a white civilization that had grown "psychically, religiously, socially, and esthetically shattered." This was rather a lot to ask of a people struggling merely to live on the fringe of the civilization that had overwhelmed them; it was even more to ask acceptance of such notions from a Congress that had demonstrated little faith in the belief that white civilization had anything much to learn from the Indians—it was rather the other way around, in the view of most members, particularly a growing cadre of conservative dissidents who tended to look upon such ideas as the spawn of a collectivist devil.

The upshot was an increasingly hostile relationship between the Indian Affairs committees of the House and Senate and Collier's administration and a willingness to heed the complaints of individual Indians and Indian groups who were antagonistic toward the bureau—often without reference to whether or not these were justified or even rational—and to promote the interest of the white constituency when its desires clashed with the welfare of Indian groups. Over the years, a dossier of discontent slowly fattened the archives of both committees.

The forty-five thousand Navajo Indians, for instance, occupying about twenty-five thousand square miles of land in Arizona and New Mexico, remained a thorn in Collier's side throughout his administration. The problem had begun early in 1933, when a joint committee from Interior and Agriculture had visited the reservation to study the condition of its soils. The committee found that the 1.3 million sheep and goats on reservation land had overgrazed it to the point that several hundred thousand acres had been all but destroyed and millions more severely damaged—so much so that erosion from the Navajo Reservation was contributing an estimated 60 percent of all silt carried by the Colorado River. A program of stock reduction was put in place, but it was so badly administered and so bitterly resented by the Indians—who found not only subsistence but a measure of personal worth in the possession of livestock—that they rejected the Indian Reorganization Act. Continued stock reduction and administrative blundering, coupled with the absence of any firm Indian governmental structure, had contributed to a condition of persistent poverty, land abuse, intratribal conflict, and societal disintegration that made the administration of the Navajo one of the major failures of the New Deal.

However grim, the story of the Navajo's disaffection at least had a basis in reality. Not as much could be said for the machinations of the American Indian Federation, a group of about four thousand Indians from various tribes that had been organized in August 1934 by its president, Joseph Bruner, a full-blood Creek Indian from Oklahoma. Bruner was fully assimilated, a successful businessman with interests in oil, real estate, and insurance, and he wanted all Indians to repudiate their tribal pasts and to embrace "American civilization and citizenship." The Indian Reorganization Act, he maintained, was designed to establish "Russian communistic life in the United States," and during hearings before the House Indian Affairs Committee in 1935, Bruner demanded the removal of Collier on the grounds that the Commissioner was an atheist promulgating "Communism instead of Americanism."

Bruner was joined in his crusade by the federation's vice president, Jacob Morgan, a member of the Navajo Tribal Council and a missionary for the Christian Reformed Church, and by Alice Lee Jemison, a mixed-blood Seneca who was a district president of the federation and a woman whom Ickes once described as "a dangerous agitator." Mrs. Jemison was particularly agitated over the question of communism, it seemed, pointing out to the members of the House committee, who listened solemnly, that one powerful piece of evidence that communism was rampant in the bureau was the fact that Ickes, Anna, Collier, and Nathan Margold were all card-carrying members of the American Civil Liberties Union.

Even long after it became commonly known that the federation had powerful ties to and support from the American Nazi movement, particularly William Dudley Pelley's Silver Shirts and the German-American Bund, such charges would continue to be made regularly, and continue to be taken seriously by such House committee members as Abe Murdock of Utah, Usher Burdick of North Dakota, and John McGroarty of California—hard-line conservatives all—and even by Senator Burton K. Wheeler, chairman of the Senate Committee on Indian Affairs, a generally liberal Democrat who had experienced a violent falling-out with Roosevelt over the question of the Supreme Court.

The repeated accusations of communism, while demonstrably ridiculous, nevertheless contributed to an attitude in Congress that, in the spring of 1937, helped defeat legislation to create an Indian Claims

Commission to begin the process of satisfying historic claims against the government for the loss of land.* This same attitude gave weight to Senator Wheeler's determination that year to have the Reorganization Act and its companion legislation repealed, and in February he introduced legislation to that effect. The senator himself was not always entirely rational by now, and when someone apparently told him that Collier had accused him of acting in the interests of whites who wanted to exploit Indian land (a statement Collier never made or implied), Wheeler flew into a rage during the commissioner's appearance before his committee on April 5, 1937, to testify on the bill for repeal.

"My only reason for trying to get this Act repealed," Wheeler told the astonished Collier,

> is because the Indians don't like it. All over the state they tell me they don't like it. That's the only reason I am opposing it, and anybody who says anything else is a damned liar. If you said these things—if you said what I think you said—then all I can say is you are a low cowardly liar. There is not one word of truth in the things I think you said. I haven't read your statement myself. But I want to know from you—all I want to know—is on what grounds you said or implied that I was motivated by pressure from local interests; because—don't interrupt me—it is a dirty lie; it is a damned low thing to do and just about what I expect from you, Collier. . . . You can't tell me you didn't say these things. I know you so well, Collier. I know just how you have gone about this thing. No one is better able to cast implications than you are. I know you through and through. You deliberately said things about me that aren't true and that you know aren't true. You haven't any respect for anybody on God's earth.

Collier formally denied Wheeler's accusations by letter that same day. "I could not at the hearing meet your animus with a like animus," he said with Christian forbearance, "because I did not feel it. . . . No word of mine has been personal or invidious. And surely I have not been, as your remarks at the hearing seemed to imply that I ought to be, deterred by dread of your wrath."

Nor was a majority of the Senate, which defeated Wheeler's bill expeditiously a few weeks later.

By the beginning of World War II, the most ambitious plans that Collier, Ickes, and the rest of the New Dealers had entertained for the hapless

---

* This legislation, which Nathan Margold had been working on even before joining the Interior Department, was not successfully passed until 1946, after Collier's departure from the BIA and Ickes's from Interior.

American Indian had been trimmed back at best and entirely thwarted at worst. What injury Wheeler and the other opponents could not accomplish by legislation they did through the appropriations process. In 1934, before opposition had set like concrete, the bureau had received an appropriation of $52,879,328; in 1937, that had been cut to $37,741,622, and while it increased somewhat in each of the next five years, during the last three years of the war it would be sliced to less than $30 million a year (though by then, this was as much the doing of the Bureau of the Budget as it was of Congress). During the war years, struggling because of budget cuts and the removal of his offices from Washington to Chicago to make room for the military, Collier was left with a skeleton agency, which he departed with some real relief on January 22, 1945, complaining to Roosevelt that the move to Chicago had created "all but insurmountable difficulties and problems" and that declining appropriations had all but nullified the purposes of the Indian Reorganization Act and had cut out the heart of the Indian New Deal.

Felix Cohen left a more positive memory of those years—in both his work and his words. Having cut his legislative teeth on the Indian Reorganization Act, as well as other early New Deal legislation, in 1939 he was appointed special assistant to the Attorney General and assigned to direct an "Indian Law Survey." The result, published in 1942 by the Interior Department as the *Handbook of Federal Indian Law,* was the first attempt by anyone to codify, analyze, and rationalize the more than four thousand laws related to Indian matters that had been passed over the whole sweep of American history. "Only a ripe and imaginative scholar with a synthesizing faculty," Justice Felix Frankfurter would write more than a decade later, "would have brought luminous order out of such a mish-mash. . . . It required realization that any domain of law, but particularly the intricacies and peculiarities of Indian law, demanded an appreciation of history and understanding of the economic, social, political, and moral problems in which the more immediate problems of that law are entwined."

The *Handbook,* revised twice and still considered the bible of Indian law, is one of the most enduring legacies of the age of Roosevelt, and Cohen's remarks in his acknowledgments for the first edition of the work summarize eloquently the depth of conviction and commitment that for all their failings the best and brightest of New Dealers embodied. It was a kind of nobility, and it should be remembered as such:

> What has made this work possible, in the final analysis, is a set of beliefs that
> form the intellectual equipment of a generation—a belief that our treatment

of the Indian in the past is not something of which a democracy can be proud, a belief that the protection of minority rights and the substitution of reason and agreement for force and dictation represent a contribution to civilization, a belief that confusion and ignorance in fields of law are allies of despotism, a belief that it is the duty of the Government to aid oppressed groups in the understanding and appreciation of their legal rights. . . . These beliefs represent, I think, the American mind in our generation.

CHAPTER

· 40 ·

Keeper of the Jewels

O N THE MORNING of Tuesday, November 19, 1934, all of the country's national park superintendents, many of their assistants, and various other park personnel gathered in the auditorium of the old Interior Building on C Street in Washington. They were there for a conference on the problems and prospects of the National Park System, and the first speaker to be heard from was their boss. "Gentlemen," Ickes told them, "I do not have any formal remarks to make; I just have some general observations which may give you something to discuss and to think about. As you will observe, I am sitting down instead of standing up." Then, sitting down, the Secretary proceeded to extemporize a few general observations that took up the better part of an hour and effectively summarized his own conclusions on a subject to which he had given considerable thought himself. The talk indicated that if Ickes consistently maintained a light touch on Collier's operations at the Bureau of Indian Affairs, his interest in the functions of the National Park Service was proprietary from the beginning. The parks, often called the "crown jewels" of America's public lands, were close to the Secretary's heart, and he intended to leave the National Park System bigger and better than when he found it. This, of course, is a sentiment common to most newly arrived secretaries of the Interior; unlike most, however, Ickes accomplished much, if not all, of what he wanted.

"I suspect that my general attitude on what our national parks ought to be is fairly well known," he told his superintendents.

> I do not want any Coney Island. I want as much wilderness, as much nature preserved and maintained as possible. . . . I recognize that a great many people, an increasing number every year, take their nature from the automobile. I am more or less in that class now on account of age and obesity. But I think the parks ought to be for people who love to camp and love to hike and who like to ride horseback and wander about and have . . . a renewed communion with Nature. . . .
>
> I am afraid we are getting gradually alienated from that ideal. We are becoming a little highbrow; we have too many roads. We lie awake nights wondering whether we are giving the customers all of the entertainment and all of the modern improvements that they think they ought to have. But let's keep away from that, because if we once get started, there will be no end.

He had, he said, nothing against the concessionaires—such businesses as the Yosemite Park and Curry Company in Yosemite or the Fred Harvey Company in Grand Canyon—who provided hotels, cabins, food, transportation, and other tourist facilities. "Certainly with our acquiescence, and probably as the result of our urgent representations in many cases," he said, "they have gone into the parks and invested their money. . . . I have a lot of sympathy for them. I wish we had the statutory power and the money to take over all of those concessions and run them ourselves." But they did not, he added. Still, however legitimate the need of the concessionaires to make back their investments and even enjoy a little profit, "we must not yield to that pressure" by caving in to every touristic whim that might be satisfied by concessionaires.

As for the big, expensive hotels like the Old Faithful Inn in Yellowstone, the Ahwahnee Hotel in Yosemite, or El Tovar on the South Rim of Grand Canyon, he said,

> I think there was a wrong concept to begin with. I think accommodations of that sort ought to be simple. The parks can perform a wonderful service in showing people that there is something more to life than jazz, and even radios. I think you should cut them out and let people sleep in peace, if they can sleep, and eliminate all of the hectic overliving that all of us have indulged in to too great an extent during these last jazz years. The greatest service that we can do the people who come to our parks is to get them back to the simpler things of life. . . . [W]e can give people generally a renewal of the fundamentals of life and the worthwhile things in life. That is what our parks are for. They are to be the great outdoor temple. And we ought not to desecrate them or permit them to be desecrated.

And in their spartan quest for spiritual renewal, he said, park visitors should generally be left to their own devices. "On the question of nature study," he told his audience, "I suspect that we are overdoing that. . . . If people are genuinely interested, we ought to satisfy that interest. But don't let's drum up trade." Let visitors go back to nature on their own, if that is what they want, he said. "And don't let's force the issue as to people being educated. . . . Don't force it upon people. . . . [D]on't go upon the theory that a park is a factory, and that the human material comes in one end and goes through certain processing and goes out the other end like so many sausages."

Finally, he returned to a theme that already was old with him—that of vehicular transportation and its place in the parks—this time adding a particularly modern variation: "I think if we make it too easy for airplanes to go whizzing over our parks that we destroy a great deal of their value. . . . If we encourage the airplane business, we will see Glacier, Yellowstone, and Yosemite from the air at a hundred miles an hour. I don't see any sense in catering to that sort of thing." Then, the automobile again:

> I know that when I ride in an automobile, in the modern automobile, I am not able to see from it. . . . There is less window space in the automobiles year after year. Now they have the animated beetles that look like prison cells. And I anticipate the time in the future, at the rate they are developing automobiles, when we will have to run a periscope up through the top in order to see the scenery. It is ridiculous. You can't see the scenery from automobiles.

With the exception of his comments regarding nature study—generally promoted today—there was little in his talk with which modern conservationists, and even professional park managers, would not be inclined to agree—though it would take another forty years for the philosophy of management he expressed to become an acknowledged part of official National Park Service policy. (Even today the idea that the national parks should be maintained primarily as natural systems with as little human alteration or interference as possible is less than perfectly realized.) The Park Service, like most bureaucracies, resisted change as a matter of course, and ever since the days of Mather's spectacular reign it had been devoted to the pursuit of tourism as the foundation on which the future of the parks rested: the more happy tourists there were, the more pressure could be brought upon Congress when appropriations time rolled around or when other concerns important to the service arose. As well, just as it was in most land-managing agencies, the Park Service superintendents on the spot were uncommonly vulnerable to local influence, and local people linked development with jobs and other income.

Ickes's difficulties in this regard had begun at the top, however. Horace Albright, director of the National Park Service after Mather's retirement, had been offered a job as president of the United States Potash Company shortly after Roosevelt's inauguration. He held off accepting until he had secured from both Ickes and Roosevelt a commitment to have the national military parks—most of them Civil War battlefield sites—and other historic sites taken out of the War Department, which had been neglecting them for years, and placed in the Department of the Interior under the aegis of the National Park Service. He also wanted the Park Service to assume control of the parks and historic monuments of Washington, D.C. (at that time administered by an independent body called the Office of Public Buildings and Public Parks of the National Capital), as well as the national monuments under the control of the U.S. Forest Service. Ickes was by no means averse to the idea of expanding the department's responsibility, and Roosevelt was a devoted history buff. On June 10, 1933, the President signed an executive order that more than doubled the size of the National Park System by transferring to it sixty-four national monuments, military parks, battlefield sites, cemeteries, and memorials from the other agencies.

With the assurance that this development was going to take place, Albright had tendered his resignation early in May, naming as his most qualified successor Arno B. Cammerer, a civil service career man who had worked himself up to assistant director under Mather and associate director under Albright, even though Cammerer was not in the best of health, and, according to Albright, did not really want the responsibility. For his part, Ickes did not like Cammerer, considering him lazy, slow-witted, and pure bureaucrat, with little gumption and irritating personal habits. ("As usual," Ickes noted in a diary entry after one meeting with Cammerer, "he sat by my desk vigorously chewing gum in an openmouthed manner.") When Albright mentioned Cammerer, he remembered, "the Secretary flatly refused to consider him. Ickes said he didn't want someone who was 'lock step in the Civil Service,' and I couldn't change his mind."

Albright did talk Ickes into letting him name an advisory committee to choose a successor. The committee, which included Albright, Horace C. McFarland of the American Civic Association, John C. Merriam of the National Parks Association (brother to Ickes's Chicago colleague Charles Merriam), and others, came up with the name of Newton B. Drury of California, a nationally known and respected conservationist who was then president of the Save-the-Redwoods League. Ickes offered the job in July, but Drury turned it down. ("He told me at the time," Drury's friend Robert Sterling Yard remembered in 1940, "that it was too political to suit him.") Ickes then told Albright to "Get your boys together again, and see who else you can come up with." After several hours of discussion in an office adjacent to that of the Secretary, the group finally concluded that the only name on which it could agree was that of the reluctant, gum-snapping Cammerer. Albright marched into the Secretary's office with the news; Ickes was not pleased, but with no other choice before him accepted what he could not avoid, and Cammerer became director in August.

While Cammerer was too good a bureaucrat to openly defy his Secretary's wishes, the two men were clearly poles apart in their philosophy of what the national parks were supposed to be all about—particularly when it came to roads. Two days after Ickes's address to the superintendents on November 19, Cammerer presided over a meeting of park concessionaires at Washington's Powhatan Hotel. After a disclaimer that "Road-building is zealously guarded against" and that such caution was "becoming a more and more important item" (he had been present during Ickes's remarks, after all), Cammerer went on with discernible pride to devote most of his own presentation to a discussion of all the money the Park Service had invested in various development projects over the previous few years—especially roads. "In the West," he said,

> we have put in $41 million since the first of July, 1929. . . . Most of this has gone for modernizing the road system. . . . We are slowly and carefully building up the finest system of scenic roads of any nation on earth, and the cream of them all is in the national parks. The Bureau of Public Roads knows more about road-building than any other similar agency in the world, and I feel that it has done its finest work for us. . . . So rapidly have developments forged ahead in the East that twenty-five and a half million dollars have been allotted, or authorized, for developments in the areas now under our jurisdiction. Nineteen and a half millions of this have gone for roads and trails. This makes a grand total of almost $67,000,000 for roads and trails and other improvements that has been expended by this bureau on the national park system of the United States, covering the past five-year period.

Such pride in purely physical developments did not augur well for the preservation of the national parks as wilderness places where, as Ickes had put it, people might learn "that there is something more to life than jazz, and even radios." During Ickes's term as Secretary of the Interior, very few new roads would be built in the parks after those already authorized had been finished, but in the day-to-day operations of the system, the fondest objectives of the Secretary were consistently undercut at the top by the lack of commitment (or even sympathy) on the part of Cammerer and his assistants, and in the field by park superintendents who were used to doing things the way they had always done them. It would take a stronger individual than Cammerer to effect any substantial change—and while Ickes himself certainly could have served that function, he did not have the time, most of the time. The situation inspired confusion in at least some of the conservation leadership in the country. "There seem to be two policies on the part of the . . . administration," Benton MacKaye, a planner with the TVA and a cofounder of The Wilderness Society, wrote Robert Marshall in May 1935.

> One of these, which is somewhat sketchily expressed by the higher authority Mr. Ickes, appears to be one with our own objective; the other, being put to tangible operation . . . just the opposite of our objective. . . . Outdoor organizations generally are in favor of the National Park administration in the belief and tradition that it is a true guardian of the primeval. But under its present Director and staff, and under the pressure of commercial influence, said administration, so far as I have observed it, is a despoiler of the primeval; and while this is so in one place the Wilderness Society should be wary indeed of endorsing its extension anywhere.

Robert Sterling Yard tended to agree with MacKaye, particularly after paying a visit to the director's office in the summer of 1936 to promote a Wilderness Society and National Parks Association proposal for the designation of a special class of park—the National Primeval Park. This concept arose in reaction to the establishment of such national parks as Shenandoah in the Blue Ridge Mountains of Virginia, very little of which had not been logged over or otherwise exploited at one time or another in the history of the region.* Because of this, in the view of Yard and other purists, its inclusion in the National Park System had degraded the whole idea of the national parks—as had the expansion of the system with the acquisition of the military parks and other nonnatural sites in June 1933. National Primeval Parks, as an antidote to this, would be carved out of entirely roadless and undeveloped regions and would be managed in much the same way as today's National Wilderness Preservation System—no roads or vehicles of any kind allowed, no permanent structures, no commercial use whatever.

Yard found little sympathy for his idea in Cammerer's office. "Last week . . . we indirectly ran up against Cam," he wrote a Wilderness Society member on July 6, 1936.

> Wharton, Jim Foote and myself called on the Big Chief to find him busy with a delegation, and we went in to sit with Ben Thompson. Ben, you know, is special assistant to Cam and is reflecting his views more and more, as is natural. He at once attacked us on our attitude. He called it unbecoming for a

---

* It should be noted that Shenandoah was not the creation of the Roosevelt Administration. The lands that went into it had been acquired from private holdings through state money and private subscription, including money from John D. Rockefeller, Jr.

single organization to assume to create Government policy. He said that he personally would never give up the dream to have all national parks held in like esteem by Congress and the people. He also said we were creating classes and discords. . . . The importance of the incident is that it shows what we have to expect from Cam.

Yard would have done better to beard Ickes himself, probably, for if he and others had been able to put aside their mistrust of the Secretary's motives long enough to recognize his commitment to preservation and support him in the attainment of his highest ambitions, they might have forged an alliance that could have transformed the history of public land management in this country. As it was, by operating at the highest levels of power, Ickes surmounted both their opposition and the frequently recalcitrant behavior of his own staff to achieve more along the lines of what both he and they wanted than anyone had during any other period in the history of the country.

Even during Roosevelt's first term, punctuated by demands coming at it from every direction, there had been room found for the growth of the National Park System—not merely the military sites, city parks, and monuments encompassed in Horace Albright's design, but large units whose designation was meant to provide either recreation opportunities or the preservation of large natural systems, and, where appropriate, both. Like Shenandoah, some of these parks had been proposed and even authorized before the Roosevelt administration, but it took the New Deal to finally bring them forth. Great Smoky Mountains National Park, officially folded into the system in 1934, was one example. In 1926 Congress had authorized the Secretary of the Interior to accept deeds of land for the park from the states of North Carolina and Tennessee. Ten million dollars of the money it would take to purchase the 521,000 acres of land, most of it privately owned, that would be incorporated into the park had been raised through appropriations by the two states and by private subscription, including dimes from schoolchildren and, from John D. Rockefeller, Jr., five million. Ten million dollars had not been quite enough, however, and in August 1933 Roosevelt had allocated $1.55 million in federal funds to complete the purchases. While nothing in the act establishing the park specifically stipulated that it was to be managed essentially as wilderness, that philosophy prevailed during the Roosevelt era and the years that followed—so much so that decades later most of the park survived as almost entirely wild, roadless country.

There was no question about the wilderness character of Everglades

National Park, proposed in the 1920s but not established until FDR's first term. The act of May 30, 1934, spelled it out precisely when it authorized the Secretary of the Interior to accept state deeds to about two thousand square miles of the Everglades in Dade, Monroe, and Collier counties, Florida (which deeds were forthcoming in 1935): "The said area or areas shall be permanently reserved as a wilderness, and no development of the project or plan for the entertainment of visitors shall be undertaken which will interfere with the preservation intact of the unique flora and fauna and the essential primitive conditions now prevailing in this area." The essential primitive condition of 559,960 acres of Joshua Tree National Monument in southern California, established by Executive Order in 1936, would not have been argued by anyone, nor did management practices seriously alter that quality. Lake Mead National Recreation Area—nearly 1.5 million acres of land and water in and around the reservoir created by Boulder Dam in Arizona—also was established by Executive Order in 1936; it was the first of its kind, and its purposes were unashamedly recreational in nature. Big Bend National Park in Texas, another essentially primitive reserve and the last major park unit to be gotten under way during Roosevelt's first administration, was authorized on June 20, 1935; like those for Shenandoah and Great Smoky Mountains, the lands for this park were obtained via private funding, and it would be several years before it was completed and placed in the National Park System.

In just four years, then, Ickes had seen his national park domain show promise of growing by another five million acres in addition to the expansion of June 1933—all of this with very little effort expended on his part. In the years to come, however, he would embrace plans to amplify the system even more by adding the kinds of parks that would earn him membership in the pantheon of heroes whom even Robert Sterling Yard might revere, and this ambition would not be so easily satisfied—for it became snarled in the complexities and frustrations that attended his parallel crusade to engineer the creation of a Department of Conservation and seat firmly within it the 162 million acres of the national forests of the United States.

This time around, the Secretary took heart from the fact that to all appearances his obsession with the forests had been fully and officially endorsed as part of a program initiated and vigorously promoted by the President himself. In March 1936, Roosevelt had named a body called the President's Committee on Administrative Management, headed by Louis Brownlow of the Brookings Institution, Charles Merriam, and Luther

Gulick, director of the Institute of Public Administration in New York. Their task had been to study and make recommendations for a major reorganization of the Executive Branch, and in November of that year they presented their report to the President. On Sunday, January 10, 1937, just a few days after his second inauguration, Roosevelt called his legislative point men in the House and Senate—led by Representative Sam Rayburn and Senator Joseph Robinson—and laid before them a reorganization bill based on the committee's recommendations, announcing that he wanted it introduced and flogged through Congress.

It was quite a package. Simply outlined, the reorganization bill would have given the President six executive assistants; would have raised government salaries and expanded the merit system in the civil service, while at the same time eliminating the Civil Service Commission—which Rexford Tugwell had once described as a body that guaranteed that "barring revolution, war or economic disaster, the chosen dullards could have a long, uneventful, thoroughly secure working life"—and replacing it with a single strong administrator; would have established the National Resources Planning Board as a permanent agency in control of all government planning; would have created two new cabinet posts—the Department of Welfare and the Department of Public Works—and would have renamed the Department of the Interior the Conservation Department; would have brought every one of sixty-three Executive agencies—dozens of them independent of any other Executive department—into one or the other of the twelve cabinet-level departments; and, finally, would have given the President the power to move agencies in and around the Executive Branch until he got the mix he wanted.

Those portions of the bill that elicited Ickes's administrative cupidity, of course, were those renaming the Interior Department and empowering the President to shift agencies from one department to another. As early as the middle of November 1936, Roosevelt apparently had discussed specific transfers with Ickes and had given him reason to hope, though the President did not unveil the plan to the rest of the cabinet until December 22. Even then, FDR played his cards close to his vest, but according to Ickes's diary, the Secretary of Agriculture was swift to grasp the implications of the plan for his own department:

> Henry Wallace pricked up his ears at the suggestion made of the new name for this department and the statement of the duties with which it would be charged. Plainly, he was fearful that Forestry and perhaps one or two other of his bureaus would be transferred to the new Department of Conservation. . . . The President refused to discuss any details, insisting that he might do anything or nothing under the plan. Finally Henry had to be

content with the general observation that on his part he would regret it if any of the agricultural activities of his Department should be taken away. Of course, I know that the President has in mind to send Forestry, Biological Survey, Fisheries, and the CCC administration to the new Department of Conservation. I know, too, that minds can change. I hope this will not occur in this instance.

At a press conference on the day after his January 10 meeting with congressional leaders, FDR remained coy, warning reporters to "Keep away from saying that this is going to be transferred there and the other thing somewhere else, because, heavens, we haven't even approached that and haven't a thought on it. In other words, you ask me, 'Where is X bureau going?' I say, 'The Lord only knows, I don't.' That is a thing I will not say anything about. I will keep a completely open or blank mind, if you choose, until after the bill is passed. And guesses will be, as usual, 90 percent wrong." Nevertheless, Ickes recognized this opportunity as the best chance he would likely ever have of getting his Department of Conservation, and to that end he would devote every resource of energy at his disposal. To head off any opposition from within his own department, he called his bureau chiefs into his office early in January to explain the situation, telling them "that the President would shortly cause to be introduced in Congress a bill giving him power to reorganize the executive departments. I warned them that that would be an Administration bill and that it would have the cordial support of the Interior Department. I cautioned them that any lobbying against that bill would be the occasion for suspension under charges."

He had no such control over the Department of Agriculture, however, and from the beginning Henry Wallace made it clear that he would fight transfers just as furiously as Ickes would promote them. During a meeting on January 8 to consider calling a governors' conference to discuss conservation matters in the various states (Ickes was for it, Wallace against it on the grounds that everyone had plenty to do as it was), the two men clashed over the question of relations between the two departments and the potential transfers of Agriculture agencies. After what he considered a harmless observation that "we ought to keep conservation before the people," Ickes reported,

> Henry turned on me savagely. Apparently he thought that what I meant was that I was going to try to build up a conservation department at the expense of Agriculture. I had meant nothing of the sort, although it had never been a secret that I am in favor of such a department. Before I realized what was happening I found myself under a very bitter attack. I was careful to hold on to my self-control and answer as quietly and disarmingly as possible. . . .

Until the end I did my very best to avoid a discussion that plainly was becoming hotter and hotter, but evidently Henry had a lot on his chest that he was determined to blow off. He could not be stopped. . . .

Altogether it was a heated and unpleasant session. Perhaps I said some things that I should not have said, but, after all, what I had said was not personal. Henry's attack on me was personal and it was bitter. It was rather an extraordinary thing for one Cabinet member to accuse another of disloyalty to the President and to question his veracity in the presence of witnesses. But that is precisely what Henry did. When I could not stop him, naturally, I did make some points of my own, but they were points of policy and not of personality.

Given the fact that he was still suffering the effects of his automobile accident of December, we can assume that even when under restraint Ickes gave pretty much as good as he got during this quarrel. Whatever he said, it was enough to cause him to pen that same afternoon a handwritten note that came perilously close to an apology: "My Dear Henry: I regret the unfortunate incident of this afternoon. . . . I have regarded you as a friend, even when we have differed on policies and principles, and I shall continue to do so regardless of whether the President shall add, subtract, or divide as between our two Departments." Wallace's own handwritten reply was stiff by comparison, but he was by nature a reserved man:

Dear Harold: I am glad to have your note of January 8. Our frank speaking seems to me to have been fortunate, not unfortunate. It was and is my hope that we can perfect a co-operative formula for the general welfare between our Departments. After the President has obtained the powers which we both hope he will get, I trust the problem will be carefully examined from every point of view and that the solution found will serve the public interest in the long run.

It would be a long time before so friendly an exchange between the two men would again take place, for over the next several months, as the reorganization bill was slowly and painstakingly escorted by the administration's soldiers through the minefield of the Seventy-fifth Congress (many of whose members disliked it as one more grasp for Presidential power), the controversy over the transfers would grow so virulent as to effectively poison an already troubled relationship, with neither man giving an inch. The full force of the Forest Service lobby—from the field to the offices of the Agriculture Department in Washington, D.C., one of the most powerful and experienced in the nation—was brought to bear against the idea, and before the dust settled, no fewer than 250 organizations would go on record as being opposed.

It was not long before Gifford Pinchot offered himself as the principal, if unofficial, defender of the Forest Service.* For months—indeed, for years ahead—he would inveigh against what he insisted, in a speech before the Izaak Walton League on April 30, 1937, was "the most dangerous attack that has been made upon the National Conservation policy since it was first laid before the people of the United States by Theodore Roosevelt." Then, in that same speech, he got nasty: "What is behind all this? The ambition of one man is behind it. . . . [T]he man who has been my friend for more than a quarter of a century has allowed his ambition to get away with his judgment." Great power, he said, had "bred the lust of greater power." Finally, a certain sepulchral note: "Secretary Ickes will protest, as he has protested before, that under him the Interior Department is pure as the driven snow, and that it is not fair to lay old faults against it. It is not pure as the driven snow, but suppose it were. Secretary Ickes will not live forever."

Ickes was more than a match for him, replying in kind with a press release on May 2:

> Gifford Pinchot, who is a persistent fisherman in political waters, exemplifies more than anyone else in American public life how the itch for public office can break down one's intellectual integrity. . . .
>
> In 1934 this piscatorial politician sent to see me in my office in Washington a special emissary—the closest possible special emissary [it was Amos, of course]. This emissary suggested that the way to solve the Pennsylvania political situation at that time was to . . . make up a ticket composed of George H. Earle for Governor and Gifford Pinchot for Senator. Later Mr. Pinchot himself came personally to beg for support that was denied him.
>
> Mr. Pinchot did not then see in the head of the Department of the Interior a man with a "lust for greater power." He had not discovered at that date in the President of the United States one whom he now damns for every forward-looking measure that he advocates. If Gifford Pinchot had been substituted in 1934 as a candidate for Senator from Pennsylvania . . . he would not have made the speech that he did before the Izaak Walton League.

---

* His brother Amos also was opposed, so the falling out between the Pinchots and Ickes was complete. Amos, who had turned on the New Deal because in his view it had abandoned its liberal principles, was one of the leaders of a group called the National Committee to Uphold Constitutional Government, formed to oppose the President on the Supreme Court issue and other points of administration policy. The reorganization bill was one of these points, and in early May, 1937, Amos was anxious to get his hands on a copy of the legislation, apparently being kept under tight security by Roosevelt's congressional people. He turned to none other than Ickes's former investigator Louis Glavis in this quest—and sure enough, on May 21, Amos wrote his brother: "Finally, a copy appeared mysteriously, in a manila envelope, at my house." "It's pretty hot," he told a colleague.

The discourse between Ickes and Pinchot rarely ascended above this level of invective throughout the debate, exchanges interrupted only by Ickes's heart attack in June and worthy of neither man. Occasionally, however, matters of substance did get raised, as in Pinchot's May 31 speech before the American Forestry Association, during which he accused the Interior Department of mismanaging the 2.5 million acres of revested Oregon & California Railroad lands it owned in southwestern Oregon. The forests here—some of the most valuable stands of old-growth Douglas fir and spruce anywhere in the Pacific Northwest—had been wrecked by uncontrolled logging, Pinchot said, a fact that "makes it perfectly clear that the Departmental leopard has not changed his spots."

Pinchot's criticism, which drew heavily on an article that had appeared in *American Forests,* was at best an exaggeration. Up until about 1935, in fact, there had been little demand for timber from the "O & C lands" because of generally depressed conditions throughout the lumber industry; Interior's operations in the region had been minimal since the department got the land in 1916, and very little out of some fifty billion board-feet available had ever been touched. Some of the sting was taken out of the argument also by the fact that the Interior Department, possibly as a response to the *American Forests* article, had fashioned legislation to establish management policy for these forests that was designed to put in place for the first time on *any* federal forest lands a mandated program of sustained yield management.* The legislation, under consideration by Congress even as Pinchot spoke, was passed and signed into law in August—and stood as a model for similar programs that in time would be instituted on almost all federal lands, including those of the Forest Service.

Such relatively intelligent arguments aside, for the most part disagreement between Ickes and his opponents on the question of a Forest Service transfer proceeded along lines that were savage even by the standards of the often feral world of Washington bureaucracy. The conflict not only put a major strain on the foundations of the New Deal throughout most of Roosevelt's second term, it served to exacerbate the already convoluted difficulties involved in achieving what are generally regarded as two of the most important preservation victories in the twentieth-century history of conservation—the acquisition of Olympic and Kings Canyon national parks, two particularly splendid jewels for the American diadem.

---

*Simply defined, sustained yield means cutting no more timber than can be replaced by natural regrowth or reforestation within a given period of time. It is the preferred system of federal resource management today—enshrined in the Multiple Use and Sustained Yield Act of 1960.

卐卐卐卐

Gifford Pinchot's observations regarding the Interior Department's management of the O & C lands took on an added fillip of interest for those closest to the controversy because these lands contained much the same kinds of magnificent old-growth forests that were at stake in another, often equally malignant conservation battle: the fight to create Olympic National Park in northwestern Washington State.

On Washington's Birthday, 1897, President Grover Cleveland had established a 2.18-million-acre forest reserve on the Olympic Peninsula as one of the last acts of his administration. In addition to hundreds of thousands of acres of some of the oldest and biggest trees on this continent, the reserve was home to herds of Olympic elk, in the view of many people the most stately and beautiful of the species in this country; their teeth were attractive, too, especially to members of the Benevolent and Protective Order of Elk, and the animals were being killed so wantonly by professional hunters for their teeth that as early as the turn of the century, Representative Francis Cushman of Tacoma had proposed legislation that would have created a national park out of the whole reserve. It did not succeed. Neither did attempts by Representative William Humphrey to establish the area as a federal game refuge in 1906 and 1908. Finally, in 1909 Humphrey used the elk slaughter as the means of persuading President Theodore Roosevelt to establish Mount Olympus National Monument on 620,000 acres of the reserve and ban hunting as well as logging.

In 1915 the Forest Service—which, until Franklin Roosevelt's Executive Order of June 1933, administered all national monuments—persuaded President Woodrow Wilson that much of the land in the Mount Olympus region contained rare deposits of manganese, a metal essential to the manufacture of armaments. With the probability of war growing with every passing week, Wilson removed from the monument 292,000 acres of "manganese lands" chosen by the Forest Service. As it happened, no significant deposits of manganese were ever discovered in these lands. But there were a lot of Douglas fir, spruce, and western red cedar present, and they were soon in the mills of the timber industry. Cynics maintained that this was what the Forest Service had had in mind all along, particularly when they noticed that virtually all of the "manganese lands" had been found in the heavily forested lower slopes and river valleys of the mountains. Willard Van Name of the Emergency Conservation Committee was one of the cynics, noting that "most of the timber still left in the Monument is small, scrubby high mountain stuff, worthless commercially. . . . The Forest Service took all the meat and left the bone for the public."

In October 1933 the Washington State Game Commission announced a four-day elk-hunting season in Olympic National Forest (the monument itself remained closed to hunting). Most of the animals killed (estimates range from 150 to 230) were big bulls, depleting the future strength of the herd by an estimated 20 percent. In April 1934 the Emergency Conservation Committee issued a pamphlet written by Willard Van Name that expressed outrage over both the hunt and the continued logging of old growth just outside the monument, and proposed that the monument be restored to its original size and the whole region be established as a national park. In response to the pamphlet, the Washington State Planning Council formed a committee to study the proposal, and in spite of objections from the supervisor of Olympic National Forest (who said that while the pamphlet was "so inaccurate that it deserves no consideration," it still had been "read by many and is believed by the gullible and may do this country great harm"), there was enough support for the idea to cause Park Service director Arno Cammerer to appoint his own committee.

The Park Service committee's report was issued in October and concluded that while a park of the size advocated by proponents was impracticable because the proposed additions included "much valuable timber," the monument at least could be enlarged by about 110,000 acres and a park created out of this expansion. On February 20, 1935, Cammerer submitted a memorandum to Ickes noting that "several towns on the Peninsula and conservationists throughout the country are in favor of the establishment of a national park to preserve this wilderness area. Congressman Wallgren [Monrad C. Wallgren of Seattle] is also very much interested. It is recommended that in order to crystallize public sentiment, necessary legislation be drawn up, subject to your approval, for the establishment of this area as a national park." Cammerer had also included a map of the proposed park boundaries; it had embraced only one complete river system, that of the Bogachiel, but in his notation on the memorandum, Ickes himself added the river corridor of the Quinault as well.

A few days later, Willard Van Name met with Ickes and emphasized the desire of the Emergency Conservation Committee that the original monument boundaries be used for a park, not those of Cammerer's smaller proposal. On March 15, Arthur A. Demaray, Cammerer's assistant, apparently at Ickes's urging, sent Van Name a map of the proposed park, adding that "the map will be submitted to Congressman Wallgren who expressed his intention of introducing a Mount Olympus National Park bill during the current session of the Congress." Wallgren did so on March 28, calling for the creation of an even larger park that would include

328,000 acres in the present monument and add some 400,000 acres from Olympic National Forest. Local opposition from Forest Service officials and towns and organizations dependent upon the timber industry was stiff enough to keep the bill from moving during 1935—and to inspire Henry Wallace, after a visit to the area in October, to issue a statement that he would not yield any area under the administration of the Forest Service without local consent.

That was the situation when newspaperman and Emergency Conservation Committee officer Irving Brant interested himself in the project early in 1936. In February, while in Washington, D.C., during a research trip for a biography of President James Madison, he had been granted a long meeting with Wallace and Silcox, the subject being the question of protecting the old-growth forests around the monument. Afterward, he reported on the meeting to Roosevelt. On coming out of the President's office, Brant encountered Ickes waiting to go in. The Secretary apparently asked for a report himself, and on February 13, Brant gave him a written summary of what he had been up to:

> I had made some comment to Secretary Wallace about the unwillingness of the Forest Service to let go of any of its lands, and he asked me to have lunch with himself and Mr. Silcox to talk about the Olympus situation. . . . Silcox (who seems to have a genuine desire to protect virgin timber) said that if the facts were as I stated he would support a move to have additional areas (he did not say how extensive) permanently protected. But he said he would not sanction the transfer of a single acre to the "administrative methods" of the Park Service. . . .
>
> Silcox said the Forest Service could be trusted to guard these forests in perpetuity. I told him that in 1927 or thereabouts the Forest Service officials in Portland had told me they were going to make these forests into a wilderness area to be preserved forever, but now they were planning to run roads and railroads in and log them off. Silcox then said he would be willing to see the Olympic [*sic*] National Monument extended if administration of it were transferred to the Forest Service, or if administration of the added area were left to the Forest Service.

With this communication, Brant began a second career as a kind of ambassador without portfolio for the Interior Department, not only keeping both Ickes and Roosevelt informed on developments attendant on this and other conservation matters, but in many respects acting as their emissary and agent—without authority but with considerable influence nevertheless. "It turned out that I put in so many hours on the Olympic park project—by this time an administration affair," he remembered, "that I was working half-time for the White House without being paid for it." That would change; in the meantime, his role as ombudsman for the

President Franklin D. Roosevelt takes the hands of well-wishers at Warm Springs, Georgia, in December 1933. The first one hundred days were well behind him by now, and most of the cards of the New Deal were on the table. These people, at least, liked what they saw there. (*UPI/Bettmann Newsphotos*)

Above, Roosevelt's first cabinet meets for the first time, March 5, 1933. Clockwise, beginning from the President's left: William H. Woodin (Treasury), Homer S. Cummings (Attorney General), Claude Swanson (Navy), Henry A. Wallace (Agriculture), Frances Perkins (Labor), Daniel C. Roper (Commerce), Harold L. Ickes (Interior), James A. Farley (Postmaster General), George H. Dern (War), and Cordell Hull (State). (*UPI/Bettmann Newsphotos*) At the right is Harold in front of his rented Georgetown house sometime in the summer of 1933. (*Raymond Ickes*)

At the right, Ickes and Roosevelt share a lunch at the Civilian Conservation Corps camp in Shenandoah National Park, August 12, 1933. The young man forking out the fried chicken probably was chosen for the task as much for his clean good looks as for any waiterly skills; the CCC was one of the most relentlessly publicized programs of the New Deal. (*The Franklin D. Roosevelt Memorial Library*)

For the official photograph of a Presidential cruise through the Panama Canal and the Caribbean in October 1935 (top of the opposite page), Roosevelt put a disgruntled Ickes at his right hand and an equally disgruntled Harry Hopkins at his left. During a fishing trip two years later (top of this page), both seem to have cheered up considerably. At the bottom of the opposite page, Ickes delivers the Flag Day address before a hometown crowd in Altoona, 1935. Directly right, the body of Anna Wilmarth Ickes is carried out of the side door of the house in Hubbard Woods, September 3, 1935. (All, *The Franklin D. Roosevelt Memorial Library*)

On the road again—and again, and again . . . Ickes spent an astonishing amount of time traveling. At the top of the opposite page he is forced to share a backseat (and Roosevelt's presence) with Henry Wallace during the 1936 Presidential campaign; above, he has the President to himself on the back end of a train during the same campaign. At the bottom of the opposite page, he chats it up with reporters during a western rail junket in 1935. (All, *The Franklin D. Roosevelt Memorial Library*)

At the top of the opposite page, Ickes shares a backseat joke with friend and ally Thomas Corcoran, 1938. At the bottom of the page, he lays the cornerstone of the new Interior Building on April 16, 1936, while Roosevelt looks on. So does someone else: the impish face peeking out of the crowd just behind the President's head is that of Jane Dahlman, ever the Ickes's constant companion. Above, the Secretary surveys his domain, 1938. (All, *The Franklin D. Roosevelt Memorial Library*)

Ickes may have been the most frequently cartooned Interior Secretary in our history—at least before James Watt. He enjoyed most of these lampoons, including these four, which he liked so much that he included them in his *Autobiography of a Curmudgeon*.

Jane and Harold Ickes, bride and groom—at the top of the page on their return from their elopement and European honeymoon, June 2, 1938; at the bottom, in Rainier National Park later that same year. (Top, *The Franklin D. Roosevelt Memorial Library;* bottom, *Elizabeth Ickes*)

There were nearly forty years between them, but all the evidence suggests that Harold and Jane made a good life and a good marriage of it in spite of the handicap. The family portrait above, with one-year-old Elizabeth on the left and three-year-old Harold on the right, was taken in 1942; that on the top of the opposite page was shot in 1947. At right, on the opposite page, is the main house at Headwaters Farm in the winter of 1938. (All, *Elizabeth Ickes*)

At the top of this page, Ickes poses with senators Alva Adams (left) and Key Pittman (right) during hearings to make E. K. Burlew (standing next to Ickes) his assistant in 1938. At the left, Ickes and Jane stand with Abe Fortas, another assistant, and his wife during the fourth Roosevelt inaugural, 1945. At the top of the opposite page, Ickes looks appropriately shaken after viewing his President lying in state at the White House in April 1945. Below that, the former Secretary jokes with reporters after his resignation in February 1946. (All, *The Franklin D. Roosevelt Memorial Library*)

Ickes waves good-bye to reporters in the auditorium of the Interior Department after announcing his resignation at what was called the biggest press conference in Washington history up to that time, February 13, 1946. (*The Franklin D. Roosevelt Memorial Library*)

park could not have been more useful. "He is all the more effective," Ickes would write, "because he is not connected with the Department or the Government in any way. He has been quite willing to cooperate."

Brant's effectiveness was felt almost immediately. Shortly after he had been in to see Roosevelt in February 1936, the President sent a note to Ickes and Wallace: "I understand that there is a forest area immediately adjacent to the [Olympus] national monument. Why should two Departments run this acreage? If the forest portion is not to be used for eventual commercial forestation and cutting, why not include the forest area in the national monument?" After discussions on Roosevelt's questions between Cammerer and Silcox took place with no firm resolution, Ickes drafted a proclamation that Roosevelt might issue that would pull more than 100,000 acres out of Olympic National Forest and add them to the national monument as interim protection under the stipulations of the Antiquities Act of 1906. When Roosevelt passed the proclamation on to Homer Cummings for a legal opinion, however, the Attorney General was skeptical:

> I deem it advisable . . . to invite your attention to the statutory provision that the land reserved as a part of a monument shall in all cases be confined "to the smallest area compatible with the proper care and management of the objects to be protected." The area proposed to be included in the national monument consists of approximately 429,630 acres. Although there is no statutory limit upon the size of national monuments, the area in this instance is so extensive that it raises the question whether . . . the whole of it is needed for the purposes stated.

Meanwhile, the pressure being exerted by the Forest Service was having its effect. When his first bill died in the last session of the Seventy-fifth Congress, Representative Wallgren asked the Park Service to endorse a compromise that would reduce the size of the proposed park to about 648,000 acres. The Park Service recommended endorsement and passed it on to Ickes. On February 4, 1937, perhaps on the theory that this proposal was as good as they were likely to get—particularly since Cummings had strongly advised against protection by proclamation— Ickes approved the compromise. On February 15, Wallgren introduced the new bill.

While the Forest Service and the timber industry were partially (though by no means completely) mollified by the compromise, the Emergency Conservation Committee was outraged. "The power of the Forest Service over the Park Service is clearly demonstrated by the introduction of this new bill of Congressman Wallgren," Rosalie Edge wrote Ickes on February 19. "May I ask you a direct question? Will you fight?" It is probably fortunate that Ickes was too preoccupied with the steadily deteriorating situation in Puerto Rico to give her a direct answer to her direct question, but if her letter angered him—and it almost certainly did—there is no question but that he was ready to be prodded in the direction of a larger park in spite of his earlier endorsement of the Wallgren compromise. By early June he apparently had changed his mind entirely. "As you know," Harry Slattery wrote in a memorandum to Assistant Park Service Director Arthur Demaray on June 11, "there have been a great many protests against the proposed boundaries of the present Wallgren bill. . . . The Secretary wants the matter looked into and does not agree that the boundaries proposed by the present Wallgren Bill will be sufficient."

Irving Brant played a part in this turnabout by keeping Ickes informed of his own gambits following the introduction of the revised Wallgren legislation. Among these was a letter to Henry Wallace calling the new bill "a shocking retreat" that would "make a mockery of the movement to save the last primeval stand of Douglas fir and Sitka spruce on our Pacific Coast." He could not believe, he said, that "the Department of Agriculture will become a partner in this wanton commercialism. . . . Knowing you as I do, I hope that you will not hold the pen that dooms [the trees] to destruction."

Five weeks later, Wallace sent him the unsigned *draft* of a reply, probably written by Silcox, asking for his comments. "Silcox and I are just as determined as you are that adequate and representative portions of our remaining virgin forests, in the Northwest and elsewhere, shall be preserved for posterity," the letter said, then went on to offer an analysis of the region's potential for timber production and jobs that Brant found deranged. "According to the Forest Service ratio," he recalled, "the entire acreage of the original Wallgren bill would sustain 9,585 persons instead of 860. The entire Grays Harbor timber area would sustain a population of 191,700. . . . The whole proposition was preposterous." He returned the Wallace draft with a number of comments to that effect, concluding, "I do not believe that Mr. Silcox would tolerate the course he has approved if he were free from the myopic effects of the rivalry between the Forest Service and the Park Service."

After a summer of impasse (and, for Ickes, a heart attack and recovery), the movement for a large park took on new life when Roosevelt himself became an active player. At the end of September he made a tour of the Olympic Peninsula, including the lands proposed for the new park. On his arrival at Port Angeles, he pointed to a sign erected by the children of a local schoolhouse—"Please, Mr. President, we need your help. Give us an Olympic National Park"—and proceeded to extemporize as only he could: "Mr. Mayor and friends of Port Angeles, that sign on the school house is the appealingest appeal that I have seen in all my travels. I am inclined to think it means more to have the children want that park than all the rest of us put together, so, you boys and girls, I think you can count on my help in getting that national park. Not only because we need it for us old people and you young people, but for a whole lot of young people who are going to come along." He followed that announcement by meeting with both opponents and proponents of a large park and, according to a report furnished Brant by Irving M. Clark of Seattle (a member of The Wilderness Society's governing council), calmly demolished the arguments put forward by regional forester C. J. Buck. He made his feelings additionally clear during his automobile tour of the national forest when he spotted an old clear-cut area that had never recovered: "I hope the son-of-a-bitch who logged that is roasting in hell!"

On February 8, 1938, Roosevelt went even further, calling a meeting in the White House among all interested parties, including Cammerer, Silcox, Wallgren, and both of Washington's senators, and demanded they hammer out the details of a large park. Meeting again on February 12, they came up with substitute legislation that increased the size of the park proposal to 898,292 acres. On March 26, Henry Wallace, finally giving up his opposition, notified the Bureau of the Budget that his department would not oppose the new bill or any amendment that might be made to it, and when the bureau approved the legislation, Wallgren introduced it on March 28 as a substitute for his 1937 bill.

The bill was reported out of committee in the House and passed on May 16, but stalled in the Senate. Added pressure was supplied by Ickes, who recorded a speech, broadcast on the CBS affiliates in Seattle and Tacoma on May 17, that was written by Brant and that lambasted the timber industry for having "made a shambles" of the environment already and now wanting to move on to "destroy the last wilderness." Reporting to Brant, Clark said that the speech "was all that could be desired and I feel sure will be tremendously helpful," but the bill still threatened to die in the Senate as the adjournment date of June 16 approached. Roosevelt then suggested a compromise that would allow for the designation of a smaller park with an amendment to the effect that, with the consultation of the state's governor and other parties, the President would be empowered to add national forest and selected private lands up to the maximum size desired.

That did it. On June 11 the bill was amended by the Senate Committee on Public Lands to establish a park of 648,000 acres and give the President authority to add as much as another 250,292. In this form it passed and was sent back to the House for concurrence. After a few more housekeeping details stalled it long enough to give its proponents small strokes, Speaker of the House William Bankhead finally slammed his gavel down at 6:30 P.M. on Thursday, June 16, the last minute of the last day of the session. "Bang! That was over," Brant, who was in the House gallery with his wife and a few supporters, recalled. "I let out a yip, and we left before anybody called the police."

The Secretary was so impressed by the energy and competence of his *sub rosa* lieutenant that after passage of the Olympic National Park legislation he asked Brant to become director of the National Park Service. "The Secretary," Brant recalled, "had taken a strong dislike to Director Arno Cammerer, about whom he used epithets associated with excessive weight. But the reasons were only symbolically physiological. 'Cammerer,' he said, 'has no guts. He is afraid to disagree with me. He tries to guess my position and support it.' Cammerer's attitude," Brant added, "was in harmony with an impression widely held in the Interior Department that it was dangerous to disagree with the ardent secretary." What Ickes might have done with the substantial avoirdupois of civil service careerist Cammerer was not mentioned, but in any case Brant turned the offer down.

He did agree, however, to go on the payroll part-time as a consultant to the National Resources Board, and his first assignment was to make a trip to the Olympic Peninsula, spend a few weeks studying the land, and return to submit a report recommending which of the areas adjacent to the new national park should be added to it by Presidential proclamation, as stipulated by the June legislation. Gathering a team of Park Service specialists about him, Brant began his investigations in July 1938; by the middle of December he had produced a 114-page book, complete with photographs, recommending that ten specific areas be included in the Presidential additions. It took another year of consultation and negotiation with state officials, Forest Service people, sundry politicians, and industry representatives, but on January 2, 1940, all but 62,881 acres of Brant's original recommendations were officially added to Olympic National Park.*

Long before that happy outcome, Brant was deeply involved in a

---

* This acreage included a corridor to the ocean along the Queets River, a nine-mile corridor on the Bogachiel River, and a fifty-mile strip of shoreline on the Pacific Ocean—lands encumbered by various administrative difficulties (including the necessity of purchasing private inholdings) that prevented their addition for several years. By the middle of the 1950s, however, the park was finally completed.

second park proposal whose economic and political intricacies were every bit as tangled as those that had accompanied the creation of Olympic— Kings Canyon, an almost entirely wild region of more than half a million acres in the Sierra Nevada range of California adjacent to the northern border of Sequoia National Park. The first proposal to make this region a national park had been offered as early as 1881 and echoed ten years later by John Muir; and in 1893, Interior Secretary John W. Noble had gone so far as to put the matter before Congress. Nothing came of this, but in that same year the area was embraced within the Sierra Forest Reserve established by President Benjamin Harrison. In 1911 and for each of several years thereafter, legislation was introduced for the enlargement of Sequoia National Park to take in the Kings Canyon region, but even then disagreements between the Forest Service and the National Park Service had left bills stranded in Congress.

The situation was muddied in 1920, when the Federal Power Act opened national parks to hydropower development; in response to pressure from Park Service director Stephen Mather and his well-entrenched lobby, the act was amended in 1921 to exclude existing parks, but it still left such potential areas as Kings Canyon open, even if they should become parks. Power and irrigation interests in the San Joaquin Valley were adamant that they would need the watersheds of the Kings River drainage for future development and forced a compromise in 1926 that enlarged Sequoia National Park but left Kings Canyon out of the equation. Since then, a preponderance of local opinion had held that Kings Canyon and its rivers should be left in the hands of the Forest Service.

John R. White, who had been superintendent of Sequoia National Park both before and after its enlargement and who was not a man who enjoyed controversy, tended to agree. As early as May 12, 1933, he had cautioned Cammerer against reviving the national park idea: "There is no doubt whatever that the San Joaquin Valley has expressed itself against further park extension, and I hope this will settle the matter so far as the National Park Service is concerned for a good many years to come. It is most unhealthy and it is against the best interests of the National Parks to have this Kings Canyon proposition constantly coming up and constantly inviting invidious comparisons between the parks or the forests."

This level of timidity was a bit much even for Cammerer, however, and later that year he let White know that the National Park Service was keeping an open mind on the subject: "There is a good deal of difference between respecting and recognizing the present feeling and considering the matter closed for all time. In fact, from what I glean here and there,

there is already a perceptible change in the attitude of some of the people."
One suspects that the person from whom Cammerer was getting most of
his attitudinal readings was Ickes, for the Secretary was not long in
putting the Kings Canyon park on his own agenda. In March 1935,
Assistant Director Arthur Demaray finished a task Ickes had assigned
him—draft legislation for a Kings Canyon National Park bill—and the
Secretary persuaded Senator Hiram Johnson to introduce it. In September
he followed up on this with a memorandum to Cammerer that outlined
his intended policies for the management of the park, should it come to
pass: "This park will be treated as a primitive wilderness. Foot and horse
trails to provide reasonable access will be encouraged, but roads must be
held to the absolute minimum. The state road now being constructed
should never be extended beyond the floor of Kings River Canyon. . . .
Accommodations provided must be of a simple character and the rates
moderate. No elaborate hotels shall be constructed."

The Forest Service had other plans for the region, which it began to
develop even as Ickes's park bill languished in Congress, stalled by
opposition in California so immediate and forceful that Hiram Johnson
never seriously pushed the legislation after introducing it. Though it is
not likely that it was designed as a direct response to Ickes's somewhat
premature directive, the Forest Service proposal, issued in December
1936, served the purpose well enough: it would have placed the highest
peaks and mountain valleys of the region in the High Sierra Primitive
Area, but virtually everything else would be left open to "multiple-
purpose" management—including logging, mining, summer home developments, intensive recreation use, many roads and developed trails,
and, especially, dams and reservoirs for water storage, power generation,
and irrigation in two of the area's most spectacular canyons, Tehipite
Valley on the Middle Fork of the Kings River and Cedar Grove on the
South Fork. Robert Marshall, by then chief of lands and recreation for the
Forest Service, was appalled. "If I was outside the government," he wrote
in an official comment on the report, "and was shown this plan of the
Forest Service, I would swallow all my prejudices against the Park Service
and root for a Kings River National Park merely to keep out these
commercial desecrations and the roads which will go wit'ı them from as
glorious a wilderness as remains in the United States. . . . If the Forest
Service was to keep the Kings River country as a National Forest, I think
it should burn this Kings River report and write a radically new one."

While the Forest Service made its plans (and ignored Marshall's objections) and his park legislation finally died aborning, Ickes calmly included the Kings Canyon proposal among his future goals in each of the

Interior Department's annual reports. This alone was enough to cause the somewhat paranoid San Joaquin Valley Council of the California State Chamber of Commerce to call a meeting in Fresno in October 1937 to discuss rumors that the Park Service had more specific plans in mind. Among the sixty-five people in attendance were representatives of local chambers of commerce, irrigation districts, power companies, farm bureaus, and sportsmens' associations, as well as Charles Dunwoody, director of the Conservation Department of the California State Chamber of Commerce; C. B. Morse, assistant regional forester for the Forest Service; Frank Kittredge, the National Park Service's California Region director; and a number of private citizens. Each of the government men was asked to outline his agency's plans for the Kings Canyon area. Kittredge said he had no specifics to give them, since he was new on the job. Morse was a good deal more vocal, outlining in loving and enthusiastic detail the service's 1936 plan. A resolution was then offered that requested the board of directors of the California State Chamber of Commerce "in the full spirit of its adopted National Park Policy to oppose the creation of the proposed Kings River National Park." After general discussion, and to no one's surprise, the motion was adopted.

This action, like Ickes's memorandum of 1935, was a bit premature— but the meeting of October 1937 served to illustrate both the depth and character of the opposition that would coalesce swiftly and ride at full gallop against every effort to create Kings Canyon National Park for the next three years. The opposition's first chance came in the spring of 1938, when Ickes apparently felt it was time to test the waters again; at his request Congressman René De Rouen of Louisiana, chairman of the House Committee on Public Lands, introduced yet another bill for a Kings Canyon National Park of a little over 450,000 acres in size. Not especially well drawn, the bill probably was meant to serve notice to the Forest Service that the Interior Department remained determined to obtain the area and to sound out opposition and support as a beginning toward fashioning workable legislation. This was the bill under consideration when Irving Brant put aside his duties on the Olympic National Park matter in August 1938 and took a six-day pack trip into the Kings Canyon country at Ickes's behest, accompanied by Frank Kittredge and Joel Hildebrand, president of the Sierra Club. As a result of the trip, Brant remembered, he concluded:

> The problem of Kings Canyon boundaries . . . was 99 percent political. From the standpoint of national-park standards, one could put markers anywhere along hydrographic ridges, and if the markers were far enough apart, they would produce a park of superb beauty. The political problem was double: the

contest between the Forest Service and National Park Service for custodian-ship, and the contest between the environmentalists and the irrigationists for Cedar Grove and Tehipite. . . . Had the two bureaus been united, they could have saved both scenic gems by persuading the irrigationists of the truth—that better power sites existed on the North Fork of the Kings River, outside the proposed park. Instead, the Forest Service backed the demand for dams at these two points.

Brant also returned convinced that the active support of the Sierra Club was going to be necessary for the success of any kind of legislation affecting its native state of California. At his urging, then, Ickes met with the Sierra Club directorate in San Francisco's Bohemian Club on October 21 during a trip west. After an informal dinner, Ickes talked for more than an hour, assuring the club's officers of the Interior Department's passion for a wilderness park and otherwise wooing and winning them in a burst of candor and charm. "The whole thing was a grand triumph, on both sides," Joel Hildebrand declared in a letter to Brant two days later.

While Ickes courted the aid of the Sierra Club and Brant continued to knit up the strands of support in Congress and among other conservation groups, S. Bevier Show, regional director for the Forest Service, marshaled his own forces and launched an attack before there really was anything substantial to be attacked. On October 11 he had issued a statement to the press announcing that proper development of the Kings Canyon region would require that "The water must be impounded back in the mountains. Many reservoirs, not a single one, will be required to fully regulate and use the water." Flood control, too, the announcement said, "will undoubtedly require a comprehensive series of reservoirs throughout the drainage. . . . A permanent flood control program can hardly be carried out if the land is dedicated to a single purpose [a park], as is now proposed." Another press release on December 2 made his position even clearer:

> The Forest Service will fight any proposed extension of national parks in California that will lock up national forest resources vital to the welfare and prosperity of the people and the State. This applies to the proposed Kings Canyon National Park and any other new parks which under National Park Service policy would be permanently closed to all economic use and develop-ment and managed solely for special classes of recreation. California already has more national parks and monuments than any other State in the Union. . . . This is surely an adequate reservation.

Show apparently loathed both Roosevelt and Ickes with a depth of feeling that was still running strong nearly thirty years later when he wrote that "the amoral national administration and the conscienceless leader operating within it" had forced "this innate, built-in Agriculture-Interior conflict of aim, method and morality from the series of skirmishes and localized battles into the status of a general war." Ickes himself, Show said, was determined "to expand, without bounds, the single-purpose parks and grazing districts at the expense of the national forest system, and to capture control of the latter through transfer to his tender care," then went on in an attempt to eviscerate the Secretary personally: "If anyone doubts Ickes' overweening ambition, the sublimity of his valorous and ignorant self-confidence, his ready and eager embrace of any method, however mean, venal or ruthless, calculated to further his ends, his intolerance of and contempt for opposition, his egocentric imposition of his will on subordinates who accepted or else, let such a doubter read the record."

Show himself was not subjected to the "egocentric imposition" of anyone's will but his own. Like many regional foresters, he seemed to operate with near autonomy. Wallace, according to Brant, admitted at one point that "I can't control the Forest Service," citing the powerful ties to local interests his regional foresters—particularly in the Northwest and in California—enjoyed and which they exploited to strengthen their positions and further their ambitions. Keeping an angry, arrogant man like Show in line would have been difficult even if Wallace and Silcox had actively tried; they had not, and over the next several weeks California's regional forester would spend much of his time both overtly and covertly in a stubborn campaign against the Kings Canyon proposal.

The struggle took on real substance when Congressman Bertrand W. Gearhart of Fresno, whose district embraced two-thirds of the area that would fall within the proposed park, announced that he planned to introduce his own park bill immediately after the opening of the new Congress in January 1939. At Gearhart's request, Cammerer and De-maray fashioned park legislation and sent it around for comment; the Sierra Club people, Brant, and Ickes all disliked it, mainly because it made no provision for wilderness management. At Ickes's direction, Brant and Demaray got to work on a revision. The new version designated the park the "John Muir–Kings Canyon National Wilderness Park" in honor of the Sierra Club's founder, and stated the principle that the park would be managed as wilderness, with a minimum of roads and no hotel or other unseemly concessionaire facilities. It sought to satisfy the desires of the irrigation lobby by excluding the Tehipite Valley and Cedar Grove areas from the park as potential reservoir sites, providing, however, that the two areas would be managed essentially as wilderness by the Park Service until such time as the Bureau of Reclamation might be authorized by Congress to build dams in either place and that all lands above the high-water mark of either completed reservoir would remain in Park Service management. If the two sites were ever deemed not suitable for reservoirs by the Bureau of Reclamation by official notice, the bill said, they would immediately be folded into the park by proclamation. Finally, in one of the few noncontroversial sections of the bill, it stated that the existing 2,548-acre General Grant National Park—established to preserve a grove of especially fine sequoias—would be absorbed by the new park.

In a further effort to dissipate the opposition of the irrigationists, the previous spring the Interior Department had announced its support of legislation that would authorize the Bureau of Reclamation to build a large irrigation, flood-control, and public power dam at Pine Flat well outside the bounds of the proposed park. This support, together with the Park Service's promise to exclude the Tehipite and Cedar Grove sites from the park, had gone a long way toward getting the Kings River Water Association, a major coalition of irrigation interests, to formally with-draw its objection to a Kings Canyon National Park. Roosevelt himself had attempted to stem Forest Service opposition by issuing an order specifically prohibiting it. "I am told," Wallace wrote the President on January 13, "that your instructions to the Forest Service to refrain from public opposition to the proposed park have been conveyed to the Re-gional Forester at San Francisco, and I have no reason to believe that they are being violated." He soon would have, for on January 17 Roosevelt learned that Show's assistant forester had gone before the California state legislature with the local office's objections. "I am told," FDR wrote in an angry note to Wallace, "that at the Senate Rules Committee meeting of the State Senate in Sacramento, California, Regional Forester J. H. Price of San Francisco appeared in opposition to establishing the Kings Canyon National Park. How long are the orders of the President, the Secretary of Agriculture and the Chief Forester to be disobeyed?" He ordered Wallace to have Price transferred out of the California office immediately, and the insubordinate forester ended up in Milwaukee.

All the bases, then, seemed to have been covered when Gearhart's bill was introduced on February 7, 1939, and referred to the House Commit-tee on Public Lands, where hearings were scheduled for the middle of March. A few days after the bill's introduction, Ickes traveled to Califor-nia and on February 13 attended a morning conference on the bill held in the Mark Hopkins Hotel. "This conference was well attended by both proponents and opponents of the park," he wrote in his diary.

> The leader of the opposition was a man who had been one of the organizers of Farmers, Inc. [Associated Farmers, Inc.], the labor-baiting, fascist minded group that constitutes a front for the antilabor bankers and businessmen of his state. I let everyone have his say, either for or against, and then I summed up

the arguments pro and con, giving my reasons for the park and meeting the objections of those who are fighting it. Since the facts were with me, it wasn't difficult to meet these arguments, and at the end of the meeting I had the distinct impression that we had made a good deal of headway.

Two days later he gave another speech before the Commonwealth Club, California's admirable forum of public opinion. Written by Brant and broadcast by NBC over most of its California affiliates, it reiterated the arguments in favor of the bill, reemphasized the intent to manage the new park as wilderness, then included a slightly barbed gesture of conciliation toward Wallace and the Forest Service. After announcing that Wallace had written him an official letter stating the Department of Agriculture's support of the national park proposal, he added:

> At this point let me express my appreciation of the attitude that has been taken by the United States Department of Agriculture and the Washington office of the Forest Service. . . . The letter from Secretary Wallace to me . . . did not represent a change of policy on the part of the Department of Agriculture. On the contrary, Secretary Wallace adhered to a long-established and consistent record. This national park project had been supported by the Secretary of Agriculture and by the Chief of the Forest Service on every occasion when their opinion has been sought by committees of Congress, beginning about 1920. . . .
>
> In other words, when some of the minor employees [how Show would have hated that characterization!] of the Forest Service were so busy in California, making speeches and getting articles in newspapers opposing a national park . . . their superiors in Washington were taking the precisely opposite position.

If Wallace ever read this speech, he probably would not have been pleased to learn that Ickes had managed to praise him for his support while simultaneously reminding him that one of his biggest agencies was out of control. Nevertheless, the last obstacle in official Washington seemed removed, and with the stated support of the Kings River Water Association, the Sierra Club (not to mention most, though not all, of the rest of the conservation organizations in the country, including the Emergency Conservation Committee and the Izaak Walton League), most of the state's newspapers, and a probable majority of those who lived in the districts affected, the hearings on the bill in the House seemed assured of fairly smooth going. In the middle of the session being held on March 29, however, Congressman Gearhart rose to a point of privilege and announced that the Kings River Water Association had renounced its support of both the park bill and the bill authorizing the construction of a dam at Pine Flat. "In view of this startling information," Gearhart said, "and in view of the fact that it is the irrigationists alone whom I desire to serve," he requested that the committee delay its hearings until the new development could be investigated. Chairman De Rouen refused, and the testimony continued.

Throughout the hearings Ickes took an active role; and during the last of his three appearances before the committee, the Secretary thoroughly discredited the Water Association's motives by submitting strong evidence that the organization had changed its mind primarily because the California State Chamber of Commerce, the Associated Farmers, and other pro–private-power groups had persuaded the association's leadership that the U.S. Army Corps of Engineers wanted to build the dam at Pine Flat and that if it did, the irrigationists would not have to abide by the stipulations of Reclamation Law (true)—nor would they have to pay anything for the delivery of federal water to their lands (not true). Suddenly, Ickes said, the irrigation interests now wanted Pine Flat and any other dam project in the region taken out of the hands of the Bureau of Reclamation and given to the Corps of Engineers.

The hearings finally ground to an end after twenty-three straight days. The private-power lobby tried one more trick to keep the bill as submitted from reaching the floor, persuading Clyde L. Seavey, acting chairman of the Federal Power Commission, to ask President Roosevelt for an amendment that would permit the wholesale development of all power sites in the proposed park should it be found necessary in order to satisfy California's power needs in the future. Roosevelt rejected this proposal. The bill was subsequently reported for passage on May 25, though along the way it had suffered some damage: the name "John Muir" was removed and all specific references to the intent to manage the park as wilderness were stripped away (even so, De Rouen got the proposal designated the "Kings Canyon Wilderness National Park," thus at least establishing the clear intent of Congress). Finally, after fighting off one more amendment that would have opened the whole park to hydropower development, the House passed the revised Gearhart bill on July 18, after which Congress adjourned for the remainder of the summer.

One important casualty in an otherwise acceptable bill was the excision of Section 5, that part of the legislation that had stipulated that the Tehipite Valley and Cedar Grove would not be included in the park proposal but that they would be administered by the Park Service. Instead, Section 3 now made reference only to "the lands withdrawn" without naming them specifically, although these unnamed lands were still to be administered by the Park Service. The bill was less than Ickes and its other promoters had wanted, Demaray admitted in a letter to Brant the next day, but explained the Secretary's determination to push it in spite of its shortcomings: "I have just had the opportunity to discuss the bill with the Secretary, who states that he would prefer that the bill be passed in its present form by the Senate, if that can be done without Senate Public Lands Committee hearings. It is his view that if the bill can be thus handled, we can seek legislation next year to provide for Park Service administration of the reclamation withdrawals for recreation purposes."

It was a gamble to let the bill go forward without making some specific recommendation about the two areas, and not everyone was happy about such a long shot. The National Parks Association had been against the Gearhart bill from the beginning because of the withdrawals and believed the final House version to be even worse. Robert Sterling Yard of The Wilderness Society had been equally opposed, although Robert Marshall had persuaded the organization's governing council, by a vote of five to one, not to actively oppose the bill but to concentrate its efforts on an attempt to save the two withdrawn sites, "which can be properly safe-guarded only through the creation of a Park." For his part, Yard had no faith at all in Ickes or the Park Service. "I'm quite sure," he had written at one point to Anne Newman of the Izaak Walton League, "that the Park Service would be glad to accept the park filled with power dams from the glacial lakes down rather than leave it safe with the Forest Service."

In spite of the split in the conservation movement, the bill had taken on strength and a kind of momentum now. When the Senate reconvened in November, the Public Lands Committee reported the Gearhart bill without hearings and with no changes, calling for a vote of unanimous consent. But Senator Key Pittman of Nevada, a lurid Ickes despiser, refused consent, and the bill was laid over. By the time it was put back on the calendar for February 19, 1940, Pittman apparently had decided that he had made his point; that afternoon, after delivering a thirty-minute speech in denunciation of Ickes on general principles, the senator sat down without making objection to unanimous consent and the bill was read into the record and passed. On March 4, 1940, Roosevelt signed it into law, and one of the most beautiful regions in the United States found safety in the National Park System.

If Robert Sterling Yard remained skeptical, others found reason for celebration. William Colby of the Sierra Club had been pursuing the goal of a Kings Canyon National Park ever since the death of his mentor, John Muir, in 1914. "I feel now that I can 'die in peace,' " he wrote Ickes on February 20, the day after the bill passed the Senate. "At least you have added the greatest possible joy to my remaining years." It is unfortunate that neither he nor Ickes would live to see the final victory: in 1965, after several years when it became increasingly clear that the irrigation and power needs of the Central Valley were never going to require exploitation of Tehipite Valley and Cedar Grove, Congress vindicated Ickes's gamble by passing legislation adding these still essentially wild sites to the national park.

Ickes lost his best conservation lieutenant after the Kings Canyon fight; shortly after passage of the act, Irving Brant resigned his consultancy to devote most of his time to his multivolume biography of James Madison, although he would remain active with the Emergency Conservation Committee and return to the barricades regularly as a private citizen for the rest of his long life. "Just a word of appreciation," Ickes had written him on his departure, "to convey to you my very real thanks for the tremendous and tireless help that you gave in support of the bill to establish the Kings Canyon National Park."

Ickes also lost Arno Cammerer that year—though it gave him no comparable regret. The Park Service director had suffered a heart attack in 1939 (caused, Cammerer's friends and Ickes's enemies believed, by being overworked by his boss), and after the director's recovery Ickes began casting about for a replacement. Brant had made it clear in 1938 that he was not interested, but among the other names that Ickes seriously considered were those of Gerard Swope, former president of General Electric, and Robert Moses, the park czar of New York State. Swope took a job as director of the New York Housing Authority before the Secretary could offer him the job, and Roosevelt was worried that Moses "would run the Park Service without reference to me," if the President appointed him, Ickes reported in his diary. "I don't think that he would," Ickes added, "and even if he should, I can't see that any harm would come to the Park Service. A year of vigorous administration by someone other than a bureaucrat would do the parks a lot of good." But Roosevelt, who still entertained a cordial hatred of Moses, was adamantly against it. A third name was that of Ferdinand Silcox, whom Ickes had grown to like and respect in spite of his Forest Service connections and the fights over Olympic and Kings Canyon. He had been determined to make Silcox an undersecretary with responsibility for the parks and forests if his hopes for reorganization were ever fulfilled, but any plans Ickes may have contemplated for the chief forester became moot when Silcox died suddenly just before Christmas of 1939.*

---

* His friend and fellow forester Robert Marshall had also died suddenly, just a little more than a month before.

Ickes finally settled on Newton B. Drury, the Save-the-Redwoods League leader who had turned down the job six years before. The Californian's worries over the political aspects of the position apparently had dissipated over the years, for on June 17, 1940, Drury accepted the offer after negotiating an agreement with Ickes that would assure him of a little more autonomy than Cammerer had enjoyed. Cammerer, probably with relief, resigned and was installed as regional director in Richmond, Virginia, a much less demanding job (though it would not prevent Cammerer's death after another heart attack a year later). Robert Sterling Yard, an admirer of Drury, but still sharpening his knives for Ickes, did not know quite what to make of this development. "I was amazed," he wrote a friend on June 21,

> when the announcement appeared in the *Evening Star* on June 19. Not because Cam had resigned. We had been expecting that for years. He and the Secretary never had got on very well together.
>
> What amazed me was that his successor is one of the highest-minded conservationists in the United States. I have known Newton Drury intimately for years. He is not only the executive secretary of the Save-the-Redwoods League, in California, but an active member of the Wilderness Society. . . . He is a writer on parks, always from their idealistic point of view. All the fine redwoods publications you have seen came from his office at 114 Sansome Street, San Francisco. . . .
>
> Why Ickes should name an idealist, without warning . . . must be explained. How the appointment came about must also be explained. . . . Sooner or later I'll discover the inside story.

No, he would not, because there was none. Ickes had wanted a strong man as director of the National Park Service, a man with a powerful interest in preserving as much of the wilderness character of the parks as was possible. In Drury, whose interest in "primeval parks" was no less intense than that of Robert Sterling Yard, he had found him. End of story. And among Drury's first and most significant actions was the institution of a general policy of wilderness management for both Olympic and Kings Canyon national parks—a policy that survives to this day—not only vindicating the Secretary's faith in him, but giving weight to the words put in Ickes's mouth by Irving Brant in February 1939: "The United States, rich beyond all other countries in the variety and beauty of its mountains and forests, can afford to set aside and protect some of its mountains and forests, not merely from commercial exploitation, but from a too intensive use for recreation. In dealing with some spot of supreme beauty, let us not, like a boy holding a butterfly, destroy it by a too ardent laying on of hands."

CHAPTER

· 41 ·

*In the Arms
of Disappointment*

W ITH THE APPOINTMENT of Drury and the designation of Olympic
and Kings Canyon national parks, the most expansive era of growth
in the National Park System since the days of Stephen Mather came to a
close. In conjunction with the more than 1.3 million acres involved in the
Olympic and Kings Canyon proposals, there were less dramatic but no
less significant additions made during Roosevelt's second term. Land
purchases and exchanges for Isle Royal National Park—a 115,643-acre
wilderness island in Lake Superior, authorized in 1931—were completed
in 1938. Organ Pipe Cactus National Monument, a 330,689-acre desert
enclave in southwestern Arizona, was established by Executive Order in
1937. Cape Hatteras National Seashore—the first national seashore—
was authorized as a 30,319-acre "primitive wilderness" in 1937. One way
or another, by executive fiat, purchase, trade, or assumption of lands
authorized in earlier administrations, during the first seven years of Ickes's
tenure as Secretary of the Interior the National Park System had grown
from 8.2 million acres to more than twenty million.

Ickes had wanted more. He had wanted a Green Mountains National
Park in Vermont, and in 1938 had fashioned legislation to that effect,
which moved not at all in a reluctant Congress. He wanted a White
Mountains National Park in New Hampshire, but legislation introduced
in 1939 had never gotten out of committee. He wanted a Katahdin

National Park in Maine, but the Maine delegation was violently opposed and legislation was killed in 1939. He wanted a Cascades National Park in northern Washington, but disputes over whether or not there were valuable mineral deposits that would be "locked up" kept that proposal from reaching even the stage of draft legislation. He wanted more national seashores, outlining the country's needs in a speech of 1938:

> When we look up and down the ocean fronts of America, we find that everywhere they are passing behind the fences of private ownership. The people can no longer get to the ocean. When we have reached the point that a nation of 125 million people cannot set foot upon the thousands of miles of beaches that border the Atlantic and Pacific Oceans, except by permission of those who monopolize the ocean front, then I say it is the prerogative and the duty of the Federal and State Governments to step in and acquire, not a swimming beach here and there, but solid blocks of ocean front hundreds of miles in length. Call this ocean front a national park, or a national seashore, or a state park or anything you please—I say the people have a right to a fair share of it.

But Cape Hatteras National Seashore was the only one he got.

He had wanted an expansion of Rocky Mountain National Park as a trade-off for the intrusion of the Colorado–Big Thompson Project, a tunnel beneath the park designed to deliver water from the west slope of the Colorado Rockies to the east slope. The interbasin diversion—the first in the history of federal water projects—had been specifically authorized in the organic act that had established the park in 1915, but proposals for so major an effort were not put forth actively until the 1930s. Like the Park Service, Ickes worried that the diversion would violate the sanctity of the park, not only by tunneling beneath it, possibly threatening its own water supplies, but by constructing various works—including a parkway along the route of the tunnel—in and near the park. Working with Congressman Edward Taylor, whose district included many west-slope constituents who objected to the siphoning of their water eastward, Ickes had tried to get the law amended to stifle the project, but had failed.

On August 9, 1937, Congress had authorized the expenditure of $900,000 to begin construction. On the theory that his hands were tied—though in truth hard put to fight vigorously a project whose presumed social values were so similar to those he was promoting in the basins of the Colorado, Columbia, and Missouri rivers—the Secretary had tried to get concessions from the Congress for expansion of the park, particularly to the south, where some thirty-five thousand acres of national forest land called the "Arapaho Addition" were particularly appealing. All he got, as he explained to the President, was "the right of the Park

Service to pass upon plans and specifications where lands authorized to be added to the park are involved."

In short, not much, and that he was not entirely comfortable with the situation was evident when he called a conference of conservation groups and other interested parties to his office on November 12, 1937. After hearing objections to the project from Robert Sterling Yard of The Wilderness Society, James Foote of the National Parks Association, Frederick Delano of the National Parks and Planning Commission, and others, Ickes got up to say that he was personally opposed to the project, but that he could not

> follow my own will in this matter. I have to follow the law and I tell you very frankly that between the Bureau of Reclamation and the Park Service, I am for the Parks, but I am sworn to obey the law. Congress definitely appropriated $900,000 to start that Reclamation project. Now suppose I, for some trivial reason, would have to find that it was infeasible—I am afraid it would have to be trivial—would I be performing my duty? Are you not asking me to usurp powers that clearly belong to Congress? . . .
>
> Now, if I do this, I will probably go to the guillotine, but if I do go to the guillotine, how many of you would go with me? . . . I have to follow the law. I wish the baby had not been laid on my doorstep, but it is there.*

On December 20, however reluctantly, Ickes recommended to the President that he approve the Colorado–Big Thompson project. In doing so, he earned one more arrow in the quivers of those in the conservation community who did not trust him—and he never did get the Arapaho Addition.

Ickes had wanted to create the largest national park unit in the lower forty-eight states—the Escalante National Monument in southeastern Utah, a 4.4 million-acre reserve that would have encompassed the magnificent slick-rock canyon country on both sides of the Colorado River from just above the Arizona border to the lower stem of the Green River nearly 150 miles to the north. Virtually all of this was federal public land, and at Ickes' direction the Park Service began studying the possibilities of such a monument in 1936. Utah state officials had been thinking more along the lines of a national park of maybe thirty-five thousand acres; grazing, mining, irrigation, and other commercial interests were barely able to swallow that and had no interest at all in anything bigger. When they made their complaints known to the Park Service, Cammerer had cut the study area down to a more narrow band of about 1.5 million acres

---

* Robert Sterling Yard, for one, was not impressed by either Ickes's apologia or his plight. "Asking each other why we had been summoned to argue again a project already unalterably adopted by Congress," he reported tersely, "we lunched briefly in the department restaurant."

along both sides of the Colorado up to and including part of the Green. The compromise was not enough for the westerners, who were particularly worried that they would lose control of water resources by the presence of what they perceived to be too prehensile a federal grip on "their" land. During the annual National Reclamation Association meeting in Denver in 1939, a resolution was passed stating that no further national parks or monuments would be made in any of the seventeen western states without the consent of the people and the governors involved.

To get around this reluctance, Ickes asked his people to draft legislation that would amend the Antiquities Act of 1906, exchanging the Executive power to establish national monuments by proclamation for the power to establish national recreation areas that would be more readily available for mining, grazing, and other commercial uses than were monuments. In answer to an article in *Mining World* critical of the legislation, Ickes claimed that "the real question involved in the bill is a very simple one: do you want recreational reservations set up by Executive Order that are closed to prospecting and mining, water conservation projects, hunting, and grazing, or do you want them open to these activities?" Western commercial interests were not deceived, recognizing fully the fact that administrative restrictions on such recreation areas could close them just as effectively as those applying to national monuments. Given a choice, the westerners wanted *no* reservations, thank you very much, and probably would have abolished the Antiquities Act itself if they could. Failing that, the Utah congressional delegation joined with other western delegations to bring the amendment to a dead halt and forged so unified a front against the creation of a national monument under existing law as to force Ickes and Roosevelt to back off until the beginning of World War II rendered the question moot.

Another legislative proposal close to the secretary's heart at about this time suffered a similar fate. In 1939, at his behest, Senator Alva B. Adams of Colorado and Congressman René De Rouen had introduced companion bills that would empower the President to set aside, by proclamation, wilderness areas in national parks and monuments, places in which roads, automobiles, commercial developments, hotels, cabin camps, or any other permanent human structures would be banned. "If this bill for national park wilderness areas becomes a law," Ickes declaimed in his Commonwealth Club speech of February 15, 1939,

> the eastern forests of the Great Smoky Mountains National Park . . . can be held as wilderness, in contrast with the more highly developed western slope in Tennessee. It will enable us to protect more effectually the areas that still remain roadless in Mount Rainier National Park. Under this proposed legis-

lation, a proclamation by the President will establish a wilderness area, and
once it is established, only an act of Congress can change its status. . . .

In asking Congress for the passage of this bill to set aside wilderness areas,
I am requesting that the discretionary power of my own Department be cut
down. I suppose that is something new in the annals of government, for the
head of a department to ask that part of his own power be shorn away. But that
is what I desire. I want those wilderness areas so protected that neither I, nor
any future Secretary of the Interior, can lower their guard merely by signing
an administrative order.

This proposal (quite deliberately, it is almost certain) went far beyond the
administrative regulations that had allowed the designation of wilderness
areas on the national forests by the Forest Service—too far for its time, as
it happened. The Secretary did not get his Wilderness Act, which died
quietly in the public lands committees of the House and Senate; it would
be a quarter of a century before the Congress of the United States would be
ready for so revolutionary an idea.

While the Secretary's wilderness and recreation area proposals were immobilized by opposition in Congress, the President's reorganization bill
was barely staggering along, losing some of its substance and a great deal
of its own revolutionary character in the process. Everyone, it seemed, was
in favor of simplifying and rationalizing government operations, particularly if some money could be saved along the way. But not, of course, if
simplification, rationalization, and economizing threatened the continued power—or even survival—of those agencies in which one or another
special interest had a stake. Veterans disliked the bill because they feared
that a single administrator in civil service might overhaul a system that
had traditionally given them preference. The medical profession did not
want the Public Health Service taken out of the Department of the
Treasury and put in a new Department of Welfare; it might mean social-
ized medicine. The American Federation of Labor was against the bill
because a single civil service administrator would be a "dictatorial authority" over government employees. The business community grew to hate it
because, in the words of the New York Chamber of Commerce, it would
give the President "such tremendous control over the economic and social
activities of the people of this Nation, that it would be only a short step to
a dictatorship, and a form of government similar to that prevailing under
the Communist, Fascist or Nazi systems."

The bill was a feast of anger for lobbyists of all stripes. The question of
agency transfers continued to lie at the center of the conflict, none more so

than the matter of the Forest Service and its shift to the proposed Department of Conservation. On his side, Ickes had the Emergency Conservation Committee, the Sierra Club, and, somewhat lukewarmly, the National Audubon Society, together with scattered support in Congress, chiefly from Senate minority leader Charles L. McNary of Oregon. Combined, they were still not much of a match for the experienced and widely based Forest Service lobby, which continued a relentless agitation against the bill, at one point persuading the California Chamber of Commerce to send Charles G. Dunwoody—one of the Forest Service's most effective allies in the fight over Kings Canyon—to Washington as a special lobbyist against the legislation. The General Federation of Women's Clubs joined in the opposition, as did The Wilderness Society, the Society of American Foresters, and even J. N. "Ding" Darling, the editorial cartoonist who had been an Ickes supporter when Darling was director of the Department of Agriculture's Bureau of Biological Survey. The bureau—which he had left in September 1935—was almost certainly going to be one of the agencies that the new Department of Conservation would get if the reorganization bill passed, and Darling had changed his mind about Ickes. By the middle of 1937 he was campaigning actively against reorganization. "I have come to the conclusion," Ickes wrote in his diary for July 1, "that 'Ding' Darling is just a congenital double-crosser. Two or three times, when he was Chief of the Biological Survey, he told me that he would like to have his bureau brought into Interior. He has told me on more than one occasion, not only orally but in writing, that he regarded me as the 'fightingest' conservationist in government. He pretends one thing to me and then tried to prevent the accomplishment of the thing that he says he is in favor of."

But the chief dog robber of the antitransfer coalition remained Gifford Pinchot. "I call your attention," he told an audience at an Izaak Walton League dinner in October 1937, "to the fact that, with the possible exception of the national parks, and I underline the word 'possible,' the Interior Department has never had control of a single publicly owned natural resource that it has not devastated, wasted, and defiled." Ickes came back at him immediately in a press release whose level of fury is remarkable even for this master of invective: "This is an outrageous statement, a libelous charge, a deliberate prevarication of the truth, a reckless manhandling of the known facts. No man has any right to bring such a charge against the thousands of devoted and patriotic members of the staff of the Interior Department during the eighty-odd years of its existence."

Such was the language of debate that accompanied Roosevelt's attempt to rationalize his complicated and sometimes helplessly confused government bureaucracy, and Roosevelt himself did not help matters by playing Wallace and Ickes off against each other, never really letting either of them know precisely how committed he was to the idea of the Forest Service transfer. In later years, Wallace speculated that it all satisfied some basic—perhaps even distorted—need of the President's. "Roosevelt surrounded himself with people forever vying for his favor—courtiers," he said. "He *loved* that. Farley always claimed that it was a sadistic impulse—that he loved to see people suffer. It may have been a balance of power instinct of some kind. . . . I don't know whether he perceived the confusion that resulted or not. He may have been completely opaque to the confusion which it produced."

Ickes was suffering, that much was certain. "As to the present reorganization bill," he noted in his diary on January 29, 1938, "I fully believe that the president is getting ready again to let me down. I have talked to him. So has Henry Wallace, and I know that Wallace has been carrying word up to the Hill that the President doesn't care anything about a Department of Conservation." But if Ickes was suffering, he was not going to suffer alone, and during one session with Roosevelt managed to wrench something very like anguish out of the President by pushing at him with righteous ferocity. "I told him that in every issue between Henry Wallace and me from the beginning," he wrote,

> he had decided in favor of Wallace. . . . The President said that he couldn't take any sides as between Henry and me; that he loved us both. I insisted that he was taking sides and then I told him that I would not be interested if there was not to be a Department of Conservation. At this point he cried out, in an agitated voice, "You musn't say such things, Harold. You and I have a lot of things to do together yet. You have been with me a thousand per cent. I haven't been able to accomplish everything that I set out to do, but we have done some things, haven't we, and we must go on and try to do some more things."
>
> At some point during this remark he reached over and put his hand on my right arm. . . .
>
> My nerves were raw when I went in to see the President. . . . The result was that I became emotional. From this point on I said nothing more about the Department of Conservation, knowing that the President's mind was made up. He tried to make me feel better but I made no response. I sat there feeling grim and, I suspect, looking even grimmer.

There was soon enough reason to look and feel grim. After rancorous hearings and lively debate, the Senate passed the reorganization bill on March 28, 1938, by a vote of forty-nine to forty-two—but any feeling of triumph that may have followed was short-lived. On April 8, even after a number of amendments had watered it down substantially, the House nevertheless voted to recommit the legislation, 204–196—an action quite as good as outright rejection. Nor was there much comfort to be found when the Seventy-seventh Congress convened in January 1939 and a new reorganization bill was put in the legislative hopper. Compared to the weighty measures included in the legislation of 1937, the reorganization bill of 1939 was made of gossamer; it gave the President an Executive Office and six administrative assistants, but any reorganization proposals were subject to the veto of Congress and everything else was gone—civil service reform, the power to move agencies around by Executive Order, the creation of new departments, including, to Ickes's sorrow, a Department of Conservation. In this form, the bill was passed by the House on March 8 and by the Senate two weeks later. On April 3, Roosevelt signed the Reorganization Act into law.

"Now it remains to be seen," Ickes wrote, his gaze still fixed on the national forests, "whether the President will transfer Forestry to Interior. Congressman [John J.] Dempsey . . . told me that he thought if the President made this transfer, it would not be upset. . . . Senator [Burton K.] Wheeler, who led the fight against the bill, told Senator [Robert] Wagner that Forestry belonged in Interior. Congressman [James W.] Mott, who is a Forestry man, said to me that he believed Forestry would be transferred to Interior, and I think that this is the general expectation." The expectation was not fulfilled with the first reorganization order sent up by FDR for congressional approval on April 21. The order, Ickes said, "hit me harder than any other man in the Administration. It took from me PWA, the National Resources Committee, the Office of Education, the management of Federal buildings in the District of Columbia and the United States Housing Authority, and it gave me nothing. . . . I was very low indeed in my mind."

He got lower. The Public Works Administration was not only to be taken out of Interior, but severely reduced in size and power and renamed the Federal Works Authority. Ickes asked for the job of administrator, but did not get it, the position going instead to John M. Carmody, then head of the Rural Electrification Administration. Something finally came Ickes's way on May 9, when the second reorganization order transferred the Biological Survey from Agriculture, the Bureau of Fisheries from the Department of Commerce, and the Bureau of Insular Affairs (whose main responsibility was the Philippine Islands) from the War Department. It also restructured the Coal Commission as a separate bureau within Interior. But still no Forest Service.

"How about Forestry?" Ickes asked six weeks later, after the President had discussed with him a scheme to transfer authority over the TVA to Interior (it never happened).

"I intend to do the same thing," FDR replied. "I will give you Forestry."

"When?"

"At the same time I give you TVA and on the same principle."

"Mr. President, I have been hearing for five years that I was going to get Forestry and I am getting older every day."

"I intend to give you Forestry."

The next day Ickes sent Roosevelt a long complaint in the form of a valedictory with regard to the PWA:

> For six years I have been Administrator of PWA. A newly born child was laid on my doorstep and I have taken care of and loved that child as if it were my own. I had hoped that I would be permitted to continue a relationship that was prized by me, at least until there should be entrusted to my care other interests that would make up the loss. . . .
>
> But instead of complaining, I ought to be thanking you for allowing me to be Public Works Administrator during the past six years, even if, as I have always suspected, you haven't thought a great deal of PWA.

"My Dear Harold," Roosevelt replied almost immediately,

> I wish you would not make assumptions which have absolutely no basis in fact. If, as you say, you have been conscious that PWA has not been a favorite at the White House, you are just utterly and one hundred per cent wrong. If you have been puzzled and distressed, it is your own fault for imagining things that do not exist. You and the fine staff of PWA have not been "outside," but just as much inside as any other branch of the government. . . .
>
> Work with me, please, to build up the Interior Department into a real Conservation Department, as we both looked forward to. . . . And for the hundredth time, I am *not* forgetting Forestry.

Perhaps not, but he was not doing much about it, either, nor would he do much about it over the next several months. So little was done, in Ickes's view, that the opposition had been given time to build up an almost impregnable wall in Congress against the transfer. In an effort to shake Roosevelt into action, finally, the Secretary wrote him on February 7, 1940, to say that the political situation was such that he could not "conscientiously ask that you transfer Forestry," but pointing out that since "Forestry has become a symbol to me," he was forced to resign as Secretary of the Interior, effective February 29. "The President," Ickes noted with visible satisfaction in his diary, "hit the ceiling. He had Miss

LeHand get me at once on the telephone and I could tell from his voice that he was highly excited and troubled. He shouted at me that I was making life miserable for him." Roosevelt refused the resignation with a short note to the effect that "We—you & I, were married 'for better, for worse'—and it's too late to get a divorce & too late for you to walk out of the home—anyway. I need you! Nuff said."

"It is pretty difficult to do anything with a man who can write such a letter," Ickes remarked, and did not repeat his offer.

As the contretemps continued, picking up occasional ink in the press, it seemed to some of those who were truly on the outside that the struggle for the control of the national forests had taken on dimensions that echoed the larger world. "As I watch the unfolding pageant of the Great War among conservation bureaus," Aldo Leopold—now heading up the Forest Products Laboratory at the University of Wisconsin—wrote Robert Sterling Yard on April 29,

> I am struck by the deadly parallels with international politics. All or most of the bureaus have a power complex, but Interior seems to display the worst case, and the Park Service is rapidly assuming the Himmler ruthlessness. The conservation public is alternately wheedled, bribed, and kicked, like other "small neighbors." To dominate "recreation" is the major strategy of all and sundry, and for this noble end any means is justified. . . . It makes one think again that there must be some cosmic infection of the human mind. "It can't happen here?" It is happening here.

But it was not. Roosevelt's only serious attempt to transfer the Forest Service and the national forests to Interior was swiftly scotched by his own supporters in Congress even before a reorganization order making the transfer could be sent up to the Hill. In 1939, in order to get Key Pittman's support for the reorganization bill, Roosevelt had let the senator from Nevada understand that he would not transfer the Forest Service to Interior. FDR may actually have forgotten his promise, but Pittman had not, and according to Gifford Pinchot, still operating *in medias res,* when the senator heard that Roosevelt planned to issue a transfer order at the end of March 1940, he told Roosevelt that it "would smash the whole legislative situation," and that if Roosevelt sent it out, Pittman "would be off the reservation for foreign affairs and everything else." It took no more than that to persuade Roosevelt to tear up the order.

Although he would try again with a new Congress in 1941 and even during the war years would continue to explore avenues and devices that might bring the Forest Service his way, the aborted Executive Order of March 1940 was as close as Ickes ever came to achieving his oldest, largest dream. There would never be a Department of Conservation; he would never be permitted to have the national forests. Still, he had acquired the Biological Survey, with its authority over hundreds of wildlife refuges, and the Bureau of Fisheries, with its authority over such commercial fishing operations as the salmon industry of Alaska. These two agencies, together with the National Park Service and the Grazing Division, combined to make at least the skeleton of something that might have been called a Department of Conservation. It would have to do, in any case.

Ickes got some vindictive pleasure in May when an article he had dictated was finally published in the *Saturday Evening Post.* In January he had gone down to Florida to spend a few days with Margaret and Raymond Robins. While visiting these old friends—Raymond confined to a wheelchair now, but "his mind as clear as ever and as vigorous," Ickes wrote—he had read Henry Pringle's recent *The Life and Times of William Howard Taft.* "I was particularly struck by Pringle's interpretation of the Ballinger-Pinchot controversy," the Secretary noted in his diary. "If he is right, and his statement sounds convincing, I have been very unjust to Ballinger all these years, and Pinchot and Glavis have much to answer for." They certainly did, in the Ickesian view, and not just for the 1910 imbroglio with Interior Secretary Richard Ballinger. Upon his return to Washington, Ickes had assigned one of his speech writers, Saul K. Padover, to do some research on the question, and when the evidence in favor of Ballinger was gathered, Ickes had dictated the *Saturday Evening Post* piece, "Not Guilty, Richard A. Ballinger—An American Dreyfus," emphasizing throughout the singularly manipulative role Pinchot had taken in forcing Taft to fire him. Interior Secretary Richard Ballinger had been innocent of any wrongdoing with regard to the Cunningham coal claims, Ickes said. He was the victim of Pinchot's "sadistic hate" and his "overweening and ruthless ambition." And, in conclusion, just in case the readers did not make the connection, the author made it for them: "The war waged by the Forest Service against the Department of the Interior, as disclosed by the record of the Pinchot-Ballinger episode, has been one of more than 30 years. It is still being carried on in the open and under cover and even in defiance of orders from the White House."

For all the bitterness, for all the fact that he was once more in the arms of disappointment, there was much good he could have remembered from the past seven years as Interior Secretary. He had been reminded of some of the best of it on June 26, 1939, when he held his last staff meeting of the PWA. It was, he wrote at the time, "a pretty lugubrious gathering. I was so emotional that I could hardly talk at all and others in the group were in almost as bad shape as I was. I feel this severance of old ties very deeply indeed."

So did most of his employees, apparently. They gave him a plaque. There was nothing unusual in this, but the grace and eloquence of the plaque's handwritten language suggested a level of pride and sorrow not common among government bureaucracies:

> You have done a job as Administrator of Public Works which has never before been done, and you have done it without blame from friend or foe. You drew the thousands of us from all walks of life, from all corners of the country, and you have welded us into a vital organization of which we are all proud. You have shown neither fear nor favor; you have neither asked nor tolerated any bending of the knee or any concessions to undue influence; and you have asked of us only one thing: that our job be well and truly done for the good of the Nation.

That would do to take along.

PART VIII

Curmudgeon's Way

As I see it, this issue will be the fundamental one of whether we want to go forward along democratic lines or whether we prefer to undertake a kind of American Fascism. Willkie talks about civil liberties in a democracy, but his associations and predilections have been what they have been and they do not have for me the odor of democratic sanctity.

—Letter to Raymond Robins, July 5, 1940

CHAPTER

· 42 ·

Love at the Headwaters

H AROLD'S LIFE in the last crowded years of the decade was not all work, insomnia, wrecked nerves, disappointed hopes, and heart attacks—although it sometimes appeared that way. He had little gift for play, but an enormous capacity for love and the wounding that often accompanies it, as both his marriage and his fevered infatuation with "Mrs. X" had demonstrated. The personality that lurked behind all the hard-boiled posturing in many ways remained as sensitive to pain as that of a young girl, and as ready to embrace it when it came. This tender relict of an emotionally pinched childhood remained at his center, for all the fact that he was now well into his sixties. Only partially obscured by the fury of energy that possessed his life, there remained a childlike questing in him that may explain why there were women who were profoundly attracted and dedicated to this driven, irascible, pear-shaped, bespectacled man whose face most often given to the world was that of a righteous scold. And in 1938, in his sixty-fourth year, his yearning ended with an unlikely, impractical, hopelessly romantic marriage that brought him the fullest measure of happiness he had ever known.

In his memoirs, Ickes is uncharacteristically demure about any sexual adventuring he might have enjoyed in the months following Anna's death; he was either bored with the subject or there was precious little to report. But not all his closest relationships were purely sexual. There was May

Conley, for example, who remained at his side for most of his professional life, patiently scribbling down and typing up the oceans of words that spilled from him—not just letters and memoranda, but many of his weekly diary entries, as well as the harshly intimate stream-of-consciousness memoirs he began dictating shortly after becoming Secretary of the Interior and continued at intervals for most of the decade. In the course of events, she also had tended to many of the frequently messy details of his daily life, arranging travel plans, keeping his personal and professional accounts, arranging schedules, bringing the gift of order to his existence. "She has always stood by me loyally in many difficult situations," he said in one snatch of memoirs (probably calmly taken down by the subject herself), "and, naturally, she came to know practically everything that there was to know about my personal and family affairs. It was a great comfort to know that I could trust her discretion. . . . She is the only person to whom I feel I can dictate such an intimate recital as this personal biography." The trust was not misplaced; May Conley remained a faithful shadow in his life, so discreet as to be nearly without shape or form. Leona B. Gerard (then known as Leona Graham), who had worked in both the PWA and the Division of Territories and Island Possessions, remembered her "as a small person, pastel-colored, blue-eyed, I think, and blond to grey haired. A rather soft but efficient woman." That is as clear a description as exists anywhere.

There was Ruth Hampton, for another example. In his memoirs, he describes her only as an old friend from the Illinois days, and there is nothing to suggest that there was anything in their relationship that drifted beyond platonic bounds. Nevertheless, she was important to him. He had given her a job in the Division of Territories and Island Possessions, where she had swiftly risen from field representative to assistant director, a position she held until 1946—taking full responsibility for the agency during the frequent gaps between directors. Ruth, he notes in his memoirs, was the only other person besides May Conley who knew the whole story of his troubled marriage; it was Ruth whom he had called to pick out the clothes in which Anna was buried, and Ruth whose opinion he sought a few weeks later when Henry S. Hubbel delivered portraits of Anna that had been commissioned before her death. ("They are terrible," he reported in his diary, noting that Ruth "had the same feeling about them that I did.") Finally, Raymond Ickes remembers that his father once told him that if anything ever happened to him, his son should turn to Ruth Hampton for anything he might need.

Then, odd as it may have seemed, for quite a while there was Cissy Patterson—Eleanor Medill Patterson, editor of William Randolph

Hearst's *Washington Herald.* Strong of will and sharp of tongue and by all accounts one of the best editors in the business, Cissy Patterson had come out of the Chicago newspaper traditions established by her grandfather, Joseph Medill, and carried on by her cousins Robert and Medill McCormick and her brother, Joseph Patterson, who had since left the *Chicago Tribune* to found the *New York Daily News.* Nearly fifty by the time she met Ickes, she had survived a brief and violent marriage to Count Josef Gizycki of Russian Poland, though not without difficulty; when she left him in 1908, the count kidnapped their child, Felicia, and it had taken the personal intervention of President William Howard Taft with Czar Nicholas himself to get the child released to her mother's custody in 1909. Felicia had since married newspaperman Drew Pearson, coauthor of the "Washington Merry-Go-Round" column. After divorcing Count Gizycki, Cissy herself had married Chicago lawyer Elmer Schlesinger, but after his death in 1929 had returned to her maiden name and remained single, while accumulating a number of men in her life.

It was not long after the inauguration that Harold was pulled into the orbit of this powerful woman, who, while not beautiful in the accepted sense of the term, was unquestionably handsome and possessed of considerable charm when she cared to exercise it. She exercised it at their first meeting during a dinner party at Dower House, her seventeenth-century country estate in Maryland, in May 1933. "Mrs. Patterson," Ickes wrote in his diary for May 19, "is a very interesting and vivacious hostess. She is brilliant, has lived an interesting life, and has had wide experiences." While apparently confined to formal occasions, their relationship over the next several months began to ripen into something that went beyond casual acquaintance. "Dear Mr. Secretary," she wrote him on September 22, apparently after he had confessed his weariness and insomnia to her.

> I didn't wake up at one o'clock this morning—but I did wake up before daybreak and had plenty of time to think about plenty of things. You are slathering your energy and reserve strength all over the place. God made you a "willing horse," and, looking on as an innocent bystander, it seems to me that you are set to pull your load until you drop in your traces. Personally, I can't see any sense to this. Your load won't get to its ultimate destination, and there you will be—down on your haunches, your head on your knees.
>
> Incidentally, what I believe about your wanton waste of your life is a great inspiration to me personally. That is because I am naturally the most lazy, poor white trash "critter" you ever knew. Instead of forever babying myself and complaining the whole time, I think from now on I will go out and do a little work for a change. And this will be due to you.

Ickes's reply was equally warm:

Dear Cissy:

It was sweet of you to write me as you did. . . . I suppose you are right about me. I have hardly a trace of religion left in my makeup, but when I analyze myself I am conscious that generations of Presbyterian ancestors have left me an ineradicable impress on my character. You have had the same sort of ancestors yourself and so you will understand what I am driving at. . . .

You may be all that you say that you are, but I don't believe it. Anyhow, I do know that you have the capacity for making friends and I know that one of the things that I chiefly treasure as a result of my brief sojourn in Washington is that you have made me feel that you are my friend, while at the same time making me keenly aware that I want to be yours.

After Anna's death in 1935, Ickes became a frequent Patterson guest, including long weekends at her home on Long Island and intimate dinners at both Dower House and her Italianate mansion at 15 Dupont Circle in Washington. The friendship had become sturdy enough to endure in spite of a growing political difference between them. Like her brother, Joseph Patterson, Cissy was personally in favor of much of what the Roosevelt administration was up to during the early years of the New Deal— although her newspaper judiciously reflected the prejudices of her boss. By 1936, however, many of Hearst's prejudices had become her own, and she supported the Landon candidacy. Nevertheless, she and Ickes remained close even during the heat of the campaign, and her fondness and concern for him continued. In August 1936, during a dinner party at Dower House, Ickes reported:

Cissy noticed that I was pretty tired and after dinner she took me down by the swimming pool, where we sat and talked for quite some time. She told me how foolish she thought I was to work so hard and allow things to worry me. . . .

I was impressed again with Cissy's gentleness and friendly understanding. I have come to be very fond indeed of her. I have found in her the best friend I have made in Washington. She seems to me to be a very genuine person with broad sympathies.

They would continue to see each other off and on over the next several months, but if there had ever been the possibility of something more profound than friendship developing between them, it had been thoroughly scotched as early as the spring of 1936. For by then, Harold was in love, as completely, deeply, and insanely as any adolescent boy who ever mooned over any adolescent girl.

The young woman in question, as it happened, was not all that far removed from adolescence, a fact that would not escape the attention of the world.

In one of the photographs taken during the laying of the cornerstone of the new Interior Building on April 14, 1936, the Secretary is shown touching up with a trowel. In the crowd behind him is the partially obscured face of a gamine who is grinning straight at the camera. Her name was Jane Dahlman, she was twenty-three years old, a recent graduate of Smith College in Massachusetts, and she was present at the invitation of the secretary himself. He was, in fact, her boss—but had hopes of becoming something more. Jane was the youngest of the Dahlman sisters, the oldest of whom, Betty, had married Wilmarth. With the middle sister, Ann, Jane had been a frequent visitor to the Ickes's enclave at Hubbard Woods since childhood, and the two girls had come to see the Ickes family in Spring Valley at least once, earning a brief and noncommittal reference in Ickes's diary for April 6, 1934. There was no diary reference at all made to another meeting that took place in the fall of 1935, after Anna's death. At that time, he says in his unpublished memoirs, "I had a note from Jane from Belchertown, Massachusetts.

> She wanted my advice on something important to her and would I see her if she came to Washington? It rather bored me. I was not keen about the prospect of having to play host to a young girl. However, the family relationship had been such that I could not say "no." . . .
>
> I went down to the station and when the train pulled in I started down the platform. In the distance I saw an attractive young woman with beautiful red hair struggling toward the gate, attended by a couple of porters, all of them loaded with a large number of bundles and suitcases. And before we ever reached each other I knew that I was in love. I kissed her formally and took her back to the office.

Ickes kept his sudden burst of emotion to himself. What Jane wanted, he learned during the course of a two-day visit, was a job so that she would not have to return to her family in Milwaukee. Life there had always been unhappy for her. Her mother, while still living at home, remained mentally ill—a few surviving, incoherent letters from her suggest some variety of schizophrenia—and her father gave every indication of being the kind of doting, demanding parent whose love sucks the vitality from his children. Her sister Ann was about to leave home, and the prospect of taking on the full weight of her father's dominance had little appeal. She also was engaged to a young man in Belchertown, she told Ickes, but was not certain that she loved him and wanted time to think about it.

Harold gave her a job as a historical researcher in the Park Service in

November (transferring her to the Bureau of Reclamation a few weeks later) and she took an apartment. It is not entirely clear when they began to see each other seriously, but he did have Jane out to the Spring Valley house with a few friends on Thanksgiving, 1935, after which he took her to the movies. On New Year's Eve, he informed his diary, "Jane Dahlman and I had dinner . . . with Ruth Hampton and Bess Beach in their apartment, and the four of us had a very good time. Ruth is enthusiastic about Jane. I did not feel much like working on New Year's Day and I largely yielded to my inclination. . . . Jane and I went to the movies at night. We saw *Captain Blood* and both of us thought it was very poorly done."

On January 27, her birthday, he gave her a small dinner party ("Tom Corcoran brought his accordion and guitar and kept things going after dinner") and the next night arranged that she receive an invitation to one of the Presidential musicales at the White House. "Jane was happy to get the invitation," he wrote, "but said that she wouldn't go unless I went with her. That I was glad to do," he added, even though he had gone on record a number of times as hating those musicales in the East Room. He was clearly proud of her and not unwilling to flaunt their relationship a little: ·

> I don't think I am exaggerating at all when I say that she was the most striking looking woman at the White House last night. She has the freshness of youth and her coloring is superb. Her hair is really beautiful.* She was happy and it was evident that many people found her interesting. I took malicious pleasure in introducing her to Mrs. Homer Cummings, Mrs. J. Fred Essary, and one or two other women who I knew would be burning up with curiosity as to who she was and why I happened to have her at the White House. . . . Captain Brown, the naval aide of the President . . . commented upon Jane's appearance, and so did the President when I was in with him. Both of them thought that she was not only very good looking but that she was sweet and attractive. They were right on all these propositions. She is with me a good deal and I have never had anyone in the house, man or woman, who creates such a genuinely happy atmosphere, who is so companionly and so pleasant to get along with.

By this time, Jane had broken the engagement to her young man in Belchertown after a painful confrontation. Significantly, she had moved in with Ickes for a couple of days during the crisis and had let the fiancé have her apartment, where, Ickes says in his memoirs, "They had a terrible

---

* So it was. A lock has survived, tucked into an envelope in the papers in the possession of her son. It is dark red, with hints of gold, and must have been nothing short of stunning when formally dressed.

time discussing the situation . . . and both of them were badly broken up. . . . It was hard for her to do it, but Jane told him finally that she could never marry him. . . . He was a nice boy . . . but not nearly as mature as Jane."

"But still," he adds, "I was far from winning Jane." Confused and emotionally shaken, Jane quit her job at Interior and went back to Milwaukee sometime in May 1936. By then, he had declared himself and she had responded, at least tentatively. "Jane, dearest," Ickes wrote her on May 16, "I love you with all my heart. Please go on loving me because I can't live without it." As with her previous relationship, Jane decided she needed time to mull this one over. She persuaded her father (who as yet had no idea of what was blooming between his daughter and her father-in-law, once removed) to give her enough money to finance a trip to Europe for the summer, where she wanted to hear the Vienna opera and travel about Germany. "I know you love me deeply," Ickes wrote on the eve of her departure,

> but I know too that you are fighting it and that a principal reason for your going to Vienna is the hope that you may be able to overcome your love. I doubt whether you would be going if it were not for this. In the circumstances what is my duty to the person whom I profoundly love? Obviously it is to make it as easy as possible for you to get over your love, even if I have not the strength actively to help you. . . .
>
> Oh, my Jane, I want to do what is best for you, at whatever cost to myself.

She did not write to dissuade him of this conviction, and the cost to him, in fact, was considerable as he helplessly let her disappear across the sea. "This was the worst summer that I have ever spent," he remembered. "I went through hell. . . . In the middle of the Summer I arranged to talk with her by telephone when she was in Munich, but neither of us could hear a word of what the other said and then we frantically cabled and wrote each other. I did much letter-writing that Summer that deliberately laid siege to her heart. The poor girl was greatly harassed."

But clearly leaning in his direction, for all the fact that there were nearly forty years between them. In July she wrote him from Vienna in a letter hardly calculated to put the damper on his passion. She had just read *Lady Chatterley's Lover,* she informed him ("unexpurgated, my dear!"). D. H. Lawrence, she had decided,

> understands the peculiarities of a woman's mind—that strange mixture of cold calculation (realism, you would call it) and self-deception—whether willfully or in ignorance I cannot say. We like to think that we can do without physical passion in sexual relations. We are inclined to feel superior to the man in that respect. But goodness me—suddenly we are quite as much at the

mercy of that irresistible force—and we know the physical sensation of all ecstasy; *feel* what we have before looked down upon with a coldly intellectual eye.

In September she returned, Ickes meeting her in New York and bringing her back to stay with him at Spring Valley. This was in the aftermath of Wilmarth's suicide and in the heart of the Presidential race, a period that must have provided great emotional stress for both of them. "She had been in Washington only a few days," he remembered,

> when I came home one night to find that she had already shipped the substantial part of her belongings to Milwaukee and had everything else packed and ready to leave. I had known that she was going back to Milwaukee, but I thought that it would be for only a few days to see her family. Now she announced that she was going for good.
>
> Once again I found myself in hell, but I did not try to hold her back. I knew that she was right. I saw her off at the airport and I turned back to try to reconcile myself to the thought that she had passed out of my life for good and all.

If Harold could not hold her, neither could her family. By December she had moved to New York, taken rooms at the Barbizon Hotel, that Manhattan refuge for Respectable Young Single Women, and begun studying photography, when not opening, reading, and responding in kind to the storm of fervent letters Ickes sent her way. Whenever the press of business allowed him, he sent himself, too, and by the spring of 1937 the fact of the love between them had been firmly settled even if what to do about it had not. No one in either family as yet knew anything about it, and of his friends only Ruth Hampton had been taken into Harold's confidence.

Jane returned to the Washington area sometime in the spring, early enough to be on hand in May when a real estate agent took Ickes out to Olney in Montgomery County, Maryland, to look at the estate of L. C. Probert, the former president of the Chesapeake & Ohio Railroad, who that February had died, leaving no heirs. The visits to Cissy Patterson's Dower House estate, which impressed him greatly, may have kindled a desire to become propertied on a generous scale or had stirred powerful memories of his happy childhood days on the farm at Newry, Pennsylvania. Then, too, he was enraptured and may have wanted to make some kind of spectacular offering to the new woman in his life. Whatever his motives, Harold fell in love with the Probert land, which included a ten-room house only a little over a decade old, a servants' cottage, a two-bedroom farmhouse, a good barn, and a little over 220 acres, forty of them wooded, with the option to buy another forty acres adjoining the property. On May 25 he signed a contract to buy the place and he and Jane began making plans to get him moved out of the Spring Valley house as soon as possible.

Before he could do more than think about the move, however, he was interrupted by his heart attack on May 27. Throughout his recovery, Jane was rarely absent from his side, visiting him daily in the hospital and reading to him for hours. Her constant attendance gave rise to speculation that she and Ickes were engaged, but when a *Herald* reporter asked her if the rumor was true, she tearfully denied it, while admitting that she was "awfully fond of the Secretary."

On July 15, Jane and Ann—who was now living in an apartment on N Street in Northwest Washington—went with him when he moved from his makeshift apartment in the Interior Building to his new home in Olney, which he had decided to christen Headwaters Farm. "I was so glad to get here," he wrote in his diary, "that I experienced a positive physical lift. There are many things about the house that I do not like and which I would change if I could, but, on the whole, it is quite satisfactory and the country is lovely. . . . I am sure that I am going to like it here and be quite happy and comfortable."

Jane came and went regularly for the rest of the summer and fall, staying usually with her sister or at the Wardman Park Hotel, and as soon as he was able to do so comfortably, they began being seen together at various functions. At Thanksgiving she returned to Milwaukee to spend time with her family—and almost immediately was felled by an attack of asthma (from which she, like Anna, would suffer periodically all her life). The illness kept her bedridden for weeks, doctors and nurses coming and going regularly to give her injections of Adrenalin, but it did not keep her from telephoning Harold regularly and writing long letters to him almost daily, sending them in fat, pink envelopes addressed either to Headwaters Farm or the Interior Department and invariably marked "personal."

As indeed they were. "Harold, dearest Harold," she wrote on December 30, "it hurts to love you so much. I feel on pins and needles. I want you—lustfully, passionately—oh—not at all nicely. A pity to waste one's youth sleeping alone!" Or one's old age, Ickes might have reflected. By then, the two of them had talked their way through the thirty-nine years that separated them and even the sobering implications of his heart attack. At some point during her visit home, Jane informed her parents and her sisters that she intended to marry Harold. They did not take it well, Ickes remembered:

For days at a time neither her father nor her mother would go into her bedroom. . . . And her father was trying to win her away from me by haranguing her and trying to bully her. Meanwhile . . . Betty and Ann were working hard in the same direction and Ann even undertook to do something about it with me. My position always was that, while they were dead right in insisting that Jane ought not to marry me, on account of the difference in our ages, and while I would not urge Jane to marry me, if she really did not want to, it was, after all, a matter for her to decide.

Jane, who could be as strong-willed as her intended, did not give an inch, and by the early spring of 1938 it was no longer a question of whether they would marry, but when and how. "As to my side of the family," Ickes says, "I didn't care what any of them thought, except Raymond. I told Raymond what my plans were. He was not surprised. He was perfunctory in his expressions, but it could be seen that he was not too happy about the situation." This did not deter his lovestruck father.

In April it was settled. They would marry as secretly as possible in order to avoid the inevitable press ballyhoo. Jane would slip off to Dublin, where her uncle, John Cudahy, served as the American ambassador to Ireland. After an appropriate interval, Ickes would join her, traveling first to England, then hopping across the Irish Sea for the wedding. Jane left, according to plan, on April 13, Harold seeing her off in New York. "I want you to know," she wrote from shipboard that day, "that you made me very happy yesterday and last night and this morning. In addition to [being] dear and sweet, you are a thrilling lover." A week later, arrived in Dublin, she wrote to pour out her frustrations over her uncle's recalcitrance (he, too, did not approve) and the difficulties of getting anything arranged as a result—though she finally was able to schedule the wedding in a Presbyterian church: "My God in heaven—did two people ever have such fiendish difficulty getting married? I do love you so very much, dearest one—but let's get this over—I really cannot stand much more. . . . Oh Harold *how* ARE you? I haven't heard for so long! All my love—all of it, dear—all. Please come soon."

Her father entered one more objection on May 19: "I regret that you are of the same mind but I will say nothing further," he wrote, then went on to say something further. "It seems too bad that a girl of your capabilities and youth should, for a few years of apparent security, sacrifice so much. I have always had the feeling that if the home here were adequate you would not consider it, but even with its inadequacy I do not think it sufficient reason for your determination." Too late—and too wrong—by far. That she may have wanted to escape a family life for which the word "inadequate" probably is too weak seems likely, but that this and a search for security were the sole reasons for her decision to marry Harold were the fond delusions of a jealous father. The passionate intensity of her letters to Harold is unmistakably genuine; she was in love, remained in love, and continued to describe the relationship, their son Harold remembers, "as a great love affair" long after Ickes's death.

Ickes himself certainly was willing to take her word for it. He had his heart checked out in the middle of May, and reported in his diary that his doctor thought that he was "better in this respect than I probably was before my break last summer. Lately I have been feeling better than I can remember. This is probably due, in large part at least, to my state of mind." He had told the President of his plans, and noted that "I found him perfectly fine about the whole thing. . . . He told me that his father was almost sixty years old when he married his mother, who was a young woman at the time, and that it did not matter if I was over sixty." Secretary of State Cordell Hull helped him to arrange for passport and visas on the sly for their honeymoon trip and E. K. Burlew made arrangements for Ickes to sail on the *Normandie* under the name of John L. Williams, a long-deceased cousin.

After leaving word with Mike Straus, his press secretary, that if anyone asked after him they were to be told that he was in Chicago and would be unavailable for a few days, Ickes flew to New York, then boarded the *Normandie* for Southampton. After an uneventful crossing, he arrived at Southampton the evening of May 23, almost too late for the boat train to Liverpool—which, if he had missed it, would have made him miss the wedding, too, scheduled for 9:00 A.M. the next morning. With the help of the American vice consul, he was able to shuttle himself and baggage into and out of customs at breakneck speed and onto the boat train with five minutes to spare. He arrived in Liverpool at six in the morning, hopped the boat for Dublin, and arrived at the Adelaide Street Presbyterian Church at nine, Jane already there with the license in her purse. The Reverend Dr. R. K. Hanna presided, not knowing precisely who it was he was joining together, with three witnesses, an organist, and the sexton. John Cudahy did not attend, claiming that it would put him in an embarrassing position to attend a Protestant wedding in a Catholic country. ("Of course, I scoffed at this as the flimsiest kind of alibi," Ickes told his diary. "It is no concern of the Irish Free State where I was to be married and, after all, John Cudahy is representing the United States of America at Dublin, not the Catholic Church.") A telegram from Roosevelt probably took some of the sting out of this snub (for which Jane never forgave her uncle): "AFFECTIONATE GREETINGS AND CONGRATULATIONS TO YOU BOTH ABILITY OF AMERICAN GOVERN-

MENT TO KEEP A SECRET FIRMLY ESTABLISHED FOR FIRST TIME IN HISTORY."

Ickes cabled Mike Straus to release a previously prepared statement to the press, and the couple fled to a small hotel outside Cork, where for the night they were able to escape the newspaper people who immediately began looking for them when word came from Washington to Dublin about the marriage. The next day a pride of newsmen caught up with them as they waited to catch the boat to Wales, and another contingent was waiting for them when they got off the train at Waterloo Station in London. In both instances, the couple endured lengthy interviews and photo sessions patiently, but when reporters began following their cab in London, Ickes had the driver stop, got out, and begged them to leave him and his wife in peace; if they didn't, he threatened, they would sit in the cab right where they were for as long as it took for the reporters to lose interest. The tactic worked, and for the rest of their stay in the city they were let alone.

Through the good offices of the American ambassador, Joseph P. Kennedy, the couple got a full dose of London society and politics over the next fortnight, rubbing elbows with the Duke and Duchess of Kent, Prime Minister Neville Chamberlain, the American-born Lady Astor ("I did not care for her," Ickes wrote. "She seemed nervous and fussy, quite in contrast to the English women present."), Lord and Lady Halifax, Winston Churchill ("a dumpy-looking person with decidedly bowed shoulders but with a very alert expression"), Lloyd George, Clement Atlee, and, among the Americans present, John D. Rockefeller, Jr., Arthur Sulzberger of *The New York Times,* and young John F. Kennedy, about whom he had nothing to say.

They then flew to Paris for two weeks, being taken under the wing of Ambassador William C. Bullitt, who would become a fast friend of both of them. The time here was a good deal less crowded than in London. "From our hotel," Ickes wrote in his diary, "we sallied forth every day to gorge ourselves on wonderful French food at various restaurants and hotels. We were so charmed with Paris that we just lived in it without doing too much sightseeing. I don't like to travel with an open Baedeker in one hand," he added, probably remembering the militantly organized excursions with Anna during the difficult trip of 1911, "and, as it happily developed, Jane doesn't like to either." Happy, if probably a little more plump than when they had started, they boarded the *Île de France* for New York on June 15, arriving to a flutter of press attention on June 21. "I never came to America in such a happy state of mind," Ickes told reporters. The next day Cissy Patterson ran two columns of text and a photograph of Ickes beaming at his bride on the front page of the *Herald.*

Cissy, in fact, had reached them on the ship's radiophone to offer the use of her apartment if they planned to spend any time in New York, but they decided to fly down the next day and get ensconced at Headwaters Farm. There, *Herald* reporter Carol Frink was given an exclusive interview on June 22. "Are you happy?" she asked the couple as they walked around the property, still dressed in their traveling clothes. "What a ridiculous question!" Ickes said. "Just look at us." Then, after one of those "alone at last looks," Frink reported, "Secretary and Mrs. Ickes strolled slowly, hand in hand, toward the house that looks so much like Mount Vernon, except that it is bigger and more luxurious."

"I have thanked God more than once," Ickes informed his diary the next Sunday, "that I had not married a flapper or a flibbertigibbet. Jane is young, but she is not immature. Both of us since our marriage have been perfectly sure that we did the right thing. There has not been so much as a flyspeck to mar our happiness." Well, perhaps just a speck. One of the questions Carol Frink had asked Jane during her interview had been how she planned to spend the summer. "I expect to spend my time trying to keep cool," Jane had answered ruefully. The temperature was 82 degrees Fahrenheit, with 77 percent humidity, and the newspapers were reporting it as one of the most ghastly June days in the region's memory. With her asthma problems, Jane had little physical tolerance for swamp weather, and it may have been during this first season at Headwaters Farm, as she later related the story to her son, that the heat drove her to the basement of the house in search of relief. There, she said, she rested her forehead against the cool surface of a big water tank they kept there, and wept in misery.

CHAPTER
· 43 ·

Inside Passages

PROBABLY TO HER DELIGHT, Jane did not have to endure her first summer at Headwaters Farm for long. On July 3, Ickes had a visit at his office from Anna Roosevelt, FDR's daughter, and her husband, John Boettiger. He knew Anna slightly from having met her at various official functions, and knew John even less well—though they may have encountered each other in the Chicago years, when Boettiger was becoming one of the *Tribune*'s leading reporters, and certainly had met since Boettiger's promotion to the *Tribune*'s Washington Bureau. (Among other incidents, Boettiger had interviewed him in 1933 with regard to the Malmin affair.) After a brief sojourn in New York working for Will Hays at the Motion Picture Producers Association, Boettiger had since become editor and publisher of the *Post-Intelligencer,* Hearst's struggling Seattle newspaper, while Anna had signed a contract as a feature writer for the paper's women's pages. They had come to Ickes to urge that he and Jane join them for a tour of Alaska. Seattle had always considered Alaska to be within its sphere of interest, since the city was its nearest port of entry to Outside (which was how Alaskans tended to describe the states of the Mother Country), and Boettiger probably thought it would do the territory some good to have the Secretary of the Interior come and have a look.

Ickes agreed, though it was nearly a month before he could clear his desk of work that had accumulated during his honeymoon—a task made more difficult by the fact that Harry Slattery, who had been confirmed as undersecretary during his absence, had undergone an operation and was recuperating at his old home in Greenville, South Carolina. This left Ickes and an exhausted E. K. Burlew, who had been promoted to assistant secretary in April, with the bulk of the work to do. Slattery's absence, Ickes reported to his diary, "has thrown a terrific burden on Burlew. I found him nervous and terribly overworked. I told him that he must get away during July because unless he gets hold of himself he will soon reach a stage where he will lose a good deal of his effectiveness. I don't like the thought of having to hold the lines with only Chapman to help, but even this is better than allowing Burlew to break down."

By the end of July, Slattery was back to work and Burlew returned from a restful vacation, so Ickes and Jane could safely board the train for Chicago, then change to the Great Northern for the fine, rattling trip across the northern tier of states to Seattle. There was a brief stopover in Glacier National Park, Ickes's first visit to what may have been his favorite park since a cross-country journey as part of Roosevelt's entourage on a "nonpolitical" junket in 1934. (A contingent of Blackfeet Indians had made him and the Roosevelts honorary members of the tribe and had given him a war bonnet and christened him "Omuc Ki Yo," or "Big Bear.") There was a group of Blackfeet on hand for the 1938 visit, too, but only Jane got adopted this time, under the name of Princess Mountain Bird Woman.

John and Anna met them at the station in Seattle, accompanied by Major Owen A. Tomlinson, superintendent of Rainier National Park. From Seattle, the party flew over Puget Sound and the Olympic Peninsula to Port Angeles on the Strait of Juan de Fuca. It was a beautiful, clear day, and Ickes could look down for the first time on the snow-smothered mountains and darkling forests of the newly authorized Olympic National Park, which to his eyes vindicated all the time and energy he and his people had put into its designation. "It did not take more than a superficial glance," he wrote in his diary, "to determine that these mountains should be in a national park where they could be preserved for all time." At Port Angeles, they were met by Irving Brant, just beginning his survey of areas that should be added to the park under the terms of the legislation that had just been passed. A drive south into the park took them to a grove of old-growth Douglas fir, some of the trees hundreds of years old, where they picnicked. "It is the intention to keep this park," he noted in a later entry, "so far as is possible, in a wilderness area. It is truly a wonderland of nature and it is more than I can understand how people who pretend to be interested in conservation could be opposed to its creation into a national park."

That evening, they flew to Seattle, spending the next two nights with
the Boettigers. The two couples were well on the way toward an abiding
friendship by then, possibly linked emotionally by the romantic circumstances of their respective marriages. John and Anna had met and fallen in
love during Roosevelt's campaign for the Presidency in 1932, when both
were still married to other people (Anna had two children by her marriage, Boettiger two stepchildren by his). They had done little to camouflage their relationship, and the affair had been the talk of Washington
until their marriage in 1934. Whatever the reason, as Ickes noted in his
diary, the four of them got along beautifully, and he found Anna particularly appealing, "a delightful person—simple and unaffected but interesting and attractive. She and Jane seemed to fall for each other from the
start. At any rate, Jane came away with a very real liking for her." Jane was
indeed taken with the older, sympathetic woman, and this visit began a
particularly deep and mutually rewarding friendship between them that
would last all their lives, surviving the Boettigers' later move to Phoenix,
their divorce in 1949, and John's suicide in 1950.

Newspaper business would keep the Boettigers in Seattle, so on
August 4, Jane and Harold sailed off on the Alaska Steamship Company
liner *Mt. McKinley* without their new friends, steaming up through the
Inside Passage past the mountains, glaciers, and scores of misty, forested
islands of the Alaska panhandle, one of the most spectacularly beautiful
sea routes anywhere in the world and for Ickes a fine introduction to the
largest and least troublesome of the territories under the control of the
Interior Department. With a population of only a little over seventy-one
thousand people—including more than thirty-two thousand native
Athabascan, Thlingit, Aleut, and Inuit (Eskimo) peoples—and a land
mass of more than 591,000 square miles, virtually every acre of it
federally owned, the Great Land was an unlikely arena for the kinds of
political, economic, and environmental conflicts common to Outside.
Not that it was entirely free of problems, a fact Ickes discovered soon
enough—although, as was often the case, the Secretary's view of precisely
what they were and what ought to be done about them differed somewhat
from that of the local population.

Their first stop was Ketchikan, a sturdy village whose physical characteristics were typical of the outposts Jane and Harold would see clinging
to the edge or pocketed in the middle of tens of thousands of square miles
of wilderness unmatched anywhere on the continent. The town was
succinctly described by travel writer Harry A. Franck, who had preceded
them to the territory by just a month: "Ketchikan," he wrote,

is built on an island forty miles in diameter, and is pushed almost into the sea by steep, wooded mountains. Not only does the town itself stretch long and narrow at the foot of its mountains, but houses are scattered far out along heavily wooded shores in both directions. . . . The business section is built on piles; the rest of the town on rock. Water pipes, perforce on the surface, are allowed to trickle if it is very cold. . . . Modern business blocks . . . well, modern buildings, at least, give it the familiar American aspect. Without exception, as far as we saw, the homes are frame structures. . . . Flowers grew in profusion about them. The big new concrete post-office and Federal Building is beautified, if that is the word, by a huge brass plaque bearing the names of our current President, Postmaster General and lesser fry, in letters proportionate to their political importance. It was reassuring to realize that we were still at home.

The Secretary (whose name probably was among the "lesser fry" of the plaque, since the town's Federal Building had been constructed with PWA money) and his party were greeted by a large crowd, then taken out to an Indian day school and after that for a tour of a local salmon canning factory. Continuing north, the party reached Juneau, the territorial capital, on August 7, where Ickes spent a few hours with then Governor John W. Troy (he would be replaced by Ernest Gruening in the summer of 1939).

The next stop was Seward, and after that Anchorage, the southern terminus of the government-owned and -operated Alaska Railroad and as such the only coastal town that gave access to the interior at Fairbanks, the railroad's northern terminus on the Tanana River 250 miles away. Anchorage was "a typical Alaskan town," Ickes curtly noted, and even Franck gave it short shrift as "a government-built railroad town of little architectural pretensions," but both found more of interest a few miles north of the town at Palmer, the hub of the New Deal's northernmost experiment in socioeconomic planning—the Matanuska Colony.

In the summer of 1934, Jacob Baker, Harry Hopkins's assistant director of the FERA, made a quick tour of Alaska to discover its peculiar needs, and had been told again and again by those he interviewed that what the territory had to have was more settlement. O. F. Ohlson, general manager of the Alaska Railroad, had been particularly vociferous in this regard, outlining an ambitious scheme to colonize the arable and comparatively mild (by Alaskan standards) valley of the Matanuska River with destitute farmers from Outside. "It has been ascertained," Ohlson wrote Baker upon the FERA man's return to Washington, "that an active settler can clear, cultivate and put under crop twenty acres during the first three years, which will make him self-supporting. Great care should be exercised and only the hardier type of settlers should be selected."

The idea caught the imagination of the FERA's Division of Rural Rehabilitation, and with the cooperation and consultation of Interior's Division of Territories and Island Possessions, 202 rural families from the so-called cut-over counties of northern Minnesota, Wisconsin, and Michigan were ultimately enticed north by the promise of being able to own and cultivate their own forty-acre farms—each complete with farmhouse, barn, well, and necessary outbuildings—with thirty-year, 3 percent government loans and liberal repayment policies. The FERA estimated that at the end of five years of work, each farm would achieve a net annual income of $500, after which families could start making installment payments on their debt to the government. In the summer of 1938, at the end of four years, it was clear that things were not quite working out according to plan. Many colonists had found the work and the living conditions harder than anticipated, even for stump farmers from northern Minnesota, and had defaulted; and only a handful of those who had stuck it out had hopes of being able to begin making payments on their loans anytime soon.

Nevertheless, the colony remained a going concern, with about 170 families remaining. The village of Palmer, although measurably smaller than even most Alaskan towns, still had a diesel-powered generating plant, as well as a school, a gymnasium, a dormitory and office building for the colony's government staff, and a hospital. In keeping with the social instincts of the New Deal, the berries, wheat, barley, oats, hay, potatoes, eggs, poultry, and "Matanuska Maid" dairy products produced by the colony were all marketed through the Matanuska Valley Farmers Cooperative Association, to which all colonists were required to belong. Travel writer Franck professed to find in all this some sinister weakness. "The trouble," he wrote, "is that if a man makes a success at Matanuska he finds he is not entirely a free man. He cannot sell his forty without government permission, even if it is free and clear. That, they say, is to keep out speculators. Four colonists were ordered out just the other day because they refused to join the cooperative marketing association." It all "smells faintly of Russia," he decided.

After touring the colony with Jane, Ickes himself concluded that while "it has been a failure in one or two respects . . . in so far as the underlying principle is concerned, it has proved to be a great success. . . . Enough of these settlers are already self-supporting to prove that the experiment was soundly conceived." Responsibility for most of the failures, he felt, could be laid at the door of the FERA's "sentimental social-service people" who had chosen colonists on the basis of need rather than willingness or ability to produce. When "the lazy settlers who won't work any more than they have to . . . are ruthlessly weeded out," he said, "this ought to be a very prosperous section of Alaska." His interest was more than academic, more even than might have been expected from him as the individual with ultimate responsibility for the fate of the territory. Harry Hopkins, it seemed, had made it clear that he would be happy to turn the colony over to the Interior Department. "I am willing to accept it," Ickes wrote in his diary, "but only on certain conditions. I will want all outstanding expenditures taken care of and I will want an over-all sum of not less than $350,000 to put the colony firmly on its feet. I will want the right to weed out the drones and replace them with men and women who are willing to work when they have such a fine opportunity."*

On August 11, Ickes and Jane boarded the Alaska Railroad for Mt. McKinley National Park and, after that, Fairbanks. The continent's tallest mountain remained hidden behind an impenetrable mantle of clouds (as it did 80 percent of the time), and Ickes had nothing to say in his diary about their brief stay at the new hotel the railroad had constructed at the entrance to the park. Jane kept a journal herself for part of the trip, however, and was scandalized: "Rolling into the park siding, an atrocious sight greeted us—an elongated pile of bastard-modern, dun-colored boards, pierced by niggardly slits of windows. . . . Without exception, it is the most appalling monstrosity. Tiny cells of rooms; no view; no sitting space; a power plant blocking the approach. . . . A typical example of criminal inefficiency on the part of bureaucrats. Harold was simply frantic." (And angry enough to insist on some changes, an outcome gleefully seized upon by Franck as one more example of New Deal largess: "[The hotel] is larger than was at first planned," he wrote in 1939, "because last August the Secretary of the Interior came along and said, 'Here, you are not spending enough. Add another twenty rooms.'")

Above Fairbanks, along the numerous creeks that fed into the Tanana River (itself one of the main tributaries of the great Yukon River), they found the modern version of the mining booms that had given birth to the territory's first American settlement of consequence. It was gold mining, but on a scale and of a character that few of the sourdoughs of forty years before would have recognized or understood. Hoses with nozzles the size of howitzers sent screaming jets of water against cliffsides and the banks of

---

* After his return in September, the transfer was made according to his specifications, Hopkins maintaining that the $350,000 payment should be enough to finance the colony until fiscal 1941, when, as Ickes put it, "all the colonists ought to be self-supporting or thrown out on their own." Not all the colonists, in fact, had become self-supporting by 1941, but in spite of all the tough talk, neither were many of them ever foreclosed upon—and after the Japanese attack on Pearl Harbor in December, the question no longer seemed important.

streams that had been dammed and turned out of their courses, the mud cascading down through ditches to settle in enormous man-made lakes across which gold dredges as big as Mississippi riverboats chewed their way, steadily and noisily scooping up the treasure-laden muck, separating the gold from it, then depositing the residue behind them in windrows like the endless excreta of unimaginable prehistoric creatures.

A good deal of the deposited muck, in fact, contained bits and pieces of prehistoric creatures—the tusks of mastodons, for example, or the hooves of eohippi, the jawbones of saber-toothed tigers, bones from the feet of ancient dromedaries. It was these relics that had brought Ickes up to Fairbanks, but a look around at the great mess of the mining operations, most of them controlled by such large operators as the Fairbanks Exploration Company, a subsidiary of the U.S. Smelting and Refining Company in the Outside, also must have reinforced his convictions about the self-defeating transience of such enterprises. "The chief drawback to Alaska, as I see it," he reflected later,

> is that the people here, generally speaking, think of everything in terms of mining, and those of us who do not live in Alaska think of mining too when we think of this Territory. . . . People have come to Alaska to exploit a nonrenewable resource, such as gold or copper, and then take the wealth back to the United States in order to live an easy life. . . . This great universal wealth has gone and is going to stockholders in the United States and abroad, and Alaska has not even collected a decent share of it by taxation. At the same time, it is clamoring for more Federal money. Alaskans won't tax themselves or their exportable wealth. They think Uncle Sam ought to build and maintain highways, extend and improve the Alaska Railroad, and supply the Territory with public works of all nature while they continue exploring every crack and crevice for precious metal which will make them rich and enable them to go back to the United States to live in luxury.

"I have taken occasion to talk along these lines to people I have met here," he added. "I have told them that their psychology is wrong. I very much doubt whether they have understood what I was talking about." They may or may not have understood his psychological points, but they understood him clearly enough when he started talking about money. One of the themes he established in his little homilies was the necessity of raising the territorial tax on extracted minerals, presently set at 3 percent of gross profit, to at least 8 percent and that each mining operation should post a bond of $2,500 against the possibility that it might skip the territory without paying said tax. Franck, who maintained that most people in the territory referred to Ickes as "Alaska's Dictator" and purported to speak for the oppressed, wrote in 1939:

That is the usual politician's idea of business, say the miners of Alaska, who claim they hardly make a reasonable profit under the present tax; say that it should be lowered. . . . Alaskans say that an 8 percent tax would promptly kill mining in Alaska; that the bond for $2,500 would probably cost at least $300 and would be hard for most and impossible for some miners to get. . . . Alaska's Legislature introduced at this year's session a bill based on the dictator's demands, "merely to show respect to the Secretary of the Interior," but turned it down in twelve minutes flat. But that perennial raiding of producers by politicians calls for eternal vigilance even in Alaska.

Back in Seward, Alaska's Dictator and his wife took passage on the U.S. Coast Guard cutter *Spencer* for the return trip through the Inside Passage to Seattle, with a number of stops along the way. They were given a tour of Glacier Bay National Monument by B. Frank Heintzelman, chief forester for Alaska, who astonished Ickes by insisting that the monument ought to be enlarged with Forest Service lands to make a national park. "I was delighted with what I saw," Ickes noted in his diary. "The new park limits would be extended so that some of the original forests, including one of the finest stands of virgin timber in Alaska, and a number of glaciers, bays, estuaries, and rivers would be included. This would constitute a wonderful park. I think I am safe in saying that it would be the most outstanding park in the whole national park system."*

Hooniah, a small Thlingit village, by contrast, Ickes found a disgrace, "ramshackle, squalid, dirty, and apparently poverty-stricken," with a population of tubercular and alcoholic natives. He made alcohol and Indians one of the subjects of discussion during a second visit with Governor Troy in Juneau a few days later, telling him that "I was shocked with the ease with which whisky could be bought by the Indians. I told him that whisky was demoralizing and that the Territorial Legislature ought to do something about it." He also delivered himself of his standard lecture regarding Alaska's exploitation by Outside interests and the need for an increased minerals tax, then debated the point with J. A. Hellenthal, a member of the Democratic National Committee and local attorney for the Alaska-Juneau Company. The governor and Hellenthal made polite noises through all of this, but doubtless were greatly relieved when the secretary and his pretty wife got back on board the *Seward*.

---

* There are those who would agree that it is—although the upper echelons of the Forest Service combined with Alaskan mining interests to block Glacier Bay's designation as a national park until the Alaska National Interest Lands Conservation Act of 1980. So little appreciated was the monument in the latter 1930s, in fact, that it took all of Ickes's powers of persuasion just to keep Roosevelt himself from opening the monument to mining operations that would have severely damaged its appeal as a park. Heintzelman became governor of the territory in the 1950s.

A final stop in Alaska was made at Metlakatla in the Annette Islands south of Ketchikan, where a colony of Tsimshean Indians from British Columbia had been established in 1887. Under the stewardship of the Reverend William Duncan, the Indians had prospered, and Ickes found the place one of the few native communities which had taken full advantage of the Alaska Reorganization Act of 1936, operating its own fishing fleet, canning factory, and sawmill. "It is the best built, cleanest, and most prosperous Indian village I have seen in these parts," he wrote in his diary. "Their houses are fairly modern and on the American style. They have built their own sidewalks and a very large, well-constructed and well-appointed community center where they can have music, amateur theatricals, basketball, etc. They have built their own schools, and at least one of the two large churches was built completely by these Indians."

With this pleasant encounter and the unfolding beauty of the Inside Passage as their last memories of Alaska, they docked in Seattle on August 23. They were met again by John and Anna Boettiger, this time with their children, and were driven out to the newly built Sunrise Camp in Mount Rainier National Park for a two-day rest. "Three months ago, in Dublin, we were married," Jane wrote in her journal on August 24. "And what a glorious day on which to celebrate our third anniversary—bright hot sun in a cloudless sky—the dry mountain air tingling in our lungs. Mt. Rainier a great frozen white mass towered above us. . . . No cares; no office; no telephones. . . . Nervousness and pique dropped away—he was sun-burned and happy."

Reality with the bark on presented itself a few hours after they came down from the mountain and drove into Tacoma the morning of August 26. Here, they were met by Congressman John F. Coffee, who was running for reelection and had urgently requested some help. Ickes gave it by addressing a luncheon meeting of the Young Men's Business Association. About four hundred people showed up for the speech, which was broadcast locally over both the CBS and Mutual affiliates. "I spoke extemporaneously and I think that I did a pretty good job," Ickes wrote later.

> I took a fling at the Dies Committee which is on one of the periodic Red hunts that Congress is addicted to. From the *Post-Intelligencer* of the day before, in Raymond Clapper's column, it appeared that this committee had discovered that Shirley Temple, the child movie star, had Red affiliations, and I referred in my speech to a burly Congressman leading a *posse comitatus* in a raid upon Shirley Temple's nursery to collect her dolls as evidence of her implications in a Red plot. . . . In general I made a New Deal speech, putting in some boosts for Coffee at intervals, and there is no doubt that the speech went over well.

Both Coffee's appeal for help and the attention Ickes paid to Martin Dies's newly formed House Un-American Activities Committee were symptomatic of a profoundly changed political atmosphere in the country since the campaign of 1936. As Jane and Ickes boarded the Great Northern the night after his speech and began the return trip to the East, he might have done well to reflect on the fact that a number of New Deal chickens had come home to roost—and that some of them were his.

CHAPTER

· 44 ·

Reductive Politics

T HE TRANSFORMATION HAD begun with the Supreme Court—or, more accurately, with Roosevelt's plans for the Supreme Court. The resentment among the most ardent New Dealers over what the "nine old men" had done to FDR's legislative program in 1935 had been muffled during the 1936 campaign, but it had not vanished—certainly not from the breast of Harold L. Ickes, who had been thinking about it in some detail even while Roosevelt was being sworn in on Inauguration Day behind a curtain of driving rain: "It was noted," the Secretary told his diary,

> that the Chief Justice, when he came to that part of the oath which required the President to protect and defend the Constitution of the United States, spoke slowly and with especial emphasis. It was noteworthy also that . . . the President gave the full answer and he, too, spoke with slowness and particular emphasis when he declared that he would protect and defend the Constitution of the United States.
>
> This whole incident was quite significant. The Chief Justice was asking the President to swear that he would protect and defend the Constitution of the United States and the President was obligating himself to do so, and yet what was the Constitution to the Chief Justice was not the Constitution to the President, at least in some very vital particulars. And that poses the question that is becoming more clamorous in this country today. Just what is the Constitution of the United States? Is it what five out of nine Justices of the Supreme Court say it is, or is it what the President and millions

of Americans believe it to be, namely, not a restrictive force but a broad charter designed to permit the people under changing conditions to advance the general welfare and to accomplish the greatest good of the greatest number of the people?

Ickes may or may not have been hearing more than met the ear as he observed the ceremony, but that Roosevelt had been thinking about the question himself was made clear at ten o'clock in the morning of February 5, when the President convened a special cabinet meeting. Also called in were Joseph Robinson, Senate majority leader, and Henry Ashurst, chairman of the Senate Judiciary Committee; Speaker of the House William Bankhead; the newly elected House majority leader, Sam Rayburn; and Hatton Sumners, chairman of the House Judiciary Committee. Roosevelt wasted little time in putting on the table a proposal he was going to offer Congress in a message that afternoon. Over the past few days, in extraordinary secrecy, the proposal had been put together by Roosevelt and a team of advisers headed up by Attorney General Homer Cummings, who had come up with its general structure; Samuel I. Rosenman, now serving as a justice on the New York State Supreme Court but still FDR's chief speechwriter; Donald Richberg, who had gone into private practice but was still available for special services; and Stanley Reed, solicitor general in the Justice Department.

There was not much discussion on the proposal. Roosevelt simply read the message, doubtless with one eye peeled to observe its effect. It proposed that legislation be enacted that would enable the President to appoint an additional judge for every judge in the federal judiciary system who had reached the age of seventy or more without availing himself of the opportunity to retire at full salary (the Economy Act of 1933 had cut it to half salary, but Representative Sumners was currently pushing legislation to restore the full amount of $20,000).

While couched in language that made it applicable to the whole federal system, there was no question in anyone's mind that the plan was meant primarily for the Supreme Court, six of whose justices were at or over the age of seventy already. Under the proposed legislation, the President could appoint a maximum of six additional justices—which, conceivably, could bring the number of sitting justices up to fifteen. The message pointed out that the present structure of the Court was hardly sacrosanct: between 1789 and 1869, the number had gone from six to five to seven to nine to ten to seven and, finally, back to nine again, where it had since remained.

One of the primary reasons for making this proposal, the message emphasized, was that the justices were overworked, citing the fact that in the previous year, the Supreme Court had declined to review 695 out of 803 cases brought before it. "Many of the refusals were doubtless warranted," the message granted, "but can it be said that full justice is achieved when a court is forced by the sheer necessity of keeping up with its business to decline, without even an explanation, to hear 87% of the cases presented to it by private litigants?" Decrepitude, the message strongly implied, may have had something to do with it: "In exceptional cases, of course, judges, like other men, retain to an advanced age full mental and physical vigor. Those not so fortunate are often unable to perceive their own infirmities. They seem to be tenacious of the appearance of adequacy."

When Roosevelt was finished reading the message, the room was, according to Ickes, subdued, if not stunned. "The Vice President said not a word during the entire discussion," he noted in his diary. "This is the first time that I have ever seen him at a Cabinet or any other meeting sit entirely silent."* The face of Speaker Bankhead, he said, was "pokerish," while Senate Majority Leader Robinson indicated "mild assent" (as well he might have, given the fact that Roosevelt had already promised him a seat on the Court at the next available vacancy). Sam Rayburn sat silent, like his mentor Garner. Ashurst, Ickes said, was downright enthusiastic, and if Sumners was as quiet as Rayburn and Garner, "his pleasure was apparent when the President in his message endorsed the idea of retiring Supreme Court justices at full pay."

"Pokerish" was probably the most accurate of the Secretary's adjectives used to describe the historic cabinet meeting of February 5, for none of the congressional leaders in attendance were pleased that they had not been taken into Roosevelt's confidence earlier—it was they, after all, who were going to have to muscle the radical proposal through to passage. For all the "pleasure" that Ickes may have discerned in his countenance, Chairman Sumners was livid. "Boys," he told the others when they got back to the Capitol from their White House meeting, "this is where I cash in," and from that point forward refused to support the plan, when not opposing it outright. Speaker Bankhead maintained a position that some might have described as bordering on the neutral, while Rayburn, who was less than enthusiastic himself, nevertheless did his best to gather signatories or at least willing sympathizers for the legislation in the House. When he was certain that only about a hundred votes could be

---

* Many years later, Garner would claim that he told Cummings during the meeting that "Mr. Attorney General, before that law comes back up here for the Boss's signature, many, many moons will pass." It is not likely that Ickes would have missed such a good line; Garner probably was just "remembering big," as Max Baer's wife once said of her husband.

counted on, however, Rayburn persuaded Roosevelt's people to concentrate on getting a bill through the Senate first, where Robinson's power might be more effective. Even here, the legislation was strenuously opposed from the outset by a powerful minority, led by Senator Burton K. Wheeler, the early New Dealer from Montana who was becoming increasingly convinced that the Executive Branch had acquired a lust for power that had to be stopped.

Wheeler made his feelings known immediately after the President's formal presentation of the Court plan in his congressional message later in the afternoon of February 5. Thomas B. Corcoran—who, like most of the President's men, had stifled any resentment he may have felt at being left in the dark—went to see Wheeler to sound out the President's old ally.

"Do you remember Huey Long?" Wheeler asked him in what Corcoran described as "one of his passionate furies."

Corcoran said that, yes, he did remember the late senator from Louisiana.

"Did you see what Roosevelt did to Huey?" Wheeler shouted.

"You don't think Roosevelt had him killed?" Corcoran asked, incredulously.

"I say did you see what he did to Huey?" Wheeler repeated ambiguously. "Now I've been watching Roosevelt for a long time. Once he was only one of us who made him. Now he means to make himself the boss of us all. Well, he's made the mistake we've been waiting for a long time— and this is our chance to cut him down to size."

"But, Burt, the Court."

"Your Court plan doesn't matter: he's after us."

"So now the Kingdom was at stake," Corcoran remembered thinking as he carried this disturbing reaction back to the White House. "It wasn't the Court issue—the Barons were at Runnymede. At the very beginning of Roosevelt's second term his own friends who had made him were now determined to destroy him. Women's jealousy was a peanut compared to male envy."

More and more Democrats were coming to agree with Wheeler— though none went on record, even obliquely, to suggest that FDR had hired the death of Huey Long. They were backed by most of the press, which immediately identified the proposal as FDR's "Court-packing" scheme and described it in terms of abhorrence. "Its objective," the *Chicago Tribune* editorialized with uncharacteristic restraint but with unmistakable opposition, "is to enable Mr. Roosevelt to command a majority of the Supreme Court. The question raised . . . Shall the Supreme Court be turned into the personal organ of the President . . . is fundamental because, if Congress answers yes, the principle of an impartial and independent judiciary will be lost in this country. In all probability it will be abandoned for all time." Walter Lippmann was as close to ferocity as that studiously rational man ever got in print, saying that Roosevelt was "drunk with power," was trying to engineer a "bloodless coup d'état which strikes a deadly blow at the vital center of constitutional democracy," and whose nefarious purpose was nothing less than "to create the necessary precedent, to establish the political framework for, and to destroy the safeguards against, a dictator."

The President's friends had their work cut out for them—and in spite of the fact that to varying degrees most harbored doubts about the wisdom of his action and were unhappy at not having been consulted by the President during the days preceding the message, they joined forces behind him and gave their best efforts to drum up support with the public and the Congress. These included the "young Turks" on whose shoulders most of the work of the "Second New Deal" had rested—including Corcoran, Ben Cohen, Robert Jackson (an assistant Attorney General in the Justice Department's Antitrust Division), William O. Douglas (a member—and soon to be chairman—of the Securities and Exchange Commission), and Joseph L. Rauh, Jr. (a special assistant to Corcoran and Cohen). There were a few old Turks, too, among them Felix Frankfurter at Harvard, who allowed his love of Roosevelt (and possibly his hope of a Supreme Court appointment for himself) to overcome his distaste for the proposal itself. Without being specific, FDR had warned Frankfurter on January 15 that he would give him "an awful shock" in a couple of weeks. After the public announcement, Frankfurter replied:

> Dramatically and artistically you did "shock" me. But beyond that—well, the momentum of a long series of decisions not defensible in the realm of reason nor justified by settled principles of Constitutional interpretation had convinced me, as they had convinced you, that means had to be found to save the Constitution from the Court, and the Court from itself. . . . There was no perfect way out. . . . But I have, as you know, deep faith in your instinct to make the wise choice.

Ickes also had some reservations about the proposal—not concerning its wisdom, but its restraint in not going as far as the Secretary would have liked: he wished the President had challenged the Court's very right to impose constitutional interpretations in the first place (an opinion that would have won Ickes few supporters then and even fewer today, and one he confined to his diary). Nevertheless, while the Puerto Rican situation and other departmental matters had kept him from the fight for most of the spring of 1937, he did strike a blow on April 10 before five or six thousand people at the Chicago Stadium and to several million over the NBC Blue Network. The speech was entitled "Odd Man Wins." Four judges, the Secretary explained,

> of an average age of approximately 75 years have served notice on the nation that they are on a sit-down strike and will not help the people of the United States work out their modern problems. . . . [U]nless the present personnel of the Court is enlarged, every new and debatable constitutional issue will come before the Court with four justices definitely hostile to any theory that would permit the Constitution to be adapted to the needs of the time. Four out of nine votes are loaded—*packed* against the people.

This would leave five presumably unprejudiced justices, he went on, but if even one of the five voted with the four intransigent conservatives on any given issue, liberalism would be "nullified." Under the present system, then, he concluded, "Whether democracy can be made to work depends upon a single peripatetic vote."

After the speech, Ickes joined Harry Hopkins in Florida for a brief fishing trip on the U.S.S. *Houston* that Roosevelt had arranged and had all but ordered them to take in an effort to give them both some rest and the opportunity to cultivate the still rough territory between them. ("National budget almost balanced," FDR wired them on April 20. "If you both stay away another week debtor nations will pay war debt and we can all head for Samoa.") As always, when taken out of the context of Washington and put on a purely personal footing, the two rivals got along fine. Ickes, who was by then seriously contemplating marriage with Jane, was particularly interested to learn during this trip that Hopkins had stood his first marriage "for as long as he could. Then he made up his mind that he had twenty-five years ahead of him and that he wasn't going to let them all go to pot." He had divorced his wife and remarried quite happily—although Barbara, his new wife, had recently undergone surgery for breast cancer. The Supreme Court and Roosevelt's plans for it also provided a good deal of the conversation during the ten-day vacation, and Ickes was, he noted in his diary, astonished when Hopkins "remarked that he supposed I would be one of the first men to be considered by the President for one of the places. I told him that this was news to me and that I had never even thought of such a matter. . . . I am not going to speculate about what I regard as an outside possibility. I am not even going to reflect whether I would care for such an appointment."

It was just as well that he did not spend much time thinking it over, for FDR never once hinted at anything like this, and Hopkins may well have been teasing him. In any case, by the time they returned from the trip on April 23—in fact, as early as Ickes's Chicago speech—Roosevelt's threat of judicial revolution was beginning to lose validity rapidly. The first blow had been dealt by Wheeler during hearings before the Senate Judiciary Committee on March 22. Wheeler opened his remarks with a summary of FDR's message, emphasizing in particular the President's contention that under the present system, the justices were overworked with a consequent backlog of cases on the docket. He then held up a sheaf of papers and announced, "I have here now a letter from the Chief Justice of the Supreme Court, Mr. Charles Evans Hughes, dated March 21, 1937, written by him and approved by Mr. Justice Brandeis and Mr. Justice Van Devanter."

This stopped conversation immediately. Chief Justices of the United States Supreme Court do not write to congressional committees; it had never been done, and those in the room were suddenly aware of history. Wheeler read the letter, which declared emphatically that

> The Supreme Court is fully abreast of its work. . . . An increase in the number of justices of the Supreme Court, apart from any question of policy, which I do not discuss, would not promote the efficiency of the Court. It is believed that it would impair that efficiency so long as the Court acts as a unit. There would be more judges to hear, more judges to confer, more judges to discuss, more judges to be convinced and to decide. The present number of justices is thought to be large enough so far as the prompt, adequate, and efficient conduct of the work of the Court is concerned.

Having gutted one of the President's most forceful arguments, over the next several weeks the Court proceeded to obliterate systematically the charge that it was generically backward when it came to social issues— whether as a result of FDR's attack or simply as a matter of course is still a point of contention among Supreme Court scholars. On March 29, in a decision that effectively reversed its 1935 ruling invalidating a minimum wage law for women in New York State, the Court upheld the constitutionality of a minimum wage law in Washington State. On April 12, it declared the Wagner National Labor Relations Act to be valid, and on May 24 came down in favor of a Wisconsin law that prohibited injunctions designed to interfere with labor picketing and on the same day declared the Social Security Act constitutional. As one cynic noted, "A switch in time saved nine."

In the meantime, on May 18, the same day that the Senate Judiciary Committee, by a vote of 10–8, sent the Court bill to the floor with a "Do not pass" recommendation, Justice Van Devanter tendered his resignation. Early in August, Roosevelt would name the liberal senator from Alabama, Hugo L. Black, to occupy Van Devanter's chair. The President now had the chance of a clear majority on any given liberal issue that might come before the Court. But he still would not give up on his plan. Among other reasons—including plain stubbornness—he felt trapped in his promise to Joseph Robinson, who continued to fight for the legislation manfully. When Robert Jackson pointed out to him that Robinson, an old-line southern Democrat and hence essentially conservative, was hardly likely to enhance the liberal cast of the Court, Roosevelt replied, "The trouble, Bob, is that I've promised it to him. The first vacancy, I'll give to him. I don't know any way I can get out of it, if he gets that through." Faced with apparently insurmountable opposition from Wheeler and his allies, Robinson did talk FDR into compromise legislation that would have limited him to appointing not more than one additional justice per year for each unretired justice over the age of seventy-five. But before he could negotiate this bargain with the Senate, Robinson was found dead of a heart attack on his apartment floor the morning of July 14. Without its most dedicated supporter, the bill was just as dead. On the afternoon of July 22, the Senate voted 70–20 to recommit the legislation to the Judiciary Committee. A week later, a substitute measure instituting a number of minor reforms in the lower judiciary was passed. It was done, Vice President Garner said, so as "not to bloody the President's nose."

Harold Ickes professed to find comfort in the fact that even if the Court plan had been rejected, notice had been served on the Supreme Court. In a speech entitled "The Federal Constitution—May It Always Live!" the Secretary had instructed a crowd regarding this point at Forbes Field in Pittsburgh the afternoon of September 17: "However much the people may have acquiesced in arrogated power of the courts to veto the acts of direct representatives of the people, the people may still say even to the Supreme Court: 'We may be willing to permit you to continue to exercise the power which you have usurped to pass upon the constitutionality of our laws but we are prepared to modify your power or modify *you* unless you act in the interest of the people as a whole.'"

In the course of events, the Supreme Court did get modified, though not quite as Roosevelt had planned it. In January 1938, Justice George Sutherland retired and Roosevelt replaced him with liberal Stanley Reed; in July 1938, Justice Benjamin Cardozo died and was replaced by liberal Felix Frankfurter; in February 1939, Justice Louis Brandeis retired and was replaced by liberal William O. Douglas (at thirty-nine, the youngest member of the Court); in November 1939, Justice Pierce Butler died and was replaced by liberal Frank Murphy, former governor of Michigan and, after Cummings's resignation at the end of 1938, attorney general; in January 1941, Justice James McReynolds retired and was replaced by liberal James F. Byrnes, former senator from South Carolina and one of the few southern Democrats to remain loyal to the administration; and finally, in June 1941, Chief Justice Charles Evans Hughes retired, Roosevelt naming Justice Harlan Fiske Stone Chief Justice and filling the empty chair with liberal Robert Jackson, who had been appointed Attorney General in 1939 after Murphy's leap to the Supreme Court. With Justice Hugo Black already in place, Roosevelt now had a solid liberal block of seven votes on the Court.

But the defeat of the summer of 1937 ate at Roosevelt. He not only resented the defections of those old reliables like Wheeler in the Senate; he was legitimately worried over the coalition that was beginning to take place between Republicans and a growing number of conservative southern Democrats. He was losing the solid South for the first time, a situation that pushed him, Corcoran remembered, "into a position of political impotence and antagonism incredible to him." He did not deal with it well, and Eleanor Roosevelt was convinced that both the Court fight and subsequent political ineptitude could be ascribed to the loss of Louis Howe. "After Louis' death," she wrote in *This I Remember,* "Franklin never had a political advisor who would argue with and give him unquestioned loyalty. Louis gave Franklin the benefit of his sane, reasoned, careful political analysis and even if Franklin disagreed and was annoyed, he listened and respected Louis' political acumen."

Without Howe, Roosevelt was inclined to plunge ahead on the strength of his own instincts—which were good, but not infallible. And his instincts, after the humiliation of the summer, took him down the precarious byways of vengeance. "Immediately after the defeat," James Farley remembered,

he began summoning Senators and Congressmen down to the White House to discuss various matters. Almost invariably he would drop some suggestion that those who had opposed him had better be on guard. It was not so much what he said as what he left unsaid. What he left unsaid lost nothing in being relayed to Capitol Hill. There they were searched for hidden meanings. Various members of Congress came to me seeking enlightenment which I was unable to give.

The President enjoyed his little game thoroughly. On August 1, 1937, I found him chortling over the uneasiness he was creating. . . .

"I've got them on the run, Jim," he cried. "They go out of here talking to themselves, memorizing my lines to repeat them up on the Hill. I'd like to see the faces sag over my mumbo-jumbo. They have no idea what's going to happen and are beginning to worry. They'll be sorry yet."

In fact, as yet he did not have any specific program of attack in mind, save torturing them with uncertainty, although during a trip west in early September he managed to pointedly snub defecting senators Edward Burke of Nebraska, Joseph O'Mahoney of Wyoming, and, of course, Wheeler of Montana—while making a large and public fuss over Republican senator William E. Borah of Idaho, a progressive supporter of the administration.

The deteriorating Roosevelt alliance experienced even more pressure as 1937 drew to a close and something that smacked of Depression began to be felt—though it was more often referred to as a recession. The stock market had taken a sharp fall in August, and over the next two months the Dow Jones average had slid from 190 to 115. Unemployment figures were on the rise, creeping toward twenty million. Investments, production, and sales were all down. Roosevelt professed not to be worried. "I have been around the country and know conditions are good," he told his cabinet on October 8, as reported by Farley. "I am sure the situation is just temporary. Everything will work out all right if we just sit tight and keep quiet. The whole situation is being manufactured on Wall Street."

The downturn refused to go away no matter how studiously it was ignored, and by early November Roosevelt had decided two things: one, to call Congress into special session to deal with the problem that was not a problem; and, two, it really *was* Wall Street's fault. "Organized wealth," he told the cabinet on November 6, as Ickes recorded it in his diary, "which has controlled the Government so far, seizes this opportunity to decide whether it is to continue to control the Government or not." According to Farley's recollection, the President was a little sharper in his comments. "I know who's responsible for the situation," he said. "Business, particularly the banking industry, has ganged up on me. They are trying to use this recession to force me to let up on some of my program. They want to get back the control they had in the past, to get back what they feel is theirs."

The special session was called the following week, though the proposals Roosevelt put before it were less than revolutionary in character. They included a housing bill, a wages and hours bill, and a revival of the reorganization bill. All of these measures immediately began to suffer the

effects of the increasingly nasty undercurrent of antagonism that was
beginning to typify relations between the White House and Capitol Hill.
The conservatives on both sides of the aisles in both houses of Congress
took full advantage of the situation, and the special session ended with
nothing accomplished.

The New Dealers saw in the impasse the echo of Roosevelt's conviction
that the business class had joined with the conservative element in
Congress in an effort to regain its lost power. They found ammunition for
this argument not only in personal observation and opinion, but in a
richly detailed and relentlessly doctrinaire study published earlier that
year—*America's Sixty Families,* by Ferdinand Lundberg, a former financial
reporter for the *New York Herald-Tribune.* Lundberg made no bones about
his thesis, stating it flatly at the beginning of the book and spending the
rest of its considerable length marshaling evidence from history, politics,
and economic theory to document his accusation:

> The United States is owned and dominated today by a hierarchy of its sixty
> richest families, buttressed by no more than ninety families of lesser wealth.
> Outside this plutocratic circle there are perhaps three hundred and fifty other
> families, less defined in development and in wealth, but accounting for most
> of the incomes of $100,000 or more that do not accrue to members of the
> inner circle.
>
> These families are the living center of the modern industrial oligarchy
> which dominates the United States, functioning discreetly under a *de jure*
> democratic form of government behind which a *de facto* government, absolut-
> ist and plutocratic in its lineaments, has gradually taken form since the Civil
> War. This *de facto* government is actually the government of the United
> States—informal, invisible, shadowy. It is the government of money in a
> dollar democracy.

This model of the conspiracy theory of history at work was prey to all the
weaknesses of the form, but its arguments were supported by a higher
level of scholarship than most such polemics. That was good enough for
the New Dealers, at any rate, including Ickes, who used the book's
assumptions as the text for a thirty-minute address on the NBC Blue
Network on December 30. Entitled "It Is Happening Here" as a play on
the title of Sinclair Lewis's popular novel, and written by Corcoran and
Ben Cohen, rewritten by Ickes, then revised again by Corcoran and
Cohen, the speech was given as—and appropriately taken for—a kind of
invocation for the election year of 1938. ("For some time it has been in the
President's mind to make this the issue in the 1938 elections," Ickes
remarked in his diary. "If he doesn't, I don't know what issue we are going
to run on.") Its tone would set the scene for what may fairly be described

as one of the least elegant periods, politically speaking, in the history of the Roosevelt era:

> To Franklin Roosevelt and the overwhelming millions who have three times approved his policies [the Sixty Families] have made a threat like that which Nicholas Biddle of the Bank of the United States one hundred years ago made to Andrew Jackson—a threat they will refuse to do business at all unless the President and the Congress and the people will repeal all that we have gained in the last five years and regrant them the suicidal license they had enjoyed in 1929.

And, like Jackson, Ickes would later advise the President, the only way to deal with this kind of opposition was to challenge it head-on. But after the turn of the year, Roosevelt seemed to maunder. "The President appears to have lost all his fight since he was beaten on his Court bill," Ickes complained on March 2. "It looks to me as if all the courage has oozed out of the President. Except for a brief assertion of leadership in his message to Congress in January, he has let things drift. . . . Quite sad to state, the political situation, so far as the Democratic Party is concerned, is in a mess and if we go into the election next fall as we are now, there may be serious inroads made into the Democratic party's strength." Roosevelt in fact was drifting, apparently still hoping that the economic situation would improve without major new federal spending programs—programs that Harry Hopkins and others had been urging on him as necessary to "prime the pump." Morgenthau, who still dreamed of a balanced budget, approved. "As I see it," he said to the President at lunch in mid-March, "what you are doing now is just treading water . . . to wait to see what happens this spring."

"Absolutely," Roosevelt said.

Unfortunately, what happened was that on March 25 the stock market took another dive, and while Morgenthau was out of town, Hopkins and his allies persuaded Roosevelt to commit his administration to a brand new spending program. The Secretary of the Treasury did not approve at all. "I don't mind telling you gentlemen," he fretted to his staff after a talk with the President the night of April 10. "The way it was put up to me last night just scared me to death—worse than I've been scared—and the thing hasn't been thought through. . . . They have just stampeded him during the week I was away. He was completely stampeded. They stampeded him like cattle." On April 14, just a week after the House had voted to recommit—and thus kill—his reorganization bill, Roosevelt offered up a spending program that would amount to $3.75 billion.

By then, the growing contingent of the most militant New Dealers—dubbed the "White House Janizaries" by Hugh Johnson in one of his newspaper columns—had also convinced Roosevelt that he must couple his vigorous new spending program with an equally strenuous effort not merely to support the administration's friends in the upcoming primary elections but to defeat those Democrats who had joined his enemies to kill both the Court plan and reorganization. Those who got targeted called it an attempted "purge," and while those responsible insisted it was nothing of the kind, the term came into general use simply because it was precisely accurate. The "Janizaries"—with Hopkins, Corcoran, Cohen, Ickes, and James Roosevelt, the President's son and personal secretary, operating as the core group—wanted nothing less than the complete restructuring of the Democratic Party, and that meant ridding it of conservatives wherever possible.

The effort began in Florida, where Senator Claude Pepper had already distinguished himself as the only southern senator to support openly the wages-and-hours legislation introduced during the special session of 1937. He got his reward on February 6, when James Roosevelt issued a statement from the White House saying that "we hope that Senator Pepper will be returned to the Senate." In the primaries, Pepper beat his principal opponent, conservative Mark Wilcox, by more than 100,000 votes—largely because of FDR's endorsement, Pepper believed. Roosevelt's crew agreed, and with this encouragement, FDR prepared for a long "vacation" trip that incidentally would take him through a number of states with primary elections in the offing. Before leaving, he called Rosenman, Corcoran, and Cohen in to work up a fireside chat to explain a thing or two. Ickes, who had just gotten back from his honeymoon trip in time to hear it delivered on June 24, called it a "fine speech" that "served notice that, as leader of the Democratic party, he proposed to interest himself in primary contests between liberals and reactionaries." In fact, the speech was a little less incendiary than that, although it remained a clear and unmistakable challenge:

> Never in our lifetime has such a concerted campaign of defeatism been thrown at the heads of the President and Senators and Congressmen as in the case of this Seventy-fifth Congress. Never before have we had so many Copperheads—and you will remember that it was the Copperheads who, in the days of the War Between the States, tried their best to make Lincoln and his Congress give up the fight, let the nation remain split in two and return to peace—peace at any price. . . .
>
> As the head of the Democratic Party . . . charged with the responsibility of carrying out the definitely liberal declaration of principles set forth in the 1936 Democratic platform, I feel that I have every right to speak in those few

instances where there may be a clear issue between candidates for a Democratic nomination involving these principles, or involving a clear misuse of
my own name.

The purge was a political disaster. Only in New York, where James Fay
won out over John J. O'Connor, did a candidate favored by a statement—
and often a speech—of support from FDR win against one opposed by the
administration. James A. Farley, who, with Vice President Garner and
other old-line Democrats had been against the purge (though none,
including Farley, had possessed the gumption to express himself openly
on the point), could not restrain a note of satisfaction in a summation
written ten years later. "I knew from the beginning," he said,

> that the purge could lead to nothing but misfortune, because in pursuing his
> course of vengeance Roosevelt violated a cardinal political creed which de-
> manded that he keep out of local matters. Sound doctrine is sound politics.
> When Roosevelt began neglecting the rules of the game, I began to have
> doubts. When he persisted in violating the rules, I lost faith in him. I trace
> all the woes of the Democratic party, directly or indirectly, to this interference
> in purely local matters.

Farley's analysis probably was pretty close to the mark; more important, however, it demonstrated with precision the permanence of the split
between the hard-liners of both the left and right of the Democratic Party.
From this point forward, no political decision, no political campaign, no
political question of any stripe would be made or addressed that was not
affected by this internal struggle for power.

One symptom of the new Democratic malaise was the success of Congressman Martin Dies of Orange, Texas. Dies was a protégé of Vice President
Garner, whose influence had gotten him a seat on the powerful House
Rules Committee, from which perch he had been one of the most effective
voices against passage of the wages-and-hours bill. He had larger ambitions, however, and had been trying to get his own investigating committee since the spring of 1937, when he had introduced a resolution asking
for an investigation of sit-down strikes, which, he said, were a craze
"sweeping the nation and threatening the very foundations of orderly
government." This had been rejected by the House, but a few months
later he introduced another resolution, this one calling for

> a special committee to be composed of seven members for the purpose of
> conducting an investigation of (1) the extent, character, and objects of un-
> American propaganda activities in the United States, (2) the diffusion within
> the United States of subversive and un-American propaganda that is insti-

gated from foreign countries or of a domestic origin and attacks the principle of the form of government as guaranteed by our Constitution, and (3) all other questions in relation thereto that would aid Congress in any necessary remedial legislation.

Over the next several months, armed with the support of Vice President Garner, Speaker of the House William Bankhead, and Majority Leader Sam Rayburn—and the virtual assurance of the southern bloc that came with that support—Dies quietly maneuvered his resolution past the objections raised against it by such liberals as his fellow Texan, Congressman Maury Maverick, by putting most of his emphasis on the need to investigate the growing Nazi movement in the country. In truth, he had less interest in fascism than in communism; in 1932 he had introduced a bill to exclude and expel alien communists from the United States on the theory that the "ultimate objective" of the Communist Party was "the seizure of governmental power by an armed uprising led by the Communist party and the establishment, under a regime termed 'the dictatorship of the proletariat,' of a soviet republic which will be a member of a world union of soviet republics."

He had not changed his mind by 1937, but he did understand that to emphasize this early version of an Evil Empire would be to obviate any support he might expect from the House liberals. "I am not inclined to look under every bed for a Communist," he informed the House when his resolution finally was called up on May 26, 1938. A few days later, then, by a vote of 191 to 41, the House created a Special Committee to Investigate Un-American Activities, stipulating that it "ought to" end its work at the end of the current session of Congress and giving it an appropriation of $25,000. On June 7, Speaker Bankhead named seven congressmen to the new body: Dies, who was appointed chairman; republicans Noah Mason of Illinois and J. Parnell Thomas of New Jersey; conservative Democrat Joe Starns of Alabama; and liberal Democrats Harold Mosier of Ohio and John J. Dempsey of New Mexico. Various liberal Democrats would come and go through the years, but Dies, Mason, Thomas, and Starns were a continuing foursome, the two southern Democrats joining with the two Republicans to form a conservative majority as solid as that which had characterized the Supreme Court in the days before Roosevelt's attack.

Fully authorized now, the House Un-American Activities Committee got to work with a flurry of publicity, most of it provided by the furious efforts of J. Parnell Thomas, who was swiftly recognized as one of the most dedicated Red-baiters the nation had ever seen. He made no secret of his beliefs; even before the Dies Committee had been authorized, he had gone on record with his assessment of the real threat facing the country. "I hope that this committee will not devote all its time to nazi-ism," he told his colleagues in the House. "We have another problem in this country which is more acute and far-reaching than even the Nazi problem, and that is the issue of communism. The communists outnumber the Nazis at least five to one. They are right in our government," he concluded in an alarum that would become part of the American political vocabulary. They were in the Federal Theatre Project, for example, he said, and with the chairman's blessing he went after that WPA program like a virago. They were in the Labor Department, he said, and it was they—if, indeed, Madam Secretary Perkins was herself not part of the plot—that saw to it that Australian-born Harry Bridges, the demonstrably radical leader of the International Longshoremen's and Warehousemen's Union, could not be deported for his subversive activities, as ought to have been done without a second thought. Impeachment proceedings were clearly in order, he said (most of his colleagues did not agree with this particular charge, and efforts to institute impeachment proceedings against Frances Perkins failed).

Thomas garnered his share of publicity, but there were others willing to claim the light. No one was happier to see the committee formed than Joseph Bruner and Alice Lee Jemison of the American Indian Federation, that thundering foe of John Collier's New Deal for the Indian. Jemison was a welcome witness to the Dies committee hearings on numerous occasions, the members listening solemnly while she openly declared both Collier and Ickes himself to be communists. Ickes had been contemptuous of the committee at the end of August when he took his first shot at it over the question of Shirley Temple's un-American activities. After Dies let the Jemison woman slander him repeatedly, his contempt combined with a cold and consistent anger that would make him the committee's most diligent antagonist for the rest of his life. During a press conference on November 22 after one of Jemison's testimonials, a reporter asked him to comment. He was willing. Dies, he said, "has proved himself to be probably the outstanding zany in our political history. But even he ought to have some of the decencies that obtain primarily between right-minded people, assuming they are right-minded, but he seems to have left all that behind him in the state of Texas."

"What is a zany?" the reporter asked.

"It is a good word."

"How do you spell it?"

"Look it up in your dictionaries. It isn't libelous."

The committee was beginning to worry him by the end of the year, particularly when a Gallup poll in December showed that public opinion generally favored what it was up to. "Some people now feel that no one can control Dies," he remarked in his diary on December 18.

> He is publicity mad and the unfortunate Gallup poll will make him worse than ever. . . . It is doubtful whether many people understand the extralegal high-handed things that he is doing or appreciate the fact that, without conclusive evidence or without even giving the accused a chance to defend himself, it is heralded to the world that a man is a communist when he is nothing of the sort. Miss Perkins, Harry Hopkins, and I have been the special targets of this blatherskite.

Having characterized the enemy, the Secretary prepared to go after him even as Dies began gathering his arguments to push a House resolution in January that would reauthorize his committee for a full year and give it at least $150,000 with which to bring to light all the subversion (most of it communistic, a little of it fascistic) that it had found gnawing at the vitals of the Republic. Ickes was scheduled to deliver an address to the American Congress for Peace and Democracy on January 6 and decided to make the Dies committee the subject of his discourse. Entitled "Playing with Loaded Dies," the speech would have been one of his best efforts. "The proceedings of Congressman Dies would disgrace the lowest type of police court," he had written (and he did in fact write most of this speech).

> He mocks justice. . . . Prejudice is at a premium over fairness, prevarication blankets truth, innuendo occupies an honored seat, and opinion is accorded the sanctity of fact. . . .
>
> Alice Lee Jemison, the gentle lady who accepts a dollar per head from live Indians not only for themselves but for dead Indians as well, in return for which she holds out the representation that the Congress will vote $3,000 to every Indian, alive or dead, for whom a dollar shall have been paid, volunteered as a witness before the Dies Committee. She was received with great acclaim and shown great consideration. Mrs. Jemison recited glibly the accusation that Commissioner John Collier of the Bureau of Indian Affairs and the Secretary of the Interior were communists. And it did not require much cleverness to know what epithet to apply in order to find favor in the eyes of witch-hunting Martin Dies. She was quite willing to play in the game where the "Dies" were loaded if she were given loaded "Dies" with which to play.

He never got to deliver this polemic. On Monday, January 2, Steve Early, Roosevelt's press secretary, telephoned him. "The President," he said, "has just called me from the White House to ask you about it and to tell you for God's sake not to do it." Dies's strength in the House was growing, Roosevelt later told Ickes, a power fueled by fear. His hope was that House leaders might be able to limit the committee's impact by underfunding it and limiting the amount of time it could function. But, he said, Rayburn and the rest had told him that if Ickes went ahead with his attack they would not be able to hold Dies back. Ickes vehemently disagreed. "The reason Dies has made so much headway," he said in his diary, "is because we have not fought him. To be sure, the President has made one or two critical comments, and I have taken a couple of pot shots at him, but this is not the same as a well-thought-out frontal attack." Nevertheless, Roosevelt insisted, and Ickes canceled the speech.

The fear was real enough. "Legislators admitted privately," *The New York Times* editorialized on January 8, "that they cannot afford, for political reasons, to vote against [the committee's] continuance." A good part of the reason for this conclusion could be laid at the door of the national press, which had helped to make something of a popular hero of Dies—and the public had responded with letters, the weather vanes of a congressman's life. The *Chicago Tribune* was particularly enamored of the committee's work, which seemed to vindicate suspicions it had been harboring for a long time now. "Links Perkins Aid to Plot to Keep Red in U.S.," one of its news-story headlines had explained on August 15, 1938, while an editorial on October 17 had gloated: "The New Deal master-minds have pawned themselves out to the Communist strategists until now they are so far out on a limb it is practically impossible for them to get back." The still noisy and still powerful Father Charles Coughlin liked Dies, too, and on September 12 had made him his "Man of the Year."

Combined with the poisoned relationship between the White House and a large part of the Congress, this kind of pressure proved too much: on February 3, 1939, the House voted 344–35 to give Congressman Dies another year and another $100,000. Congressional leaders, Ickes snorted, had "abjectly surrendered to the blatant and demagogic Dies." Then he delivered himself of a prediction:

> I cannot forget that Mussolini rose to absolute power in Italy as a result of a "Communist" hunt; that Hitler did the same thing in Germany; that Japan invaded China in order to suppress "communism"; that England has groveled on its belly before Hitler because it is afraid of communism. Dies can put his pieces together in the same pattern. It is not unlikely that, as a result of his efforts, a communist scare will be fomented and kept fanned in this country, following which some man on horseback may arise to "protect" us against this fancied danger. The result here in that event will be fascism.

If the danger of communism was fancied, so was this darkly pessimistic vision; America was not Italy, or Germany, or England, and certainly not Japan. But this was an era that validated the old Oriental curse—"May you live in interesting times"—and Ickes was not alone in his paranoia. Furthermore, it could have been little comfort to him or to any of the other New Dealers to acknowledge that this viper had been born of their own party and had come to power just as the great liberal coalition that was to have saved the Republic seemed almost certain to totter. In such a context, one grasped at every moment of grace that might present itself; and in the spring of 1939 such a moment came in the form of a young black woman whose nearly total ignorance of political matters did not for one minute hamper her symbolic value—not merely as someone who represented the pain and hope of her own people, but as someone whose needs could move the great heart that still pulsed beneath the tattered fabric of the New Deal.

CHAPTER
· 45 ·

Once in a Hundred Years

B Y 1939, ROOSEVELT and his people had done an astonishing thing: they had taken the black vote away from the Republican Party and given it to the Democrats. They had accomplished this in spite of the fact that FDR's initial strength had been fortified by a coalition with the supremely racist Democratic South and in spite of the initial reservations of most of the traditional black leadership, which had been wedded to the Republican Party for decades. They did it by making it obvious that in the New Deal black Americans had better reason to hope than at any other time since Reconstruction. "Your forgotten man has become a famous symbol, Governor Roosevelt," a black reporter had said to the candidate in September 1932. "Is the Negro included in the plan you have to aid the plight of the mass of the people?"

"Absolutely and impartially," Roosevelt had replied without hesitation.

Roosevelt's commitment was earnest enough, and if the particular plight of the mass of black people in the country was not at the forefront of his mind or at the top of the New Deal's list of things to do, his clear sympathy for their needs had earned him their votes and an encomium given him by Melvin J. Chisum of the National Negro Press Association in September 1936: "President Roosevelt is by-and-large the best friend of the Negro who has been in the presidency in twenty-five years and the blacks of this country know it."

At the same time, Roosevelt was not an activist in civil rights matters. He could be persuaded to do the right thing when the right thing needed to be done—but only when he felt it *could* be done. As important as the black vote became to the New Deal, it was never important enough in Roosevelt's judgment to overcome the political disadvantages that would have followed had he been more strenuous in his efforts; he governed, it should be remembered, from a city which itself remained widely segregated throughout his era. His hesitancy to move too visibly or vocally to challenge the status quo was perhaps most clearly demonstrated by his somewhat dithering support of antilynching legislation.

Like any other right-thinking human being, Roosevelt deplored what he had described as "that vile form of collective murder," and in his annual message in January 1934 had declared that lynching, kidnapping, and other violent crimes required "the strong arm of Government for their immediate suppression." There was reason enough for action of some kind: between 1930 and 1934, more than sixty black men had been shot, hanged, and/or burned to death by lynch mobs. Early in 1934, Senators Edward P. Costigan of Colorado and Robert F. Wagner of New York introduced a federal antilynching law. Without visible support from the administration, it died in committee. Costigan and Wagner reintroduced it early in the first session of the next Congress in 1935, and this time— given impetus by the fact that an average of one black a month had been murdered by mobs during 1934—the bill was reported to the floor of the Senate in the spring and Costigan made a motion for its consideration. His motion met with an instant filibuster on the part of southern members that continued into the summer, Roosevelt using none of his persuasive arts to cut it short. He was not against the legislation so much as afraid to touch it, he told Walter White, secretary of the NAACP: "I did not choose the tools with which I must work. But I've got to get legislation passed by Congress to save America. The Southerners by reason of the seniority rule in Congress are chairmen or occupy strategic places on most of the Senate and House committees. If I come out for the antilynching bill now, they will block every bill I ask Congress to pass to keep America from collapsing. I just can't take that risk." Deprived of the President's active support, Costigan's motion was still lost in the murk of the filibuster when a motion to adjourn was made, seconded, and carried. While never officially killed, the Costigan-Wagner bill was doomed to remain on the shelf indefinitely.

Since Roosevelt hesitated to make himself too visible on the issue, questions of civil rights and equal opportunity for black people were left to the mercies of the New Deal's system—which, however ideally conceived, was, like all systems, no better than those who set and carried out its policies. The results were mixed: at its best, the system gave blacks a degree of participation in their own fate that would have been unthinkable a few short years before; at its worst, it raised expectations that were never really fulfilled—not only because some expectations were politically and culturally impossible to achieve at the time, but because too many of the New Deal's functionaries simply would not challenge bigotry.

The best of what the New Deal had to offer was represented by the National Youth Administration. Established in June 1935 as part of the Works Progress Administration, the NYA was designed to help young women, who were excluded from the programs of the CCC, and those young men who could not meet the strict physical requirements of CCC work. NYA work programs were provided to enable those in high school and college to complete their educations and to give a living to those between the ages of sixteen and twenty-four who were already out of school. As its executive director, Roosevelt appointed the WPA's deputy director, Aubrey Williams, a southern social worker with a radical bent and a determination to include black youth in the agency's programs to the fullest extent possible. To that end, a Division of Negro Affairs was set up in the agency and Mary McLeod Bethune, a black woman, was appointed by Roosevelt to administer it. Mrs. Bethune was by then perhaps the best-known and most respected black woman in the country. She was the founder of the Daytona Educational and Industrial School for black women in Daytona, Florida (which by 1935 had merged with a black men's school to become Bethune-Cookman College), a leader in virtually every black organization available, from the National Association of Teachers in Colored Schools to the NAACP; and, significantly, a close acquaintance of Eleanor Roosevelt, whom she had met in 1924. An imposing woman whose determination matched her presence, she took full advantage of the access to the President provided by her friendship with his wife, and if she was rarely able to persuade him to become more vocal on behalf of black people, her very presence in his company was something in which the black community could and did take pride. Her stature within the administration was a beacon of possibility.

And in spite of its decentralized nature and its reliance on state administrators for the dispensation of its favors, with Williams's encouragement and the dogged work of Mrs. Bethune and her staff, black participation in the NYA's programs was more consistent, more orderly, and more fruitful than in any others the New Deal had to offer. This was true even in the Deep South. In Georgia, for instance, as much as 37 percent of those being aided in the high school and college programs during any given year were black. Much of the employment—like that in other portions of the WPA—was largely make-work, not the "dignified, constructive, and needful" work that Mrs. Bethune held out as the ideal. But any work was better than no work at all, and by the time the NYA was closed out in 1943 it had helped at least half a million young black people survive with dignity—and tens of thousands to finish school or learn new skills. No other federal program in the history of the United States had done as much for black people—at least not since northern troops had kept southern voting booths open to them at the point of a gun during Reconstruction.

Nor did any other program of the New Deal do as much, for that matter, even those that might have contributed the most to the improvement of the Negro's lot. In the Department of Agriculture, for example, Henry Wallace was reluctant to give the plight of the black farmer special treatment, arguing that the creation of a Negro bureau or even a special adviser would "seem to be patronizing" and in the long run might do the black agricultural community "more harm than good." He explained himself further—though no more persuasively—in a letter to Congressman Fred Hildebrandt of North Dakota early in 1933: "I believe the most progressive among our Negro population and those who have the best interests of this group at heart would prefer that the Department of Agriculture render to them the same service, through the same organizations, that is rendered to our entire rural population." The department's Extension Service—the field arm of its educational program—was employing 425 black field agents in the sixteen southern states by 1939 (contrasted with 3,248 white agents), but almost all of these were confined to counties where the population of blacks was highest. Elsewhere in the department, the percentage of black employment was even lower. The total number of employees came to about fifty-two thousand; of these, there were only eleven hundred blacks, and with the exception of the field agents in the Extension Service all but a handful of these held custodial or other low-level jobs.

Until the Bankhead-Jones Farm Tenant Act of 1937 attempted to redress some of the inequities, even the most radical of Wallace's farm programs worked against the black farmer because of the Secretary's refusal to interfere with local customs and administration. The most egregious example of this was the farm tenant program established by the Agricultural Adjustment Act of 1933, in which southern white farm landlords promised so far as possible not to disturb the present tenants on their land, most of whom were black, and were further entrusted with the disbursement of government checks in a fair and impartial manner to these tenants. That these agreements were honored more often in the breach than in the observance was substantiated by investigations sponsored by the Department of Agriculture itself, but this was not sufficient to persuade Wallace to interfere. Enforcement of the provisions was left up to local production boards, which uniformly serviced the desires of the white landowning class. As a consequence of what might be called racism by inanition, for years thousands of black tenant farmers were forced off the land or systematically cheated of their share of federal support.

If the Department of Agriculture could be described charitably as administratively neutral on the question of black needs, the attitude of the Civilian Conservation Corps might sometimes have been mistaken for outright hostility. This failing was perhaps the only major weakness in what was arguably the New Deal's most admirable and effective single program, but it was enough to leave the CCC's work sullied by the memory of bigotry. This outcome probably was inevitable, given the structure of the agency, which had the Department of Labor recruiting the workers, the army building and running the camps, Interior's Office of Education supervising school programs, the departments of Interior and Agriculture furnishing most of the work projects, and the whole business coordinated by Robert Fechner, director of Emergency Conservation Work. "Oh, that doesn't matter," Roosevelt had remarked when someone worried that such a division of responsibility might lead to problems. Everything would be fine, the President said; the various departments involved would organize the program and Fechner would " 'go along' and give everybody satisfaction and confidence."

But the division of responsibility did matter, particularly when it came to racial considerations. Fechner, a white man born and reared in Georgia and a vice president of one of the several trade unions that specifically excluded blacks from membership, was more inclined to "go along" with local prejudices and the army's long-established traditions than with any sentiments for reform that anyone in any of the other agencies might express. So it was, then, that young black men found it difficult to be enrolled in the CCC in some states—often being told that the program was for whites only or that they simply did not qualify on a variety of spurious grounds. The situation was aggravated when Fechner instituted a quota system, which gave bigoted recruiters the opportunity for another lie—and even when it was not deliberately discriminatory, the quota system was operated in an arbitrary and inconsistent manner throughout the program, all of which tended to militate against blacks.

Furthermore, Jim Crow reigned; this was the way the army always had done things, and this was the way it did things in the CCC. Fechner approved wholeheartedly, giving his agreement to an army order sent out to the adjutant general and area commanders in the summer of 1935. "Colored companies," the order stated, were to be "employed in their own states" and "complete segregation" was to be maintained except in those few states in which there simply were not enough black enrollees to make up a full company (a condition largely confined to New England and a few western states). Much of the time, segregation alone was not enough to quell white sensitivity. When citizens of Gettysburg, Pennsylvania, objected to the placement of a black CCC camp near their town, Fechner immediately had it moved. The CCC did the same for white citizens living near Abraham Lincoln State Park in Illinois, as well as those in Long Island, rural New York, portions of New Jersey, a number of southern states, and nearly anywhere else that local communities complained. Scores of black camps consequently were confined to national forests, national parks, and even a few army bases to avoid the objections of whites—and in such areas as the national forests of the Southern Appalachians, even this device did not stifle complaint.

Bigotry found other expression, too. Part of each camp's structure was to include an army reservist as commander and a reservist as his assistant, together with a resident doctor, a resident educational adviser, resident teachers, teaching assistants, coaches and recreation directors, clerks, typists, secretaries, and storekeepers. This would seem to have offered a rich opportunity for the employment of qualified black people in the CCC system, particularly in the segregated camps. Not so, as it happened. It was not army policy to employ blacks in any capacity in which they might—even inadvertently or only in special circumstances—command or minister to whites. Black reserve officers (of which there were not very many to begin with) were therefore excluded as candidates for command or assistant command. Fechner endorsed this strategy. Similarly, the army simply did not use black doctors and was not about to change policy for the CCC. Once again, Fechner bowed to tradition. Even for those positions in which the army itself had no particular interest, however, Fechner still resisted hiring black people, including college graduates fully qualified to handle any job that might be placed in their way.

That left the five-million-dollar CCC educational program as a potential field of employment. This was outside Fechner's jurisdiction, but George F. Zook, director of Interior's Office of Education, whose jurisdiction it was, proceeded immediately with a whites-only hiring program. When this became apparent, Zook's office began getting letters of query and complaint on an almost daily basis from scores of black educational institutions around the country. Still, nothing was done about the situation until it was brought to the attention of Secretary Ickes himself, who in March 1934 called Zook in and demanded an explanation for what appeared to be a clear case of discrimination. It was the army's fault, Zook told him. C. S. Marsh, director of the CCC educational program, Zook said, had reported to him that army officials did not want to put up with any "complications" that might result in the hiring of black teachers and educational advisers.

Ickes instantly fired off a letter to Secretary of War George Dern, objecting to this policy. "I trust," he concluded stiffly, "that you will see that the objections to such appointments on the part of certain officers of the War Department is withdrawn." Dern replied that no such prejudice existed, insisting that "the policy of nondiscrimination . . . is well known throughout the service"—a statement that probably derived more from ignorance of War Department traditions than any desire to misrepresent the situation. Still, no matter how well entrenched discrimination was, at no point had the army actually gone on record as being against the hiring of black teachers or the appointment of black educational advisers. Either Zook lied to Ickes or Marsh had lied to Zook. Marsh's own attitudes were revealed clearly enough when he went to see Louis Howe about the matter. Marsh, Howe told Fechner, was "very much opposed to having colored teachers." While Howe himself, he said, "didn't give a darn about this thing," he did hope that Fechner could inform him "as to who wants what."

Fechner was saved the trouble. Zook had no desire to earn the wrath of Harold Ickes (well established by the spring of 1934 as something to be avoided whenever possible), and in April the policy of white-only hiring was officially discontinued and the heads of black colleges were invited to submit names of candidate advisers and teachers. Even so, it was a reluctant concession, and since Ickes could not personally watchdog the program on a regular basis, throughout the life of the CCC there never was a fair and proportionate number of black teachers hired or advisers appointed. Like other racial inequities, this failing marred the otherwise exemplary record of the New Deal's happiest experiment.

In the same 1936 pamphlet in which he praised FDR, Melvin J. Chisum had singled out some other New Dealers for comment on the question of black rights:

The Hon. Harold L. Ickes has led in the matter of giving broad consideration to the needs of the colored people; Mr. Harry L. Hopkins has shown a disposition to recognize the need for placing Negro key men and women where they could assist in getting the policy of fair dealing through, out in the provinces where the local officials are unwilling to give just consideration to the claims of the Negro citizen; and Dr. Rexford Guy Tugwell has done a great deal in this same direction.

All three kudos were well earned. Throughout his tenure at both the FERA and the WPA, Hopkins had gone out of his way to see that relief got to blacks on an equitable basis. He also directed his staff to be diligent in its efforts to surmount local resistance to the hiring of black men and women for work programs and the various arts projects the WPA fostered—from the Federal Writers' Project, which had given young black writers like Ralph Ellison and Richard Wright employment on WPA guidebooks, to the Federal Theater Project, which provided the first hint of stardom to actors like Dooley Wilson and Edna Thomas.* Tugwell, too, had worked as best he could to circumvent the Department of Agriculture's disinclination to do anything directly for black farmers, both when he directed the AAA and later when he took over the Subsistence Homestead program from Interior and structured it with the Resettlement Administration. Among other programs Tugwell either initiated or at least supported were the all-black communities of Aberdeen Gardens near Newport News, Virginia, and Gee's Bend outside Camden, Alabama, together with twelve government-sponsored integrated communities, all of them in the South.

Of the three men, however, it can be said that Ickes had done—or at least had attempted—more for black people than any other high official in the administration; what is more, he often had done so militantly, vocally, and visibly (as he did most things). Among his first acts as Interior Secretary had been a directive specifically banning all segregation in the Department of Interior building and discrimination in hiring practices throughout his domain. He had encouraged the hiring of black architects and engineers in the PWA and black field agents (including, for a time, Melvin J. Chisum himself) in Glavis's Division of Investigations. He had brought in William Hastie as assistant solicitor for Interior (and later backed him as a federal judge in the Virgin Islands). Nor was he above interesting himself in the affairs of other cabinet departments in the pursuit of fair treatment for blacks. In fact, that became one of the perceived functions of his position.

* At least until the Dies Committee persuaded the rest of Congress to cut off the project's funding in 1939 on the grounds that it was infested with black and white Reds.

In the summer of 1933, the director of the Julius Rosenwald Fund* had come to Roosevelt suggesting that someone in the Executive Department be appointed to oversee equal treatment for blacks in the various government services and agencies. FDR agreed and suggested that such an individual be attached to the Interior Department, Ickes's past presidency of the Chicago NAACP giving him more direct experience and sympathy with black issues than most government men (however frustrating that experience had proved to be). Ickes was more than willing, but had no money for the operation. That was quickly solved by a grant from the Rosenwald Fund, and the Secretary immediately hired Clark Foreman, the fund's director of studies, to act as coordinator, liaison, and troubleshooter for Negro affairs in all departments of government on which the operations of the Department of the Interior touched, however lightly. (Since that included everything from the Department of Labor to the Department of War, Foreman's responsibilities ultimately included a wide spectrum of government operations.)

If Ickes was expecting huzzahs from the black community, he was disappointed. Foreman, however sympathetic to black concerns, was, like Robert Fechner, a white man born and reared in Georgia, and Roy Wilkins, assistant secretary of the NAACP, wrote to take issue with the appointment. Ickes defended Foreman faithfully, calling him a man who had "devoted his life to the Negro," and chided Wilkins by noting a little arrogantly that the NAACP ought to be glad to have a "sympathetic government" composed of people who were "honestly interested in the Negro." Wilkins was not convinced. "The colored citizens," he wrote Harry Slattery on September 22, 1933, had

> looked with more hopefulness than the average American upon the coming of Mr. Roosevelt's administration into power. They believed his promise of a New Deal. They were encouraged in their optimism when the President named Mr. Ickes to a post in his cabinet. . . . They felt that certainly here was the time when they would receive better treatment and here was the man who, of all other men in the administration, would be sure to give them that square deal.
>
> The appointment by Mr. Ickes of Mr. Clark Foreman to advise upon the economic problem of Negroes was the first jolt received by colored Americans. Here was the same kind of treatment they had been receiving over all the other years and throughout all the other administrations. There was nothing new about it.

---

* Julius Rosenwald, it will be remembered, was the Chicago philanthropist who had financed Ickes's participation in the Lazar Averbuch murder case in 1908. His fund, which provided financial aid to minority groups, had been established in 1919.

Wilkins was mollified somewhat when Slattery sent him a copy of the Secretary's order banning discrimination in hiring and management practices on PWA projects and mollified further in November when Ickes appointed a young black lawyer named Robert C. Weaver as Foreman's assistant. Weaver began working with a network made up of other black officials in the various departments of the Executive Branch—among them Mary McLeod Bethune of the NYA; Robert L. Vann, publisher of the *Pittsburgh Courier,* now working in the Attorney General's office; Henry Hunt of the Farm Credit Administration; Forrester B. Washington, a social worker in the FERA; Eugene Kinckle Jones, an official in the Urban League who had taken a position in the Commerce Department; and Lawrence A. Axley of the Department of Labor.

In January 1934, Ickes appointed Vann, Weaver, Hunt, Washington, and Jones to an entity of the Secretary's creation called the Interdepartmental Group Concerned with the Special Problems of Negroes. White representatives from the Extension Service, the AAA, the CCC, the NRA, the TVA, and the Treasury, Navy, and War departments joined the group for its first meeting in February. Ickes had hoped that the body would facilitate the coordination of efforts to assure equal treatment for blacks in the government, but the Interdepartmental Group lasted only four months and met only four times. Criticism of inequities in the AAA and the Extension Service by the black members of the group caused the Department of Agriculture to pull out its representatives. The NRA (whose director, Hugh Johnson, had fired the NRA's only black employee in December 1933) reacted similarly to complaints that it fostered lower wage agreements for blacks. Neither the TVA nor the CCC took criticism with better grace, and the departments of War and Navy would not countenance it. By the time of the fourth meeting on June 1, 1934, the group was down to a small clutch of frustrated members. It never convened again.

Weaver, who in 1936 would take over Foreman's position when the white man went to work in the Power Division of the PWA, became a charter member of the "Black Cabinet" put together by Mary McLeod Bethune in 1935. This band of black professionals, which had taken its name from that given by the press to a similar group during Theodore Roosevelt's administration, was to a large degree made up of those who, like Weaver, had served on the short-lived Interdepartmental Group. It had no official status. "The group was not a cabinet in the usual sense of the word," Weaver remembered many years later,

since none of its members save Mrs. Bethune had more than sporadic, if any, contact with the President. . . . In contrast to the earlier . . . Interdepartmental Group, the Black Cabinet did not have white participants; it had no official standing and kept no minutes. The meetings of the group continued on an irregular schedule, but we were always subject to being called in an emergency. . . .

The Black Cabinet provided a forum where problems could be discussed and potential solutions developed. The members often made concrete decisions and carried out assignments concerning matters such as preparing memoranda for future meetings, presenting ideas to government officials or black leaders, and assembling information for release to the press.

Ickes's efforts to knit an interagency unit devoted to the needs of blacks had thus come down to a kind of *sub rosa* black constituency inside the government with, at best, limited power. He was more effective in enforcing the policies he had laid down for his own department and frequently took a hand himself to see that they were carried out. When Roy Wilkins complained in the summer of 1933 that out of a work force of more than four thousand men on the Boulder Dam project only eleven were black, that these eleven were not allowed to live in the government town of Boulder City with the rest of the workers, and that they were "transported to and from the dam in buses separately from white workers, and on the job . . . were humiliated by such petty regulations as separate water buckets," Ickes had Glavis launch an investigation. The charges, he discovered, were true enough. He could do nothing to force the Six Companies to employ blacks, since the government's contract with the construction consortium had been signed long before the creation of the PWA and Ickes's nondiscriminatory regulations, but he could and did immediately order that the few blacks that were employed be allowed to live in Boulder City. When a report came to him that black tourists had been forced to the end of the line while going on a tour through Carlsbad Caverns, he ordered Cammerer to look into the matter and take any necessary action against the superintendent. When William Pickens, the field secretary of the NAACP, was told to step aside and wait while a group of whites got on an elevator at Boulder Dam, Ickes had Glavis investigate; when Pickens's complaint was verified, Ickes demanded the resignation of the ranger responsible. When Glavis reported that there had been discrimination against blacks in several PWA projects in Illinois, the Secretary made himself clear in a terse letter to the state engineer: "I hereby direct you to bring this matter to the attention of the violating contractors and to see to it that the existing discrimination against Negroes is remedied at once. I should like to have a report from you within the next week telling me of the steps which you have taken."

Ickes made his determination felt in similarly unmistakable ways throughout Interior. And even if he could not effect any substantial change in other departments, the Secretary's moral weight was considerable, giving him the character of "an informal Secretary of Negro Relations," as historian Arthur M. Schlesinger, Jr., once described him. Ickes was not unaware of this stature. "[M]y stand on the Negro question," he informed his diary on December 20, 1936, "is well known. I have been in advance of every other member of the Cabinet, and the Negroes recognize this." However self-serving, the statement was true enough. Even after Congress had stifled the antilynching bill, for example, he remained in favor of it, joining with Vice President Garner and Secretary of Commerce Daniel Roper in a fruitless campaign to persuade Roosevelt to engineer its revival. Even though he read too much potential into the fact that Garner, a Texan, and Roper, a South Carolinian, were in favor of the bill, the sincerity of his reaction was unquestionably genuine: "It begins to look as if real justice and opportunity for the Negro at long last might begin to come to him at the hands of the Democratic party."

There were some things which even Ickes could not bring himself to accomplish, however. "I think it is up to the states to work out their own social problems if possible," he ruminated in April 1937, adding that

> while I have always been interested in seeing that the Negro has a square deal, I have never dissipated my strength against the particular stone wall of segregation. I believe that wall will crumble when the Negro has brought himself to a higher educational and economic status. After all, we can't force people on each other who do not like each other, even when no question of color is involved. Moreover, while there are no segregation laws in the North, there is segregation in fact and we might as well recognize this.

A good part of the *de facto* segregation he mentioned could have been found under his own nose, a fact with which he could not have been comfortable. When the parks of Washington came under the jurisdiction of the National Park Service in June 1933, Ickes had desegregated those facilities he felt he could, but not those in which blacks might be "forced" on whites—including swimming pools and public golf courses. Separate but a good deal less than equal swimming and golfing facilities were maintained by the Park Service for several years.*

Ickes was hardly alone among New Deal liberals in falling back on the

---

* To Ickes's credit, however, it should be noted that when it came down to cases, he refused to enforce segregation. In the summer of 1941 tickets were sold to a few blacks on the East Potomac Park golf course, causing a near riot of white players. Ickes ordered in the park police to quell the disturbance and remarked in his diary that black people "are taxpayers, they are citizens, and they have a right to play golf on public courses." He then announced that it would

easy rationalization that the black population was not quite "ready" for integration in many areas; very few white people of any stripe were themselves ready to allow black people true equality. And if he, too, demonstrated some timidity in this area, by comparison to nearly any other white person in the national government, his record was quite sufficient for him to claim, when addressing the annual convention of the NAACP in the summer of 1936, that "I feel at home here." That record was both enhanced and given a permanent place in the national memory nearly three years later by his happy participation in a moment that stands like an epiphany in the history of black Americans.

In the fall of 1935 a black American contralto named Marian Anderson gave a concert of songs by Schubert, Brahms, Beethoven, and other composers in the ballroom of a hotel in Salzburg, Austria. During the intermission, the thirty-three-year-old singer was approached by Arturo Toscanini. "The sight of him caused my heart to leap and throb so violently that I did not hear a word he said," Miss Anderson remembered. What the great conductor had said, she learned later, was "Yours is a voice such as one hears once in a hundred years."

After years of dedication to her art, Miss Anderson already was well established as one of the premier contraltos in the United States; after Toscanini's well-publicized remark, she became one of the most famous singers in the world. She had given her first concert in the White House at Eleanor Roosevelt's request in February 1936, and three years later her manager, impresario Sol Hurok, had booked her to appear in Washington again under the sponsorship of the Howard University Concert Series. Her fame was such by now that a huge turnout was expected, but before the concert's scheduled date in the spring of 1939, the theater that had been reserved for the performance was destroyed in a fire. Officials of the university's School of Music asked the District of Columbia Board of Education for the use of the all-white Cardozo High School, one of the few places with an auditorium big enough to hold the expected audience. But the concert was to be open to people of both races, and the Board of Education turned down the request. The university then asked for the use of Constitution Hall, owned and operated by the Daughters of the

---

henceforth be Interior Department policy to allow blacks to play on all park courses, and when a black man and his wife were subsequently harassed a few days later by a mob of whites when they tried to play, Ickes sent the police in with strict orders to "protect the Negro players and to lose no time in making arrests of those who were conducting themselves in an improper manner."

American Revolution. The DAR also said no. Moreover, the organization's president, Mrs. Henry M. Robert, Jr., later vowed to a reporter that neither Marian Anderson nor any other black would ever be allowed to perform in that hallowed white space.

For her own sake and for that of the DAR, Mrs. Robert probably should have kept her mouth shut. The reporter, Mary Johnston, promptly went to Walter White, secretary of the NAACP, for his reaction. He pointed out that indignation from him would be expected; why not telegraph the news to a selected list of musical artists for their feelings on the matter? Reporter Johnston did as he suggested, and her story the next day was replete with exclamations of dismay and outrage from people like Leopold Stokowski, Lawrence Tibbett, Walter Damrosch, and Geraldine Farrar. Someone even more famous than these musical luminaries made her own feelings clear a few days later. Eleanor Roosevelt, a longtime member of the DAR, resigned from the organization in protest. "The question is," she explained to the readers of "My Day," her regular newspaper column, on February 28,

> if you belong to an organization and disapprove of an action which is typical of a policy, shall you resign or is it better to work for a changed point of view within the organization? In the past when I was able to work actively in any organization to which I belonged, I have usually stayed in until I had at least made a fight and then been defeated. . . . But, in this case I belong to an organization in which I can do no active work. They have taken an action which has been widely talked of in the press. To remain as a member implies approval of that action, and therefore I am resigning.

Mrs. Roosevelt's resignation set the scene for one of the most colorful events in the Capital's history. Sol Hurok, who was not reluctant to cash in on the sudden publicity for his client, suggested to Walter White that an outdoor concert be staged somewhere in the city on Easter Sunday, April 9. The site finally selected could not have been more appropriate symbolically, but accounts vary as to whose idea it was. Marian Anderson, who was in the middle of a tour at the time—constantly pursued now by reporters who wanted the mystified singer's reaction to Eleanor Roosevelt's resignation—remembered that it was Sol Hurok. Walter White implied that he may have come up with it, although Assistant Interior Secretary Oscar Chapman later told historian Joseph Lash that he himself had first suggested both the time and place. White, Chapman claimed, had come to him and asked whether Lafayette Park could be made available. Chapman replied that the park across from the White House did not really lend itself to a concert.

"What can you do?" White asked him.

Had any thought been given, Chapman said he answered, to the effect it would have "if we used Lincoln Memorial on Easter?"

"Oh, my God," White gasped, "if we could have her sing at the feet of Lincoln!"

Whether he thought of it first or not, Chapman did take the idea to Ickes, who not only seconded it, but kept President Roosevelt from leaving on a scheduled trip to Warm Springs until he had listened to the Secretary and given his blessing to the use of the Memorial. Congresswoman-at-large Caroline O'Day of New York was then persuaded to act as chair of a sponsoring committee, and numerous distinguished individuals in and out of the government were asked to lend their names to the cause. Among these were Henry Wallace, Vice President Garner, and Postmaster James Farley, all of whom were by now eyeing the prize of the 1940 Presidential nomination and were consequently reluctant to get involved in the controversy. None of the three replied to the letter of solicitation. Ickes, already certain that Roosevelt should run for a third term, was not above taking advantage of the situation to make them squirm a little and had Chapman follow up with telegrams—and when these, too, went unanswered, another set of telegrams was sent. To pin them down even more firmly, Ickes and Chapman had the manager of the telegraph office obtain certifications that all three telegrams had been received. The news of all this, of course, was not hidden from the press, and Ickes took more than a little satisfaction out of seeing all three of the erstwhile Presidential candidates making lame excuses to reporters.

The concert was scheduled for five o'clock on the afternoon of Easter Sunday. As he drove down from New York the day before, Walter White was appalled to encounter sleet, then snow as he neared the city. "Weeks of thought and all our hard work seemed about to be thwarted by nature," he remembered. "I was almost afraid to look out of the window when I awoke early the next morning. I shouted with happiness to see the sun." By four o'clock of what turned out to be a clear, cool, and windy day, every parking place for blocks around the Lincoln Memorial had been taken and an estimated seventy-five thousand people spilled out from the base of the memorial and up both sides of the long Reflecting Pool that stretched toward the Washington Monument. To the east, across the Tidal Basin, they could see the white marble dome of the Jefferson Memorial, then under construction. Some had driven from towns and villages within a radius of hundreds of miles. Many probably could remember the bitter irony of the day in 1922 when the Lincoln Memorial had been dedicated; then, the black people whose ancestors the Great Emancipator had freed from slavery had been segregated off in a small section of the audience to the left of the memorial. Not this day. Most of the seventy-five thousand in the audience were black, but there was a substantial contingent of whites who mixed indiscriminately with no apparent fear of contamination.

Roosevelt, who felt he should remain above such things, was not present. Neither was Eleanor, who feared that the publicity would center on her rather than Marian Anderson if she attended. The Secretary of the Interior, however, was there to introduce the singer. While the wind noisily hammered at a bouquet of microphones (including two for the NBC radio network) and a plane from Washington Airport just across the Potomac River growled in the sky overhead, Ickes raised his flat prairie voice in what he later described as "the best speech I have ever made." It was not quite that, but it was very good indeed: "In this great auditorium under the sky, all of us are free," he began, a phrase that brought forth the first of many interruptions, as applause and even cheers repeatedly washed up from the sea of people before him.

> When God gave us this wonderful outdoors and the sun and the moon and the stars, He made no distinction of race, creed, or color. And one hundred and thirty years ago He sent forth one of His truly greats in order that he might restore freedom to those from whom we had disregardfully taken it. In carrying out this great task, Abraham Lincoln laid down his life, and so it is as appropriate as it is fortunate that today we stand reverently and humbly at the base of this memorial to the Great Emancipator while glorious tribute is rendered to his memory by a daughter of the race from which he struck the chains of slavery.
>
> Facing us down the Mall beyond the Washington Monument . . . there is rising a monument to that other great democrat in our short history— Thomas Jefferson, who proclaimed that principle of equality of opportunity which Abraham Lincoln believed so explicitly and took so seriously. You know, these times there are many who pay mere lip service to these twin planets in our democratic heaven. There are those even in this great capital of our democratic republic who are either too timid or too indifferent to lift up the light that Jefferson and Lincoln held aloft.
>
> Genius, like Justice, is blind. For Genius with the tip of her wings has touched this woman, who, if it had not been for the great mind of Jefferson, if it had not been for the great heart of Lincoln, would not be able to stand among us today a free individual in a free land. Genius draws no color line. She has endowed Marian Anderson with such a voice as lifts any individual above his fellows and is a matter of exultant pride to any race. And so it is fitting that Marian Anderson raise her voice in tribute to the noble Lincoln whom mankind will ever honor.

Miss Anderson then emerged from the small anteroom next to the enormous statue of the sitting Lincoln and made her way to the microphones, flanked on either side by Caroline O'Day and Oscar Chapman. Her accompanist, Franz Rupp, was seated at the piano, waiting. "All I knew . . . as I stepped forward," she remembered in her autobiography, "was the overwhelming impact of that multitude. There seemed to be people as far as the eye could see. . . . I had a feeling that a great wave of good will poured out from these people, almost engulfing me. And when I stood up to sing . . . I felt for a moment as though I were choking." And, in an even later memory: "It was a tremendous thing and my heart beat like mad—it's never beat like that before—loud and strong and as though it wanted to say something."

What she wanted to say blossomed with the words and music, the unearthly voice conquering the wind and history with "America," "O Mio Fernando" from Donizetti's *La Favorita,* Schubert's "Ave Maria," and two spirituals, "Gospel Train" and "Trampin'." Less than twenty minutes later, she mumbled a few words of thanks while the cheering, beatified crowd swelled with noise and movement, threatening to engulf the singer. Walter White stepped to the microphones to calm them. As he did so, he caught sight of a slender black girl. "Her hands were particularly noticeable as she thrust them forward and upward," he recalled, "trying desperately, though she was some distance away from Miss Anderson, to touch the singer. They were hands which despite their youth had known only the dreary work of manual labor. Tears streamed down the girl's dark face. Her hat was askew, but in her eyes flamed hope bordering on ecstasy. . . . If Marian Anderson could do it, the girl's eyes seemed to say, then I can, too."

CHAPTER

· 46 ·

Family Business

E ARLY IN THE WEEK," Ickes wrote in his diary on September 2, 1939,
"I predicted to Jane that Hitler would not really move against Poland
until September because he regards September as his lucky month." Sure
enough, for the United States and most of the rest of the world, the central
event of 1939 had taken place at approximately 5:20 A.M. on September
1, when a German Stuka bomber dropped a load of explosives on Puck, a
Polish fishing village and air base on the Baltic Sea. It was the first
eruption of a Nazi blitzkrieg that would destroy the armed forces of
Poland within a matter of weeks—and the beginning of World War II, for
at eleven o'clock in the morning of September 3, Great Britain declared
war on Germany, honoring a commitment she and France had made to the
Polish government by a treaty signed in April. France followed suit with
her own declaration six hours later.

It was in the shadow of these world-changing disruptions that the
central event of 1939 in the lives of Harold and Jane Ickes took place: at a
little after 3:00 P.M. of the day after the start of World War II, Jane gave
birth to a son. That the child was a boy was a relief to his mother, who,
like most new wives (at least in those days), had been anxious to produce a
son for her husband. "I am busily engaged in fulfilling my function as a
woman and a mother of men," she had written Anna Roosevelt Boettiger
in March; "—at least, it had better be a man (please God, not men!) if

654

it doesn't want to be exposed upon the nearest, highest, chilliest mountain top." Gestation had proceeded without incident, although Jane's timing could have been better: some of the travails of pregnancy in the heart of a Washington summer were suggested when she wrote Anna again in the middle of June. Temperature readings ultimately overwhelmed her wide-eyed delight regarding the state dinner at the White House she and Harold had just attended in honor of the visiting King George V and Queen Elizabeth of England:

> Our impression was one of great admiration for two genuine, nice, gallant people who were doing their damnedest for the old Empire. The Queen seemed to me the more complex—and possibly the less genuine of the two, although, of course, I had no real opportunity to judge them. The Queen has learned the technique of meeting many people without wearing herself out. She doesn't look at them, tho most people think that she does. Twice when I was presented, I beetled straight at her. She has nice blue eyes with a kind of myopic gaze—she simply didn't see me, but she smiled charmingly. . . .
>
> But oh, dear Lord, was it hot! I nearly swooned away at the State Dinner, seriously. There I was, shrouded in a mandarin coat—which was the only garment tentlike enough to cover the acreage—simply sweating. Men's shirts buckled in the middle and collars wilted. Women, including the unfortunate Queen, turned beetlike. Anna, I give you my word that it must have been 97 or 98 in that place. If I ever see your father, I have ready for delivery a short but concise dissertation upon why the White House should be air-conditioned NOW.

Ickes had left a cabinet meeting when word came that the child had been born. Jane was still sleeping when he got to the hospital, so he went in to see his son. "No new-born baby ever looks particularly attractive or husky," he wrote in a touchingly unguarded moment, "but when it is your own, you have a feeling of great interest and love for him. I was particularly glad it was a boy because Jane wanted a boy, and with the short span of life that is ahead of me, as compared with Jane's expectation, I, too, very much wanted it to be a boy so that as she grows older Jane will have what I hope will turn out to be a sturdy, fine young man to depend upon and to love her." The child was named Harold McEwen after his paternal grandmother's family name, corrected from the McCune version that had come into use during the nineteenth century.

There is no evidence to suggest that the sixty-five-year-old father spent much time reflecting on the astonishing fact that his first son, Raymond, had just passed the bar in 1938 at the age of twenty-six, had taken a job on the staff of John Cahill, the U.S. District Attorney for Manhattan, would himself soon marry Miralotte Sauer, the daughter of Dr. Louis

Sauer, the discoverer of a serum for whooping cough—and, by all that was right and logical, should have been the one looking forward to raising a family (and in fact would soon be doing so, making the new father a grandfather as well). Nor did the fact that he was once again a family man slow Ickes down appreciably. It was soon one of the few bones of contention between him and Jane. "Harold and I lead two very separate existences—necessarily," she complained to Anna in October.

> But, necessary tho it is, I do not like it. Sometimes it seems as tho I scarcely see him, and since he happens to be the center of my universe I rebel against the inevitability of what I think is one of the worst ills of society. . . . My fat little husband loves to sound off in true masculine fashion about how the poor American husband slaves to keep his wife in ribbons and fripperies while she, the harridon [sic], lolls all day and then makes him go out stepping at night. I maintain that men are so naturally acquisitive both of power and material goods that they pursue their occupations madly . . . leaving the old lady out on a limb unless she joins women's clubs in self protection. It is a vicious circle.

Over the years Jane would resign herself to the fact that her husband belonged, if not to the ages, at least to the times, and would soon fill her life with the details of running a household and supervising what would become a demanding chicken-and-egg operation at Headwaters Farm. And, besides, Ickes took such simple, open delight in his new child that it made up for much. "He is adorable with the baby," she told Anna. "It makes me feel all warm inside to see the little fiend in his arms."

Not all his family matters held such satisfaction for Ickes. Before the end of the year was out, he had written Robert out of his will. His ward had driven Ickes to distraction from time to time throughout the decade. The boy had managed to graduate from Lake Forest College in 1935, but after that had gone through the allowances Ickes gave him like a prodigal and could not seem to hold any jobs, including those Ickes had gotten for him in the PWA and the National Park Service. He drank too much and did it too publicly. In the middle of August 1936 he had been arrested in Woburn, Massachusetts, for driving under the influence. While he was acquitted of the charge two weeks later, anti-Roosevelt newspapers (which included most of the nation's press) had made such an embarrassment of the incident that Ickes took pains to make it clear to inquiring reporters that Robert, while a ward of the family during his childhood, was in no sense his legally adopted son.

At some point after Wilmarth's suicide, Robert had gotten into trouble again, this time in Wheeling, West Virginia. There was nothing minor about it. He had been driving while drunk again, had struck a man and slightly injured him, then had fled. He was soon tracked down and arrested for drinking while driving and for leaving the scene of an accident. Ickes hired a good attorney, he remembered, but it looked very much as if Robert would be facing a penitentiary term. "So I did something that I have ever since been ashamed of doing," Ickes wrote in his unpublished memoirs. "I got in touch with the Congressman from that district and learned that the judge before whom Robert would be arraigned had formerly been his law partner. I don't know what the Congressman said or did, but the result was that the Prosecuting Attorney withdrew the felony charge and substituted one charging a misdemeanor." Ickes paid the fine and settled a civil suit brought by the injured man. After that, Robert disappeared into a job with the Duquesne Lighting Company in Pittsburgh and little was heard from him until Ickes spotted a news item about him in the spring of 1939. He had gotten married. Ickes sent him one hundred dollars and his congratulations.

If the Secretary hoped that would be the end of it, he was dead wrong. Not long after the birth of young Harold, Ickes began to hear rumors that Robert was going about claiming that he had been cheated out of his fair share of Anna's estate, which, he said, had been worth at least a million dollars. Ludicrous rumor was soon followed by a letter from a Chicago lawyer by the name of Henry S. Blum, who informed Ickes that it would be a good idea for the two of them to discuss "circumstances surrounding the execution of the will" and "collateral matters that might throw light" on what, Blum said, "seems, to Robert at least, so unexpected and bewildering." When Ickes refused to meet, that letter was followed by another that outlined what Blum said was Robert's legal claim to a present share in the estate.

Ickes was not bewildered; he was angry. He immediately revised his own will and turned Blum's letter over to Nathan Margold. Margold read the letter as well as Anna's will and ventured the opinion that Robert's claim had no legal standing. Ickes replied to Blum to that effect. Blum was not deterred, and filed suit, challenging Anna's will. From then until 1944, when—after endless, repeated communications, the trading of threats, and accusations of blackmail—the Illinois Supreme Court finally decided the question in Ickes's favor, this ugly little contretemps nagged at the Secretary's public and private life, breaking into print from time to time and destroying forever any love Ickes may have had left for the man who as a troubled little boy had been taken into the life of the house in Hubbard Woods so casually nearly a quarter of a century before.

༺༒༒༒༒༺

Even in the Interior Department there was a certain amount of unpleasant family business that the Secretary had to deal with before 1939 was done. This was the matter of Harry Slattery. For some time now, Ickes and his undersecretary had not been getting on well. Part of the difficulty, though it was not stated openly by either man, was Slattery's long friendship with Gifford Pinchot, which he had managed to maintain even during the ignoble debate between Pinchot and his boss regarding ownership of the national forests. There is no evidence to suggest that Slattery ever betrayed Ickes in this fight, but the relationship could not have helped coloring Ickes's regard. More directly, however, he apparently had been undercutting his boss in another area in which Ickes had developed an interest—namely, the acquisition of the Rural Electrification Administration. During the long reorganization struggle, Roosevelt had more than once dangled this Department of Agriculture agency before Ickes as one of those he might expect to administer someday, along with the TVA and any other federal facilities that had anything whatever to do with the generation and distribution of electricity. Ickes liked the idea, but Slattery, who had specialized in public power issues back in the days when he worked for Pinchot's National Conservation Association, apparently was convinced that the REA should remain in Agriculture and had let his feelings be known here and there—particularly to his longtime sponsor, Senator George Norris, the father of the TVA and no fan of the idea of having Harold Ickes administer it.

Then there was the question of Slattery's physical condition and emotional state. He was given to periodic bouts of apparently stress-related gastrointestinal attacks that immobilized him for a week or more at a time. Further, hints that he was not as stable as he might have been were revealed when he threatened to sue novelist Margaret Mitchell in 1936. One of the more reprehensible characters in Miss Mitchell's flamboyant novel, *Gone With the Wind,* had been named Slattery. Since her husband, John Marsh, was an employee of the Georgia Power Company, against which Slattery had once filed complaints on behalf of the National Conservation Association, he, his brother, and—especially—his aged and infirm mother, whose father had been a Confederate naval officer who died in battle, came to the conclusion that the choice of the Slattery name for the character of a pillaging carpetbagger in the novel was done with malicious intent. Slattery wrote Miss Mitchell to that effect, made noises during subsequent newspaper interviews about a lawsuit over this gross miscarriage of justice, and generally gave the whole business an overblown importance until the novelist was able to convince him that her husband (who in spite of rumors to the contrary, had not been the book's coauthor) had no connection with any dealings Slattery may have had with Georgia Power and that she had chosen the name for her character out of the Manhattan telephone book.

Even more revealing, if true, was a story related by Claude R. Wickard, who was a desk man specializing in corn and hog matters in the Department of Agriculture when Slattery was Undersecretary of the Interior. Slattery, according to Wickard, at one point had told associates that he had punched and knocked down a well-known general during a Washington cocktail party for making slurs against Roosevelt. Curious, Ickes had the story checked out and discovered that the general in question had been out of the country at the time of the alleged incident. This, among other stories, may have been behind Ickes's later remark in his diary that

> Harry has a perfect Alice-in-Wonderland imagination when it comes to himself. As time goes on he discovers more and more outstanding affairs in Washington with which he was intimately and prominently connected. When run down his connection is found to be non-existent. But Harry goes on building himself up not only with newspaper correspondents but publicly in formal statements and speeches. I suppose Harry finds some compensation in this for his mediocrity and his distinct inferiority complex.

By the spring of 1939, Ickes had become thoroughly disenchanted with Slattery. As was his wont with those high-level officials in his department whom he was ready to wash his hands of but whose political connections were such that they were next to impossible to dismiss on anything less than the most heinous moral charges, he resorted to a tactic designed to encourage resignation: he moved Slattery to a smaller, remoter office, stopped calling him in for consultations, and sent him almost no work to do.*

For all his fragile health (which Ickes tended to dismiss as largely imaginary) and emotional instability, Slattery proved to be fairly tough— although native laziness, for which he had acquired a reputation, may have helped. He survived life in durance vile until John Carmody left the REA to head up the new Federal Works Administration which Roosevelt

---

* According to Warner W. Gardner, an assistant in the Interior Solicitor's Office at the time, Ickes had tried a related device on Slattery's predecessor, Charles O. West. After West returned to his office from one of his many political junkets, Gardner recalled, he found "all furniture, all drapes, all rugs, removed, except for one desk and one straightbacked chair sitting in the middle of the largest room." West still refused to leave until Ickes managed to persuade the President himself to request his resignation.

had created out of Ickes's old PWA. He then went to Norris and asked him
to persuade Roosevelt to appoint him administrator of the REA. Carmody
thought he knew why. Under his administration, he remembered, REA
"had achieved quite a considerable reputation throughout the country and
here in Washington among government people who knew something
about it as an effective, popular program that was moving along pretty
smoothly. . . . I had sort of a notion that Harry Slattery thought that it
was a pretty easy job . . . that it would not require too much attention."
Whether motivated by dreams of sloth or simply anxious to get out of
the Interior Department, Slattery pursued the REA job until he got it in
the fall of 1939.*

While he was waiting for the resolution of the Slattery problem, the
Secretary took care of another, less onerous, housekeeping chore. After the
Supreme Court had invalidated the Guffey Coal Act in May 1936, John L.
Lewis, the florid and powerful president of the United Mine Workers of
America and founder and president of the supremely radical Committee
for Industrial Organization (later renamed the Congress of Industrial
Organizations and known in both incarnations as the CIO), who had been
one of the coauthors of the 1935 Guffey Act, persuaded Roosevelt to
prepare a substitute bill. The result, the Guffey-Vinson Bituminous Coal
Act, was subsequently signed by FDR on April 26, 1937. The new act
eschewed the controversial wage-and-hour provisions that had brought
down the original act, but did establish a Coal Commission to establish
and administer price codes, put a tax of one cent on every ton of coal sold
at code prices and a tax of 19.5 cents on every noncode ton, exempted
participating coal operators from the antitrust laws, and made provision
for a consumers' counsel to protect the public interest. Lewis had wanted
the legislation even without wage-and-hour provisions because he believed
it would at least stabilize a volatile industry, which in the long run would
benefit labor (this, as it turned out, the law never did quite do). The new
agency was nominally placed in the Department of Interior, but because
Ickes had never been given clear authority over it, the commission and its
counsel had in fact existed in a kind of administrative no-man's-land,
becoming little more than a convenient dumping ground for the payment
of political debts through the appointive process (each of the seven commissioners got a salary of $10,000 a year, no mean sum in 1937).

In July 1939 this tiny rotten borough went to Harold Ickes and the
Interior Department on an official basis with Roosevelt's second reorgani-

---

* Claude Wickard, who inherited the increasingly troublesome Slattery when he became
Secretary of Agriculture in 1941, once accused Ickes of wishing Slattery off on the REA.
"Believe me," he said Ickes replied, "I don't think that little of anybody."

zation order. The Secretary was not especially pleased by the gift. "It has been one of the worst managed and most malodorous organizations in the entire national Administration," he complained in his diary, and the depth of his irritation at getting it is suggested by his claim to Budget Director Harold Smith that "I would not have had any feeling about it at all if the thing had gone to Harry Hopkins for administration." But it had not, so he set about doing the best he could with it. Among his first acts was to meet with Lewis, who, Ickes said, "made no demands on me with respect to the Coal Commission. He said that he wanted it to work and that he thought I could bring order out of disorder. I told him that I would be glad to confer with him at any time or to have his advice. I suspect that when we really get under way it won't be all smooth sailing as far as Lewis is concerned because he is a domineering individual, who is interested not only in coal and labor but in politics as well." He was correct in his suspicions that Lewis was going to be trouble (though not quite in the way in which Ickes had anticipated), but in the meantime Lewis kept his peace, not even raising an objection when Ickes removed Lewis's old colleague (some would say flunky), Colonel Percy Tetlow, as director of the Coal Commission, putting in his place Howard A. Gray from the staff of the dismantled PWA, with Dan Wheeler, also of the old PWA, as Gray's administrative assistant.

For chief counsel, he selected one of the Interior Department's newest, most energetic young lawyers—Abe Fortas, who had been William O. Douglas's director of the SEC's Public Utilities Division until, on Douglas's recommendation, Ickes had appointed him general counsel to the PWA when Douglas went to the Supreme Court in April. "Fortas is one of the most brilliant lawyers in Washington," Ickes had noted in his diary at the time, then had gone on to utter one of those startling remarks that crop up from time to time in both his unpublished diary and in private correspondence: "While he is a Jew, he is of the quiet type and gives the impression of efficiency as well as legal ability."

The condescending, genteelly anti-Semitic sentiment suggested by such a statement was hardly unusual among those of the Secretary's age and station. Roosevelt himself, when among gentile colleagues, had a way of using the word "Hebrew" with such a tone of arch superiority that across all the decades it still has the effect of fingernails on a blackboard; hearing it at the time would have made any self-respecting Jew go rigid with anger. Furthermore, the pleasure the President took in teasing Henry Morgenthau had the unpleasant character of overt (if almost certainly unconscious) anti-Semitism. But such impulsive remarks by Ickes are startling because all his life he had cultivated and sincerely prized such

Jewish friends and colleagues as Julius Rosenwald, Ben Cohen, and Nathan Margold (and he would ultimately feel much the same about Fortas, who in time would be given more real responsibility at the Department of the Interior than anyone else who had ever worked for the Secretary). The contradiction, one of the most dominant and puzzling in the whole web of his life, is even more striking when placed against the record of a lifetime of deeply felt public acts and statements that validated him as one of the most outspoken, most consistent, and most effective Gentile opponents of anti-Semitism in the history of his time. And at no period was this paradox demonstrated more vividly than during the blighted era of the thirties, when a cloak of terror fell over the Jews of Europe, an undiluted barbarism that in Ickes's view defined institutionalized fascism quite as precisely as the aggression against nations that had started war: it was part of the same vile fabric.

CHAPTER
· 47 ·

Cycles of Darkness

Aʟʟ ʜɪs ʟɪFE, Ickes hated a bully. It probably would not be stretching reality to suggest that this antipathy stemmed from years of being pummeled by his loutish and sometimes brutal older brother when they both were children. In any event, the sight or suggestion of the strong imposing their will upon the weak could produce a righteous fury in him that he was rarely long in translating into action of one kind or another. In 1908, for instance, while still living in Chicago, he had heard that a Jewish peddler had knocked on the door of Ickes's Phi Delta Theta fraternity house one morning only to have a pail of cold water thrown in his face when the door was opened, a prank that evoked gales of laughter among the residents. Ickes was not amused and immediately wrote the house officers the kind of letter that normal people often think of sending under similar circumstances but rarely do. "It is not only cowardly," he said,

> but contemptible, to make the weakness of another the occasion for sport. I would not have believed that there was any man in the Fraternity of such caliber as to take part in, or condone, the baiting of an old Jew, whose only apparent misfortune seems to be that he finds it necessary to carry his goods from house to house in an effort to make an honest living. I am frank to say, that if I had to choose between being circumstanced as the Jewish peddler was in this case, and being the "man" who was the instigator of this offense, I would, without much consideration, choose to be the former.

While it is probably not quite true that Ickes tended to view the politics of fascism in terms of the unfortunate Jew of Chicago, the character of his reaction to what was happening in the world—and, for that matter, in the United States—was not much more complex than that earlier, visceral burst of anger. And if his response got him into trouble or made him appear the simpleton from time to time, the potential for incurring wrath or looking foolish rarely stopped him, and, if nothing else, endeared him permanently to the oppressed themselves.

At the heart of his anger lay the conviction that fascism was the seedbed in which such hatred blossomed, and he reserved his highest contempt for it wherever he believed he found it, whether on domestic or foreign ground. "The raids of the nightshirt nations," he said in his address before the ACLU in New York on December 8, 1937, "constitute the greatest threat to civilization since the democratic principle became established. . . . There is a world-wide struggle on today between the forces of absolutism and those of democracy. If we are to preserve our dearly won, our highly cherished freedom, we must be on the alert against any abhorrent system of government that is alien to our traditions, to our desires, and to our aspirations." On January 23, in a speech before the United Palestine Appeal at the Mayflower Hotel entitled "Cycles of Darkness," he got a little closer to specifics: "No civilized man who values the sacrifices made by his own ancestors in the long struggle for human liberty can pretend that the cruel assaults made upon your people are not his concern. No friend of human liberty can be indifferent because his own liberty has not yet been attacked."

No one else in the administration was yet saying such things, and there were those who were made nervous by them. One of these was Secretary of State Cordell Hull, who tended to look upon the European scene, not without justification, as a tinderbox which any vagrant spark might set into flame. Roosevelt himself had been holding back, but in March 1938 made it clear that he was not averse to having Ickes speak, however unofficially and unspecifically, for him. Ickes had been asked to make the address on the occasion of the fiftieth anniversary of the *Jewish Daily Courier,* the most widely read and respected Jewish newspaper in the United States. "The only reason I accepted this assignment," Ickes noted in his diary on March 30, "was because I could get a national hookup which would give me an opportunity to say something to the country about recent developments of fascism, particularly with reference to the persecution of the Jews in fascist countries in Europe."

A draft of his prepared speech had been sent to the State Department for review. Hull had complained to FDR about specific references to the

Nazi Party, as well as to Hitler and Mussolini. Roosevelt asked Ickes to "make Cordell happy," so he had cut out all proper names. But Hull wanted all references even to the term "fascism" removed as well and Ickes balked at this. Roosevelt backed him up, and at the Sherman House in Chicago on April 3, Ickes had gone on the CBS radio network with a speech that, even watered down, still included the strongest statement yet made by anyone in the administration on the question of atrocities against the Jews. He did not mention Germany, Italy, or the Nazis by name, but he did not have to: "It happens that in practically all of the nations in Europe that have gone fascist the Jews constitute the racial minority against which bitter hate is fanned into a searing flame. It seems that the false god of fascism must have its devil upon which it can pour out its objurgations, wreak its bloody vengeance."

Having Roosevelt's tacit support was welcome, but it hardly consti-tuted the all-out diplomatic assault that Ickes would have had the admin-istration pursue. When fascist dictator Benito Mussolini sent Italian troops into Ethiopia in September 1935, Roosevelt and Hull had used the stipulations of a Neutrality Act that a largely isolationist Congress had forced on them in the summer of 1935 to impose what Hull called a "moral embargo"; while ostensibly neutral, this tactic was designed to deprive the sophisticated Italian war machine of essential supplies. A series of Presidential proclamations specifically prohibited the sale of arms or munitions to either of the belligerents, as the Neutrality Act man-dated, but beyond that merely warned Americans that they traveled to either country at their own risk and chided any American corporation which might think of profiteering by the sale of oil and other natural resources. ("I do not believe," the President announced on October 30, "that the American people will wish for abnormally increased profits that temporarily might be secured by greatly extending our trade in such materials.")

The announcements had little effect, and while it is hard to see what more the President could have done in the face of a Congress that rejected all foreign entanglements, Ickes and others fretted that the action was not strong enough—mainly because the shipment of oil, gasoline, refined copper, and other useful materials to Italy, which had doubled by October 1935, showed very little inclination to decline after the President's moral embargo began. On November 21, Ickes had been asked at a press conference to comment on the fact that oil shipments to Italy seemed to be on the rise and had replied with what for him passed for circumspection, saying only that "everyone should comply both in letter and in spirit with the efforts of the Government to prevent shipments of munitions to belligerents." There must have been something in his tone of voice, however, for the *Washington Post* chose to interpret this seemingly bland statement as a call for an end to the shipment of oil, and the alarmed Italian ambassador, Augusto Rosso, told Hull during a confrontation the next day that the manner in which the United States was conducting the embargo discriminated against Italy. Hull refused to apologize for the statement and during his session with Rosso was as firm as one would expect of a man from the hill country of Tennessee: "The charge of discrimination," he told the ambassador, "does not apply. . . . Your Government might well have thought of all these and other unsatisfactory phases before getting into the war. These trading incidents about which your Government complains are trivial compared with the real problems and deep concern which your war causes this Government."

Nevertheless, the United States, Britain, and France all continued to pursue such a devout policy of neutrality that the problem of what to do about Ethiopia was "solved" when Italian troops all but destroyed the army of Emperor Haile Selassie and occupied the country's capital of Addis Ababa in May 1936. Spain soon offered another arena where fascism might have been faced down, but was not. In February, a coalition government made up of Republicans, communists, and socialists had established itself after King Alfonso had fled the country. In July an opposing coalition of royalists, clerics, and conservative businessmen backed a revolt led by Francisco Franco. It was the beginning of a civil war that over the next three years would foreshadow the horror to come, as Franco's efforts were soon supported by arms, men, and munitions— including trained Italian infantry and fighter planes with German pilots—supplied by both Hitler and Mussolini.

In spite of the open violations of neutrality demonstrated by the two fascist countries, the United States, following the lead of Britain and France, maintained an unsullied strategy of nonintervention—even when sympathy for the Loyalist cause embraced nearly the entire liberal spectrum, ranging from old-line progressives like William Allen White, who called the Franco forces "the rats of Spain" from his desk at the *Emporia Gazette,* to radical young journalists like black poet Langston Hughes, who covered the war on the spot for the *Amsterdam News* of New York. Among hundreds of young Americans, the struggle was seen as an apocalyptic conflict between good and evil, freedom and slavery, and they hurried to join the little army of American radicals called the Abraham Lincoln Battalion, one of several "International Brigades" that joined in the fighting. Sympathy ran strong within the government as well, finding expression in such disparate voices as Henry Wallace, Henry Morgenthau,

Harold Ickes, Claude Bowers (U.S. ambassador to Spain), and even Assistant Secretary of State Sumner Welles, who eight years later would write, "In the long history of the foreign policy of the Roosevelt Administration, there has been, I think, no more cardinal error than the policy adopted during the civil war in Spain."

Unlike the situation with regard to the Ethiopian conflict, the struggle in Spain was internal and thus not covered by the stipulations of the Neutrality Act, which had been revised slightly, then reauthorized, early in 1936. It would have been legally possible, then, to provide arms to the Loyalist government during the first few months of the war. Not even so eager an interventionist as Ickes, of course, had advocated that such a move be made before the elections in November, but in the months after Roosevelt's second term was secured, Hull and Roosevelt still would not help the Loyalists—Hull because he feared that intervention would put the United States in direct conflict with Germany and Italy, Roosevelt because he did not want to jeopardize his efforts to enlarge the Supreme Court. Neither did anything to block passage of yet another Neutrality Act; signed into law by Roosevelt in January 1937, this one not only repeated most of the restrictions imposed by the acts of 1935 and 1936, but specifically outlawed aid to either side in Spain. The Secretary of State, Ickes felt, was willing to carry the spirit of the new law a good deal too far. In March, Hull refused to issue passports to an American ambulance unit that wanted to serve the Loyalist government. "There was no general discussion of this matter," Ickes wrote in his diary after the cabinet meeting at which Hull's decision was announced,

> because no opinions were asked for, but I certainly do not agree with this policy. I do not think that ever before have a voluntary ambulance corps or persons who propose to go as doctors and nurses been refused passports, especially when they were going to help out on the side of a regularly constituted and recognized Government. It makes me feel bad that we should adopt such a policy. It seems to me to be really an unneutral act rather than one in the interest of neutrality. Some time ago we refused to permit the shipment of munitions of war to the Spanish Government and now we prevent doctors and nurses and medical supplies from going. I have been a great admirer of Secretary Hull's foreign policies, but this makes me ashamed.

There was not much that Ickes could do about the Spanish situation but complain, which he was willing to do. In May 1938 he told the President that the country's refusal to sell arms to the Loyalists "constituted a black page in American history," and that Congress should be browbeaten into lifting the embargo. Roosevelt told him that he had been assured by congressional leaders that if Congress did such a thing, the pro-Franco Catholic vote would rise up in the upcoming November elections and strike down any congressman who had favored revision of the Neutrality Act. "This was the cat that was actually in the bag," Ickes wrote in disgust, "and it is the mangiest, scabbiest cat ever." This admission probably contributed to Ickes's resolve not to back down in one area in which he felt he could strike a blow, however minor, against fascism.

On the evening of May 6, 1937, the German airship *Hindenburg,* filled with hydrogen gas, had exploded at Lakehurst, New Jersey, in one of the most memorable disasters of the twentieth century. Shortly thereafter, to help prevent any such terrible accidents in the future, Congress passed legislation allowing the Secretary of the Interior to sell helium, a natural gas that was almost completely inert, to foreign countries, provided that it was not used for military purposes; the sales would be licensed by the National Munitions Control Board, of which Hull was chairman. At first, Ickes was all in favor of the scheme, writing FDR that "With adequate safeguards against the military use of exported helium, it would appear to be the duty of this country as a good neighbor to share any unneeded surplus it may have with other countries for the promotion of commerce and science, alleviation of human suffering, and safeguarding the lives of passengers on airships." When the American Zeppelin Transport Company, as agent for the Zeppelin Company of Germany, requested 17.5 million cubic feet of the gas in October 1937, Ickes agreed to the sale. Hull processed the license, and a contract was sent to the Secretary for his signature. Ickes suggested a number of revisions, including a penal bond of half a million dollars against the use of the helium for military purposes. The contract was so changed and sent back to Ickes's office in early March.

And there it sat, Ickes refusing to sign it. On March 13, 1938, the Nazis seized the Austrian government in the bloodless but nevertheless brutally arrogant coup called the *Anschluss.* "In view of Germany's ruthless and wanton invasion of Austria I doubt whether it is right for us to sell any helium gas to Germany under any pretext," the Secretary declared in his diary, and on March 18 announced his reluctance at a cabinet meeting. Hull objected strongly on the grounds that for the United States to back out of a sale to which it had agreed in principle would strain relations between the two countries. For his part, FDR believed that the country had a "moral obligation" to make the sale, but probably to save himself the irritation of a cabinet room squabble, the President postponed any decision until after he returned from a trip to Warm Springs.

Roosevelt subsequently called a meeting of interested parties on May

12. The President had brought in Admiral William Leahy and the army chief of staff, General Malin Craig, to testify to the uselessness of helium for military purposes, hoping that this would quell the Secretary's fears. No such luck. Ickes disputed the opinions of the military men by pointing out that their own experts had once testified to the contrary before the House Military Affairs Committee. So long as there was the slightest chance of military use for the stuff, he said, he could not legally sign the contract, as it would violate the 1937 Neutrality Act (which had been extended). He rejected a proposal from the President that a guarantee not to use the helium for military purposes be extracted from Hitler himself. "Who would take Hitler's word?" he asked. (Apparently no one tried to answer that one.) Finally, Ickes played his trump card by having Solicitor General Robert Jackson, who was also present, summarize his opinion that the contract was invalid because the meeting of the Munitions Board that had unanimously approved it had been attended entirely by proxies and that under the statute authorizing helium sales, the power to vote on the question could not be delegated. "Mr. President," Jackson concluded, "under the law I do not think anything can be done so long as you have such a stubborn Secretary of the Interior with so much information in his brief case."

The meeting ended in laughter—and an impasse. Roosevelt made one more try during a cabinet meeting a few days later, but Ickes still refused to sign. The President was left with two choices: to go along, since he could not by law supersede Ickes's authority in the matter, or fire his Secretary of the Interior, a move that would have had immeasurable political implications even if he had been willing to lose a man whose resignations he had been turning back with boring regularity for nearly five years. The President gave up.

The persecutions against which Ickes already had been speaking were as nothing compared to the beast that was let out of its cage following the *Anschluss* on March 13. Throughout the spring, summer, and fall of 1938, economic reprisals, the plundering of Jewish businesses, mass arrests, beatings, death, and deportations mounted throughout the growing German empire—which by the fall included Czechoslovakia as well as Austria. *The New York Times* estimated that as many as 170 Jews a day were committing suicide in despair. Then, on November 7, after hearing that twelve thousand Polish Jews living in Germany had been rounded up in a single night, transported to the Polish border, then left to starve and freeze to death, a Polish Jew living in Paris shot Ernst vom Rath, the

German ambassador to France. The ambassador died of his wounds two days later, and that evening—called forever after *Kristallnacht,* the Night of Broken Glass—virtually all of Germany became a caldron of violence against Jews. Store windows were smashed, their contents looted, the stores set on fire. Synagogues and temples, as well as Jewish schools, hospitals, nursing homes, and residences were wrecked or put to the torch. Somewhere between twenty thousand and sixty thousand Jews were arrested and put in concentration camps; hundreds were shot or beaten to death. Not since the pogroms of the Middle Ages had there been such systematic, concentrated violence directed against Jews over so wide a territory in so short a time.

The civilized world was aghast. Harold Ickes was aghast. "The intelligence and culture of a humane people," he told the attendees of the annual Hanukkah banquet of the Cleveland Zionist Society on December 18, "by a sudden, swift revulsion, has been sunk without trace in the thick darkness of pre-primitive times." Probably drafted by Saul Padover, Ickes's resident historian and speechwriter, this powerful piece of work, rather than his introduction of Marian Anderson, may have been the best speech he ever made:

> Tolerance and sympathetic understanding have given way to brutal deeds. The milk of human kindness has become a corroding acid. Witchcraft has been reenthroned. Superstition once more rules the minds of men and modern dictators have set themselves up as high priests of a more cruel, if a more refined voodooism. . . .
>
> Today the Jew in certain areas is a political eunuch, a social outcast, to be dragged down like a mad dog. Deprived of their property without even a pretense of equitable right or legal form; brutally told that they are no longer wanted in their homeland and yet denied the right to leave even if they had a place to which they could go; tortured; herded with other unfortunates into concentration camps; killed, many of them; deprived of civil rights and the opportunity to make a living, until finally driven into ghettos that are reminiscent of the Middle Ages, these people may well wonder what they have done to bring down upon their heads such condign and savage punishment. Just as a Christian may well wonder how a civilization founded upon the doctrines of the gentle Jew of Nazareth is entitled to call itself Christian when it does such things.

Ickes was wrong when he said that the German and Austrian Jews were being denied the right to leave. In 1938, even after the *Kristallnacht,* the solution to the "Jewish problem" still being applied by the Nazis was simply to make life so miserable for the victims that they would seek to get out by whatever means and at whatever cost (most certainly including the forfeiture of any assets or property they might own in the homeland).

It would be a few years yet before the distilled evil of the "final solution" would be implemented. The Secretary was entirely correct, however, when he noted that the exiles, by and large, had nowhere to go. It was a concern that he had felt for some time. After the *Anschluss* in March, he had wondered during a cabinet meeting whether it would not be possible to get Congress to raise or even temporarily remove some of the immigration quotas imposed by the McCarran Act of 1924 in order to admit refugees. "I pointed out," he said in his diary,

> that we stood to get a fine class of citizen, similar to the type that we got after the abortive revolution of 1848. . . . [W]ith men of ability and culture committing suicide in Austria, as the result of the annexation of that country by Germany, it seems terrible that our doors are closed. Apparently also the time is at hand when many of the Spanish Loyalists will have to seek asylum in other countries if they are to escape the vengeance of General Franco. The Loyalist cause . . . appears to be at the point of total collapse.

(Not quite; in spite of the odds, the Loyalists would hold on until April 1939.)

Concern for the refugees was shared by most of those around the table. At the same time, it was conceded as reality that Congress was so driven by a combination of isolationism, anti-Semitism, and a presumed threat to native American jobholders that if any changes at all were made in the immigration law they were more likely to reduce quotas than raise or eliminate them. Nevertheless, the Roosevelt administration did move to do something. In the last week of March, FDR had invited twenty-seven European and Latin American countries to a conference in July to discuss the situation and see what could be done about the tens—and soon to be hundreds—of thousands of European refugees seeking new homelands. As the U.S. representation, he formed a seven-person Presidential Advisory Committee on Political Refugees, a poorly financed and nearly powerless little agency that would remain the core of the administration's refugee program for the rest of the Roosevelt years.

The conference accomplished precious little. At the outset, Roosevelt had assured the invited nations that "no country would be expected or asked to receive a greater number of immigrants than is permitted by its existing legislation," and Myron C. Taylor, the main administration representative, fortified that assurance when he opened the conference by announcing that for its part the United States would make available its entire quota of 27,370 openings for Germany and Austria. "The time has come when governments . . . must act and act promptly," he said. But, as a reporter for *Newsweek* wrote, "Most governments represented acted promptly by slamming their doors against Jewish refugees." There was very little room at anyone's inn—not even Canada or Australia, neither of which would seem to have been overpopulated. Britain went so far as to close off even the most logical choice: it refused to allow the consideration of emigration to Palestine, which had been a British Protectorate since the end of World War I. As is usual in such circumstances, what the conference did was create a committee—a permanent Intergovernmental Committee on Refugees whose duty it would henceforth be to investigate and where possible implement refugee-placement programs. Given almost no money with which to operate and constantly frustrated by the inflexible closed-door policies of most nations, the Intergovernmental Committee amounted, as Sumner Welles would put it, "to little more than nothing."

One of the possibilities explored by the Intergovernmental Committee was that of mass colonization, and it explored without profit colonization schemes for Kenya, the Orinoco Plains of Brazil, French Guiana, Northern Rhodesia, and other regions whose appeal to the principals involved was not very great—at least according to a sardonic writer for the *Jewish Workers' Voice:* "Powerful nations, enjoying sovereignty and freedom, have only their own countries to fall back upon. But Jewish refugees have a choice of many lands to pick from. If one prefers the humid heat of the jungles of Guiana, he is welcome to it. If someone else's taste runs to tsetse flies and similar blessings of East Africa, they are at his disposal. Verily, it is good to be a refugee." With the exception of tiny outposts in British Guiana and the Dominican Republic, nothing came of the project.

For a time, though, the American Secretary of the Interior and his staff thought his own domain might harbor two possibilities. Why not offer the Virgin Islands, for example, as a temporary refuge for those waiting their turn to enter the States legally under the quota system? As many as two thousand refugees might be accommodated in any given year. In April 1938, an Executive Order fashioned by the Interior Department allowed the governor of the Virgin Islands in emergency cases to allow some aliens to enter the islands without visas. After the violence of November 1938, the Legislative Assembly of the Virgin Islands expressed its own approval by passing an official resolution offering the islands as a haven. One obstacle remained: a stipulation in immigration law that prevented anyone who had already entered a territory of the United States to qualify for entry under the quota system—a proviso that, if enforced, would void the Virgin Islands plan.

In October 1939, Ickes and the Interior Department's Solicitor's Office entered negotiations with the Labor, State, and Justice departments in an effort to gain approval for an exception to the law. Labor went along with the idea, but both the State Department and the Justice Department disapproved. Congress would have to revise the law, they said, before anything could be done. Margold and Ickes apparently still felt that an agreement somehow could be worked out with the State Department and over the next several months began making plans to accept about two thousand refugees. Operating in the same hope, in November 1940, as one of his last acts as governor of the islands, Lawrence Cramer signed an executive order allowing the entrance of refugees without benefit of either passports or visas. But the State Department still would not relent, and on December 10, Roosevelt himself received an angry letter of opposition to the idea from Ward Canaday, a member of the board of the Willys-Overland Company and one of the major landowners in the islands. That and the proposal's shaky legal standing effectively killed it. "Interior," Roosevelt said in a memorandum to the Secretary on December 18, "should find some unoccupied place not now a social and economic problem." Ickes and Margold continued to push for the idea in spite of the President's own opposition, but when it became clear in the spring of 1941 that the State Department was going to remain quite as stubborn as Ickes had been with regard to the sale of helium to Germany, they finally capitulated.

Alaska presented itself as another possibility, and not long after the *Kristallnacht*, Ickes got his people to work on a settlement plan for the territory that would include provisions for the settlement of European refugees. The result was *The Problem of Alaskan Development*, issued in August 1939. This document—often called the "Slattery Report," since the undersecretary had signed its letter of transmittal before moving on to the REA—was a detailed and complex blueprint for encouraging and guiding immigration to Alaska that outlined the opportunities for economic growth the territory presented, sketched out proposed federal/private cooperative development agencies called "public purpose corporations," and stipulated that while hundreds of thousands of the anticipated pioneers would come from the ranks of the unemployed in the United States, immigration quotas should be revised to allow the inclusion of an unspecified percentage of "skilled labor from the four corners of the earth" on the grounds that the special needs of Alaskan development would require a pool of technologically sophisticated craftsmen.

Ickes sent the report to Roosevelt with a covering letter for the President's signature that could be used to present the thing to the Intergovernmental Committee on Refugees in October 1939. Roosevelt sent the proposed letter and the report over to Sumner Welles at the State

Department. "Do you think I should sign this?" he asked Welles. By no means, said Welles in a sentence that was uncommonly long and orotund even for a government communication:

> I have spoken with the Secretary of State and we both agree that if you sent the suggested letter and the report on Alaska were presented in this manner to the [Committee] a great deal of unnecessary excitement would be stirred up in this country because of the mistaken belief that would arise that Alaska offered in reality an extensive field for resettlement of refugees, with the inevitable implication that great quantities of refugees would soon be pouring from Alaska into the United States proper over and above the number now permitted by law.

Roosevelt neither signed nor sent the documents, though he did encourage Ickes in his plan to have legislation drawn up that would revise the immigration law along the lines outlined in the report. The legislation, a "Bill to Provide for the Settlement and Development of Alaska," was completed in February 1940 and in March was introduced in the Senate by Senator Robert Wagner of New York, acting for Senator William King of Utah and in the House by Congressman Franck Havenner of California. In May hearings were held by a special subcommittee of the Senate Committee on Territories and Insular Possessions. Ickes was the first witness, and his testimony emphasized the need for the kind of specialized talents much of the refugee population could provide:

> I know that most refugees cannot meet those requirements; perhaps 90 percent of the refugees of Europe cannot meet them. But the ten percent who can meet such requirements—technicians, scientists, inventors, factory owners and managers, skilled craftsmen—people who know the world markets where Alaskan products could be sold—people of these types can help us get Alaska settled. . . .
> I know that the word "humanitarian" is in bad odor these days, but I don't suggest that this Committee take any action at all on humanitarian grounds. I do propose that, if a proposition is good for business and good for the national defense and good for the American people, we ought not to turn it down merely because it has some humanitarian by-products.

He then brought forth a series of experts from the Bureau of Mines, the U.S. Geological Survey, the Division of Alaska Fisheries, and other Interior Department offices to support the bill.

Only four witnesses appeared in opposition, but four was all it took. They were the mayor of Seward, Alaska's territorial delegate to the Congress, a representative of the American Legion, and one from the American Coalition of Patriotic Societies, and none of these worthies was fooled for one minute by the Secretary's high-minded phrasing, they wanted the committee to know, or by the sea of facts and figures put forward by his experts. What this legislation meant was that there would be a lot of Jews coming to Alaska, and from Alaska probably to the United States, and they wanted no part of either likelihood. Neither did the subcommittee, as it turned out; in the absence of any noticeable support for the idea outside the precincts of the Department of the Interior, the Senate subcommittee allowed the bill to die where it sat. In the House, the measure never even got the benefit of hearings.

Even if both of the Secretary's schemes of rescue had been approved and enthusiastically supported by the government, the Congress, and the people of the United States, of course, they would have provided sanctuary for only a pitiful few of the millions whose fate we know so well now—a destiny that, even at the distance of more than two generations, seems too malevolent to be believed, much less endured. And yet, something must be said for these efforts: in a world in which it sometimes seemed as if all the lights of human history were winking out one by one, the power of even two weak candles like these must have been like sunbursts. For a time until the darkness overcame the world, Harold L. Ickes, this flawed and troubled American bureaucrat, illuminated a small corner of what was left of hope.

CHAPTER
· 48 ·

Celebrating the Sphinx

O N JUNE 1, 1939, Ickes wrote Anna Boettiger in response to a letter asking him to give her and John his assessment of the coming Presidential race. "I am not happy about 1940," he said, "but I have one deep conviction. This conviction is not a new one, because I have been harping on it now for many months, and you know what it is from what I said when we four wise people discussed the affairs of the Nation in Seattle last Summer. It is that unless the President runs again, there won't be a liberal in the White House for the four years beginning in 1941. Further, it will mean the end of a significant and vital era in our history." He then went on to analyze with considerable astuteness the quandary the Democratic Party found itself in because of Roosevelt's unwillingness or inability to make a decision about 1940: whether to run and become the first President in history to ignore the tradition that there should never be a third term, or, if not, whom to name as his successor. Politics, like nature, will not tolerate a vacuum, and as Ickes outlined the situation, all manner of flotsam was beginning to drift in to fill the empty place.

Vice President Garner, whom Ickes had once described as having "the real welfare of the country at heart," was dismissed now as "a traitor," who had enjoyed "his long-distance peek into the promised land but . . . has had to use powerful glasses to get that peek and he is already slipping." James Farley, on the other hand, "is now making his supreme try, and it is not beyond the bounds of possibility that he may succeed in winning the nomination. . . . The astonishing thing to me is that Jim should have the effrontery to regard himself as qualified to be President of the United States. . . . He is a boxing commissioner occupying the office of Postmaster General." As for Harry Hopkins, Ickes said, "At one time there was much talk of Hopkins as being the choice of your father. The President never said or intimated to me that Harry . . . was in his mind for President but I understand that he has said so to others. I never was able to take seriously the possibility of Harry becoming President. I like him personally; he has an engaging way about him, but I don't believe that he could be either nominated or elected."

"Frank Murphy in his heart expects to be the first Catholic President of the United States," Ickes went on, "but he does not think that a Catholic can be elected at this time. . . . I understand that the great and good Joe Kennedy [Joseph Kennedy, former Boston bootlegger, now American ambassador to Great Britain], that international statesman of renown, who loves to call royalty by their first names, also believes that he is going to be the first Catholic President of the United States." Henry Wallace, Ickes was sure, "has been a candidate ever since 1936 but he does not seem to me to have gathered any real strength. . . . Moreover, Henry is cold and aloof and transcendental, the latter quality being a strange thing for a Scotchman to have." Cordell Hull "has greater possibilities as a compromise candidate than probably anyone else who has been mentioned. But I know that he is not a liberal. . . . He, too, is cold and aloof and Mrs. Hull is Jewish, which is not a political asset, even in free America, at this time." Finally: "Bob Jackson would make a fine President. He is not only a thoroughgoing liberal, he is a convinced liberal. He knows what it is all about and he has poise and strength and character. If he had made the grade for the Governorship of New York, I believe that Bob would offer the way out and make it unnecessary for your father again to assume a grueling task from which he is entitled, in all conscience, to be relieved. But Bob did not make the grade and I can't see him for 1940."*

The one person he did not mention as a potential candidate was Harold L. Ickes. This is not to say that he had not thought about it. The Presidential Bug, a peculiar insect that tends to seek out and inhabit the ear of any politician or bureaucrat who has achieved a station high enough to attract it, had first started buzzing around the Secretary of the Interior as early as January 1935, when Congressman William I. Sirovich, a very

---

* Jackson had made an attempt to win the backing of the Democratic machine in New York for the governorship in 1938 but had failed; among those most rigidly opposed was James B. Farley, still a power in his home territory.

wealthy New York surgeon-politician, came to see him. Sirovich let it be known that he and a few other congressmen had been discussing a scenario that would see Ickes nominated as Roosevelt's running mate in 1936, then in 1940 to be nominated and elected as President. "I listened to all of this with a straight face," Ickes archly noted in his diary, "because Sirovich was undoubtedly quite in earnest. If anyone can think of me as Vice President two years from now and candidate for President four years from now, he ought to be allowed to dream on without being awakened rudely." Sirovich was still dreaming two years later, by then advocating that Ickes go straight for the Presidential nomination in 1940. He also had gotten support for the idea from Congressman Maury Maverick of Texas, the state's most liberal politician, who in January 1937 had actually told reporters that he intended to organize Ickes for President clubs around the nation. (Maverick, unfortunately, was defeated the next year in his bid for reelection and no Ickes clubs ever sprang up on the political landscape.) Again, in his diary, Ickes disclaimed any real interest, saying only that "the Maverick statement was ill-advised and badly timed, but since I am not a candidate, and don't expect to be, no harm after all has been done." He may not have been a candidate, but this statement was a long distance removed from saying that the idea was entirely preposterous, and Ickes continued to listen with understandable interest when the subject came up—as it did again in March, when Burlew reported to his boss that during a dinner at Sirovich's home in New York, the congressman had turned to the guest of honor, Generoso Pope, owner of a string of Italian-language newspapers across the country, and asked the publisher whether he would be willing to give $50,000 to an Ickes campaign. "Sure!" Pope had replied.*

He was attentive again in the fall, when Colonel "Pa" Watson told him that his and Ross McIntire's guess was that "there are probably four men whom the President might be considering—Henry Wallace; Governor [George] Earle, of Pennsylvania; former Governor Paul McNutt, of Indiana; and myself. 'Pa' said that I was the only man in the Administration who could make a good speech and the only one who was a liberal along the lines of the President. He admitted that I might be a little old in 1940. It was all very pleasant and agreeable and flattering," Ickes said.

It also was the last apparent word on the subject. This abortive little movement never achieved even the stature of a boomlet, and while Ickes was undoubtedly sincere when he insisted that he was not a candidate and

---

* Pope's son, also named Generoso, became the founding publisher of the *National Enquirer,* probably the most successful supermarket weekly in the history of the world.

did not want the "killing" job, he could not have helped feeling some disappointment when his support dribbled away so swiftly. He may have found some solace in the more substantial movement that would have had him run for mayor of Chicago in 1939. One of those pushing most forcefully for this was none other than Charles Merriam, his old companion of the urban campaign trail, who told him in the middle of July 1938, according to Ickes, that "He believes that Chicago is ready for a thorough housecleaning and that I can do the job." The Secretary had mixed feelings:

> The primaries will probably be held in February. I do not have to make a decision yet but, frankly, the thought of leaving Washington for the hurlyburly of a Chicago mayoralty fight and the turbulence of a reform Chicago administration does not appeal to me. And yet I cannot turn this proposition aside lightly. My first interest in politics was one local to Chicago. For more than an average lifetime I have tried to help Chicago get a decent mayor. . . .
>
> The question is whether in the end I shall feel it my duty to give up something that I want to do, and the doing of which I consequently enjoy, for a task that ought to be done but the doing of which I do not want to undertake.

Nothing more had been heard on the subject from Merriam or anyone else until the end of November, when John Fewkes, head of the powerful Chicago Teachers Union, came to see him and urged him to run. Ickes repeated what he had said to Merriam, that he was very uncertain about the idea and tending toward rejection of it, but did not attempt to dissuade Fewkes when he said he was going to talk to William Green, president of the AF of L, and ask him to encourage the rest of the Chicago unions to support an Ickes candidacy. When the story was leaked to *The New York Times* (Ickes maintained it was Green's office that let it out), it added not only spice to Washington's ever-simmering stew of gossip, but enough favorable support that for a few days it seemed entirely possible to Ickes that if he chose to announce for the mayoralty there was a good chance he could get it. Then, on December 3, his young Chicago friend, Paul Douglas, called to say that someone had discovered an ancient Chicago statute that prohibited anyone from running for city office who had not lived in the city for at least a year preceding his election.

That information killed any temptation Ickes might have had (though Douglas assured him that the Board of Election Commissioners could be persuaded to make an exception), but while it lasted, the Secretary had thoroughly enjoyed the twitches of agitation he had inflicted on not only "Boss" Kelly and Colonel Robert McCormick of the *Chicago Tribune,* but Harry Hopkins, whose candidacy for the Democratic Presidential nomination, in Ickes's view, was dependent upon an alliance with Kelly and his Chicago machine.

That Hopkins was a candidate by now was certain; what was not certain was whether or not Roosevelt himself endorsed the idea. According to Hopkins's own interpretation, he had. All three of Hopkins's biographers—beginning with Robert Sherwood, the Presidential speech-writer who had known and worked with him—have accepted as valid the handwritten notes that Hopkins made after a meeting with the President in April 1938. During this meeting, Hopkins said in the notes, FDR had stated flatly that only the outbreak of war could persuade him to run for a third term—and possibly not even under those circumstances would he do it—then had gone down the same list of candidates that Ickes would include in his June 1939 letter to Anna and had dismissed each of them by turn (adding the name of Ickes, and rejecting that, too). That left Hopkins. The President, who had already asked Hopkins to sit in on most cabinet meetings, then said he would appoint him Secretary of Commerce at the end of the year, when Daniel Roper was expected to leave—this in order to give Hopkins Presidential stature and to provide him the opportunity to persuade the business community that he was not some kind of socialistic ogre. FDR then had ended the meeting with, Hopkins's notes say, "assurances and hopes."

It hardly seems likely that Hopkins would have made such notes if the conversation had not taken place, but according to the recollection of Thomas Corcoran, in the days to follow Hopkins acted in a manner that only intensified the mystery. Sometime that summer, Corcoran remembered, Hopkins had come to him late one night and had asked him to help suppress his name in connection with the death of a woman who had just jumped out of a New York hotel window. Corcoran had called his friend Bernard Baruch, who had called his friend and personal publicist, New York newspaperman Herbert Bayard Swope; Corcoran did not know whom Swope had called, but Hopkins's name did not in fact show up in any newspaper accounts of the woman's suicide. The next morning, Corcoran said, Hopkins came to him again and thanked him, then said, "Tommy, I will be the first to tell you—the President wants me to succeed him." He then said that the President also wanted Corcoran to ask his friend Edward Noble, inventor of Life Saver candy and chairman of the Civil Aeronautics Board, for a fifty-thousand-dollar nut for the Hopkins campaign. Corcoran said he would do what he could—but only if the President asked him directly. This, Corcoran remembered, horrified Hopkins, who exclaimed, "But you mustn't talk to the President about me or about money. I'm acting for the President but he doesn't want to be asked about it. You will have to do this on faith." Corcoran refused, a betrayal which may have led to Hopkins's later description of him as "that little Jesuit."

Corcoran, like Ickes, was a Robert Jackson man, and, like Ickes, did not think Hopkins was electable even if he did have Roosevelt's support. Hopkins's first wife had divorced him on grounds of adultery in 1930 (though the cause was not generally known) and had been Jewish, which, as Ickes so bluntly pointed out with regard to Hull's wife in his June 1, 1939, letter to Anna Boettiger, was not an advantage. Hopkins's second marriage had been a happy one, but on October 7, 1937, his wife Barbara had died of the breast cancer that had been discovered the previous spring. Ickes, as he often did in the presence of death, had risen above any bitterness between them. "I liked Barbara Hopkins," he wrote in his diary on Saturday,

> and her death made me sad because she and Harry were one of the few couples that I have known who were really happy together. . . . I took Harry home to dinner with me last night. He looked pretty much shaken. I let him talk about Barbara when he wanted to, but otherwise I tried to keep the subject on indifferent matters of mutual interest. I am afraid that he is going to feel her loss very heavily. They have been married only six years and she left a little daughter five years old.

A little over two months later, Hopkins had gone to the Mayo Clinic in Rochester, Minnesota, to have chronic stomach pains investigated, had been diagnosed as having cancer, and on December 7 nearly two-thirds of his stomach was removed. He had recovered well enough since then, and the doctors had told him that the odds were very good that there would not be a recurrence of the cancer. Still, his health was certain to become an issue in any campaign—a situation that could not have been helped by the fact that in the best of health he was still one of those individuals who managed to *look* sick much of the time. What is more, as soon as he felt sufficiently recuperated, he had gone through a period of high living that had not gone unreported in the press. (Among other items, he apparently had been seeing enough of the woman who killed herself that summer of 1938 to have gotten his name linked with hers before her death, if not after.)

In spite of these disadvantages, Roosevelt did appoint Hopkins Secretary of Commerce in December 1938, Attorney General Homer Cummings administering the oath of office on Christmas Eve. When Hopkins and his daughter spent the rest of the holidays with the Roosevelts at the White House, it fueled further speculation. But Roosevelt was not saying anything specific to anyone, and would remain as maddeningly noncommittal as a Sphinx about the political future for months to come while his lieutenants gossiped and wondered and bickered among themselves and worried increasingly about the fate of the Democratic Party. "All of the men here who are devoted to your father," Ickes told Anna in his letter of June 1, 1939, uttering a political *cri de coeur* that would have been seconded by many,

> . . . are utterly in the dark as to what course he may adopt in 1940, although everyone is becoming more and more firmly convinced that it is either Roosevelt or reaction in 1940. And if we are in the dark as to what your father might do in the end, we are greatly disturbed by what seems to be a policy of drifting in the political field. . . .
>
> Once in a while a group of us will get together—Frank Murphy, Harry Hopkins, Bob Jackson, Tom Corcoran . . . Ben Cohen and one or two others, and we will talk without having anything to talk about [Hopkins and Corcoran presumably keeping mum about Roosevelt's ostensible plans for the new Secretary of Commerce]. . . . Word comes to us that the President is going to call us all over to the White House but the call never comes. . . .
>
> While we are willing to do the best that we can, we must have leadership, and only your father can furnish that. Perhaps subconsciously he is trying to disassociate himself from the whole mess, and for that reason is letting things drift. . . . [M]eanwhile precious days and weeks and months are slipping by, representing a loss of time and effort that is likely to be keenly regretted before we are through.

If he was hoping that Anna would persuade her father to declare himself, he was disappointed. Roosevelt remained coy even when Ickes, unable to contain himself any longer, became the first major figure to burst into print with the third-term proposal. "If it is admitted, as seems to me to be self-evident," he wrote in an article for *Look* magazine on July 4, 1939, "that only a liberal Democratic ticket can hope to win in 1940, then the next question is: What liberal can be nominated on the Democratic ticket? There is only one certain answer to this question. The liberal who can most surely be nominated and, therefore, elected on the Democratic ticket, is the man who was overwhelmingly elected in 1932 and re-elected by an even greater vote in 1936."* Roosevelt's only

---

* Entitled "Why I Want Roosevelt to Run Again," the piece was actually Ickes's second article on the subject to appear in *Look*. The first, "Why I Want Roosevelt for a Third Term," which had been published in the magazine's June 20 issue, had been heavily edited and revised—or "mutilated, supplemented, and transposed," according to the furious author. After the article's appearance he so harassed the editors of the magazine—threatening, among other things, an injunction that would force the publisher to recall every issue it could get its hands on—that they capitulated and ran his original version on July 4.

response to the article was a request that Ickes send him a copy. Ickes never learned whether the President read it.

It seems likely that Roosevelt maintained his teasing silence for two reasons. First, if he let it be known that he would not be a candidate, as those who hungered for his job would have liked, he would immediately become a lame duck with all the political frailty that condition implied. Second, if he did announce his candidacy, as Ickes, Corcoran, and the other recalcitrant New Dealers wanted, he probably would have loosed such a storm of rage in opposition that it would have made it just as impossible to function effectively as if he had made himself a lame duck. So he waited, his intent and his desire unknown to anyone but himself (and it is not impossible that he simply did not know himself what he wanted to do yet).

The Sphinx finally began to hint at his intentions in the spring of 1940, when a combination of domestic politics and foreign disasters gradually persuaded him to make some overt moves. In March, while retaining a semblance of disinterest, he had given his tacit approval to efforts by those whom Adolf Berle, now an assistant Secretary of State, called "the Corcoran-Ickes crowd" to get a clear Roosevelt victory in the California primary and work out a compromise with Garner's people in Texas. On March 9, Ickes had gone to California to see if he could knit up the state's warring Democratic factions into a solid front for the third term. Over a period of two hard days in San Francisco, the Secretary met and talked with—and at—most of California's Democratic leadership, including Governor Culbert Olson, former senator William G. McAdoo, Lieutenant Governor Ellis E. Patterson, several state senators, and clots of lower-echelon Democrats both in and out of state government, including actor Melvyn Douglas from southern California, who was swiftly becoming one of the most respected Democratic workhorses in the state. (Ickes had met Douglas and his wife, actress Helen Gahagan, during his trip to California in 1938; she would enter politics herself as a member of Congress in a few years and she and Melvyn would remain among Harold's best political friends for the rest of his life.) In the end, a coalition strong enough to beat back any major delegate bids by Garner or Farley had been patched together. "All told," Ickes wrote in his diary, "I didn't find Democratic politics in a very healthy condition, although everyone seemed to think that Roosevelt would carry the state if he were nominated."

During the last week of March 1940, he had taken Jane with him for a quick trip to Texas. Roosevelt had specifically said that he wanted no overt politicking in Garner's home territory; without coming right out with it, the implication was clear enough that he did not want local politicians offended because, while it was clear by now that Garner's support was much too thin for him to get the nomination, his people in Texas might throw their weight behind a movement to stop Roosevelt at the convention if they and their man were not treated with sensitivity. During a press conference while on a tour of the oilfields outside the east Texas boomtown of Kilgore, Ickes confined himself to generalized discussions regarding his personal advocacy of Roosevelt for a third term. "So far as Garner was concerned, I disappointed them," he wrote. "I did not mention his name. One or two questions were asked about Jim Farley, but these I parried. . . . The newspapers treated me fairly and gave the impression that I was neither talking nor advocating delegates on my trip into the state." After his return, he and Corcoran worked with freshman Texas congressman Lyndon Baines Johnson and Johnson's mentor, Texas attorney Alvin J. Wirtz—whom Roosevelt had appointed Undersecretary of the Interior to replace Harry Slattery on January 2 (another no-help political appointment with which Ickes had been burdened)—to engineer a deal that enabled Garner to save face in his home state while guaranteeing that the state's delegation would ultimately go for Roosevelt during the nominating convention in July. The compromise was laid out in a telegram issued from the White House but cosigned by Sam Rayburn, House majority leader and Garner's main political backer in Washington, and Congressman Johnson, who was rapidly becoming a force that threatened the hegemony of the old-line Texas Democrats: "TEXAS ROOSEVELT SUPPORTERS SHOULD ENDORSE NATIVE SON JOHN GARNER AND SEND DELEGATION INSTRUCTED TO VOTE FOR HIS NOMINATION FOR THE PRESIDENCY. . . . GARNER ORGANIZATION AND HIS SUPPORTERS WILL INSIST THAT STATE CONVENTION APPROVE AND ACCLAIM ADMINISTRATION RECORD AND WILL REFUSE TO BE A PARTY TO ANY STOP-ROOSEVELT MOVEMENT."

On May 7, Roosevelt's delegate slate in the California primary beat those of Garner, Farley, and all others combined by more than three to one. This victory, coupled with the successful deal with the Texas delegation, put the President in a singularly jocular mood. "Optimistically," Ickes wrote on May 11 after a meeting with Roosevelt on the day after the California primary, "he said to me that California now meant control, which would result in liberal candidates and a liberal platform. At this point he looked at me and said: 'Don't look at me so quizzically.' My reply was: 'The Democratic convention will be for one particular liberal candidate and for such a platform as he wishes.' "

Events across the Atlantic were also beginning to contribute to Roosevelt's increasing interest in going after the nomination openly—or at least in putting together a scenario in which the convention would draft him with such overwhelming unity that he could not in good conscience refuse. The impasse called the "phony war" that had settled on the European conflict since the invasion and conquest of Poland in September 1939 had ended that spring with sudden force and clarity. On April 8, Germany attacked Norway and within a few days had effectively conquered the country. On April 9, Denmark was "asked" by the German government to accept its "protection." With little real choice, the Danish cabinet and King Christian agreed, and German troops soon occupied the country. On May 10, with their positions in Denmark and Norway secured and Sweden out of the conflict by way of a declaration of neutrality, the Germans launched simultaneous blitzkriegs against Luxembourg, the Netherlands, and Belgium, and by the end of the month all three countries had surrendered.

On May 13 newly elected prime minister Winston Churchill had presented his cabinet to Parliament. "I have nothing to offer but blood and toil and tears and sweat," he told the members. "We have before us an ordeal of the most grievous kind. We have before us many, many long months of struggle and of suffering. If you ask me what is our policy I will say it is to wage war—war by air, land and sea, war with all our might and with all the strength that God can give us, and to wage war against a monstrous tyranny never surpassed in the dark and lamentable catalogue of human crime." He did not exaggerate the dimensions of the struggle. On June 4, in what Churchill called "a miracle of deliverance," three hundred thousand British troops were safely evacuated from the French coast at Dunkerque; the escape was a cause for celebration, but a retreat was a retreat, and with the aid of Italian forces striking from the south, Germany turned its attention to France with little resistance from anyone but a rapidly disintegrating French army. By the end of the month, that job, too, was done: Under the leadership of Marshal Philippe Pétain, the country had sued for an armistice and the German-dominated government of Vichy France had been organized. After that, the Battle of Britain began in earnest, and for the next several months the skies of England were corrupted by the smoke and fire and death of the most furious air combat in the history of warfare.

With Hitler now threatening England from his position comfortably astride the Continent, bolstered by military alliance with Italy and a nonaggression pact with Russia; and with Japan, the subjugator of China and Hitler's ally in spirit (and soon to be in fact), poised to strike somewhere in the Pacific Basin, though no one knew where or when (including, at this point, the Japanese), the world had grown to be a more dangerous place than perhaps at any other time in its history. In the United States, all political decisions and all political acts were now made within the inescapable context of war—and, among many, with the conviction that it was only a matter of time before America would be among the combatants.

"All bad, all bad," Roosevelt was said to mutter about the daily news from Europe. In May he called for a massive military buildup for defense purposes, and over the next several months Congress would give him $1.7 billion for it. In that same month, he formed the seven-member National Defense Advisory Commission, chaired by William S. Knudsen, president of General Motors (not a move cheered by the New Dealers, who worried that war might become just another profit-making enterprise, as many still believed World War I to have been). On June 12 he asked Congress for $4 billion to build a "two-ocean" navy of 257 ships, including twenty-seven aircraft carriers. Later that month, and even more forcefully as the summer wore on, he let it be known that he would like some kind of selective service law from Congress.

On June 20, not merely to bring consternation to the Republicans on the eve of their nominating convention in Philadelphia (although the hope of this certainly dictated his timing) but also to strengthen the quality of bipartisanship he felt his cabinet would have to have in this angry new world, he announced that he was appointing two Republicans. For Secretary of War, replacing Harry Woodring, who had resigned in protest of what seemed to be a sure third term, the President chose the seventy-three-year-old Henry Stimson, who had been Herbert Hoover's Secretary of State and, before that, William Howard Taft's Secretary of War. For Secretary of the Navy, replacing Claude Swanson, who had died on July 7, 1939, he picked Frank Knox, editor of the *Chicago Daily News,* a man who was not only a contemporary of Harold Ickes but also one of his oldest and friendliest political rivals.

There was nothing revolutionary about either choice. Both of these men could reasonably have been described as Progressive Republicans of the old school and thus were by no means totally outside the ring of liberalism that encircled the New Dealers; furthermore, while neither man was a warmonger, the instincts of both were too aggressive to accept the tenets of isolationism—they would be comfortable in an administration that would grow closer and closer to active participation in the European conflict as the months wore on. Ickes, whose high and repeated recommendations of Knox had carried considerable weight with the

President, was pleased by the choice of his old friend. And in spite of the fact that for some time he had thought of himself for the job—and had even done some quiet lobbying for it—he thoroughly approved of Stimson, too. "Even if I had had any hope that the President would make me Secretary of War," he wrote in his diary when he got the news of the appointments, "I would have had to admit, as I still do, that the Stimson appointment was excellent. . . . He has always had a fine reputation for character and ability, and his standing on the international situation has been both right and courageous."

Steadily now, coming out of the long political trance he seemed to have occupied for months, Roosevelt also got his ducks in a row for the Democratic National Convention in Chicago. The plan was still that he would not let himself be seen as actively pursuing the nomination; rather, he would respond to a draft, preferably by unanimous choice of the delegates, this to avert as much criticism of his Caesarian ambitions as possible (though he would never fully escape the accusation that he was intent on making the Presidency his personal fiefdom). As the man designated to achieve this result, he settled on Harry Hopkins, in spite of the fact that Hopkins had become something of a periodic invalid.

In September 1939, Hopkins had been taken ill again with a still undiagnosed illness (though it was not a recurrence of his cancer), and it had taken him months to recuperate. He was no longer a candidate for President now, even in his own mind, but well on his way to becoming another Louis Howe. On May 10, 1940, he had attended a dinner at the White House. He was still feeling poorly, and after dinner Roosevelt had talked him into staying the night. While he eventually recovered most of his strength, he remained a White House resident off and on for the next three and a half years. Until he formally resigned the position on September 15, 1940, to become, in effect, the President's chief of staff (no formal position was ever quite created), he was Secretary of Commerce in name only, the business of the agency being handled by his undersecretary, Edward J. Noble. (Despite Noble's yeoman service, after Hopkins the Commerce job went to former RFC director Jesse Jones.) Hopkins's true function now was as Roosevelt's liaison and general political factotum, and in this capacity he would soon replace Corcoran in the President's entourage.

By the time the President's plans and Hopkins's place in them had become general knowledge among the New Dealers, the name of the Republican candidate had been settled in Philadelphia. For quite a few months, it had appeared that it would be Thomas E. Dewey, the young Manhattan district attorney who had been making a name for himself prosecuting organized and disorganized crime in the city (some of it, incidentally, committed by Tammany politicians). By the last week of March, Dewey had worked his way so far to the front that he earned a wingshot by Ickes in the March 26 issue of *Look:*

> When Tom Dewey first accepted the role of Clamor [*sic*] Boy for the Republican Party, I remarked that he had tossed his diaper into the ring. As the result of subsequent education in infant's intimate garments, I hereby make a public correction. I shouldn't have said diaper. A diaper has to be pinned up both front and back. And Tom Dewey doesn't need any fixing up in front. He puts up a pretty good front all by himself.
>
> Apparently what I should have said was rompers. Because, for all Tom Dewey's smooth front, he has to have somebody to button him up from behind. And by his buttoners-up-behind shall ye know him!

But after stunning primary victories in Wisconsin (where he beat the still-powerful La Follette machine), Nebraska, Maryland, and New Jersey (where his popularity had been such as to scare off Robert Taft), Dewey's strength had begun to fade in the face of a brilliant, grass-roots campaign being waged by Wendell Willkie—the gravel-voiced, homespun-appearing private-utility lawyer from the Middle West who had gone from Firestone Tire & Rubber Company in Akron, Ohio, to the presidency of the Commonwealth & Southern Company, and along the way had crossed swords with the New Deal over the question of public power in the TVA. Dewey, a professional politician backed and guided by professionals, ultimately was done in by a man who had been registered as a Republican only for a year and, according to *New York Times* columnist Arthur Krock, was so little experienced in convention politics that when Krock asked him if he had a floor leader for the convention, "He didn't seem to know what I meant, and asked in turn if one was needed." Perhaps because of that very amateurishness—or a political skill more subtle and effective than Krock or anyone else imagined—Willkie captured the Republican nomination on June 25 after six ballots.

Probably one of Willkie's greatest advantages over Dewey was his age and experience. At thirty-eight, Dewey was hardly a youngster (no matter what Ickes might say), but in a world being shaped by the events in Europe, a man of forty-eight who had directed corporations might be safer. And, as Ickes had been among the first Democrats to notice, Willkie was a man of presence, if nothing else. He had first met the candidate in February during an Economic Club dinner at which Ickes had delivered a speech. "Willkie is undoubtedly a man of affairs and ability," Ickes wrote at the time. "He makes a distinctly favorable impression and he is no man's fool. He handles himself well on his feet and has the self-confidence that a successful man ought to have." Ickes would not be so kind in the months to come, but it was clear from the beginning that Willkie would be a candidate not easily dismissed.

In keeping with his predetermined scheme, Roosevelt did not go to Chicago (blessedly cool for a change) for the Democratic convention when it opened on Monday, July 15. He would wait until the convention called for him. Hopkins was there well ahead of opening day, however. Ickes, supremely irritated at having been left out of Roosevelt's confidence and certain that he had been systematically ignored by Hopkins, became downright surly when he and Jane arrived Saturday and he found Hopkins

> fully established in supreme command of the Roosevelt strategy. . . . I got in touch with both Hopkins and [Robert] Jackson by telephone on Saturday. There seemed to be no immediate occasion for a conference. As a matter of fact, there was never any occasion for a conference because Harry was running things to suit himself and he doesn't like to share any possible credit with anyone else. There was a sardonic aspect to this in view of the fact that it was a long time after I had announced for the President for a third term before Harry Hopkins emitted a supporting note. . . . As a matter of fact, when I declared for the President, Hopkins was still nurturing his own sickly and absurd boom. . . . But here he was sitting at the throttle and directing the movement that I had started.

His injured feelings not only gave birth to this rather bloated evaluation of his role in the third-term movement, but colored his whole view of the convention as it progressed. He saw very little of Hopkins, and then only to fight with him about procedure. Ickes, Jackson, and a few others worried that Farley and his forces would either manage to block the draft movement or muck it up with so much dissension that it would weaken both the party and the campaign. Farley already had made it clear to Roosevelt and everyone else that he was not going to agree not to have his name presented in nomination. At one point, the dissidents advocated having the Rules Committee suspend the rules, after which they would take Roosevelt's nomination directly to the floor for a vote by acclamation. But Hopkins told them that the word from Roosevelt was to let it alone. They still worried, and on Tuesday afternoon Ickes sent Roosevelt a telegram telling him that his friends were "convinced, as am I, that this convention is bleeding to death and that your reputation and prestige may bleed to death with it," and urging him to take leadership directly: "Here in Chicago are more than nine hundred sheep waiting for the inspiration of leadership that only you can give them."

Roosevelt ignored the telegram and refused to budge from the White House. He was waiting for his moment—which he had arranged, or had instructed Hopkins to arrange, with Chicago mayor Ed Kelly. What that moment was became abundantly clear Tuesday night, when Senator Alben Barkley of Kentucky, taking over as the convention's permanent chairman, unexpectedly announced that "at the specific request and authorization of the President" he was letting it be known that "The President has never had, and has not today, any desire or purpose to continue in the office of the President, to be a candidate for the office, or to be nominated by the Convention for that office. He wishes in all earnestness and sincerity to make it clear that all the delegates to this Convention are free to vote for any candidate." After a few seconds of uncomprehending silence among the delegates, loudspeakers began a chant of "We want Roosevelt! We want Roosevelt!" Delegates around the floor began to pick it up, a parade started, and soon there was exhibited in full force that peculiarity of American convention politics—the absolutely genuine planned spontaneous demonstration. It took nearly an hour to restore order, and by then the deed was done. The next night, after the names of Farley, Garner, Tydings, and Hull were dutifully introduced in nomination, the first and only ballot was taken: Roosevelt got 946 votes, Farley 72, Garner 61, Tydings 9, and Hull 5. Farley bowed to the inevitable, stepped to the microphone, and asked that the vote be made unanimous. It was. However tainted by manipulation, Roosevelt had his draft.

There remained the Vice-Presidential nomination. On the eve of the convention Roosevelt had announced his choice: Henry Wallace. It was not a popular selection. Ickes, as might be expected, hated the idea. So did many others. *Chicago Tribune* reporter Walter Trohan, who was there, remembered that at one point Governor E. D. Rivers of Georgia turned to Governor Leon C. Phillips of Oklahoma and asked what Phillips thought of Wallace.

"Why, he's my second choice," Phillips replied.

"Who's your first choice?" Rivers asked.

"Any son of a bitch—red, black, white or yellow—who can get the nomination."

There were plenty who wanted it, and in an episode of what can only be adequately characterized as a kind of temporary insanity, Ickes decided that he was one of them. Encouraged by Oscar Chapman, who actually went around trying to drum up support, and—especially—by Jane, who was caught up in the indescribable excitement of her first convention, Ickes went so far as to compose and send a telegram to the President offering either Robert M. Hutchins of the University of Chicago ("a liberal and one of the most facile and forceful speakers in the country") or himself ("I have the confidence of liberals generally") as alternates to the troublesome Wallace, whom Hopkins was having difficulty jamming down the convention's throat. Roosevelt never answered the telegram and stubbornly insisted on Wallace in spite of the anger that at times threatened to turn the proceedings even more ugly than conventions tend to get under the best of circumstances; at one point he went so far as to write out a statement declining the nomination, which he intended to deliver if Wallace was rejected. That did not become necessary. In the end, grumbling and backbiting all the way and only after a seesaw battle for the first-ballot lead between Wallace and Speaker of the House William Bankhead, the Democrats did their duty and gave Roosevelt the running mate of his choice.

Willkie opened his campaign on August 17 by making his acceptance speech before a crowd of about twenty thousand (and a radio audience of millions) at a park in his hometown of Elwood, Indiana. The standard complaints and promises the country had come to expect by now in the aging debate between Republican principles and New Deal excesses were enlivened this time around by talk of the possibility of war. Willkie said he agreed with the President that the nation must be prepared to defend itself. He agreed that so far as possible, the United States should "extend to the opponents of force the material resources of this nation." He even agreed that "some form of selective service is the only democratic way in which to secure the trained and competent manpower we need for national defense." But, he said, "There have been occasions when many of us have wondered if [the President] is deliberately inciting us to war. . . . He has dabbled in inflammatory statements and manufactured panics. . . . He has courted a war for which the country is hopelessly unprepared—and which it emphatically does not want." With this as one of his principal battle cries, then, Willkie launched himself on the Roosevelt administration like a Derby horse bursting out of the gate. It was the beginning of the most energetic individual effort since William Jennings Bryan's tornadolike crusades of 1896 and 1900, a one-man "amateur's" campaign that would take the candidate to scores of cities and to half a dozen or more major speeches a day.

Roosevelt opened his campaign on August 19 with Harold L. Ickes. The President had explained in his own acceptance speech that he would be much too busy with matters of statecraft and domestic emergencies to engage in a fruitless debate with the Republican candidate. Ickes, over his sulk by now, had been tapped as Roosevelt's principal surrogate, and fell to with a will. He bore no fondness for Willkie, but harbored no illusions that he would not be a strong opponent. "He is attractive and able and very plausible," he had written Raymond Robins on July 5.

> That he will make an effective campaign cannot be doubted. Of course he has the weakness of talking to everybody, of talking at the drop of the hat and of talking on all subjects at any hour of the day or night. He is likely either to talk himself into the presidency or out of it. . . . We are not fooling ourselves that we are going to have anything short of a tough fight, but I am positive that the President will run and we ought to win if we put up the right kind of case to the people. . . .
>
> As I see it this issue will be the fundamental one of whether we want to go forward along democratic lines or whether we prefer to undertake a type of American Fascism. Willkie talks about civil liberties in a democracy, but his associations and predilections have been what they have been and they do not have for me the odor of democratic sanctity.

On NBC for the first attack on August 19, Ickes made much of the fact that back in the days when Willkie had been a Democrat, he had found it convenient to join Tammany Hall, that paradigm of corruption, and had never formally resigned his membership (the information was provided by Mayor Fiorello La Guardia in New York; when Willkie denied the charge the next day, Ed Flynn, now the Democratic national chairman, magically produced photostatic copies of Willkie's Tammany records). Ickes also laid into the candidate for his devotion to the interests of private utilities, the needs of Wall Street, and what Ickes characterized as his vacillating stand on the European danger: "For a time, Mr. Willkie thought and spoke like a lion; then the weasel, which has replaced the elephant as the Republican symbol, asserted itself."

After a three-week vacation on Mount Desert Island in Acadia National Park, Maine—the first of increasingly long summer escapes from the steaming caldron of Middle Atlantic heat that the asthmatic Jane would take to this cool place of dunes, rocks, and sea—Ickes and his wife returned to Headwaters Farm, left baby Harold with his nanny, then joined Roosevelt in New York for one of the several well-publicized "inspection trips" to various defense installations the President was making in lieu of campaign junkets. This one took them on a swing through Tennessee, North Carolina, and West Virginia, during which the President officially dedicated Great Smoky Mountains National Park as well as Chickamauga Dam, the latest TVA project; toured an ordnance factory in South Charleston, West Virginia; and announced the sale of fifty vintage World War I destroyers to England in exchange for American military bases in Newfoundland, Bermuda, the Caribbean, and British Guiana— getting around the Neutrality Act (renewed once again in 1939) by describing this deal as "the most important action in the reinforcement of our national defense . . . since the Louisiana Purchase."

Ickes took advantage of this time with the President to come to the defense of Thomas Corcoran, with whom Roosevelt had become disaffected. Corcoran's cronies believed that Hopkins had poisoned the President against his old adviser, but Corcoran's didactic style may have had as much to do with the falling out as any efforts put forth by Hopkins. As James Rowe, a Corcoran friend and fellow Frankfurter protégé, explained it, "The problem between Tom and the President was that Tom would stand in front of the President and insist on a course of action and pound on the desk. Now, you know, no one ever pounded the desk with Roosevelt."

Ickes had already written the President from Maine, saying, "My heart aches for Tom Corcoran so I am venturing to write you about him without his having the slightest intimation that I am doing so. . . . As I look back over these last two years I can honestly say that Tom has been invaluable. Some of us could speak and write for the cause . . . but it was Tom who did most of the practical work." Corcoran had since disappeared into the Maine woods for a vacation, and as the Presidential train rattled through the Appalachians, Ickes gave it one more try, telling Roosevelt "that I hoped he would telegraph for Tom Corcoran to come back. I pointed out how valuable Tom had been on occasions when Jim Farley was holding back in the traces, and I said that he was badly needed in the campaign." Roosevelt agreed to send a telegram. At the same time, Ickes noted, "The President seemed to me a little vague about Tom. He thinks that Tom ought to resign from the legal staff of the RFC and then, after the election, either come back into the government or do whatever he may feel like doing."

Ickes's attempt to heal the breach was not particularly effective, and Corcoran never did take much part in the campaign.* The Secretary's own position with the President remained secure enough, however, and after his return he was worked like a draft horse, particularly when the contest began to take on heat in October. By then, even Henry Wallace, normally a reluctant campaigner at best, was in the middle of it and giving such a good account of himself—"Whether it knows it or not," he repeatedly intoned in perhaps his most effective line, "the Republican Party is the

---

* The break was complete. After the election, when FDR did not give him the job of solicitor general of the United States—which the President had been promising him since early January 1940—Corcoran left government service, entered private practice with offices in New York and Washington, and by utilizing his political and administrative connections became one of the most sought-after lobbyists in the country and a reasonably wealthy man.

party of appeasement"—that he earned praise even from Ickes. Since the middle of September, Roosevelt, the master of timing, had defied his advisers and held off any direct campaigning until the last three weeks— when he, Wallace, and Ickes finally combined for a major assault. While the train called the "Willkie Special" steamed around the country, the candidate operating at an increasingly frantic pace, and his throat beginning to give out, Ickes opened fire. On October 15 in Akron, Willkie's own territory, Ickes pounded at the theme of Willkie's financial connections with unforgiving rigor. "Wendell Willkie," he told Democratic Akronites with the gravid sarcasm that had become his style, "graduated from your Main Street to Wall Street of the great financial interests of America" to become "the greatest crusader since Peter the Hermit. If there is anything that you want—from a bag of peanuts to a shooting star—Wendell Willkie will provide it to you, *after* the election." In St. Louis three days later, he called Willkie a "simple, bare-foot, Wall Street lawyer"—a label that would stick—and after a week off was at him again in Chicago: "If Willkie has proved anything in this campaign, it is that he is thoroughly irresponsible. The truth is not in him if any deviation from the truth will serve his purposes." He was particularly contemptuous of Willkie's own claim that he was nominated by acclamation in Philadelphia during a convention that Ickes said was replete with "such skullduggery, such threats, such deception" that the claim of "the people's" overwhelming support was ludicrous:

> Out of the mess comes Willkie, the chest-beating Willkie, the Willkie of personal pronouns, declaring that he was nominated because of a genuine and "spontaneous" demand on the part of the people; on the part of the people, if you please, who had never heard of him; on the part of the people who detest Wall Street because they have been fleeced by Wall Street; on the part of the people who had been overcharged for electric power by private utilities until the Government, through its public power projects such as TVA and Bonneville, came to their rescue.

The evening of that same day—October 25—the United Mine Worker's president, John L. Lewis, went on the air over all three networks with an announcement that insiders had been expecting for some time but which came as a surprise to the twenty-five to thirty million estimated radio listeners who had tuned in. By then, Lewis had become completely divorced from the Roosevelt administration. Part of the reason was the New Deal's inability to do much about the continuing high rate of unemployment, part was what isolationist Lewis perceived to be Roosevelt's determination to take the nation into war, and part—not the least part—was Roosevelt's appointment of Lewis's rival Sidney Hillman of the

Garment Workers' Union to the National Defense Advisory Council as labor's representative. The words poured like vitriolic syrup from the fabric-covered fronts of American radios that night, surpassing in raw hatred the worst that Ickes or any of Roosevelt's other political voices might have attempted.

Roosevelt, the most powerful President in our history, Lewis said, was exhibiting "the spectacle of a President who is disinclined to surrender that power, in keeping with traditions of the Republic. . . . Personal craving for power, the overweening abnormal and selfish craving for increased power, is a thing to alarm and dismay. . . . America needs no superman." The country had had its fill of the "economic and political experiments of an amateur, ill-equipped practitioner in the realm of political science." Willkie was the man the country needed, Lewis said, and if the nation rejected him in favor of Roosevelt, it would be "a national evil of the first magnitude." If UMW members did not vote for Willkie, he, Lewis, would resign from the organization he had created. On September 14, Congress had passed legislation that authorized the President to call up the National Guard and created a Selective Service System for men between the ages of twenty-one and thirty-five. Under the circumstances, Lewis warned, if the young men of America voted for Roosevelt, they would regret it: "You who may be about to die in a foreign war, created at the whim of an international meddler, should you salute your Caesar?" Finally, he hoped that on election day the mothers of America would "with the sacred ballot, lead the revolt against the candidate who plays at a game that may make cannon fodder of your sons."

Like Lewis himself, those who opposed him believed him to possess more real power than he did in fact own. His alarmist declarations about Roosevelt's flirtation with war sent ripples of worry through the Democratic ranks. Still, Roosevelt made no direct response. In his first speech following Lewis's outburst, he concentrated instead on Republican failure to endorse national defense efforts early on. "But now," he told a huge audience at Madison Square Garden on October 28, "in the serious days of 1940, all is changed! Not only because they are serious days, but because they are election days as well. On the radio these Republican orators swing through the air with the greatest of ease; but the American people are not voting this year for the best trapeze performer." He then hit upon a happy phrase by playing off the last names of three of Willkie's most vocal isolationist supporters in Congress—House Minority Leader Joe Martin (also Willkie's campaign manager) and representatives Bruce Barton and Hamilton Fish of New York. "Martin, Barton, and Fish," repeated in tones of high derision, became one of the most famous and effective political slogans in American history. However, a less felicitous—but no less memorable—phrase uttered in Boston on October 30 almost certainly was a response to the accusations of warmongering from Lewis and others and would come back to haunt him. He delivered it at the end of a segment of his speech directed to worried parents: "And while I am talking to you mothers and fathers, I give you one more assurance. I have said this before, but I shall say it again and again: Your boys are not going to be sent into any foreign wars." The President had made this same promise before, Samuel Rosenman remembered, but had always added to it the words, "except in case of attack."

"I suggested that he add the same words this time," Rosenman said, "but he suddenly got stubborn about it—I could not understand why.

" 'It's not necessary,' he said. 'It's implied clearly. If we're attacked it's no longer a foreign war.' "

Nevertheless, in the years to come, critics would remind him of what he had said that day in Boston.

Ickes, in the meantime, had been out to Salt Lake City on October 28 to tell an audience that Willkie was a man who "herds sheep in the canyons of Wall Street," then back to Wilkes-Barre, Pennsylvania, on November 1, where he assured another audience that if Willkie was elected the money men would determine the future, not the man in the White House: "Willkie keeps telling us that he will keep us out of war. Willkie will have no more to say about this than did Chamberlain in England. . . . In America it will be what we know as Wall Street that will determine the issue of peace or war—if Willkie is elected President. And Wall Street will determine it on the basis of whether there is more profit in war than in peace." Finally, on November 2 in Springfield, Massachusetts, he pointed out that for the same reason John L. Lewis should not expect too much in return for his support of Willkie:

> Lewis can get little, if anything, from Willkie because Willkie has nothing left to give. Henry Ford made a special trip to Rushville for a secret conference with Willkie. The next day Ford declared his support of Willkie. What did Willkie agree to deliver in that deal? Ernest T. Weir, head of Little Steel, agreed to collect the money to finance Willkie's campaign. What did Willkie agree to come across with for that service? . . . What has Willkie agreed to deliver to the bankers, the industrialists, the economic royalists who have been pouring untold millions into the Willkie campaign despite their bitter complaints that the "New Deal" has reduced them to penury?

Both Roosevelt and Willkie closed out their campaigns that same night, Roosevelt from Cleveland, Willkie from Madison Square Garden in New York. While each of the candidates—and those who spoke for them—had dipped into and hurled his share of mud in a campaign that was at least as inelegant as any that had gone before it, parts of each man's closing speech possessed a sometimes stirring eloquence. "I see an America," Roosevelt said, "whose rivers and valleys and lakes—hills and streams and plains—the mountains over our land and nature's wealth deep under the earth—are protected as the rightful heritage of all the people. . . . I see an America with peace in the ranks of labor. . . . I see an America devoted to our freedom—unified by tolerance and by religious faith—a people consecrated to peace, a people confident in strength because their body and their spirit are secure and unafraid."

And Willkie, his voice somewhat recovered now but still harsh with a rasp that somehow gave it authenticity: "This is the battle of America. The drums of victory are rolling, rolling, rolling. The thunderous drums of an aroused electorate are beating in the nation tonight. Victory, victory is on the march. . . . A free people now arise to write a single word across the vast American sky: Liberty, Liberty, Liberty!"

But there were other drums to be heard this November of 1940, and on Tuesday, November 5, a little under five million more people rose up for Roosevelt than for Willkie. It was the narrowest plurality of any winning candidate since 1916, but enough—and with 449 electoral votes to Willkie's 82, more than enough—to give the President a mandate which he would not hesitate to use as the drums of war became ever more clear, ever more close.

CHAPTER
· 49 ·

A Distant Fire

I T COULD BE argued that sometime between the first week of November
1940 and the middle of March 1941, the United States entered World
War II, for in that span of a little over five months the nation's commitment to the defense of Britain—and, to a lesser extent, China—grew to
such dimensions that we were in effect an active and vigorous, if undeclared, ally in the war against the Axis powers of Germany, Italy, and
Japan. Two months after the outbreak of war in Europe, Roosevelt had
managed to engineer a revision of the Neutrality Act that allowed the
United States to sell war goods on a strict "cash-and-carry" basis, but
this was as nothing compared to Lend-Lease, a scheme that started to
percolate in Roosevelt's mind in early December 1940, when, during a
postelection vacation cruise aboard the *Nourmahal,* he received a direct
appeal for aid from Winston Churchill. "The decision for 1941,"
Churchill cabled him, "lies upon the seas. Unless we can establish our
ability to feed this island, to import . . . munitions of all kinds . . .
unless we can move our armies to the various theatres where Hitler and
his confederate Mussolini must be met . . . we may fall by the way, and
the time needed by the United States to complete her defensive preparations may not be forthcoming." A solution, the prime minister said,
would be "the gift, loan, or supply of a large number of American vessels of war" which could be used to convoy the shipment of all the

planes, tanks, artillery, and small arms the small nation also needed from the United States in ever-growing numbers.

Unfortunately, in spite of the "cash-and-carry" provisions of the revised Neutrality Act, Great Britain probably was not going to be able to pay for any of it, Churchill said:

> The moment approaches when we shall no longer be able to pay cash for shipping and other supplies. While we will do our utmost, and shrink from no proper sacrifice to make payments across the exchange, I believe you will agree that it would be wrong in principle and mutually disadvantageous in effect if at the height of this struggle Great Britain were to be divested of saleable assets, so that after the victory was won with our blood, civilisation saved, and the time gained for the United States to be fully armed against all eventualities, we should stand stripped to the bone. Such a course would not be in the moral or economic interests of either of our nations.

This play upon guilt and mutual interest had its desired effect, and during the cruise FDR came up with the program called Lend-Lease. While the plan itself was entirely Roosevelt's conception, both the term and the way in which Roosevelt chose to characterize it owed a great deal to a letter Ickes had written the President on August 2 to express his enthusiastic support of FDR's plan to sell the fifty World War I destroyers to Great Britain in exchange for military bases in British possessions. "It seems to me," Ickes had emphasized, "that we Americans are like the householder who refuses to lend or sell his fire extinguishers to help put out the fire in the house that is right next door even though that house is all ablaze and the wind is blowing from that direction."

Ickes's little conceit must have been in Roosevelt's mind when Lend-Lease was announced and outlined by the President during his press conference of December 17. "There is," he said, "absolutely no doubt in the mind of a very overwhelming number of Americans that the best immediate defense of the United States is the success of Britain in defending herself." The United States, then, must supply Britain with what she needed. Describing them as "banal," he said he had dismissed both the notion of loans and the idea of simply giving the goods away. He had, he said, another solution:

> Now, what I am trying to do is eliminate the dollar sign. That is something brand-new in the thoughts of everybody in this room, I think—get rid of the silly, foolish, old dollar sign.
>
> Suppose my neighbor's home catches fire, and I have a length of garden hose four or five hundred feet away. If he can take my garden hose and connect it up to his hydrant, I may help him to put out his fire. Now, what do I do? I don't say to him before that operation, "Neighbor, my garden hose cost me

fifteen dollars; you have to pay me fifteen dollars for it." What is the transaction that goes on? I don't want fifteen dollars. I want my garden hose back after the fire is over.

Three days later, while Ben Cohen, Edward H. Foley, and other specialists worked up language for legislation that would enable him to furnish the British government with millions of tons of "garden hoses" (or even fire extinguishers), Roosevelt invoked the powers granted him under the limited state of emergency he had declared on September 8, 1939, to put the National Defense Advisory Commission under the wing of a brand new agency—the Office of Production Management (OPM). The OPM would be run by a four-member board consisting of Secretary of War Henry Stimson, Secretary of the Navy Frank Knox, and, from the Advisory Commission, Sidney Hillman and William Knudsen. The new bureau's purpose would be nothing less than "to increase, accelerate, and regulate the production and supply of materials, articles, and equipment and the provision of emergency plant facilities and services required for the national defense, and to insure effective coordination of those activities of the several departments, corporations, and other agencies of the government which are directly concerned therewith." It was Roosevelt's first major step toward the building of a bureaucracy specifically designed to find and meet the needs of a wartime economy, and while at first limited in power it still provided the basic framework of a structure that would be capable of waging total war when the time for total war came.

In the meantime, the President began efforts to win public approval of his Lend-Lease program even before the members of the Seventy-seventh Congress, who would take their seats for the first session on January 3, 1941, had a chance to consider it as a piece of legislation. Four days after Christmas, he went on the radio with a "fireside chat" that was not calculated to make his listeners feel particularly comfortable. "Never before since Jamestown and Plymouth Rock," he began, "has our American civilization been in such danger as now. . . . If Great Britain goes down, the Axis powers will control the continents of Europe, Asia, Africa, Australasia, and the high seas—and they will be in a position to bring enormous military and naval resources against this hemisphere. It is no exaggeration to say that all of us, in all the Americas, would be living at the point of a gun—a gun loaded with explosive bullets, economic as well as military."

He continued his educational program on January 6 with his State of the Union address. Only through the elimination of dictatorships, he said, could the "Four Freedoms" dear to all human hearts be realized: "The first is freedom of speech and expression—everywhere in the world.

"The second is freedom of every person to worship God in his own way—everywhere in the world.

"The third is freedom from want—everywhere in the world.

"The fourth is freedom from fear—anywhere in the world."

On January 8, he submitted his annual budget for FY 1941 to Congress, calling for total expenditures of $17.4 billion, of which $10.8 billion was earmarked for defense. Two days later, Senator Alben Barkley in the Senate and Congressman John W. McCormack in the House introduced identical versions of a Lend-Lease bill (in the House, the legislation was deliberately designated H.R. 1776, a number whose implications were clear to all). Isolationist sentiment against the proposal was every bit as pungent as the administration had expected, but no more bitterly expressed than by Senator Burton K. Wheeler. "Never before," he said on the floor of the Senate on January 12, "has the Congress of the United States been asked by any President to violate international law. Never before has this nation resorted to duplicity in the conduct of its foreign affairs. Never before has the United States given to one man the power to strip this Nation of its defenses. Never before has a Congress coldly and flatly been asked to abdicate." The highly respected historian Charles A. Beard, testifying before the Senate Foreign Relations Committee, was so outraged that he allowed passion to unhinge reason; he insisted that the title of the bill was imprecise and should be revised to read:

> All provisions of law and the Constitution to the contrary notwithstanding, an Act to place all the wealth and all the men and women of the United States at the free disposal of the President, to permit him to transfer or carry goods to any foreign government he may be pleased to designate, anywhere in the world, to authorize him to wage undeclared wars for anybody, anywhere in the world, until the affairs of the world are ordered to suit his policies, and for any other purpose he may have in mind now or at any time in the future, which may be remotely related to the contingencies contemplated in the title of the Act.

The isolationists in both Houses did their best, but on March 11, a Lend-Lease bill passed the Senate 60–31 and the House 317–71. The next day, Roosevelt asked Congress for an appropriation of seven billion dollars to carry out the act's provisions, and on March 15 took the occasion of an address before the annual banquet of the White House Correspondents' Association to deliver a message via shortwave radio to all the people of Europe. "I remember a quarter of a century ago," he said, "that

the German Government received solemn assurances from their representatives that the people of America were disunited; that they cared more for
peace at any price than for the preservation of ideals and freedom; that
there would even be riots and revolutions in the United States if this
nation ever asserted its own interests. Let not dictators of Europe or Asia
doubt our unanimity now."

Over the horizon the war intensified throughout the spring of 1941.
The Battle of the Atlantic, Hitler's relentless U-boat slaughter of British
shipping, had been under way since the beginning of the winter and
continued strong; German forces overwhelmed Yugoslavia in just eleven
days, drove the British east of Tobruk in North Africa, forced the evacuation of British forces from Greece, occupied that country, then invaded
and finally overwhelmed British soldiers on the island of Crete. In the
United States, war-related Executive Orders, treaty agreements, letters,
proclamations, and statements slid out of the White House like a spilled
deck of cards—setting up a National Defense Mediation Board, establishing Defense Areas on and around Kodiak Island, Alaska, and the
Philippines, declaring the Red Sea open to ships of the United States,
recognizing war between Yugoslavia and the Axis, including Greenland
in the U.S. System of Hemispheric Defense, calling up units of the
National Guard, asking Congress for power to acquire foreign merchant
vessels, endorsing an agreement between the United States and Mexico for
the reciprocal movement of aircraft, pledging help to Greece, urging the
U.S. Maritime Commission to secure two million tons of merchant
shipping for defense, establishing an Office of Price Administration and
Civilian Supplies (OPACS) to prevent war profiteering and unwarranted
price increases for military goods and appointing Securities and Exchange
commissioner Leon Henderson to head it up, prodding industry to produce more and more bombers and fighter planes, creating an Office of
Civilian Defense and naming Mayor Fiorello La Guardia as its director,
putting Harry Hopkins in charge of administering Lend-Lease and sending him off to England as the President's personal representative on the
first of many exhausting shuttles across the Atlantic Hopkins would make
to meet with Churchill and other Allied leaders.

Not since the Hundred Days of 1933 had there been so much activity
packed into so short a period of time; it was a war of paper, of words, but
one made frighteningly real by a Presidential proclamation of May 27:
"Now, therefore, I, Franklin D. Roosevelt, President of the United States
of America, do proclaim that an unlimited national emergency confronts
this country, which requires that its military, naval, air and civilian

defenses be put on the basis of readiness to repel any and all acts or threats of aggression directed toward any part of the Western hemisphere."

The people of the United States had, in effect, been put on alert. "We say good-bye now to the land we have known," Raymond Clapper, the newspaper columnist and radio commentator, said in his broadcast that night.

> Like lovers about to be separated by a long journey, we sit in this hour of mellow twilight, thinking fondly of the past, wondering. . . . It's been a grand life in America. We have had to work hard. But usually there was a good reward. We have had poverty, but also the hope that if the individual man threw in enough struggle and labor he could find his place. Man has gained steadily in security and dignity, in hours of leisure, in those things that made his family comfortable and gave lift to his spirit. Under his feet, however rough the road, he felt the firm security of a nation fundamentally strong, safe from any enemy, able to live at peace by wishing to. In every one of us lived the promise of America. Now we see the distant fire rolling toward us. . . . It is still some distance away, but the evil wind blows it toward us.

The Secretary of the Interior got his own marching orders the next day in an official letter from the President:

> One of the essential requirements of the national defense program, which must be made the basis of our petroleum defense policy in the unlimited national emergency declared on May 27, 1941, is the development and utilization with maximum efficiency of our petroleum resources and our facilities, present and future, for making petroleum and petroleum products available, adequately and continuously, in the proper forms, at the proper places, and at reasonable prices to meet military and civilian needs. . . . In order to provide the desired coordination, I am hereby designating you as Petroleum Coordinator for National Defense.

"The letter of the President," Ickes noted with satisfaction in his diary, "is both very sweeping and very specific. This is what I wanted it to be. If I am to have power, I do not want any doubt to exist that I have it." The Secretary certainly had no doubt. On June 4 he appointed Ralph K. Davies his deputy administrator. He had met Davies a few months before through Edwin A. Pauley, an independent California oilman and a friend of Edward J. Flynn, the Bronx political boss and head of the Democratic National Committee. Davies was a vice president of Standard Oil of California, but he had impressed Ickes at that first meeting by advocating a federal law to conserve oil in the state of California. ("In this," Ickes had noted admiringly, "he is an exception among oil men.") On June 19, Ickes and Davies called a meeting with representatives of the oil industry and among other things told the fifteen hundred who assembled in Washington that the Office of Petroleum Coordination (OPC) would be "organized along functional lines paralleling the principle functions of the petroleum industry itself, and staffed by men possessing practical experience in these areas." If this reassured those who remembered the Secretary's whipsaw passage through their industry in the summer of 1933, so did the announcement that an industry committee would be created "to advise and assist the Government and to insure full cooperation of industry members. At the same time, orders and regulations [would] be kept to a minimum, and the greatest possible reliance placed upon voluntary compliance and support."

That done, the two men then set up an agreement with William Knudsen's people at the OPM to coordinate the supply of materials necessary to the petroleum industry, worked out an understanding with Leon Henderson at the OPACS that the OPC would have a voice in determining pricing structures for oil and gasoline, and Ickes himself negotiated an arrangement with Attorney General Francis Biddle (who had replaced Robert Jackson when Jackson moved on to the Supreme Court), whereby Biddle agreed to relax antitrust procedures whenever he was convinced that group action within the industry was being pursued strictly as a mobilization effort and not as an attempt to control production, prices, or profit. Finally, Ickes and Davies divided the country up into five regions, established district offices and suboffices, and began the process of staffing—some 75 percent of the employees coming out of the oil industry, as promised. Within a month, the Office of Petroleum Coordination was ready for action.

The appointment as petroleum coordinator was the Secretary's first official connection with the prewar defense effort, though he had been involved in some skirmishing already. There was, for example, an ongoing fight with the Aluminum Company of America (ALCOA), which appeared bent on stepping to the aid of its country in this national emergency by assuring itself of a monopoly in the production of a metal necessary to the manufacture of airplanes and other vehicles of war. The company had first moved to get this accomplished in January, when it made application to the Bonneville Power Authority for virtually all of the available power left at that Pacific Northwest generating site. Both the OPM and the War Department were anxious to give it to them, but Ickes had reservations that soon would become convictions. "There is no doubt that we will need a great deal more aluminum for defense purposes," he wrote in his diary, "but if we give the company all of the power that it wants, it is bound to cause criticism later because the Aluminum Company will have what might be charged as being a monopoly." He began to investigate such alternatives as the R. J. Reynolds Company or even Henry J. Kaiser, whom Ickes had learned to respect on the Boulder Dam project, and was soon adamant that ALCOA should not get the power. The company was just as determined that it should, however, and used every pound of influence available to it, including W. Averell Harriman, who was working for the OPA at the National Defense Advisory Commission. Harriman came into Ickes's office to plead ALCOA's case in the middle of February; with him was Undersecretary of War Robert Patterson, who, Ickes said, "was almost hysterical in expressing himself. He felt that we ought to overlook anything in view of the national emergency. I believe that he would turn over every kilowatt of power if Alcoa wanted it. . . . I stood firmly on my decision that there should be no further contract for power for Alcoa at Bonneville unless there were no other way out." Even Secretary of War Henry Stimson put in a word for ALCOA, but in the end R. J. Reynolds was awarded the contract.

One of the most surprising allies Ickes found in this conflict had been Jesse Jones, an old friend of Arthur Davis, chairman of the board of ALCOA. In spite of this relationship, Jones had called Ickes late in February and told him that he was all in favor of awarding the contract to R. J. Reynolds and that the RFC would be happy to give the company financing to build a plant. "This means that Alcoa will get no additional firm power at Bonneville and that we are really setting up a rival to Alcoa," Ickes concluded. "I hope that this not only will result in reducing the prices of finished aluminum but will be an effective check on this monopoly." He underestimated his opponent. Even as the Reynolds deal was being concluded, Arthur Davis was working out a sweetheart of a contract with Jones and the RFC that would have given ALCOA just as solid a monopoly as it would have enjoyed if it had won exclusive rights to Bonneville power. (This may have explained Jones's sudden willingness to cooperate with Ickes on the question of power—it put him on the Secretary's good side while in reality it cost his friend Davis nothing.) Under the terms of this agreement, the RFC would provide the money for the construction of government-owned plants, all of them to be operated by ALCOA under renewable, five-year leases; the company would reserve the right to cut back on the production of aluminum any time demand fell below a certain level in order not to affect production in its privately owned plants; and finally, the government guaranteed that the sale price of the aluminum would be anything that ALCOA said it should be.

Unfortunately for ALCOA, one of Jesse Jones's subordinates in the RFC was mortally offended by this giveaway and had seen to it that both Thurman Arnold, head of the antitrust division of the Justice Department, and Abe Fortas, now head of Interior's new Power Division, got a look at the contract. (Electricity to run the new government plants would have to be allocated from public power sources.) Arnold, Fortas, and Fortas's assistant, Arthur Goldschmidt, kicked up such a cloud of objections over this agreement that it came to the attention of the Senate's Special Committee to Investigate the National Defense Program, chaired by Harry S. Truman of Missouri. It still took several months of agitation and committee hearings before the contract finally was abrogated, and then not until Ickes himself had been brought into the mess, testifying before the Truman Committee that "When the story of this war comes to be written, it may have to be written that it was lost because of the recalcitrance of the Aluminum Company of America. It is just as simple as that."

Long before that, another crisis had been met—not with industry now but with labor. For a time in April it had looked as if Roosevelt would have to invoke the powers of national emergency and seize American coal mines in order to end a strike that had begun on April 1—one complicated not only by John L. Lewis's continuing hatred of Roosevelt but by dissension between the operators of the North and those of the South (contrary to his threat before the election, Lewis had not resigned from the CIO—although he had lost power in that organization to Sidney Hillman and other moderates, while retaining his presidency of the UMW). On Thursday, April 24, Roosevelt had told Ickes that he was going to give the operators until the coming Monday night to come to a settlement with both the striking miners and themselves; in the meantime, plans should be laid for a seizure. The Secretary had gotten his people on the job of drawing up papers and plans for operating the mines through Interior's Bureau of Mines, and for each of the next several days the lights had burned for nearly twenty-four hours in the Interior Building's legal department. By Monday afternoon, however, enough progress in the negotiations had been made to persuade the President to call off his plans, even though full settlement would not come until July.

In the interim, Ickes had declared war on Japan. He had looked with increasing antagonism toward that nation ever since December 12, 1937, when Japanese planes had attacked and destroyed the American gunboat *Panay,* stationed on the Yangtze River in China to protect U.S. shipping. One American civilian and two sailors had been killed and eleven badly wounded. The State Department had been swift to accept Japanese explanations that the attack had been a terrible mistake. Not Ickes. "World peace seems a long way off these days," he had written Raymond Robins on December 27. "The situation resulting from the apparently deliberate and wanton sinking of the *Panay* by the Japanese is most disquieting. If ever there was an outlaw nation that nation is Japan today." His opinion had not mellowed by the summer of 1941. He had barely been appointed petroleum coordinator and chosen Ralph Davies to help him before he informed the President that he was not happy about the situation with regard to the shipment of oil to Japan. During the cabinet meeting on June 6, he reported to his diary, "I had with me a quantity of editorials and cartoons raising hell about continuing to ship oil and gasoline to Japan while talking of rationing our own people on the Atlantic Coast. I said that while the difficulty on the Atlantic Coast was one of transportation, and not a lack of supplies, still the people who could not buy oil for their oil burners next winter would not be able to understand it. I stirred both the President and Hull."

"Give Cordell three or four days' more time, Harold," the President said.

"If Hull moves that fast," Ickes remarked to his diary, "it will be a new speed record for him." He gave the Secretary of State five days before writing to Brigadier General Russell L. Maxwell, administrator of export control:

> Information obtained from the Office of Merchant Ship Control, Treasury Department, shows that 826,283 barrels of petroleum, an average of 118,040 per day, were shipped to Japan from United States ports during the week ended May 31. From the same source, it has been learned that 4,654,029 barrels were shipped from the United States to Japan in the eleven weeks between March 15 and May 31. . . . It may be important to note that the shipments of the past eleven weeks included 1,397,024 barrels of blended or California high octane crude from which by commercial distillation there can be separated more than 3 percent of aviation motor fuel.

He wanted, he told General Maxwell, information on all export licenses authorizing the shipment of oil that had been granted by the State Department, "as I am recommending to the Secretary of State that no additional licenses covering petroleum shipments to Japan be approved until I have received this information and have had an adequate opportunity to study it."

Once again he did not give Hull much chance to react. On June 16 he received a telegram from a manufacturer in Philadelphia complaining that oil his company needed to produce defense materials was currently being loaded aboard the Japanese tanker *Azuma Maru* in Philadelphia. In his capacity as petroleum coordinator, Ickes promptly issued a hold on the shipment, claiming to Stephen Early the next day that "I was not stopping the shipment because it was headed for Japan, but because it was headed away from the Atlantic seaboard, where oil and gasoline will undoubtedly be scarce this summer and winter." That may or may not have been, but Hull and Roosevelt were both appalled and furious. For months, Hull had been doing everything possible to prevent any kind of open break with Japan which that country's military faction could use as an excuse for launching some kind of military excursion—against a U.S. possession or the Dutch East Indies. "Japan's willingness to make war, plus the far greater state of her military preparedness," Hull wrote in his memoirs,

> provide full explanation for our holding off as long as we did on applying embargoes on the shipment of petroleum, scrap iron, and other strategic materials to Japan. The President and I saw eye to eye on this policy. We felt that Japan might well retaliate in a military way if we cut off such shipments. . . .
>
> I often stated . . . that I did not believe in making a threat unless the nation was prepared to back up the Government; that if the Navy could accompany our policy in the Far East we would have no hesitation in embargoing Japan in any manner or at any time. But any half-informed person should have known that our Navy during those years of armament by the aggressor nations was not satisfactorily prepared. . . . Furthermore, at the very intimation that the Navy would be sent to the other side of the earth to back up what we knew was a threat that might lead to dangerous complications with Japan, a large section of the American public would have almost crucified the Government officials advocating such a policy.

Roosevelt was buying time, which he feared Ickes might now have stolen from him. "Lest there be any confusion whatever," he wrote the Secretary on June 18, "please do not issue any directions, as Petroleum Coordinator, forbidding any export or import of oil from or to the United States. . . . The reason for this is that exports of oil at this time are so much a part of our current foreign policy that this policy must not be affected in any shape, manner or form by anyone except the Secretary of State or the President."

This was clear enough to thoroughly offend Ickes, and in his reply, after stating that he would "implicitly follow the directions conveyed to me by your letter of June 18," the Secretary went on for another two thousand words in defense of his action, noting particularly his belief that

> if we permitted oil of any nature to be shipped from the Atlantic Seaboard to Japan, we would be making a political mistake of the first order. . . . I have

no hope that I can persuade the State Department that the taking of fuel oil from the Atlantic Coast is adding fuel to a flame of resentment. . . . The State Department is too ostrich-like sure of itself even to listen to the words of anyone who does not belong to the esoteric brotherhood of international statesmen. But I do beg of you, Mr. President, that you will not stick your chin out.

He was even more insistent three days later, after Hitler abrogated the 1939 German-Russian treaty of nonaggression by suddenly invading Russia. "There will never be so good a time," Ickes wrote, "to stop the shipment of oil to Japan as we now have. Japan is so preoccupied with what is happening in Russia and what may happen in Siberia that she won't venture a hostile move against the Dutch East Indies." In response to this astonishingly arbitrary—and utterly groundless—assurance, FDR trifled with sarcasm: "I have yours of June 23rd recommending the immediate stopping of shipments of oil to Japan. Please let me know if this would continue to be your judgment if this were to tip the delicate scales and cause Japan to decide either to attack Russia or to attack the Dutch East Indies."

Two days later, Roosevelt sent another, longer letter, this one in direct answer to Ickes's lengthy communication of June 20. The letter was prepared at FDR's request by Sumner Welles in the State Department— and if Ickes, who despised Welles, had known this, his reaction might have been even more explosive than it was. "This is a matter not of oil conservation," the communication scolded,

but of foreign policy, a field peculiarly entrusted to the President and under him to the Secretary of State. The considerations in this particular situation are peculiarly delicate and peculiarly confidential. They were not and could not be fully known to you or to anyone but the two persons charged with the responsibility. . . .

For this reason I insisted to you in my letter of June 18 that your writ did not run in the field of export control policy. Whenever and wherever your investigations disclose the threat of shortage to any section of the country, you may count on the cooperation of the Department of State. . . . That Department must equally count upon your co-operation in refraining from any act or statement which may embarrass it in carrying out under my direction policies in our foreign relations.

The Secretary probably deserved this, but it had the effect that might have been expected: he offered his resignation as petroleum coordinator— a job he had held for only a little over three weeks. "I have not attempted to interfere with the policy of the State Department," he remarked in a surly manner, "but I did not know that I am not supposed to have an opinion with respect to it and some of its policies." Roosevelt turned the resignation down (as Ickes surely knew he would) with "There you go again!"—sweetening the rejection further with a bit of inside information the United States had gleaned from intelligence operations and the decoding breakthrough called MAGIC:

> I think it will interest you to know that the Japs are having a real drag-down and knock-out fight among themselves and have been for the past week— trying to decide which way they are going to jump—attack Russia, attack the South Seas (thus throwing in their lot definitely with Germany), or whether they will sit on the fence and be more friendly with us. No one knows what the decision will be, but, as you know, it is terribly important for the control of the Atlantic for us to help to keep peace in the Pacific. I simply do not have enough Navy to go around—and every little episode in the Pacific means fewer ships in the Atlantic.

"The President's letter seemed to me to be more than a little disingenuous," Ickes wrote in his diary, "but now the atmosphere has been cleared." Since in the interim Roosevelt and Hull had begun putting restrictions on oil shipped from anywhere on the Atlantic seaboard to anywhere in the Pacific Basin, he chose to view this entire episode as a victory—though it is likely that the new restrictions had been planned all along. "I suspect that [the President] will be very friendly and gracious now until he accumulates another grouch," he wrote, "which may not be so long after all, with Harry Hopkins needling me, as I am certain that he does."

Ickes now attributed most of his troubles with Roosevelt to Harry Hopkins, who from his intimate position as the President's personal assistant, the Secretary was convinced, was engaged in a conspiracy against him. This belief solidified when, after months of pleading his case for a central authority, Ickes was not able to persuade Roosevelt to appoint him power coordinator, with responsibilities similar to those he was developing as petroleum coordinator. Only Hopkins, he was sure, could have put the knife to so logical and salutary an idea. The Secretary was encouraged in his belief by Bernard Baruch, whom Ickes had first gotten to know fairly well during the campaign of 1940. The old speculator had since taken to dropping by Ickes's office on a regular basis, where the two men fed each other's suspicions.

Baruch, who had been head of the powerful War Industries Board during World War I, thought both the OPM and the OPACS to be inadequate to the task of administering war production in the new crisis and had been urging Roosevelt to create the modern equivalent of the War Industries Board; he did not openly suggest himself as the head of the proposed agency, but he did not object when his new friend Ickes sent Roosevelt a letter recommending Baruch as a replacement for William Knudsen at the OPM (which, rumor had it, Roosevelt was thinking of reorganizing), nor did he question the implications of a Bureau of the Budget report in the summer of 1941 that called for the creation of an "Emergency Supply Board" with "a vigorous chairman" at the helm. "This proposed plan for the determination of priority policies and the administration of priority activities is supported by World War activities," the report went on. "The key to the successful working of the World War plan was the strong hand who served as chairman of the War Industries Board." No one, including Harold Smith of the Budget Bureau, needed to be told who that had been.

As with his touchy Secretary of the Interior, Roosevelt listened to Baruch patiently, giving him to understand that he quite agreed with him, then went ahead to do what he wanted to do. He did not make Ickes a power czar. He not only did not make Baruch a war production czar, he went in the opposite direction of the centrality that Baruch had been advocating. In August he created yet another agency and did so much shuffling of responsibilities among the groups and individuals of his defense structure that one is tempted to wonder if the President was less interested in rationalizing the mobilization effort than in trying to confuse the enemy.

The new agency was called the Supply Priorities and Allocation Board (SPAB). The SPAB would take over policy decisions from the OPM and would be headed by former Sears, Roebuck executive Donald M. Nelson, who continued to serve the OPM as its purchasing director; this made Nelson William Knudsen's superior in one function and his subordinate in another. The new agency also cut the "old" OPACS (it had only been around since April) in two, making the Office of Price Administration a separate outfit reporting only to the Office of Emergency Administration (OEA)—the executive department under whose wing all war-related functions operated—and putting civilian supplies into the OPM; Leon Henderson continued to operate both, however, which made him head of an independent agency in one capacity and a subordinate of Knudsen in the other. The President also pulled Edward Stettinius out of the industrial supplies section of OPM and named him administrator of Lend-Lease; Harry Hopkins was ill again, and Roosevelt wanted him to reserve his waning strength to serve as his personal liaison, troubleshooter, and surrogate on a wide variety of prewar fronts.

There had already been contention between the radical Henderson and the conservative former General Motors executive Knudsen—particularly when Henderson wanted to curtail automobile production severely and retool the industry for vehicles of war. Now it would occur on a regular basis, and, as Bruce Catton wrote seven years later, "What all of this meant, of course, was that the deep, fundamental split in the government—or at least in that part of the government that was getting the country ready for war—had come out in the open in such a way that nobody could fail to notice it or think about it."

Baruch certainly did not approve. "No one has final authority," he told reporters who asked him what he thought of the new defense setup. "It always gets back to that. You have seven excellent men there, any one of whom is capable of doing a swell job, but none has the final word. It's a faltering step forward." Ickes—a man who enjoyed the possession of final authority if anyone ever did—would have agreed. He also sympathized with Baruch over having had his advice ignored. "I think that the President has given Bernie a particularly rotten deal," he told his diary. "He called on him for help, which was cheerfully and loyally rendered. But the President apparently could not go along with Bernie and, at the same time, keep certain people, including myself, in their places."

His interest in these developments was high and his sympathy for Baruch genuine (not least because Jane had grown especially fond of the financier), but he had troubles of his own to occupy him. In May, Roosevelt had met the pleas of Churchill for shipping by calling on American owners and operators to lend fifty oil tankers to Great Britain. That had left somewhere between 200 and 250 tankers to serve the American East Coast from ports in California and on the Gulf Coast. Ickes and Davies worried that there would soon be a shortage of oil and gasoline on the eastern seaboard. Ickes had made public requests for the voluntary conservation of gasoline as early as June. These were not particularly effective, but he tried it again on July 20, issuing a recommendation for a voluntary 33.3 percent reduction in nonessential gasoline consumption, noting that while "people haven't fallen into line as fast as they should in conserving gasoline . . . it does no harm to hope, so I am hoping that voluntary curtailment will succeed." But it didn't, and ten days later he sent forth another recommendation, asking eastern service stations to close between 7:00 P.M. and 7:00 A.M. Many complied, but motorists got around that by coming in more frequently during the day to fill their tanks. Finally, on August 13, Ickes and Davies decided to order the suppliers of gasoline along the eastern seaboard to cut deliveries to service stations by 10 percent. Since Ickes had no specific power to issue such an order, it had to come from Leon Henderson's civilian supplies operation. It took two days of legal work with the soon-to-be-dismembered OPACS, but the order finally was issued on August 15, after which the Secretary got out of town.

Harold had been promising Jane all summer he would get her out of the city to relieve her asthma. They both needed a vacation. "I don't suppose there ever is a good time for me to be away from Washington," he wrote in his diary, "but there could scarcely have been a worse one than this." Nevertheless, he assured himself, "I have been so desperately tired . . . that I realized that unless I got away for a while I might have a nervous breakdown. I have never been so tired in my life. Each morning when I get up I have wondered how I would get through the day and each evening when I got home I wondered whether I would be able to repeat the following day."

For her part, Jane had been working nearly as hard as her husband in her efforts to get Headwaters Farm in good operating condition— including her chicken-and-egg enterprise, which by now had grown to the dimensions of a small village, with about five hundred capons, one thousand laying hens, two thousand pullets, and four thousand chicks occupying eight poultry houses and two brooding sheds. There were also cows, pigs, sheep, a cornfield, a wheat field, flower gardens which Harold was attempting to make superior even to the glory he had created at Hubbard Woods twenty years earlier, and a huge vegetable garden, which was also his responsibility, since he insisted on setting their table with vegetables that had been picked and cleaned only minutes before cooking and consumption.

In the midst of all this, Jane had brought forth their second child on May 14—a girl they named Jane Elizabeth but who was known thereafter only as Elizabeth. Once again, Jane had refused to let her husband come to the hospital. "She seemed to be quite sincere about this," Ickes had written in his diary. "Some women want to have the assurance of a husband in close proximity; others want their husbands present so that they can be made aware how great a sacrifice the woman is making for the man. I have never forgotten the fact that when Raymond was born, Anna insisted on my being present in the room all of the time. As she put it in advance, she wanted me to know just what happened and what torment a woman went through for the man—as if a woman wanted a child merely to please the man." He was somewhat startled to see that the baby had a healthy thatch of black hair. "I prefer a bald baby, myself," he wrote. "A newly born baby with a mop of hair is a queer object to me. . . . Her skin is dark too. I told Jane that she looked like a Japanese. I teased Jane about its being a girl and asked whether she was going to take it home with her. She thought that since she had been to so much trouble in the matter she might as well take the girl home."

In addition to work and childbearing, the summer had brought the young mother some emotional anguish from an unexpected quarter. Her uncle, Ambassador John Cudahy, a devout isolationist, had been recalled from his final post in Belgium in 1940 when he declared in an interview that German soldiers had conducted themselves quite decently during the invasion and occupation of the little country. He had since become a leading light in the America First Committee, the largest isolationist group in the country, among whose most active spokesmen were Senator Burton K. Wheeler and Colonel Charles Lindbergh (who in May had testified against Lend-Lease on the grounds that Great Britain could not possibly win the war even with American aid). Cudahy's new alliance was troubling enough to the solidly interventionist Mrs. Ickes, but her uncle had compounded that offense on June 4 when *The New York Times* and other newspapers carried an article he had written based on an interview Hitler had granted the former ambassador on May 23. The article was made up almost entirely of long, uninterrupted quotations from the dictator, among them the warning that if British convoys were accompanied by American ships, those ships would be sunk by German submarines. "It was an outrageous bit of propagandizing," Ickes had written in his diary, "and John has come in for a pretty thorough spanking, even by the newspapers that had printed his stuff. Why they should have fallen for this sort of thing, I do not understand." Ickes himself responded by dictating a quick article that was distributed by the North American News Alliance syndicate on June 8 and was distinguished by the use of the word "senile."*

Harold's words would have been stronger and Jane's distress greater if they had known the full truth—that in Berlin on May 5 Cudahy had told German Foreign Minister Joachim von Ribbentrop that the Germans *should* make threats against American ships if any were used with British convoys. He had repeated his recommendation during the interview with Hitler himself on May 23, telling the dictator that such a warning "would

---

* It was not the Secretary's first—or last—public assault on the isolationists of the country. He had singled out Lindbergh for special attention. In 1938, while he was living in Paris, the "Lone Eagle" had been given the Service Cross of the German Eagle by none other than Reichsmarschal Herman Goering in commemoration of Lindbergh's solo flight across the Atlantic in 1927. He had not been in a position to reject the award even if he had wanted to, but Ickes took full advantage of the incident to characterize Lindbergh—whom he had already called "a peripatetic appeaser"—in a number of speeches as a "Knight of the German Eagle." Lindbergh complained to Roosevelt, but got no satisfaction.

even at this time establish publicly the responsibility of the American Government for drawing the United States into the war. This clear realization, however, would produce such a reaction among the American people who are against the war that it would defeat the resolution to provide American protection for trans-Atlantic convoys." As the published article demonstrated, Hitler had taken Cudahy's advice by furnishing him with precisely such a threat.

Jane's anger and unhappiness was sufficient even without knowing precisely how close to the thin ice of treason her uncle was skating. "Harold thinks I am gallant," she had written Anna Boettiger on July 4,

> but I know that I am not at all gallant. I have retched over this row and have wept gallons of salty tears that he will never know about. I feel exhausted and old, older and more exhausted each day that I see hatreds and bitterness bubbling and seething. That they are doing just that, Anna, is undeniable. Every day the tide seems stronger against us. Lindbergh and Wheeler appear to be gaining more strength, and in their wake travels confusion and fear. . . .
>
> Harold promises that we will leave here about the 15th of August, to stay west until about the 15th of September. Dear Lord, if you knew how much we wanted to see you and John. I am hungry for the sight of a friendly and understanding face.

She got her wish when she and Harold left the children at Headwaters Farm with the servants right on schedule, boarded a connection to the Great Northern, and arrived at Spokane, Washington, on August 19. After a visit to Grand Coulee Dam, a luncheon in Spokane, and a radio address on the subject of public power, they were picked up at the railroad station in Seattle on the twentieth by the Boettigers. They spent the next two days with their friends at their new home in Lake Washington on Mercer Island—which, Ickes was happy to report, they had to get to by crossing a bridge that John Boettiger had persuaded Ickes to authorize as a PWA project three years earlier. After this happy interlude, they ferried down to Olympic National Park, then drove in to the Storm King Ranger Station, where they idled the next three weeks away in relative peace and quiet—although Davies, Baruch, Fortas, Burlew, and others called and wrote regularly, filling him in on business back in Washington. ("It is really hopeless for me even to try to cut myself off from official matters," he complained later, "or to have the privacy that I really like.") In spite of these interruptions and the misty weather typical of the park even in the summer, he had thoroughly enjoyed the respite and was not happy when they left on September 13. "I didn't feel the least like going back," he wrote, "and I became lower and lower in my mind the nearer I got to Washington."

Not the smallest part of his depression was worry over his relationship with Roosevelt. They had always had their differences, sometimes bitter ones, but even in the middle of an ongoing argument the two of them had always been able to talk it through because they saw so much of each other. Now, with war rising like a cloud and the President beset by a swarm of considerations about which Ickes knew nothing, could know nothing, with Harry Hopkins seeming to take up more and more of Roosevelt's time (and putting in a bad word for Ickes whenever possible, the Secretary was sure), with crowds of new people filling up the new agencies and with fewer and fewer of the New Dealers still left, Ickes felt isolated for the first time from the very government he had helped to create—and even more important, from the man in whose name it had all been done. His increasing inability to see Roosevelt at anything but cabinet meetings, to spend time talking with him, was a complaint that would ring in his diary like a set of changes for the next four years.

He was also worried because he was coming home to a storm of consumer protest over the 10 percent reduction in oil and gas supplies to the eastern seaboard he and Davies had set in motion on August 15.* Congress had responded, as it often did, by setting up a committee to look into the matter. This one was established in the Senate and was called the Special Committee to Investigate Gasoline and Fuel Oil Shortages, chaired by Senator Francis Maloney of Connecticut. It had gone into action while Ickes was on vacation. Deputy Coordinator Ralph Davies testified that the loss of fifty oil tankers to Lend-Lease meant that there were not enough railroad tank cars available in the country to move the 200,000 gallons a day from west to east to meet the demand, particularly in the winter months, when the need for heating oil would be at its height. The committee then took testimony from John J. Pelley, president of the Association of American Railroads, and Ralph Budd, transportation commissioner for the National Defense Advisory Commission; both assured the committee that there were at least twenty thousand tank cars immediately available should they be needed. That was good enough for the committee, which hurriedly got out a preliminary report and released it to the President and the press on September 11. "The committee believes," the report said,

> that in the handling of the petroleum problem unnecessary alarm was created. We are of the opinion that this was caused by an over-enthusiasm on the

---

* He also returned to find the following limerick from Roosevelt on his desk: "There was a lady of fashion / Who had a terrific passion; / As she jumped into bed / She casually said, / 'Here's one thing that Ickes can't ration.' "

part of those charged with the direction of the petroleum situation. The committee . . . feels duty bound to make the observation that had an adequate analysis been made, by those to whom the responsibility of coordination was delegated, the confusion of the past few months might have been avoided.

The committee furthermore has now concluded that there is no shortage of transportation facilities. This conclusion is based upon the studied opinion and serious "promises" of Mr. John J. Pelley . . . and Mr. Ralph Budd. . . . Their testimony favorably impressed and satisfied the committee—although it should be pointed out that the Acting Petroleum Coordinator [Davies], and at least one or two others who testified, were reluctant to accept the accuracy of the statements of Mr. Budd and Mr. Pelley.

Reluctant, indeed. Ickes may have been depressed at returning to Washington, but once he had a copy of the committee's hasty report in hand, depression was displaced by fury. If the committee had hoped to avoid confrontation with the Secretary by issuing the report before his return, they were disappointed. In a formal letter to Maloney he immediately demanded that the committee reconvene long enough to hear *his* testimony on the subject. There was no easy way to refuse such a request, and on October 1, doubtless bracing themselves in their chairs, they sat to hear him. "I went at the committee with both fists," he said in his diary, "although I tried to be as polite as possible."

After reiterating what he said was the unvarnished truth about the shortage of supplies on the East Coast to meet the anticipated needs of the winter, he took on Pelley's claim of twenty thousand available tank cars to move the oil from where it was to where it was needed:

With the supply, demand and transportation facts as they stand today, it is obvious that we must hedge against the uncertain future. The committee admits that it cannot guarantee the future, and I admit that I cannot. An optimist today is a person who says the future is uncertain. Even if you admit my premises, you are probably disinclined to accept my conclusions, which are not based upon the extraordinary testimony of the extraordinary Mr. Pelley, about the extraordinarily mythical 20,000 empty and usable tank cars which, according to his testimony, he could mobilize "easily within a week's time" and "have solid trains of oil moving from Texas and Louisiana."

Instead of taking the uncorroborated word of Pelley—who, after all, was a lobbyist for the railroads and mainly worried about competition from cheaper means of transportation, the Secretary said—the committee should have called for testimony from those in a position to supply real information. But, he intoned with deliberate emphasis, "*Not a single witness from the railroads, from the tank car companies, which own the great majority of tank cars, or from the oil companies supplying the eastern coast States, was called.*" If any or all of these had been called, he indicated, they might have given the committee the same facts that Ickes himself had been given by W. Alton Jones, former president of the Cities Service Company, who was acting as chairman of the transportation committee for OPC's District 1, which comprised the states of the eastern seaboard. On September 7, Jones had sent a telegram to 188 tank car owners and operators to ask them to tell him how many cars out of a total fleet of 147,838 could be made available. All had responded within ten days. The total of available cars, this response showed, was actually 5,146, not the twenty thousand of Pelley's dreams. And that, as it happened, was the good news. On September 20, T. W. Tutwiler, president of Cities Service, had sent his own telegram, this one to seventy-six leasing companies, railroad companies, and shipper-owner companies telling them that Cities Service would be needing about one thousand tank cars over the coming months to move oil into and around the eastern states. Sixty-four replies from companies owning 125,337 cars had brought in promises of only 160. "Did ever a giant mountain," Ickes asked when introducing these two pieces of evidence, "conceive so small a mouse? Mr. Pelley's twenty thousand tank cars . . . have actually shrunk to 160. In all candor, gentlemen of the Committee, Mr. Pelley owes not only you but the American people, whom he has wantonly and maliciously deceived, an abject apology."

Pelley was called before the committee the next day. He did not apologize. Instead, he now claimed the existence of not twenty thousand available tank cars but twenty-two thousand. The committee dismissed him with its thanks and did not revise its estimates of the situation. Neither did the newspapers, which, from the beginning, had assumed that the petroleum coordinator had been exaggerating the gravity of the situation and were not about to let the facts get in the way of their preconceptions.

Unfortunately, even the facts soon turned against the Secretary. It was an unusually warm fall. Oil stocks in the east were not drawn down nearly as far as had been predicted. By the middle of October, representatives of eastern oil and refining companies had convinced him that the restrictions on the amount of oil and gasoline supplied to the retailers of the East Coast were no longer needed. What was more, by then several thousand tank cars had finally appeared—not as many and not as fast as Pelley had predicted, but enough to be carrying more than 140,000 gallons into the East every day. Finally, Ickes had gotten word that the British were ready to return twenty-five of the oil tankers they had borrowed and promised even more within a few weeks. On October 17 he told Davies that it was time to "beat a graceful retreat as rapidly as possible. We can't insist that there is an oil shortage and that restrictions are necessary if such companies as the Standard of New Jersey, Socony-Vacuum, and the Sun Oil Company say there is no shortage. And we can't say there is a shortage in transportation when the British are ready to give back some tankers." The problem now, he said, "is largely a question of public relations," and when he announced, on Thursday, October 23, that he was lifting all restrictions on the movement of oil and gasoline to eastern retailers, it was with the clear implication that it was possible to do so mainly because of the cautionary action that had been taken back in August when the restrictions were imposed.

"Now I feel that I am out of the woods in this oil matter," he reported with bitter relief to his diary. "Now we can breathe freely and I have told my people that there won't be any more restrictions . . . until people drive their cars to the filling stations and find empty pumps. I am not going to kid myself ever again that the dear American people will voluntarily ration themselves or even cut out waste in the public interest in order to prevent a scarcity."

Soon enough, they would have little choice.

All November long, most of the diplomatic saraband between the United States and Japan was kept secret, but enough information emerged from time to time to give the public the strong whiff of impending war. On November 5 the tens of millions of Americans who regularly tuned in to Lowell Thomas's daily CBS news broadcast at 6:00 P.M. learned that Japan's militant prime minister, General Hideki Tojo, had sent Saburo Kurusu, former ambassador to Berlin, to Washington to help Kichisaburo Nomura, their ambassador to the United States, in negotiating an agreement with Secretary of State Cordell Hull that would keep the two countries from going to war. "The way his mission is being described in Tokyo," Thomas said, "it's an eleventh-hour effort to preserve the peace between Japan and the United States." On November 18 they learned from Thomas that Tojo "appeared before his parliament today and declared that the armed forces of the Mikado are fully prepared to meet any eventualities. Meanwhile, Ambassador Nomura and Special Envoy Kurusu were closeted for two hours and three quarters with Secretary Hull." On November 19, he told them that "The special emissary from Tokyo and the Japanese Ambassador to Washington are waiting for fresh instructions from their government after their conferences with President Roosevelt and Secretary of State Cordell Hull," and the next night reported that the instructions had been received and "diplomatic parleys were renewed at once."

What Americans did not learn from Thomas or anyone else that month was that the Japanese had offered a deal that Hull would later describe as "preposterous." Agreeing to their proposal, Hull wrote, would have meant "condonement by the United States of Japan's past aggressions, assent to future courses of conquest by Japan, abandonment of the most essential principles of our foreign policy, betrayal of China and Russia [by now an official U.S. ally], and acceptance of the role of silent partner aiding and abetting Japan in her effort to create a Japanese hegemony over the western Pacific and eastern Asia." From that point forward, though Hull and the Japanese went through the motions, "Diplomatically, the situation was virtually hopeless."

Americans did not know this, but they were beginning to suspect it. "From official sources in the capital," Thomas reported on November 28, "we learn that Uncle Sam demands that Japan must consent to get out of China and Indochina and renounce all policies of aggression. The belief is that Tokyo can hardly accept these conditions. So the Japanese-American negotiations would seem to be at the point of collapse." December 1: "At Singapore [a British possession] a state of emergency was proclaimed for the entire Straits Settlements, including the great naval base. From Manila comes a report that a fleet of Japanese warships, sixteen heavy cruisers, and several aircraft carriers, is concentrated around the southern Caroline Islands." December 2: "A British fleet steamed into Singapore today, including a brand-new thirty-five-thousand-ton man-of-war, H.M.S. *Prince of Wales*." December 4: "Tomorrow morning at eleven o'clock the Japanese reply to the United States will be presented." December 5: "The White House has just released the contents of the Japanese message. Tokyo flatly denies that the recent landing of troops in Indochina has any aggressive significance. It is evident that the Japanese want to keep on talking. And this may be the old dodge of sparring for time— stalling."

That was Friday night. Saturday night, in an action that even he deemed useless, Roosevelt sent a message directly to Emperor Hirohito, asking for the withdrawal of all of Japan's forces from territory not her own as the only means of keeping the peace. "This son of man," he remarked to friends after the message, "has just sent his final message to the Son of God."

And at 7:40 A.M., Sunday, December 7, 1941, one world ended and another began in the skies over ninety-six ships of the American Pacific Fleet sitting at rest in Pearl Harbor on the distant, dreaming island of Oahu, Hawaii. Like all wars, it sounded at first like thunder.

PART IX

The Last Adventure

As I was interested in the war, so am I interested in the peace—rather fearfully interested at times. We are on the verge of a great spiritual adventure—the greatest in history—and you have been chosen by the people to be the leader of the world in the direction of peace.

—Letter to President Franklin D. Roosevelt,
December 13, 1944

CHAPTER

· 50 ·

Metamorphosis

D ECEMBER 7 in Washington was a clear, cold, beautiful Sunday. At a
little after two-thirty in the afternoon, Stephen Early, the President's
press secretary, speaking to all three press associations via a conference
call, made this terse announcement: "This is Steve Early at the White
House. At 7:35 A.M., Hawaiian time, the Japanese bombed Pearl Harbor.
The attacks are continuing and—No, I don't know how many are dead."
He did not have much else to tell them at that point. No one yet knew
precisely how bad it was, though it was clear enough already from the
messages flashing into the War Department and the White House that it
was going to be the most devastating attack on an American possession by
a foreign power since Washington itself was burned during the War of
1812. Messengers were dispatched to the links to bring in generals and
admirals who had defied the brisk weather and were playing golf on the
various courses around the city. In Griffith Stadium, where the Redskins
were playing the Philadelphia Eagles in the last home game of the season,
the attention of the twenty-seven thousand fans was diverted when loudspeakers started methodically paging the names of high-level government
officials and army and navy officers who, one by one, got up and left the
stands. When reporters began to catch the drift of things, they, too, got
up and left.

I. F. Stone, the Washington correspondent for the *Nation,* went to the public relations office of the War Department, where he was refused any information on the relative strengths of United States and Japanese forces. The Navy Department was a little more relaxed, he found, giving out data already on the record, which at least saved reporters a trip to the Library of Congress. The mood there, he wrote, was not at all glum: "In the Navy Department reference room women employees, hastily summoned from their homes, sent out for sandwiches and coffee and joked about Japanese bombers. There as elsewhere one encountered a sense of excitement, of adventure, and of relief that a long-expected storm had finally broken."

Out at Headwaters Farm that Sunday, Harold and Jane Ickes were giving a luncheon. On hand were Justice Hugo Black; Ann Dahlman; two new secretaries at the Interior Department, Ellen Downes and Evangeline Bell; Senator Tom Connally of Texas; and Donald Nelson, director of SPAB and purchasing director for the OPM, a man whom newsman David Brinkley described as "an economist who could not control his weight, his shirttail, his hair, his shoelaces or his temper." Ickes was inclined to approve of the bearlike bureaucrat. "I found that he used to live west of me in Hubbard Woods," he wrote, then added, perhaps in reference to shirttails or shoelaces, "I don't know what impression he would have made if I had attempted to judge him on his appearance dissociated from the good job he has been doing with OPM. He seemed energetic and forceful but lacking somewhat in background. Doubtless he has worked hard all of his life and has gotten ahead solely by his energy and ability." These were qualities with which the Secretary could identify.

Most of the guests left when Ickes got a call at about three-thirty from Mike Straus, his press secretary, telling him of the attack. He and Jane and the remaining guests seemed to take the news calmly enough. Later, while Jane, Ann Dahlman, and Ellen Downes were strolling about the farm and Harold was napping, Grace Tully telephoned to say the President had called for a cabinet meeting that night at eight-thirty. Ickes had a light supper, then packed his bag for what might turn out to be an overnight stay in his office bedroom.

All afternoon, a crowd had slowly grown around the front gate of the White House on Pennsylvania Avenue. Some had pulled themselves to the top of the fence to get a better look. Another bunch was packed into West Executive Avenue between the White House grounds and the State Department. As darkness slowly settled on the city, people spoke quietly among themselves and stared at the lighted windows of the White House as if some sort of message would be flashed to them. It did not matter what it might be; they wanted something—anything. They were still there when Ickes arrived at a little after eight for the cabinet meeting. "The people were quiet and serious," he wrote. "They were responding to that human instinct to get near a scene of action even if they could see or hear nothing. The iron gates to the White House grounds were open to admit only those who had a right to be inside. This included a large group of newspaper correspondents who stood on the north portico . . . in the hope that someone would drop an item of important news."

There was plenty of that, as Ickes and the rest of the cabinet—including Harry Hopkins ("He looked pale and ill," Ickes wrote)—learned when they had gathered in a circle around the President's desk and he had been wheeled in. "The President was quite serious," Ickes told his diary.

> There wasn't a wisecrack or a joke or even a smile that was not strained.
>
> As the President told us the story, four of our battleships had been fully or completely sunk. Two of the remaining four were seriously damaged. In addition, lighter craft were sunk or damaged. It was the worst naval disaster in American history. While the Japanese bombers were mainly interested in the fleet, they did not overlook the Army flying fields. These were badly battered and a large but unknown number of our airplanes were put out of commission.

All afternoon, between conferences with State Department people and military personnel, Roosevelt had been working on a speech he planned to give before a joint session of Congress on Monday, asking for a declaration of war against Japan. He read it to the cabinet now, including the line that was to become part of the national lexicon: "Yesterday, December 7, 1941, a date which will live in infamy, the United States was suddenly and deliberately attacked by naval and air forces of the Empire of Japan."

At nine-thirty congressional leaders were called into the room, including Vice President Henry Wallace, Senator Alben Barkley, Representative Sam Rayburn, and Senator Hiram Johnson, who had been one of the stalwarts of the isolationist wing in Congress. The cabinet members pulled back from the President's desk so that the delegation could hear him outline the situation. "The President asked the Congressional leaders when they would be ready to receive him," Harry Hopkins wrote in a memorandum before turning in that night,

> and it was agreed he would appear personally at 12:30 tomorrow. They asked him whether he wanted a declaration of war and what was going to be in the message and he said he had not as yet decided. As a matter of fact the President, of course, knew that he was going to ask for a declaration of war but he also knew that if he stated it to the conference that it would be all over town in five minutes, because it is perfectly footless ever to ask a large group of Congressmen to keep a secret.

When the conference was over, Ickes decided to return to Headwaters Farm in spite of the hour. "With such important news," he wrote, "I felt that I really ought to go home. I had promised Jane to call her up if I should make up my mind to stay in town but I knew that if I called her up I would have to tell her something of what had transpired and she would have a bad night."

Many Americans would, but apparently not Roosevelt, who slept soundly before arising the next morning and getting ready to deliver the most important message twentieth-century Americans had yet heard from one of their Presidents. Before Congress and an estimated sixty million radio listeners (the biggest audience in radio history) he would demonstrate that afternoon the unwavering confidence on which it sometimes seemed the country's own resolution depended—even when the President's strength was sometimes more imagined than real, even when he was in fact beginning to fail. He had been a symbol throughout the troubled, sometimes terrifying years of the thirties—a different symbol to different people, to be sure, serving the convenience of prejudice and engendering as much hate as love—but he would be even more of a symbol in the years to come, when it seemed to millions of Americans that the future of the world was carried on the wide shoulders covered by the flowing blue naval officer's cape he had taken to wearing like a uniform. It was in this perceived strength that even so profound a realist as I. F. Stone—who had hammered the President and his policies on a fairly regular basis in the *Nation*—found his own hope. "My . . . confidence springs from a deep confidence in the President," he wrote when the dark week following Pearl Harbor was done, after Roosevelt had called for and been given his declaration of war, after Guam and the Philippines had been invaded and the Japanese had begun their seemingly inexorable sweep of conquest through most of the Pacific Basin, after Hitler and Mussolini had both declared war on the United States in support of Japan. "I hate to think what we should do without him, and when I drive down to work early in the morning past the White House I cannot help thinking with sympathy of the burdens that weigh him down. On the threshold of war, and perhaps ultimately social earthquake, we may be grateful that our country has his leadership."

Another symbol: on December 9, the light that had illuminated the Capitol with a soft, democratic glow every night for as long as anyone could remember was turned off and would remain off until war's end, a vaguely disturbing reminder for Washingtonians that things were never going to be the same again. Not that they really needed another reminder. The New Deal had changed this enormous southern village; World War II would obliterate it. The impact had begun as early as the summer of 1940, when the fall of France finally demonstrated the full power of Hitler's domination of the Continent and the dimension of England's peril. As the structure of a bureaucratic machine capable of waging war was pieced together by Presidential proclamation and congressional appropriation, it was swiftly accompanied by a population explosion in the ranks of the civil service and an apparent geometric increase in the numbers of hungry entrepreneurs and their representatives who arrived like ants at a picnic determined to carry away with them fat crumbs in the form of government contracts.

Cissy Patterson, who in 1939 had bought both the *Times* and the *Herald* from her old boss, William Randolph Hearst, and merged them into one round-the-clock newspaper, the *Times-Herald,* was not happy. She, like her brother Joseph Patterson at the *New York Daily News* and her cousin Robert McCormick at the *Chicago Tribune,* had been an isolationist, and as the country drew closer to war her contempt for Roosevelt and what remained of the New Deal reached such an acidic level that even the friendship between her and Ickes had been irredeemably corroded (although Jane always maintained that Cissy's antagonism was caused more by jealousy than politics; the imperious doyenne of Dupont Circle, she said, had never forgiven Harold for marrying). Cissy looked around at the new Washington and did not like what she saw. "The once sleepy southern town of charm and grace on the Potomac," she editorialized in the *Times-Herald,*

> has burgeoned into the frenzied capital of the world. Where money pours, power reigns. Here is being enacted a spectacle of imperial waste. It is being enacted on a scale that would have been considered grandiose even in the days of Xerxes, most lavish of the kings of man. . . .
>
> Into this city to direct, touch, fight for or carry away a bit of this money, now tumble 45,000 people a day by train, 1,000 by plane. An almost equal number tumble out again, many with a fistful of arms contracts, many with broken hopes and illusions. Here a conglomerate army of government workers holds forth. As armaments become more of an octopus, so the multitude swells. With this army of jobholders, who hurry down the streets and sidewalks morning, noon, and evening, is a camp-following of amazing proportions. Lobbyists, propagandists, experts of every species, wealthy industrialists, social climbers, inventors, ladies of uneasy virtue and pickpockets infest the city.

What Cissy Patterson saw and hated in 1940 was little more than a hint of the metamorphosis that was to come. In that year there were 139,000 government workers; by 1945 the number would grow to 265,000. Nearly a third of these were women, most of them young women drawn from all quarters and corners of the continent in a search for jobs, excitement, and, with any luck, men. What they found, most of them, was more work than could have been imagined. Daylight saving time—"war time"—was instituted throughout the country, and in Washington working hours were staggered to ease congestion in the streets and offices. The town that had once gone to bed at nine with the rest of Main Street America was now open all night. Official government hours went to forty-four a week in January 1942, then to forty-eight in December. Some agencies instituted fifty-four-hour work weeks. Overtime was a constant even with these hours. "The men may have started this war," a young typist told Sally Reston of *The New York Times,* "but the women are running it." If so, it was at a cost suggested by reporter Scott Hart's memory of a typical scene in lunch-counter restaurants that now stayed open late to accommodate exhausted war workers:

> During the evenings as the war progressed, government girls sat on the counter stools hunched over plates of the first thing they could think of to order without thinking, because thinking hurt. Many raised their forks or spoons slowly. The stains of ink from typewriters discolored their fingers. The fingernails were unattended and their hair straggly. The eyes were staring. Outside, the night turned bronze under dimmed street lights. To the girls, the night was a time of day, and the day wasn't ended. This was war, and they felt themselves in it, but they didn't know exactly what it was all about except that the Japanese had attacked the United States. . . . They knew they were tired, and something screamed for release of the mind and the body. A few broke under the strain. Others stepped into their places, and little was made of it beyond murmurings.

Five thousand new people were added to the city's population every month, until by the end of 1943 the number reached a wartime high of 839,013. Trees were ripped up and streets widened to accommodate automobile traffic that choked the city in spite of the staggered hours. The Chesapeake and Potomac telephone system urged people to use their telephones as little as possible; the company's lines could not handle the flow of communications. Housing was impossible. The owners of the city's 104,000 private homes were encouraged, as a patriotic gesture, to rent "decent living accommodations" to government workers; many did, often at rents that were unpatriotically exorbitant for accommodations that mutilated the definition of decency. Cheaper but inexpressibly depressing were the scores of TDUs (temporary dwelling units) slapped together by the Defense Homes Corporation for government workers, primitive hives with cell-like apartments that encrusted every vacant space not occupied by similarly crude buildings hastily being assembled by private contractors. Suburban populations were bloated far beyond the ability of communities to provide necessary services, particularly across the Potomac River in Arlington, where the world's largest office building was rising with incredible speed; begun in August 1941, the War Department's Pentagon Building would be ready for occupancy throughout most of its hundreds of offices by the summer of the following year.

Other wartime government offices were less impressive. On Constitution Avenue and the Mall, where a few "temps" still remained from World War I, ugly rows of transitory office buildings spread, and other clusters appeared along both sides of the Reflecting Pool in front of the Lincoln Memorial and all over the grounds of the Washington Monument. In most neighborhoods throughout town, similar growths bloomed, and what the government did not build it tended to take, moving into 358 office buildings, small hotels, and other structures—including homes and apartment houses—that previously had been used or occupied by private citizens. Basketball arenas, concert halls, and skating rinks were seized and converted into enormous typing pools. The most voracious portion of the government in this regard was the military, and the most voracious portion of the military was the navy, secure in FDR's admiration. Two weeks after Pearl Harbor, the navy moved into the fashionable Mount Vernon Seminary, a school for young women, while its students were still on their Christmas break, explaining to school officials and the Washington Planning Commission in the maddeningly arrogant fashion of military folk everywhere that zoning regulations did not apply to the United States Navy and that the communications facility it intended to establish on the Mount Vernon campus was "vital to the war effort and its nature should not be publicized." When the school's administrator asked what he was expected to do with the girls when they returned, the navy replied that that was his problem, not theirs. The property was worth $5 million; the navy paid $1.1 million for it. The girls ended up going to school on the vacant top floor of the nearby Garfinckel's department store.

The military's presence dominated the city in other ways as well. Washington had always possessed a vaguely military look, what with all the Civil War statues and cannon scattered around its parks and traffic circles and the presence of uniforms and military bands at nearly all civic events of any stature. But there had been a sort of genteel, officer-class feeling about it that could not be taken quite seriously; it was not exactly Gilbert and Sullivan, but it was close. No more. The military was everywhere, and everywhere it was clear that this was serious business. Fully armed military guards stood at the entrances to the most sensitive wartime agencies and after government haberdashers managed to overcome the uniform shortage at the beginning of the war, the streets and public buildings of the town bristled with army, navy, and marine officers dressed for business. Not all the uniforms were worn by men; women in the olive drab of the army's WAC and the air force's WAFS, the blue of the navy's WAVES, and the forest green of the female marines blossomed like muted flowers. Khaki-colored army vehicles crowded the avenues and machine guns with antiaircraft capabilities ornamented the tops of many government buildings—including the Interior Department, where a gun accidentally discharged one afternoon. Walton Onslow, a Washington reporter who worked for Ickes as a speechwriter for a time during the early part of the war, told the story: "We all knew a gun was atop our building, and my office was just under the roof. This day, I heard a chuff, chuff, chuff from overhead, and I said to myself, 'My God, they're firing that gun!' It occurred to me that just maybe they were testing the thing with blanks. But the next thing we heard was that a frightened guard at the Lincoln Memorial had yelled into a telephone, 'They're bombing the Memorial!' " Damage to the Memorial a quarter of a mile away was not serious, but Ickes was not pleased that his building had been used to launch a barrage against one of his monuments and the army was made to pay.

As usual, the portion of the city's population that felt most profoundly the impact of all this change was the black community. Some of it, in fact, disappeared, as housing for white government workers and government office buildings crowded black people out of such traditional neighborhoods as Foggy Bottom and parts of Georgetown (fated someday to be among the most fashionable white enclaves in the District of Columbia). No one seemed to know (and most did not care) where the displaced blacks went, but it certainly was not into government-sponsored housing; the National Capital Housing Authority—successor to the old Alley Dwelling Authority—would build only one-fourth as much housing for blacks as for whites during the war (even that built for whites was not enough) and of the 30,700 dwelling units private contractors had been authorized to build, only two hundred had been put up for blacks. Rigid discrimination in nongovernment housing, of course, kept them out of all-white residential areas and apartment buildings even when they could afford the prices.

For those black people who could find a place to live in and around the District, there was plenty of work. As early as February 1941, the Family

Service Association reported that virtually all of the city's semiskilled workmen had found jobs, and for the next four years a sizable contingent of the "government girls" who occupied the typing pools and cubbyholes of Washington were black women. For both men and women, of course, discrimination in placement and promotion in and out of government prevailed; the jobs they got were consistently at the lower end of the scale in both wages paid and responsibilities assumed.

Early in the summer of 1941, A. Philip Randolph, head of the Brotherhood of Sleeping Car Porters, the most powerful black union in the country, had joined with Walter White of the NAACP and Eugene Davidson of the relatively militant New Negro Alliance (it had staged a few lunch-counter sit-ins around the city) to call for a July 4 march on Washington of at least fifty thousand blacks to protest job discrimination. This had gotten the government's attention, as it was designed to do. Late in June of the year, Randolph and White were asked to the White House to discuss the situation with William Knudsen and Sidney Hillman of OPM, Aubrey Williams of the National Youth Administration, and Mayor Fiorello La Guardia, acting as a go-between. In exchange for calling off the march, the government men promised, the President would appoint a commission to investigate discrimination and recommend an appropriate Executive Order. Not good enough, Randolph and White said. At a second meeting on the morning of June 24, La Guardia offered a plan that would assure that no government contractors would be allowed to discriminate. Still not good enough, the black representatives said. That afternoon, in total surrender to the inevitable, the White House people prepared the language for a sweeping Executive Order regarding fair employment practices that established rules ensuring nondiscrimination in all federal offices and agencies and all plants with defense contracts. On June 25 Roosevelt signed it.

It was a historic document—but, like many such, limited by reality. Prejudice and resentment on the part of unions and independent employees alike undercut the law and the War Manpower Commission's ability to enforce it, and antagonism from southern congressmen and senators who knew all too well how to use the weapon of appropriations to get their way stifled it at many turns. What is more, the law did not apply to most of the private sector, where old habits continued. As the most grievous example, the Manpower Commission's unsuccessful four-year effort to force the District's Capital Transit Company—privately owned, but a public utility nonetheless—to start hiring black bus and trolley operators was punctuated throughout by company intransigence, employee resistance, the threats of strikes and boycotts, general discontent, and irritation between the races, all of this coupled with the fear that riots like those which exploded in Detroit in the summer of 1943 would erupt in Washington, too. No riots took place, but once again expectations had been raised without being fully satisfied, and resentment continued through the war years—along with a rise in the crime rate and a strain of frustration among blacks that would be carried intact into the postwar years.

Black Washingtonians might or might not have taken comfort from the fact that at least the documents of freedom were safe. A little over two weeks after Pearl Harbor, Librarian of Congress Archibald MacLeish had supervised proceedings as the original Declaration of Independence, in which all men were declared to be created equal and endowed by their Creator with certain unalienable rights, and the original Constitution, whose Thirteenth Amendment had freed the slaves and whose Fourteenth and Fifteenth amendments had guaranteed blacks basic citizenship rights, were carefully removed from their display cases in the Library of Congress, placed between sheets of acid-free manila paper, bound tightly with Scotch tape between all-rag, neutral millboards, and slid into a bronze container, which was then padlocked shut after the documents had been heated to drive all moisture from them. The bronze container was then sealed with lead and put in a metal-bound box surrounded by rock wool. The whole package, by now weighing about 150 pounds, was taken by armed convoy to Union Station, where it was placed in a special compartment in an otherwise empty car on the Baltimore & Ohio Railroad and carried off to Louisville, Kentucky. Here, the box was put in an army truck, carried out to Fort Knox, and locked in a vault where the minions of the Axis would never find it.

CHAPTER

· 51 ·

Oil, Arms, and the Man

T HE SECRETARY OF THE INTERIOR started his own wartime service as a belligerent and remained one for the duration. His enemy was generic German and Japanese aggression, of course, but there were other enemies closer to home. There was Harold Smith in the Bureau of the Budget, for instance. One of the duties Smith had assumed was the responsibility for finding room to put all the expanding war agencies. One solution, he decided in December, was decentralization—move agencies that had little or nothing to do with the war effort to other cities, thereby making room in Washington for war work. Roosevelt agreed, and over the next several months eleven federal agencies with more than twenty thousand employees occupying two million square feet moved to places like Richmond, Chicago, Philadelphia, and Kansas City to wait out the war.

There was not a single head of a single affected agency in Washington who did not resist these moves with all the energy at his command, but none fought more bitterly than Harold L. Ickes. In the middle of December, while the Secretary was at home recovering from a cold, Smith had called him and said he was going to recommend the removal of the Bureau of Indian Affairs, the National Park Service, and the Fish and Wildlife Service. "I told him," Ickes reported in his diary, "that if we were treated fairly with other departments I wouldn't let a squawk out of me, but I insisted that the first agency that ought to be taken out of Interior was the

Office of Education." Smith maintained that the Office of Education had wartime importance, but Ickes ascribed its favored status to the friendship between the commissioner of education, John W. Studebaker, and Eleanor Roosevelt. Studebaker, Ickes told Smith, "had been running to Mrs. Roosevelt to keep his organization in Washington and Smith admitted that this was probably true. I told Smith that it made me damned tired to have to submit to this kind of influence."

When the conversation ended, the Secretary's understanding was that they would talk again before any final decisions were made—but that same afternoon the order went out from Smith's office to move National Parks, the BIA, and Fish and Wildlife to Chicago. Education could stay where it was. Burlew called Ickes to tell him that his people in the affected agencies felt that their boss had let them down. This and Smith's arbitrary decision put a fire under the Secretary. "I hope that I can go to the office tomorrow," he wrote on Sunday, December 21, "and, if possible, I am going to start in and bombard Smith. I shall insist that, in order to save my face with my own employees, I am at least entitled to have the Office of Education not only chased out of my building, but out of the City of Washington. It makes my gorge rise that petticoat influence can be effective in an instance where the argument for transferring the agency out of Washington is overwhelming."

He did make it to work and he did start to bombard Smith in a campaign that lasted for more than three months. He obligingly offered up a list of other agencies that might be moved instead of his (always excepting the Office of Education)—the Veterans Bureau, for instance, or the Federal Trade Commission or the Federal Housing Administration. "They don't have to operate in Washington at all," he said. Smith, as tough as his petitioner, did not buy the idea. Ickes offered to build temporary buildings at the Wildlife Refuge in Patuxent, Maryland, to house Fish and Wildlife Service people. No deal. He offered to remodel an old CCC barracks in Rock Creek Park for the use of some war agency. No, thank you, Smith said. Ickes offered to let the Park Service, the Bituminous Coal Division, and other agencies go if he could keep BIA and Fish and Wildlife. No.

By the middle of March 1942, the Secretary had worn himself out on the subject. Smith was adamant. On Friday, March 20, Ickes called all employees of the three affected bureaus into the Interior Department auditorium to announce his capitulation. "I wanted to tell them how sorry I was," he wrote in his diary, "and how I had done my best to have this order either amended or repealed. I tried to make the best out of a bad situation for them. I appealed to their loyalty, telling them that we were all soldiers and that this was an order from the Commander-in-Chief. I was successful in putting a light enough touch into my remarks to make them laugh on three or four occasions so that I think they left the auditorium in better spirits than they were in when they came."

Smith also was embroiled in Ickes's second (and simultaneous) great conflict of 1942—one which might have been called the Battle of Economic Warfare. It, too, began in December 1941. On the seventeenth Roosevelt had restructured a prewar agency called the Economic Defense Board into a new entity, this called the Board of Economic Warfare. Vice President Henry Wallace was named its chairman, and Wallace appointed Milo Perkins BEW's director. On the twenty-third a letter over FDR's signature went to Wallace, instructing him to set up a "policy subcommittee under the Board of Economic Warfare" in order to "provide and to safeguard an adequate oil and gasoline supply for the use of our Country and our allies in the Far East and in other areas of the world outside of the United States."

The Secretary got word of this move soon enough, and on the twenty-ninth wrote Roosevelt to point out that the directive subverted the order given to Ickes on May 28 making him petroleum coordinator for national defense:

> I do not see how it can be gainsaid that your letter of authority to Henry Wallace distinctly and substantially diminishes the powers indicated in your letter to me of May 28. Of course, I do not question your power to modify the power heretofore granted to me. I wish, however, that it might have been done after consulation with me. I would have liked, at the very least, to have had the opportunity to demonstrate to you that my operations as Petroleum Coordinator have not been such a failure as would justify the public rebuke that your delegation of some of my most important functions to the Economic Warfare Board so clearly means.

"However," Ickes added blithely, "until you tell me so directly, I will refuse to believe that you intended the result that your letter to Henry Wallace will effectuate unless it is withdrawn or modified." He suspected conspiracy: "That certain persons in Washington . . . have been looking for an opportunity to acquire power for themselves, even at the expense of the war effort," he told the President, "I am fully aware. I do not think that I would need even a second guess to disclose the name of the draftsman of the letter that you signed to Henry Wallace."

The draftsman in question was Harold Smith, who admitted as much to Ickes a few days later—though he insisted that the Secretary was putting the wrong interpretation on the letter. If so, Ickes wanted to know, why was Henry Wallace acting as if he was now in charge of all foreign distribution of oil? Ickes told Smith that immediately after Ickes and Davies had called a conference of oilmen into the Interior Department to discuss the foreign oil situation on December 26, the same executives had gone off to meet secretly with Max Thornburg, a vice president of the California-Texas Oil Company and the State Department's petroleum expert. Ickes believed that Thornburg was a front man for Henry Wallace, and he may have been right. When Thornburg was done with them, Wallace had then sent telegrams to each of the oil representatives thanking them for their cooperation. This action suggested that Wallace was in charge of foreign petroleum issues, and Ickes was determined to scotch that idea. "I made it clear to Smith," Ickes recorded in his diary, "that I was not going to stand for this . . . without protest."

Smith tried for compromise. On January 5, at his behest, Ickes and Davies met with him and Milo Perkins. Ickes was deliberately nasty. "I went out of my way to make some harsh remarks about Wallace," he wrote, "in the hope that Perkins would carry them back to him. This was on the theory that Wallace would avoid an open fight with me if he could. Among other things, when Perkins remarked, 'You do not like Wallace, but I do,' my reply was 'No, I do not. I do not like any man whose path in Washington is strewn with the maimed bodies of men who were his friends.' I also remarked that it was characteristic of Wallace to sneak up on a man in the dark and stick a knife into his back." Ickes was nevertheless willing to cooperate, he said. While he refused to be part of the Board of Economic Warfare's policy subcommittee in any way, he would go so far as to follow strict policy guidelines established by that subcommittee as to which country was to get which amount of oil at which time—so long as his agency remained in charge of the actual distribution. "I saw a sharp distinction," he said,

> between foreign policy with respect to oil and the implementing of such policy. Smith swung more and more to our point of view. But Perkins would have none of it. . . . He insisted that I should appoint a member of his proposed sub-committee. I told him that I would do no such thing. Toward the end he became pretty angry. He said "Your refusal to name a man means one of two things: either that the President will have to withdraw or revise his letter of December 23, or that there will have to be a new Petroleum Coordinator." My answer to this was that he was precisely right.

When the meeting broke up two hours after it had begun, Smith, who was still in search of a compromise, took Ickes and Davies aside and told them that they should continue to administer distribution in the foreign field—which for the most part meant exports to Great Britain, Russia, and the South American nations—until some kind of agreement could be reached with the Board of Economic Warfare. Ickes took this to mean that at least he had gotten the upper hand in the struggle.

It was with some discernible relief that he wrote to Anna and John Boettiger on January 7 to report that Jane had come through a painful operation at Johns Hopkins on January 2 for the removal of her tonsils and adenoids—"The doctor found a very bad condition, including even pus in the tonsils, but Jane is coming along fast now. She was able to give me orders over the telephone today." Family business taken care of, he then outlined the situation with regard to the "raid" on his petroleum adminis-tration by Wallace and Perkins. "All that they proposed to do," he wrote, perhaps unconsciously carrying out the medical theme,

> was to cut a sound and living organism out of a well-functioning body. . . . I have been fighting with my back to the wall ever since. It looks today as if I would come out all right, but one never knows. Sometimes I am glad I am as old as I am because if I were not I might be damned fool enough to want to stay on in public office. It is certainly something to be avoided at all costs, unless one wants to be a comfortable fat cat, who never makes any trouble for anyone and for whom, therefore, no one makes any trouble.

No one (including the Secretary) could or would accuse Ickes of making no trouble for anyone, and, as it turned out, the one man who did not want any part of trouble was Wallace. On January 19, Max Thorn-burg, now acting openly as an intermediary, told Ickes that Wallace had authorized him to work out a compromise. He had written a memoran-dum that established lines of authority much as Ickes had outlined them during the acrimonious meeting of January 5. He showed it to Ickes, who cheerfully scrawled on it, "Accepted in principle, HLI," after which the memorandum was passed on to Wallace for his response. That took another week, but the Vice President finally wrote Ickes directly to say that he, too, had initialed the Thornburg memorandum as representing his understanding of the powers of his agency versus those of the Petro-leum Coordinator. "As this was a complete victory for my position," Ickes graciously told his diary, "I had to regard the matter as settled."

Not quite. Ickes had authority over the acquisition and distribution of petroleum products for the war effort, but he was still operating under the mandate of the Petroleum Administration for National Defense. On January 17, contrarily, Roosevelt had changed the name of the Office of Production Management to the War Production Board (WPB), had abol-ished the Supply Priorities and Allocation Board, folding it into the WPB, and had placed Donald Nelson in charge of the whole business, with a new set of regulations and responsibilities (Leon Henderson would remain—at least for a while—as the head of the still autonomous Office of Price Administration). Ickes wanted a similar name change and restructured organization for his petroleum job, particularly with respect to its relationship with the Bureau of Economic Warfare and the other federal war agencies. A reasonable request, certainly, and Roosevelt agreed with it in principle. Easier agreed upon than done, however. Working out the stipulations of an applicable Executive Order that would satisfy Ickes, Smith, Nelson, Henderson, Wallace, Perkins, Jesse Jones of the Department of Commerce and the RFC, Cordell Hull and Sumner Welles of the State Department, Henry Stimson of the War Department, Frank Knox of the Navy Department, Attorney General Francis Biddle, and the oil company executives serving as advisers on the Petroleum Industry Council for National Defense (whose own name would soon be changed to the Petroleum Industry War Council)—not to mention a very busy President of the United States—took more than eleven months of negotiating and revision among all parties before a final Executive Order establishing the Petroleum Administration for War was approved and signed by Roosevelt.

It was not until December 2, 1942, then, that Ickes officially became petroleum administrator for war and Davies deputy administrator. In fact, the two men had been operating as such for months. They had no choice—and if the bureaucratic conniving, manipulation, and bad spirit that had gone into the effort to establish his authority showed Ickes at his most infuriatingly stubborn, it should be noted that what he managed to do with that authority helped to win a war. Within a month of Pearl Harbor, Admiral Karl Dönitz of the German navy had launched a major submarine campaign against American shipping off the East Coast. The result, naval historian Samuel Eliot Morison would write, was "one of the greatest merchant-ship massacres in history." Between January and July, Nazi U-boats sank more than three hundred merchant ships along the eastern seaboard, off Bermuda, and in the Caribbean. Fifty-five of these had been oil tankers, reducing the supply of oil to the East Coast to about 173,000 barrels a day—less than 10 percent of the region's requirements and one-fifth the amount that had arrived by tanker daily in December 1941.

To make up the difference, Ickes and Davies worked around the clock with railroads and suddenly cooperative tank-car owners and operators, and by July 1942 were moving about 800,000 barrels a day into District 1. Existing pipeline systems and barge carriers along the Inland Waterways system brought in another 200,000 barrels a day. It still was not enough, could not be enough. As early as the middle of February, Ickes had already decided it was time to revive an idea left over from the previous year. In September 1941 a "pipeline committee" of the Petroleum Industry Council for National Defense, headed by W. Alton Jones, had recommended the construction of two pipelines from the oil-producing areas of the Southwest to eastern refining areas. The first—twenty-four inches in diameter and dubbed the "Big Inch"—would run north from Longview, Texas, to Norris City, Illinois, and east from there to Phoenix City, Pennsylvania, for a total of 1,254 miles. The second—twenty inches in diameter and called the "Little Big Inch"—would run from Beaumont, Texas, to Norris City, and then to Linden, New Jersey, for a total of 1,475 miles. The Big Inch could handle up to 300,000 barrels a day, the Little Big Inch 235,000.

Unfortunately, the amount of steel that would be needed for both lines amounted to nearly 650,000 tons, which would build a great many tanks, planes, jeeps, and other vehicles of war. Donald Nelson at the SPAB had turned down Ickes's first request for the material. Now, with ships sinking within sight of Miami Beach and the New Jersey shore, Ickes applied for the steel again, this time to the WPB, but on February 24 Nelson turned him down again. Ickes refused to give up. In April he wrote directly to Roosevelt to plead his case; Roosevelt passed the letter on to Nelson. The WPB director met with Ickes, the Secretary noted in his diary, and

> argued strenuously that it simply wasn't possible to allocate so much steel. He told, in some detail, about other demands for steel. I argued that without the pipeline we could not supply New England industries and that if these industries couldn't get fuel they couldn't turn out essential war materials. I insisted that oil was indispensable; that without it tanks and ships and airplanes, however many we might have of them, were useless. Nelson continued to shake his head and insist that no steel was available. He believed that sufficient oil could be transported by other means but he didn't tell me by what other means.

Ickes applied again in May. On June 10, Nelson finally, if reluctantly, parted with enough steel to build the first leg of the Big Inch from Longview to Norris City. Construction of the line began on June 23, 1942, and on February 19, 1943, the first Texas oil reached Norris City, where it was loaded into trains of tank cars. By then, the remaining segment of the Big Inch had been approved and it was completed to Phoenix City in August. In January 1943 the Little Big Inch got its own approval. Construction got under way on April 21, and the first oil reached Linden in December. By war's end, an average of 390,000 barrels of oil a day were pouring through the gullets of the Big Inch and Little Big Inch lines. The cost of the two, financed by the RFC through the

Defense Plant Corporation, came to nearly $150 million—but from the moment of the Big Inch's completion, the problem of supply to the East Coast ended.

Until then, of course, supply remained far below need—or at least demand, a problem for which Ickes and Davies were hard put to find ready solutions. Early in February they had recommended to the WPB that the hours of operation be reduced for eastern service stations and that a massive public relations effort be made to persuade people to conserve on gas and fuel oil voluntarily—and never mind the fact that this device had not worked the previous year. The WPB helped things along in March by cutting shipments of gasoline to service stations and bulk plants by 20 percent, then a month later by a full one-third. It still was not enough, and on April 22 Leon Henderson announced that a rationing system for the seventeen states of the eastern seaboard would go into effect on May 15. Motorists would be limited to three gallons of gas a week as a basic allowance. In spite of the fact that there was, as Bruce Catton later described it, "a confusion of tongues and a blowing of great winds" in opposition, the system went into operation on schedule.

The District 1 rationing program was a stopgap measure at best. As the weeks went by, it was becoming more and more clear to those willing to admit it that nationwide rationing sooner or later would have to be put into effect no matter how much oil might be moved from one part of the country to the other. Quite aside from the fact that even during the first two months of the war the military's need for regular gasoline, high-octane aviation fuel, kerosene, lubricants of varying weights, and fuel oil would more than triple, and quite aside from the fact that the United States was still supplying its allies with much of their oil, there was the question of rubber consumption.

As early as the summer of 1940, it had been clear that any kind of Japanese expansion into such rubber-producing areas of the Far East as Java and the Malay Peninsula would effectively cut off supplies of that necessity to the United States. With that likelihood in mind, on June 25, 1940, Congress passed legislation creating the Rubber Reserve Company as a subsidiary of Jesse Jones's RFC. The new agency was empowered to start stockpiling raw rubber from whatever sources it could find. Most of those sources in the years before Pearl Harbor were controlled by a British-Dutch cartel, and Jones maintained that the cartel's reluctance to cooperate (it feared the Americans would dump supplies on the market once the war was over), together with consumer demand in the United States for 900,000 tons of automobile tires a year, prevented him from piling up more than 630,356 tons by December 1941.

But the Rubber Reserve Company also had been authorized to finance the construction of synthetic rubber plants. In 1940 private industry was producing about five thousand tons of synthetic rubber a year from neoprene and butadiene—derivatives of alcohol and petroleum—but Edward R. Stettinius and William L. Batt of the National Defense Advisory Committee estimated that 100,000 tons a year would have to be produced in wartime and that one hundred million dollars ought to be spent to finance the plants necessary to maintain that level of production. Jones took their recommendation to the President, who, the Commerce Secretary reported in his memoirs, was not concerned:

> He told me that we could always build the necessary plants in a year's time and that we would always have ample notice if it should become necessary. Either the President thought there would be no necessity for building a synthetic rubber industry or he was woefully ignorant of the problem. I advised Messrs. Stettinius and Batt of the President's attitude. They were greatly disappointed and concerned. Mr. Batt pounded my office table with his fist and said he would have to do it (meaning the President would have to O.K. it). To that I replied that I had been working for and with President Roosevelt for a good many years and had not yet seen anyone make him do anything that he did not want to do.

Roosevelt authorized the expenditure of no more than twenty-five million dollars. In truth, Jones did not push as hard as he might have, for the business worried his banker's mind. "The whole idea of setting up what amounted to an untried industry," he wrote, "was greatly speculative, involving processes still in the experimental stage." (Not quite true: Du Pont had been producing neoprene on a small but commercially viable scale since 1933.) What is more, most of the major oil and chemical companies had developed various processes which they guarded from one another jealously, and getting them to cooperate, Jones knew, was going to be nettlesome. Finally, the British-Dutch rubber cartel viewed the automobile-addicted United States as its biggest potential customer for raw rubber after the war (no matter who won) and exerted what influence it could to discourage the development of a competitive synthetic rubber industry in this country.

For various reasons, then, the rubber situation was at a critical point when the Japanese attacked Pearl Harbor, and only an effort of uncommon magnitude was going to make enough of the stuff available to wage war. Jones deservedly took most of the heat for the shortage. "The rubber failure was his failure," Ickes would write old friend Stacey Mosser in April 1942. "I haven't any hesitation in saying to you, as I have said to some of my friends here, that Jones should have been fired long ago. If you want a real example of what big business will do for the country in a time of crisis, regard Jones' record." It was a judgment shared by many observers at the time—although one of them, Bruce Catton, would later dilute the criticism by dividing the responsibility. "[I]f apportioning the blame was important," he wrote, "it was obvious that Jesse Jones didn't deserve all of it; OPM was entitled to some, too, for it had failed to push through either an adequate synthetic program or a proper stockpiling program."

In any case, once the United States entered the war, Jones moved with admirable speed. In February he brought eighteen executives from such companies as Phillips Petroleum, Dow Chemical, Standard Oil of New Jersey, and Monsanto Chemical into Washington, where they met one morning at ten o'clock and worked almost straight through until the following afternoon on a program to pool their secrets and their finances and operate under the aegis of the Rubber Reserve Company to produce the goal of 400,000 tons of synthetic rubber a year at a cost of about a thousand dollars a ton. (By the end of the war, annual production would in fact top 865,000 tons.)

Meanwhile, until such time as supplies sufficient to satisfy both domestic and military needs were available (a happy state that was never quite achieved), something had to be done about consumption. Arthur Newhall, whom Donald Nelson had installed at the WPB as rubber coordinator, had already made it clear that the tires on which the average American was driving were the only tires he could expect to have legally for as long as the war continued. There had not been much outcry at this news—perhaps because people could not quite imagine a time when something they had always had for the asking would not be available; by the time their tires wore out, something else surely would come along as a substitute. There was not much chance of that, however, and one obvious option open to the government was to ration gasoline to cut down on domestic automobile driving and thus prolong the life of tires. As early as May 1942 both Roosevelt and Nelson had mentioned this as a possibility in public statements.

Rationing was something Americans could imagine easily enough— and imagining it, dislike intensely. They voiced their dislike to their representatives in Congress. This was the first war year, but it also was an election year, and the voice of the people was attended to with that gravity which members of Congress reserve for those biennial moments when their jobs are on the line. Hearing that voice, Congress itself began to grumble, a sound to which Roosevelt's own ear was exquisitely sensitive. He changed his tune. During a press conference at the end of May, he announced that there had been a great deal of "overexcitement" about the rubber situation and that much progress was being made in the development of synthetics. This encouraged some hundred members of Congress to adopt a resolution opposing gasoline rationing "until such time as Congress was convinced" that it was necessary.

Nelson, Henderson, and the WPB's rubber man, Arthur Newhall, were appalled. They requested a meeting with the President to outline the real situation and on June 5 gathered with Roosevelt, Ickes, Joseph B. Eastman, coordinator of transportation, and Librarian of Congress Archibald MacLeish, who was doubling as head of the Office of Facts and Figures. Nelson, Henderson, and Newhall offered their best estimates of the situation. Roosevelt remained unconvinced. Ickes chose this moment to announce that, according to figures he had seen, there were about a million tons of scrap rubber available in the country. Why not institute a scrap rubber drive? Ickes doubtless thought of this as an interim measure, but Roosevelt seized upon it as the solution to his political dilemma: he immediately told the Secretary to set up an appropriate structure under the supervision of the Petroleum Industry War Council, and on June 12, during one of his fireside chats, urged Americans to bring old tires, rubber raincoats, gloves, shoes, garden hoses, and anything else they could spare to their local gasoline stations for collection. They would be paid a penny a pound, or twenty dollars a ton (the oil companies would then sell it to the RFC for twenty-five dollars a ton, the difference of five dollars going to various war-related charities).

This was perfectly fine, as far as it went; it just did not go far enough. The estimate of one million tons—which Ickes may have gotten from the copy of a letter that Jones had sent to Nelson on February 27 claiming the presence of that much—apparently was greatly exaggerated. After the two-week drive was over, the total brought in was so embarrassing that Ickes snapped at a press conference that "we suspect that there are people hoarding rubber, and there may even be people in official life who are doing a little hoarding."* Roosevelt extended the drive for another two weeks, but all the campaign ever produced was 454,000 tons. Nevertheless, in a March 8, 1943, letter to William R. Boyd, Jr., then chairman of the Petroleum Industry War Council, Ickes put the best face he could on the effort (and provided the President with a copy as a matter of courtesy—or to remind FDR what he had gotten the Secretary into):

---

* Ickes became a little unhinged by frustration, if a story told by Bruce Catton is on the mark. The Secretary, he wrote in 1948, "tried to contribute to the campaign the rubber floor mats from the Interior Department buildings. These mats were owned, however, by the Public Buildings Administration, over which Ickes had no control, and the Public Buildings

It was, in a sense, just a part of the morning report when Deputy Administrator Davies told me the other day that March 10 was to be the deadline for shipment by the oil companies of the remainder of the scrap rubber which they collected during last summer's campaign. But, to me, it was much more than merely that. To me, it was a reminder of an outstandingly important job that was done outstandingly well. . . . The results are now history: approximately 454,000 tons of scrap rubber added to the Nation's stockpile. My thought at this time, however, is that I earnestly hope that, because it is history, the campaign will not be forgotten.

It was, though. By the end of July 1942 even Roosevelt was beginning to realize that he was going to have to do something drastic. Congress had just passed a bill to set up an independent agency for the manufacture of synthetic rubber from alcohol. This would take responsibility away from the WPB and, as Ickes noted in his diary, "could create hell generally and the worst of the bill is that it could set a precedent by which Congress might set up any number of authorities with respect to the war." Roosevelt would have to veto the bill, Ickes believed, and furthermore endorsed an idea that had come from Bernard Baruch to set up a special committee to look into the whole situation and make a report to the President he could then use to persuade the nation that gasoline rationing was the only answer. Roosevelt had already asked Chief Justice Harlan Fiske Stone if he would head up such an investigation. Stone had turned him down, and Roosevelt probably was already thinking along the same lines as his Secretary of the Interior when Ickes called him on July 29 to propose that he

commandeer Bernie for this job. I pointed out that Bernie had the confidence of the people. He isn't a Government official and he commands the respect of Congress on the whole more than any man in public life. He has far more prestige than most men in public life. He also knows how to get results. The President thought well of the suggestion and asked me what I thought of associating with Bernie President [James B.] Conant of Harvard and Lyman J. Briggs, director of the Bureau of Standards. I thought that this would work out all right.

That settled, events moved swiftly. The next day, Roosevelt sent Baruch a note that managed to appeal to the old speculator's vanity, his

---

Administration stopped him. . . . Visiting the White House one day, Ickes seized a rubber mat at the doorway to the Executive Offices, rolled it up, handed it to his chauffeur, and told him to take it to the nearest scrap rubber collection center. White House Secretary Early told reporters this was perfectly okay; nobody at the White House would try to get the mat back." In any event, it should be added, most floor mats were made of rubber that had already been reclaimed and were thus good only for making *new* floor mats.

patriotic duty, and his previous experience in one fell swoop: "Because you are 'an ever present help in time of trouble' will you 'do it again'?" Baruch would—and so would Conant and Briggs. On August 6, Roosevelt vetoed the synthetic rubber bill and a little over a month later Baruch's Rubber Survey Committee made its report. Its conclusions came as no surprise to anyone (including, by now, Roosevelt):

> We find the existing situation to be so dangerous that unless corrective measures are taken immediately this country will face both a military and civilian collapse. The naked facts present a warning that dare not be ignored. . . .
>
> Therefore this committee conceives its first duty to be the maintenance of a rubber reserve that will keep our armed forces fighting and our essential civilian wheels turning. This can best be done by "bulling through" the present gigantic synthetic program and by safeguarding jealously every ounce of rubber in the country. . . . To dissipate our stocks of rubber is to destroy one of our chief weapons of war.

The report recommended the wholesale expansion of the synthetic rubber program, the enforcement of a thirty-five-mile-an-hour speed limit, and nationwide gasoline rationing—and had precisely the effect that had been hoped for it. Before it was issued, a Gallup poll asked a sampling of Americans, "Are you in favor of nationwide gasoline rationing to conserve tires?" Forty-nine percent had favored it, 44 percent opposed it, and 7 percent had expressed no opinion. After the Baruch report, the results were 73 percent, 22 percent, and 5 percent, respectively. And on December 1, 1942, under the aegis of Leon Henderson at the OPA, gasoline rationing finally began.*

With the question of domestic allotments finally settled, Ickes and Davies could concentrate on meeting the needs of war. Those were not merely considerable, they were historic in dimension. No other war in history—no other *event* in history—had ever required so much of a single product. Like the activities of the Public Works Administration during the first six years of his New Deal career, the accomplishments of the Petroleum Administration for War in meeting this need made for a record in which the Secretary could, and did, take a full measure of justifiable pride. Like those for the PWA, the logistics involved in the job of

* Rationing lasted longer than Henderson, who resigned a few weeks later—pleading poor eyesight and a bad back. In fact, pressure on the admittedly radical price administrator (who occupied an unpopular job in the first place) from such reactionary members of Congress as Martin Dies and J. Parnell Thomas and the constant pillorying he got from their friends in the press finally wore him down. He was replaced by Chester Bowles, a more moderate but no less dedicated administrator, who drove the enemies of the OPA to distraction by remaining inconveniently in the middle of the political road.

providing oil for the war effort were staggering. When the war began, Ralph Davies estimated, the army alone possessed fifty-seven different kinds of trucks, jeeps, armored cars, and other machines—1.5 million American soldiers, he said, would "ride to battle in 300,000 vehicles." At the end of the first year of the war, it would be taking two gallons of gasoline a day to support every soldier in uniform. That need was met. So was the need for more than 200,000 barrels a day of aviation fuel and thousands of additional barrels of diesel fuel and residual fuel oil for navy vessels, as well as all other forms of refined petroleum used for everything from lubrication to explosives. In 1941 total military procurement accounted for a mere 25.1 million barrels out of the country's total domestic production of more than 1.4 billion barrels; at war's end, the military was taking 588.1 million barrels out of total production of 1.7 billion— almost precisely one-third. All of it, one way or another, was produced and distributed under the supervision of the Petroleum Administration for War—and if neither Ickes nor Davies could actually claim to have stood over every well as every barrel got sucked out of the ground for nearly four years, they deserved their fair share of the credit given the PAW and the oil industry by the Joint Chiefs of Staff at the end of the war:

> The achievement of this gigantic task was without question one of the great industrial accomplishments in the history of warfare. The urgent demands of the Army and Navy for unprecedented volumes of aviation gasoline, motor gasoline, diesel oil, fuel oils, lubricants and countless other petroleum products vital to victory were unending and often appeared impossible of fulfillment. It is a very special tribute, therefore, that at no time did the Services lack for oil in the proper quantities, in the proper kinds, and at the proper places.

Production and distribution for war were the most important considerations during these years, of course, but already many people were beginning to discern the outlines of a future in which even the peacetime needs of the United States would outstrip the industry's ability to supply it from domestic sources. It was even possible to imagine a time when the supplies from Mexico and Venezuela would not be enough. With that in mind, in February 1943 "Star" Rodgers, chairman of the board at Texaco, and Harry Collier, president of Standard Oil of California, called upon Ickes in Washington and entangled him in a long, portentous addendum to the story of World War II and oil. Several years before, the executives reminded Ickes, they had won a valuable oil concession from King Ibn Saud of Saudi Arabia and had formed a partnership with the king called the Arabian-American Oil Company (Aramco). But now the British Petroleum Company was pouring millions of dollars on the king's head in an effort to undercut the influence of the two American companies. The United States could not afford to lose dominance in a region of the world in which a thin layer of sand seemed to cover an immeasurable pool of oil. Would Ickes persuade Roosevelt to throw some Lend-Lease money the king's way?

He would and did, and within a few weeks enough American money was coming into Saudi Arabia to inspire "a further orgy of extravagance and misarrangement, accompanied by the growth of corruption on a large scale in the highest quarters," according to Harry St. John Philby, a former officer in the British Colonial Service, a dedicated Arabist, and now one of King Ibn Saud's principal advisers. The companies wanted more. They wanted the U.S. government to enter into exclusive contracts with them for the delivery of oil to build up U.S. reserves. They went to the State Department with this proposal and won the support of Cordell Hull and the people in his Committee on International Oil Policy. In the meantime, William C. Bullitt, now serving as Assistant Secretary of the Navy, offered another idea to the President. The United States, Bullitt said, should set up a Petroleum Reserve Corporation along the lines of the British Petroleum Company in England. This government corporation would then buy a controlling interest in Aramco and construct a refinery on the Persian Gulf. The country, Bullitt emphasized, was "forty years late in starting—but we are not yet too late."

Over the objections of Hull and his advisers but with the enthusiastic encouragement of Harold Ickes, Roosevelt embraced this idea and on June 30 authorized the creation of the Petroleum Reserves Corporation. The secretaries (or, as was more often the case, their appointed representatives) of the Navy, War, and State departments would serve as the corporation's board of directors, while the role of the Secretary of the Interior was described by Ickes in a letter to Roosevelt on July 27: "In the selection of officers we will, of course, be guided by your wishes. At the meeting in your office it was indicated by Frank Knox, Bob Patterson [Assistant Secretary of War] and Dr. Feis [Herbert Feis, an economic adviser for the State Department and Hull's surrogate on the corporation's board] that I was agreeable to them for President. . . . I want you to know," he added, perhaps hoping to stave off charges of self-aggrandizement, "that this suggestion was entirely voluntary on the part of those who made it." It was also suggested, he said, that "I ought to bring this corporation over to Interior and run it from here—this, of course, because I have had more experience with oil than anyone else in the Administration." Roosevelt concurred in Ickes's presidency, but wanted him to keep the corporation independent of any other agency, including the Interior Department.

As secretary of the new organization, Ickes installed Abe Fortas, who was by now the second Undersecretary of the Interior actually chosen by the Secretary of the Interior himself (Harry Slattery having been the first). Undersecretary Alvin J. Wirtz had resigned abruptly in the spring of 1941 to return to Texas and run Lyndon B. Johnson's campaign for the Senate (Johnson lost). His replacement, former New Mexico representative John J. Dempsey, another political appointee, had resigned in May 1942 to go back to New Mexico to run for governor (he, too, would lose). Because Roosevelt had no unemployed politicians on hand to put into the job at that point, Ickes asked for and got Fortas.

Ever since he had appointed the young man to the Power Division in 1939, Ickes had grown to depend upon Fortas both officially and as an understanding listener—at times seeming to look upon him as a surrogate son. In March 1942, when Ickes was going through one of his increasingly numerous periods of estrangement with Roosevelt, it was Fortas he called in to his office. "I sent for Abe Fortas twice Friday afternoon," he wrote in his diary at the time. "I told him that I did not see how I could stand it much longer to stay with the Government in view of the evident distaste of the President for me. I more or less wept on his shoulder. Abe is understanding and sympathetic."

And ambitious and hardworking and good at his job, which, as the years passed, would include functioning as Acting Secretary at cabinet meetings when Ickes was ill or out of town—the first assistant to whom Ickes had ever accorded that much trust. In the fall of 1943, after Fortas made an abortive attempt to serve in the navy (he would be discharged a few weeks later because of chorioretinitis, a tubercular condition of the retina), Ickes wrote him a letter of extraordinary praise:

> I am prepared to commit myself on the proposition and to maintain that you are the best Under Secretary who has ever worked in this Department. I feel at a loss without you. It was so natural for me to ring your bell and have you in my office before really getting settled for the day and then to see you two or three times during the day. I must confess that I wasn't always happy to see you push your way through the swinging door when I was trying to clean my desk and start for home, but there was always a reason for your behavior, and it strengthened my faith that I could go away, even for a comparatively long period, and not have to worry about how the work was going if you were Acting Secretary.

Fortas would return to Interior and remain until December 1945, when he left to form a legal partnership with former Assistant Attorney General

Thurman Arnold, thus going on record as not only serving better but longer than any other undersecretary Ickes had enjoyed.

This is not to say that the two men did not have their bad moments. Fortas could be manipulative and devious when it served his purposes, was slightly hypochondriacal, and was given to fits of paranoia, anger, and depression that were sometimes a match for those of his boss. At one point, Fortas's biographer notes, Ickes first used cardboard to block the door connecting their two offices, then removed the doorknobs—both in an attempt to keep the undersecretary from bursting in on him. Furthermore, Fortas and Davies did not get along from the outset. "I hope you don't mind my speaking so bluntly," Fortas wrote Ickes a little over two months after taking his position, "but I have a feeling that the superb job you are doing in oil and rubber is suffering unnecessarily because of Davies' unfamiliarity with Washington personalities and tactics; and because he does not have an innate feeling for what makes people tick." This brash contempt for his colleague (and, Davies would insist, equal) in time would bring Fortas and the Secretary to the brink of their only real split.

Meanwhile, he was invaluable in freeing Ickes from many of the most time-consuming and irksome details the Secretary's still enormous and varied responsibilities entailed, allowing him to focus his energies on one major project at a time—or as close to that ideal as Ickes's omnifarious personality would allow. For a while, this included the Petroleum Reserves Corporation. Shortly after the agency's first official meeting on August 9, 1943, it hired the renowned oil geologist Everett de Golyer to make a survey of the estimated oil reserves in Saudi Arabia. De Golyer returned with a prediction that positively thrummed: "The centre of gravity of the world of oil production is shifting from the Gulf-Caribbean areas to the Middle East, to the Persian Gulf area, and is likely to continue to shift until it is firmly established in that area." This was a vision of the future, and Ickes struggled for weeks to persuade Rodgers and Collier of Aramco to sell control of the Saudi Arabia concession to the government. They were just as able to make out the future as the Secretary, however, and had no intention of giving up control over what would certainly become billions of dollars; the best they would offer was a one-third interest. By early November, negotiations had broken off.

In the meantime, Ickes had begun exploring other ideas, among them a partnership with the Anglo-Iranian Oil Company in which the United States would build a pipeline from the British-controlled Iraqi oilfields to the Mediterranean in exchange for a share in the oil thus produced; this would give the U.S. government a foothold in the Middle East and assure a continuous supply for its reserves. Cordell Hull at the State Department objected strenuously. "We believe," he wrote Ickes on November 13, "that strong criticism will develop if British petroleum facilities in the Middle East are further expanded for American purposes and with American materials, for to do so will retard the development of American enterprises, jeopardize their holdings, and so tend to make this country dependent on British oil in the future." Ickes thought it preferable to be dependent on a proven ally than on an untried nation like Saudi Arabia, but could not get the cooperation of the State Department.

He then turned back to Aramco, offering to build a thousand-mile government-owned but privately operated pipeline from the company's Saudi Arabian fields to some point on the Mediterranean in exchange for a guaranteed reserve of a billion barrels of oil in the ground for the use of the armed forces of the United States, this oil to be made available at a permanent discount of 25 percent. The proposal was a bargain for the oil companies, and they readily agreed. However, since the pipeline would have to cross territory under the sphere of influence of the British government (and would compete directly with British Petroleum as well), some sort of treaty agreement regarding the future exploitation of Middle Eastern oil by both countries would have to be worked out before the project could proceed. Hull, who had only reluctantly acquiesced in the Aramco contract, thought negotiations for an agreement with the British should be handled strictly by the State Department. Ickes insisted in a letter to Roosevelt on December 29, however, that "This is my baby." Roosevelt agreed, and Ickes, with Ralph Davies assisting, became one of the key negotiators on the American team. After sundry details of protocol and procedure were worked out with the British, preliminary talks began early in April 1944.

This was the point at which Fortas and Ickes clashed. From the beginning, the undersecretary had objected to the participation of Davies, who was still a vice president (on paper, at least) of Standard Oil of California and thus had an interest in the outcome of the pipeline deal. "I do not believe that your principal representative on the grave issues of foreign and domestic policy," he wrote Ickes on April 8,

> should be a person who is in the position in which Mr. Davies finds himself. He should be a person who believes himself ready to urge whatever policy may seem to be the most desirable in the circumstances, whether or not that policy is likely to be acceptable to the oil industry or any part of it. . . . I recommend that Mr. Davies confine himself to his work as deputy head of the Petroleum Administration for War; that the formulation of foreign and domestic policy—particularly post-war problems—be placed under the direction of another individual.

Davies, predictably enough, objected to the Fortas objection, writing Ickes on April 10 that

> What Mr. Fortas contends, it seems to me, is that to have sound judgment on national oil policy one must be completely devoid of viewpoint at the moment and be altogether ignorant on the subject of oil. . . . We have not done badly over the past three years, but we face disintegration now. I am either totally qualified or I am not. I either have or have not the full confidence of the Administration in acting as your Deputy for petroleum. I could not function effectively on a partial basis—any more than you could yourself—and I should be unwilling to undertake to do so. I see no disqualifying "fundamental conflicts" as a reality; imaginary ones scarcely justify serious consideration.

That afternoon, the three men talked over the problem in Ickes's office, and Fortas apparently came away with the idea that everything was put on hold until after Ickes's return from a brief trip to California. While the Secretary was gone, however, Fortas saw the copy of a signed letter from Ickes to Hull designating Davies as a participant on the "technical committee" for discussions with a counterpart committee of Britishers. Fortas felt betrayed, and when Ickes returned he found the undersecretary's resignation as secretary of the Petroleum Reserves Corporation ready to be passed on to the board.

Ickes was no Roosevelt; he turned over the resignation and on April 25 it was formally accepted by the board. The Secretary also sat down and dictated an eight-page, single-spaced memorandum to Fortas denying that he had misled his undersecretary and defending Davies's integrity. Given the character of memoranda written on similarly volatile subjects in the past, the Secretary's exegesis was a marvel of restraint—another indication of the depth of affection he felt for the impetuous young man. "Speaking personally," the memorandum concluded, "I would say that I regret deeply what I regard as a lack of friendliness in your approach to this whole matter and the intolerable manner in which you have dealt with it. I do not like to deal at arm's length with members of my staff for whom I have both a feeling of respect and one of personal friendliness."

The quarrel was patched up soon enough—though a certain coolness remained in their relationship—and the talks with the British proceeded without the participation of Fortas (and with the participation of Davies). On August 22 a tortuously vague and voluntary agreement was reached whereby, in effect, each country agreed not to interfere openly with the operations of the other in the Middle East or any other foreign country in which the two might be vying for oil and called for the creation of an International Petroleum Commission that would prepare long-term estimates of world oil demand and make recommendations to participating countries.

That was about that, but even this triumph of imprecision was too much for the U.S. Senate, which feared the postwar domination of two parties—Great Britain and Harold L. Ickes. When the treaty had been sitting without movement for several weeks, the Roosevelt administration asked that it be returned for revision. It was diluted even more, and in the spring of 1945, Ickes took the revised document to London and got British approval of the changes. It was then resubmitted to the Senate for ratification. There it remained until July of 1947, when it was finally rejected. The Aramco pipeline project died at the same time, and with it the last easy chance the government of the United States would ever have to establish an official presence in the heart of a region whose future domination of world oil supplies would dictate the economic health of entire continents—including our own. *

---

* Another postwar development should be mentioned here: when Ralph Davies wanted to go back to work for Standard Oil, the company broke its promise and refused to rehire him—in spite of furious letters from Ickes. Davies went on to form his own company, one of whose executives would be Raymond Ickes.

CHAPTER

· 52 ·

The Portals and Seams of Compromise

O IL WAS NOT the only fuel occupying the Secretary's attention during the war years. At the same time he made Ickes petroleum administrator for war, Roosevelt had conferred upon him a similar role for solid fuels—which is to say, coal. Normally, this responsibility was a good deal less complicated a business than overseeing the production and distribution of oil, but it had its moments.

The most disruptive of these episodes occupied much of 1943 and centered on the lion-maned leader of the United Mine Workers of America, John L. Lewis. Lewis had not been precisely docile since July 1941, when an eleventh-hour settlement had eliminated the possibility that Ickes might have to take over operation of the nation's coal mines. In October 1941, in an effort to force the steel companies to accept union shops in the "captive" coal mines they owned, he had called out fifty-three thousand miners. After two months of confrontation—much of it between Lewis and the President, noisily played out in the public press— the government had forced a settlement favorable to the union. After the attack on Pearl Harbor, Lewis and most of his miners had joined the chorus of patriotism. He committed his union to support a no-strike pledge signed by other labor leaders and promised to cooperate with the newly formed National War Labor Board (NWLB). "Our nation is at war and coal production must not cease," he had lectured a group of miners engaged in a wildcat strike in July 1942.

By 1943, that solemn unanimity no longer applied. Rank-and-file workers in many industries now were going out on short-lived but no less unsettling wildcat strikes on a fairly regular basis, some of them calling for an official end to the unofficial no-strike pledge. (Even so, during the war years as a whole, only about half as many man-hours were lost from strikes every year as had been lost in the prewar years.) No group was more fractious than the UMW, which had become convinced that it was being discriminated against in the matter of wages. In July 1942, responding to pressure from the OPA to hold wages at January 1941 levels in order to combat inflation, the NWLB had developed what it called the "little steel formula" (based on a settlement reached between steelworkers and the steel industry that month). Under this ruling, workers were entitled to a 15 percent increase from levels in effect on January 1, 1941, since the cost of living had gone up that much. Wages would then be frozen at the new levels until the end of the war. But UMW members were not included in the ruling. In July 1941, the settlement they had agreed upon had given them a 16 percent increase in wages—which had been based on a parallel rise in the cost of living since April 1939. Now, because of that increase, the NWLB ruled that the UMW had already received what it was entitled to and would not be allowed any further raises, in spite of the fact that the cost of living had, by the NWLB's own admission, gone up another 15 percent.

Uncertain over what Roosevelt might do during the first few months of the war if Lewis openly challenged the ruling, the UMW president held off until the spring of 1943, then finally made his position clear: a two-dollar increase in daily wages, a demand he brought to contract talks with mine owners and operators at the beginning of March. "When the mine workers' children cry for bread," he wrote in the March 15 issue of the *United Mine Workers Journal,* "they cannot be satisfied with a 'Little Steel Formula.' When illness strikes the mine workers' families, they cannot be cured with an anti-inflation dissertation. The facts of life in the mining homes of America cannot be pushed aside by the flamboyant theories of an idealistic economic philosophy." Unimpressed by the rhetoric, the coal producers were convinced that Lewis would not dare to call a strike; they refused to consider the two-dollar increase. Lewis—who in truth did not want to go on strike—then began discussions with a federal conciliator to look for the establishment of portal-to-portal pay instead of an outright raise (in current practice, a miner's pay period began only when he had walked from the portal of the mine to the face of the coal seam he was working; portal-to-portal pay would have compensated him for the time it took to walk to and from the seam).

Roosevelt, who had learned to despise Lewis as much as Lewis loathed the President, put an end to that possibility on April 8 when he issued an order to the NWLB not to allow *any* kind of increase that did not correct substandard wages as measured by the Little Steel Formula; furthermore, he ordered that all decisions of the NWLB would be subject to the review and approval of the director of stabilization—which ended the independence of the board and, in effect, gave the President immediate control. Lewis tried one more gambit, offering to drop the demands for an hourly increase if the operators would guarantee six days of work a week. They refused and petitioned the President to send the matter to the NWLB for resolution. On April 22, with contracts due to expire on May 1 (they had already been extended for a month on April 1), Secretary of Labor Frances Perkins certified the dispute to the NWLB.

The NWLB's chairman, William H. Davis, made the board's position clear at the outset, announcing on April 24 that its earlier ruling held. On April 26, apparently acting on their own initiative, sixteen thousand workers walked off the job. By April 28, the number of striking workers had grown to seventy-five thousand and the NWLB suspended hearings on the dispute, turning the matter over to the President. On April 29, Roosevelt issued a statement calling for an immediate end to the strike; if "work at the mines is not resumed by ten o'clock Saturday morning [May 1]," he warned, "I shall use all the power vested in me as President and as Commander-in-Chief of the Army and Navy to protect the national interest and to prevent further interference with the successful prosecution of the war." In response, another ninety-seven hundred miners took a walk.

Up to this point, the solid fuels administrator for war had been relegated to the status of an interested observer in what was essentially a showdown between Roosevelt and Lewis; the President had made it clear that he intended to follow his own counsel in the conflict. "As usual," Ickes wrote Margaret Robins on the deadline morning of May 1,

> I haven't heard from anyone at the White House on coal since long before this crisis developed. My guess is that the President will issue an order to someone to take over the mines and run them and my further guess is that he won't name me this time. I know that the War Labor Board is strongly opposed to my taking over. It wants either the Army or the Navy. This is characteristic of that board. . . .

He was dead right about what the President would do, but dead wrong about who would not be told to run the mines. That evening Roosevelt ordered Ickes to seize the thirty-three hundred affected pits. The Secretary did so immediately, operating under contingency plans developed in the summer of 1941, and just to make the situation clear to anyone who might be watching, he ordered that an American flag be raised and flown every day at the front of every mine. On Sunday, May 2, Ickes met with Lewis at the Interior Building. Making it clear that he had little regard for the fairness of the little steel formula and little more than contempt for the NWLB, Ickes persuaded Lewis to send the workers back to the mines, beginning on May 4.

The implication seemed clear that further negotiations would take place between Ickes and Lewis—a situation much to Lewis's liking, since he respected the Secretary. But Roosevelt refused to allow it; the union was going to have to deal directly with the owners, he said, and do so under the supervision of the NWLB. Lewis issued accusations of double cross. "Lewis is, as you say," Ickes wrote Raymond Robins on May 8,

> "poisoned by his own bile." He hates the President and I think that either one would like to destroy the other. He hates the War Labor Board and it hates him, especially the labor members on that Board. Notwithstanding, I wish that the Board were more interested in digging coal than in destroying Lewis. It is unnecessarily and foolishly priggish about its own authority and jurisdiction at this time, it seems to me.
>
> I don't know how the coal thing will end. I had a hunch that if I could persuade Lewis to get the men back to their jobs it would not be so easy to get them out again. But there are walkouts today as I write.

On May 14 the NWLB ordered the union and the operators to start negotiations and the workers to stay on their jobs until a settlement was reached. (Again, the little steel formula was emphasized as the proper framework for discussion.) Lewis refused to have anything to do with the Board at this point, holding that only Ickes, as official custodian of the mines now, was authorized to deal with him. He did voluntarily extend the back-to-work order until June 1, however, which irritated the members of the board because he announced his decision to Ickes, not them. The board forthwith prohibited any further direct dealings between Ickes and Lewis. Even so, on May 31, Ickes attempted a wildcat compromise, suggesting to Lewis and Charles O'Neill, the representative of the operators, that the workers be given an extra $1.50 a day in portal-to-portal pay while the matter was taken under consideration by a specially appointed presidential commission; final pay rates would be based on recommendations of the commission. But O'Neill refused to talk with Lewis before the midnight deadline, and on June 1 more than 500,000 workers went out. On June 2, Roosevelt ordered the miners to return to work by

June 7. Lewis complied with a back-to-work order, but set a deadline of June 20 for a settlement with the operators.

Meanwhile, Congress entered the fracas by passing the Smith-Connally bill on June 15. Officially called the War Labor Disputes Act, the legislation gave broad authority to the NWLB—including the power to compel the appearance before the board of any parties in a dispute and the right to make binding settlements in any such dispute. The bill also affirmed the President's power to seize war-related industries and provided criminal penalties for anyone who ordered a strike or otherwise disrupted production in any such industries after a settlement had been reached. Roosevelt recognized the fact that while the fight with Lewis had prompted the bill, it reflected a growing antilabor sentiment in the increasingly conservative Congress and would hurt all of labor, not just Lewis and the UMW. Acting on the advice of Ickes and Frances Perkins, among others, he vetoed the legislation, but the veto was swiftly overridden and the War Labor Disputes Act became law.

On June 18 the War Labor Board issued a directive that gave the miners an increase in vacation pay, ordered that charges for equipment and other production-related supplies be assumed by the company, and raised some wages for workers on the lower end of the scale. This, the board declared, was to be the contract under which coal miners were to operate until March 31, 1945 (when, presumably, the war would be over—a date that was remarkably close to the fact). Lewis called the directive an "infamous yellow-dog contract" and on June 20 half a million coal miners were again on strike. The mine owners, comfortable in the settlement imposed by the board and confident that they would get their mines back from the government within sixty days after the resumption of normal production, as the War Labor Disputes Act stipulated, refused to negotiate. Lewis then played what was very nearly his last card: he ordered the miners back to work, stating that his men would dig coal "for the Government itself under the direction of the custodian of mines. The mine workers have no favor to grant the coal trust, but will make any sacrifice for the Government, the well-being of its citizens, the upholding of our flag, and for the triumph of our war effort." What is more, he said, they would remain on the job until October 31—but only if the mines continued to be operated by the government. By this tactic, he hoped that the operators would be driven back to the negotiating table out of a fear that after a long enough period of time, the government might just decide that permanent wartime nationalization was the best thing all around.

Ickes, who by now was interested only in getting the coal out, did his best to add to the pressure. As his coal mine administrator he appointed Carl Newton, president of the Chesapeake & Ohio Railroad—an enterprise that needed coal to haul—and a colleague of industrialist Cyrus Eaton, who was a close friend of Lewis's. While going about the business of running the mines, Newton quietly nourished fears of potential nationalization among the operators. In the meantime, Ickes put as strict an interpretation on the meaning of the term "normal production" as he reasonably could, holding off the return of individual mines until the last possible moment—all of this to give Lewis time to talk with individual mine owners. As a result, the last of the mines did not go back to private operation until the middle of October.

The tactic almost worked. In July the UMW president managed to negotiate a contract with the Illinois Coal Operators Association which, among other things, granted portal-to-portal pay and a forty-hour work week. The contract was submitted to the NWLB. On August 25 the board rejected it. Lewis took the contract back to the Coal Operators Association and the parties worked out a revised agreement. On September 23 the new contract was submitted to the board; a month later, it, too, was rejected.

On November 1, after Lewis's October 31 deadline had passed, 530,000 coal miners once again went on strike. Roosevelt struck quickly himself. At eight o'clock that night he ordered Ickes to seize the mines again—but this time with a significant codicil: he put aside his hatred of Lewis and told the Secretary to start negotiating with him to come up with a contract. It would have to be submitted to the NWLB, but there was little chance that the board would challenge an agreement worked out by a member of the Cabinet appointed to the task by the President himself. Ickes and Lewis met on November 2, and the Secretary described the outcome in a letter to Margaret Robins four days later:

> I asked [Lewis] to come to my office where he and I discussed the situation alone. I do not think that we talked an aggregate of more than an hour and a quarter at three interviews. Then we had more in on both sides in order to discuss details and agree upon the memorandum that both of us finally signed. . . . Everyone was taken by surprise by the speed with which the matter was handled. Lewis and I signed the agreement less than 48 hours after the President had authorized me to take over the mines. Of course it was bitter medicine for the War Labor Board but my guess was that it had to take the dose whether it wanted to or not.

Ickesian self-satisfaction aside, the board did take the dose that Ickes and Lewis had prescribed—largely a minor revision of the second agreement that Lewis had worked out with the Illinois Coal Operators. As each of the mine owners—individually and in association—grudgingly signed contracts with the union according to the agreement's stipulations, the mines were returned to private operation one by one (though it was not until May 31, 1944, that the last of them was turned over by the government). Coal production was not seriously interrupted again during the war years, although short strikes in August 1944 and May 1945 did cause the government to seize a number of mines for a brief time.

The Secretary would never be known as the Great Compromiser; more often than not during his government career, it had been others who had engineered the settlement of sundry disputes in which Ickes had found himself (or, just as often, had created for himself). But in the case of the 1943 coal dispute, the Secretary had pulled Roosevelt's chestnuts out of the fire in splendid fashion, rescuing his President from a situation in which his own hatred and stubbornness had ensnarled him. Roosevelt almost acknowledged the debt, Ickes told Margaret Robins. At the beginning of the Cabinet meeting on November 5, he related, Roosevelt had made only one oblique reference to the events of the previous few days: "When I got well of the flu," he had announced to the room in general, "I learned that Harold was getting coal out of the ground again."

CHAPTER
· 53 ·

Interludes
of Ink and Cowboys

T HE YEAR OF the coal settlement also saw the acquisition of other feathers for the Secretary's cap. This was the year, for instance, when he became something of a literary presence with the publication of *Autobiography of a Curmudgeon.* It was not the first book with his name on it, of course, but most of the others had been little more than inspirational boilerplate welded together by one or another of his assistants from internal reports, press releases, speeches, even transcripts from press conferences, then worked over to a greater or lesser degree by the Secretary before publication. *The New Democracy,* a screed in defense of the New Deal published in 1934, had possessed that character, as had *Back to Work,* the little history of the PWA that came out in 1935, and *Fightin' Oil,* another book for 1943.

Two exceptions to this general rule had come out of his ongoing feud with the American press—not so much with working reporters, with whom he maintained a generally amicable relationship (he had once been one of them, as he was willing to point out), as with their publishers and the gaggle of columnists who had never been reluctant to aim barbs tipped with journalistic curare at the numerous sensitive spots on the Secretary's person. The first and better of these two literary efforts had been *America's House of Lords,* a short indictment of the newspaper business, the first drafts of which were prepared by Saul Padover and Mike

Straus, then revised even more extensively than usual by Ickes before being published by Harcourt, Brace in November 1939. The book was unashamed polemic, but pretty vigorous polemic. "A publisher or editor sits in an impregnable fortress," he wrote in the introduction, adding that

> Common citizens whose rights he may choose to ignore and against whose interests he runs counter, the man in public life who can hope to get nothing out of the service he renders except a reputation in which he himself may take satisfaction and of which his children may be proud, are fair game to . . . attacks from these strongholds of power. . . .
>
> There have been some incongruous figures in the newspaper world, especially on the publishing side. Given money, notwithstanding its source or the method of its acquirement, with which to buy a newspaper, and the man who theretofore would have been regarded as one of the least qualified to express himself upon the morals and the manners of any class of the people, immediately becomes an oracle in the land.

He had reserved some of his most pungent remarks for columnists. After a quick disclaimer—"this is not intended to be a blanket indictment of all columnists and commentators," many of whom "serve a good purpose"— he launched into one of the most violent diatribes in his long career:

> There are columnists today who hardly, if ever, stir out of the dens in which they weave their webs of intrigue, misinformation and misrepresentation. Peeping toms, scandal mongers, "leg men," purvey to these "gentlemen" of the press choice bits of gossip or equally choice morsels of intellectual garbage which are chemically treated just to the degree necessary to make the columnist immune under the libel laws. . . . Washington is the happy hunting ground of this new fraternity. The departments are riddled with informers, private lives are spied upon, rewards are offered to the disloyal, reputations are placed in jeopardy, and all in order that a moronic mind may have some putrescent morsel over which to gloat. It is a new conception of journalism that newspapers must develop an unfailing crop of pustules in order to preserve a healthy organism.*

This antipathy also drove the Secretary to what may have been the only instance on record in which he succumbed to poetry, and definitely the only instance in which such indulgence was given the gross luminosity of print:

---

* The Secretary neglected to mention the fact that he, like most government bureaucrats, was not above furnishing a few morsels himself when it served his purposes—particularly to those few columnists like Raymond Clapper and Drew Pearson who had proved themselves friendly. He would have argued, of course, that in such instances he was acting in the public interest. So it was, so it always had been. Ours, historian Bruce Catton once wrote, "has always been a democratic government, which means that it has always been somewhat loose-jointed, which in turn means that there have always been leaks."

Wouldst know what is right and what is wrong?
Why birdies sing at break of dawn?
Ask the columnists.

Does milk come from the Milky Way?
Why do dogs bark and asses bray?
Ask the columnists.

Who pronounce decrees of fate,
And supervise affairs of State?
Who? The columnists.

Who knowing scarce their A.B.C.,
Rank doctors of philosophy?
Who, but columnists?

Wouldst learn of art, of singing males,
Of sharks and minnows, spouting whales?
Ask the columnists.

Who expound the Constitution
Adding circum to locution?
Why, the columnists!

When F.D.R. you want to sock
Page Lippmann, Johnson, Kent or Krock.
Page a columnist.

Who, knowing all from zero plus,
Right answers have to this or thus?
Only columnists.

I'd like to strut and look profound,
And order Presidents around,
I'd like to be a columnist!

The Secretary's other book about American journalism, *Freedom of the Press Today: A Clinical Examination,* published by the Vanguard Press in April 1941, remained innocent of poetry. It remained innocent, in fact, of almost any involvement on the Secretary's part. An unremarkable collection of twenty-eight solicited essays on the subjects of newspaper journalism and publishing ethics by, among others, Bruce Bliven, William Allen White, Raymond Clapper, and Harold Lasswell, the book had been inspired, Ickes noted in a brief introduction (his only contribution, Padover having gathered and properly assembled the essays), after he had assistants check the daily output of five representative newspapers—*The New York Times,* the *Chicago Tribune,* the *Pittsburgh Post-Gazette,* the *Rochester Times,* and the *Los Angeles Times*—during October 1940, at the height of the Presidential campaign. Armed with rulers, his investigators (probably Straus and Padover) had discovered that the newspapers under surveillance were found to have given a total of 2,245½ inches of their news space to Willkie and only 348 inches to Roosevelt. Just how free, he had wondered, was such a press? *Freedom of the Press Today*, it must be said, was too loosely organized, poorly presented, and predictable to provide an answer. It sold poorly and was remaindered swiftly.

Autobiography of a Curmudgeon was more respectable than these earlier efforts on all counts. The book had evolved out of two abortive projects early in 1942, each of them inspired by his need for extra cash to keep Headwaters Farm going (the farm never did make much money, in spite of Jane's exhausting labors). The first was a series of three reminiscent articles to be entitled "Biography of a Curmudgeon" which he had offered to the *Saturday Evening Post*. After due consideration, the magazine had turned them down. At the same time, he was discussing the possibility of writing a weekly column for *Collier's* magazine. Its editor, William Chenery, had been after him for some time to produce a one-page "report from Washington" of somewhere around a thousand words in length. For this he would pay Ickes the sum of $25,000 a year, an astonishing amount for the time. They could call the column "Diary of a Curmudgeon," Chenery said, and Ickes could even work in the rejected *Saturday Evening Post* material when it seemed appropriate. "Of course, the money offered is tempting," Ickes wrote with overwhelming understatement in his diary for January 18, 1942,

> and I am going to need some help to get through this year without drawing somewhat heavily upon our capital. Moreover, there are other possibilities involved in this undertaking if I go ahead with it. It will have a revivifying spiritual effect upon me and some of the people in Washington who now think that I am definitely and finally in the background may change their minds. A columnist on as influential and far-flung a magazine as *Collier's* is entitled to some respect, especially if he is a member of the Cabinet.

The irony in the fact that he was now contemplating becoming one of those scurvy creatures—a columnist—whom he had vilified with such relish in *America's House of Lords* apparently was lost on him. In any case, the trouble with these happy speculations was that he *was* a member of the cabinet, and Roosevelt was not going to permit as loose a gun as Ickes to roll around on the deck at *Collier's,* with its weekly circulation of three million. The President was sympathetic to Ickes's need for money, Steve Early told the Secretary, but refused his permission to write the column. Ickes briefly considered defying Roosevelt on the point, but thought better of it and during the course of the year began putting together the chapters of a book based on the political memoirs he had been dictating to May Conley off and on for years. In July he signed a contract with Reynal & Hitchcock in New York to produce a manuscript of seventy-five thousand to one hundred thousand words, tentatively entitled "Confessions of a Curmudgeon."

Most of the book had to do with his boyhood in Altoona, his newspaper days, and his political adventures in Chicago up to the point at which he took the job as Interior Secretary in 1933, but four of the later chapters had to do with his present employment. Anticipating censorship, Ickes carefully made these segments as general as possible, but for the chapter called "Mr. Ickes Goes to Washington," in which he wanted to lambast the press and a few politicians, he found it all but impossible to write without naming specific individuals and events. To get around the problem, he hit upon the not very happy scheme of simply blacking out the offending words and sentences and printing the chapter with the black marks boldly displayed, explaining in a footnote that "I am not able to write as freely as I might were I a private citizen." This gave birth to such sentences as "His ▬▬▬ and ▬▬▬ and ▬▬▬ and ▬▬▬ and ▬▬▬ ▬▬▬ resulted in my sending for Burlew ▬▬▬ was prepared to go to court, and asking him as a favor to me to drop the proceedings that were about to get under way."

He explained to his understandably nervous editor at Reynal & Hitchcock that "we must remember that the book would not be complete without some reference to that part of my life that has been passed in the Government Service and I can not indulge in any language that might be regarded as critical of my associates here. And to write anything in which names are used and situations alluded to might be regarded as at least indirect criticism. I do not know whether you realize how sensitive most political hides are." He was certainly correct about the thickness of hides. "I feel that I ought to give you a candid opinion on one aspect of the work," Steve Early wrote after Ickes sent him the manuscript for a reading. "There are passages in these chapters, which, in my opinion, would not promote national unity in the government's all-out effort to win the war."

In spite of Early's complaint, the publication of *Autobiography of a Curmudgeon* in the spring of 1943 did no measurable damage to the war effort, and in spite of its inclination toward archness and the kind of elephantine humor demonstrated by the chapter with the fat black stripes in it, it is an engaging, useful, and frequently moving account of his life—although, as one would expect, thoroughly sanitized in order to leave out such matters as his father's philandering and the true details of

Ickes's own relationship with Anna. And in the final chapter, "A People's Peace," in which he laid out his hopes for what the war might accomplish beyond the immediate task of defeating the Axis, he produced a liberal's credo that did not have to apologize to anyone for eloquence:

> I lay no claim to originality—only to consistency—when I record that civil liberties cannot possibly exist under an absolute form of government. . . . For untold generations . . . man has fought for the right to live in peace and harmony and understanding, not only in the world of the spirit, but with his fellow men. Above all other things he has aspired to and striven for liberty— liberty to live his own life in his own way, subject only to the right of other men also to live their lives in their own way; liberty to worship according to the dictates of his own conscience; liberty to adapt the social customs that have come down to him from his forefathers to whatever new environment he may choose for himself; liberty to think his own thoughts and give free expression to them; liberty to find for himself in the social order the niche for which he is best adapted, regardless of race, creed, or color; liberty to work at any task, suitable to his abilities and agreeable to his taste, for a sufficient wage to support himself and his family in reasonable comfort, with a modest surplus over for his periods of leisure and to carry him in decency and security through the years of his old age; liberty to follow freely his own political convictions; liberty to keep his children in school until they are equipped in their turn to put their abilities and their talents to the highest service of the State and of society.

Part of the rationale Ickes had offered to Steve Early in explanation of why he wanted to write the weekly column for *Collier's* had been that the President had frozen him out of any significant part in the planning or procedure of the war, thus leaving him "with time on my hands which I could employ in writing." The image this suggests of Harold Ickes sitting around during the war years, twiddling his thumbs and wondering what to do with himself, is ludicrous. It is true that he had slowed down over the years and would continue to do so for the remainder of his tenure at the Department, giving over more and more responsibility to Burlew and, especially, Fortas—but what this tended to mean in Ickesian terms was that he was slowly cutting back from doing the work of three men every day to doing that of only two, or possibly one and a half. Even at this level, he had no trouble occupying himself.

There were even some major conservation matters to be attended to. The most dramatic of these by far was the designation of the 220,000-acre Jackson Hole National Monument. Designating the monument, as a matter of fact, was not much of a problem—but protecting it from those who would have snatched it back out from under the umbrella of the national park system was a battle whose pyrotechnics of agitation would ornament the last two years of the war and spill over into the postwar years.

Jackson Hole, which some argued was far and away the most beautiful portion of the Snake River Valley, lay like an enormous meadow beneath the towering, snaggle-toothed peaks of the Teton Range in Wyoming south of Yellowstone National Park, its curving river slinking through the grassy, flowering fields like an uncoiled whip, feathered by the wind and burnished by the sun. Aside from its beauty, the place was an important winter habitat for one of the most extensive elk herds in the Rocky Mountain region. Most of the valley was owned and operated by the U.S. Forest Service as Teton National Forest, though there were a little over twenty-four thousand acres set aside as the National Elk Refuge under the administration of the Biological Survey, as well as fifty thousand acres held in private hands—including about thirty-five thousand acres of some of the most beautiful and ecologically significant tracts west of the Snake River.

For several years after World War I, there had been attempts made by Stephen Mather and Horace Albright of the National Park Service, together with a handful of local people, to get the boundaries of Yellowstone National Park extended to include the Jackson Hole portion of the Snake River Valley. Opposition by local stockmen and the Forest Service had managed to stifle that idea every time it was presented. Albright then joined with Struthers Burt, a local dude rancher, and other conservation-minded people in the valley to propose the designation of a national recreation area in the region. Again, opposition from stockmen and the Forest Service had blocked this move—one also complicated by the fact that it would take a great deal of money to buy up enough of the private land in the area to ensure the creation of a reserve sufficiently large and coherent to stand as a definable unit.

In the meantime, development in the valley was assuming a distinctively tacky character, as described by Horace Albright in a statement included in a Park Service report nearly twenty years later:

> By midsummer [1926] the highway between Jackson and Moran was pretty well littered with nondescript buildings. Goss had started his Elbo Ranch— Hollywood Cowboys Home—as he called it. A dance hall was built near Jenny Lake. The local Forest Service officer had built a telephone line along the new highway. Before it was built, I had suggested that the line be built east of the road in order not to cut across the view of the Tetons, but it was built as planned on the west side and in the face of the sublime mountain scene.

That summer of 1926, Albright took John D. Rockefeller and his wife on a tour of Yellowstone, then south to Jackson Hole, where the philanthropist fell in love with the valley. In 1927, under the guidance of Albright, Rockefeller set up the Snake River Land Company and quietly began buying up parcels of private land. By 1933, Rockefeller's representatives had purchased a total of 35,310 acres at a cost of $1.4 million and in August of that year the Land Company's president, Vanderbilt Webb, disclosed the purpose of Rockefeller's interest before a subcommittee of the Senate Public Lands Committee holding investigative hearings in Jackson: "Mr. Rockefeller is prepared to present to the United States Government the lands acquired by the Snake River Land Company, in order that they may be administered under an ownership, control and management best calculated to make them available for the future enjoyment of the public." The best way to assure that, Webb said, was to place the Rockefeller lands under the jurisdiction of the National Park Service and join to them all unappropriated public lands and all lands now administered by the Forest Service. Under this scheme, Teton County would be reimbursed by the federal government for the loss of about eleven thousand dollars in yearly taxes that would come with the transfer of the Rockefeller lands, and to assuage the concerns of local stockmen, they would be guaranteed the right to move their cattle across the valley floor to and from their ranches and the summer range in the mountains.

The Forest Service, of course, did not like one single thing about this idea. Nor did the stockmen of the valley, who had been serviced so long and so accommodatingly by the Forest Service that they may have been justified in feeling that the agency was designed principally for their aid and comfort. Furthermore, they neither liked nor trusted the Park Service (which did not promote grazing anywhere in the West), an antipathy encouraged by local Forest Service officials. Finally, many people in the towns of Jackson and Moran feared the loss of Rockefeller's tax money and gave little credit to the notion that the government would reimburse them for the deprivation.

In the meantime Congress had passed legislation in February 1929 creating Grand Teton National Park, which included the east slope of the Teton Range and a narrow strip of the valley at the foot of the mountains. Residents of the valley soon fell into opposing camps—one advocating that the new park be extended to include the lands involved in the Rockefeller proposal, the other resisting any change from the status quo. Olaus J. Murie, a biologist for the U.S. Biological Survey on the Elk Refuge (and a later president of The Wilderness Society), who lived in the valley hamlet of Moose with his wife, Margaret, from 1927 until his death in 1963, described the increasingly tense atmosphere of the region throughout the decade of the thirties: "Card parties, dinner parties had their embarrassments if certain ones prominent on 'the other side' were present. In some inexplicable way an atmosphere was created in which one felt inhibited from even mentioning the subject. There was no such thing as getting together and talking it over."

Largely because the Bureau of the Budget would not approve the stipulation that Teton County be reimbursed for the loss of the Rockefeller tax money, the Forest Service and its allies survived two major efforts on the part of Wyoming senators Robert D. Carey and Joseph C. O'Mahoney to get legislation through Congress to enlarge Teton National Park and take in most of the Jackson Hole region. Another proposal for enlargement, this one offered by the Park Service itself, never even got out of committee. Meanwhile, Rockefeller, exhibiting extraordinary patience, continued to pay those taxes (which ultimately brought his total investment to more than $1.5 million) until 1942, when he had had his fill of waiting. "In view of the uncertainty of the times," he wrote Ickes on November 27,

> like everyone else I am and have been for some time reducing my obligations and burdens in so far as I wisely can. In line with that policy I have definitely reached the conclusion, although most reluctantly, that I should make permanent disposition of this property before another year has passed. If the federal government is not interested in its acquisition, or, being interested, is still unable to arrange to accept it on the general terms long discussed and with which you are familiar, it will be my thought to make some other disposition of it or, failing in that, to sell it in the market to any satisfactory buyers.

There was nothing ambiguous about this statement (although the implication that Rockefeller's financial position was threatened by having to pay eleven thousand dollars a year in Snake River land taxes was ridiculous on the face of it), and Rockefeller reiterated it during a meeting with Ickes the day before Christmas, adding that he could not hold the land beyond February 28, 1944. It was not until February 27, 1943, that Ickes first broached a proposal to Roosevelt through his appointments secretary Edwin M. Watson. He probably had held off so long because in late December and early January Roosevelt had been occupied with planning the substance of upcoming talks with Churchill and his people in Casablanca, Morocco. After the talks, which had been held from January 14 to 17, Roosevelt had come down with the flu and that had kept him in bed at Hyde Park until well into February.

Ickes himself had been ready for action for some time, it was clear from his letter to Watson. "My own view," he wrote, "is that the President ought to set up a national monument before we lose an offer that will never be made again. . . . Naturally, I am anxious to move. We have the

Executive Order all drawn and it has been submitted to Director Smith of the Budget. I have Director Smith's authority to say that he is in favor of setting up this monument and doing it now. I hope for an early appointment with the President on this matter." But these were not the loose-limbed days of the early New Deal; he did not get an appointment until March 12. Roosevelt was not difficult to persuade, however, and on March 15, he signed the Executive Order establishing a national monument of 221,610 acres.

Ickes had stipulated in his letter to Watson that "There should be no publicity on this." He worried that if word got out before the proclamation was issued, the uproar over an executive fiat of such scope might dissuade the always politically sensitive President from making it. The Secretary may or may not have been right about that, but there was no gainsaying the dimensions of the subsequent agitation once the proclamation was safely on the record. Wyoming's state delegation—which included Frank A. Barrett, a rancher-lawyer out of Lusk, as the state's only representative, and Senators Edward V. Robertson and Joseph C. O'Mahoney, who had once favored the protection of the valley—was outraged. Four days after the proclamation, Barrett introduced legislation in the House to abolish the monument, Robertson began circulating a petition asking Roosevelt to rescind the proclamation (something he could not legally do), and O'Mahoney began exploring ways in which he might use the appropriations process to make it impossible for the Park Service to administer its new fiefdom.

It was the element of surprise that infuriated the Wyoming delegation as much as anything. Nor were they the only ones surprised. So was Newton B. Drury, director of the National Park Service. As he remembered it:

> [T]he first I knew about it was when I was having a staff meeting in Chicago and George Mosky, our chief attorney, came in, just having attended a meeting in Washington. He sat for quite a while through a lot of more or less inconsequential discussion; finally he interrupted and said, "I think maybe I ought to tell you that just before I left Washington this morning President Roosevelt signed the proclamation establishing Jackson Hole National Monument," whereupon I said, "The meeting is hereby adjourned." . . . [W]hat somewhat amused me and also caused consternation in our ranks was the fact that although there had been periodic discussion as to whether this action should be taken, it finally came like a bolt out of the blue. . . . It would have been very handy for us if we had known some months in advance that this was coming up, because this way we had hurriedly to be summoned to meetings and present to hearings both out there and in Congress the justification for the monument. Ideally, we could have used more time for preparation.

Ickes and Roosevelt both attempted some damage control. The Secretary wrote to O'Mahoney in an effort to reassure him that the monument would be administered benignly along the precise lines set forth in the Snake River Land Company's offer of 1933 and that no private parties need fear the federal presence:

> In the various national parks and monuments owners of private holdings have been given protection under the law and under departmental policies. Private owners in the Jackson Hole National Monument are and will be given similar protection. In establishing this monument all valid existing rights on Federal lands were protected, and the rights of private land owners are not affected. All permits, including grazing privileges and stock driveway privileges, issued by the Forest Service or other Federal agencies for use of land within the monument will be honored by the National Park Service during the lifetime of the present holders.

Nor would the local economy inevitably be made to suffer, Roosevelt told Wyoming's Governor Loren Hunt: "I am aware that national forests, wildlife refuges, Federal grazing districts and other forms of Federal land reservations, except the national parks, return a portion of their revenues to the counties in which the lands are situated. Uniformity of practice in this regard appears to be desirable, and I would favor some equitable means by which a portion of the revenues of Yellowstone, Grand Teton and Jackson Hole should benefit Teton County."

None of this seemed to have any effect at all on the opposition, which was apparently determined to believe what it was determined to believe. On May 1, as a public demonstration of their "right" to move cattle across the monument land (that privilege specifically allowed them in public pronouncements both by Ickes and by the superintendent of Grand Teton National Park, which would take over administration of the monument), a band of local ranchers and Jackson Hole citizens strapped on six-guns, grabbed rifles, mounted up, and drove 653 yearling Herefords across the monument to one of the ranches to graze. The brave cowboys went unchallenged by the Park Service. "Declaring they have seen promises of the park service broken heretofore," a story in the *Salt Lake Tribune* (Utah) reported, "the cattlemen are not trusting anything park service employees or Secretary Harold L. Ickes might say, they asserted. In the words of Mr. Kratzer: 'The ranchers are bound and determined that they can protect themselves, asking no sympathy, charity nor assistance.' "

Among those asking no sympathy was popular film star Wallace Beery, who had ridden, fully armed, with the others across the flowering valley, much to the delight of the local and national press. The burly actor had starred in numerous westerns and probably enjoyed this somewhat deranged slice of reality, but in August, Struthers Burt put the whole incident in perspective in a letter to an associate editor of the *Saturday Evening Post* (which, in an editorial, had said that Beery owned a ranch in the valley):

> Incidentally, Wallace Beery is not a Wyoming rancher, nor has he "a ranch" in here. When he is here, which is only for a few weeks of the year, he lives just below me. He has a half-acre Forest Service lease, to be renewed annually, and a cabin on Jackson Lake. His one head of stock, a milch-cow, died two months ago. Also, his "historic ride" across the Monument, armed to the teeth and on a borrowed horse, and in the face of no opposition at all, and half an hour after a lady-rancher, unaware of all the fuss, had driven a hundred head of cattle across the Monument, has become a sore point even among those who rode with him. . . . I'm afraid, Wally most literally "took them for a ride" and as they now realize, a lot of free publicity.

The facts were not allowed to interfere with a good cause. On May 13 the Wyoming state attorney general's office filed suit in the U.S. District Court against Paul R. Franke, representing the Department of the Interior as superintendent of Grand Teton National Park, challenging the validity of the President's action. While that suit started through the slowly grinding wheels of federal justice, the House Committee on Public Lands held a series of hearings on Barrett's bill to abolish the national monument. Among those testifying was Secretary Ickes, who calmly outlined the legality of Roosevelt's action under the authority of the Antiquities Act of 1906 (which, he reminded the committee members, had been used by two Republican presidents—Theodore Roosevelt and William Howard Taft—to establish such enormous reserves as the 615,000-acre Olympus National Monument). The Secretary then repeated his guarantees of existing private rights and privileges:

> Long before movie actor Wallace Beery and his picturesque associates made their widely publicized, desperate and daring dash across Jackson Hole with not even a jack rabbit to oppose them, I stated publicly to the Governor of Wyoming and to the members of Congress from that State, and it appeared in the Jackson Hole newspaper, that the privilege of driving cattle across the monument would be continued. . . . The rights of those cattlemen who have ranches outside of the monument but who have crossed the area for years to reach their present summer range in the National Forest will be continued. This is surely a reasonable position to take. It is fair to the cattlemen and to Teton County. . . . This whole campaign to discredit and nullify the Jackson Hole National Monument originated in the minds of a few self-seeking

individuals who feared that in an orderly and logical administration of these Federal lands they might lose their special privileges to trespass on the public domain which they have long enjoyed and which they had hoped to perpetuate forever.

He might later have been tempted to add that by their allies could one know them, for on June 16, none other than Westbrook Pegler, the clamoring Roosevelt hater, took up the cudgel of his prose to defend the helpless folk of Wyoming. "President Roosevelt and Harold Ickes," he reported in his syndicated column for June 16, "have recently perpetuated in the state of Wyoming an act of annexation which follows the general lines of Adolf Hitler's seizure of Austria. They anschlussed a tract of 221,610 acres for Ickes' domain by a subterfuge." Ickes, he added, was now reveling in a position which "corresponds to that of the Nazi governor of Poland."

In spite of this kind of high-minded support, no action on Barrett's bill took place before the first session of the 78th Congress adjourned, but it was reported favorably out of committee on March 28, 1944, in the second session. The allies of the President and the Interior Department managed to keep it from coming up for a vote until December, but on the eleventh of the month the House passed it, 178 to 107 (142 abstaining). The administration had fewer friends in the Senate, where the Committee on Public Lands and Surveys reported favorably on the House bill after a single day of hearings. On December 19, by unanimous consent, the bill passed, with no objection and no roll call. The Senate then adjourned. The President (as the proponents of the bill in both Houses knew he would) pocket-vetoed the legislation on December 29. Even if the timing had been right, the vote in the House had made it clear that there would not have been enough support to override such a rejection. The antimonument forces got another setback on February 10, 1945, when U.S. District Court Judge T. Blake Kennedy ordered the state of Wyoming's suit against the federal government dismissed. The dispute, he said, was "a controversy between the legislative and executive branches of the Government in which . . . the court cannot interfere."

Nevertheless, when Ickes asked Rockefeller (who had been holding on to his land pending the outcome of the suit and Barrett's bill) to make the formal transfer of the Snake River Land Company properties to the government, the philanthropist decided to wait until the administration's contretemps with Congress was settled; he did not want his $1.5 million gift wasted. Ickes did not argue the point with him, and it was just as well. In the Interior Appropriations Act of 1945, Senator O'Mahoney managed to get accepted an amendment that prohibited any funding for the administration of the monument—a device he and his allies would use repeatedly during the decade to cripple the Park Service's ability to manage the new park. And two days after Judge Kennedy's February decision, Barrett introduced yet another bill to abolish the monument— then followed that with two more bills: one that would transfer grazing management of all lands in the monument from the Park Service to the Forest Service, and another to repeal the Antiquities Act of 1906. These new measures did not even make it so far as a vote, but that did not deter Barrett. He would continue to introduce similar measures for as long as he remained a member of Congress, and while none succeeded in killing the monument, the agitation they stirred up in session after session would keep the final disposition of the Rockefeller lands and the integrity of the park unsettled for years. Like Wallace Beery, Congressman Barrett had found himself a good horse and was determined to ride it as far as it would take him.

While the defense of Jackson Hole National Monument was played out in such high drama (or low comedy) as Wallace Beery's ride for freedom, two other rescue efforts were engineered more quietly, but with more unequivocal success. One brought Irving Brant into the conservation fray again. He was still writing his multivolume biography of James Madison and was now working as an editorial writer for the *Chicago Sun* as well, but he remained an active legman and propagandist for the Emergency Conservation Committee and continued to funnel information to the White House and to Ickes at the Interior Department when it seemed appropriate. Brant retained a special interest in Olympic National Park, whose designation and configuration owed so much to his work in the 1930s, and when word came to him that the park was threatened shortly after the beginning of the war, it did not take him long to move.

Timber industry people had begun to express an interest in the timber resources of the Morse Creek watershed above the city of Port Angeles early in 1942, using as an excuse the need for high-quality spruce in the construction of airplanes for the war effort. Morse Creek was one of the areas that Brant had recommended be added to the park. No action had yet been taken, but when the timber companies proposed that the Forest Service let them start cutting, Brant and his allies in Port Angeles had managed to persuade city officials that to let logging take place in their principal watershed would be criminally stupid, and on March 2, Brant wrote Roosevelt urging him to issue a proclamation adding twenty thousand acres of the Morse Creek area to the park immediately. He also warned that "sawmill interests in the Olympic peninsula are making a heavy drive on the WPB and Secretary Ickes to get the national park opened to lumbering on the plea of war necessity."

Roosevelt would add the Morse Creek watershed to the park in May 1943, but Brant's warning about the broader threat was well taken. Ever since the beginning of Lend-Lease, in fact, the industry had urged that it be allowed to log such parts of the park as the Hoh and Bogachiel valleys, whose ancient forests of uncut spruce, hemlock, and Douglas fir were enough to bring tears of avarice to the eyes of any timber company executive. In response, Park Service director Drury had issued a memorandum to then-undersecretary Dempsey in November 1941 setting forth his conviction that "Legislation to permit logging in Olympic National Park should be resisted" and that "In order to insure an adequate supply of airplane spruce, and at the same time to relieve the pressure on the Olympic National Park, the possibility of utilizing the large spruce resources in Alaska should be investigated at once, with a view to making this large body of spruce available for purposes of national defense."

After the war began, F. H. Brundage, western log and lumber administrator for the WPB, had ignored that recommendation, turning a sympathetic ear instead to the pleas of industry that the park be opened to logging. Early in 1943, in the hope of relieving some of this pressure, Ickes reluctantly authorized the sale and selective cutting of about three million board feet of Sitka spruce and eight hundred thousand board feet of Douglas fir in a portion of the Queets River Corridor, not yet an official part of the park but managed by the Park Service as if it were. ("Fortunately," Brant remembered, "no sale made then did any serious injury to the corridor.") This concession had little effect. Encouraged by Brundage's inclinations, the Port Angeles Chamber of Commerce (its own watershed safely tucked into the park) passed a resolution in April 1943 asking the President to open the Hoh and Bogachiel valleys and other areas to logging, adding that "Should it be legally impossible . . . for this elimination to be made by the president, we urgently request our Senators and Representatives to request Congress to pass an Act to transfer from the jurisdiction of the U.S. National Park Service to the jurisdiction of the U.S. Forest Service the area herein described, to be administered by them under their Sustained Yield Policy."

Other Olympic Peninsula communities were making similar statements, and in May, Newton Drury took a trip to Port Angeles to assess the situation and share Park Service thinking with local interests. "They were advised," he summarized in a report made to Presidential secretary Marvin McIntyre at Ickes's request early in June

> that the cutting of any of the live timber within the national park under any system of logging, however restrictive, would be contrary to the principles upon which the park was established; that, once logging of timber is introduced, the area no longer exists as a superlative virgin forest; and that, if it eventually should be determined that the cutting of part of the timber within the national park is essential to the successful prosecution of the war, then undoubtedly steps would be taken to permit such logging, but the Nation would have to accept the fact that . . . the qualities that justified the establishment of the national park will be sacrificed.

One possibility Drury left open was that some of the most recent additions to the park (not including the Morse Creek area) might be made available if absolutely necessary, a contingency he included in an official report sometime later. Brant, who apparently managed to see everything that passed into, through, and out of the National Park Service offices in Chicago, was distressed when he read Drury's comments. "While I understand from him that they outline concessions to which he is opposed, but which he fears may become necessary later," he wrote Ickes on July 7, "I can't help feeling that this is a time for an 'offensive defensive' rather than the charting of a line of retreat." Ickes replied that he agreed with Brant's feeling that it was time to go on the offensive. "I agree with you about Newton Drury, too. He is a good man but not a fighter."

In the middle of July, Rosalie Edge of the Emergency Conservation Committee checked in with a welcome bit of ammunition. The Washington State treasurer, Otto A. Case, had asked her to tell Ickes that studies his office had completed showed nearly 2.5 billion board feet of spruce available on private land in the state and another billion or so available on state and national forest land. The claim that the war required the opening up of the park was nonsense, he said, alarmist propaganda spread by the "same old crowd" that had fought the designation of the park in the first place and was now determined to get its hands on the locked-up timber—driven less by a commitment to the war effort than by a desire to get in position for an anticipated postwar building boom. "There is plenty of timber available without spoiling the beauties of the great Olympic National Park," he insisted. Another arrow in the quiver of Ickes, Brant, and their allies was supplied by Reino Sarlin, assistant forester for the National Park Service, who testified before a hearing in Seattle on the lumber industry's war needs. Just ahead of him, Chief Forester William B. Greeley of the Forest Service had claimed that Olympic National Park contained three billion board feet of spruce. Sarlin's calculations put the figure at closer to 758 million board feet—and as little as eighty million of that, he told Irving Clark of the Wilderness Society after his testimony, was commercially loggable.

When stacked up against the Washington state treasurer's calculations of timber available everywhere else in the state, such figures made Olympic National Park a singularly minor source of wing struts and propellers. By one means or another—possibly through the good offices of Bruce Catton, one of Donald Nelson's chief assistants and a good friend of Brant's—this and the ulterior motives of the timber industry were made clear to the WPB, one of the few government agencies in Washington impervious to the influence of western politicians. And by the fall of 1943, the importance of the park's timber to the war effort was further diminished by the growing use of aluminum for airplane construction, by an increase in timber production from Alaska, and by the importation of logs from British Columbia. All these factors combined to lay the matter to rest during hearings before the House Subcommittee on Lumber Matters in October, when J. Philip Boyd, director of the Lumber and Lumber Products Division of the WPB (and Brundage's superior), put the coffin lid on the hopes of the timber industry by telling the committee that the logging of Sitka spruce from the park was not necessary to meet war needs and that the Department of the Interior had been so notified.

Then there was the matter of federal water. The Bureau of Reclamation had never been one of the Secretary's favorite agencies. Like the National Park Service during the days of Stephen Mather, the bureau had always assumed greater autonomy within the Interior Department than the law had predicated—an independence of mind and spirit that had been perpetuated under strong administrators like Elwood Mead and, after Mead's death in 1936, John C. Page. These men were engineers, not social scientists; they were interested in projects like Boulder, Grand Coulee, and Bonneville dams as demonstrations of American engineering know-how in the conquest of rampaging nature and in the electric power they could be made to produce. So was Ickes, whose longtime interest in public power development, especially, tended to dominate his attitudes toward Reclamation projects. So long as the bureau did not challenge him on those aspects of the agency's job in which he was interested, he did not challenge it—or interest himself in supervising its day-to-day operations, most of the responsibility for which had fallen to his various undersecretaries.

From top to bottom, then, the Department of the Interior and the Bureau of Reclamation had conspired to ignore one of the most significant parts of the 1902 legislation that had created the bureau: the 160-acre limitation law. On Ickes's part, at least, the ignorance may have been real; there is no indication that he even was aware of the stipulations of the law until the 1940s. Having been systematically spurned for more than three decades, the 160-acre law was one of the least known and understood in the land, and neither Mead nor Page nor anyone else in the Bureau of Reclamation had ever brought it to his attention, possibly fearing that if they did he would make them enforce it—a prospect that doubtless appalled them. Ickes's assistants had been no more forthcoming. Both E. K. Burlew and Alvin J. Wirtz, for example, had routinely authorized two major exceptions to the limitation law—Burlew with regard to the Colorado–Big Thompson Project in 1938 while Ickes was on his honeymoon, and Wirtz for a project on the Truckee River in Nevada in 1940. Neither had bothered to tell the Secretary about their actions.

It is not difficult to understand why. The law stipulated that each farm serviced by a Reclamation project could receive cheap federal water on only 160 acres (320 acres for a man and wife); any lands in excess of the limitation had to be sold at prewater prices within ten years of receiving federal water; further, the farmers in question had to live on and cultivate the land themselves. The law was designed to perpetuate the small family farm, already suffering a decline, but from the beginning a great deal of the federal water had been going to corporate farming operations whose control over local politics and economies in the western states often surpassed even that of the livestock industry. The enforcement of the 160-acre limitation law was a potato much hotter than the bureau and most Interior bureaucrats cared to handle, and they simply had not done so.

Tradition was not insurance enough for the corporate farming interests, however, especially not when a reorganization in the administration of the Bureau of Reclamation in 1943 threatened to set in motion enforcement proceedings for the first time—and do so on the Central Valley Project, the largest single Reclamation project still under construction. There were a great many family farms in the region that would benefit from reclamation water obtained under the stipulations of the law; there were also a great many corporate farms which would not get the cheap water if the law was enforced—namely, the Southern Pacific Railroad, with 109,000 acres; Standard Oil of California, with 79,844 acres; Will Gill & Sons, with 29,926 acres; the Bellridge Oil Company, with 25,544 acres; the Anderson & Clayton Company, with 19,144 acres; the J. G. Boswell Ranch Company, with 16,700 acres; the DiGiorgio Company, with 10,000 acres; and other businesses whose "factories in the field," to use author Carey McWilliams's phrase, far exceeded the limits of reclamation law.

These industries began to look to their knitting when John C. Page, who had demonstrated sympathy with their cause on more than one occasion, retired in 1943 and Harry Bashore was hired to take his place. Bashore reported to Michael Straus, who had been raised from his position as Ickes's press secretary to that of assistant secretary, and both Bashore and Straus were unknown quantities; they might decide to take reclamation law more seriously than any officials had in the past. Their first move suggested the possibility: they established a regional office in Sacramento and put Charles E. Carey in charge. Virtually his entire responsibility would be to oversee the development of the Central Valley Project.

Carey, an engineer with expertise in hydroelectric development, had little knowledge of irrigation law, but he was a fast learner, according to Paul Schuster Taylor, an economist and social scientist at the University of California who had been hired as a consultant to the Interior Department's Power Division by Arthur Goldschmidt. (Goldschmidt had taken the position vacated by Abe Fortas when the Interior Department's continuing game of musical chairs had made Fortas undersecretary in 1942.)* "I met Charles Carey one afternoon in his office in the old Post Office building in Sacramento," Taylor remembered.

> Carey was in Sacramento on his first trip to take over his new position. The office was in complete lack of order. The telephone was still on the floor because there was no desk, but there were two chairs. We talked for a long time. He told me the story of public power; I told him the story of acreage limitation of which he had never heard. His response was fully in sympathy with it. . . .
>
> Not long after—in weeks or a month or so—Carey was invited to speak before the California Farm Bureau Federation convention and was asked the question: would he apply the acreage limitation? His response was, yes, of course; it was the law.

---

* Taylor, who would go on to become the leading scholar (and proponent) of reclamation law in the country, had already achieved a measure of fame. A field researcher for the Farm Security Administration on the migrant labor problem, he had teamed up with his wife, photographer Dorothea Lange, to produce one of the three great books of 1939 on migrant laborers: *American Exodus: A Record of Human Erosion*. The other two 1939 books, of course, were Carey McWilliams's *Factories in the Field: The Story of Migratory Farm Labor in California* and John Steinbeck's novel, *The Grapes of Wrath*. Little wonder that the Associated Farmers of California and other conservative organizations were convinced there was a leftist conspiracy against them in California. Each of the books, however, was produced quite independently of the others, and Steinbeck and McWilliams had never even met.

No federal official had talked like that in California for decades, and it worried the corporate farmers and their spokesmen in Congress. In the spring of 1944, Alfred J. Elliott, a farm-owning congressman from Tulare County in the San Joaquin Valley, quietly introduced a rider to the appropriations bill for rivers and harbors that exempted the state of California from enforcement of the 160-acre limitation law. The stipulation rode through to passage with no particular opposition—in fact, it had taken the Bureau of Reclamation completely by surprise, and it was not until the Senate Commerce Committee scheduled hearings on the House bill for May 8 that the agency began to take action. It was pretty timid action—at least in the beginning. Straus and Bashore were not at all sure that the rider could be defeated in the Senate and worked with Congressman Jerry Voorhis to come up with a compromise amendment that would exempt those farms already getting water from portions of the project that had been completed by 1944.

Taylor and Goldschmidt opposed this. "Now the question was," Taylor said they told Straus, "should a concession be offered in the Senate? Or should there be an out-and-out no-compromise fight to retain the law?"

"I tell you, boys," Straus said, "you're right—*if* you can win."

Taylor thought they could and took that message to Ickes. "I was called in to speak to Ickes a couple of times," he recalled, "so that he could get his personal impressions of me as a source of information and as a guide to what the position of the department should be." The position should be one of no compromise, Taylor told the Secretary. "He responded beautifully. . . . Secretary Ickes was a man who relied upon his own judgment, after careful examination of the subject and consultation with those in whom he had confidence. . . . After learning the meaning of the issue, and that his subordinates had been allowing its circumvention . . . he became a staunch and effective supporter of the law and its enforcement."

The Secretary ordered the agency to resist any compromise measure and to testify against the Elliott amendment. Taylor brought in witnesses from the AF of L, the CIO, the National Grange, the Veterans of Foreign Wars, and other interested citizens, among them John Swett, director of the Contra Costa Farm Bureau and a man who made a decent living off 170 acres of land:

> Vast haciendas, great plantations, land baronies, latifundia, may provide caviar and champagne for the barons, their associates, and their knights in legal armor, but their men who do the work on the acres, in the past, have had rather meagre fare. . . . We hope [the Senators] will not be seduced by the powerful few who aspire to the domination of the "agricultural empire" that they would create in the Central Valley. Do we need more emperors or

dictators of empires? Don't we need, for the safety of California, agricultural commonwealths, with family farms?

The weight of testimony against the amendment was too much for the committee to resist. It reported the bill out unfavorably, and in December the whole package was defeated and sent to conference committee to be rewritten. Senator Sheridan Downey, the leading spear carrier for the pro-amendment forces, managed to get the rider grafted back on to the bill, but the committee chairman then recommended that the Senate reject the conference report. This was done, and the assault against the 160-acre limitation law was repulsed.

Which is not to say that the law was suddenly enforced with a vigor that would have gladdened the heart of Francis Newlands, who had given birth to the Reclamation Act of 1902. By the time Central Valley Project water became available to most of the contested lands, Michael Straus had been appointed head of the Bureau of Reclamation by President Harry S. Truman and after Ickes's departure soon proved himself no match for the political muscle Downey and the corporate farmers were able to exercise. While they were never quite able to get the limitation law repealed, they frustrated attempts at enforcement at every turn and during one period even managed to cut off his salary through the appropriations process, forcing him to work without pay for fiscal year 1948. Straus left the agency during the Eisenhower administration and the law never would be enforced with any regularity. In 1970, Paul Schuster Taylor could still complain that "with the passing of time it becomes ever clearer that while the desert may blossom as the rose, the political power of giant land-owners has taken precedence over people. Law observance is a victim, honored in the breach." And to all intents and purposes, the walls of limitation came tumbling down altogether in 1982, when Congress amended the Reclamation Act for the first time since its passage, raising the number of eligible acres to a minimum of 960 and emasculating several of the stipulations that had once given it the character of revolution.

CHAPTER
· 54 ·

A Species of Redemption

THROUGH IT ALL, now muted, now pitched high enough to interrupt thought, but forever present, was the threnody of war. It was so commonplace now as to be both banal and incomprehensible, a matter of headlines, newsreels, reports, statistics, and casualty lists whose sterile march down all the pages was a kind of shorthand for levels of horror that could not truly be understood by anyone who was not there to witness or experience them personally.

Harold L. Ickes was as insulated from the reality of war as most Americans—although he got more than his share of the paper that the engines of war produced, since the Interior Department's Division of Territories and Island Possessions was still the principal civilian authority in Hawaii and Alaska, each of which was feeling the impact of the conflict in varying degrees. In addition, in September 1942, after General Douglas MacArthur's forces had been defeated in the Philippines and the general himself had escaped to Australia, Roosevelt issued an order to Ickes transferring all the duties of the High Commissioner of the Philippines to the Secretary: "While the work of the High Commissioner's office has been materially changed in character as a result of military action and the occupation of the Philippines by Japanese forces," the order said with bland understatement, we must be ready to deal with the many new problems that will confront us when the enemy is ousted from Philippine soil. . . . It will be your duty to undertake the conduct of such studies and investigations as may be necessary to enable us to deal with these problems when the time arrives. . . .

In the conduct of your studies and investigations you will consult with the President of the Philippines and other officials of the Philippine Government to the extent that you find it necessary or advisable.

Most of the planning for the future in the Philippines was done in the cubbyholes of the Division of Territories and Island Possessions, as well as the Interior Department's legal division. Ickes's contacts with Manuel L. Quezon, the president of the Commonwealth of the Philippines, and his government-in-exile were limited. Quezon was a dying man and was obsessed with seeing the promise of the Philippines Independence Act of 1934—a promise Roosevelt reiterated in August 1943 when he said that "the Republic of the Philippines will be established the moment the power of our Japanese enemies is destroyed." From his sickbed in a sanitarium at Saranac Lake, New York, he petitioned Ickes, Roosevelt, Secretary of War Stimson, and anyone else in the government who would listen to him.

But it was not until the end of September 1943, when Senator Millard Tydings—he who had been giving Ickes fits over territorial matters for years—announced his intention to introduce legislation granting immediate independence to the islands, that the administration made its move. Roosevelt asked Samuel Rosenman, still acting as one of the President's many uncategorized special assistants, to get Ickes, Stimson, and Tydings together with Quezon to work out the details of a Presidential message to Congress requesting authority to proclaim a free Philippine Republic. Quezon came down to Washington for the meetings, which were held around the dying man's bedside at the Shoreham Hotel during the first week in October.

Rosenman forgot neither the occasion nor Quezon's intensity: "These conferences were among the most dramatic episodes of my years in Washington," he remembered. "His small body, his tiny, emaciated, flushed face seemed to make his large bed seem larger. . . . He was tensely holding on to life, determined to carry on in the cause to which he had dedicated his whole career." Ickes and Stimson (who had served as governor-general of the Philippines himself during the Coolidge administration) resisted the Tydings plan, feeling that there was not enough structure to support an independent government-in-exile. They believed it would be better to wait until the reconquest of the islands and the beginning of a suitably coherent rehabilitation effort. Quezon and his vice president, Sergio Osmena, of course, supported immediate independence, believing that it would give the most comfort to the hard-pressed Philippine guerrillas and the greatest discomfort to the puppet government the Japanese had installed. After three days of discussions, compromise language for the request to Congress was worked out that stopped just short of granting outright independence. It stipulated the use of the phrase "independence after the Japanese have been expelled," while giving the American President the latitude to declare full independence at any earlier date that seemed feasible, after consultation with the commonwealth government. In exchange, Quezon would agree to grant the American government such military bases in the islands as "necessary for the mutual protection of the Philippine Islands and of the United States." The agreement was signed by Roosevelt and sent to the Congress on October 6; living up to his part of the arrangement, Tydings then shepherded it through to approval.

Ten months later, in July 1944, Quezon died. A little over three months after that, MacArthur's invasion of the island of Leyte marked the first step toward the reconquest of the Philippines. Manila would be retaken in February 1945, and by that summer, the Philippines would be fully secured. But Roosevelt, too, was dead by then and both Ickes and Stimson would be gone from the cabinet before Roosevelt's promise could be fulfilled by another President on July 4, 1946.

If the Japanese military occupation of the Philippines was the chief obstacle to the Secretary's proper administration of affairs for those islands, the American military occupation was Ickes's biggest headache in the governing of Hawaii. Within hours of the attack on Pearl Harbor, martial law was declared arbitrarily and quite illegally by the local military authorities (but was swiftly confirmed by order of the President). All hotels were seized for military purposes. Liquor stores, bars, dance halls, arcades, and whorehouses were closed. A curfew was established and universal blackouts instituted. *Habeas corpus* was suspended; Japanese aliens deemed suspicious—including a number of Buddhist priests—were rounded up and several hundred sent to the mainland for the duration. Civilian courts and police stations were closed down and justice, including the enforcement of traffic laws, was meted out by the Provost Marshal's office. The press was censored. The Hawaiian Territorial Guard, made up largely of nisei, American-born Japanese, was dissolved. Citizens and noncitizens alike were required to get and carry identification cards. A forty-four-hour work week was instituted, wages were frozen, and labor strikes forbidden—in fact, any worker who left his job without permission of the military for any reason was subject to fine and imprisonment. Not since Lincoln had closed down Washington, D.C., during the Civil War had an entire region of the United States been so completely militarized.

While some minor restrictions were lifted in the coming months (liquor stores and bars would be reopened, for example), Hawaii became an occupied territory—and stayed that way long after even the military conceded that any threat of invasion or further attack by the Japanese was unlikely. Among other reasons for the long military reign, some of the more cynical pointed out, was the fact that the executives who ran the Big Five companies enjoyed the presence of a thoroughly subdued and controlled labor force and encouraged the authoritarian instincts of the territory's military governors—particularly those of Lieutenant General Robert C. Richardson, Jr., by all accounts a genuine martinet.

The civilians of the islands needed someone in the government to stand up for them, Ickes was convinced. Governor Joseph B. Poindexter, whom Ickes and Roosevelt had so reluctantly appointed in March 1934, was too ineffectual to be a match for the army, but territorial law still prevented Ickes from appointing any governor who had not lived in the islands for at least five years. As the next best thing, in February 1942 he sent Ben W. Thoron to Hawaii to act as a special representative of the Secretary of the Interior, reporting directly to Ickes. "Thoron is just the right man for the job," the Secretary noted in his diary on February 7.

> He has been in the government service a long time, practically all of it under me. . . . He is highly intelligent, incisive and firm. He isn't afraid to make up his mind and I don't believe that he will let the Army officers run over him, although he will do his best to cooperate. I told him that, in effect, I wanted him to take over the duties of the Governor but to do it tactfully, and allow Poindexter to feel that he is really functioning. I told him also that he was to resist any improper demands on the part of the Army.

Thoron, no matter how intelligent, incisive, and firm he may have been, was, like Ickes himself, powerless to do more than complain about the military's abridgment of civil rights. Only Roosevelt, as Commander-in-Chief, could order a change, and after the debacle of Pearl Harbor, FDR was not about to take any unseemly chances with the security of the islands. Even a visit to Honolulu in July 1944 for strategy discussions with MacArthur, Admiral Nimitz, and Admiral Leahy did not change his mind. It was not until October 24, 1944, just hours before the Battle of Leyte Gulf finished off what was left of the Japanese navy, that the President was finally persuaded to issue a proclamation terminating martial law and restoring *habeas corpus*.

Hawaii at least remained uncorrupted by battle—after the Pearl Harbor attack, at any rate. Not as much could be said for Alaska, whose position gave it strategic importance to both sides in the Pacific War—though it had taken quite a while for Congress to be convinced of this. As early as 1935, Anthony Dimond, Alaska's nonvoting congressional delegate, had pointed out to his colleagues the fact that unfortified Alaska was even more vulnerable to attack than fortified Hawaii: "What is the use of locking one door and leaving the other one open? It is only too obvious that a hostile force moving across the Pacific could avoid Hawaii entirely and seize the coast of Alaska and as much of the mainland as required, establishing there speedily a base of attack on the northwestern and western part of the United States." Two years later, he would repeat himself on the point, and do so again in the spring of 1940.

By then, however, the navy had already started construction of air bases at Kodiak Island and Sitka, together with a radio station at Dutch Harbor on Unalaska Island in the eastern Aleutians. In July 1940, the army sent Lieutenant General Simon Bolivar Buckner, Jr., to Anchorage as head of the Alaska Defense Command, and after that the militarization of Alaska got under way in full force, so that, by December 7, 1941, there were about twenty-two thousand army troops, twenty-two hundred army and navy pilots and support personnel, and 550 navy people stationed in Alaska.

Jean Potter, a reporter for *Fortune* magazine, toured the territory in the summer of 1941. At Fort Richardson outside Anchorage, she wrote,

> where there was nothing but wilderness, a great city of soldiers, busier and more populous than Anchorage itself, has sprung into being. Huge hangars have been built, and all day and all night, bombers and fighters roar up off the new concrete runways of nearby Elmendorf Field. Many thousands of men in uniform are living in the miles of tents and hastily constructed barracks at Fort Richardson. . . .
>
> As fast as boats could be loaded, they steamed to Alaska jammed to bursting with defense workers and supplies. Over twenty thousand construction workers migrated north in two years. Soldiers swarmed up faster than barracks could be built to house them. The towns near the bases were thronged with officers and privates from all over the States. . . . It seemed as if Alaska were one great army camp, with most of its population in uniform.

The military boom reached even greater heights after the attack on Pearl Harbor, but unlike Hawaii, martial presence here was never quite translated into martial law—though Ickes had to spend some time in the spring of 1942 working to prevent its equivalent. Early in March 1942, Alaska's governor, Ernest Gruening—whose career at the Division of

Territories and Island Possessions and as administrator of the Puerto Rican Reconstruction Administration had complicated the Secretary's life so colorfully in the previous decade—came to see him in Washington. The governor had lately been stirring things up in his new position, principally by pushing for a coastal route for a highway connection between Alaska and the United States through Canada. Some kind of road had been under consideration by the two governments for years before the war brought a new urgency to the idea. Of the routes considered, the Army Corps of Engineers, which would be building the road, had chosen an interior one and Ickes's department had agreed. But Gruening continued to press for a shorter coastal route, which would, however, be vulnerable to military attack and harder to build. Ickes finally had to shut him up with a direct order. (Construction on the Alcan Highway began early in February 1942 and was completed in a little over eight months.)

Gruening, quite as stubborn as his boss, made one more brief complaint about the route during his meeting with Ickes on April 8, but he had other things on his mind, as well. "He has picked up rumors," Ickes told his diary, "that it is the plan to replace him with a retired general or admiral. According to him, and he gets about a lot, Dempsey [still Ickes's undersecretary at that time] has been spreading this story." As a matter of fact, Ickes noted in that same entry, he had heard from Budget Director Harold Smith that Roosevelt was not sure Gruening was the right man for Alaska during a war. Smith had asked Ickes whether he could suggest a replacement. "I reminded him that Gruening had been the President's selection, not mine," Ickes wrote. "I had given no thought to a replacement of Gruening and I have no one to suggest. I am not so sure that I think it would be wise to make a change now." He did not tell Gruening on April 8 of the President's thinking, but "I did tell him that I had no such plans and that he might know that, in any event, I would not be in favor of a general or an admiral." Unlike most of their encounters, this one ended amicably.

A little over a week later, Ickes learned that not only Gruening's job but the entire civilian government of Alaska was in jeopardy. Two analysts from the Bureau of the Budget and one from the National Planning Board came to see Ickes and Burlew on April 17, armed with a proposed order from the President regarding the military government of Alaska. "We were given copies of the proposed order," Ickes wrote.

> It simply wiped out the civilian administration and turned it all over to the War Department. . . . I won't even attempt to set down the substance of our

conversation, but I tore this order apart and told these young chaps just what I thought of their methods and of their purposes. . . . I told them that I would not take lying down any such proposal. . . .

When I asked for specific instances of things not done properly . . . [all] that they could say was that Gruening was unpopular. We assured them that of course he was. He was unpopular because he was an outside man [who] believed that the Alaskans should pay some local taxes instead of milking the Treasury all the time. . . .

When they asked me to suggest what I thought ought to be done, my proposal was that some sort of a war council be set up under the chairmanship of the Governor. On this should be represented the various Departments that have large interests in Alaska, as well as the War and the Navy Departments. They finally retreated in a good deal of disorder and said that they would try to work out something along the line of my suggestion.

Ickes won the battle but lost the war. While the civilian government remained functional in Alaska, there was never any question about who was in charge. Less rigidly but no less unmistakably than in Hawaii, military considerations took precedence over civilian matters whenever a conflict between the two arose. The relationship became even more firmly established after June 1942, when in an attempt to draw American carrier forces north from the American-held island of Midway, which the main Japanese force was preparing to attack, the Japanese navy sent two small carriers into waters off the Aleutian Islands, then launched an air attack on Dutch Harbor—by then built into a good-sized air and submarine base—on June 3.

The attack was not much of a blow to the American military effort. Nor did it succeed in distracting the American fleet from its full concentration on Midway, where on June 4, after hours of the most intense naval and air fighting yet seen in the Pacific theater, the Japanese were defeated. But two days later Japanese planes once again bombed and strafed the base at Dutch Harbor, this time to somewhat greater effect, and the following day, Japanese infantry landed on the islands of Attu and Kiska in the western Aleutians, quickly capturing the ten sailors manning a weather station on Kiska and the thirty-nine Aleut villagers on Attu (after killing an American missionary). The Japanese would occupy both islands until the middle of 1943, when American assault forces finally took them back.

Under the circumstances, Alaska's place in the war machine could hardly be argued, but Ickes nevertheless did what he could to maintain a strong civil presence, for he hoped that the postwar years would see a resurgence of settlement in the territory—careful settlement, planned settlement, the kind that had been dreamed of by those who had started the Matanuska Colony north of Anchorage back in the early days of the New Deal. He believed—as he had from the moment he first saw the place in 1938—that Alaska's most important function would always be as the permanent repository of some of the most compellingly beautiful country and richest wildlife populations left anywhere in the world; he was convinced that most of it should remain protected in national parks, wildlife refuges, and other federal reserves. At the same time, he knew that commercial development was both inevitable and to a certain degree desirable. He wanted to help shape the outlines of that development so that the use of the territory's abundance of natural resources would not replicate the work of unfettered greed that had made a wreckage of so much of the American continent already.

Since he did not fully trust the reports he got from Gruening, Ickes had hired his own correspondent to keep him informed about the territory and its promise. She was Ruth Gruber, a young Ph.D., whose book, *I Went to the Soviet Arctic,* had caused something of a sensation (including accusations of communistic leanings) when it was published in 1940. In the summer of 1941, Ickes hired her as a special assistant to snoop around in Alaska and keep him informed about anything she deemed appropriate or interesting, a job she would perform off and on until the summer of 1944.

The Secretary was particularly interested in learning as much as possible about the attitudes and feelings of the people—not merely those who had lived in the territory for a long time, but those military personnel and civilians who had been called north to prepare for war—and who might remain to become the core of a new generation of Alaskans. In that regard, he must have been disappointed in what Ruth Gruber was uncovering. Just before Pearl Harbor, she had reported from Anchorage that "The question of morale, serious enough in the States, is really acute here. There have been a distressing number of suicides and insanities among the soldiers. . . . Evenings hang heavy; new saloons open almost over night; the red light districts spread and flourish while men and women search desperately for time-killers. . . . The boys look upon the territory as a prison, a place of exile. The general attitude is, 'If the Germans get Alaska, they deserve it.' " Three months after the American entrance into the war, the situation had not improved. From Dutch Harbor, then in the throes of construction, Gruber reported on March 2, 1942, that she had been

> talking to all the leaders and as many of the men as possible trying to learn
> their mental attitude toward the territory. . . . For the most part, their

mental attitude toward Alaska is about the attitude of prisoners in a work camp. They dislike Alaska and they hate the base. . . . The superintendent of the construction job here at Dutch Harbor told me frankly that he assumes that most of his thousand odd men (who come and go at a sickening pace) come here only to get the money and get out. . . . One of the navy officers . . . expressed the general navy sentiment: "Why do they evacuate only the women? Why don't they evacuate all of us, and give this country back to the Russians?" And a grand old army man crystallized about 95% of the army feeling: "I wish the Japs would take Alaska; then we could go home and feel sorry for them."

Those were the sentiments of the leaders, she said, and they were reflected by the men they commanded or bossed. "There ain't nothin' here but prostitutes and saloon keepers," one civilian worker in Kodiak told her. "There ain't nothin' here at all. You get sick of movies every night— and there ain't no girls to talk to except klooches." In her own "very small and wholly insignificant way," she reported, she had been trying to build morale by giving talks and slide shows to illustrate the glorious scenery the territory possessed. "I've tried to show them why they were sent to Alaska," she said, "what Alaska's importance is, what its future may be like if they build it properly, and how the work that they are doing is speeding the development of the territory by fifty, perhaps even a hundred years." Something had to be done to change attitudes, she said, "since this war may very well set the pattern for the future development of the territory. Alaska's entire economy is being uprooted now, convulsively uprooted. Fishing villages like Kodiak have swollen from 450 to about 10,000; sleepy native villages like Unalaska may be plowed under by army garrisons and disappear . . . while interior towns like Anchorage are booming into cities."

This was exactly what Ickes was afraid of: unplanned, uncontrolled growth and exploitation. It was, in fact, an accurate forecast of precisely what would happen. Some of the estimated 300,000 soldiers and fliers and naval men who were stationed in Alaska during the war would remain or return in spite of their wartime experience; the territory's total nonnative population in 1940 had been thirty-nine thousand, and by 1950 it would grow to ninety-three thousand. But neither Ickes nor his young assistant would be on hand to help direct matters by then, and the economy perpetuated by these new Alaskans—many of whom would stay for only so long as it took to get what it was they came for—was a scaled-down version of wartime frenzy coupled with the boom-and-bust syndrome as experienced on all American frontiers. And while Ruth Gruber in the field and Harold Ickes with his planners in Washington spent much of the rest of the war trying, their efforts to change the character of a history as old as the nation itself were as ineffective as they were noble.

Gruening knew better than to fight history; he stayed in Alaska, helped to nurture the boom as the territorial governor until 1953, became one of the most effective proponents of statehood, and, when that blessing was bestowed in 1959, became a U.S. senator, serving until his defeat in 1968.

The war was not entirely a matter of paper for Ickes, not all of it. One portion of its true face was revealed to him in February 1944 when he assumed one more job—perhaps the single most distressing assignment he had ever taken on for the government: the final responsibility for tens of thousands of Japanese Americans who had found themselves the pawns of circumstance, greed, and prejudice. To a measurable degree, he had his old friend Secretary of the Navy Frank Knox (who would die suddenly of a heart attack in April) to thank for this, for Knox's public statements following the attack on Pearl Harbor had been among the most credible of all the effusions of hysteria that had spewed forth in the first few irrational days after the attack. "I think the most effective Fifth Column work of the entire war was done in Hawaii," he had told the wire services on December 15, 1941. Japanese spies on Hawaii had been responsible for the success of the raid, he said, and he still was saying it on March 24, 1942, this time to a congressional committee:

> There was a considerable amount of evidence of subversive activity on the part of the Japanese prior to the attack. This consisted of providing the enemy with the most exact possible kind of information as an aid to them in locating their objectives, and also creating a great deal of confusion in the air following the attack by the use of radio sets which successfully prevented the commander in chief of the fleet from determining in what direction the attackers had withdrawn and in locating the position of the covering fleet including the carriers.

There was not, in fact, one bit of evidence to support any such claim—not in 1942, not ever. It did not matter, particularly on the West Coast of the United States, where more than 110,000 nisei (American-born), issei (Japanese-born), and kibei (American-born, but educated in Japan) lived. Anti-Oriental sentiment on the coast had been endemic ever since the days of the Gold Rush, but it had blossomed with a particular virulence in the weeks following Pearl Harbor. Hearsay and the most preposterous rumors had taken on the weight of documented fact: Japanese farmers were plowing and planting their fields in the shape of arrows pointing to military and industrial targets; Japanese fishermen were in reality officers and enlisted men in the imperial Japanese navy; Japanese field hands were militiamen; Japanese gardeners, household workers, laundrymen, butchers, bakers, and candlestick makers were actually intelligence agents in a vast espionage network that blanketed Oregon, Washington, and California, financed by Tokyo through Japanese banks and other Japanese businesses; all were waiting for the day of invasion, when they would rip off their benign, inscrutable masks and attack those who had welcomed them to these shores. The Japs had to be removed, taken away from the sensitive, vulnerable coast, taken somewhere else. Now.

Although there had not been one single verified incident of Japanese-American espionage in Hawaii or on the mainland, millions of people in the three West Coast states wholeheartedly believed this indictment, encouraged in their delusions by such explosions of hatred as those of Hearst columnist Harry McLemore in the *San Francisco Examiner* on January 29, 1942:

> Everywhere that the Japanese have attacked to date, the Japanese population has risen to aid the attackers. Pearl Harbor, Manila. What is there to make the Government believe that the same wouldn't be true in California? Does it feel that the lovely California climate has changed them and that the thousands of Japanese who live in the boundaries of the state are all staunch and true Americans?
>
> I am for the immediate removal of every Japanese on the West Coast to a point deep in the interior. Herd 'em up, pack 'em off and give 'em the inside room in the Badlands. Let 'em be pinched, hurt, hungry and dead up against it.

And so it was done. West Coast politicians like California governor Culbert Olson, California state attorney general Earl Warren, and Mayor Fletcher Bowron of Los Angeles; civic groups like the Native Sons of the Golden West and the California State Grange; military men like Colonel Karl Bendetsen and Lieutenant General John L. DeWitt of the Western Defense Command; most of the congressional delegations of all three West Coast states; the secretaries of the Navy and War departments, Frank Knox and Henry L. Stimson—pressure from all these and more simply collapsed the feeble defense of the Constitution put up briefly by Attorney General Francis Biddle. On February 20, 1942, he sent to President Roosevelt the final draft of Executive Order 9066, authorizing the War Department to remove any and all Japanese from the military zone that embraced most of the West Coast. "The President is authorized in acting under his general war powers without further legislation," Biddle assured Roosevelt in a covering note. "The exercise of the power can meet the specific situation and, of course, cannot be considered as any punitive measure against any particular nationalities. It is rather a precautionary measure to protect the national safety."

Within the next several months, this "precautionary measure" had forced 110,000 Japanese Americans from their farms and homes and businesses; had shuttled men, women, and children of all ages into "assembly centers" (former racetracks, fairgrounds, livestock exhibition halls, and the like) with no more personal belongings than they could carry on their backs, stuff under their arms, or hold in their hands; had held them in these overcrowded, unsanitary places for weeks; then had transported them by bus and train to jerry-built "relocation centers" in ten singularly nonstrategic locations, ranging from Tule Lake in northern California to Jerome, Arkansas, from Minidoka, Idaho, to the banks of the Gila River in Arizona. Housed in overcrowded, thin-walled, and poorly heated barracks, surrounded by barbed wire, watched over by guard towers (complete with searchlights and armed sentries), the evacuees may not have been hungry or hurt, but they were inescapably pinched and dead up against it.

Placed under the administration of yet another federal agency—an independent executive bureau called the War Relocation Authority, whose first director was Milton Eisenhower, followed by Dillon Myer—these isolated little communities may have been called Relocation Centers by the government, but Harold Ickes described them for what they were: "Fancy-named concentration camps." He had been against relocation even before it became policy. "The Hearst newspapers are putting on a typical Hearst campaign for the removal and sequestration of all the Japanese along the Pacific Coast," he had noted in his diary on February 1, 1942. "This would be a cruel and unnecessary step." He felt even more strongly about it a month later, when relocation had become policy, calling it "both stupid and cruel. At vast expense and with a total disregard of any considerations due any Japanese, these people will be torn from their homes and transported to inland camps, there to be maintained by the Government until drum-head court martials shall decide whether it is safe for them to return."

Nevertheless, he did little more than occasionally carp to his diary about this abridgment of civil rights until the spring of 1943, when he and Jane hired two Japanese farm workers and their wives to come work on Headwaters Farm. The couples had come from the Arizona camp, having been among the roughly twenty-five hundred who had applied for indefinite leave permits and had satisfied the requirements: that they have the offer of a job or some other visible means of support, that there was evidence that the community to which they were going would accept them, that there was no evidence that they were a security risk to the nation, and that they agreed to keep the War Relocation Authority informed of their whereabouts. (All permittees were forbidden to return to the West Coast.) The Secretary had a personal interest now, and on April 13, 1943, wrote to Roosevelt himself to voice his concern:

> Information that has come to me from several sources is to the effect that the situation in at least some of the Japanese internment camps is bad and is becoming worse rapidly. . . . The result has been the gradual turning of thousands of well-meaning and loyal Japanese into angry prisoners. I do not think that we can disregard, as of no official concern, the unnecessary creating of a hostile group right in our own territory consisting of people who are engendering a bitterness and hostility that bodes no good for the future.

"Like you," Roosevelt replied on April 24, "I regret the burdens of evacuation and detention which military necessity has imposed upon these people. I am afraid some measure of bitterness is the inevitable consequence of a program involving direct loss of property and detention on grounds which the evacuees consider to be racial discrimination." The only solution, the President said, "lies in encouraging the relocation of the Japanese-Americans throughout the country and in turning as many as possible of the relocation centers over to the War Department for use as prisoner-of-war camps. Your own recent action in employing a Japanese family on your farm seems to me to be the best way for thoughtful Americans to contribute to the solution of a very difficult and distressing problem."

The notion that tens of thousands of Japanese were somehow going to be gathered to the bosoms of American families scattered across the land was ridiculous, of course. At best, such arrangements could have disposed of only a few people. In a March 11, 1943, letter to Secretary of War Henry Stimson that outlined various alternatives for the program, WRA director Dillon Myer had estimated that under the present indefinite-leave program—which he called Plan A—he might be able to relocate somewhere between 10 and 25 percent of the evacuees outside the restricted zone in four to six months. "If we can obtain the proper degree of public acceptance and if a sufficient number of evacuees are willing to face the public in unfamiliar areas," he had added, "the volume may be somewhat larger. But in any case . . . I feel certain we shall have to maintain ten relocation centers for some time to come."

So much for Roosevelt's solution. But Myer's letter had offered another idea: remove the ban on the return of evacuees to the West Coast except those unable to pass a security muster before a joint board representing the War Department, the Department of Justice, and the Office of Naval Intelligence. These would be reinterned or excluded from entering specific areas. This, which he called Plan B, would greatly accelerate the relocation process. A third alternative—Plan C—would involve a compromise between the two extremes. "My recommendation," he wrote, "is that we adopt Plan C or something similar to it immediately and that we move toward the adoption of Plan B as soon as real danger of West Coast invasion seems to be eliminated."

Stimson rejected Plans B and C, suggesting instead that the morale problem be met by taking malcontents and other undesirables out of the individual camps and putting them all together in one. Then, perhaps, the War Department would entertain the other alternatives. Myer complied, setting up the Tule Lake, California, camp as a "segregation center" for about nine thousand people who had requested deportation to Japan, or had refused to sign a loyalty oath, or who had intelligence records that suggested them as security risks. That still was not good enough for the War Department—which was being influenced in its thinking by the Western Defense Command, which in turn was being influenced by West Coast politicians, businessmen, and others who had no desire at all to see the Japanese return. The level of hatred remained high, as Ickes himself had learned. "Am I to understand that you are *Molly Coddling* Japs," one Stan C. Jackson of El Cerrito in northern California had written the Secretary when he heard of the Japanese farm workers Ickes had hired. "Just who gives you the authority to remove Japs from concentration points. . . . Why don't you move out there yourself and live with them and make sure they get plenty of sugar for their coffee, ALL JAPS ARE HERE ILLEGALLY BORN FROM PICTURE BRIDES."

Such was the situation in December 1943 when the War Department released information regarding Japanese atrocities against American prisoners of war. The flames of prejudice on the West Coast took on new life. "The bitterest witches' brew since the black days of the Reconstruction is boiling on the Pacific Coast," a reporter for *PM* wrote in January 1944. "A campaign is under way to make lynching popular, and the vast majority of the press, the politicians, the profiteers, and the patriotes 's have enlisted for the duration." The WRA, independent but alone, suddenly seemed very exposed, and on December 30, Attorney General Biddle advised the President to tuck it under somebody's wing: "Some of [WRA's] difficulties with the press and some elements of Congress might be lessened if, instead of being required to meet these pressures as a small new independent agency, WRA were part of a permanent department of the Government under the supervision of a member of the Cabinet and could rely on the relations of such a department with the public and Congress."

Roosevelt agreed and, remembering who had been complaining most loudly about the inadequacies of the whole relocation program, gave it to the Secretary of the Interior on February 16. Ickes met the hysteria head-on, as was his wont, declaring at his first press conference on the subject that under his direction the WRA "will not be stampeded into undemocratic, bestial, inhuman action" by what he characterized as the "vindictive, bloodthirsty onslaughts of professional race-mongers." On June 2, after Stimson finally conceded the lack of any possible danger to the war effort, the Secretary urged Roosevelt to revoke the order forbidding the return of released evacuees to the West Coast:

> It is my understanding that Secretary Stimson believes that there is no longer any military necessity for excluding these persons from the State of California and portions of the States of Washington, Oregon and Arizona. Accordingly, there is no basis in law or in equity for the perpetuation of the ban. . . . I will not comment at this time on the justification or lack thereof for the original evacuation order. But I do say that the continued retention of these innocent people in the relocation centers would be a blot upon the history of this country.

There may have been no basis in law or equity for the continued ban, but there was a definite basis in politics; 1944 was an election year and Roosevelt did not intend to make so dramatic a move until after the polls closed in November. He did not put it that way, of course. What he said to Ickes on June 12 was that "the more I think of this problem of suddenly ending the orders excluding Japanese Americans from the West Coast the more I think it would be a mistake to do anything drastic or sudden." He could not be persuaded to change his mind, and it was not until December 17, with the elections safely behind him, that he issued the directive rescinding the exclusion order.

Myer and his people set about establishing twenty-five relocation offices on the West Coast to facilitate the reentry of the evacuees. Hostels in most of the major cities were established as "halfway houses" for those who would have to look for new homes. There were 150 of these halfway houses in California alone. Various public housing projects in Los Angeles, San Francisco, Sacramento, and other cities were made available. The War Department turned over Fort Funston in San Francisco for evacuee housing. Other military installations and unused barracks were found and utilized. House trailers were rounded up.

None of it was enough. There were simply too many people dumped back into the population too soon. By October 1945, all of the relocation centers except that at Tule Lake had been closed and most of their people taken back to the West Coast. Thousands were living in greater squalor than they had experienced in the centers. "Hostels are nothing but flophouses," a letter given to Congresswoman Helen Gahagan Douglas in October reported. "The San Jose hostel, originally planned for 80, now must accommodate 300. In Cortez and Livingston, housing is particularly pitiful. Reportedly, 25 or 30 are crowded in one large room of the Christian Church at Livingston. In Cortez, family groups are housed in tents supplied by the WRA. Because there is no flooring, occupants cannot remain clean, nor are their facilities kept neat. There is no heating and the chilly nights are distressing to women and children."

"Can a man like Harold Ickes condone the action of the federal government toward these helpless people?" the man who passed the information on to Mrs. Douglas asked. She gave a copy of his letter to the Secretary, whose reply to her is redolent with a level of frustration and sorrow not common with him:

> The job that was handed to this Department was distasteful from every point of view. I believe that Dillon Myer has tried to do a good job but I have been afraid that he was attempting the impossible in carrying out an evacuation schedule that apparently has disregarded the human rights of the Nisei. We were confronted with the alternative of pushing many of the Japanese out or of maintaining them in what really were concentration camps for months or years to come. It was not an easy or a pleasant choice to make. . . .
>
> Mr. Hewes' letter has made me very uncomfortable in my conscience. I wish to hell that people would quit doing that because it has been belabored enough both voluntarily and involuntarily. But I willingly admit that I have a responsibility.

A responsibility, but not a solution. There were no solutions. The Japanese Relocation Program, begun in hatred, fear and anger, ended in fumbling, frustration, and guilt. Slowly, sometimes over a period of years, on their own or with government aid that was never enough, people drifted out of the hostels and interim housing, edged back into society, endured the hatred that still greeted many of them, found work, built homes and restitched families, survived.

There was one ironic grace note in the long, sordid story of Japanese relocation: it gave Ickes the opportunity to provide a small measure of redemption for his country by helping to save some European Jews. By the summer of 1944, the "final solution" to the "problem" of Jews under the reign of Adolf Hitler had become common knowledge throughout most of the world—although it would not be until the liberation of the death camps themselves that the true, immeasurable, nearly inconceivable dimensions of the pathology would be revealed.

Reliable news that Germans had developed a plan for the systematic elimination of Europe's Jews had first reached the United States in August 1942 from a prominent German industrialist who had given the information to Dr. Gerhart Riegner in Switzerland. Riegner, a refugee from Germany himself, was a representative of the World Jewish Congress in Geneva. He took his information to the American and British embassies in Geneva and Bern, which in turn cabled it to London and Washington. The cable from the American legation in Bern to the State Department concluded: "Informant stated to have close connections with the highest German authorities generally speaking reliable."

The informant was reliable; the information was accurate. Corroboration came less than three weeks after the Riegner disclosure had made its way around the State Department and finally into the hands of Rabbi Stephen Wise, at that time the best-known Jewish leader in the United States. The new information, cabled from a representative of the Agudath Israel World Organization in Switzerland to the group's president in New York, Jacob Rosenheim, said that the plan was not merely under consideration—it was under way and at least 100,000 Polish Jews had already died. "The mass murders are continuing," the communication said. "The corpses of the murdered victims are used for the manufacturing of soap and artificial fertilizers. Similar fate is awaiting the Jews deported to Poland from other occupied territories. Suppose that only energetic steps from America may stop these persecutions. Do whatever you can to cause an American reaction to halt these persecutions."

Wise and Rosenheim tried. On the day he received his message, Rosenheim sent it by telegram to the President, then met the next day with James G. McDonald, chairman of the nearly moribund President's Advisory Committee on Political Refugees. McDonald sent a copy of the Rosenheim message to Eleanor Roosevelt. Neither of the Roosevelts ever responded. For his part, Wise went to Sumner Welles at the State Department, who urged him to keep the Riegner disclosure away from the press until he and his people had had a chance to substantiate it. Wise did not show it to the press, but he did share it with a few friends in the government. One of them was Harold Ickes. Reminding Ickes of the 1940 scheme to bring Jewish refugees to the Virgin Islands, Wise asked if that idea could be revived, at least for perhaps a thousand Jewish children. Ickes wrote to Roosevelt on October 7 suggesting the plan once again, adding that in addition to the children, the islands might also be made a refuge "for some adults who, failing this, are likely to be murdered by Hitler's brutes."

Roosevelt's reply was oblique, but amounted to a rejection: "In regard to the Jewish children, I wish you would speak to Sumner Welles about it. I think he is definitely planning to accept a certain number of Jewish refugees from France."*

Roosevelt did not deal directly with the new development until December. By then there was no way to avoid it, had he wanted to. Near the end of November, Sumner Welles had called Wise to his office and handed him documentation gathered by State Department intelligence sources that fully confirmed the news of the extermination effort. In fact, it indicated that as many as two million people were already dead. "For reasons you will understand," Welles told him, "I cannot give these to the press, but there is no reason why you should not. It might even help if you did." Wise did release the documents on November 24, and on December 8 Roosevelt met with Wise and a delegation of Jewish leaders. He expressed dismay at the idea of two million deaths and assured the people gathered in his office that while "the mills of the gods grind slowly . . . they grind exceedingly small. We are doing everything possible to ascertain who are personally guilty." He also promised to issue a strong warning against war crimes, with specific reference to the Jewish situation.

If he intended to make such a statement independently, circumstances intervened. The British government, under considerable pressure from Parliament, was pushing for a joint declaration of promised retribution from Great Britain, the United States, Russia, and representatives of the eight countries now occupied by the Germans. Some officials in the middle levels of the State Department—a region in which many people believed the odor of anti-Semitism was detectable—briefly attempted to block or dilute to the point of vapidity any such statement. The effort failed, and the joint declaration was issued on December 17, condemning the German government's "intention to exterminate the Jewish people in Europe," a program it called a "bestial policy" in response to which the signatory nations promised to take all "necessary practical measures" to see to it that those who were guilty of such war crimes would be prosecuted and punished after the war.

---

* He was referring to the State Department's agreement, made in September, to relax its regulations enough to allow five thousand Jewish children trapped in France to enter this country; the Vichy government stalled, however, and when the Allies invaded North Africa in November, it broke off diplomatic relations with the United States, ending any hope for the children—and the last real effort at rescue the State Department would make.

That was all to the good. It also was nearly all there would be for the next two years, the odds against rescue, almost impossibly high to begin with, being fortified by a combination of indifference, competing priorities, and both passive and active anti-Semitism. The American press would give the news of the Holocaust only occasional attention. The President, preoccupied with the war and, some of his harsher critics would claim, not all that interested in the fate of the Jews to begin with, gave the question only intermittent attention, declaring it his belief that the best and quickest way to save the Jews of Europe was to win the war. Over at the State Department, Secretary Cordell Hull and Undersecretary Sumner Welles sympathized with the victims, but they had other things on their minds and the functionaries below them—particularly Assistant Secretary Breckinridge Long—did everything they could to close American doors to refugees. The War Department had little official interest in the question beyond Secretary of War Henry Stimson's general dislike of immigration. Among those with regular access to the President's ear, only Treasury Secretary Henry Morgenthau and (on those rarer and rarer occasions when he was able to see Roosevelt) Harold Ickes ever took advantage of it to urge the relaxation of refugee laws—and as long as Roosevelt refused to be pinned down, their power to do anything more was limited. After a time, Ickes no longer bothered to discuss it with him. Congress, with the exception of a handful of militant Jewish members like Emanuel Celler of New York, did little but keep a sharp eye out for any relaxation of the immigration laws.

What, then, of the American Jewish community? Riven by a conflict of philosophies and purposes between Zionists and anti-Zionists, Orthodox and Reform, rich and poor, eastern European and western European, divided into a polyglot collection of competing and mutually exclusive organizations, each of which was fiercely jealous of its prerogatives and place in the world, at once cautious and fearful and impetuous and belligerent, the Jews of America were trapped in their own terrible humanity and were rendered impotent. There were those among them who raged in protest. Judah Piltch, for example, wrote in the Hebrew-language weekly *Hadoar* on January 15, 1943:

> And what will happen when my son asks me tomorrow: "What did you do while your brothers were being exterminated and tortured by the Nazi murderers?" What will I say and what will I be able to tell him? Shall I tell him that I lived in a generation of weaklings and cowards who were neither moved nor shocked when they heard of hundreds and thousands of their brothers being led to the slaughter hour by hour, day by day, year by year?

Shall I describe this chapter in the annals of American Jewry and admit that
our people did not meet the test of history?

There was plenty of guilt for the sharing. It was not merely the Jewish
community that was failing the test of history. Nothing would be done in
even a limited way to save the Jews until January 1944, when Roosevelt
was finally persuaded by Henry Morgenthau to sign an Executive Order
establishing a War Refugee Board, to be headed up by Morgenthau,
Secretary of War Stimson, and Secretary of State Hull. In cooperation
with private groups and whatever foreign government agencies were
already involved in rescue work (a short list), special attachés with full
diplomatic status appointed by the board were to find and help organize
programs for the rescue, transportation, maintenance, and relief of the
victims of Nazi oppression wherever possible, and to establish temporary
havens of safety for those smuggled out of danger. Funded by an appropriation of one million dollars, the War Refugee Board was something
around which even the disunited Jewish community could coalesce—or at
least to which it could give financial support. (During the board's life,
Jewish organizations would contribute more than $15 million to its
work.) Before war's end, the work of the board would be directly or
indirectly responsible for the saving of approximately 200,000 lives. It
was a record worth the noting, although the *National Jewish Monthly* for
March 1944 was among those who brought up a subject that was still not
a comfortable one: "American generosity may have to face the fact that
some of the rescued may have to be given at least temporary refuge in the
United States. We can't undertake a job of rescue and expect our allies to
shelter all the rescued. The responsibility of a rescuer includes giving the
rescued a place of refuge in his own house if that is necessary."

Not in the American house, not if the State Department had anything
to do with it—and it did. Breckinridge Long and his associates were the
most consistent voices raised against one of the War Refugee Board's most
creative ideas, the designation of "free ports" in this country that would
provide for the temporary shelter of refugees until the war was over. We
did this sort of thing for trade goods, the reasoning went; why not for
human beings? The Jewish community, especially, seized this idea as the
one thing that the United States could do to make a real difference, and its
disappointment was huge when the only response was a Presidential
Executive Order on June 8, 1944, establishing exactly one such haven—
Fort Ontario outside the town of Oswego in upstate New York, which,
the President said, would be ordered to accommodate up to one thousand
people, including "a reasonable proportion of various categories of per-

secuted peoples." The word "Jew" was not used, Roosevelt fearing the political consequences of an anti-Semitic uprising if he put any emphasis on the fact that it was Jews who were being rescued. He also promised an antagonistic Congress that the refugees would be sent back to Europe just as soon as practicable after the cessation of hostilities. "Is this the act of salvation for which we waited with such longing?" the editor of *Hadoar* asked. "Whence will help come? Who will save those who can still be saved? A dreadful question—for the world, for America, for ourselves." And I. F. Stone called the gesture "a kind of token payment to decency, a bargain-counter flourish in humanitarianism."

It was indeed not much, but it was all that the President was prepared to do in an election year, encouraged in his timidity by the State Department and political advisers. The question remained as to which government agency would assume responsibility for the Oswego sanctuary. The War Department was willing to contribute the facility at Fort Ontario, but that was all. The State Department wanted nothing to do with any part of the project. The War Refugee Board would oversee the operation, but the only department with practical experience in the care and feeding of people in a camp setting was the Department of the Interior, proprietor of the War Relocation Authority's operations for the interned Japanese Americans. And it was the Department of the Interior that was given the responsibility for the care of the 984 Yugoslavian refugees, most of them Jews, who were to be taken out of Italy and brought to Fort Ontario.

Among those who received the news of this rescue mission with uncommon interest was Ickes's assistant Ruth Gruber, the young woman who had been acting as a kind of intelligence agent in Alaska since 1941. She was working in Washington in June 1944 when she read of the President's decision. She went immediately to her boss with the suggestion that he send her over to Italy to bring the refugees back. They were coming to a strange land, frightened and alone, she said. It would help if a sympathetic American Jew were on hand to help them through the ordeal. It did not take the Secretary long to act, she recalled in *Haven,* her story of the Oswego refugees. "It's a great idea," Ickes exclaimed, and put in a call to Dillon Myer. "Myer," he said, "I want to send someone over to Italy to bring back those refugees. What? You've already selected someone? A man? You send your man. I'm sending her. That's right. It's a woman. A young woman. What's that?" His jowls, Gruber remembered, were now trembling with anger. "What has being young got to do with this job? Being young didn't stop her from getting a Ph.D. in literature when she was twenty. . . . And she took it in Germany—an exchange student from America. I know her capabilities. She's been working for me now"—he turned to Gruber—"how long is it?" Three years, she told him. "Three years," he continued. "With all kinds of jobs. And this one is right for her. Those refugees are from the Balkans and Central Europe. They probably speak mostly German. She speaks German and Yiddish. There'll be a lot of women and children. She'll know how to speak to them; she'll understand them. You better come in at two-thirty today; I want to talk to you about her."

Gruber got the assignment, in spite of some further complaining from Myer about her sex and age, and joined her charges on board the army troopship *Henry Gibbons* in Naples late in July. Half the ship was given over to the tattered refugees, most of whom had with them little more than the clothes they wore, the other half to a contingent of American soldiers wounded during the Italian campaign. During the voyage, she attempted to soothe the fears of the refugees, many of whom were convinced that they were on their way to another concentration camp. She settled squabbles, acted as a go-between for people from different villages in different regions of different countries whose only commonality was their Jewishness and their peril. She organized English-language lessons and helped put together a musical-comedy revue written and performed by the refugees for the soldiers. She comforted the frightened women and children during the blackouts when there was fear of air attack and the long hours of silence when the ship lay dead in the water in order to avoid submarine attack. Above all, she listened, listened to all the terrible stories the refugees carried with them like burdens that could never quite be put down.

Once the refugees were safely across the Atlantic and placed in the confinement of the Fort Ontario settlement, Gruber made regular visits to the community as Ickes's representative, bringing back reports of the situation there as the refugees struggled to adjust to the limbo in which they found themselves. Their circumstances were never comfortable. They were fed, clothed, and maintained decently, but were allowed to leave the camp only six hours a day. The tensions that were inevitable when people of diverse origins are thrown together against their will multiplied as the months passed. Depression and other mental disorders plagued the camp. Not the least of the problems was uncertainty as to the future. Would Roosevelt stick by his pledge to Congress that they would be deported when the war was over? For most of them, that would be a return to the scene of a nightmare they had no desire to relive. What was more, as the war crawled slowly to an end, it was becoming increasingly clear that Europe was so ravaged that it would not be able to support the millions of refugees it already possessed, much less nearly a thousand more returned from the United States. How would they live?

The refugees were not alone in asking such questions. It was not long after the establishment of the Fort Ontario settlement that Dillon Myer suggested to Ickes releasing the refugees into the general population under a kind of sponsorship program in which private agencies would assume the responsibility for individual refugee families. Ickes supported the idea immediately, finding it "intolerable that anti-Nazis should be kept under lock and key." But the Justice Department and the War Refugee Board refused to allow it, with Morgenthau going along with Stimson and Hull because he feared repercussions that would make life for the released refugees intolerable. Ickes and Myer then pressed Roosevelt to let the refugees be transported to Canada, where they could then apply for visas under the existing quota system and be returned to the United States. The President had every legal right to make such a move, if he chose to. But just as the refugees had feared, Roosevelt would not go back on his promise to Congress, not even after the elections in 1944. The Oswego internees remained at Fort Ontario. They were still there when the war ended, even when the War Refugee Board was dissolved and full responsibility for the Fort Ontario camp was placed in the hands of the Interior Department. For months they waited, as Congress and a new administration decided what to do about them.

Finally, on December 5, 1945, the State Department and the Justice Department collaborated on a letter to the chairmen of the House and Senate committees on Naturalization and Immigration. This letter, which the departments suggested be signed by Ickes, Attorney General Tom C. Clark (who had replaced Francis Biddle), and Secretary of State James F. Byrnes (who had replaced Cordell Hull), recommended that the Oswego refugees be deported. Ickes refused to sign it. Instead, Ruth Gruber remembered, "he asked me to draft a letter to Undersecretary of State Dean Acheson, explaining our position. Secretary of State James Byrnes was out of town."

She did, and on the strength of that letter Acheson met with Gruber and a delegation of supporters for the release of the Fort Ontario refugees on December 14. They handed him a long legal brief outlining the case for release and acceptance under the immigration laws. "I have nothing to report to you now," Acheson said. "I'm going to see the President tomorrow and I'll get back to you." Acheson did not get back to them, but perhaps it was because he soon knew what President Truman was going to announce on December 22. That announcement was called the Truman

Directive, designed to expedite the full use of American immigration quotas to relieve the plight of Europe's "displaced persons," as the universal victims of war were called, and among its stipulations was an order that allowed the Oswego refugees to apply for residence in the United States immediately. "It would be inhumane and wasteful," Truman said, "to require these people to go all the way back to Europe merely for the purpose of applying there for immigration visas and returning to the United States."

"We won," Ickes told Gruber a few days later.

They had won—a tiny victory, certainly, but in a context in which the face of war had been revealed with such squalid power that even a tiny victory gave a measure of solace, one small demonstration of humanity to stand in the shadow of the larger indictment outlined by Elie Wiesel: "The killers killed, the victims perished, and the world, though at war, did not intercede. Marriages and parties were held, daily prayers were recited, dinners and balls were organized: all this as though no flames were consuming the heavens above a small Polish village named Auschwitz.

"Yet in America they knew. Oh, yes, they knew."

CHAPTER
· 55 ·

The Scent of Lilacs

I NTIMATIONS OF MORTALITY: The year 1944, quite aside from what it held for him in the matter of interned Japanese Americans and of European Jews escaping the Holocaust, brought a string of casualties that struck especially close to home and must have intensified the Secretary's awareness of time passing. He endured them with a superficial stoicism probably learned from all the deaths that had punctuated his youth, demonstrating a fatalistic acceptance that may have cloaked considerable inner travail.

The first to go was William Allen White, the great and gentle editor of the *Emporia Gazette* who had stood with Ickes on the crowded Progressive barricades in 1912, who had shared the pain of 1916, when Theodore Roosevelt ripped the hopes of the Bull Moosers to tatters with his last-minute refusal to accept the Republican nomination. They had remained friends in spite of their political differences in the twenties and even during the Franklin Roosevelt years, when White continued to vote Republican in every Presidential election in spite of the fact that he supported most of what FDR and the New Deal were up to. "Bill is with me," Roosevelt had quipped, "three and a half years out of every four." White had been particularly important to Roosevelt in the months just before the war, when, as chairman of the Committee to Defend America by Aiding the Allies, he had become the leading Republican spokesman

for the virtues of Lend-Lease. As for Ickes, White's friendship might best
be seen in a letter he wrote in 1937, when Ickes and Pinchot were at their
snarling worst over the question of possession of the national forests, and
the editor was trying to patch things up between the two old friends. In
the course of the letter to Pinchot, White delivered a eulogy for a time
long past that may have sentimentalized their common struggle, but was
no less touching for its romanticism:

> The other day Mrs. White saw something in a New York paper which
> indicated you were taking a crack at Harold for something or other. I was hurt
> a little. For I know whatever comes, Harold will be honest and imbued with a
> high and noble purpose. He has not changed, no more than you have
> changed, and we who were once so near and dear should not let anything
> come into our lives to lessen the bond of respect and affection which held us
> together so happily in another day. For it was a good day, and the fighting was
> worth while. God knows I didn't do much except stand around and cheer, but
> you boys who were fighting pushed the line forward or we could not be where
> we are now. *

On January 29, 1944, Kansas Day, a little short of his seventy-sixth
birthday, one of the last important lights of the Progressive Era winked
out. "I have been a little worried about Will since he went to the Mayo
Hospital a few months ago for another abdominal operation," Ickes wrote
in his diary the day after White's death. "I was very fond of Will White
and wish that I might have seen more of him during the last few years
than I found myself able to do. I regarded him as one of America's really
great men and the country will miss his high qualities and his intellectual
probity. I have never known anyone like him."

In April, Secretary of the Navy Frank Knox was felled by his heart
attack, and at the end of July, Missy LeHand, Roosevelt's personal secretary, died. Ickes was particularly affected by Missy's death, for like most
of those who had worked for the President he had grown very fond of her
warm and constant presence throughout the years of the New Deal, bright
and efficient and clearly in love with her boss—although no one ever knew

---

* It probably pleased White when Ickes and Pinchot did, in fact, become reconciled—though
not at White's direct intervention. In 1939, Pinchot almost died from a heart attack. When
the old forester recovered enough to receive visitors, Ickes paid a call. On April 29, he wrote in
his diary that he was "glad to be there again on friendly terms with him. I have always liked
him very much indeed in spite of our temporary breaking away from each other." They would
still clash whenever the subject of the forests came up for contention, but never again with the
old bitterness—and in the fall of 1939, Ickes went so far as to offer Pinchot's name to
Roosevelt as a possible head of territories and island possessions when Gruening went to Alaska
as governor. Roosevelt dismissed the idea on the grounds that Pinchot would be too hard to
control.

(apparently even she) just how deeply Roosevelt may have cared for her. She had suffered a stroke in the summer of 1941 and had never fully recovered, though she was well enough to survive for more than three years in the care of her sister in Massachusetts. Ickes had written her from time to time during the years of her illness, sending along chatty, uncomplicated letters about things going on in the White House and with the President she had worshiped. "I was devoted to Missy and I admired her," he told her sister after receiving news of Missy's death. "I have often said that her disability constituted the greatest loss that the President has suffered since his inauguration. She was so wise and so discreet, and she never failed to be helpful when one went to her with his difficulties."

In October, Clinton Hazard, his sister Julia's husband, died after struggling through many years of intermittent illness and deprivation, during which Harold had propped the couple up from time to time. Assuming an old and familiar responsibility, Ickes settled Clinton's affairs for Julia after her husband's burial in Fairview Cemetery in Altoona, where so many of the Ickes family lay, then set up a small annuity that would keep his sister comfortably off for the rest of her life.

By then, the Secretary had been experiencing reminders of his own advancing years. These were anything but abstract. His heart, fully recovered from the attack of 1937, remained strong, but he was still suffering from a staggeringly chronic insomnia. In order to get any sleep at all, he had become increasingly dependent on healthy shots of bedtime whiskey—the taste of which he disliked—almost always taken with some kind of powerful soporific like Seconal.

Frequently, however, even these doses were not enough to keep him down for an entire night; they were merely enough to make him disoriented when he awoke. He began to fall down during the night from time to time now, occasionally with damaging results. "Some time before midnight," he wrote in his diary after one such incident in the middle of May 1944, "I thought that I heard one of the youngsters calling. I got out of bed without waiting to turn on the light or to put my robe on and before I knew it I was in a violent collision with something. I found myself bleeding profusely from my forehead." Jane was in the city for the evening, but Florence Henderson, the housekeeper, and an overnight guest managed to get him to Bethesda Naval Hospital, where three stitches were taken. "It was not a serious accident," he insisted.

Perhaps not, but it was not the only such accident he would have. On sporadic occasions, he would struggle to conquer his dependence on the whiskey-drug combination, and sometimes would stay off the stuff for weeks at a time, but sooner or later the agony of sleeplessness would always drive him back to it. The strain on his mind and body was terrific, and it is a testament to his strength of will that he continued to perform more than a normal day's work most of the time during these years. What is more, not long after his seventieth birthday he found the resources to gallop full-tilt into perhaps the most demanding campaign tour of his life.

As he had for Anna Roosevelt Boettiger back in 1940, Ickes analyzed the 1944 political situation in a letter to his old Chicago friend, Stacey Mosser, in January. "The political situation is far from satisfactory," he wrote.

> Take the Republican side first. I believe that Willkie is talking himself to death, if he has not already done so. In any event, he is erratic and unpredictable. I would have no confidence in him. . . .
>
> I regard Dewey as the strongest candidate and the most likely nominee. I regard him as a miniature fascist, and therefore, dangerous. . . .
>
> On the Democratic side I don't know any more than you do. The President is undoubtedly still the strongest man in his party, but the politicians, especially those in Congress, are getting badly out of hand. Whether he can call them to heel again, I do not know. I have not been asked for any advice and I have volunteered none. I doubt whether even the President knows whether he will be a candidate. I know that I don't. . . . My feeling is that Wallace is not likely to be renominated. That, too, is in the lap of the Gods. If Roosevelt should not run, the result is likely to be a shambles.

Ickes was generally correct in his assessment of Willkie's position. Ever since the outbreak of war, the Republican candidate of 1940 had found himself and his party growing further and further apart. His whole-souled support of Roosevelt's foreign policy during the war had alienated the increasingly conservative core of the Republican leadership. In 1942, with FDR's blessing, Willkie had traveled some thirty thousand miles as a kind of ambassador without portfolio, learning what he could of those parts of the world not dominated by the Axis powers, bringing back with him a message of internationalism that was articulated in a forceful if simplistic little book called *One World,* published in 1943. Among other things, he saw as one of the purposes of the war the political independence of what we now call "Third World" countries: "Are the thirty-one United Nations now fighting together agreed that our common job of liberation includes giving to *all* peoples freedom to govern themselves as soon as they are able, and the economic freedom on which all lasting self-government inevitably rests?"

Such sentiments made the Republicans in America nervous, at best.

But Willkie repeated the message constantly as he traveled around the country in the months following publication of the book, coupling it now with more and more forceful demands that this country liberate the oppressed within its own borders—the blacks—and a growing disenchantment with traditional notions of free enterprise and the capitalistic system. He also committed the cardinal sin of politics: he let his contempt for the party regulars show. During one speech before a hostile audience of Republican rank-and-filers in October, he announced that "I don't know whether you are going to support me or not, and I don't give a damn. You're a bunch of political liabilities anyway." As he still believed they had done in 1940, he was convinced that "the people" would rise up to sweep him into the Republican nomination—but in the Wisconsin primary in April 1944 the people rose up to give him not a single delegate to the Republican National Convention, scheduled for the Chicago Coliseum in June. Not so blind that he would not see, Willkie pulled out of the race (he would die of a coronary thrombosis in October).

The big winner in Wisconsin was Dewey—now governor of New York—and, as Ickes had predicted, Dewey was the choice of the convention in June, his running mate the junior senator from Ohio, John Bricker ("a reputable Harding," Ickes had called him). And if Ickes was convinced that the Democratic Party would be in a "shambles" if Roosevelt did not run, the President generally agreed (without telling Ickes, of course)—although he continued to make noises of coy reluctance in public until July 11, when during a press conference he released the contents of a letter he had written to Robert E. Hannegan, the new chairman of the Democratic National Committee. "All that is within me," the President had said to Hannegan, "cries to go back to my home on the Hudson River." But if the convention chose him, he conceded, he would serve "like a good soldier." United Press reporter Allen Drury was covering a Senate committee hearing when the content of the letter was published. "I shall never forget the expressions on the faces of three Democratic Senators in committee this morning when they heard the news," he wrote in his journal. "It was as though the sun had burst from the clouds and glory surrounded the world. Relief, and I mean relief, was written on every face. The meal ticket was still the meal ticket and all was well with the party."

There may have been a kernel of truth in Roosevelt's claims of reluctance. At sixty-two, he probably was an even frailer man than his seventy-year-old Secretary of the Interior. He certainly looked worse, and had for some time. David Brinkley had seen the President from a few feet away for the first time during a press conference sometime in 1943. "It was a shock, unnerving," he remembered.

Here was the most famous face in the world, one . . . seen a thousand times. In newspaper and magazine and newsreel pictures it was the face of a handsome man with strong, well-formed features displaying a smiling, good-natured manner, chin tilted high, ivory cigarette holder pointed to the sky. Those were the pictures. Here was the reality—a man who looked terribly old and tired. No doubt youth was too quick to notice the effects of age, but this man's face was more gray than pink, his hands shook, his eyes were hazy and wandering, his neck drooped in stringy, sagging folds accentuated by a shirt collar that must have fit at one time but now was two or three sizes too large.

"He's just tired," press secretary Steve Early said when questioned. "Running a world war is a hell of a job." It was, and it was not one Roosevelt could ever have abandoned—especially not after June 6, when with the Normandy invasion the Allies began grinding inexorably across France and ultimately into Germany itself, fighting hedgerow-to-hedgerow, while plans were laid for the final assaults in the Pacific theater and out on a windy mesa top near Los Alamos, New Mexico, and in the converted doubles squash court of Stagg Field at the University of Chicago, and in the laboratories at Oak Ridge, Tennessee, scientists were establishing the quanta of a new and even more dangerous age.

Nevertheless, Roosevelt was more than tired; a physical examination in March 1944 would reveal high blood pressure and progressive enlargement of the heart. The President did not ask to see the results of the examination because he probably knew that he would not like what he would be shown. He would run, and having announced his willingness, knew that he would be nominated.

Henry Wallace, who was quite as determined to run, had no such assurances. There was a new Democratic National Committee now, a powerfully conservative one dominated by such men as its treasurer, Edwin Pauley, the oilman from California, together with such machine eminences as Mayor Ed Kelley of Chicago, Tom Pendergast of Kansas City, and Tammany ward boss Edward Flynn of the Bronx. They did not want Wallace and they spent a good deal of time and effort letting Roosevelt know that they did not want Wallace—aided in this crusade by the work of Steve Early and Edwin Watson in the White House, both of whom disliked Wallace, and given a golden opportunity when Wallace departed in late May for a seven-week trip to Russia and China.

By the time Wallace returned to Washington on July 10, his candidacy was dead. Roosevelt had been convinced that there would be a terrible convention fight if he put forward Wallace's name. "I am just not going to go through a convention like 1940 again," he told Samuel Rosenman in

June. "It will split the party wide open, and it is already split enough between the North and South; it may kill our chances for election this fall, and if it does, it will prolong the war and knock into a cocked hat all the plans we've been making for the future." Roosevelt, who hated to be the bearer of bad tidings, was not about to tell Wallace this himself. He enlisted Ickes and Rosenman for that job.

The three men met in Wallace's apartment in the Wardman Park Hotel at midday on July 10. "Wallace's face can be as immobile as stone when he wants it to be," Rosenman remembered, "—and he certainly wanted it to be during that conference. Both Ickes and I tried our best to explain the reasons in back of the President's determination. He seemed not even to be listening." Apparently, he was not, or Rosenman was not nearly as forceful as he thought he had been. "Ickes said how much I had grown in his esteem," Wallace wrote in his own diary.

> That I was a true liberal and that he and I were the only two real liberals left in the government. . . . Ickes then made it clear that I had made many enemies, that I was a bone of contention in the convention and that I ought not to let my name be presented.
>
> Before Ickes made this presentation, however, Sam made it clear that the President preferred me as a running mate. In other words Sam created the impression that the President wanted me but he either did not think I could win in the convention nor help him win in the fall."

Armed with the certainty that he could talk the President around, Wallace met with FDR later that same day. Roosevelt gave every impression that Wallace's interpretation of the situation was right. "He said I was his choice as a running mate," Wallace remembered, "that he was willing to make a statement to that effect. I asked him if he would be willing to say, 'If I were a delegate to the convention I would vote for Henry Wallace.' He said, 'Yes, I would.'"

Roosevelt kept his word—in his fashion. He did write to Senator Samuel E. Jackson, permanent chairman of the convention, to make his feelings known regarding Wallace: "I personally would vote for his renomination if I were a delegate to the Convention." So far, so good—but there was an addendum: "At the same time I do not wish to appear in any way as dictating to the Convention. Obviously the Convention must do the deciding." Even worse than this flimsy statement of support was another letter he sent to Hannegan at about the same time: "You have written me about Harry Truman and Bill Douglas. I should, of course, be very glad to run with either of them and believe that either one of them would bring real strength to the ticket." The combination of the two letters constituted a death warrant for Wallace's hopes.

But Wallace did not know this, and when the convention opened—again in Chicago—in the third week of July, he fought vigorously for votes, stepping up his efforts after Roosevelt's nomination by acclamation on July 20. He found himself with an ally in Harold Ickes, at least briefly. The Secretary was attending in his usual capacity as a delegate-at-large in the Illinois contingent and had been pushing the cause of Douglas. When Douglas's name faded badly after the first ballot for the Vice-Presidential nomination had been taken, Ickes switched his support to Wallace. Whatever else he may have felt about Wallace, he had never denied that the Vice President was a strong liberal, as he had emphasized during the meeting in Wallace's Wardman Park rooms earlier that month, and the Secretary was absolutely convinced that anything less than a powerful liberal on the ticket would be a disaster. He was not persuaded that Truman filled the bill, particularly when it came to racial matters (not an entirely accurate judgment, as time would prove). Even worse were Truman's connections to the Kansas City machine of Tom Pendergast, which, as an old antagonist in the Chicago wars, Ickes distrusted at the very marrow of his being. He was so worried, in fact, that he wired Roosevelt on July 21 to say that "The issue of the city bosses in the event of Truman's nomination, in my judgment, will cut deeply into the election and may very well mean the return of an opposition Congress." Roosevelt, who was on his way to Pearl Harbor for his meeting with the commanders of the Pacific theater, never replied.

Truman himself was the only man who now stood between himself and the nomination. He had made a commitment to the candidacy of James F. Byrnes, former senator from South Carolina and now head of the Office of War Mobilization. He remained faithful to that pledge until word was passed to him that Roosevelt, speaking from San Diego just before boarding ship for Pearl Harbor, had said to "tell the Senator that if he wants to break up the Democratic party by staying out, he can, but he knows as well as I what that might mean at this dangerous time in the world."

"I guess I'll have to take it," Truman finally said, and asked Byrnes to release him. He won the nomination on the second ballot.

"Wallace himself took the result beautifully," Ickes noted approvingly in his diary two days later. "He sent me a note to the hotel . . . expressing appreciation of what I had done for him, and asking me to call him up. I did call him up and I think that he appreciated it. I told him that he had come out of the convention a bigger man than Truman and congratulated him generally on the way in which he had conducted himself." (Wallace's graciousness would later be rewarded with the Department of Commerce.)

As he had in 1940, Roosevelt busied himself with matters of statecraft for the first several weeks of the campaign, and Dewey himself did not officially open his own campaign until September 6. Ickes, who had been asked once again by Roosevelt to be one of his major spear carriers, was on stage before either of the candidates, beginning his own effort early in August, then, after his usual summer holiday at Bar Harbor with Jane and the children, taking up the spear again in September and not letting up until the eve of the election. It was the most impressive campaign in his career—not merely because he did it at the age of seventy, but that it was done with such enthusiasm, such energy, such visible pleasure in the performance. The joy of combat was on him from the beginning and never left him.

His opening move was a speech on August 10 before the unashamedly leftist American Labor Party in New York. During his acceptance speech in Chicago, the Republican candidate had claimed that the administration was being run by decrepit leftovers from the New Deal, a movement, he said, that had grown "old and tired and quarrelsome." Dewey would emphasize—often not even that subtly—over and over again the issue of age, clearly aiming to foment doubt regarding Roosevelt's health. Ickes picked up on the tactic immediately and proceeded to turn it around by chopping away at Dewey's youth and inexperience with the ponderous ax of his wit:

> The Dragon with dragging feet . . . has included me, I am sure, in his category of "tired old men." Well, I don't feel tired, and as to age, I acknowledge that I am well through the period of adolescence. I don't have to pretend to a maturity that is not mine or supply myself with an adventitious makeup to act a part for which I have been prematurely cast. . . . It is a great pleasure for me to be permitted to emerge from the home for the aged to which your effervescent Governor so graciously consigned me.

And, just in case his audience did not get the point, he added: "I believe that Governor Dewey is still in the formative stage. I would no longer say, as I did in 1940, that Governor Dewey has tossed his diaper into the ring. I would have to admit that he has reached the jumper stage. He is undoubtedly growing up."

A month later, after the Maine vacation, he was at Dewey again, this time in Grand Rapids, telling the audience at the ninth annual convention of the International Union of United Automobile, Aircraft and Agricultural Workers of America that "Mr. Dewey's well-financed, well-groomed, well-oiled and well-advertised campaign is now under way, although some of you may not have noticed it. The candidate in the blue serge suit made his opening bow in Philadelphia last Thursday night. For one, I regret that there were so many empty seats in Convention Hall on that occasion. My own belief is that the more people who see and hear the Republican candidate the easier our task will be."

Roosevelt opened his own campaign on September 23, speaking at a Teamsters Union banquet after a conference with Churchill in Quebec. The story had been spread that on his return from his Pacific trip in August, the President had sent a destroyer back to Alaska to pick up his Scotch terrier, Fala, who had been inadvertently left behind. The story was nonsense, but at the conclusion of one of the most effective speeches he ever gave, Roosevelt seized the accusation and wrung every ounce of political juice out of it he could—and that was considerable: "These Republican leaders have not been content with attacks on me, or my wife, or on my sons. No, not content with that, they now include my little dog, Fala. Well, of course, I don't resent attacks, and my family doesn't resent attacks, but Fala *does* resent them. . . . He has not been the same dog since." Like his "Martin, Barton, and Fish" refrain of 1940, the "Fala speech" became a hallmark of the 1944 campaign.

Dewey was not silent during all this, and in one of his efforts hit upon a theme that probably did as much as anything to make the popular vote as close as it was. "Let's get this straight," he told Republicans in Oklahoma City.

> The man who wants to be President of the United States for sixteen years is, indeed, indispensable. He is indispensable to Harry Hopkins, to Madame Perkins, to Harold Ickes . . . to America's leading enemy of civil liberties— the mayor of Jersey City. He's indispensable to those infamous machines in Chicago, in the Bronx, and all the others. He's indispensable to Sidney Hillman and the [CIO's] Political Action Committee, he's indispensable to Earl Browder, the ex-convict and pardoned Communist leader. Shall we, the American people, perpetuate one man in office for sixteen years? Shall we do that to accommodate this motley crew?

He might have gotten more mileage from this message if he had used it with greater consistency. As the fight intensified in October, however, he chose instead to put increasing emphasis on Roosevelt's age and health and on the perceived communist influences at work in the administration, particularly in the persons of Earl Browder and Sidney Hillman. Roosevelt countered by appearing in public as often as possible, moving about the country briskly and with evident vigor; at one point during the campaign, he insisted that the top be left down on his car during a rainstorm in order to illustrate his healthy indifference to the weather. By some miracle, he did not come down with one of the colds to which he was ordinarily susceptible.

Ickes, in the meantime, had been hammering away at his own set of themes. When Dewey announced at one point that one of the first things he would do as President would be to fire the Secretary of the Interior, Ickes sent him a well-publicized "letter of resignation" on September 28. Among the reasons for his "resignation," the Secretary cited a few of Dewey's more colorful supporters:

> I realize . . . that when you become our Never-Never President you will be besieged for favors by the hordes of hungry politicians who are supporting you. Gerald L. K. Smith, who has recently announced his support of the Dewey-Bricker ticket, will be pressing his face against the window. Bertie McCormick of the *Chicago Tribune* may have claims that cannot well be ignored. "Cissy" Patterson may insist that the women of the country should be represented in your cabinet in her person. Ham Fish and "Curley" Brooks and Stephen Day and Werner W. Schroeder, staunch isolationists all, who have their own persuasive reasons for supporting you, will demand the recognition to which their efforts on your behalf will entitle them. As you probably surmise, Mr. Dewey, I would not be comfortable in such company.

On the road then, where he would remain for most of the next five weeks—to Los Angeles, where on October 8 he told the members of the Hollywood Democratic Committee at the Ambassador Hotel that

> I understand that my admirer, Mr. Dewey, has been out this way. . . . The Wild West spectacle in which the young hopeful from the East starred here was staged by none other than Cecil B. DeMille [DeMille had orchestrated a rally on September 15 at the Los Angeles Coliseum that featured live elephants], who, as I remember it, enhanced his reputation by including in every movie that he made a scene of the heroine taking a bath. Imagine the enthusiasm if DeMille had rolled his candidate onto the platform in a bright and shining tub.

To Salt Lake City on October 10, where he reminded his audience of the great public works projects and conservation efforts the Roosevelt administration had instituted in the West, a record that had "not been written in forgettable words but in unforgettable facts, such as great dams and reservoirs, roads and bridges, power lines and aqueducts, restored range and protected forests." To Newark, New Jersey, on October 16, in a radio address before the Independent Committee for Roosevelt, during which he declared that he was "glad that Governor Dewey is going to follow me on the air tonight. I understand that he proposes to talk about 'Honesty in Government.' This will be a double adventure into the unknown by Mr.

Dewey. He knows little if anything about the Government and, judging by his campaign speeches, he is totally unfamiliar with honesty."

To New York then and an NBC "Town Meeting of the Air" broadcast on October 26, where he claimed "I never heard a candidate for a high public office talk so recklessly. This campaign has proved that Thomas E. Dewey is no George Washington when it comes to telling the truth. He has a hatchet and he has tried his best to cut down the cherry tree, but be will never, never say, 'Yes, Pa, I did it.' " To New York again on November 1 to address several hundred Harlem residents at the Golden Gate Ballroom and remind them of "the progress America has made during the past twelve years, in terms of our progressive recognition of the dignity and rights of American Negroes," then to Madison Square Garden the next night, where an "Everybody for Roosevelt" rally was told that "In a last desperate effort . . . Governor Dewey has called on the ragged balance of his reserves and has thrown them into the trenches equipped with the only kind of weapons that he possesses—hate, vilification, prejudice, misrepresentations, distortions, and lies." To Baltimore on November 3, where the Maryland Committee for Roosevelt and Truman had Dewey described for them as "the 1944 edition of Warren G. Harding," and finally, on November 5, to Milwaukee, where a gathering of the United Labor Committee of Wisconsin was informed that "Great issues are at stake, but Governor Thomas 'Elusive' Dewey has refused to meet those issues. Instead, he has sung a hymn of hate against President Roosevelt."

He was home in time to vote, and with 25.6 million other citizens cast his ballot for Roosevelt on November 7. Dewey received twenty-two million. The margin was the narrowest yet recorded for Roosevelt. But it was enough, even if Dewey did not concede defeat until after three o'clock the following morning. Nor did he send the traditional message of congratulations to Roosevelt at that time (it would come three days later), even though the President had stayed up to receive it. Dewey offered his congratulations instead over the radio. Roosevelt sent his thanks by telegram, then headed for bed at four. Just before wheeling himself into his private elevator for the trip upstairs, he turned to his aide, William D. Hassett, and uttered the final words of the campaign: "I still think he's a son of a bitch."

The President, who understood precisely how important Ickes's campaigning had been, had kinder words for his Secretary of the Interior. "Dear Harold," he wrote on November 27, "this is just a personal note to send my compliments to The Curmudgeon on the greatest performance of his career. There is, I understand, some complaint from pieces of Republicans that I have a buzz saw for Secretary of the Interior. I can't say I blame them and I must say I like it." Ickes was grateful, but in both conversation with the President and in his *pro forma* letter of resignation he had indicated a willingness to step down—and for the first time seemed to mean it. Roosevelt would have nothing to do with the idea. "In spite of our conversation—in spite of your letter of resignation," he wrote on December 9, "—you will, if you say anything more about it, find a Marine Guard from Quantico dogging your footsteps day and night. . . . Of course, I want you to go along at the old stand where you have been for twelve years. We must see this thing out together."

"Your letter of December 9 makes me feel all fluttery," Ickes replied on December 13. "To have you write about me as you did is like an accolade to my spirit. No one can be so generous as you and from no one else would what you wrote mean so much." Nevertheless, he insisted, he was tired and time inevitably was running out for him. He felt a need to write in the cause of peace:

> I was one of the first to see this war coming. When Jane and I came back from London and Paris in 1938, we both had the conviction that war was impending over Europe and we did not see how it could be averted from the United States. . . .
>
> As I was interested in the war, so am I interested in the peace—rather fearfully interested at times. We are on the verge of a great spiritual adventure—the greatest in history and you have been chosen by the people to be the leader of the world in the direction of peace. The Secretary of the Interior, although he holds an honorable and eye-filling job, would not be any closer to the peace and its evolvement than if he were a surf-fisherman casting for blue fish off the coast of Cape Cod. And so it has been running in my mind that if I could get myself a job as a writer I might have more to say about and do with the peace than as a frustrated Secretary of the Interior.

Roosevelt did not send a marine guard around, but he would not let Ickes go. The Secretary would have to remain as a witness to the last great adventure.

The year just past had possessed its fill of death for Ickes, and 1945 showed signs of becoming another such. First, Margaret Dreier Robins died. Throughout the decade of the thirties, after Raymond's terrible fall and consequent paralysis, Harold had grown increasingly close to the couple, though they were able to see one another only on rare occasions. There was a steady stream of letters, however, heartfelt and often very moving, and many of them must have brought Ickes comfort in difficult times—including a particularly touching one from Margaret during his convalescence after the heart attack in 1937: "We are both distressed beyond words," she wrote on July 19,

> to think that you still have to spend so much time in bed and are practically living in your beloved Department of the Interior—if only it could be on one of your great mountain tops with the view of the world at your feet. However, I am certain that your imagination can bring both mountain tops and views to you in a moment's notice. And for all the great gifts you have brought the people of our country in making possible to them mountain tops, and the wilderness, and beauty past compare, many are blessing you, and I for one do so with all my heart.

Both Margaret and Raymond had taken Jane to their capacious hearts, and the two couples had sustained a relationship that by all the evidence was as intimate and mutually satisfying as any Ickes had ever enjoyed. They had last seen Margaret in the summer of 1941, when she had stayed with them for a few days on her return to Chinsegut Hill after her own annual excursion to Southwest Harbor, Maine. From then on, she had been generally confined to home, suffering from pernicious anemia and rheumatic heart disease and growing slowly weaker through the war years. She died on February 21, 1945, and was buried at Chinsegut Hill, beneath an enormous tree she and Raymond had christened the Altar Oak. "According to the papers," Ickes wrote in his diary on February 25, "Margaret was 76. I had guessed her age at about that but I had not really known, although I did know that she was somewhat older than Raymond, who is about my age. No one has come into Jane's and my life who has made such an impression on Jane as did Margaret. She cared for her dearly and was terribly grieved by her death."

Then, just two weeks after Margaret's passing, death's wing brushed even closer. Harold's son Raymond had enlisted in the marines and on February 19, 1945, was a second lieutenant and platoon leader when the marines invaded Iwo Jima, the island shaped like a pork chop just seven hundred miles south of Japan. On March 8 he took a sniper's bullet that tore through his back and out his left armpit, puncturing and collapsing a lung in its passage. More dead than alive, he was carried to an aid station on a litter, then put on board a hospital ship a few days later.

On March 9, Ickes got a message from Admiral Chester Nimitz telling him that Raymond had taken a burst of shrapnel in the chest that broke three ribs but had done no other serious damage. It would be several days before the family learned the real nature of his wound and that it was going to be weeks before he was out of danger of death. In the meantime, Ickes called Miralotte, Raymond's wife, told her what he knew, then had her and the two grandchildren picked up from their home in Maryland and brought to Headwaters Farm to stay until they could be sure that Raymond would recover.

Ickes performed these necessary duties with his usual brusque dispatch, betraying nothing on the surface to the little family huddled at Headwaters Farm to indicate that he had felt much of anything even when death had come so near to his firstborn. But his chronic insomnia got suddenly worse. "I have had two pretty bad nights," he reported in his diary for March 11. "Last night, although I did not take as much whisky as usual, I did take more Seconal than I had been taking." And he had fallen in the bathroom during the night, hitting his face against the bathtub spigot and blackening his right eye so badly that his doctor wanted him to go to the hospital. He refused, but he did stay at home for a few days.

By the first week of April, Raymond was on his way to the Oak Knoll Naval Hospital in San Francisco and it was reasonably certain that he was going to pull through. The Secretary had recovered from his fall by then, too, although probably there still was some soreness. (He had hit the spigot with such force, his son Harold remembers, that it had been bent completely over.) Early in the evening of April 12, he was just getting ready to leave his office to meet Jane, who was joining him for dinner at the home of Felix Frankfurter, when the White House called and asked him to come over right away. "I asked what was up but was given no information," he reported to his diary more than two weeks later. As he prepared to go downstairs, word came to him "that there had been a flash . . . to the effect that the President had died. This flash seemed to me to be confirmed by my summons to the White House so that I went over prepared for the news which was forthcoming."

Roosevelt had gone down to the "Little White House" in Warm Springs, Georgia, for a rest on March 30. He had needed it. The campaign had taken far more out of him than he knew, and at the beginning of March he had returned badly worn out by the Yalta Conference, eight days of intense discussions during which he, Churchill, and Stalin had settled the postwar dismemberment of Europe. During the first several days of his Warm Springs vacation, the President's mental and physical health both seemed to be improving. On the morning of the twelfth, he had felt up to sitting for several hours for a portrait by Madame Elizabeth Shoumatoff, who had been commissioned by his old friend Lucy Mercer Rutherford. Mrs. Rutherford was among those with him in the afternoon when the President suddenly announced "I have a terrific headache," slumped forward, then fell into a snoring unconsciousness that lasted until his heart finally stopped and he was pronounced dead at 3:35 P.M. of a cerebral hemorrhage.

While Mrs. Rutherford was hustled out of the Warm Springs complex and preparations were made to ready the President's body for the trip to Washington, Ickes and other government officials gathered in the Cabinet Room. Vice President Truman had been told of the President's death by Eleanor Roosevelt and Anna Roosevelt Boettiger less than an hour before. "Is there anything I can do for you?" he had asked Eleanor. She had smiled briefly and looked down at the floor before answering: "Is there anything we can do for you? For you are the one in trouble now." He and his daughter, Margaret, came into the Cabinet Room from the Oval Office a little after six-thirty. "The Vice President," Ickes wrote, "expressed his very deep concern and his regret even that the duties of the Presidency had devolved upon him. I could well understand his feeling about it." At 6:45 P.M., Chief Justice Harlan Stone administered the oath of office.

Jane was waiting for him with Abe Fortas, Oscar Chapman, and Mike Straus when Ickes got back to his office after the ceremony. "I was very glad indeed to take a good stiff drink of whisky," he said. "Jane had called Felix Frankfurter and he had expressed the wish that we come to dinner as we had planned. So we went."

No one wanted to be alone this night.

The body was placed in a casket and shipped north by train the next morning, winding through the soft spring countryside at half speed all the way to Washington. People lined the tracks in and out of all the little towns to watch the train rattle slowly by, the cars swaying gently on the curves. Early on the morning of April 14, the train pulled into Union Station, coming to rest on platform number one. The casket was carried out of the funeral car and placed on a black caisson. Then began the long, slow, parade to the White House through streets lined with weeping citizens, two miles of marching soldiers, sailors, WACs and WAVES, the Marine Band, armored cars, motorcycle policemen, all led by the flag-draped caisson drawn by six white horses, trailed by one black, riderless horse. It was a dark parallel to the wintry day in 1933 when Roosevelt had watched another parade with such fierce pleasure. Now, on the radio, Arthur Godfrey was struggling to keep the tears from choking his voice.

The funeral service in the Blue Room of the White House that afternoon was brief, beginning at four o'clock and ending at four-twenty-three. The body lay in state in the East Room until nine-thirty, when its casket was placed on the caisson again and taken back to Union Station by the six white horses. Everyone, it seemed, wanted to ride to Hyde Park with Franklin Roosevelt, and two trains had to be made up—one for the body and the Roosevelt family and the President's closest friends and associates, another for members of the cabinet, other departments, congressmen and senators, and the press. With remarkable efficiency, given the confusion natural to such an occasion, the two trains got under way on schedule, pulling out of the station into the dark night for the journey home. "I'll never forget that train trip to Hyde Park for the burial," Anna Roosevelt Boettiger wrote years later.

> The private car that Father had used for so many years was once more the last car on the train. As usual, the Secret Service had assigned staterooms and berths to each individual. I've never known who assigned it to me, but I was given Father's stateroom. All night I sat on the foot of that berth and watched the people who had come to see the train pass by. There were little children, mothers, fathers, grandparents. They were there at eleven at night, at two in the morning, at four—at all hours during that long night.

The train arrived at Hyde Park at 8:40 A.M., and the guests were ferried by automobile up to Springwood, the Roosevelt estate, then ushered into the Rose Garden, a large square surrounded by towering hedges. It was here that the burial service began at 10:00 A.M., conducted by the Reverend George W. Anthony, rector of St. James's Episcopal Church in Hyde Park, where Roosevelt had worshiped since he was a boy. The Reverend Anthony intoned the ancient, comforting words: "Unto Almighty God we commend the soul of Thy brother departed. . . ." Three volleys were fired by a cadre of West Point cadets as the casket was slowly lowered into the grave, then a single cornetist played the agonizing notes of taps.

Ickes and Jane were there to hear it, standing with the group that included the cabinet members and members of the Supreme Court. "The air was clear and cool," he reported in his diary, noting with calm approval that "everything was in dignified and simple good taste." He tells us nothing of what he was feeling at the moment the casket sank into the grave. It is possible he felt what millions of Americans felt when the news of Roosevelt's death came, something not unlike what *New York Times* reporter William S. White felt:

> It seemed not simply that a Man of History had died, but that history itself had lost its attribute of immortality, that history itself had died, in a little town I had never seen, a little town in Georgia called Warm Springs.
>
> It was a kind of grief, both personal and institutional, that I had never known and would never know again. It was one of the unspeakable memories of wartime, unique, never to change and never to end, forever imprinted on mind and heart. . . . This death was an unbridgeable, an irreparable point of

breakage between past and future. This was the end of glory and maybe even of hope, the most utterly final end that one would ever see.

Perhaps a snatch of Walt Whitman's poem written in tribute to another President's springtime death drifted into Ickes's mind, as it did into the minds of many: "When lilacs last in the dooryard bloom'd, / And the great star early droop'd in the western sky in the night, / I mourn'd, and yet shall mourn with ever-returning spring." Perhaps only the unarticulated memories occupied his mind in that sunlit patch of garden lost in a sea of lawn on a hill above the Hudson River, memories of the man who was too young to have been a father to him, but was a father, of the hero who was both larger than life and all too humanly imperfect, of the man who plucked him from nowhere, used him, manipulated him, drove him to exhaustion, appealed to the worst and the best in him, preached to him, lied to him, brought him visions of power and fits of despair, inspired him, enraged him, gave him friendship and betrayal, dominated the troubled center of his life for thirteen years, and gifted him with a share in the greatness of an age.

We do not know what went through his mind because, unlikely as it may seem, he never recorded it. We do know that for the first and last time in his public life, Harold L. Ickes cried.

CHAPTER

· 56 ·

The Rawest Proposition

I N *WITNESS TO POWER,* newsman Marquis Childs told a story: sometime after Harry S. Truman became President, Childs and several other reporters were invited for a luncheon cruise on board the Presidential yacht, then called the *Williamsburg* (now called the *Sequoia*). "We sat before lunch on the afterdeck in warm sun," Childs remembered.

> The President was in a somber mood and appeared to be oppressed by his heavy responsibilities. One of us asked a question about Ickes. "Are you referring," Truman asked, his voice charged with emotion, "to shitass Ix?"
>
> For the time being this put a damper on further discussion of the Secretary of the Interior. In fact, it dampened any exchange until, finally, the President said in a slightly more cheery vein, "Well, it must be five o'clock somewhere; let's have a drink."

The harshest name Roosevelt had ever given the Secretary was that of Donald Duck, and then it was bestowed (never in front of him) in a kind of exasperated affection. But there was no affection and less humor in Truman's choice of words; he spoke in both anger and contempt, and the depth of his feeling was a measure of the relationship between the two men at the beginning of Truman's administration.

It may or may not have been a specific incident that had triggered Truman's outburst. Just as likely, it simply illustrated a general level of irritation. Truman did not take well to being nagged, and Ickes had a talent for hectoring that he had rarely attempted to stifle. Even when he did not nag, he had a way of letting his dissatisfaction show, and ever since the Democratic convention of 1944, which he had characterized as being dominated by the machine politics of Democratic National Committee Chairman Robert Hannegan, he had been dissatisfied with Truman. "I have felt very much depressed since President Roosevelt's death," he reported in his diary on April 29, 1945.

> I suppose that my friends are right when they insist that I should not get out but if I had little heart for my job before President Roosevelt died I certainly have none now. It appalls me to think of trying to educate Truman all over again. Roosevelt had a real grasp of Interior Department matters and policies from the very beginning. We understood each other and, generally speaking, we were in accord on policies even though we did differ in some particulars when it came to the organizational setup. When Jane and I got home the Thursday night following the President's death I drank a lot of whiskey— more than I had for a long time.

Altogether, then, it is less astonishing that Ickes ultimately would leave Truman's cabinet than that he remained the length of time he did. He certainly did not expect to be around for very long. Truman had asked all cabinet members to stay on after his somber inauguration the evening of April 12, but by the end of June, four had already dropped like autumn leaves from the administration's tree—Attorney General Francis Biddle, replaced by Assistant Attorney General Tom Clark; Secretary of Agriculture Claude Wickard, replaced by Congressman Clinton Anderson of New Mexico; Secretary of Labor Frances Perkins, "Madame Secretary," replaced by U.S. District Court Judge Lewis Schwellenbach; and Secretary of State Edward Stettinius (who had succeeded Hull when he resigned in 1944), replaced by James F. Byrnes, head of the Office of War Mobilization. (Secretary of the Treasury Henry Morgenthau would resign in July, replaced by Frederick Vinson, and Secretary of War Henry Stimson would step down in September, his place taken by Assistant Secretary Robert Patterson—leaving Ickes and Henry Wallace, now Secretary of Commerce, as the last relics of the old New Deal cabinet.)

As the weeks passed and there was no word from Truman as to exactly what he had in mind for Ickes, rumors abounded. One was that he would soon be replaced by Senator Joseph O'Mahoney of Wyoming, another that the replacement would be Edwin Pauley, the California oilman and treasurer of the Democratic National Committee. In fact, it appears that Truman may simply have had too much on his mind to think seriously about the problem of replacing Ickes, knowing full well that it was likely to be a good deal more complicated a business than, say, getting rid of Frances Perkins.

Roosevelt, after all, had left his Vice President standing just a little ahead of absolute ignorance about goings-on in the administration, and there were far more important matters to attend to than the fate of the nettlesome Secretary of the Interior; that could wait. After American and Russian troops entered Berlin and Hitler committed suicide, what was left of the German army surrendered to the Allies on May 7. Once the national bacchanal of V-E Day on May 8 had sputtered out, Truman and his advisers began plans for a meeting with Churchill and Stalin at Potsdam to discuss the nature of the postwar world, a conference scheduled to begin on July 17. Out in San Francisco, meanwhile, representatives from fifty nations met on April 24 to draw up the United Nations Charter, a document designed to establish an international organization intended to make another world war unlikely; Truman welcomed the delegates to San Francisco via radio that night. On April 25, Truman met with Secretary of War Stimson and General Leslie Groves, director of the Manhattan Project, to learn for the first time in any detail of the bomb that would come to make world war unthinkable.

The new President, in short, had a good deal on his plate already. Which is not to say that he had ruled out the possibility of getting rid of Ickes when time and opportunity might present themselves. When Senator Carl Hatch wrote the President on June 24 to object to the idea of putting Senator O'Mahoney in the job, Truman's reply was at least ambivalent: "That is the first I have heard of this proposal, and I don't blame you for being somewhat interested in it. I have made no move to make a change in that office, and I am sure that I wouldn't want to take a Democratic Senator into the Executive Department now, because I think every good Democrat is needed in the Senate."

Ickes did not know what the President was thinking, but was preparing his ground, just in case. His friends were pretty generally convinced that his days were numbered, including Justice William O. Douglas, who lunched with the Secretary on May 31. "He feels quite pessimistic about the political situation generally," Ickes wrote in his diary, adding that

Bill is perfectly sure that Truman will want to get rid of me and he expressed the same view that Biddle had, namely, that I ought to wait until I am fired. In the meantime, he thinks that I ought to document everything possible so that I can make out a case against Truman. . . . I don't agree with this view. As I still see it, I ought to get out firmly and as gracefully as possible either when there arises an issue that would seem to call for my resignation or when

I suspect that Truman is getting ready to move. I do not see anything to be gained by waiting to be fired if I can anticipate it.

With that anticipation in mind, he began working on a letter of resignation and would continue working on versions of it until August, when Truman finally decided that he might as well keep Ickes around. The Secretary was convinced that Truman's decision was based only on the fact that he had not been able to find someone to replace him. "This he told me himself when I saw him the day before he left for Potsdam," Ickes wrote John Boettiger on August 28. "The result is that, last Tuesday [August 23], he told me that he wanted me to stay and that this had always been his wish. . . . I consented to stay on the condition that if he ever felt that he wanted someone else for Secretary of the Interior he would tell me so frankly while on my part I would stay until I came to a different conclusion."

A superficial peace settled over the two men—as it had over the world. On August 6 an atomic bomb was dropped on the Japanese city of Hiroshima and three days later one was dropped on Nagasaki. On September 2 the Japanese formally surrendered during ceremonies held on board the *U.S.S. Missouri* in Tokyo Bay. The period saw another kind of watershed for Ickes, one more link to the past cut away with the death of Senator Hiram Johnson. The old man's isolationism had ended with the Japanese attack on Pearl Harbor, and while Ickes and the senator never regained the warmth for each other they had once shared, Johnson earned Ickes's enduring respect when he had turned about and voted for war. His last years in the Senate had been marked more by absence than any substantive contributions, but a lifetime of integrity had given him a certain presence that commanded obeisance even from colleagues who no longer consulted him. Allen Drury, covering the Senate for United Press, had seen Johnson in this incarnation in the summer of 1944 and recorded it in his journal entry for June 19:

Hiram Johnson came back to the Senate today after six months in Florida. Clad in a cream-colored suit, with a heavy dark tan setting off his snow-white hair and distinguished face, the old man looked fit and well. Across to his desk from all parts of the chamber came other Senators to shake his hand and welcome him back. The man who lives on in the heart of California as "the greatest governor the state ever had," possesses still at 77 a great prestige among his colleagues. He carries virtually no weight any more when it comes to voting, he influences no decisions, he takes very little part in debate or committees, he contributes nothing but his presence, but in that an undeniable force still remains. This is Hiram Johnson, it seems to say: he has been a power in his time.

On August 6, 1945, the day the first atomic bomb was dropped, effectively ending the war Johnson had spent most of the 1930s trying to persuade his countrymen was none of America's business, the man who had stood at Armageddon with Theodore Roosevelt in 1912 quietly died. Ickes made no mention of the death in his diary; perhaps too many had died by then, perhaps FDR's death had taken the weight from that of anyone else.

His son Raymond, at least, remained among the living. He had gone through his final phase of recovery at Bethesda Naval Hospital, then joined the team of military lawyers who accompanied Justice Robert H. Jackson to Germany, where Jackson would serve as prosecutor for the United States at the Nuremberg war crimes trials. Ickes himself made plans for a trip to London with Ralph Davies, where, as one of his last acts as petroleum administrator for war, he would negotiate the final details of the Anglo-American Oil Treaty and bring it back to the United States for submission to the Senate, where it would linger for another two years.

He returned to find that Undersecretary Abe Fortas was making plans, too. For several months he had talked about resigning, citing the need for more money than his government job could pay him. But he had been having trouble finding a job remunerative enough to match that of his wife, Carolyn Agger, a very successful New York attorney. "She makes more money than he does," Ickes remarked in his diary, "and she may even be a better lawyer, although there is no doubt that Abe is an able lawyer." Finally, Thurman Arnold made Fortas an offer to join his Washington law firm, and on December 17, he formally resigned, effective February 1. Ickes had grown more than a little irritated over the length of time it had taken his undersecretary to make up his mind, but his response was still colored by the affection he had always felt for the ambitious young man: "Our association has been long and intimate. I have never failed to recognize your ability and your high-minded devotion to the public welfare. The Government needs the services of men like you and it does itself an ill-service in failing to make such positions as yours sufficiently attractive and secure so that men, especially those who are young and able like yourself, have no thought except to stay with the Government throughout their effective lives."

Fortas cleared out his desk and started work with Arnold on January 21, 1946, ten days ahead of schedule. Ickes would not be far behind him, although he would not leave quite so sedately. The wheels of his departure had begun to turn on January 9, when Secretary of the Navy James Forrestal (who had been appointed upon Frank Knox's death in 1944) came to lunch and told him that Truman was about to nominate Edwin

Pauley for Secretary of the Navy, after which Forrestal intended to resign. Speaking unofficially for the President, Forrestal asked Ickes if he would actively work against the nomination. "I told him that I would not on my own initiative; that I owed it to the President not to oppose one of his nominations," Ickes wrote in his diary. "I added, however, that if the Senate Committee should call me and ask me questions I would answer the questions truthfully, adding that my answers to certain questions would not do Pauley any good." Forrestal apparently did not ask what the problem might be. Just as incredibly, Ickes did not volunteer to tell him.

The problem was oil, as one would have expected it to be with Pauley, who was president of his own oil company. The oil in question was offshore oil, petroleum deposits that lay beneath the surface of the continental shelf, that underwater fringe of land which extended to varying widths off the shores of the Pacific Coast, the Gulf Coast states, and the Atlantic seaboard. The ownership of these continental shelf lands had never been formally asserted by the federal government and once oil exploration and discovery began to take place in these regions in the late 1930s, the individual states involved had proceeded on the assumption that they owned the underwater land and its resources—and accordingly charged royalties to those few oil companies drilling off the coasts. In 1942, citing the present and future need of oil reserves to prosecute the war, Ickes had talked to Attorney General Francis Biddle about getting Justice Department lawyers to file suit in U.S. District Court and assert title for the federal government. But on May 15, as he told his diary, "A short time ago I got word from Biddle that the President had told him not to go ahead with these suits just now. Biddle thought that Pauley had something to do with the President's decision. This proved to be the case. Pauley, himself, is interested in some of these oil lands. His company was among the first to drill." Pauley's apparent fear was that the oil companies would not be able to operate with as free a hand or negotiate royalty contracts as favorable to their interests if the lands were administered by the Interior Department instead of by more easily influenced state governments (in this, at least so long as Ickes remained Interior Secretary, he was certainly correct).

The issue had lain at rest for another two years, but in April 1944 Ickes started to talk about the district court suit again and Pauley came to the rescue of the companies immediately. "I told Davies," Ickes wrote, "that I thought it was a scandalous situation for an oil man, especially one who has oil interests that may be adverse to the Government, being Treasurer of the Democratic National Committee. A scandal could easily break that would involve Pauley and the Administration in a serious way that could not very well be explained away." Memories of Teapot Dome, the *bête noir* of Interior's past, had haunted him for years, and this time he was not going to back down. He had continued to push the Justice Department in the direction of a suit and by the fall apparently had Pauley seriously worried, for during a meeting with Ickes and Abe Fortas early in September he had revealed himself occupying a position only a cut or two above that of bagman for the oil industry. The Democratic Party was having trouble raising money for the Presidential campaign, he reminded Ickes, then proceeded to talk himself into the permanent record of the Ickes diary:

> He had talked with the President, he said, and the President had told him to talk to me. Pauley said that he could raise $300,000 from the oil men in California, who have interests in off-shore oil, if they could be assured that the Federal Government would not try to assert title to these oil lands. I told him that I could not give any such assurance. . . . I explained to him that if these titles were in the state of California no harm would be done by us having a court pass upon the question. On the other hand, if title actually was in the United States, as some lawyers believed that it was, it would make a pretty scandal involving not only me, but the President and himself, if I should agree not to try to assert title. . . .
>
> This is the rawest proposition that has ever been made to me. I doubt whether the President will bring it up, but if he does I will have to tell him that I can't go along. I don't intend to smear my record with oil at this stage of the game even to help to win the reelection of the President.

Roosevelt had continued to make it clear even after the election was safely over that he did not want the suit brought. He had compounded this failing when he, too, took Pauley's name into consideration as Assistant Secretary of the Navy, foreshadowing Truman's move by more than a year. This first time, as later, it was Secretary Forrestal who had discussed the possibility with Ickes on November 25. "I told Forrestal," Ickes wrote, "that in my judgment this would not be a good appointment nor a safe one. As a matter of fact, this would not be proper so long as the Navy has the great interest that it has in oil lands, especially in California." The appointment had not been made, but Pauley would not give up his quest to get Ickes to leave offshore oil alone, nagging at the Secretary again in February 1945: "He told me that he had raised $500,000 during the campaign and $300,000 had come from oil interests in California. He thought that it would be a great mistake to disturb those interests. I told him very frankly that it was my intention to cause a lease to be issued. Here was a question for the courts to decide." Then, as the grisly climax to Pauley's lobbying, the oilman had taken the occasion of the train ride back from Hyde Park after Roosevelt's burial to ask Ickes once more what he intended to do about offshore oil. The Secretary reiterated his determination to file suit and closed the discussion. "I could just about ruin him," Ickes wrote, "by relating the pressures that he has tried to exert on me with respect to offshore oil in California."

When Truman assumed office, he had made it clear that he did not object to the suit being launched, and on May 29, 1945, it had been entered before the U.S. District Court in Los Angeles. Even better, from Ickes's point of view, Truman had taken another step in the right direction when on September 28 he signed an order prepared by the Department of the Interior and the State Department that arbitrarily asserted title to all offshore lands and resources. It would take months for the suit already filed by the federal government and the suits that were ultimately filed by the tideland states in response to Truman's order to be sorted out, but for the moment the ownership of the continental shelf lands was in federal hands and would remain in federal hands until and if the government's grip could be pried loose by the courts.

That was where the situation rested when Forrestal had come to him on January 9. Since his principal objection to Pauley now was the continued security of the naval oil reserves under a potential Pauley secretaryship, Ickes attempted to persuade Truman to transfer responsibility for them back to the Interior Department, where they had resided in the years before World War I. Truman seemed to agree, but made no moves to that end before sending Pauley's nomination to the Senate on January 18 without further consultation with his Secretary of the Interior. Ickes was miffed, but intended to stick by his promise not to actively oppose the nomination. "This is my position to which I think that I must adhere while I am a member of the Cabinet," he declared in his diary. He almost told Truman the full story behind his objections to the nomination during a meeting with the President on January 30. One word of inquiry from Truman would have brought the tale of the implied bribe out into the open. "In connection with Pauley," Ickes wrote, "I told the President that I did not intend to initiate any attack on him and that I would not plant anything." Truman did not ask what he meant by "anything." Then, Ickes said, he added that "if I should be called up to the Senate I would have to answer questions honestly. Even with this lead, the President did not ask me what, if anything, I knew to Pauley's discredit."

As he had anticipated, Ickes was asked to testify before the Senate Naval Affairs Committee, to which the Pauley nomination had been referred. His testimony was scheduled for the morning of February 1 following a cabinet meeting. As the meeting was breaking up, Ickes went up to Truman at the head of the table, explained that he had been summoned, and gave the President one more chance to ask the right questions. Instead, Ickes said, the President "told me that of course I must tell the truth but he hoped that I would be as gentle with Pauley as possible. I said that this was my intention."*

Throughout his diary, Ickes insists that he leaked no information about the conversations he had had with Pauley regarding the offshore oil situation and the financial bind of the Democratic National Committee. Nevertheless, *someone* certainly had been turning a spigot somewhere, for Edwin A. Harris, a reporter for the *St. Louis Post-Dispatch,* had enough information to give to Senator Charles Tobey, a Republican of New Hampshire and the committee member who had called for Ickes's testimony, to guarantee himself a good story. Ickes had just seated himself when Senator Tobey leaned forward and asked the key question in a scene later described by correspondent Tris Coffin, who was covering the story for CBS News:

> "Did Mr. Pauley ever tell you the filing of the government suit to claim the tidelands was bad politics, that it might cost several hundred thousand dollars in campaign donations?"
>
> There was a long, complete silence.
>
> The Secretary looked unhappy. He answered slowly, "This line of questioning is embarrassing to me. But you are entitled to an answer. . . . My answer is *Yes.*"
>
> A faint, sick smile replaced the jaunty look on Pauley's face.
>
> "What was your answer?" Senator Tobey asked in his dry New England twang.
>
> Ickes answered firmly, "That I would not let that enter my consideration."

Pauley took the stand that afternoon, and when presented with Ickes's testimony replied, "I am sure Mr. Ickes was very much confused this morning. I only asked him to help raise money for the Democratic Party."

Calling Ickes "confused" was a bad idea. When he heard about Pauley's remark, the Secretary told Harris that he had excerpts from his diary that he would be more than willing to share with the world should he be called before the committee again. Tobey learned of this and did indeed call the Secretary back for an addendum on February 5. When given the opportunity, Ickes delivered a very slightly condensed reading of his diary entry for September 9, 1944, when Pauley had specifically mentioned the availability of $300,000 if the government did not press its suit. He also brought up the conversation on board the funeral train.

---

* This was one of the few points on which the two men agreed. In his memoirs, written nine years later, Truman said that his remark was "Tell 'em the truth and be gentle to Ed."

All this made for sensational news over the next two days and was one of the main subjects of the President's press conference on February 7. Truman defended Pauley vigorously, then was asked whether the conflict was going to change his relationship with his Secretary of the Interior. "I don't think so," the President replied. "Mr. Ickes can very well be mistaken the same as the rest of us."

Perhaps it was the tone of voice, but this otherwise seemingly mild response set off an explosion in the Secretary, who discussed the situation over the weekend with Jane, Thomas Corcoran, Justice Douglas, and others, then worked up a long letter of resignation (which like most of those of the past was a combination of indictment and brief for the defense) and sent it over to the White House on the afternoon of February 12. In it, he declared that he did not care to "commit perjury for the sake of the party," inquired of Truman just what the President had meant when he asked Ickes to be "gentle" with Pauley, then gave the date of March 31 as his official day of departure. He also went on the Interior Department radio station that night to say that "I could no longer, much as I regret it, retain my self-respect and stay in the Cabinet of President Truman."

Truman turned it right around on him the next day, leaking his answer to the press before giving it to Ickes himself: "My dear Harold: I have your letter of February twelfth tendering your resignation as Secretary of the Interior. The letter leaves me but one choice of action. I therefore accept your resignation, effective at the close of business on Friday, February fifteen next. I also consider that this terminates all of your other governmental activities." So much for the departure date of March 31.

"I deeply appreciate the generosity and graciousness displayed by your letter of February 13," Ickes replied immediately. "What particularly appeals to me is your statement 'I also consider that this (my resignation) terminates all of your other governmental activities.' You will pardon me if I remark that this is in the nature of supererogation. I assure you that I have had no secret design, having resigned as Secretary of the Interior, to hold on to any other office under your jurisdiction."

Ickes, who had no intention of going gently into that good night of forced retirement, immediately called the press in for a final news conference. The auditorium in the Interior Building, Tris Coffin reported, "was jammed. Every chair was taken. Correspondents stood two deep along the walls. Men who had not wandered three feet from the Press Club bar in months were there. Columnists who usually meditate in solitary dignity sat primly in their chairs. They looked a little surprised to be rubbing elbows with the masses."

"Ickes shambled down the aisle like an old bear," Coffin wrote.

"Beside him was his tall, younger wife. He climbed up on the stage with the agility of a man forty years his junior. . . .

"His jaw was thrust forward. His rimless glasses rested halfway down his nose. He looked over them at the crowded auditorium. There was a gleam of pride in his sharp eyes. These men and women had come to see HIM. It was the biggest damn news conference ever held in Washington."

It did not take long. "This is not a tentative resignation," Ickes said, emphasizing "tentative."

> My mind was made up. The immediate cause of my resignation was, of course, the Pauley incident. I don't care to stay in an Administration where I am expected to commit perjury for the sake of a party. . . . As soon as I read the report of the President's last news conference when he said I might be mistaken about Pauley, I knew what I had to do. He knew I was opposed to Pauley. Not once did he ask for my reasons. I gave him opportunities. All he had to do was ask me.
>
> I didn't like the President's statement that I might be mistaken about Pauley. I couldn't possibly be mistaken. Even the President of the United States has no right to prejudge me on that kind of an issue. He should have ascertained the facts. He should have read the record.

After a few minutes of the kind of good-natured bantering that had always characterized his best press conferences and a little less kindly give-and-take with a few reporters who had been hectoring him for years (that, too, had been common), a reporter called out for the last time, "Thank you, Mr. Secretary." The room burst into loud, sustained applause. The Secretary stood smiling for a moment in the harsh light of the newsreel cameras, then waved an arm at the standing reporters, called out a good-bye, and walked off the stage and out of the auditorium of the building he had made.

CHAPTER
· 57 ·

Final Barricades

TRUMAN ALWAYS CHARACTERIZED the 1946 resignation of Ickes as nothing more noble than the grandstand play of a man who loved the limelight almost as much as he did power. " 'Honest' Harold Ickes," was how he characterized his opponent in an unsent letter to Jonathan Daniels in 1950, "who was never for anyone else but Harold, would have cut F.D.R.'s throat—or mine for his 'high-minded' ideas for a headline—and did."* It was a sentiment shared by most of Ickes's enemies, and it must be said that his behavior before, during, and after the Pauley hearings lacked, at best, a certain candor. His departure possessed more flamboyance than was usual even for him, and the nature of the split had a contrived quality to it. His little dance with Edwin Harris of the *St. Louis Post-Dispatch,* for one thing, suggests something of manipulation of the news. For another, one is left to wonder why Ickes did not simply tell Truman the facts in the matter instead of playing the reluctant virgin. And the charge that Truman had indicated that he wanted Ickes to perjure himself during his testimony in order to protect Pauley was stretching the known evidence about as far as it could be stretched—it is a long journey

---

* Writing vituperative screeds to vent a blast of fury, then often never sending them, was one of Truman's most useful habits. It let off some of the pressure without causing permanent damage. Ickes, on the other hand, almost always sent such letters and the consequences were frequently injurious to someone's peace of mind—occasionally his own.

from "be as gentle with Pauley as possible" to "lie for him," and nothing in the record suggests that Truman wanted Ickes to take quite so long a trip.

That a large part of the whole affair was ego gotten out of hand cannot be denied; Ickes was not a man to hide his light under a bushel and he did enjoy being in the middle of a good, noisy fight. There also was a measurable touch of the vindictive in the pleasure he clearly took in having put Truman on the spot. But what tends to get lost when such an interpretation of his behavior is used to explain away the whole thing is the fate of Edwin Pauley. With good and sufficient reasons, Ickes neither liked nor trusted Pauley, despised him as just one more grifter trying to get his hands and the hands of his friends on the resources of the public domain. He was genuinely appalled at the idea that this man would be given responsibility for a good part of the nation's oil reserves, was honestly worried (as were many people) about Truman's susceptibility to influence from Pauley, Hannegan, and the President's other cronies, and was quite willing to do anything he needed to do to see to it that Pauley's nomination would be foiled. One way to accomplish this, certainly, would be to make such a stink about it that the political repercussions would make it impossible for Truman to go through with it—and if Ickes came out of the fight looking like St. George standing over an oil-smeared and very dead dragon, well, that would be all right, too.

That, in any case, is how things turned out. Before the fight was over, *The New York Times,* among others, was editorializing against the nomination. As early as February 7, it pointed out, "There has been an unceasing fight through the years to defend from private exploitation the oil reserves that the Navy needs. . . . We believe Mr. Pauley's oil interests disqualify him for a post in the Navy Department." And after the resignation, most of the liberal press came down solidly on Ickes's side. "One has the feeling," the *New York Post* said, "that a poorer and poorer cast is dealing desperately with a bigger and bigger story." Writing in the *Nation,* Freda Kirchwey sniffed the "unsavory odor of oil politics," and went on to remind her readers of an even more unsavory past: "The greater intelligence and probity of Mr. Truman does not suffice to wipe out an unhappy resemblance to Mr. Harding." The *St. Louis Post-Dispatch* complained that Truman had "raised distressing doubts whether he considers public office as sacred and inviolate." And the *Chicago Sun* spoke for an even earlier era than that of Harding: "Here is the old struggle between the machine politician and the independent; between those who hold office for its own sake and those who see it as a means to public ends; between expedience and progressive principles."

Truman, who owned a core of stubbornness that matched that of the former Secretary of the Interior, might have been tempted to hold out for a considerable period under this kind of pressure. Pauley was made of less willful stuff, and a month after Ickes's resignation, he asked Truman to withdraw his name. Truman did so on March 13, reassuring Pauley at the same time that "you stand before your countrymen after vicious and unwarranted attacks with integrity unscathed, with ability unquestioned, with honor unsullied." He was still furious more than two months later when Senator Charles Tobey—who had asked Ickes to testify back in February—had the poor judgment to write Truman asking for a favor for his constituents in New Hampshire. "Your unwarranted attacks on Mr. Pauley almost ruined a good public servant," the President wrote, turning him down. "Between you and Mr. Ickes you have made it exceedingly difficult for me to get good men to fill the necessary places in the Government."

Truman was not the first President (and certainly would not be the last) to blame his troubles on his critics, and he can be forgiven if at times he seemed to be looking for targets. He was attempting to operate in the wake of a man who had cast perhaps the longest shadow of any president in our history after Jefferson, and as historian William E. Leuchtenberg has pointed out, no administration that has followed those of the Roosevelt years has ever been entirely free of that legacy—which, like all political legacies, was a mixed blessing. It had left behind it a spectacular residue of hope and every reason on earth for confidence—we had licked the worst depression in modern times and the most powerful enemy of human civilization since Attila, had we not? The great public works of the New Deal had transformed the physical landscape of the continent, its social programs had changed forever the relationship between the government and the people, its economic revolution had razed and rebuilt our financial institutions; the armies of democracy had proved themselves in blood throughout both hemispheres, and with the most powerful weapon in history at our command, the American Colossus now bestrode the world. At home, the standard of living for most Americans already had risen higher than that of any peoples who had ever inhabited the earth, and every indication was that very soon it would reach even higher plateaus, as the machinery of growth that had been set in motion by the imperatives of global warfare did not seem to slow, but only to hesitate briefly before starting to accelerate as never before. The end of the war was, Henry Luce proclaimed in *Life* magazine, the beginning of the American Imperium.

But not everyone was comfortable in this *Pax Americana*. Somewhere, something seemed to have gone awry, Bruce Catton felt. In 1948 he wrote:

> The end of the war did not leave us on a high mountain top, looking ahead to a limitless vista, with horizon lying beyond horizon to the end of time. Instead it left us in a mysterious valley, cloaked by an eerie fog and swept by confused alarms. We came out of the war timorous, uncertain, confused, not quite clear just what it was we had done and everlastingly perplexed as to exactly what we ought to do next. We had won the war but we had done nothing more than that, and we began to see that a good deal more than that was urgently required.

Truman had inherited this confusion and would never quite feel in control of it—for all his brisk, businesslike moves and the no-nonsense delivery of his Missouri-bred diction. Forever chastised for falling short of the expectations of the Presidency established by his predecessor, he was challenged by difficulties that might have frustrated even Roosevelt in his prime, and Truman was simply not equipped with either the vision or the intellect to prevail. Fear, frustration, and expedience became the watchwords of the new age. Demobilization slid into chaos as the National Association of Manufacturers and the American Farm Bureau lobbied successfully for the swift dismantlement of nearly all the wartime agencies. Only price controls lingered for any length of time, and legislation so eviscerated their effectiveness that it loosed wave after wave of inflation. Housewives—many of them recently booted off their defense jobs by returning veterans and none too pleased about it, either—organized in protest, picketing, directing letter-writing campaigns, and holding rallies against inflation. Even with price restraints all but eliminated and wartime necessities satisfied, it took industry and agriculture time to retool and raise production levels; rationing ended, but shortages continued for a time, contributing to the general air of impatience. For years, housing especially was at a premium in a fecund era when postwar coupling was producing children at an unprecedented clip.

The grotesque leap in the number of unemployed that had been anticipated for the postwar years—some analysts predicting that as many as five million would be out of work—never quite developed, but overtime all but disappeared and take-home pay consequently shrank. The labor movement, the restraints of wartime patriotism and federal regulation (however inconsistently effective) removed, took on new and belligerent life with major strikes in the railroad, automobile, steel, and coal industries that drove Truman to briefly seize coal mines and the railroads under the stipulations of the War Powers Act—still technically in effect in 1946—and to advocate legislation that would give him virtually dictatorial powers to induct labor into the army and determine wage levels in all industries. (The legislation passed the House, but Truman had the wit to abandon the bill when the Senate made it clear that it was political suicide; on the other hand, its sentiments, if not its precise structure, would be reflected in the later Taft-Hartley Act.) The civil rights movement, fortified now by the injection of veterans who believed that they had earned a new place in the American scheme, showed signs for the first time of becoming a national force whose power would change the face of politics and already was helping to disturb the always fragile alliance between northern and southern Democrats.

Politically, the disaster that Roosevelt and the Democrats had managed to hold off for years finally happened—the elections of 1946 gave the Republican Party a thin majority in the Senate, a large majority in the House, and most of the nation's governorships. Congress had not been precisely a pushover for the White House since 1938, but now it would be openly and consistently antagonistic. And as the postwar world shook down into what was seen as an ideological struggle to the death between the forces of democracy and those of international communism, the succubus of anticommunism, never quite dormant even during the war years, rose again to haunt the land and provide meal tickets for the otherwise unemployable. Martin Dies had not run for reelection in 1944, but his House Un-American Activities Committee was alive and well and came to glory in the postwar years under the leadership of its next two chairmen, John Rankin of Mississippi and J. Parnell Thomas of New Jersey. Hollywood, which had been under suspicion even before the war, now was discovered to have been one of the major spawning grounds of domestic communism, and for the next several years the committee was able to reel in trophy-sized headlines on a regular basis by fishing those waters. In Washington the confrontation between Whittaker Chambers and Alger Hiss brought sustenance to committee member Richard M. Nixon, who had obtained his California seat by defeating the liberal Democrat Jerry Voorhis largely on charges that Voorhis was, at best, a dupe of the communists and, at worst, a willing ally.

The White House expressed a legitimate concern over the security of the nation's military and foreign affairs in the midst of the Cold War, but overreacted with Truman's Loyalty Order of March 1947. It set up a complicated system for establishing the loyalty of federal employees and penalizing them not only for membership in but "sympathetic association" with any organization or movement the Justice Department (in the person of J. Edgar Hoover of the FBI) determined to be subversive, and designated the House Un-American Activities Committee's files as a splendid source of such information. Legislatures, school systems, municipal governments, and even private businesses in many states across the country suddenly discovered the utility of loyalty oaths, and for a while they were all the craze. Meanwhile, the Senate did not begin to make a major contribution to the effort until the arrival of Senator Joseph R. McCarthy, who, like Richard Nixon in the House, was not so dense that he could not see a wave of the future when one washed up over his feet; in 1948, McCarthy magically unearthed dozens of subversives in the State Department, the army, and other branches of the federal government and, armed with pieces of paper he tended to wave around in front of the cameras but never quite released for publication, began his brief but gaudy passage across the political firmament.

Behind all the domestic and international posturing and manipulation lay the shadow of annihilation, a potential for destruction that lent an existential character to the age. The Truman administration, in one of its better efforts, had managed to wrest control of the atomic bomb and the future development of nuclear power from the hands of the military, but not without a struggle in the Senate, where in the fall of 1945 the newly created Senate Atomic Energy Committee had begun to hold hearings on a bill to set up a civilian agency for atomic power. Secretary of the Navy James Forrestal, for one, had wanted the military to keep power over the bomb. "I do not want it to come to pass," he had told the committee, "that someone will be able to say to the military, 'This is as far as you can go.' . . . We must not limit the military until the world has reached the pattern we all hope for." Forrestal's testimony had been followed by that of Interior Secretary Harold Ickes. "A democracy cannot afford to keep secrets from itself," Ickes said.

> I object to making a scientist get permission from an army officer to analyze an atom. I hope the day will never come when scientific thinking can be hedged about with petty restrictions. If the push of a button can destroy a city, no nation can allow this button to be in private hands. . . . We have only a little time to negotiate for world security, and we can't get it with a monopoly of knowledge. The military is suspicious. If you look through military eyes, all you can see is wreckage. And the answer, more wreckage.

"We need to have civilian control," Ickes insisted. "I hope our victory will not lead to military control of science and industry."

"Do you think we should disclose to *all* the atomic bomb secret?" Senator Thomas Hart of Connecticut had asked.

"If that means the nations that fought with us to win the war, *yes.*"

In the summer of 1946, Congress passed legislation creating the Atomic Energy Commission, a civilian agency, leaving the military with only a Division of Military Control within the new bureau to exercise its influence. The question of sharing or not sharing, of course, was rendered moot when the Russians developed and detonated their own bomb in 1949, and when the Truman administration later went all out for the development of the hydrogen bomb, even the military was given solace. By then, too, the armed services were busy with another war—although the Korean War was officially described as a "police action" on the part of a multinational force drawn from the cooperating countries of the United Nations, General Douglas MacArthur presiding.

It was not a particularly elegant age, the Truman era, but it could not have been described as boring, either. The former Secretary of the Interior did not find it so, in any case, and to observe the goings-on at close range had purchased a small house on Prospect Avenue in Washington, to which he now commuted as he had to his old job in the Interior Building, often staying over. Ickes may have lost power with his departure as Secretary of the Interior, but he had acquired another podium by taking up a career in a field he had once professed to loathe. Beginning on April 1, 1946, he was Harold L. Ickes, columnist. Ever since his resignation, the *New York Post,* which in those days still boasted the reputation of being a generally liberal institution, had been after him to contribute a column called "Man to Man" three times a week. The column would appear both in the *Post* and in papers nationally via distribution through the *Post* syndicate. He signed on in March, and his first six-hundred-word effort appeared on April 1—a date about which he resisted the temptation of making a joke. "I have read a good many columnists in my time," he wrote, "some with approval and some with aversion, notwithstanding which I do not know the etiquette in connection with the debut . . . of a columnist. Should I bow from the waist with a self-conscious smile or jump overboard into a deep pool in the hope that I may be able to swim ashore, but knowing surely that if I do not a lot of people will be edified?"

There was nothing demure about this debutante. He relished the role of gadfly to the Republic, and for three days a week for the next three years, he got to say what he wanted to say in the public prints without the intercession or approval of anyone; by the terms of his contract, no editor was allowed to revise or expurgate any given column—the only choice was to run or not run it (Ickes had never forgotten what the editors at *Look* magazine had done to him in 1939). Most of those who subscribed ran most of the columns, but when the *Post*'s own editors began letting some of them drop, he turned to the *New Republic,* which signed him on to do a weekly column in the spring of 1949. "Harold Ickes is old enough to be called an Elder Statesman," the editors wrote to introduce his first column on May 2, "but he is too salty for that label. He himself has cheerfully accepted the epithet of Curmudgeon, which likewise is insufficient to his case. A more accurate description would be that he is America's most venerable progressive and one of the stoutest fighters, at any age, for justice and good government."

His *Post* and *New Republic* columns were not the only writing he did in these last years—although "dictating" might have been a closer description of the process. He had always dictated his material, and when Dictaphones came into general use had seized the technology with enthusiasm. He had one with him at almost all times now, in his Prospect Avenue house, in his study just off the living room at Headwaters Farm, even at the house the family rented for the summer at Southwest Harbor, Maine (having had to give up the Bar Harbor house, which was owned by the National Park Service as part of Acadia National Park). For hour after hour, day after day, he kept the red lights on those machines glowing. The secretaries who came and went during the years then transcribed the tapes, and Ickes worked them over carefully and put them into final form.

This was how he produced his only significant published account of his career as Secretary of the Interior, "My Twelve Years with Roosevelt," an eight-part series that ran in the *Saturday Evening Post* through the months of June and July 1948. With his diary and copies of his voluminous correspondence as his basic references, he cobbled a rambling, discursive, often self-serving, and irrepressibly one-sided account of the Roosevelt years for which the *Post* paid him a fee of $60,000. That sum, remarkable for its time, may have mellowed him a little, for he proved himself amenable to suggestions for revision from editor Ben Hibbs throughout the production of the series—at one point even agreeing to delete a potentially libelous reference to Charles Lindbergh's prewar activities. "There can be no doubt . . . how I feel about this gentleman," he wrote Hibbs on March 11, 1948. "To my mind, he is beneath contempt. However, since you seem to feel strongly on the matter, I am willing to eliminate all reference to him although, frankly, I do it with great reluctance." As Ickes took on such characters as General Hugh Johnson— "General Johnson, for all his undoubted ability and energy, ran through

official life in Washington like a Model T Ford with a missing cylinder"—
and Harry Hopkins—"both irresponsible and arrogant"*—Hibbs continued to display a certain nervousness from time to time, at one point
appending an editorial note: "Mr. Ickes' views on issues and personalities
in the foregoing article are his own and not necessarily those of the
Saturday Evening Post."

Ickes continued to produce his diary, although in later years he was not
quite so religious about making weekly entries as he had been during his
time with the government. It nevertheless continued to mount, page after
page, like leaves in the Book of Judgment. In addition, he began to put
together a more formal account of the Roosevelt years than his *Saturday
Evening Post* series. This would thereafter be referred to as "the book" in his
correspondence, and it was something he was always promising himself to
get down to in a serious way just as soon as he found the time, but in fact
worked on only sporadically over the years. It never did get finished.

Most of his time, now, was taken up in the writing of his columns, in
keeping up an incredible correspondence, and in the monitoring of all the
political and social concerns that continued to inspire his attention—and,
more often than not, the three functions coincided. In his "Man to Man"
column in 1947, for example, he repeatedly pushed for ratification of the
Anglo-American oil treaty he had negotiated in 1945, citing in particular
the opposition of Harry Sinclair, the Texas oilman who had been involved
with Albert Fall in the Teapot Dome scandal. "Just why Mr. Sinclair is
working against the public interest this time, I do not know," Ickes wrote
on June 18. "Nor is he likely to take the public into his confidence. He is
known in the oil industry as a contumacious person who is instinctively
opposed to any policy that his competitors approve. He just naturally
opposes anything that does not produce a business advantage or money
profit to Mr. Harry F. Sinclair." He also went to considerable effort and
expense to write and privately print "An Oil Policy: An Open Letter by
Harold L. Ickes to the Members of the Congress of the United States" in
May. "I would like to present the case of oil for the American people
against oil for reckless exploitation for private profit," he wrote. "I want to
argue the case of oil available to the United States for the protection of its
people as against oil permitted to be exploited quickly and wastefully for
less important purposes." And argue he did—although opposition from
such oil producers as Sinclair and such political allies of the oil industry as

* Hopkins could not have answered this charge even if he had wanted to. After filling Truman
in on the background of the upcoming Potsdam Conference with Stalin and Churchill,
Hopkins resigned on July 2, 1945. His health, never very good, deteriorated rapidly, and on
January 29, 1946, he died.

Senator Tom Connally was more than enough to keep the treaty from ratification until its final demise in 1948.

He also retained a powerful interest in the tidelands oil question. When Senator Pat McCarran introduced legislation in the spring of 1946 that would have voided the claim of the federal government to the title in offshore lands that Truman had put forth in 1945 (a question still pending before the Supreme Court in 1946), Ickes assured the readers of "Man to Man" that Truman was certain to veto the legislation if it passed, for "President Truman knows that it is his duty to safeguard all of the wealth of the United States, particularly that in the public domain. He knows that it is the prerogative of the Supreme Court to decide who has legal title to this disputed land and until the Supreme Court decides that the United States has no right, title or interest, he is going to hold on to it." The bill did pass and Truman did veto it without the opposition being able to come up with enough votes for an override. The Supreme Court eventually upheld the federal right to title, but legislation similar to McCarran's 1946 bill would come up again near the end of Truman's second term, when Ickes once again worked against it so effectively through both his *New Republic* column and a vigorous letter-writing campaign that his efforts brought a note of thanks from Truman himself on July 10, 1951:

> I appreciate most highly yours of the ninth regarding the bill which affects the Tidelands oil titles. Every effort is being made to give away the oil resources adjacent to the continental United States and the most peculiar thing in connection with it is that members of the Congress from inland states are perfectly willing to give away their birthright without a qualm. I don't understand it. I really don't think they have enough votes to pass the "big steal" over my veto.

(They didn't; it was not until the first administration of Dwight D. Eisenhower in 1953 that legislation transferring title of the tidelands to the states was passed and signed into law.)

Over the nearly six years of their production, both the "Man to Man" and the *New Republic* columns came in handy for the expression of opinion on a kaleidoscopic variety of subjects whose only common element was a strain of old-fashioned liberalism that Ickes refused to let time diminish. It translated well into the new age, even when it came up against the testing of atomic bombs in the Bikini atolls of the South Pacific during the summer of 1946: "[I]t seems to me to be shocking that the United States, or any other nation for that matter, should at this time give any indication, however remote, that it is preparing for atomic warfare. This is not a time for martial gestures; it is not a time for public exercises in the art of modern war." Or when he decided to lambaste John L. Lewis, who, Ickes wrote, "started his career in the mines by beating a mule over the rear end to persuade it to draw out a coal car. He has not changed his tactics except that now he wants the mule to pull, not a coal car, but his own chariot up the hill to personal power and glory." Or when he laid bare the continuing existence of racial prejudice in the nation's Capital: "Discrimination against minority groups in Washington is deeply embedded. It is the hydrogen in the social atmosphere. As to government jobs, discrimination against Negroes has become notorious. Some government agencies hardly go to the trouble to conceal their malignant prejudice."

The Ickes editorial net was cast wide enough to include the recognition of the state of Israel in 1948 (he was for it), the supplying of enough arms to that new state to enable it to defend itself against its Arab neighbors (he was for that, too), legislation limiting the President of the United States to two terms (he was against it), the effort on the part of American banking and manufacturing interests to restore and promote the industrial power of the Ruhr valley in Germany in spite of Roosevelt's promises to dismantle it (he was against the restoration effort), the firing of General MacArthur by President Truman on April 11, 1951. (He was for it, and in fact had been advocating it since December 1950, writing in the *New Republic* that "To be sure, there was one brilliant interlude for which MacArthur has been given high credit. But that one stroke which drove the North Koreans out of Pyongyang was more than matched by the rout of the UN armies with terrific casualties. U.S. prestige has been damaged to an extent that will be difficult to rebuild.")

The Dictaphone was kept glowing by sundry controversies in the field of conservation, as well—including Congressman Frank Barrett's repeated introduction of bills to abolish Jackson Hole National Monument and to turn over all national forests to the individual states. These were systematically rejected, but not without concerted effort on the part of the conservation community and a few powerful private voices like Bernard DeVoto, the "Easy Chair" columnist for *Harper's* magazine. The monument itself was not rendered entirely safe until 1950, when it was finally tucked into the boundaries of Grand Teton National Park, where it remains. Even more dramatic was an attempt by lumber interests in the Pacific Northwest to get at more than fifty-six thousand acres of Olympic National Park for logging in 1947. Three separate bills to take the land and give it to the Forest Service for management were introduced early that year, and Park Director Newton Drury and Julius A. Krug, Ickes's successor as Secretary of the Interior, at first decided not to contest the

action. Informed of these proceedings by Rosalie Edge of the Emergency
Conservation Committee, Ickes waxed sarcastic in his "Man to Man"
column of April 10, 1947, pointing out that "in reaching out to grab
56,000 acres of the Olympic National Park," timber interests "cannot be
charged with a statutory crime inasmuch as the Dept. of the Interior is
well beyond the age of consent. And apparently Secretary Krug and
Director Drury . . . were eager to consent."

Ickes wrote another stinging column on the same subject eight days
later and sent both to Irving Brant, suggesting that Brant work up a third
one for him. Brant was happy to oblige, and with Ickes's continued
exposure of the attempted rape as one of his principal weapons, was able to
persuade Krug and Drury to change their minds, Truman to oppose the
idea, and Congressman Henry M. Jackson, whose district encompassed
most of the park, to ask that his bill for the taking of the parkland be
withdrawn when a new Congress opened for business in January 1948. A
similar fight for the preservation of the Calaveras groves of enormous old
ponderosa pine and sugar pine trees in the Sierra Nevada also came to
victory in 1951, when, largely through the intervention of Ickes and
Brant, the Forest Service was forced to open negotiations for the acquisition of these groves from their private owners via a land exchange—later
rendered unnecessary when John D. Rockefeller came up with a grant of
one million dollars to buy them outright.

The former Secretary also objected to the growing dominance of the
stockmen's advisory boards established by the Taylor Grazing Act of
1934, particularly after the first of Truman's two executive reorganiza-
tions incorporated the functions of the Grazing Service and the old
General Land Office into a single agency called the Bureau of Land
Management in 1946. He especially disliked the artificially low fees the
bureau continued to charge for the grazing of cattle and sheep on public
lands, fees established and maintained at the behest of the livestock
industry: "These lands," he wrote Krug on September 23, 1947, "belong
to the general public and they should bring in a return similar to that
received from comparable lands in private ownership." (The fees remained
at bargain-basement levels, where they sit today.) And after Herbert
Hoover's congressionally mandated Commission on Organization of the
Executive Branch of Government recommended that the Bureau of Land
Management be taken out of Interior and placed in the Department of
Agriculture, Ickes wrote Truman early in 1951 to object; while he was at
it, he also took the occasion to make one last plea that the national forests
be taken out of Agriculture and given to Interior. (In the end, the Bureau
of Land Management stayed put, but so did the national forests.)

He even managed to get in a few licks against what would become one of the major conservation battles of modern history—the attempt to build reclamation and hydropower dams in Echo Park and Split Mountain Canyon that would flood most of Dinosaur National Monument. The dams had been approved by Oscar Chapman, who succeeded Julius Krug when he left Interior in the fall of 1949. Ickes had cheered the appointment of Chapman when it was announced—"President Truman could not have done better than he did," he had written in the *New Republic* on November 28, 1949—but Chapman's action in approving the dams for Dinosaur outraged him. "If Dinosaur National Monument is to be sacrificed to Reclamation," he wrote to Bernard DeVoto at *Harper's,* "why not the Yellowstone and other National Parks and Monuments? As you apprehend, it is an entering wedge. Having established such a precedent, Chapman will be besieged for other concessions. I am against them all." So saying, he devoted what time and space he could to this conflict, whose resolution would not come until the middle of the decade (the dams would be defeated in Congress). Had he been there to see it, he would have joined his voice in thanks to that of a new generation of conservationists—who owed more to him and his work than most of them ever knew.

Ickes took a lot of pleasure in the writing of his *New Republic* column. "It keeps me out of the rut and I really have fun with it," he wrote Raymond Robins in December 1949. "I select my own subjects and have an absolutely free hand." No subject gave him the opportunity to exercise that free hand with greater imagination and stylistic vigor than the anticommunist hysteria of the time. He had warmed up to the subject in his old "Man to Man" column, particularly when the House Un-American Activities Committee fell under the control of J. Parnell Thomas in 1947, predicting as early as January 30 that things were going to get increasingly ugly:

> The committee starts off by fracturing a fundamental American principle— that a man is to be regarded as innocent until he is proved guilty. The committee operates on the reverse theory that a man is guilty until he is proved innocent. The injustice of this procedure lies in the fact that many who are assumed to be guilty never get a chance to prove their innocence. Sometimes the hurt that is done is so great that it is impossible to repair it. As the battle lines between communist and non-communist are drawn more tightly in this country, the harm that will be done to the innocent will become greater.

He would be proved correct, and never more so than when the name of his former assistant Ruth Gruber was mentioned during the trial of Judith

Coplon, a Department of Justice employee who had been arrested for spying, in the summer of 1949. Miss Gruber, it seemed, had been identified in a third-hand FBI report as a "contact" of F. A. Garanin of the Soviet Embassy in Washington—all members of the Soviet embassy being assumed to be practicing spies, as indeed some were. She knew Garanin casually, as many people did, Ickes reported angrily in his *New Republic* column for June 20, but to proceed from this knowledge to the presumption of some kind of guilty relationship was foul play: "Thus, thanks to some feckless FBI agent, whom Mr. Hoover should immediately direct to earn his living more honestly, a surmise and a lie are married and set loose, hand in hand, to march through headlines and the text of newspaper articles. Unfortunately, from such a miscegenation can be born a teeming progeny of distorted and misshapen monstrosities. Is it for playing fast and loose with the characters of honorable citizens that Congress votes money so generously?"

The FBI came in for a blast again six months later when it was revealed that the agency had been tapping the telephones of private citizens in its quest for subversives: "If the FBI so disregards legal propriety—to say nothing of common decency—as to tap telephone wires in order to hear what a lawyer and a client may say to each other, then it is time for a free people who never have and, it may be hoped, never will, tolerate a secret police, to abolish the FBI, if nothing short of that will keep it within proper bounds."

Ickes reserved his highest umbrage, however, for "Tailgunner Joe," Senator Joseph R. McCarthy, whose career as a blatherskite was in full flower the last three years of Ickes's life. "If it is a practice of Marshal Stalin to recognize outstanding services to the Soviet Union, then he is doubtless already aware that Senator Joseph R. McCarthy of Wisconsin has earned the biggest and shiniest medal of them all," he wrote on April 10, 1950. "It is expected that the aim of the Communists would be, deliberately and persistently, to undermine and discredit our democratic institutions," he added. "But that a Senator of the United States, however lacking he may be in intellectual integrity, should deliberately undertake to achieve the same result is a sad commentary upon the type of public servant in this country that blathering Joe typifies. Unfortunately, there are a few feckless ignoramuses who applaud him." In June, Ickes went after McCarthy's scalp, writing, "He should be impeached, and promptly. But, without waiting for the result of unnecessarily slow and cumbersome impeachment proceedings, the Senate should unseat him as unworthy to associate with patriotic and scrupulous Senators." Ickes was not around in 1954 to see the Senate finally censure the raucous opportunist from Wisconsin, but he did take some satisfaction from events in the late summer of 1950, when a Senate subcommittee under the chairmanship of Millard Tydings, Ickes's old antagonist, found that McCarthy's charges of communist infiltration of the State Department constituted "a fraud, a hoax, and a deceit," as Ickes reported on August 7 in one of the most orotund and pungent passages of his public life:

> Bumbling, babbling Joe McCarthy with his own hands has so stripped himself of the few rags of decency that he possessed that, intellectually and morally, he stands hideously nude before the American people. . . . He has already done incalculable injury to his country, and there would have been no limit to the harm that he seemed willing to do if a majority of the subcommittee . . . had not courageously exposed McCarthyism for what it is—a putrescent and scabious object that is obnoxious to the senses of sight, smell and hearing—a thing obscene and loathsome, and not to be touched, except with sterilized fire tongs.

Ickes managed to produce a fury of prose on numerous subjects in these years, but it must have been a sadness to him that his steadily declining physical abilities prevented him from getting more actively involved in political stumping. Nevertheless, he joined the Truman campaign for election in 1948 and gave it the best that he could, given the fact that he was now seventy-four. Truman certainly welcomed it, in any case.

Ickes did not support the President out of any sudden discovery of virtue in the former haberdasher from Independence. In fact, he had joined a short-lived effort by the radical Americans for Democratic Action to draft Dwight D. Eisenhower, the architect of the Allied invasion of France and now president of Columbia University, to run on the Democratic ticket, with Justice William O. Douglas as his running mate. Eisenhower let the Democrats play for a while, then on July 5 had formally announced his refusal to allow his name to be entered into the competition. Ickes did not attend the Democratic National Convention on July 12 (it was the first he had missed since 1932), and when Truman succeeded in capturing the nomination—with Senator Alben Barkley of Kentucky as his running mate—Ickes accepted the conventional wisdom that the ticket "has practically no chance of winning," as he wrote in his diary. "Whether the Democrats can make a respectable showing is not clear at this date."

But Truman's opponent was Thomas Dewey again, who had gotten the Republican nomination in June, with Governor Earl Warren of California at his side. Ickes still could not abide Dewey and particularly did not trust his judgment about conservation matters that were important to the former Secretary. Furthermore, Henry Wallace had decided to challenge the two-party system. He resigned as Secretary of Commerce early in 1948 and announced his candidacy for the nomination of the Progressive Party. He got the nomination, with the "singing senator," former cowboy showman Glen Taylor of Idaho, as his running mate. The Progressive Party, populated by radicals of every stripe, was too vulnerable to charges of communist infiltration to have been a serious contender, but it was widely believed that it would draw off a substantial number of Democratic votes. So would the States' Rights Democratic Party—the "Dixiecrats"—a recalcitrant group of southern Democrats led by Governor Strom Thurmond of South Carolina. These two disaffections alone, it was believed, would give the Republicans a clear shot at the Presidency for the first time since 1928.

With that dread possibility in mind, Ickes and Truman each swallowed old angers and agreed to meet on October 4, after Ickes, Jane, and the children returned from the annual Maine vacation in the last week of September. It was the first meeting between the two men since Ickes's resignation. "When I was shown into the President's office," he reported to his diary,

> I walked to his desk and he stood up to shake my hand. He expressed pleasure at seeing me and said, in effect, "You never should have left me. I did not want you to go and I have never been critical of you." Of course, this was not true. . . . I had reason to believe, from what I have heard from time to time, that the air of the White House is nothing short of sulphurous whenever my name has been mentioned. However, I was not there to argue with him. . . .
>
> Then I told him that, after a long period of doubt as to what I would do in the campaign, I had decided to support him. I gave as my reason, Dewey's side-stepping of all the conservation issues in which I was interested. I told President Truman that I took it for granted that his position on these issues had not varied. . . .
>
> At the end, he said that he was glad that I had come back and that I must never leave him again. As I thought about this interview during subsequent days, I could not but feel that Truman presented something of a pathetic figure, which is something that a President of the United States ought not to do in any circumstances.

Compared to previous campaigns, the Ickes contribution this time around was minimal, if briefly splashy. On October 11 he held a press conference at the Cabinet Room of the Willard Hotel to announce his support of the Truman-Barkley ticket. On October 14, over the ABC radio network via WMAL in Washington, he gave the first of the two speeches he would make in the campaign, this one sponsored by the AF of

L–CIO. It was a journeyman effort, but not up to his old standards. "I am here to talk about Mr. Dewey, Thomas Elusive Dewey, the Candidate in Sneakers. Mr. Dewey is tripping to and fro about the country talking about 'Unity,' " he intoned, referring to Dewey's low-key campaign strategy, one based on the fact that nearly every pundit in the land worthy of the name had conceded the election to him. "For the past month he has gone North and South, East and West—riding in every direction at once—telling us How Beautiful Everything Is. . . . Mr. Dewey reminds me of the title of that popular song on the 'Hit Parade'—'You Call Everybody Darling.' " He used a musical image again in his second speech, this one given at Madison Square Garden in New York on October 28:

> *Has anybody here seen Dewey? D-E-W-E-Y?*
> *Has anybody here seen Dewey? Have you seen his smile?*
> *His hair is sleek, his shine is new,*
> *And he is Wall Street through and through.*
> *Has anybody here seen Dewey? Dewey of the lullaby?*

He wrote a few letters in support of Truman, made a few telephone calls, but it was all *pro forma*. As he had told a friend when he decided to announce his support, "I had no illusions as to who would be elected but . . . I felt, from my own point of view, it was important to begin to build up a body of opinion with which to oppose the attempt that I foresaw to cause the country to reverse itself on its conservation and power program."

The pollsters certainly would have applauded his lack of illusions. Roper, Gallup, Crossley—all showed Dewey winning by at least five percentage points. David Lawrence, Arthur Krock, Walter Lippmann, James Reston—the premier columnists of the day all picked Dewey to win with no trouble.

He lost—though not by much, as the electoral vote was counted. Truman garnered 24.2 million popular votes to 22 million for Dewey, while Wallace and Thurmond each brought in about 1.2 million. However, a shift of only thirty thousand votes portioned out among the states of California, Ohio, and Illinois could have given Dewey enough electoral votes for a majority. Nevertheless, a win was a win. Ickes was as astounded as anyone. "It actually took two or three days for me to become accustomed to the idea of all predictions, especially those of the polltakers, having gone so far astray," Ickes told his diary. "I hope that the professional polltakers will meet the fate of the *Literary Digest* which, in 1936, predicted the election of Landon over Roosevelt. . . . Commentators, newspaper editors, polltakers and all others have been trying to explain away predictions that were utterly ridiculous in the light of the result."

This particular pundit, it is worth noting, did not include himself among the soul-searchers—but he was.

Truman had beaten the odds and the odds-makers. Two years later, Ickes's old friend, Congresswoman Helen Gahagan Douglas, would not be so lucky. In 1950, Douglas faced a powerful challenge for the California U.S. Senate seat from the upstart Republican Richard Nixon. As early as the spring of the year, she had been confident that she would be able to win the Democratic nomination for the Senate, and thought that with Ickes's help she might also be able to win the Republican nomination as well. (California, the Great Exception, as Carey McWilliams once called the state, practiced cross-filing in primary elections.) Her chief opponent for the Republican nomination would very likely be Richard Nixon, who had parlayed his work on the House Un-American Activities Committee into national prominence. Douglas had asked Ickes to come out in April and campaign as much against Nixon as for her. "I am becoming a little wary," he wrote Anna Roosevelt on March 20, "of the Democratic high command taking me off the museum shelf and dusting me off and sending me out to make a speech or two and then returning me to the museum."* He declined Douglas's request—though without telling her all of his reasons. "You expressed the idea that, by concentrating on Nixon, it might be possible for you to win the Republican nomination for Senator," he wrote her on April 13. "I do not concur in this and those with whom I have talked here think that it is too much to expect. After all, Nixon will be running on a ticket with [Governor Earl] Warren and it is to be expected that Republicans will make every effort to put across a big vote for both."

He was right in that prediction. Nixon and Warren won the Republican nominations for senator and governor respectively with no trouble. Douglas won the Democratic Senate nomination, as expected, and James Roosevelt, FDR's son, won the Democratic nomination for the governor's race.

Douglas asked Ickes to come out to speak again in the fall, but he had to turn her down, this time with genuine regret. He did, however, consent to make his first and only television "spot," a one-minute film in which he told the voters of California that if he were able to he would vote for her "because she is a statesman and not a policeman. She has made a distinguished record during her three terms in the House of Representatives. She has convictions and the courage to fight for them. She has not

* Anna and John Boettiger had separated after attempting to run a newspaper together in Phoenix for a while after the war. She was now living in Los Angeles with the children. John Boettiger committed suicide in October.

spent your time or my time hunting for a Red under the bed. She has fought Communism in the only way in which it can be effectively fought—by improving the economic and social conditions of the under-privileged." He also sent her money and used his *New Republic* column on October 16 in an appeal for more: "In order to cover her huge state adequately, Mrs. Douglas needs money. She needs it quickly. Unfortunately, it has always been true in this country that those candidates who honestly believe in the people and would unselfishly serve them very often have to run impoverished campaigns." None of it did any good. Nixon had learned to use the weapon of anticommunism with a skill and persistence unmatched by any other politician of his time, and he won the election in November by a margin of 680,947 votes.

The Douglas race for the Senate seat in California was Ickes's last campaign. He had a fairly comfortable winter that year, and in the spring of 1951 took his usual delight in watching the flowers around the grounds of Headwaters Farm begin their annual blossoming. He had planted them with the same careful attention to detail he had given the flowers around Hubbard Woods all those years before—peonies here, dahlias there, roses, daisies, gladioli, gardeners kept hopping to maintain the celebration of flowers that had always marked his life. He had his vegetable gardens to supervise, too. Meals at Headwaters Farm were accompanied by fresh vegetables grown on his own ground—and when he said fresh, he meant fresh, picked and cleaned just minutes before being cooked and placed on the table. No exceptions. "The farm was my mother's territory," his son Harold remembers, "but the flowers and the vegetables were my father's responsibility. God knows where he got the time to supervise all of that and do everything else he seemed to do, but he did."

Both children loved the farm. Young Harold enjoyed what he was able to do of the work itself (and would get quite serious about it in later years). Elizabeth was too young to participate at that level, but "I got my love of the land and animals from that experience," she says. "I suppose it was not entirely a good thing to have grown up in such an isolated way. But we did love it there, both of us."

In some ways it was a lonely life for the children. Ickes and Jane did not exactly shut the children out of their own sphere, but it was an old-fashioned family in many respects, Elizabeth remembers. Their father was at the center of things when he was home; the household revolved around his needs and Jane did not ordinarily challenge that relationship. The children usually ate their meals alone and for the most part lived a schedule separate from that of their parents. The most persistent images both children have of their father in these years is of him working, talking into his Dictaphone, hunched over a desk, giving instructions to the secretaries and stenographers who came and went like messengers in a field campaign. Harold does not remember much physical contact with his father (nor did his first son, Raymond). "I'm sure he loved me," he says, "but I have no real memory of that kind of close physical relationship." Elizabeth does: "I have the very distinct memory of sitting in his lap, being read to, feeling warm and loved and protected," she remembers. But even that memory was one of rare moments, not as a regular part of her father's routine.

It is possible, of course, that Ickes was unconsciously insulating the children against the sense of loss that would come when he died. In March 1951 he started feeling an occasional twinge of pain in his side that he ascribed to lumbago. A little painkiller took care of it at first, but it got worse as the spring progressed. His temperature started registering a little over a degree below normal, and he found himself exhausted much of the time. On Sunday, May 27, he reported to his diary that he had had such a painful night on the previous Tuesday that his usual dose of whiskey and two grains of Nembutal (his sleeping potion of choice now) was not enough to keep him asleep. He had risen at eleven to take more whiskey. "I was awake again at 3:30 and . . . I felt wild and strange." The next day, he dosed himself with Dexadrine, and the next day "practically all day, I had a terrific headache and, particularly in the morning, my legs ached."

The pain subsided later that spring, and according to a letter from Jane to Anna on August 31, the summer at Southwest Harbor was satisfying for both of them. "Harold continues to be in quite good shape," she wrote.

> There is no question, however, but that he tires more easily than he did even a year ago. But if he sticks to his routine, he is all right and even in good spirits. We ceased to be man and wife and became merely male and female pillars of authority when the children came home [they spent part of each summer in camp]. Inevitable, I suppose, but nonetheless a blight. That is the reason for disposing of the young each year for a breather, a matrimonial "refresher" course, as we say in the government. We have had no outstanding crises and so, of course, I began to get fat. . . . I did venture to suggest that he get something done on the book, whereupon he rose up and blasted me quite effectively. He certainly was going to do just that; he only needed this weekend in order to clean off his desk. There were also a few pointers about how to mind my own business, which I suppose I asked for. . . . We will be home by Sept. 24, worse luck, but it has been a good summer.

On October 27 she told Anna that "Harold has just come through a really dreadful week. He had a nerve being pinched by his vertebrae, and he was in great pain for a whole week before his difficulty could be diagnosed. When the doctor made up his mind about it, the nerve decided to go back where it should have stayed, because the pain diminished immediately and he can now resume his normal routine." But it was not a pinched nerve. What Ickes had was a degenerative form of arthritis that gave him greater and greater periods of terrible pain. He had lived with pain all his life, and it stalked him now at the end more relentlessly than ever before. Sometime before Christmas he went into Georgetown University Hospital for treatment. While there, on December 27, 1951, he made his final diary entry:

> The weather has been unusually cold for this time of the year, and, also for this time of the year, we have had a good deal of rain and snow. Jane brought the children in to see me early the afternoon of Christmas. During the last two or three days, I have had really excruciating pain. I had Dr. Minor in for consultation purposes last Tuesday and next Saturday, Dr. Francis Grant will come down from Philadelphia. He is head of neurology at the University of Pennsylvania. It has put an almost intolerable burden upon Jane, who is showing the strain.

He was still in the hospital on January 4, 1952. He had wanted badly to testify at an Interior Department hearing on some regulations that Dillon Myer, now commissioner of Indian Affairs, wanted to change regarding contracts between Indians and their lawyers. The changes would be to the Indians' detriment, Ickes believed, and he wrote Secretary Chapman to "respectfully suggest that the hearing be kept open until I shall have had a chance to appear before you and present my views on the impending lawyers' code, which I would like to do at as early a date as possible." (As it happened, on January 24 Chapman decided not to issue the proposed new regulations.) Ickes also had made arrangements to have Dean Albertson of the Oral History Research Office at Columbia University come down to Washington and start a series of interviews for the university's oral history program. He could not keep that appointment, Helen Cunningham, one of his most recent secretaries, informed Albertson on January 24, because "He only returned to his home on Friday of last week. He is still confined to his bed for the most part and has suffered a great deal of pain." On February 2, after showing some signs of improvement, he lapsed into unconsciousness and was rushed to Emergency Hospital with a heart attack.

On May 6, 1948, he had written Jane a letter and sealed it in an envelope to be opened in the event of his death. After a few instructions regarding his preferences as to burial, he summed up their life together and offered a measure of comfort:

> I have loved you and you have loved me, but we faced the inevitable, before you ever agreed to marry me, that, considering the difference in our ages, I would go first. You will have to be brave and strong, both for yourself and those two wonderful children of ours. . . .
>
> With a love that has never abated and an admiration that has grown with the years, I have died as I have lived, during these last wonderful years, deeply grateful to you for that which you alone have been able to give to me and that which I so desperately needed and craved.

And for Raymond he had left another letter. On May 16 of that same year, he wrote: "Any husband, and especially an old one, of a young wife, who at the same time is the father of small children, cannot be but anxious when he thinks of the days to come. I have tried to deal justly and affectionately as between you and Jane and Harold and Elizabeth. . . . May you close the ranks after I have gone and march on, all of you, steadily and ever forward, remembering that if you all stand together nothing need daunt you. But you, dear Raymond, will have to be the captain to carry the standard for the little Ickes clan after I am no longer here."

Now, on February 3, sometime after 6:00 P.M., there was another heart attack and he drifted into a deeper coma, farther from the pain. It would be good to know that his memory moved through fields of flowers as his troubled spirit finally was given the blessing that had evaded it all his life: at 6:35 P.M., February 3, 1952, Harold L. Ickes slept.

Epilogue

H E WAS BURIED in a grave surrounded by generations of Millers. The plot was a small patch of unoccupied ground given to Jane by Francis Miller, a local banker and friend of the family. The cemetery itself was an old graveyard next to the Friends Meeting House on the edge of the tiny village of Sandy Spring in suburban Maryland, just minutes away from Headwaters Farm. There had been no free space left, except for that in a few family plots; this was one of them. Though Harold had expressed no preference for his final resting place—save that it not be among all the rest of the Ickes clan in that crowded hilltop cemetery in Altoona, or with Anna and her people in Memorial Park, Chicago—he probably would have liked it here. He had always passionately admired the Friends, believing them to possess strength of character and moral conviction uncommon among the human species—as well as little of the hypocrisy he found so repellent about most institutionalized religions. He would have liked the character of the place, too—a quiet spot that might have reminded him of some of the bosky dells he had known as a boy. Dappled with shade and sunlight and ornamented with weathered stones and markers, a grassy slope rose gently perhaps two hundred feet from his gravesite to the top of a hill overlooking the countryside. Ancient lindens and white oak trees spread their branches over the site. There were clumps of ivy, vagrant patches of flowers. Like many old graveyards, it was slightly unkempt, but comfortable.

Only the family and a few friends had been on hand for the burial here on February 6—just a fragment of the enormous crowd that had filled the interior of All Souls' Unitarian Church in Washington that morning for the brief funeral service. President Truman had been a little late, bustling into the already packed church with a contingent of Secret Service men and the accompaniment of popping flash bulbs just as the ceremony was scheduled to begin. The disruption was brief, but characteristic of the relationship between the two men—as was the President's official statement after the announcement of Harold's death. "Mr. Ickes was preeminent as an administrator," Truman had said, damning with faint praise every step of the way. "Although he was often irascible and could be intolerant of the opinions of others, his sharpest critics never doubted his integrity and were quick to concede that he was always efficient in a single-minded purpose: to get on with the work." True enough, as far as it went, but hardly the sort of eulogy one expects to hear from the lips of sitting Presidents.

The Reverend Palfrey Perkins of King's Chapel, Boston, a friend from the summer vacations at Southwest Harbor, had officiated at the service, and his words had possessed more seemly, if somewhat predictable, warmth. "This company come to pay tribute to Harold Ickes is his unspoken eulogy," the Reverend Perkins had intoned, going on to praise Ickes's "unwavering integrity, passionate honesty, scorn of meanness and tender solicitude for all those whose needs were greater than his own. . . . We love him and honor him as a man who never turned his back but marched breast forward." Also true enough, as far as it went.

He had been the subject of such mixed feelings for most of his public and private life, and the same kind of split decision might have been found among the honorary pallbearers—some of the best known and even most important names in American life: Secretary of State Dean Acheson, financier Bernard Baruch, columnists Walter Lippmann and Drew Pearson. Governor Adlai Stevenson of Illinois was one of them; so was Speaker of the House Sam Rayburn. Three associate justices of the Supreme Court—Robert Jackson, Hugo Black, and William O. Douglas—were listed, as were a quartet of senators—Joseph O'Mahoney, Robert Taft, Charles Tobey, Paul H. Douglas. Two of his oldest and closest friends, Benjamin Cohen and Thomas Corcoran, the quintessential New Dealers, were there, as were three of the remaining members of Franklin Roosevelt's first cabinet—Frances Perkins, Henry Morgenthau, and Henry Wallace. Few men had been borne from their biers, figuratively speaking, on so prestigious a collection of shoulders.

Things might have been left at that, with a brief flurry of newsreel attention, a few words at the church, a short black caravan of hearse and limousines gliding out of the city, a few more words spoken in the graveyard, then the sound of falling earth. That would have satisfied Harold, certainly, who had already attended too many funerals. But someone recognized that a door had closed, that with Ickes's death the end of something important had been entered in the books of the nation and that the necessary rituals had not been fully served by the funeral itself. A memorial service was planned.

No one had ever quite forgotten the Easter Sunday afternoon in April 1939 when about seventy-five thousand people had put aside the wretched baggage of prejudice and freely joined at the steps of the Lincoln Memorial to witness the glory of a woman's voice. Ickes had helped to make that moment possible, and it was in his memory that some ten thousand came again to the Memorial on the Sunday afternoon of April 20, 1952. Up on the platform in front of the Memorial were Jane, young Harold, and Elizabeth, surrounded by Interior Secretary Oscar Chapman and other notables. President Truman had not been able to attend, pleading an accumulation of work, but his press secretary, Joseph Short, represented him.

More than twenty-four hundred people had been lucky enough to find seats in the folding chairs that had been assembled on the steps; the rest spread out to bracket the western end of the Reflecting Pool. Most of them had been there thirteen years before and most of them, like Jane Ickes, were remembering that day. "I'll never forget it," she told a reporter for the *Washington Evening Star*. "I wasn't sitting up here on the platform, but down there with the crowd. It was a beautiful day—like this one, but a little cooler. I remember looking up and seeing Harold and Miss Anderson." She looked out over the pool, where the reflected image of the Washington Monument wavered gently as a soft breeze wrinkled the surface of the water. Thirteen years ago, the organizers of the 1939 concert had worried that several days of bad weather would persist and ruin the affair; but that Easter Sunday had been sunny, cool, and clear. Jane remembered: "Today . . . this sun . . . we've had such rainy weather and now it's so beautiful. You know, I'm a little superstitious."

At 4:00 P.M. the Reverend Frederick E. Reissig, executive secretary of the Washington Federation of Churches, offered the invocation, speaking of the "rough-hewn but gentle" man whose memory they had come to honor. "For his life of integrity," the minister prayed, "for his impatience with racial barriers, for his courageous championship of unpopular but good causes; for his warm friendship and for his selflessness, we are a grateful people."

Secretary Chapman then spoke briefly. "We meet again," he said, "at the foot of Lincoln's shrine, where thirteen years ago Harold L. Ickes presided at an open-air concert demonstrating that America's faith in its basic ideals remains strong." Then from behind one of the great pillars of the Monument stepped Marian Anderson. Dressed in a sweeping blue taffeta gown and carrying an armful of blood-red roses against her breast, she strode to the microphone as a standing ovation filled the air. When it subsided, her accompanist began the opening bars of Bach's "Come, Sweet Death," and soon that extraordinary voice rolled out over the crowd once again. After "Come, Sweet Death," she sang "Ave Maria" as she had in 1939, then the same bittersweet spirituals, and finally, the whole audience on its feet now to sing it with her, "America, the Beautiful." When the last notes of that simple, moving song had been carried away by the wind, the audience cheered for a very long time, perhaps recognizing in this moment a final gift from the irascible, righteous old pilgrim whose dedication to the protocols of liberty had done so much to shape the world of their inheritance. Our world.

Acknowledgments

This book was my wife Joan's idea. Back in the summer of 1983, Les Line, editor of *Audubon* magazine, called and gave me the assignment of a piece on Harold Ickes; the noisome career of then–Secretary of the Interior James Gaius Watt was in full swing, and Les thought an article about a *good* Interior Secretary would be welcomed by his readers. During the course of a research job done under deadline (and a lot of it consequently accomplished by Joan), I was appalled to discover how little had been written about Ickes since his death. Joan, on the other hand, was intrigued by the fact. One evening, after having lugged home an armful of books for me, she remarked with characteristic bright conviction that I ought to do a book. By the time the article was finished, I agreed with her.

Joan's participation did not end there. Over the next six years, she accompanied me on numerous occasions to the manuscript reading room of the Library of Congress—surely one of the Seven Wonders of Democracy—to help me paw over the awesome treasures that incomparably valuable trove contains. She did considerable digging on her own, as well; it was she, for instance, who went through the microfilmed version of the Margaret Dreier Robins Papers buried in the collection of the Women's Trade Union League, pulling out eminently useful nuggets. Joan also contributed more than a fair portion of proofreading, critical commentary, and good-humored patience; early one morning I found the following couplet taped to the wall above my work table:

> *We are a* ménage à *three,*
> *My husband, Clair Ickes, and me.*

I have been similarly favored by the full and enthusiastic cooperation of the members of the Ickes family. That cooperation came, first of all, from Raymond

Ickes, the Secretary's first son, who endured hours of personal interviews and numerous inquiries by mail and telephone and who met my impertinent and often painful inquiries about his mother and father with meticulous honesty; he also supplied me with a collection of family photographs and read the entire manuscript of the book faithfully. So did Ickes's second son (and literary executor), Harold McEwen Ickes, who submitted cheerfully to an interview, provided photographs, and not only was good enough to give me permission to quote from the unpublished diaries, but allowed me to prowl through and copy previously unknown primary material in his personal collection. Harold's sister, Elizabeth—who first discovered the cache of new materials and sent them to her brother—also read the manuscript, furnished her own set of photographs, and was very helpful during a long telephone interview. Finally, I must thank Wilmarth Thompson Ickes's daughter, Anne Ickes Carroll, who went far out of her way to provide me with photographs from her side of the family and to share her own memories.

There was not a single attempt on the part of any member of the family, I should emphasize, to influence my judgment or conclusions. All biographers should be so lucky; most are not.

"Author's queries" placed in the book review sections of various newspapers brought forth a small flood of cards and letters, many of which proved indispensable (and one of which, written not to me but to Raymond Ickes by an acquaintance of his who had spotted my plea in the pages of the *Albuquerque Journal,* inspired Raymond to write me and offer his help). Chief among these: Edward T. James, editor of the Papers of the Women's Trade Union League and Its Principal Leaders, now on deposit at the University of Florida; Jean C. Byrd, currently at work on a biography of John Collier, who was helpful in my interpretation of that difficult man; Elmo Richardson, a prolific historian and biographer of Dwight D. Eisenhower, who pointed me in some useful directions; Mrs. Mary Grace Schulze, who passed on memories of her friendship with Frances Thompson Bryant; James W. McNally, who put me in touch with his niece, Anne Ickes Carroll; Leona B. Gerard, who as Leona Graham was employed by Ickes at both the PWA and the Division of Territories and Island Possessions; and Guy Fringer, who kindly gave me access to his work on Olympic National Park. Special thanks here must go to Walter Roth of Chicago for contributing material from his own research on the Jeremiah (Lazar) Averbuch affair of 1908.

Even more special is the thanks due to the late Robert Cochran, a longtime Washington newsman, who had shared with me his own work on the relationship between Ickes and Harry Truman, and to his wife, Gloria, who after Bob's death was generous enough to send me the great pile of original materials that he had acquired from the Truman Memorial Library in Independence, Missouri; I hope this book measures up to Bob's expectations of it.

In this regard, I owe a very large debt to Linda J. Lear, who not only possesses a profound knowledge of the era and the politics with which this book is concerned, but also a willing generosity. In spite of the fact that five years ago she discovered me rummaging around in the tailings of an intellectual claim she had staked out and developed herself, she has from the first given tremendous support to this work, and her own book, *Harold L. Ickes: Aggressive Progressive, 1874–1933,* provided a beacon of insight and analysis in a too often murky political landscape.

As my bibliographic note makes clear, most of the archival material for this book resides in the collections of the Library of Congress, and to all the rotating "Saturday crews" in the library's splendid Manuscript Reading Room who guided me through a bewildering wealth of documents during the years of research, I extend my earnest gratitude. Similar thanks goes to the staffs of the Bancroft Library at the University of California, Berkeley; the Blair County Historical Society in Altoona, Pennsylvania; the Chicago Historical Society; the Archives of the University of Chicago; the Manuscript Department of the Perkins Library, Duke University; the Superintendent's Office of King's Canyon National Park, California; the Oral History Department and Manuscript Room of the Butler Library, Columbia University, New York; the National Archives and Records Service in Washington, D.C., and Kansas City, Missouri; the Western History Collection of the Denver Public Library; and the Franklin D. Roosevelt Memorial Library in Hyde Park, New York—whose director, William R. Emerson, was especially helpful.

A number of people read major parts of the work in progress, and for their critical acumen and guidance I would like to thank Kenneth S. Davis, Geoffrey C. Ward, Frederick Turner, and John G. Mitchell. Both Tim Jacobson, former editor of *Chicago History,* and David Plowden, a friend and longtime resident of Winnetka, were helpful in getting me around and about in Chicago, and my friend John Frantz was kind enough to track down and bring me to Ickes's burial spot in Sandy Spring, Maryland. Carol Lee Short was instrumental in putting a large part of this book into a word processor and guided me with superhuman patience through my own tumultuous introduction to the witchery of bytes and bits called WordPerfect, while Linda Hengerson and Patricia Harris typed early versions of the manuscript during more primitive times.

For eight years, The Wilderness Society has provided me with financial support and profoundly satisfying work to do—not to mention the latitude to pursue my other writings—and I would be remiss not to thank my friends and fellow workers at the Society for their help and understanding, especially George T. Frampton, Jr., president, and Gaylord Nelson, counselor. An extra measure of thanks goes to Mary Hanley, director of the Public Affairs Department, for helping to put me in touch with Harold McEwen Ickes.

To Wallace Stegner I owe much, not the least of which is the fact that for thirty years his own work has been a model for my aspirations as a writer. He also was one of those brave few who read the entire book in manuscript, as he has so many others of mine, and his commentary on and enthusiasm for the project throughout its production has been a tonic for the mind and heart.

To my agent, Carl Brandt, I owe an investment of confidence and encouragement that can't be adequately measured. To my editor, Marian Wood, I owe a relentless eye, a generous heart, a cheerful spirit, expert guidance, and the patience of Job's wife (consider what *she* had to put up with).

None of the individuals or organizations mentioned so inadequately above should be held accountable for any errors of fact, interpretation, commission, or omission that this book may contain; these are the sole and exclusive property of the author.

Finally, while *Righteous Pilgrim* may be dedicated to the late W. H. Hutchinson, of Hutchinson Plaza, California State University at Chico, the dedication alone is not enough to express what he meant to me. Quite aside from the fact that he, too, read the entire book in manuscript (as he did just about everything I have ever written), for more than a quarter of a century Hutch was an intellectual mentor, a spiritual adviser, and a loving friend who taught me much of what I know about what it is to be a man. If this book is "for" anyone, it is indeed for him.

—T. H. Watkins
Washington, D.C.
March 1984–March 1990

Notes

ABBREVIATIONS

BL	Bancroft Library, University of California, Berkeley
CHMI	Collection of Harold McEwen Ickes
FDR	Franklin D. Roosevelt
FDRL	Franklin D. Roosevelt Memorial Library, Hyde Park, New York
HLI	Harold L. Ickes
HLIP	Harold L. Ickes Papers, Manuscript Reading Room, Library of Congress, Washington, D.C.
HSTL	Harry S. Truman Memorial Library, Independence, Missouri
KCNPA	Kings Canyon National Park Archives, Kings Canyon National Park, California
NAKC	National Archives and Records Service, Kansas City, Missouri
OHCU	Oral History Research Office, Butler Library, Columbia University, New York
PWTUL	Papers of the Women's Trade Union League and Its Principal Leaders, University of Florida, Gainesville
SPDU	Harry Slattery Papers, William E. Perkins Library, Duke University, Durham, North Carolina
TWS/DPL	Papers of the Wilderness Society, Western History Collection, Denver Public Library, Denver, Colorado
UCA	University of Chicago Archives

Prologue

1   My description of the old Grand Central Station (razed in 1971) is from David S. Lowe, *Lost Chicago* (New York: Crown Publishers, 1985), p. 57; and Carl W.

Condit, *Chicago, 1910–1929: Building, Planning, and Urban Technology* (Chicago: University of Chicago Press, 1973), pp. 45–46.

2   "I am for experimenting": Quoted in William E. Leuchtenburg, *Franklin D. Roosevelt and the New Deal, 1932–1940* (New York: Harper and Row, 1963), pp. 344–45.

PART I: THE ORPHANED SPIRIT

1. Passions in a Small Place

The Ickes family history is from HLI, Unpublished personal memoirs, Speeches and Writings file, Folder 2, Container 432, HLIP; from HLI, *Autobiography of a Curmudgeon* (New York: Reynal & Hitchcock, 1943); and from Africa J. Simpson, *A History of Huntington and Blair Counties, Pennsylvania* (Philadelphia: Louis J. Everts, 1883; reprint, Huntington County Historical Society and Blair County Historical Society, 1975). The history of Altoona is from Simpson, *A History of Huntington and Blair Counties, Pennsylvania* (as above); Edgar A. Custer, *No Royal Road* (New York: H. C. Kinsey and Company, 1937); Jesse C. Sell, *A 20th Century History of Altoona and Blair County, Pennsylvania, and Representative Citizens* (Chicago: Richmond-Arnold Publishing Company, 1911); and contemporary files of the *Altoona Weekly Tribune* in the Blair County Historical Society.

PAGE

11   "To understand the fashion of any life": Mary Austin, *The Land of Little Rain* (Boston: Houghton Mifflin Company, 1903), p. 103.

12   "industrious, frugal, well-informed": Sell, *A 20th Century History*, p. 9.

13   "I believe that when I left Altoona": HLI, Folder 2, Unpublished personal memoirs, HLIP, pp. 16–17.

14   "Of course there isn't any doubt": HLI to William Allen White, 6/28/21, General Correspondence, Container 41, HLIP.
     "I don't recall the circumstances": HLI, Folder 2, Unpublished personal memoirs, HLIP, p. 5.
     "I do remember my grandfather's last illness": *Ibid.*

15   "In those days Altoona": Edgar A. Custer, *No Royal Road*, p. 27. Lest the reader's gorge threaten to rise here, it should be pointed out that this delicacy could have been nothing less than ancestral chicken-fried steak, which, in this writer's opinion, is one of the unsung glories of the culinary arts.
     "I have always had a tremendous": HLI, Folder 2, Unpublished personal memoirs, HLIP, p. 18.
     "numerous moral and beneficial associations": Simpson, *A History*, p. 158. The list of Jesse's memberships was discovered on a business card he apparently carried around with him to impress his drinking companions and probably the occasional woman; Scrapbooks, Container 542, HLIP.

16   "It was a major family feat": HLI, *Autobiography*, p. 8.

"He drank": HLI, Folder 6, Unpublished personal memoirs, HLIP, p. 140.

17 "It is not fair": *Ibid.*, p. 141.

18 Dressing up in his father's regalia: HLI, Folder 1, Unpublished personal memoirs, HLIP, pp. 17–18.

"They don't make buggies any more": HLI, Folder 2, Unpublished personal memoirs, HLIP, p. 10.

19 "I loved this life": *Ibid.*, p. 31.

"I found real pleasure there": *Ibid.*, p. 32.

"I cultivated": *Ibid.*

"Between the house": *Ibid.* The full name of Amelia was Mary Amelia, and in later years she would prefer "Mary"; so it is that HLI refers to her as "Mary" throughout his memoirs, but—as we shall see—as "Amelia" in his college diaries.

2. *"Queen and guttersnipe of cities . . ."*

Material for this sketch of Chicago comes largely from Emmett Dedmon, *Fabulous Chicago* (New York: Random House, 1953); Lowe, *Lost Chicago*; Harold M. Mayer and Richard C. Wade, *Chicago: Growth of a Metropolis* (Chicago: University of Chicago Press, 1969); Barbara C. Schaaf, *Mr. Dooley's Chicago* (New York: Doubleday and Company, 1977); and various numbers of *Chicago History*. Other sources as noted.

PAGE

22 "Queen and guttersnipe of cities": Quoted in Dedmon, *Fabulous Chicago*, pp. 191–92.

"This singing flame of a city": Theodore Dreiser, *The Titan*, p. 8; in *Trilogy of Desire: Three Novels by Theodore Dreiser* (New York: World Publishing Company, 1972).

"Having seen it": Quoted in David Plowden, *Industrial Landscape* (Chicago Historical Society in association with W. W. Norton and Company, 1985), v.

"come and show me": *Ibid.*, quoted.

23 "Halsted Street is thirty-two miles long": Jane Addams, *Twenty Years at Hull-House: With Autobiographical Notes* (New York: New American Library, 1961), p. 81.

24 "steam, dirt, blood and hides": Quoted in Carl S. Smith, *Chicago and the Literary Imagination, 1880–1920* (Chicago: University of Chicago Press, 1984), p. 157.

"360 acres of land": Quoted in Mayer and Wade, *Chicago*, pp. 122–23.

25 "This town of ours": Quoted in Smith, *Chicago and the Literary Imagination*, p. 22.

26 "There was built and completed": Quoted in Mayer and Wade, *Chicago*, p. 120.

"Tall buildings will pay": *Ibid.*, quoted, p. 128.

"one of the final monuments": *Ibid.*, quoted, p. 132.

27   "Player with Railroads": Quoted in Plowden, *Industrial Landscape*, v–vi.

3. Prescribed Care

PAGE

29   "I didn't like any of it": HLI, *Autobiography*, p. 12. It should be noted that much of the narrative in the *Autobiography* must be discounted by about 20 percent for hyperbole and wishful remembrance and that his statements of fact are sometimes confused. His fond memory of Lakemont is an example; this little man-made resort was not opened until 1893, three years after Ickes's departure. The description of Englewood is from Mayer and Wade, *Chicago*, pp. 160–64.

31   "Your Poor Miserable Father": Jesse B. W. Ickes to HLI, n.d., Family Papers, Correspondence, Container 27, HLIP.
"Well, I guess I will have to go": HLI, Folder 2, Unpublished personal memoirs, HLIP, p. 39.
"I don't believe that you can possibly realize": HLI to Agnes Rogers, 5/1/29, General Correspondence, Container 38, HLIP.

32   "Kindly, considerate, and jolly": HLI, Folder 2, Unpublished personal memoirs, HLIP, p. 58.
"one of the dearest women": *Ibid.*, p. 57.

33   Uncle's cheating: HLI, Folder 1, Unpublished personal memoirs, HLIP, pp. 49–50.

34   "Of course I was keen to try it": HLI, Folder 2, Unpublished personal memoirs, HLIP, p. 50.
"Even when I think back now": HLI, *Autobiography*, p. 18.

4. In the Days of Fried Ham

Most of the discussion of the World's Columbian Exposition is from Dedmon, *Fabulous Chicago*, and Frank A. Cassell and Marguerite E. Cassell, "The White City in Peril: Leadership and the World's Columbian Exposition," *Chicago History* (Fall 1983), pp. 10–27. My treatment of the University of Chicago is based on Richard J. Storr, *A History of the University of Chicago: Harper's University—The Beginnings* (Chicago: University of Chicago Press, 1966), which is a splendid book in spite of the fact that its title seems to have been a compromise agreed upon by faculty committee.

PAGE

35   "My father was not interested": HLI, *Autobiography*, pp. 19–20.

36   "If I had a vacancy": J. E. Armstrong to Chicago Board of Education, 9/20/93, Scrapbooks, Container 542, HLIP.

37   "Genius is but audacity": Quoted in Dedmon, *Fabulous Chicago*, p. 220.

38   "Service for mankind": Quoted in Storr, *A History of the University of Chicago*, p. 59.

39   "It has been a subject of general comment": *Ibid.*, quoted, p. 111.
     "I have often said": HLI, Folder 3, Unpublished personal memoirs, HLIP, p. 22.
     "A nicer lot of people": HLI, College Diary, 1/27/96, CHMI.

40   "I put in another very busy day": *Ibid.*, 4/3/94.
     "Pittsburg is the dirtiest city in creation": *Ibid.*, 7/10/94.

41   "While the past year had many disappointments": *Ibid.*, 12/31/94.
     "A notice was sent you": William Rainey Harper to Jesse B. W. Ickes, 3/11/95, Scrapbooks, Container 542, HLIP.

42   "He declined to help": HLI, Folder 4, Unpublished personal memoirs, HLIP, p. 19.
     "Her food was good": *Ibid.*, p. 20.
     "I despair of myself": HLI, College Diary, 3/28/95, CHMI.
     "I was listless": *Ibid.*, 3/29/95.

43   "The Democratic politicians are thicker": *Ibid.*, 7/6/96.

44   "I was nearly steamed": *Ibid.*, 7/8/96.
     "How the *Chicago Tribune* and others": HLI, *Autobiography*, p. 81.

45   "She was said to be": HLI, Folder 7, Unpublished personal memoirs, HLIP, p. 32. The details of Anna's background are gleaned from a biographical sketch on file at the Chicago Women's Club during her membership there and furnished me by her son, Raymond. Additional material came from Leonard J. Bates, "Anna Wilmarth Thompson Ickes," in *Notable American Women* (Cambridge, Mass.: Belknap Press of Harvard University Press, 1971), pp. 251–52.

46   "seemed to pay no attention": HLI, Folder 7, Unpublished personal memoirs, HLIP, p. 14.
     "We danced until nearly one o'clock": HLI, College Diary, 3/12/96, CHMI.
     "We had an out of sight time": *Ibid.*, 3/28/96.

47   "I . . . will go if I have to walk": *Ibid.*, 7/3/96.
     "This afternoon we managed to row": *Ibid.*, 7/26/96.
     "I flatter myself": *Ibid.*, 8/9/96.
     "I am horribly blue": *Ibid.*, 8/29/96.
     "went home and went to bed": *Ibid.*, 8/30/96.

48   "I can recommend no more satisfactory": William Rainey Harper to Susan Harding, 8/12/96, William Rainey Harper Papers, UCA.
     "This rather broke me up": HLI, College Diary, 9/28/96, CHMI.
     "frightfully blue": *Ibid.*, 9/29/96.
     "I sent her six": *Ibid.*, 10/25/96.
     "The men are improving in tackling": *Chicago Weekly*, 10/1/96, UCA.

49   "Herschberger is making too many": *Ibid.*, 10/8/96.
     "I cannot understand why": HLI, College Diary, 2/25/97, CHMI.
     "I cannot understand it and will write": *Ibid.*, 3/4/97.
     "I got a letter yesterday from father": *Ibid.*, 3/12/97.

50   " 'You have doubtless heard it reported' ": *Ibid.*, 3/25/97.
     "I . . . tried to read myself to sleep": *Ibid.*

51 "They don't seem to know how to run things": *Ibid.*, 4/3/97.
52 "marched up with the rest": HLI, Folder 4, Unpublished personal memoirs, HLIP, p. 3.

PART II: AT THE CENTER OF THE WEB

5. *On the Street*

PAGE

56 "In some heat I went on": HLI, Folder 7, Unpublished personal memoirs, HLIP, p. 54.
57 "We are a curious and not a very pleasant family": *Ibid.*, p. 112.
Ickes makes no mention of Thompson's intercession in *Autobiography of a Curmudgeon*; in fact, he makes no mention of Thompson at all. The story is told only in the unpublished memoirs (*ibid.*, pp. 21–22). The world of journalism in Ickes's time is nicely outlined by Bernard Weisberger in *The American Newspaperman* (Chicago: University of Chicago Press, 1961), pp. 156–84.
"I was at large": *Ibid.*, quoted, p. 157.
58 "My years in Chicago": Ben Hecht, *A Child of the Century: The Autobiography of Ben Hecht* (New York: Simon and Schuster, 1954), p. 113.

6. *Urban Blights*

My discussion of Chicago politics in this period is taken from Dedmon, *Fabulous Chicago*; Harold F. Gosnell, *Machine Politics: Chicago Model* (Chicago: University of Chicago Press, 1937); Addams, *Twenty Years at Hull-House*; Schaaf, *Mr. Dooley's Chicago*; Lloyd Wendt and Herman Kogan, *Lords of the Levee: The Story of Bathhouse John and Hinky Dink* (New York: Bobbs-Merrill Company, 1943; reprinted by Indiana University Press, Bloomington, 1967); HLI, *Autobiography*; and various numbers of *Chicago Weekly*. Other sources as noted.

PAGE

59 "There was nothing gentle about big city politics": HLI, *Autobiography*, pp. 33–34.
60 "built upon bribery": Quoted in Dedmon, *Fabulous Chicago*, p. 257. Graft payments took all the usual forms—protection, special favors, liquor licenses, and the like—but the aldermen of Chicago displayed uncommon enterprise along these lines. One favorite tactic was the creation of dummy traction (streetcar) corporations, which were then granted streetcar franchises (gratis, of course). In order to build real lines, genuine traction companies had to "buy" the dummy corporations from the owners—who were, of course, the aldermen who had engineered the whole thing. An even more dramatic instance was the case involving a group of eastern speculators who wanted to

build a system of underground freight lines in the Loop and thus gain a monopoly over inner-city transportation of goods. The electorate turned back an enabling ordinance, so the entrepreneurs (with the connivance of a few aldermen) set up their own dummy corporation, a "telephone" company that forthwith requested passage of an ordinance that would allow it to bore holes beneath the streets to carry its telephone lines. This eminently reasonable law was passed, arrangements were made with selected aldermen to doctor the ordinance before it was legally recorded, and before anyone noticed anything out of the ordinary, several miles of tunnels twelve feet wide and fourteen feet high had been excavated and rail lines, not telephone lines, installed. The underground freight line served the city for many years. Dedmon, *Fabulous Chicago*, pp. 258–59.

"from lack of interest": *Ibid.*, quoted, p. 258.

"He is not safe": *Ibid.*, quoted, p. 260.

61   "Why should I?" In slightly different forms, this wonderfully arrogant statement appears in both Dedmon, *Fabulous Chicago*, p. 260, and in Perry Duis, "Whose City? Part Two," *Chicago History*, Summer 1983. Since the remark was verbal, I have chosen to combine the two versions here.

"Now Alderman Kenna is a straight man": Quoted in Gosnell, *Machine Politics*, note, p. 28.

62   "Mr. Mayor, I was talkin' a while back": Quoted in Dedmon, *Fabulous Chicago*, p. 261.

"It happened that the Republicans": HLI, *Autobiography*, pp. 34–35. Among his other distinctions, Henry L. Hertz was well on his way toward accumulating the fleet of horse-drawn taxicabs that was the foundation of his fortune— and the ancestral expression of today's Hertz Rent-A-Car empire.

63   "I confess that I liked": *Ibid.*, p. 35.

7. *Exuberance and Wrath*

The basic sources for this chapter were Addams, *Twenty Years at Hull-House*; Harry Barnard, *Eagle Forgotten: The Life of John Peter Attgeld* (New York: Duell, Sloan & Pearce, 1938); Ray Allen Billington, *Westward Expansion: A History of the American Frontier* (New York: Macmillan Publishing Company, 1974); Paul H. Boese, *The Rhetoric of Protest and Reform, 1878–1898* (Athens: Ohio University Press, 1980); Daniel J. Boorstin, *The Americans: The Democratic Experience* (New York: Random House, 1973); Bernard J. Brownell, *Eugene V. Debs: Spokesman for Labor and Socialism* (Chicago: Charles H. Kerr Publishing Company, 1978); Dedmon, *Fabulous Chicago*; Ray Ginger, *The Bending Cross: A Biography of Eugene Victor Debs* (New Brunswick: Rutgers University Press, 1949); Eric F. Goldman, *Rendezvous with Destiny: A History of Modern American Reform* (New York: Alfred A. Knopf, 1953), one of the truly great works of modern American history; Richard Hofstadter, *Social Darwinism in American Thought* (Philadelphia: University of Pennsylvania Press, 1944); Walter Johnson, *William Allen White's America* (New York: Henry Holt and Company, 1947); Howard Mumford Jones, *The Age of Energy: Varieties of American Experience, 1865–1915* (New York: The Viking Press, 1971); Justin Kaplan, *Lincoln Steffens: A Biography* (New

York: Simon and Schuster, 1974); Margaret Leech, *In the Days of McKinley* (New York: Harper and Brothers, 1959); Sidney Leus, *The Labor Wars: From the Molly Maguires to the Sitdowns* (Garden City, N.Y.: Doubleday and Company, 1973); Kathleen D. McCarthy, *Noblesse Oblige: Charity and Cultural Philanthropy in Chicago, 1849–1929* (Chicago: University of Chicago Press, 1982); Edmund Morris, *The Rise of Theodore Roosevelt* (New York: Coward McCann and Geoghegan, Inc., 1979); Allan Nevins, *The Emergence of Modern America, 1865–1878* (New York: The Macmillan Company, 1927); Carl S. Smith, *Chicago and the Literary Imagination*; U.S. Strike Commission, *Report on the Chicago Strike of June–July 1894* (Washington, D.C.: Government Printing Office, 1895); and William Allen White, *The Autobiography of William Allen White* (New York: The Macmillan Company, 1946). Other sources as noted.

PAGE

64   "It was as if": Jones, *The Age of Energy*, xii.
65   "Land of Opportunity, you say": Quoted in Goldman, *Rendezvous with Destiny*, pp. 35–36.
     "Corruption dominates the ballot-box": From the "Preamble" to the Populist Party Platform (largely written by Donnelly) in Henry Steele Commager, ed., *Living Ideas in America* (New York: Harper & Row, 1964), pp. 459–60.
     "God has intended the great": Quoted in Goldman, *Rendezvous with Destiny*, p. 89.
66   "The American Beauty rose": Quoted in Hofstadter, *Social Darwinism*, p. 32.
67   "It is not merely schoolgirls": Quoted in Morris, *The Rise of Theodore Roosevelt*, pp. 552–53.
68   "Chicago has chosen a star": Quoted in Dedmon, *Fabulous Chicago*, p. 237.
69   "that such advantages and surroundings": *Ibid.*, quoted, p. 239.
     "We are born in a Pullman House": Quoted in McCarthy, *Noblesse Oblige*, p. 100. The information on rents is from U.S. Strike Commission, *Report on the Chicago Strike*, xxxv.
70   "A man who won't meet his men": Quoted in Goldman, *Rendezvous with Destiny*, pp. 69–70.
     "I tried to go home this afternoon": HLI, College Diary, 7/6/94, CHMI.
     "I could not get home today": *Ibid.*, 7/7/94.
     "I . . . got out of Chicago today": *Ibid.*, 7/8/94.
71   "modern Lear": Quoted in McCarthy, *Noblesse Oblige*, pp. 100–101. A particularly good discussion of the Pullman strike appears in Sidney Leus, *The Labor Wars*, especially "The Debs Revolution," pp. 80–109. See also U.S. Strike Commission, *Report on the Chicago Strike*.
     "a little charity, a lot of culture": Helen Lefkowitz Horowitz, "Hull-House as Women's Space," *Chicago History*, Winter 1983–84.
72   "The idea underlying our self-government": Addams, *Twenty Years at Hull-House*, pp. 81–82.
     "the only saint": Quoted by Henry Steele Commager in the Foreword to Addams, *Twenty Years at Hull-House*, xvi.

8. Tinkering with the Machine

At this point, as HLI is about to throw himself body and mind into the political arena for the first time, I should emphasize once again my great indebtedness to Linda Lear's *Harold L. Ickes: The Aggressive Progressive, 1874–1933* (New York: Garland Publishing Company, 1981). While she and I do not always agree on minor points of interpretation and emphasis, her work remains the authoritative source by which to track HLI's tortuous path through the politics of his city, as well as his complex relationship with the Progressive movement. I am less indebted to Graham White and John Maze, *Harold Ickes of the New Deal: His Private Life and Public Career* (Cambridge, Mass.: Harvard University Press, 1985), which is much thinner in its history, while replete with psychological speculation. The other main source for this chapter is HLI, *Autobiography of a Curmudgeon.*

PAGE

74 "Don't any of you realize": Quoted in Morris, *The Rise of Theodore Roosevelt*, p. 724.

75 "He was delighted": HLI, Folder 6, Unpublished personal memoirs, HLIP, p. 146.
"I was so hot": HLI, *Autobiography*, p. 47.
Speeches: Morris, *The Rise of Theodore Roosevelt*, pp. 730 and 862, note.

76 "As Mullaney and I loitered": HLI, *Autobiography*, p. 49.
"Personally, Hanna was a likable man": *Ibid.*, pp. 50–53.

78 "My name appeared nowhere": *Ibid.*, p. 92.

79 "I became a human sponge": *Ibid.*
"Busse was fundamentally yellow": *Ibid.*, p. 95.

80 "If there had been a band": HLI, *Autobiography*, p. 97.
"delivered to Graeme Stewart": *Ibid.*, p. 98.

81 "the same as John Harlan's": *Ibid.*, p. 99.

9. Triangulations

PAGE

83 "My servants are *not* allowed company": Anna W. Thompson to James W. Thompson, 8/4/03, Family Papers, Correspondence, Container 28, HLIP.

84 "If by the 16th I do not hear from you": *Ibid.*
"As there was not the slightest prospect of my marrying": HLI, Folder 7, Unpublished personal memoirs, HLIP, p. 19.
"This is as good an occasion as any": *Ibid.*

85 Ickes first mentions his suspicions that the marriage was unhappy on pp. 21–23, *Ibid.*
"As for Mr. Ickes": Anna W. Thompson to James W. Thompson, n.d., Family Papers, Correspondence, Container 28, HLIP.

"It does no good to say": Wayne Thompson to Anna W. Thompson, 9/19/03, Family Papers, Correspondence, Container 27, HLIP.

"For the sake of a woman in trouble": *Ibid.*, Wayne Thompson to HLI, 9/24/03.

86   "she was telling me": HLI, Folder 7, Unpublished personal memoirs, HLIP, p. 25.

87   "such mastery of these": Quoted in Boorstin, *The Americans*, p. 63.

88   "The Republicans had reached the conclusion": HLI, *Autobiography*, p. 101.

"A fight was, after all, a fight": *Ibid.*, p. 102.

"I pleaded with him": *Ibid.*, p. 112.

89   Ickes's growing involvement with Anna is told in detail in HLI, Folder 7, Unpublished personal memoirs, HLIP, pp. 24–39.

"My sole claim to your consideration": Anna W. Thompson to James W. Thompson, n.d., Family Papers, Correspondence, Container 28, HLIP.

90   "We Want Seats": Scrapbooks, Container 543, HLIP.

Biographical information on Raymond and Margaret Robins is taken from Elizabeth Robins, *Raymond and I* (New York: The Macmillan Company, 1956); Mary Dreier, *Margaret Dreier Robins: Her Life, Letters, and Work* (New York: Island Press, 1950); William Appleton Williams, "Raymond Robins," in *Dictionary of American Biography* (Supplement 5, 1951–1956), pp. 578–80; David Brody, "Margaret Dreier Robins," *ibid.*, 638–39; and "Margaret Dreier Robins," *New York Times*, February 22, 1945 (obituary).

91   "the mighty reforms": Quoted in Williams, "Raymond Robins," p. 578.

92   "Beyond these is the incentive": Quoted in *New York Times*, February 22, 1945.

"When I started in that first morning session": HLI, Folder 6, Unpublished personal memoirs, HLIP, p. 139.

10. The Case of the Missing Brain

PAGE

93   "I simply hated to render bills": HLI, Untitled autobiographical draft, Container 435, HLIP, p. 2. An examination of his legal file in the Library of Congress (Containers 381–394) demonstrates his lack of ambition with regard to the law. Between 1907 and 1920, for instance, it shows only sixty-seven items of adjudication or other legal proceedings; many of these involved friends and relatives, few of them seem to have called for much court time, and none of them brought in very much money.

94   "I have not started seriously to practice law": HLI to D. K. Woodward, 2/5/08, Letterbooks, Container 26, HLIP.

95   "foreign cast of features": Chief Shippy's suspiciously articulate memories of the incident were most exhaustively reported in the *Chicago Evening Post*, March 2, 1908, quoted in A. James Rudin, "From Kishinev to Chicago: The Forgotten Story of Lazar Averbuch," *Midstream* (August–September 1972). The death certificate issued by the Cook County coroner's office puts the boy's

age at nineteen and notes that he died from "Gun shot wounds, said wounds inflicted by bullets fired from revolvers held in the hand of Geo. M. Shippy and Jas. Foley"; the certificate, for some unknown reason, was not signed by Coroner Peter Hoffman until April 17 (certificate courtesy of Walter Roth).

"the greater proportion of anarchists": Quoted in Rudin, "From Kishinev to Chicago."

96   "It was, to our minds . . . most unfortunate": Addams, *Twenty Years at Hull-House*, pp. 285–86.

"She . . . said, 'I am afraid of trouble' ": Quoted in Rudin, "From Kishinev to Chicago."

97   "He went perfectly white": HLI, Untitled autobiographical draft, HLIP, p. 15.

98   "At the request of your daughter Olga": HLI to "Mrs. Averbuch" (no other name is given), 3/28/08, CHMI.

"The already savage press": Rudin, "From Kishinev to Chicago."

11. Travesties and Triumphs

PAGE

100   "All of us—young men and young women": HLI, Untitled autobiographical draft, HLIP, p. 15.

101   "It must have been fairly early in 1909": HLI, Folder 7, Unpublished personal memoirs, HLIP, p. 44.

"it had happened on another occasion": *Ibid.*

102   "She has refused to talk": HLI to Mary Wilmarth, 6/24/09, Letterbooks, HLIP.

"There are two separate questions": Henry Pratt Judson to James Westfall Thompson, 8/30/09, James Westfall Thompson Papers, BL.

103   "DEMOCRATIC LEGISLATOR CONFESSES": Quoted in Joseph Geis, *The Colonel of Chicago: A Biography of the Chicago Tribune's Legendary Publisher, Colonel Robert McCormick* (New York: E. P. Dutton, 1979), p. 37. Geis also tells the story of Lorimer's downfall in good detail, pp. 37–39.

105   "The police would sound riot calls": HLI, Untitled autobiographical draft, HLIP, p. 8. An excellent discussion of the strike is in Matthew Josephson, *Sidney Hillman: Statesman of American Labor* (New York: Doubleday and Company, 1952), and I have drawn heavily on this source for the facts in the matter.

"were careful to keep their hands off": HLI, Untitled autobiographical draft, HLIP, p. 9.

"She looked like a pygmy": *Ibid.*, p. 12.

106   "The trouble with our movement": HLI to Charles R. Crane, 11/23/10, General Correspondence, Container 29, HLIP.

"the one in a million": HLI, *Autobiography*, p. 122.

107   "one of the finest pieces of strategy": James Hamilton Lewis to HLI, 3/1/11, General Correspondence, Container 35, HLIP.

108   "on the one hand": Quoted in Lear, *Harold L. Ickes*, p. 98.

"if we hewed to our own line": HLI, *Autobiography*, p. 134.

"I have always thought": *Ibid.*

"If a candidate wins": *Ibid.*, p. 142.

"We were still talking": HLI, Folder 7, Unpublished personal memoirs, HLIP, p. 118.

"I have often had a bitter and caustic tongue": *Ibid.*, p. 117.

109 "People will think that we got married": *Ibid.*, p. 126.

"Well, what if they do?": *Ibid.*

PART III: TATTERED GUIDONS, PROUDLY BORNE

12. *Progressive Declensions*

The first part of this chapter relies on a number of standard sources, among them Judith Icke Anderson, *William Howard Taft: An Intimate History* (New York: W.W. Norton and Company, 1981); Archie Butt, *Taft and Roosevelt: The Intimate Letters of Archie Butt, Military Aide*, in two volumes, (Garden City, N.Y.: Doubleday and Company, 1930); Samuel P. Hays, *Conservation and the Gospel of Efficiency: The Progressive Conservation Movement, 1890–1920* (Cambridge, Mass.: Harvard University Press, 1959); William Manners, *TR & Will: A Friendship That Split the Republican Party* (New York: Harcourt Brace Jovanovich, Inc., 1969); and Gifford Pinchot, *Breaking New Ground* (New York: Harcourt, Brace and Company, 1947; reprinted by Island Press, Washington, D.C., 1988).

My general discussion of the birth of the Progressive Party owes its usual debt to Goldman, *Rendezvous with Destiny*. Other important sources include Lawrence F. Abbott, ed., *The Letters of Archie Butt, Personal Aide to President Roosevelt* (Garden City, N.Y.: Doubleday and Company, 1924); Claude G. Bowers, *Beveridge and the Progressive Era* (Boston: Houghton-Mifflin Company, 1932); Herbert Croly, *The Promise of American Life* (New York: The Macmillan Company, 1909); Kenneth R. Davis: *FDR: The Beckoning of Destiny, 1882–1928* (New York: G.P. Putnam's Sons, 1972); Richard Hofstadter, *The Age of Reform: From Bryan to FDR* (New York: Alfred A. Knopf, 1965); Johnson, *William Allen White's America*; Kaplan, *Lincoln Steffens*; David W. Levy, *Herbert Croly of the New Republic: The Life and Thought of an American Progressive* (Princeton, N.J.: Princeton University Press, 1985); Arthur S. Link, *Woodrow Wilson and the Progressive Era, 1910–1917* (New York: Harper and Row, 1954; reprinted 1963); George E. Mowry, *The Era of Theodore Roosevelt, 1900–1912* (New York: Harper and Row, 1958); Otis Pease, ed., *The Progressive Years: The Spirit and Achievement of American Reform* (New York: George Braziller, 1962); Donald R. Richberg, *The Tents of the Mighty* (New York: Willet, Clark, and Colby, 1930) and *My Hero: The Indiscreet Memoirs of an Eventful but Unheroic Life* (New York: G.P. Putnam's Sons, 1954); Theodore Roosevelt, *Theodore Roosevelt: An Autobiography* (New York: Charles Scribner's Sons, 1929); Clinton Rossiter and James Lare, eds., *The Essential Lippmann: A Political Philosophy for Liberal Democracy* (New York: Random House, 1963); Ronald Steel, *Walter Lippmann and the American Century* (New York: Random House, 1980); Thomas R. Vadney, *The Wayward Liberal: A Political Biography of*

Donald R. Richberg (Lexington: University Press of Kentucky, 1970); and White, *The Autobiography of William Allen White.*

PAGE

113   "Yea, I hated all my labor": Quoted in Manners, *TR & Will*, pp. 68–69.

114   "Jim, something has come over Will": Quoted *ibid.*, p. 74.

       "He thinks, that if we were cast away": Quoted in Butt, *Taft and Roosevelt,* vol. I, p. 384.

116   "I am convinced": Quoted in Manners, *TR & Will*, p. 114.

       "There is no other question before": *Ibid.*, quoted, p. 117.

       "most vigorous defender" and "almost unparalleled in the history": Quoted in Butt, *Taft and Roosevelt*, p. 386.

117   "Hurrah!": Quoted in Pinchot, *Breaking New Ground*, p. 451.

       "It would be offensive": HLI to Amos Pinchot, 1/14/10, General Correspondence, Container 37, HLIP.

       "We have reached a point": *Ibid.*, Pinchot to HLI, 1/17/10.

118   "Exposure forms the typical current literature": Quoted in Mark Sullivan, *Our Times: The United States, 1900–1925*; Volume III: *Pre-War America* (New York: Charles Scribner's Sons, 1930), p. 84.

       The list of magazine articles is in Goldman, *Rendezvous with Destiny*, pp. 173–74.

       "the average man got": Sullivan, *Our Times*, p. 88.

119   "no more than moral and political purification": Croly, *The Promise of American Life*, p. 145.

       "Reform exclusively as a moral protest": *Ibid.*, pp. 149–50.

       "more severe, more unscrupulous": *Ibid.*, p. 106.

       "an economic mechanism": *Ibid.*, p. 115.

120   "lost in a maze of admiration": Quoted in Levy, *Herbert Croly*, p. 137.

       "the most remarkable book": *Ibid.*, quoted.

121   "education and sound chastisement": Quoted in Goldman, *Rendezvous with Destiny*, p. 164.

       "If I am fighting against plutocracy": *Ibid.*, quoted, p. 162.

       "the Man with the Muckrake": Quoted in Sullivan, *Our Times*, p. 94.

122   "no public duty of mine": Quoted in Manners, *T.R. & Will*, p. 191.

       "Combinations in industry": Quoted in Levy, *Herbert Croly*, p. 141.

123   Ballinger's resignation: After the Alaska coal lands incident, Taft's advisers considered Ballinger a liability to the administration, even though the congressional investigation had exonerated him, and convinced him to resign. Poor Ballinger, whose nerves had almost been destroyed by the conflict, was both appalled and confused by Fisher's appointment. "The circumstances of the appointment of Mr. Fisher as my successor," he wrote to Taft, "in view of his attitude toward your enemies and my enemies, was, I frankly confess, hard to bear." (As quoted in Anderson, *William Howard Taft*, p. 185.)

       "to prevent any movement": Quoted in Manners, *T.R. & Will*, p. 203.

"too energetic": Quoted in Anderson, *William Howard Taft*, p. 200.

"Roosevelt Was Deceived": Quoted in Manners, *T.R. & Will*, p. 200.

"Taft was a member of my Cabinet": *Ibid.*, quoted, p. 201.

124   "If you were to remove Roosevelt's skull": *Ibid.*, quoted, p. 205.

13. The Road to Armageddon

PAGE

125   "I argued that": HLI, Folder 7, Unpublished personal memoirs, HLIP, p. 132.

126   Medill McCormick had served as treasurer and as vice president of the *Tribune* until a drinking problem forced his resignation and he turned to politics. In spite of his alcoholism, he would enjoy an astonishingly long political career. See Geis, *The Colonel of Chicago*, pp. 26–29.

"I will accept the nomination": Quoted in Manners, *T.R. & Will*, p. 217.

127   "En route to Chicago": HLI, *Autobiography*, p. 159.

"was packed to suffocation": *Ibid.*, p. 160.

"There never was such a national political convention": Edna Ferber, *A Peculiar Treasure* (New York: The Literary Guild of America, 1939), p. 195. Ferber was working as a stringer for the George Matthew Adams Newspaper Service at the time. So was William Allen White, who had taken time away from his own *Emporia* (Kansas) *Gazette* to cover the convention. They and the other Adams correspondents—including cartoonist J. N. "Ding" Darling—set up shop in a suite at the Stratford Hotel. Ferber, young and ebullient, became the darling of the bunch, especially of the avuncular White, who called her "the angel child," and through him she eventually met all the leading lights of the Progressive movement, including Harold Ickes. In 1921 it would be Ferber and Ickes who would meet White's train in Chicago one afternoon to tell him that his daughter Mary had died after falling from her horse. White's subsequent editorial/obituary in the *Gazette*, "Mary White," became one of the most anthologized pieces of writing in modern American journalism.

128   "We have fought with you five days": Quoted in Manners, *T.R. & Will*, p. 261.

"A clear majority": *Ibid.*, quoted, pp. 261–62.

"He sat on a couch . . . tossing whisky after whisky down his gullet": Hecht, *A Child of the Century*, p. 171.

129   "He came not out of any stage wings": *Ibid.*, pp. 172–73.

"I dearly wanted to be at least a spectator": HLI, Folder 7, Unpublished personal memoirs, HLIP, p. 133.

131   "We were hopping-mad": White, *The Autobiography of William Allen White*, p. 483.

"Reporters asked Colonel Roosevelt": *Ibid.*, p. 482.

"I want to be a Bull Moose": Quoted in Bowers, *Beveridge and the Progressive Era*, p. 425.

132   "Here were the successful middle-class": *Ibid.*, p. 483.

"The great question of the day": Quoted in Goldman, *Rendezvous with Destiny*, p. 207.

"My observation and reasoning": *Ibid.*, quoted, p. 206.

133   "the concentration of modern business": *Ibid.*, quoted, p. 211.

134   "Perhaps this new and all-conquering": *Ibid.*, quoted, p. 215.

"Six weeks ago, here in Chicago": Theodore Roosevelt, "A Confession of Faith," in Pease, ed., *The Progressive Years*, pp. 340–41.

135   "The moose has left the wooded hill": *Ibid.*, quoted in Pease introduction to "A Confession of Faith," p. 309.

14. Diminishing Returns

PAGE

136   "I won't pretend that we didn't awaken": HLI, *Autobiography*, p. 164.

"The Nation has been deeply stirred": Quoted in Goldman, *Rendezvous with Destiny*, p. 217.

137   "the present Congress should be credited": Quoted in Levy, *Herbert Croly*, p. 237.

"Everyone knew that the Progressive Party was disintegrating": HLI, *Autobiography*, p. 171.

138   "I am not dead": Richberg, *The Tents of the Mighty*, pp. 38–39.

139   "During the transition period": Quoted in Vadney, *The Wayward Liberal*, p. 26.

"My father was a man of strong convictions": Richberg, *My Hero*, p. 61.

"For what you did today": Donald R. Richberg to HLI, 2/26/15, General Correspondence, Container 38, HLIP.

140   "The organization was in our hands": HLI, *Autobiography*, p. 167.

"The matter has been made the subject of": HLI to William Sullivan, 10/15/13, General Correspondence, Container 39, HLIP.

141   "Now that your decision": *Ibid.*, HLI to Raymond Robins, 4/24/14, Container 38.

"He loved to go in state": HLI, "On My Interest in Politics and Public Affairs," Container 433, HLIP, p. 219.

"My disgust was unbounded": HLI, *Autobiography*, p. 175.

142   For the garment workers' strike of 1915, as for that of 1910, Josephson's *Sidney Hillman* provides the best summary of events.

"The Progressive party was tottering": HLI, *Autobiography*, p. 178.

"falling more and more into the hands": Amos Pinchot to HLI, quoted in Lear, *Harold L. Ickes*, p. 117.

143   "our chief danger as a party": *Ibid.*, HLI to Amos Pinchot, 12/2/12.

"No, White, I just musn't": Quoted in White, *The Autobiography of William Allen White*, p. 521.

144   "infernal skunk": Quoted in Manners, *TR & Will*, p. 296.

"The just war": Quoted in Hofstadter, *The Age of Reform*, p. 274.

"impartial in thought as well as deed": Quoted in Davis, *FDR: The Beckoning of Destiny*, p. 383.

"President Wilson has earned for the nation": Quoted in John Milton Cooper, *The Warrior and the Priest: Woodrow Wilson and Theodore Roosevelt* (Cambridge, Mass.: Harvard University Press, 1983), p. 315.

145 "Roosevelt . . . would not desert them": White, *The Autobiography of William Allen White*, p. 523.

146 "The last words": *Ibid.*, pp. 526–27.

"to keep in touch": HLI to Chester A. Rowell, 7/24/16, Chester A. Rowell Papers, BL.

"Hiram Johnson will be the one man": *Ibid.*, HLI to Chester A. Rowell, 11/10/16.

15. The House in Hubbard Woods

147 "I told Anna some time ago": HLI to Raymond Robins, 4/24/14, General Correspondence, Container 38, HLIP.

148 "Anna had one advantage": HLI, Folder 8, Unpublished personal memoirs, HLIP, pp. 136–37.

"We quarrelled about everything": *Ibid.*, Folder 9, pp. 3–4.

149 "Psychologically there seems to be": *Ibid.*, Folder 8, p. 136.

"I have always been repelled": *Ibid.*

"this life was playing havoc": *Ibid.*, Folder 9, p. 5.

150 "if Raymond loved me": *Ibid.*, p. 11.

"was Anna herself": *Ibid.*, p. 14.

151 "never . . . a very friendly place": *Ibid.*, Folder 10, p. 3.

"While building this house": *Ibid.*, p. 1.

"Every Sunday morning": *Ibid.*

152 Ickes expressed his litany of complaints in a series of letters to the unfortunate Perkins from January to June, 1916; General Correspondence, Container 32, HLIP. Most of the seven acres Ickes purchased have long since been sold off and developed, but the garage (now a separate residence) and the house itself remain. The house is an elegant place still, and in spite of the emotional strain its construction put upon him, Perkins could have been proud of it.

"I have never seen anywhere": HLI, Folder 10, Unpublished personal memoirs, HLIP, p. 5.

153 "Anna had learned nothing": *Ibid.*, Folder 9, p. 14. Additional material for this section was provided by an interview with Raymond Ickes, 2/21/85.

154 "There is much to be said": Richberg, *My Hero*, p. 63.

"I slept apart from Anna": HLI, Folder 9, Unpublished personal memoirs, HLIP, pp. 13–14.

155 "some such movement as ours": HLI to James Garfield, 12/29/16, quoted in Lear, *Harold L. Ickes*, p. 163.

156 "willing to go ahead": HLI to Hiram Johnson, 2/2/17, *Ibid.*, quoted, p. 169.

16. Escape to Paris

The discussion of Samuel Insull's life and accomplishments in Chicago is taken from Forrest McDonald, *Insull* (Chicago: University of Chicago Press, 1962). Material on troop movements, battles, and other military matters during World War I is from S. L. A. Marshall, *World War I* (New York: American Heritage, 1985).

PAGE

157   "was a wonderful statement": HLI to Newton D. Baker (Secretary of War), 4/16/17, quoted in Lear, *Harold L. Ickes*, p. 171.

        "for the emotional drunkenness": HLI to Emergency Peace Federation, 4/2/17, *ibid.*, quoted, p. 175.

158   "ever since the war": HLI to Ingram D. Hook, 5/18/17, *ibid.*, quoted, p. 171.

160   "He was at great pains to sell himself": HLI, "On My Interest in Politics and Public Affairs," HLIP, p. 353.

        "I had no desire": *Ibid.*, p. 355.

        "That man Itches": Quoted in McDonald, *Insull*, p. 171.

        "It is not an army": Quoted in Marshall, *World War I*, p. 316.

        "The Neighborhood Committee was organized": HLI to Samuel Insull, 4/15/18, General Correspondence, Container 32, HLIP.

161   "not thrilling": HLI, Untitled autobiographical draft, HLIP, p. 48.

        "Anna was really expert": *Ibid.*, p. 44.

        "He has a bully captain": HLI to Clinton Hazard, 4/22/18, Letterbooks, HLIP.

162   "But she had built up": HLI, Untitled autobiographical draft, HLIP, pp. 34–35.

        "We sat and talked": *Ibid.*, pp. 35–36.

        "Not only, like Frances": *Ibid.*, p. 40.

163   "We spent a few days": *Ibid.*, p. 56.

        "really a mess": *Ibid.*, p. 59.

164   "would not desert her post": *Ibid.*, pp. 103–4.

        "The sound of the artillery": HLI to Anna Ickes, 6/20/18, General Correspondence, Container 27, HLIP.

165   "I continued to lie there": HLI, *Autobiography*, p. 197.

        "I am very happy over this assignment": HLI to Anna Ickes, n.d. This is from a selection of his World War I letters to Anna that was typed up separately, deleting all personal material, and inserted into his Untitled autobiographical draft, Container 435, HLIP.

166   "I was in Frances' room": *Ibid.* HLI also tells this story in *Autobiography*, pp. 204–5.

        "Here Henry and I were": *Autobiography*, p. 200.

167   "I have just heard that Wilmarth's division": HLI to Anna Ickes, 9/3/18, General Correspondence, Container 27, HLIP.

        "Among these troops, no time was allowed": Marshall, *World War I*, pp. 430–31.

168   "they sluiced large doses": HLI, *Autobiography*, p. 208.
       "I saw not one exhibition of ill nature": HLI to Anna Ickes, 11/12/18, General
       Correspondence, Container 27, HLIP.
       "When I come home to you": *Ibid.*, 7/3/18.

169   "I love you my dear wife": *Ibid.*, 6/2/18.
       "At this hour you are probably": *Ibid.*, 6/9/18.
       "My Loved One": *Ibid.*, 7/3/18.
       "Dear, dear Anna": *Ibid.*, 9/9/18.
       "Dearest, no one could influence me": *Ibid.*, 7/3/18.
       "How could you feel": *Ibid.*, 7/9/18.

170   "Dear, dear Anna, I wonder why": *Ibid.*, 9/9/18.
       "I never said, implied or meant": *Ibid.*, 11/19/18.
       "I carried it with me": HLI, Untitled autobiographical draft, HLIP,
       p. 190.
       "Anna had written that she would meet me": *Ibid.*

171   "Here was hell with a vengeance": *Ibid.*, pp. 193–94.

PART IV: THE MAKING OF A HAS-BEEN

PAGE

173   "I don't believe anything can be done": HLI to S. J. Duncan-Clark, 11/6/29,
       General Correspondence, Container 31, HLIP.

17. *Cutting Through the Smoke*

175   "Make no little plans": Quoted in Dedmon, *Fabulous Chicago*, p. 301. An
       excellent discussion of Burnham's not-so-little plan for Chicago is in Carl W.
       Condit, *Chicago, 1910–1929: Building, Planning, and Urban Technology*, pp.
       63–85. Burnham did not confine his urban visions to the city of Chicago. In
       1905 he had presented the Association for the Improvement and Adornment of
       San Francisco with *Report on a Plan for San Francisco*, a similarly grandiose
       scheme to rebuild the entire town. The city fathers studiously ignored his
       suggestions—expensive!—even when the earthquake and fire of 1906, by
       obliterating much of the city, gave them the opportunity to incorporate them.
       Burnham also contributed plans for all or part of such other cities as Washing-
       ton, D.C., Cleveland, Minneapolis, and Manila.

176   "empire crying glory in the mud": Dreiser, *The Titan*, p. 8.
       "consideration is given": Quoted in Condit, *Chicago*, p. 65.
       "Caesar Augustus found Rome": Quoted in Dedmon, *Fabulous Chicago*,
       p. 288.

177   "A booster is better than a knocker!": *Ibid.*, quoted.
       "All hats off to our mayor": *Ibid.*, quoted.
       "Like an old fire horse": HLI, *Autobiography*, p. 219.
       "He was hearing a case": HLI, "On My Interest in Politics and Public Affairs,"

HLIP, pp. 2–3 of an insert for p. 357. On page 357 the Judge's architectural reference is to a "backhouse," but on the insert this has been revised to "shithouse." Being of a crude disposition myself, I have chosen to use the second version.

178   "Chicago is disgraced": Quoted in Geis, *The Colonel of Chicago*, p. 84.

179   "I find with respect to these": HLI to Will Hays, 12/12/19, General Correspondence, Container 32, HLIP.
      "Most earnestly urge": *Ibid.*, Will Hays to HLI, 1/1/20.
      "I appreciate compliment": *Ibid.*, HLI to Will Hays, 1/2/20.
      "Much to my surprise": HLI, *Autobiography*, pp. 222–23.

180   A good brief discussion of the League of Nations and the controversy over Article Ten appears in William Leuchtenberg, *The Perils of Prosperity, 1914– 1932* (Chicago: University of Chicago Press, 1958), pp. 50–65.

181   "hold their noses and vote": HLI to Hiram Johnson, 6/4/19, General Correspondence, Container 33, HLIP. The United States never ratified the Treaty of Versailles.

182   "The standpatters don't respect anything": HLI to Henry Allen, 12/19/19, General Correspondence, Container 29, HLIP.

183   "We went into session": HLI, "On My Interest in Politics and Public Affairs," HLIP, p. 4 of an insert for p. 390.
      "We might just as well have had a tortoise": Margaret Robins to Raymond Robins, 5/1/20, Margaret Dreier Robins Papers, PWTUL.
      "The total and net result": HLI, *Autobiography*, p. 225.

184   "the sun beat down": Ferber, *A Peculiar Treasure*, pp. 250–51.
      "There I saw the brewing": *Ibid.*, p. 250. The best single account of this poisonous brew is Francis Russell, *The Shadow of Blooming Grove: Warren G. Harding in His Times* (New York: McGraw-Hill Book Company, 1968), pp. 355–96. With exceptions as noted, my treatment of the 1920 convention is based on that of Russell.

185   "fearfully and wonderfully made": White, *The Autobiography of William Allen White*, p. 585.
      "After reading these nominating speeches": Quoted in Russell, *The Shadow of Blooming Grove*, p. 375.
      "clinched and set like a bone": White, *The Autobiography of William Allen White*, p. 586.

186   "I don't expect Senator Harding": Quoted in Robert K. Murray, *The Harding Era: Warren G. Harding and His Administration* (Minneapolis: University of Minnesota Press, 1969), p. 36.
      "disheveled"; "a two-days' beard": White, *The Autobiography of William Allen White*, p. 584.
      "However many times": Russell, *The Shadow of Blooming Grove*, p. 381.
      "There ain't any first-raters": *Ibid.*, quoted, p. 383.

187   "I believe now that the death of Theodore Roosevelt": White, *The Autobiography of William Allen White*, pp. 587–88.
      "Now, in the trumped-up fanfare": Ferber, *A Peculiar Treasure*, p. 252.

"No!": Quoted in Russell, *The Shadow of Blooming Grove*, p. 395.

"that we either had to go along": HLI, *Autobiography*, p. 234.

188 "keeping up any further pretense": HLI, "On My Interest in Politics and Public Affairs," HLIP, p. 399.

"complascent [*sic*] instrument ready for manipulation": HLI to Henry Allen, 6/30/20, General Correspondence, Container 29, HLIP.

The account of the Democratic convention is from Gene Smith, *When the Cheering Stopped: The Last Years of Woodrow Wilson* (New York: William Morrow and Company, 1964), pp. 162–65.

189 "Cox didn't measure up to my conception": HLI, *Autobiography*, p. 241.

"was a distinct shock to the progressive thought": Quoted in the *Chicago Daily News*, August 19, 1920.

190 "To date, I have received 256 letters": HLI to Hiram Johnson, 9/11/20, Container 33, HLIP.

The Red Scare of 1919–20 is treated in detail in Leuchtenburg, *The Perils of Prosperity*, pp. 66–83. Davis, in *FDR: The Beckoning of Destiny*, tells the story of the bespattered front steps of the Roosevelt home, p. 580.

191 "I hope these reports are inaccurate": HLI to George White, 9/17/20, General Correspondence, Container 41, HLIP.

192 "Too much has been said": Quoted in Leuchtenburg, *The Perils of Prosperity*, p. 81.

"America's present need is not heroics": Quoted in Russell, *The Shadow of Blooming Grove*, p. 347.

"Here was reaction": HLI, "On My Interest in Politics and Public Affairs," HLIP, p. 399.

18. Keeping the Faith

PAGE

194 "a world of Nevertheless": Gene Fowler, *Skyline: A Reporter's Reminiscences of the Twenties* (New York: The Viking Press, 1961), p. 10.

"future is coming; it is in sight": Quoted in Kaplan, *Lincoln Steffens*, p. 268.

"Dr. W. at the University of Chicago wanted me": Quoted in McCarthy, *Noblesse Oblige*, pp. 167–68.

195 "I made a bully good talk on Lenin": Raymond Robins to Margaret Robins, 11/10/23, Margaret Dreier Robins Papers, PWTUL.

My description of the dismal state of affairs in Chicago at the beginning of the twenties is based largely on Dedmon, *Fabulous Chicago*, pp. 290–95, and on Wendt and Kogan, *Bosses in Lusty Chicago*, pp. 328–44.

196 "dealer in second-hand furniture": Quoted in Wendt and Kogan, *Bosses*, p. 343.

197 "progressive movement . . . that was halted": Quoted in Lear, *Harold L. Ickes*, p. 232.

198 "a plain liar": *Ibid.*, quoted, p. 246.

"I am very tired tonight": Raymond Robins to Margaret Robins, 4/2/23, Margaret Dreier Robins Papers, PWTUL.

"I wish you were here": *Ibid.*, 4/3/23.

"We were standing in the front rank" (note): Raymond Ickes, interview, 2/21/85.

199   Neither Geis, in *The Colonel of Chicago*, nor Wendt, in the *Chicago Tribune*, states outright that McCormick committed suicide, but Ralph G. Martin in *Cissy*, a biography of McCormick's cousin, Eleanor "Cissy" Patterson (New York: Simon and Schuster, 1979), makes no bones about it: "It was announced that he had suffered a gastric hemorrhage, but in fact he had committed suicide" (p. 200).

"I think the idea is a good one": HLI to Frank O. Lowden, 8/2/19, General Correspondence, Container 29, HLIP.

"So far as I have been able": HLI to Jane Addams, 11/1/22, General Correspondence, Container 29, HLIP.

200   "I have little time": Undated note written at bottom of HLI to Mrs. Irwin Rosenfels, 9/23/22, General Correspondence, Container 36, HLIP.

"that Chicago should have at least": *Ibid.*, Robert W. Bagnall to HLI, 9/27/22.

"I don't know what is the matter": *Ibid.*, HLI to Robert Bagnall, 11/6/24.

202   Anna's asthma was neither organic nor psychosomatic (as one might expect from someone in that troubled household), nor was it the salubrious air of New Mexico that cleared it up when she traveled there. The asthma, it turned out, was allergenic. It was not an allergy common to your everyday American household, then or now, but Hubbard Woods was not your average everyday American household. In addition to Anna, Harold, the children, Tom Gilmore, and all the servants, Hubbard Woods also had been home to two monkeys, and it was monkey fur that brought on Anna's seizures. It took many, many trips to New Mexico before this was discovered by the doctors. By then, one of the monkeys had died; the other was given to the Lincoln Park Zoo when the doctors ordered it out of the house. Raymond Ickes, interview, 2/21/85.

My sketch of John Collier is taken from John Collier, *From Every Zenith: A Memoir, with Some Essays on Life and Thought* (Denver: Sage Books, 1963), a self-serving and irritatingly coy reminiscence that should be used with caution, and from Lawrence C. Kelly, "John Collier," in Howard R. Lamar, ed., *The Reader's Encyclopedia of the American West* (New York: Thomas Y. Crowell Company, 1977), pp. 237–39.

203   "A more moving tale of wrongs": HLI to Hiram Johnson, 1/12/23, General Correspondence, Container 33, HLIP.

204   "stupid and shortsighted": HLI to John Collier, 8/3/23, General Correspondence, Container 32, HLIP.

205   "Here was a great man": Collier, *From Every Zenith*, p. 293.

My summary of conditions in the mid-twenties is largely from Leuchtenburg, *The Perils of Prosperity*, pp. 178–203.

206   Russell, *The Shadow of Blooming Grove*, pp. 551–603, provides as good a discussion as any of the Albert Fall affair, as well as other aspects of the sordid goings-on in the Harding administration, and I have relied on it for much of my own treatment of these years. See also M. R. Werner and John Starr, *Teapot Dome* (New York: The Viking Press, 1959).

207   "My God, this is a hell of a job!": Quoted in White, *The Autobiography of William Allen White*, p. 619.

"All my life's buried here": Quoted in Russell, *The Shadow of Blooming Grove*, p. 563.

"It is my dearest wish to see": HLI to Hiram Johnson, 4/10/23; quoted in Lear, *Harold L. Ickes*, p. 247.

208   "There are three purgatories": Quoted in Russell, *The Shadow of Blooming Grove*, p. 622.

Daugherty's resignation did not end it. Over the next several years, further hearings, followed by flurries of indictments and trials, would enliven the columns of the nation's press on a regular basis. In the end, Fall, Sinclair (for contempt of Congress, not bribery), Gaston Means, and William J. Burns all did time in jail or prison. The Sinclair and Doheny leases at Teapot Dome and Elk Hills were both canceled and neither has ever since been leased. Altogether, it was the worst Presidential scandal since that of the Grant administration fifty years before, and would not be matched again until that of the second Nixon administration fifty years later.

209   "take a chance on some wide awake": HLI to Hiram Johnson, 8/31/23; quoted in Lear, *Harold L. Ickes*, p. 254.

"I am for Johnson": HLI to Henry Allen, 11/24/23, General Correspondence, Container 29, HLIP.

210   "Hitchcock has been determined from the start": HLI to Hiram Johnson, 1/29/24; quoted in Lear, *Harold L. Ickes*, p. 282.

"I don't mind being licked": HLI to Raymond Robins, 1/29/24, General Correspondence, Container 38, HLIP.

211   "The business of America": Quoted in Davis, *FDR: The Beckoning of Destiny*, p. 748.

"The Republican Party is the party of reaction": HLI to George Payne, 6/13/24, General Correspondence, Container 36, HLIP.

"Harold does not come out": Raymond Robins to Margaret Robins, 8/11/24, Margaret Dreier Robins Papers, PWTUL.

212   "I have never seen such a peculiar campaign": HLI to Hiram Johnson, 9/9/24, General Correspondence, Container 33, HLIP.

"I don't know when I have spent": Raymond Robins to Margaret Robins, 10/3/24, Margaret Dreier Robins Papers, PWTUL.

"I challenge these former Progressives": Statement of Harold L. Ickes, 10/4/24, General Correspondence, Container 35, HLIP.

19. A Wall Against Despair

214 "Mediocrity is king": HLI to Hiram Johnson, 11/11/24, General Correspondence, Container 33, HLIP.

216 "I told her the other day": *Ibid.*
"I never ran a more helpless": HLI, Untitled autobiographical draft, HLIP, pp. 361–62.
"As a matter of fact": *Ibid.*, p. 364.

217 "I don't believe anything can be done": HLI to S. J. Duncan-Clark, 11/6/29, General Correspondence, Container 31, HLIP.

218 "I don't think he *had*": Raymond Ickes, interview, 2/25/85.

219 "They are bum hosts!": Raymond Robins to Margaret Robins, 4/16/23, Margaret Dreier Robins Papers, PWTUL.
"I can only consent to your return": Anna Ickes to HLI, 9/14/25, Scrapbooks, HLIP.

220 "I agree that responsibility to my home": *Ibid.*, HLI to Anna Ickes, n.d.
"Very perceptive, very warm individual": Raymond Ickes, interview, 2/25/85.
"young and pretty": HLI, Untitled autobiographical draft, HLIP, p. 227.

221 "Robert was always pretty much": Raymond Ickes, interview, 2/25/85.

222 "At the time that Raymond was called": HLI, Untitled autobiographical draft, HLIP, p. 300.

223 "I am very much worried about Clinton": George W. Smith, Jr., to HLI, 11/7/28, Letterbooks, HLIP.

224 "Dear Clair: Your letter of recent date": Julia Ickes Hazard to HLI, 4/10/29, Letterbooks, HLIP. HLI's letter to her is one of the few that has not survived.
"I hope you are psychologist enough": HLI to Agnes Rogers, 5/1/29, General Correspondence, Container 38, HLIP. As noted earlier, after HLI became Secretary of the Interior Miss Rogers and he reopened communications on a regular basis and continued writing each other quite fondly until her death (this correspondence currently is in the collection of Harold McEwen Ickes).

225 "We developed our own varieties": HLI, Folder 10, Unpublished personal memoirs, HLIP, p. 5. Except for a small patch alongside the road that now cuts through the property, these flower beds are long since gone.

226 "Like Ferdinand the Bull": HLI, *Autobiography*, p. 299.
"He'd come home from the office": Raymond Ickes, interview, 2/25/85.

PART V: IN THE CRUCIBLE OF FEAR

227 "Few people seem to be aware": HLI, speech, 3/12/31, Speeches and statements, Container 407, HLIP.

20. Snuffing Out the Decade

Material on Insull's later career and on the Opera Building comes from McDonald, *Insull*; Mayer and Wade, *Chicago*; Dedmon, *Fabulous Chicago*; and Condit, *Chicago, 1910–1929*. My discussion of the stock market frenzy and collapse is based on material gleaned from a number of sources, chief among them Frederick Lewis Allen, *Only Yesterday: An Informal History of the 1920s* (New York: Harper and Brothers, 1931; reprinted by Harper and Row, New York, 1964); Kenneth S. Davis, *FDR: The New York Years* (New York: Random House, 1985); John Kenneth Galbraith, *The Great Crash, 1929* (Boston: Houghton Mifflin Company, 1955); Paul Johnson, *Modern Times: The World from the Twenties to the Eighties* (New York: Harper and Row, 1985); Leuchtenburg, *The Perils of Prosperity*; Joe Alex Morris, *What a Year!* (New York: Harper and Brothers, 1956); Lloyd Morris, *Postscript to Yesterday: America, the Last Fifty Years* (New York: Random House, 1947); Cabell Phillips, *From the Crash to the Blitz, 1929–1939* (New York: Macmillan Company, 1969); Arthur M. Schlesinger, Jr., *The Crisis of the Old Order, 1919–1933* (Boston: Houghton Mifflin Company, 1957); Page Smith, *A People's History of the 1920s and the New Deal* (New York: McGraw-Hill Book Company, 1987); and Edmund Wilson, *The American Earthquake: A Documentary of the Twenties and Thirties* (Garden City, N.Y.: Doubleday and Company, Inc., 1964). Other sources as noted.

PAGE

230   "My God. A hundred and fifty million dollars!": Quoted in McDonald, *Insull*, p. 282.

231   "Today, American prosperity exists": Quoted in Davis, *FDR: The New York Years*, p. 113.
      "We grew up founding our dreams": Quoted in Leuchtenburg, *The Perils of Prosperity*, p. 242.
      "Everybody ought to be rich": *Ibid.*

232   "the safest form of investment": Quoted in *Time Capsule/1929* (New York: Time-Life Books, 1967), p. 213.
      "It was during those terrible days": HLI, Untitled autobiographical draft, HLIP, p. 366.

233   "I was frightened": *Ibid.*, p. 367.
      "When the great boom days came": *Ibid.*, p. 369.
      "I would have cashed in": *Ibid.*, p. 370.

234   "Stock prices have reached": Quoted in Leuchtenburg, *The Perils of Prosperity*, p. 244.
      "retained hopeful features": Quoted in Davis, *FDR: The New York Years*, p. 147.
      "Bankers, brokers, clerks": Allen, *Only Yesterday*, pp. 276–77.

235   "Never was a decade": Leuchtenburg, *The Perils of Prosperity*, p. 269.
      In *The Great Crash*, John Kenneth Galbraith lays to rest the suicide talk: "In the United States the suicide wave that followed the stock market crash is . . . part of the legend. In fact, there was none" (p. 133).

"Anna and I had been having": HLI, Untitled autobiographical draft, HLIP, p. 370.

236   "I feel morally certain": *Ibid.*, pp. 370–71.
        "It was on my way back": *Ibid.*, pp. 371–72.

237   "I was devoted to him": *Ibid.*, p. 223.
        "not only every convenience": *Ibid.*, pp. 222–23.

238   "A hot discussion developed": *Ibid.*, p. 330.
        "Of course Anna had the right": *Ibid.*

239   "I was anxious to get back": *Ibid.*, p. 332.

21. ". . . at least 90% damn fool"

PAGE

240   "Insull is the supreme utility and political boss": HLI to Raymond Robins, 7/28/30, General Correspondence, Container 38, HLIP.

241   "had to be in the politics": William Allen White to William E. Chenery, 6/13/32, in Johnson, *Selected Letters of William Allen White*, p. 325.

242   "The valuation of $167 million claimed": Paul H. Douglas, *In the Fullness of Time: The Memoirs of Paul H. Douglas* (New York: Harcourt Brace Jovanovich, Inc., 1972), p. 56.

243   "We even reached into the political sepulchre": HLI to Raymond Robins, 7/28/30, General Correspondence, Container 38, HLIP.
        "I was given the roles of": Douglas, *In the Fullness of Time*, p. 57.
        "the city is now emancipated": Quoted in Donald R. Richberg to HLI, 8/1/29, Donald R. Richberg Papers, Library of Congress. Oddly enough, neither Richberg in *My Hero* nor Ickes in *Autobiography of a Curmudgeon* mentions his participation in this fight against the Insull interests, though both devote considerable ink to earlier and similar struggles. Ickes, in fact, does not even make note of it in his *unpublished* political and personal memoirs. I have no idea why.
        "The right to lock the stable door": *Ibid.*

244   "Judge Wilkerson, on behalf of the security holders": HLI press release, 7/23/29, in the Charles E. Merriam Papers, UCA.
        "Quixotic crusaders": Gosnell, *Machine Politics*, p. 143.
        "Since I am not ready to join": HLI to Board of Directors, City Club of Chicago, 6/16/30, General Correspondence, Container 37, HLIP.
        "I never felt so much alone": HLI to Raymond Robins, 7/28/30, General Correspondence, Container 38, HLIP.

245   "We are urged to accept": Quoted in Lear, *Harold L. Ickes*, p. 341.
        "so long as our traction situation": *Ibid.*, quoted, p. 339.
        "I never had any illusions": HLI to Raymond Robins, 7/28/30, General Correspondence, Container 38, HLIP.

246   "I have realized for several years": *Ibid.*
        "Few people seem to be aware": HLI, speech, 3/12/31, Speeches and statements, Container 407, HLIP.

247   "I owed nobody an explanation": HLI, *Autobiography*, p. 254.
       "was too clever for her": *Ibid.*, p. 239.
       "Tony, where is your pushcart at?": Quoted in Gosnell, *Machine Politics*, p. 13.
       "good executive": HLI to Hiram Johnson, 4/28/31, quoted in Lear, *Harold L.
       Ickes*, p. 328.
248   "You can't go on buying": Quoted in McDonald, *Insull*, p. 292.
       "Well, gentlemen, here I am": *Ibid.*, quoted, p. 304.

22. No Foundation

The statistics cited at the beginning of this chapter were pulled from many sources, but most from the following: Frederick Lewis Allen, *Since Yesterday: The Nineteen-Thirties in America, September 3, 1929–September 3, 1939* (New York: Harper and Brothers, 1940); Davis, *FDR: The New York Years*; Johnson, *Modern Times*; Robert S. McElvaine, *The Great Depression: America, 1929–1941* (New York: Times Books, 1984); Phillips, *From the Crash to the Blitz*; Gilbert Seldes, *The Years of the Locust: (America, 1929–1932)* (Boston: Little, Brown and Company, 1933); Richard Norton Smith, *An Uncommon Man: The Triumph of Herbert Hoover* (New York: Simon and Schuster, 1984); U.S. Bureau of the Census, *The Statistical History of the United States: From Colonial Times to the Present* (New York: Basic Books, Inc., 1976); and Dixon Wecter, *The Age of the Great Depression, 1929–1941* (Chicago: Quadrangle Books, 1971). Other sources as noted.

PAGE

249   "In other periods of depression": Quoted in Steel, *Walter Lippmann*, p. 286.
251   "The suddenly idle hands": Studs Terkel, *Hard Times: An Oral History of the
       Great Depression* (New York: Random House, 1970), p. 6.
       "The Depression was a way of life": *Ibid.*, quoted, p. 444.
       "A marvelous investment": *Ibid.*, quoted, p. 442.
       "While sitting in the Landlord and Tenants Court": *Ibid.*, quoted,
       pp. 471–72.
252   "every available dry spot": Quoted in Mayer and Wade, *Chicago*, p. 360.
       "You can ride across": *Ibid.*, quoted, p. 358.
       "All around the social workers of Hull House": Wilson, *The American Earth-
       quake*, p. 454.
       "an old man . . . dying of a tumor": *Ibid.*, p. 455.
       "faces that are shocking": *Ibid.*, pp. 459–60.
       "seven stories, thick with dark windows": *Ibid.*, pp. 460–61.
253   "There is not a garbage-dump in Chicago": *Ibid.*, p. 462.
       "spontaneous expression of the pride": Quoted in Dedmon, *Fabulous Chicago*,
       p. 443.
       "He saw himself walking in the rain": James T. Farrell in Harvey Swados, ed.,
       The American Writer and the Great Depression (Indianapolis: The Bobbs-Merrill
       Company, 1966), pp. 261–62.

23. Waiting for Something to Turn Up

255 "No sooner is one leak plugged up": Quoted in Gene Smith, *The Shattered Dream: Herbert Hoover and the Great Depression* (New York: William Morrow and Company, 1970), p. 62. For material on Hoover and his reaction to the Depression, see also Donald J. Lisio, *The President and Protest: Hoover, Conspiracy, and the Bonus Riot* (Columbia: University of Missouri Press, 1974); McElvaine, *The Great Depression*; Eliot A. Rosen, *Hoover, Roosevelt, and the Brain Trust: From Depression to New Deal* (New York: Columbia University Press, 1977); and Smith, *An Uncommon Man*.

256 "The most dangerous animal": Quoted in Smith, *An Uncommon Man*, p. 113.

257 "Never before has so dangerous": *Ibid.*, quoted, p. 126.

"any lack of confidence": Quoted in McElvaine, *The Great Depression*, p. 66.

"What this country needs is a great poem": Quoted in Smith, *The Shattered Dream*, p. 67.

"I did, and that was the only time": HLI, *Autobiography*, p. 191.

258 "Your whole plan": HLI to Russell Doubleday, 12/12/30, General Correspondence, Container 31, HLIP.

"facilitate exports by American agencies": Quoted in Jesse H. Jones, with Edward Angley, *Fifty Billion Dollars: My Thirteen Years with the RFC* (New York: The Macmillan Company, 1951), ix.

"It used to be the wage earner alone": Quoted in Smith, *An Uncommon Man*, p. 79.

259 "There is no hope": Quoted in Johnson, *William Allen White's America*, p. 425.

"I feel the capitalistic system is dead": Quoted in Schlesinger, *The Crisis of the Old Order*, p. 265.

"When despite every effort": Quoted in McElvaine, *The Great Depression*, p. 91.

260 "This marks a new era": Quoted in Smith, *The Shattered Dream*, p. 146.

"Un-American as it sounds": Anne O'Hare McCormick in Marion Turner Sheehan, ed., *The World at Home: Selections from the Writings of Anne O'Hare McCormick* (New York: Alfred A. Knopf, 1956), p. 84.

"Dear Chief": HLI to Hiram Johnson, 1/22/32, General Correspondence, Container 34, HLIP.

261 "Dear Hiram": HLI to Hiram Johnson, 2/16/32, *ibid.*

"Just between you and me": HLI to William Allen White, 3/18/32, General Correspondence, Container 41, HLIP.

"a pure waste of money": Gifford Pinchot to HLI, 5/5/32, General Correspondence, Container 38, HLIP.

"the stupidest and most boresome ever": Quoted in Smith, *An Uncommon Man*, p. 141.

"Well, it was not wholly unexpected": *Ibid.*, quoted.

262 "From my hotel": Jones, *Fifty Billion Dollars*, p. 73. The rescue efforts, as it

turned out, were only temporarily effective. By August the constant drain of withdrawals forced Central Republic into receivership—although Jones took pains to note in 1951 that "the loan has panned out well. The RFC has collected the entire $90,000,000 loan plus more than $10,000,000 interest, in addition to several millions in connection with the liquidation" (p. 72).

263   "To the politicians who like action": James A. Farley, *Behind the Ballots: The Personal History of a Politician* (New York: Harcourt, Brace and Company, 1938), pp. 113–14. Farley, with Davis, *FDR: The New York Years*, provides the best discussion of FDR's nomination, and I rely heavily on both for my own. For FDR's earlier career see Davis, *FDR: The Beckoning of Destiny, 1882–1928*, and Geoffrey C. Ward's two volumes of biography, *Before the Trumpet: Young Franklin Roosevelt, 1882–1905*, and *A First-Class Temperament: The Emergence of Franklin Roosevelt* (New York: Harper and Row, 1985, 1989).

265   "When cynics ask what is the use": Quoted in Steel, *Walter Lippmann*, p. 169. "I am now satisfied": Walter Lippmann to Newton D. Baker, 11/24/31, in John Morton Blum, *Public Philosopher: Selected Letters of Walter Lippmann* (New York: Ticknor and Fields, 1985), p. 280. "A pleasant man who": Quoted in Steel, *Walter Lippmann*, p. 292. "a man who thinks": *Ibid.*, quoted, p. 291. "It was Thursday afternoon": Farley, *Behind the Ballots*, p. 137.

266   "I learned something on that occasion": *Ibid.*, p. 140. "On the night they took three ballots": Quoted in D. B. Hardeman and Donald C. Bacon, *Rayburn: A Biography* (Texas Monthly Press, Austin, 1987), p. 141. "bucket of warm spit": Quoted in Davis, *FDR: The New York Years*, p. 327.

267   "California came here to nominate": Quoted in Smith, *The Shattered Dream*, p. 119. "Roosevelt, gripping the parallel bars": Bess Furman, *Washington By-line: The Personal History of a Newspaperwoman* (New York: Alfred A. Knopf, 1949), p. 120. "The appearance before a national convention": The first portion of FDR's speech as quoted is from Furman, *Washington By-line*, p. 120; the second portion is from Davis, *FDR: The New York Years*, p. 335. Arthur M. Schlesinger points out in *The Crisis of the Old Order* (p. 403) that "new deal" was not a conceit original with Roosevelt's speechwriters; it had most recently been used in the current issue of the *New Republic* by economist-philosopher Stuart Chase in an article called "A New Deal for America." And as Davis points out in *FDR: The New York Years* (note, p. 335), it was political cartoonist Rollin Kirby who first recognized the magic in the phrase. On Sunday, July 3, hundreds of newspapers across the country carried his drawing of a farmer leaning on his hoe, looking up at Roosevelt's plane on its way to Chicago with "New Deal" emblazoned on the bottom of its wings.

24. Hung for a Secretary

PAGE

268   "I had been head over heels": HLI, *Autobiography*, p. 260.
      "I told him that . . . I was through": *Ibid*.
269   "Busse and I nearly came to blows": HLI, "On My Interest in Politics and
      Public Affairs," HLIP, pp. 475–76.
      "Deneen was not man enough": *Ibid*.
270   "I had always been as irregular": HLI, *Autobiography*, p. 262.
271   "Recent and exhaustive investigations": Ray Lyman Wilbur and William
      Atherton Du Puy, *Conservation in the Department of the Interior* (Washington,
      D.C.: U.S. Government Printing Office, 1932), p. 112.
      "Our Indians are already suffering": Anna Ickes to Margaret Robins, 9/23/31,
      Margaret Dreier Robins Papers, PWTUL.
272   "cooperate fully with the . . . police": Quoted in Lisio, *The President and
      Protest*, p. 200.
      "the first bloodshed": *Ibid*., quoted, p. 155.
273   "incipient revolution in the air": *Ibid*., quoted, p. 193.
      "bivouac under the guns": *Ibid*., quoted, p. 214.
      "a great and glorious end": HLI, *Autobiography*, p. 265.
274   "All I can say" (note); HLI to William Allen White, 9/23/32, General
      Correspondence, Container 41, HLIP.
      "At the top of my list": Collier, *From Every Zenith*, p. 169.
275   "his personal idiosyncracies unfit him": Quoted in Lawrence C. Kelly, "Choos-
      ing the New Deal Indian Commissioner," *New Mexico Historical Review*,
      Winter 1974.
      "personally impracticable": *Ibid*., quoted.
      "The notion came to me": HLI, *Autobiography*, p. 265.
276   "It was, of course, too much for me": HLI to Hiram Johnson, 1/30/33,
      General Correspondence, Container 34, HLIP.
277   "showed real concern about a third group": R. G. Tugwell, *The Brain Trust*
      (New York: The Viking Press, 1968), pp. 489–90.
      "I discussed this with Louis Howe": Raymond Moley, *The First New Deal* (New
      York: Harcourt, Brace and World, Inc., 1966), p. 94.
278   "Of course I could"; "I called on Senator Cutting": HLI, Unpublished Cabinet
      Memoirs, No. 1, Container 436, HLIP, pp. 27–28.
      "Am persuaded Roosevelt": HLI memorandum for the record, 2/27/33, Gen-
      eral Correspondence, Container 38, HLIP.
      "in effect asked me": *Ibid*., Donald R. Richberg to HLI, 2/24/33.
279   "We had all been standing": HLI, Unpublished Cabinet Memoirs, HLIP,
      p. 30.
280   "All during my life": *Ibid*., p. 31.
      "I was as nervous as could be": *Ibid*., p. 32.
      "badly needed"; "a delicious dinner": *Ibid*.

"On the way up to 65th Street": *Ibid.*
"one of the most casual appointments": Moley, *The First New Deal*, p. 94.

PART VI: POWER AND AUTHORITY

285   "If this administration plan": HLI, *The Secret Diary of Harold L. Ickes,* Volume I: *The First Thousand Days, 1933–1936* (New York: Simon & Schuster, 1953), p. 348.

25. "What Has This Man to Say to Us Today?"

Background on the city of Washington is taken from James Borchert, *Alley Life in Washington: Family, Community, Religion, and Folklife in the City, 1850–1970* (Urbana: University of Illinois Press, 1980); H. P. Caemmerer, *Washington: The National Capital* (Washington, D.C.: U.S. Government Printing Office, 1932); Melanie Choukas-Bradley and Polly Alexander, *City of Trees* (Washington, D.C.: Acropolis Books, 1981); Constance McLaughlin Green, *Washington: Capital City, 1879–1950* (Princeton, N.J.: Princeton University Press, 1963), and, by the same author, *The Secret City: A History of Race Relations in the Nation's Capital* (Princeton, N.J.: Princeton University Press, 1967); Federal Writers' Project, Works Progress Administration, *Washington, City and Capital* (Washington, D.C.: U.S. Government Printing Office, 1937); Erle Kaufmann, *Trees of Washington, The Man—The City* (Washington, D.C.: The Outdoor Press, 1932); other sources as noted. Most of the story of inauguration day, 1933, is based on various numbers of the *Washington Herald*; the oral memoirs of Frances Perkins at Columbia University; Kenneth S. Davis, *FDR: The New Deal Years, 1933–1937* (New York: Random House, 1986); Frank Freidel, *Launching the New Deal* (Boston: Little, Brown and Company, 1973); and Richard Norton Smith, *An Uncommon Man: The Triumph of Herbert Hoover* (New York: Simon & Schuster, 1984).

288   "where a mighty forest": Quoted in Choukas-Bradley and Alexander, *City of Trees*, p. 34.
"Today in Washington,": Erle Kauffmann, *Trees of Washington* p. 57.

289   "The noble scheme": Federal Writers' Project, *Washington: City and Capital*, pp. 109–10.
"Long live King Baseball": Quoted in Green, *The Secret City*, p. 202.

290   Statistics on Washington's financial state are from *ibid.*, p. 221, and Green, *Washington: City and Capital*, pp. 378–80.

291   "I am not bitter": *Washington Herald*, February 22, 1933.

292   Cermak's impending demise was not the only death haunting the inauguration. The other was that of Senator Frank Walsh, who had been chosen by FDR as his attorney general. Walsh, seventy-four, had married a Cuban widow in

February, and while on the train to Washington a few days after his honeymoon had suffered a heart attack, dying on March 2. Homer Cummings had been chosen in his stead.

"Members find it necessary": *Washington Herald*, March 3, 1933.

"unwarranted and undemocratic": *Ibid.*, February 23, 1933.

294   "Mr. Roosevelt"; "It's been very pleasant": Quoted in Smith, *An Uncommon Man*, p. 161.

"a freight train full": *Washington Herald*, March 4, 1933.

"I do not know how": Quoted in William E. Leuchtenberg, *Franklin D. Roosevelt and the New Deal* (New York: Harper & Row, 1963), pp. 39–40.

295   "We are at the end": Quoted in Smith, *An Uncommon Man*, p. 162.

"O Lord . . . we heartily beseech Thee": Quoted in Davis, *FDR: The New Deal Years*, p. 27.

296   "I said to myself": Quoted in Grace Tully, *FDR, My Boss* (New York: Scribner's, 1949), p. 68.

297   "You get your seat": *Washington Herald*, March 5, 1933.

"The famous smile": *Ibid.*

"This is a day": In Samuel I. Rosenman, *The Public Papers and Addresses of Franklin D. Roosevelt*, Volume II: *The Year of Crisis, 1933* (New York: Random House, 1938).

298   "It was very, very solemn": *New York Times*, March 5, 1933.

"Well, he's taken the ship of state": Quoted in George Martin, *Madam Secretary: Frances Perkins* (Boston: Houghton Mifflin, 1976), p. 11.

"thrilled us into forgetfulness": Olive Ewing Clapper, *Washington Tapestry* (New York: McGraw-Hill, 1946), p. 26.

"full of weasel words": Quoted in Schlesinger, *The Crisis of the Old Order*, p. 8.

"one reads them later": Wilson, *The American Earthquake*, p. 478.

299   "We heard Roosevelt's speech": Beatrice Bishop Berle and Travis Beal Jacobs, eds., *Navigating the Rapids, 1918–1971: From the Papers of Adolf A. Berle* (New York: Harcourt Brace Jovanovich, 1973), p. 84.

Details of radio coverage are from a feature in the *Washington Herald*, March 4, 1933.

"It was a talk the nation had not heard": John R. Tunis, quoted in Frank Freidel, *FDR: Launching the New Deal*, p. 207.

300   "fighting planes": *Washington Herald*, March 5, 1933.

"I hope you don't mind": Quoted in Perkins, oral memoirs, vol. IV, p. 66, OHCU.

301   "As I looked about the Oval Room": HLI, "My Twelve Years with FDR," *Saturday Evening Post*, June 12, 1948.

"No cabinet has ever been": Quoted in Martin, *Madam Secretary*, p. 14.

"By this informal little touch": Farley, *Behind the Ballots*, p. 209.

"The inaugural ball that night": Furman, *Washington By-line*, pp. 151–52.

"pleasure mad crowd": *Washington Herald*, March 5, 1933.

26. The Inheritance

My summary of the history of the Interior Department and American public land policy calls upon numerous secondary sources, but to my knowledge the most comprehensive and reliable study of the subject ever accomplished is Paul W. Gates, *The History of Public Land Law Development* with a chapter on mining law by Robert W. Swenson (Washington, D.C.: U.S. Government Printing Office, 1968). Other important works include Billington, *Westward Expansion*; William C. Everhart, *The National Park Service* (Boulder, Colo.: Westview Press, 1983); Ronald A. Foresta, *America's National Parks and Their Keepers* (Washington, D.C.: Resources for the Future, 1984); Michael Frome, *Whose Woods These Are: The Story of the National Forests* (Garden City, N.Y.: Doubleday, 1962); Samuel P. Hayes, *Conservation and the Gospel of Efficiency: The Progressive Conservation Movement, 1890–1920* (Cambridge, Mass.: Harvard University Press, 1959); John D. Leshy, *The Mining Law: A Study in Perpetual Motion* (Washington, D.C.: Resources for the Future, 1987); Richard G. Lillard, *The Great Forest* (New York: Alfred A. Knopf, 1947); Ernest Staples Osgood, *The Day of the Cattleman* (Chicago: University of Chicago Press, 1970); Louise Peffer, *The Closing of the Public Domain* (Palo Alto, Calif.: Stanford University Press, 1951); Marc Reisner, *Cadillac Desert: The American West and Its Disappearing Water* (New York: The Viking Press, 1986); Roy Robbins, *Our Landed Heritage: The Public Domain, 1776–1970* (Lincoln: University of Nebraska Press, 1976); Alfred Runte, *National Parks: The American Experience* (Lincoln: University of Nebraska Press, 1987); Wallace Stegner, *Beyond the Hundredth Meridian: John Wesley Powell and the Second Opening of the West* (Boston: Houghton Mifflin, 1954); T. H. Watkins, *Gold and Silver in the West: The Illustrated History of an American Dream* (Palo Alto, Calif.: American West, 1971); T. H. Watkins and Charles S. Watson, Jr., *The Lands No One Knows: America and the Public Domain* (Sierra Club, 1975); Walter Prescott Webb, *The Great Plains* (Boston: Houghton Mifflin, 1936); Donald Worster, *Rivers of Empire: Water, Aridity, and the Growth of the American West* (New York: Pantheon Books, 1985); William K. Wyant, *Westward in Eden: The Public Lands and the Conservation Movement* (Berkeley: University of California Press, 1982); Dyan Zaslowsky and The Wilderness Society, *These American Lands: Parks, Wilderness, and the Public Lands* (New York: Henry Holt, 1986). Gifford Pinchot's *Breaking New Ground* (New York: Harcourt Brace, 1947) pleads a special case but is nevertheless an essential source for the birth of the Forest Service and modern forest policy. The same is true of Horace M. Albright (as told to Robert Cahn), *The Birth of the National Park Service: The Founding Years, 1913–33* (Salt Lake City: Howe Brothers, 1985). Not as much can be said for Lyman F. Wilbur and William Du Puy's *Conservation in the Department of the Interior* (Washington, D.C.: U.S. Government Printing Office, 1932), one of the most shamelessly self-serving and obfuscating documents in the long history of such things issuing from government presses; it is useful, however, as the demonstration of a point of view and as the source of some otherwise elusive statistics. Finally, I had recourse to Eugene F. Trani's unpublished manuscript, "The Secretaries of the Department of the Interior, 1849–1969" (Washington, D.C.: National Anthropological Archives, 1975).

PAGE

302 "President Roosevelt called the members": HLI, *Diary*, vol. I, p. 3.

"I . . . remember that you insisted" (note): HLI to Paul H. Douglas, 8/17/43, Secretary of Interior File, Container 160, HLIP.

303 "dog tired": HLI, *Diary*, vol. I, p. 3.

"They filed past me": *Ibid.*

304 "Perhaps I had aspired": HLI, "My Twelve Years with FDR," June 12, 1948.

305 "Cultivators of the earth": Quoted in Watkins and Watson, *The Lands No One Knows*, p. 37.

307 "Secretary Ewing's great concern": Quoted in Eugene Trani, "The Secretaries of the Department of the Interior," p. 62.

309 "It invited corruption": Billington, *Westward Expansion*, p. 608.

310 "care and custody": Quoted in Frederick Turner, "The Language of the Forest," *Wilderness*, Summer 1983.

"a public opinion, looking with indifference": Quoted in Pinchot, *Breaking New Ground*, pp. 84–85.

"That the President of the United States may": Act of March 3, 1891, 26 Stat. 1095.

311 "vitally important though it was": Pinchot, *Breaking New Ground*, pp. 85–86.

"to improve and protect the forest": Act of June 4, 1897, 30 Stat. 34–36.

313 "The land was a mere barren waste": Quoted in Morris, *The Rise of Theodore Roosevelt*, p. 372.

"are today more competent to manage": Quoted in Gates, *History of Public Land Law Development*, p. 608.

314 "The law is at once highly specific"; "a statute so inadequately conceived": Leshy, *The Mining Law*, pp. 19, 21.

317 "be obliged to repurchase": Quoted by Robert W. Swenson in Gates, *The History of Public Land Law Development*, p. 732.

"a belated effort to safeguard": Robert Engler, *The Politics of Oil: Private Power and Democratic Directions* (Chicago: University of Chicago Press, 1961), p. 81.

318 "It took a man to break": Stegner, *Beyond the Hundredth Meridian*, p. 221.

"Not one dollar will be invested": Quoted in Worster, *Rivers of Empire*, p. 173.

320 "The destiny of man is": *Ibid.*, quoted, p. 188.

321 "Dear Steve: If you don't like": Quoted in Zaslowsky, *These American Lands*, p. 21.

"promote and regulate the use": Act of August 25, 1916, 39 Stat. 535.

322 "consolidate our gains": Quoted in Zaslowsky, *These American Lands*, p. 28.

323 Information on Alaska, Hawaii, and the Virgin Islands in this section is largely taken from Wilbur and Du Puy, *Conservation in the Department of the Interior*; information on the Office of Education and other Department of Interior responsibilities is taken from Caemmerer, *Washington: The National Capital*.

324 "not only willing to undertake": HLI, "My Twelve Years with FDR," June 12, 1948.

27. The Hundred and Twenty-two Days

As the notes for this and subsequent chapters make clear, some of the most useful sources for the years of the New Deal are the oral histories on file at Columbia University, particularly those of Frances Perkins and Henry Wallace. The Perkins memoirs are particularly helpful; at thirteen manuscript volumes, they are lengthy enough to include almost anything one would want to cover (Ickes and others were quite right about her volubility!), and they display a sharp eye and a sometimes eloquent tongue. Any list of the best secondary sources must begin with the second and third volumes of Arthur M. Schlesinger's *The Age of Roosevelt—The Coming of the New Deal* (Boston: Houghton Mifflin, 1957) and *The Politics of Upheaval* (Boston: Houghton Mifflin, 1960); it has been more than a generation since their first publication, but anyone who wants to challenge Schlesinger's interpretations had better do his homework. Frank Freidel in *FDR: The Launching of the New Deal* and Kenneth S. Davis in *FDR: The New Deal Years, 1933–1937* do not so much challenge as build upon Schlesinger's work—as do we all. Another welcome addition to the literature is Joseph P. Lash's *Dealers and Dreamers: A New Look at the New Deal* (New York: Doubleday, 1988). Other sources as noted.

PAGE

325 "What happened on March 4"; "are vivified by a strong undercurrent": Sheehan, *The World at Home*, pp. 174, 195–96.

326 "The speed with which the government": T.R.B., "Washington Notes," *New Republic*, March 22, 1933. "T.R.B." was the pseudonym of whoever turned out any given issue's "Washington Notes" column; in this case, it probably was Frank R. Kent.

327 "is more entertaining than I have ever known it": Wilson, *The American Earthquake*, p. 536.

"These are grand days": William Allen White to HLI, 5/23/33, in Walter Johnson, ed., *Selected Letters of William Allen White, 1899–1943* (New York: Henry Holt and Company, 1947), p. 335.

"The first thing to do": HLI, "My Twelve Years with FDR," June 12, 1948.

328 "I was under very great pressure": HLI, *Diary*, vol. I, p. 9.

329 "He was an extremely hard person": Milburn L. Wilson, oral memoirs, p. 1363, OHCU.

330 "Many friends of mine": Harry Slattery, "From Roosevelt to Roosevelt: A Story of Forty Years in Washington," pp. 138–39, SPDU.

"proposal thoroughly dismayed me": Collier, *From Every Zenith*, p. 171. Collier's single-minded pursuit of the appointment to the Bureau of Indian Affairs is superbly laid out in Kelly, "Choosing the New Deal Indian Commissioner."

"unlawful cohabitation, fornication": Quoted in Kenneth R. Philp, *John Collier's Crusade for Indian Reform, 1920–1954* (Tucson: University of Arizona Press, 1977), p. 67.

331 "My concern is to bring about the appointment": HLI to Mr. and Mrs. Charles de Young Elkus, 2/28/33, Container 56, General Correspondence, HLIP.

"I think you know that I have": HLI to Francis Wilson, 4/18/33, Container 168, Secretary of the Interior File, HLIP.

"I was willing to be at ease": HLI, "My Twelve Years with FDR," June 12, 1948.

332 "After tea had been served": *Ibid.* All of the Robinson episode is from this source.

333 "This, of course, will be of no benefit": George Norris to HLI, 5/26/33, Container 162, Secretary of the Interior File, HLIP.

"dog robber to the New Deal": *Time*, September 15, 1941.

"His office was in one of the wings": Milburn L. Wilson, oral memoirs, p. 1229.

334 "The fact is": HLI, *Diary*, vol. I, p. 308.

"Customarily, the President was wheeled": HLI, "My Twelve Years with FDR," June 5, 1948. Ickes's descriptions of Hull, Woodin, Morgenthau, Swanson, Farley, Cummings, and Wallace are all from this source.

336 "in a perfect torrent"; "pushed in ahead of everybody else": HLI, *Diary*, p. 407.

337 "a pretty substantial and sturdy character": *Ibid.*, p. 316.

"tough guy": Quoted in John Morton Blum, *From the Morgenthau Diaries: Years of Crisis, 1928–1938* (Boston: Houghton Mifflin, 1959), p. 87.

"was often quite far to the left": Cordell Hull, *The Memoirs of Cordell Hull* (New York: Macmillan, 1948), vol. I, p. 209.

"peculiarly twisted man": Henry Wallace, diary entry for 7/1/41 in oral memoirs, p. 1224, OHCU.

"I liked Ickes": Perkins, oral memoirs, vol. IV, pp. 83–84.

338 "So this will be a military training": Quoted in Perkins, oral memoirs, vol. IV, p. 485.

"I thought it would be better": Wallace, oral memoirs, p. 243.

"coordinate the plans for": FDR to the secretaries of War, Interior, Agriculture, and Labor, 3/14/33, in Edgar B. Nixon, ed., *Franklin D. Roosevelt and Conservation, 1911–1945* (Washington, D.C.: U.S. Government Printing Office, 1957), vol. I, p. 138.

"We are of the opinion": Cabinet committee to FDR, 3/15/33, *ibid.*, pp. 141–42.

339 "of a civilian conservation corps": FDR message to Congress, 3/21/33, *ibid.*, p. 143.

"work-camps fit into": Quoted in Freidel, *Launching the New Deal*, p. 261.

"Oh, that doesn't matter": Quoted in Frances Perkins, *The Roosevelt I Knew* (New York: The Viking Press, 1946), p. 181.

340 My discussion of the "hot oil" controversy relies most heavily on J. Stanley Clark, *The Oil Century: From the Drake Well to the Conservation Era* (Norman: University of Oklahoma Press, 1958); Carl Coke Wister, *Oil! Titan of the Southwest*, a much better book than its title would suggest (Norman: University of Oklahoma Press, 1949); and Harold F. Williamson, Ralph L. An-

dreano, Arnold R. Daum, and Gilbert C. Klose, *The American Petroleum Industry, 1899–1959: The Age of Energy* (Evanston, Ill.: Northwestern University Press, 1963).

"Hoover sent the army" (note): Quoted in Freidel, *Launching the New Deal*, p. 264.

342 "SUCH ISSUES AS REVOLVE": J. Edward Jones, *And So—They Indicted Me* (privately printed, New York, 1939), p. 24.

343 "the courage with which President Roosevelt": Quoted in Freidel, *Launching the New Deal*, p. 427.

"certainly all hot and bothered": HLI, *Diary*, vol. I, p. 10.

"As Mr. Ickes listened": Jones, *And So—They Indicted Me*, p. 44.

344 "On two or three occasions": HLI, *Diary*, vol. I, pp. 10–11.

"The only concrete suggestion"; "were beginning to feel neglected"; and "Then we went down": *Ibid.*, pp. 11–12.

345 "even the iron hand": Quoted in Freidel, *Launching the New Deal*, p. 427.

"The last two or three days": HLI, *Diary*, vol. I, pp. 12–13.

"had made more progress": *Ibid.*, p. 13.

"The President of the United States": FDR to governors of oil-producing states, 4/3/33, in Rosenman, *The Public Papers*, vol. II, pp. 103–4.

346 "When former civilizations": Quoted in Schlesinger, *The Coming of the New Deal*, p. 35.

"Franklin, in common with": Tugwell, *The Brain Trust*, p. 309.

347 "proceeded to rip that list": HLI, *Diary*, vol. I, p. 28.

348 "I said that I had known him": *Ibid.*

349 "almost continuously for several days": Richberg, *My Hero*, pp. 164–65.

"the evolution of Section 7a": Vadney, *The Wayward Liberal*, p. 118.

350 "Well, what difference does it make": Quoted in Perkins, oral memoirs, vol. V, p. 18.

"I remember that it was hot": *Ibid.*, pp. 21–22.

"I think he's a good number-three man": Perkins, *The Roosevelt I Knew*, pp. 200–201.

351 "Oh, mercy no": The entire Perkins version of the Johnson-Ickes appointment is from her oral memoirs, vol. V, pp. 146–71.

352 "It was clear that General Johnson was taken quite aback": HLI, *Diary*, vol. I, p. 54.

353 "Howe called": *Ibid.*, p. 59.

"Harold L. Ickes to exercise": FDR, Executive Order No. 6198, in Rosenman, *The Public Papers*, vol. II, p. 270.

28. The X Factor

Ickes tells the story of his love affair in the portion of his unpublished recollections labeled "Untitled autobiographical draft," Container 35, pp. 384–410, HLIP. Unless otherwise cited, all quotations regarding his entanglement with "X" are from this source. In *Harold Ickes of the New Deal*, Graham White and John Maze state flatly that the identity of the woman "can be deduced from other writings" (p. 121). Such a feat is possible, I suppose, though they do not go on to tell us the results of their deductions. For the purposes of this book, I have done no more than keep a weather eye out for a hint of her presence elsewhere in the papers, and have found nothing.

PAGE

354   "When it was suggested to Mrs. Ickes": *Washington Herald*, March 6, 1933.
355   "one of those ageless women": *Ibid.*, March 9, 1933.
356   "Quiet, loyal, and devoted": HLI, "My Twelve Years with FDR," 6/12/48.
357   "Colonel Howe assured me": HLI, *Diary*, vol. I, pp. 82–83.
358   "that he would not enter into": *Ibid.*, p. 89.
       "Is this Mr. Slattery?": Related in Harry Slattery memorandum to HLI, 10/13/33, SPDU. The Judge Malmin story is told in some detail in HLI, *Diary*, vol. I, pp. 64–65, 88–90, 155, 167.
359   "I know you": Quoted in *ibid.*, p. 122.
       "Naturally I demurred strongly": *Ibid.*
360   John Boettiger would soon marry FDR's daughter, Anna, and within a few years would become one of Ickes's closest friends.
361   "I am tremendously enthusiastic": *Washington Post*, October 8, 1933.
       "Poised and friendly": *Ibid.*
364   "There was more preoccupation with sex": Walter Trohan, *Political Animals: Memoirs of a Sentimental Cynic* (Garden City, N.Y.: Doubleday, 1975), pp. 132–33.
       "There were many young ladies": *Ibid.*, p. 140.
       "as obtrusive": HLI, *Diary*, vol. I, p. 197.
       "mere stenographer"; "more than a stenographer"; and "Boys": The Unofficial Observer (Jay Franklin), *The New Dealers* (New York: The Literary Guild, 1934), p. 36.
       "Bobby Straus reported": Quoted in Berle and Jacobs, *Navigating the Rapids*, p. 102.
365   "A somewhat similar situation": *Ibid.*
       "As the matter now stands" (note): HLI, *Diary*, vol. I, p. 220. See also Vadney, *The Wayward Liberal*, pp. 144–45.
       "I have never had contact": HLI, *Diary*, vol. I, p. 127.
366   "I continued to work hard": *Ibid.*, p. 133.
       "I had a tough argument": *Ibid.*, p. 134.

29. Cheops Redux

Material for this outline of the PWA's accomplishments has been drawn from numerous sources. The most useful of the published works include John Braeman, Robert H. Bremner, and David Brody, eds., *The New Deal*—Volume I: *The National Level*; Volume II: *The State and Local Level* (Columbus: Ohio State University Press, 1975); Robert Caro, *The Power Broker: Robert Moses and the Fall of New York* (New York: Alfred A. Knopf, 1974); HLI's own *Back to Work: The Story of PWA* (New York: Macmillan, 1935); Judson King, *The Conservation Fight: From Theodore Roosevelt to the*

Tennessee Valley Authority (Washington, D.C.: The Public Affairs Press, 1959); Richard Lowitt, *The New Deal and the West* (Bloomington: Indiana University Press, 1984); and C. Herman Prichett, *The Tennessee Valley Authority: A Study in Public Administration* (Chapel Hill: University of North Carolina Press, 1943). Other sources as noted.

PAGE

367   "Probably no member": HLI, *Back to Work*, pp. 56–57.

368   "proceeded to surround himself with engineers": *Ibid.*, p. 58.

     Details on the PWA's complex structure and equally complicated approval process are taken largely from HLI, *Back to Work*, and John Carmody, oral memoirs, OHCU.

370   "The device that Mr. Ickes had set up": Carmody, oral memoirs, p. 604.

     "I went to Secretary Ickes' office" (note): Jones, *Fifty Billion Dollars*, p. 181.

371   "The resultant search": HLI, *Back to Work*, pp. 61–62.

     "have not and, in my opinion": *Ibid.*, p. 217.

     "Ickes was completely constipated": Wallace, *New Frontiers*, p. 350.

372   "What PWA sought to do": HLI, *Back to Work*, p. 216.

     "The duty of Public Works": HLI, "My Twelve Years with FDR," 6/12/48.

373   "a builder to rival Cheops": Leuchtenberg, *Franklin D. Roosevelt and the New Deal*, p. 133.

     "Including dependents of those": HLI, *Back to Work*, p. 256.

374   "Jesus Christ": Quoted in Caro, *The Power Broker*, p. 426.

375   "I don't know Moses": HLI, *Diary*, vol. I, pp. 267–68.

     "Ickes Backs Down": Quoted in Caro, *The Power Broker*, p. 440.

     "There can be no doubt" (note): *Ibid.*

377   "the goal of the greatest happiness"; "Utopian goals?": HLI, "Where Is the Nation Heading?," *New York Times Magazine*, May 27, 1934.

     "We have been going ahead": Quoted in Schlesinger, *The Coming of the New Deal*, p. 350.

378   "to prepare and present": FDR, Executive Order 6777, in Rosenman, *The Public Papers*, vol. III, p. 335.

     "develop a plan for": FDR to HLI, 7/5/34, in *ibid.*, pp. 339–40.

     "Today it is builders": David Lilienthal, *TVA: Democracy on the March* (New York: Harper & Brothers, 1944), p. 3.

379   "Muscle Shoals is more today": FDR, "Informal, extemporaneous remarks," 1/21/33, in Rosenman, *The Public Papers*, vol. I, pp. 888–89.

     "construct dams, reservoirs": Quoted in Pritchett, *The Tennessee Valley Authority*, p. 34.

381   "the biggest dam built": Quoted in "The Earth Movers," *Fortune*, August 1943. The discussion of Boulder/Hoover Dam and other river basin projects relies most heavily on Linda Lear, "Boulder Dam: A Crossroads in Natural Resource Policy," *Journal of the West*, October 1985; George A. Pettit, *So Boulder Dam Was Built* (The Six Companies, Inc., 1935); Joseph E. Stevens, *Hoover Dam: An American Adventure* (Norman: University of Oklahoma Press,

1988); Frank Waters, *The Colorado* (New York: Rinehart and Company, 1946); and T. H. Watkins, *et al.*, *The Grand Colorado: The Story of a River and Its Canyons* (Palo Alto, Calif.: American West, 1969). Marc Reisner, *Cadillac Desert*, and Donald Worster, *Rivers of Empire*, were useful for other river basin projects.

382   "except for a variation": HLI, *Diary*, vol. I, p. 32.
        "The name Boulder Dam": HLI to Robert P. Crane, 5/20/33, quoted in Stevens, *Hoover Dam*, p. 174.
383   "Every reason to believe": Henry J. Kaiser to HLI, 3/18/35, SPDU.
384   "a telegraphic bombardment": Quoted in Stevens, *Hoover Dam*, p. 234.
        "Here behind this massive dam": *Ibid.*, quoted, pp. 245–46.
        "With its completion": Lear, "Boulder Dam."
386   "that I have every confidence": HLI, *Diary*, vol. I, p. 130.
        "Very frankly, the clique": Harry Slattery to HLI, 7/13/34, SPDU.
387   "that since he was an extremely busy": Milburn L. Wilson, oral memoirs, p. 1362.
        "Sparing no expense": Quoted in Schlesinger, *The Coming of the New Deal*, p. 366.
        "I said to Colonel Howe": Milburn L. Wilson, oral memoirs, p. 1362.
388   "I am afraid": HLI, *Diary*, vol. I, p. 129.

30. Sorting Out the Public Weal

There are three major biographies of Harry Hopkins: Henry H. Adams, *Harry Hopkins, A Biography* (New York: G.P. Putnam's Sons, 1977); George McJimsey, *Harry Hopkins: Ally of the Poor and Defender of Democracy* (Cambridge, Mass.: Harvard University Press, 1987); and Robert E. Sherwood, *Roosevelt and Hopkins: An Intimate History* (New York: Harper & Brothers, 1948). For the purposes of this and following chapters, the Adams and McJimsey books are better than Sherwood's—which is best in his discussion of Hopkins's astonishing service just prior to and during World War II—and of these two, McJimsey's is the better. Among other virtues, McJimsey does not automatically assume, as so many do, that Ickes was *ipso facto* the villain in the struggle between the two. Harry L. Hopkins, *Spending to Save: The Complete Story of Relief* (New York: W.W. Norton, 1936), is a succinct outline of FERA and the beginning of the WPA, as well as a good outline of Hopkins's own philosophy of relief.

PAGE

389   "Mr. President! Mr. President!": Quoted in Perkins, oral memoirs, vol. IV, p. 471.
        "a suggestion of quick cigarettes": Quoted in Schlesinger, *The Coming of the New Deal*, p. 266.
390   "It was a good plan": Perkins, oral memoirs, vol. IV, p. 472.
        "work out in the long run": Quoted in Sherwood, *Roosevelt and Hopkins*, p. 52.
        "Every department of government": Quoted in McJimsey, *Harry Hopkins*, p. 54.

"As a nation": Hopkins, *Spending to Save*, p. 109.

391 "There is a great deal to be said": FDR press conference, 11/3/33, in Rosenman, *The Public Papers*, vol. II, pp. 445–46.

"Approved it, hell": Quoted in McJimsey, *Harry Hopkins*, p. 58.

"would put a serious crimp in": HLI, *Diary*, vol. I, p. 116.

"This organization will undertake": *Ibid.*, p. 119.

392 "The big boss is getting ready": Quoted in McJimsey, *Harry Hopkins*, pp. 76–77.

"Boys—this is our hour": Quoted in Sherwood, *Roosevelt and Hopkins*, p. 65.

393 "demanded definitions": Blum, *From the Morgenthau Diaries: Years of Crisis*, p. 235.

"With the Treasury staff reduced": Marriner S. Eccles, *Beckoning Frontiers: Public and Personal Recollections* (New York: Alfred A. Knopf, 1951), p. 184.

394 "in a very emphatic and rather angry": Quoted in Blum, *From the Morgenthau Diaries: Years of Crisis*, p. 237.

"I have no respect at all": HLI, *Diary*, vol. I, p. 264.

"and if he and I will": *Ibid.*, p. 265.

395 "He gives himself absolutely all": *Ibid.*, pp. 340–41.

For background on Corcoran and Cohen, see Lash, *Dealers and Dreamers*.

396 "He said that I was the last hope": HLI, *Diary*, vol. I, p. 342.

397 "I have always thought" (note): HLI, "My Twelve Years with FDR," 6/12/48.

"terrible" (note): Quoted in McJimsey, *Harry Hopkins*, p. 79.

398 "assure that as many"; "Recommend and carry on": FDR, Executive Order No. 7034, 5/6/35, in Rosenman, *The Public Papers*, vol. IV, p. 166.

"If this administration plan": HLI, *Diary*, vol. I, p. 348.

"Of course, in the end": *Ibid.*, p. 351.

"not without embarrassment": HLI, "My Twelve Years with FDR," 6/19/48.

"It was a long meeting": Rexford Tugwell, Diary, pp. 87–88, Tugwell Papers, FDRL.

399 "I have no money": Quoted in McJimsey, *Harry Hopkins*, p. 80.

"Ickes wants to get": *Ibid.*, quoted, p. 84.

400 "Hopkins holds up": HLI, *Diary*, vol. I, p. 410.

"I am more disposed": *Ibid.*, p. 422.

"I am writing to inform you": FDR to HLI, 8/26/35, *ibid.*, quoted, p. 424.

401 "Ickes Is Shorn": *Ibid.*, quoted.

"He said the newspapers were cockeyed": *Ibid.*, p. 425.

31. The Mourned and Unmourned Dead

PAGE

403 "I was terribly shocked": HLI, *Diary*, vol. I, p. 63.

"I saw Harold": Raymond Robins to Margaret Robins, 4/24/35, PWTUL.

404 "Congratulations! I have just finished": Raymond Robins to HLI, 7/31/35, Container 162, HLIP.

"The hotel management said": HLI, *Diary*, vol. I, p. 356.

405   "I made a great hit": *Ibid.*, p. 367.

"Dean Gilkey gave a good talk": *Ibid.*

406   "It really is one of the ugliest": *Ibid.*, p. 377.

"I am no stranger": HLI speech, 6/14/35, Container 276, Secretary of the Interior File, HLIP.

407   "Letters from Anna": HLI, "Untitled autobiographical draft," pp. 412–16, Container 435, HLIP. Except where otherwise noted, this is the source for all quotes regarding Anna's death and funeral.

408   Note: The scrapbook is in Container 467, HLIP.

Details of the accident are from *The New York Times*, September 1, 1935.

32. Apostleship and Dissidence

PAGE

410   "near the end of my": HLI, *Diary*, vol. I, p. 433.

411   "I would not worry about that": Hopkins press conference, 9/5/35, Hopkins Papers, FDRL.

"has received many complaints": HLI, *Diary*, vol. I, p. 433.

"reported dispute": HLI press conference, 9/10/35, Hopkins Papers, FDRL.

412   "I told him that": HLI, *Diary*, vol. I, p. 436.

"I was pretty sore": *Ibid.*, p. 437.

413   "I know there has been a leak": *Ibid.*, p. 438.

"vote of confidence": Walter Lippmann to FDR, 12/7/34, in Blum, *Public Philosopher*, p. 320.

414   On Huey Long, Father Coughlin, *et al.*: Alan Brinkley, *Voices of Protest: Huey Long, Father Coughlin, and the Great Depression* (New York: Alfred A. Knopf, 1982); T. Harry Williams, *Huey Long: A Biography* (New York: Alfred A. Knopf, 1970); and Wallace Stegner, "The Radio Priest and His Flock," in Isabel Leighton, ed., *The Aspirin Age, 1919–1941* (New York: Simon & Schuster, 1949).

Note: HLI on Long, *Diary*, vol. I, p. 346; Long on HLI, *et al.*, quoted in Davis, *FDR: The New Deal Years*, p. 502.

415   "an articulate, organized lobby": Quoted in Brinkley, *Voices of Protest*, p. 175.

"I don't disagree with Father Coughlin": *Ibid.*, quoted, p. 211.

"I expressed the opinion": HLI, *Diary*, vol. I, pp. 195–96.

"They speak with nothing of learning": Quoted in Brinkley, *Voices of Protest*, p. 6.

"steal Long's thunder": Quoted in Davis, *FDR: The New Deal Years*, p. 503.

416   "The President has been living in a fool's paradise": Quoted in Lash, *Dealers and Dreamers*, p. 254.

"We have been relegated": Quoted in Davis, *FDR: The New Deal Years*, p. 520.

417   "The spirit of violence": FDR, press conference, 9/9/35, in Rosenman, *The Public Papers*, vol. IV, p. 358.

"I was very glad to have had": HLI, *Diary*, vol. I, p. 446.

418 "The Blue Bonnet is anxious to pay"; "The feud between Hopkins and Ickes": *The Blue Bonnet*, 10/16/35, Hopkins Papers, FDRL.
"I slept better": HLI, *Diary*, vol. I, p. 460.

419 "Harry Hopkins fitted in": *Ibid.*, p. 461.
"One day when Thomas G. Corcoran": HLI, "My Twelve Years with FDR," June 19, 1948.
"It distresses me to learn": HLI to Margaret Robins, 10/25/35, Container 162, Secretary of the Interior File, HLIP.

420 "I have had a couple of letters": HLI, *The Secret Diary of Harold L. Ickes*, Volume II: *The Inside Struggle, 1936–1939* (New York: Simon and Schuster, 1954), pp. 76–77.
"I feel that I am a burden": Quoted in Vadney, *The Wayward Liberal*, p. 168.
"unscrupulous money-changers": FDR, Annual Message, 1/3/36, in Rosenman, *The Public Papers*, vol. V, p. 14.

421 "There isn't any doubt": HLI, *Diary*, vol. I, p. 530.
"just as much a local activity": Quoted in Davis, *FDR: The New Deal Years*, p. 613.
"Congress would pass a law": HLI, *Diary*, vol. I, pp. 529–30.

422 "the President who faced this issue": *Ibid.*, p. 530.
"I was struck": *Ibid.*, p. 526.
"It is all right with me"; "It was perfect": Quoted in Schlesinger, *The Politics of Upheaval*, p. 519.

423 "a gibbering political jackanapes": *Ibid.*, quoted, p. 520.
"the swellest party ever given": *Ibid.*, quoted, p. 519.
"His Chain-Gang Excellency": HLI, press conference, 1/21/36, Hopkins Papers, FDRL.
"The record shows that this enormous": Walter Lippmann to Lewis Douglas, 4/16/36, in Blum, *The Public Philosopher*, p. 350.

424 "the most regrettable thing": Quoted in Brinkley, *Voices of Protest*, p. 252.
"They indulged in cries" (note): *Ibid.*, quoted, p. 259.

425 "I think four more years": Quoted in Schlesinger, *The Politics of Upheaval*, p. 536.
"Has this clean-living, simple man": Quoted in Martin, *Cissy*, p. 349.
"Fundamentally, he has nothing bad": William Allen White to HLI, 7/24/36, in Johnson, *Selected Letters*, pp. 366–67.

426 "he would be re-elected": HLI, *Diary*, vol. I, p. 533.
"took a pad of paper": *Ibid.*, p. 546.
"I was given a list": *Ibid.*, p. 565.

427 "I said that it was not fair": *Ibid.*, p. 578.
"The President agreed with me": *Ibid.*, p. 583.
"I don't know who": *Ibid.*, p. 589.

428 "I did not think it was quite fair": *Ibid.*, p. 591.
"I find myself differing": HLI to FDR 5/14/36, *ibid.*, quoted, p. 592.
"looked at me": *Ibid.*, p. 593.

429 "Dear Harold": FDR to HLI, undated, *ibid.*, quoted, pp. 593–94.

"I read this communication": *Ibid.*, p. 594.

"I said that": *Ibid.*, p. 595.

"While PWA doesn't get": *Ibid.*, p. 620.

33. On the Attack

PAGE

430   Philadelphia merchants: "Jim Farley," Davis writes, ". . . deemed it 'good politics' to assure the merchants of a profit on their investment." *FDR: The New Deal Years*, p. 627.

      "Under a cloud-veiled moon": *New York Times*, June 27, 1936.

431   "The royalists of the economic order": FDR, acceptance speech, 6/27/36, in Rosenman, *The Public Papers*, vol. V, pp. 233–34.

      "it was the greatest political speech": HLI, *Diary*, vol. I, p. 627.

432   "profound satisfaction": *Ibid.*, p. 641.

      "I am beginning to suspect": HLI memorandum to Harry Slattery, 11/22/34, SPDU.

433   "The story was": HLI, *Diary*, vol. I, p. 260.

      Wiretapping (note): HLI, "Statement before Senate Committee on Public Lands, 1938," Container 140, Secretary of the Interior File, HLIP.

434   "driven crazy"; "besmudged": Quoted in Blum, *From the Morgenthau Diaries: Years of Crisis*, p. 89.

      "very excited and demanded": *Ibid.*, quoted.

      "Don't you understand, Henry": *Ibid.*, quoted.

      "The President succeeded": HLI, *Diary*, vol. I, p. 296.

435   "that they ought to be very careful": *Ibid.*, p. 466.

      "very frankly as a friend": *Ibid.*, pp. 480–81.

      "So far as Glavis' doing me": *Ibid.*, p. 551.

      "Considerable argument took place": Harry Slattery, "Memorandum for Secretary Ickes," 9/9/36, SPDU.

436   "This has created": HLI, *Diary*, vol. I, p. 550.

      "I am willing to continue": *Ibid.*, p. 551.

      "There seems to be considerable conjecture": HLI press conference, 4/7/36, Hopkins Papers, FDRL.

      "As a matter of fact": HLI, *Diary*, vol. I, p. 555.

437   "In conversation with the President": J. Edgar Hoover, "Confidential Memorandum," 8/24/36, Item number nine in Director's Personal Files, archives of the Federal Bureau of Investigation. This may be the place to discuss a personal disappointment. Since J. Edgar Hoover and Ickes grew to cordially despise each other over the years—particularly during the postwar "Red Menace" era—I assumed that Hoover, as was his wont with other people who offended him, would have amassed an "enemies" file on the secretary. I applied for material on Ickes; his second wife, Jane; Glavis; and other likely candidates from the director's personal files under the stipulations of the Freedom of

Information Act. After several months of waiting, this little note and one vapid item regarding Ickes and Wendell Willkie is all my hopeful quest ever unearthed.

"There can be no doubt": HLI speech 7/14/36, Container 282, Secretary of the Interior File, HLIP.

"The people should beware": HLI speech 7/17/36, *ibid.*

Statistics (note): From Wattenburg, ed., *The Statistical History of the United States*, pp. 126, 224.

438   "take out after Alf Landon": James. A. Farley, *Jim Farley's Story: The Roosevelt Years* (New York: McGraw-Hill, 1948), p. 63.

"I think this is downright silly": HLI, *Diary*, vol. I, p. 639.

"WE WISH TO URGE": James Farley to FDR, 7/21/36, Container 35, Farley Papers, Library of Congress.

"is the platform": HLI speech, 8/4/36, Container 282, Secretary of the Interior File, HLIP.

"It is notorious": HLI speech, 8/27/36, Container 283, *ibid.*

439   "Chairman Farley is apparently": Quoted in undated, unidentified news clipping, *ibid.*

Wilmarth's decline and death are recounted in HLI, "Untitled autobiographical draft," pp. 328–44. Unless otherwise specified, all quotes are from this source.

Details of Anna's will are from a report entitled "The Probate Proceedings" in Miscellany, Container 537, HLIP.

440   "but what I don't see": HLI, *Diary*, vol. I, pp. 438–39.

441   "The suicide note is copied": Quoted in unpublished HLI diary entry, 9/2/36, HLIP. To spare the family distress, I have chosen not to reproduce it here.

442   "The task on our part": FDR speech, 9/29/36, in Rosenman, *The Public Papers*, vol. V, p. 383.

443   "queer combination . . . hatred of Roosevelt": HLI speech, 10/9/36, Container 285, Secretary of the Interior File, HLIP.

"Landon's Angels": HLI speech, 10/19/36, Container 286, *ibid.*

"Governor Landon is a changeling": HLI speech, 10/20/36, *ibid.*

"You people who suffer": HLI speech, 10/21/36, Container 287, *ibid.*

"It is nothing short of tragic": HLI speech, 10/27/36, *ibid.*

444   "What manner of man is this": HLI speech, 10/28/36, Container 288, *ibid.*

"we expect a tremendous landslide": James A. Farley to Claude G. Bowers, 10/23/36, Container 35, Farley Papers, Library of Congress.

"It is all over now": HLI, *Diary*, vol. I, p. 703.

PART VII: A DEPARTMENT OF CONSERVATION

PAGE

445   "In a very real sense": HLI to Henry Wallace, 6/25/35, Container 261, Secretary of the Interior File, HLIP.

34. The House That Ickes Built

Except where otherwise noted, all material for this chapter is from *The Interior Building: Its Architecture and Its Art*, by David W. Look and Carole L. Perrault (Washington, D.C.: U.S. Department of the Interior, National Park Service, 1986).

PAGE

448 "I did talk it over": HLI, *Diary*, vol. I, p. 222.
"This should clear up": Quoted in Blum, *From the Morgenthau Diaries: Years of Crisis*, p. 88.
450 "The Secretary expressed": Edward Rowen to Millard Sheets, 7/2/37, Collection of Interior Department Museum.
"It seems to me pretty revolting": Edward Bruce to Millard Sheets 7/20/37, *Ibid*.
451 "gold and blue marble": Quoted in Look, *The Interior Building*, p. 17.
"As I view this": FDR, "Address at the Dedication of the New Department of Interior Building, Washington, D.C.," 4/16/36. In Rosenman, *The Public Papers*, Vol. V, p. 170.
"This new building": HLI, dedication speech, 4/16/36, Speeches and Writings, Container 280, Secretary of the Interior File, HLIP.

35. Cries in the Wilderness

The literature of conservation is, of course, enormous, although there is not yet a single comprehensive history of the whole movement. The closest thing we have to that is *John Muir and His Legacy: The American Conservation Movement*, by Stephen Fox (Boston: Little, Brown, 1981), and I borrow freely from that source throughout much of this chapter. Roderick Nash's seminal *Wilderness and the American Mind*, 3rd ed. (New Haven: Yale University Press, 1981) is still the most complete history of the literary, social, psychological, and spiritual background of the preservation movement, although it is surpassed in many respects by Frederick Turner's more general work, *Beyond Geography: The Western Spirit Against the Wilderness* (New York: The Viking Press, 1980). *These American Lands: Parks, Wilderness, and the Public Lands*, by Dyan Zaslowsky and The Wilderness Society, provides a good capsule history of the character and conservation of each of the major federal public land systems. *American Sportsmen and the Origins of Conservation*, by George Reiger (Lincoln: University of Nebraska Press, 1975), and *Theodore Roosevelt: The Making of a Conservationist*, by Paul Russell Cutright (Urbana: University of Illinois Press, 1985), both provide excellent companions to Pinchot's *Breaking New Ground* and Samuel P. Hayes's *The Gospel of Efficiency*. Of the several Muir biographies available, the best is the most recent: *Rediscovering America: John Muir in His Time and Ours*, by Frederick Turner (New York: The Viking Press, 1985). The two central figures of the wilderness movement in this century have finally been given their biographies: *A Wilderness Original: The Life of Bob Marshall*, by James M. Glover (Seattle: The Mountaineers, 1986), and *Aldo Leopold: His Life and Work*, by Curt Meine (Madison: University of

Wisconsin Press, 1988). The posthumously published memoirs of Irving Brant, *Adventures in Conservation with Franklin D. Roosevelt* (Flagstaff, Ariz.: Northland Publishing, 1989), have been long awaited—and now that they are available, are merely indispensable. So also are the two volumes of *Franklin D. Roosevelt and Conservation, 1911–1945*, compiled and edited by Edgar B. Nixon (Hyde Park, N.Y.: General Services Administration, National Archives and Records Service, Franklin D. Roosevelt Library, 1957).

PAGE

453 "The real trouble with the conservation": HLI, speech before annual Game Conference banquet, 1/22/35, Speeches and Writings, Container 274, Secretary of the Interior File, HLIP.

454 "The first duty": Pinchot, *Breaking New Ground*, p. 505.
"Conservation is the application": *Ibid.*, p. 507.

455 "The West of which I speak": Henry David Thoreau, "Walking," in *Henry David Thoreau: The Natural History Essays*, Literature of the American West Series (Layton, Utah: Peregrine Smith Books, 1984), pp. 112–17.

456 "lies the hope of the world": Quoted in Turner, *Rediscovering America*, p. 290.

457 "The battle we have fought": Quoted in Fox, *John Muir*, p. 107.
"wouldn't let me kill it": Pinchot, *Breaking New Ground*, p. 103.

458 "The destruction of the charming groves": Quoted in Dewitt Jones and T. H. Watkins, *John Muir's America* (Palo Alto, Calif.: American West, 1976), p. 132.

459 "as a barrier between": Quoted in Fox, *John Muir*, p. 154.
"work for the preservation": Quoted in Reiger, *American Sportsmen*, p. 119.

461 "I am weary": Quoted in Fox, *John Muir*, p. 159.
"The sportsmen are led": *Ibid.*, quoted, p. 167.

462 "in the belief": *Ibid.*, quoted, p. 172.
"bird sanctuaries should be": Brant, *Adventures in Conservation*, p. 5.
"which owing to entangled": Quoted in Fox, *John Muir*, p. 174.
"The Museum is": Quoted in Brant, *Adventures in Conservation*, p. 15.
"I presented the Audubon": *Ibid.*, p. 15.

463 "My entrance made a stir": Quoted in Fox, *John Muir*, pp. 174–75.
"impressed by her keen mind": Brant, *Adventures in Conservation*, p. 15.
"Slowly, painfully": *Ibid.*, p. 22.

464 "The committee fully deserved": *Ibid.*, p. 15.
"was, how far shall the Forest Service": Quoted in Meine, *Aldo Leopold*, p. 178.

465 "When the national forests were created": *Ibid.*, quoted, pp. 195–96.
"in order to preserve": *Ibid.*, p. 205.
"A Wilderness, in contrast" (note): Wilderness Act, 78 Stat. 890 (1964), 16 U.S.C.

466 "environment, transportation, habitation": Quoted in Zaslowsky, *These American Lands*, p. 208.
"A greatly increased program": Quoted in Glover, *A Wilderness Original*, p. 113.

"the Commanding General": Quoted in Meine, *Aldo Leopold*, p. 248.

467   "Just a few years more of hesitation": Robert Marshall, "The Problem of the Wilderness," *Scientific Monthly*, February 1930.

"a greatly increased amount": Robert Marshall, "The Forest for Recreation," in *A National Plan for American Forestry* (Washington, D.C.: Department of Agriculture, U.S. Forest Service, 1933), pp. 475–76.

468   "There is just one hope": Marshall, "The Problem of the Wilderness."

"The Wilderness Society does not plan": Robert Sterling Yard, "A Summons to Save the Wilderness," *The Living Wilderness*, September 1935.

"the propaganda spread": Quoted in Glover, *A Wilderness Original*, p. 182.

469   "so far ahead of any": *Ibid.*, quoted, p. 154.

"A forest is not solely": FDR to the Society of American Foresters, 1/29/35, in Nixon, *Franklin D. Roosevelt*, vol. I, p. 346.

470   "the smell of the woods": FDR, "We Seek to Pass On to Our Children a Richer Land—a Stronger Nation," address at dedication of Shenandoah National Park, 7/3/36. In Rosenman, *The Public Papers*, vol. V, p. 239.

"need for recreational areas": *Ibid.*

"It looks dead": Quoted in Fox, *John Muir*, p. 199.

"I love nature": HLI, NBC address, 3/3/34, Speeches and Writings, Container 272, Secretary of the Interior File, HLIP.

471   "I am not in favor of building": HLI speech before the State Park Authorities, 2/25/35, Speeches and Writings, Container 275, *ibid*.

472   "We are making a great mistake": Quoted in Glover, *A Wilderness Original*, p. 207.

36. The Dust Cloud That Voted

Literature on the Dust Bowl abounds. The best single history of the phenomenon is Donald R. Worster's *Dust Bowl: The Southern Plains in the 1930s* (New York: Oxford University Press, 1979). Two very different but equally interesting contemporary experiences are offered in *Dust Bowl Diary*, by Ann Marie Low (Lincoln: University of Nebraska Press, 1984), and *An Empire of Dust*, by Lawrence Svoboda (Caldwell, Id.: Caxton, 1940). Of the various accounts of the refugee experience, my personal preference includes two by Paul Schuster Taylor: *An American Exodus: A Record of Human Erosion*, with Dorothea Lange (New York: Reynal & Hitchcock, 1939), and *On the Ground in the Thirties* (Salt Lake City: Peregrine Smith Books, 1983); another good contemporary account is *America's Own Refugees: Our 4,000,000 Homeless Migrants*, by Henry Hill Collins, Jr. (Princeton, N.J.: Princeton University Press, 1941). The Taylor Grazing Act gets its best history in Louise Peffer's *The Closing of the Public Domain*, though Paul Gates's *History of Public Land Law Development* and Roy M. Robbins's *Our Landed Heritage* both have additional information to offer.

PAGE

474   "Their houses had gone": Quoted in Richard Lowitt, *The New Deal and the West* (Bloomington: Indiana University Press, 1984), p. 10.

"Approximately 35,000,000 acres": Milton S. Eisenhower, ed., *Yearbook of Agriculture, 1934* (Washington, D.C.: Department of Agriculture, 1934), p. 78. The statistics, prices, etc. in this chapter are from this edition of the *Yearbook*, as well as *Conservation in the United States*, A. F. Gustafson, *et al.* (Ithaca: Comstock Publishing Co., 1939); Gates, *History of Public Land Law Development*, and "Vacant Public Lands on July 1, 1932," General Land Office Circular No. 1282 (Washington, D.C.: Department of the Interior, 1932).

475   "An evil that is the twin": HLI, speech at dedication of first delivery of water from Hetch Hetchy Reservoir, 10/28/34, Speeches and Writings, Container 274, Secretary of the Interior File, HLIP.

"By mid-morning a gale was blowing": R. D. Lusk, "Life and Death of 470 Acres," *Saturday Evening Post*, August 13, 1938.

476   "Life in what the newspapers call": Low, *Dust Bowl Diary*, p. 98.

"I am half inclined to agree": HLI, *Diary*, vol. I, p. 259.

"I have not taken this matter up": Donald R. Richberg to FDR, 2/28/35, in Nixon, *Franklin D. Roosevelt*, vol. I, p. 358.

"I have the feeling": Henry A. Wallace to FDR, 3/7/35, in *ibid.*, p. 362.

477   "I have no disposition": HLI, *Diary*, vol. I, p. 326.

"This, gentlemen": Quoted in Worster, *Dust Bowl*, p. 213.

"Listen. If this country": *Ibid.*, quoted, p. 224.

"because the citizens": Quoted in Peffer, *The Closing of the Public Domain*, p. 217.

478   "pending its final disposal": Quoted in Ferdinand A. Silcox to Henry A. Wallace, 6/21/34, in Nixon, *Franklin D. Roosevelt*, vol. I, p. 308.

"within or near a district": *Ibid.*, p. 313.

479   "shall be denied": Quoted in note, *ibid.*, p. 294.

"heretofore enacted": Quoted in note, *ibid.*, p. 313.

"*Provided*, however, that": *Ibid.*

"It is not now": Silcox to Wallace, in Nixon, *Franklin D. Roosevelt*, vol. I, pp. 308–13.

480   "a graduate of Harvard": HLI, *Diary*, vol. I, p. 229.

"naively said that he had told": *Ibid.*, p. 230.

481   "I want to emphasize": HLI, speech before conference of western officials, 2/12/35, Speeches and Writings, Container 275, Secretary of the Interior File, HLIP.

482   "I am of the philosophy": Quoted in Watkins and Watson, *The Lands No One Knows*, p. 119.

"set up an Advisory Committee": HLI, *Diary*, vol. II, p. 101.

"free-loading on the public domain": Quoted in Wyant, *Westward in Eden*, p. 312.

37. Stewardship and Strife

There are two excellent studies of the reorganization effort in Roosevelt's administration, and I have used both to guide me through this singularly nasty patch of history—not only in this chapter, but in parts of chapters 40 and 41 as well. Barry

Karl's studious *Executive Reorganization and Reform in the New Deal: The Genesis of Administrative Management, 1900–1939* (Cambridge, Mass.: Harvard University Press, 1963), as its title suggests, is not for the general reader. Richard Polenberg's *Reorganizing Roosevelt's Government, 1936–1939: The Controversy Over Executive Reorganization* (Cambridge, Mass.: Harvard University Press, 1966) is equally authoritative but much more accessible—even lively at times. Other sources as noted.

PAGE

484   "all bureaus primarily devoted": Brant, *Adventures in Conservation*, p. 36.

485   "Before any man enters": Quoted in Polenberg, *Reorganizing Roosevelt's Government*, p. 7.

      "instead of the National Forests": HLI, *Diary*, vol. I, p. 23.

      "I heard the disturbing rumor": HLI, speech before the American Civic Association, 4/19/33, Speeches and Writings, Container 269, Secretary of the Interior File, HLIP.

      "Should the Park Service go": Quoted in Richard Polenberg, "The Great Conservation Contest," *Forest History*, January 1967.

486   "I told him that I believed": HLI, *Diary*, vol. I, p. 151.

      "The old quarrel": Rexford Tugwell, Diary, pp. 35–36, Tugwell Papers, FDRL.

487   "discussed with him": HLI, *Diary*, vol. I, p. 161.

      "I visited in May": Henry Wallace, oral memoirs, p. 306, OHCU.

      "still of the same mind": Tugwell, Diary, pp. 154–55.

488   "had made it so clear": HLI to Henry Wallace, 6/25/35, Container 155, Secretary of the Interior File, HLIP.

      "if we are in the highest": HLI, speech before American Game Conference dinner, 1/22/35, Speeches and Writings, Container 274, *ibid.*

      "It seemed that Secretary Ickes": Wallace, oral memoirs, pp. 321–22.

      "authorized me to say": *Ibid.*, pp. 325–26.

      "like to have all": HLI, *Diary*, vol. I, p. 328.

489   "All right, go ahead": *Ibid.*, p. 344.

      "all right": *Ibid.*, p. 347.

      "a metaphysical discussion": HLI, *Diary*, vol. I, pp. 364–65.

      "I told him": *Ibid.*, p. 385.

490   "pre-eminent in conservation matters": Quoted in Polenberg, *Reorganizing Roosevelt's Government*, p. 7.

      "The committee had to adjourn": HLI, *Diary*, vol. I, p. 386.

      "discretion and finesse": Quoted in Polenberg, *Reorganizing Roosevelt's Government*, p. 7.

491   "There isn't any doubt": HLI, *Diary*, vol. I, p. 418.

      "because your views": HLI to H. H. Chapman, 8/19/36, Container 261, Secretary of the Interior File, HLIP.

      "Congress will be in session": HLI to Harry Slattery, 9/30/35, SPDU.

492   "Secretary Ickes is pushing it": Robert Sterling Yard to Charles C. Moore, 1/25/36, TWS/DPL.

492   "I at once called": HLI, *Diary*, vol. I, p. 597.
       "the real student of history": HLI, NBC address, 5/16/36, Speeches and
       Writings, Container 280, Secretary of the Interior File, HLIP.
493   "I do not believe it": HLI, *Diary*, vol. I, p. 602.
       "broken faith": *Ibid.*, p. 605.

38. Territorial Imperatives

Ruth Tabrah's *Hawaii: A History* (New York: W. W. Norton, 1984) provides a good
general history of the islands. The first few chapters of *Revolt in Paradise: The Social
Revolution in Hawaii After Pearl Harbor*, by Alexander MacDonald (New York:
Stephen Daye, 1944), were useful in establishing the economic structure of the place.
The Massie trial is covered in considerable detail—and remarkable objectivity, given
the fact that he was involved—by Lawrence M. Judd in his autobiography, *Lawrence
M. Judd & Hawaii* (Rutland, Ver.: Charles E. Tuttle, 1971). As the page notes
indicate, the level of participation in Hawaiian matters on the part of Ickes was
limited once the decision had been made to name the new governor—and the impact
of the New Deal in general was light. There was a good deal more going on in the
Virgin Islands, however, and a particularly valuable guide through that particular
jungle was John Frederick Grede's unpublished dissertation, "The New Deal in the
Virgin Islands, 1931–1941" (University of Chicago, August 1962). Thomas G.
Mathews's own dissertation, "Puerto Rican Politics and the New Deal" (Columbia
University, 1957), was similarly invaluable for Puerto Rican matters, which, if
anything, were more difficult to unravel than those of the Virgin Islands. Further
guidance came from *Puerto Rico: A Political and Cultural History*, by Arturo Morales
Carrión (New York: W. W. Norton, 1983), and *Transformation: The Story of Modern
Puerto Rico*, by Earl Hanson (New York: Simon and Schuster, 1955), which is useful
and entertaining in spite of the sound of an ax being ground.

PAGE

496   "Despite all this mingling": Wilbur, *Conservation in the Department of the
       Interior*, p. 198.
497   "On the upper crust": Quoted in Millicent Bell, *Marquand: An American Life*
       (Boston: Little, Brown, 1977), p. 192.
       "the beachcombers and the bums"; "the slum dwellers": *Ibid.*, p. 193.
       "Honolulu is not safe": Quoted in Judd, *Laurence M. Judd*, p. 176.
498   "We, as members of": *Ibid.*, quoted, p. 201.
       "very conservative senators": *Ibid.*
499   "feeling of personal guilt": *Ibid.*, p. 203.
       "very delicate situation": HLI to Dean Harry Bigelow, 3/31/33, Container
       167, Secretary of the Interior File, HLIP.
500   "In a fine old prayer": FDR, "Extemporaneous Remarks in Hawaii," 7/28/34,
       in Rosenman, *The Public Papers*, vol. III, p. 350.
       "there cut the terrible swift sword": Tabrah, *Hawaii*, p. 153.
503   "an effective poorhouse": Quoted in Grede, "The New Deal," p. 87.

505   Note: The undated communication is in SPDU.
      "I, together with other loyal": Quoted in Grede, "The New Deal," p. 114.
      "I am responsible only to": Ibid., quoted, p. 115.
506   "Judas and Benedict Arnold": Ibid., quoted.
      "more strongly than ever": HLI, Diary, vol. I, p. 298.
      "I thought I would have it out": Ibid., p. 301.
507   The hallway fight (note) is recorded in Grede, "The New Deal," p. 126.
      "we ought to fight": HLI, Diary, vol. I, p. 393.
      "very suave and unctuous": Ibid., p. 391.
      "Have you plans": HLI, press conference, 7/9/35, Hopkins Papers, FDRL.
      "whitewashing": Quoted in Grede, "The New Deal," p. 128.
      "If in the future": Ibid.
508   "went after Tydings": HLI, Diary, vol. I, p. 395.
      "I told him": Ibid., p. 401.
509   "My respect for Pearson": Ibid.
510   "a fine person": Diary, vol. II, p. 94.
      "Tydings will be a candidate": Ibid.
511   "I hope that time will prove": Quoted in Grede, "The New Deal," p. 247.
      "a tragic joke": HLI, The Secret Diary of Harold L. Ickes, Volume III:
      The Lowering Clouds, 1939–1941 (New York: Simon & Schuster, 1954),
      p. 443.
      "Never in my ten years": Quoted in Grede, "The New Deal," p. 234.
      "Certainly . . . had the appearance": HLI, Diary, vol. I, p. 508.
512   "the worst slums": Ibid., p. 504.
513   "The Puerto Rican is said": Ibid., p. 505.
514   "are beyond doubt the dirtiest": Quoted in Mathews, "Puerto Rican Politics,"
      p. 50.
      "Puerto Rico . . . has been": HLI to Duncan N. Fletcher, 1/15/35, Container
      255, Secretary of the Interior File, HLIP.
515   "to the ownership and control": Quoted in Mathews, "Puerto Rican Politics,"
      p. 312.
516   "chews gum": Ibid., quoted, p. 82.
      "They hate this new governor": Ibid., quoted, pp. 147–48.
      "I hope that mere politics": Ibid., quoted, p. 167.
518   "full control over": Nathan Margold to HLI, undated, Container 255, Secre-
      tary of the Interior File, HLIP.
519   "a southern gentleman": Hanson, Transformation, p. 164.
      "frequent suggestions, recommendations": Ernest Gruening to HLI, 7/15/35,
      Container 255, Secretary of the Interior File, HLIP.
520   "it would have been much better": Quoted in Mathews, "Puerto Rican
      Politics," p. 391.
      "although I am convinced": Ernest Gruening to HLI, 3/13/36, SPDU.
521   "I strongly urged": HLI, Diary, vol. I, p. 547.
      "double and triple": Quoted in Mathews, "Puerto Rican Politics," p. 377.
522   "The picture is this": Luis Muñoz Marín to Ruby Black, 10/26/36, Container
      255, Secretary of the Interior File, HLIP.

"such amazing incompetence": Quoted in Mathews, "Puerto Rican Politics," p. 450.

"if there should be": *Ibid.*, quoted.

524   "that you request me": HLI to Blanton Winship, 5/21/37, Container 257, Secretary of the Interior File, HLIP. The radiogram was sent in naval code; for the curious, a portion of the undeciphered message reads as follows: "ISUHDHUMUA SESAWEPH CABNIEAZ FAVOMHUMUI EGZELKEG DYBACK. . . ."

"Did you get my radiogram?": HLI conversation with Blanton Winship, 5/24/37, Container 257, Secretary of the Interior File, HLIP.

525   "There isn't any doubt": HLI, *Diary*, vol. II, p. 13.

"Governor Winship said": *Ibid.*, p. 149.

"What is happening": HLI to Harry Slattery, 6/2/37, Container 257, Secretary of the Interior File, HLIP.

526   "This is flagrant insubordination": HLI to Harry Slattery, 6/4/37, *ibid.*

"At this particular time": FDR to HLI, 6/9/37, *ibid.*

"I hope that we do not find ourselves": HLI to FDR, 6/9/37, *ibid.*

"the entire staff of the PRRA": Hanson, *Transformation*, p. 191.

527   "I asked Gruening": HLI, *Diary*, vol. II, pp. 160–61.

528   "planners must control the people": Walter Lippmann, "Planning in an Economy of Abundance," in Howard Zinn, ed., *New Deal Thought* (Indianapolis: Bobbs-Merrill, 1966), pp. 101–2.

529   "Five years have seen the New Deal": Raymond Clapper, *Watching the World* (New York: McGraw-Hill, 1944), p. 129.

39. The Most Forgotten American

The best general survey of the cultural history of the American Indian through the nineteenth century remains Peter Farb's *Man's Rise to Civilization as Seen in the Indians of North America from Primeval Times to the Coming of the Industrial State* (New York: E. P. Dutton, 1968); a revised edition, with the title shortened to *Man's Rise to Civilization*, was issued by the same publisher in 1978. Alvin Josephy's *The Indian Heritage of America* (New York: Alfred A. Knopf, 1968) gives excellent summaries of the clash of white and Indian civilizations, while S. Lyman Tyler's *A History of American Indian Policy* (Washington, D.C.: Department of the Interior, Bureau of Indian Affairs, 1973), for all the fact that it is a government publication, is a clear and objective discussion of the largely idiotic fumbling that characterized official Washington's relationship to the Native American population. *A Century of Dishonor*, by Helen Hunt Jackson (reprint edition, New York: Harper & Row, 1965), even though it was written and published in 1881 amid the white heat of nineteenth-century reformism, remains both an accurate and an astonishingly powerful indictment. *The Problem of Indian Administration*, edited by Lewis Meriam (Baltimore: Johns Hopkins University Press, 1928), is the best single source regarding the condition of the Indians just prior to the New Deal years, while for both that period and all the years that followed, John Collier's *From Every Zenith* (cited above), as noted earlier, must be used with extreme caution. An excellent guide in this respect is Kenneth R. Philps's *John Collier's Crusade for Indian Reform, 1920–1954* (Tucson:

University of Arizona Press, 1977), the best study of the man and his Indian work available. The Byzantine world of congressional committees and American Indian policy in the Collier years is examined in exquisite detail in "The New Deal for Indians: A Study in Bureau-Committee Relations in American Government," a dissertation by John Leiper Freeman, Jr. (Princeton, N.J.: Princeton University Press, 1952).

PAGE

530   "It is the nature of human ecology": John Greenway, *Folklore of the Great West* (Palo Alto, Calif.: American West, 1968), p. 132.

       "The progress of our settlements": Quoted in Watkins and Watson, *The Lands No One Knows*, pp. 209–10.

531   "The utter absence of": Quoted in Jackson, *A Century of Dishonor*, p. 341.

532   Land and population statistics are derived from "Dawes Severalty Act," by Fred Niklason in Howard Lamar, ed., *The Reader's Encyclopedia of the American West*, (New York: Thomas Y. Crowell, 1977), pp. 290–91; and U.S. Bureau of the Census, *The Statistical History*, pp. 14, 430.

533   "grossly inadequate": Meriam, *The Problem of Indian Administration*, p. 33.

       "resulted in much loss": *Ibid.*, p. 44.

534   "a pickle and let it howl": *Washington Star*, March 21, 1929.

       "The Indian should be developed": Wilbur and Du Puys, *Conservation in the Department of the Interior*, p. 125.

       "Even after twenty-five years": William Zimmerman, Jr., "The Role of the Bureau of Indian Affairs Since 1933," *The Annals*, May 1957.

       "The discovery that came to me": Collier, *From Every Zenith*, p. 126.

535   "No interference": Quoted in Tyler, *A History of American Indian Policy*, p. 128.

       "a powerful stimulus": Zimmerman, "The Role of the Bureau."

       "It was urged": HLI, *Diary*, vol. I, p. 51.

539   "It will be properly asked": Quoted in Freeman, "The New Deal for Indians," pp. 142–43.

540   "It was anticipated": *Ibid.*, quoted, pp. 203–4.

543   "if native communities are to": Quoted in *The State of Alaska: A Definitive History of America's Northernmost Frontier*, by Ernest Gruening (New York: Random House, 1968), p. 365.

       "would have a massive and dramatic": Quoted in Philp, *John Collier's Crusade*, p. 140.

       "new collective advantages": *Ibid.*, quoted, p. 161.

       "The Indian folk-life has not": *Ibid.*, quoted, pp. 270–71.

544   "must be a collaboration"; "psychically, religiously, socially": Quoted in Philps, "John Collier's Crusade," p. 140.

545   "American civilization and citizenship"; "Russian communistic life"; "Communism instead of Americanism": *Ibid.*, quoted, p. 172.

       "a dangerous agitator": HLI, *Diary*, vol. II, p. 507.

546   "My only reason for trying": In "Excerpts from Remarks by Senator Wheeler at the Senate Indian Affairs Committee Meeting, April 5, 1937," SPDU.

"I could not at the hearing": John Collier to Burton K. Wheeler, 4/5/37, SPDU.

547 "Only a ripe and imaginative scholar": Quoted in introduction to *Felix Cohen's Handbook of Federal Indian Law*, revised edition (Charlottesville, Vir.: The Michie Company, 1982), viii.

"What has made this work possible": *Ibid.*, xi.

40. Keeper of the Jewels

The best studies of the evolution of national park policy are Ronald A. Foresta, *America's National Parks and Their Keepers* (Washington, D.C.: Resources for the Future, 1984); Alfred Runte, *The National Parks: An American Experience* (Lincoln: University of Nebraska Press, 1979); and Joseph Sax, *Mountains Without Handrails: Reflections on the National Parks* (Ann Arbor: University of Michigan Press, 1981). William C. Everhart's *The National Park Service* (Boulder, Colo.: Westview Press, 1983) is a good, straightforward history of the agency itself. The story of the transfer of military parks and national monuments is told in some detail in Horace Albright's *The Birth of the National Park Service*. For the continuing reorganization fight, Karl's *Executive Reorganization and Reform*, Polenberg's *Reorganizing Roosevelt's Government*, and Polenberg's article "The Great Conservation Fight," in *Forest History* (January 1967) were essential. On the Olympic and Kings Canyon park battles, I relied heavily on the greatly detailed firsthand accounts in Irving Brant's memoirs, *Adventures in Conservation with Franklin D. Roosevelt*. Important sources for the story of Olympic include Robert E. Ficken, *The Forested Land: A History of Lumbering in Western Washington* (Durham, N.C.: Forest History Society; Seattle: University of Washington Press, 1987); Guy Fringer, "Olympic National Park," an unpublished manuscript written for the National Archives and Records Service (Washington, D.C., 1985); and Murray Morgan, *The Last Wilderness* (New York: The Viking Press, 1955; Seattle: University of Washington Press, 1976). My discussion of the creation of Kings Canyon National Park was given a new dimension by the discovery of a cache of primary materials in the collection of the park itself (cited here as KCNPA), material that had not yet been incorporated in the National Archives. In the understanding of these and all other conservation subjects, Edgar B. Nixon's *Franklin D. Roosevelt and Conservation* was immeasurably important.

PAGE

549 "Gentlemen, I do not have": In "Address of the Honorable Harold L. Ickes," transcribed remarks in "Proceedings of National Parks Superintendents' Conference," November 19, 1934, TWS/DPL. All of Ickes's remarks to the superintendents are from this source.

552 "As usual, he sat by my desk": HLI, *Diary*, vol. II, p. 584.

"the Secretary flatly refused": Albright, *The Birth of the National Park Service*, p. 306.

"He told me at the time": Robert Sterling Yard to Harvey Broome, 6/20/40, TWS/DPL.

553   "Road-building is zealously guarded against": In "Proceedings of National Park Service Superintendents' Conference," November 22, 1934, TWS/DPL.

554   "There seem to be two policies": Benton MacKaye to Robert Marshall, 5/10/35, TWS/DPL.

      "Last week . . . we indirectly ran": Robert Sterling Yard to Waldo G. Leland, 7/6/36, TWS/DPL.

556   "The said area or areas": In *Laws Relating to the National Park Service*, Supplement 1 (Washington, D.C.: Department of the Interior, 1944), p. 35.

557   "barring revolution": Quoted in Polenberg, *Reorganizing Roosevelt's Government*, p. 22.

      "Henry Wallace pricked up his ears": HLI, *Diary*, vol. II, p. 23.

558   "Keep away from saying": Quoted in Polenberg, *Reorganizing Roosevelt's Government*, p. 29.

      "that the President would shortly": HLI, *Diary*, vol. II, p. 33.

      "we ought to keep conservation": *Ibid.*, pp. 39–42.

559   "My Dear Henry": HLI to Henry A. Wallace, 1/8/37, Container 261, Secretary of the Interior File, HLIP.

      "Dear Harold": Henry A. Wallace to HLI, 1/9/37, *ibid.*

560   "the most dangerous attack": Copy of Pinchot speech in Container 226, *ibid.*

      "Gifford Pinchot, who is": Container 226, Secretary of the Interior File, HLIP.

      "Finally, a copy appeared" (note): Quoted in Polenberg, *Reorganizing Roosevelt's Government*, p. 67.

561   "makes it perfectly clear": Quoted in Polenberg, *Reorganizing Roosevelt's Government*, p. 108.

562   "most of the timber still left": Quoted in Brant, *Adventures in Conservation*, p. 72.

563   "so inaccurate that it deserves": Quoted in Fringer, "Olympic National Park," p. 91.

      "much valuable timber": *Ibid.*, quoted, p. 92.

      "several towns on the Peninsula": *Ibid.*, quoted, p. 95.

      "the map will be submitted": *Ibid.*

564   Irving Brant: The Olympic National Park project was only one conservation crusade Brant was involved with at the time. He was also spending considerable energy in trying to save a ninety-six-hundred-acre grove of ancient sugar pines in California. The "Carl Inn Grove," situated on the southern border of Yosemite National Park, had been left out of the park in 1890 because of the cost of purchasing the land from its private owner and because in those years the supply of sugar pines seemed inexhaustible. By the 1930s, however, logging had eliminated most of the oldest sugar pines left in the Sierra Nevada and now threatened this grove of particularly magnificent specimens. In spite of objections from the Forest Service—Wallace complaining over the cost—Brant, with Ickes's enthusiastic cooperation and some arm-twisting help from Roosevelt, spearheaded a successful drive to get Congress to authorize the purchase of the grove for $1.5 million in August 1937, whereupon it was finally added to the national park. Brant tells the story in *Adventures in Conservation*, pp. 55–68.

"I had made some comment": Irving Brant to HLI, 2/13/36, in Nixon, *Franklin D. Roosevelt*, vol. I, p. 484.

"It turned out that I put": Brant, *Adventures in Conservation*, p. 97.

565   "He is all the more effective": HLI, *Diary*, vol. II, p. 338.

"I understand that there is": FDR to HLI and Henry A. Wallace, 2/18/36, in Nixon, *Franklin D. Roosevelt*, vol. I, p. 485.

"I deem it advisable": Homer Cummings to FDR, 5/22/36, in Nixon, *Franklin D. Roosevelt*, vol. I, p. 525.

"The power of the Forest Service": Quoted in Fringer, "Olympic National Park," p. 106.

566   "As you know, there have been": *Ibid.*, quoted, p. 109.

"a shocking retreat": Quoted in Brant, *Adventures in Conservation*, p. 79.

"Silcox and I are just": *Ibid.*, quoted, p. 80.

"According to the Forest Service.": *ibid.*, pp. 80–81.

"I do not believe that Mr. Silcox": *Ibid.*, p. 81.

"Please, Mr. President"; "Mr. Mayor and friends of Port Angeles": Quoted in Fringer, "Olympic National Park," pp. 114–15.

567   "I hope the son-of-a-bitch": Quoted in Morgan, *The Last Wilderness*, p. 185.

"made a shambles": Quoted in Brant, *Adventures in Conservation*, p. 105.

"was all that could be desired": *Ibid.*, p. 105.

568   "Bang! That was over.": *Ibid.*, p. 113.

"The Secretary had taken a strong": *Ibid.*, pp. 115–16.

569   "There is no doubt whatever": John R. White to Arno B. Cammerer, 5/12/33, KCNPA.

"There is a good deal of difference": Arno B. Cammerer to John R. White, 11/18/33, KCNPA.

570   "This park will be treated": HLI to Arno B Cammerer, 9/20/35, KCNPA.

"If I was outside the government": Quoted in Glover, *A Wilderness Original*, p. 234.

571   "in the full spirit of its adopted": In "Minutes of Kings River Meeting Called by San Joaquin Council, California State Chamber of Commerce, October 25, 1937," KCNPA.

"The problem of Kings Canyon": Brant, *Adventures in Conservation*, p. 151.

572   "The whole thing was": *Ibid.*, quoted, p. 156.

"The water must be impounded": *Ibid.*

"The Forest Service will fight": In "Forest Service Will Fight National Park Extensions," press release from California Region office, U.S. Forest Service, 12/2/38, KCNPA.

"the amoral national administration": S. Bevier Show, oral memoirs (interview by Amelia Fry, 1965), pp. 195–96, courtesy, the BL.

573   "I can't control the Forest Service": Brant, *Adventures in Conservation*, p. 161.

574   "I am told that your instructions": *Ibid.*, quoted, p. 161.

"I am told that at the Senate": *Ibid.*, quoted, p. 162.

"This conference was well attended": HLI, *Diary*, Vol. II, p. 578.

575   "At this point let me": In "A National Park for Kings Canyon," speech before Commonwealth Club, 2/15/39, KCNPA.

"In view of this startling information": Quoted in Brant, *Adventures in Conservation*, pp. 184–85.

577 "I have just had the opportunity": *Ibid.*, quoted, p. 211.

"which can be properly safeguarded": Quoted in Glover, *A Wilderness Original*, p. 256.

"I'm quite sure": Robert Sterling Yard to Anne Newman, 6/2/39, TWS/DPL.

"I feel now that I can": Quoted in Fox, *John Muir*, pp. 216–17.

578 "Just a word of appreciation": Quoted in Brant, *Adventures in Conservation*, p. 219.

"would run the Park Service": HLI, *Diary*, vol. III, p. 103.

579 "I was amazed": Robert Sterling Yard to Mrs. C. C. Marshall, 6/21/40, TWS/DPL.

"The United States, rich beyond all other": In "A National Park for Kings Canyon," speech before the Commonwealth Club, 2/15/39, KCNPA.

41. In the Arms of Disappointment

PAGE

581 "When we look up and down": Quoted in Zaslowsky, *These American Lands*, pp. 31–32.

"the right of the Park Service": HLI to FDR, 12/20/37, in Nixon, *Franklin D. Roosevelt*, vol. II, p. 158.

582 "follow my own will": HLI, statement of 11/12/37, *ibid.*, pp. 160–61.

"Asking each other why" (note): Robert Sterling Yard to Catherine Mitchell, 11/15/37, TWS/DPL.

583 "the real question involved": HLI to *Mining World*, 8/7/40, in Nixon, *Franklin D. Roosevelt*, Vol. II, p. 463. The story of the attempt to set aside the canyon country of southern Utah is most comprehensively told in Elmo R. Richardson, "The Escalante National Monument Controversy of 1935–1940," *Utah Historical Quarterly*, Spring 1965.

"If this bill for national park wilderness": HLI, "A National Park for Kings Canyon," speech before Commonwealth Club, 2/15/39, KCNPA. To the best of my knowledge, this was the first legislative attempt to create a wilderness system ever proposed—not to be repeated until 1956, when Senator Hubert Humphrey introduced a wilderness bill crafted by Howard Zahniser of The Wilderness Society. Revised sixty-six times, the bill culminated in the Wilderness Act of September 3, 1964.

584 "dictatorial authority": William R. Green, president of the AF of L, quoted in Polenberg, *Reorganizing Roosevelt's Government*, p. 84.

"such tremendous control": New York State Chamber of Commerce, *ibid.*, quoted, p. 88.

585 "I have come to the conclusion": HLI, Unpublished Diary Segment, 7/1/37, HLIP.

"I call your attention": Gifford Pinchot, speech before Izaak Walton League, 10/11/37, Container 226, Secretary of the Interior File, HLIP.

"This is an outrageous statement": HLI, press release, 10/12/37, *ibid.*

586   "Roosevelt surrounded himself": Henry A. Wallace, oral memoirs, p. 434, OHCU.

"As to the present reorganization bill": HLI, *Diary*, vol. II, p. 305.

"I told him that in every issue": *Ibid.*, pp. 308–9.

587   "Now it remains to be seen": *Ibid.*, p. 603.

"hit me harder than any other man": *Ibid.*, p. 623.

588   "How about Forestry?": This and rest of dialogue quoted *ibid.*, p. 660.

"For six years"; "My Dear Harold": *Ibid.*, pp. 667–74. Both Ickes's letter and FDR's reply are reproduced in their entirety in the *Diary*.

"conscientiously ask that you transfer": *Ibid.*, quoted, vol. III, p. 127.

"The President hit the ceiling": *Ibid.*, p. 128.

589   "We—you & I": *Ibid.*, quoted, p. 131.

"As I watch the unfolding pageant": Quoted in Meine, *Aldo Leopold*, pp. 402–3.

"would smash the whole legislative situation": Gifford Pinchot, quoted in Richard Polenberg, "The Great Conservation Contest."

590   "his mind as clear as ever": HLI, *Diary*, vol. III, p. 110.

"I was particularly struck": *Ibid.*, p. 111.

"sadistic hate"; "overweening and ruthless ambition"; "The war waged by the Forest Service": In HLI, "Not Guilty, Richard A. Ballinger—An American Dreyfus," *Saturday Evening Post*, May 25, 1940.

"a pretty lugubrious gathering": HLI, *Diary*, vol. II, p. 664.

591   "You have done a job": CHMI.

PART VIII: CURMUDGEON'S WAY

PAGE

593   "As I see it": HLI to Raymond Robins, 7/5/40, Container 162, Secretary of the Interior File, HLIP.

42. Love at the Headwaters

My story of the love affair and marriage of Ickes and Jane Dahlman is taken mostly from that portion of Ickes's personal memoirs designated "Untitled Autobiographical Draft," Container 435, HLIP; personal letters and memorabilia in the collections of Harold McEwen Ickes (CHMI); and various parts of the three published diaries. Eleanor Patterson's life has been most handsomely chronicled in Ralph Martin's *Cissy*. See also Paul F. Healy, *Cissy: The Biography of Eleanor M. "Cissy" Patterson* (Garden City, N.Y.: Doubleday & Co., 1966).

PAGE

596   "She has always stood by me": HLI, "Untitled Autobiographical Draft," pp. 1–4 of insert for p. 27.

"as a small person": Leona Graham Gerard to author, 9/14/84.

"They are terrible": HLI, *Diary*, vol. I, p. 440.

597 "Mrs. Patterson is a very interesting": *Ibid.*, p. 44.

"Dear Mr. Secretary": Eleanor Patterson to HLI, 9/22/33, CHMI.

598 "Dear Cissy": HLI to Eleanor Patterson, 9/26/33, CHMI.

"Cissy noticed that I was": HLI, *Diary*, vol. I, p. 662.

599 "I had a note from Jane": HLI, "Untitled Autobiographical Draft," pp. 424–25. There is a curious inconsistency in his recollection of the date of this encounter. In the unpublished memoirs cited here he says that the meeting took place in the spring of 1936. In his published *Diary* (vol. II, pp. 400–401), however, he says it took place in the *fall* of 1936. Both are impossible. Since other evidence indicates that she was already working for the Park Service as early as November 1935—and since he contradicts himself again in the diary itself when he mentions that they went to the movies together after Thanksgiving dinner in 1935—the only logical time for her to have come down from Massachusetts seems to be fall 1935, not 1936. It is possible that he got confused about his dates (though it was rare for him to get *this* confused), but I think he may have been a little nervous about letting the world (even Miss Conley) know just how soon after Anna's death he had become interested in Jane, and I think further that for much the same reason Jane may have let the little deception stand in her edited version of the diaries.

600 "Jane Dahlman and I had dinner": HLI, *Diary*, vol. I, p. 499.

"Tom Corcoran brought his accordion": *Ibid.*, p. 527.

"Jane was happy to get": *Ibid.*, p. 528.

"They had a terrible time": HLI, "Unpublished Autobiographical Draft," p. 427.

601 "Jane, dearest, I love you": HLI to Jane Dahlman, 5/16/36, CHMI.

"I know you love me deeply": HLI to Jane Dahlman, 5/20/36, CHMI.

"This was the worst summer": HLI, "Untitled Autobiographical Draft," p. 428.

"unexpurgated, my dear!": Jane Dahlman to HLI, 7/17/36, CHMI.

602 "She had been in Washington": HLI, "Untitled Autobiographical Draft," p. 429.

603 "awfully fond of the Secretary": *Washington Herald*, May 25, 1938 (in a news story about their marriage).

"I was so glad": HLI, *Diary*, vol. II, p. 160.

"Harold, dearest Harold": Jane Dahlman to HLI, 12/30/37, CHMI.

"For days at a time": HLI, "Untitled Autobiographical Draft," p. 431. Jane had recovered enough by January 18 to meet him in Chicago and drive him out to pick up a few things from the house in Hubbard Woods, now unoccupied and up for sale. "The house does look rather gaunt and bare," he wrote in his diary. "I have had no nibbles for it. One thing comforts me, however, and that is that there is very little desirable vacant land left in Winnetka, and if the worst comes to the worst I can tear down the house and sell off the land at a good price. . . . It would well nigh break my heart, however, to tear down a house that not only is beautiful and livable but was built to stand a thousand years" (*Diary*, vol. II, p. 299). In the end, the house found a buyer and he did not have to tear it down.

604 "As to my side of the family": HLI, "Untitled Autobiographical Draft," p. 432.

"I want you to know": Jane Dahlman to HLI, 4/13/38, CHMI.

"My God in heaven": Jane Dahlman to HLI, 4/21/38, CHMI.

"I regret that you are": Frederick Dahlman to Jane Dahlman, 5/19/38, CHMI.

605 "as a great love affair": Interview with Harold M. Ickes, 5/27/89.

"better in this respect": HLI, *Diary*, vol. II, p. 401.

"I found him perfectly fine": *Ibid.*

"Of course, I scoffed": *Ibid.*, p. 403.

"Affectionate greetings": FDR to HLI, 5/24/38, President's Personal File, FDRL.

606 "I did not care for her": HLI, *Diary*, vol. II, p. 407.

"a dumpy-looking person": *Ibid.*, p. 406.

"From our hotel we sallied forth": *Ibid.*, p. 406.

"I never came to America": *Washington Herald*, June 22, 1938.

607 "Are you happy?": *Ibid.*, 6/23/38.

"I have thanked God": HLI, *Diary*, vol. II, p. 410.

43. Inside Passages

Alaska's history is competently told by its former governor (and later senator) Ernest Gruening, in *The State of Alaska: A Definitive History of America's Northernmost Frontier*, though it is both irritating and amusing to note the author's prejudices against the New Deal (with which the former head of the Division of Territories and Island Possessions had become thoroughly disenchanted over the years). With that borne in mind, it is still a useful history. Harry A. Franck's brief junket to the Great Land was recounted in the somewhat slapdash travelogue style of the time in *The Lure of Alaska* (New York: National Travel Club, 1939). The remarkable story of the Matanuska Colony is admirably documented in Orlando W. Miller, *The Frontier in Alaska and the Matanuska Colony* (New Haven: Yale University Press, 1975). The love affair and marriage of Anna Roosevelt and John Boettiger is told in their son's touching and lovingly honest memoir, *A Love in Shadow*, by John R. Boettiger (New York: W. W. Norton & Co., 1978). The journal that Jane Ickes kept during their Alaska travels fills only a few pages of a bound notebook in the Harold M. Ickes collection. It is too bad that she was not as resolute about "journaling" as her husband—she wrote with wit, style, and most of the time with a sharp and telling eye for detail.

PAGE

609 "has thrown a terrific burden": HLI, *Diary*, vol. II, p. 411.

"It did not take more than a superficial glance": *Ibid.*, p. 437.

"It is the intention": *Ibid.*, p. 438.

610 "a delightful person": *Ibid.*, p. 439.

"Ketchikan is built": Franck, *The Lure of Alaska*, p. 5.

611   "a typical Alaskan town": HLI, *Diary,* vol. II, p. 441.

"a government-built town": Franck, *The Lure of Alaska*, p. 53.

"It has been ascertained": Quoted in Miller, *The Frontier in Alaska and the Matanuska Colony*, pp. 37–38.

612   "The trouble is that": Franck, *The Lure of Alaska*, p. 45.

"it has been a failure": HLI, *Diary*, vol. II, p. 442.

"sentimental social service people": *Ibid.*

"lazy settlers who won't work": *Ibid.*, p. 443.

613   "I am willing to accept it": *Ibid.*

"Rolling into the park": Jane Ickes journal, August 1938, CHMI.

"[The hotel] is larger": Franck, *The Lure of Alaska*, p. 24.

"all the colonists" (note): *Ibid.*, p. 461.

614   "The chief drawback": HLI, *Diary*, vol. II, pp. 444–45.

615   "That is the usual politician's": Franck, *The Lure of Alaska*, p. 279.

"I was delighted": HLI, *Diary*, vol. II, p. 447.

"ramshackle, squalid": *Ibid.*

"I was shocked": *Ibid.*, p. 449.

616   "It is the best built": *Ibid.*, p. 452.

"Three months ago, in Dublin": Jane Ickes journal, August 1938, CHMI.

"I spoke extemporaneously": HLI, *Diary*, vol. II, p. 455.

44. Reductive Politics

Virtually everyone who had anything to do with the New Deal had a story to tell and an opinion to offer and often an ax to grind regarding Roosevelt's attempt to expand the Supreme Court and his later effort to purge the Democratic Party. The second volume of Ickes's published diary provides an excellent running account of these proceedings, and most of the New Deal memoirs and histories already cited deal with them at various lengths—though it should be said that Joseph Lash's *Dealers and Dreamers* is purely indispensable here. To this list should be added, first, James A. Farley, *Jim Farley's Story: The Roosevelt Years* (New York: McGraw-Hill, 1948); written in bitterness (and with the help of newsman Walter Trohan, a Roosevelt hater) but with a fortunate reliance on the extensive notes he took on an almost daily basis in his dealings with Roosevelt, it can generally be relied upon for fact, if not always for interpretation of fact. Two other very useful sources are Eugene C. Gerhart, *America's Advocate: Robert H. Jackson* (Indianapolis: Bobbs-Merrill, 1958), and Gerald T. Dunn, *Hugo Black and the Judicial Revolution* (New York: Simon & Schuster, 1977). On other fronts, Walter Goodman demonstrates remarkable objectivity in his history, *The Committee: The Extraordinary Career of the House Committee on Un-American Activities* (New York: Farrar, Straus and Giroux, 1968). So does Lewis H. Carlson in his "J. Parnell Thomas and the House Committee on Un-American Activities, 1938–1948" (Ph.D. dissertation, Michigan State University, 1967). On the other hand, William Gellerman did not even attempt objectivity in his furious little book,

Martin Dies (New York: John Day, 1944), but since it is richly ornamented with well-documented quotations from the chairman, the hearings, the victims, the press, and other sources, the book is both useful and great good fun to read. Other sources as noted.

PAGE

618   "It was noted that": HLI, *Diary*, vol. II, p. 52.
620   "Many of the refusals": Quoted in Morgan, *FDR*, p. 470.
        "The Vice President said not a word": HLI, *Diary*, vol. II, p. 66.
        "Boys, this is where I cash in": *Ibid.*, p. 222.
        "Mr. Attorney General" (note): Quoted in Hardeman and Bacon, *Rayburn: A Biography*, p. 221.
621   "Do you remember Huey Long?": This whole strange episode is based on Corcoran's autobiographical notes and is presented in Lash's *Dealers and Dreamers*, p. 298.
        "Its objective is to": Quoted in Lloyd Wendt, *Chicago Tribune: The Rise of a Great American Newspaper*, p. 596.
622   "drunk with power": Quoted in Steel, *Walter Lippmann*, p. 319.
        "an awful shock"; "Dramatically and artistically": Quoted in Lash, *Dealers and Dreamers*, p. 62.
623   "of an average age": HLI, Speeches and Writings, Container 414, Secretary of the Interior File, HLIP.
        "National budget almost balanced": FDR to HLI, 4/20/37, President's Personal File, FDRL.
        "for as long as he could": HLI, *Diary*, vol. II, p. 119.
        "remarked that he supposed": *Ibid.*
624   "I have here now": Quoted in Nathan Miller, *FDR: An Intimate History* (New York: Doubleday, 1983), p. 400.
        "The Supreme Court is fully": Quoted in Gerhart, *America's Advocate*, p. 113.
        "A switch in time": Quoted in Rosenman, *Working with Roosevelt*, p. 161.
625   "The trouble, Bob": Quoted in Gerhart, *America's Advocate*, p. 117.
        "not to bloody the President's nose": Quoted in Morgan, *FDR*, p. 478.
        "However much the people": HLI, Speeches and Writings, Container 414, Secretary of the Interior File, HLIP.
626   "into a position of political": Quoted in Lash, *Dealers and Dreamers*, p. 313.
        "After Louis' death": Eleanor Roosevelt, *This I Remember* (New York: Harper & Bros., 1949), pp. 167–68.
        "Immediately after the defeat": Farley, *Jim Farley's Story*, p. 96.
627   "I have been around the country": *Ibid.*, quoted, p. 101.
        "Organized wealth": HLI, *Diary*, vol. II, p. 243.
        "I know who's responsible": Quoted in Farley, *Jim Farley's Story*, p. 106.
628   "The United States is owned": Ferdinand Lundberg, *America's Sixty Families* (New York: Vanguard Press, 1937), p. 3.
        "For some time": HLI, *Diary*, vol. II, p. 285.

629   "To Franklin Roosevelt": HLI, Speeches and Writings, Container 414, Secretary of the Interior File, HLIP.

"The President appears to have lost": HLI, *Diary*, vol. II, pp. 325–26.

"As I see it": Quoted in Blum, *From the Morgenthau Diaries: Years of Crisis*, p. 415.

"I don't mind telling you": *Ibid.*, pp. 420–21.

"White House Janizaries": Quoted in Lash, *Dealers and Dreamers*, p. 355.

630   "we hope that Senator Pepper": Quoted in Pepper, *Pepper: Eyewitness to a Century*, p. 73.

"fine speech": HLI, *Diary*, vol. II, p. 414.

"Never in our lifetime": Quoted in Rosenman, *Working with Roosevelt*, p. 178.

631   "I knew from the beginning": Farley, *Jim Farley's Story*, pp. 146–47.

"sweeping the nation": Quoted in Goodman, *The Committee*, p. 15.

"a special committee": Quoted in Gellerman, *Martin Dies*, p. 61.

632   "ultimate objective": *Ibid.*, quoted, p. 47.

"I am not inclined to look": Quoted in Goodman, *The Committee*, p. 21.

"I hope that this committee": Quoted in Carlson, "J. Parnell Thomas," p. 14.

633   "has proved himself to be": Container 157, Secretary of the Interior File, HLIP.

634   "Some people now feel": HLI, *Diary*, vol. II, p. 529.

"The proceedings of Congressman Dies": Container 157, Secretary of the Interior File, HLIP.

"The President has just called": Quoted in HLI, *Diary*, vol. II, p. 546.

635   "The reason Dies has made": *Ibid.*, p. 547.

"Legislators admitted": Quoted in Carlson, "J. Parnell Thomas," p. 30.

"Links Perkins Aid": *Ibid.*, quoted, p. 31.

"The New Deal masterminds": *Ibid.*

"Man of the Year": *Ibid.*, p. 32.

"abjectly surrendered": HLI, *Diary*, vol. II, p. 574.

45. Once in a Hundred Years

The story of the somewhat ambiguous place black citizens occupied in the architecture of the New Deal is most amply documented in Ailen Kifer's Ph.D. dissertation, "The Negro Under the New Deal" (University of Wisconsin, 1961), and I have relied on this account for most of the general discussion here. Other useful material was found in Constance Green's *The Secret City*. Of the New Deal historians, Arthur M. Schlesinger in *The Politics of Upheaval* deals with the subject in the most felicitous detail. The story of the Marian Anderson concert is well covered in her autobiography, *My Lord, What a Morning* (New York: The Viking Press, 1956), while Eleanor Roosevelt's part in the event is nicely rendered by Joseph Lash in *Eleanor and Franklin*. Other sources as noted.

PAGE

637   "Your forgotten man has become": Quoted in Kifer, "The Negro Under the New Deal," ix.

"President Roosevelt is by-and-large": Melvin J. Chisum, "Why the Negro Is for Roosevelt," pamphlet in HLI, Speeches and Writings, Container 154, Secretary of the Interior File, HLIP.

638 "that vile form": Quoted in Schlesinger, *The Politics of Upheaval*, p. 437.

"the strong arm of Government": *Ibid.*, quoted.

"I did not choose the tools": *Ibid.*, quoted, pp. 437–38.

640 "dignified, constructive, and needful": Quoted in Kifer, "The Negro Under the New Deal," p. 106.

"seem to be patronizing"; "more harm than good": *Ibid.*, quoted, p. 144.

"I believe the most progressive": *Ibid.*, quoted, p. 146. Wallace remained ambivalent about the situation. As late as 1940 he could still ask a black colleague, "Will, don't you think the New Deal is undertaking to do too much for the Negro?" Quoted in Lash, *Eleanor and Franklin*, p. 528.

641 "Oh, that doesn't matter": See Notes for p. 339.

642 "Colored companies": Quoted in Kifer, "The Negro Under the New Deal," p. 20.

643 "complications": *Ibid.*, p. 54.

"I trust that you will": HLI to Secretary of War George Dern, 3/25/34, *ibid.*, pp. 54–55.

"the policy of nondiscrimination": Secretary of War George Dern to HLI, 3/26/34, *ibid.*, p. 55.

"very much opposed": Louis Howe to Robert Fechner, 4/7/34, *ibid.*

"The Hon. Harold L. Ickes": Chisum, "Why the Negro Is for Roosevelt."

645 "devoted his life to the Negro": HLI to Roy Wilkins, 8/31/33, Kifer, "The Negro Under the New Deal," p. 219.

"The colored citizens": Roy Wilkins to Harry Slattery, 9/22/33, SPDU.

646 "The group was not": Quoted in Katie Louchheim, *The Making of the New Deal: The Insiders Speak* (Cambridge, Mass.: Harvard University Press, 1983), pp. 262–63.

647 "transported to and from": Quoted in Stevens, *Hoover Dam*, p. 177.

"I hereby direct you": HLI to Illinois State Engineer Osborne, 10/18/34, SPDU.

648 "an informal Secretary of Negro Relations": Schlesinger, *The Politics of Upheaval*, p. 435.

"stand on the Negro question": HLI, *Diary*, vol. II, p. 20.

"It begins to look": *Ibid.*

"I think it is up to the states": *Ibid.*, p. 115.

"are taxpayers, are they citizens" (note): *Ibid.*, vol. III, p. 563.

649 "I feel at home": Quoted in Schlesinger, *The Politics of Upheaval*," p. 435.

"The sight of him": Anderson, *My Lord, What a Morning*, p. 158.

"Yours is a voice": *Ibid.*, quoted.

"protect the Negro players" (note): *Ibid.*

650 "The question is": Eleanor Roosevelt, "My Day," 2/28/39, quoted in Lash, *Eleanor and Franklin*, p. 526.

"What can you do?": Chapman's version of how the Lincoln Memorial got chosen is from footnote in Lash, *ibid.*, p. 527.

651 "Weeks of thought": Walter White, "Marian Anderson and the D.A.R.," in
Don Congdon, ed., *The 30s: A Time to Remember* (New York: Simon & Schuster,
1962), p. 623.

652 "the best speech I have ever made": HLI, *Diary*, vol. II, p. 615.
"In this great auditorium": This version of HLI's speech is taken from a
transcribed recording of the NBC radio broadcast of the event: "Marian
Anderson 'Live'—Lincoln Memorial Concert, Washington, D.C." (Legendary
Recordings, LR 126, n.d.).

653 "All I knew": Anderson, *My Lord, What a Morning*, p. 191.
"It was a tremendous thing": Quoted in Barbara Klaw, "A Voice One Hears
Once in a Hundred Years: An Interview with Marian Anderson," *American
Heritage*, February 1977.
"Her hands were particularly": White, "Marian Anderson," p. 624.

46. Family Business

PAGE

654 "Early in the week": HLI, *Diary*, vol. II, p. 709.
"I am busily engaged": Jane Ickes to Anna R. Boettiger, 3/26/39, Anna
Roosevelt Papers, FDRL.

655 "Our impression was one": Jane Ickes to Anna R. Boettiger, 6/15/39, *ibid*.
"No new-born baby": HLI, *Diary*, vol. II, p. 715.

656 "Harold and I lead": Jane Ickes to Anna R. Boettiger, 10/24/39, Anna
Roosevelt Papers, FDRL.
"He is adorable": *Ibid*.

657 "So I did something": HLI, Untitled autobiographical draft, Container 435,
p. 28, HLIP.
"circumstances surrounding the execution of the will": Quoted in HLI,
unpublished diary segment, 12/3/39, HLIP.

658 Harry Slattery's brief contretemps with Margaret Mitchell is documented in
the Slattery Papers in the collections of the Perkins Library, Duke University.

659 Claude Wickard tells this story on Slattery in his oral memoirs, OHCU.
"Harry has a perfect": HLI, Unpublished Diary Segment, 6/9/40, HLIP.
"all furniture, all drapes" (note): Quoted in Clayton R. Koppes, "Oscar L.
Chapman: A Liberal at the Interior Department, 1933–1953" (Ph.D. dissertation, University of Kansas, 1974), note, p. 30. Ickes grew to cordially
despise the opportunistic West and was not particularly surprised when in
June 1942 he received a letter from a man who had had the misfortune of
getting involved with West in a business deal. West had left him holding the
bag and had disappeared somewhere in Mexico City, apparently kiting checks
as he went, and the man wondered if Ickes might know of his whereabouts.
The Secretary did not. "If you had written to me your letter of June 8," he
replied, "omitting the name but describing the events, I could have filled in
the name without any difficulty. Mr. West at one time, unfortunately, was
Under-Secretary of this Department, but as soon as I got onto him I got rid of

him. . . . In short, I wouldn't believe him under oath, and if he left a trail of
hot checks behind him that wouldn't be the first time that he has done that
sort of thing." HLI to Wayne D. Phillips, 6/10/42, Container 164, Secretary
of the Interior File, HLIP.

660   "had achieved quite a considerable": Carmody, oral memoirs, p. 535.
      "Believe me, I don't think" (note): Claude Wickard, oral memoirs, OHCU.
661   "It has been one": HLI, *Diary*, vol. II, p. 630.
      "I would not have had": *Ibid.*, p. 631.
      "made no demands": *Ibid.*, p. 638.
      "Fortas is one": HLI, Unpublished Diary Segment, 4/8/39, HLIP.

47. Cycles of Darkness

The unedifying story of the desperate inability of the United States to rationalize
politics, foreign policy, and conscience in such a way that might have led to the
rescue of the Jews before and after the outbreak of war in 1939 is recounted in
relentless detail in David S. Wyman's two important studies, *Paper Walls: America
and the Refugee Crisis, 1938–1941* (Amherst: University of Massachusetts Press,
1968), and *The Abandonment of the Jews: America and the Holocaust, 1941–1945* (New
York: Pantheon Books, 1984). The first title was of particular use to me in this
chapter.

PAGE

663   "It is not only cowardly": HLI to Chicago Phi Delta Theta Chapter, 10/31/08,
      General Correspondence, HLIP.
664   "The raids of the nightshirt nations": HLI, "Nations in Nightshirts,"
      12/8/37, Speeches and Writings, Container 414, Secretary of the Interior File,
      HLIP.
      "No civilized man": HLI, "Cycles of Darkness," 1/23/38, *ibid.*
      "The only reason I accepted": HLI, *Diary*, vol. II, pp. 347–48.
665   "It happens that in practically": HLI, "Progress by Purges," 4/3/38, Speeches
      and Writings, Container 414, Secretary of the Interior File, HLIP.
      "I do not believe that": FDR, "Presidential Statement Against American
      Profiteering in Italian-Ethiopian War," 10/30/35, in Rosenman, *The Public
      Papers*, vol. IV, p. 440.
      "everyone should comply": HLI, *Diary*, vol. I, p. 472.
666   "The charge of discrimination": Hull, *The Memoirs*, vol. I, p. 438.
      "the rats of Spain": Quoted in Walter Johnson, *William Allen White's America*
      (New York: Henry Holt & Co., 1947), p. 513.
667   "In the long history": Sumner Welles, *The Time for Decision* (New York: Harper
      & Bros., 1944), p. 61.
      "There was no general discussion": HLI, *Diary*, vol. II, p. 93.
      "constituted a black page": *Ibid.*, p. 389.
668   "This was the cat": *Ibid.*, p. 390.
      "With adequate safeguards": Quoted in Hull, *The Memoirs*, I, p. 597.
      "In view of Germany's ruthless": HLI, *Diary*, vol. II, p. 344.

669   "Who would take Hitler's word?": *Ibid.*, p. 392.
      "Mr. President, under the law": Quoted in Eugene C. Gerhart, *America's Advocate: Robert H. Jackson* (Indianapolis: Bobbs-Merrill Co., 1958), p. 148.
670   "The intelligence and culture": HLI, "Esau, the Hairy Man," 12/18/38, Speeches and Writings, Container 415, Secretary of the Interior File, HLIP.
671   "I pointed out": HLI, *Diary*, vol. II, 343.
      "no country would be expected": Quoted in Wyman, *Paper Walls*, p. 43.
      "The time has come": *Ibid.*, quoted, p. 50.
      "Most governments represented": *Ibid.*
672   "to little more than nothing": *Ibid.*, quoted, p. 51.
      "Powerful nations, enjoying sovereignty": *Ibid.*, quoted, p. 58.
673   "Interior should find": FDR to HLI, 12/18/40, quoted in Grede, "The New Deal in the Virgin Islands," p. 245.
      "public purpose corporations": Quotations from and outline of Slattery Report are from Wyman, *Paper Walls*, pp. 99–101.
674   "Do you think I should sign this?": Copy of handwritten memorandum from FDR to Sumner Welles, 10/19/39, President's Personal File, FDRL.
      "I have spoken": Sumner Welles to FDR, 10/19/39, *ibid.*
      "I know that most refugees": HLI, "Testimony Before Subcommittee of Senate Committee on Territories and Insular Affairs," 5/13/40, Speeches and Writings, Container 415, Secretary of the Interior File, HLIP.

48. Celebrating the Sphinx

As with the court-packing scheme and the attempted purge of 1938 (see notes for Chapter 44, "Reductive Politics," above), almost everyone connected with the New Deal who left anything behind in the way of published or unpublished memoirs had something to say about Roosevelt's third term, as do all the standard histories and biographies, including Mary Earhart Dillon's useful *Wendell Willkie: 1892–1944* (Philadelphia: J. B. Lippincott Co., 1952). Two titles should be singled out for very special mention: Melvyn Dubofsky and Warren Van Tyne's excellent work, *John L. Lewis: A Biography* (New York: Quadrangle Books/The New York Times Book Company, 1977), far and away the best biography of that strange, important man ever written and one of the best books available on the modern labor movement in general; and Robert Dallek's brilliant analysis, *Franklin D. Roosevelt and American Foreign Policy, 1932–1945* (New York: Oxford University Press, 1979), which supplants and surpasses everything on the subject that has gone before. It is indispensable to an understanding of how foreign affairs affected Roosevelt's political actions—including the decision to run for a third term. Once again, however, the best single source for day-to-day developments during this period are volumes II and III of the Ickes diary: *The Inside Struggle* and *The Lowering Clouds*.

PAGE

676   "I am not happy": HLI to Anna R. Boettiger, 6/1/39, Anna Roosevelt Papers, FDRL.

678 "I listened to all of this": HLI, *Diary*, vol. I, pp. 263–64.

"the Maverick statement": HLI, *Diary*, vol. II, p. 29.

"Sure!": *Ibid.*, quoted, pp. 101–2.

"there are probably four": *Ibid.*, p. 237.

679 "killing": *Ibid.*

"He believes that Chicago": *Ibid.*, pp. 428–29.

680 "assurances and hopes": Quoted in Henry H. Adams, *Harry L. Hopkins: A Biography* (New York: G. P. Putnam's Sons, 1977), p. 131.

"Tommy, I will be the first to tell you": This quotation, the story of the suicidal woman, and the episode regarding Noble are taken from Corcoran's own notes for his biographer as presented in Lash, *Dealers and Dreamers*, pp. 366–67.

681 "that little Jesuit": *Ibid.*, quoted, p. 367.

"I liked Barbara Hopkins": HLI, *Diary*, vol. II, pp. 224–25.

682 "All of the men here": HLI to Anna R. Boettiger, 6/1/39, Anna Roosevelt Papers, FDRL.

"If it is admitted": HLI, "Why I Want Roosevelt to Run Again," *Look*, July 4, 1939.

"mutilated, supplemented, and transposed" (note): HLI, undated memorandum, Container 106, Secretary of the Interior File, HLIP.

683 "the Corcoran-Ickes crowd": Berle and Jacobs, *Navigating the Rapids*, p. 225.

"All told, I didn't find": HLI, *Diary*, vol. III, p. 153.

684 "So far as Garner was concerned": *Ibid.*, p. 156.

"Texas Roosevelt supporters should": Quoted in Robert A. Caro, *The Years of Lyndon B. Johnson: The Path to Power* (New York: Alfred A. Knopf, 1982), p. 592.

"Optimistically, he said to me": HLI, *Diary*, vol. III, p. 172.

685 "I have nothing to offer": Quoted in Leon Bryce Bloch and Lamar Middleton, eds., *The World Over in 1940* (New York: Living Age Press, 1941), p. 164.

686 "All bad, all bad": Quoted in Nathan Miller, *FDR: An Intimate History* (New York: Doubleday, 1983), p. 446.

687 "Even if I had had": HLI, *Diary*, vol. III, pp. 214–15.

688 "When Tom Dewey first accepted": HLI, "Dewey, the Clamor Boy," *Look*, March 26, 1940.

"He didn't seem to know": Arthur Krock, *Memoirs: Sixty Years on the Firing Line* (New York: Funk & Wagnall's, 1968), p. 193.

"Willkie is undoubtedly": HLI, *Diary*, vol. III, p. 137.

689 "fully established in supreme command": *Ibid.*, pp. 240–41.

"convinced, as am I": *Ibid.*, quoted, p. 249.

690 "at the specific request": Quoted in James MacGregor Burns, *Roosevelt: The Lion and the Fox* (New York: Harcourt, Brace & World, 1956), p. 427.

"Why, he's my second choice": Quoted in Trohan, *Political Animals*, p. 48.

"a liberal and one of the most"; "I have the confidence": Quoted in HLI, *Diary*, vol. III, p. 257.

691 "extend to the opponents": Wendell L. Willkie, "Acceptance Speech," in

Campaign Text Book of the Republican Party, 1940 (Washington, D.C.: Republican National Committee, 1940), p. 8.

"some form of selective service": *Ibid.*

"There have been occasions when": *Ibid.*, pp. 8–9.

692   "He is attractive and able": HLI to Raymond Robins, 7/5/40, Container 234, Secretary of the Interior File, HLIP.

"For a time, Mr. Willkie": HLI, "What Willkie Did Not Say," 8/19/40, Speeches and Writings, Container 415, *ibid.*

693   "the most important action": Quoted in Dallek, *Franklin D. Roosevelt*, p. 247.

"The problem between Tom and the President": Quoted in Lash, *Dealers and Dreamers*, p. 446.

"My heart aches": HLI to FDR, 8/23/40, Container 235, Secretary of the Interior File, HLIP.

"that I hoped": HLI, *Diary*, vol. III, p. 311.

"Whether it knows it or not": Quoted in Russell Lord, *The Wallaces of Iowa* (Boston: Houghton Mifflin, 1947), p. 481.

694   "Wendell Willkie graduated": HLI, "All This and Heaven Too," 10/15/40, Speeches and Writings, Container 416, Secretary of the Interior File, HLIP.

"simple, bare-foot": HLI, "The Dispensable Mr. Willkie," 10/18/40, *ibid.*

"If Willkie has proved": HLI, "Willkie's Gallery Gods," 10/25/40, *ibid.*

695   "the spectacle of a President": Quoted in Dubofsky and Van Tyne, *John L. Lewis*, p. 358.

"But now, in the serious days": Quoted in Rosenman, *Working with Roosevelt*, p. 240.

"Martin, Barton, and Fish": *Ibid.*

696   "And while I am talking": *Ibid.*, p. 242.

"except in case of attack": *Ibid.*

"herds sheep in the canyons": HLI, "When Ignorance Is Not Bliss," 10/28/40, Speeches and Writings, Container 416, Secretary of the Interior File, HLIP.

"Willkie keeps telling us": HLI, "Short Wave from Berlin," 11/1/40, *ibid.*

"Lewis can get little": HLI, "Willkie Merges, Lewis Submerges," 11/2/40, *ibid.*

697   "I see an America": Quoted in Rosenman, *Working with Roosevelt*, pp. 251–52.

"This is the battle of America": Quoted in Dillon, *Wendell Willkie*, p. 221.

49. A Distant Fire

In addition to Dallek's study (cited above), a number of sources were particularly useful in tracing out the convoluted steps by which the United States finally edged into war. Two attempt to prove the contention that the President deliberately connived to get the nation involved from the very beginning: Charles A. Beard's *President Roosevelt and the Coming of the War, 1941: A Study in Appearances and Realities* (New Haven: Yale University Press, 1948); and Charles Callan Tansill's *Back Door to War: The Roosevelt Foreign Policy, 1933–1941* (Chicago: Henry Regnery Co., 1952); neither makes much of a case for the theory—particularly when stacked up against Dallek—but each provides insight into isolationist thinking. More rational investigations can be found in Henry H. Adams, *Years of Deadly Peril: The Coming of the War,*

1939–1941 (New York: David McKay Co., 1969); T. R. Fehrenbach, *FDR's Undeclared War, 1939 to 1941* (New York: David McKay Co., 1967); Saul Friedlander, *Prelude to Downfall: Hitler and the United States, 1939–1941,* translated from the French by Aline B. and Alexander Werth (New York: Alfred A. Knopf, 1967); Eric Larrabee, *Commander in Chief: Franklin Delano Roosevelt, His Lieutenants, and Their War* (New York: Harper & Row, 1987), whose early chapters are as good a compression of events leading up to Pearl Harbor as can be found anywhere; and Joseph P. Lash, *Roosevelt and Churchill: The Partnership That Saved the West* (New York: W. W. Norton & Co., 1976). Other sources as noted.

PAGE

698 "The decision for 1941": Quoted in Dallek, *Franklin D. Roosevelt,* p. 254.
699 "It seems to me": HLI to FDR, 8/2/40, President's Personal File, FDRL.
"There is absolutely no doubt": Quoted in Adams, *Years of Deadly Peril,* pp. 369–70.
700 "to increase, accelerate, and regulate": Quoted in *Roosevelt's Foreign Policy, 1933–1941: Franklin D. Roosevelt's Unedited Speeches and Messages* (New York: Wilfred Funk, Inc., 1942), p. 325.
"Never before since Jamestown": Quoted in Adams, *Years of Deadly Peril,* pp. 370–71.
701 "Four Freedoms" speech quoted *ibid.,* p. 373.
"Never before has the Congress": Quoted in Beard, *President Roosevelt and the Coming of the War,* p. 17.
"All provisions of law and the Constitution": Quoted in Adams, *Years of Deadly Peril,* pp. 374–75.
"I remember a quarter": Quoted in *Roosevelt's Foreign Policy,* pp. 342–47.
702 "Now, therefore, I": *Ibid.,* p. 394.
703 "We say good-bye now": Clapper, *Watching the World,* pp. 274–76.
"One of the essential": FDR to HLI, 5/28/41, Container 164, Secretary of the Interior File, HLIP.
"The letter of the President": HLI, *Diary,* vol. III, p. 529.
"In this he is an exception": *Ibid.,* p. 456.
704 "organized along functional lines": Quoted in Williamson, *et al., The American Petroleum Industry,* p. 754.
"There is no doubt": HLI, *Diary,* vol. III, p. 420.
705 "was almost hysterical": *Ibid.,* pp. 431–32.
"This means that Alcoa": *Ibid.,* p. 446.
706 "When the story of this war": Quoted in I. F. Stone, *A Non-Conformist History of Our Times: The War Years, 1939–1945* (Boston: Little, Brown & Co., 1988), p. 87.
707 "World peace seems": HLI to Raymond Robins, 12/27/37, Container 162, Secretary of Interior File, HLIP.
"I had with me": HLI, *Diary,* vol. III, p. 537.
"Information obtained": HLI to Brigadier General Russell L. Maxwell, 6/11/41, President's Personal File, FDRL.

708 "I was not stopping": HLI to Stephen Early, *ibid.*
"Japan's willingness to make war": Hull, *The Memoirs*, vol. II, pp. 1102–3.
"Lest there be any confusion": This and subsequent correspondence between HLI and FDR on the subject of oil and the Japanese are from HLI, *Diary*, vol. III, pp. 553–67.

711 "a vigorous chairman": Quoted in Jordan A. Schwarz, *The Speculator: Bernard M. Baruch in Washington, 1917–1965* (Chapel Hill: University of North Carolina Press, 1981), p. 375.

712 "What all of this meant": Bruce Catton, *The War Lords of Washington* (New York: Harcourt, Brace & Co., 1948), p. 61.
"No one has final authority": Quoted in Schwarz, *The Speculator*, p. 376.
"I think that the President": HLI, *Diary*, vol. III, pp. 607–8.
"people haven't fallen": Quoted in Williamson, *et al.*, *The American Petroleum Industry*, p. 758.

713 "I don't suppose there ever is": HLI, *Diary*, vol. III, p. 603.
"She seemed to be quite sincere": *Ibid.*, p. 515.
"I prefer a bald baby": *Ibid.*, p. 516.

714 "It was an outrageous bit": *Ibid.*, p. 539.
"a peripatetic appeaser" (note); "Knight of the German Eagle": Quoted in Walter S. Ross, *The Last Hero: Charles A. Lindbergh* (New York: Harper & Row, 1968), pp. 301–2.

715 "would even at this time": Quoted in Lash, *Roosevelt and Churchill*, p. 323.
"Harold thinks I am gallant": Jane Ickes to Anna R. Boettiger, 7/4/41, Anna Roosevelt Papers, FDRL.
"It is really hopeless": HLI, *Diary*, vol. III, p. 606.
"I didn't feel the least": *Ibid.*, p. 608.

716 "The committee believes": *Preliminary Report of the Special Committee to Make a Full and Complete Investigation with Respect to the Shortage of Gasoline, Fuel Oil, and Other Petroleum Products*, U.S. Senate, 9/11/41, Container 164, Secretary of the Interior File, HLIP.
"There was a lady of fashion" (note): FDR to HLI, 9/15/41, Container 265, Secretary of Interior File, HLIP.

717 "I went at the committee": HLI, *Diary*, vol. III, p. 622.
"With the supply": HLI, "Statement of Petroleum Coordinator for National Defense Harold L. Ickes, Before the Senate Special Committee to Investigate Gasoline and Fuel Oil Shortages," 11/1/41, Container 164, Secretary of the Interior File, HLIP.

718 On September 7, Jones had sent: Figures here are from a letter of W. Alton Jones to Ralph K. Davies, 9/17/41, *ibid.*
On September 20, T. W. Tutwiler: Figures here are from a letter of T. W. Tutwiler to HLI, 9/23/41, *ibid.*
"Did ever a giant mountain": HLI, "Statement of Petroleum Coordinator."
"beat a graceful retreat": HLI, *Diary*, vol. III, p. 631.

719 "Now I feel that I am": *Ibid.*, p. 634.
"The special emissary from Tokyo": This and all subsequent quotations from the Thomas broadcasts are from Lowell Thomas, *History as You Heard It*

(Garden City, N.Y.: Doubleday & Co., 1957), pp. 179–82.

720 "preposterous"; "condonement by the United States": Hull, *The Memoirs*, vol. II, p. 1070.

"Diplomatically, the situation": *Ibid.*, p. 1071.

"This son of man": Quoted in Dallek, *Franklin D. Roosevelt*, p. 309.

PART IX: THE LAST ADVENTURE

PAGE

721 "As I was interested": HLI to FDR, 12/13/44, Container 265, Secretary of the Interior File, HLIP.

50. Metamorphosis

Information on the atmosphere in Washington during Pearl Harbor and the transformation of the city during the war years is taken largely from two sources—Scott Hart's amalgam of memory and history called *Washington at War: 1941–1945* (Englewood Cliffs, N.J.: Prentice-Hall, 1970), and David Brinkley's own version of much the same kind of book, *Washington Goes to War* (New York: Alfred A. Knopf, 1988). Although both men were young reporters in Washington during the war and both are amateur historians, they have managed to write two very different books, each both readable and useful on its own merits. Neither book is annotated, though judging from the "Note on Sources" at the end of the Brinkley book (Hart has merely a short listing of titles), Brinkley seems to have dug a little deeper into the midden of the city's life during this period; on the other hand, I am particularly indebted to Hart for having uncovered the story of how the Declaration of Independence and the Constitution were moved. Material on the situation with regard to black people during the war years is taken from Brinkley and from Constance Green's two books, *Washington: Capital City, 1879–1950*, and *The Secret City: A History of Race Relations in the Nation's Capital*. Other sources as noted.

PAGE

723 "This is Steve Early": Quoted in Lyle C. Wilson, "World War II," in Cabell Phillips, *et al.*, eds., *Dateline: Washington: The Story of National Affairs Journalism in the Life and Times of the National Press Club* (Garden City, N.Y.: Doubleday & Co., 1949), p. 184.

724 "In the Navy Department": Stone, *A Non-Conformist History*, p. 92.

"an economist who could not": Brinkley, *Washington Goes to War*, p. 52.

"I found that he": HLI, *Diary*, vol. III, p. 661.

725 "The people were": *Ibid.*, pp. 661–62.

"He looked pale and ill": *Ibid.*, p. 662.

"The President was quite serious": *Ibid.*, pp. 662–63.

"Yesterday, December 7": Quoted in Rosenman, *Working with Roosevelt*, p. 307.

"The President asked": Quoted in Sherwood, *Roosevelt and Hopkins*, p. 433.

726   "With such important news": HLI, *Diary*, vol. III, p. 665.

"My . . . confidence springs": Stone, *A Non-Conformist History*, p. 94.

727   "The once sleepy southern town": Quoted in Hart, *Washington at War*, p. 40.

728   "The men may have started": Quoted in Brinkley, *Washington Goes to War*, p. 243.

"During the evenings": Hart, *Washington at War*, p. 91.

"decent living accommodations": Quoted in Chalmers M. Roberts, *The Washington Post: The First Hundred Years* (Boston: Houghton Mifflin, 1977), p. 243.

729   "vital to the war effort": Quoted in Brinkley, *Washington Goes to War*, p. 118.

730   "We all knew a gun": Quoted in Hart, *Washington at War*, p. 74.

51. Oil, Arms, and the Man

Background on the move of the three Interior agencies to Chicago is from the unpublished Ickes diary in the Library of Congress. The diary and other primary materials in the Library of Congress manuscript collection were also important in the discussion regarding wartime gasoline rationing, rubber shortages, and oil policy and Ickes's part in them, but a number of additional sources were essential to various aspects of the story: John Morton Blum, *V Was for Victory: Politics and American Culture During World War II* (New York: Harcourt Brace Jovanovich, 1976); James Mac-Gregor Burns, *Roosevelt: The Soldier of Freedom, 1940–1945* (New York: Harcourt Brace Jovanovich, 1970); Bruce Catton, *The War Lords of Washington* (cited above), the great Civil War historian's first book, this one written as a journalist and participant; J. Stanley Clark, *The Oil Century: From the Drake Well to the Conservation Era* (Norman: University of Oklahoma Press, 1958); Robert Dallek, *Franklin Roosevelt and American Foreign Policy, 1932–1945*; Cordell Hull, *The Memoirs of Cordell Hull*, Volume II; Jesse H. Jones, with Edward Angly, *Fifty Billion Dollars: My Thirteen Years with the RFC*; Richard R. Lingeman, *Don't You Know There's a War On? The American Home Front, 1941–1945*; Bruce Allen Murphy, *Fortas: The Rise and Ruin of a Supreme Court Justice*; Geoffrey Perrett, *Days of Sadness, Years of Triumph: The American People, 1939–1945* (Madison: University of Wisconsin Press, 1973); Cabell Phillips, *The 1940s: Decade of Triumph and Trouble* (New York: Macmillan Publishing Co., Inc., 1975); Carl Coke Rister, *Oil! Titan of the Southwest*; Anthony Sampson, *The Seven Sisters: The Great Oil Companies and the World They Shaped* (New York: The Viking Press, 1975); Jordan A. Schwarz, *The Speculator: Bernard M. Baruch in Washington, 1917–1965*; and Harold F. Williamson, *et al.*, *The American Petroleum Industry, 1899–1950*.

PAGE

733   "I told him": HLI, unpublished diary, 12/21/41, HLIP.

734   "I hope that I can go": *Ibid.*

"They don't have to operate": *Ibid.*, 12/27/41.

"I wanted to tell them": *Ibid.*, 3/22/42.

735   "policy subcommittee under the Board": *Ibid.*, quoted, 1/4/42.

"I do not see how": *Ibid.*, quoted.

736   "I made it clear": *Ibid.*

"I went out of my way"; "I saw a sharp distinction": *Ibid.*, 1/11/42.

737   "The doctor found a very bad": HLI to John and Anna Boettiger, 1/7/42, Container 159, Secretary of the Interior File, HLIP.

"Accepted in principle": HLI, unpublished diary, 1/25/42, HLIP.

"As this was a complete": *Ibid.*, 2/1/42.

738   "one of the greatest": Quoted in Larrabee, *Commander in Chief*, p. 176.

739   "argued strenuously that": HLI, unpublished diary, 4/26/42, HLIP.

740   "a confusion of tongues": Catton, *The War Lords*, p. 156.

741   "He told me that": Jones, *Fifty Billion Dollars*, pp. 403–4.

"The rubber failure": HLI to Stacey Mosser, 4/16/42, Container 162, Secretary of the Interior File, HLIP.

742   "[I]f apportioning the blame": Catton, *The War Lords*, p. 153.

743   "overexcitement": *Ibid.*, quoted, p. 160.

"until such time": *Ibid.*, quoted, p. 161.

"we suspect that there are": *Ibid.*, quoted, p. 163.

"tried to contribute" (note): *Ibid.*

744   "It was, in a sense": HLI to William R. Boyd, Jr., 3/8/43, President's Personal File, FDRL.

"could create hell": HLI, unpublished diary, 8/4/42, HLIP.

"commandeer Bernie": *Ibid.*

745   "Because you are": Quoted in Schwarz, *Liberal*, p. 394.

"We find the existing situation": *Ibid.*, quoted, pp. 394–95.

"Are you in favor": *Ibid.*

746   "ride to battle": Quoted in Rister, *Oil!*, p. 353.

"The achievement of this gigantic task": Quoted in Williamson, *et al.*, *The American Petroleum Industry*, p. 794.

747   "a further orgy": Quoted in Sampson, *The Seven Sisters*, p. 95.

"forty years late": *Ibid.*, quoted.

"In the selection of officers": HLI to FDR, 7/27/43, President's Personal File, FDRL.

748   "I sent for Abe Fortas": HLI, unpublished diary, 3/1/42, HLIP.

"I am prepared to commit myself": HLI to Abe Fortas, 11/17/43, Container 161, Secretary of the Interior File, HLIP.

749   "I hope you don't mind": *Ibid.*, Abe Fortas to HLI, 8/24/42.

"The centre of gravity": Quoted in Sampson, *The Seven Sisters*, p. 97.

750   "We believe that strong criticism": Quoted in Hull, *The Memoirs*, vol. II, p. 1521.

"This is my baby": *Ibid.*, quoted, p. 1522.

"I do not believe": Abe Fortas to HLI, 4/8/44, Container 161, Secretary of the Interior File, HLIP.

751 "What Mr. Fortas contends": Ralph K. Davies to HLI, 4/10/44, *ibid.*
"Speaking personally": HLI to Abe Fortas, 4/24/44, *ibid.*

52. The Portals and Seams of Compromise

Most of the secondary sources that cover the years of World War II (see notes for Chapter 51, above) deal with the coal strikes of 1943 to a greater or lesser degree. Both the standard biographies of John L. Lewis, of course, treat them in considerable detail, but Melvyn Dubofsky and Warren Van Tyne's *John L. Lewis* is a much more authoritative and balanced account than Saul Alinsky's *John L. Lewis: An Unauthorized Biography* (New York: G. P. Putnam's Sons, 1949), and I have relied on it for my discussion of the confrontation between Lewis and Roosevelt.

PAGE

753 "Our Nation is at war": Quoted in Dubofsky and Van Tyne, *John L. Lewis*, p. 415.

754 "When the mine workers' children cry": *Ibid.*, quoted, p. 419.

755 "work at the mines": *Ibid.*, quoted, p. 427.
"As usual, I haven't heard": HLI to Margaret Robins, 5/1/43, Container 162, Secretary of the Interior File, HLIP.

756 "Lewis is, as you say": HLI to Raymond Robins, 5/8/43, *ibid.*

757 "infamous yellow-dog"; "for the Government": Quoted in Dubofsky and Van Tyne, *John L. Lewis*, p. 433.

758 "I asked [Lewis] to come": HLI to Margaret Robins, 11/6/43, Container 162, Secretary of the Interior File, HLIP.

759 "When I got well of the flu": *Ibid.*, quoted.

53. Interludes of Ink and Cowboys

Harold Ickes was not indulging in paranoia when he accused the American press of being more than slightly one-sided in its treatment of the New Deal in general and of him and FDR in particular. For an excellent overview of the alliance between the newspaper press and Roosevelt's political enemies, see George Wolfskill and John A. Hudson's *All But the People: Franklin D. Roosevelt and His Critics, 1933–1939* (New York: Macmillan, 1969). See also Graham White's shorter but trenchant little study, *FDR and the Press* (Chicago: University of Chicago Press, 1979). Even in his own time, Ickes was not alone in his criticisms. *America's House of Lords* owed much of its tone and some of its opinions (not to mention its title) to a close reading of Gilbert Seldes's *Lords of the Press*, a vigorous indictment published in 1938 (New York: Julian Messner). In fact, Ickes had furnished Seldes with some of the material that he put in his book and Seldes had furnished some of the material that Ickes put in his—a symbiosis from which both profited. Seldes was a little less scurrilous (and much less poetic) in his criticism of columnists, but in speaking of the press and the election of

1936, demonstrated a similar antipathy: "Nineteen thirty-six also showed up the place of that new power in American journalism, the columnist. The Washington correspondents, those several hundred men who write the politics of the nation, were overwhelmingly on the side of Roosevelt and Reform, although overwhelmingly their papers were opposed. Most of the columnists, however, had no compromise to face, no conscience to trouble them: they as well as big business, the millionaire oil man of Kansas, Hearst, the manufacturers' association, the Liberty League, were all on the same side" (p. 331).

The story of the designation of Jackson Hole National Monument is told briefly but well in David J. Saylor's history, *Jackson Hole, Wyoming: In the Shadow of the Tetons* (Norman: University of Oklahoma Press, 1971, 1977). A personal view of the struggle is given in Olaus J. and Margaret Murie's *Wapiti Wilderness* (New York: Alfred A. Knopf, 1966). See also Irving Brant's "The Fight Over Jackson Hole" in the *Nation* (July 7, 1945) and Robert W. Righter's "The Brief, Hectic Life of Jackson Hole National Monument," in *The American West* (November–December 1976). The Jackson Hole story and the story of the assault on Olympic National Park are also done up at considerable length in Brant's *Adventures in Conservation*. The Olympic fight is also covered briefly in Murray Morgan's *The Last Wilderness*.

The fate of the 160-acre limitation law is discussed somewhat in Paul Gates's *History of Public Land Law Development* and in greater detail in Marc Reisner's *Cadillac Desert*. The source on which I have relied most heavily in this segment, however, is Donald Worster's exhaustive history of reclamation in the West, *Rivers of Empire*. See also Sheridan Downey's *They Would Rule the Valley* (privately printed, San Francisco, 1947), a highly biased account that should be used with extreme caution; Robert W. De Roos's *The Thirsty Land* (Palo Alto, Calif.: Stanford University Press, 1948); and four articles by Paul Schuster Taylor: "The Excess Land Law: Execution of a Public Policy," *Yale Law Journal*, February 1955; "The Excess Land Law: Legislative Erosion of Public Policy," *Rocky Mountain Law Review*, June 1958; "Water, Land, and People in the Great Valley," *The American West*, March 1968; and "Reclamation: The Rise and Fall of an American Idea," *The American West*, July 1970.

PAGE

761   "A publisher or editor sits": HLI, ms. copy of *America's House of Lords*, pp. 13–15. Container 128, Secretary of the Interior File, HLIP.
      "this is not intended": *Ibid.*, pp. 4–5.
      "has always been" (note): Bruce Catton, "The Inspired Leak," *American Heritage*, February 1977.
762   "Wouldst know what is right": HLI, *America's House of Lords,* pp. 104–5.
763   "Of course, the money is offered": HLI, unpublished diary, 1/18/42, HLIP.
764   "I am not able to write": HLI, *Autobiography*, p. 272.
      "His ———": *Ibid.*, p. 278.
      "we must remember": HLI to John A. Reed, 11/9/42, Container 129, Secretary of the Interior File, HLIP.
      "I feel that I ought to give": Stephen Early to HLI, 11/9/42, *ibid*.
765   "I lay no claim to originality": HLI, *Autobiography*, p. 326.

"with time on my hands": HLI, unpublished diary, 2/1/42, HLIP.

766   "By midsummer the highway": Quoted in National Park Service, "Jackson Hole National Monument," p. 3, ms. in Record Group 79, NAKC.

767   "Mr. Rockefeller is prepared": *Ibid.*, quoted, p. 8.
      "Card parties, dinner parties": Murie, *Wapiti Wilderness*, p. 121.

768   "In view of the uncertainty": John D. Rockefeller to HLI, 11/27/42, in Record Group 79, NAKC.
      "My own view is": HLI to Edwin M. Watson, 2/27/43, in Nixon, *Franklin D. Roosevelt*, vol. II, pp. 570–71.

769   "There should be no publicity": *Ibid.*
      "[T]he first I knew about it": Newton B. Drury, oral history memoirs, vol. II, pp. 490–91, courtesy, the BL.

770   "In the various national parks": HLI to Joseph C. O'Mahoney, 4/8/43, in Record Group 79, NAKC.
      "I am aware": FDR to Governor Loren Hunt, 4/29/43, in National Park Service, "Jackson Hole National Monument," p. 22, Record Group 79, NAKC.
      "Declaring they have seen": *Salt Lake Tribune*, May 3, 1943, Record Group 79, NAKC.

771   "Incidentally, Wallace Beery is not": Struthers Burt to Stuart Rose, 8/24/43, Record Group 79, NAKC.
      "Long before movie actor": HLI, "Statement of the Secretary of the Interior Before the House Public Lands Committee, June 1, 1943," Record Group 79, NAKC.

772   "President Roosevelt and Harold Ickes": Westbrook Pegler column, 6/16/43, Record Group 79, NAKC.
      "a controversy": Quoted in Saylor, *Jackson Hole*, p. 201. According to Irving Brant in "The Fight Over Jackson Hole," a certain animosity between agencies attended the transfer of authority: "When the Jackson Hole employees of the Forest Service obeyed the President's order to turn government lands, buildings, and equipment over to the monument staff, every particle of plumbing and telephone equipment was torn out of the buildings. They did this, it is explained, by mistake."

774   "sawmill interests": Irving Brant to FDR, 3/2/42, President's Personal File, FDRL.
      "Legislation to permit logging": Quoted in Fringer, "Olympic National Park," pp. 139–40.
      "Fortunately, no sale made": Brant, *Adventures in Conservation*, p. 234.
      "Should it be legally impossible": Port Angeles Chamber of Commerce, "Resolution Adopted, April 12, 1943," President's Personal File, FDRL.

775   "They were advised": Irving Brant to Marvin H. McIntyre, 6/8/43, President's Personal File, FDRL.
      "While I understand": Irving Brant to HLI, 7/7/43, President's Personal File, FDRL.
      "I agree with you"; "same old crowd": Quoted in Brant, *Adventures in Conservation*, p. 236.

777 "Farm acreage figures from Reisner, *Cadillac Desert*, pp. 349–50.
778 "I met Charles Carey": Paul Schuster Taylor, oral history memoirs, vol. II, p. 169, courtesy, the BL.
779 "Now the question was": *Ibid.*, pp. 180–181.
"Vast haciendas": Quoted in Worster, *Rivers of Empire*, p. 252.
780 "with the passing of time": Taylor, "Reclamation: The Rise and Fall of an American Idea."

54. A Species of Redemption

My account of the negotiations leading to the President's request of Congress that he be given powers to declare independence for the Philippines is based on that in Samuel I. Rosenman's *Working with Roosevelt*. Both Ruth Tabrah's *Hawaii: A History* and Alexander MacDonald's *Revolt in Paradise* give good summaries of wartime conditions in Hawaii, though MacDonald's book is better detailed. In addition to the primary material cited, Alaska on the eve of war is illuminated by Jean Potter's solid journalistic account in *Alaska Under Arms* (New York: Macmillan, 1942), while the war years are well documented by *The Forgotten War: A Pictorial History of World War II in Alaska and Northwestern Canada*, by Stan Cohen (Missoula, Mont.: Pictorial Histories Publishing Company, 1981). The story of the relocation of Japanese Americans is told in a number of studies, but never more movingly than in Michi Weglyn's *Years of Infamy: The Untold Story of America's Concentration Camps* (New York: William Morrow, 1976); see also Dillon Myer's slightly self-serving but very well documented *Uprooted Americans: The Japanese Americans and the War Relocation Authority During World War II* (Tucson: University of Arizona Press, 1971). Accounts of the Holocaust are, of course, voluminous, but two deal in particularly significant detail with the American response to the phenomenon: *Were We Our Brothers' Keepers? The Public Response of American Jews to the Holocaust, 1938–1944*, by Haskell Lookstein (New York: Random House, 1985, 1988), and *The Abandonment of the Jews: America and the Holocaust, 1941–1945*, by David S. Wyman. The story of the Fort Ontario refugees is narrated best by Ruth Gruber's *Haven: The Unknown Story of 1,000 World War II Refugees* (New York: Coward-McCann, 1984; New American Library, New York, 1985), and from another viewpoint by Dillon Myer in *Uprooted Americans*.

PAGE

781 "While the work of the High Commissioner's": FDR to HLI, 9/16/42, President's Personal File, FDRL.
782 "the Republic of the Philippines": Quoted in Rosenman, *Working with Roosevelt*, p. 389.
"These conferences were among": *Ibid.*, p. 391.
783 "independence after the Japanese": *Ibid.*, quoted, p. 392.
"necessary for the mutual protection": *Ibid.*, quoted, p. 390.
784 "Thoron is just the right man": HLI, unpublished diary, 2/7/42, HLIP.
785 "What is the use"; "Alaska is today": Quoted in Potter, *Alaska Under Arms*, p. 33.
"where there was nothing": *Ibid.*, pp. 38–40.

786   "He has picked up rumors": HLI, unpublished diary, 4/11/42, HLIP.

"We were given copies": *Ibid.*, 4/19/42.

788   "The question of morale": Ruth Gruber to HLI, 12/2/41, Container 93, Secretary of the Interior File, HLIP.

"talking to all the leaders": *Ibid.*, Ruth Gruber to HLI, 3/2/42. In her Alaskan travels, Gruber managed to incur the wrath of Lieutenant General Simon Bolivar Buckner when she made public suggestions that the soldiers be allowed to fraternize more freely with the Eskimos and other Alaska natives. Buckner wrote Assistant Secretary of War John J. McCloy in objection to this idea on July 29, 1943, and the letter is worth quoting at length as an illustration of the military mind at work in Alaska: "Whether a white oak tree is superior, equal or inferior to a willow is a matter of opinion depending upon what they are to be used for. At all events, they are different and must be treated differently. . . . Similarly, the Lord in His infinite wisdom has, for reasons beyond our knowledge, created in the Indian a human being differing in many respects from a white man. . . . Profiting by the experience of the Department of the Interior and other agencies in Alaska, certain post commanders have found that, as a matter of common sense and general welfare, it has become desirable to place certain restrictions upon intercourse between white soldiers and Indian girls. . . . In some cases, native girls are encouraged to come to supervised soldier dances but discouraged from associating with soldiers without supervision. No distinct color line is drawn anywhere. Indian soldiers eat, sleep, play, fight and live with white soldiers. In no case are Indian soldiers forbidden to associate with white women. Even Dr. Ruth Gruber will probably testify that she had no difficulty in fully satisfying her desires for associating with Indian soldiers.

"Unfortunately, attempts have been made by certain classes of our white population to arouse indignation and stir up dissatisfaction among the Indians. . . . Among such persons may be found: shyster lawyers and others who get money out of it, politicians who get votes out of it, fifth columnists who seek to destroy our national unity by it, innocent individuals who are misled by one or more of the foregoing classes and persons who see no appreciable differences between the Chinese, the Caucasians, the Japs, the Negroes, the Papuans, the Indians and the Australian Bushmen and who would be happy to intermarry with any of them." Container 93, Secretary of the Interior File, HLIP.

790   "I think the most effective": Quoted in Weglyn, *Years of Infamy*, p. 29.

"There was a considerable amount": *Ibid.*, quoted, p. 30.

791   "Everywhere that the Japanese": Quoted in Myer, *Uprooted Americans*, p. 18.

"The President is authorized": Quoted in Weglyn, *Years of Infamy*, p. 71.

792   "Fancy-named concentration camps": *Ibid.*, quoted, p. 218.

"The Hearst newspapers": HLI, unpublished diary, 2/1/42, HLIP.

"both stupid and cruel": *Ibid.*, 3/1/42.

793   "Information that has come to me": HLI to FDR, 4/13/43, Container 376, Secretary of the Interior File, HLIP.

"Like you, I regret": FDR to HLI, 4/24/43, *ibid.*

"If we can obtain": Quoted in Myer, *Uprooted Americans*, p. 168.

794　"Am I to understand": Stan C. Jackson to HLI, 6/1/43, CHMI.

　　　"The bitterest witches' brew": Quoted in Weglyn, *Years of Infamy*, p. 218.

　　　"Some of [WRA's] difficulties": *Ibid.*

795　"will not be stampeded": *Ibid.*

　　　"It is my understanding": Quoted in Myer, *Uprooted Americans*, pp. 178–79.

　　　"the more I think": Quoted in Morgan, *FDR*, p. 630.

796　"Hostels are nothing": Quoted in Lawrence I. Hewes to Helen Gahagan Douglas, 10/19/45, Container 376, Secretary of the Interior File, HLIP.

　　　"Can a man like Harold Ickes": *Ibid.*

　　　"The job that was handed": HLI to Helen Gahagan Douglas, 11/12/45, *ibid.*

797　"Informant stated": Quoted in Lookstein, *Were We Our Brothers' Keepers?*, p. 108.

　　　"The mass murders are continuing": Quoted in Wyman, *The Abandonment of the Jews*, p. 45.

798　"for some adults": HLI to FDR, 10/7/42, President's Personal File, FDRL.

　　　"In regard to the Jewish children": FDR to HLI, 10/10/42, *ibid.*

　　　"For reasons you will understand": Quoted in Lookstein, *Were We Our Brothers' Keepers?*, p. 110.

　　　"the mills of the Gods": *Ibid.*, quoted, p. 112.

　　　"intention to exterminate": Quoted in Wyman, *The Abandonment of the Jews*, p. 75.

799　"And what will happen": Quoted in Lookstein, *Were We Our Brothers' Keepers?*, pp. 214–15.

800　"American generosity may have to face": *Ibid.*, p. 182.

　　　"a reasonable proportion": *Ibid.*, p. 194.

801　"Is this the act": *Ibid.*

　　　"a kind of token payment": Quoted in Wyman, *The Abandonment of the Jews*, p. 266.

　　　"It's a great idea": Quoted in Gruber, *Haven*, pp. 14–15.

803　"intolerable that anti-Nazis": Quoted in Myer, *Uprooted Americans*, p. 114.

　　　"he asked me to draft": Gruber, *Haven*, p. 205.

　　　"I have nothing to report to you": *Ibid.*, quoted, p. 207.

804　"It would be inhumane": Quoted in Myer, *Uprooted Americans*, p. 120.

　　　"We won": Quoted in Gruber, *Haven*, p. 209.

　　　"The killers killed": Elie Wiesel in Foreword to Lookstein, *Were We Our Brothers' Keepers?*, p. 11.

55. *The Scent of Lilacs*

The brief "alliance" between Roosevelt and Willkie is discussed in some detail in Mary Earhart Dillon's *Wendell Willkie*, and is nicely analyzed by John Morton Blum in *V Was for Victory*. The betrayal of Henry A. Wallace (which is how he viewed it, and some historians have agreed) is well documented in John Morton Blum, ed., *The Diary of Henry A. Wallace, 1942–1945* (Boston: Houghton Mifflin, 1973); Samuel I. Rosenman, *Working with Roosevelt*; and Edward L. and Frederick H. Schapsmeier, *Prophet in Politics: Henry A. Wallace in the War Years* (Ames: Iowa State University

Press, 1970). The standard Roosevelt biographies cover the campaign of 1944 with varying levels of detail, as does Richard Norton Smith in *Thomas E. Dewey and His Times* (New York: Simon & Schuster, 1982). Information on Raymond Ickes's Iwo Jima experience is from a telephone interview with the author, 8/24/89. Roosevelt's death and burial are covered in great detail in Joseph Lash's *Eleanor and Franklin.*

PAGE

805 "Bill is with me": Quoted in Johnson, *William Allen White's America,* p. 331.
806 "The other day Mrs. White": William Allen White to Gifford Pinchot, 5/17/39, in Johnson, *Selected Letters of William Allen White,* p. 376.
     "I have been a little worried": HLI, unpublished diary, 1/30/44, HLIP.
     "glad to be there" (note): HLI, *Diary,* vol. II, p. 625.
807 "I was devoted to Missy": HLI to Mrs. Ann Rochon, 8/1/44, Container 162, Secretary of the Interior File, HLIP.
     "Some time before midnight": HLI, unpublished diary, 5/20/44, HLIP.
808 "The political situation": HLI to Stacey Mosser, 1/6/44, Container 162, Secretary of the Interior File, HLIP.
     "Are the Thirty-one United Nations": Wendell Willkie, *One World* (New York: Simon & Schuster, 1943), p. 180.
809 "I don't know whether": Quoted in Blum, *V Was for Victory,* p. 271.
     "a reputable Harding": HLI to Stacey Mosser, 1/6/44, Container 162, Secretary of the Interior File, HLIP.
     "All that is within me": Quoted in Miller, *FDR,* p. 499.
     "I shall never forget the expressions": Allen Drury, *A Senate Journal, 1943–1945* (New York: McGraw-Hill, 1963), p. 216.
     "It was a shock": Brinkley, *Washington Goes to War,* p. 252.
810 "He's just tired": *Ibid.,* quoted, p. 253.
     "I am just not going": Quoted in Rosenman, *Working with Roosevelt,* p. 439.
811 "Wallace's face can be": *Ibid.,* p. 442.
     "Ickes said how much": in Blum, *The Diary of Henry A. Wallace,* p. 361.
     "He said I was his choice": *Ibid.,* p. 362.
     "I personally would vote": Quoted in Schapsmeier, *Prophet in Politics,* p. 103.
     "You have written me": Quoted in Rosenman, *Working with Roosevelt,* p. 446.
812 "The issue of the city bosses": Quoted in HLI, unpublished diary, 7/23/44, HLIP.
     "tell the Senator": Quoted in Rosenman, *Working with Roosevelt,* p. 451.
     "Wallace himself took": *Ibid.*
813 "old and tired and quarrelsome": Quoted in Smith, *Thomas E. Dewey,* p. 404.
     "The Dragon": HLI, "The Eager Man Who Was Somewhere Else," 8/10/44, Speeches and Writings, Container 350, Secretary of the Interior File, HLIP.
     "Mr. Dewey's well-financed": HLI, untitled address before the Ninth Convention of the International Union of United Automobile, Aircraft and Agricultural Workers of America, 9/12/44, *ibid.*
814 "These Republican leaders": Quoted in Rosenman, *Working with Roosevelt,* p. 477.

"Let's get this straight": Quoted in Smith, *Thomas E. Dewey*, p. 424.

815 "I realize . . . that": HLI to Governor Thomas E. Dewey, 9/28/44, Container 238, Secretary of the Interior File, HLIP.

"I understand that": HLI, "Don't Change a Trojan Horse in the Middle of a War," 10/8/44, Speeches and Writings, Container 351, *ibid*.

"not been written": HLI, "Gullible's Travels," 10/10/44, *ibid*.

"glad that Governor Dewey": HLI, "Ananias Rides Both on and in the Trojan Horse," 10/16/44, *ibid*.

816 "I never heard a candidate": Quoted in "Town Meeting of the Air: For a Sound National Administration—Roosevelt or Dewey," published by *Reader's Digest* (Columbus, Ohio, October 26, 1944), Container 352, *ibid*.

"the progress America has made": HLI, "Promise Versus Performance," 11/1/44, *ibid*.

"In a last desperate effort": HLI, untitled, 11/2/44, *ibid*.

"the 1944 edition of Warren G. Harding": HLI, "Dewey: The Man Nobody Is For," 11/3/44, *ibid*.

"Great issues are at stake": HLI, "Dewey: Apostle of Hate," 11/5/44, *ibid*.

"I still think he's": Quoted in William D. Hasset, *Off the Record with FDR, 1942–1945* (New Brunswick, N.J.: Rutgers University Press, 1958).

"Dear Harold": FDR to HLI, 11/27/44, Container 265, Secretary of the Interior File, HLIP.

817 "In spite of our conversation": FDR to HLI, 12/9/44, *ibid*.

"Your letter of December 9": Quoted in HLI, unpublished diary, 12/16/34.

818 "We are both distressed": Margaret Robins to HLI, 7/19/37, Container 162, Secretary of the Interior File, HLIP.

"According to the papers": HLI, unpublished diary, 2/25/45, *ibid*.

819 "I have had two": *Ibid*., 3/11/45.

"I asked what was up": *Ibid*., 4/28/45.

"I have a terrific headache": Quoted in Bishop, *FDR's Last Year*, p. 580.

820 "Is there anything I can do for you?": *Ibid*., p. 598.

"The Vice President": HLI, unpublished diary, 4/28/45.

"I was very glad indeed": *Ibid*.

821 "I'll never forget that train trip": Quoted in Boettiger, *A Love in Shadow*, p. 261.

"The air was clear and cool"; "everything was in dignified and simple good taste": HLI, unpublished diary, 4/29/45.

"It seemed not simply": William S. White, *Majesty and Mischief: A Mixed Tribute to FDR* (New York: McGraw-Hill, 1961), p. 14.

822 It was Frances Perkins who made a note of the fact that Ickes was weeping during the funeral. Oral history memoirs, vol. VIII, pp. 808–9, OHCU.

56. *The Rawest Proposition*

The best published account of the events that led up to the Ickes resignation is Robert J. Donovan's *Conflict and Crisis: The Presidency of Harry S. Truman, 1945–1948* (New York: W. W. Norton, 1977), although Tris Coffin's more nearly contemporary *Mis-*

souri Compromise (Boston: Little, Brown, 1947) is a remarkably knowledgeable and fair-minded treatment of the incident, if clearly leaning in Ickes's favor. Leaning in Truman's direction all the way is his own *Memoirs of Harry S. Truman*, Volume I: *Year of Decisions* (New York: Doubleday & Co., 1955; New York: Da Capo Press, 1986).

PAGE

823 "We sat before lunch": Marquis Childs, *Witness to Power* (New York: McGraw-Hill, 1975), pp. 44–45.
824 "I have felt very much depressed": HLI, unpublished diary, 4/29/45, HLIP.
825 "That is the first": Harry Truman to Senator Carl A. Hatch, 6/24/45, President's Secretary's File, HSTL.
    "He feels quite pessimistic": HLI, unpublished diary, 6/2/45, HLIP.
826 "This he told me himself": HLI to John Boettiger, 8/28/45, Anna Roosevelt Papers, FDRL.
    "Hiram Johnson came back": Drury, *A Senate Journal*, p. 200.
827 "She makes more money": HLI, unpublished diary, 10/13/45.
    "Our association has been": HLI to Abe Fortas, 12/24/45, Container 161, Secretary of the Interior File, HLIP.
828 "I told him that": HLI, unpublished diary, 1/12/46.
    "A short time ago": *Ibid.*, 5/17/42.
    "I told Davies": *Ibid.*, 4/29/44.
829 "He had talked": *Ibid.*, 9/9/44.
    "I told Forrestal": *Ibid.*, 11/26/44.
    "He told me that": *Ibid.*, 4/4/45.
830 "I could just about ruin": *Ibid.*, 4/29/45.
    "This is my position": *Ibid.*, 1/20/46.
    "In connection with Pauley": *Ibid.*, 4/3/46.
831 "told me that of course": *Ibid.*
    "Did Mr. Pauley ever tell you": Quoted in Coffin, *Missouri Compromise*, p. 48.
    "I am sure Mr. Ickes": *Ibid.*, p. 49.
    "Tell 'em the truth" (note): Truman, *Memoirs*, vol. I, p. 554.
832 "I don't think so": Quoted in Donovan, *Conflict and Crisis*, p. 181.
    "commit perjury"; "I could no longer": *Ibid.*, p. 182.
    "My dear Harold": Quoted in HLI, unpublished diary, 2/17/46.
    "I deeply appreciate": *Ibid.*
    "was jammed": Coffin, *Missouri Compromise*, p. 48. This entire account of the Ickes farewell press conference is based on Coffin, pp. 54–61.

57. Final Barricades

My overview of the postwar years is based largely on Coffin's *Missouri Compromise*, Donovan's *Conflict and Crisis*, Alonzo F. Hamby, *Beyond the New Deal: Harry S. Truman and American Liberalism* (New York: Columbia University Press, 1973); and Eric F. Goldman's *The Crucial Decade and After: America, 1945–1960* (New York:

Alfred A. Knopf, 1956). The 1948 Presidential election is treated in detail in a variety of sources—John Morton Blum's edited version of *The Diary of Henry A. Wallace*; Merle Miller's *Plain Speaking: An Oral Biography of Harry S. Truman* (New York: Berkley, 1974), which should be used with full knowledge of the fact that Truman took advantage of these interviews to get even with a few people; Edward L. and Frederick Schapsmeiers' *Prophet in Politics*; Richard Norton Smith's *Thomas E. Dewey*, Richard J. Walter's *Henry Wallace, Harry Truman and the Cold War* (New York: The Viking Press, 1976); and two recent articles: Robert H. Ferrell, "The Last Hurrah," and Alonzo L. Hamby, "The Accidental Presidency," both in *The Wilson Quarterly*, Spring 1988. Conservation matters in the immediate postwar years are covered well in Irving Brant, *Adventures in Conservation* and in Stephen Fox's *John Muir and His Legacy*. The literature of postwar anticommunism is monstrous; here are a few useful titles: Bert Andrews, *Washington Witch Hunt* (New York: Random House, 1948), a militantly radical view of the proceedings written in the glare of events; Lewis H. Carlson, "J. Parnell Thomas"; Walter Goodwin, *The Committee*; Robert L. Griffith, *The Politics of Fear: Joseph R. McCarthy and the Senate* (Amherst: University of Massachusetts Press, 1987); Thomas C. Reeves, *The Life and Times of Joe McCarthy: A Biography* (New York: Stein and Day, 1982); Peter L. Steinberg, *The Great 'Red Menace': United States Prosecution of American Communists, 1947–1952* (Westport, Conn.: Greenwood Press, 1984). Helen Gahagan Douglas's adventures with Richard Nixon are told in her autobiography, *A Full Life* (Garden City, N.Y.: Doubleday, 1982).

PAGE

834   " 'Honest' Harold Ickes": Harry S. Truman to Jonathan Daniels 2/26/50 (not sent), in Robert H. Ferrell, ed., *Off the Record: The Private Papers of Harry S. Truman* (New York: Harper & Row, 1980), p. 174.

835   "There has been an unceasing fight": Quoted in Donovan, *Conflict and Crisis*, p. 181.
        "One has the feeling": *Ibid.*, p. 183.
        "unsavory odor": Quoted in Hamby, *Beyond the New Deal*, p. 73.
        "raised distressing doubts": *Ibid.*
        "Here is the old": *Ibid.*

836   "you stand before": Harry S. Truman to Edwin A. Pauley, 3/13/46, Official File, HSTL.
        "Your unwarranted attacks": Quoted in Donovan, *Conflict and Crisis*, p. 183.

837   "The end of the war": Catton, *The War Lords*, p. 307.

839   "I do not want it to come": Quoted in Coffin, *Missouri Compromise*, p. 223.
        "A democracy cannot afford": *Ibid.*, pp. 223–24.

840   "I have read a good many": HLI, "Man to Man," 4/1/46, Speeches and Writings, Container 458, HLIP.

841   "Harold Ickes is old enough": Editorial note, *New Republic*, May 2, 1949.
        "There can be no doubt": HLI to Ben Hibbs, 3/11/48, Speeches and Writings, Container 442, HLIP.

"General Johnson": HLI, "My Twelve Years with Roosevelt," *Saturday Evening Post*, March 12, 1948.

842   "both irresponsible and arrogant": *Ibid.*, March 19, 1948.

"Mr. Ickes' views": *Ibid.*, March 12, 1948.

"Just why Mr. Sinclair": HLI, "Man to Man," 6/18/47, Container 43, HLIP.

"I would like to present": HLI, "An Oil Policy: An Open Letter to the Members of the Congress of the United States," May 1947, *ibid.*

843   "President Truman knows": HLI, "Man to Man," 7/19/46, Speeches and Writings, Container 458, HLIP.

"I appreciate most highly": Harry S. Truman to HLI, 7/10/51, Container 87, HLIP.

[I]t seems to me": HLI, "Man to Man," 7/15/46, Speechs and Writings, Container 458, HLIP.

844   "started his career": HLI, "Man to Man," 4/8/46, *ibid.*

"Discrimination against": HLI, "Man to Man," 10/28/47, Container 457, HLIP.

"To be sure": HLI, "MacArthur Home for Christmas," *New Republic*, December 25, 1950.

845   "in reaching out": Quoted in Brant, *Adventures in Conservation*, p. 279.

"These lands belong": HLI to J. A. Krug, 9/23/47, Container 77, HLIP.

846   "President Truman could not have": HLI, "Farewell, Secretary Krug," *New Republic*, November 28, 1949.

"If Dinosaur National Monument": HLI to Bernard DeVoto, 12/12/50, Container 78, HLIP.

"It keeps me out of the rut": HLI to Raymond Robins, 12/7/49, Container 82, HLIP.

"The committee starts off": HLI, "Man to Man," 1/30/47, Speeches and Writings, Container 458.

847   "Thus, thanks to": HLI, "Guilt by Non-Association," *New Republic*, June 20, 1949.

"If the FBI": HLI, "A Dirtier 'Dirty Business,'" *New Republic*, January 9, 1950.

"If it is a practice": HLI, "A Decoration for Mr. McCarthy," *New Republic*, April 10, 1950.

"He should be impeached": HLI, "And a Woman Shall Lead Them," *New Republic*, June 19, 1950.

848   "Bumbling, babbling Joe": HLI, "McCarthy Strips Himself," *New Republic*, August 7, 1950.

"has practically no chance": HLI, unpublished diary, 7/16/48.

849   "When I was shown": *Ibid.*, 10/23/48.

850   "I am here to talk": HLI, untitled speech, 10/14/48, Speeches and Writings, Container 409.

"Has anybody here": HLI, untitled speech, 10/28/48, *ibid.*

"I had no illusions": HLI, unpublished diary, 10/23/48, *ibid.*

"It actually took": *Ibid.*, 11/6/48.

851 "I am becoming": HLI to Anna Roosevelt, 3/20/50, Anna Roosevelt Papers, FDRL.

"You expressed the idea": HLI to Helen Gahagan Douglas, 4/13/50, Container 55, HLIP.

"because she is": HLI, untitled script for telecast, 11/11/50, Speeches and Writings, Container 410, HLIP.

852 "In order to cover": HLI, "Helen Douglas and Tobey," *New Republic*, October 16, 1950.

853 "I was awake again": HLI, unpublished diary, 5/27/51, HLIP.

"Harold continues to be": Jane Ickes to Anna Roosevelt, 8/31/51, Anna Roosevelt Papers, FDRL.

854 "Harold has just come through": Jane Ickes to Anna Roosevelt, 10/27/51, *ibid*.

"The weather has been": HLI, unpublished diary, 12/27/51, HLIP.

"respectfully suggest": HLI to Oscar Chapman, 1/4/52, Container 50, HLIP.

"He only returned": Helen Cunningham to Dean Albertson, 1/24/52, *ibid*.

855 "I have loved you": HLI to Jane Ickes, 5/6/48, CHMI.

"Any husband": HLI to Raymond Ickes, 5/16/48, CHMI.

Epilogue

PAGE

858 "Mr. Ickes was preeminent": Quoted in *Washington Times-Herald*, February 4, 1952. The disruption in the service caused by Truman's entrance was described to me in an interview with Elizabeth Ickes, August 1989.

"This company come to pay": Quoted in *Washington Evening Star*, February 7, 1952.

859 "I'll never forget it": *Ibid.*, April 21, 1952.

"rough-hewn but gentle": *Ibid.*

"We meet again": *Ibid.*

Sources

PRIMARY MATERIALS

Harold LeClair Ickes never threw anything away, and most of what he and his family kept out of the nearly seventy-eight years of an incredibly busy life now resides in the papers deposited in the Library of Congress—an estimated 150,000 items in 589 containers occupying 225 feet of linear space. In volume, the material is divided nearly evenly between that confined to the Secretary of the Interior File and that which encompasses the years before and after his government service. Superbly catalogued and accessible, it is one of the richest and most complete records of a single human life that exists anywhere and has been the source for most of my discussion of his personal and professional existence.

By far the best known and most frequently used portion of the Ickes Library of Congress collection is the diary that he began the first week of his tenure as Secretary of the Interior and continued until his death—a little under five million words in length, roughly 800,000 words of which were published as *The Secret Diary of Harold L. Ickes* in three volumes in the early 1950s: *The First Thousand Days, 1933–1936* (1953), *The Inside Struggle, 1936–1939* (1954), and *The Lowering Clouds* (1954), which ended with the attack on Pearl Harbor. All three were edited by Ickes's widow, Jane Dahlman Ickes, who had planned a fourth and final volume, but became ensnarled in a fight with the publisher, Simon & Schuster, over portions of the diary she refused to have published. "S & S," she wrote to her old friend Anna Roosevelt on April 17, 1955, revealing a streak of angry determination worthy of her husband's memory, "is raising hell and bandying threats of suits to make me divulge the parts of the diary which have been edited out of the post-Pearl parts. I can tell you now that NEVER will they get them" (Anna Roosevelt Papers, FDRL). They did not get the excised portions, nor did the volume ever get published. She was regretful but still firm when word came to her that Eleanor Roosevelt was unhappy over the publication of some of Ickes's references to her and her husband, as well as the Roosevelt children—even though Jane had let Anna delete any portions of the diary that she might find offensive (Harold McEwen Ickes remembers, in fact, that Anna erred on the side of honesty, if anything, often putting material back in that Jane had taken out). "I regret not going to your mother at the outset," she wrote Anna on April 22, 1954, to explain to her that I was complying with Harold's wishes in regard to publication and that, quite independently of Harold, I regarded the diary, in its totality, as a real asset for our side. I should have warned her that there would be observations critical of her and of her sons and even that the President's feet of clay, as seen by Harold, would appear. This is my one deep regret, because I feel that it is too late to do this now, without seeming to apologize for Harold which, of course, I am not willing to do. [Anna Roosevelt Papers, FDRL]

However abbreviated and incomplete, the published diaries earned encomiums even from those who, like Richard Rovere in *The New Yorker*, professed to find their author personally repugnant: "The second volume of Harold L. Ickes' 'Secret Diary,' he wrote in the July 5, 1954 issue of the magazine,

makes it plain that what we have here is not only the fullest and most instructive of all inside accounts of the Roosevelt administration but an addition of some importance to the main body of our literature. Ickes is not just one more political diarist, interesting because strategically placed; he is one of the great journal-keepers, in certain respects the peer of another narcissistic bureaucrat, Samuel Pepys. As often as not, Ickes is dealing with matters about which most of us nowadays couldn't care less. . . . Ickes, however, generates an interest in whatever he is writing about. The truth is that he has *created* something, or at least has fashioned a work that has some of the attributes of creativeness. His Washington, like Dickens' London, Balzac's Paris, and Faulkner's Jefferson, is a community in which one can settle down and lead a life of one's own.

The remaining four million unpublished words of the diary, gossipy, self-absorbed, observant, obtuse, angry, wise, ridiculous, colorful, boring, meticulously—indeed, obsessively—detailed, validate Rovere's opinion. The diary, published and un-published, is nothing less than essential to an understanding of the entire Age of Roosevelt.

The Library of Congress Ickes collection also holds the kind of thing every biographer must dream of and almost never finds (and, in fact, this particular cache of material was not opened to the public until 1977 because of family restrictions). In 1933, simultaneously with the diary, HLI began to dictate a set of personal memoirs that at first were designed to be a perfectly ordinary narrative of his background and life up to that point for the benefit of his children and grandchildren—but which, out of some immeasurable compulsion, quickly evolved into something similar to the life histories modern psychotherapists attempt to extract from their patients. By my count, there were more than 800,000 words of dictation that spilled from him before the purgation ended. Unhappily, the memoirs are not nearly as coherent as one would like, since they were dictated at odd snatches of time and in varying moods, and quite often Ickes wandered indiscriminately from one subject to another at any given dictation—often paying little attention to chronology along the way. While the intensely personal nature of these memoirs makes it unlikely that Ickes ever intended to publish them, the typed transcript that the inconceivably patient and accommodating May Conley made is replete with revisions, corrections, and in-sertions scratched in with pen by his own hand. Miss Conley did her best to keep all this in some kind of order in her typed transcripts, and the archivists of the material have followed suit, but even if Ickes had stuck to one version of his personal life, the job would have been difficult. In fact, there are two distinct (though often overlapping) versions. He began to dictate the first in 1933 and continued to add to it until sometime in 1939; it is labeled "Unpublished personal memoirs" and is divided into twenty-six individual folders (each with its own pagination) found in Container 432 of the Ickes Papers. The second version, apparently begun sometime in 1939 and continued for perhaps a year, is labeled "Untitled autobiographical draft" and is found, with its own pagination, in Container 435.

In addition to the strictly personal memoirs, sometimes simultaneously, sometimes after long gaps of time, he also managed to dictate two additional sets of reminiscences, these generally confined to a discussion of his professional and political careers, but which, from time to time, also reveal a broad patch of his emotional life. The first, "On My Interest in Politics and Public Affairs," which may or may not have been meant for publication, was begun in 1933 and finished in 1937; it covers his public career up to 1933 and is found, with its own pagination, in Container 433. "I made no effort to give to this political autobiography a literary flavor," he wrote at its end.

> Moreover, unfortunately, I made the mistake of letting many years elapse before I undertook to write it at all and even after I had begun I found that I could not push it through quickly to completion after I had started it. . . . I make this explanation because, if any one should read this document, he might wonder why there have been so many omissions and repetitions. . . . Considering the circumstances in which I have written it, it will perhaps be easy to understand why the narrative lacks continuity and even why events sometimes are not set down in their chronological order. [Pages 481–82]

The disclaimer aside, parts of this memoir did find their way into his published reminiscence, *Autobiography of a Curmudgeon* (1943).

The fourth and final reminiscence is entitled "Unpublished cabinet memoirs" and is found, again with its own pagination, in Containers 436–441. Well organized and very neatly done up, this unfinished work almost certainly was the book which kept him occupied intermittently during the last years of his life. It was based on information from his own diary, for the most part, and some of it found its way into his published series of articles in the *Saturday Evening Post* in 1948, "My Twelve Years with FDR."

I know of nothing in the archives of anyone, anywhere—certainly of no major American political figure—that compares with the length, candor, and obsessively revelatory quality of these four extraordinary documents. Because this kind of material is by its very nature susceptible to all kinds of readings, I have used direct quotation, sometimes at length, whenever the literary quality of the material seemed to justify it—and even when it did not, but the information itself was important enough. It seems to me that if a man chooses to expose his own frailties or reveal some dark truth or suspicion about someone else, it is generally a good idea to let him do it himself and not attempt to explain to the reader what it is he is trying to say. By the same token, I have tried to keep my own analysis of the material and the man behind it within the limits imposed by the fact that I am, at best, a writer and a historian, not a psychoanalyst, and at worst, just as capable of misreading him as any other biographer (or psychoanalyst, for that matter) would be who was separated from his subject by the nearly forty years years since Ickes's death. Prudence and a decent respect for the sanctity of the individual human mind seem to be called for under such circumstances, and I have tried to exercise both without abdicating my responsibility to present the truth as I perceive it to have been. What was most astounding about these memoirs (aside from the fact that he felt compelled to produce them) was that, in spite of considerable repetition from one to another version, I found no evidence of one flatly contradicting another—Ickes did not correct these memories so much as elaborate upon them; in that respect, at least, he does not confuse the hapless biographer.

In addition to the Ickes collection, the Library of Congress also holds the papers of Benjamin Cohen, Thomas B. Corcoran, James A. Farley, Gifford Pinchot, Donald R. Richberg, and Henry A. Wallace, among other New Dealers, and I had frequent recourse to these as well. Finally, the microfilm version of the Margaret Dreier Robins papers in the Papers of the Women's Trade Union League (University of Florida) is available through services in the public reading room of the library.

However rich, the personal and public material in the Library of Congress is not all that exists. I was about halfway through this project when I learned that Elizabeth Ickes, HLI's daughter from his second marriage, had discovered several boxes of materials that had never found their way into the Library of Congress. She sent them to her brother, Harold McEwen Ickes (also born of the second marriage), where at this writing they remain. Mr. Ickes, as noted in the acknowledgments, kindly gave me access to this new material in the course of my work, and among its most valuable treasures was a previously unknown letter written by HLI to the mother of Jeremiah (Lazar) Averbuch in 1908; four diaries that the young Ickes kept during his college years, starting something he would carry to extremes in later life; scores of love letters between HLI and Jane Dahlman that left no doubt that theirs was a love affair of endearingly old-fashioned intensity; and HLI's instructions to Jane and Raymond on various matters to be attended to upon his death.

Other primary sources included the manuscript, correspondence, and Oral History Office collections at the Bancroft Library, University of California, Berkeley (the papers of Hiram Johnson, Chester Rowell, and James Westfall Thompson, and the oral memoirs of Horace Albright, William Colby, Newton Drury, S. Bevier Show, and Paul S. Taylor); a miscellany of materials at the Blair County Historical Society in Altoona, Pennsylvania; the map and photographic collections of the Chicago Historical Society; the archives of the University of Chicago (the papers of William Rainey Harper, Amos Alonzo Stagg, and Charles Merriam, and the files of the *Chicago Weekly*); the collections of the Oral History Research Office at Butler Library, Columbia University (the memoirs of John Carmody, Frances Perkins, Henry A. Wallace, Claude Wickard, and Milburn Wilson); the Western History Collection of the Denver Public Library (the papers of The Wilderness Society); the Manuscript Department of the William R. Perkins Library, Duke University (the papers of Harry Slattery); the archives of Kings Canyon National Park (materials on the history and creation of the park); National Archives and Records Service, Kansas City, Missouri (materials on the history of the Jackson Hole National Monument controversy and operational matters in National Park Service Chicago headquarters during World War II); the Franklin D. Roosevelt Memorial Library, Hyde Park (the papers of Harry Hopkins, Henry Morgenthau, Anna Roosevelt, Franklin D. Roosevelt, and Rexford G. Tugwell); and the Harry S. Truman Memorial Library, Independence, Missouri (materials on the relationship between Ickes and Truman in the President's Official File and the President's Secretary's File).

INTERVIEWS

Personal interviews were held with Raymond Ickes, HLI's firstborn son, in Berkeley, California, in March 1985 and March 1986. We also held numerous telephone conversations and kept up a lively correspondence. An interview with Anne Ickes Carroll, Wilmarth Thompson Ickes's daughter, took place in May 1985. Harold McEwen Ickes, Harold's son by his second marriage, was interviewed in May 1989. Elizabeth Ickes, Harold's daughter, was interviewed by telephone in August 1989. Telephone interviews were held in the summer of 1985 with Mrs. J. Frederick Schoellkopf, a friend of the family during the Hubbard Woods days.

NEWSPAPERS

Scattered issues of the following newspapers were consulted during the course of research: the *Altoona Tribune*, 1874–1897; the *Chicago Daily News*, 1920–1933; the *Chicago Herald-Examiner*, 1927–1933; the *Chicago Tribune*, 1897–1952; the *Chicago Weekly* (University of Chicago student newspaper), 1894–1897; *The New York Times*, 1920–1952; the *Washington Evening Star*, 1952; the *Washington Herald*, 1932–1939, the *Washington Times-Herald*, 1939–1952, and the *Washington Post*, 1932–1952.

DISSERTATIONS AND UNPUBLISHED MANUSCRIPTS

Carlson, Lewis H. "J. Parnell Thomas and the House Committee on Un-American Activities, 1938–1948." Ph.D. dissertation. Michigan State University, 1967.

Freeman, John Leiper, Jr. "The New Deal for Indians: A Study in Bureau-Committee Relations in American Government." Ph.D. dissertation. Princeton University, 1952.

Fringer, Guy. "Olympic National Park." Unpublished manuscript. National Archives, Washington, D.C., 1985.

Grede, John Frederick. "The New Deal in the Virgin Islands, 1931–1941." Ph.D. dissertation. University of Chicago, 1962.

Kifer, Allen Francis. "The Negro Under the New Deal, 1933–1941." Ph.D. dissertation. University of Wisconsin, 1961.

Koppes, Clayton R. "Oscar L. Chapman: A Liberal at the Interior Department, 1933–1953." Ph.D. dissertation. University of Kansas, 1974.

Mathews, Thomas G. "Puerto Rican Politics and the New Deal." Ph.D. dissertation. Columbia University, 1957.

Trani, Eugene P. "The Secretaries of the Department of the Interior, 1849–1969." Unpublished manuscript. National Anthropological Archives, Washington, D.C., 1975.

BOOKS

Abbott, Lawrence F., ed. *The Letters of Archie Butt, Personal Aide to President Roosevelt.* Garden City, N.Y.: Doubleday, 1924.

Acheson, Dean. *Present at the Creation: My Years in the State Department.* New York: W.W. Norton, 1969.

Adams, Henry H. *Harry L. Hopkins: A Biography.* New York: G. P. Putnam's Sons, 1977.

————. *Years of Deadly Peril: The Coming of the War, 1939–1941.* New York: David McKay Co., 1969.

Addams, Jane. *Twenty Years at Hull-House: With Autobiographical Notes.* New York: Macmillan, 1910; reprinted, with foreword by Henry Steele Commager, 1961.

Albertson, Dean. *Roosevelt's Farmer: Claude R. Wickard in the New Deal.* New York: Columbia University Press, 1961.

Albright, Horace, and Robert Cahn. *The Birth of the National Park Service: The Founding Years, 1913–1933.* Salt Lake City: Howe Brothers, 1985.

Alinksy, Saul. *John L. Lewis: An Unauthorized Biography.* New York: G. P. Putnam's Sons, 1949.

Allen, Frederick Lewis. *Only Yesterday: An Informal History of the 1920's.* New York: Harper & Brothers, 1931; reprinted, Harper & Row, 1964.

————. *Since Yesterday: The Nineteen-Thirties in America, September 3, 1929–September 3, 1939.* New York: Harper & Row, 1940.

Allen, Robert S., and William V. Shannon. *The Truman Merry-Go-Round.* New York: The Vanguard Press, 1950.

Alsop, Joseph. *FDR, 1882–1945: A Centenary Remembrance.* New York: The Viking Press, 1982.

Altoona City Directory, 1886.

Anderson, Judith Icke. *William Howard Taft: An Intimate History.* New York: W. W. Norton & Co., 1981.

Anderson, Marian. *My Lord, What a Morning.* New York: Viking Press, 1956.

Andrews, Bert. *Washington Witch Hunt.* New York: Random House, 1948.

Baker, Leonard. *Brandeis and Frankfurter: A Dual Biography.* New York: Harper & Row, 1984.

Baldwin, Hanson W., and Shepard Stone, eds. *We Saw It Happen: The News Behind the News That's Fit to Print—by Thirteen Correspondents of The New York Times.* Cleveland: World Publishing Co., 1938.

Bargeron, Carlisle. *Confusion on the Potomac: The Alarming Chaos and Feuds of Washington.* New York: Wilfred Funk, Inc., 1941.

Barnard, Harry. *Eagle Forgotten: The Life of John Peter Altgeld.* New York: Duell, Sloan & Pearce, 1938.

Baruch, Bernard. *Baruch: The Public Years.* New York: Holt, Rinehart and Winston, 1960.

Bates, J. Leonard. "Ickes, Anna Wilmarth Thompson, Jan. 27, 1873–Aug. 31, 1935." In *Notable American Women, 1607–1950*. Cambridge: Belknap Press of Harvard University Press, 1971.

Beard, Charles A. *President Roosevelt and the Coming of the War, 1941: A Study in Appearances and Reality*. New Haven: Yale University Press, 1948.

————, and Mary R. *America in Midpassage*. New York: The Macmillan Company, 1939.

Bell, Jack. *The Splendid Misery: The Story of the Presidency and Power Politics at Close Range*. Garden City, N.Y.: Doubleday & Co., 1960.

Bell, Millicent. *Marquand: An American Life*. Boston: Little, Brown, 1977.

Berle, Beatrice Bishop, and Travis Beal Jacobs, eds. *Navigating the Rapids, 1918–1971: From the Papers of Adolf A. Berle*. New York: Harcourt Brace Jovanovich, 1973.

Beschloss, Michael R. *Kennedy and Roosevelt: The Uneasy Alliance*. New York: W. W. Norton, 1980.

Billington, Ray Allen. *Westward Expansion: A History of the American Frontier*. New York: The Macmillan Co., 1974.

Bird, Caroline. *The Invisible Scar*. New York: David McKay, 1966.

Bishop, Jim. *FDR's Last Year: April 1944–April 1945*. New York: William Morrow, 1974.

Blair County Historical Society. *Blair County's First Hundred Years, 1846–1946*. Altoona, Penn.: The Mirror Press, 1945.

Bloch, Bryce, and Lamar Middleton, eds. *The World Over in 1940*. New York: Living Age Press, 1941.

Blum, John Morton, ed. *The Diary of Henry A. Wallace, 1942–1945*. Boston: Houghton Mifflin, 1973.

————. *From the Morgenthau Diaries: Years of Crisis, 1928–1938*. Boston: Houghton Mifflin, 1959.

————. *From the Morgenthau Diaries: Years of Deadly Urgency, 1938–1941*. Boston: Houghton Mifflin, 1965.

————, ed. *Public Philosopher: Selected Letters of Walter Lippmann*. New York: Ticknor & Fields, 1985.

————. *V Was for Victory: Politics and American Culture During World War II*. New York: Harcourt Brace Jovanovich, 1976.

Boase, Paul H. *The Rhetoric of Protest and Reform, 1878–1898*. Athens: Ohio University Press, 1980.

Boettiger, John R. *A Love in Shadow*. New York: W. W. Norton, 1978.

Boorstin, Daniel J. *The Americans: The Democratic Experience*. New York: Random House, 1973.

Borchert, James. *Alley Life in Washington: Family, Community, Religion, and Folklife in the City, 1850–1970*. Urbana: University of Illinois Press, 1980.

Bowers, Claude G. *Beveridge and the Progressive Era*. Boston: Houghton Mifflin, 1932.

Bowles, Chester. *Promises to Keep: My Years in Public Life, 1941–1969*. New York: Harper & Row, 1971.

Braeman, John, Robert H. Bremner, and David Brody, eds. *The New Deal—Vol. I,*

The National Level; Vol. II, The State and Local Level. Columbus: Ohio State University Press, 1975.

Brant, Irving. *Adventures in Conservation with Franklin D. Roosevelt*. Flagstaff: Northland Publishing, 1989.

Brinkley, Alan. *Voices of Protest: Huey Long, Father Coughlin, and the Great Depression*. New York: Alfred A. Knopf, 1982.

Brinkley, David. *Washington Goes to War*. New York: Alfred A. Knopf, 1988.

Brownell, Bernard J. *Eugene V. Debs, Spokesman for Labor and Socialism*. Chicago: Charles H. Kerr, 1978.

Bullitt, Orville H., ed. *For the President: Correspondence Between Franklin D. Roosevelt and William C. Bullitt*. Boston: Houghton Mifflin, 1972.

Burns, James MacGregor. *Roosevelt: The Lion and the Fox*. New York: Harcourt, Brace & World, 1956.

―――――. *Roosevelt: The Soldier of Freedom, 1940–1945*. New York: Harcourt Brace Jovanovich, 1970.

Butt, Archie. *Taft and Roosevelt: The Intimate Letters of Archie Butt, Military Aide*. 2 volumes. Garden City, N.Y.: Doubleday, 1930.

Byrnes, James F. *Speaking Frankly*. New York: Harper & Brothers, 1947.

Caemmerer, H. P. *Washington: The National Capital*. Washington, D.C.: U.S. Government Printing Office, 1932.

Campbell, Carlos C. *Birth of a National Park: In the Great Smoky Mountains*. Knoxville: University of Tennessee Press, 1969.

Caro, Robert A. *The Power Broker: Robert Moses and the Fall of New York*. New York: Random House, 1974.

―――――. *The Years of Lyndon B. Johnson: The Path to Power*. New York: Alfred A. Knopf, 1982.

Carrion, Arturo Morales. *Puerto Rico: A Political and Cultural History*. New York: W.W. Norton, 1983.

Catton, Bruce. *The War Lords of Washington*. New York: Harcourt, Brace & Co., 1948.

Chambers, John Whiteclay II. *The Tyranny of Change: America in the Progressive Era, 1900–1917*. New York: St. Martin's Press, 1980.

Childs, Marquis W. *I Write from Washington*. New York: Harper & Brothers, 1942.

―――――. *Witness to Power*. New York: McGraw-Hill, 1975.

Choukas-Bradley, Melanie, and Polly Alexander. *City of Trees*. Washington: Acropolis Books, 1981.

Clapper, Olive Ewing. *Washington Tapestry*. New York: McGraw-Hill, 1944.

Clapper, Raymond. *Watching the World*. New York: McGraw-Hill, 1944.

Clark, J. Stanley. *The Oil Century: From the Drake Well to the Conservation Era*. Norman: University of Oklahoma Press, 1958.

Coffin, Tris. *Missouri Compromise*. Boston: Little, Brown, 1947.

Cohen, Felix. *Felix Cohen's Handbook of Federal Indian Law*. Revised edition. Charlottesville: The Michie Company, 1982.

Cohen, Stan. *The Forgotten War: A Pictorial History of World War II in Alaska and Northwestern Canada*. Missoula, Mont.: Pictorial Histories Publishing Co., 1981.

Coit, Margaret L. *Mr. Baruch*. Boston: Houghton Mifflin, 1957.

Collier, John. *From Every Zenith: A Memoir with Some Essays and Thought*. Denver: Sage Books, 1963.

Collins, Henry Hill, Jr. *America's Own Refugees: Our 4,000,000 Homeless Migrants*. Princeton, N.J.: Princeton University Press, 1941.

Condit, Carl W. *Chicago, 1910–29: Building, Planning, and Urban Technology*. Chicago: University of Chicago Press, 1973.

Congdon, Don, ed. *The Thirties: A Time to Remember*. New York: Simon & Schuster, 1962.

Conklin, Groff. *The New Republic Anthology, 1915–1935*. New York: Dodge, 1936.

Cooper, John Milton. *The Warrior and the Priest: Woodrow Wilson and Theodore Roosevelt*. Cambridge, Mass.: Harvard University Press, 1983.

Croly, Herbert. *The Promise of American Life*. New York: The Macmillan Co., 1909.

Custer, Edgar A. *No Royal Road*. Pittsburgh: H. C. Kinsey & Co., 1937.

Cutler, Phoebe. *The Public Landscape of the New Deal*. New Haven: Yale University Press, 1985.

Cutright, Paul Russell. *Theodore Roosevelt: The Making of a Conservationist*. Urbana: University of Illinois Press, 1985.

Dallek, Robert. *Franklin D. Roosevelt and American Foreign Policy, 1932–1945*. New York: Oxford University Press, 1979.

Daniels, Jonathan. *Frontier on the Potomac*. New York: The Macmillan Co., 1946.

————. *Washington Quadrille: The Dance Beside the Documents*. Garden City, N.Y.: Doubleday & Co., 1968.

Davis, Kenneth S. *FDR: The Beckoning of Destiny, 1882–1928*. New York: G. P. Putnam's Sons, 1972.

————. *FDR: The New York Years, 1928–1933*. New York: Random House, 1985.

————. *FDR: The New Deal Years, 1933–1937*. New York: Random House, 1986.

Davis, Maxine. *They Shall Not Want*. New York: The Macmillan Co., 1937.

Dedmon, Emmett. *Fabulous Chicago*. New York: Random House, 1953.

Degler, Carl N. *The New Deal*. Chicago: Quadrangle Books, 1970.

De Roos, Robert W. *The Thirsty Land*. Palo Alto, Calif.: Stanford University Press, 1948.

Dillon, Mary Earhart. *Wendell Willkie: 1892–1944*. Philadelphia: J.B. Lippincott, 1952.

Donovan, Robert J. *Conflict and Crisis: The Presidency of Harry S. Truman, 1945–1948*. New York: W.W. Norton, 1977.

————. *Tumultuous Years: The Presidency of Harry S. Truman, 1949–1953*. New York: W.W. Norton, 1982.

Douglas, Helen. *A Full Life*. Garden City, N.Y.: Doubleday, 1982.

Douglas, Paul H. *In the Fullness of Time: The Memoirs of Paul H. Douglas*. New York: Harcourt Brace Jovanovich, Inc., 1972.

Douglas, William O. *The Autobiography of William O. Douglas. Go East, Young Man: The Early Years*. New York: Random House, 1974.

————. *The Autobiography of William O. Douglas: The Court Years, 1939–1975*. New York: Random House, 1980.

Downey, Sheridan. *They Would Rule the Valley*. San Francisco: privately printed, 1947.

Dreier, Mary. *Margaret Dreier Robins: Her Life, Letters, and Work*. New York: Island Press, 1950.

Dreiser, Theodore. *Trilogy of Desire: Three Novels by Theodore Dreiser—The Financier, The Titan, The Stoic*. New York: World Publishing, 1972.

Drury, Allen. *A Senate Journal, 1943–1945*. New York: McGraw-Hill, 1963.

Dubofsky, Melvin, and Warren Van Tyne. *John L. Lewis: A Biography*. New York: Quadrangle Books/The New York Times Book Company, 1977.

Dunn, Gerald T. *Hugo Black and the Judicial Revolution*. New York: Simon & Schuster, 1977.

Eccles, Marriner. *Beckoning Frontiers: Public and Personal Recollections*. New York: Alfred A. Knopf, 1951.

Eisenhower, Milton S., ed. *Yearbook of Agriculture, 1934*. Washington, D.C.: U.S. Department of Agriculture, 1934.

Engler, Robert. *The Politics of Oil: Private Power and Democratic Directions*. Chicago: University of Chicago Press, 1961.

Everhart, William C. *The National Park Service*. Boulder, Colo.: Westview Press, 1983.

Farb, Peter. *Man's Rise to Civilization: The Cultural Ascent of the Indians of North America*. New York: E.P. Dutton, 1978.

Farley, James A. *Behind the Ballots: The Personal History of a Politician*. New York: Harcourt, Brace and Co., 1938.

————. *Jim Farley's Story: The Roosevelt Years*. New York: McGraw-Hill, 1948.

Farr, Finis. *FDR*. New Rochelle, N.Y.: Arlington House, 1972.

Federal Writers' Project, Works Progress Administration. *Washington: City and Capital*. Washington, D.C.: U.S. Government Printing Office, 1937.

Fehrenbach, T. R. *FDR's Undeclared War, 1939 to 1941*. New York: David McKay Co., 1967.

Feis, Herbert. *1933: Characters in Crisis*. Boston: Little, Brown, 1966.

Ferber, Edna. *A Peculiar Treasure*. New York: The Literary Guild of America, 1939.

Ferrell, Robert H. *Off the Record: The Private Papers of Harry S. Truman*. New York: Harper & Row, 1980.

Ficken, Robert E. *The Forested Land: A History of Lumbering in Western Washington*. Durham and Seattle: Forest History Society and the University of Washington Press, 1987.

Filler, Louis, ed. *The Anxious Years: America in the Nineteen Thirties—A Collection of Contemporary Writings*. New York: G.P. Putnam's Sons, 1963.

Foresta, Ronald A. *America's National Parks and Their Keepers*. Washington, D.C.: Resources for the Future, 1984.

Fowler, Gene. *Skyline: A Reporter's Reminiscences of the Twenties*. New York: The Viking Press, 1961.

Fox, Stephen. *John Muir and His Legacy: The American Conservation Movement*. Boston: Little, Brown, 1981.

Franck, Harry A. *The Lure of Alaska*. New York: The National Travel Club, 1939.

Franklin, Jay (the Unofficial Observer). *The New Dealers*. New York: The Literary Guild, 1934.

Freidel, Frank. *Launching the New Deal*. Boston: Little, Brown, 1973.

Friedlander, Saul. *Prelude to Downfall: Hitler and the United States, 1939–1941*. Translated from the French by Aline B. and Alexander Werth. New York: Alfred A. Knopf, 1967.

Frome, Michael. *Whose Woods These Are: The Story of the National Forests*. Garden City, N.Y.: Doubleday, 1962.

Furman, Bess. *Washington By-line: The Personal History of a Newspaperwoman*. New York: Alfred A. Knopf, 1949.

Fussell, Paul. *Wartime: Understanding and Behavior in the Second World War*. New York: Oxford University Press, 1989.

Galbraith, John Kenneth. *The Great Crash, 1929*. Boston: Houghton Mifflin, 1955.

Garrett, Charles. *The La Guardia Years: Machine and Reform Politics in New York City*. New Brunswick, N.J.: Rutgers University Press, 1961.

Gates, Paul. *The History of Public Land Law Development*. With a chapter on mining law by Robert W. Swenson. Washington, D.C.: U.S. Government Printing Office, 1968.

Gellerman, William. *Martin Dies*. New York: John Day, 1944.

General Land Office. *Vacant Public Lands on July 1, 1932*. General Land Office Circular No. 1282. Washington, D.C.: U.S. Department of the Interior, 1932.

Gerber, Larry G. *The Limits of Liberalism: Josephus Daniels, Henry Stimson, Bernard Baruch, Donald Richberg, Felix Frankfurter and the Development of the Modern American Political Economy*. New York: New York University Press, 1983.

Gerhart, Eugene C. *America's Advocate: Robert A. Jackson*. Indianapolis: Bobbs-Merrill, 1958.

Gies, Joseph. *The Colonel of Chicago: A Biography of the Chicago Tribune's Legendary Publisher, Colonel Robert McCormick*. New York: E.P. Dutton, 1979.

Ginger, Ray. *The Bending Cross: A Biography of Eugene Victor Debs*. New Brunswick, N.J.: Rutgers University Press, 1949.

Glover, James M. *A Wilderness Original: The Life of Bob Marshall*. Seattle: The Mountaineers, 1986.

Goldman, Eric F. *The Crucial Decade and After: America, 1945–1960*. New York: Alfred A. Knopf, 1956.

————. *Rendezvous with Destiny: A History of Modern American Reform*. New York: Alfred A. Knopf, 1953.

Goodman, Walter. *The Committee: The Extraordinary Career of the House Committee on Un-American Activities*. New York: Farrar, Straus & Giroux, 1968.

Gosnell, Harold F. *Machine Politics: Chicago Model*. Chicago: University of Chicago Press, 1937.

Graham, Otis L., Jr., and Meghan Robinson Wander. *Franklin D. Roosevelt, His Life and Times: An Encyclopedic View*. Boston: G.K. Hall & Co., 1985.

Green, Constance. *Washington: Capital City, 1879–1950*. Princeton, N.J.: Princeton University Press, 1963.

————. *The Secret City: A History of Race Relations in the Nation's Capital*. Princeton, N.J.: Princeton University Press, 1967.

Greenway, John. *Folklore of the Great West*. Palo Alto, Calif.: The American West, 1968.

Griffith, Robert L. *The Politics of Fear: Joseph R. McCarthy and the Senate*. Amherst: University of Massachusetts Press, 1987.

Gruber, Ruth. *Haven: The Unknown Story of 1,000 World War II Refugees*. New York: Coward-McCann, 1984; reprint, New American Library, 1985.

Gruening, Ernest. *The State of Alaska: A Definitive History of America's Northernmost Frontier*. New York: Random House, 1968.

Gunther, John. *Roosevelt in Retrospect: A Profile in History*. New York: Harper & Brothers, 1950.

Gustafson, A. F., et al. *Conservation in the United States*. Ithaca, N.Y.: Comstock Publishing, 1939.

Hamby, Alonzo F. *Beyond the New Deal: Harry S. Truman and American Liberalism*. New York: Columbia University Press, 1973.

Hanson, Earl. *Transformation: The Story of Modern Puerto Rico*. New York: Simon & Schuster, 1955.

Hardeman, D. B., and Donald C. Bacon. *Rayburn: A Biography*. Austin: Texas Monthly Press, 1987.

Hart, Jeffrey. *From This Moment On: America in 1940*. New York: Crown Publishers, 1987.

Hart, Scot. *Washington at War: 1941–1945*. Englewood Cliffs, N.J.: Prentice-Hall, 1970.

Hassett, William D. *Off the Record with FDR, 1942–1945*. New Brunswick, N.J.: Rutgers University Press, 1958.

Hays, Samuel P. *Conservation and the Gospel of Efficiency: The Progressive Conservation Movement*. Cambridge: Harvard University Press, 1959; reprinted 1988.

Healy, Paul F. *Cissy: The Biography of Eleanor M. "Cissy" Patterson*. Garden City, N.Y.: Doubleday & Co., 1966.

Hecht, Ben. *A Child of the Century: The Autobiography of Ben Hecht*. New York: Simon and Schuster, 1954.

Hofstadter, Richard. *The Age of Reform from Bryan to FDR*. New York: Alfred A. Knopf, 1965.

————. *Social Darwinism in American Thought*. Philadelphia: University of Pennsylvania Press, 1944.

Hoover, Irwin H. (Ike). *Forty-two Years in the White House*. Boston: Houghton Mifflin, 1934.

Hopkins, Harry L. *Spending to Save: The Complete Story of Relief*. New York: W. W. Norton, 1936.

Hull, Cordell. *The Memoirs of Cordell Hull*. 2 volumes. New York: The Macmillan Co., 1948.

Hurd, Charles. *When the New Deal Was Young and Gay*. New York: Hawthorn Books, Inc., 1965.

Ickes, Harold L. *America's House of Lords*. New York: Harcourt, Brace & Co., 1939.

————. *The Autobiography of a Curmudgeon*. New York: Reynal & Hitchcock, 1943.

————. *Back to Work: The Story of PWA*. New York: The Macmillan Co., 1935.

_____, ed. *Freedom of the Press Today*. New York: Vanguard Press, 1941.

_____. *The Secret Diary of Harold L. Ickes*: Vol. I, *The First Thousand Days, 1933–1936*; Vol. II, *The Inside Struggle, 1936–1939*; Vol. III, *The Lowering Clouds, 1939–1941*. New York: Simon & Schuster, 1953–1954.

Jackson, Helen Hunt. *A Century of Dishonor*. Reprint, New York: Harper & Row, 1965.

Johnson, Paul. *Modern Times: The World from the Twenties to the Eighties*. New York: Harper and Row, 1985.

Johnson, Walter. *William Allen White's America*. New York: Henry Holt and Co., 1947.

_____. *Selected Letters of William Allen White, 1899–1943*. New York: Henry Holt and Co., 1947.

Jones, Dewitt, and T. H. Watkins. *John Muir's America*. Palo Alto, Calif.: The American West, 1976.

Jones, Howard Mumford. *The Age of Energy: Varieties of American Experience, 1865–1915*. New York: The Viking Press, 1971.

Jones, J. Edward. *And So—They Indicted Me*. New York: privately printed, 1939.

Jones, Jesse H., with Edward Angly. *Fifty Billion Dollars: My Thirteen Years with the RFC (1932–1945)*. New York: The Macmillan Co., 1951.

Josephson, Matthew. *Sidney Hillman: Statesman of American Labor*. Garden City, N.Y.: Doubleday & Co., 1952.

Josephy, Alvin. *The Indian Heritage of America*. New York: Alfred A. Knopf, 1968.

Judd, Lawrence. *Lawrence M. Judd and Hawaii*. Rutland, Ver.: Charles E. Tuttle, 1971.

Kaplan, Justin. *Lincoln Steffens: A Biography*. New York: Simon & Schuster, 1974.

Karl, Barry. *Executive Reorganization and Reform in the New Deal: The Genesis of Administrative Management, 1900–1939*. Cambridge, Mass.: Harvard University Press, 1963.

Kaufmann, Erle. *Trees of Washington, The Man—The City*. Washington, D.C.: The Outdoor Press, 1932.

Kelly, Lawrence C. "Collier, John (1884–1968)." In Howard R. Lamar, ed., *The Reader's Encyclopedia of the American West*. New York: Thomas Y. Crowell Co., 1977.

Kiplinger, W. M. *Washington Is Like That*. New York: Harper & Brothers, 1942.

Klehr, Harvey. *The Heyday of American Communism: The Depression Decade*. New York: Basic Books, 1984.

Kobler, John. *Capone: The Life and World of Al Capone*. New York: G.P. Putnam's Sons, 1971.

Koppes, Clayton R., and Gregory D. Black. *Hollywood Goes to War: How Politics, Profits, and Propaganda Shaped World War II Movies*. New York: The Free Press, 1987.

Krock, Arthur. *In the Nation: 1932–1966*. New York: McGraw-Hill, 1966.

_____. *Memoirs: Sixty Years on the Firing Line*. New York: Funk & Wagnalls, 1968.

Lamar, Howard R. *The Reader's Encyclopedia of the American West*. New York: Thomas Y. Crowell, 1977.

Larrabee, Eric. *Commander in Chief: Franklin Delano Roosevelt, His Lieutenants, and Their War*. New York: Harper & Row, 1987.

Lash, Joseph P. *Dealers and Dreamers: A New Look at the New Deal*. New York: Doubleday, 1988.

_____. *Eleanor and Franklin: The Story of Their Relationship, Based on Eleanor Roosevelt's Private Papers*. New York: W.W. Norton, 1971.

_____, ed. *From the Diaries of Felix Frankfurter*. New York: W.W. Norton, 1975.

_____. *Roosevelt and Churchill: The Partnership that Saved the West*. New York: W.W. Norton, 1976.

Lawrence, David. *Diary of a Washington Correspondent*. New York: H.C. Kinsey & Co., 1942.

Lear, Linda J. *Harold L. Ickes: The Aggressive Progressive, 1874–1933*. New York: Garland Publishing Co., 1981.

Leech, Margaret. *In the Days of McKinley*. New York: Harper and Brothers, 1959.

Leighton, Isabel, ed. *The Aspirin Age: 1919–1941*. New York: Simon & Schuster, 1949.

Lens, Sidney. *The Labor Wars, From the Molly Maguires to the Sitdowns*. Garden City, N.Y.: Doubleday, 1973.

Lerner, Max. *Public Journal: Marginal Notes on Wartime America*. New York: The Viking Press, 1945.

Leshy, John D. *The Mining Law: A Study in Perpetual Motion*. Washington, D.C.: Resources for the Future, 1987.

Leuchtenburg, William E. *Franklin D. Roosevelt and the New Deal*. New York: Harper & Row, 1963.

_____, ed. *Franklin D. Roosevelt: A Profile*. New York: Hill & Wang, 1967.

_____. *The Perils of Prosperity, 1914–32*. Chicago: University of Chicago Press, 1958.

Levy, David W. *Herbert Croly of the New Republic: The Life and Thought of an American Progressive*. Princeton, N.J.: Princeton University Press, 1985.

Lilienthal, David. *TVA: Democracy on the March*. New York: Harper & Brothers, 1944.

_____. *The Journals of David E. Lilienthal*. Volume I: *The TVA Years, 1939–1945*. New York: Harper & Row, 1964.

Lillard, Richard. *The Great Forest*. New York: Alfred A. Knopf, 1947.

Lindbergh, Anne Morrow. *War Within and Without: Diaries of Anne Morrow Lindbergh, 1939–1944*. New York: Harcourt Brace Jovanovich, 1980.

Lindley, Ernest K. *Half Way with Roosevelt*. Revised edition. New York: The Viking Press, 1937.

Lingeman, Richard R. *Don't You Know There's a War On? The American Home Front, 1941–1945*. New York: G.P. Putnam's Sons, 1970.

Link, Arthur S. *Woodrow Wilson and the Progressive Era, 1910–1917*. New York: Harper & Row, 1954; reprinted 1963.

Lisio, Donald J. *The President & Protest: Hoover, Conspiracy, and the Bonus Riot*. Columbia: University of Missouri Press, 1974.

Logan, Rayford W. *Howard University: The First Hundred Years, 1867–1967*. New York: New York University Press, 1969.

Look, David W., and Carole L. Perrault. *The Interior Building: Its Architecture and Its Art*. Washington, D.C.: U.S. Department of the Interior, National Park Service, 1986.

Lookstein, Haskell. *Were We Our Brothers' Keepers? The Public Response of American Jews to the Holocaust, 1938–1944*. New York: Random House, 1985; reprinted 1988.

Lord, Russell. *The Wallaces of Iowa*. Boston: Houghton Mifflin, 1947.

Lord, Walter. *The Good Years: From 1900 to the First World War*. New York: Harper and Brothers, 1960.

Louchheim, Katie. *By the Political Sea*. Garden City, N.Y.: Doubleday & Co., 1970.

_____. *The Making of the New Deal: The Insiders Speak*. Cambridge, Mass.: Harvard University Press, 1983.

Low, Ann Marie. *Dust Bowl Diary*. Lincoln: University of Nebraska Press, 1984.

Lowe, David. *Lost Chicago*. New York: American Legacy Press, 1985.

Lowitt, Richard. *The New Deal and the West*. Bloomington: Indiana University Press, 1984.

Luce, Robert B., ed. Commentary by Arthur M. Schlesinger, Jr. *The Faces of Five Decades: Selections from Fifty Years of the New Republic, 1914–1964*. New York: Simon and Schuster, 1964.

Lundberg, Ferdinand. *America's Sixty Families*. New York: The Vanguard Press, 1937.

MacDonald, Alexander. *Revolt in Paradise: The Social Revolution in Hawaii After Pearl Harbor*. New York: Stephen Day, 1944.

McCarthy, Kathleen D. *Noblesse Oblige: Charity and Cultural Philanthropy in Chicago, 1849–1929*. Chicago: University of Chicago Press, 1982.

McCutcheon, John T. *Drawn from Memory*. New York: Bobbs-Merrill Co., 1950.

McDonald, Forrest. *Insull*. Chicago: University of Chicago Press, 1962.

McElvaine, Robert S. *The Great Depression: America, 1929–1941*. New York: Times Books, 1984.

McIntyre, Ross T., in collaboration with George Creel. *White House Physician*. New York: G.P. Putnam's Sons, 1946.

McJimsey, George. *Harry Hopkins: Ally of the Poor and Defender of Democracy*. Cambridge, Mass.: Harvard University Press, 1987.

McKenna, Marian C. *Borah*. Ann Arbor: The University of Michigan Press, 1961.

Maney, Patrick J. *"Young Bob" La Follette: A Biography of Robert M. La Follette, Jr., 1895–1953*. Columbia: University of Missouri Press, 1978.

Mann, Arthur, ed. *The Progressive Era: Liberal Renaissance or Liberal Failure?* New York: Holt, Rinehart and Winston, 1963.

Manners, William. *TR and Will: A Friendship That Split the Republican Party*. New York: Harcourt Brace Jovanovich, 1969.

Marshall, Robert. *The People's Forests*. New York: Harrison Smith and Robert Haas, 1933.

Marshall, S. L. A. *World War I*. New York: The American Heritage Library, 1985.

Martin, George. *Madam Secretary: Frances Perkins*. Boston: Houghton Mifflin, 1976.

Martin, Ralph G. *Cissy: The Extraordinary Life of Eleanor Medill Patterson*. New York: Simon & Schuster, 1979.

Mason, Alpheus Thomas. *Brandeis: A Free Man's Life*. New York: The Viking Press, 1946.

Mayer, Harold M., and Richard C. Wade. *Chicago: Growth of a Metropolis*. Chicago: University of Chicago Press, 1969.

Meine, Curt. *Aldo Leopold: His Life and Times*. Madison: University of Wisconsin Press, 1988.

Meriam, Lewis. *The Problem of Indian Administration*. Baltimore: Johns Hopkins University Press, 1928.

Merriam, Charles E. *Chicago: A More Intimate View of Urban Politics*. New York: Macmillan, 1929.

Miller, Merle. *Plain Speaking: An Oral Biography of Harry S. Truman*. New York: Berkley, 1974.

Miller, Nathan. *FDR: An Intimate History*. New York: Doubleday, 1983.

Miller, Orlando W. *The Frontier in Alaska and the Matanuska Colony*. New Haven: Yale University Press, 1975.

Millis, Walter, ed., with the collaboration of E. S. Duffield. *The Forrestal Diaries*. New York: The Viking Press, 1951.

Moley, Raymond, and Eliot A. Rosen. *The First New Deal*. New York: Harcourt, Brace & World, Inc., 1966.

Montgomery, Ruth. *Hail to the Chiefs: My Life and Times with Six Presidents*. New York: Coward-McCann, 1970.

Morgan, Murray. *The Last Wilderness*. New York: The Viking Press, 1955; reprint, Seattle: University of Washington Press, 1976.

Morgan, Ted. *FDR: A Biography*. New York: Simon and Schuster, 1985.

Morison, Elting E. *Turmoil and Tradition: A Study of the Life and Times of Henry L. Stimson*. Boston: Houghton Mifflin, 1960.

Morris, Edmund. *The Rise of Theodore Roosevelt*. New York: Coward, McCann & Geoghegan, Inc., 1979.

Morris, Joe Alex. *What a Year!* New York: Harper & Brothers, 1956.

Morris, Lloyd. *Not So Long Ago*. New York: Random House, 1949.

————. *Postscript to Yesterday: America—The Last Fifty Years*. New York: Random House, 1947.

Mowry, George E. *The Era of Theodore Roosevelt, 1900–1912*. New York: Harper & Row, 1958.

Murie, Olaus J., and Margaret E. *Wapiti Wilderness*. New York: Alfred A. Knopf, 1966.

Murphy, Bruce Allen. *Fortas: The Rise and Ruin of a Supreme Court Justice*. New York: William Morrow and Company, 1988.

Murray, Robert K. *The Harding Era: Warren G. Harding and His Administration*. Minneapolis: University of Minnesota Press, 1969.

Myer, Dillon. *Uprooted Americans: The Japanese Americans and the War Relocation Authority During World War II*. Tucson: The University of Arizona Press, 1971.

Nash, Roderick. *Wilderness and the American Mind*. 3rd ed. New Haven: Yale University Press, 1981.

Nesbitt, Henrietta. *White House Diary*. Garden City, N.Y.: Doubleday & Co., 1948.

Nevins, Allan. *The Emergence of Modern America, 1865–1878*. New York: The Macmillan Co., 1927.

————. *The New Deal and World Affairs: A Chronicle of International Affairs, 1933–1945*. New Haven: Yale University Press, 1950.

Nixon, Edgar B., ed. *Franklin D. Roosevelt and Conservation, 1911–1945*. 2 volumes. Hyde Park: General Services Administration, National Archives and Records Service, Franklin D. Roosevelt Library, 1957.

Norris, George W. *Fighting Liberal: The Autobiography of George W. Norris*. New York: The Macmillan Co., 1945.

O'Neill, William L. *A Better World: The Great Schism: Stalinism and the American Intellectuals*. New York: Simon & Schuster, 1982.

Osgood, Ernest Staples. *The Day of the Cattleman*. Chicago: University of Chicago Press, 1970.

Pease, Otis, ed. *The Progressive Years: The Spirit and Achievement of American Reform*. New York: George Braziller, 1962.

Peffer, Louise. *The Closing of the Public Domain*. Palo Alto, Calif.: Stanford University Press, 1951.

Pells, Richard H. *Radical Visions and American Dreams: Culture and Social Thought in the Depression Years*. New York: Harper & Row, 1973.

Pepper, Claude Denson, with Hays Gorey. *Pepper: Eyewitness to a Century*. New York: Harcourt Brace Jovanovich, 1987.

Perkins, Dexter. *The New Age of Franklin Roosevelt, 1932–45*. Chicago: University of Chicago Press, 1957.

Perkins, Frances. *The Roosevelt I Knew*. New York: The Viking Press, 1946.

Perrett, Geoffrey. *Days of Sadness, Years of Triumph: The American People, 1939–1945*. Madison: The University of Wisconsin Press, 1973.

Pettit, George A. *So Boulder Dam Was Built*. Berkeley: The Six Companies, Inc., 1935.

Phillips, Cabell. *From the Crash to the Blitz, 1929–1939*. New York: The Macmillan Co., 1969.

————. *The 1940s: Decade of Triumph and Trouble*. New York: The Macmillan Co., 1975.

————, et al., eds. *Dateline Washington: The Story of National Affairs Journalism in the Life and Times of the National Press Club*. Garden City, N.Y.: Doubleday & Co., 1949.

Philp, Kenneth R. *John Collier's Crusade for Indian Reform, 1920–1954*. Tucson: University of Arizona Press, 1977.

Pilat, Oliver. *Drew Pearson: An Unauthorized Biography*. New York: Harper's Magazine Press, 1973.

Pinchot, Gifford. *Breaking New Ground*. New York: Harcourt, Brace, 1947; reprinted Washington, D.C.: Island Press, 1988.

Plowden, David. *Industrial Landscape*. New York: W.W. Norton & Co., 1985.

Polenberg, Richard. *Reorganizing Roosevelt's Government, 1936–1939: The Controversy over Executive Reorganization*. Cambridge, Mass.: Harvard University Press, 1966.

Potter, Jean. *Alaska Under Arms*. New York: The Macmillan Co., 1942.

Powers, Richard Gid. *Secrecy and Power: The Life of J. Edgar Hoover*. New York: The Free Press, 1987.

Prichett, C. Herman. *The Tennessee Valley Authority: A Study in Public Administration*. Chapel Hill: University of North Carolina Press, 1943.

Reiger, George. *American Sportsmen and the Origins of Conservation*. Lincoln: University of Nebraska Press, 1975.

Reisner, Marc. *Cadillac Desert: The American West and Its Disappearing Water*. New York: The Viking Press, 1986.

Republican National Committee. *Campaign Text Book of the Republican Party, 1940*. Washington, D.C.: Republican National Committee, 1940.

Richberg, Donald R. *My Hero: The Indiscreet Memoirs of an Eventful but Unheroic Life*. New York: G.P. Putnam's Sons, 1954.

————. *The Tents of the Mighty*. New York: Willett, Clark, and Colby, 1930.

Rister, Carl Coke. *Oil! Titan of the Southwest*. Norman: University of Oklahoma Press, 1949.

Robbins, Roy. *Our Landed Heritage: The Public Domain, 1776–1970*. Lincoln: University of Nebraska Press, 1976.

Roberts, Chalmers M. *The Washington Post: The First Hundred Years*. Boston: Houghton Mifflin, 1977.

Robins, Elizabeth. *Raymond and I*. New York: The Macmillan Co., 1956.

Roosevelt, Eleanor. *This I Remember*. New York: Harper & Brothers, 1949.

Roosevelt, Elliott, ed. *F.D.R.: His Personal Letters, 1928–1945*. 2 volumes. New York: Duell, Sloan and Pearce, 1950.

————, and James Brough. *A Rendezvous with Destiny: The Roosevelts in the White House*. New York: G.P. Putnam's Sons, 1975.

Roosevelt, Franklin D. *Roosevelt's Foreign Policy, 1933–1941: Franklin D. Roosevelt's Unedited Speeches and Messages*. New York: Wilfred Funk, Inc., 1942.

Roosevelt, James, with Bill Libby. *My Parents: A Differing View*. Chicago: Playboy Press, 1976.

Roosevelt, Theodore. *Theodore Roosevelt: An Autobiography*. New York: Charles Scribner's Sons, 1929.

Rosen, Eliot A. *Hoover, Roosevelt, and the Brain Trust: From Depression to New Deal*. New York: Columbia University Press, 1977.

Rosenau, James N. *The Roosevelt Treasury*. Garden City, N.Y.: Doubleday & Co., 1951.

Rosenman, Samuel I. *The Public Papers and Addresses of Franklin D. Roosevelt*. 5 volumes. New York: Random House, 1938.

————. *Working with Roosevelt*. New York: Harper and Brothers, 1952.

Ross, Walter S. *The Last Hero: Charles A. Lindbergh*. New York: Harper & Row, 1968.

Rossiter, Clinton, and James Lare, eds. *The Essential Lippmann: A Political Philosophy for Liberal Democracy*. New York: Random House, 1963.

Royster, Vermont. *My Own, My Country's Time: A Journalist's Journey*. Chapel Hill: Algonquin Books, 1983.

Runte, Alred. *The National Parks: An American Experience*. Lincoln: University of Nebraska Press, 1979.

Russell, Francis. *The Shadow of Blooming Grove: Warren G. Harding in His Times*. New York: McGraw-Hill, 1968.

Sampson, Anthony. *The Seven Sisters: The Great Oil Companies and the World They Shaped*. New York: The Viking Press, 1975.

Satterfield, Archie. *Home Front: An Oral History of the War Years in America, 1941–1945*. Chicago: Playboy Press, 1981.

Sax, Joseph. *Mountains Without Handrails: Reflections on the National Parks*. Ann Arbor: University of Michigan Press, 1981.

Saylor, David J. *Jackson Hole, Wyoming: In the Shadow of the Tetons*. Norman: University of Oklahoma Press, 1971, 1977.

Schaaf, Barbara C. *Mr. Dooley's Chicago*. Garden City, N.Y.: Anchor Press/Doubleday, 1977.

Schapsmeier, Edward L., and Frederick H. *Prophet in Politics: Henry A. Wallace and the War Years, 1940–1965*. Ames: Iowa State University Press, 1970.

Schlesinger, Arthur M., Jr. *The Age of Roosevelt:* Vol. I, *The Crisis of the Old Order, 1919–1933*; Vol. II, *The Coming of the New Deal*; Vol. III, *The Politics of Upheaval*. Boston: Houghton Mifflin Co., 1957, 1958, 1959.

_____. *The Cycles of American History*. Boston: Houghton Mifflin Co., 1986.

Schwarz, Jordan A. *Liberal: Adolf A. Berle and the Vision of an American Era*. New York: The Free Press, 1987.

_____. *The Speculator: Bernard M. Baruch in Washington, 1917–1965*. Chapel Hill: University of North Carolina Press, 1981.

Seldes, George. *Lords of the Press*. New York: Julian Messner, Inc., 1938.

_____. *Witness to a Century: Encounters with the Noted, the Notorious, and Three SOBs*. New York: Ballantine Books, 1987.

Seldes, Gilbert. *The Years of the Locust (America, 1929–1932)*. Boston: Little, Brown & Co., 1933.

Sell, Jesse C. *A 20th Century History of Altoona and Blair County, Pennsylvania, and Representative Citizens*. Chicago: Richmond-Arnold Publishing Co., 1911.

Severn, Bill. *Frances Perkins: A Member of the Cabinet*. New York: Hawthorn Books, 1976.

Sheehan, Marion Turner, ed. *The World at Home: Selections from the Writings of Anne O'Hare McCormick*. New York: Alfred A. Knopf, 1956.

Sherwood, Robert E. *Roosevelt and Hopkins: An Intimate History*. New York: Harper & Brothers, 1948.

Simon, Rita James. *As We Saw the Thirties: Essays on Social and Political Movements of a Decade*. Chicago: University of Chicago Press, 1967.

Simpson, Africa J. *A History of Huntington and Blair Counties, Pennsylvania*. Philadelphia, 1853; reprinted Altoona: Huntington County Historical Society and Blair County Historical Society, 1975.

Smith, Alston J. *Chicago's Left Bank*. Chicago: Henry Regnery Co., 1953.

Smith, A. Merriman. *Thank You, Mr. President: A White House Notebook*. New York: Harper & Brothers, 1946.

Smith, Carl S. *Chicago and the American Literary Imagination, 1880–1920*. Chicago: University of Chicago Press, 1984.

Smith, Gene. *The Shattered Dream: Herbert Hoover and the Great Depression*. New York: William Morrow and Co., 1970.

————. *When the Cheering Stopped: The Last Years of Woodrow Wilson*. New York: William Morrow and Co., 1964.

Smith, Geoffrey S. *To Save a Nation: American Countersubversives, the New Deal, and the Coming of World War II*. New York: Basic Books, 1973.

Smith, Page. *Redeeming the Time: A People's History of the 1920s and the New Deal*. New York: McGraw-Hill, 1987.

Smith, Richard Norton. *An Uncommon Man: The Triumph of Herbert Hoover*. New York: Simon & Schuster, 1984.

————. *Thomas E. Dewey and His Times*. New York: Simon & Schuster, 1982.

Spector, Ronald H. *Eagle Against the Sun: The American War with Japan*. New York: The Free Press, 1985.

Stearns, Harold A. *America Now: An Inquiry into Civilization in the United States by Thirty-six Americans*. New York: Charles Scribner's Sons, 1938.

Steel, Ronald. *Walter Lippmann and the American Century*. New York: Random House, 1980.

Steffens, Lincoln. *The Autobiography of Lincoln Steffens: Volume II*. New York: Harcourt, Brace and World, Inc., 1958.

Stegner, Wallace. *Beyond the Hundredth Meridian: John Wesley Powell and the Second Opening of the West*. Boston: Houghton Mifflin, 1954.

Steinberg, Peter L. *The Great Red "Menace": United States Prosecution of American Communists, 1947–1952*. Westport, Conn.: Greenwood Press, 1984.

Sternsher, Bernard. *Rexford Tugwell and the New Deal*. New Brunswick, N.J.: Rutgers University Press, 1964.

Stevens, Joseph E. *Hoover Dam: An American Adventure*. Norman: University of Oklahoma Press, 1988.

Stone, I. F. *A Non-Conformist History of Our Times: The War Years, 1939–1945*. Boston: Little, Brown, 1988.

Storr, Richard J. *A History of the University of Chicago: Harper's University—The Beginnings*. Chicago: University of Chicago Press, 1966.

Sullivan, Mark. *Our Times: The United States, 1900–1925; III: Pre-War America*. New York: Charles Scribner's Sons, 1930.

Svoboda, Lawrence. *An Empire of Dust*. Caldwell, Id.: Caxton Press, 1940.

Swados, Harvey, ed. *The American Writer and the Great Depression*. Indianapolis: The Bobbs-Merrill Co., 1966.

Swisher, Carl Brent, ed. *Selected Papers of Homer Cummings, Attorney General of the United States, 1933–1939*. New York: Charles Scribner's Sons, 1939.

Tabrah, Ruth. *Hawaii: A History*. New York: W.W. Norton, 1984.

Tansill, Charles Callan. *Back Door to War: The Roosevelt Foreign Policy, 1933–1941*. Chicago: Henry Regnery Co., 1952.

Taylor, Paul Schuster. *On the Ground in the Thirties*. Layton, Utah: Gibbs Smith, Publisher, Peregrine Smith Books, 1983.

————, and Dorothea Lange. *American Exodus: A Record of Human Erosion*. New York: Reynal & Hitchcock, 1939.

Terkel, Studs. *Hard Times: An Oral History of the Great Depression*. New York: Random House, 1970.

Thomas, Hugh. *The Spanish Civil War*. New York: Harper & Row, 1961.

Thomas, Lowell. *History as You Heard It*. Garden City, N.Y.: Doubleday & Co., 1957.

Thoreau, Henry David. *Henry David Thoreau: The Natural History Essays*. Layton, Utah: Gibbs Smith, Publisher, Peregrine Smith Books, 1984.

Time-Life Books. *Time Capsule/1923, 1929*. New York: 1967. *1939, 1940, 1941, 1942, 1943, 1944, 1945*. New York: 1969.

Trohan, Walter. *Political Animals: Memoirs of a Sentimental Cynic*. Garden City, N.Y.: Doubleday, 1975.

Truman, Harry S. *The Memoirs of Harry S. Truman. Vol. I, Year of Decisions*. New York: Doubleday & Co., 1955.

_____. *The Memoirs of Harry S. Truman. Vol. II, Years of Trial and Hope*. New York: Doubleday & Co., 1956.

Tugwell, R. G. *The Brain Trust*. New York: The Viking Press, 1968.

_____. *The Democratic Roosevelt: A Biography of Franklin D. Roosevelt*. Garden City, N.Y.: Doubleday & Co., Inc., 1957.

Tully, Grace. *FDR, My Boss*. New York: Scribner's, 1949.

Turner, Frederick. *Beyond Geography: The Western Spirit Against the Wilderness*. New York: The Viking Press, 1980.

_____. *Rediscovering America: John Muir in His Time and Ours*. New York: The Viking Press, 1985.

Tyler, Lyman S. *A History of American Indian Policy*. Washington, D.C.: U.S. Department of the Interior, Bureau of Indian Affairs, 1973.

U.S. Bureau of the Census. *The Statistical History of the United States: From Colonial Times to the Present*. New York: Basic Books, 1976.

U.S. Congress. House. *Biographical Directory of the American Congress, 1774–1961*. 85th Cong., 2d sess. H. Doc. 442, 1961.

U.S. Department of Agriculture. *A National Plan for American Forestry*. Washington, D.C.: Department of Agriculture, U.S. Forest Service, 1933.

U.S. Department of the Interior. Bureau of Indian Affairs. *A History of Indian Policy*. Prepared by S. Lyman Tyler. Washington, D.C., 1973.

_____. National Park Service. *Laws Relating to the National Park Service, the National Parks and Monuments*. Washington, D.C.: U.S. Government Printing Office, 1933.

_____. *Laws Relating to the National Park Service, Supplement 1*. Washington, D.C.: U.S. Government Printing Office, 1944.

U.S. Strike Commission. *Report on the Chicago Strike of June–July 1984* . . . Washington, D.C., 1895.

Vadney, Thomas E. *The Wayward Liberal: A Political Biography of Donald R. Richberg*. Lexington: University Press of Kentucky, 1970.

Waldrop, Frank C. *McCormick of Chicago: An Unconventional Portrait of a Controversial Figure*. Englewood Cliffs, N.J.: Prentice-Hall, 1966.

Wallace, Henry. *New Frontiers*. New York: Reynal & Hitchcock, 1934.

Walter, Richard J. *Henry Wallace, Harry Truman and the Cold War*. New York: The Viking Press, 1976.

Ward, Geoffrey C. *Before the Trumpet: Young Franklin Roosevelt, 1882–1905*. New York: Harper & Row, 1985.

_____. *A First-Class Temperament: The Emergence of Franklin Roosevelt*. New York: Harper & Row, 1989.

Waters, Frank. *The Colorado*. New York: Rinehart, 1946.

Watkins, T. H. *Gold and Silver in the West: The Illustrated History of an American Dream*. Palo Alto, Calif.: The American West, 1971.

_____, et al. *The Grand Colorado: The Story of a River and Its Canyons*. Palo Alto, Calif.: The American West, 1969.

_____, and Charles S. Watson, Jr. *The Lands No One Knows: America and the Public Domain*. San Francisco: The Sierra Club, 1975.

Wattenburg, Ben J., ed. *The Statistical History of the United States from Colonial Times to the Present*. New York: Basic Books, 1976.

Webb, Walter Prescott. *The Great Plains*. Boston: Houghton Mifflin, 1936.

Wecter, Dixon. *The Age of the Great Depression, 1929–1941*. Chicago: Quadrangle Books, 1971.

Weglyn, Michi. *Years of Infamy: The Untold Story of America's Concentration Camps*. New York: William Morrow, 1976.

Weisberger, Bernard A. *The American Newspaperman*. Chicago: University of Chicago Press, 1961.

Welles, Sumner. *The Time for Decision*. New York: Harper & Brothers, 1944.

Wendt, Lloyd. *Chicago Tribune: The Rise of a Great American Newspaper*. Chicago: Rand McNally and Co., 1979.

_____, and Herman Kogan. *Big Bill of Chicago*. New York: Bobbs-Merrill, 1953.

_____. *Lords of the Levee: The Story of Bathhouse John and Hinky Dink*. New York: Bobbs-Merrill, 1943; reprinted Bloomington: Indiana University Press, 1967.

Werner, M. R., and John Staff. *Teapot Dome*. New York: The Viking Press, 1959.

White, Graham. *FDR and the Press*. Chicago: University of Chicago Press, 1979.

_____, and John Maze. *Harold Ickes of the New Deal: His Private Life and Public Career*. Cambridge, Mass.: Harvard University Press, 1985.

White, William Allen. *The Autobiography of William Allen White*. New York: The Macmillan Co., 1946.

_____. *Forty Years on Main Street*. New York: Farrar and Rinehart, Inc., 1937.

White, William S. *Majesty and Mischief: A Mixed Tribute to FDR*. New York: McGraw-Hill, 1961.

Wilbur, Lyman, and William Atherton Du Puy. *Conservation in the Department of the Interior*. Washington, D.C.: U.S. Government Printing Office, 1932.

Williams, William Appleton. "Robins, Raymond (Sept. 17, 1873–Sept. 26, 1954)." *Dictionary of American Biography*, Vol. 5:1951–1955.

Williamson, Harold F., Ralph L. Andreano, Arnold P. Daum, and Gilbert C. Klose. *The American Petroleum Industry, 1899–1959: The Age of Energy*. Evanston: Northwestern University Press, 1963.

Willkie, Wendell. *One World*. New York: Simon & Schuster, 1943.

Wilson, Edmund. *The American Earthquake: A Documentary of the Twenties and Thirties*. Garden City, N.Y.: Anchor Books/Doubleday and Co., 1964.

Wister, Carl Coke. *Oil! Titan of the Southwest*. Norman: University of Oklahoma Press, 1949.

Wolfskill, George, and John A. Hudson. *All But the People: Franklin D. Roosevelt and His Critics, 1933–1939*. New York: The Macmillan Co., 1969.

Worster, Donald. *Dust Bowl: The Southern Plains in the 1930s*. New York: Oxford University Press, 1979.

——————. *Rivers of Empire: Water, Aridity, and the Growth of the American West*. New York: Pantheon, 1985.

Wyant, William K. *Westward in Eden: The Public Lands and the Conservation Movement*. Berkeley: University of California Press, 1982.

Wyman, David S. *Paper Walls: America and the Refugee Crisis, 1938–1941*. Amherst: University of Massachusetts Press, 1968.

——————. *The Abandonment of the Jews: America and the Holocaust, 1941–1945*. New York: Pantheon Books, 1984.

Zaslowsky, Dyan, and the Wilderness Society. *These American Lands: Parks, Wilderness, and the Public Lands*. New York: Henry Holt, 1986.

Zinn, Howard, ed. *New Deal Thought*. Indianapolis: Bobbs-Merrill, 1966.

PERIODICALS

Brant, Irving. "The Fight Over Jackson Hole." *Nation*, July 7, 1945.

Cassell, Frank A., and Marguerite E. Cassell. "The White City in Peril: Leadership and the World's Columbian Exposition." *Chicago History*, Fall 1983.

Catton, Bruce. "The Inspired Leak." *American Heritage*, February 1977.

Duis, Perry. "Whose City? Part Two." *Chicago History*, Summer 1983.

"The Earth Movers." *Fortune*, August 1943.

Ferrell, Robert H. "The Last Hurrah." *Wilson Quarterly*, Spring 1988.

Fraser, Hugh Russell. "One Man Beats 150—Donald R. Richberg of Chicago, and His Fight in the Greatest Lawsuit of Our Times—The Railroad Valuation and Rate Case." *Outlook*, October 1927.

Hamby, Alonzo L. "The Accidental Presidency." *Wilson Quarterly*, Spring 1988.

Horowitz, Helen Lefkowitz. "Hull-House as Women's Space." *Chicago History*, Winter 1983–84.

Ickes, Harold L. "And a Woman Shall Lead Them." *New Republic*, June 19, 1950.

——————. "A Decoration for Mr. McCarthy." *New Republic*, April 10, 1950.

——————. "A Dirtier 'Dirty Business.' " *New Republic*, January 9, 1950.

——————. "Farewell, Secretary Krug." *New Republic*, November 28, 1949.

——————. "Guilt by Non-Association." *New Republic*, June 20, 1949.

——————. "Helen Douglas and Tobey." *New Republic*, October 16, 1950.

——————. "McCarthy Strips Himself." *New Republic*, August 7, 1950.

——————. "MacArthur Home for Christmas." *New Republic*, December 25, 1950.

——————. "My Twelve Years with FDR." *Saturday Evening Post*, June 5–July 24, 1948.

————. "Not Guilty: Richard A. Ballinger—An American Dreyfus." *Saturday Evening Post*, May 25, 1940.

————. "Where is the Nation Heading?" *New York Times Magazine*, May 27, 1934.

Kelly, Lawrence C. "Choosing the New Deal Indian Commissioner: Ickes vs. Collier." *New Mexico Historical Review*, Winter 1974.

Klaw, Barbara. "A Voice One Hears Once in a Hundred Years: An Interview with Marian Anderson." *American Heritage*, February 1977.

Lear, Linda. "Boulder Dam: A Crossroads in Natural Resource Policy." *Journal of the West*, October 1985.

Lusk, R. D. "Life and Death of 470 Acres." *Saturday Evening Post*, August 13, 1938.

Marshall, Robert. "The Problem of the Wilderness." *Scientific Monthly*, February 1930.

Polenberg, Richard. "The Great Conservation Contest." *Forest History*, January 1967.

Richardson, Elmo R. "The Escalante National Monument Controversy of 1935–1940." *Utah Historical Quarterly*, Spring 1965.

Righter, Robert W. "The Brief, Hectic Life of Jackson Hole National Monument." *The American West*, November–December 1976.

Rudin, A. James. "From Kishinev to Chicago: The Forgotten Story of Lazar Averbuch." *Midstream*, August–September 1972.

Taylor, Paul Schuster. "The Excess Land Law: Execution of Public Policy." *Yale Law Journal*, February 1955.

————. "The Excess Land Law: Legislative Erosion of Public Policy." *Rocky Mountain Law Review*, June 1958.

————. "Reclamation: The Rise and Fall of an American Idea." *The American West*, July 1970.

————. "Water, Land, and People in the Great Valley." *The American West*, March 1968.

Van Zanten, Ann Lorenz. "The Marshall Field Annex and the New Urban Order of Daniel Burnham's Chicago." *Chicago History*, Fall and Winter 1982.

Watkins, T. H. "The Terrible-Tempered Mr. Ickes." *Audubon*, March 1984.

Weiler, N. Sue. "Walkout: The Chicago Men's Garment Workers Strike, 1910–1911." *Chicago History*, Winter 1979–1980.

Yard, Robert Sterling. "A Summons to Save the Wilderness." *The Living Wilderness*, September 1935.

Zimmerman, William Jr. "The Role of the Bureau of Indian Affairs Since 1933." *The Annals*, May 1957.

Index

Aberdeen Gardens (Vir.), 644
Abraham Lincoln Battalion, 666
Acadia National Park, 692, 841
Acheson, Dean, 803, 858
Adams, Alva B., 583
Adams, Samuel Hopkins, 118
Addams, Jane, 3, 4, 23–24, 45, 70–72, 91, 96, 100, 105, 130, 131, 138, 199, 200, 252, 404–5
Ade, George, 57, 74
Adirondack Park and Forest Preserve, 466
Adjusted Compensation Act (1924), 259
Adkinson, Henry, 31–32, 35, 42, 48
Adkinson, Ruth, 32
Adler, Alfred, 118
Adler, Dankmar, 26
Advisory Committee on Allotments, 397, 398, 401
AFL-CIO, 849–50
Agger, Carolyn, 827
Agricultural Adjustment Act (1933), 421, 640
Agricultural Adjustment Administration (AAA), 346, 537, 644, 646
Agricultural Marketing Act, 256
Agriculture Department, U.S., 115, 226, 311–12, 388, 460, 477, 484–94, 566, 572, 659, 845
    blacks and, 640–41, 644, 646
    Civilian Conservation Corps and, 339, 476
    grazing rights and, 479
    new building for, 290
    reorganization and, 558, 585, 587, 658
    Robins and, 403

territories and, 517
Agudath Israel World Organization, 797
Aïda (Verdi), 229
Alaska, Territory of, 322, 323, 480n, 495, 527, 542–43, 608–16, 673–74, 774, 776, 781, 785–90, 801
Alaska-Juneau Company, 615
Alaska National Interests Lands Conservation Act (1980), 615
Alaska Reorganization Act (1936), 542, 616
Alaska Steamship Company, 610
Alaska Syndicate, 115
Albertson, Dean, 854
Albizo Campos, Pedro, 518, 520
Albright, Horace M., 321, 322, 458, 551–52, 555, 766
Aleutian Islands, 785, 787
Aleuts, 323, 610
Alexander & Baldwin, 496
Alfonso, King of Spain, 666
Alger, George W., 118
All-American Canal, 382
Allen, Frank, 408
Allen, Frederick Lewis, 234–35
Allen, Henry, 128, 130, 133, 162, 165–68, 178, 180–83, 195, 209, 212, 213
Allen, Robert S., 505, 507n
Alley Dwelling Authority, 730
All Pueblo Council, 203
Altgeld, John P., 44–45, 61, 67, 68
Altoona (Pa.), 4, 11–21, 29, 33, 35, 40, 41, 55–56, 75–77, 88, 152, 405–7, 470, 807, 857

Aluminum Company of America (ALCOA), 704–6
Amalgamated Clothing Workers of America, 404, 695
America First Committee, 714
American Automobile Association, 468
American Bankers' Association, 397
American Bar Association, 96
American Broadcasting Corporation (ABC), 849
American Civic Association, 485, 552
American Civil Liberties Union, 275, 502, 520, 523, 545, 664
American Coalition of Patriotic Societies, 674
American Congress for Peace and Democracy, 634
American Conservation League, 454
American Earthquake, The (Wilson), 252
American Exodus: A Record of Human Erosion (Taylor and Lange), 778n
American Factors, 496
American Farm Bureau, 837
American Federation of Labor, 91, 259, 339, 584, 679, 779
American Forestry Association, 454, 561
American Forests, 561
American Game Protective Association, 460–62
American Indian Defense Association (AIDA), 204–5, 274, 330, 533, 537
American Indian Federation, 545, 633
American Labor Party, 813
American Legion, 292, 674
American Liberty League, 422, 425
Anschluss, 668, 669, 671
Anthony, George W., 821
Antiquities Act (1906), 320, 460, 565, 583, 771, 773
Anti-Saloon League, 215, 216
Arabian-American Oil Company (Aramco), 747, 749–50, 752
Arbeiter Zeitung, 68
Arctic Village (Marshall), 468n
Armour, Philip, 65
Armour & Company, 25
Armstrong, J. E., 36
Armstrong, Louise, 294
Army, U.S., 338, 339

Corps of Engineers, 376, 378, 381, 384, 397, 455, 489, 576, 786
    segregation in, 641–43
    women in, 730
    in World War II, 746, 755, 784, 785
Arnold, Thurman, 706, 749, 827
Ashurst, Henry, 487, 539, 619
Ashwater v. Tennessee Valley Authority (1936), 421
Associated Charities of Atlanta, 202
Associated Farmers, Inc., 574, 576
Associated Press, 480
Association of American Railroads, 716, 717
Astor, Lady, 606
Athabascans, 323, 610
Atlantic, Battle of the, 702
Atlantic Monthly, 118, 528
Atlee, Clement, 606
Atomic Energy Commission, 840
Atwood, Stella M., 203, 275
Audubon Societies, 459–63
Auschwitz, 804
Austin, Mary, 362
Australia, 672
Austria, Nazi seizure of power in, 668, 671
Autobiography of a Curmudgeon (Ickes), 16, 29, 31, 43, 59, 63, 75, 87, 127, 136, 137, 141, 165, 178, 179, 183, 194, 226, 268, 270, 275, 367n, 760, 763–65
Averbuch, Lazar, 4, 95–100, 645n
Averbuch, Olga, 95–98
Axley, Lawrence A., 646
Azuma Maru (tanker), 707

Back to Work (Ickes), 367, 371–73, 390, 404, 760
Baer, Eli, 505–7
Baer, Max, 620n
Bagnall, Robert W., 200
Baker, Jacob, 611
Baker, Newton D., 263, 265, 422
Baker, Ray Stannard, 57, 118, 277
Baldwin, Roger, 520, 523
Ballinger, Richard Achilles, 114–16, 123, 245, 332, 333, 457, 590
Baltimore Sun, 57
Bankhead, William B., 387, 568, 619, 620, 632, 691

Bankhead-Jones Farm Tenant Act (1937), 640

Banking Act (1935), 416

Barcelo, Antonio, 514

Barkley, Alben, 690, 701, 725, 848

Barrett, Frank A., 769, 771–73, 844

Barton, Bruce, 695

Baruch, Bernard M., 279, 348, 350, 680, 710–12, 715, 744–45, 858

Bashore, Harry, 778, 779

Bass, John, 138

Batt, William L., 741

Beach, Bess, 600

Beale, Joseph H., 87

Beard, Charles A., 701

Beebe, Lucius, 184

Beecher, Henry Ward, 65

Beery, Wallace, 770–71, 773

Beiter, Alfred F., 426

Bell, Alexander Graham, 497

Bell, Daniel W., 412

Bell, Evangeline, 724

Belgium, German invasion of, 685, 714

Bellamy, Edward, 68

Bellridge Oil Company, 77

Beman, Solomon S., 1

Bendetsen, Colonel Karl, 791

Benevolent and Protective Order of Elk, 562

Bennett, Edward H., 175

Bennett, Hugh Hammond, 476, 477

Berle, Adolf A., 264, 299, 364, 365, 683

Berle, Beatrice, 299

Bethesda Naval Hospital, 366, 432, 525, 526, 807

Bethune, Mary McLeod, 639, 646

Bethune-Cookman College, 639

Beveridge, Albert J., 133

Beverly, James, 515

Biddle, Francis, 704, 738, 791, 794, 803, 824, 825, 828

Biddle, Nicholas, 629

Big Bend National Park, 556

Big Five, 496, 498–500, 784

Big Inch pipeline, 739–40

Bikini atomic bomb tests, 843

Billington, Ray Allen, 309

Biological Survey, U.S., 460, 491, 585, 587, 590, 766, 767

    Migratory Waterfowl Division, 491

Bird-Lore, 463

Bituminous Coal Commission, 317, 587, 660–61, 734

Bituminous Coal Conservation Act (1935), 416, 421

Black, Hugo, 347, 436, 625, 626, 724, 858

Black, Ruby, 515, 522

Blackfeet Indians, 609

Blacks

    in Chicago, 178, 190, 199–201

    in Washington, D.C., 289–90, 648–50, 652–53, 844

    during World War II, 730–32

"Black Sox" scandal, 177n

Blaine, Anita McCormick, 73

Blair, Henry, 241

Blair County Radical, 12

Bliven, Bruce, 762

Blount, Fred, 63

Blum, Henry S., 657

Bly, Nellie, 57

Boettinger, Anna Roosevelt, 608–10, 616, 654–56, 680–82, 715, 737, 808, 820, 821, 851, 853, 854

Boettinger, John, 360, 608–10, 616, 715, 737, 851n

Bolshevik revolution, 190

Bonneville Dam, 384

Bonneville Power Authority, 704, 705

Bonus Army, 259–60, 272–73, 290, 292, 340n

Bookman, The, 120

Boone and Crockett Club, 459, 460

Borah, William E., 327, 424, 627

Boston police strike, 190

Boston Transcript, 185

Boswell, J. G., Ranch Company, 777

Boulder Canyon Project, 319

Boulder Dam, 381–85, 417, 491, 556, 647, 705

Boulder Dam Association, 329

Bowen, Louise de Koven, 73

Bowers, Claude G., 444, 667

Bowers, John C., 245

Bowles, Chester, 745n

Bowron, Fletcher, 791

Boyd, J. Philip, 776

Boyd, William, 342

Boyd, William R., Jr., 743

Boyer, Professor, 36

Braden, Tom, 63

Brant, Irving, 462–64, 484, 485, 489, 564–68, 571–73, 575, 576, 578, 579, 609, 773, 775, 776, 845

Brandegee, Frank, 186–87

Brandeis, Louis, 137, 396, 416, 624, 625

Breaking New Ground (Pinchot), 311, 454, 457

Brennan, George, 188, 189, 212, 215

Brewer, C., & Company, 496

Bricker, John, 809, 815

Bridges, Harry, 633

Briggs, Lyman J., 744, 745

Brinkley, Alan, 424*n*

Brinkley, David, 724, 809–10

Brisbane, Arthur, 425

Britain. *See* Great Britain

British Petroleum Company, 747, 750

Bronx Zoo, 461, 462

Brookings Institution, 275, 330, 347, 533, 556

Brooks, "Curley," 815

Brotherhood of Railway Workers, 197, 209

Brotherhood of Sleeping Car Porters, 731

Broun, Heywood, 57

Browder, Earl, 814

Brown, Captain Wilson, 417, 600

Brown, Herbert, 502–3

Brown, Walter, 179

Brownlow, Louis, 556

Bruce, Edward, 449, 450

Brundage, F. H., 774, 776

Bruner, Joseph, 633

Bryan, William Jennings, 4, 44, 62, 67, 74, 75, 91, 133, 691

Bryant, Requa, 220

Bryce, James, 322

Buck, C. J., 567

Buckner, Lieutenant General Simon Bolivar, Jr., 785

Budd, Ralph, 716, 717

Budget, Bureau of the, 547, 567, 711, 733, 768, 769, 786

Bullitt, William C., 606, 747

Bull Moose Party, 131–34, 137, 138, 144, 212, 424, 805

Bunyan, John, 121

Burdick, Usher, 545

Burke, Edward, 627

Burke Act (1906), 533

Burlew, Ebert Keiser ("E.K."), 329, 387, 395, 428, 433, 451, 508, 525, 526, 605, 609, 678, 715, 734, 765, 777, 786

Burnham, Daniel H., 26, 37, 175, 229

Burns, John, 72

Burns, William J., 207

Bursum, Holm Olaf, 203, 205

Burt, Struthers, 766, 771

Burton, Ernest D., 38

Busby, Leonard, 241

Busse, Fred A., 63, 78–80, 90, 94, 97, 103, 106–8, 198, 269

Busse, William, 269

Butler, Pierce, 626

Butt, Archie, 114

Byrnes, James F., 762, 803, 812, 824

Byrns, Joseph, 492, 493

Cahill, John, 655

California, University of, 778, at Berkeley, 103

California Farm Bureau Federation, 778

California State Chamber of Commerce, 571, 576, 585

California State Grange, 791

California State Immigration and Housing Commission, 202

California State University at San Francisco, 202

California-Texas Oil Company, 736

Cammerer, Arno B., 552–55, 563, 567, 568–70, 573, 578, 579, 582, 647

Campbell, Daniel A., 107

Canada, 672

Canaday, Ward, 673

Canton Evening Repository, 44

Cape Hatteras National Seashore, 580, 581

Capital Transit Company, 731

Capone, Al, 196, 199, 215

Cardozo, Benjamin J., 2, 300–301, 625

Carey, Charles E., 778

Carey, Robert, 183, 768

Carhart, Arthur, 464–65

Carlsbad Caverns, 647

Carmody, John M., 370, 587, 659

Caroline Islands, 720

Carpenter, Farrington R., 480, 482

Carter, Boake, 299

Carter, E. C., 164, 165

Carter, Orrin N., 73
Case, Otto A., 775
Castle & Cooke, 496, 500
Catton, Bruce, 712, 740, 742, 743*n*, 761*n*, 776, 837
Celler, Emmanuel, 799
Census Bureau, 307, 322
Central Pacific Railroad, 308
Central Republic Bank, 262–63
Central Uptown Chamber of Commerce, 245
Central Valley Project, 385–86, 777–80
Century magazine, 321, 456
Century of Progress, 253, 282
Cermak, Anton, 247, 268, 278*n*, 292, 399
Chamberlain, Neville, 606, 696
Chamberlain, Thomas, C., 38
Chambers, Whittaker, 838
Chapman, H. H., 491
Chapman, Oscar, 327, 328, 503, 506, 517, 525, 609, 650–51, 653, 690, 820, 846, 854, 858, 859
Chardon, Carlos, 516, 519
Chardon Plan, 516, 518
Chase National Bank, 234
Chatauqua movement, 503
Chenery, William, 763
Cherokee, 530
Chesapeake & Ohio Railroad, 758
Chicago, 22–28, 37
    bank failures in, 262–63
    blacks in, 178, 190, 199–201
    Board of Education, 91, 94
    during Depression, 2, 251–53
    dust storm in, 476
    gangsters in, 195–96, 199, 229
    Grand Central Station, 1
    Ickes closes office in, 281–82
    Ickes moves to, 7, 20–22, 29–30
    Interior Department agencies in, 547, 734, 769, 775
    Jewish community of, 95–99, 663–64
    politics in, 50–51, 59–63, 73, 78–81, 88–90, 103–4, 106–9, 140, 141, 176–78, 188, 197–99, 215, 229, 247, 268–69, 679
    plutocracy in, 65
    progressivism in, 71–73
    public works in, 175–76
    streetcar companies in, 241–46

strikes in, 68–71, 104–5, 142
suit against People's Gas Light and Coke Company by, 140
utilities in, 140, 159–60, 230
working class in, 65
Chicago, University of, 4, 35–43, 45–52, 55, 58, 62*n*, 83, 90, 102–3, 106, 194, 203, 222, 242, 281, 365*n*, 368, 690, 810
    Law School, 87, 405
    Press, 101
Chicago American, 23, 243
Chicago Athletic Club, 461
Chicago Board of Trade, 294
Chicago Boosters Club, 176
Chicago Chronicle, 23, 77
Chicago City Club, 90
Chicago Consolidated Traction Company, 51
Chicago Daily Globe, 25
Chicago Daily News, 25, 177, 243, 424, 686
Chicago Defender, 200
Chicago Edison Company, 159, 230
Chicago Evening Post, 23, 217
Chicago Federation of Labor, 107
Chicago Herald-Examiner, 243
Chicago Home for the Friendless, 101
Chicago Indian Rights Association, 204, 205
Chicago Inter-Ocean, 23, 61, 77
Chicago Municipal Lodging House, 91
Chicago National Bank, 63
Chicago Progressive Republican League, 108, 126, 130
Chicago Record, 25, 57–58, 73, 74, 77
Chicago Record-Herald, 95, 104
Chicago Sanitary District, 373
Chicago School of architecture, 27
Chicago Sun, 773, 835
Chicago Teachers Union, 679
Chicago Times Herald, 23, 76, 77
Chicago Tribune, 25, 44, 58, 103, 104, 126, 176, 178, 296, 357, 360, 364, 443, 597, 608, 621, 635, 679, 690, 727, 762, 815
Chicago Tuberculosis Institute, 73
Chicago Weekly, 42, 43, 48–49, 51, 52, 57
Chicago White Sox, 177*n*
Chicago Women's City Club, 45

Chickasaw, 530

Child of the Century, A (Hecht), 128–29

Childs, Marquis, 823

China, 635, 685, 706
  Wallace in, 810
  in World War II, 698, 720

Chisum, Melvin J., 637, 643–44

Christian, King of Denmark, 685

Christian Reformed Church, 545

Choctaw, 530

Churchill, Winston, 606, 685, 698–99, 702, 712, 768, 814, 819, 825, 842*n*

Cicero (Ill.), 199

Cities Service Company, 718

Citizens' Association, 78, 244

Citizens' Traction Settlement Committee, 241, 244, 248*n*

City Club, 73

City College of New York, 329

City of Memphis (ship), 156

Civic Federation, 73

Civic Opera, 229–30

Civil Aeronautics Board, 680

Civilian Conservation Corps (CCC), 326, 337–40, 476, 504, 536, 639, 641–43, 646

Civilian Defense, Office of, 702

Civil Service Commission, U.S., 67, 479, 557

Civil War, 12, 64, 191, 302*n*, 552, 630, 784

Civil Works Administration (CWA), 391–92, 537

Clapper, Olive, 298

Clapper, Raymond, 298, 529, 616, 703, 761*n*, 762

Clark, Champ, 133

Clark, George Rogers, 451

Clark, Irving M., 567, 776

Clark, Tom C., 803, 824

Clayton Anti-Trust Act, 137

Cleveland, Grover, 70, 311, 455, 562

Cleveland Zionist Society, 670

Coal Act (1864), 315

Coal Commission. *See* Bituminous Coal Commission

Coast Guard, U.S., 376, 615

Cobb, Charles, 209

Cobb, Henry Ives, 37, 38

Cobb, Irwin S., 322

Cochran, Elizabeth, 57

Cochran, John J., 489

Coffee, John F., 616

Coffin, Tris, 831–33

Cohen, Benjamin V., 368, 395, 396, 416, 419, 622, 628, 630, 662, 682, 700, 858

Cohen, Felix, 329–31, 537, 538, 542, 547

Colby, Bainbridge, 145, 188, 277

Colby, Everett, 146

Colby, William E., 458, 577

Colcord, Joanna Carver, 503

Cold War, 838

Collier, Harry, 746, 749

Collier, John, 202–6, 274–75, 330–32, 361, 469, 472, 533, 534–47, 549, 633, 634

Collier's magazine, 118, 763, 765

Colorado–Big Thompson Project, 581–82, 777

Colorado River Project, 381–84, 386

Colosimo, Big Jim, 176, 195

Columbia Broadcasting System (CBS), 299, 415, 438, 443, 444, 567, 616, 665, 719, 831

Columbia Institution for the Deaf, 324

Columbia University, 264, 536, 848
  Oral History Research Office, 854
  School of Journalism, 514

Columbus, Christopher, 37

Commerce Department, U.S., 290, 322, 348, 587, 646, 738, 812

Commercial Club, 175

Commission on Conservation and Administration of the Public Domain, 256, 313–14

Commission on Organization of the Executive Branch of Government, 845

Committee for Industrial Organization (CIO), 660

Committee for the Relief of Belgium, 181, 255

Committee of Public Information, 257

Committee on International Oil Policy, 747

Committee to Defend America by Aiding the Allies, 805

Commonwealth and Southern Corporation, 380*n*, 688

Commonwealth Club, 575, 583

Commonwealth Edison, 159, 230, 248
Communist Party, 191, 259, 272, 632, 635
Conant, James B., 744, 745
Condit, Carl, 26
Conference for Progressive Political Action, 211
Congress, U.S., 119, 203, 205, 275, 288, 291, 296, 324, 683. *See also* House of Representatives, U.S.; Senate, U.S.
  Bonus Army and, 260, 272
  Boulder Dam and, 381, 383–85
  budget cuts in, 290
  civil rights legislation in, 638, 648
  conservation policies and, 457, 462, 467, 477–78, 481, 486, 487, 489, 491–93, 561
  Coolidge and, 290
  FDR and, 277, 298, 326, 336, 339, 345, 347, 349, 394, 395, 413–14, 416, 420, 426, 508, 626–30, 635, 808, 812
  Hoover and, 258
  immigration quotas set by, 671, 673
  Indians and, 532, 533, 535–36, 538–47
  isolationists in, 181, 665, 667–68, 671, 695
  national parks and, 551, 555, 563, 565, 569, 572, 575–76, 578, 580–84, 767–69, 771, 772, 774, 845
  public housing and, 376
  public lands and, 305–7, 310–11, 313–14, 316, 317, 319–22
  PWA and, 370n
  refugees and, 799, 801–3
  reorganization proposals in, 557–59, 584–89
  Supreme Court and, 421–22, 619, 621–25
  and Teapot Dome scandal, 206–7
  territories and, 323, 497, 499, 502, 509, 515, 517, 520–22, 782–83, 785
  Theodore Roosevelt and, 121
  Truman and, 838, 843
  water-use policy and, 779–80
  Wilson and, 137, 156
  World War II and, 686, 695, 701, 702, 716, 725, 726, 740, 742–44, 745n, 757

Congress of Industrial Organizations (CIO), 660, 706, 779, 814
Conley, May, 221, 281, 402, 451, 525, 595–96, 764
Connally, Tom, 724, 843
Connally Act (1935), 416
Conservation in the Department of the Interior (Wilbur and Du Puy), 270
Constitution, U.S., 190–91, 326, 421, 460, 618, 622, 632, 732, 791
  Seventeenth Amendment, 141n
  Eighteenth Amendment, 193
  Nineteenth Amendment, 196
  Twentieth Amendment, 444
Consumer Price Index, 250
Consumers' League, 45
Contra Costa Farmer Bureau, 779
Cooke, Jay, & Company, 66
Coolidge, Calvin, 181, 187, 190, 208, 210, 212, 214, 233, 249, 260, 264, 273, 290, 313, 330, 420, 533, 782
Cooper, Judge, 526
Cooper Union, People's Institute of, 202
Copeland, Royal, 467
Copeland Report, 467
Coplon, Judith, 846–47
Corcoran, Thomas G., 395–96, 411, 416, 419, 600, 621, 622, 626, 628, 630, 680–84, 687, 693, 832, 858
Cornell University, 32, 35
Corporation Securities Company of Chicago, 231, 248
Cosmopolitan, 118
Costigan, Edward, 327, 347, 390, 638
Coughlin, "Bathhouse John," 61, 62, 195
Coughlin, Father Charles Edward, 415, 424, 425, 443, 635
Courtney, Thomas J., 268–69, 273
Court of International Justice, 413
Couzens, James, 300
Cox, James M., 188–92, 264, 268, 273
Craig, General Malin, 669
Cramer, Charles, 207
Cramer, Lawrence, 503, 504, 509–11, 673
Crampton, Louis, 322
Crane, Charles R., 73, 106, 130, 245
Crane, Richard Teller, 25, 65, 73
Crater Lake National Park, 320
Creek Indians, 530, 545

Creel, George, 257
Crete, 702
Crisis in Conservation, A (Van Name), 462
Croly, Herbert, 119–22, 132, 137, 159, 194, 202, 204
Crowe, Frank, 381
Cuba, 512
Cudahy, John, 604, 605, 714–15
Culver, Helen, 72
Cummings, Homer S., 303, 335–36, 351, 358, 383, 432, 479, 505, 506, 508, 509, 511, 565, 619, 620*n*, 626, 681
Cummings, Mrs. Homer, 600
Cunningham, Clarence, 115
Cunningham, Helen, 854
Curry, John Steuart, 450
Curtis, Charles, 296
Curtis, William E., 74
Cushman, Francis, 562
Custer, Julia, 20, 40
Customs Office, 323
Cutting, Bronson, 275–80, 347
Czechoslovakia, 669

Dahlman, Ann, 220, 328, 599, 603, 604, 724
Dahlman, Betty. *See* Thompson, Betty Dahlman
Dahlman, Jane. *See* Ickes, Jane Dahlman
Damrosch, Walter, 650
Daniels, Jonathan, 834
Daniels, Josephus, 206
Danish Bank, 504
Danish West India Company, 504
Darling, Jay Norwood ("Ding"), 490–91, 585
Darrow, Clarence, 3, 93, 105, 197, 498
Darwin, Charles, 66
Datil National Forest, 465
Daugherty, Harry M., 185–86, 207, 208
Daughters of the American Revolution (DAR), 649–50
Davidson, Eugene, 731
Davies, Morgan, 140, 209
Davies, Ralph K., 703, 704, 707, 712, 715–18, 736, 738, 740, 745, 746, 749–51, 752*n*, 827, 828
Davies, Theo. H., Company, 496
Davis, Arthur, 705

Davis, Elmer, 265
Davis, John W., 211–14, 422
Davis, Kenneth S., 430
Davis, William H., 755
Dawes, Charles G., 258, 262
Day, Stephen, 815
Daytona Educational and Industrial School, 639
Debs, Eugene V., 70, 192
Declaration of Independence, 732
Defense Homes Corporation, 729
Defense Plant Corporation, 740
de Golyer, Everett, 749
Delano, Frederick, 377, 378, 582
Demaray, Arthur A., 563, 570, 573
DeMille, Cecil B., 815
Democracia, La, 514, 516
Democratic Party, 2, 17, 67, 119, 123, 139, 203, 204, 215, 307, 335, 505, 545, 615, 703, 828, 829, 831, 851
  anticommunism and, 632
  blacks and, 637, 648
  in Chicago, 51, 60, 62, 78, 88, 103, 107, 108, 188, 197, 247
  1896 convention of, 43–44
  League of Nations and, 180
  in 1896 elections, 44–45, 67
  in 1900 elections, 74, 75
  in 1920 elections, 188–89, 191
  in 1924 elections, 211
  in 1932 elections, 262–71, 300
  in 1934 elections, 413
  in 1936 elections, 423, 425–26, 430–41, 438, 442–43
  in 1938 elections, 630–31
  in 1940 elections, 676–84, 686–87, 689–97
  in 1944 elections, 808–16, 824
  in 1946 elections, 838
  in 1948 elections, 848–50
  patronage and, 328
  progressives and, 133, 136–37, 212
  in Puerto Rico, 514*n*, 516
  right wing of, 422–23
  Southern, 625, 626
Democratic Roosevelt, The (Tugwell), 346
Dempsey, John H., 409, 587, 632, 748, 774, 786
Denby, Edwin N., 206

Deneen, Charles S., 32, 63, 107, 108, 247, 269
Denmark, German occupation of, 685
Dent, Newton, 22
Dern, George, 335, 338, 347, 439, 643
De Rouen, René, 571, 576, 583
Desert Land Act (1877), 308
Des Moines Register, 491
Detroit
    during Depression, 258
    riots in, 732
Dever, William E., 197–99, 215, 218, 223
DeVoto, Bernard, 308, 844, 846
Dewey, Chauncey, 103
Dewey, John, 38
Dewey, Thomas E., 686–87, 808, 809, 813–16, 848–50
DeWitt, Lieutenant General John L., 791
Dickinson, John, 348, 349
Dies, Martin, 617, 631–35, 745n, 838
DiGiorgio Company, 777
Dilg, Will H., 461, 462
Dimond, Anthony, 785
Dinosaur National Monument, 320, 846
District Bankers' Association, 291
Dix, Dorothy, 408n
Dixon, Arthur, 63
Dixon, Maynard, 450
Dobyns, Fletcher, 106
Dodge, Mabel, 202
Doheny, Edward, 206–8
Donitz, Admiral Karl, 738
Donnelly, Ignatius, 65
Doubleday, Russell, 257
Douglas, Helen Gahagan, 683, 796, 851–52
Douglas, Lewis, 347–49, 393, 412, 423–24
Douglas, Melvyn, 683
Douglas, Paul H., 3, 242–43, 302n, 679, 858
Douglas, William O., 622, 626, 661, 811–12, 825–26, 832, 848, 858
Dow Chemical, 742
Dow-Jones Industrials, 235, 627
Downes, Ellen, 724
Downey, Sheridan, 780
Drake, Edwin L., 340
Dreier, John, 403
Dreier, Mary, 91

Dreiser, Theodore, 22, 62n, 176, 461
Drury, Allen, 809, 826
Drury, Newton B., 552, 579, 580, 769, 774–75, 844–45
Duck Stamp Act (1934), 491
Duffy, Sherman, 57, 58
Duncan, William, 616
Duncan-Clark, S. J., 173, 217
Dunne, Edward F., 88, 90, 91, 130, 197, 243
Dunwoody, Charles, 571, 585
Du Pont, Pierre S., 422–24
Du Pont Corporation, 741
Du Puy, William Atherton, 270, 496, 500
Duquesne Lighting Company, 657
Dutch East Indies, 708, 709
Dutch Harbor, 785, 787–89
Dutcher, William E., 459, 460, 463

Earle, George H., 560, 678
Early, Stephen, 344, 401, 417, 438, 505, 634, 723, 744n, 763–65, 810
Eastern Sugar Associates, 518
Eastman, Joseph B., 743
Easton, Cyrus, 233, 248, 758
Eaton brothers, 100
Eccles, Mariner, 393
Economic Club, 688
Economic Defense Board, 735
Economic Warfare Board, 735–38
Economy Act (1933), 334, 347, 485, 495, 619
Edge, Rosalie, 462–64, 565, 775, 845
Edison, Thomas Alva, 140, 158
Edison General Electric Company, 158
Education, Office of, 323, 339, 449, 587, 641–43, 734
Efficiency, Bureau of, 502–3
Eisenhower, Dwight D., 273, 780, 843, 848
Eisenhower, Milton, 792
Eliot, Charles, II, 377
Elizabeth, Queen (wife of George V), 655
Elkus, Charles de Young, 274, 275, 331
Elliott, Alfred J., 779
Elliott, John B., 342–44, 343
Ellison, Ralph, 644
Ely, Robert, 204
Emergency Administration, Office of (OEA), 711

Emergency Conservation Committee, 463, 464, 491, 562–65, 575, 578, 585, 773, 775, 845
Emergency Conservation Work, 641
Emergency Peace Federation, 157
Emergency Relief Appropriation Act (1935), 394, 395, 401
Emerson, Rupert, 511, 527
Emporia Gazette, 666, 805
"End Poverty in California" (EPIC) program, 414
England. *See* Great Britain
Enlarged Homestead Act (1909), 308
Erisman, Ida, 109, 153
Eskimos, 323, 468*n*, 495, 542, 610
Essary, Mrs. J. Fred, 600
Ethiopia, Italian invasion of, 665–67
Ettleson, Samuel, 240
Evanston (Ill.), 151
Everglades National Park, 555–56
Everleigh, Ada, 26
Everleigh, Minna, 26
Everybody's Magazine, 118
Ewing, Thomas, 307
Extension Service, 640, 646

Fabian socialism, 117
Factories in the Field: The Story of Migratory Farm Labor in California (McWilliams), 778*n*
Facts and Figures, Office of, 743
Fahy, Charles, 329, 330, 537, 538
Fairbanks (Alaska), 611, 613
Fairbanks Exploration Company, 614
Fajardo Sugar Company, 513
Fall, Albert B., 203, 205–8, 371, 447, 490, 533, 842
Family Service Association, 730–31
Farley, James A., 280, 293, 301, 374, 403, 414*n*, 433, 434, 515, 586, 626–27, 631, 693
  at cabinet meetings, 335
  at Democratic convention of 1932, 263–66, 270
  and 1936 reelection campaign, 431, 432, 438, 439, 444
  Presidential candidacy of, 651, 676–77, 683, 684, 689, 690
Farm Credit Administration, 646
Farmers' Holiday Association, 259

Farm Relief Act (1933), 346
Farm Security Administration, 778*n*
Farrar, Geraldine, 650
Farrell, James T., 253–54
Fascism, 120, 663–69
Favill, Henry Baird, 731
Fay, James, 631
Fechner, Robert, 339, 641–43, 645
Federal Bureau of Investigation (FBI), 207, 358, 437, 838, 847
Federal Emergency Relief Administration (FERA), 326, 390–92, 504, 517, 537, 611–12, 644, 646
  Division of Rural Rehabilitation, 612
Federal Employment Stabilization Board, 352
Federal Housing Administration, 734
Federalist Papers, 305
Federal Oil Conservation Board, 317, 340
Federal Parole Board, 508
Federal Power Act (1920), 569
Federal Power Commission, 378, 576
Federal Reserve Board, 137, 231, 294, 348, 393
Federal Theater Project, 633, 644
Federal Trade Commission, 137, 378, 734
Federal Triangle, 290
Federal Works Authority, 587, 659
Federal Writers' Project, 644
Federation of Citizens' Associations, 287
Feis, Herbert, 747
Ferber, Edna, 3, 127, 184, 187, 283, 377
Fergusson, Miriam, 341
Fernández Garcia, Rafael, 519
Ferris, George, 37
Festich, Roscoe, 269, 279
Fewkes, John, 679
Field, Eugene, 57
Field, Marshall, 37, 60, 159
Field & Stream, 459
Fifty Billion Dollars (Jones), 370
Fightin' Oil (Ickes), 760
Fillmore, Millard, 307
Financier, The (Dreiser), 62*n*
Firestone Tire & Rubber Company, 688
First National Bank of Chicago, 73, 236
Fish, Hamilton, 695, 815
Fish and Wildlife Service, 733, 734
Fisher, Irving, 233–34
Fisher, Walter L., 106, 123, 245, 454

Fisheries, Bureau of, 587, 590
Fitzgerald, F. Scott, 231
Fitzgerald, Zelda, 231
Five Civilized Tribes, 530, 542
Flynn, Edward J., 692, 703, 810
Foley, Edward H., 395, 700
Foley, James, 95
Folks (Murdock), 14
Food Administration, 181
Foote, James, 554, 582
Forbes, Colonel Charles R., 207
Ford, Henry, 193, 379, 696
Ford Motor Company, 259
Foreman, Clark, 645–46
Foreman National Bank, 236
Forest and Stream, 459, 462
Forest Organic Act (1897), 311
Forest Reserve Clause, 310–11, 320, 460
Forest Service, U.S., 336, 397, 464–67,
        478, 484–88, 490–93, 552, 562,
        569–78, 584, 615, 766, 767, 844,
        845
    Civilian Conservation Corps and, 339
    Division of Lands and Recreation, 465,
        472
    lumber industry and, 455, 564–66,
        585–90, 773–76
    under Pinchot, 114, 115, 121, 312,
        329, 457
    reorganization and, 557–61
Forness, Norman, 307
Forrestal, James, 827–30, 839
Fortas, Abe, 661, 662, 706, 715, 765,
        778, 820, 827, 829
Fortescue, Mrs. Granville, 497, 498
Fort Knox, 732
Fort Ontario, 800–804
Fort Peck Dam, 384
Fortune magazine, 785
"Four Freedoms," 701
Fowler, Gene, 57, 194
France, 527
    and Italian invasion of Ethiopia, 666
    and Spanish Civil War, 666
    in World War I, 162–68
    in World War II, 654, 685, 727, 798,
        810, 848
Franck, Harry A., 610–15
Franco, Francisco, 666, 668, 671
Frank, Bernard, 468

Franke, Paul R., 771
Frankfurter, Felix, 275, 277, 329, 368,
        396, 547, 622, 625, 693, 819, 820
Frankstown (Pa.), 9–10, 18
Fred Harvey Company, 550
*Freedom of the Press Today: A Clinical Exam-
        ination* (Ickes), 762–63
French, Daniel Chester, 37
Freud, Sigmund, 118
Frick, Henry Clay, 122
Frink, Carol, 607
Fuel Administration, U.S., 317
Fuller, Henry Blake, 25
Furman, Bess, 267, 301
Future in America, The (Wells), 61

Gadsden Purchase, 304
Gage, Lyman, 73
Gallaudet College, 324
Garanin, F. A., 847
Garden, Mary, 229
Garden, Oliver Max, 359–60
Gardner, Warner W., 659n
Garfield, James, 114, 123, 130, 146, 155,
        182, 212, 256, 457
Garner, John Nance, 263, 266–68, 296,
        300, 302, 336–37, 389, 430, 431,
        507–8, 620, 625, 631, 632, 648,
        651, 676, 683–84, 690
Gary, Elbert, 122
Gearhart, Bertrand W., 573–77
Gee's Bend (Ala.), 644
General Allotment Act (1887), 532, 533,
        542
General Electric, 158, 234, 250, 404, 578
General Federation of Women's Clubs, 533,
        585
    Indian Welfare Committee of, 202, 203
General Grant National Park, 320, 574
General Land Office, 114, 115, 305–13,
        315, 317, 464, 473, 845
General Mining Act (1872), 115, 314, 539
General Motors, 686, 711
General Printing Company, 221, 233, 238
General Reorganization Act (1891), 121
Geological Survey, U.S. (USGS), 315–18,
        322, 674
George, Henry, 68
George V, King of England, 655
Georgetown University Hospital, 854

Georgia Power Company, 658–59
Gerard, Leona B. *See* Graham, Leona
Gerhard, Ashley, 409
German-American Bund, 545
Germany, 376, 635, 665
    Austria seized by, 668, 669
    persecution of Jews in, 665, 669–75, 796–804
    postwar, 844
    and Spanish Civil War, 666, 667
    in World War I, 156, 162, 164–67
    in World War II, 654, 685, 698, 702, 709, 710, 714, 733, 738, 798, 810, 825
    zeppelins of, 668, 673
Grand Canyon National Park, 320, 470, 550
Gibbons, Floyd, 299
Gibson, George H., 504–5, 507
Gila Wilderness Area, 465
Gilkey, Dean, 405
Gilmore, Tom, 153, 222
Gizycki, Count Josef, 597
Gizycki, Felicia, 597
Glacier Bay National Monument, 615
Glacier National Park, 320, 470, 551, 609
Glassford, Pelham D., 272
Glavis, Louis Russell, 115–16, 332–33, 358, 360, 361, 368, 369, 375, 387, 432–37, 505, 508, 560*n*, 590, 644, 647
Glenn, Otis F., 215
Godfrey, Arthur, 299, 820
Goering, Herman, 714*n*
Goldschmidt, Arthur, 706, 778
Gone With the Wind (Mitchell), 658
Good Neighbor League, 443
Gore, Robert, 515–16
Gosnell, Harold F., 244
Graham, Leona, 522, 596
Grand Coulee Dam, 385
Grand Teton National Park, 767, 768, 770, 771, 844
Grant, Francis, 854
Grapes of Wrath, The (Steinbeck), 473, 778*n*
Gray, Howard A., 661
Grazing Service, U.S., 478–80, 482, 492, 590, 845
Great Britain, 635
    Ickes in, 606

and Italian invasion of Ethiopia, 666
Palestine and, 672
and Spanish Civil War, 666
in World War II, 654, 685, 692, 698–700, 702, 712, 714, 719, 720, 727, 736, 747, 749–52, 798
Virgin Islands and, 500, 510
Great Depression, 249–60, 377, 414, 424, 437*n*
    bank failures during, 262–63, 292
    Chicago during, 2, 251–53
    Dust Bowl during, 473–75
    in Hawaii, 496
    Hoover's attempts to deal with, 255–59
    in Virgin Islands, 502
    Washington during, 287, 289–92
Great Northern Egg Company, 94
Great Northern Railroad, 609
Great Smoky Mountains National Park, 322, 471–72, 555, 556, 583, 692
Greece, German occupation of, 702
Greeley, William B., 455, 464, 775–76
Green, William, 259, 339, 679
Greenland, 702
Greenway, John, 530
Gregory, S. S., 96
Grey, Zane, 461
Grinnell, George Bird, 459–60, 462
Grosscup, Peter S., 88
Groves, General Leslie, 825
Gruber, Ruth, 788–89, 801–4, 846–47
Gruening, Ernest, 495, 506, 517–22, 525–27, 785–88, 806*n*
Guadalupe-Hidalgo, Treaty of, 203, 304
Guam, 726
Guaranty Trust, 234
Guffey Act (1935), 416, 421
Guffey Coal Act (1936), 660
Guffey-Vinson Bituminous Coal Act (1937), 660
Guggenheim banking interests, 115
Gulick, Luther, 557
Guthrie, Woody, 475

Hadoar (weekly), 799, 801
Hahneman Medical College, 32
Halifax, Lord and Lady, 606
Hamilton, Alice, 72, 404
Hampton, Ruth, 328, 409, 596, 600, 602
Hampton's magazine, 118

Hand, Learned, 120
Handbook of Federal Indian Law, 547
Hanna, Marcus A., 70, 74–76, 425
Hanna, R. K., 605
Hannegan, Robert E., 809, 811, 824, 835
Hanson, Earl, 521, 526
Harcourt, Brace publishers, 761
Harding, Susan, 48
Harding, Warren G., 181, 185–93, 203,
    205–8, 213, 256, 264, 273, 330,
    420, 835
Hard Times (Terkel), 251
Harlan, John, 90, 94, 130
Harlan, James Maynard, 51, 60, 73, 78–
    81, 83, 89–90, 94, 99, 102, 106,
    130, 218, 245, 269
Harper, William Rainey, 4, 36, 38, 41, 73,
    102
Harper's magazine, 844, 846
Harriman, E. H., 65
Harriman, W. Averell, 705
Harris, Edwin A., 831, 834
Harrison, Benjamin, 310, 311, 455, 569
Harrison, Carter H., 37, 69
Harrison, Carter H. II, 51, 60–62, 78, 81,
    88, 107, 108, 140, 204, 243
Harrison, Pat, 505, 506, 508
Harrison, William Henry, 307
Hart, Scott, 728
Hart, Thomas, 839
Hart, Schaffner and Marx, 104–5, 142
Harvard University, 527, 744
    Harvard Forest, 466
    Law School, 87, 90, 275, 329, 368, 396,
        480, 622
    Medical School, 72, 404
Harwood, Charles, 511
Hassett, William D., 816
Hastie, William, 509–10, 644
Hatch, Carl, 825
Hatch Act (1939), 328
Haven (Gruber), 801
Havenner, Franck, 674
Hawaii, Territory of, 322, 323, 334, 494–
    500, 512, 528, 781, 783–85, 787,
    790, 791
Hawaii Sugar Planters Association, 498
Hawley-Smoot tariff act (1930), 256
Hayden, Carl, 343, 427
Haymarket bombing, 68, 95, 96

Hays, Arthur Garfield, 523
Hays, Will H., 178–79, 182, 183, 608
Haywood, William D. ("Big Bill"),
    91, 191
Hazard, A. Clinton, 56, 161, 223–24,
    406, 442, 807
Hazard, Harold, 161–62, 442
Hazard, Julia Ickes, 11, 20, 35, 40, 161,
    223–24, 328, 406, 440, 442, 807
Hearst, William Randolph, 118, 243, 244,
    296, 424, 425, 438–39, 441n,
    596, 598, 608, 727
Hecht, Ben, 57–59, 128
Heintzelman, B. Frank, 615
Hektoen, Ludvig, 38
Held, John, Jr., 461
Hellenthal, J. A., 615
Heller, Samuel A., 251
Hemispheric Defense, U.S. System of, 702
Henderson, Florence, 807
Henderson, Leon, 702, 704, 711–12, 737–
    38, 740, 743, 745
Henry, Francis, 277
Henry Gibbons (ship), 802
Herrick, Genevieve, 407, 408
Hertz, Henry L., 63
Hibbs, Ben, 841–42
Hickok, Lorena, 474
High Sierra Primitive Area, 570
Hildebrand, Joe, 571, 572
Hildebrandt, Fred, 640
Hillman, Sidney, 142, 404, 694–95, 700,
    706, 731, 814
Hindenburg, 668
Hirohito, Emperor of Japan, 720
Hiroshima, 826
Hiss, Alger, 838
Hitchcock, Ethan Allen, 311
Hitchcock, Frank, 209, 210
Hitler, Adolf, 376, 635, 654, 665, 666,
    669, 685, 698, 702, 709, 714–15,
    726, 727, 772, 796, 798, 825
Hodson, William, 389–90
Hoffman, Peter, 97
Hollywood Democratic Committee, 815
Holmes, Oliver Wendell, 396
Holocaust. *See* Jews, Nazi persecution of
Homestead Act (1862), 308, 317–18, 319,
    479, 480n
Hooniah (Alaska), 615

Hoover, Herbert, 181, 185, 208, 295–97, 299–300, 383, 403, 420, 424, 845

presidency of, 215, 255–62, 270, 272–73, 290, 293, 294, 313–14, 327, 340n, 341, 370, 502–3, 533, 686

Hoover, J. Edgar, 190, 358, 437, 838, 847

Hoover Dam. *See* Boulder Dam

Hopkins, Barbara, 623, 681

Hopkins, Harry, 2, 378, 389–95, 474, 517, 519, 611, 613, 629, 630, 634, 661, 682, 687, 689–91, 693, 716, 814, 842

at Anna's funeral, 409

blacks and, 643–44

on *Houston* cruises, 417–19, 623

Indians and, 537

presidential candidacy of, 677, 679–81

public works and, 391–92, 397–400, 410–13, 426, 429

during World War II, 702, 710, 711, 725

Hornaday, William T., 461–63

Horton, Benjamin, 517, 518

Hough, Emerson, 461

Houghton Mifflin, 354

House of Representatives, U.S., 203, 246, 259, 263, 307, 414, 426, 427, 429, 498, 523, 557, 567–68, 838, 851

Appropriations Subcommittee for Interior, 322

Bonus Bill in, 260

conservation legislation in, 478, 490–92

Democratic majority in, 413

Expenditures Committee, 490

immigration legislation in, 674, 675

Indian Affairs Committee, 538, 539, 542, 544, 545

Judiciary Committee, 619

Lend-Lease bill in, 701

Lumber Matters Subcommittee, 776

Military Affairs Committee, 669

Naturalization and Immigration Committee, 803

Public Lands Committee, 571, 574, 584, 771, 772

reorganization bill in, 587, 629

Rules Committee, 493, 631

Un-American Activities Committee, 617, 631–35, 644n, 838, 839, 846, 851

Housing Authority, U.S., 376, 587

Houston (cruiser), 417–19, 623

Howard, Edgar, 538

Howard University, 323–24, 334, 450, 503

Concert Series, 649

Howe, Louis McHenry, 264, 265, 277–78, 296, 330, 353, 357, 374, 387–88, 395, 432, 626, 643, 687

Hubbard Woods (Ill.), 151–54, 162, 163, 166, 182, 211, 219–20, 222, 225, 233, 237, 246, 281, 405, 409, 439–41, 447, 599, 713, 724, 852

Hubbell, Henry Salem, 447, 596

Hughes, Charles Evans, 144–46, 181, 297, 624, 626

Hughes, Langston, 666

Hull, Charles, 72

Hull, Cordell, 266, 300, 335, 337, 605, 664–68, 677, 681, 690, 707–8, 710, 719–20, 738, 747, 749–51, 799, 800, 803, 824

Hull, Mrs. Cordell, 677

Hull-House, 4, 45, 71–73, 91, 96, 104, 105, 201, 252, 404, 405

Humphrey, William, 562

Hunt, Henry T., 368, 646

Hunt, Loren, 770

Hunt, Richard Morris, 37

Hurley, Patrick J., 272, 273

Hurok, Sol, 649, 650

Hutchins, Robert M., 222, 365n, 690

Hutchinson, W. H., 319

Husing, Ted, 299

Ibn Saud, King, 746–47

Ickes, Ada Katrina (sister), 11, 14, 17

Ickes, Amelia (sister), 11, 20, 29, 32, 40, 41, 56, 83, 222–23

Ickes, Anna Wilmarth (first wife), 1, 4, 94, 96, 183, 197, 222, 237, 603, 606, 765, 857

in Altoona, 405–7

birth of Raymond to, 125–26, 129, 131, 713

conflicts with Harold, 147–51, 168–71, 219–20

courtship of, 45–50
death of, 408–10, 439, 442, 595, 596, 598
estate left by, 439–40, 657
first marriage of, 57, 82–90, 101–3
and garment workers' strike, 105
and Harold's mistress, 356–57, 361–63
honeymoon of, 109, 113
Hubbard Woods house of, 151–54
in Illinois assembly, 3, 215–16, 242, 247, 268–70, 273, 280, 354, 402
at inauguration, 295, 301
and Indians, 202–4, 270, 271, 354, 361–62, 402, 407, 537, 545
inheritance of, 238
marries Harold, 108–9
in New Mexico, 202, 235–36
and Progressivism, 73, 201
Robinses and, 130, 219
spending by, 233
supports FDR's candidacy, 272
in Washington, 280, 287, 293, 354–55, 359, 361, 402, 404
and Wilmarth's marriage, 220–21, 239
during World War I, 161, 162, 164, 166–68
Ickes, Elizabeth (daughter), 713, 852–53, 855, 858
Ickes, Felix (brother), 11, 20, 35, 40, 41, 56, 88
Ickes, Harold
  Anna and, 45–50
    Anna's death, 408–10
    Anna's first marriage, 57, 82–90, 101–3
    Anna's political career, 215–16, 268–70, 273
    Anna's will, 439–41
    conflicts, 147–51, 168–71, 219–20, 237
    finances, 238–39
    honeymoon, 109, 113
    marriage, 108–9
    in New Mexico, 235–36
  birth of, 7, 11, 12
  births of children of, 125–26, 129, 131, 654–56, 713–14
  books by, 760–65, see also titles of specific works

in Chicago politics, 60, 62–63, 73, 140–42, 177, 178
  Averbuch affair, 95–100
  Dever campaign, 197–99
  Harlan campaigns, 51, 78–81, 88–89
  Insull and, 240–41
  Merriam campaign, 106–9, 178–79
  Republican precinct captain, 104
  streetcar companies, 242–46
childhood of, 13–20
as columnist, 840–48
on Coolidge, 214
death of, 853–55
deaths of friends of, 805–7, 817–18, 826–27
and Democratic Party politics, 630
  Cox-Roosevelt ticket endorsed, 188–92
  FDR's candidacy supported, 268–73
  FDR's reelection campaigns, 423, 425, 430–32, 437–39, 442–44, 682–84, 686–94, 696, 808–17
  1940 Presidential race, 676–82
Dies Committee and, 616–17, 633–35
at Eaton ranch, 100–101
education of
  high school, 30–34
  law school, 87–88, 90
  University of Chicago, 35–36, 38–43, 45–52, 55
family relations of, 220–24, 852–53
fascism abhorred by, 663–69
and FDR's death, 819–22
first exposures to politics, 43–45, 67
friendships with women, 595–98
funeral of, 857–58
gardening by, 225–26
goes to Washington, 1–4, 280–82, 287
health problems of
  broken ribs, 366
  depression, 154–55
  heart disease, 525, 603
  insomnia, 807–8, 819
  in old age, 853–54
Hoover and, 257–58
on Houston voyage, 417–19
Hubbard Woods house of, 151–54, 233, 246, 281, 447, 852
in Illinois politics, 140, 209

Ickes, Harold (*cont'd*)
  Lowden supported, 179–81, 185
  proposed constitution, 196–97
  state race of 1926, 214–15, 218
  at inauguration, 293, 295, 301
  and Indians, 202–6, 274–76
  and Jane Addams's funeral, 404–5
  Jews and, 661–62
  last political campaign of, 851–52
  last summer in Altoona, 55–56
  law practice of, 93–94, 100, 104–5,
      131, 138–40, 160, 209–10, 230
  and League of Nations, 180, 181
  Long and, 414*n*, 415
  Malmin and, 357–59
  memorial service for, 858–59
  mistress of, 355–57, 359–65
  mother's death, 20
  moves to Chicago, 7, 20–22,
      29–30
  NAACP and, 199–201
  as newspaper reporter, 57–59, 62, 73–
      78
  oligarchy denounced by, 628–29
  passes bar exam, 92
  physical appearance of, 1–2
  Progressives and, 73, 126, 130–31, 133,
      137–38, 140–47, 155–57, 178–
      79, 182–84, 240–41, 454
    garment workers' strike, 104–5
    Harding nomination, 187–89
    Johnson's candidacy, 207–12, 214,
      217, 260–61
    La Follette, 212–13
    1931 Washington conference, 227,
      246–47
    Peoria conference, 104
  and Pullman strike, 70
  returns to Altoona, 405–7
  Robert disowned by, 656–57
  Robinses and, 90, 92, 129–30, 140–41,
      218–19, 403–4, 419, 590
  second marriage of, 595, 598–608
  as Secretary of Interior, 2, 285, 302–4,
      317, 320, 322–24, 354, 355, 402,
      658–61
    blacks and, 643–49, 651–52
    at cabinet meetings, 334–37, 348,
      427–28, 434–35, 619, 620, 627,
      724–25

  and Civilian Conservation Corps,
      338–40
  conservation and, 452, 453, 458,
      469–72, 475–82, 484–94, 556–
      61, 585–90, 765, 768–80
  construction of new building, 447–52
  Glavis as problem for, 432–37
  Indians and, 534–37, 540, 543, 545,
      546
  Jewish refugees and, 670–75
  national parks and, 549–53, 555–56,
      561, 563–68, 570–84
  official portrait, 447
  oil production and, 340–46
  Public Works and, 347, 350–53,
      367–78, 382–89, 394–95, 398–
      401, 410–13, 426–29, 455, 590–
      91, 715
  resignation by, 832–36
  Roosevelt's appointment by, 275–80
  staff appointed by, 327–34
  swearing in of, 301
  territories, 495, 499, 503–15, 517,
      518, 520, 522–27, 608–16, 622
  under Truman, 823–32, 839–40
  work-relief program and, 390–98
  during World War II, 699, 703–12,
      715–18, 721, 724–25, 730, 733–
      41, 743–53, 755–59, 765, 781–
      90, 792–97, 801–4
  stamp collection of, 225
  stock market and, 232–33, 235–38
  and Supreme Court, 421, 422, 618–20,
      622–25
  and Taft administration, 117
  Theodore Roosevelt and, 126–27, 136,
      218
  in Truman campaign, 848–51
  in Warm Springs, 365–66
  and Wilmarth's death, 439–42
  during World War I, 157–58, 160–69
Ickes, Harold M. (son), 605, 654–56, 692,
      819, 852–53, 855, 858
Ickes, Jane Dahlman (second wife), 220,
      328, 599–607, 623, 683, 692,
      712, 714–15, 724, 726, 727, 763,
      792, 807, 813, 817, 832, 849,
      852–53
  on Alaska trip, 608–10, 612, 613,
      615–17

birth of children to, 654–56, 713–14
at Democratic convention of 1940, 689, 690
and FDR's death, 819–21, 824
and Harold's death, 854–55
at Harold's funeral and memorial service, 857–59
marries Harold, 604–6
Robinses and, 818
surgery on, 737
Ickes, Jesse Boone Williams (father), 10–11, 14–17, 19, 20, 31, 34–36, 40–42, 48, 50, 55, 56–57, 75–77, 87
Ickes, Jesse Merrill (brother), 11, 20, 33
Ickes, John (brother), 11, 16–18, 20, 35, 40, 56, 223, 399
Ickes, John (grandfather), 10, 11, 14, 15
Ickes, Julia (sister). See Hazard, Julia Ickes
Ickes, Martha (Mattie) McCune (mother), 10–11, 14–20, 30, 35
Ickes, Miralotte Sauer, 655, 818–19
Ickes, Raymond (son), 1, 46n, 147, 149, 150, 153, 154n, 198n, 218, 220–22, 226, 237, 238, 281, 596, 752n, 853, 855
    and Anna's death, 409
    and Anna's will, 440
    birth of, 125–26, 129, 131, 201, 713
    and father's second marriage, 604
    in law school, 405
    marriage of, 655–56
    in New Mexico, 235–36
    at Nuremberg trials, 827
    in Washington, 287, 293, 410, 417
    in World War II, 818–19
Ickes, Robert (ward), 1, 221, 235, 238, 281, 287, 293
    adoption of, 153–54
    and Anna's death, 409
    and Anna's will, 440
    disowned, 656–57
    in Interior Department, 328
Ickes, Wilmarth (stepson), 82–85, 89, 94, 103, 109, 149–50, 220–21, 233, 237–39, 363, 599
    and Anna's death, 409
    death of, 439–42, 602, 656
    in World War I, 161, 162, 167
Iglesias, Santiago, 513

Île de France (ship), 606
Illinois (ship), 156
Illinois, University of, 216
Illinois Bar Association, 358
Illinois Birth Control League, 100
Illinois Coal Operators Association, 758
Illinois Commerce Commission, 240, 243
Illinois Progressive Party, 140–41
Illinois Progressive Republican League, 108, 126
Illinois Public Utilities Commission, 214
Illinois State Assembly, 3, 196, 216, 247, 268, 354, 402
Illinois State Utilities Board, 140
Illinois Steel Company, 31, 40
Illinois Supreme Court, 358, 657
Independent magazine, 118
Independent Petroleum Association of America, 342
Independent Petroleum Association Opposed to Monopoly, 344, 345
Indian Affairs, Bureau of (BIA), 271, 275, 307, 308, 330–32, 469, 486, 531, 533–47, 549, 634, 733, 734
    Applied Anthropology Unit, 543
Indian Arts and Crafts Board, 543
Indian Commissioners, Board of, 536
Indian Emergency Conservation Work (IECW) program, 536
Indian Reorganization Act (1934), 538–43
Indians, 202–4, 270, 271, 354, 361–62, 402, 407, 530–48. See also specific tribes
    Alaskan, 610, 615, 616
Indian Wars, 530
Indochina, 720
Industrial Relations Committee, 500
Industrial Revolution, 12
Institute for Government Affairs, 329
Institute for Government Research, 533
Institute of Public Administration, 557
Insular Affairs, Bureau of, 513, 587
Insull, Samuel, 140, 158–60, 197, 214, 215, 229–33, 240–45, 247–49, 262, 302n, 396
Insull Utilities Investments (IUI), 230, 248
Inter-Departmental Committee for the Economic Rehabilitation of Puerto Rico, 517

Interdepartmental Group Concerned with the Special Problems of Negroes, 646

Intergovernmental Committee on Refugees, 672, 673

Interior Appropriations Act (1945), 772

Interior Department, U.S., 115, 205–6, 303–4, 355, 356, 363, 365, 371, 407, 658–61, 724. *See also specific agencies and programs*
appointments to, 327–34
blacks in, 644–46, 648, 649n
Civilian Conservation Corps and, 338–40
conservation policy and, 457, 484–94, 556–61, 584–90, 773, 776, 777
creation of, 307
Division of Investigations, 332, 369, 432–37, 644
Division of Territories and Island Possessions, 322–23, 495–528, 596, 610, 612, 613, 781, 782, 758–86, 806n
educational responsibilities of, 323–24
land management by, 308–22
new building for, 447–52
Petroleum Division of, 416
Power Division of, 706, 778
Public Works and, 351–53
refugees and, 672–75
Solicitor's Office, 537, 659n, 672
during Truman administration, 824, 828, 830, 832, 844–46, 854
during World War II, 730, 733–36, 743n, 748, 801

Internal Revenue Bureau, 290

International Association of Machinists, 339

International Brigades, 666

International Council of Religious Education, 215

International Harvester Company, 24, 132

International Ladies' Garment Workers Union (ILGWU), 105

International Longshoremen's and Warehousemen's Union, 633

International News Service, 368

International Union of United Automobile, Aircraft and Agricultural Workers of America, 813

Interstate Commerce Commission (ICC), 90, 94, 121

In the Dark (Richberg), 138

Inuits. *See* Eskimos

Iowa Farmers' Union, 259

Iowa Game Commission, 491

Ireland, 605–6

Isle Royal National Park, 580

Israel, 844

Italy, 635, 665–66
and Spanish Civil War, 666, 667
in World War II, 685, 698, 801–2

I Went to the Soviet Arctic (Gruber), 788

Izaak Walton League, 461, 491, 560, 575, 577, 585

Jackson, Andrew, 629

Jackson, Henry M., 845

Jackson, Robert, 622, 625, 626, 629, 669, 677, 681, 682, 689, 704, 858

Jackson, Samuel E., 811

Jackson, Stan C., 794

Jackson Hole National Monument, 765–73, 844

Jameson, John Franklin, 38

Jamieson, T. N. ("Doc"), 63

Japan, 635
in World War II, 613n, 685–86, 698, 706–10, 719–20, 723–26, 728, 733, 740, 781, 783, 784, 787, 794, 826

Japanese-Americans, internment of, 790–96, 801, 805

Java, 740

Jefferson, Thomas, 67, 137, 305, 532, 652, 836

Jemison, Alice Lee, 545, 633, 634

Jenkins, Newton, 278

Jenney, William LeBaron, 27

Jewish Daily Courier, 664

Jewish Workers' Voice, 672

Jews
in Chicago, 95–99, 663–64
Nazi persecution of, 665, 669–75, 796–805

Johns Hopkins University, 466, 737
Press, 533

Johnson, General Hugh, 348–52, 364–65, 415, 432, 630, 646, 841–42

Johnson, Hiram, 3, 119, 130, 131, 155, 156, 203, 216, 218, 247, 274–80, 326, 401, 570
  death of, 826–27
  isolationism of, 181, 413, 725, 826
  Presidential candidacy of, 146, 179–81, 185, 190, 205, 207–12, 260–61
  Theodore Roosevelt and, 128, 134, 144–45
Johnson, Lyndon Baines, 684, 748
Johnson, Mordecai, 503
Johnson, Robert, 295
Johnson, Robert Underwood, 456
Johnson, Tom, 118
Johnston, Mary, 650
Joint Chiefs of Staff, 746
Jones, Andrieus Aristieus, 203, 204
Jones, Eugene Kinckle, 646
Jones, Howard Mumford, 63
Jones, J. Edward, 342–44
Jones, Jesse, 262, 370, 429, 504, 687, 705–6, 738, 740–43
Jones, Walter Clyde, 126
Jones, W. Alton, 718, 739
Joshua Tree National Monument, 556
Joslin, Theodore, 255
Journal of Forestry, 465
Judd, Lawrence M., 498–500
Judson, Henry Pratt, 102
Julius Rosenwald Fund, 645
Juneau (Alaska), 611, 615
Jung, Carl, 3, 118
Justice Department, U.S., 122, 190, 207, 307, 322, 396, 509, 511, 619, 672–73, 803, 828, 829, 838, 847
  Antitrust Division, 622, 706

Kahahawai, Joseph, 498
Kaiser, Henry J., 383–84, 705
Kaltenborn, H. V., 299
Kansas City Board of Trade, 294
Kauffman, Earle, 288
Kelly, Ed, 399–400, 409, 679–80, 690, 810
Kelly, Florence, 72
Kenna, Michael ("Hinky-Dink"), 61, 62, 195
Kennedy, John F., 606
Kennedy, Joseph P., 606, 677
Kennedy, T. Blake, 772, 773

Kenney, Mary, 72
Kent, Duke and Duchess of, 606
Kent, William, 245
Kent College of Law, 223
Ketchikan (Alaska), 610–11
Kew Indians, 542
King, William, 674
Kings Canyon National Park, 561, 569–80
Kings River Water Association, 574–76
Kipling, Rudyard, 22
Kirchwey, Freda, 835
Kittredge, Frank, 571
Klamath Indian Agency, 536
Kneipp, L. F., 465
Knight, Thomas D., 198
Knox, Alex, 19
Knox, Frank, 424, 425, 443, 686, 700, 738, 747, 790, 791, 806, 827
Knox, Sam, 19, 20
Knudsen, William S., 686, 700, 704, 711, 731
Kodiak Island (Alaska), 702, 785
Kohlsaat, Herman H., 77, 104
Korean War, 840, 844
Kristallnacht, 670, 673
Krock, Arthur, 430–31, 688, 850
Krug, Julius A., 844–45
Ku Klux Klan, 197–98, 201
Kurusu, Saburo, 719

Labor Department, U.S., 290, 329, 338, 339, 347, 365n, 633, 641, 645, 672–73
Lacey Art (1900), 459
Lady Chatterley's Lover (Lawrence), 601
Ladies' Home Journal, 231
La Follette, Robert M., 3, 118–19, 123, 128, 133, 157, 207, 210–13, 268, 277
La Follette, Robert M., Jr., 277, 347, 390
La Follette Act, 137
La Guardia, Fiorello, 374–75, 462, 692, 702, 731
Lake Forest College, 281, 656
Lake Mead National Recreation Area, 556
Lamont, Thomas W., 234
Land Classification Board, 316
Landers, Martha, 109
Landis, Kenesaw Mountain, 3, 177
Land Management, Bureau of, 845

Landon, Alf, 341–45, 424–25, 431, 438–39, 443–44, 598, 850
Lane, Franklin K., 321, 329, 457
Langdell, Christopher Columbus, 87
Lange, Dorothea, 473, 474, 778n
Lardner, Ring, 57
Lasker, Albert J., 183, 209
Lasswell, Harold, 762
Lathrop, Julia, 72
Lawrence, David, 299, 850
Lawrence, D. H., 601
Lawson, Thomas, 118
Lawson, Victor, 57, 73, 74, 77, 177
League of Nations, 181, 185, 187, 189, 195
Leahy, Admiral William D., 527, 669, 784
Legal Aid Society, 45
LeHand, Marguerite ("Missy"), 331–32, 364, 412, 417, 428, 588–89, 806
Lehman, Herbert, 294
Lemke, William, 424
Lend-Lease program, 699–702, 711, 714, 716, 747, 774, 806
Lenin, V. I., 195, 259
Leopold, Aldo, 464–65, 468, 470, 471, 589
Leuchtenberg, William E., 235, 373, 836
Levitt, Albert, 509, 510
Lewis, David J, 343
Lewis, James Hamilton, 107, 247, 489
Lewis, John L., 343, 423, 660–61, 694–96, 706, 753–58, 844
Lewis, Meriwether, 451
Lewis, Morris, 200, 201
Lewis, Sinclair, 628–29
Lewis, William Draper, 277
Leyte Gulf, Battle of, 784
Libby, McNeill & Libby, 25
Liberal Party, Puerto Rican, 513–14, 516, 521, 522, 527
Library of Congress, 289, 724, 732
Life and Times of William Howard Taft, The (Pringle), 590
Life magazine, 836
Lilienthal, David, 378, 379, 381
Lincoln, Abraham, 191, 630, 652, 784
Lindbergh, Charles A., 714, 715, 841
Lindbergh kidnapping, 273n
Lindley, Ernest, 433
Linton, Ralph, 536

Lippincott, Jane, 22
Lippmann, Walter, 194, 202, 264–65, 413, 423–24, 528, 850, 858
Literary Digest, 850
Little Big Inch pipeline, 739
Little Egypt, 37
Little Steel, 696
Living Wilderness, The, 468, 471
Lloyd George, David, 606
Lodge, Henry Cabot, 181, 185, 186, 187
London
  Ickes in, 606
  slums of, 71
Long, Breckinridge, 799, 800
Long, Huey, 332, 414–17, 424, 433–35, 621
Look magazine, 682, 688, 841
Lord, John S., 140, 209
Lorimer, George Horace, 322
Lorimer, William, 62, 103–4, 107, 108
Los Angeles Times, 762
Louisiana Purchase, 304
Lowden, Frank, 160, 178–81, 185, 199, 210
Lowell, Lawrence, 329
Loyalty Order (1947), 838
Luce, Henry, 836
Lueder, Arthur C., 197, 198
Luhan, Antonio, 202, 203
Lummis, Charles F., 362
Lundberg, Ferdinand, 628
Lusitania (ship), 144
Luxembourg, German invasion of, 685

McAdoo, William Gibbs, 188, 211, 266–67, 683
MacArthur, Charles, 57
MacArthur, General Douglas, 272–73, 292, 781, 783, 784, 840, 844
McCarran, Pat, 479, 482, 843
McCarran Act (1924), 671
McCarthy, Joseph R., 839, 847–48
McClure's Magazine, 118
McCormack, John W., 701
McCormick, Anne O'Hare, 260, 325
McCormick, Cyrus, 24, 73
McCormick, Medill, 126, 130, 138, 140, 141, 162, 176, 185, 197–99, 247, 597

McCormick, Robert, 126, 296, 443, 597, 679, 727, 815
McCormick, Ruth Hanna, 140, 212, 213, 247, 269
McCormick Harvesting Machine Company, 24, 68
McCosh, David, 451
McCrillis, William, 409
McCune, Joseph, 9
McCune, Julyanna, 10, 14
McCune, Sam, 31, 34, 35, 40, 56
McCune, Seth Robert, 9–10, 14, 18, 406
McCutcheon, John T., 74, 204
McDonald, James G., 797
McDowell, Malcolm, 58, 74
McDowell, Mary, 200
McFarland, Horace C., 552
McGroarty, John, 545
McIntire, Ross, 678
McIntosh, Leonard, 505–7
McIntyre, Colonel Marvin H., 353, 359, 365, 438, 493, 775
McIntyre, Colonel Ross, 417
Mack, Theodore, 358, 402, 451
MacKaye, Benton, 468, 554
Mackenzie, Frank J., 451
MacLeish, Archibald, 732, 743
McLemore, Harry, 791
McKim, Charles, 37
McKinley, William, 44, 67, 70, 74–76, 182
McNamee, Graham, 299
McNary, Charles L., 585
McNutt, Paul, 678
McReynolds, James, 626
McWilliams, Carey, 777, 778n, 851
Madden, Martin B., 51
Madison, James, 305, 564, 578, 773
Mafia, 196
Magee, Sylvia, 32, 40–42
MAGIC, 710
Magill, Hugh S., 126, 215, 218
Magnuson, Eric, 153
Magnuson, Ruth, 153
Malay Peninsula, 740
Malmin, Lucius J. M., 357–59, 608
Maloney, Francis, 716, 717
Mammoth Oil Company, 206
Man and Nature (Marsh), 309, 454, 455
Manhattan Project, 381, 825

Manley, Basil, 268, 269
Margold, Nathan, 275, 328–31, 344, 479, 518, 537, 545, 546n, 657, 662, 673
Marion (Ohio) Star, 186
Maritime Commission, U.S., 702
Markham, General, 489
Marquand, John P., 496–97
Marsh, C. S., 643
Marsh, George Perkins, 309, 453–56, 473
Marsh, John, 658–59
Marshall, Louis, 466
Marshall, Robert, 466–72, 492, 536, 543, 554, 570, 577, 578n
Marshall, S. L. A., 167
Marshall Field and Company, 25, 26, 241
Martin, Joe, 439, 695
Marx, Fred, 359, 408
Marx, Karl, 68, 118
Mason, Billy, 62
Mason, Noah, 632
Massachusetts Audubon Society, 459
Massie, Lieutenant Thomas, 497, 498
Massie, Thalia, 497
Masters, Edgar Lee, 204
Matanuska Colony (Alaska), 611–13, 788
Mather, Stephen, 320–22, 458, 551, 552, 569, 580, 766, 776
Maverick, Maury, 632, 678
Maxwell, General Russell L., 707
Mayo Clinic, 681, 806
Mazur, Paul M., 231
Mead, Elwood, 776, 777
Means, Gaston Bullock, 207
Medill, Joseph, 597
Men and Religion Forward movement, 90
Mencken, H. L., 57, 261
Mental Hygiene Society, 45
Mercer, Lucy, 364
Merchant Ship Control, Office of, 707
Meriam, Lewis, 275, 330, 533
Meritt, Edgar B., 330–32
Merriam, Charles H., 90, 94, 103, 106–9, 130, 138, 140, 160, 162, 177–78, 196, 197, 218, 242, 245, 280, 377, 378, 405, 552, 556, 679
Merriam, John C., 552
Mesa Land: The History and Romance of the American Southwest (Ickes), 354, 361–62

Mesa Verde National Park, 320
Metlakatla (Alaska), 616
Metro-Goldwyn Meyer (MGM), 300
Metropolitan Life Insurance Company, 230
Metropolitan Water District of Southern California, 382
Mexican War, 304, 305
Mexico, 702, 746
Meyer, Eugene, 294, 357
Middle West Utilities Company, 159, 229, 233, 235, 248
Midland Utilities Company, 230
Midway, Battle of, 787
Miller, Francis, 857
Mills, Ogden, 183
Mineral Leasing Act (1920), 317
Mines, Bureau of, 317, 322, 349, 674, 706
Mining Law (1866), 314
Mining World, 583
Minor, Dr., 854
Mission Gardens, 225, 226
Mississippi Valley Committee, 377
Missouri (ship), 826
Mitchell, Charles E., 234
Mitchell, Jonathan, 424n
Mitchell, Margaret, 658–59
Mitchell, Wesley C., 377, 378
Moley, Raymond, 264, 277–80, 293, 296, 298, 303, 347–48, 350, 503
Moline Implement Company, 348
Monroe, James, 530
Monsanto Chemical, 742
Montgomery Ward, 25
Moore, Charles H., 175
Moran, William H., 357
Morgan, Arthur H., 380, 381
Morgan, H. A., 380
Morgan, Jacob, 545
Morgan, J. P., 65, 122, 123, 158
Morgan banking interests, 115, 132, 234, 248
Morgenthau, Henry, 335, 337, 392–94, 433–35, 448, 629, 661, 666, 799, 800, 803, 824, 858
Morison, Samuel Eliot, 738
Morley, Christopher, 257
Morrill Land Grant Act (1862), 308, 309, 323
Morse, C. B., 571
Moser, Charlie, 14, 18, 32

Moser, "Muzzy," 14
Moses, Robert, 374–76, 388, 578
Mosier, Harold, 632
Mosky, George, 769
Mosser, Stacey, 78, 83, 109, 197, 409, 741, 808
Motion Picture Producers and Distributors of America, 178, 608
Mott, James W., 587
Moulton, Richard G., 38
Mt. McKinley National Park, 613
Mt. McKinley (ship), 610
Mount Rainier National Park, 320, 583, 609, 616
Mount Vernon Seminary, 729
Muir, John, 312, 456–58, 461, 471, 473, 569, 573, 577
Mullaney, Bernard J., 76
Mullen, Arthur, 266, 270, 279
Multiple Use and Sustained Yield Act (1960), 561n
Municipal Voters League, 73
Munõz Marín, Luis, 514, 516–17, 521, 522, 527
Munsey, Frank, 132, 133, 142
Munsey's magazine, 22, 118, 132
Murdock, Abe, 545
Murdock, Victor, 13–14
Murie, Margaret, 767
Murie, Olaus J., 767–68
Murphy, Frank, 258–59, 626, 677, 682
Murray, William H. ("Alfalfa Bill"), 341
Mussolini, Benito, 635, 665, 666, 698, 726
Mutual Broadcasting Company, 616
Myer, Dillon, 792, 795, 796, 801–3, 854
My Hero (Richberg), 139

Nagasaki, 826
Nancy (France), 166, 167
Nation, 404, 495, 514, 517, 723, 726, 835
National Archives, 290
National Association for the Advancement of Colored People (NAACP), 199–201, 329, 502, 503, 638, 639, 645, 647, 650, 731
National Association of Manufacturers, 837
National Association of Teachers in Colored Schools, 639

National Audubon Society, 463–64, 585
National Broadcasting Company (NBC), 299, 404, 406, 422–23, 438, 453, 470, 488, 492, 575, 623, 652, 692, 816
National Business Survey Conference, 257
National Capital Housing Authority, 730
National City Bank, 234
National Committee to Uphold Constitutional Government, 560n
National Conservation Association, 206, 329, 454–55, 658
National Conservation Congress, 455
National Council of Defense, 160
National Defense Advisory Commission, 686, 695, 700, 705, 716, 741
National Defense Mediation Board, 702
National Elk Refuge, 766, 767
National Emergency Council, 397, 476
National Enquirer, 678n
National Farmers' Union, 259
National Forest Reservation Commission, 334
National Geographic, 288
National Grange, 779
National Guard, 695, 702
National Industrial Recovery Act (NIRA) (1933), 349, 351, 353, 368, 377, 387, 401, 416
National Industrial Recovery Board, 365
National Irrigation Congress, 318
Nationalist Party, Puerto Rican, 514, 516, 518, 520, 522, 523, 526
National Jewish Monthly, 800
National Labor Relations Act (1935), 395, 416, 624
National Labor Relations Board, 500
National Munitions Control Board, 668, 669
National Negro Press Association, 637
National Parks and Planning Commission, 582
National Parks Association, 458, 552, 554, 577, 582
National Parks Organic Act (1916), 321
National Park Service, 458, 464, 471, 485, 491, 492, 549–55, 563, 566, 571–73, 576, 581–82, 766–79, 773, 776, 841. See also names of specific parks

Brant and, 568–69, 578
Civilian Conservation Corps and, 337
creation of, 320–22
Drury appointed head of, 579, 580
Jane employed at, 599
reorganization and, 589–90
Robert employed at, 656
segregation of facilities of, 648
during World War II, 733, 734, 774, 775
Yard and, 492, 577, 582
National Planning Board, 786
National Power Policy Committee, 378, 396
National Press Club, 334
National Progressive League, 272, 277
National Progressive Republican League, 106, 119, 126, 138
National Public Health Service, 373, 584
National Reclamation Association, 583
National Recovery Administration (NRA), 350, 352, 364–65, 420, 421, 646
National Resources Committee, 587
National Resources Planning Board, 377–78, 577, 568
National Union for Social Justice, 415, 424
National War Labor Board (NWLB), 753–58
National Wilderness Preservation System, 554
National Youth Administration (NYA), 639–40, 646, 731
Native Sons of the Golden West, 791
Navajo Indians, 202, 361, 537, 541, 544–45
Navy, U.S., 376, 497–98, 502, 708, 729
women in, 730
in World War II, 746, 755, 785
Navy Department, U.S., 646, 724, 738, 747, 787, 791, 829, 835
Nazis, 654, 665, 668, 670, 800
American, 545, 632, 633
Neighborhood Committee, 160–61, 163, 257
Nelson, Donald M., 711, 724, 737–39, 742, 743, 776
Nelson, John N., 211
Netherlands, German invasion of, 685
Neutrality Act (1935), 665, 667–69, 692, 698, 699

New Deal, 2, 333, 340, 368, 373, 377, 388, 396, 415, 418, 423, 433, 473, 560n, 561, 598, 628, 629, 636, 688, 745, 769, 788, 805, 813. *See also specific agencies and programs*
  blacks and, 637–41, 643, 645
  conservation and, 469, 477, 484
  critics of, 413, 696
  Dies Committee and, 616–17, 635
  first hundred days of, 334, 337
  Ickes's book on, 760
  impact on Washington of, 727
  Indians and, 530, 534, 536, 538, 541, 543, 545–47, 633
  limitations of, 386
  National Parks and, 555
  and 1936 elections, 430, 432, 437
  optimism of, 378–79
  original cabinet of, 336, 824
  sex and, 363, 364
  social programs of, 381, 425, 836
  Supreme Court and, 416, 421, 422, 618, 621
  territories and, 496, 500, 503, 504, 509–11, 515, 516, 519–21, 523, 528–29, 611–12
  unemployment and, 694
  World War II and, 686, 691, 727
New Democracy, The (Ickes), 760
Newell, Frederick, 318
New Freedom, 134, 144
Newhall, Arthur, 742, 743
Newlands, Francis, 318, 780
Newlands Act (1902), 121, 317, 318
Newman, Anne, 577
New Nationalism, 120, 122, 134, 144
New Negro Alliance, 731
New Republic, 137, 194, 204, 326, 424n, 514, 841, 843, 844, 846, 847, 852
Newsweek, 671–72
Newton, Carl, 758
New York Chamber of Commerce, 584
New York City
  bombings in, 190
  dust storm in, 475
  PWA projects in, 373–76, 433–34, 436
New York Economic Club, 204
New York Daily News, 296, 439, 597, 727
New York Emergency Public Works Commission, 374

New York Herald-Tribune, 375, 433, 462, 628
New York Housing Authority, 578
New York Life Insurance Company, 132
New York Post, 495, 835, 840–41
New York Power Authority, 330
New York State College of Forestry, 466
New York State Council of Parks, 374
New York State Senate, 263
New York State Temporary Emergency Relief Administration, 389
New York Stock Exchange, 231, 232, 234, 248, 294
New York Times, The, 123, 132, 430, 439, 606, 635, 669, 679, 688, 714, 728, 762, 821, 835
New York Times Magazine, The, 377
New York Transit Commission, 329
Nicholas II, Czar, 597
Nietzsche, Friedrich, 202
Nimitz, Admiral Chester W., 784, 818
Nixon, Richard M., 838, 839, 851–52
Nobel Peace Prize, 72
Noble, Edward, 680, 687
Noble, John W., 310, 569
Nomura, Kichisaburo, 719
Normandie (ship), 605
Norris, George W., 119, 157, 270, 272, 276, 277, 330, 333, 379, 380, 658, 660
North American Light and Power Company, 230
North American News Alliance, 714
North Chicago Rolling Mills, 24
Northwestern Mutual Life Insurance Company, 441
Northwestern University, 220, 237, 443
Northwestern University Settlement House, 91
Norway, German invasion of, 685
Norwell, Betty, 291
Nourmahal (ship), 698
Nuremberg war crimes trials, 827

Oak Knoll Naval Hospital, 819
O'Connor, John J., 493, 631
O'Day, Caroline, 651, 653
Oglesby, Richard, 68
Ohlson, O. F., 611

Oklahoma Corporation Commission, 341, 349
Oklahoma Welfare Act (1936), 541
"Old Age Revolving Pensions" movement, 414
Olmsted, Frederick Law, 37
Olson, Cuthbert, 683, 791
Olympic National Park, 561–68, 571, 579, 580, 609, 715, 773–76, 844–45
O'Mahoney, Joseph, 627, 768, 769, 772, 824, 825, 858
O'Neill, Charles, 756
One World (Willkie), 808
Onslow, Walton, 730
Oregon & California Railroad, 561, 562
O'Reilly, James D., 2
Organic Act (1916), 459, 499, 513
    for Virgin Islands (1936), 509, 510
Organ Pipe Cactus National Monument, 580
Origin of Species (Darwin), 66
Osmena, Sergio, 783
Oswego (N.Y.), 800–804
Otis and Company, 233
Ottawa Indians, 542
Outdoor America, 461
Outlawry of War, 195, 210
Outlook magazine, 126
Ovington, Mary White, 199

Pacific Railroad Act (1862), 308
Padover, Saul K., 590, 670, 760, 762, 763
Page, John C., 776–78
Palmer, A. Mitchell, 188, 190–91, 272
Palmer, Mrs. Potter, 73
Panama Canal Zone, 511
Pan-American Petroleum and Transport Company, 206
Panay (gunboat), 706–7
Papago Indians, 539
Paris
    assassination of German ambassador in, 669–70
    during World War I, 163–66, 168
Parker, John M., 145
Parker Dam, 382
Parliament, British, 685
Parrington, Vernon L., 308
Patent Office, 307, 322
Patman, Wright, 260

Patterson, Bob, 747
Patterson, Eleanor ("Cissy"), 296, 415, 425, 596–98, 602, 606–7, 727, 815
Patterson, Ellis E., 683
Patterson, Joseph, 126, 296, 597, 598, 727
Patterson, Robert, 705, 824
Pauley, Edwin A., 703, 810, 824, 828–36
Pawnee Indians, 542
Peabody, Endicott, 295
Peabody, George Foster, 503
Pearl Harbor, 496, 812
    Japanese attack on, 613n, 720, 723–24, 726, 729, 732, 738, 741, 753, 784, 785, 790, 826
Pearson, Drew, 503, 505, 597, 761n, 858
Pearson, Paul, 503–9, 511
Pearson, T. Gilbert, 460–63
Pease, James, 63, 107
Peculiar Treasure, A (Ferber), 283
Pegler, Westbrook, 772
Pelley, John J., 716–18
Pelley, William Dudley, 545
Pendergast, Tom, 810, 812
Pennsylvania, University of, 854
Pennsylvania Railroad, 223, 373
Penrose, Boies, 127
Pension Office, 307
Peoples, Admiral Joy, 394
People's Forests, The (Marshall), 468
People's Gas Light and Coke Company, 140, 159, 160, 230, 248
People's Protective League, 196–97
People's Traction League, 242–44
Peoria Conference, 104–5
Pepper, Claude, 630
Perkins, Dwight, 109, 151–52
Perkins, Frances, 278, 280, 295, 298, 300, 336–39, 343, 347, 349–53, 389–91, 633–35, 755, 757, 814, 824, 825, 858
Perkins, George W., 132, 133, 138, 142–46, 155–56, 179
Perkins, Lucy, 109
Perkins, Milo, 735–38
Perkins, Palfrey, 858
Perkins, Fellows & Hamilton, 151
Permanent Wild Life Protection Fund, 461
Pétain, Marshal Philippe, 685
Petroleum Administration Board, 349

Petroleum Administration for National Defense, 737
Petroleum Administration for War (PAW), 738, 745–46, 750
Petroleum Coordination, Office of (OPC), 704, 705, 710–11, 718
Petroleum Industry Council for National Defense, 738, 739
Petroleum Industry War Council, 738, 743
Petroleum Reserves Corporation, 747, 749, 751
Philby, Harry St. John, 747
Philippines Independence Act (1934), 782
Philippines, 495, 497, 587
  in World War II, 702, 726, 781–83
Phillips, David Graham, 118
Phillips, Leon C., 690
Phillips Petroleum, 742
Pickens, William, 647
Pilch, Judah, 799
Pilgrim's Progress, A (Bunyan), 121–22
Pinchot, Amos, 3, 117, 130, 133, 138, 142, 143, 277, 560n
Pinchot, Gifford, 3, 133, 143, 182, 183, 188, 212, 276, 278, 329, 330, 403, 454–57, 465, 470, 473, 490, 560–62, 585, 658, 806
  fired by Taft, 114–17, 123, 312, 332, 590
  Forest Service under, 114–16, 121, 261, 311–12, 464
  as governor of Pennsylvania, 206, 261, 466
  Landon supported by, 443–44
Pittman, Key, 577
Pittsburgh, 40
Pittsburgh Courier, 646
Pittsburgh Post-Gazette, 762
Placer Act (1870), 314, 316
PM magazine, 794
Poindexter, Joseph B., 499, 784
Poland, 654
  German invasion of, 685
Polk, James K., 307
Ponca Indians, 542
Pond, Allen Bartlit, 71, 72
Ponselle, Elsa, 251
Pooler, Frank, 465
Poor, Henry Varnum, 450
Pope, Generoso, 678

Popular Democratic Party, Puerto Rican, 527
Populist Party, 66–67, 117, 205
Porter, Gene Stratton, 461
Post Office Department, 433
Potsdam Conference, 825, 826, 842n
Potter, Jean, 785
Potter, William C., 234
Powell, Major John Wesley, 316, 450
Pre-Emption Act (1830), 306, 308
Presbyterianism, 10, 17, 134
President's Advisory Committee on Political Refugees, 671, 797
President's Committee for Unemployment Relief, 256
President's Committee on Administrative Management, 556
Price, J. H., 574
Price Administration, Office of (OPA), 711, 745, 754
Price Administration and Civilian Supplies, Office of (OPACS), 702, 704, 710–12, 738
Prince of Wales (ship), 720
Princeton University, 133
Pringle, Henry, 590
Probert, L. C., 602
Problem of Alaskan Development, The, 673
Problem of Indian Administration, The (Meriam), 275, 330, 533
Production Management, Office of (OPM), 700, 724, 731, 737, 742
Progressives, 2, 3, 71–73, 117–23, 126, 137–38, 140–47, 155–57, 177, 184, 187, 189, 196, 197, 201, 209, 240–41, 260, 318, 424, 805
  conservation and, 276, 454, 457, 481
  FDR and, 276–78, 328, 396–97, 805–6
  of La Follette, 211–13
  Landon and, 438, 443
  and 1912 presidential election, 126–36, 138
  in 1920 elections, 179–80, 182–84, 187–88
  1931 Conference of, 227, 246–47
  in 1948 election, 849
  during World War I, 157, 165, 178
Prohibition, 193, 215, 269, 532
  repeal of, 504

Promise of American Life, The (Croly), 119–20, 130, 132, 159

Prosperity: Its Causes and Consequences (Mazur), 231

Proudhon, Pierre Joseph, 68

Public Buildings Act (1926), 290

Public Buildings Administration, 743*n*

Public Buildings and Public Parks of the National Capital, Office of, 552

Public Roads, Bureau of, 471, 553

Public Service Gas and Electric, 248

Public Utility Holding Company Act (1935), 395–96, 416

Public Works Administration (PWA), 257, 367–78, 386–88, 395, 396, 403–4, 416, 418, 426–29, 476–77, 493, 596, 660, 661, 715, 745, 760

   in Alaska, 611

   blacks and, 644, 646, 647

   Civil Works Administration and, 391–92

   dams built by, 380, 381, 383–86, 455, 471

   funding of, 367–68

   Glavis and, 432–36

   Housing Division of, 376, 412, 508

   Indians and, 537

   Interior Department building constructed by, 448

   military program of, 376

   in New York City, 374–76

   number of projects undertaken by, 373

   Power Division of, 646

   reorganization of, 587, 588, 590–91

   Robert employed by, 656

   staffing of, 368–69

   Subsistence Housing Division of, 387, 403, 433, 486, 644

   in Virgin Islands, 504, 505, 510

   Works Progress Administration and, 397*n*, 410–13, 427, 429, 432

Pueblo Indians, 202–3, 205, 329, 361, 534, 537

Puerto Rican Reconstruction Administration (PRRA), 518–19, 522, 525–28, 786

Puerto Rico, 'Territory of, 323, 412, 495, 512–28, 566, 622

Puerto Rico, University of, 516

Pullman, George, 24, 65, 69–71

Pullman Car Company, 24

   1894 strike against, 3, 69–70

Quezon, Manuel L., 782–83

Quinn, Davis, 463, 464

Radio Corporation of America (RCA), 234

Railroad Retirement Act, 421

Rainey, Henry T., 302

Raisa, Rosa, 229

Rand, McNally & Company, 27

Randolph, A. Philip, 731

Rankin, John, 838

Raskob, John J., 231, 264, 270, 422

Rath, Ernst vom, 669–70

Rauh, Joseph L., Jr., 622

Rayburn, Sam, 266, 619–21, 632, 635, 684, 725, 858

Reclamation, Bureau of, 319, 322, 334, 378, 381, 382, 385, 412, 455, 464, 471, 486, 573–74, 576, 582, 600, 776–80

Reclamation Act (1902), 576, 780

Reclamation Fund, 383

Reclamation Service, 318–19

Reconstruction Finance Corporation (RFC), 258, 262, 287, 370–71, 390, 396, 429, 504, 687, 693, 705–6, 738–40, 743

Reconstruction Finance Corporation Act (1932), 258

Red Cross, 90, 162, 165, 503

Red Scare, 190

Reed, Stanley, 619, 625

Reedsville (W. Va.), 387–88

Reissig, Frederick E., 859

Reno, Milo, 259

Reorganization Act (1939), 587

Republican Party, 10, 16, 17, 32, 38, 67, 113, 119, 162, 168, 195, 205, 383, 505, 536, 851

   Anna in, 216

   anticommunism and, 632

   blacks and, 637

   in Chicago, 51, 62–63, 73, 78–81, 88, 90, 103, 106–8, 176–78, 197, 215

   in 1896 election, 44–45

   in 1900 election, 73–76

Republican Party (cont'd)
  in 1920 election, 179–89
  in 1924 election, 211
  in 1932 election, 260–61, 263, 268, 269, 273n, 490
  in 1936 election, 422, 424–25, 438–39, 443
  in 1940 election, 686–88, 691–97
  in 1944 election, 808–9, 813–16
  in 1946 election, 838
  in 1948 election, 848–50
  Progressives and, 108, 126–29, 131, 134, 137, 138, 140, 143–45, 155–56, 165n, 178–80, 182–84, 212–13, 379, 627, 805
  Southern Democrats and, 626
  split in, 117
  and World War II, 686
Resettlement Administration, 387, 398, 537, 644
Reston, James, 850
Reston, Sally, 728
Review of Reviews, 60
Reynal & Hitchcock, 764
Reynolds, R. J., Company, 705
Rhoads, Charles J., 271, 534, 536
Rhoads, Cornelius, 514
Ribbentrop, Joachim von, 714
Rice, Grantland, 57
Richardson, General Robert C., Jr., 784
Richberg, Donald, 90, 130, 131, 138–40, 144, 145, 154, 160, 182, 183, 197, 209–11, 230, 243, 245, 278, 348–50, 364–65, 380, 394, 420, 476–77, 619
Richberg, John Carver, 139
Richberg, Ickes & Richberg, 139
Riegner, Gerhart, 797
Riggs, Colonel E. Francis, 520, 526
Rivers, E. D., 690
Rivers and Harbors Act (1899), 504
Robert, Mrs. Henry M., Jr., 650
Roberts, Chip, 433–34
Robertson, Edward V., 769
Robins, Margaret Dreier, 90–92, 94, 109, 129–30, 142, 182, 183, 195, 197, 198, 211, 212, 216, 219, 271, 403, 419–20, 590, 755, 758, 759, 817–18
Robins, Raymond, 90–92, 129–31, 140–

41, 182, 183, 202, 218–19, 402–4, 590, 817–18
  and Anna's political career, 216
  back injury of, 419–20, 817
  in Bull Moose Party, 131, 138, 144, 145
  and Chicago politics, 94, 107, 197, 198
  disappearance of, 273n–74n, 402, 403
  at Harold and Anna's wedding, 109
  Ickes's correspondence with, 111, 141, 147–48, 154, 210, 240, 243–46, 593, 692, 707, 756, 846
  La Follette and, 211–13
  in NAACP, 200
  in Russia, 195, 402
  during World War I, 162
Robinson, Frances ("Robbie"), 364
Robinson, George, 506
Robinson, Joseph T., 331–32, 423, 508, 510, 619, 620, 625
Rochester Times, 762
Rockefeller, John D., 38, 66
Rockefeller, John D., Jr., 322, 555, 606, 766–68, 772, 773, 845
Rockefeller Foundation, 514, 533
Rocky Mountain National Park, 320, 581
Rogers, "Star," 746, 749
Rogers, Agnes, 31–33, 36, 224–25
Rogers, Will, Jr., 542, 543
Rolph, James ("Sunny Jim"), 341
Roosevelt, Betsy, 294
Roosevelt, Eleanor, 188, 263, 294, 295, 298, 300, 301, 340n, 358, 387, 388, 404, 409, 433, 626, 639, 649, 650, 652, 734, 797, 820
Roosevelt, Franklin Delano, 183, 190, 283, 312, 333, 357, 358, 396, 404, 409, 413–14, 448, 527, 529, 598, 600, 609, 615n, 659, 660, 714n, 763, 823, 825, 834, 837, 841, 842, 851, 858
  annual cabinet dinners of, 361
  assassination attempt on, 278n, 292
  attempted purge of Democratic Party by, 630–31
  and bank holidays, 293–94, 302–3, 326
  blacks and, 637–39, 643, 645, 646, 648, 651, 652
  cabinet meetings, 334–37, 341, 359, 389, 427–28, 434–35, 619–20, 627, 680, 724–25

conservation policies of, 469–71, 476–80, 484–90, 493–94, 556–59, 586–89, 768–74
death of, 819–22, 824, 827, 830
dedication of Interior Building by, 451
Dies Committee and, 634–35
elected President, 253–68, 270–73, 610
fascism and, 664–69
Glavis and, 433–37
Hopkins and, 390–95, 397–400, 411–13, 680–81
on *Houston* voyage, 417–19
Hundred Days of, 325–27, 334, 338–39, 343–53, 485
and Ickes's remarriage, 605
inauguration of, 2, 280, 292–301, 325, 389
Indians and, 536, 540, 547
Jews and, 661
legacy of, 836
Long and, 414–17
Missy LeHand and, 806–7
mistress of, 364
National Planning Board appointed by, 377–78
national parks and, 552, 554n, 555, 556, 564–68, 572, 574, 576–78, 580, 581, 583
and NRA, 350–52, 364–65
patronage and, 328, 330–32
as President-elect, 274–80
Progressives and, 276–78, 328, 396–97, 805–6
PWA and, 368–72, 374–75, 378, 385–88, 400–401, 412–13, 426–29
reelection campaigns of, 411, 420, 422–27, 430–32, 437–39, 442–44, 676, 682–84, 686–97, 762–63, 808–17, 829, 850
refugee program of, 671, 673–74
reorganization plan of, 557–59, 584–87, 629, 658, 660–61
special session of Congress called by, 627–28
Supreme Court and, 415–16, 420–22, 424, 426, 545, 618–26, 629, 632
territories and, 495, 499–500, 503, 506–11, 515–19, 522, 523, 526
and TVA, 379–80

as Vice-Presidential candidate, 188–89, 191, 263–64
Warm Springs retreat of, 365
and World War II, 686, 698–703, 706–12, 716, 720, 761, 723–26, 731, 733, 735–39, 741–45, 747, 748, 750, 752–59, 768, 781–84, 786, 791, 793–95, 797–803
Roosevelt, James, 294, 297, 630, 851
Roosevelt, Theodore, 3, 67–68, 116, 120–24, 143–46, 152, 181, 188–89, 209, 212, 213, 218, 256, 263, 276, 278n, 293, 646, 805, 827
conservation policies of, 312, 313, 315, 316, 318, 320, 455, 457, 459, 469, 560, 562, 771
death of, 171, 187
elected Vice President, 74–76
in 1912 Presidential election, 126–29, 131–34, 136
presidency of, 113–16, 121–22
Roosevelt, Theodore, Jr., 189
Roosevelt and Hopkins (Sherwood), 390
Roosevelt-Garner Club, 508
Root, Elihu, 127, 185
Root, John Wellborn, 26
Roper, Daniel C., 336, 353, 648, 680
Rosenfeld, Mrs. Irwin, 200
Rosenheim, Jacob, 797
Rosenman, Samuel I., 264, 296, 619, 630, 696, 782, 810–11
Rosenwald, Julius, 73, 96, 99, 106, 107, 130, 645n, 662
Rothstein, Arnold, 473
Rough Riders, 74
Rowe, James, 693
Rowell, Chester, 130, 138, 146, 182
Rowen, Edward, 450
Rubber Reserve Company, 740–42
Rubber Survey Committee, 745
Runyon, Damon, 57, 297
Rupp, Franz, 653
Rural Electrification Administration, 587, 658–60, 673
Rural Resettlement program, 412
Russell, Charles Edward, 118
Russell, Francis, 186
Russia, 185, 190, 194, 195, 402
atomic bomb and, 840

Russia (cont'd)
  German nonaggression pact with, 685,
    709
  and postwar anticommunism, 847
  Wallace in, 810
  in World War II, 709, 710, 720, 736,
    798
Russo, Augusto, 666
Rutherford, Lucy Mercer, 819–20

St. Elizabeth's Hospital, 324
Saint-Gaudens, Augustus, 37
St. Louis Post-Dispatch, 831, 834, 835
St. Mihiel (France), 167
St. Valentine's Day Massacre, 229
Salt Lake Tribune, 770
Sandburg, Carl, 22–23, 27
San Francisco Examiner, 791
San Francisco State Teachers' College,
    202
San Joaquin Valley Council, 571
Sarlin, Reino, 775–76
Saturday Evening Post, 193, 322, 327, 334,
    372, 397n, 419, 590, 763, 770,
    841–42
Saudi Arabia, 746–47, 749–50
Sauer, Louis, 655–56
Saulxures (France), 166
Save-the-Redwoods League, 552, 579
Sawyer, Donald H., 352
Schaffner, Joseph, 105, 142
Schecter v. United States (1935), 416
Scheel, Fred, 248
Scheutler, Herman F., 98
Scheville, Ferdinand, 38, 46
Schlesinger, Arthur M., Jr., 648
Schlesinger, Elmer, 597
Schnepfe, Fred E., 400
Schofield Barracks, 496
School Life, 323
Schroeder, Werner W., 815
Schurz, Carl, 310
Schwellenback, Lewis, 824
Scientific Monthly, 466, 468
Scott Stamp & Coin Company, 225
Sears, Roebuck, 25, 73, 96, 711
Seattle, bombings in, 190
Seattle Post-Intelligencer, 608
Seavey, Clyde L., 576
Secret Service, 293, 357, 360, 821, 857

Securities and Exchange Act (1934), 396,
    421
Securities and Exchange Commission, 622
  Public Utilities Division, 661
Selassie, Haile, 666
Selective Service System, 695
Seminole, 530
Senate, U.S., 104, 107, 203, 204, 214–15,
    218, 242, 247, 277, 296, 414,
    498, 509, 513, 626, 748, 752,
    826, 827, 838, 851
  Agriculture and Forestry Committee, 116
  Appropriations Committee, 427–29
  Atomic Energy Committee, 839
  Bonus Bill in, 260
  civil rights legislation in, 638
  Commerce Committee, 779
  confirmation of Roosevelt appointees by,
    328, 390, 534
  conservation legislation in, 478, 492
  Court packing and, 621
  Democratic majority in, 413
  Expenditures Committee, 489
  Finance Committee, 505
  Foreign Relations Committee, 701
  Glavis and, 433–36
  Harding and, 186
  immigration legislation in, 674–75
  Indian Affairs Committee, 538–40,
    544–46
  Indian Investigating Subcommittee,
    332–33
  Judiciary Committee, 619, 624, 625
  Lend-Lease bill in, 701
  McCarthy censured by, 847–48
  National Parks and, 567
  Naturalization and Immigration Com-
    mittee, 803
  Naval Affairs Committee, 335, 830–31
  Public Lands Committee, 207, 208,
    567, 577, 584, 767, 772
  reorganization bill in, 557, 586, 587
  Robins runs for, 141
  Roosevelt and, 300
  Special Committee to Investigate Gas-
    oline and Fuel Shortages, 716–18
  Special Committee to Investigate the
    National Defense Program, 706
  Territories and Insular Possessions Com-
    mittee, 505–7, 674

Truman and, 825, 828, 830, 838
Versailles Treaty in, 180–81
and World War I, 157
Seneca Indians, 542, 545
Sequoia (yacht), 823
Sequoia National Park, 320, 569
Seventh Inter-American Conference (1933), 495
Seward (Alaska), 611, 615
Seyfullah, Ibrahim, 408
Shadow Man, The (Richberg), 138
"Share the Wealth" program, 414, 424
Sheets, Millard, 450
Shell Oil, 341
Shenandoah National Park, 322, 469, 554–56
Sheperd, Alexander Robey ("Boss"), 288
Sherman Anti-Trust Act (1890), 121, 122, 133
Sherwood, Robert, 390, 680
Shippy, George, 95, 97, 98
Short, Joseph, 858
Shoumataoff, Elizabeth, 819
Show, S. Bevier, 572–75
Sierra Club, 456–58, 461, 464, 571–73, 575, 577, 585
Sierra Forest Reserve, 569
Signal Corps, 164–65
Sikes, George, 57
Silcox, Ferdinand A., 479, 481, 489, 490, 564, 566, 567, 573, 578
Silver Shirts, 545
Simmons, Henry Harriman, 232
Simpson, James, 241
Simpson, John A., 259
Sinclair, Harry F., 206–8, 842
Sinclair, Upton, 414
Sinclair Oil, 341
Singapore, 720
Sioux Indians, 334, 531
Sirovich, William I., 677–78
Sitka Air Base, 785
Six Companies, 381–84, 647
Slattery, Harry, 206, 329–30, 358, 386–87, 395, 428, 432, 435, 451, 455n, 480, 491, 525, 455n, 480, 491, 525, 526, 609, 645, 658–60, 673, 684, 748
Slaughter, A. O., and Company, 233, 235, 236, 359

Smith, Alfred E., 211, 215, 263, 264, 300, 422–24, 426, 443
Smith, Frank, 214–15
Smith, George, 20
Smith, Gerald L. K., 414, 424, 443, 815
Smith, Harold, 661, 711, 733–36, 738, 769, 786
Smith, Jess, 207
Smith College, 599
Smithsonian Institution, 290
Smoot, Reed, 317
Smulski, John P., 107
Smyth, John M., 63
Snake River Land Company, 767, 770, 772
Socialist Party, Puerto Rican, 513, 514, 517, 518, 521, 522
Social Security Act (1935), 395, 416, 421, 624
Society of American Foresters, 469, 491, 585
Socony-Vacuum, 719
Soil Erosion Act (1935), 477
Soil Erosion Service, 476–77
Southern California Edison Company, 382
Southern Pacific Railroad, 119, 250, 308, 777
Soviet Union. *See* Russia
Spanish-American War, 181, 223, 495, 513
Spanish Civil War, 666–68, 671
Special Board for Public Works, 352, 370
Spencer (ship), 615
Spencer, Herbert, 66
Spending to Save (Hopkins), 390–91
Spies, August, 68
Spoon River Anthology (Masters), 204
Stackpole, Ralph, 450
Stagg, Amos Alonzo, 3, 38, 43, 51, 106, 197
Stalin, Josef, 819, 825, 842n, 847
Standard Oil, 118, 177, 341, 342
Standard Oil of California, 703, 746, 750, 752n, 777
Standard Oil of New Jersey, 719, 742
Standards, Bureau of, 744
Stanley, Augustus O., 123
Stannard, Amy, 508
Stanton, Henry, 203
Staples, Bertram I., 202
Starns, Joe, 632

Starr, Ellen Gates, 45, 71, 72, 105
Starr, Frederick, 38, 52
State Bank of Chicago, 236
State Department, U.S., 304, 307, 664, 672–74, 706, 709, 724, 725, 736, 738, 747, 749–50, 797–801, 830, 848
States' Rights Democratic Party, 849
Stead, William T., 60
Steffens, Lincoln, 57, 118, 194, 195
Stegner, Wallace, 155, 318
Steinbeck, John, 473, 778n
Stettinius, Edward, 711, 741, 824
Stevenson, Adlai, 858
Stewart, Graeme, 63, 79, 81
Stimson, Henry L., 298, 686, 687, 700, 705, 738, 782, 783, 791, 793, 799, 800, 803, 824, 825
Stock-Raising Homestead Act (1916), 308, 479, 480n
Stoic, The (Dreiser), 62n
Stokowski, Leopold, 650
Stone, Harlan Fiske, 626, 744, 820
Stone, I. F., 723–24, 726, 801
Straight, Dorothy, 204
Straight, Willard, 204
Strap Hangers' League, 79, 90
Straus, Bobby, 364
Straus, Michael W., 368, 439, 441, 442, 606, 724, 760, 763, 778–80, 820
Straus, Oscar, 121, 146
Studebaker, John W., 734
Studs Lonigan (Farrell), 253–54
Success on Irrigation Projects (Widstoe), 320
Sullivan, Louis, 26–27, 37, 38
Sullivan, Mark, 118
Sulzberger, Arthur, 606
Sumners, Hatton, 619, 620
Sun Oil Company, 719
Supply Priorities and Allocation Board (SPAB), 711, 724, 737, 739
Supreme Court, U.S., 137, 144, 290, 350, 396, 415–16, 420–22, 424, 426, 533, 545, 618–26, 629, 632, 660, 661, 667, 704, 821, 843
Sutherland, George, 421, 625
Swamp Land Act (1850), 308
Swanson, Claude, 335, 686
Swarthmore College, 243
Sweden, 684

Swett, John, 779–80
Swift & Company, 25
Swope, Gerard, 404, 578
Swope, Guy J., 257
Swope, Herbert Bayard, 680

Taft, Lorado, 37
Taft, Robert, 688, 858
Taft, William Howard, 113–17, 120, 123–24, 126–28, 134, 181, 206, 245, 312, 315, 317, 320, 329, 332, 457, 460, 590, 597, 686, 771
Taft-Hartley Act, 838
Talmadge, Eugene, 423, 426
Tammany Hall, 264, 375, 688, 692, 810
Tanner, John R., 45
Tarbell, Frank, 38
Tarbell, Ida, 57, 118
Tariff Commission, U.S., 336
Taussig, Charles W., 503
Taxi Commission, 295
Taylor, Edward, 477–78
Taylor, Glen, 849
Taylor, Harry, 511
Taylor, Myron C., 671
Taylor, Paul Schuster, 474, 778–80
Taylor, Zachary, 307
Taylor Grazing Act (1934), 479–82, 487, 845
Teamsters Union, 814
Teapot Dome scandal, 206–8, 304, 842
Temple, Shirley, 616, 633
Tennessee, University of, 380
Tennessee Coal and Iron Company, 122, 123
Tennessee Valley Authority (TVA), 379–81, 384, 386, 421, 455, 468, 554, 588, 646, 658, 688, 692
Terkel, Studs, 251
Tetlow, Colonel Percy, 661
Texaco, 746
Texas Railroad Commission, 341, 342
Texas Tech, 374
Theodore Roosevelt Memorial Association, 218
This I Remember (Roosevelt), 626
Thlingits, 323, 610, 615
Thomas, Edna, 644
Thomas, John William Elmer, 542
Thomas, J. Parnell, 632–33, 745n, 838, 846

Thomas, Lowell, 719–20
Thomas, Norman, 339
Thompson, Anna Wilmarth. *See* Ickes, Anna Wilmarth
Thompson, Ben, 554
Thompson, Betty Dahlman, 220–21, 233, 239, 328, 409, 441, 599, 604
Thompson, Dorothy, 57
Thompson, Frances, 101, 103, 109, 150, 153, 162, 164, 166, 170, 171, 220, 238, 274n, 409, 440
Thompson, James Westfall, 4, 47, 50, 57, 82, 89, 101–3, 109
Thompson, John R., 107
Thompson, J. Walter, advertising firm, 203
Thompson, Wayne, 85–86, 439–40
Thompson, William Hale ("Big Bill"), 141, 142, 176–78, 195, 197, 199, 215, 229, 240, 244, 247, 251
Thoreau, Henry David, 455–56
Thorn, Ben W., 784
Thornburg, Max, 736, 737
Thurmond, Strom, 849, 850
Tibbett, Lawrence, 650
Timber and Stone Act (1878), 308–10
Timber Culture Act (1873), 308
Time magazine, 333
Titan, The (Dreiser), 62n
Tobey, Charles, 831, 836, 858
Tojo, General Hideki, 719
Tolstoy, Leo, 68
Tomlinson, Major Owen A., 609
Torrio, Johnny, 195–96
Toscanini, Arturo, 649
Townsend, Francis, 414, 424, 443
Toynbee Hall Settlement (London), 71
Trading with the Enemy Act (1917), 303
Treasury, U.S., 393, 400, 532
Treasury Department, U.S., 304–7, 323, 396, 517, 584, 646, 707
    Procurement Division, 394, 433–34, 448, 449
Triborough Bridge Authority, 374–75
Trohan, Walter, 364, 690
Trout, Bob, 299
Troy, John W., 611, 615
Truckee River Project, 777
Truman, Harry S., 706, 780, 803–4, 811–12, 820, 823–40, 842n, 843–46, 848–51, 857–58

Truman, Margaret, 820
Tsimshean Indians, 616
Tugwell, Rexford G., 264, 277, 346–49, 398–99, 412, 486–89, 503, 517, 527–28, 537, 557, 644
Tully, Grace, 296, 417, 724
Tumacacori National Monument, 320
Tutwiler, T. W., 718
Twenty Mule Borax Company, 321n
Twenty Years at Hull-House (Addams), 23
Tydings, Millard, 434, 505–10, 520, 521, 526, 690, 782–83, 848
Tyler, John, 307

Udall, Stewart, 472
Unione Siciliano, 196
Union Pacific Railroad, 308
Union Party, 424
Union Party, Puerto Rican, 513–14
Union-Republican Party, Puerto Rican, 513, 517, 518, 521, 522
Union Stock Yards, 24–25
United Charities of Chicago, 105
United Garment Workers of America, 105
United Labor Committee, 816
United Mine Workers (UMW), 343, 660, 694, 695, 706, 753–59
United Nations, 825, 840, 844
United Palestine Appeal, 664
United Press International (UPI), 184, 282, 480, 529, 809, 826
United States Marshals, 422
United States Potash Company, 552
United States Steel Corporation, 122, 123, 132, 223, 234, 250
Urban League, 252, 502, 646
U.S. Chamber of Commerce, 347
U.S. Council of Mayors, 397
U.S. Smelting and Refining Company, 614
U.S. v. Butler (1936), 421

Vandenburg, Arthur H., 424
Van Devanter, Justice, 624–25
Vanguard Press, 762
Van Name, Willard G., 462–63, 562, 563
Vann, Robert L., 646
Vaughan, L. Brent, 43, 50
Veblen, Thorstein, 38
Venezuela, 746
Versailles Treaty, 180–81

Veterans' Bureau, 207, 734
Veterans' National Liaison Committee, 292
Veterans of Foreign Wars, 779
Vichy France, 685, 798
Villard, Oswald Garrison, 404
Vinson, Frederick, 824
Virginia, University of, 525
  Institute of Public Affairs, 437
Virginia State College for Negroes, 373
Virgin Islands, 322, 323, 357, 495, 500–
  514, 528, 644, 672–73, 797
Virgin Islands Company (VICO), 503–4,
  510, 516–17
Virgin Islands National Bank, 504
Voices of Protest (Brinkley), 424n
Volstead Act (1919), 193
Voorhis, Jerry, 779, 838

Wagner, Robert, 257, 347, 348, 390, 587,
  638, 674
Wagner Act. See National Labor Relations
  Act
Waite, Colonel Henry M., 368, 386
Walker, Frank, 270, 397, 399
Walker, Robert J., 306–7
Walker, Stanley, 57
"Walking" (Thoreau), 455
Wallace, Henry A., 183, 328, 338, 346,
  371–72, 404, 414n, 422, 503,
  810–12, 824
  blacks and, 640–41
  and Civil Works Administration, 391
  conservation issues and, 445, 467, 469,
    476, 479, 481, 484–94, 564, 566,
    567, 573–75
  at Ickes's funeral, 858
  at inauguration, 295
  Indians and, 536–37
  Presidential candidacy of, 651, 677, 849,
    850
  in reelection campaigns, 432, 693–94
  and reorganization plan, 557–59, 586
  and Spanish Civil War, 666
  as Vice President, 336, 678, 690–91,
    725, 735–38, 808
Wallace, Henry C., 183
Wallgren, Monrad C., 563, 565–67
Walsh, Frank, 442
Walsh, John R., 63, 77
Walsh, Thomas J., 207, 208, 278

Walters, Theodore A., 327
War Department, U.S., 304, 307, 338,
  347, 380, 489, 531, 537, 552, 704
  blacks and, 643, 645, 646
  territories and, 323, 495, 513, 516,
    520, 587
  during World War I, 379
  during World War II, 723, 724, 729,
    738, 747, 786–87, 791, 793–95,
    799, 801
War Industries Board, 348, 710, 711
War Labor Disputes Act (1942), 757
War Manpower Commission, 731
War Mobilization, Office of, 812, 824
Warneke, Heinz, 451
War of 1812, 305, 723
War Powers Act, 837
War Production Board (WPB), 737, 739,
  742, 744, 774, 776
War Refugee Board, 800, 801, 803
War Relocation Authority, 792–96, 801
Warren, Earl, 791, 848, 851
Washington, Booker T., 121
Washington: City and Capital (WPA guide),
  288
Washington, D.C.
  blacks in, 289–90, 648–50, 652–53,
    844
  bombing in, 190
  Bonus Army in, 260, 272–73, 290, 292
  during Civil War, 784
  conference of Progressives in, 246, 277
  during Depression, 287, 289–92
  dust storms in, 475, 477
  Ickes arrives in, 287
  local administration of, 288
  train from Chicago to, 1–4
  in War of 1812, 723
  during World War II, 726–34
Washington, Forrester B., 646
Washington Board of Trade, 289, 291
Washington Daily American, 289
Washington Evening Star, 401, 428, 534,
  859
Washington Herald, 287, 291, 294, 296,
  297, 300, 301, 354, 425, 597,
  603, 606–7, 727
Washington Planning Commission, 729
Washington Post, 294, 357, 361, 666
Washington Senators, 289

Washington State Game Commission, 563
Washington State Planning Council, 563
Washington Times, 727
Washington Times-Herald, 727
Waters, Walter, 259
Watson, Colonel Edwin M. ("Pa"), 417,
    678, 768–69, 810
Wealth Tax Act (1935), 416
Weaver, Robert C., 646
Webb, Beatrice, 118
Webb, Sidney, 118
Webb, Vanderbilt, 767
Weir, Ernest T., 696
Welles, Gideon, 302*n*
Welles, Sumner, 667, 672–74, 709, 738,
    797–99
Wells, H. G., 61
West, Charles F., 411, 426–27
West, Charles O., 659*n*
West, Roy B., 511, 525, 526
West Coast Lumbermen's Association, 455
Western Federation of Miners, 91
We Too Are the People (Armstrong), 294
Wheeler, Ada, 20, 29, 30, 33, 34, 40,
    224
Wheeler, Burton K., 208, 266, 538, 539,
    545–47, 587, 621, 624–27, 701,
    714, 715
Wheeler, Dan, 661
Wheeler, Felix, 20, 29–33, 36, 39–41, 48,
    224
Whig Party, 10, 307
White, Charles, 104
White, George, 191
White, John R., 569
White, Walter, 503, 638, 650, 651, 653,
    731
White, William Allen, 3, 5, 123, 138,
    155, 183, 195, 241, 259, 327,
    762
    death of, 805–6
    fascism denounced by, 666
    Harding and, 186, 187, 207
    Ickes's correspondence with, 7, 13–14,
        130, 261, 274*n*
    League of Nations supported by, 180,
        185
    New Deal and, 425, 805
    on Republican National Committee,
        178, 182

    Theodore Roosevelt and, 123, 131, 133,
        143, 145, 146
    during World War I, 162, 165*n*
White, William S., 821–22
White House Correspondents' Association,
    701
White Mountain National Forest, 464–65
Whitman, Walt, 22, 822
Whitney, Richard C., 234
Wichita (Kan.), 14
Wickard, Claude R., 659, 660*n*, 824
Wickensham, George, 123
Widstoe, John, 320
Wiesel, Elie, 804
Wiggin, Albert H., 234
Wilbur, Ray Lyman, 270–71, 340, 345,
    382, 383, 496, 500, 505, 533–34
Wilcox, Max, 630
Wilde, Oscar, 207
Wilderness Act (1964), 465*n*
Wilderness Society, The, 468–69, 492,
    554, 567, 577, 579, 582, 585,
    767, 776
Wilkerson, James, 241, 244, 248*n*
Wilkins, Roy, 645–47
Will Gill & Sons, 777
Williams, Aubrey, 639, 731
Williamsburg (yacht), 823
Willkie, Wendell, 380*n*, 688–89, 691–92,
    694–97, 763, 808–9
Willys-Overland Company, 673
Wilmarth, Anna. *See* Ickes, Anna Wilmarth
Wilmarth, Henry W., 45
Wilmarth, Mary Hawes, 45–46, 87, 96,
    102, 105, 109, 131, 201
Wilson, Dooley, 644
Wilson, Edmund, 252, 298–99, 327
Wilson, Francis, 203, 205
Wilson, Milburn, 329, 333–34, 387
Wilson, T. Webber, 505–9
Wilson, William Otis ("Billy"), 48, 52, 57,
    329
Wilson, Woodrow, 133–34, 136–37, 144,
    156, 157, 160, 180, 181, 188–90,
    206, 256, 257, 263, 299, 315,
    317, 320, 321, 326, 457, 499,
    502, 562
Winchester Repeating Arms Company,
    460
Winesburg, Ohio (Anderson), 14

Winnetka (Ill.), 151, 221, 225, 439–41.
    See also Hubbard Woods
Winship, Blanton, 516, 518, 519, 521,
    523–27
Wirtz, Alvin J., 684, 748, 777
Wisconsin, University of, 456
    Forest Products Laboratory, 465, 589
Wise, Stephen, 797, 798
Witherspoon, Carl, 356, 405, 410
With the Procession (Fuller), 25
Witness to Power (Childs), 823
Women's City Club, 201
Women's International League for Peace and
    Freedom, Anniversary Committee
    of, 404
Women's Municipal League of New York,
    91
Women's Trade Union League, 91–92, 94,
    104–5, 142, 201
Wood, General Leonard, 181, 185, 186
Wood, Waddy B., 448
Woodin, William H., 293, 300, 303, 335
Woodring, Harry H., 335, 686
Woolhiser, H. L., 439
Work, Hubert, 553
Works Progress Administration (WPA),
    288, 397–400, 410, 426, 427,
    429, 432, 504, 519, 537, 633,
    639, 640, 644
    Federal Arts Project of, 449
World Court, 413
World Jewish Congress, 797
World's Columbian Exposition, 4, 37, 60,
    68, 253
World War I, 90, 144, 156–58, 160–69,
    176, 257, 273, 317, 348, 379,
    458, 474, 501, 562, 672, 686,
    710, 729
    agricultural expansion during, 250, 313
    Hoover during, 255
    Ickes in France during, 163–69
    veterans of, 259, 340*n*, *see also* Bonus
        Army
World War II, 339, 380, 381, 495, 500,
    504, 511, 536, 546, 547, 583,
    685–86, 691, 698–99, 714–15,
    727, 733–59, 764–65, 808, 817

end of, 825–27, 836
internment of Japanese-Americans dur-
    ing, 790–96, 801
Jewish refugees during, 796–804
Lend-Lease program in, 699–702
Normandy invasion, 810
outbreak of, 654
preparation for, 686, 695, 702–12,
    716–19, 805
territories during, 528, 781–90
U.S. entry into, 719–20, 723–26
Washington, D.C., during, 726–34
Wounded Knee, Battle of, 530
Wright, Luke, 114
Wright, Richard, 644
Wrigley, William, Jr., 209
Wyzanski, Charles, 365*n*

Yale University, 233
Yalta Conference, 819
Yard, Robert Sterling, 321, 322*n*, 458,
    468, 492, 552, 554–56, 557, 579,
    582, 589
Yates, Paul C., 505, 507
Yellowstone National Park, 320, 321, 409,
    459, 550, 551, 766, 770
Yerkes, Charles T., 28, 51, 60–62, 65, 77,
    79, 88, 107, 158, 241
Yosemite National Park, 320, 321, 456,
    457, 550, 551
Young, James W., 203
Young Men's Business Association, 616
Young Men's Christian Association
    (YMCA), 162–70
Young Men's Progressive Republican Club,
    106, 108
Yugoslavia, German invasion of, 702

Zangara, Anthony, 278*n*
Zeppelin Company of Germany, 668
Zimmerman, William, 332
Zimmerman, William, Jr., 534, 535,
    538
Zion National Park, 320
Zook, George F., 642–43
Zuni Indians, 202